The Romans

FOR

DUMMIES®

by Guy de la Bédoyère

JOHN WILEY & SONS, LTD

The Romans For Dummies®

Published by
John Wiley & Sons, Ltd
The Atrium
Southern Gate
Chichester
West Sussex
PO19 8SQ
England

E-mail (for orders and customer service enquires): cs-books@wiley.co.uk

Visit our Home Page on www.wiley.com

For general information on our other products and services, please contact our Customer Care Department within the U.S. at 800-762-2974, outside the U.S. at 317-572-3993, or fax 317-572-4002.

For technical support, please visit www.wiley.com/techsupport.

Wiley also publishes its books in a variety of electronic formats. Some content that appears in print may not be available in electronic books.

British Library Cataloguing in Publication Data: A catalogue record for this book is available from the British Library

ISBN-13: 978-0-470-03077-6 (P/B)

Printed and bound in Great Britain by Bell & Bain Ltd, Glasgow.

10 9 8 7 6 5 4 3 2

WILEY

About the Author

Guy de la Bédoyère is a freelance writer and broadcaster who took a history and archaeology degree at Durham University, followed by a history degree at the University of London specialising in Roman history, with papers in US history. Next came an MA in Roman Empire archaeology at University College, London. He has written many books on his specialist field of Roman Britain and is well-known for his numerous appearances on television, especially Channel 4's *Time Team* in Britain. He has also written books on a variety of other historical subjects, including the papers of Samuel Pepys, and is a Fellow of the Royal Numismatic Society. His other interests include playing the piano, travelling in the United States, and studying genealogy. He lives in Lincolnshire, England.

Author's Acknowledgements

I can't list all the Roman experts I've met and talked to over the years who have made a difference to this book whether they know it or not, but I would like to make a special mention of Richard Reece and Neil Faulkner, both of whose idiosyncratic and original perspectives on Roman history have made me think more than they know. I'd also like to thank Daniel Mersey, Samantha Clapp, and Martin Tribe at Wiley for their comments along the way on assembling the text, and Wejdan Ismail for her help. Special mention for Tracy Barr for her editorial work in developing the text through to its final form. I'm also grateful to all those people I've worked with in television archaeology and history, and the viewers, for their comments and observations which have helped me cut through the waffle to see things more clearly. Finally to my wife who endured several fourteen-hour days tramping round Rome and Ostia during the research for this book, and who has put up with the Roman Empire for nearly thirty years.

Publisher's Acknowledgements

We're proud of this book; please send us your comments through our Dummies online registration form located at www.dummies.com/register/.

Some of the people who helped bring this book to market include the following:

Acquisitions, Editorial, and Media Development

Project Editor: Daniel Mersey

Development Editor: Tracy Barr

Content Editor: Steve Edwards

Commissioning Editor: Samantha Clapp

Copy Editor: Christine Lea

Proofreader: Charlie Wilson

Technical Editor: Cassian Hall

Executive Editor: Jason Dunne

Executive Project Editor: Martin Tribe

Cover Photos: © Caesar: Bettmann/ CORBIS; Hadrian's Wall: The National Trust Photolibrary/ Alamy; gladiator: Christie's Images/ CORBIS; clock face: Jupiterimages; all other images Guy de la Bédoyère.

Cartoons: Rich Tennant (www.the5thwave.com)

Composition Services

Project Coordinator: Jennifer Theriot

Layout and Graphics: Lavonne Cook, Stephanie D. Jumper, Barbara Moore, Barry Offringa, Heather Ryan, Alicia South

Proofreaders: Jessica Kramer, Charles Spencer

Indexer: Techbooks

Brand Reviewers: Zoë Wykes, Jan Withers

Publishing and Editorial for Consumer Dummies

    Diane Graves Steele, Vice President and Publisher, Consumer Dummies

    Joyce Pepple, Acquisitions Director, Consumer Dummies

    Kristin A. Cocks, Product Development Director, Consumer Dummies

    Michael Spring, Vice President and Publisher, Travel

    Kelly Regan, Editorial Director, Travel

Publishing for Technology Dummies

    Andy Cummings, Vice President and Publisher, Dummies Technology/General User

Composition Services

    Gerry Fahey, Vice President of Production Services

    Debbie Stailey, Director of Composition Services

Contents at a Glance

Table of Contents

Introduction

When I was about 12 years old, my father came home from work with a Roman coin he'd bought for me. It was very worn, with a barely visible profile of a Roman emperor's head on one side. But I was totally fascinated by the sudden realisation that this coin had existed for a length of time I was struggling to imagine. It belonged to a truly amazing world of emperors, vast buildings, epic wars, villains, and heroes. And I could hold a part of it in my hand!

Roman history is a hotch-potch made up from every, or indeed, any source that historians and archaeologists have been able to get their hands on. There's no one-stop ancient source of Roman history, no great Roman textbook that we can pick up and start with. Even the Romans were more than a bit hazy about how their world had come together. They had historians, but most of what got written down hasn't survived. Even the works we do have are usually incomplete. What we do know is that the further the Romans looked back into their past, the more they had to fill in the gaps with myth and hearsay.

If you think back to learning about the Romans at school or watching a documentary on TV, you'd probably have come across things that sounded really exciting, like Mount Vesuvius erupting and burying Pompeii in AD 79. But you probably also got the idea that the Romans were also dreadfully serious. Some museums don't help either because rows and rows of dusty pots aren't very inspiring, especially if you had to troop around with a question sheet while on a school trip.

But the truth is that the Roman Empire is one of the most exciting periods in all history. Not only is it packed with real people living real lives, but it also has an unending series of remarkable events that mark the rise of a little village in Italy all the way from total prehistoric obscurity into the greatest of all ancient civilisations.

The Roman world is all around us. In Europe, North Africa, and the Near East, the debris is there to see wherever you go. From the crumbling line of Hadrian's Wall in northern England all the way to the rock-cut tombs of Petra in Jordan, the Romans left their mark everywhere they went and created the world's first superstate. The very fact that it's long gone is why we should use it as a mirror for our own age. 'All Things Must Pass,' said George Harrison, and when it comes to empires, he couldn't have been more correct.

About This Book

Teaching Latin goes back right to the Middle Ages. In the nineteenth century, the Victorians loved the Romans and used them as a kind of justification for what they were doing: conquering the world, basically. So Latin and ancient history were major subjects, and things didn't change for years. Generations of schoolchildren – actually, in the 1960s I was one of them – had to learn Latin so that they could translate lines like 'Caesar attacked the enemy's fortifications'. The upshot was that the Romans looked like a rather boring master-race of generals and politicians, who did a lot of standing around in togas when they weren't massacring other people. Hardly thrilling stuff and apparently completely irrelevant to today, but thanks to archaeology, cinema, and TV, they're now enjoying something of a revival.

The story's miles more interesting than that, so the idea behind this book is to tell it like it was: a rollercoaster of a drama packed with amazing events and amazing people. Now it's easy to get the idea that all the Romans came from Rome, and it was just them who made the Roman Empire what it was while everyone else watched. Not a bit of it. The Romans were very clever at what they did. They turned being Roman into an idea, a way of life, that anyone could have – under certain conditions of course, like being prepared to accept the emperor's authority without question. The fact is that millions of people did just that. They adopted Roman names, lived the Roman way, and they did that wherever they lived. There were Syrian Romans, North African Romans, Spanish Romans, and British Romans.

I can't pretend I don't think the Romans were brilliant, but that's not the same as thinking they were all good, and I'd like to think I've acknowledged the downside to Roman life. After all, it's difficult to defend the horrors of the amphitheatre, slavery, or the brutal massacre of innocent civilians during the wars of conquest. This book is undoubtedly my spin on the Roman world, but I've tried to give a balanced account, both the good and the bad.

It also goes without saying I've had to leave a lot out, so I chose the key events and people that made Rome what it was, those things that reflect what the Roman Empire and being Roman mean to us. Of course, the events related are entirely my choice, which you might not agree with, but that's always been the historian's luxury.

Foolish Assumptions

In writing this book, I've had to make a few assumptions about you:

 ✔ You have a vague idea about the Romans from school.

 ✔ You've probably been dragged to one or two Roman places on holiday.

> ✔ You basically thought the Romans came from Rome.
>
> ✔ You love the idea of reading history packed with murderers, megalomaniacs, mayhem, corruption, swindles, decadence, heroic valour, and crazy weirdo gods.

How This Book Is Organised

I could very easily have started at the beginning of Roman history and written about nothing thing else until I stopped, but where's the fun in that? The Roman Empire was an ancient civilisation, full of exciting events and interesting people. In this book, you get the best of both worlds: Information about what it meant to be Roman *and* a rundown of Roman history. The following sections show you what you can expect to find in each part.

Part 1: Romans – The Big Boys of the Ancient World

The first part is all about putting the Romans into context. The Romans might be popular today, but in fact they've been pretty popular ever since ancient times. Many rulers and governments along the way spotted that the Romans were good at being in charge. This part introduces you to how and why the Romans have had such an impact on later civilisations and the legacy of some of their ideas. Of course, Romans weren't just armour-clad brutes. The Romans kept their world together through a mixture of the sword and a straightforward acceptance of the structure of their society and its laws. Part I also examines Roman society: the class system, from senator to slave; the Roman fantasy about their identity; the sheer hard practicalities of being in the army; and more. Unlike almost all other ancient civilisations in the western world, the Romans really got a handle on creating a system that actually worked, even if the man in charge was sometimes a raving lunatic.

Part 11: Living The Good Life

This bit is all about daily life as a Roman in the Roman Empire. This part includes lots of things that you'll have heard of, like gladiators in the Colosseum, chariot-racing, and roads. But there's loads more besides, and the idea is that this part explains how people in the Roman Empire enjoyed themselves, how they got around, where and how they lived, and the gods they prayed to in the hope that they'd be protected from all the nasty things that nature could throw at them. It's also got a bit about the Roman economy – no, not pie charts and statistics – but the international marketplace the Romans created for themselves.

Part III: The Rise of Rome

Rome was once just one of thousands of nondescript villages in Italy, so it seems almost impossible to understand how just one of them could have become so powerful. Needless to say, it didn't happen overnight. Like many great success stories, the Roman Empire had a very rocky ride to begin with. Not only that, it also started submerged in the misty obscurity of ancient legends. This part takes you from the very earliest beginnings through the succession of wars and struggles that gradually won the Romans control of Italy. Naturally, no-one gets that powerful without others noticing, and this part also discusses the first major international wars, such as the Punic Wars when the Romans beat the Carthaginians. By the end of this part, the Romans are the most powerful people in ancient Europe, poised on the brink of total domination of the Mediterranean.

Part IV: When Romans Ruled the World

Power corrupts – we all know that – and it also breeds a sense of injustice. This part starts off with the massive struggle and crisis of the late Roman Republic when a succession of military leaders like Marius, Pompey, and Julius Caesar jockeyed for power in a conflict that climaxed in a civil war. The outcome was the Roman Empire, when for the first time one man ruled the whole show: Augustus.

Of course, nothing is ever straightforward, and the story takes us through the shenanigans of the Twelve Caesars of the first century AD and the reigns of maniacs like Caligula and Nero, with occasional bouts of sanity under the rule of Vespasian and Titus. Despite the internal problems, this was the time when the power of the Romans extended over more area than ever before. The last bit is the brilliant success of the 'Five Good Emperors' of the second century when the system worked, and it was once said this was the happiest time in human history.

Part V: Throwing the Empire Away

It's tragic, isn't it? Just when human beings start to get something right, they have to ruin it. In a way, it wasn't the Romans' fault. Other people wanted a slice of the action and wanted to invade the Empire. Unfortunately, the Roman Empire was now so big that governing and defending it was almost impossible. So Part V is all about how it started to go horribly wrong. The Romans didn't help, though, because they had a succession of military adventurers, thugs, and lunatics for rulers, most of whom died a violent death after short, turbulent reigns. But in the fourth century emperors like

Dioclectian and Constantine the Great made a good stab at holding everything together. But the other problems, like barbarians rattling at the gates, didn't go away, and the coming of Christianity cut right to the very core of Roman tradition, and changed society forever. So in the end, Rome fell, though what she stood for and what she meant clung on in the Eastern Empire for another thousand years.

Part VI: The Part of Tens

This is the bit of the book where you can find the low-down on ten points in Roman history when things changed. Because that's how it is in history. There might be long-term changes afoot, but things really change when something dramatic happens, like the Battle of Actium in 31 BC. That didn't just change the history of the Roman Empire; it changed the history of the whole world. Next, I've picked out ten unusually interesting Romans whose contribution to their world and ours has marked them out as people to be reckoned with. After them come ten bad Romans because like all villains the baddies are often the most interesting people of their times. I've also chosen ten people who gave the world's first superpower a monumental runaround. These are the anti-Romans. Finally, because I know by this stage in the book you'll be champing at the bit to go and see the Roman Empire for yourself, I've made a list of ten unmissable places that have some of the most sensational remains there are.

Icons Used in This Book

When you flick through this book, you'll notice little icons in the margins. These icons pick out certain key aspects of the Roman world:

This icon marks key decisive events, which helped define the shape of things to come. Sometimes these affected just Rome's future history, but some went on to influence directly the world we live in today.

The Romans lived in the same world we do. This icon marks out events, places or things that have come down to us directly from them.

Movie-makers have often found that the Roman world is a fertile source of great stories for epic films. This icon marks out movie versions of events.

This icon indicates quotes from the Romans, things said in their own words which we can read today.

Occasionally points pop up in the text which are important to bear in mind because of what comes next. This icon marks the most important.

Technical stuff in a Roman context includes things like the staggering dimensions of an amphitheatre, or other remarkable facts, which I've popped in along the way.

Where to Go from Here

There are several different ways you can go with this book. You can start at the beginning and work your way through to the end. Or you could remember that in 1773 Dr Samuel Johnson was asked if he had read a book from cover to cover. He replied, 'No, Sir, do you read books through?' Dr Johnson would be pleased with this book (at least I hope he would have been) because you can read any part you want when you want, and as many times as you want. So if you want to know about the emperor Nero, you can dive right in at Chapter 16, but if it's soldiers you're after then Chapter 5 will set you up, while chariot-racing is lurking in Chapter 8. There's no need to read any chapter you don't want to. And one of the nicest things of all is that you can read about any bit of the Romans you want without having to learn a single Latin verb!

Part I

Romans – The Big Boys of the Ancient World

The 5th Wave   By Rich Tennant

"Oh great–an invitation to another toga party."

In this part . . .

Rome started out as nothing more than a village, but
the Romans and their Empire became one of the
most important – possibly the *most* important – of the
ancient civilisations. The Romans made an enormous contribution to the whole meaning of power, law and order,
and political thought that has affected in some way almost
every country that has existed since. More than that, the
Romans came up with the very letters I'm writing this
down with, and even the whole idea of cities as places
where people live together and expect all kinds of public
services.

They created such a powerful and compelling sense of
identity and protective power that neighbouring villages,
then the rest of Italy, all wanted a share. Although their
society was organised into a hierarchy of social divisions
based on wealth, starting with senators at the top and
going all the way down to the slaves at the bottom, it was
a flexible and mobile system. New people could be
absorbed from all round the Roman world, while others
could move themselves up the social ladder.

The Romans also became powerful because of their intoxicating sense of who they were and what Rome's destiny
meant to them, based on their love of their rural fantasy
past.

And, of course, let's not forget the Roman army. There's
no getting away from the fact that a vital part of Rome's
power was her army and its incredibly systematised way
of working that meant even in defeat, it always came back
for more to wear its enemies down.

Chapter 1

The Romans: Shaping Their World and Ours

*O*ne of the most famous comedy sketches set in the ancient world was dreamed up by the 1970s Monty Python team in their movie *The Life of Brian* (1979). Set in ancient Judaea, a remote province of the Roman Empire, Reg, leader of the rebellious anti-Roman Peoples' Front of Judaea, is holding a morale-boosting meeting. He announces in a careworn and cynical voice, 'What have the Romans ever done for us?' His fellow rebels nod in agreement and then one after another of them pipes up:

- ✔ Aqueducts
- ✔ Sanitation
- ✔ Roads
- ✔ Irrigation
- ✔ Education
- ✔ Medicine
- ✔ Public order

Before long, the list is as long as your arm and Reg is forced to redraft his opening gambit by asking, 'Apart from law and order, water, roads (etc) what have the Romans ever done for us?' Silence follows until a wag adds 'Peace'.

Of course, that's a laugh and it's far too simple just to say 'oh the Romans were brilliant because they brought nice things like running water, sanitation, and nice roads'. But Reg's rebels did have a sort of point. The Romans, despite the fact that their Empire could also be brutal and oppressive, contributed a great deal to the world. Their influence was so profound, in fact, that it continued long after the Romans and their Empire had vanished. You can see evidence of this influence even today.

This chapter gives you a quick overview of who the Romans were and what they did. It also answers Reg's question, 'What have the Romans ever done for us?' from a twentieth-century perspective.

Being Roman

The key thing about the Romans is that you didn't have to come from Rome to be one. Of course, the original Romans did, but over time their Empire became made of conquered peoples who were awarded Roman status and privileges and who often fought to get them. People in the Roman Empire saw themselves as Roman, while they proudly maintained their own national and ethnic heritages. It was rather like people in the United States being proudly American and also proudly Native American, Polish, German, or Mexican, and so on. But it was the Roman bit that held them all together, just as it's the American bit that keeps the USA together now.

You can find out more information about what it meant to be Roman in the remainder of this part and in Part II.

The Roman national identity

With the Romans, it was all about image. The Romans maintained a fantasy that they were all no more than country villagers and farmers; simple hardy folk whose rural origins had given them the steely discipline and strength to win an Empire. This Empire, they believed, was their reward from the gods for being such a worthy people (for more about the gods, see Chapter 9).

This myth is true, to a point. In Rome's earliest days, around 1000 BC, it was just one of the many little villages – which were nothing more sophisticated than a collection of thatched cottages – dotted around Latium, a region in central Italy on the west coast.

Yet despite its modest origins, Rome became the biggest city in the whole of Europe and the Mediterranean area. At its climax, Rome had well over a million inhabitants. (To put this in perspective, consider that most other cities of the time would have had a struggle to find 10,000 people to call their own.) More important than its size, however, was its meaning: Rome wasn't just a place to live – it was a concept, a state of mind, as explained in more detail in Chapter 6.

The Romans never lost sight of their origins. Even though those origins were really long-lost in the mists of time, they saw themselves as peasant farmers and were constantly fantasising about returning to their roots (see Chapter 4 for more on this).

The Roman myth of destiny

The Romans very definitely believed that not only were they superior to everyone else, but that they had a preordained destiny to rule the world. They set the rules and the others had to play by them. Those who went along with this arrangement were welcome to join in. And the truth is that quite a lot of people did. All over the Roman world men and women happily called themselves Roman Spaniards, Roman Africans, Roman Gauls, and so on. This only reinforced the Romans' belief in their destiny.

The Romans believed their superior virtues had won them all this power and were very upset that all the wealth had brought decadence and corruption and lousy, violent sexual perverts for emperors and aristocrats (like Nero – see Chapter 16). This corruption of the Roman ideal flew right in the face of everything the Roman world was supposed to be: honest, law-abiding, self-disciplined. But it didn't dent the myth one bit. It only made them all the more determined.

The Golden Age

In Roman myth, Jupiter's father was the god Saturn. Romans believed that Saturn had taught the ancient peoples of Latium, whom he ruled over, how to farm. He also instructed them in liberal arts. Saturn was popular and his reign gentle, and this mythical age was called 'The Saturnian kingdoms', which is the Roman equivalent of 'The Golden Age'. That's what the Romans believed in – their Golden Age as farmers. One of the Romans' most famous poets, Virgil, popped this into one of his most well-known poems, called the *Fourth Eclogue*, an allegory about the rule of Augustus (see Chapter 16). In his poem, Virgil said 'The Saturnian kingdoms are back'. In other words, 'The Golden Age is back'. Blatant propaganda, but it sounds good.

Other ancient civilisations

Roman civilisation lasted from about 753 BC up to AD 476 in the West. That's pretty remarkable when you think about it, but where do the Romans fit into world history? After all, the Romans didn't exist in some sort of historical isolation. Although the Romans thought they were the be-all and end-all, there *were* other civilisations about. So here's a potted look at the ancient civilisations who existed before, during, and after the time of the Romans.

✔ **Egypt:** By the time the Romans got up and running, the Egyptian civilisation had been going for nearly 5,000 years. By around 2700 BC, what you and I think of as ancient Egypt really got going – that's about 2,000 years before Rome was founded. During this period, the pyramids, built by the pharaohs, first started to appear. By about 1550 BC, Egypt had the astonishing pharaoh Akhenaten, and Tutankhamun, whose tomb is for sure the most famous ancient burial ever found. This period, called the New Kingdom, was the age of the Valley of the Kings, the great temple at Karnak, and other massive monuments like Abu Simbel, built by Ramesses II, the most famous of all pharaohs. But Egypt was already past her peak: Divided by rival dynasties, Egypt was invaded, first by the Assyrians, then by the Persians, and finally by Alexander the Great who established a Macedonian dynasty of pharaohs, whose last ruler, Cleopatra VII, had affairs with Julius Caesar and Mark Antony. Antony's defeat at Actium in 31 BC brought ancient Egypt to an end and the longest-established of all civilisations ever became just another Roman province.

✔ **Mesopotamia:** Mesopotamia is the land between the rivers Tigris and Euphrates in what is now modern Iraq. The Sumerians (3500–2300 BC), who wielded their power from the cities of Ur, Eridu, and Uruk, had palaces and built temples on the top of towers called *ziggurats*. By 3000 BC, they had made a vast stride that set them apart from the hundreds of thousands of years of human development: They invented writing. After the Sumerians came the Akkadians (2300–2150 BC), who were highly skilled in bronze sculpture. But Mesopotamian civilisation came to a climax with the Assyrians (1400–600 BC), whose kings commissioned magnificent relief sculptures. Then came the Babylonians (625–538 BC), whose most famous ruler is Nebuchadnezzar II, who built the Hanging Gardens of Babylon.

✔ **The Phoenicians and Carthaginians:** Phoenicia was where the coast of Lebanon and Syria is today, at the eastern end of the Mediterranean. The Phoenicians were brilliant seafarers, which incidentally the Romans never were, and one story is that they might even have sailed right round the coast of Africa. Major traders, the Phoenicians shipped their products, which included cloth, dye, and timber, everywhere they could and set up colonies all round the Mediterranean, including Spain, Malta, and Sicily. The most important Phoenician settlement was Carthage, which became Rome's most deadly rival. Founded by the ninth century BC in what is now modern Tunisia on the north coast of Africa, Carthage's wealth and influence spread north into Sicily and Italy, providing the biggest threat Roman expansion faced. It took the three Punic Wars to wipe out Carthage, finally destroyed in 146 BC, leaving the way open to the Romans to take total control of the Mediterranean. (See Chapter 12 for information on the Punic Wars.)

✔ **The Greeks:** Greece, called Achaea in ancient times, was always the story of city-states dotted about the mainland and the various islands across the Aegean Sea. The first phase of Greek civilisation is called Minoan, after Minos, the mythical king of the island of Crete who lived at Knossos. Minoan civilisation started around 3000 BC and lasted till about 1400 BC when a natural disaster seems to have seriously damaged many settlements. Meanwhile, in Greece itself, famous strongholds like Mycenae and Tiryns had developed. On the north-west coast of Turkey was Ilium, or Troy. Somewhere around the time Minoan civilisation collapsed, the famous Trojan War took place, but no-one really knows how much of the story is myth or true. All we do know is that by 800 BC Homer's poems, the *Iliad* and the *Odyssey,* had been composed. They set the pace for Greek literature, while Greek art was being developed, too. During this time, the Greek city states like Athens and Sparta developed. By the fifth century BC, Athens had reached its climax with the development of a sophisticated democracy and political theory in the age of Pericles. Greek colonies were dotted all round the Mediterranean, including southern Italy and Sicily. But the Greek city-states were forever fighting with one another. Athens and Sparta brought each other to virtual ruin in the Peloponnesian War. Weakened, Greece was easy prey first for Philip II of Macedon (357–338 BC) and then the Romans in 146 BC (see Chapter 12). But Greek art, culture, literature, and sport remained immensely popular in the days of the Roman Empire. Today, the Greeks are still heralded as the fathers of modern democracy and civilisation.

✔ **The Etruscans:** The Etruscans lived in what is now Tuscany and Umbria in Italy. Most of what is known about them comes from the excavation of their magnificent painted tombs and the grave goods, which were designed to make the afterlife as much like home life as possible. They were particularly good sailors and traders, but to this day scholars know little about them because their language still cannot be read properly. It was thanks to the Etruscans that Rome got off to a good start. The Etruscans built Rome's first walls, its temple to Jupiter, and also the great sewer called the Cloaca Maxima. Some of Rome's first kings were Etruscans too, including the last one, Tarquinius Superbus (more on him in Chapter 10).

✔ **Macedonians and Alexander the Great:** Ancient Macedonia was just a small mountainous area of northern Greece and part of what is now Bulgaria. In 338 BC, the Macedonian king, Philip II, took control of Greece, setting the pace for things to come. In 336 BC he was succeeded by his son Alexander, who proceed to conquer a vast swathe of territory across the area of modern Turkey, Iraq, and Iran by defeating the Persian Empire and reached as far as the Indus valley on the fringes of India. He then seized Egypt and made one of his generals, called Ptolemy, pharaoh. Alexander died in 323 BC from a fever in Babylon at the height of his powers. But his empire was built totally around his own personality and with him gone it fell apart quickly, with his various generals ruling different parts of it. Along with the rest of Greece, Macedonia fell to Rome in 146 BC (see Chapter 12), with Egypt and Asia Minor following afterwards.

Roman history, blow by blow

Rome's early life was more about internal social struggles, beginning with the kings. With the kings gone, the Republic was created, and Rome gradually accumulated local allies in her bid to ensure her own security. As Rome's power grew, these allies came to want to share the same social privileges the Romans enjoyed. As she grew in power and prestige, Rome increasingly came into contact with international rivals like Carthage. A seemingly endless series of wars followed, which were far from conclusive, yet Rome prevailed simply because she constantly came back for more and ultimately wore down her opponents. By the first century BC, Rome was the most powerful state in the Mediterranean. (You can read the details about this early period in Rome's history in Part III.)

Rome then started falling apart because immensely powerful generals used their armies to pursue their own political ambitions. Decades of political chaos followed until Octavian brought the wars to an end and took over supreme power. He 'restored the Republic', so he said, but he really created himself as emperor – a spin most accepted in return for peace. Ruling as Augustus, the stability he brought made Rome even more powerful. By the early second century AD, Rome under the emperors was at her zenith, controlling the whole Mediterranean area, north-west Europe, central Europe, North Africa, Egypt, and the Middle East. (This period of Roman history is covered in Part IV.)

In the third and fourth centuries AD, with barbarians battering down the frontiers, it became impossible for one emperor to control it all. So by the fourth century, it was usually the case that at least two, and sometimes more, emperors ruled different parts of the Roman Empire. The basis of the division was between the East and the West. The Eastern Empire managed to survive until 1453 but it was a mere shadow of its former self. The Western half had really ceased to exist by the mid-400s, a thousand years earlier. (To find out about the events that led to the eventual fall of Rome, go to Part V.)

After the end of the Roman Empire in the West, Europe fragmented into numerous little kingdoms, principalities, and duchies. Imagine the United States falling apart and the governor of each state becoming the head of a local dynastic monarchy. To make things worse, each king had to constantly fight for his kingdom against rivals. Borders were always changing, and the threat of invasion was never far away. In England, for example, King Alfred of the Saxons in Wessex (AD 871–899) had to fight back the Viking invaders. In medieval Italy, even cities fought one another.

Today, what was once the Roman Empire is now dozens of independent countries. It's quite remarkable to think that an area once ruled by Roman emperors even to this day is broken up into so many parts. Only with the coming of the European Union have many European countries started co-operating again.

Discovering the Romans

You might very well wonder why anyone would need to discover the Romans, what with their ruined buildings all over the place and one medieval king after another falling all over himself trying to copy the Romans. Well, one of the reasons is the Dark Ages, when a lot of what Rome was all about was forgotten. Apart from a few exceptions, books and libraries were destroyed, and buildings fell down.

When the Renaissance came during the fifteenth century, European thinkers started to rediscover the classical world: They rediscovered Greek and Roman teachings, and printing made Greek and Roman books more widely available. Inspired by what they found, Renaissance men became interested in new forms of art, ancient books on politics and philosophy, and the whole idea of learning for learning's sake.

Even though the ancient Empire fell, it left behind ruins and literature that made the people throughout the ages – including our own – marvel at what the Romans had been able to accomplish.

Great ruins and ruined cities

All over the Roman world, great cities fell into ruin, but those ruins were so enormous that people wondered at them. In far-off Britain, a poem was written about the tumbled-down ruins of the great temple of Sulis Minerva and baths complex at Bath. The poet called the ruins the work of 'giants' because he, like most of his contemporaries in the Dark Ages, couldn't imagine who else apart from a giant could possibly have built anything like that.

Many of the mighty cities of North Africa like El Djem in what is now Tunisia were left to decay in peace. Even today they have massive ruins. El Djem has its vast Roman amphitheatre. Orange, in southern France, has a Roman theatre and an aqueduct. Athens has a vast Roman temple of Zeus and a library built by the emperor Hadrian (AD 117–138), who passed this way on his travels (see Chapter 17). Baalbek in the Lebanon has two colossal temples, and one of them – the temple of Bacchus – is still practically intact.

Rome itself remained home to some of the most enormous ruins: The Colosseum, the city's biggest amphitheatre, is still largely in one piece (see Chapter 8); the ruins of the imperial palaces still cluster across the Palatine Hill, and the baths of Caracalla look like a giant's cave complex. The Aurelian walls of Rome, built in the 270s (see Chapter 19 for information on the emperor Aurelian), still surround most of Rome.

The survival of Roman books

Roman writers were all hugely influential in different ways, but it's thanks to the survival of their texts that we know what we do about the Roman world. Consider these examples:

- ✔ **Cicero (Marcus Tullius Cicero) (106–43 BC):** Cicero was a great orator, lawyer, and statesman. Well aware of his importance, he published his speeches, treatises on government *(De Re Publica),* duty *(De Officiis),* the nature of gods *(De Deorum Natura),* and also a vast collection of his private correspondence. A great deal survives and he had a huge influence on thought and literature in early modern times.

- ✔ **Caesar (Gaius Julius Caesar) (100–44 BC):** Caesar wrote his own account of his war in Gaul *(Bellum Gallicum),* and also part of his civil war with Pompey *(Bellum Civile).* The texts are famous for sounding objective (though they aren't at all), and for their spare, terse style, but are exceptional historical resources for the time. To find out more about Julius Caesar, go to Chapter 14.

- ✔ **Catullus (Gaius Valerius Catullus) (84–54 BC):** Catullus was a young man when he died, and his passionate poetry of a new type for the age reflects that in his choice of subjects, particularly his interest in wine, life, and women. Catullus's poems are filled with his frustrations at his relationship with Lesbia, a married woman (probably Clodia Metelli) who was believed to have murdered her husband and was denounced by Cicero as a scandalous prostitute, a woman beyond his capacity to cope with.

- ✔ **Virgil (Publius Vergilius Maro) (70–19 BC):** Virgil was the great state propaganda poet of the Augustan age. His most famous poem is the *Aeneid (Aeneis),* modelled on Greek Homeric epic poems like the *Odyssey,* which trace the adventures of Aeneas, the legendary founder of Rome, and include prophecies about the coming of Augustus. His other surviving works, the *Eclogues (Eclogae)* and the *Georgics (Georgica),* were designed to reinforce the Roman fantasy about their rural origins by creating an image of a world of primeval rural bliss. The *Fourth Eclogue* included a description of a messianic coming, which was, in fact, written to anticipate Augustus's dynasty, but which early Christians spotted as a possible prophecy of the coming of Christ.

- ✔ **Horace (Quintus Horatius Flaccus) (65–8 BC):** The son of an ex-slave (a freedman; see Chapter 2 for information on social classes) and a friend of the poet Virgil, Horace used his writing to support the Emperor Augustus. After Virgil's death, Horace replaced him as the poetic voice of the state. Horace's works include the *Satires (Saturae* – works of social criticism), the *Odes (Carmina* – poems about state events and everyday things), and the *Secular Song (Carmen Seculare* – which celebrated the Secular Games of 17 BC).

- ✔ **Livy (Titus Livius) (59 BC–AD 17):** Livy wrote a vast history of Rome from its foundation *(Ab Urbe Condita).* The work took most of his adult life, and unfortunately only about a quarter has survived. Although his history relied in part on myth and legend in its early parts, Livy's an invaluable source for Rome's struggle against Carthage and other aspects of early Roman history.

✔ **Ovid (Publius Ovidius Naso) (43 BC–AD 17):** Ovid's *Metamorphoses* is one of the most popular poems to survive from antiquity. A compendium of Greek and Roman myths, it tells the whole complicated story of which god did what and when and to whom, all in one place. Ovid was also a scoundrel who loved telling good stories about picking up girls in the circus.

✔ **Pliny the Elder (Gaius Plinius Secundus) (AD 23–79):** Pliny the Elder's vast *Natural History (Historia Naturalis)* is the Roman world's equivalent to a modern one-stop encyclopedia of Everything You Ever Wanted To Know Plus A Whole Lot More. Pliny was an equestrian, the second grade of Roman top society (see Chapter 2), and served in the army. A relentless and tireless enthusiast for knowledge, Pliny described everything from geography to gemstones, and medicine to monuments. Curiosity killed the cat – Pliny was asphyxiated taking a close-up look at the eruption of Vesuvius in AD 79.

✔ **Pliny the Younger (Gaius Plinius Secundus) (c. AD 61–113):** Pliny the Younger was Pliny the Elder's nephew who got promoted to senatorial status. Pliny the Younger's chief value to us is as a letter-writer. Many of his letters survive, covering all sorts of fascinating aspects of life at the top in the early second century. Pliny provides an eyewitness account of the eruption of Vesuvius in AD 79, a complete description of his villa, and numerous other priceless anecdotes. The letters he exchanged with the emperor Trajan (AD 98–117 – see Chapter 17 for his reign) are the most important record of the management of a Roman province to have survived.

✔ **Suetonius (Gaius Suetonius Tranquillus) (c. AD69–120+):** Suetonius wrote several works, but the only one to survive in full is an all-time classic of antiquity: the *Twelve Caesars,* which is a series of potted biographies of Julius Caesar (who wasn't an emperor) and then the first 11 emperors who came next, up to AD 96. Packed with scandal, intrigue, downright salacious gossip, and priceless historical detail, the *Twelve Caesars* is still a racy read and a not-to-be-missed chance to find out about some of the most extraordinary men in human history.

✔ **Tacitus (Cornelius Tacitus) (c. AD 55–117):** Tacitus wrote two major works: the *Annals (Annales),* and the *Histories (Historiae),* as well as an account of the German tribes *(Germania)* and a biography of his father-in-law *(Agricola).* The *Annals* covers the period AD 14–68, which is the reigns of Tiberius, Claudius, Caligula, and Nero. Most of the work survives. The *Histories* pick up where the *Annals* left off, but only the first section exists today. Tacitus was a genius of a historian who provides an unparalleled account of the first century AD. He was undoubtedly biased, but his terse style is a model of economy and his work is filled with damning and magnificent observations.

> ✔ **Cassius Dio, or Dio Cassius (Cassius Dio Cocceianus) (*c.* AD 150–235):**
> Dio was a senator in Rome but came from Nicaea in Asia Minor (Turkey).
> He wrote a history in Greek of Rome that started with Aeneas and the
> Trojan War. Sadly only a chunk from the middle survives, covering the
> period 68 BC–AD 47. Some of the rest is made good by summaries writ-
> ten by later authors. But it's still vitally important.

The reason we know about any Roman authors at all is because people
copied their works. The people we have most of all to thank for that are the
monks in the monasteries of the Middle Ages. Thanks to their work, scholars
ever since have been able to analyse some of the greatest Roman literature,
poetry, philosophy, and history. Unfortunately, a huge amount has been lost
and of what there is, it's sometimes obvious that the copyists made mistakes.
Who wouldn't? Imagine spending your day in a freezing monastery copying
out thousands of lines of a Roman epic poem!

Although various copies of the same text turn up in different monasteries,
they usually all go back to just one manuscript that survived antiquity. Here's
a for-instance. The Roman poet Catullus is well-known today. But his entire
life's work survived in just one copy that was in Verona in Italy in the early
fourteenth century. Within a few decades it was lost – forever. Fortunately,
two copies were made before that date. If they hadn't been, we'd know nothing about Catullus today apart from one or two other fragments.

Bringing the Romans home: Roman artifacts

Part of the whole Renaissance experience was exploring the remains of the
ancient world as part of a broader cultural education. The Grand Tour, the
name given to the practice of sending out wealthy young men to explore
Europe and its sights, reached its climax in the eighteenth century. A Tour
could last a few months or even several years. Funded by his nobleman
father or a wealthy patron, a young man toured the capitals of Europe, but
the ultimate object of the exercise was always to reach Italy and see the
ancient ruins of Rome. Here the young men would have been instructed to
buy manuscripts, books, paintings, and antiquities to ship home to decorate
their fathers' stately homes.

Some of the Grand Tour men became wildly enthusiastic collectors and today
Europe's great houses and museums are packed with the results of the
buying. The collections stimulated interest at home and helped encourage
growing tourism into the nineteenth century.

Charlemagne and the monks

The Holy Roman Emperor Charlemagne (AD 742–814) did a lot to get the ball rolling at Aix-la-Chapelle (Aachen) where he had his palace. This became the centre of what is known as the Carolingian Renaissance. Charlemagne also encouraged the copying of ancient Roman books in his library at Aachen. The copies his men made survived long enough to be copied again by monks centuries afterwards, until printing arrived in Europe and changed everything forever. Under Charlemagne's rule, a new sort of handwriting called 'Carolingian minuscule' was developed to make copying easier. That's the basis of modern English handwritten characters today.

Roman excavations: The Pompeii sensation

On 24 August AD 79, Mount Vesuvius, near Naples, erupted catastrophically. Many settlements around the volcano were buried by falling pumice or drowned by a surge of pyroclastic mud filled with ash, rock, and pumice. The two most famous places destroyed were the towns of Pompeii and Herculaneum. Yet many of the towns' buildings, complete with their contents and in some cases even their inhabitants, were preserved pretty much as they were on the day that Vesuvius erupted. Scavengers recovered what they could, but the towns and villas in the area were simply abandoned and forgotten about.

Centuries later, in 1594, Pompeii was rediscovered when work to divert a river near Pompeii uncovered some inscriptions; unfortunately nothing was done. It wasn't until 1748 that excavation began and has continued on and off ever since.

Pompeii caused a sensation amongst scholars, collectors, and wealthy men with an interest in the ancient world. The Emperor of Austria declared in 1769 that 3,000 men should be employed to clear Pompeii of its pumice covering. Once much of the town had been cleared, people could at last walk from room to room in an original house and admire the mythological and fantasy architectural scenes painted on the walls. They could walk from the house down a Roman street and visit the amphitheatre.

Pompeii stimulated other men to look for Roman remains in their own countries. In England Samuel Lysons (1763–1819) excavated the remains of a Roman villa at Bignor and published the colourful mosaic floors in a magnificent hand-painted volume. The designs influenced decorations in the houses of the rich and famous.

The Portland Vase

The Portland Vase is just one example of many great art treasures from the Roman world. Made of blue glass and decorated with white cameo classical figures, it's believed to have been made at the end of the first century BC and survived largely intact. By 1601, it was in the collection of a church cardinal. Then an Italian family acquired it. In 1778 it was bought by Sir Alexander Hamilton, a great collector of antiquities, but he sold it to the family of the Dukes of Portland two years later. They lent it to the potter Josiah Wedgwood, and it provided the direct stimulus for a style of fine pottery that has been made by Wedgwood ever since. Unfortunately, it was broken badly in 1845 but has been repaired and is now in the British Museum.

Actually, some people believe the Portland Vase was made in the Renaissance but it's impossible to prove. It doesn't matter anyway. The point is, it was thought to be Roman and was very influential on art and design in the eighteenth century, like many other Roman artefacts at the time like sculpture, coins, jewellery, and ceramics.

What happened to the Herculaneum ruins? In the early eighteenth century, deep tunnelling near the town uncovered the perfectly preserved theatre. The tunnellers ransacked the theatre for its statues, keeping no record of exactly where they found them. They also hacked tunnels through some houses, badly damaging walls as they went. Modern excavations have opened up a small part of the town, and exposed some spectacularly well-preserved buildings. But the rest, along with the theatre, remains deeply buried to this day.

What the Romans Did for Us

Whenever we think of the Romans, we tend to think of men in togas and sometimes with a crown made of laurel wreaths. That's not at all inappropriate. On the whole, that's how Roman emperors posed on their coins and on their statues. But there was far more to the Roman image of power, and it was so successful an image it's been echoing down the ages ever since.

Yet probably the main reason the Romans had such an impact on themselves and everyone else wasn't just because they had the most efficient army. It had much more to do with language, the rule of law, and the whole concept of thinking about government and what it meant. These have all had a dramatic effect on the world since the Romans. Of course, they weren't completely original – actually, some people think that the Romans had scarcely an original thought in their heads – but they were extremely good at taking all sorts of ideas from elsewhere and putting them into practice. And in the end, it was the practice that counted.

The Roman image of power

It's as if the Romans had created the template for power: If you want to be a ruler, you have to pose as a Roman. That was the Roman genius – getting people to want to be Roman – and it worked just as well centuries after their time as it did in their own. As a result, there's a relentless parade of later European rulers who wanted to be Holy Roman Emperors, or who dressed up like an original Roman emperor for paintings and statues.

Charlemagne, the Holy Roman Emperor

Ever since the Roman Empire collapsed in the West European, rulers have often gone out of their way to model themselves on Roman emperors. The first great exponent of this was Charlemagne (AD 742–814), who became King of the Franks in what is now France in 768. He actively tried to recreate the Roman Empire by conquering parts of Italy, some of Spain, and even added Hungarian territory to his domains. Charlemagne actually tried to pretend that ever since Rome had fallen to barbarians in the year 410, the post of Roman emperor had simply been vacant and now it had passed down to him, the next in line. So he had himself crowned Holy Roman Emperor in Rome by the pope in 800.

After Charlemagne's death his kingdom was divided up amongst his three sons, so his Empire fell apart almost as soon as it had started. In 962 Pope John XII made Otto I, King of Germany (AD 936–973), a new Holy Roman Emperor even though his territory was outside the old Roman Empire. The revived Holy Roman Empire staggered on until the reign of Francis II (1792–1806).

Napoleon

Francis II gave up his title when Napoleon conquered most of Germany. Napoleon Bonaparte (1769–1821) was crowned Emperor of the French in 1804, at the climax of a military and administrative career that had gone from success to success. In paintings and on medals, Napoleon was shown as if he was a Roman emperor, complete with the laurel wreath.

The Fascists

The Nazis, under Hitler, got some of their ideas about image of empire from the Romans, while Italy's fascist dictator Benito Mussolini (1883–1945) was determined to revive Rome's ancient power. He had the ancient Forum in Rome excavated and other important sites exposed to public display as part of his propaganda campaign.

The German and Russian words for their emperors, *Kaiser* and *Czar/Tsar,* both come from the Roman word *Caesar,* the family name of the first emperors (see Chapter 16).

The Victorians

During the nineteenth century, Great Britain controlled one of the largest empires the world has ever seen. Britain's dominions included Canada, Australia, New Zealand, and South Africa. The climax of the British Empire was under Queen Victoria (reigned 1837–1901), and the Victorians looked back to the days of the Roman Empire not only as their inspiration, but also as an outright justification of using force to seize territory and then impose what they believed were superior values and customs.

That's pretty much what the Romans did. Just as the Romans left Latin behind them and all the infrastructure of their world like roads and public buildings, so the Victorians littered the Empire with railways, government buildings, and the English language. Today India has long been independent from Britain, but the language of government there is still English and the nation is dependent on the railways originally laid out by the British.

The USA today

The British Empire is long gone. These days, we often hear the term 'the American Empire' because in the twenty-first century, the United States of America is the most powerful nation on Earth. Actually, it's an Empire like no other, because the USA does not seek to conquer other territories and keep a hold on them. If that's the case, then why am I banging on about the American Empire having anything to do with the Roman Empire? Well, if you look at any piece of American coinage you'll see this phrase and this word:

> *E Pluribus Unum (Liberty)*

E Pluribus Unum is a motto of the United States. It's Latin for 'One out of many' and that means there's one nation made out of the many states (or people). So the United States uses the ancient language of the Romans to express its central identity. Liberty is the main aspiration of the constitution of the United States. And that comes from the Roman Empire, too, where Libertas was a goddess used on coins by Roman emperors to show off that that's what they were protecting.

The reason the United States has symbols of the Roman world is not because the United States want to be the Roman Empire of today, but simply because the Romans set the template for the image of power. And the ultimate symbol is the eagle, used by the Romans on their standards, and today the eagle sits proudly in the middle of the Great Seal of the United States of America, together with the motto *E Pluribus Unum* clamped in its beak.

The European Union

Much of Europe is today organised into the European Union. Unlike the Roman Empire, the European Union is dedicated to the peaceful development of Europe's political, commercial, and social interests. But the Roman Empire was the first time Europe was governed as a single entity. So that's why, when the European Union was first created, the treaty was not only signed in 1957 in Rome but also on the very Capitoline hill itself, the spiritual centre of the Roman Empire.

Language

If you've read up to this point in the book, you've taken it for granted that you could do so. If you dropped in here right at this point, you're taking it for granted that you can read this section. Whichever you did, you've been using Roman letters. You've also been using some words that have their origins in the Latin language.

Alphabet soup

Latin comes from the ancient name for the part of the Italy where Rome lies: Latium. The earliest Latin inscription dates to around the end of the seventh century BC. The Etruscans, whose civilisation came before the rise of Rome (see the sidebar 'Other ancient civilisations'), had their own alphabet but very little is known about their language. However, it's very clear that the Latin-speaking peoples used some of the Etruscan letters and letters from Greek, to create their own alphabet, which went like this:

A B C D E F G H I K L M N O P Q R S T V X Z

And of course that's pretty much the same alphabet we use today. Latin doesn't have the letters *J, W,* or *Y.* The Romans used *I* to represent sounds we'd use *I* or *J* for, and they used *V* to represent sounds we'd use either *U* or *V* for. Otherwise, it's basically the same. Of course, we now use all sorts of different fonts for these letters, but the basic design hasn't altered.

Official languages

When the Romans conquered their Empire, they found people speaking a vast array of languages and local dialects. You can't run an empire with everyone speaking different words. That's why the British ruled their Empire by using English as the official language, and that's why English is the official language of the United States. So the Romans imposed Latin as the language of government across the Empire. Although everyone continued using local languages, in the West, Latin became everyone's second language, and in the East, Greek was used. What this all means is that the whole Roman Empire was managed with just two main languages: Latin and Greek.

Any self-respecting educated Roman would have been able to use both. Imagine if you set off on a journey from New York or London today to explore all the countries round the Mediterranean and all you needed was English and, say, Spanish. But today you'd need English, Spanish, Italian, Arabic, Turkish, and plenty of others.

Spreading a language like that had a colossal impact on local languages, and that's where you can see the effect of the Romans to this day. The so-called 'Romance' languages like French, Italian, and Spanish, owe a huge amount to the Latin of the Romans. English originally grew out of the Germanic languages, but when the early English-speaking peoples advanced south and west, they adopted Latin words which have ended up in English today. The other way Latin has found its way into English is when a new word is needed and Latin terms are used to make a new one.

Law 'n' order

The Romans had a fully-fledged legal system. They had laws, judges, lawyers, courts, and punishments. Men were tried, with the case being put for the prosecution and the case for the defence. Laws were not only written down, but the Romans also kept a record of case law which means when a law was tested before a court. It all went back to the Law of the Twelve Tables in 449 BC which first set out written law, though all it actually did was modify existing customary laws which weren't written down (see Chapter 10 for information about the Twelve Tables). This type of law is called civil law, and it has had a huge influence on European law.

In about 300 BC, Gnaeus Flavius is supposed to have published legal formulae for the first time. Until then, only priests knew them and had jealously guarded them as secrets. Gnaeus Flavius wasn't the only man who actively treated the law as something to be written about and analysed. Quintus Mutius Scaevola produced a textbook of Roman law which later lawyers made great use of. Men like these established the Roman tradition of seeing the law and its practice as a formal profession in its own right.

Over the next ten odd centuries, all sorts of new laws were passed and it became increasingly complicated. The Western Empire finally collapsed in AD 476, but the Eastern half of the Empire carried on and in AD 530 the Emperor Justinian I (527–565) had the whole lot codified into a single book of law (see Chapter 21 for information on Justinian's reign).

Justinian's book is called the *Codex Iuris Civilis,* or the *Book of Civil Law.* It became the basis of civil law throughout most of Europe right up until the end of the eighteenth century. These are some of the divisions of law it contained:

✔ **Citizen law:** Common laws that applied to Roman citizens

✔ **Law of Nations:** Common laws applied to foreigners in their dealings with Roman citizens

✔ **Private law:** Laws to protect private individuals

✔ **Public law:** Laws to protect the state

✔ **Singular law:** Laws covering special provisions for people in special circumstances that differ from normal situations

✔ **Unwritten laws:** Laws that had become customary over time

✔ **Written laws:** Laws made by the decisions of magistrates, the emperor's declarations, and the Senate's decisions

Civil law isn't the same as common law. In England the law is based on common law, which has been made along the way by countless decisions in courts. These decisions were made on three criteria: custom, precedent, and tradition.

Even so, English law has been influenced by Roman law, and so has law in Scotland, which is based on both common and civil law. In the United States, law also has a mixed tradition and it varies from state to state. Louisiana, for example, has laws based on the Roman civil law tradition and so does Canada. So while nowhere today has a legal system exclusively based on Roman law, almost everywhere has been affected by it to some degree.

Philosophy

This probably looks like a rather heavy, deep, and meaningful section. Well, I suppose it is, but plenty of people treat philosophy, and how it should affect the way we live and govern ourselves, as seriously today as the Romans did. The Romans took a lot of their ideas from the Greeks, and it wasn't really until the first century BC that Roman philosophy really started to get written down.

Roman philosophy came in two popular flavours: Epicureanism and Stoicism.

Epicureanism

The Epicureans were devoted to the idea of sensual pleasure with the ultimate aim being complete peace of mind. They took their name from a Greek philosopher called Epicurus (341–270 BC). It was generally believed that the Epicureans were all out for indulging in bodily pleasures, when in reality they were much more interested in pleasing their souls. Physical indulgences were favoured because they stopped the soul from being pained by denial. Epicureans also believed that matter was made up of indestructible atoms moving about in a void, controlled by natural forces: Change comes about when atoms are rearranged.

Lucretius (99–55 BC) is the most famous Roman Epicurean. He put his ideas about the soul, sensation, and thought, as well as the universe and its workings, into his massive poem called *de Rerum Natura* ('On the Nature of Things'), which has survived. Lucretius influenced many later philosophers such as Pierre Gassendi (1592–1655), a Frenchman. Gassendi accepted Lucretius's ideas about the atomic basis of matter and believed this should form the foundations of scientific research. But he also believed this should be compatible with Christianity. Much more recently the English philosopher Alfred North Whitehead (1861–1947) followed the same principles of trying to associate facts found in physics into a philosophical structure – which was pretty much exactly what Lucretius had started to do 2,000 years earlier.

Stoicism

Stoicism was much more popular than Epicureanism, and it was all about accepting things as they are – which was right up the Romans' street as there was nothing they admired more than manly virtues (which they called *virtus*) and being tough even in the worst possible circumstances. Stoics believed that only things that have a physical presence actually exist. The Stoics left a valuable legacy in their construction of a system of morality based on pure reasoning. They also anticipated the way in which the mind is thought to work today because they believed that the body and the mind must obey the laws of physics like everything else, and that, therefore, the state of mind was the result of that.

Marcus Aurelius (AD 161–80) was a Stoic Roman Emperor. He, like other Stoics, was dedicated to accepting life the way it is and responding to difficulties with self-sufficiency. Marcus Aurelius composed 12 books of Meditations, all of which have survived. Here's one of his thoughts, which gives you a good idea of his mindset:

'Consider yourself to be dead, and to have completed your life up to the present; and live the remaining time allowed you according to nature. Love only what happens to you and is spun with the thread of your destiny. For what is more suitable?'

The idea of city

Many of us today live in cities, far more than in ancient times. The Romans really established the idea, not just of a city as a place to live, but also as a place that was a centre of government with public services, security, and identity. For sure, cities had existed before the days of the Roman Empire, but on nothing like the same scale, nor were they anything like so widespread.

The very basis of the whole Roman world was the city. Where the Romans found cities, especially in places like Greece, Asia Minor (Turkey), and North Africa, they adapted them into Roman cities. In the West, they often had to build cities and link them into the infrastructure of the rest of the Roman world. Roman cities, while individually unique, were all modelled on a similar idea of what a city should be. So anyone travelling around the Roman world had a fairly good idea of what to expect wherever he or she went.

Norman architecture

The Normans, from Normandy in northern France, became the most powerful force in western Europe in the eleventh century. They understood what power was all about. Although they had nothing like the resources of the Roman Empire, they did what they could to copy the power of Roman architecture by using arches and vaults to create their castles and cathedrals. The style is called Romanesque for obvious reasons, and it heralded the great age of medieval architecture that followed.

Although the styles of cathedrals changed over later centuries, many have their origins in the massive and heavy Norman arches of the original structures. Sometimes the churches and cathedrals were built out of Roman masonry that was still lying around. Take a look at St Albans Abbey church in England if you ever get a chance. It's built out of Roman brick and tiles taken by the monks from the ruined Roman city just down the hill. At the other end of the Roman world, the Roman Christian churches in Constantinople (now Istanbul) provided a template for the later mosque builders, who were amazed at the vast church of Santa Sophia built by the sixth-century Emperor, Justinian I (AD 527–565).

Many of the major cities of Europe today are a direct legacy of the Roman Empire. Consider London, capital of the United Kingdom, for example. It must be the most remarkable of all. London sits on the river Thames in England, but until the Romans came in AD 43, there was no London at all, or any kind of settlement apart from scattered farmsteads. The Romans spotted the potential of the river and an ad hoc trading settlement sprang up around a bridgehead that they built. Within a few generations, London had grown into the biggest Roman city with the biggest public buildings north of the Alps. Although it fell into disrepair when the Romans left, by the Middle Ages it was well on the way to being one of the largest cities in all of Europe.

The Roman influence on cities goes beyond Europe. Take a look at the great buildings of Washington DC, the US capital. When Pierre L'Enfant (1754–1825) produced his plans for the city in 1791, he got some of his inspiration from the classic Roman model of a street grid system. The Supreme Court (1928) uses the architectural model of a great Roman temple. Washington's Capitol (begun 1793) uses Roman types of architecture throughout, and, of course, most of the other state capitols are modelled on Washington's. Designed by Daniel Burnham, Washington DC's Union Station (opened 1907) owes its main design to the Baths of Diocletian (built AD 298–306) and its entrance to the Arch of Constantine (built 315), both in Rome.

A Long Time Ago but Not That Far Away

The Roman Empire in the West started to fall apart permanently about 1,600 years ago. In the broader history of the world, which runs into billions of years, that's no more than a pipsqueak of time. So it's not really that surprising that the Romans have had such a substantial effect on the world we live in today because they weren't very long ago.

There have been plenty of other influences along the way, and, of course, we do things the Romans could never have imagined. It's also true that there isn't a single person around today who can reliably trace his or her family tree all the way back to the Romans. But that's just because it's too long for the records to have survived.

The truth is that lots of us, millions and millions of us, have the genes of people who lived in the world of the Romans. And if you plucked a Roman out of his world and brought him to ours in a time machine, yes sure, he'd be amazed by our technology and how many of us there are. But once our Roman had settled down, he'd recognise huge amounts of his world in ours, right from the streets we drive down to the law courts where lawyers battle it out, and even to the lettering on our buildings and books. So if the Romans ever seemed irrelevant, they shouldn't do so now, wherever you live in the world today.

Chapter 2

It's the Cash That Counts: Roman Social Classes

In This Chapter

▶ How Roman society was divided up

▶ Tensions between nobles and the mob

▶ Slaves and freedmen

▶ Women and children in the Roman pecking order

*R*oman society was ultimately based on wealth – and how much you had of it – and what family you'd been born into. At rock bottom were those with nothing: the men and women who didn't even own themselves. They were the slaves, the engines that drove the Roman world, often treated like a disposable resource constantly replenished through conquest. Above them came the freed slaves (freedmen), then freeborn Roman citizens, and at the top was the two-tiered aristocracy of equestrians and senators.

This chapter explains how Roman society was divided up, and what qualified a man to be at any level within the structure. It's absolutely fundamental to understanding how Roman society worked. Another key to understanding Roman society is to remember that this was primarily a man's world. It was men who did the voting and who held the jobs. But it's important to bear in mind that these traditions grew out of the old days of the Republic. In the days of the Empire, society gradually started changing and by the fourth century many of the old ways and distinctions had fallen into decline.

First Things First: The Roman Family

The core component of Roman society was the family *(familia)*. The Roman family was a private and public affair. In both respects, total loyalty from members was expected and given, though more than a few of the emperors set an appalling example – the emperor Caracalla murdered his brother Geta to make sure he had sole power (see Chapter 18).

A Roman *familia* was much more than a married couple and their children. It was the whole extended family, overseen by the senior male, the *pater familias* ('master of the household' – he had to be a Roman citizen), even if members were living in different houses. It also included a man's adopted sons, who were treated legally as blood members of the family. The senior male had total power over all the members of his family *(patria potestas)*, which means he made all the decisions over what happened to any one of them, including marriage and punishments, and also acted as family priest. He controlled and even legally owned all their property, and also had the power to sell his son into slavery or kill him. The family was *sub manu*, 'under his hand'. The familia also included the slaves of the household, and any freedmen, too, and were linked to other families by marriage into clans called *gentes* (singular *gens*). The clan leaders became the most important controlling members of the state (more on this in the section 'Being on Top – Upper-crust Romans').

Romans were sticklers for tradition, and tradition meant unswerving loyalty to one's family and respect for precedent and authority. Roman society was *paternalistic,* based on the principle of the head male in a family, known as pater familias.

That word *pater* is the basis of many Latin terms related to families, land, inheritances, and the state, and therefore also the word patrician:

- ✔ *Patrimonium:* An inheritance
- ✔ *Patria:* One's native land (or fatherland)
- ✔ *Patriarch:* Tribal chief
- ✔ *Pater Patriae:* 'Father of the Country', a title awarded to Augustus and his successors

---

A family day

Family life was reinforced by the daily routine. Roman days were divided into 12 hours, measured by a sundial. This is how a typical day panned out:

- ✔ **First hour:** light breakfast *(jentaculum)* and pater familias says the morning prayers with the household

- ✔ **Second hour:** Everyone gets about their work and the pater familias greets his clients (see below)

- ✔ **Sixth hour:** Lunch *(prandium)* followed by a siesta *(meridiatio)*

- ✔ **Eighth hour:** Back to work. Affluent men headed for the baths

- ✔ **Ninth hour (mid-afternoon) or later:** The main family meal *(cena)*

Being on Top – Upper-crust Romans

Early Roman society was made up mostly of free citizens, but there was a core group of aristocratic families. The distinction between the general free population and the aristocrats gradually became clearly defined into 'orders' known as the *plebeians* (the majority) and the *patricians* (the aristocrats). There doesn't seem to have been any ethnic basis for the division. Instead, the distinctions came about through wealth founded on land.

The original patrician families became organised into clans *(gentes)* of families tied together through marriage and by owning so much land they ended up controlling Roman society. In Rome's early days, the patricians had total control of all political privilege and all high offices including the priesthood. They achieved this out of a powerful sense of social solidarity. They were absolutely determined to hang on to their power and exclude the rest, the plebs, from sharing in it.

As you can imagine, this was an arrangement that the plebs – especially the wealthier and more educated ones – resented. A political struggle between patricians and plebs, called the Conflict of the Orders, ensued (you can read about this struggle in Chapter 10). Essentially, the plebeians fought to end the patricians' monopoly on political power and all the chief offices of state. One of the most significant changes came in 455 BC when the ban on inter-marriage between plebs and patricians was lifted. In practice what happened was that patrician families accepted marriage with wealthy pleb families because one of the key ways to keep power was to marry money. These wealthy plebs really became indistinguishable from the patricians and had little in common with the rest of the plebs.

Pets

The animal-killing frenzies that went on in the arena (Chapter 8) doesn't mean Romans were totally unsentimental about animals. Some did have pets, or at least working animals that were part of the family household. Dogs and cats were essential for the control of rodents, and dogs were useful guards. There's a fourth-century AD dog tag from Rome inscribed 'Hold me, lest I flee, and return me to my master Viventius on the estate of Callistus'. A doorway mosaic in a house at Pompeii has an inscription reading *Cave Canem,* 'beware of the dog!' A wall-painting from another house at Pompeii shows a terrier-like dog that must have been a household pet. One of the most famous relics from Pompeii is the cast of a dog, tied up and unable to flee his post as the pumice and lava rained down during the eruption of AD 79 (the dog's remains decayed, leaving a void in the packed pumice and ash which was filled with plaster by archaeologists). For a curious use of dogs, see Chapter 9.

The word *plebs* just means everyone else apart from the aristocracy. It started out meaning something like the 'majority' or 'all the rest' but came to mean the 'mob' or 'common rabble', and included everyone except those wealthy plebs who had gained a foothold in Rome's upper class. You can read about them in the section 'Ordinary Citizens'.

The old patrician families struggled for survival as intermarriage and the growing power of the wealthy plebs eroded them. By Augustus's reign (27 BC–AD 14) only about 15 patrician families were left, and by Trajan's (AD 98–117) just six. In Constantine I's time (AD 307–337) the title 'patrician' had come to mean anyone who held high office in the imperial court.

Because the patricians controlled Roman society, the rest of the population became totally dependent on them, working as labourers or tenants on their land. Out of this developed the patron-client relationship:

✔ The patron acted like a father figure to his clients, who were often his freedmen (former slaves): He took a personal interest in their careers, financial concerns, and any legal or business problems.

✔ The client had a duty of loyalty to his patron, which meant helping with money if his patron was in public office or had been fined, for example, or if he was captured in war and held to ransom, and generally offering him support.

Patrons and clients could never appear against one another in a court of law, even as witnesses. Having plenty of clients was a sign of status and especially useful to politically-ambitious nobles.

Nobles (Nobiles)

By the third century BC, the mixture of old patrician families and wealthy plebs had become the new aristocracy *(nobiles)* of rich landowners – the only respectable source of wealth for a Roman aristocrat. The nobles took no part in trade or anything commercial (at least directly). Simply because they were wealthy, they fulfilled the property qualification to enter the Senate (one million sesterces by the time of Augustus) and serve in the magistracies as aediles, praetors, and so on, because all these positions were unpaid and were regarded as a public honour *(honor)*. Noble families were regarded as those who had had consuls amongst their number and who expected later generations to follow in those footsteps, serving in the magistracies of the *cursus honorum* ('the succession of honours'), the career ladder for up-and-coming Roman politicians and statesmen. So although plebs had won the right to stand for office, in practice those without a substantial income couldn't consider it. (To find out about political positions, go to Chapter 3.)

The Toga

The toga was a piece of clothing unique to the Romans. A toga was a woollen sheet made in the form of a rather stretched semicircle around 6 metres wide. It was worn by free-born Roman males as a mark of distinction. But an incredible piece of irony is that the only women who wore togas were prostitutes, making it a badge of shame for them. A toga was worn over the left shoulder with the rest gathered up into folds around the back and then hung over the left arm. It was only suitable for special occasions because it was completely useless for any sort of action or physical effort and had become almost redundant when Augustus revived it as part of restoring Roman traditions. Domitian (AD 81–96) said anyone attending the games had to wear togas. There were several different types:

✔ *Toga virilis* or *toga pura:* Plain off-white toga worn by adult male citizens

✔ *Toga praetexta:* Off-white toga with a broad purple border, worn by magistrates of aedile or senior status (see **cursus honorum** in Chapter 3), and also by free-born boys until they were old enough to wear the *toga virilis*

✔ *Toga candida:* A specially whitened toga worn by nobles standing for magistracies to suggest their purity

✔ *Toga picta:* Purple toga decorated with gold thread worn during victory parades by generals, and by emperors on special occasions

✔ *Toga pulla:* A dark toga for mourning

In theory, the whole citizen body could vote for the magistrates. In the real world, though, the only people who could vote were those who were in Rome at the time. What's more, the powerful noble families used their influence over their clients, as well as bribery and other means, to make sure the magistracies only went to their own. The result was that office became as good as hereditary because the key families manipulated elections to make sure the positions were handed down from generation to generation.

Nobles wore tunics with a broad vertical purple border *(laticlavius)* on either side, and togas, a traditional piece of Roman clothing (see the sidebar on 'The Toga'), with a broad purple border. Some nobles clung to the habit of wearing an iron finger ring, as an ancient symbol of simpler times.

The nobiles families possessed the right of *ius imaginum. Ius* means 'law' or 'right'. Certain high offices allowed the holder the right to sit in public in a special chair inlaid with ivory called the *Sella Curulis.* Descendants of such men were allowed to make figures with wax faces of their ancestors *(imagines)* and display them in the public rooms of the family house for all to see. The more such figures a noble family had, the greater its esteem and dignity. Men who came from families without the ius imaginum, but had managed to obtain high office, were called 'new men' *(novi homines)* and were treated with great hostility (see Chapter 7 for the experience of Marius as a new man).

Equestrians (Equites)

Equestrians went back to the days of the kings when Roman society was divided into classes according to ability to pay for military service (see Chapter 3). The top class was made up of men who could afford to field a horse and were known as the equestrians (*equites* from *equus*, 'a horse').

Over the years, as Rome's wealth grew, there were far more men with the necessary qualification to be equestrians than were needed for war, especially as Rome came to rely on allies and provincials to do the bulk of the fighting. The equestrians became more and more involved with commerce, from which the senatorial *nobiles* were excluded. By the days of the Second Punic War (218–202 BC), government contractors were supplying the Roman army, and these must have been equestrians. After the War, anyone who had the property qualification of 400,000 sesterces was counted an equestrian. These included some municipal aristocracies in Italian cities with Roman citizen status as well as the businessmen 'financier equestrians' in Rome. In the late Republic, equestrians formed an important rival political force to the senators, especially in Rome after 122 BC, when Gaius Gracchus brought in a law that said judges in jury trials had to be equestrians.

By the first century BC, equestrians were becoming recognised in their own right *(ordo equester)*, and were united as a single order in the year AD 22 under the emperor Tiberius. There was no longer any connection with military service. To mark their status and distinguish them from nobles, equestrians wore a gold finger ring and their tunics had a narrow vertical purple stripe *(angusti-clavius)* on either side. Equestrians could be promoted to senatorial status en masse to bump up the Senate's numbers or as individuals.

By the days of the Empire, equestrians were used to fill lots of administrative posts, such as the financial affairs of provinces, or the governorship of lesser provinces. The most famous equestrian of all is Pontius Pilate, who became governor of Judaea. You can find more about the important role equestrians played in Roman society in Chapter 3.

Ordinary Citizens

The world of senators and equestrians was very different from the one spent by the ordinary citizens in the Roman world, who fell into various types: Roman citizens, Latin citizens, and the rest (apart from slaves). These people passed their time working desperately hard to earn a living. As they were practically ignored by historians of the time, we only know about them from their tombstone inscriptions, graffiti, and archaeological remains.

These tell us that the Roman world was heaving with all sorts of service industries like clothes dyers and launderers, teachers, civil servants, and money collectors and lenders. There were manufacturers of clothing and shoes and repairers, artisans who made metal tools, implements, architectural fittings, and furniture. There were also builders, plasterers, sculptors, carpenters, and brick-makers. Food was supplied by shippers and traders, cooks, bakers, restaurant owners, fishmongers, butchers, and farmers. Some jobs were done by both slaves and freedmen.

These people led hard, short, and dangerous lives in a world where protective health and safety legislation were non-existent. But it was also these people that the nobles entertained in the circus and amphitheatre, and were fed with the corn and oil dole. The nobles might have looked down on the Roman mob, but they knew they could not do without them.

Roman citizens

Although some of the plebs had grown wealthy and joined the ranks of the aristocracy whether as senators or equestrians, the vast majority of the Roman population were just ordinary citizens.

The important thing about being a Roman citizen was that each man had the right to vote *(suffragium)* and also had duties *(munera)* to the state, which meant paying taxes and military service (women had none of these rights or duties). People power came through the *Concilium Plebis Tributum* (Council of Plebeians arranged by tribes) and its officials: the tribunes and their assistant aediles (more about this and other assemblies in Chapter 3). A man could lose his citizenship under certain conditions, for example, if he deserted the army, mutilated himself so he could not serve, or dodged a census to evade taxation.

Roman citizens were immune from summary arrest and imprisonment. In the city of Philippi in the mid-first century AD, the future St Paul was sentenced to a flogging after having been at the centre of a riot. Paul asked the man about to whip him, 'Is it lawful for you to scourge a man that is a Roman citizen and not condemned?' The commanding officer told Paul his own citizenship had cost him a great deal of money. Paul retorted, 'I was free-born', and was promptly released.

Tribal membership

It wasn't until the time of Servius Tullius (579–535 BC) and his census (see Chapter 10) that the Roman people were divided into 30 tribes, with one tribe per region. Servius Tullius did this because, until that date, the plebs were just a confused mass of people, which made them difficult to govern. Four of the new tribal regions were in Rome (the *Tribus Urbanae*) and the other 26 (originally 16) were in the countryside around Rome *(Tribus Rusticae)*. Landowners were allocated to the tribe of the region where their land was. People without land were allocated to one of the city tribes.

What's in a name?

Roman citizens had a triple name, the *tria nomina* made up of:

- ✔ *praenomen* (forename)
- ✔ *nomen* (name of clan)
- ✔ *cognomen* (family surname)

Some had an *agnomen* (additional surname), too. So, Publius Cornelius Scipio Africanus was a member of the Cornelii clan, of the Scipio family, with the forename Publius. His additional name Africanus helped distinguish him from other family members with the same names.

As Rome's territory increased, more tribes were added until, by 241 BC, there were 35. Despite a short-lived plan in 90–89 BC to add 10 more, 35 was all there ever were. So any new citizens, wherever they lived in the Roman Empire, were allocated to one of the existing tribes, but, of course, unless they were close enough to Rome to vote, the privilege wasn't much use.

Universal citizenship

In the early days of Rome, to be a citizen, you had to be the child of a Roman father and mother, or of a Roman parent married to someone from an approved place. Later on, citizenship could also be held by:

- ✔ The adopted children of such men
- ✔ Those who bought citizenship or earned it through membership of a city or an auxiliary army unit privileged with a grant of citizenship
- ✔ Those who had been honourably discharged from an auxiliary unit of the Roman army after serving for 25 years
- ✔ Those granted citizenship by petition to the emperor

Being a Roman citizen was a jealously guarded privilege, at least until AD 212 when the emperor Caracalla issued his famous *Constitutio Antoniniana* which made all freeborn men of the Empire into Roman citizens (see Chapter 19).

Latin citizens

Latin rights were originally dreamed up as a sort of halfway house for some of Rome's allies in Italy during the third century BC. Men from these towns were called Latin citizens and were allowed to conduct law suits in Roman courts on the same terms *(commercium)* as a Roman citizen. If they moved to Rome, they became Roman citizens. A Latin woman could marry a Roman citizen and her sons would become Roman citizens *(conubium)*.

Towns instituted with similar rights were called *municipia* with a legal status called *civitas sine suffragio* ('community without the vote'). These towns had to provide troops. After 89 BC, they got the right to vote and *municipium* came to mean any self-governing Italian town except colonies. Outside Italy, municipia with Latin rights came first, and later Roman citizen rights were created as special privileges.

To discourage people from moving en masse to Rome, a law of 150 BC made magistrates of these towns into Roman citizens. It was a handy way of easing provincials into becoming Roman citizens. In 89 BC, Transpadane Gauls were made into Latins, with full citizenship following in 49 BC. Obviously after AD 212 and the edict of universal citizenship, the distinction between Roman and Latin citizens ceased to exist.

Everyone else: Provincials

Because people moved fairly freely around the Roman Empire until Diocletian's time (AD 284–305), even in the remotest areas, a traveller would find Roman citizens in the form of soldiers and administrators, Latin citizens in the army or trading, and local citizens. These non-Roman and non-Latin citizens were known as *peregrinae* ('foreigners'), and had to fulfil all the local responsibilities of their own communities. Peregrinae had no civil rights under Roman law unless they were represented by a citizen *patronus,* couldn't exercise any political function in Roman assemblies or magistracies, and were banned from wearing togas in case they tried to enter a Roman assembly.

Any such man could be granted Roman citizenship, after the reign of Augustus, though such men still had to take care of their own local responsibilities. Sometimes units of provincial soldiers in the Roman army (see Chapter 5) were rewarded with Roman citizenship en masse for acts of valour. Normally such soldiers had to wait until their term of service was up to be made citizens.

Trading insults

There was a strict protocol in Roman society about insults. Vespasian (AD 69–79) ordered that no-one should insult a senator with foul language, but if a senator insulted an equestrian, then the victim was perfectly entitled to insult the senator back the same way. In other words, any citizen could respond to an insult from another citizen in the same way, regardless of whether they held different status.

Are You Being Served?

Slavery was endemic in the Roman world, as it was throughout antiquity. As Rome grew more powerful, the numbers of slaves increased, and Roman society became increasingly dependent on them. The slave revolt of 73–71 BC, led by Spartacus (see Chapter 14) and which had nearly devastated southern Italy, preyed on Roman minds. The Senate once considered forcing slaves to wear distinctive dress until someone pointed out that then the slaves would realise how many of them there were. But if slaves made up a huge part of the population, so also did the freedmen – ex-slaves freed by their masters.

Slaves

Anyone conquered by the Romans was liable to be enslaved, and so were rebellious provincials. Their children were automatically slaves. There were other sources of slaves, like people convicted of capital crimes.

Tiberius Sempronius Gracchus (c. 210–150 BC), the Roman commander in Spain 180–179 BC (see Chapter 14), crushed a rebellion in Sardinia in 177 BC. He captured so many slaves there that the Roman slave market was flooded with cheap Sardinian captives. *Sardi venales,* 'Sardinians for sale', was the cry, and it became an everyday Latin expression for any commodity available in abundance and cheap as a result – a bit like our 'Made in China'!

A slave's life

Slaves could have desperately hard lives, like those sent to work in the mines or on large agricultural estates, but educated slaves owned by rich masters often lived better than poor free people. Slave marriages existed but had no legality so either partner could be sold if his or her master decided. Female slaves were liable to be sexually abused by their masters or overseers, but they also could be freed and married by their former owners (see the sidebar 'Regina the freedwoman', later in this chapter, for just such an example). Punishments were arbitrary and down to the master or mistress's whims. Slaves were expensive to buy, clothe, and feed and that could encourage meaner masters to scrimp.

Slaves in the household of a wealthy man could have a relatively pleasant life, especially if they came from parts of the Roman world thought civilised, like Greece. Pliny the Younger mentions walking and talking with educated slaves of his. Many of his slaves might have been born in the household and were treated as part of the home.

One of the reasons for better treatment was that the smarter members of the free population realised abusing slaves was likely to backfire. Largius Macedo was a praetor around the beginning of the second century AD, but his father

was a freedman. As was so often the case with men who came from lowly origins, Largius Macedo went over the top to show how upper class he was and
treated his own slaves cruelly. So one day, while he was bathing at his villa,
some of his slaves attacked and beat him and left him for dead. Other faithful
slaves revived their master and a hunt went out for those who had escaped.
Most were recaptured and punished, but Macedo died a few days later.

Slave rights

Slaves also had some rights, which were steadily increased in the days of the
emperors. It became illegal to kill a slave or get rid of a slave simply because
he or she was ill. There were strict laws against castrating slaves or abusing
their bodies in other ways. Antoninus Pius (138–161 AD) even made it possible to prosecute the murderer of a slave.

In Egypt in the year AD 182, during the days of Marcus Aurelius, an 8-year-old
slave boy called Epaphroditus rushed up to the roof of his master Plution's
house to watch a procession of dancers go by. He fell off in the excitement
and was killed. He might only have been a slave boy, but the papyrus document that records the disaster also records how his master's father-in-law
Leonidas made arrangements for the boy's proper burial.

Slaves, wherever they lived, had no freedom. One of the ironies of the way
Roman society evolved into the Dominate established by Diocletian at the
beginning of the fourth century (refer to Chapter 20), is that many ordinary
citizens found themselves effectively enslaved to their jobs and homes with
no right to move away or change profession.

Freedmen

Slaves in the Roman world, unlike most other slave-owning societies from
ancient to early modern times, could always hope they might one day be
freed. There were millions of freedmen and women in the Roman Empire,
found in all provinces at all times and in all walks of life. As free people, they
were entitled to the privileges of citizenship and some rose to positions of
high status. The emperor Claudius notoriously relied on freedmen to run the
Empire for him (flick to Chapter 16 for more on this).

Freeing a slave

A slave could be freed by his master in the master's will (the most usual) or
as a gift during his master's lifetime, which meant going before a magistrate
who touched the slave with a rod after his master had given him a pretend
slap as a symbol of his last punishment as a slave. Slaves could even save up
money from casual earnings or gifts and purchase their own freedom, but
that usually meant negotiating a deal with their master to compensate him
for the original purchase price.

The technical term for freeing a slave is *manumission,* which comes from two Latin words: *manus* ('hand') and *emittere* ('to let go').

Even though he was now free, a freedman had a duty of obligation to his former master and that meant becoming his client and remaining tied to him in that mutually-advantageous relationship. In fact, the new client might even carry on in his old job. Refer to the earlier section 'Being on Top – Upper-crust Romans' for details of the patron-client relationship.

The advantage to the old master is pretty clear: He no longer had to feed and clothe his former slave, who now had to deal with all that for himself. An ex-slave could vote on his old master's behalf, too. If a court case blew up, then his ex-slave could now serve as a witness on his behalf. The disincentive was the tax levied on freeing each slave at 5 per cent of his or her value.

Freedmen usually took their former master's name. A centurion of the XX legion called Marcus Aufudius Maximus visited the shrine and spa centre of Bath in Britain where two of his personal freedmen, Marcus Aufidius Lemnus and Aufidius Eutuches, set up dedications on their former master's behalf as he was now their patron and they his loyal clients.

Stigma

Freedmen could never become equestrians or reach senatorial rank; they suffered the social stigma of having been slaves, and were looked down on as coarse and vulgar. But it wasn't a prejudice many Romans could afford to have because so many people were descended from slaves at some point in their ancestries, even a few emperors. The emperor Pertinax (AD 193), for example, was the son of a freedman called Helvius Successus who had made his money in the timber trade; you can read more about Pertinax in Chapter 18.

The most average freedmen could hope for was to serve in the administration of their city or on the imperial service, or become modest businessmen like merchants. If successful enough, a freedman could afford to become a member of the *seviri Augustales* ('the board of six priests in the cult of Augustus'), which was monopolised by freedmen. As Pertinax's example shows, unlike their fathers, the *sons* of freedmen could rise as high as any man from a free family, without any obligations to their father's old masters.

Regina the freedwoman

Regina (Latin for 'queen') was a slave girl from the British tribe called the Catuvellauni. She was owned by a Syrian called Barates who fell in love with her, freed her, and moved her with him to South Shields on the northern frontier in Britain. Sadly she died when only 30, in the early years of the third century AD. Barates invested in a magnificently carved tombstone to his beloved wife, which has survived. You can see it in the museum there today.

Women and Children Last!

Women and children naturally made up the bulk of the population, but in theory, they were totally subject to men. Although women could be citizens, they couldn't vote.

Women

Women could have citizenship status, but they had no formal role in Roman society. Women couldn't serve in any of the capacities men served in as magistrates, politicians, or soldiers. A woman couldn't even be an empress in her own right, though they were used for family alliances, such as when Augustus made his daughter Julia marry Marcellus, then Agrippa, and finally Tiberius (see Chapter 16) in an effort to establish a dynasty through his only descendant. If an emperor left only a daughter, then the succession passed to a male relative or another man altogether.

Women had almost no legal identity other than as a man's daughter, sister, wife, or mother. Vespasian (AD 69–79) passed a law that said any woman who had become involved with a slave man should be treated as a slave herself. Real slave women had even less of an identity, if that's possible to imagine.

Barbarian women didn't think much of Roman women. When Septimius Severus campaigned in Britain in AD 208–211, he made a treaty with the Caledonians from Scotland (refer to Chapter 18). During the negotiations, the empress Julia Domna made fun of the wife of a chieftain called Argentocoxus about how British women slept with lots of different men. Argentocoxus's wife snapped back: 'We fulfil nature's demands in a much better way than you Roman women do because we consort openly with the best men, whereas you let yourself be debauched by the vilest men in secret.'

Education

Women were generally excluded from education, which was biased towards boys. But some girls from good families were taught to read and write and were known as *doctae puellae,* 'educated girls'.

Here's an exceptional case of an educated woman in the public eye. After Caesar's assassination in 44 BC, heavy taxes were imposed by the Second Triumvirate on anyone implicated with the conspirators. A woman called Hortensia (whose father was an orator called Quintus Hortensius) made a speech to the Triumvirs in 42 BC on behalf of the wives of the men affected. It was written down and studied in later years as an example of an outstanding speech and not just because it was by a woman.

Women in the home

In the man's world of the Roman Empire, women were theoretically confined to running the home and having children. The wife of a *pater familias* was known as the *mater famiilias domina* ('mistress mother of the household'), and she was supposed to be entirely subject to her husband and, before him, her father. In general though, Roman society (which means basically men), reserved their admiration for women renowned for their upright moral virtues who were regarded as the guiding force behind teaching their sons the value of honourable behaviour in public and private life. In 215 BC, during the Second Punic War, the *lex Oppia* imposed limits on women's right to own gold, wear elaborate dresses, or ride in fine carriages. It was repealed in 195 BC much to the annoyance of moral diehards like Marcus Porcius Cato (whom you can read about in Chapter 23).

By the first century BC women's rights were improving. Those over the age of 25 could have their own property and divorce their husbands if they chose. Women could also play a more important role in society, though they were still never allowed to take on any official jobs. But women were still primarily seen as wives and mothers. Augustus penalised unmarried women and men (for example, bachelors were prevented from inheriting legacies), but he rewarded those who did marry and had children.

Even so, Roman women could be legally beaten by their husbands. In fact, it was even considered a reasonable way to treat a woman if her husband thought she had misbehaved. As a result, it was not unusual for women to bear scars on their faces from the treatment they had received. One of the most horrible cases was that of Egnatius Mecenius, who beat his wife to death for drinking wine. No-one criticised him, all thinking she had deserved it.

Women's clothing and beauty treatments

Women's clothing, like most Roman clothing, was much simpler than today's:

- Breasts were supported by a strapless band *(strophium)*.

- Instead of panties or briefs a sort of bandage *(feminalia)* was often used instead, though panties very like modern ones have been found.

- A slip *(tunica interior)* was worn over these undergarments.

- On top was a woollen gown *(stola)* tied in round the waist and perhaps a shawl *(palla)*.

Wealthy women could afford silk and a Greek woman called Pamphile invented a way to weave silk so fine that the clothing made women look nude. Bronze (or silver and gold for the rich) brooches, like our safety pins, were used to hold the clothing in place. Shoes were like open leather sandals today, sometimes elaborately decorated with patterned cut-outs. Cosmetic treatments included using ass's milk on the skin or even a jelly made by boiling a bull-calf's bone for 40 days to avoid wrinkles, antimony as an eyebrow make-up, and kaolin as a face-powder.

Women and their children

Roman women had no legal rights over their children. Unwanted children could be *exposed* (abandoned in the open air), which might mean death or enslavement, depending on where the child was found and whether the mother wanted that or not. If her husband died, then the estate passed to the son and a woman could find herself with nothing at all.

Women who kept their children faced all the worry and tragedy of a very high level of infant mortality and all the pressure to produce a healthy son who lived to adulthood and could inherit his father's estate.

Special women

Apart from being confined to special jobs like serving as Vestal Virgins (refer to Chapter 9), the limitations on women didn't affect some in powerful families from having a huge amount of influence on the men around them. Agrippina the Younger, Caligula's sister and Nero's mother, was effectively in total charge until Nero had her murdered (see Chapter 16). Some of the women of the Severan dynasty – Julia Maesa, Julia Soaemias, and Julia Mamaea – were the real power behind the thrones of Elagabalus and Severus Alexander (refer to Chapter 19). Under special circumstances, women from more modest origins could also play an important role in the lives of their communities. Here are some of them:

- **Eumachia of Pompeii** was one of the city's most important business-women in the mid-first century AD; she dedicated a building in Pompeii's forum to the corporation of dyers, weavers, and launderers. Her building was used as a wool market, and Eumachia was able to afford a substantial tomb outside the city gates but no-one knows much about her. She may have been a widow who took over her husband's businesses or she may have been wealthy in her own right.

- **Sempronia** lived around the time of the Catiline Conspiracy of 62 BC (see Chapter 14). A former prostitute, Sempronia was a supporter of Lucius Sergius Catalina. Extremely good-looking and a talented musician and dancer, she had even managed get married and have children. But she was notorious for being as bold as a man in daring and wasn't the slightest concerned about her reputation. She was lustful and would approach men directly, she'd been an accessory to murder, and was constantly in debt due to her extravagant lifestyle. But according to the historian Sallust, she was witty, charming, excellent company, and a talented poet.

- **Volumnia Cytheris** was a freedwoman actress and probable prostitute in the mid-first century BC. A poet called Cornelius Gallus wrote poetry dedicated to her. Her sexual status gave her access to relationships at the top end of Roman power politics and she found time to be Mark Antony's and Brutus's mistresses. Cicero was disgusted by how she moved in such circles. Unfortunately for women like Volumnia, age was their enemy and they could easily lose favour and disappear . . . and that's what happened to her.

Children

Children were immensely important to Roman families, not just as potential heirs or wives to make family alliances but as individuals, too. The tombstones of children show that their loss was mourned just as in all societies. Children had hard lives though, even if they were born into wealthy households. Firm discipline was routine and was thought to toughen them up for adulthood and improve their character.

Upbringing and education

The better off a family, the more likely the children would be handed over to the care of a nurse when small and then male slaves *(paedagogi)* who accompanied the child everywhere: to school, or on outings to public places like the baths and theatre. They were more than just protectors: Nurses and paedagogues had to take care of their charges' moral education, manners, and behaviour.

Education was simply a matter of family wealth, but rich or poor, it was often only boys that had any real chance of a serious education. There was no system of public education in Rome or anywhere else in the Empire, though Vespasian (AD 69–79) was the first emperor to hire teachers of rhetoric at the state's expense in Rome.

Boys from wealthy families could expect the best education, which was designed to prepare them for a career in military and public life so that they could take their place amongst the movers and shakers in the Roman world. That meant grammar, rhetoric, music, astronomy, literature, philosophy, and oratory, rather than subjects we would recognise today, though, of course, reading and writing were an essential foundation.

Educating the enemy

In order to get conquered provincials 'on side', a tried-and-trusted Roman technique was to educate the sons of local rulers at Rome so that they grew up within the Roman system and took Roman ideas and customs home with them. It's just what the British did with their Empire in places like India nearly 2,000 years later. A good example is Juba II who was educated in Rome and made client King of Mauretania in 25 BC (see Chapter 16 for more on client kings) by Augustus. Juba ruled till AD 23 and introduced all sorts of Greek and Roman customs to his part of north-west Africa. It didn't always work. See Chapter 21 for Attila the Hun, who was brought up in the court of the emperor Honorius.

Children's charities

Charity was all-important in a world with no proper social services. Alimenta worked like this: The emperor lent money at low rates of interest to farmers. The farmers paid the interest, which went into a pot to pay for the upkeep of a predetermined number of children. But charity could also be private. Pliny the Younger gave half a million sesterces (equal to the annual pay of 417 legionaries) in his lifetime for the support of girls and boys in Rome. Sometimes wealthy men would leave a capital sum in their wills, so that the interest could be used to take care of poor children. Publius Licinius Papirianus of the city of Cirta in North Africa left 1.5 million sesterces to earn 5 per cent interest annually to pay for the upkeep of 300 boys and 300 girls.

Teaching was conducted in a schoolmaster's house, apartment, or even in a public place, while the rich had their own personal tutors. Basic schooling just involved literary and familiarity with literature, myth, and law. Better schools included more in-depth study as well as a grounding in Greek, while the boys from the top families went on to be taught by a *rhetor* (a teacher of oratory) to prepare them for public life.

Some examples of writing exercises have survived, showing that children could expect to find themselves copying out passages from works by Virgil or other poets, regardless of where they lived in the Roman Empire. Most of the time the students had to listen to their teachers and memorise passages because writing materials were costly. But many children went without, and only perhaps picked up reading and writing in later life if they were lucky. It's clear from archaeological evidence of graffiti and other surviving written evidence that soldiers and veterans were on the whole more literate than most of the rest of the population.

Poor children

Poor children had far fewer opportunities, though under Nerva (AD 96–98) and Trajan (AD 98–117) the imperial system of *alimenta* was introduced to provide funds to educate poor Italian children (see below).

All this presupposes poor kids were even allowed to grow up. Poor families were used to the idea that another unwanted mouth to feed, especially a girl, would be cast out *(exposed)* in the hope that they would die or be picked up by someone else. In the East anyone who found an exposed child could enslave it until Trajan outlawed the practice. Constantine I (AD 307–337) started state assistance to prevent exposure – the Empire simply couldn't afford the loss of any additional labour, though it wasn't actually banned until 374.

Children were liable to be orphaned if their mothers died in childbirth, which meant they had to hope their fathers or other relatives would take them on. The best hope for slave children was being brought up in the household where their parents worked, as nothing stopped them being sold off. Children born with congenital ailments or other serious birth defects had little or no chance of survival.

Chapter 3

Stairway to the Stars: The Greasy Path to Power

In This Chapter

▶ The assemblies that ruled Rome

▶ The emperor's power and succession

▶ Climbing up the Roman career ladder

*T*he Roman Empire was all about power: getting it, keeping it, and exercising it. In the days of the Republic, the whole system was designed with a whole series of checks and balance, such as the various assemblies and always having more than one of any magistrate, to prevent any one man having supreme power. But the Romans realised that under extreme circumstances, a man in sole charge was essential for getting out of serious scrapes, so the office of *dictator* was created. (Keep in mind that the Roman term *dictator* means a magistrate temporarily elected to supreme power in an emergency. It didn't mean what it has come to mean today, thanks to men like Hitler and Mussolini.)

Despite these safeguards, various men like Marius and Sulla showed that a general who had a loyal army at his disposal could toss the Republic's system aside (refer to Chapter 14). Then Julius Caesar was created dictator for life, and the Republic collapsed as a result (see Chapter 15). What emerged was a system in which one man – the emperor – had supreme power within the Republican system.

This chapter explains how Roman power worked: who had it, how it was exercised, and how the emperors took power for themselves. It's also about the whole career structure of the elite in the Roman world: how a man's career in power politics started and where it went.

Roman Assemblies

The Roman people had several assemblies, important at different times and with different powers. They reflected the divisions of Roman society between patricians and plebs (refer to Chapter 2). Some of these assemblies had their origins in advisory bodies under the kings, like the Senate. Once the kings had been expelled, the assemblies became the basis of government. Under the Republic, the plebs challenged the patricians' control in the Senate by creating their own assembly, the *Concilium Plebis Tributum* (described later in this chapter).

Over succeeding centuries, enormous tensions built up between the various bodies, as the plebs' representatives, the tribunes, constantly challenged the aristocrats (which now included wealthy plebs) in the Senate. This tension had a dramatic effect on Roman history, contributing to the collapse of the Republic and leading to rule by one man as an emperor. Under the emperors, the assemblies remained intact but their powers were all vastly reduced.

The Comitia Curiata ('Assembly of the Divisions')

The *Comitia Curiata* was only important in the very early days of Rome. It was an ancient assembly of Roman citizens from the three original patrician tribes (Ramnes, Tities, and Luceres). These tribes were divided into 30 *curiae* ('divisions' – ten per tribe), probably consisting of family groups in *gentes* ('clans', see Chapter 2 for families and their clan groupings). The assembly had few powers, and its main role was to ratify the choice of a king, who had already been ratified by the Senate, and the appointment of magistrates.

The Comitia Centuriata ('Assembly of the Centuries')

The *Comitia Centuriata* was the assembly of the army. The 35 tribes of the Roman people were divided into the equestrians (see Chapter 2) and five classes (*classes* – yep, our word's the same as the Roman one). Classes were organised, according to wealth and subdivided into blocks called centuries (*centuriae*) of 100 men. The centuries served as infantry, with the top class having a full set of armour, a sword, and spear. Each class that followed had less equipment, until you reached the bottom class, which had pretty much nothing at all to offer except an able-bodied man who could turn up for war.

The centuries gathered in their individual classes at the Comitia Centuriata to elect magistrates such as the consuls (see the section, 'A career ladder for senators', later in this chapter). In practice, the two top classes usually voted together and effectively out-voted the rest. This system was created in Rome's early days. By the time of the Empire, the division into tribes still existed, but it was really just a formality.

The Concilium Plebis Tributum ('Council of the Plebeians arranged by Tribes')

In 471 BC during the Conflict of the Orders (refer to Chapter 14 for more on this), the patricians were forced to accept the plebeian assembly now known as the *Concilium Plebis Tributum,* which had its origins in the *Comitia Tributa* ('tribal assembly', a plebeian counterpart to the patrician Comitia Curiata – see the earlier section). The assembly passed laws (known as *plebiscita*), elected representatives called tribunes of the plebs *(tribuni plebis)* and their assistants, the *aediles plebeii* ('plebeian aediles').

Tribunes pop up throughout Parts III and IV of this book, showing how they steadily increased their power so that eventually they could do almost anything they wanted on the pretext that they were protecting the rights of the people.

The power of the tribunes

Tribuni plebis, 'tribune of the people' (first heard of in 494 BC), could convene the Senate, but his main power came from the right to interfere on behalf of a pleb who was being oppressed by a patrician (see the sidebar, 'The tribunes' power of veto'). Because the tribune was the one to decide whether someone was being oppressed, it was a great power: Tribunes could disrupt magistrate elections, stop troops, supply levies, and even suspend Senate business. Tribunes did all these things to wear down the patrician monopoly on power, so that, for example, in 367 BC plebs were admitted to the consulship. In the late Republic, rival factions exploited tribunes and their powers, causing the political chaos of the age, helped by the fact that tribunes were usually treated as sacred and inviolable.

Under Sulla, the power of tribunes was seriously reduced until Crassus and Pompey restored it (see Chapter 14). Caesar used the excuse that the Senate had infringed the tribunes' prerogative to justify his crossing of the Rubicon and marching on Rome in 50 BC.

The tribunes' power of veto

Veto means 'I forbid (this)' in Latin. If a tribune thought a law or a magistrate was against the interests or freedoms of the plebs, he could use his veto because he had the right of interference *(ius intercessionis)*. Strictly speaking there wasn't any law that gave tribunes this power. It came about simply because of the sheer force of the plebs' support for their tribunes and their sworn protection of the tribunes. In other words, the Senate couldn't afford to ignore it. So if a tribune felt inclined to obstruct a measure and use his veto, the Senate had to accept it. While we're on the subject, the tribune's power to defend the common people this way was something Augustus took advantage of when he 'restored' the Republic but, in reality, made himself supreme ruler.

Tribunes under the Empire

From Augustus's time onwards, the tribunes took care to do only what the emperor wanted. Not surprising seeing as the emperors routinely served as one of the tribunes in order to give them rights over legislation and the Senate. Not many men wanted to serve as tribune alongside an emperor, so Augustus had to have a law passed that tribunes be selected by lot from men who had served as quaestors (see the later section, 'Senatorial careers'). Even though it was really no more than just an honorific post, tribunes still existed in the fifth century at Rome and carried on even later at Constantinople.

The aediles

In the beginning, the only job the aediles had was to take care of tablets on which laws passed by the Concilium Plebis and decrees of the Senate had been written. The tablets were stored in the Temple of Ceres *(aedes* means a temple, hence the word *aedile)*, and the plebs were naturally concerned that the patricians would alter the tablets without the aediles around. By the late 400s BC, aediles could arrest people and take care of administration in the city. They also had various responsibilities for using public revenue to pay for public services. See the section 'A career ladder for senators' for what aediles did under the Empire.

The Latin word *plebiscitum* (plural *plebiscita*) is made up of two words: *plebs* and *scitum* ('law' or 'ordinance'). From it, we get our word *plebiscite,* which means a vote by all electors on an important issue, like a change in the Constitution of the United States. It can also mean an expression of opinion by vote, without having the binding force of law.

The Senate

The Senate was manned by the *nobiles* (discussed in Chapter 2), mainly those who had held magistracies in the career ladder. By the reign of Augustus, a senator had to have a personal estate of at least 1 million sesterces (compared to 400,000 sesterces for an equestrian).

Origins of the Senate

The Senate had its origins as a Council of Elders (*senex*, 'an old man'), made up of the head man from each of the leading clans *(gentes)*. They were the men early kings of Rome called on for advice, and they met in the *senaculum*, an open area in the Forum. Roman tradition claimed that Romulus had created a Senate of 100 members and that by the end of Tarquinius Superbus's reign in 509 BC there were 300 senators. It's very unlikely the numbers are true, but it does suggest the Senate gradually grew in size and influence under the kings, even though in those early days it had no actual legal power. A small number of families dominated the Senate, and in the last days of the Republic, this caused a huge amount of tension when rivals started using personal armies or the plebeian assembly to jockey for power.

New recruits

Equestrians (see Chapter 2 for more on these) were the prime source of new recruits to the Senate. Sulla chose 300 equestrians to bump up the Senate's numbers after the Civil War. Caesar allowed Italians and some Gauls to enter the Senate. By 29 BC, the Senate had around 1,000 members, many of whom were former equestrians, and Augustus had to get around 190 of them to withdraw voluntarily. Individual men could seek promotion to the Senate if they could stump up the money. The future emperor Vespasian secured his own promotion that way and made himself eligible for a political career. As emperor, Vespasian promoted others and even gave them the money if they were suitable but short of cash (see Chapter 16 for more on Vespasian). Over the centuries that followed, provincials from almost all over the Empire became members. Britain is one of the places not yet known to have produced a single senator. That could have been deliberate exclusion, or it could be that the province was so poor no-one ever became wealthy enough to qualify.

The powers of the Senate

The Senate had various powers. It could:

- Approve laws passed in the assembly
- Approve treaties
- Appoint governors to provinces
- From 121 BC, declare anyone an enemy of the state and support any magistrate's action against that person: effectively martial law through the power of *Senatus Consultum Ultimum* (see Chapter 14)

A Senatorial resolution (*Senatus Consultum*, abbreviated by the Romans to SC) was not a law, but it came to be as powerful as a law. The emperor generally ruled through Senatorial resolutions. Emperors placed SC on their brass and bronze coins to make it appear the small-change coinage at least was being issued with the Senate's approval. One expression of the identity of the Roman state was *Senatus Populusque Romanus* (SPQR), meaning 'The Senate and the People of Rome'. It's still used by the present-day government of the city of Rome.

The *Curia* (Senate House) in Rome's Forum is one of the most intact Roman buildings to have survived. Built in 29 BC by Augustus, and rebuilt in AD 284 by Diocletian, it could seat about 300.

The Emperors

From the time of Augustus, emperors ruled not because they had been declared supreme rulers and a formal office of 'emperor' created, but because they possessed a unique set of qualifications, titles, and prestige within what was essentially (on paper at least) the old Republican system of magistracies, and which allowed them great power over the assemblies.

The emperor's titles

When Augustus effectively became emperor in 27 BC, he'd arranged things so that the Senate awarded him his powers. This way it didn't appear that he had taken them by force or any other means (see Chapter 16 for the details). All other emperors down to the time of Diocletian's Dominate maintained this fiction, though as time passed it became increasingly obvious that it was a formality.

Some of the titles taken by emperors included the following:

✔ **Augustus:** Octavian was given this name in 27 BC by the Senate. It means 'the Revered One' or 'the One Worthy of Honour'. The month of Sextilius was renamed August, a name, of course, it still bears today. Augustus was really a kind of religious title and conveniently elevated him from just being the former Octavian of the Second Triumvirate. Augustus became a name for any reigning emperor, but if there was a junior emperor the Augustus was the senior partner (see the next bullet).

✔ **Caesar:** This was part of the family name of the Julio-Claudians (all the emperors from Augustus to Nero) and showed their actual (or adoptive, in the case of Tiberius) descent from Julius Caesar's father.

After Nero's suicide in AD 68, the Julio-Claudians had died out, so later emperors took Caesar as part of their names to maintain the fiction of a family succession. But Caesar became a way of indicating an imperial successor – usually a son or adopted son of the Augustus. Under Diocletian and later, it became *nobilissimus Caesar,* 'most noble Caesar'.

IN THEIR WORDS

'Veni, vidi, vici...'

✔ *Imperator:* This means 'Commander (of the army)' and has the same origins as the word *imperium* (see the next bullet), used to describe the military authority endowed on a man by the Senate. Augustus came to use this as part of his name, not as a title. Because he had, effectively, supreme control, it came to mean a broader sense of supreme power which is why it has survived as our word 'emperor'. Later emperors, mainly from Vespasian on, did use imperator as a title.

Emperors greeted the Senate with the words: 'If you and your children are in health, it is well; I and the legions are in health.' The greeting reinforced the emperor's position as the head of the armed forces and maintained the formality of respect to the Senate as the senior and traditional basis of the Roman state.

✔ *Imperium: Imperium* means 'Military Command' and 'Supreme Authority'. A holder of imperium had control of war and the law, and thus he had power over armies. In the remote past, the early kings of Rome had held this title. In later times, it was reserved for dictators and magistrates. In the Republic, the title was awarded to men like Pompey the Great. Consuls and praetors also held imperium (see the section 'A career ladder for senators', later in this chapter). Amongst magistrates, there were degrees of imperium depending on individual seniority. It was normally awarded for a restricted period. The emperors had *imperium maius* 'greater imperium', to mark them at a level above the rest.

✔ **Military titles:** Emperors adopted a variety of military titles to commemorate the wars they had taken part in. These usually named the location, like Parthicus and Dacicus for Trajan's wars in Parthia, and Dacia or Armeniacus for Marcus Aurelius's Armenian war; but the title Germanicus was a more generic military title and went back to the general Germanicus, father of Caligula, who had campaigned so brilliantly in Germany during the reign of Tiberius.

✔ *Pater Patriae:* Augustus was awarded this title in 2 BC. It means 'Father of the Country' and was a sort of religious patriotic term that acknowledged his pre-eminent role in making the Roman world what it was. Many later emperors held the title, too.

✔ *Pontifex Maximus:* This title means 'Chief Priest', a position held for life and usually conferred when an emperor came to power, though Augustus did not receive it till 13 BC (14 years after he became emperor). The holder was in supreme charge of everything to do with Roman religion and ceremony. The closest equivalent today is probably the pope, who even calls himself *Pontifex Maximus.*

> ✔ ***Princeps:*** From the Latin words *primus* and *capio,* which mean literally 'I take first place'. This title went along with another phrase – *Primus Inter Pares,* which means 'First Among Equals'. Being Princeps simply awarded Augustus the premier authority in Rome. Indeed, the sheer force of his personal influence was described as being in possession of *auctoritas* ('authority'), reinforced by the strength of his *dignitas* ('worthiness'). This was transferred to his successors, so today the Roman Empire from the reign of Augustus until the reign of Diocletian is known as the Principate. Naturally the word is the source of our 'prince' and 'principality'.
>
> ✔ ***Dominus Noster:*** This title means 'Our Lord'. From Diocletian's time on (AD 284–305), this title gradually supplanted imperator, and marks the transition to the Dominate.

Multitasking: The emperor's jobs

Augustus and his successors took on a number of Republican magistracies and other jobs, including the position of tribune, consul, and censor. By holding these positions, they could be seen to be working *within* the Republican system, which made their power legal. After all, Augustus's great claim was that he had *restored* the Republic, not wiped it out.

The tribunician power

An emperor's tribunician power was the most important (refer to the earlier section 'Concilium Plebis Tributum' for an explanation of what a tribune is).

Augustus made being tribune the basis of his power: He could pose as defender of the people, with powers over the Senate like being able to convene it and veto anything it did. Having tribunician power also had the value-added extra of making an emperor sacred and inviolable. So in 19 BC, Augustus became tribune for life, but it was awarded annually – just a formality, of course. All his successors did the same.

The consulship

The office of consul was held much more infrequently by the emperors, so it's covered below in the career ladder of men of senatorial rank (see the section 'Climbing to the Top', later in this chapter), along with the key qualities all Roman men of rank needed to have: dignity, authority, and virtue.

Censor

This was an old Republican magistracy. The censor was in charge of public morals and from *c.* 443 BC oversaw censuses of citizens. The position was almost redundant by the end of the Republic, but some emperors like Vespasian (AD 69–79) and his son Domitian (81–96) held it.

The line of succession

Because, in theory, there was no monarchy, there was no system of succession for the emperors. In practice, though, from the time of Augustus onwards, any emperor who could tried to nominate a suitable male heir to assume the various positions and titles he had. Wherever possible, this heir was the emperor's son, but often there wasn't one available.

The hereditary principle

Augustus had no sons or surviving (or suitable) grandsons. If he was going to establish a dynasty (see Chapter 16 for the tortuous line of descent which followed down to Nero), he totally depended on marrying his daughter Julia to a suitable male successor (Marcellus, Agrippa, and finally his stepson Tiberius). But just about all the emperors from Vespasian on maintained the dynastic principle, through the second century mainly by adoption. Thereafter emperors constantly tried to have their biological or adopted sons succeed them until the reign of Diocletian (AD 284–305). If no successor was available, then the best available man for the job would be lined up, assuming someone else hadn't already decided to appoint himself emperor.

Jumping the gun

The Romans amply proved to themselves over and over again how the power of the sword ruled because when an emperor died without a clear successor, there was usually no shortage of would-be emperors with soldiers behind each one. That's how the civil wars of AD 68–69 and 193–197 started, and it's also why the third century saw such a reckless cavalcade of soldier emperors who fought and murdered their way into power before being (usually) murdered themselves (Chapter 19 goes into detail on this period).

But even this gang of cut-throats tried to install their own sons as successors, and they invariably adopted all the titles an emperor was supposed to have. Maximinus I (AD 235–238) was a Thracian peasant who rose through the ranks until he overthrew and killed Severus Alexander (222–235). Maximinus was immediately given the power of a tribune for life, awarded the titles of Augustus, Pontifex Maximus, and Pater Patriae, and served as Consul in the second year of his reign.

The only time the succession was based purely on merit was under Diocletian's Tetrarchy (refer to Chapter 19) where two senior emperors (each an *Augustus*) appointed two junior emperors (each a *Caesar*) who would succeed them, and then appoint their own Caesars and so on. The system soon crumbled when the biological sons of some of the Tetrarchs objected to being cut out. Basically, blood is thicker than water.

Climbing to the Top

Nobles and equestrians had their own career paths to climb. By the days of the Empire, these had become fairly well-defined, being based on status, wealth, and age.

A career ladder for senators

Men from noble families of senatorial rank were expected to follow a career through a succession of magistracies, mostly elected by the assemblies, and generally held for one year each. Once a man had held the first magistracy, he could enter the Senate. The senatorial career ladder was called the *cursus honorum*, 'the succession of honours [magistracies]'.

Theoretically, all the magistracies in a career were elective. In practice, they were often sold by emperors or their associates. Vespasian (AD 69–79), who loved money, sold offices, and under Commodus, the freedman Cleander did a roaring trade (see Chapter 18), but they were far from being the only culprits.

Whatever position a Roman held in the career ladder, he was expected to have several key qualities, which also applied to the emperors. Those were:

- **Authority (*auctoritas*):** The authority to command founded on personal prestige.

- **Dignity (*dignitas*):** This means being a man of honour, trust, and reliability, which meant he was faithful (*fides*) and stuck to his guns and his principles (*constantia*).

- **Manly values (*virtus*):** A Roman man was measured by his excellence, his goodness, and his personal virtue.

The magistracies

In the first and second centuries AD, senators could take on the following roles, usually in this order, as they worked their way up:

- **Quaestors (*Quaestores*):** The most junior magistracy, quaestors took care of public finance and the treasury (*aerarium*), receiving all tax income and taking charge of public expenditure. This post was usually held between the ages of 27 and 30, often after being a military tribune attached to a legion (see Chapter 5 for information on the Roman army). After serving as quaestor, a man on the make might become tribunus plebis (for this exceptional post, see the section 'Roman Assemblies', earlier in this chapter), or aedile. Neither was a compulsory post on the career ladder, and by imperial times, being a tribune was just honorific (see the sidebar on 'Gnaeus Julius Agricola's career').

✔ **Aediles *(Aediles)*:** Aediles had responsibility for the corn dole, streets, public order, water supply, weights, measures, and even aspects of religious practice. Aediles started out as assistants to each of the two tribunes of the plebs, but in 367 BC, they were increased to four and became a normal magistracy. Serving as an aedile wasn't essential for the *cursus honorum,* but it was useful because an aedile could win popularity and earned the right of *ius imaginum* for his family (see Chapter 2 for this prestigious social status).

✔ **Praetor *(Praetores)*:** Praetors were mainly involved with justice. The *praetor urbanus* ('city praetor') dealt with justice in Rome, while a *praetor peregrinus* ('provincial praetor') dealt with cases involving foreigners. Praetors had *imperium* (the power of military command). By the days of the emperors, there were 12 annual praetorships, held by men who were normally at least 30 years old. Men who had served as praetors had earned propraetorian status (see the following section, 'Legionary commanders and provincial governors', for details).

✔ **Consul *(Consules)*:** Consuls were the senior civil and military magistrates and were the heads of state. Like praetors, consuls had imperium, but the position was of much greater prestige. Men who had been consuls ennobled their families and descendants, making them the nobiles. The first two consuls were elected in 509 BC, when the kings were expelled. Election was by the Comitia Centuriata (see the section 'Roman Assemblies' earlier). A consul had to be at least 42 for the first time, and wait ten years for re-election (ignored by Marius, see Chapter 14). But under the emperors, all these restrictions were thrown aside, and it was the emperor who usually recommended the men to be consuls, sometimes standing as one himself annually (Domitian was consul ten times in his 16-year reign). By then, several pairs of consuls were elected annually, instead of just one pair under the Republic. The first two consuls of each year were the senior pair and were called *consules ordinarii.* Later pairs in each year were called *consules suffecti* ('substitute consuls'). By increasing the numbers this way, more qualified men became available for jobs like governing provinces.

All the senatorial posts described in the preceding list really belong to the first and second centuries AD, but had their origins in the Republic. By the third century, things were changing: Equestrians were being increasingly used for jobs senators had once done. By Diocletian's Dominate, the whole system was very different. You can find out the details of that in Chapter 20, where I explain how Diocletian reorganised the Empire.

Legionary commanders and provincial governors

Ex-praetors were eligible for jobs of *propraetorian* status (commanding legions or governing less important provinces), and ex-consuls for those of *proconsular* status (governing the most senior or militarily-demanding provinces). Because emperors had almost invariably served as consuls, they also had proconsular status. The word *pro-* meant that the holder had all the powers and status of a praetor, or a consul, in the new job.

- ✔ *Proconsul:* Governor of a senatorial province, a man who had served as consul (these were the older provinces, mostly around the Mediterranean, such as Greece).

- ✔ *Praefectus urbi:* Prefect of Rome with imperium and in charge of keeping order in Rome; usually held by a senator who had been consul.

- ✔ *Legatus Augusti pro praetore:* Governor of an imperial (the emperor's) province (mostly the frontier provinces like Britain and Germany); could be of proconsular or propraetorian status. The most troublesome provinces like Britain had the senior men, but the job was always rated propraetorian so that the governor did not have technically the same status as the emperor, for whom the governor was serving as his delegate.

- ✔ *Legatus iuridicus* ('judicial legate'): Created by Vespasian to ease the workload on governors by hearing court cases, the judicial legate could hear lawsuits and deal with any legal issues while the governor was tied up with other work like fighting wars.

- ✔ *Legatus legionis:* Commander of a legion; usually a man of propraetorian status.

Gnaeus Julius Agricola's career

Agricola (AD 40–post 97) was the historian Tacitus's father-in-law. Tacitus wrote a biography of Agricola, so we know an exceptional amount about his career (there's no equivalent account for anyone else). Agricola was born in Forum Julii (Fréjus) in the province of Gallia Narbonensis. Both his grandfathers were equestrians and served as Procurators, but his father, Julius Graecinus, was promoted to senator. Everyone's career was unique, but Agricola's gives us a good example of a man at the top of Roman society.

- ✔ Aged 20: A Military Tribune at the Governor's HQ in Britain in *c.* AD 60

- ✔ Aged 23–24: Returned to Rome, got married and became *c.* 63–64 quaestor for the proconsular governor of Asia

- ✔ Aged 24–25: A year off *c.* 64–65

- ✔ Aged 26–27: Tribunus Plebis *c.* 66–67

- ✔ Aged 27–28: Praetor *c.* 67–68

- ✔ Aged 29–30: In Britain again as Propraetorian Legatus Legionis (Commander) of the XX legion by 69–70

- ✔ Aged 33–36: Propraetorian Legatus Augusti (governor) of Gallia Aquitania *c.* 73–76

- ✔ Aged 37: Consul in Rome in 77

- ✔ Aged 37–44: Proconsular Legatus Augusti (governor) of Britain, leading a major war of conquest *c.* late 77–83/4

Following his stint as governor of Britain, Agricola should have become proconsul (governor) of Asia or Africa but for political reasons declined. He held no further office.

The status of these jobs didn't stay fixed forever. During Gallienus's reign (253–268), the command of legions was increasingly given to equestrian prefects, probably experienced soldiers who had risen up through the ranks, and reflecting the needs of the age (Chapter 19).

The equestrian career ladder

Most equestrians spent their lives working as bankers and merchants. But there was a sort of elite equestrian career ladder. This was more flexible than the senatorial ladder and didn't necessarily involve passing through a standardised series of hoops. The big difference from senatorial careers is that these elite equestrians were directly dependent on the emperor for their positions.

An equestrian might progress through the commands of a series of auxiliary army units, starting perhaps with a minor administrative job like deputy manager *(promagister)* of harbour dues, before going to be *praefectus* ('prefect', a person placed in command) of an infantry unit, and rising to command a cavalry unit before being promoted to command an arm of the Roman fleet. Next he might be made *procurator* of a province, managing its financial affairs (to prevent the governor having too much control). Another equestrian could serve in a variety of civilian procuratorships, managing imperial estates or other interests (see Chapter 4 for imperial estates and Chapter 7 for mines). By the second century, these various jobs were all rated according to a pay scale based on how important the job was.

A highly successful equestrian could rise to become any one, or in succession, all of these top jobs:

- **Praefectus aegypti:** The governor of the province of Egypt, the emperor's personal possession (usually held by a former *praefectus annonae*).

- **Praefectus annonae:** Responsible for managing the grain supply to Rome and the handouts to the mob.

- **Praefectus civitatium:** An equestrian governor of a province.

  The most famous equestrian governor today is Pontius Pilate. Pilate was an equestrian prefect who governed Judaea between AD 26–36 in the time of Christ's crucifixion. Judaea was one of several small but very annoying provinces (others were Raetia and Noricum) to which the emperor allocated equestrian governors.

- **Praefectus praetorio:** Responsible for commanding the garrison of Rome.

- **Praefectus vehiculum:** In charge of Rome's roads.

- **Praefectus vigilum:** Commander of Rome's fire brigade.

Vespasian's equestrian sponges

It was said that Vespasian (AD 69–79) used to appoint the most rapacious men to the most lucrative equestrian posts so that if he condemned them later on, he could confiscate more cash. They were called his sponges because he soaked them in money when dry and then squeezed them when they were wet.

The reason these were equestrian posts was so that the emperor could keep these immensely powerful offices out of the hands of the senatorial nobiles. Not all prefects were equestrian though, and things did change. The *praefectus urbi,* effectively the mayor of Rome, was a senatorial post. Under Severus Alexander (discussed in Chapter 19), the post of praetorian prefect became senatorial, too. Conversely, command of legions went to equestrian prefects under Commodus (Chapter 18) and Gallienus (Chapter 19), instead of senators.

Because the ranks of the equestrians were used from the late Republic on to provide new recruits to the Senate, it's no surprise that many senators and even emperors, such as Agricola and Vespasian respectively, had equestrian ancestors. By Commodus's reign, some legionary commanders were equestrians, and the process carried on thereafter. The emperor Macrinus (AD 217–218) was still an equestrian when he made himself Emperor, which was unprecedented and did him no favours (see Chapter 19 for more on Macrinus). The division of Roman aristocratic society into senators and equestrians lasted until the reign of Constantine (Chapter 20), by which time the distinction had ceased to have any practical relevance.

Chapter 4

Rural Bliss – Roman Dreamland

. . . .

In This Chapter

▶ The Roman love of the countryside

▶ Roman textbooks on how to be farmers

▶ What villas meant to the Romans

▶ How the rest of the Empire picked up the villa habit

. . . .

*A*ll across the Roman world, from remote parts of Gaul to the Rhine frontier, North Africa, and by the Black Sea, untold millions of farmers and peasants toiled for their whole lives on the land, producing the vast quantities of produce that were transported to Rome to feed the mob and the populations of the Empire's cities. But to the Romans, agriculture was more than a business enterprise. Despite the fact that Roman power and identity were tied up in Rome the city, the Romans always felt that living in and off the countryside was the only means to find inner peace. Even when they couldn't be in the countryside, they adorned the walls of their townhouses with mythical pastoral scenes. The works of Roman poets and writers include literary descriptions of rustic topics, which were seen as patriotic symbols of Roman austerity, restraint, and hard work: the very qualities that had turned Rome into a powerful city with a vast Empire. Even conquered provincials started buying into the same fantasy. In short, if the heart of the Roman world was the city (see Chapter 6), its soul – at least to the Romans themselves – was the countryside.

This chapter is all about the Romans' fanciful image of the countryside, the authors who helped create and promote that idea, and the way rich Romans tried to live out their rural dream in country villas. But it's also about the everyday reality of living in a townhouse or apartment block, or eking out a life as an estate worker supporting the Roman rural dream.

The Roman Fantasy Self-image: We're Farmers at Heart

Even though the Empire only functioned because of the army, cities, communications, assemblies, magistracies, and the way the emperors ruled, the Romans permanently fantasised about an idyllic Italian rural past. Romans believed that Rome had become so powerful because of their origins as peasant farmers with the hard work and discipline that involved.

The great textbooks on Roman rural life were written by three stalwarts of the tradition: Cato (234–149 BC), Varro (116–27 BC), and Columella (first century AD). These men were very influential in their own time, mainly amongst educated men (it's unlikely the average farmer even knew the books existed, let alone had the opportunity to read or own a copy). But what matters more than that is what they tell us about the Roman self-image and the value Roman thinkers attributed to farming.

The Roman scholar Cato (full name Marcus Porcius Cato) grew up on his father's farm near the Sabine town of Reate (modern Rieti) about 60 kilometres (40 miles) north-east of Rome. He came to love the soil for its purity and the simple, straightforward life of a farmer and saw the farming life as the ultimate gesture of Roman patriotism. In his *De Agri Cultura* ('On the Cultivation of Fields'), which was supposed to be a farmer's handbook, Cato conveys the sense that farming is the only honest way to earn a living. Money-lending and trade might offer a chance of more cash, but according to Cato, they were dishonourable and full of hazards. Cato also claimed that the 'bravest and sturdiest' soldiers came from farming stock. In his work, Cato helped to reinforce the Roman tradition that the Empire was the reward and fruit of an army whose origins lay in tilling the fields.

Marcus Terentius Varro was born in Reate (Rieti) and had a successful career working for Pompey the Great (discussed in Chapter 14). In later life, he spent most of his time writing. He was almost 80 when he started his *Res Rusticae* ('Country Matters'), which was supposed to be a handbook for his wife Fundania who had just bought a farm. Varro wrote his work as a series of dialogues between various characters with appropriate rustic names like Scrofa (which also means 'breeding sow') and Stolo (which means 'a shoot growing out of a plant or tree'). In addition to providing a lot of basic technical information for farmers, Varro's work also inspired the Roman poet Virgil's *Georgics,* poems that celebrated rural idealism and were used by Augustus and later emperors to reinforce Roman self-belief.

Lucius Junius Moderatus Columella came from Spain but lived and farmed in Italy. He wrote his *Rei Rusticae* ('On Agriculture') in about AD 60–65 to encourage agriculture. He was very worried about what he considered the decline of Italian agriculture due to absentee landlords who had no interest in promoting farming. As Italy became more and more dependent on imported food, Columella was desperate to encourage landowners to take more interest, but he knew only hard graft would turn things around. The point of *Res Rusticae,* which discussed the farm buildings, crops, fruit, animals, staff duties, and trees, was to provide the essential information to work from and to make a farm a successful and profitable investment.

Life in the City; Dreams in the Country

London, Washington, and New York are full of people from every social tier. The movers and shakers at the top come to the city for business reasons, for government, to be part of the action. Other people come because of the availability of work, and the security and convenience of a city. Rome was just the same. It was the centre of power and commerce, and it attracted people like a magnet. But one of the great paradoxes of city life is that city dwellers spend a lot of time wishing they lived somewhere else.

As the Romans became more dependent on the advantages of urban life and a cosmopolitan economy, they agonised over what they had lost, just as we do. Cities are noisy, busy, dirty places, and plenty of Romans yearned for the wide open spaces away from the crowds. Educated Romans read Virgil's *Georgics* poems to dream of a past paradise, as we go and watch movies of Jane Austen novels filmed in soft focus on eighteenth-century country estates and moan about the loss of our countryside to motorways, interstates, car parks, and shopping malls.

Escaping the city

Everyone knows what happens when human beings live in close proximity, especially those who live in cities. The poet Juvenal, who lived in Rome in the early second century AD, slated city life for the horrendous noise of traffic that kept him awake at night. When he tried to move around, he found his way barred by traffic jams, accidents, crowds of people, and he dodged falling roof tiles, drunks fighting, and muggers.

For the average super-rich Roman, then, a country estate offered a blissful escape from Rome's public life and stinking racket. Rich Romans needing to escape the city raced off to extravagant country houses they called *villae* ('farms'). In exceptional cases, villas were like villages or small towns, manned by small armies of slaves, where their owners pretended they were 'downshifting' to a country lifestyle. You can read more about Roman villas in the section 'Villas: Bedrock of Roman Agriculture', later in this chapter.

Happy Horace and others

In 39 BC the poet Horace was given a farm by his friend and patron, Maecenas. Horace was delighted, and you can see from his excitement how much it meant to him:

'It's just what I had been praying for: a modest-sized plot of land, where there might be a garden, and not far from the house a spring with a ceaseless flow of water, and above these a small piece of woodland. The gods have given me all this but more of it and even better. I am happy. Mercury, I ask nothing more from you except that you ensure these blessings last the rest of my life.'

Seneca (5 BC–AD 65), Nero's tutor, got sick one day and decided to escape to his country

estate, desperate to get out of Rome. He wrote to a friend to rave about the experience. He sounds like someone who's managed to escape from Manchester or Chicago for the weekend:

'As soon as I had left behind that crushing air in Rome and that stink of smoky cooking hearths which belch out, along with all the ashes, all the poisonous fumes they've stored inside whenever they're fired up, than I noticed an immediate improvement in my condition. You can just imagine how invigorated I felt when I reached my vineyards. I ploughed into my dinner – you might as well be talking about cattle sent out into spring pastures!'

Buying and investing in land

For a noble Roman, which mean the senatorial class (refer to Chapter 2), owning land and storing wealth in land was the only acceptable way to earn a living. So a noble villa owner would always be on the lookout to increase his land holding, which meant buying up neighbouring estates if they came on the market. (Trade was regarded as vulgar, a snobbery that made it easy for the equestrians to corner the commercial markets, often earning enough to buy their own villas.)

Buying more land meant thinking about all sorts of considerations: Was the villa house in good repair? Did it even need to be kept or could it be demolished? Was the land productive and good quality? How had it been run in the past? Were the tenants reliable and well looked after? Would more slaves be needed to get the estate up to scratch and turn a good profit? If the harvest was bad, would the rents need to be put down for the tenants?

For wealthy aristocratic Romans, these were the primary considerations in life – we know they were because they wrote about them. A large and healthy estate enriched such men and their immediate families but also, and perhaps more importantly, became what they could leave to their heirs and descendants, which was a huge matter of prestige as well as security. Of course, the more prestigious the villa, the more attractive it was to bad or resentful emperors who looked for excuses to confiscate the wealthiest estates (for example, Constantius II did quite a business in this regard; see Chapter 20); so the very thing that made a Roman secure – wealth – also put him at risk.

Tour du jour: Pliny the Younger's villa

Pliny the Younger (*c.* AD 61–113) (full name, Gaius Plinius Caecilius Secundus) was a Senator from Comum (Como) who became Governor of the province of Bithynia and Pontus under Trajan (98–117). He's famous for the letters he sent to friends and colleagues. One of the best-known is his description of his Laurentine villa about 25 kilometres (15 miles) from Rome in a letter he wrote in the late first century AD. It's so important and so vivid the best thing I can do is let Pliny tell you about it himself with some excerpts I've picked out. Bear in mind his villa was a luxury home despite his claims about its modesty. Now over to Pliny to take us round his place:

✔ **Entering the villa:** 'My villa is the right size for me but inexpensive to maintain. The front hall is plain, without being mean, through which you come to D-shaped colonnades which enclose a small and cheerful intermediate courtyard . . . [which] leads through to a well-lit and pleasing inner hall. From there it leads into an elegant dining room which runs down to the seashore, so that when the wind blows from the south-west it is gently splashed by the waves which work themselves out at its base.

'On every side of this dining room there are folding doors or windows of a similar size through which you have a view of three different seas, as it were, from the front and the two sides. From the back you can see through to the inner hall, the courtyards and the colonnades and from the entrance hall through to the distant woods and mountains.

'To the left of this dining room, a bit farther back from the sea, is a large bedroom and beyond that another one, but smaller, which has one window facing the rising sun, and another the setting sun. This room also has a view of the sea, but from a safer distance. In the angle formed between this bedroom and the dining room is a corner where the sun's warmth is retained and concentrated. This forms the household's winter quarters and the gymnasium because it is sheltered from all the winds except the one which brings rain and it can still be used after the weather has broken.'

✔ **The library and accommodation for slaves and guests:** 'Joining this angle is an apsidal room, with windows so arranged that the sun shines in all day. One wall is fitted with bookcases containing the works of authors I never grow tired of. Next to this is a bedroom opposite a corridor fitted with a raised floor fitted with pipes which take in hot steam and circulate it at a fixed temperature. The other rooms on this side of the villa are set aside for my slaves and freedmen but the majority of these are smart enough to put guests in.'

✔ **The baths and sea views:** 'Next comes the bath suite's cold bath. This is large and roomy and has two curved baths built into opposite walls which are quite sufficient considering that the sea is so close. Next is the oil and massage room, the furnace chamber, the boiler room, then two sanctuaries which are tasteful and very sumptuous. This leads to the hot swimming pool from which bathers survey the sea. Near

(continued)

(continued)

this is the ball-court which the sun warms as it goes down. From here you go up to a tower which is a two-up, two-down, arrangement of rooms, as well as a dining room which has a panoramic view of the sea, the coast, and all the beautiful villas along the shore. At the other end is a second tower with a room lit by the sun as it rises and as it sets. Behind here there is a large wine cellar and granary, and underneath a roomy dining room where the sea can only just be heard, even when it is rough. It looks out across the garden and the drive.'

✔ **The garden:** 'The drive is marked out with a box hedge, or rosemary where the box has gaps, because box grows very well if the buildings give it shelter but withers when exposed to the wind or sea spray, even from some distance. The inner part of the drive has a shady vine pergola where the path is so soft and forgiving that you can walk on it barefoot. The garden is mainly planted with mulberries and figs, which this soil favours as much as it repels everything else. Over here there is a dining room which despite being away from the sea has a garden view which is equally pleasant. Two rooms run round the back part of it, through the windows of which the villa entrance and a fine kitchen garden can be seen.'

In another letter Pliny tells us about what he did at his villa. As you'll see, he doesn't seem to have spent any of his time farming. Despite what men like Cato wanted Romans to do, the truth is that wealthy Romans regarded getting hands dirty as something for their tenants and slaves:

'I get up when I feel like it, normally when the sun rises, and often before that but never later. The shutters stay closed because the darkness and peace help me meditate. Freed from all those external distractions I am left to my own thoughts and my eyes don't make my mind wander. With nothing to see, my eyes are controlled by my imagination.

'Anything I am working on can be sorted out, chosen, and corrected, in my head. What I get done depends on how well I can concentrate and remember. Then I call my secretary, open the shutters, and dictate to him what I have knocked into shape. Then I send him away, call him back, and send him away again. At the fourth or fifth hour after sunrise (I don't stick to an exact time) I take a walk on the terrace or portico where I carry on thinking about or dictating whatever is outstanding on the topic I am working on. Once that's done, I go for a drive where I carry on as before when I was in my study or walking. I find the change of scene revives me and helps me concentrate.

'When I get home I have a rest and then a walk. Then I read out loud a Greek or Latin passage with proper enunciation. The reason is more for my digestion than for the good of my voice, though both are improved by the activity. Another walk follows before I am oiled, do my exercises, and have a bath. If I dine alone with my wife, or with a few friends, we have a reading during the meal. Once we have eaten we either listen to music or a comedy. When that's over I take a walk with members of the household, several of whom are well educated. So, the evenings pass with all sorts of conversations and even when the days are at their longest, they end very pleasantly.'

Villas: Bedrock of Roman Agriculture

The bedrock of the Roman agricultural world was the villa estate. *Villa* means farm, and the term was applied to almost everything from a fairly reasonable farmhouse right up to vast palatial country estates that looked as much like a farm as the White House does Abraham Lincoln's (so-called) wooden hut birthplace in Kentucky. But that didn't stop the owners pretending they were farmers in the best Roman tradition. They were encouraged by writers like Cato, who told his readers to build a villa they'd want to go and stay in often so the farm could benefit from the attention and interest. That's key: Roman villa owners rarely lived in villas the whole time; they usually split their time between a place in town and the country villa. Sometimes they even had several villas.

Rome's grain supply, and the grain used by towns and forts all over the Empire, was grown on these vast agricultural estates (for the grain supply and trade, see Chapter 7). In reality, villas were like agricultural factories, mass-producing food to make their owners wealthier.

Here a villa, there a villa . . .

Villas have been found all over the Roman world, usually on the best land, evidence for farming on an industrial scale. The biggest estates included not just thousands of slaves but whole villages of tenanted communities working vast expanses of land. Many very rich villa owners had several villas, visiting them only occasionally, and normally used resident staff like a bailiff and slaves to run the farm. It's quite possible that modest villas were parts of huge estates owned by big landlords and lived in only by tenants.

As Rome's power and influence spread across the Roman Empire, the villa tradition and the Roman love of simpler rural origins spread, too. Rome's great genius had always been to make others want to 'be Roman', rather than regarding themselves as conquered subject peoples. These villa owners picked up the Roman literary tradition as well and absorbed it into their ideas of who they were.

Imperial and giant estates

The most important landowner of all was the emperor, who had more land than anyone else thanks to his inheritances, what he had conquered himself, and what had been confiscated from his enemies. These were the imperial estates, and they were managed by imperial procurators (usually freedmen) who rented land to tenant farmers *(coloni)* or sublet it to lessees. The tenants had to hand over some of their produce (as much as one third) to the landlord, lessee, or the procurator.

Houses in the Roman Empire

There were two main types of Roman house: the country *villa,* and the townhouse *(domus).* Villas tended to sprawl out with various wings surrounding courtyards, while townhouses were compact, inward-looking buildings where the rooms faced enclosed gardens (as can best be seen at Pompeii in Italy today). Townhouses and villas were similar in having public rooms for receiving guests, clients, and business visitors, and private family rooms. These are the main ones:

- ✔ **Prothryum:** Entrance corridor.

- ✔ **Atrium:** Entrance hall with a central opening in the roof and below it a small rain-catching pool called the *impluvium.* This was the public reception hall and it also held the household shrine (*lararium* – see Chapter 9).

- ✔ **Tablinum:** A corridor room connecting the atrium to the peristylium.

- ✔ **Peristylium:** A garden surrounded by a covered walkway supported by a colonnade.

- ✔ **Oecus:** Reception room opening off the peristylium.

- ✔ **Cubicula:** Bedrooms, opening off the atrium and peristylium.

- ✔ **Triclinium:** Dining room, also usually opening off the atrium or peristylium, and often more than one, designed for summer and winter use.

- ✔ **Xystus:** A bigger enclosed garden.

- ✔ **Others:** Other rooms were used for storage, kitchens, or perhaps a library. Some street-facing rooms or suites were sublet as self-contained shops to tenants (perhaps the owner's freedmen and their families). Some townhouses had an upstairs level but these rarely survived, even at Pompeii and Herculaneum.

Needless to say only people with money could afford villas or townhouses with all these facilities.

The walls in affluent Roman villas and townhouses were painted in panels and borders of bright colours, including pictures of mythological scenes and fantasy architecture. The floors in the best rooms would have had mosaic pavements featuring geometric designs, pictures of mythological beasts, gods, and heroes, as well as a variety of rural everyday activities like hunting. The quality of the flooring and wall painting always reflected the owner's tastes, pocket, and the date. Rich people could also afford glass windows instead of an iron grille, but they were small by our standards and made of an opaque greeny-blue glass. The constant increase in luxury and extravagance in wealthy townhouses in Rome was considered by Pliny the Elder to be a mark of how excessive Roman culture had become. The smartest house in Rome in 78 BC wasn't even in the top 100 by 43 BC and by Pliny's time they'd all been surpassed by houses elsewhere.

Meanwhile, ordinary people in towns had to make do with renting rooms in apartment blocks (sometimes several storeys high) or as self-contained parts of the rich houses let out to rent. In the countryside, simple stone farmhouses might be all a peasant farmer could afford, and in remoter provinces like Britain, thatched roundhouses of an ancient Iron Age design were still used by the poorest people.

Giant villa estates weren't much different, merely that the owner was a private landlord. In Nero's time (AD 54–68), just six landlords owned half of the province of Africa, which most of them managed by constantly buying up neighbouring land. These vast slave-operated estates were called *latifundia* ('extended estates'), and by the days of the Empire, smallholdings on them were increasingly let out to free tenants, who provided additional seasonal labour.

Melania the Younger was a hyper-wealthy Christian heiress in the year AD 404. She had estates in Italy, Sicily, North Africa, Spain, and Britain. We know about her because as part of her faith she toured her property, giving it away, but it shows how the super-rich of the Roman world were truly international millionaires, despite belonging to a culture that thought it was maintaining the simple country life.

Villas in the later years of the Empire

By the fourth and fifth centuries AD, the world of Pliny the Younger and his villa seems a very long way back in the past. Some provinces had been overrun with barbarians. When Britain was abandoned in 410, the collapse of a financial system, provincial government, and a trading and communications infrastructure, as well as barbarian raids, soon saw her villas falling into ruin by the early fifth century. But in other provinces, the wealthy landowners carried on as if nothing had changed. Ausonius (AD 310–395), the Gallo-Roman poet and tutor to the emperor Gratian (367–383), wrote many poems, but one of his best-known was about the river Moselle near where he had grown up. Copying the style of Roman classical poetry from writers like Virgil, Ausonius described the Moselle as a rural paradise of abundant produce including fish, and peopled it with ancient Roman gods.

Even Gaius Sidonius Apollinaris (AD 430–*post* 475), who became Bishop of Auvergne and helped lead the Gaulish resistance against the Visigoths, wrote about his villa and rural life almost as if he was personal friend of Virgil's and had lived 500 years before his own time. Sidonius also talks about his friends' villas, showing that fifth-century southern Gaul still had plenty of senatorial aristocrats who enjoyed traditional Roman villa life.

Living in villas meant being dependent on a colossal amount of tied labour, safe and reliable communications to ship supplies in and produce out, and access to reliable markets in towns. In the Eastern Empire, this system lasted a lot longer, but in the Western Empire, as order collapsed and as provinces were lost, it became impossible to maintain villa estates and the Roman fantasy rural way of life.

A Quick Rural Reality Check

Don't be fooled by the Romans' self-image. The reality for most people in the Roman Empire was a life of endless toil in the fields, coming back from war to find your smallholding had been absorbed into a huge slave-run estate, struggling against natural disasters, bad weather, pests, tax collectors, and the economic chaos caused in the third and fourth centuries by civil war and barbarian invasions, or scraping a living in a crowded apartment block in a city. Many of these people worked as slaves or tenants on vast villa or imperial estates and had no chance at all of ever experiencing the kind of villa life men like Pliny the Younger and Ausonius banged on about.

But it's also true that the rich villa owners set the social standard for top-class living and less-well-off people did whatever they could to copy them. That's why archaeologists dig up small and modest villas with maybe just a couple of mosaic floors laid by a second-rate mosaicist, because to the less-well-off villa owner, a bad mosaic was better than no mosaic at all – a bit like people today buying cheap copies of designer clothing worn by film stars. As ever, people are pretty much the same whatever time or place you look at!

Chapter 5

When We Were Soldiers

*I*f you ask someone to describe a Roman, the first thing that'll come to mind is a Roman soldier, and most probably a Hollywood-style Roman soldier complete with extravagant breastplate, plumed helmet, red cloak, and waving an enormous sword. It's not entirely inappropriate because in much of the world conquered by the Romans the first thing local populations saw was the Roman army.

The Roman army was the driving force of Roman power. In Chapter 4, I mention the Roman writer Cato who said that it was Roman farming stock that produced the best soldiers. These were men with staying power, and it's certainly true that throughout the wars that won the Romans their Empire (see Parts III and IV of this book), it was the ability of the Roman army to cope with defeat, to be adaptable, and to keep coming back for more that wore the Romans' enemies down. So this chapter is all about the Roman army: how it worked, who fought in it, and what a soldier's life was like.

Mastering the Universe: The Fighting Men

There wasn't really 'a Roman army' with a high command nerve centre in Rome and generals gathered round a map of the Roman world directing their troops. Roman armies were put together as the need arose for different campaigns, and they were under the local command of their individual generals. That went right back to Rome's early days when citizens were classified according to what they could provide for military service.

In the days of the late Republic, armies could be official or unofficial, because they were created simply by the sheer force of circumstance. It all boiled down to the prestige and power of generals like Marius, Sulla, Pompey, and Caesar. Awarded *imperium* by the Senate to defend the state's interests, these men, unlike earlier generals, created their own armies and also pursued their own political ambitions. Unlike the earlier armies, these armies were loyal to their generals first and Rome only second. After those days, the commander-in-chief was the emperor.

Army units were stationed all round the Roman Empire, mainly in the most troublesome places. Perhaps the most remarkable thing at all, however, is that in total the Roman army probably didn't amount to more than 300,000–350,000 troops at its climax, which is an amazingly small total given the vast amount of territory the army controlled. To put it into perspective, consider this: At the outbreak of the First World War in 1914, Britain had 740,000 soldiers (including reservists and others), while France and Germany had armies of nearly 1 million troops each, making a combined total around nine times the entire Roman army. Yet most of these troops were fighting in a far smaller area than the Roman army controlled (though to be fair, the population of Europe in 1914 was much higher than in Roman times).

As a very rough estimate, around half the Roman soldiers were citizen infantry soldiers who fought in *legiones* (singular: *legio,* a legion made up of just under 5,500 soldiers). The rest were called the *auxilia* ('assistant' or 'auxiliary troops'): hired provincials who were divided up into infantry, cavalry, and mixed units sometimes with specialised forms of warfare.

It took a long time for the Roman army to evolve into the system I describe in this section; see Chapter 14 for a little more detail about how the early army operated. From its relatively humble origins as a Roman citizen army, made up of men from Rome and Latium, the Roman army grew into a large force spread out across the Roman world. It was made up of men from every last province: citizens who entered the legions, and provincials who entered the auxiliary units. It also included men from beyond the frontiers, 'barbarians' by any other name, who played an increasingly important role in the Empire's defence.

Legions and legionaries

The Roman historian Tacitus, writing around the end of the first century AD, listed 27 legions dispersed around the Roman Empire for the year AD 23. By Trajan's reign (98–117), there were about 30 legions. At the beginning of the third century, there were only 19. The number of legions fluctuated as new ones were formed and others were lost, or cashiered. Legions were stationed where they were most needed. As a result the Rhine – one of the most dangerous frontiers – had eight legions, while the whole of North Africa and Egypt had only four between them. Britain, one of the smallest provinces but one of the most troublesome, never had less than three legions.

Legionaries had to be Roman citizens. In AD 92, a soldier in the III Legion Cyrenaica was accused of not being a citizen and faced instant dismissal. The man had to call three witnesses, two soldiers and a veteran, to testify that he was a citizen.

Organising a legion

Back in the Republic, around the time of the Third Punic War (151–146 BC), a legion varied in number from 4,200 to 5,000 infantry, depending on circumstances, with 300 cavalry. The legion was divided into *maniples,* each of which was made up from two centuries of troops. Maniples of young men made up the front line. Behind them came slightly older troops and at the back were the old, experienced soldiers.

A century used to mean what it sounds like, literally 100 soldiers. Over time, however, the term became less precise, and in practice a century had 80 soldiers. Those 80 soldiers were divided up into ten 'tent parties' *(contubernia)* of eight men each. Each tent party was garrisoned together in the permanent fort, and on campaign they marched together, bringing their tent and equipment on their allocated mule.

The legions went through a lot of changes, but by the late first century AD, they'd reached the form in which they existed for most of the great years of the Roman Empire: one legion totalling 5,120 infantry Roman citizen soldiers. The legion was made up like this:

Men	*Total*
6 centuries of 80 men	480 (one cohort)
10 cohorts made up a legion thus:	
9 cohorts of 480 men	4,320 men

The first cohort was double-sized and made up of ten centuries of 800 men.

$$800 + 4{,}320 = 5{,}120 \text{ men}$$

That wasn't all. Each century had a *centurion* to command it, and his assistant called an *optio.* There were about 128 of these, bringing the total to 5,248.

A legion in the days of the Empire had just 120 cavalrymen used as scouts and couriers, making the final total (not including officers) of 5,368. To that you can add other ad hoc staff like doctors.

Don't imagine if you turned up to a legionary base you'd only see soldiers. Officers and some centurions could afford servants, freedmen, and slaves, and there were also sometimes officers' families, and the unofficial families of soldiers (who lived outside the fortress in the civilian settlement). When the general in Germany called Quinctilius Varus set off to his doom in AD 9 (see Chapter 16), his three legions went out on campaign with women, children, and servants, who all helped slow him down.

Legionary emblems

Various standard-bearers carried emblems on parade and into battle:

✔ **Aquila:** A gold eagle, only carried when the whole legion was on the march

✔ **Imago:** An image of the emperor or a member of his family

✔ **Signa:** A standard for an individual century

✔ **Vexilla:** A flag on a pole naming the legion or a detachment *(vexillatio)*

The loss of standards was the worst thing that could happen to the Roman army. The general Crassus was killed and lost his at Carrhae in 53 BC (Chapter 14). Varus lost his in AD 9 (Chapter 16).

The command structure

A legion was usually commanded by *legatus legionis* ('commander of the legion'), a man of senatorial rank who had served as a praetor (refer to Chapter 3). He had six military tribunes to assist him. The most senior (*tribunus laticlavius*, 'tribune with a broad purple stripe', meaning a man of senatorial rank) was one who would one day command a legion himself. The other five (*tribuni angusticlavii*, 'tribunes with narrow purple stripes') were equestrians and had usually already commanded auxiliaries and might go on to command auxiliary cavalry units.

Then there was the *praefectus castrorum* ('prefect of the camp') who was normally a former senior centurion who had risen through the ranks. Unlike the officers, he had a lifetime's experience in the army. The senior centurion in each cohort commanded his cohort. The senior centurion in the first cohort was called *primus pilus* (probably meaning 'the first spear'). He was the legion's top centurion and had the position all the junior centurions hoped to reach one day. But the truth is no-one knows exactly how the centurions' promotion system worked.

If this all sounds jolly neat and organised, you can forget it. For a start, we know that legions were often split into detachments called *vexillationes* ('wings'). Centurions were frequently sent off to command auxiliary units. We also know that legions, like every other collection of human beings since the world began, were prone to sickness and desertion, quite apart from soldiers legitimately being away from base (see the section following this to find out what duties, military and otherwise, legionaries performed).

Jack-of-all-trades: Legionary duties

Legionaries were used by the Roman state for a whole variety of tasks from putting up fortresses, forts, and civilian public buildings to building bridges, mending roads, collecting taxes, and acting as policemen. In a new province, especially one in the West like Spain or Britain, Roman soldiers would be the only men with all the necessary skills to establish Roman civilization. Their architects, engineers, carpenters, masons, and blacksmiths were invaluable and played a huge part in developing these areas.

One of our sources is a duty roster for the III Legion Cyrenaica in Egypt in the late first century AD. The duties listed include being on guard duty at the local market, road patrol, road cleaning, latrine detail, and detachment to the harbour.

By imperial times, legionaries served for about 25 years, but plenty carried on for longer. They could hope for a grant of land from the emperor on discharge, perhaps in or around a Roman colony of other veterans, and run a business or farm. Augustus claimed that he personally settled 300,000 veterans. At an uncertain later date, a legionary called Vitalinius Felix served in the I Legion Minervia on the Rhine frontier. When retired, he moved to Lugdunum (Lyons) in Gaul where he sold pottery until he died at the age of 59 years, 5 months, and 10 days.

The auxiliaries

The idea of auxiliaries was to add muscle to the Roman army by using the provincials the Romans had once fought. By tapping into their fighting skills, the Romans formed units of Gauls, Spaniards, Thracian cavalry, Sarmatian archers (from an area north of the Black Sea), and a host of others. The auxiliaries were mostly divided into infantry, cavalry, or mixed units. Even if originally hired in one province, new soldiers were often later recruited from places where units were stationed, but the unit's original ethnic title was kept. Here are some examples of auxiliaries:

- ✔ The First Ala (cavalry) of Thracians (northern Greece).
- ✔ The Third Ala of Arabians.
- ✔ The Eighth Ala of Palmyrenes.
- ✔ The First Thousand-strong Mounted Cohort of Vardullians (mixed infantry and cavalry). Vardullians came from Spain.
- ✔ The Fourth Cohort of Gauls (infantry).
- ✔ The First Cohort of Hamian (Syrian) Archers.

And that's only a tiny fraction of them!

There's no better description of the auxiliaries than that by a Roman military historian called Vegetius:

'[Auxiliaries] are hired corps of foreigners assembled from different parts of the Empire, made up of different numbers, without knowledge of one another or any tie of affection. Each nation has its own peculiar discipline, customs and manner of fighting . . . it is almost impossible for men to act in concert under such varying and unsettled circumstances. They are, however, when properly trained and disciplined, of material service and are always joined as light troops with the legions in the line. And though the legions do not place their principal dependence on them, they still look on them as a very considerable addition to their strength.'

Organising auxiliaries

Auxiliaries didn't serve in legions. They were arranged in much smaller units, based on the cohort. They were commanded by equestrian prefects or tribunes, or sometimes by legionary centurions on detachment. This is how they were divided up:

- Infantry auxiliaries were organised into cohorts of 480 or 800, divided into centuries like the legions.

- Cavalry auxiliaries were organised into wings *(alae)* of about 500 or 1000, divided up into *turmae* (squadrons) of 16 troopers each.

- There were also mixed units where blocks of 128 or 256 cavalry were added to infantry units. These were called *cohorts equitatae* ('mounted cohorts').

Fighting fodder and frontline soldiers: Auxiliaries' duties

Auxiliaries marched alongside the legionaries and even camped with them, but were paid less. Crucially, auxiliaries always bore the brunt of the fighting. The idea was that it was much better to lose provincials than Roman citizens. So in most set-piece battles, the auxiliaries would be thrown in first. Sometimes the legionaries just stood and watched.

The reason auxiliaries put up with such a raw deal was that they could earn citizenship that way, not just for themselves but for their families. Citizenship was awarded after 25 years' service (in theory – often they were kept hanging on). Yet again, Rome had an advantage because other people wanted to be Roman, too. Of course, after AD 212 and the grant of universal citizenship under Caracalla (see Chapter 18), this distinction ceased to mean anything anyway.

The Romans also hired an unending series of more casual ad hoc auxiliaries, often from barbarian tribes on or near the frontier, who were even less well paid and who had no chance of citizenship. Handy for propping up the borders, these units were treated as totally disposable and were much more loosely organised and much more unreliable as a result. These units, sometimes generally referred to as *foederati* (federates), played an increasingly important and sometimes decisive part in Rome's later history.

The Praetorian Guard: Rome's garrison

The prefect of the Praetorian Guard constantly pops up in the history of the Roman Empire (see Chapters 16 through to 19). The Praetorians were the garrison of Rome, so they were right on hand to influence the imperial succession.

The origins of the Guard went back to the days of Publius Cornelius Scipio Aemilianus Africanus the Younger (c. 184–129 BC) who took a personal bodyguard of 500 troops to Spain with him in the Third Punic War (151–146 BC) because the soldiers in Spain were unreliable.

Under Augustus, the Praetorians were organised into nine cohorts of about 500 men, three of which were based in barracks outside Rome and the rest in various Italian cities. Praetorians were commanded by the equestrian *praefectus praetorio* (refer to Chapter 3), were paid more than legionaries, and served for much less time (16 years only). They occasionally took part in military campaigns, could be promoted to be centurions in legions, and in AD 61, a few were even sent to find the source of the Nile.

The fleet: Rome's navy

Even though the Roman world was held together by lying around the Mediterranean, the Roman fleet *(classis)* or navy was really just an extension of the army. The Romans weren't natural sailors and had no great skills in navigation or seamanship, despite Italy's extensive coastline. When Julius Caesar invaded Britain in 55 and 54 BC, he lost ships on both occasions to storms and the tides, having no idea how extreme they could be.

The big naval successes for the Romans came earlier in the Punic Wars when Rome learned to sail ships in such a way that they could use them as platforms for landing soldiers (Chapters 12 and 13 explain the Punic Wars). Pompey's destruction of the Cilician pirates was a major triumph, but of course the decisive event that ended the Republic was the naval battle between Antony and Octavian in 31 BC (see Chapter 15 for that tale).

The first permanent naval bases were built at Forum Julii (Fréjus) in Gaul, and in Italy at Misenum and Ravenna by Augustus's time. They were designed to protect Italy and the grain fleets. Misenum became the main naval headquarters not far from where today the US Navy, the world's most powerful, has a major base at Naples. Various other Roman fleets were installed around the Empire, for example in Alexandria, the Black Sea, Syria, Germany, and Britain, where they protected commerce or supported invasion forces by bringing up supplies, reconnoitring the land, building advance bases, and carrying marines *(nauticus miles)*.

Fleets were generally commanded by equestrian prefects. Sailors, who came mostly from the east, turned up doing all sorts of other jobs from supplying recruits for new legions to building a granary on Hadrian's Wall. The most notorious fleet event came in Britain in 286 when the commander of the British fleet, Carausius, used his naval power to rebel against the emperors Diocletian and Maximian (see Chapter 20).

The Roman siege of Syracuse between 213–211 BC in the Second Punic War (covered in Chapter 12) was a powerhouse of ingenuity. The Roman general Claudius Marcellus doubled up eight of his war galleys so they could carry siege ladders right up to the city walls. The idea was that attackers could launch themselves off the top onto the Syracusan defenders. Unfortunately, the Syracusans had the brilliant mathematician Archimedes (287–211 BC) on hand. Amongst the defensive weapons he devised was one that used a grappling iron to lift Roman ships up by the bows till they were vertical. The bottoms of the ships were then tied up and the grappling irons let go, causing the ships to fall back and sink. A far less reliable and much later source says Archimedes told the Syracusans to reflect sunlight with hexagonal mirrors onto the wooden ships. This supposedly set them on fire, but modern experiments have suggested this would have been extremely difficult if not impossible. Either way, Claudius Marcellus abandoned the assault by sea, but with a combination of land forces and a Syracusan traitor, he fought his way in and seized the city. Archimedes was killed in the battle, even though Marcellus had ordered his capture.

Having the Right Equipment

Regardless of how the Roman army was organised, none of that would have mattered a jot if soldiers hadn't had the right gear. At its climax, the Roman army was the best equipped and best supplied force in the ancient world.

Uniforms and weapons

Until the mid-first century AD (around the reign of Claudius), the average legionary's equipment consisted of the following:

- Helmet (with cheek and neck guards) *(galea)*.
- Mail shirt *(lorica hamata)*.
- Dagger *(pugio)*.
- Sword *(gladius)*.
- Shield *(scutum)*.

✔ Spear *(pilum)*.

✔ Open leather boots with hobnails *(caligae)*. (These are the boots the young Caligula, emperor AD 37–41, wore and were how he got his name.)

After the mid-first century AD, a legionary was more likely to have armour made of overlapping strips of iron *(lorica segmentata)* and a more elaborate helmet with deeper neck-guard and bigger cheek-pieces. But it's plain from excavated examples that all this kit was liable to be handed down and used by many different soldiers over the years, so the likelihood is that any Roman army line-up would have looked distinctly ad hoc.

Not as ad hoc as the auxiliaries though, who used an almost unlimited array of weaponry and armour depending on their specialisations, where they came from, and what was available. The biggest show-offs were the auxiliary cavalry who loved fitting out their horses with decorative medallions on the harnesses. For special occasions, they had parade armour with face masks so that they could pose as mythical heroes in mock display battles.

The Roman army's tradition was as an offensive, not a defensive force. Scipio Africanus the Younger once saw a soldier showing off his shield and told him, 'It is a very fine one, my boy; but a Roman soldier must have more trust in his right arm than in his left', meaning his sword arm, of course.

Artillery

The Romans were experts at artillery, though, of course, with no gunpowder, it was all done by sheer brute force and tensioned ropes. This is some of what they had, and it was especially suitable for siege warfare:

✔ **Ballista:** Rather like a medieval crossbow, a *ballista* (or *cheiroballista*) fired iron darts.

✔ **Onager:** A catapult sitting in a frame. A throwing arm, tensioned with ropes wrapped round the axle, was pulled back and let go, hurling rocks and other ammunition at the enemy.

✔ **Aries:** The name means both a male sheep and a battering ram and is named because that's what male sheep do. So like the Romans, we use the same word for both. The Romans used rams housed in vehicles with wheels. Inside, men pulled the ram back and forth on rollers. There was also a similar vehicle housing a drill, turned by a winch.

The best possible Roman battle in the movies is in the opening few minutes of *Gladiator* (2000). You get to see authentic-looking Roman soldiers caked in grime after years of campaigning on the German frontier, complete with artillery, archers, and an axe-wielding barbarian enemy. It's amazingly realistic, though, in fact, it was filmed just outside London.

Holding the Fort

The Roman fort was like a miniature town. No matter where a Roman fort was built, or how big, it always conformed to the same basic design, though no two forts were identical. The biggest were legionary fortresses, accommodating more than 5,000 men, while the smallest full-sized forts housed auxiliary infantry cohorts of about 500 men. Even the fleet used coastal forts built to the same design. But smaller ones are known, right down to fortlets accommodating a dozen men.

The permanent fort was based on the marching camp, and the idea was to maintain discipline and organisation: Every Roman soldier should know exactly where he was supposed to be in the fort, whether the home base or an overnight marching camp. Permanent forts really came into being in the late first century AD and into the second century, once the Empire's frontiers became fairly static.

Fort defences

Forts were generally planned in playing-card shapes with curved corners, and flush gateways (one in each side, opposite one another). Even the biggest fortresses were larger versions of the same basic layout (see Figure 5-1).

Turf and timber ramparts were about 4–5 metres in height and supported a walkway with a timber parapet. Planks were inserted in the turf to strengthen it. Stone walls could be as high as 4.5 metres (15 feet), with a 1.5 metre (5 foot) parapet above, and were often built as facings to existing turf ramparts. Beyond the walls a huge V-shaped ditch *(fossa)* was dug, and if the location was especially dangerous, extra ditches were added, sometimes with sharpened stakes dug into the sides.

Gateways were the weak link, but the Romans heavily protected them with flanking gate-towers. Interval towers around the walls added additional viewpoints. A grid of streets divided up the inside into various zones. The most important bit was the central zone *(latera praetorii)* where the administrative buildings were.

A Roman fort could be built in timber and turf, or in stone, or even a combination. Turf and timber was quick, easy to obtain, and extremely effective. The labour in the form of soldiers was available anyway, so it's common for archaeologists to find several different builds of a fort, erected within a few years of each other on the same site, especially from the first century AD or earlier. After that date, forts were more usually built in stone because with settled frontiers, units were far less likely to move on from permanent bases.

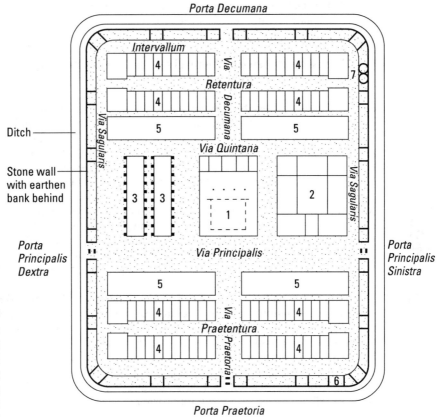

Porta Decumana

Ditch

Stone wall with earthen bank behind

Porta Principalis Dextra

Porta Principalis Sinistra

Porta Praetoria

Figure 5-1: A typical small Roman fort for housing about 480 auxiliary infantry troops and 128 cavalry.

1 The headquarters (principia)	5 Storebuildings or stables
2 Commander's house (praetorium)	6 Latrine
3 Granaries (horrea)	7 Rampart ovens
4 Barracks (centuriae)	

Fort buildings

Forts had every facility necessary for daily life in the Roman army, including armouries and workshops to make and repair everything the soldier needed, from a humble buckle to a piece of artillery:

- **Barracks *(contubernia):*** Filled out most of the fort area, with one block for each century (80 men).

- **Commander's house *(praetorium):*** Next door to the headquarters. Legionary fortresses had houses for the tribunes nearby, too.

- **Granaries *(horrea):*** Usually built in pairs close to the headquarters building and heavily buttressed to withstand the pressure from settling grain.

> ✔ **Headquarters** *(principia):* The nerve centre where standards, valuables, and admin records were stored.
>
> ✔ **Hospital** *(valetudinarium):* Not always built.
>
> ✔ **Workshop** *(fabrica):* Where all the fort's needs like carpentry, blacksmithing, and clothing could be seen to (not always built).

A large gap always existed between buildings and the defences so that soldiers could rush to defend the fort walls and to protect the buildings. The only structures found around the edge were usually cooking ovens (kept away from the barracks because of the danger of fire) and latrines. Baths were such a fire risk they were often built outside the fort at some distance, but legionary fortresses usually had their baths within the walls.

Roman fort layouts are so similar that if an archaeologist finds a few key reference points by excavation, the rest of the plan can usually be worked out from that. Forts are at the heart of the Roman genius: It was all about system. Military architects could lay things out easily and quickly, and every soldier knew what he had to do and where he belonged once the fort was finished.

Sometimes legions built specialised works depots, which were industrial centres, especially useful when the legion was in a way-out place where pottery and other manufactured goods couldn't be bought in. The XX legion at Chester in Britain had a works depot nearby at a place called Holt. Here the legion made its pottery, brick, and roof tiles, amongst other things, and then shipped them downriver to their fortress at Chester. But the army had vast needs for food and resources. It also bought in goods, or simply requisitioned them as tribute from conquered territories.

Marching camps

Marching camps were simply forts built on the move, though it'd probably be better to say that forts were permanent versions of marching camps. An army on campaign obviously needed an overnight stop. A suitable place on raised ground with access to water was chosen, and the fort systematically laid out, starting with the commanding officer's tent *(praetorium)*. Once the streets were laid out with all the places for the troops, the soldiers produced their spades and dug out a ditch around 1 metre deep and used the spoil to create a rampart. Each man carried wooden stakes so an instant palisade could be set up. Troops were then allocated various details like rampart guard duty or protecting supplies. In the morning, or as soon as the army moved on, the camp was packed up and the rampart flung back into the ditch.

Hadrian's Wall

Hadrian's most famous monument was his 76-mile-long frontier in Britain. A complex of stone wall, forts, fortlets spaced at 1-mile intervals with lookout towers at one-third-mile intervals between, together with forward and rearward defensive earthworks, it created a ribbon of Roman military life across northern Britain. One Roman historian said it was 'to separate barbarians and Romans', but it's plain that crossing the Wall was allowed. Its real purpose was probably to control movement to prevent trouble and enforce taxation, rather than stop it altogether. Since Hadrian visited Britain around the time the Wall was begun, it's almost certainly the case that he helped designed it. A bronze pan, inscribed with the names of several of the Wall's forts, recently found in Britain also carries the words *Val(l)i Aeli,* which gives us the ancient name for the frontier: 'The Aelian Frontier', named after Hadrian (his full name was Publius Aelius Hadrianus). The Wall went through many repairs, restorations, and rethinks, but it remained a more or less permanent fixture until Britain was abandoned by the Empire in the early fifth century. Large stretches of the Wall can still be seen today. The Wall is studied by Roman military scholars from all over the world and visited by millions of tourists.

Keeping the enemy out: Frontier fortifications

Protecting the frontiers wasn't strictly in the Roman tradition as the Romans had generally assumed they'd be forever expanding. But by Hadrian's day (AD 117–138), the decision had been taken to stop conquering new territory (see Chapter 17). Frontiers were settled, and the Romans had to find ways of permanently protecting their troops and the borders. Wherever possible rivers, like the Rhine in Germany, or other natural boundaries were used. Watchtowers were built and acted like modern-day CCTV cameras, where troops could watch out for barbarians trying to sneak across. Warning could then be sent by beacon or mounted messenger to the nearest fort.

In some places, there just weren't the natural boundaries so the ever-practical Romans had to make their own. The most extreme and the most famous is Hadrian's Wall in Britain, but it wasn't the only one. Other frontiers joined the Rhine and Danube, for example, and out in Egypt's desert a chain of remote forts protected the Empire's richest province.

The Late Army

From the reign of Marcus Aurelius (AD 161–180) on, the Empire was under attack on the borders. Not all the time, and not everywhere, but the assaults gradually increased and got much worse in the third century during the age of short-lived 'soldier emperors' (see Chapter 19). Cavalry became especially important. Gallienus (253–268) was the first to create an independent cavalry army under its own commander and put the legions under the command of equestrians rather than senators.

The really big changes started under Diocletian (284–305) and the Tetrarchy (Chapter 20). Diocletian increased the number of legions to about 60. They were installed in pairs along the frontiers, together with cavalry units, but a few were attached directly to the mobile imperial court *(comitatus)* along with the highest grade cavalry troops.

Dividing the army

Under Constantine (307–337), the emphasis on mobility became the first priority, though the change began under Gallienus (253–268). The army now became fully divided into the following:

- *Comitatenses* **(from *comes* meaning a member of the emperor's retinue):** The *comitatenses* fought the wars around the Empire, and were highly trained, well-paid, quality troops based on around a dozen 500-strong cavalry units which created the core of the emperor's mobile army. These were the men who would race to confront any invading army of barbarians.

- *Limitanei* **(from *limes*, 'frontier'):** The mainly infantry static frontier garrisons, the *limitanei* held the restored frontier defences and were lower grade in every respect. In fact, they were frontier spear fodder, a hotch-potch of long-established auxiliary units, ad hoc bands of hired provincials, and even barbarians. As a result they were variable in their fighting ability and, even worse, in their loyalties.

Meanwhile, the legions were pulled back from the frontiers to create fortified strongholds and military centres within the Empire, which would protect civilians and military resources in the event of an invasion.

New forts for the late army

The frontier garrisons continued to occupy their old forts, but a new form of military architecture was developed that resembled medieval castles. With bigger walls and huge projecting towers and gates that supported defensive artillery, the new forts were really massive defensive compounds. The same features are often found on Roman city walls like those built by Aurelian for Rome (see Chapter 19).

The end of the Roman army in the West

The trouble is that with the army divided up into local frontier garrisons, it was easier for would-be emperors to cash in on local loyalty and rebel. There was also a huge setback in 378 when the emperor of the Eastern Empire Valens (364–378) was killed at Hadrianopolis trying to push back the Ostrogoths and Visigoths (explained in Chapter 21).

By the early fifth century, the West faced three key problems:

- ✔ So much territory had been lost, the West couldn't support or provide the army it needed.
- ✔ A succession of rebellions inside the Roman Empire had taken troops away from frontiers and allowed forts and defences to become rundown.
- ✔ The West became more and more dependent on hiring barbarian troops known as *foederati,* who were only loyal if they were being paid. They could turn against the Empire without warning.

Meanwhile, the East had suffered far less from invasions and was able to support the army it needed. In the end, what did it for the army in the West was simply that there weren't enough resources or money to keep it going. The very last unit from the old days recorded was the Ninth Cohort of Batavians, which nearly 400 years earlier had been responsible for some of the writing tablets found at the fort of Vindolanda in northern Britain (see Chapter 17). Some of the unit's soldiers tried to get back pay during the reign of Romulus Augustus (475–476). The troops were killed and thrown in the river. The Roman army in the West was no more.

Part II
Living the Good Life

The 5th Wave   By Rich Tennant

"Tell the emperor if he has any trouble with it, just try jiggling the handle a little."

In this part . . .

The Roman world was a system – in fact, the first system in human history – that affected almost everyone who was part of the Roman Empire. That system included living in or visiting cities where you could marvel at Roman architectural achievements and enjoy the fruits of international trade and even on-demand running water; enjoying the first mass leisure industry the world had ever seen, complete with amphitheatres and circuses and more; and finding solace in the gods in an age of extraordinary religious tolerance.

It's important to remember that, in addition to all the wonders it offered, the Roman world was also a brutal place which enslaved untold millions of people and which made a few people very rich and powerful at the expense of the many.

The good life came at a heavy price.

Chapter 6

The Urban Jungle

*T*he Roman Empire was an empire of cities. Rome was a city, and she used cities to run the Empire. If we look at what Rome became, we can understand a huge amount about what made the Romans tick. It's no exaggeration to say that without cities, Roman power couldn't have existed. Throughout this book, there's a constant theme: The Romans were geniuses at persuading other people that 'being Roman' was a good thing. Cities impressed people with Roman power, but they also created a sense of order, permanence, and security, and were an essential part of government and the economy.

This chapter is about getting to grips with the essence of Rome the city and its part in Roman society, the architectural techniques that made Rome's buildings possible, how those buildings functioned and what they were used for, and how all across the Roman Empire every town of consequence resembled a miniature Rome. It's also about the communications that held the Roman world of cities together: the roads.

The Idea of City

The essence of the Roman world was the city. Rome herself was often known as simply *Urbs*, 'the City'.

In the ancient Mediterranean world of the early first millennium BC, the idea of a city was already synonymous with a community. Egypt's mighty and much older civilisation was ruled from great cities like Thebes and Memphis, which were home not just to large numbers of people with their homes and businesses but which also gave over vast areas to temple complexes and royal palaces. Greece was divided up into city states where places like Athens ruled their hinterlands. The Phoenician colony of Carthage in North Africa was an important trading city, destined to become Rome's greatest rival.

Rome itself had grown out of a collection of villages that were drawn together under the early kings thanks to their shared culture and their common interest in defending themselves against enemies in the region. These early kings introduced the ideas of public services and government to the early Romans and were inspired by the cities that already existed in the Mediterranean area including the Greek colonies in Sicily and southern Italy.

The Romans also believed that their city was divinely ordained in the myth of Aeneas and his descendants Romulus and Remus (see Chapter 10 for information on the founding of Rome). So Rome wasn't just a practical facility, it was also a place with a spiritual identity whose people were destined to rule the world. This provoked an intoxicating sense of community summed up in the way the Romans portrayed the city as a female figure seated on a suit of armour, wearing a helmet, and holding a Victory (a winged goddess) in her hand.

The effect in ancient times was to create the idea that Roman urban civilisation was the bedrock of security. The natural world is dangerous and unpredictable. Cities provide man's response – it's why so many of us live in them today. For the Romans, this created a paradox: They felt that Rome and her Empire were the rewards from the gods for a superior civilisation, but that the comforts and easy living had softened them up and created a population that was no match for the hardy tough men who had founded Rome and built her up. As the pressure on Roman civilisation grew from barbarian invasions in the third century AD and later, the Romans grew absolutely terrified at the thought Rome herself might disappear. If that sounds weird, cast your mind back to 9/11 and remember how frightened New Yorkers were when it seemed their city's very existence hung in the balance.

St Jerome, a Christian teacher, wrote this in a letter of 413, just three years after the sack of Rome by Attila the Hun (Chapter 21). As a Christian, he thought it was all to do with the sins of the Roman people, echoing Tacitus's feelings three centuries before about the decadence of imperial times, but the point is Jerome thought he was witnessing the end of the world: 'Shame on us. The world is falling into ruin, but our sins still flourish. The glorious city that was once head of the Roman Empire has been devoured by one mighty fire.'

Rome: The urban template

Rome might have been just one of many cities in the Mediterranean area in antiquity, but no other ancient civilisation developed the city in quite the same way the Romans did. The city of Rome took centuries to grow into the sprawling monster she became in the days of the emperors, by which time Rome was a vast co-ordinated organism of government, public services, utilities, and communications.

Rome's power and wealth attracted people in vast quantities, who all needed governing, feeding, and entertaining. The more people, trade, and industry there was, the more prestigious were the men who controlled them. During the first century BC, a number of exceptionally powerful men (see Chapter 15) like Caesar and Pompey jockeyed for control of Rome, in part by providing public facilities and entertainments. When the emperor Augustus listed his lifetime achievements, he rattled off dozens of buildings which he had built or repaired to show his power and generosity (listed in the section 'Improving the model city', later in this chapter). These men wanted Rome to be the showcase of their own and Rome's power and divine backing. They succeeded brilliantly.

Even today Rome's magnificent history and majestic ruins give it a status above all other cities in the world. Rome has had an enormous influence on the development of cities ever since. New York's Grand Central Station and Washington DC's Union Station are modelled on Roman architecture. Liverpool's vast commercial wealth of the nineteenth century led to a suite of public buildings based directly on Roman designs.

The Romans had developed Rome into a huge template for her civilisation. In the centre were Rome's public buildings, forums for trade and commerce, basilicas for legal affairs, and temples to state religions as well as the imperial palaces. Scattered around these were the theatres, amphitheatres, and the Circus Maximus. A road network radiated from the centre through housing, while above the city, aqueducts carried water in, and below the city, sewers drained it away. Rome's system of civic magistrates from consuls down to aediles was used to govern not just Rome and her immediate environs but the whole Roman Empire. Various equestrian prefectures were created to control key services like the grain supply, the city garrison, the fire brigade, and the roads (for details of these positions, see Chapter 3). Although Rome had taken centuries to evolve, at its climax it had a number of key features:

- ✔ **Amphitheatres:** Home to gladiatorial and beast fights.
- ✔ **Basilicas:** Law courts and administration.
- ✔ **Baths:** Vast public bathing establishments provided by the state, as well as a host of private smaller concerns.
- ✔ **Circuses:** Home to chariot-racing.
- ✔ **Curia:** Senate house, where the senators met.
- ✔ **Forums:** Public piazzas for trade and politics surrounded by shops and businesses.
- ✔ **Public services:** Mainly defences, aqueducts, drains, fire service, and roads.
- ✔ **Temples and religious precincts:** Temples funded by emperors, rich citizens, or corporations to look after their interests and that of the Roman people, worshipping state, local, specialised and eastern cults.
- ✔ **Theatres:** For comedies, tragedies, and poetry-readings.

Strabo visits Rome

Strabo, a geographer, visited Rome in the days of Tiberius (AD 14–37). He wondered at the extraordinary public buildings, but he was also fascinated by the constant demolition and rebuilding that went on:

'There's a constant need for wood and stone for the endless construction work in Rome. This is caused by frequently collapsing houses, and because of the fires and house disposals which never seem to let up. These disposals are a kind of deliberate demolition, each owner knocking down his house and then rebuilding as the fancy takes him. To this end the huge number of quarries, forests, and rivers in the region which provide the materials, offer superb facilities.'

When Vespasian came to power in 69, he actively encouraged anyone to take over vacant sites caused by fires or collapse and put up new buildings, because he thought they made Rome look unsightly.

No wonder the natural historian Pliny the Elder said 'there has been no city in the world that could be compared to Rome in magnitude'. Writing about the year AD 73, he said Rome had 14 administrative regions, with roads forming 265 crossroads, and 60 miles of major roads within Rome radiating from a point in the Forum out to the 37 gates in 13 miles of defensive walls.

Improving the model city

The emperor Augustus (27 BC–AD 14) was particularly keen on making Rome into a showcase for Roman imperial power, but he was only following a trend. In the first century BC the general Pompey the Great built a massive theatre, and Julius Caesar was responsible for numerous buildings like the Basilica Julia.

Augustus used his friend Agrippa to organise much of the new work, and this is some of what they achieved (the ones you can still see today are marked with an asterisk):

- ✔ Finished off Julius Caesar's forum and basilica*

- ✔ Restored old temples and erected new ones, like the vast temple of Mars Ultor (the Avenger)* which fulfilled a vow Augustus had made before the Battle of Philippi in 42 BC, and another one to the deified Julius Caesar

- ✔ Built a new forum, the Forum Augusti*

The Forum in Rome is so ruinous that you might be forgiven for wondering whether the Romans were as good at building as is often claimed. Well, what happened is that in the year 667, the Byzantine emperor Constans II decided the bronze and iron clamps which held the stone blocks of the Forum buildings together would be far more useful to him melted down into weapons for his wars to defend the Byzantine Empire. So he had them all removed, which meant that subsequent earthquakes (not unusual in that part of the world) caused most of the buildings to collapse.

- ✔ Presided over the Altar of Augustan Peace *(Ara Pacis Augustae)**, ordered by the Senate and dedicated in 9 BC

- ✔ Built the Theatre of Marcellus* to commemorate Augustus's nephew (who died in 23 BC)

- ✔ Installed new aqueducts

- ✔ Built the original Pantheon (later rebuilt and redesigned by Hadrian)*

- ✔ Raised a vast mausoleum for Augustus and his family*

Many of the emperors who came after Augustus provided Rome with greater and more impressive public buildings. These are just some of them:

- ✔ Claudius (41–54) built an aqueduct.

- ✔ Vespasian (69–79) began the Colosseum*.

- ✔ Titus (79–81) finished the Colosseum and built public baths.

- ✔ Domitian (81–96) built a circus.

- ✔ Trajan (98–117) built more public baths and a vast new multi-level forum*.

- ✔ Hadrian (117–138) built the huge double Temple of Venus and Rome* and rebuilt the Pantheon*.

- ✔ Caracalla (211–217) built a vast bathing complex* which still dominates the southern part of Rome.

- ✔ Maximian (286–305) built the Baths of Diocletian. Enough survived of the great vaulted cold room *(frigidarium)* for it to be converted by Michelangelo (1474–1564) in the Renaissance into the Church of Santa Maria degli Angeli*, and today this is one of the great sights of Rome.

- ✔ Maxentius (306–312) built a vast vaulted basilica*, part of which towers over the Forum to this day.

IN THEIR WORDS

'Veni, vidi, vici...'

The map of the city of Rome

Under Septimius Severus (AD 193–211) a vast map of Rome – the *Forma Urbis Romae* – was carved on marble and displayed in the city. Measuring 18 by 13 metres, it recorded everything from shops to mighty public buildings.

Sadly, just 10 to 15 per cent survives, broken into 1,186 pieces, but those fragments preserve vital evidence, including its plan of the Theatre of Pompey, which is still buried.

Civic corruption and incompetence

There were all sorts of opportunities for incompetence and corruption to ruin public building projects. In the early second century, Pliny the Younger was governor of Bithynia and Pontus in Asia Minor. He wrote to Trajan (AD 98–117) about various problems with buildings in his province including this moan:

'The Nicaeans are also rebuilding their gymnasium (which was burned down before I arrived in the province) on a much larger scale. They have already gone to considerable expense and I'm afraid it may have been for nothing. The building is irregular and badly proportioned, and the current architect, admittedly a rival of the one who was on the project at the beginning, says that the 22-feet thick walls are not strong enough to hold up the super-structure. This is because the core is filled with rubble, and the walls have no brick facing.'

No-one knows what the outcome was. But it's plain from other excavated buildings that the Romans weren't always brilliant construction engineers, and no doubt incompetence and corruption were sometimes the reasons, just like today.

Copycat Romes

Exploring the Roman world today means visiting places like Pompeii and Ostia in Italy, Ephesus and Aspendos in Turkey, Thuburbo Majus and Dougga in Tunisia, Arles and Nîmes in Gaul, and London and Cirencester in Britain – all contain familiar Roman urban features. Every one of these towns has its own history, but in the days of the Roman Empire, they all conformed to the basic Roman urban template. The story was the same throughout the Roman Empire as provincial or regional capitals functioned like miniature Romes. Each had its own forum, basilica, temples to Capitoline Jupiter and the imperial cult, theatres, townhouses, brothels, bars, and public lavatories. Anyone from the Roman period would have recognised facilities and the layout.

REMEMBER

But don't assume everything was copied from Rome. Rome copied ideas from elsewhere. The Romans took plenty of their ideas about classical architecture from the Greeks. In southern Italy, they found cities like Pompeii, which had a stone amphitheatre, stone theatre, and a basilica long before Rome ever did. The Roman genius was combining all these with their idea of city government to create the Roman city.

In each major city, the local civic assembly was modelled on the Roman Senate, electing its local magistrates just as Rome elected her consuls, tribunes, aediles, and quaestors. Rome had her two consuls while Pompeii, like many other cities in the Empire, had her two annually elected magistrates called the *duoviri* ('the two men'). Those magistrates were often responsible for commissioning and paying for public buildings. Doing so made them and their cities look good and was a way of buying votes, so the magistrates competed with one another to be the most generous. In a tiny town in northern Britain called Brough-on-Humber, for example, there was an aedile called Marcus Ulpius Januarius who supplied the town's theatre with a stage during the reign of Antoninus Pius (AD 138–161).

In the Eastern Empire, urban life was already well-established, and cities of Greek origin like Ephesus in Asia Minor found themselves embellished with Roman additions. In the Western Empire, urban life was more of a novelty, especially in Britain and northern Gaul. Towns had to be founded by the Romans and built to conform to a general Roman theme. In remoter areas, it was probably the emperor who had to order and pay for public buildings, rather than the local bigwigs.

Two Brilliant Ideas

The Romans weren't the most original architects. Many of their designs were borrowed from the Greeks and the Etruscans. But they made exceptional use of two fundamental techniques: concrete and the arch.

Concrete

Concrete was the miracle of Roman building, called by them *opus caementicium,* and by us 'Roman concrete' (and this is the source of our word 'cement'). It had just four components:

- ✔ Water
- ✔ Lime
- ✔ Pozzolana (sandy volcanic ash, originally found near Pozzuoli near Naples in Italy)
- ✔ Aggregate (brick chips or fragments of stone)

The brilliant thing about concrete is that it can be mixed on-site from easily found ingredients and poured into moulds or shapes to create just about any sort of structure. It's also extremely strong and very durable. The Romans built walls with concrete cores and faced them with brick or stone. It allowed large and complex buildings to be erected quickly, because it was very nearly as strong as modern concrete. Concrete was in use in Rome by the second century BC at the latest.

By varying the aggregate according to requirements, this simple concrete could form the cores of massive walls or vaults (see the following section, 'Arches and vaults') and is found everywhere in the Roman Empire. In its most advanced form, Roman concrete was good enough to be the sole material used in a vault, created by pouring it into wooden moulds. This was concrete's most dramatic impact because it meant flat wooden or stone ceilings could be done away with. This discovery lay behind most distinctive Roman architecture. All across the Roman world, concrete was used to manufacture major buildings and even modest houses. Concrete used with arches, vaults, and domes made a perfect partnership.

The ultimate example of Roman concrete building is the Pantheon, built in its present form by Hadrian (AD 117–138) (see Chapter 17 for his reign), and still completely intact in Rome today. The Pantheon's main feature is a massive dome 43 metres (141 feet) wide, sitting on top of a circular drum with a total height the same as the dome's width. The secret was lightness and strength, so the dome gets thinner from bottom to top, starting at 6 metres (20 feet) where the dome meets the drum and dropping to just 1.5 metres (5 feet) at the top with decorative recesses (coffers) reducing the weight further. The materials used also got lighter towards the top, finishing with lightweight volcanic tufa. Vast wooden moulds were used to hold the dome in place while the concrete set. It's actually the biggest masonry dome ever built, and architects from all round the world have been fascinated by it ever since.

Arches and vaults

Arches and vaults were used in almost all major Roman buildings. They relieve weight, save stone, and increase a building's strength.

The Etruscans introduced the Romans to the arch, but it was the Romans who truly mastered the arch and its close relation, the barrel vault. The ideas came from a long way beyond Italy though. Arches and vaults had been used by the mud-brick builders of Assyria and Babylonia. The Greeks picked up the designs, which then found their way to Italy. By the third century BC magnificent arched and vaulted gateways were being built in Italy like the Porta Rosa at Velia (modern Elia), south of Naples.

How arches work

Arches aren't just a way of providing an entrance or a doorway that is far stronger than one with a flat top. In rows, they're the best possible way of making a whole wall lighter. Because it's curved, an arch transmits all the force from the building above down past it and through the piers that support the arch. A vault is simply a long arch and makes massive buildings far more stable and stronger than solid masses of masonry. Barrel vaults were a key part of Roman bathhouses – they were extremely strong and, unlike timber roofs, resistant to rot from hot, damp air.

Nero's palace (Domus Aurea, 'Golden House') in Rome partly survives because its vast vaulted chambers and passageways were used by Trajan (98–117) as the substructure for his baths. Incredibly, as a result, you can still walk around the very rooms Nero strutted in more then 19 centuries ago.

Using arches and vaults

The Romans used arches together with all the components of Greek architecture like columns, capitals, architraves, and pediments and created a brilliant style of architecture that made cities, villas, palaces, public buildings, forts, and all sorts of public services like sewers and aqueducts possible. I simply can't stress enough how much this changed the world, and the impact is all around today in modern architecture.

The Romans developed the whole idea of the arch and vault so brilliantly that before long they were able to erect the most extraordinary buildings. The Colosseum, built by Vespasian and Titus (69–81), is built out of multiple tiers of arches on the outside and radial barrel vaults within. The only reason it's in ruins today is because it was robbed for stone in the Middle Ages, not because it fell down. The Basilica of Maxentius in the Forum had a 35-metre-high vaulted nave, flanked by barrel-vaulted aisles. It survived until a 1349 earthquake that left just one aisle standing.

Arches just for show

Arches and vaults were beautiful and functional, but perhaps the most striking use was the triumphal arch. Emperors erected these ceremonial arches to celebrate great military victories and triumphs. Domitian (AD 81–96) was especially fond of them. Some are single arches, some have a pair of smaller arches on either side of a big one, and some were four-way arches. But they were all decorated with carved reliefs of triumphant emperors and inscriptions recording their mighty deeds. Today in Rome, the Arches of Titus (79–81), shown in Figure 6-1, Septimius Severus (193–211), and Constantine I (307–337) all survive, but there are lots of other examples all round the Roman world.

The most famous architect – Vitruvius

Marcus Vitruvius Pollio was a professional architect who took part in Augustus's reconstruction of Rome. By 27 BC, he'd already written ten books gathered together under the title *De Architectura* ('On Architecture'), dedicated to Augustus. Those ten books are packed with detail on building materials, techniques, designs, and specifications. This work was used as a standard textbook in Roman times and survived to be copied in a monastery in northern England in the eighth century AD. In the Renaissance, Vitruvius became very influential and was read by all the architects from the fifteenth to eighteenth centuries and is still available today.

Photo by the author

Figure 6-1:
The Arch
of Titus,
dedicated in
Rome's
Forum in
AD 71
during his
father
Vespasian's
reign,
now part-
restored.

All Roads Lead to Rome

If there's one thing the Romans are known for, it's for building long, straight roads. That's a misconception. They certainly built roads, but they often laid them on top of existing prehistoric tracks, and while Roman roads had long straight stretches, they also had corners and changed direction when appropriate.

Until the invention of railways and petrol engines, it was usually cheaper to go by sea, and the Mediterranean – a sort of watery super motorway or interstate – played a vital role in the transport of goods. But Roman roads were still extremely important. The quality of Roman road construction vastly improved their freight-carrying capacity. They linked cities and provinces into a vast network, which saw a continual traffic in men and goods. It really was true that all roads led to Rome.

Via Appia

The Via Appia (Appian Way) is today the most famous and best-preserved of Roman roads. Appius Claudius built the first part in 312 BC as a result of the experience of the Samnite Wars (explained in Chapter 11) – this metalled road created the Roman version of a high-speed communications link between Rome and Capua, down which troops could move quickly. It acted as the template for all the great Roman roads of the Empire to come. Originally just joining Rome to Capua, the Via Appia was later extended to Beneventum (modern Benevento) and finally by 191 BC to Brundisium (Brindisi). The Roman poet Horace wrote an account of a journey on the Appian Way, saying it was 'less tiring if you go slowly' and how he was nearly burned to death by an innkeeper who set his place on fire when roasting thrushes. The most famous user was St Paul, who came up the road from Appii-Forum (Foro Appio) to Rome in AD 61 – it's the only Roman landmark mentioned in the Bible (*Acts of the Apostles* xxviii.15–16).

Strabo, the Roman geographer, said: 'The Romans have built roads throughout the countryside, slicing through hills and filling in dips, so that now their wagons can carry the same-sized loads as boats.'

Road-building basics

The Romans weren't the first to build roads, and they weren't the first to make roads with metalled surfaces. But they were the first to build a very large number of roads, which meant that for the first time in European history many places were linked together.

Laying out a road

Laying out a road meant choosing solid ground and the shortest possible route from A to B. As the Romans loved system and order, straight lines were preferred but not always possible. Gradients were measured, and if the slope was more than about 10 per cent, then the road would have to zigzag up the incline. Some roads had curves to go round hills or followed terraces cut into higher ground. If absolutely essential, tunnels were sometimes cut to carry the road through a hill.

Roman surveyors used a groma to lay out lines. A *groma* had a central post and on top four arms at right angles, each with a plumb line. Two opposite arms could be used to sight a straight line with the help of an assistant standing at a distance and holding a staff. When building streets in a new town or fort, the four arms of a groma helped create neat right-angled junctions so that a grid based on squares (*insulae*, here meaning 'blocks') could be laid out.

Superstitious traffic control

Recent analysis of the deep ruts in Pompeii's streets show Roman traffic had to drive on the right to avoid jams. Romans were highly superstitious and feared anything to do with the left, which is why their words for left and left-hand, *sinister* and *sinistra,* have given us the modern meaning of 'sinister' as something frightening and evil.

Making a road

The real graft came with making the road. Sometimes army legionaries managed the work, but they also used slaves as well as forced local labour in provinces. The road had to remain solid in all weathers, and drain. So a raised bank *(agger)* was created by ramming wooden piles into soft ground (if necessary) followed by foundation layers of stone, gravel, chippings, clay, and then the cobbled road surface, which was built in a curved profile so that rainwater would run off into the drains on either side.

Being endlessly pragmatic, the Romans used whatever materials were to hand to build roads with. In Pompeii, huge slabs of volcanic lava were used for the road surface. In areas where iron ore was abundant, chunks of ore were used to make the surface. The iron rusted and created a rock-hard road surface.

Helping travellers: Road maps, itineraries, and more

The only way a Roman road system could be of much use was if people could plan their journeys. So the Romans had road maps – not accurate maps like today but more like the kind of schematic plans we use for city metro systems. They also had itineraries: lists of places on a particular road with distances between them. As some of the surviving manuscripts were copied in the Middle Ages, we have their texts.

The Antonine Itinerary *(Itinerarium Provinciarum Antonini Augusti)* was an itinerary probably compiled for Caracalla (211–217), though it was added to under later emperors. It's a whole series of 225 tailor-made specific road journeys throughout the Empire with a start and end point and total mileage for each. For archaeologists and historians these routes are extremely useful for finding out the ancient names of towns.

Bridges

Of course, roads can't go everywhere. Rivers and ravines get in the way. But since the Romans had mastered concrete and arches, rivers weren't much of an obstacle, though in more remote places wooden bridges were often built. Some of Rome's bridges are still intact and in use today. The Pons Fabricius was built over the Tiber in 62 BC out of volcanic tufa blocks and faced with marble. Its two main spars are 24 metres (80 feet) across.

One of the most celebrated Roman bridges ever built was put up over the Danube by Trajan (98–117) to control the Dacians beyond. It was probably designed by Apollodorus of Damascus and it's illustrated on Trajan's Column in Rome (see Chapter 17). The historian Dio described it like this:

- It had 20 stone piers 40 metres (150 feet) high

- Each pier stood 50 metres (170 feet) from its neighbours

- The superstructure was made of timber

Dio was exaggerating because this would make it far bigger than the 800 metre (0.5 mile) wide river, but there's no doubt it was still a mighty bridge. Hadrian (117–138) removed the superstructure to stop the Dacians entering the Empire and Dio says the piers were still standing in his own time a century later (in the early AD 200s).

Another way of helping people to get about was with milestones, which were set up alongside major and minor roads. These vary a lot, but most of the surviving ones are rough cylindrical stone pillars with carved inscriptions naming the current emperor, his titles for the year, and sometimes adding the distance to the next town in whole miles. Others were mass-produced with carved imperial titles and had the distance information painted on when they were set up.

Imperial post (cursus publicus)

Fast communications across the Empire were essential if the emperor was to have any chance of issuing edicts, having his orders obeyed, and keeping an eye on provincial governors and military commanders. Augustus introduced the imperial post system, which forced towns and settlements along roads to have carriages and horses permanently ready. They were a little like service stations on interstates or motorways today: They often had inns which provided travellers with beds, baths, and stabling.

Publicus means here 'the state': The service was only available to imperial messengers or anyone else on official business (though it wasn't unknown for officials to use it for private reasons – Pliny the Younger allowed his wife to use it to visit her aunt after her grandfather died). It was an expensive service and Nerva (96–98) transferred the cost to the government.

Chapter 7

Making the Roman Machine Work

In This Chapter

▶ Rome's ports and trade routes

▶ Roman water works: aqueducts, reservoirs, and sewers

▶ How the Romans stayed healthy

*T*rade and industry is essential for any city to work, because by definition the inhabitants rarely produce basics like food. So the city earns its existence by supplying goods and services the rest of the population needs.

Rome was rather different. Not only was it was the biggest city in the ancient world – with a population of more than 1 million, it was twice the size of its nearest competitors, Carthage and Alexandria, and 50 to 100 times bigger than almost all the other cities across the Roman Empire – but as the capital of a vast Empire, Rome simply took whatever resources it wanted or needed from the various regions under its control, whether that was grain from Egypt, marble from Greece, or lead from Britain. But that still meant having all the mechanisms of shipping and ports, merchants, and money, to supply not only Rome, but also the rest of the Empire and the far-flung Roman army as well.

This chapter explains how the Romans used trade routes and technology to keep the vast machinery of their Empire working. It also examines how the Romans managed urban water supplies, using their unparalleled command of hydraulics and plumbing. The water might have helped hygiene, but the Romans were endlessly preoccupied with staying fit and healthy enough to go about their daily business.

Trade Around the Empire

Aelius Aristides (AD117–181) was a Greek orator whose life spanned much of the Empire's greatest days (detailed in Chapter 17). Aristides loved Rome and wrote a eulogy singing the city's praises. He included this observation:

'Large continents lie around the Mediterranean Sea and never-ending supplies of goods flow from them to you [the Roman people]. Everything from every land and every sea is shipped to you . . . so that if anyone wanted to see all these things he would either have to travel the world or live in Rome.'

Rome managed this great influx of goods from around the Empire through its ports. This section gives you the details.

Ostia: The port of Rome

Ostia sums up Rome's commerce. Rome sits inland on the river Tiber, which is too narrow and windy to cope with all the ships and docking facilities Rome needed. From Ostia, ships could be towed upriver to Rome.

Ostia is on the coast, and by the middle of the fourth century BC, it was acting as Rome's port. In 267 BC, Ostia had its own quaestor (see Chapter 3 for details of magistracies). In 217 BC, supplies for the Roman army fighting Hannibal in Spain were shipped from Ostia. Ostia was important enough for Marius to capture the city in 87 BC, and in 67 BC, Pompey used it as his base for the fleet sent out to destroy the Cilician pirates. (You can find out about Marius and Pompey in Chapter 14.)

Ostia's Piazza of Corporations, built early in Augustus's reign (27 BC–AD 14), includes more than 70 offices that were operated by trading companies. Outside each one was a mosaic floor which tells us where the merchants came from and what they traded in, including one from the city of Sabratha (Sabart) in Libya trading in wild animals and ivory, a grain trader from Calares (Cagliari) in Spain, and Algerian traders in dates and fish.

Thanks to a freak of history, Ostia survives as a well-preserved ruin. The river Tiber silted up, leaving the port high and dry, so it was abandoned. Ostia has been excavated, and visitors can now wander round the streets of the city with its houses, shops, apartment blocks, temples, and warehouses.

International trade

Of course, Ostia wasn't the only port. All round the Roman world ports and towns developed because of the constant movement of goods. Part of being in the Roman Empire meant wanting to share in the Roman way of life, and that meant trade, whether you were in the East or the remotest corners of the north-western provinces. East Palmyra, until it was destroyed by Aurelian (AD 270–275; see Chapter 19) for getting above its station, grew into one of the wealthiest cities of antiquity on the great trade route to the Far East.

The many voyages of the Erythraean Sea

Some time in the first century AD, a merchant or seafarer who worked the trade routes between ports like Berenice on Roman Egypt's Red Sea coast to the Gulf of Arabia and India wrote down in Greek what he knew about the various ports, commodities, and routes that were available on a six-month voyage that depended on exploiting seasonal winds. It's a useful indication of the kind of knowledge traders all over the Roman Empire must have used. His account is called the *Periplus Mari Erythrae* ('The Many Voyages of the Erythraean Sea'). This is a little of what he says:

'Malao, distant a sail of about eight hundred stadia [about 100 miles]. The anchorage is an open roadstead, sheltered by a spit running out from the east . . . There are imported into this place the things already mentioned, and many tunics, cloaks from Arsinoe, dressed and dyed; drinking cups,

sheets of soft copper in small quantity, iron, and gold and silver coin, not much. There are exported from these places myrrh, a little frankincense . . . the harder cinnamon, duaca, Indian copal and macir, which are imported into Arabia; and slaves, but rarely.'

And of India: 'On [the Ganges' bank is a market-town which has the same name as the river, Ganges. Through this place are brought malabathrum and Gangetic spikenard and pearls, and muslins of the finest sorts, which are called Gangetic. It is said that there are gold mines near these places, and there is a gold coin which is called *caltis*. And just opposite this river there is an island in the ocean, the last part of the inhabited world toward the cast, under the rising sun itself; it is called Chryse; and it has the best tortoiseshell of all the places on the Erythraean Sea.'

London

London today is one of the world's greatest cities and an international financial centre. Until the Romans arrived in Britain, there was nothing on the site. But the Romans spotted this was the ideal place to bridge the river Thames. So they did. As the river is tidal, ships could come up easily. Within a few years of the Roman invasion, a trading settlement had sprung up all on its own – the very way the Roman world functioned made trading centres essential. By the 70s AD, 30 years after the invasion and despite being destroyed in the Boudican rebellion of AD 60–61 (see Chapter 16), London had a heaving port with wharves and warehouses. Goods were shipped in from all over the Roman Empire into what had become the capital of the new province. Although London shrank after Roman times, it started growing again in the Middle Ages and hasn't stopped since, though it's no longer a port.

Of course, London wasn't the only big port in the Western Roman Empire. Others included Massilia (Marseilles) and Burdigala (Bordeaux) in Gaul, and Gades (Cadiz) in Spain, but only London came from nothing to be a Roman port and then evolve into what it is today.

A universal commodity

Samianware was the name given to a red-slip pottery tableware. Originally made in Arrezzo in Italy, by the mid-first century AD, factories in Gaul had taken over the industry. They made redwares, including plain dishes and cups as well as bowls decorated with figured scenes of gods, gladiators, plants, and animal chases, in unbelievably colossal numbers in vast factory potteries. Shiploads of the finished vessels were sent out from Gaul down rivers to the coast, where traders bought consignments and despatched them across the Western Roman Empire. Places as far apart as northern Britain, the Rhine in Germany, Spain, and North Africa, all bought and used the same pottery from the first to second centuries AD. When the samian industries collapsed in the third century, new ones stepped in like the redware factories of North Africa, which copied samian forms and supplied a huge market across the Empire. Redware is a mark not just of how extensive Roman trade could be, but also how *universal* Roman culture had become. It's rather like today when places all over the world use televisions made by the same Japanese companies.

Trading posts beyond the Empire

Roman traders also went beyond the Empire's borders and set up trading posts in faraway places such as Muziris (possibly modern Kerala) in India. They made money, but it was also part of drawing in other places to a Roman way of thinking. Some of these places ended up being conquered and made into Roman provinces, and by then the local population had got used to the idea of wine from Italy, fish sauce from Spain, and fine pottery from Gaul and Italy. Roman traders and local suppliers also gathered around Roman forts and set up straggling informal settlements (called *canabae,* 'hutments') to help soldiers spend their money. Because forts usually ended up being a road junction, too, once a fort was given up (if it ever was), then these places often stayed and grew into a major settlement in their own right.

The merchants and guild system

Many merchants in Ostia and other ports were equestrians or freedmen, and they could often have personal trading interests in several different provinces – just like modern businesspeople who work in New York and London, or Paris and Munich. Marcus Aurelius Lunaris was a freedman who held office in the colonies of Lincoln and York in Britain. But he went on a business trip to Bordeaux in Gaul and set up an altar to commemorate arriving safely, which is how we know about him.

Rome's rubbish tip: Monte Testaccio

The most astonishing place in Rome isn't a ruined temple or amphitheatre, but Monte Testaccio. It's made out of nothing but millions of fragments of olive oil *amphorae* which came to Rome in the first three centuries AD from Spain and were dumped once their contents had been used. It's 35 metres (38 yards) high and 850 metres (930 yards) around the base. One estimate is that 53 million amphorae went into the hill and that these had brought 10.6 billion pints (6 billion litres) of olive oil to Rome.

Sobering isn't it? The Romans were like us because they had an international marketplace, and they were also like us because they created vast non-biodegradable rubbish dumps!

Merchants at Ostia formed themselves into guilds *(collegia)*, and other such organisations turn up all over the Empire. These guilds stuck together, helped their members out, and made sacrifices to a favoured god. In some ways they were like modern Masonic lodges. Merchants themselves were known as *negotiatores* from which, of course, comes our word 'negotiate', as in 'negotiating' a deal. They were handy for the government, too. When life became more and more controlled under the Dominate (refer to Chapter 20), the government forced guilds to cap their prices and prohibited men from leaving their jobs.

Goodies from Around the World

We can find out about what the Romans traded in from their writings and some of what archaeologists find. But foodstuffs have almost always rotted away. The next best thing is the containers used to transport it, and the commonest of all are the *amphorae* (see Figure 7-1). An *amphora* is a pottery packing case, usually cylindrical or circular in shape, with a conical base and a long neck with two handles. The base made it easy to move around by the handles and made it easier to stack. All across the Roman world amphorae bear witness to the reach of Roman traders, whether in a remote desert oasis site in Egypt or as part of a cargo of a wrecked ship found at the bottom of the sea.

Amphorae were manufactured in their millions to carry around fish sauce, grain, dates, olives, wine – you name it. Sometimes factories stamped the amphorae, or the shippers painted on what the contents were. One from Antipolis (modern Antibes on the Cote D'Azur in the south of France) but found in London where it had been shipped to reads:

Liquam(en) Antipol(itanum) exc(ellens) L(uci) Tett(i)i Africani

Translation? 'Lucius Tettius Africanus's excellent fish sauce from Antipolis.'

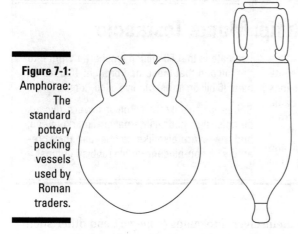

Figure 7-1:
Amphorae:
The
standard
pottery
packing
vessels
used by
Roman
traders.

Of course, the Romans traded in more than food and drink. There were plenty of other things: textiles, glass, ceramics, spices, metals like iron, copper, tin, gold and silver, exotic stone to decorate their houses and public buildings. You name it, the Romans wanted it, and what the Romans wanted they generally got.

Food, glorious food: The grain supply

At its climax, Rome had a population of 1 million people, making it the largest city in the ancient world. Feeding all those people was a mammoth task, but Rome had the power and facilities to cope. Amongst the most important were grain ships from Egypt, North Africa, and Sicily, but alongside them came in ships with olive oil from Spain, wine from numerous places in Italy and around the Mediterranean, and also luxuries like Indian spices and Baltic amber.

Roman political leaders discovered the value of buying food for free handouts. Gaius Gracchus introduced a law that guaranteed cheap grain at a fixed price. The crooked Publius Clodius Pulcher (see Chapter 14 for his other exploits) made grain free when he was Tribune in 58 BC.

By Augustus's time (27 BC–AD 14), 200,000 people in Rome were entitled to free grain (about 20 per cent of the city's population), and providing the grain was now the emperor's personal responsibility. Dozens of officials were involved in the grain handouts, and the emperor knew that if the grain supply was disrupted, he'd have riots on his hands.

The grain dole was known as the *annona,* managed by an equestrian *praefectus* whose job was one of the most important in Rome (see Chapter 3). It also came to mean the grain tax. Soldiers used to take what they needed from populations, or make compulsory purchases, and had wages deducted to pay for it. But by Septimius Severus's time (AD 193–211), buying military loyalty included giving the troops free food so the *annona militaris* was created as a new tax on the whole Empire.

Mining for metals

As the Romans expanded their Empire, the resources they were keenest on getting hold of were mineral resources. The Empire had vast needs for metals:

- **Silver and gold** were the basis of Roman coinage, because they funded the army and the imperial bureaucrats. But they were also used for luxury goods owned by the rich and the emperors, from huge collections of plates to jewellery.

- **Iron** was vital for weapons and tools.

- **Copper, zinc, and tin** were alloyed to make bronze and brass, used in countless everyday objects like taps, brooches, furniture fittings, armour buckles, horse harnesses, small-change coinage, and cheap jewellery.

- **Lead** was the Roman Empire's plastic, being used for pipes, waterproofing roofs, and lining water tanks. It was also alloyed with tin to make pewter, a cheap substitute for silver plate, and with copper and tin to make another form of bronze. Some lead deposits produce silver as well, making them doubly attractive.

New provinces were scoured for mineral resources. Often, thanks to information from traders, the Romans knew perfectly well what was available. Both Spain and Dacia's conquests were quickly followed up by organised mining. Spain was especially attractive. Gold, silver, iron, and copper were all said to be easier to get from Spain than anywhere else. Some Spanish copper mines produced 25 per cent pure copper from every load of ore dug out; in silver mines, around 26 kilograms (57 pounds) of bullion could be dug out every three days. Britain was invaded in the year AD 43. Within six years the latest lead ingots were being shipped out of the new province. Some were used for plumbing at Pompeii, and according to Pliny the Elder, British lead was so easy to mine, a law had been passed limiting production to stop the price collapsing.

Mining was mostly done by slaves, and needless to say there wasn't the slightest concern for health and safety. With so much money to be made, new slaves could be bought as required. Under the Republic, mines were operated by government contractors, but under the emperors, equestrian procurators operated the mining settlements which were about as close to towns in the days of the Old Wild West as you can get (look at those old mining settlements in South Dakota called Silver City and Lead – it's the same story). Rough and tough, they were vicious places where the equestrian procurator was judge, sheriff, town mayor, banker, and chief employer all rolled into one. Private companies could still get a slice of the action, but they had to hand over a portion of what they mined.

Money, Money, Money

The Roman trading world depended on cash (getting metals to make money was a main reason for mining; refer to the preceding section). Roman coins survive in abundance today, a mark of how they were an everyday part of commerce.

Today the money we use is token. US dollar bills and 25-cent pieces, British £1 coins, and European Euro notes and coins aren't worth their face value in terms of the paper or metal they're made from. We accept their face value because we have to by law and because we've got used to the idea.

Roman coinage, and indeed almost any coinage until early modern times, was based on the idea of *intrinsic* value. That means the coin had to be made of metal equal to its value. To look at it another way, a coin was exchangeable at the value of the metal in it. The most important metals for ancient coinage were silver and gold, but brass and copper were used for small change.

Coinage developed in Asia Minor in the first millennium BC because it was such a handy way to store wealth. The Romans first started off using huge lumps of bronze, but by Augustus's time the system had been built round a small silver coin called a *denarius*. These are the main coin types in use until the beginning of the fourth century and the metal they were made of, starting with the lowest value (refer to Figure 7-2):

> *Quadrans* (bronze) = ½ a semis
>
> *Semis* (bronze) = ½ an as
>
> *As* (bronze) = ½ a dupondius
>
> *Dupondius* (brass) = ½ a sestertius
>
> *Sestertius* (brass) = ¼ of a denarius
>
> *Denarius* (silver) = $\frac{1}{25}$ of an aureus
>
> *Aureus* (gold)

Figure 7-2: Roman coins. Top row (left to right): gold aureus, silver denarius, bronze quadrans. Middle row (l-r): brass sestertius, brass dupondius, bronze as. Bottom row (for scale): British 10-pence piece, US quarter dollar.

The important thing about the coinage system is that the coins were generally good throughout the Roman Empire. Most of it was minted at Rome and Lugdunum (Lyons) in Gaul. Egypt had its own special Roman coinage, and cities in the East were able to issue their own local bronze small change. But by and large, Roman currency was universal, and from Diocletian's reign, (284–305) mints across the Roman world produced identical issues.

Propaganda coins

In a world with no mass media, coins were a great way to publicise the emperor, his achievements, and his family. Within weeks or even just days of a new emperor taking power, coins carrying his portrait were sent out into circulation so that everyone would know who he was. Unlike today's coins, each denomination was issued in lots of versions with different reverses, depicting anything from an impressive sounding imperial virtue like *libertas* ('liberty') to pictures of great new public buildings, or commemorations of victories. Other coins might have his wife's, son's, or even mother's portrait on the obverse instead of the emperor's own. Augustus started the trend of putting his intended successor on coins to get the public used to the idea of who was coming next.

Comparative values

It's practically impossible to work out a comparison of values, but at the end of the first century AD, a legionary soldier earned a basic salary of 300 denarii a year. Half went on equipment and keep, and the rest was his. What little we know of prices suggests that ordinary labouring Romans had to work a great deal harder to buy basics than we do. A farm labourer, for example, needed to work a whole day to buy a pint (0.6 litres) of olive oil, while a pair of good quality boots could cost the equivalent of four days' work or more.

Inflation

The Romans weren't very sophisticated in their understanding of how money works. So when an Emperor like Septimius Severus (193–211) needed more silver coins to pay his troops but didn't have the bullion, he just added copper to make the silver go further. As the Empire hadn't been expanding since Trajan's time a century before, there were no new supplies of silver from conquered territory.

IN THEIR WORDS

'Veni, vidi, vici...'

Insider info, Roman style

Around the year 300, a Roman official called Dionysius in Egypt got wind that the coinage was about to be devalued by Diocletian. Before the news got out, he wrote to one of his staff on the family estate to spend all the money on goods:

Dionysius to Apio, Hail.

The divine fortune of our rulers has ordered that coinage struck in Italy shall be reduced to half the value of a nummus. Hurry and spend all the Italian cash you can and buy

any goods for me at the price you find being charged.

I'll point out from the start that if you play any tricks I'll certainly catch you out. I pray that you live long in good health, brother.

Nothing like insider information is there? Of course, the poor mugs who took the money for goods were going to wake up the next day and find it was worth a fraction of that they thought it was.

Weights and measures

Roman money generally worked because it was based on a system of weights and metal purity. This idea affected all other forms of measurement in the Roman world which were fairly consistent and enforced by law overseen by aediles (see Chapter 3 for their role). Here are some of them:

✔ **Distance** was the Roman mile, which equalled 1,536 metres or 1,680 yards, about 0.95 of a modern mile, and based on 1,000 paces of 5 Roman feet (1.48 metres each). The Romans also used the *stadium*, equal to about ⅛ mile. Subdivisions into Roman feet (*pes* = 296 millimetres or 11.65 inches)

helped the accurate design and laying out of buildings, towns, and forts.

✔ **Weights** were based on the Roman pound *(libra)*, equal to 327.5 grams (11.6 ounces), and the Roman ounce *(uncia)*, equal to 27.3 grams (0.96 ounces).

✔ **Dry measures** (for example, for grain) were based on the *modius*, equal to 8.67 litres or 15.2 pints.

✔ **Liquid measures** (for example, wine) were based on the *sextarius*, equal to 0.54 litres or 0.95 pint, and the *congius*, equal to 3.25 litres or 5.72 pints.

The average Roman soldier and the average Roman in the street soon spotted the difference and promptly hoarded the older, purer coin. Traders put their prices up to compensate for being paid in inferior coins and a vicious circle of debased coin and price rises followed. With one more soldier emperor after another trying to buy popularity, silver got rarer. By the 270s, the 'silver' coinage was no more than bronze with a silver wash.

With inflation out of control, Diocletian (AD 284–305) brought in all sorts of measure to try and control the problem (see Chapter 20), including introducing new denominations like the bronze *nummus*. Constantine (307–337) stabilised gold, using a new coin called the *solidus*, but silver virtually disappeared, and we know little about the bronze coins of the fourth century. Government came to depend on taxing in kind.

Turning on the Taps

Apart from roads, the other thing the Romans are famous for is their legendary ability to manage public water supplies. You might think being close to a river like the Tiber would solve all those problems. It doesn't. Rivers are mainly useful for transport and waste. Carrying and lifting water in quantity is incredibly difficult and labour-intensive.

Getting water into a city or a fort was all about gravity: finding a water source at a higher level than where it was needed and leading it there at a gentle gradient. The best thing to do is find a source at a higher level and run it in.

Getting water into cities: Aqueducts

Appius Claudius, who built the Appian Way (Via Appia) in 312 BC (see Chapter 6), also built Rome's first certain aqueduct, though one of the early kings (Ancus Martius, 642–617 BC) was supposed to have built one, too. Appius tapped a spring 16 kilometres (10 miles) from Rome and ran it through an underground tunnel most of the way. Only as it approached Rome was it run in a channel held above ground on masonry arches – which is probably what most people think of as an aqueduct.

Aqueduct just means 'water channel' and that includes buried tunnels, open surface channels, and channels suspended on vast masonry arches snaking across the countryside.

Once the water reached the city, it poured into a dividing tank *(castellum divisiorum)*. Silt and rubbish sank to the bottom. The tank relieved the pressure that built up from water running down a slope for miles and didn't overflow because the water ran straight out into separate pipes that fed:

- Public facilities like the amphitheatre and public baths
- Street fountains
- The houses of the rich

Because even then the pressure would have blown taps off, the water was run up into street corner cisterns suspended on towers which fed the users. These didn't overflow because the water ran off to where it was needed the whole time. It's called a *constant off-take* system. By Domitian's reign (81–96), there were about 1,350 public fountains in Rome alone.

As Rome's population grew, more aqueducts were built, bringing so much water they were, according to Strabo, like rivers. These are some of them:

- **Aqua Marcia:** Built 144–140 BC by Quintus Marcius Rex. It ran for 48 kilometres (30 miles) underground and 9.7 kilometres (6 miles) on masonry arches.
- **Aqua Vergine:** 21 kilometres (13 miles) long, it was built 19 BC by Agrippa to supply the Baths of Agrippa.
- **Aqua Claudia:** Built by Claudius in 52 AD to supply the imperial palaces. It was still running in the fifth century when the barbarian invaders finally wrecked it.

Pompeii's water worries

Just because the Romans had aqueducts doesn't mean the system worked the whole time. Pompeii, like other cities in the Bay of Naples, was supplied by water from the Aqua Augusta, built under Augustus (27 BC–AD 14). A network of underground tunnels and over-ground masonry arcades carried the water to all the cities in the area. Pompeii's arrived in a reservoir *(castellum)* at the highest point of town. Like all Roman public water supplies, the reservoir had three separate supplies: public baths and other public buildings, the houses of the rich, and public street fountains. A network of lead pipes fanned out to supply demand, with a system of street-corner tanks on towers by the street-corner public fountains.

The system worked until AD 62 when an earthquake badly damaged the city, including the reservoir and the pipes. When Vesuvius erupted in AD 79 Pompeii's water service was still being fixed. Rich householders had had to give up on gushing garden pools and bubbling fountains and install tanks to collect rainwater and use wells instead. No-one knows if the street-corner fountains were working again. Today the ruins of the city preserve the best example of a Roman civic water system, even if it wasn't operational when the city was buried by pumice.

We know a lot about Rome's aqueducts because Sextus Julius Frontinus (c. AD 35–103) was put in charge of them in 97. He wrote a report on them that survives today. Amongst other things, he was worried at how people were illegally siphoning off aqueduct water into their own homes and letting trees roots damage the aqueduct structures. But he also said that the building and maintenance of the aqueducts gave 'the best testimony to the greatness of the Roman Empire *(magnitudinis Romani imperii)*'.

Wells and reservoirs

Aqueducts weren't the only solution to providing water. Sometimes chains of buckets linked together were lowered into shafts dug down to subterranean water supplies. Driven by slaves or animals, this was one way of getting water to a small baths or maybe a factory, but it would have been hopeless for anything more.

Out in more arid places, the Romans collected any rainwater they could and used underground tunnels to supply reservoirs. There's a large masonry reservoir at the city of Thuburbo Majus in modern Tunisia. A similar system in Syria at the city of Androna (Al Anderin) that included underground irrigation channels was still functioning in the 1960s until modern water systems disrupted the water table. Using all this experience in handling water, in the sixth century AD, the Byzantines built a vast subterranean reservoir (140 x 70 metres) under Constantinople's Hippodrome. Supported by 336 columns, it's still there, and you can visit it.

Baths

Bathing was fundamental to Roman life in the days of the Empire. Vast public bathing facilities were built in Rome (such as the Baths of Titus, of Trajan, of Caracalla, and of Diocletian), in every city in the Roman Empire (Pompeii had at least three public baths), and in most small settlements. Rich people could afford to install private baths in their houses and country villas.

Bathing was a daily (usually afternoon) ritual for most people and involved a series of baths, one after the other. Although bathing was mixed in some periods, for much of Roman history, baths were segregated between men and women. The bather arrived at the baths and went through a series of rooms, and as you can see, the whole set-up was rather like a modern fitness centre or sports and social club:

- *Apodyterium:* The changing room.

- *Tepidarium:* A warm room, perhaps with a warm plunge bath, where the body started sweating.

- *Caldarium:* A hot room like a Turkish bath, where bathers sat around in clouds of steam, sweating out dirt as their pores opened in the heat. Slaves used a *strigil* to scrape the skin, and oils and perfumes could be rubbed into the skin.

- *Frigidarium:* The cold bath where bathers could swim in cool water, close the pores, and relax.

- *Palaestra:* The exercise area for running, jumping, and various sports.

IN THEIR WORDS

'Veni, vidi, vici...'

Grooming and gossip

One of the best descriptions of what happened in a bath comes from Seneca, Nero's tutor (see Chapter 16 for information on Nero). Seneca lived so close to a bath, he had to put up with all the noise and complained about it in a letter to a friend:

> 'I hear the groans as the he-men pump iron and throw those heavy weights all over the place . . . If for instance there's a lazy chap who's satisfied with a straightforward massage I can hear the slap of a hand on his shoulder . . . If a ball player comes up and starts yelling out his score – then that's me finished. Pile on top of that the row of some

cheeky so-and-so, a thief being caught, and one of those blokes who likes singing in the bath, as well as those who dive into the pool with giant splashes of water. That's as well as those with the loud voices. Think about the skinny plucker of arm-pit hair whose yells are so resonant that everyone notices him except when he's getting on with his work and making someone else yell for him. Now add on the medley of noise from drink sellers, sausage, pastry and hot-food vendors, each hawking his goods with his own individual cry.'

Roman toilets

The Romans were sociable toilet-users. Public toilets had one-piece seating platforms all round the wall with keyhole cut-outs. People marched in and sat down next to one another (no question of individual cubicles). Meanwhile, water poured into basins where users could wash their hands and soak sponges to wipe their bottoms. The water flowed out and into a channel, boosted with extra water which ran round under the seats to carry away the waste either into a sewer or into a soakaway.

Baths weren't just a place to get clean. Baths were where business was conducted, contacts made, gossip exchanged, and dinner invitations offered. In short, they were one of the most important social centres in Roman life, and the fact that they were built all over the Empire is another reflection of the impact of Roman culture.

Bathing in huge, luxurious public facilities was something of a new fad. It seems the old Romans of the Republic were above such things. In Rome's ancient days, the Romans scarcely washed at all and were proud of how they smelled of the dirt from 'the army, of farm work, and manliness'.

Getting rid of water: Rome's sewers

Baths produced waste water, and so did public latrines, industry (like laundries and fullers), and private houses. The Romans used their skills with arches, concrete, stone, and brick to build networks of underground sewers that poured the waste into the river Tiber. The system went back at least as far as Tarquinius Superbus (535–509 BC) who built the *Cloaca Maxima,* the 'Great Sewer' (refer to Chapter 10 for his reign).

Some of the sewers in Rome were big enough for boats to sail up, which is what Agrippa did in 33 BC on a tour of inspection when he was aedile. There were so many of them, Rome was called a 'city on stilts'. Other cities had sewers, too, but the quality ranged from open-air gutters to elaborate systems like Rome's. But not all Romans benefited from sewers. Many cities relied on using the streets for open sewers. That's why Pompeii's streets have huge stepping stones, to help locals make sure they didn't step in the . . . you can guess.

Keeping Well: Medicine

Naturally the Romans got sick and suffered accidents just like we do. They knew nothing about micro-organisms like bacteria and viruses, but their love of baths, clean water, and reliable sewers did mean some or parts of their cities were a lot more hygienic than their medieval equivalents. In fact, it's broadly true to say that nowhere was as hygienic as Rome was until the Victorians started building proper sewage systems in London and other Western cities.

Incidentally, it's often said that people before modern times lived shorter lives than we do. That's only partly true. What it really means is that *average* lives were shorter. Actually, the Romans were just as capable of living into their eighties and beyond as we are; it's just that fewer of them got a chance to do so and that brings the average down. Cato the Elder was 85 when he died. The emperor Gordian I (238) was in his eighties when he committed suicide. A soldier in the XX legion in Wales reached 100 years old, and there are plenty of other examples. For most people though, disease, violence, and accidents put pay to any plans for a ripe old age. None of those things stopped the average Roman from putting his or her faith in medicine.

Medical science in the Roman era

Medicine was almost totally dominated by the Greeks, so much so that if a doctor wasn't a Greek, then he would have no credibility at all – a bit like how everyone expects acupuncturists today to be Chinese. Very few Romans practised medicine, and even if they did, it was best to publish in Greek. Greek doctors turn up all over the Roman Empire and included slaves, and freedmen. There was no formal training or system of qualifications, which meant that more or less any Greek could call himself a doctor and practise medicine.

Needless to say, the way was open to quacks who toured the Empire with patent remedies which they sold to local practitioners, like eye salves (see the later section 'Medicine for the masses'). To the smarter Romans, this was all utter nonsense.

Pliny the Elder called medicine 'the vacant words of intellectual Greeks' and reminded his readers 'not everything handed down by the Greeks deserves admiration'. Pliny pointed out that no two doctors ever produced the same diagnosis, cursing a profession that changed its claims daily (doesn't that sound familiar?!). Pliny had plenty more to say, but in the end he blamed quackery on the gullibility of people who didn't have a clue about how illness and medicine worked. No wonder so many put all their faith in healing cults, which were a big part of Roman religion (see Chapter 9).

Surgeons and doctors

Roman medicine wasn't all about quacks. Pliny the Elder was just one of a number of serious Roman scientists who were interested in what really made the world tick. Cornelius Celsus, who lived in the time of Tiberius (AD 14–37) wrote an encyclopedia on just about everything. The only part which survives is his *De Medicina* ('On Medicine'). Celsus discussed the various schools of Greek medical thought:

- ✔ **The Empiricists** who believed in the value of experience in curing people, rather than worrying about what caused diseases (they thought it was impossible to answer that, so a waste of time thinking about it).

- ✔ **The Methodics** who worked on a basis of treating diseases according to types.

- ✔ **The Dogmatics** who accepted, without question, explanations of disease handed down from ancient Greeks like Hippocrates.

Celsus showed that serious Roman doctors were very well aware of the value of a good diet and physical fitness. They knew about all sorts of diseases, which they could recognise from symptoms, and they had a good idea of a patient's prognosis. A variety of treatments were known, from treating with drugs and herbs to letting blood, which, incidentally, shows just how far off the mark Roman doctors could be. This is what Celsus says about letting blood:

> 'For a broken head, blood should be preferably let from the arm . . . blood is also at times diverted when, having burst out of one place, it is let out another.'

Despite the ideas these ancient doctors got right, they still got plenty wrong. Ironically, Pliny's own *Natural History* is just as full of nonsense as some of the medical writings he criticised. And thanks to men like Celsus, doctors were still letting blood in the belief it was a good idea until the nineteenth century.

It's a wonder the Roman population survived at all, quite apart from the risk of infection from being cut open by a doctor. No wonder the poet Martial said that he'd been fine before being examined by a doctor and his medical students, but had a fever afterwards.

Practical anatomy

Roman doctors were hampered by not knowing much about anatomy – how the body worked. It wasn't for want of trying. Celsus recommended examining a wounded gladiator whose guts were hanging out because that was an ideal way of seeing how a body worked while it was still alive, instead of relying on dead bodies.

Celsus wasn't a doctor, but Claudius Galenus (AD 129–199), a Greek from Pergamum, was. Galenus was as disgusted by the quacks as Pliny the Elder was and he ended up being chased out of Rome for being so public about his views. He wrote a book in Greek called *On the Natural Faculties,* combining his own knowledge with that of earlier doctors. He was mainly interested in clinical observation and deductive reasoning drawn from that. Unfortunately, Galenus's work was also often incorrect – for example, he thought blood went to-and-fro – and proving Galenus wrong, as did the pioneer William Harvey (1578–1657) who discovered the circulation of blood, was all part of the dawn of modern science and realising the ancients weren't perfect.

Medicine for the masses

The average Roman had little or no access to quality medical care of any sort. Of course, the Romans didn't suffer from eating the over-refined, fatty foods packed with sugar that plague our society, and they were probably a great deal fitter than we are. But for most of them, a broken limb might be set badly if at all, and for all sorts of diseases and infection, there was no reliable cure at all, even if you could afford one. For these people the only options were folk cures, cheap patent remedies sold by quacks, and a trip to the nearest healing cult centre (see Chapter 9 for information about those).

Medicines were often made in small blocks or sticks. To identify them, the makers or 'doctors' pressed engraved stone stamps into them. Some of these stamps survive like one which announces: 'Tiberius Claudius M(. . .)'s frankincense salve for every defect of the eyes. Use with egg.' Another one boasts: 'Gaius Junius Tertullus's copper oxide salve for eye-lid granulations and scars.'

Chapter 8

Entertainments: Epic and Domestic

The two most famous Roman movies ever, *Spartacus* (1960) and *Gladiator* (2000), have one thing in common: the brutal world of the Roman gladiator and his short, dangerous life. They give the impression that every Roman spent his every waking hour down at the amphitheatre watching men fight to the death. Now for some Romans that might have been true, so this chapter starts with arenas and gladiators, a distinctly Italian form of entertainment with ancient origins that found a ready audience in parts of the Roman Empire.

There were also the incredible chariot races. Operated at lunatic speeds by superstar charioteers, they were the ultimate thrill for Roman boy racers. For people with politer tastes, and there were plenty of them, there were the theatres for plays and pantomimes, and little odeons for readings and poetry. And there were also the pleasures of stopping in and having dinner parties.

Introducing the Games

For most people in the Roman Empire, life was nasty, brutal, and short. In a world where war was common, where anyone could carry a lethal weapon, where appalling accidents at work happened all the time, and where people born with any kind of handicap were extremely unlikely to get medical help, physical violence and cruelty were taken for granted.

That's why most people who took part in public entertainments were slaves. If free people didn't matter much, then slaves didn't matter at all. Slaves were just a resource, and as far as the Roman authorities were concerned, one of the best ways of using them was in entertaining the mob and keeping it off the streets.

The famous phrase 'bread and circuses' *(panem et circenses)* comes from the Roman satirist Juvenal who lived *c.* AD 60–130. What he said was that the Roman people had only two interests in life: a full stomach and the action of the games. On the whole, he was probably right.

Bonding the population

Upper-class Romans originally looked down on public entertainment as a vice because games were thought undignified and nothing to do with 'proper Roman virtues' of restraint and self-discipline. So even when they put on an event in the early days, Roman aristocrats tried as hard as possible to make sure nobody enjoyed them. There weren't any seats at gladiatorial fights, for example, so everyone had to stand. When the Romans got round to putting up venues for these events to take place in, they took them apart straight-away afterwards out of a sort of shame but also because they were terrified of getting a crowd of the lower classes all together in one place.

Nevertheless, the games proved a great cultural way to bond the population, because they helped reinforce the religious connection and kept the mob out of trouble. No wonder the terrible days of the Second Punic War (discussed in Chapter 12) were when public games became more and more important.

The mob had no hang-ups about the games, so during the late Republic, men like Sulla and Caesar soon realised how putting on free games for the mob at their own personal expense could increase their popularity ratings. Later emperors followed the trend, and so did local politicians all round the Empire. A sort of free-for-all occurred, in which anyone who could afford it put on games, trying to buy political advantage and popularity. Not surprisingly, Roman historians of the day blamed the loss of 'proper Roman virtues' on all this crowd-pleasing, though they never asked themselves what the crowds would be doing if they weren't being kept busy in the arena or at the circus.

The gaming calendar

Roman public entertainments were an important part of the annual religious calendar. The *Ludi Consualia* (see the list in the next paragraph) were dedicated to Consus, another name for Neptune, god of the sea. His Greek equivalent, Poseidon, was also associated with horses. So you can see why chariot-racing might end up being associated with Neptune. Rather obscure but, as a later Roman writer called Tertullian discovered while researching the games for his book *On the Spectacles,* it was no clearer to the Romans.

By the time of the Empire, the annual religious calendar and its games were pretty well sorted out and getting on, for around half the year was allocated to religious holidays with games *(ludi)*. These games included everything from chariot-racing to animal fights and gladiatorial bouts. Some, like the *Ludi Cereales,* went back to some remote part of Rome's ancient mythical past, while others were connected with politics and war. These are the main ones, but there were others – almost any excuse would do:

- ✔ **The Megalian Games** *(Ludi Megalenses):* Celebrated 4–10 April with their origins in the introduction of the Great Mother *(Magna Mater)* of the gods, Cybele, in Rome in 204 BC.

- ✔ **The Cerealian Games** *(Ludi Cereales):* Celebrated 12– 19 April in honour of Ceres, the goddess of harvests and her children, Liber and Libera, deities of planting.

- ✔ **The Floral Games** *(Ludi Florales):* Celebrated 28 April to 3 May in honour of Flora, a goddess of flowers and also associated with licentious behaviour.

- ✔ **The Apollinarian Games** *(Ludi Apollinares):* Celebrated 6–13 July and given for the first time in 212 BC to celebrate the defeat of Hannibal at Cannae. Dedicated to Apollo.

- ✔ **The Consualian Games** *(Ludi Consualia):* Celebrated twice a year, on 21 August and again on 15 December.

- ✔ **The Roman Games** *(Ludi Romani):* Celebrated 5–19 September in honour of Jupiter Optimus Maximus, the king of the gods, and the ultimate power over Roman destiny.

- ✔ **The Plebeian Games** *(Ludi Plebei):* Celebrated 4–17 November. They were started during the Second Punic War (218–202 BC) to keep up morale amongst the public (the *plebs*).

It's very unlikely whether any of the spectators screaming with excitement gave a moment's thought to the religious origins of the games. So, let's get on with the action!

The Playing Fields: Arenas and Stadiums

In the early days, almost any open area would do for putting on games. Right down to the days of Augustus, the Forum in Rome was used. Archaeologists have discovered that temporary wooden seats were erected around an area in the middle of the Forum where there were specially designed underground tunnels equipped with lifting machinery to raise weapons, scenery, and other gear for the action. When the games were over, the seats were removed and the underground chambers closed until the next time. The Colosseum (see the section 'The Colosseum', later in this chapter) later exploited this technology to the full, but made it permanent.

Rome didn't get a stone amphitheatre until 29 BC when Statilius Taurus built one in Mars Field. Funnily enough, the oldest known permanent arena, or amphitheatre, isn't in Rome but at Pompeii. It was built in 80 BC and was large enough to hold 20,000 people. Like all amphitheatres, Pompeii's had an elliptical arena surrounded by rows and rows of seats raked at an angle so that all the spectators could get a view (see Figure 8-1). In case of any danger from the gladiators or wild beasts, a high wall separated the contestants from the public.

Figure 8-1: Pompeii's ancient amphitheatre, dating to 80 BC, and the oldest known.

Photo by the author.

Arenas could be used for several things:

- ✔ Gladiator bouts
- ✔ Animal hunts
- ✔ Re-enactments of great battles and naval events for the mob
- ✔ Displays of mock battles by army units for soldiers' entertainment
- ✔ Religious festivals

Building an arena

Arenas were usually built towards the edge of major cities or even outside the city walls. Soldiers also built them, generally just outside the walls of their forts. They also turn up sometimes at religious shrine sites in the countryside. They're generally amongst the biggest buildings put up by the Romans, but they range from colossal pieces of masonry architecture like the massive example at El-Djem in Tunisia, to ones where wooden seats were fitted to banks of earth surrounding a dug-out arena, as in Silchester in Britain. Small towns either didn't have them at all or just put up temporary wooden arenas which have left no trace.

Amphitheatres are mainly known in Italy, Gaul, parts of North Africa, Spain, and Britain, but scarcely ever appeared in the East where the Greek tradition of the theatre remained dominant. But there is the odd exception. The Romans added an amphitheatre to the great Greek city of Pergamon in Asia Minor, for instance. The most elaborate arenas had subterranean areas for storing animals, prisoners, and gladiators, and lifting gear to bring them up to ground level. They also had hydraulic equipment for flooding the arena for naval battles, and drainage systems – the water could also be used to flush out the blood and gore after the killing had finished.

Roman society was strictly hierarchical, and that was reflected in who got the best seats in the arena. The emperor, his family, and hangers-on had a kind of 'royal box'. Senators took the front rows, behind them came the equestrians, and then citizens. Their women sat behind them, and next came the lower classes in the higher rows and standing-room-only.

The Colosseum

The most famous and impressive amphitheatre of all is the Colosseum in Rome, a very large part of which still stands and dominates the middle of the city (see Figure 8-2). It was started by the emperor Vespasian (AD 69–79) who used the site of Nero's Golden Palace (see Chapter 16 for more on Nero). Since Nero (AD 54–68) had helped himself to large areas of Rome in order to build his extravagant residence, Vespasian knew that building a whopping entertainment centre on the same site was an excellent way to buy popular support.

The genius of the Colosseum was the design, and it was typical Roman: big, brash, and completely practical. Fully equipped with state-of-the-art underground chambers and hydraulics, it also had a vast sun roof that could be stretched over the crowd to keep the spectators in the shade. The underground operations took place in nine tunnel sections, with numerous workrooms branching off them. One quarter of the arena was made up of moveable flooring which acted as ceilings for the tunnels. They were pivoted at one side and were lowered by ropes and pulleys into the tunnels where scenery was prepared. Then they were raised while fighters and animals were sent up top through trap doors and elevators. Just to get an idea of the kind of killing spectacle the Colosseum could handle, as well as getting all the punters in and out in double-quick-time, under Trajan (AD 98–117), games were held to celebrate his conquest of the Dacians and an almost unbelievable 10,000 gladiators fought.

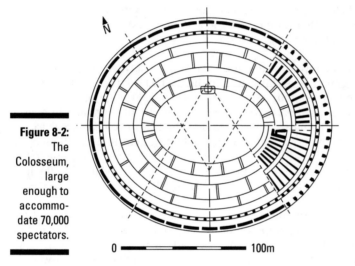

Figure 8-2:
The Colosseum, large enough to accommodate 70,000 spectators.

0 ▬▬▬▬▬▬ 100m

Stadiums

The stadium (or *circus*) was used for chariot-racing. A stadium had a long rectangular enclosure, curved at one end, with seats all round except at the straight end. Down the middle was the spine *(spina),* which the chariots hurtled around, lap after lap, trying to cut in front of each other.

Rome had eight chariot stadiums alone, and most other major cities either had a permanent stadium or an open field that could be set up as a temporary venue. Until very recently, far-off foggy Britain was thought to be an exception, but now one's been found at Colchester, putting it on a par with great cities of the East like Aphrodisias in Asia Minor (Turkey), which has one of the best-preserved.

Rome's greatest circus was the monumental Circus Maximus, ('The Greatest Circus'). It's one of, if not *the,* biggest buildings ever erected in world history for a spectator event. The first races were held here right back in the semi-mythical days of the kings of Rome. By the days of the emperors, it had been extended and enlarged. The Circus Maximus is still visible today in Rome, but most of the structures remain buried. One of the best-preserved is the Circus of Maxentius just outside Rome's walls by the Appian Way; Figure 8-3 shows its plan.

Colossal Colosseum fun facts

- It took 12 years to build the Colosseum out of thousands of 5-ton blocks of stone.

- Efficient use of arches and vaults meant only 9,198 cubic metres (325,000 cubic feet) of stone were used (the Empire State building used ten times as much).

- The blocks were held together by 300 tons of metal clamps.

- The Colosseum was 186 metres (611 feet) long and 154 metres (507 feet) wide and could accommodate 70,000 spectators, meaning it would still be in the Top Twenty stadiums in Europe today, beating the new Emirates Stadium for Arsenal in London by 10,000!

- There were 76 numbered entrances. Tickets were issued with specified entrances on them so the 70,000-strong crowd knew where to go and where to exit in an emergency.

- Estimated exit time for all 70,000 spectators was three minutes!

- The Colosseum wasn't finished until the reign of Vespasian's son Titus (AD 79–81) and was dedicated in AD 80.

- It got its name because a colossal bronze statue of Nero stood close by, later adapted into a Sun-God. Pliny the Elder described the statue, called the Colossus, as 32 metres high and 'breathtaking'. Because everyone knew where the statue was, it eventually became a kind of address tag for the new arena and the name stuck.

- In 217 the Colosseum was badly damaged by lightning. Repairs lasted until the reign of Gordian III (238–244).

- The last recorded animal hunts in the Colosseum were held in 523 by Eutharich, son-in-law of Theodoric the Great (go to Chapter 21 for details about him).

- The Colosseum still stands to its full height of 50 metres (163 feet) on one side.

- The gladiators' barracks were right next door to the Colosseum and a large part of them is still visible today.

Figure 8-3:
The Circus Maxentius. Smaller than the Circus Maximus, but the best-preserved at Rome (it's outside the city walls by the Appian Way).

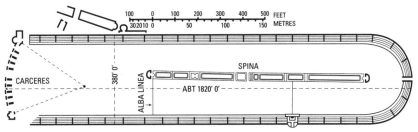

Circus Maximus fun facts

- The first stone parts were built in 174 BC.

- By the first century BC, 100,000 fans could be seated.

- By Nero's reign (AD 54–68), 250,000 fans could get in, matching today's biggest stadium: the Indianapolis Speedway (built 1909). Some believe as many as 320,000 could be crammed in later on.

- The Circus Maximus was 594 metres (1,950 feet) long and 201 metres (660 feet) wide.

- The spina down the middle had a turning post at each end.

- Each race had seven laps (about 5 miles). Seven bronze dolphins on pivots at one end of the spina and seven bronze eggs at the other were used to count them.

- Black gypsum flakes were scattered on the track to make it look bright.

- There were religious shrines along the spina.

- The spina also had obelisks shipped all the way from Egypt to show off Rome's mighty power.

- In the passageways and arches under the seats, cooks, astrologers, and prostitutes catered for the fans' other needs.

- Under Antoninus Pius (AD 138–161) overcrowding caused the deaths of more than 1,000 spectators.

- In 2006, tens of thousands of jubilant Italians gathered here once more to watch on giant screens their nation win the soccer World Cup and celebrate afterwards.

People would start gathering in the middle of the night to get the best seats. No wonder the writer Pliny the Younger looked forward to race days. He hated them, but with a quarter of a million Romans busy watching the action, it meant the streets were deserted and he could get on with his work in peace and quiet.

Fighting Men: Gladiators

Easily the best-known Roman entertainment today, gladiatorial combats were one of the most extreme forms of amusing a crowd of people in history. Specially equipped and trained fighters fought bouts in matched pairs to the death. The Etruscans probably started the idea by making prisoners fight to the death during the funerals of aristocrats, but it was the Samnites who really developed gladiator fights. They depicted bouts on their tomb walls after 400 BC. The Romans even called all gladiators 'samnites'. The first gladiator fight staged in Rome was in 264 BC when Decimus Junius Brutus made three pairs of slaves fight in honour of his dead father. It was a kind of substitute for the old human sacrifices. After that, gladiators evolved into a private form of aristocratic entertainment before becoming big-business box-office entertainment for the masses in the cities of the West and North Africa. Although amphitheatres for gladiator fights were very rare in the Eastern Empire, other venues like theatres or public squares must have been used. Ephesus in Asia Minor had no amphitheatre but the discovery of a large gladiators' cemetery (tombstone epitaphs and wounds on bones prove it) shows that even here gladiator fights were part of local entertainment.

The gladiators: Who they were

The word 'gladiator' comes from the Latin word for sword, *gladius,* so it means literally a 'swordsman'. The best way to get a man to fight to the death is to use a man who has nothing to lose, which is why slaves, criminals, and prisoners-of-war were the perfect candidates. If a man was really good, he might keep winning and get his freedom. On the whole, it was an offer he couldn't refuse even though the odds were, let's face it, not particularly good.

Slaves weren't the only gladiators, however. Some freemen volunteered, too, especially if they were down on their luck. Nero (AD 54–68), being fairly mad and with a very individual idea of what would be entertaining, once ordered that 400 senators and 600 equestrians fight as gladiators. This was a way of humiliating them, and no doubt the Roman mob thought this was extremely funny. But the most remarkable of them all was probably the emperor Commodus (AD 180–192; Chapter 18) who was a dab hand at gladiatorial fighting (not that anyone would have dared killing him). He bragged that he had fought 735 times without getting hurt and defeated 12,000 opponents.

Schools for scoundrels

There was no point in chucking just any man into the arena. Gladiatorial combat was a crowd-pleasing activity, so the action had to be good. Only men with serious fighting potential were chosen, sent to special gladiatorial schools called *ludi* that were run by businessmen called *lanistae*. The training was tough, but gladiators were well-fed and trained to the peak of physical fitness. Pompeii had a large and well-appointed gladiator school, which was buried when Mount Vesuvius erupted in AD 79. Over 60 gladiators perished there, but evidence was also found of an unexpected perk. The remains of a rich aristocratic woman were recovered – it seems she had stopped by for a 'visit' so to speak, when disaster struck. It's a reminder that successful gladiators were incredibly popular and not just for what they did in the arena.

Riot day in Pompeii

In the year AD 59, a gladiatorial contest was laid on at Pompeii by a Senator called Livineius Regulus. Rival supporters from a nearby town called Nuceria rolled up to cheer on their heroes. The locals and visitors started off by shouting at one another and then moved on to hurling stones. Soon swords were drawn, and before anyone could do anything, lots of Nucerians were being stabbed and swiped at by the Pompeians who seem to have come better equipped to cause trouble. Even women and children were cut down. The Senate in Rome was so disgusted that gladiatorial shows were banned for ten years in Pompeii as a punishment, and Regulus was forced into exile.

The fear of gladiators

Julius Caesar laid on a display of 320 gladiatorial pairs in commemoration of his dead father, but knew perfectly well it would impress people and increase his popular support. His enemies were absolutely horrified at the thought of 640 trained killers on Caesar's payroll (640 gladiators were more than a cohort of legionaries; refer to Chapter 5 for info about the Roman army) and promptly passed a law limiting the number of gladiators that could be used at any one time. The overall result was that gladiators represented a horrible, edge-of-your-seat, rabble-rousing type of glamour.

The slave revolt led by Spartacus in 73 BC started in a gladiatorial training school – remember, these boys knew how to use weapons, had nothing to lose, and terrified Italy witless (see Chapter 14 for more about the Revolt and Chapter 25 for Spartacus).

Putting on a gladiatorial show

Gladiatorial events were publicised in advance to whip up excitement to fever-pitch on the day. One painted advertisement in Pompeii announced that a total of 30 pairs of gladiators would fight each day from 8–12 April one year, together with an animal hunt. The fights were always the big event of the day. In the Colosseum, the gladiators marched in and stood before the emperor and announced *Ave Imperator, morituri te salutant* ('Hail Emperor, those about to die salute you!').

Types of gladiators

It wouldn't be much fun if all the gladiators were all the same, so the action was whizzed up by having lots of different types. This took advantage of the fact that gladiators might come from anywhere in the Roman Empire and had a whole array of specialised fighting techniques. Here are some of them:

- ✔ **Myrmillo (originally *Samnis*):** Wore a fish-like helmet and had sword and large shield.

- ✔ **Retiarius:** Fought with a trident and a net.

- ✔ **Sagitarius:** Fought with a bow and arrow.

- ✔ **Secutos:** Had a shield, sword, heavy helmet, and armour on one arm. Meaning 'pursuer', the secutores were originally based on Samnite warriors.

- ✔ **Thrax:** Armed with a curved sword and small shield (the name meaning 'Thracian').

Nor was gladiator-fighting a men-only activity. From time to time women gladiators fought. Domitian (81–96) put women into the ring, but Septimius Severus (193–211) thought that was disgusting and banned women fighting. To add to the variety, even dwarf gladiators were brought on occasionally.

Gladiators all had their own personal fans who painted slogans on walls. Two at Pompeii say 'The *thrax* Celadus makes all the girls sigh' and 'The hearththrob of all the girls is Crescens the *retiarius*'.

Winner takes all

The climax of every bout was when a gladiator was down. Then it was up to the crowd. If it had been a rubbish fight, they shouted *Lugula*, 'Kill him', but if he'd fought well, they'd shout *Mitte* for 'Let him go'. The final say-so went to the man who'd put the games on. If the downed gladiator was spared, the fight continued. If not, he was killed and his body dragged off so the next bouts could take place.

Meanwhile, the lucky winner got money and a palm leaf, a symbol of victory that went back to the Greeks when men competed in sport only for the honour of taking part. If a gladiator had done especially well, he got the ultimate prize: a wooden sword, which was a symbol of his freedom. Amazingly, some gladiators earned their freedom but carried on, obviously enjoying it too much. Or perhaps they'd forgotten how to do anything else.

Fighting Animals

Wild beasts were another deadly part of Roman entertainment. There's a mosaic from a remote Roman villa in East Yorkshire in England called Rudston. It features various scenes from the amphitheatre including wild beasts. One of the lions is called *Omicida*, meaning 'man-killing' (hence our word 'homicide'). It's almost certainly a picture of a real, and famous, lion from an arena somewhere that the mosaicist or the villa-owner knew about. Mosaics like this were especially popular in North Africa so perhaps that's where he came from.

Killing wild animals was the normal way to start a day at the arena. During the Colosseum's inaugural games in AD 80, a phenomenal 5,000 animals were killed in a single day. After his conquest of Dacia, Trajan (AD 98–117) arranged in the year 107 for 11,000 animals to fight in the arena. The whole lot were killed, even though they included tame beasts. To celebrate Rome's thousandth birthday in AD 247, the emperor Philip the Arab (AD244–249) arranged for a special display that included (amongst others):

- ✔ 60 lions
- ✔ 40 wild horses
- ✔ 32 elephants
- ✔ 6 hippos
- ✔ 1 rhinoceros

Supplying animals

Of course, part of the treat was just the display of exotica, which showed off Rome's amazing control over such a wide range of territories. Lions, rhinoceroses, and giraffes had long since disappeared from Europe, but in antiquity North Africa was a good deal more fertile than it is today. Once the Romans had control of all of North Africa, they had access to wildlife that couldn't live there today even if the Romans hadn't done such a good job of wiping them out.

Expeditions were sent out to capture wild animals and bring them to ports in North Africa from where they could be shipped to Rome. Of course, it was impossible to supply every arena with a constant supply of African wildlife, so probably most of the provincial arenas had to make do with less exciting animals like hares, wolves, and wild boar.

Animals in the arena

The animals were kept in cages in the Colosseum's underground chambers and fed with cattle, or once, under Caligula, on criminals. On the day of the games, they were lifted up to the arena and sent out to do their work. Sometimes it was – literally – easy meat, especially when the entertainment on offer was the execution of criminals or other undesirables.

Although one way of having a show was simply to set animals against one another, that didn't really make for co-ordinated and organised entertainment. To warm things up and get some serious action going, specialised animal hunters were sent into the arena to thrill the crowds. Just like gladiators, they'd been selected from the ranks of criminals, slaves, and prisoners-of-war. They were called *venatores* ('hunters'), helped by *bestiarii* ('animal fighters' from *bestia,* 'wild beast'), but were nothing like as popular as the gladiators.

Julius Caesar was the first to introduce a special type of bull-killing into the arena. The hunters rode horses alongside running bulls and killed them by twisting their heads with the horns. Most unpleasant.

Epic Shows and Mock Battles

These days, we make the most of great historical events by going to watch epic movies about them. In Rome, the epics came from great tales of heroic battles and myth. The most extravagant displays in the arena came from re-enactments of these great events, or were just made up for the sake of more action. They were another way of making use of the gladiators' talents.

Julius Caesar laid on a mock battle between two armies. Each had 500 infantry, 20 elephants, and 30 cavalry. He also laid on a mock naval battle by flooding an arena and had ships brought in with two, three, and four banks of oars, each manned by a squad of soldiers. They posed as the rival fleets of Egypt and the city of Tyre. The event was so popular that people turned up from far and wide to see the spectacle, even going to the extreme of camping by the roadside to make sure of a good view on the day.

Nero staged a sea battle with mock sea monsters swimming about amongst the ships. But he had an even better idea for making himself as popular as possible. He instituted the *Ludi Maximi,* 'the Greatest Games', and organised a continuous round of free gifts all day long, ranging from 1,000 birds, food, precious metals, and jewellery right up to handing out ships, houses, and farms.

A Day at the Races – Chariot-racing

Chariot-racing was a wildly popular sport in the Roman Empire. The tradition went right back to the very beginning. Rome's mythical founder, Romulus, is supposed to have asked his neighbours, the Sabines, to pop round and enjoy an afternoon of chariot-racing back in around 753 BC. Actually, Romulus had tricked them. While the Sabines were engrossed in the action, he got his heavies to snatch the Sabine women.

Roman chariots

Roman chariots were ultra lightweight flimsy affairs with just enough room for a man to stand on and hold the reins. In an accident, the chariot would fall to pieces in an instant and hurl the charioteer out, probably into the path of another chariot. Chariots came in (mainly) three different types:

- Two-horse chariot *(biga)*
- Three-horse chariot *(triga)*
- Four-horse chariot *(quadriga)*

If you've seen the movie *Ben Hur* (1959) forget the chariots in that – they were like battleships compared to the real ones used by the Romans. But the movie is outstanding in the way it gets across the excitement and lethal danger of the chariot race, so if you haven't seen it, make sure you do.

The charioteers

Charioteers were generally slaves, freedmen, or charioteers as no self-respecting Roman citizen would demean himself by getting his hands dirty that way. Controlling a chariot required incredible skill and quick reactions. The more horses, the more difficult it got. Because the races went one way round the stadium, the slowest horse of the team was attached to the inside. One false move, and a chariot could either turn over or veer off across the track and hit the outside wall.

Charioteers rode for one of the four main teams: the Reds *(Russata),* the Whites *(Albata),* the Blues *(Veneta),* or the Greens *(Prasina).* And being a charioteer was a bit like being James Dean: You lived fast, hard, and generally not for very long.

Fans

The city mobs across the Roman world were fanatical supporters of chariot-racing. Supporters of each team took huge pleasure in putting the boot into rival supporters. They had plenty of opportunity, and soldiers were often on hand to try and keep order. The mad emperor Caligula (AD 37–41) was a fanatical supporter of the Greens, so much so that he would eat down at their stables and sometimes even spend the night there. He even gave one of the charioteers, Eutychus, a fortune in cash.

Like gladiators, charioteers were the big stars of the day: Aristocratic women swooned at the thought of a hulking charioteer, and some became international superstars, which explains why a few carried on racing even once they'd earned their freedom.

The Roman Schumacher

One of the biggest names in chariot-racing was Gaius Appuleius Diocles, who rode for several of the teams at Rome between AD 122–148. He won a fortune in prize money by coming first in 1,462 races. The total is 35 million sesterces, which, of course, is pretty meaningless today but at the time would have paid the annual wages of about six Roman legions (about 30,000 men). In other words, it was a lot of cash.

Diocles actually took part in 4,257 races which meant he took a lot of risks. His brilliant career was cut short when he was 26 and run over by a rival called Lachesis. Maybe Lachesis did it deliberately. One charioteer in North Africa cursed four of his arch rivals, begging that a demon torture and kill their horses and then crush the charioteers to death.

Chariot-racing was one of the longest-lived of all Roman sports. In the Byzantine Eastern Roman Empire capital of Constantinople, long after the fall of Rome, circus supporters were still beating the living daylights out of each other whenever they could (head to Chapter 21 for information about Constantinople).

Pantos and Plays: Roman Theatre

Along with arenas and circuses, the average Roman city had at least one theatre and sometimes more. Just like arenas and circuses, these were originally temporary affairs. It wasn't until the days of the late Republic that massive stone theatres were built. The origins of the Roman theatre lay firmly in the Greek East where many theatres had been built by the fourth century BC, like the one at Epidauros. But the Roman establishment disapproved of theatres, believing them to be a source of disturbances and immoral influence. In 209 BC, the Censor Cassius tried to build a theatre in Rome, but he was forced to stop by one of the consuls and general opposition.

Meanwhile, Greek influence was strong in southern Italy, so Pompeii had a stone theatre by the end of the third century BC, with an *odean* (a small theatre) for poetry and speeches added right next door in 80 BC. Rome's first wooden theatre was up by 179 BC. Rome's first certain stone version, the Theatre of Pompey, was built by 55 BC, but it might have replaced an earlier stone theatre which hasn't yet been found. By the time of the emperors some of these theatres were really magnificent. But theatres were much smaller than the stadiums or arenas. According to Pliny the Elder, even the enormous Theatre of Pompey held at most about 40,000 spectators (less than one-sixth of the Circus Maximus), though some modern estimates come in rather lower.

Curio's remarkable revolving theatres

Gaius Curio, a supporter of Caesar's during the Civil War in the first century BC, was determined to come up with an ingenious way to put on costly entertainments to win votes. He came up with two wooden theatres close to one another and each built on a revolving pivot. Two separate casts put on a performance of the same play to the same audience in the afternoon before the theatres suddenly revolved and were joined together to make an amphitheatre, at which point gladiator pairs replaced the actors. Pliny the Elder was fascinated by how Curio thought to win over swaying voters by making them sway dangerously from side to side in his rickety, lethal, revolving wooden theatres.

Just like arenas and circuses, the theatres put on performances that were often part of religious festivals. So one thing you often find close to a theatre is a temple. That way sacred processions could start at one and end and finish at the other.

Theatre floor plans

Roman theatres had three parts (see Figure 8-4): the stage, the orchestra, and the auditorium. The auditorium was semi-circular with concentric rows of seats rising up from the flat semicircular chorus area at the bottom. Whenever possible, the Romans built the theatre into a hillside that made for far less complicated building. If no hill was available, then the seating area was built on top of a series of archways, vaults, and walls. The stage faced the auditorium on the far side of the orchestra. In the most extravagant theatres, the stage had a huge wall behind it, decorated with all sorts of architectural features that helped form part of the scenery.

One of the most staggering and well-preserved theatres is at Aspendos in Asia Minor (Turkey), dedicated under Marcus Aurelius (AD 161–180). Its stage is 110 metres long and 24 metres high. Many other examples survive, like the wonderful remains at Dougga in Tunisia, and Orange and Arles in France. In Rome itself part of the Theatre of Marcellus, built by Augustus, still stands.

Roman music

No-one knows what Roman music really sounded like because the Romans didn't write music down in a form we can understand or which survives. But music was everywhere: in the street, in markets, in religious festivals, and in the theatres. Musical contests were used to fill out interludes in the action at the circus and arena. Roman soldiers used trumpets in battle and at ceremonial displays. Other instruments the Romans knew included:

- Small harps called *lyrae* and the more complicated *cithara*.

- Percussion instruments like castanets, cymbals, tambourines, and the Egyptian *sistrum* (a kind of rattle).

- Wind instruments such as the double pipes, bagpipes, and flutes.

- The water organ *(hydraulus)*, invented by Ktesibios in the third century BC. It used a water pump to force air through the organ pipes. According to Pliny the Elder dolphins were especially enchanted by its sound!

Actors and impresarios

Rich upper-class Romans didn't think much of theatres and even less of actors. There was even a law that prohibited a senator, his son, grandson, or great-grandson from marrying a woman either of whose parents had been an actor. An actor's social rank was so low that he was listed along with gladiators, slaves, and criminals as the men a husband could kill if his wife committed adultery with any one of them.

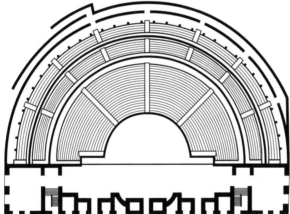

Figure 8-4: The plan of the Roman theatre at Orange in Gaul, one of the best-preserved. Most others were similar.

How to find a temple – start at the theatre

Theatres often held religious performances and were closely linked to temples. The Great Temple of Diana at Ephesus in Asia Minor (Turkey) was known to have been one of the Seven Wonders of the Ancient World but was long lost. In 1863 the British Museum sent John Turtle Wood to look for it. He started at the theatre and followed the Sacred Way from the theatre, digging it out as he went. It led all the way to the temple, now just ruined foundations in a swamp.

The only thing that was worse was an upper-class person who did like the theatre. Caligula (AD 37–41) was especially fond of an actor called Mnester and had members of the audience beaten if they made a sound while Mnester was dancing.

There was one remarkable theatre fan and impresario called Ummidia Quadratilla who died around the early second century when she was 78. Known for being on the large size even by Roman-matron standards, Ummidia owned a troupe of pantomime dancers who acted out the part of mythological characters on the stage. In her case, the dancers were freedmen, but such dancers were usually slaves. Other upper-class Romans thought her tastes were very improper for a woman of her rank. Oddly so did Ummidia, who was convinced the shows would corrupt her own grandson and prevented him from seeing them. I call that hypocrisy.

The show must go on: Performances and oratory competitions

Plays were mostly popular amongst ordinary people who were a lot less concerned about what was 'proper Roman entertainment' or not-that-snotty aristocrats. Originally there were two types of theatrical performances, called *ludi scaenici* ('plays on stage'): comedies and tragedies. The tragedies, like so much of the best of Roman culture, had been borrowed from the Greeks.

Roman comedies also borrowed ideas, and sometimes whole plots, from the Greeks but made the most of parodying Roman civilisation, especially by focusing on slaves as principal characters.

By the early second century BC the most famous comedy writer was an Italian called Titus Maccius Plautus (*c.* 254–184 BC), a failed merchant shipper. Although he got some of his ideas from the Greeks, one of his other influences was another Italian called Gnaeus Naevius. Plautus wrote at least 130 wildly popular comedies and is the only Roman playwright to have made a film in Hollywood. Well, that's not strictly true, but the famous musical and then movie *A Funny Thing Happened on the Way to the Forum* (1966), starring Zero Mostel, Phil Silvers, and Buster Keaton, was directly based on Plautus's work, as was the long-running BBC television series *Up Pompeii!*, starring Frankie Howerd as Lurcio, the slave and centre of all the action.

The Romans also enjoyed the following:

✔ **Action-adventures:** The performance of a play called *The Fire* during the reign of Nero was like watching an action movie being made. A house was put on stage and actually set on fire. As a reward for their performance and success in escaping the on-stage action, the actors were allowed by Nero to keep any furniture they'd rescued.

✔ **Re-enactments of myth:** These provided plenty of opportunities for displays of flesh. A Roman writer called Apuleius described a pantomime that took place in the second century AD. It was all about the Judgment of Paris (when Paris was supposed to choose the most beautiful goddess from Juno, Minerva, or Venus). The actress playing Venus arrived on stage with nothing on apart from a piece of silk around her hips and then took part in an erotic dance with other dancers.

✔ **Mimes and pantomimes:** By the end of the Republic, mime and pantomime were also performed on stage. The Romans weren't at all averse to livening up the proceedings with live violence, sex, and nudity. Oddly, mime actors did get to speak lines, but pantomime actors didn't.

✔ **Competition oratory:** One of the weirdest forms of cult entertainment for the Romans was the competition speech. Public speaking was a very important part of an educated Roman's repertoire, and Greek-speakers who modelled themselves on the great Athenian orators of the fifth century BC (known as the 'First Sophistic') were the most admired. The idea was to ask the audience for speech suggestions (which could be historical themes like the great days of Athens, or more down-to-earth themes like praising baldness), and then launch off into original, spontaneous, off-the-cuff speeches to riotous applause every time they said something especially learned or witty.

Theatrical performances don't seem to have remained very popular amongst the Romans, who preferred the violent action in the arena or the thrills in the stadium. The Theatre of Marcellus in Rome was falling into ruin by the early third century AD and in the fourth century was partly demolished to repair a bridge. Thanks to theatres being associated with religious festivals, the Empire going Christian didn't help either, though that doesn't seem to have affected the enthusiasm for the stadium.

A Night In: Entertaining at Home

The Romans didn't spend all their time at public entertainments. They had work to do and religious ceremonies to attend, but they enjoyed entertaining at home, too.

The best way to show off your house was at a dinner party. Dinner parties were especially popular, and it was quite common to throw one for guests who had spent the day at the amphitheatre. But the real purpose was to make a statement about who you were, who your friends were, and where you all stood in society. For example, patrons invited their clients (see Chapter 2 for an explanation of the patron-client relationship) as a kind of reward for their loyalty. As guests of lesser status, clients got inferior food and wine. But as it was customary for the host to give his guests a going-home present, attending might have turned out to be worth it.

Dinner and a show: The entertainment

Entertainment during the party included actors performing a scene from a popular play or panto, or a display by dancers. But in the more literary households, men would bore each other stiff, and no doubt their wives, too, by reading their own poetry, which they'd composed in the style of a famous poet like Ovid or Virgil. The whole point was to show off their technical expertise at constructing verses in various different rhythms (or *meters*). That this could be pretty tedious is obvious from the occasion when the poet Martial promised a dinner guest an especially good time by swearing that he wouldn't recite anything at all to his friend!

During dinner parties, guests lay on couches round three sides of the dining room which was called the *triclinium,* literally meaning 'three-sided table couch'. The idea was that slaves could bring the food into the centre through the open side so that everyone could reach out and help him- or herself. In the very richest houses, a summer dining room and a winter dining room were provided.

Party invite

One of the most famous pieces of writing from the Roman world was dug out of a waterlogged pit beside the ruins of a fort called Vindolanda in northern Britain. Dated to around the end of the first century AD, it's the earliest piece of writing in Latin by a woman ever found. A woman called Claudia Severa, wife of a commanding officer at another fort, wrote to Sulpicia Lepidina, wife of the commanding officer at Vindolanda, inviting her friend to come to her birthday party on 3 September:

> 'Claudia Severa to her Lepidina greetings. On the third day before the Ides of September, sister, for the day of the celebration of my birthday, I give you a warm invitation to make sure that you come to us, to make the day more enjoyable for me.'

It's an astonishing little document because right out on the wilds of the military frontier, hundreds of miles from Rome and all those aristocrats lolling about on couches at luxurious feasts, a couple of soldiers' wives (who'd probably never been to Rome) were doing their best to keep up Roman standards of entertainment and hospitality. Amazing.

Io Saturnalia!

The biggest booze-up of the year was the Saturnalia, the mid-winter festival. Starting on 17 December with a ceremony at the Temple of Saturn, it ended up lasting around a week, but for once it didn't matter who you were. People of all classes shared tables at a free banquet as part of the festivities and shouted *Io Saturnalia* as a greeting – it just means 'Wah-hay Saturnalia!'. Even slaves had a day off and were served by their masters. Gifts were exchanged, and everyone tried to have a good time, which was just as well because all the usual entertainments were closed for the holiday. Does some of that sound familiar? Yes, the Christians took over the Romans' great winter festival and made it into Christmas, though I'd expect you'd find a lot of people who'd tell you it's getting a lot more like the Roman Saturnalia once again.

Tableware

The very best tableware was made of gold or silver. Cups, plates, bowls, and vast dishes were all used. The most prized were those made by designer silversmiths whose individual trademarks were their own styles of decoration. Needless to say the flashiest plate was to be found in the emperor's palace. Claudius (AD 41–54) had a slave called Drusillanus who owned a silver plate that weighed about 163 kilograms (500 pounds), and he wasn't alone. Emperors gave gold and silver plates to their favourites.

If you couldn't afford silver, *pewter* (made from tin and lead) could look like silver if it was really polished up and was a passable substitute. Then there was the pottery. Romans used loads of different types, but in a dinner-party setting, pottery was very definitely only for the lower orders, even the good stuff, which was usually a lurid red colour.

Glassware was highly prized, too, especially as it was a relatively recent innovation from Egypt. The more transparent, the more it was valued.

The menu

A collection of recipes was compiled in the fourth century and published under the name of Apicius. Many of the recipes involved adding honey, vinegar, and fish sauce, which were the main flavouring-enhancers available. But the Romans also knew about salt, pepper, mustard, and fantastically expensive spices shipped in from the Far East. Romans particularly loved a sauce called *garum,* which was made from rotten fermented fish. Legend has it that this fish sauce survives today in the form of Worcestershire sauce.

You can buy a translation of Apicius today and try the recipes yourself! These are some the dishes Roman dinner guests could look forward to: Guests might have a starter of lettuce with snails and eggs, barley soup, and wine chilled with snow lugged down from the mountains, or maybe pickled tuna. Main courses could be fish, pork, sow's udders, rabbit, stuffed poultry, dormice fattened in special pots, snails so fattened with milk they couldn't withdraw into their shells, and sea urchins.

Wine was transported in from all over the Roman world. Naturally, it was priced according to quality. Sabine wine was one of the most expensive and cost nearly four times as much as the cheapest rubbish, called 'common wine'. Wine strainers removed impurities, and it could be drunk warm or chilled.

Chapter 9

Divine Intervention

. . . .

In This Chapter

▶ The ins and outs of Roman religion

▶ How the Romans used temples and shrines

▶ The amazing range of gods the Romans worshipped

▶ How the Romans assimilated other peoples' gods

▶ The impact of Christianity

▶ How the Romans went to meet their makers

. . . .

*N*ot only did the Romans believe in their divine mission to rule the world, but many also saw gods in everything, everywhere, and all the time. They believed that gods decided and controlled everything down to the last puff of wind and blade of grass. In the Roman world, places of worship existed in all shapes and sizes, from the huge temples in Rome and all other major cities, right down to tiny streetside shrines, household shrines, and even portable shrines. Even coins bore pictures of a whole array of gods and goddesses on their reverses.

Roman gods ranged from the great classical pantheon of Jupiter, Juno, and Minerva to fantastically obscure local gods (which could mean as local as being the god of the lock on your front door). They also included exotic gods from the East and strange, wild Celtic gods from the West.

The only exception was Christianity. The Romans would happily have added Christ to their list of gods (and some did), except that the Christians were having none of it. So it's remarkable that Christianity ended up as the state religion. That's also important: Religion in the Roman world was a matter of personal faith and superstition, but it was also political. Observing the state cults, including emperor worship, was part of expressing loyalty to the Empire. Anyone who refused did so at his or her peril.

Cutting a Deal: Roman Religion

Roman religion, like most ancient pagan religions, was basically about cutting a deal with a god (or gods). The average Roman wanted a service from a god, which could mean anything from support in winning a war or saving a crop, to bringing death and ruin on someone who had stolen his cloak (literally). In return for that service, the Roman promised the god a gift – usually a sacrifice or money – in return. This is how the deal worked:

- ✔ **Stage 1: The Vow.** The god was contacted and asked for a service. Depending on the god (or goddess), this could be done at a major shrine, a minor shrine, or a private shrine, often in written form on a docket which was then stored at the temple and involved specifying what was needed and what would be given in return: that's the vow *(votum)*. These are sometimes called 'curse-tablets' because they cursed the culprit and asked the god to visit violent retribution on him or her.

- ✔ **Stage 2: Fulfilling the Vow.** If the god performed the service (or was believed to have done so), the sacrifice or gift was made, and a record that the vow had been fulfilled was left at the shrine: usually a small altar of stone, earth, or wood, or a votive plaque made of bronze or silver pinned to a temple wall, which was inscribed with the person's name, the god being dedicated to, and a formula like *VSLM* which was short for *Votum Soluit Libens Merito,* 'He willingly and deservedly fulfilled the vow'.

Roman shrines ended up awash with offerings, which were buried in pits or thrown into pools. Coins were especially common, but the average Roman usually took care to throw in worn old coins of low value – well it's the thought that counts, isn't it?

Good days and bad days

A big part of religious superstition was doing things on the right day:

- ✔ **The *Kalends:*** The first day of the month was sacred to Juno.

- ✔ **The *Ides:*** The thirteenth day of short months and the fifteenth of long months were sacred to Jupiter.

- ✔ **The *Nones:*** The ninth day *before* the Ides.

Religious festivals were never held on any day before the Nones apart from an ancient one in July called *Poplifugia* (it means 'flight of the people' which might have been when everyone fled during the storm on the occasion Romulus disappeared – see Chapter 10). Similarly, religious superstition ruled when weddings could be held. The Kalends, Nones, and Ides, the first day following any of them, the whole of March, May, and the first two weeks of June were all no-nos, as were days of religious festivals.

Marriage

For most people, the marriage ceremony was a private affair starting in the bride's home with a friend presiding as *auspex* who examined entrails of a sacrificial victim to foretell the future (it's where we get our word *auspices,* meaning a forecast, from). The husband then carried his new wife into his home. Divorce was a straightforward rejection of the partner. Roman patricians had an ultra-formal wedding ceremony called *confarreatio.* The overseeing god was Jupiter Farreus, and the *pontifex maximus* ('chief priest') and *flamen dialis* ('priest of the Jupiter cult') presided. Farreus means 'made of spelt (wheat)' so a spelt cake formed a central part of the rite. Divorce for them was only possible through the ceremony of *diffarraetio.*

The key thing was ritual. Every sacrifice, every form of worship, every communication to the god had to be done exactly to a precise form of words and sequence of events. Get it wrong and the magic wouldn't work. Even if things seemed to go right, if the desired result didn't follow, then the superstitious Romans simply concluded that the ritual must have gone wrong. Less superstitious Romans, and there were plenty of them, concluded either there weren't any gods or looked around for a better one.

Divining the future

The Romans wanted to know what lay in the future. Who doesn't? But the Romans lived in a more unpredictable world than we do. Having little or no idea about impending weather catastrophes, earthquakes, disease, or their own deaths, they convinced themselves that signs must exist which foretold the future.

Omens

The Romans were obsessed with omens, good or bad. They looked out for signs of what the gods were up to. Omens counted for a lot. During the civil war of AD 68–69, the short-lived Emperor Vitellius prepared his troops to hold Italy against the approaching army of Vespasian (see Chapter 16). Vitellius got very upset by an unexpected turn of events:

- A cloud of vultures flew over and blanked out the sun.

- An ox being readied for sacrifice escaped, scattering all the ritual and sacrificial equipment, and had to be chased and killed in a non-ritual way.

Or so the story, recounted by Tacitus, went. It might have been true, but Roman historians loved being wise after the event by listing all the bad omens. Appropriately, Vitellius was defeated and killed. The Romans also saw omens of Julius Caesar's assassination (see Chapter 15). Septimius Severus concluded he was destined to be emperor, based on omens (see Chapter 18).

Being a priest was part of the official duties of men of status, which was why the emperor was also chief priest (pontifex maximus). Pliny the Younger was delighted when he was made an Omen Interpreter because (he said) it was an honour to be favoured by Trajan (AD 98–117), and also 'because the priesthood is an old-established religious office and has a particular sanctity by being held for life'.

Soothsayers

The *haruspex* was one of the specialist priests who predicted the future. There were two techniques:

- ✔ *Augurium:* The interpretation of natural phenomena like storms or animal activity
- ✔ *Extispicium:* The interpretation of the entrails of sacrificial animals

Here's an especially revolting example of soothsaying. On 15 April, special rites celebrated the sprouting seeds in the ground and the pregnancy of cows. The calves were ripped from the stomachs of their mothers, their entrails cut out for soothsaying, and the bodies burned.

Dream interpreters

Some Romans were very keen on the idea of a level of higher awareness, only reached by being profoundly intoxicated – or, basically really very, very drunk indeed. It's a similar idea to that put about by people in more modern times who believe that using mind-bending drugs gives them incredible insights to the true meaning of life (until they wake up, that is).

The lucky phallus

If you visit Pompeii today, you'll see over many of the doors into houses a representation of an erect phallus. Phalluses were connected with fertility (through Priapus, the god of procreation), but they were also symbols of good luck and were thought to ward off evil. Placing them over a door was supposed to protect the home from any evil passing in through the entrance.

Miniature phalluses were also worn as personal lucky charms as brooches or on rings. Giant phalluses were mounted in carts and wheeled around during celebrations of Bacchus. In the city of Lavinium (modern Pratica), a month was devoted to the festivities, climaxing with the phallus being displayed in the forum where matrons decorated it with flowers.

Bad day for a soothsayer

The Romans could also see the funny side of all this fortune telling and omen-reading. The poet Martial recorded what he thought was a hilarious story about a soothsayer. A billy goat was to be sacrificed to Bacchus by a Tuscan *haruspex* (soothsayer). While cutting the animal's throat, the haruspex asked a handy yokel to slice off the animal's testicles at the same time. The haruspex then concentrated on the job in hand when suddenly the yokel was shocked to see 'a huge hernia revealed, to the scandal of the rites' emerge from the goat's body – or so the yokel thought. Anxious to live up to the occasion and observe the religious requirements by removing this offensive sight, the yokel sliced off the hernia only to discover that in fact he had accidentally castrated the haruspex!

Some Roman cults grew up around this idea, with temples constructed so that the believers could drink themselves into a stupor and collapse into a drunken sleep in chambers in the temple in the presence of the god. They'd wake up the next day and recount their dreams to the resident dream interpreter who (for a fee, of course) would explain the hidden meanings. One such place was the healing shrine of a god called Mars-Nodons in Britain at a place now called Lydney. The funny thing is that the shrine was at its height when the Roman Empire was Christian, showing that some people were still keen on old pagan ideas.

Oracles

An oracle was a dedicated individual through whom a god spoke to the world. Generally oracles spoke in cryptic riddles, which needed interpreting. The most famous oracle was at Delphi in Greece, but there were many others, such as the oracle of Juno Caelestis ('Heavenly Juno') at Carthage, or the god of Carmel in Judaea. Vespasian consulted the Carmel oracle before he made a bid to become emperor in AD 69. He got a very encouraging message: Anything he wanted to, apparently, was guaranteed to happen.

Non-believers and charlatans

Not all Romans went around believing in the long-established pagan cults. Some people thought all the ritual was stuff and nonsense. Other even more cynical types spotted that fulfilling people's beliefs about religion was an excellent way of making a fast buck.

Healing cults, hot water, and dogs

The whole Greek medical tradition (refer to Chapter 7) was based on religion and went all the way back to the god Aesculapius (Greek: Asklepios). Temples of Aesculapius are found all over the Roman world and became the centres of some of the healing cults. In an age when 'real' medicine was pretty limited in its capabilities, many people put all their faith into healing cults. Hot springs were popular centres that sucked in large numbers of ailing pilgrims. They hoped for a cure in return for gifts to the presiding god or goddess. Bourbonne-les-Bains in Gaul was a major shrine and healing spring used by the Roman army, and was dedicated to a couple of local gods called Borvo and Damona.

Religious healing was big business and, until the coming of Christianity, places like this made serious money out of catering for and accommodating people desperate to get well. The most surprising element of some healing cults was the use of dogs. Dog saliva was supposed to have special healing properties, so dogs were kept at temples and encouraged to lick wounds or the eyes of blind people (eye disease was very common in antiquity).

The sceptics

Not all Romans were convinced by all this addiction to ritual, omens, and superstition:

- ✔ Cicero wondered if it didn't all amount to self-induced imprisonment, with people trapped by their fear of what omens might mean and terrified of getting ritual wrong.

- ✔ Pliny the Elder thought it was mostly superstitious self-serving nonsense and was fascinated by how people were convinced the goddess Fortuna was behind all their good luck and also responsible for their disasters and misfortune.

One of Pliny the Younger's greatest contributions to history is his letter to the historian Tacitus about the eruption of Vesuvius in AD 79. Describing the terrified crowd, he said, 'Many sought the help of the gods, but even more imagined there were no more gods left and that the universe had been plunged into permanent darkness for all eternity.'

In the motion picture *Spartacus* (1960), a politician character called Gracchus about to make a sacrifice tells the young Julius Caesar what he thought of the gods, saying, 'Privately I believe in none of them, neither do you – publicly I believe in them all.' A Hollywood script it may be, but many real Roman politicians knew how important going through the motions of belief was, regardless of what they really thought.

Religious con-artists

With so many people prepared to visit sacred shrines in search of a service from a god, it's no great surprise that there were plenty of other people interested in cashing in. A writer of the second century AD called Lucian wrote about a crook called Alexander of Abonueteichos in Bithynia and Pontus. This man cheated the credulous at his shrine by pretending to be insane and planting a goose egg in which he had placed a snake. Later he 'discovered' the egg and claimed thereby to have found the newborn Aesculapius. He also rewrote prophecies stored in the temple so he could 'prove' he'd been right all along. As far as Lucian was concerned, those who fell for this were mentally-deficient and indistinguishable from sheep. This sort of thing probably went on in a lot more places.

Roman Temples and Shrines

There were several different types of Roman temple, but in most cases the important thing to remember is that, unlike churches, pagan temples weren't places for worshippers to gather. They were sacred places to store cult statues and other cult treasures, and were only open to priests. The 'action' took place outside in the precinct, which is where altars stood for sacrifices, soothsaying, and performing ritual.

The Latin word templum for a religious precinct is now used by us just to mean the actual sacred building: that is, the temple, which the Romans called aedes or fanum.

Temples turn up in these places:

- ✔ In town centres in the forum and often near theatres because the two were closely linked in ritual. Sometimes whole towns, like Bath in Britain, grew up around a temple.

- ✔ Anywhere else in a town, often at road junctions or as part of another complex like a baths.

- ✔ At specialised rural religious centres, like a sacred tree or a sacred spring, where something special was believed to exist.

- ✔ On villa estates, tended by the villa owner for the benefit of locals.

A single precinct could have one temple, two temples, or several temples, dedicated to the same god or lots of gods in any combination. The Altbachtal sanctuary at Trier had an incredible 70 temples of various shapes and sizes. Small shrines turn up in houses, street corners, by roads, or halfway up a mountain. In short, Roman temples were everywhere and anywhere.

Classical temples

The so-called Temple of Fortuna Virilis in Rome (actually of Portumnus, the god of harbours and sea trade), shown in Figure 9-1, is what most people think of as a Roman temple: a rectangular building with columns all the way round the outside, approached up a flight of steps at the front towards columns supporting a triangular pediment filled with sculpture. At the top of the steps are one or more rows of columns before reaching a door leading into the *cella,* which makes up the bulk of the building. The cult statue stood inside the cella. Sometimes there were only columns at the front, with dummy half-columns around the walls of the cella. A few temples were circular and had columns all the way round with a central drum-shaped cella.

Classical temples could be little street-corner buildings with just four columns at the front, they could be monumental affairs, or they could be anything in between. These temples turn up all over the Roman Empire. One of the biggest was the Temple of Jupiter Heliopolitanus at Baalbek in the Roman province of Syria, now in Lebanon. Despite its vast size, the Baalbek temple was only one part of a vast religious complex of temples and courts on the site.

Figure 9-1:
The so-called Temple of Fortuna Virilis, dating in this form from the first century BC. Lying close to the Tiber, it was really dedicated to Portumnus, the god of harbours.

Photo by the author.

Fun facts about the Baalbek Jupiter temple

✔ The Baalbek Jupiter temple was 49 metres (147 feet) wide and 90 metres (295 feet) long. The Lincoln Memorial in Washington is 36 metres (118 feet) wide and 57.3 metres (188 feet) long.

✔ Some of the blocks in the temple's podium are 400 cubic metres (14,000 cubic feet) in size each.

✔ These blocks each weigh nearly 1,000 tons.

✔ Each column was 19.6 metres (63 feet) high and weighed 152 tons. Six still stand today. The columns in the Lincoln Memorial are only 13.4 metres (44 feet) high.

Regional temples

Roman classical temples appear almost throughout the Roman Empire, but they picked up influences from the places they were built in, and in some provinces almost entirely gave way to local types of temple.

Egypt was always a special case in the Roman Empire. In Egypt – unlike any-where else – Roman emperors were usually portrayed in local dress, in this case as pharaohs and in Egyptian-style carvings. They turn up most often in this form on Egyptian temples, which under the Romans were built according to traditional Egyptian forms with a series of open-air courts entered through a pair of flanking pylons before reaching the main temple structure. One of the best-preserved Egyptian temples is the Temple of Hathor at Dendarah, started under Augustus and Tiberius. It's completely Egyptian, without a hint of classical Roman style in sight.

In the north-west provinces like Gaul and Britain, the Romano-Celtic temple held sway. Unlike the classical temples, these were simple square buildings with a covered corridor all the way round a central tower which formed the cella.

Basilican temples were very different. Based on the public hall design of nave and aisles, basilicas were only suitable for religions that were congregational (that is, devotees took part in the ritual inside the building). These mainly included Mithraism and Christianity.

Shrines

Shrines could take almost any form, from an outdoor bench surrounding a few altars to little covered buildings in temple form. Romans could even carry about portable shrines with a figure of the god inside.

In the movie *Gladiator* (2000), Maximus is seen early on praying to a portable set of figures he carries around with him on campaign.

In the early second century AD, Pliny the Younger wrote a description of a religious shrine complex that surrounded the springhead of the Clitumnus, a tributary of the Tiber. Clitumnus was supposed to turn cattle which drank from the water white:

> 'At the foot of a modest hill, thickly wooded with ancient cypresses, the spring gushes out into . . . a pool as clear as glass. You can count lying on the bottom glistening pebbles and coins, which have been thrown in . . . Nearby is an ancient temple in which stands a statue of the god Clitumnus, dressed in the splendid robe of a magistrate. The oracles recorded here testify to his presence and the spirit's powers of prophecy. Around about are several little shrines to named cults with their own gods.'

The Divine Mission: Roman Gods

Roman gods existed in a hierarchy that started at the top with the pantheon of major deities headed by Jupiter, the king of the gods. He had a family of associates, many of whom were identified with Greek equivalents and also had Etruscan origins, whose worship can turn up almost anywhere in the Roman Empire. But there were many other gods ranging from lesser classical gods like the Italian woodland deity Faunus and the spirit of a city like Bourdiga, the goddess of Burdigala (Bordeaux), to the gods who represented the house and a family's ancestors, or the gods who represented a hot spring, pool, or a tree. Often Romans came across the local gods when they arrived in a region and then adopted them as their own.

Time to meet the Roman gods. I'll start with the major gods and describe more minor gods, but there were all sorts of others as well.

Public religion: Jupiter, Juno, Mars – the famous ones

The Romans saw the great gods of their classical pantheon in human form, but unlike humans, the gods were immortal and spent their time controlling the world. Jupiter was a mighty bearded old man equipped with thunderbolts. Minerva was a female warrior. Vulcan was a blacksmith. Each had a personality, particular powers, favourites, and faults – much like human beings – and some were linked by family relationships. Juno was Jupiter's wife, Mars was Juno's son, and Venus was Mars's consort, for example. They co-operated some times and rowed at others. They were shown in sculptures, on reliefs, on mosaics, and in paintings in these forms, always equipped with their identifying attributes (like Minerva's shield, or Vulcan's hammer) so that there was no doubt about who was being shown.

It was the patronage of Rome by these gods that was thought especially significant in Rome's destiny, but their essentially human traits of favouritism and squabbling add an edgy element of jeopardy and triumph over adversity: The Romans didn't take divine support for granted; it had to be sought, cajoled, and earned.

Table 9-1 lists the main Roman gods.

Table 9-1		Roman Gods
Roman God	*Greek Name*	*Description*
Jupiter	Zeus	King of the gods, also known as Jove and as Jupiter Optimus Maximus ('Jupiter the Best and Greatest') and often abbreviated to IOM on inscriptions. Husband of Juno, and father of Mercury. Worshipping Jupiter was a routine part of state and military calendars.
Juno	Hera	Queen of the gods, Jupiter's wife and mother of Mars. She was closely associated with motherly virtues. Main festivals: 1 July, 13 September.
Minerva	Athena	Inherited from the Etruscan Menrva, she was a goddess of trade and crafts as well as war (Minerva Victrix, 'the Victorious'), and is usually shown wearing a helmet and carrying a spear, with a breastplate depicting the gorgon Medusa. Main festival: 19 March.
Apollo	Apollo	The Romans adopted this Greek god and kept the name. A patron of hunting and music, he was also associated with oracles (for example at Delphi) and healing, and with the sun. Main festivals: 6–13 July (with games, see Chapter 8), and 23 September.
Ceres	Demeter	Goddess of crops (hence our word 'cereal') and natural renewal. Her festival, *Cerealia* (12–19 April), was associated with major public games (see Chapter 8).
Diana	Artemis	Goddess of hunting and the moon. Main festival: 13 August.

(continued)

Table 9-1 *(continued)*

Roman God	Greek Name	Description
Janus	(none)	The god of beginnings and doorways who rescued Saturn when he was thrown out by Jupiter. His temple was closed in times of peace, and open during war. Main festival: 17 August.
Mars	Ares	The god of war and usually shown armed. Juno's son, Mars was often associated with local gods in the north-west provinces, like hunter and warrior gods, but he was also associated with healing cults. Mars was also a god of agriculture and property boundaries. Various festivals including 1 June and 19 October.
Mercury	Hermes	Son of Jupiter and Maia (a fertility goddess). The messenger god, he also looked after trade and 'abundance'. He was extremely popular in Britain and Gaul where he was frequently associated with local gods. Main festival: 15 May.
Neptune	Poseidon	A sea god also associated with horses, so the Romans also linked him to the god of horses, Consus. Main festivals: 23 July, 1 December.
Saturn	Chronos	Father of Jupiter (Zeus). In myth Saturn ruled over a golden age and taught the Romans to farm. His name may have come from the Latin for a sower of seeds, *sator.* Saturn was thrown out by his son Jupiter and taken in by Janus. His temple in the Roman forum is one of the most ancient and best-preserved buildings there, but is a fourth-century AD reconstruction reusing bits of other buildings. Main festival: the winter solstice.
Venus	Aphrodite	Goddess of love, wife of Mars, and mythical ancestor of the Lulus clan (Julius Caesar was a member). One of her festivals was 23 April.
Vesta	Hestia	Roman goddess of the hearth fire, worshipped in every home and also in Rome itself (the latter protected by the Vestal Virgins who kept the fire going in the Temple of Vesta).
Vulcan	Hephaestus	God of fire and the smithy. Main festivals: 23 May, 23 August.

Jupiter, Juno, and Minerva form the *Capitoline Triad.* Their home temple was the Capitoline temple, the oldest temple in Rome. It was dedicated in classical form in 509 BC and restored to the same design in 76 BC. It was destroyed in AD 69 and rebuilt once more. Temples dedicated to the triad stood in the forums of most major cities of the Roman world, but these gods also had temples dedicated to them as individuals.

Household and family gods

When I say the Romans had a god for everything and everywhere, I do mean just that. If I listed them all there'd be no room for anything else in the book, so here's just a flavour.

Geniuses, Fates, and Mother goddesses

The most common of the household and family gods was the *genius,* 'guardian spirit', originally a man's guardian spirit (a little like the Christian concept of a guardian angel) but which became extended to the guardian spirit of almost anything. So the *Genius loci* was the 'Genius of the Place' which could be anything from a corner of a field to a street kerbside. There were also Geniuses of parade grounds, Geniuses of the legions, Geniuses of Our Lords (the emperors), Geniuses of any city you care to name, and Geniuses of trade guilds. Perhaps the strangest were the *Genii Cucullati,* a trio of hooded gods who have no names, recognisable facial features, or even attributes, found represented on carvings found in the north-western provinces.

Triplication was an important feature of some cults. The *Parcae* (Fates) were also worshipped in triple form, and so were the *Matres* (Mother goddesses) who were sometimes linked to the Parcae. The idea has survived into the Christian concept of the Holy Trinity.

Household gods

Every home had its resident *lares,* household guardian spirits. The head man of every household maintained a shrine for them *(lararium)* in the entrance hall *(atrium).* These gods were rather like Geniuses because there were also *lares* for road junctions and cities. Rome had lares for everyone of its 265 crossroads.

Gods for anything else

Gods could get even smaller-scale than the household gods. Believe it or not, three gods had separate protective duties over a Roman door:

- ✔ **Forculus** for the actual doors
- ✔ **Cardea** for the hinges
- ✔ **Limentinus** for the threshold

Other examples include Fabulinus, the god who helped children learn to speak. Fornax was a goddess who prevented grain being burned in driers. Robigus was the god who protected crops from mould. So you can just imagine how many gods the average household had, let alone the rest of the Roman world.

Emperor worship

Worshipping rulers as living gods was well-established in the ancient world. The whole Egyptian cycle, for example, saw the living pharaoh as the god Horus, the son of Isis and Osiris, and the dead pharaoh as the murdered Osiris, restored to life by Isis. In the Greek East, worshipping rulers as living gods had become a political fact of life. Alexander the Great asked to be worshipped as one, claiming to be the son of Ammon (Zeus).

The Romans weren't keen on the idea of living rulers being gods, and neither were most of the early emperors. Augustus (27 BC–AD 14) had to accept being worshipped in Eastern provinces because that was what the locals were used to. Tiberius wouldn't put up with it at any price. Of course, some emperors (like Elagabalus; see Chapter 19) did fancy themselves as living gods, but they usually paid for it with their lives. It's doubtful if many people seriously believed the emperor was a god, but the only ones who had a real problem with it were the Christians.

However, even Emperors like Augustus found a neat way of being associated with gods but without actually claiming to be one (until after his death). The central myth of Rome's destiny was that Aeneas was the son of Venus (see Chapter 10 for the myth surrounding the founding of Rome), one of the pantheon of classical gods. This didn't mean that her supposed descendants, the *gens* Iulus, the family of Julius Caesar, were gods. But being descended from a goddess was a thoroughly handy association and the emperors made the most of it.

This was made even more effective by making emperors into gods when they died (a process called *apotheosis,* 'to make a god of'). Cults were established in their names, like the Divus Vespasianus ('the Divine Vespasian'). What emerged for living emperors was a sort of compromise. The son of a dead emperor was thus the son of a god, and people, mainly soldiers and officials, made public displays of loyalty to the *numen* ('spirit') of the emperor and the *Domus Divina* ('the Divine Imperial House'). It was a way of treating a living emperor as if he had a kind of parallel existence as a god.

Integrating Gods from Elsewhere

The Romans were extraordinarily tolerant of religions, because they believed all gods had power, and the Romans wanted the gods to work for them and not their enemies. So they adopted cults from all over the Empire and beyond, and combined them with their own gods.

Joining Roman gods to foreign gods: Conflation

One of the reasons the Romans managed to persuade so many people that being part of the Roman Empire was a good thing was because they generally didn't try to destroy the religions of the people they came across. There were exceptions, the Jews and Christians among them, but in those situations, the problem for the Romans was mainly political, not religious.

The Romans were particularly good at creating combination-gods out of Roman ones and local ones, a process called conflation (from the Latin *conflatum,* 'a mixing together'). These are some examples:

- ✔ In Germany, the Romans came across a local healing god called Lenus. They conflated him with Mars at Trier and created the healing cult centre of Lenus-Mars.

- ✔ A Celtic god of healing called Grannus was conflated with Apollo to make Apollo-Grannus, who was worshipped in lots of places.

- ✔ The Ptolemaic pharaohs of Egypt joined the cults of Osiris and Apis and created Serapis, an underworld god who could perform miracles and heal people. The Romans liked Serapis – the Emperors Septimius Severus (193–211) and Caracalla (211–217) were very keen on him.

Provincials who brought their own gods with them when they joined the army or moved around the Empire were free to worship them as they pleased. That's how a German auxiliary army unit of Suebians brought their wildly-named goddess Garmangabis with them to Britain.

These are only a few examples, but you get the picture. There can't be many other times in human history when religious freedom was practised at this level.

Curiouser and curiouser: Mystery cults

Despite the vast array of gods available to the average Roman, whether he lived in Rome or in a remote part of Gaul or Syria, it seems that for many people, something was lacking. These people turned to the so-called 'mystery' cults which usually had secret rites, were only open to people who had qualified in some way through initiation, and which usually offered some sort of rebirth. The mystery cults usually came from the Eastern provinces and found their way round the Roman Empire thanks to the vast trading network and through soldiers posted to different destinations.

One of the most famous records of an initiation ceremony is the series of paintings on the walls of the Villa of the Mysteries outside Pompeii. The paintings concern a cult of Bacchus and involve ecstasy, flagellation, terror, and the triumph of overcoming the ordeals to join the sect, but little is known of their true significance. You can see the paintings there today.

In their own way, some of these cults challenged Roman religious tolerance. These are some of them, but you can also look at Chapter 19 and read about the Emperor Elagabalus and his sun cult.

The cult of Isis

Ancient Egypt was a source of endless fascination to the Romans, especially the gods and goddesses. Isis was closely linked to fertility and rebirth of the land through the annual flooding of the Nile, but her protection of marriage and navigation meant that her appeal became more universal. The cult of Isis reached the Roman port of Pozzuoli in Italy in 105 BC. A Temple of Isis was destroyed at Pompeii in the eruption of AD 79 and can still be seen today. By the third century AD, Isis was at the climax of her Roman popularity, often shown nursing her infant son Horus on her knee – a potent image taken over by the Christians. The furthest place Isis turned up in was London, and it's an amazing comment on the cosmopolitan Roman world that an ancient Egyptian goddess could be worshipped so far from her spiritual home.

The cult of Cybele

The cult of Cybele (or *Magna Mater,* the 'Great Mother') came from Phrygia in Asia Minor (Turkey). The Romans linked her to Ceres and even incorporated her into the official pantheon of gods. But the weirdest part of the cult was her male followers. Cybele's lover Atys had been unfaithful to her. Thoroughly ashamed of himself, Atys castrated himself as a punishment. So fanatical worshippers of Cybele castrated themselves, too. Even the normally tolerant Roman state found the frenzied carryings-on, including rowdy parades to the sound of cymbals and raucous horns and arm-slashing, too much. So laws were brought in to prevent public disorder.

The cult of Mithras

The men-only Persian cult of Mithras was extremely popular amongst sol-diers and traders, and most Mithraic temples have been found at ports or near forts. Followers, who had to go through painful initiation ceremonies, believed Mithras had been engaged in a fight to the death with a bull created at the dawn of time. Mithras killed the bull in a cave, thus releasing the blood that contained the essence of life.

Mithraic temples had no windows in order to recreate the mystery and sym-bolism of the original cave. The climax of the ceremony was a ritual meal. Theatrical props, like perforated altars through which lamps cast eerie pools of light and shadow across the congregation, enhanced the sense of being in a special place.

The tolerance of pain, the significance of bloodshed as a means to eternal life, and Mithraic hymns appalled the Christians, who spotted the similarity with some of their own beliefs. In fact, Christians were the ones most likely to attack Mithraic temples that, like churches, had a nave and aisles.

The Religion that Refused to Be Assimilated: Christianity

Theoretically, Christianity was just another of the mystery cults because in its early form, and as far as the Romans were concerned, it was just another strange cult from the East that promised eternal life to believers. In fact, until Christianity became the state religion, for many Romans the idea of Christ as *another* god to add to the list of the ones they already worshipped was a per-fectly good one. The emperor Severus Alexander (222–235) kept a collection of statues of gods of all types, even the Christian God, in his apartment and worshipped them all. So it's not surprising that some finds of early Christian worship show people apparently worshipping Christ in the old pagan way of making vows and leaving gifts (see the section 'Cutting a Deal: Roman Religion' at the beginning of this chapter).

But Christianity was different in key ways from the other religions that the Romans assimilated:

- ✔ It was open to anyone and everyone, any time and any place. This wasn't a problem for the Romans, but the next point was.

- ✔ Believers had to reject all other gods. If you've read this chapter up to this point, you'll realise this flew in the face of the general Roman atti-tude to religion.

The Roman government, therefore, got very suspicious of the Christians.

Problems with Christianity

All sorts of confused stories circulated among the Romans. When Christians consumed the bread and wine, treating them as symbolic representations of the body and blood of Christ, the word got out that they were literally practising some sort of cannibalism. Christians also made handy scapegoats for Nero (54–68) when he wanted someone to blame for the Great Fire of Rome (Chapter 16). Tacitus called Christianity a 'pernicious superstition' and said Christians were 'loathed for their vices'.

The Romans were also bewildered by the most committed followers of a cult who refused even to pay lip service to state pagan cults. Pliny the Younger, while Governor of Bithynia and Pontus under Trajan (98–117), found himself having to investigate Christians who refused to deny their beliefs and also refused to make offerings to pagan gods and to a statue of Trajan. Some actually did cave in and make the pagan offerings, but the rest refused. Pliny ordered two women deacons to be tortured to find out more, as he was very worried by Christianity's popularity. Trajan wrote to Pliny and told him not to hunt out Christians, to ignore anonymous informers, and only to punish Christians if he had to. In other words, Trajan was quite keen on the softly-softly approach.

Chi (X) and Rho (P) are the first two Greek letters of the Greek form of Christ: Χριστοζ. The two letters were placed over one another to create a symbol used by Christians on church plates, wall-paintings, and mosaics, and was also placed on coins by Christian emperors.

Persecutions

Over the next two centuries, Christianity steadily grew in popularity. Dissatisfaction with the traditional gods grew as people came to believe that all their sacrifices at temples weren't having any effect. As the Romans grew wealthier, people looked around for something with more meaning. You can see the same effect today, with people hunting around for something to believe in. Then there were the gradually increasing troubles on the frontiers. It didn't look as if the Roman system could hold up. Christianity promised a new life of eternal bliss in another world after death. It looked very attractive – except that, for the Roman state, it looked like a direct challenge to imperial authority.

Major persecutions were organised by Trajan Decius (249–251), Diocletian (284–305), and Maximian (286–305), but had been going on since Nero's time. Even Marcus Aurelius (161–180), the philosopher Emperor, authorised a persecution in 177. Persecutions took on various forms, including torture to make people give Christianity up, executions of refuseniks, confiscation of church property, banning bishops from meeting, and burning of scriptures. The persecutions had some success because some people certainly *apostatised* (gave up Christianity), but part of Christian teaching was being prepared to suffer like Christ. So the persecutors actually gave some Christians a reason to show how Christian they were by suffering under the persecution. There was even an element of competition, with Christian teachers recounting with admiration how much torture and cruelty some people had withstood without apostatising.

Tolerance and turning tables

A big change came under Constantine I (307–337). Constantine not only believed that the Christian God had been behind his own success, but he also spotted the huge political advantages of using Christianity to hold the Empire together. (You can find more about all this, and the way Christianity took hold in the Empire in Chapters 20 and 21.)

Once Christianity became legal, the church worked tirelessly to get the Romans to abandon their old customs. But as part of the job involved taking over old pagan shrines and replacing them with churches, it was tough to persuade everyone. Plenty of people decided to hedge their bets. The earliest collection of Christian silver comes from Water Newton in Cambridgeshire, England. Although covered with Chi-Rho symbols, the items include plaques exactly like those pinned to temple walls by pagans.

But paganism, or anything that smacked of it, was gradually outlawed. Even mummification in Egypt was banned. Christianity took complete hold, but if you read Chapter 21 you can see how divisions in the church rocked the Roman world to its foundations from the fourth century onwards.

Christian churches in the Roman world

Unlike pagans who worshipped their gods in specific places like shrines, Christians could worship anywhere so long as they had a priest to officiate. So early Christians often used to gather in rooms in private houses, known as house churches. One of the few to leave any traces was installed in the Roman villa at Lullingstone in Kent, England in the late fourth century. A series of rooms painted with Christian symbols served for worship and can be seen in the British Museum today. Once Christianity was legalised, the basilican hall design with its nave and aisles was used, creating the church form we know today. These were already being built in Rome by the early fourth century. Constantine (307–337) built the first Basilica of St Peter's (demolished by 1612). The best-preserved original, big Roman church is Santa Maria Maggiore, built in 366.

Burning and Burying: The Roman Way of Death

Death and burial is an appropriate way to end this chapter. The Romans lived full and extraordinary lives. It's often through the records of their lifetimes on their graves that we find out about who the Romans were and what they did. They're poignant reminders that this whole book is about real people who lived real lives. Even if we can't possibly make a direct link now, because the records don't exist, many of us can surely count them amongst our remote ancestors.

Roman afterlife: The Underworld

The spirits *(manes)* of the dead were thought by some to live in the Underworld, though the Romans also had an idea of a kind of heavenly underworld, which they called *Elysium*. (It's not very clear, and apparently the Romans weren't much clearer themselves.) According to the myth, the Underworld was ruled over by Pluto (Greek: Hades), also known as Dis, and his wife Persephone (Greek: Proserpina). To reach the Underworld, the dead were ferried across the river Styx by Charon.

Dis comes from *Dives,* 'riches', and even Pluto comes from the Greek *plouton* for rich. No-one knows why the king of the Underworld was associated with riches, unless it means the underground riches of minerals and the soil.

Cemeteries and graves

Roman funerals either involved cremation or burial of the body *(inhumation)*. Cremations tended to be earlier, but burial became more and more common. By the third century AD, it was the standard practice.

Cremation

Cremations involved burning the body on a pyre, together with personal possessions, either where the body was to be buried or in a special part of the cemetery. The ashes were packed into pottery jars, glass bottles, lead urns, wooden boxes, or even just cloth. Depending on how rich the dead person was, grave goods went in, too – usually metal, glass, or pottery vessels containing food and drink for the journey to the afterlife, and coins to pay the ferryman Charon for the trip to the Underworld.

Burial (inhumation)

Inhumation involved burying the whole body. The poorest people were buried in shrouds or nothing at all, while the wealthiest could afford lead coffins or even extravagantly carved marble *sarcophagi* (large coffins; the word means 'flesh-devouring'). Burial had become the norm by the fourth century when the Roman Empire went Christian, and didn't usually involve grave goods because that was considered a pagan custom – but plenty of Christians had them anyway. Sometimes people tried to preserve the bodies by packing them with *gypsum* (calcium sulphate) to dry the body out, or in a few cases even mummifying the bodies Egyptian-style (which was still going on in Roman Egypt until it was banned in the late fourth century, even though it wasn't done anything like as well as in Ancient Egyptian times).

Cemeteries and tombs

By law, Romans had to be buried beyond a free zone *(pomerium)* outside the settled area. It was simply a matter of hygiene though; as Roman towns grew they were often built over old cemeteries. Cemeteries usually clustered along the side of roads as they exited a town. The best visible examples today are at Rome, Ostia (see the section, 'Worshipping ancestors and burial feasts', later in this chapter), and Pompeii. On opposite sides of Roman roads at these places you can still walk down roads through the city gates and past tombs of all sorts of different shapes and sizes.

Rich people could afford elaborate architectural structures with statues or carvings of the deceased, together with detailed inscriptions that tell us the names of the people buried there, how old they were, perhaps what they did, and where they came from. Poor people were lucky to have their cremated remains stuffed into an amphora buried alongside. But all tended to bury their dead in family groups unless they belonged to a guild *(collegium),* which arranged for the burial of its members. It was common for freedmen to take care of their former master's burial.

One of the most curious tombs at Rome is the marble-faced Pyramid of Gaius Cestius, built as his tomb in 12 BC by his slaves, who were freed in his will. It's 35 metres (114 feet) high and 79 metres (260 feet) wide, and was a copy of ancient Egyptian pyramids, which had excited his imagination when he lived there for a while. It was built originally outside Rome but was incorporated into the walls built by Aurelian (AD 270–275).

Catacombs

Catacombs were subterranean cemeteries made up of multistorey tunnels with niches, chapels, and chambers cut into the side walls for burials. They became especially popular amongst Christians at Rome. The Sant'Agnese catacombs of Rome have 800 metres (half a mile) of tunnels and 8,500 tombs alone, but Rome's catacombs must originally have run into hundreds of miles.

Inscriptions on tombs

Roman tombstone inscriptions were usually for-mulaic and included a lot of abbreviations as well as the person's name. Not everyone could afford one, but those who could have left invalu-able records for us to study. Here's a few of the abbreviations:

- ✔ **DM – *Dis Manibus:*** 'To the Spirits of the Departed'

- ✔ **HSE – *Hic situs est:*** 'Is buried here'

- ✔ **HC – *Heres curavit:*** 'His/her heir took care (of the burial)'

- ✔ **FC – *Faciendum curavit:*** 'Took care of making (the tomb)'

- ✔ **V – *Vixit:*** 'Lived' (usually followed by a number, reading, for example, 'lived 29 years')

There's a tombstone of a woman called Fasiria at the city of Makhtar in what is now Tunisia in North Africa. The Christian Chi-Rho symbol is clearly carved on the stone, but so also is the pagan DM for *Dis Manibus* ('To the Spirits of the Departed'), suggesting she believed in the Christian God but wasn't prepared to risk annoying the pagan gods.

Worshipping ancestors and burial feasts

Venerating ancestors was an important part of Roman life. In the home, the family ancestors were commemorated with busts (see also *Ius Imaginum* in Chapter 3). But the Romans also made visits to graves to hold ceremonies in which they reinforced their connection with their ancestors.

Venerating and commemorating the dead was an essential part of Roman life. Two of the biggest monuments in Rome today are the Mausoleum of Augustus and the Mausoleum of the Antonines (built by Hadrian and now the Castel Sant'Angelo).

The *Parentalia* (burial feast) was held on 13–21 February. Out of respect to the dead, temples were shut, and marriages were banned. Families got together and set off for the tombs of their ancestors outside the town walls and had pri-vate feasts. The deceased were included, too: food and drink were poured down tubes to underground burials or taken into over-ground vaults to the burials there. On the last day, there was a public ceremony. The *Rosalia* was held on 10 May when Romans decorated tombs with roses, then in full bloom.

One of the best-preserved Roman cemeteries is close to the ruins of Ostia, the ancient port of Rome, at a place called Isola Sacra ('sacred island') which is incredible because now it's only about a mile from Rome's main Fiumcino air-port. It's a cluster of intact tombs, complete with dedicatory inscriptions to the deceased who once lived and worked at Ostia. You can go into the tombs and see the niches in the walls where the cremated remains of family mem-bers were stored. Outside, some the owners built copies of dining room couches for the feasts so that the family could lie down to eat with their ancestors, just like at home.

Part III
The Rise of Rome

The 5th Wave   By Rich Tennant

"Shortly after Romulus arrived, they started showing up claiming to be a relative."

In this part . . .

*I*magine you live in a small village in the English countryside, with a just a couple of hundred inhabitants, a
church, and maybe a pub. Or imagine you live in a small
town in Wyoming with a gas station and a few shops and
houses. Now imagine that same place becoming the
centre of the known universe. That's what happened to
Rome over the course of several centuries. The Romans
always looked back fondly to those times, when their
great city was just a village in and around seven small hills
on the east bank of the river they called the Tiber.

Needless to say, so much time had passed that the
Romans had really very little idea of the truth. But they
clung to the idea that this rural past contained the secret
of Rome's success. They believed that it was in Rome: the
village where toil, valour, and honour had proved that the
Romans were destined to rule the known world. This part
of the book is about the first 600 years that made Rome
what it was and took it to the brink of world domination.

Chapter 10

Kings? No, Maybe Not – Republicans

. . . .

In This Chapter

▶ Rome's mythical origins

▶ The establishment of the Republic

▶ The first written laws

▶ The struggle between the patricians and the plebs

. . . .

For a civilisation that was built around a republican system of law and government, Rome's earliest days are pretty foggy, and making sense of the first few decades is difficult. The only historical sources we have were written down much later, and the historians concerned struggled to find detailed information. But what emerged was something that the Romans would spend the rest of their days trying to prevent ever happening again: a monarchy.

Yes, that's right. Rome, the great republican state of the ancient world, had kings to begin with. But throwing the kings out for the various misdemeanours changed everything. What emerged was a class war, culminating in the rights of ordinary people (known as the *plebs*) and the first written law code in Roman history. It set the pace for the shape of things to come.

The Founding of Rome

The Romans didn't start writing history as soon as the city was founded. It wasn't until a long time afterwards that they became interested in who they were and where they'd come from. Roman historians had to hunt back through what few early records survived, and they pieced together a story that was very largely based on myth. Its most important part was linking the Romans all the way back to the gods, through the legendary hero Aeneas.

The myth

The great Roman legend about the founding of Rome goes back to the Trojan War, set in Greek Mycenaean times.

Aeneas was the mythical son of a Trojan leader called Anchises and the goddess Venus (Aphrodite is her equal in Greek mythology), and belonged to a junior branch of the Trojan royal family. According to prophecy, Aeneas would one day rule the Trojans and, according to Homer's *Iliad* (an epic poem recounting the fall of Troy), he was the only Trojan with anything to look forward to after the city was sacked by the Greeks.

After Troy fell to the Greeks, Aeneas escaped, wandered around in search of his destiny, and had grand adventures. When he finally arrived in Italy, Aeneas was greeted by King Latinus who allowed Aeneas to marry his daughter Lavinia. Aeneas founded a city called Lavinium which later became head of the Latin League, multiple cities, other than Rome, in the Latium region (see Chapter 11 for more information on the Latin League).

Aeneas's son Ascanius (who, according to one legend came with Aeneas to Italy after the fall of Troy, and in another was born after Aeneas married Lavinia) succeeded Aeneas and founded the city of Alba Longa. (Ascanius was also known as Iulus, and the family of that name claimed descent from him and thus Venus. The most famous claimant was none other than Julius Caesar, so you can see just how potent this myth was.)

Later in Alba Longa, 12 kings succeeded Aeneas's son Ascanius/Iulus. The twelfth was called Numitor, who was deposed by his brother Amulius. To make sure that Numitor's daughter Rhea Silvia wouldn't challenge him, Amulius made her into a Vestal Virgin, one of the select virgin priestesses whose main role was to guard Vesta's undying fire (which signified the permanence of Rome; Vesta was the goddess of the hearth fire). But Amulius hadn't reckoned with the god Mars, who impregnated Rhea. Rhea gave birth to the twins Romulus and Remus, who Amulius, after discovering their existence, flung into the river Tiber.

The twins were saved and suckled by a she-wolf and then brought up by a herdsman. The boys grew up to be warriors, restored their grandfather Numitor to the throne, and, in 753 BC, founded Rome. They built walls around Rome. Remus leaped over the walls, enraging his brother, who killed him. Eventually Romulus disappeared, only to reappear as the god Quirinus, a little-known ancient god who gave his name to Rome's Quirinal Hill and was once one of Rome's three principal gods along with Jupiter and Mars (he had similar powers to Mars).

How did a date as specific as 753 BC ever get assigned as the year that Rome was founded? Answer: A scholar called Marcus Terentius Varro worked back from his own time, using records, historical facts, and legend and decided that 753 BC was the date of Rome's founding. For the rest of Rome's history, 753 BC was the date from which the city's history was counted. It's a bit like Archbishop James Ussher in the seventeenth century who added up everything in the Bible and decided the world was created in 4004 BC.

The true story

Like everywhere in Europe, human history in Italy stretches back over hundreds of thousands of years, deep into the Stone Age. For millennia, early man made use of stone tools in a period called the *Palaeolithic* (the 'Old Stone Age'), a time when communities tended to move about according to the season and available resources. But around 5000 BC – which is a very approximate date – the *Neolithic* ('New Stone Age') began to spread throughout Europe. Unlike the hunter-gatherer Palaeolithic, the people of the Neolithic started establishing farms and stayed put instead of wandering about hunting.

Neolithic farmers started appearing in Italy by around 5000 BC. By about 1800 BC, some of these early Italians were making and using bronze – the Bronze Age. Meanwhile, Egypt's civilisation had already been in existence for more than a thousand years. In fact, Italy was distinctly behind the times. The Bronze Age Greeks, who had strongholds at places like Mycenae and Tiryns in Greece, were already exploring and trading around the Mediterranean. Some of these Greeks had even reached Italy and its surrounding islands.

Around 1000 BC came the Iron Age. Iron, being much stronger than bronze, was the greatest technological discovery of the era. It transformed a society's military power and made all sorts of tools possible. Iron meant far stronger weapons and equipment. Iron shovels and ploughshares lasted longer and were far more effective. Villanova, a key site in Italy, gave its name to the new culture that was making use of iron.

Early Rome: Hills with huts, and a very big sewer

Rome is famous for being on seven hills close to the river Tiber (see Figure 10-1). Those hills were called:

- ✔ Capitoline
- ✔ Palatine

- ✔ Aventine
- ✔ Esquiline
- ✔ Quirinal
- ✔ Viminal
- ✔ Caelius

Around at least 1000 BC, little farmsteads, built of *wattle and daub,* were built on some of the hills: the Palatine, Esquiline, Quirinal and Caelius. (Wattle and daub is a simple and effective way to build houses – it's a timber frame with a latticework of twigs all covered with a mixture of mud and straw.) These were no more than scattered clusters of thatched huts, just tiny villages.

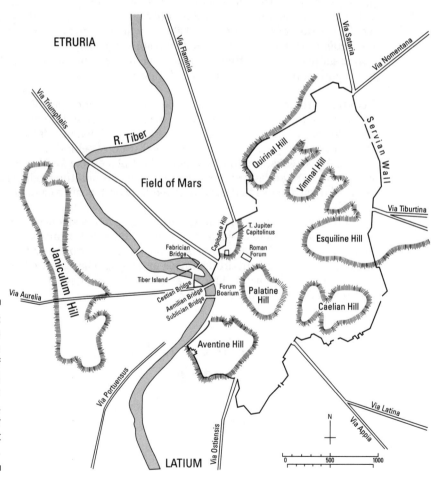

Figure 10-1:
This map shows the hills of Rome and the Servian Walls, probably built about 390 BC.

Some huts and cemeteries have been excavated, showing that by the eighth century BC the early Romans were trading with other places like Etruria and Greece, and were making their own pottery, figurines, and weapons. They grew crops like wheat and barley, raised goats and pigs, and hunted. The later Romans looked back to these simple farming times and idealised it as an era when their virtues of self-discipline, hard work, and organisation were born, and contrasted it with the riches, decadence, and indulgence of days of the Roman Empire (refer to Chapter 4 for more information on the significance of Roman myth to its rural past).

Cemeteries were dug in the marshy valleys, especially in the one that would later become the Roman Forum. The population seems to have done well because the settlements got bigger, and room soon ran out on the hills. So the marshy valleys were drained, and the settlements grew down the slopes and started to merge into one another during the seventh century BC. This was when something like a city, the earliest Rome, started to take shape.

The Romans seem to have had a folk memory of the time when Rome grew out of a collection of villages, preserved in a religious festival in which the priests and Vestal Virgins had a procession to visit shrines in the four regions of the city: the Palatine, Esquiline, Quirinal and Caelius.

During the time of the Roman kings (see the section 'The Magnificent Eight: The Kings (753–535 BC)', later in the chapter), Rome was a very primitive settlement by later standards and controlled an area of only about 150 square kilometres (60 square miles). But Rome was the most powerful state in Latium. The kings brought centralised government and organisation. Under their rule, Rome began to evolve from a cluster of villages into a city with defences, services like sewage, and religious precincts that helped foster a sense of identity.

Rome's neighbours

It's very important to remember that Rome and her inhabitants made up only one settlement of many in this part of Italy (see Figure 10-2). Some were her allies, some her rivals. Dominating this area was Rome's first step on the path to world domination.

Aequians

The ferocious Aequians lived north-east of Rome and allied themselves with the Volscians. Little is known about them because their attempts at expanding were thwarted in 431 BC. A further attempt at expanding led Rome to practically exterminate them in 304 BC.

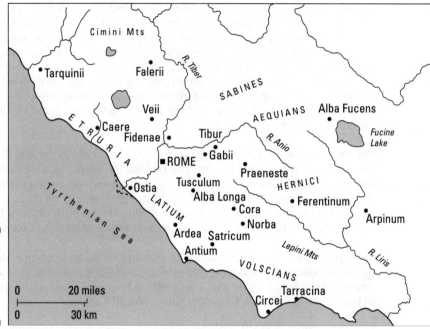

Figure 10-2:
Rome
with her
immediate
neighbours.

Etruscans

Rome's main early rivals for control of the land between the rivers Tiber and
Arno, the Etruscans lived in Tuscany and Umbria, but in the late seventh century BC, their pottery started turning up in Rome, along with their style of
housing, which was more robust and had tiled roofs rather than the thatched
huts the Romans had been building.

The Etruscans remain obscure because no-one has ever been able to make
out more than a little of their language, which is unrelated to all the main
known groups, though some words survived into Latin. But the later Roman
historians recorded what they could of this period. The incredible thing is
that their murky version of this remote period does seem to match the
archaeology. In the end, Etruscan power was squeezed by the Gaulish Celts
to the north, and Rome and the Samnites to the south. The Etruscans had
considerable influence on Roman culture. The major Roman goddess Minerva
(see Chapter 9) was once an Etruscan deity.

Sabines

The Sabines lived in villages in the Apennine hills to the north-east of Rome.
No-one knows where they came from, but they spoke an ancient language
called Oscan. Until 449 BC, they were constantly fighting the Romans, even

though they had no central leadership, but it's plain from aspects of their religious belief that they had a strong influence on Roman culture. The ancient god Quirinus (see the earlier section 'The myth') was originally a Sabine deity.

Samnites

The Samnites lived in the Appenine hills well to the south of Rome. They were made up of four tribes who formed a confederation to fight their enemies. In the fourth century BC, they became important rivals when Roman power started spreading south, leading to the three Samnite Wars. Samnium stood firm against Rome and wasn't totally defeated until the early first century BC in the Social War. Pompeii is the most famous Samnite city, becoming a Roman colony in 80 BC.

Volscians

By 500 BC, the Volscians had come out of central Italy and settled south-east of Rome. They fought against Roman expansion but hadn't reckoned on Rome's allies, who defeated them in 431 BC. Not much is known about their culture because, once they had been conquered, they comprehensively adopted Roman ways.

The Magnificent Eight: The Kings (753–535 BC)

Early Rome was ruled by kings. Their story is part myth and part true – the challenge is working out which is which. The history of Rome starts off with myth but soon turns into fact, so now you have the opportunity to meet those kings, real or mythical. Three of the first four kings were Latins (with one Sabine), but the last three were Etruscans. The Etruscan kings had a tremendous effect on early Roman culture, the city's infrastructure, and Rome's early power.

Rome's kings weren't part of a hereditary monarchy, like most lines of monarchs in world history were. Rome's kings were mostly elected or chosen by the Roman people. Incidentally, don't take the dates that follow as hard fact. They're mostly approximations, at best.

Romulus (753–716 BC)

Romulus (who founded Rome along with his twin brother Remus) was the surviving grandson of Numitor. Roman tradition credited Romulus with creating various great Roman traditions such as the Senate, which was just a myth that gave the Senate an authority founded in the city's origins.

The end of Romulus

Romulus's end is another myth, which goes as follows: A storm blew up while he was sacrificing by the river, and all the people ran for shelter. Although the senators stayed with Romulus, he somehow disappeared. Only two possibilities existed regarding his disappearance, and no-one knew which one actually occurred. Either Romulus had been killed by the senators who had then cut him up and carried off the pieces hidden under their clothing, or else the gods had gathered him up to heaven.

The big story of Romulus's reign was the rape of the Sabine women. Romulus is said to have invited a neighbouring tribe called the Sabines to share in the celebrations of the god Consus (who took care of grain storage). When the Sabines turned up, the Romans stole the Sabine women (the word used was *rapere,* 'to seize'; it doesn't mean 'rape'). The Sabines attacked Rome in revenge and seized the Capitoline Hill. The Sabine women then stepped in to prevent further bloodshed, and the peace that was negotiated made the Romans and Sabines all one people with Romulus ruling jointly with the Sabine king Tatius.

The Sabine story is a myth, but because the Romans adopted Sabine words and gods, there may be some underlying truth about the Sabines and Romans coming together.

Numa Pompilius (715–673 BC)

Numa Pompilius is an even more shadowy figure than Romulus. The Sabines in Rome said it was their turn for a king, which the Romans agreed to, so long as they were allowed to choose the candidate. Numa, son of a Sabine king called Tatius, had to be persuaded to become king but eventually agreed. He was said to have set up Rome's religious cults and priests. He was also said to have invented a 12-month calendar, rather than the 10-month one, and set up Rome's boundaries. But like the story about Romulus inventing the Senate, these stories are probably just ways of firmly setting Roman customs in the most ancient tradition they could think up.

Numa founded the temple of the two-faced god Janus, who had power over beginnings and doorways. The temple's doors were open during war and closed during peace, harking back to a time when a gate *(ianua)* was opened for the army to march out to war. In the years AD 65–7 the emperor Nero (see Chapter 16) issued coins showing the temple with closed doors to commemorate a rare time of peace.

The Vestal Virgins

Numa was said to have brought the Vestal Virgins from Alba Longa to Rome. The Vestal Virgins were women priests who tended the sacred fire of Vesta, goddess of the hearth fire. The state paid for their welfare, and they lived in the Hall of Vesta near the Forum. Originally there were two, then four, and finally six. Each virgin spent 30 years in service: 10 years learning religious rituals, 10 years performing the rituals, and 10 years teaching them to the next generation. The Vestal Virgins were ruthlessly punished by being buried alive in unmarked graves if they lost their virginity (which was particularly unfair when they were raped).

Tullus Hostilius (673–641 BC)

Tullus Hostilius was chosen from the Latins. He had to fight off an invasion by the Alba Longans and destroyed Alba Longa as a punishment. He was believed to have built the Senate house – called the Curia Hostilia – in Rome. Because this Curia Hostilia house actually existed, it's likely that Hostilius was a real person (remember, distinguishing myth from history isn't clear-cut with these early kings). What certainly did happen is that Alba Longan families moved to Rome. Amongst them were the members of the Iulus clan, the ancestors of Julius Caesar's family, who claimed descent from Aeneas's son Ascanius (see the earlier section 'The myth').

Ancus Marcius (641–616 BC)

Like Tullus Hostilius, Ancus Marcius probably was a historical personality. He is said to have taken control of salt pans south of the Tiber. Marcius may have built the first bridge over the river into Rome, called the Pons Sublicius – the name means the 'wooden-piled bridge', which has an 'early' sound to it. He was also said to have built Rome's first aqueduct and founded Rome's port at Ostia. The important thing is that Ancus Marcius increased the control Rome had over territory beyond the city.

Tarquinius Priscus (616–579 BC)

This king, also known as 'Tarquin the Elder', was an Etruscan from the city of Tarquinii, 56 miles north of Rome. He was a close friend of Ancus Marcius, and had an excellent reputation for honesty, but when Marcius died, Tarquin persuaded the dead king's sons to go hunting. While they were out of town, he presented himself as a candidate for the kingship, egged on by his ambitious wife Tanaquil. Because Tarquin was so well thought of as an honest man, he got the job.

How the Romans declared war

Ancus Marcius is credited with Rome's system for declaring war. Messengers were sent to Rome's enemy to explain what Rome was angry about and to tell the enemy what compensation Rome wanted. If Rome had to declare war, specialist priests called Fetiales threw a single spear into the enemy's territory (or into a part of the Roman Forum symbolically treated as Roman territory) before command of the army was given to a general. The idea behind this process was to make sure that the gods would back the Romans, by claiming that war had been declared because the Romans had been done an injustice or an injury by their enemies first. The Fetiales priests also approved treaties at the end of war.

Tarquin introduced a proper drainage system in Rome as well as games, both of which were Etruscan interests. He was so successful that Ancius Marcius's sons were furious with jealousy. Knowing that Tarquin's children presented a dynastic threat, Marcius's sons had Tarquin murdered.

Servius Tullius (579–535 BC)

Servius was Tarquin's son-in-law and possibly even once his slave, depending on which version of the story you read. He married Tarquin's daughter, and when Tarquin was murdered, the widowed and ever-pushy Tanaquil made sure Servius became king next. What's certainly true is that his name was *plebeian* (lower-class) and is very similar to *servus* ('slave') – which means he was almost certainly a real person. A mythical king would have had a *patrician* (upper-class) name (refer to Chapter 2 for details on Roman class structure). Servius is said to have made big changes:

✔ He introduced a census (a national register of the population) and divided the people of Rome and the countryside into new tribes according to where they lived, rather than by what family they belonged to or how much property they had. This system automatically integrated newcomers. Eighty thousand Roman citizens who could bear arms were counted in the census; those who couldn't, including all women and children, weren't included. To create the census, two censors were appointed, usually chosen from former consuls, by the *Comitia Centuriata* (a political assembly).

✔ He assessed liability for military service according to wealth by dividing landholders into classes. Each class was divided into *centuries* (groups of 100 men). Men of the richest class were given funds to buy and keep a horse, while the poorest had literally no more than sticks and stones and served as the infantry.

✔ His new military classes were the basis of the Comitia Centuriata, in which each century submitted the majority vote of its members. The votes of the centuries from the highest class counted the most, but they also had to do most of the fighting.

✔ He was said to have built Rome's earliest surviving walls (although, in reality, these came after the invasion by the Gauls in 390 BC).

✔ He began Rome's worship of Diana, equated with Artemis, the Greek goddess of the moon, hunting, and fertility.

Whether or not Servius Tullius personally created the social hierarchy for Roman society, there's no doubt that that's what emerged from this period. The Comitia Centuriata gave the richest men the upper hand because their votes took precedence, but it also gave the poorest men a voice, too. But having a voice wasn't enough. The property-owning Roman upper classes now had a clearer idea of their power, and before long they seized their opportunity and got rid of the Etruscan kings.

Tarquinius Superbus (535–509 BC)

Tarquinius Superbus ('Tarquin the Proud') was married to Servius Tullius's ambitious daughter Tullia. Tullia persuaded her husband to kill Servius, who was now an old man. Tarquin accused Servius of being a trumped-up slave and threw him out of the Senate into the street, where he was killed. As Servius was popular, this was not a good start for Tarquin, who nevertheless had two long-lasting achievements:

✔ He built the Temple of Capitoline Jupiter on the Capitoline Hill. This became the central state cult of the Roman Empire.

✔ He built Rome's biggest sewer, the Cloaca Maxima ('Great Sewer'), which still exists today, though it wasn't covered over until *c.* 390 BC.

Tarquinius was the last King of Rome and for the rest of Rome's history, the Romans fell over themselves to prevent anybody else calling himself king.

The benefits of the Etruscan kings

The kings of Rome, regardless of whether they were mythical or real, brought in some really important changes. Rome's power originally extended over only about 60 square miles in Latium. By the end of Tarquinius Superbus's reign, Rome's power was more like six times as much. The last three Etruscan kings had done a huge amount to set Rome up for the future. They introduced political and military reforms that had started to make Rome work like clockwork.

Military reforms brought in by Servius Tullius – assessing every Roman's liability for military service according to his personal financial resources, for example – meant that the state could make the most of the resources at its disposal. The drainage of the marshy valleys, especially the one that would become the Forum, made it possible for a collection of settlements on hills to grow into a city.

The Etruscans also brought in valuable skills, such as metal-working, ceramics, and carpentry, that made trade possible. The organisation of state cults and the building of temples gave the state a spiritual identity and a sense of religious destiny. Rome was becoming known as a new force in the Mediterranean world. It's obvious from the battles with Alba Longa (see the section 'Tullus Hostilius', earlier in this chapter) that, as Rome started to flex its muscles, it would run into conflict with its neighbours.

You may get the impression that Rome was on some sort of conveyor belt to world domination and that the Etruscan kings set it in motion. In reality, by the end of the sixth century BC, Rome was becoming important, but it was no more important than anywhere else. And it was a good deal less important than some of the great cities of Greece, such as Athens, Corinth, and Sparta. At this point in its history, Rome could just as easily have disappeared without trace.

The Birth of the Roman Republic

Eventually, the Romans had had enough of being ruled by Etruscans. Tarquinius Superbus was considered to be the last word in tyranny, and the Romans decided he had to go. The traditional story is that the Rape of Lucretia was the catalyst.

The story goes like this: Sextus, son of Tarquinius Superbus, was on a campaign with other young nobles, who decided to head home and see whether their wives were behaving properly. All the wives except Lucretia, wife of Sextus's cousin, Tarquinius Collatinus, were living it up. However, Sextus was overwhelmed with desire for Lucretia. When he was round for dinner at a later date, he told Lucretia she had to sleep with him or he would rape her and arrange things to look as though she had betrayed her husband by sleeping with the slaves. Lucretia gave in but told her husband. He forgave her, but in her shame she committed suicide. The rape of Lucretia provoked total outrage amongst the Roman nobles. A conspiracy was organised by Lucius Junius Brutus (c. 545–509 BC), Tarquinius Superbus's nephew. Sextus fled but was killed, and Tarquinius Superbus was ousted from the throne.

There's no way of knowing whether any of this story is true, but it's pretty clear that Etruscan influence did start to decline, even though the decline didn't happen quickly. What's more, the Etruscans didn't give up that easily, though the story of what came next (see Chapter 11) is likely to be mostly myth.

Lucius Junius Brutus

Lucius Junius Brutus was a real toughie and the traditional founder of the Roman Republic. He was unbending and ruthlessly severe, with good reason. Tarquinius Superbus was his uncle, but he killed Brutus's father and older brother so that he could steal the family estate. Brutus got his name because everyone thought he was stupid – but it was just an act so that he could survive. Not surprisingly, Brutus loathed the kings, and he even killed his own sons for trying to have the kings reinstated. Brutus was killed in a battle between the Romans and the Tarquins in 509 BC when Tarquinius Superbus's Etrsucan allies, led by Tarquinius's son Arruns, marched on Rome.

The new constitution

With no kings around any longer, a new constitution was needed. No-one knows exactly who was responsible, but Publius Valerius Poplicola (*c.* 560–503 BC), one of the first *Consuls* (powerful magistrates who ruled Rome), went down in Roman history as one of the men involved. The constitution included the following:

- ✔ **The office of king was prohibited.** No man would ever be king of Rome again (until AD 476 anyway – see Chapter 21).

- ✔ **Two senators were to be elected annually as magistrates called *consuls* (though originally called *praetors*) by the Comitia Centuriata to run the state.** The consuls had supreme power over the law or going to war, and both consuls had the power of *veto* (the right to reject the other's decision). There's no easy modern equivalent, but the tradition survives in the way each US state has two senators.

- ✔ **Some of the king's jobs, like chief priest *(pontifex maximus)* were kept on.** The pontifex maximus was in supreme charge of everything to do with Roman religion and ceremony. The closest equivalent today of this position is the Pope or Archbishop of Canterbury.

- ✔ **The constitution allowed for a dictator in times of crisis.** If things were really bad, there was no time for two consuls to fall out over what to do. When that happened a *magister populi* (dictator) was appointed to represent both consuls and to deal with the crisis. A dictator was supposed to resign after six months at the latest.

 The constitution had one very important underlying principle: In Rome's Republic no-one – and that meant no-one – was able to have permanent political power. In Part IV, you see what happened when that principle was set aside.

The fasces

The *fasces* were a bundle of rods tied up with cords with an axe in the middle. The *lictors* (assistants to magistrates) carried them. Because the bundle was very strong, the idea was to symbolise the power and unity of Rome – even though individually, the rods could be broken. However, in Rome the axe was never bundled up, a symbol of the right of appeal. The fasces first appeared in the 600s BC. Because the Italian fascists adopted the fasces as their symbol, the fasces gave their name to the fascist parties of the 1920s and 1930s.

Patricians vs. plebs

After Rome had done away with its kings, Roman society was split into two halves: the upper classes, known as the *patricians,* and the lower classes, known as the *plebs.* Great tensions existed between the two classes. Most people were plebs, and they did all the ordinary jobs. When called on, plebeian men had to serve in the army without pay. That could mean falling into debt, which could lead to financial ruin. The patricians, on the other hand, nabbed all the prestigious top jobs, like priests, and the new job of consul. (Refer to Chapter 2 for more about Roman class structure.)

The aristocrats: Consolidating power

The new constitution of the Roman Republic showed how the aristocrats were beginning to organise all the power around themselves. The Comitia Centuriata (the Assembly of the Centuries; refer to Chapter 3 for more about this group), which was made up of all men eligible to fight, may have elected the consuls, but the candidates were chosen by the senators from amongst themselves. There was no chance that a brilliant leader from a poor background was ever going to be a consul.

Also, the Senate was getting more powerful. The Senate itself was originally supposed to be just an advisory body to the kings, but after 509 BC, under the Republic, things changed. For a start, the senators were all members of the noble families. In addition, because the consuls were elected annually, no consul could get enough experience or prestige to intimidate the Senate.

The angry mob

The plebs were not particularly pleased by the new set-up at Rome. With the new constitution, it was becoming plain to them that the patricians were sewing up all the power for themselves. The situation was made worse for a variety of reasons.

The Temple of Saturn

The front six columns and part of the pediment of the 496 BC Temple of Saturn still stand in the Roman Forum. They form one of the best-preserved fragments of any building in the Forum, despite their great age. The annual winter festival of the Saturnalia's main celebrations were held here (Chapter 9 discusses Roman religious practices).

First, early Republican Rome plunged into an economic crisis. The clue is in the pottery. Imports of Greek pottery started to decline, but after *c.* 450 BC they nosedived. Various new temples were built between 500–450 BC, such as the Temple of Saturn in 496. But all this building work stopped when the money ran out.

Second, Rome was having trouble with its neighbours. Under the kings, Rome had got its hands on new territory, but that had stopped. Worse, attacks by neighbouring enemies disrupted farming, which led to famines. Special purchases of imported grain had to be made, and land had to be found for starving peasants.

Third, the general crisis was plunging people into debt. Ruinous rates of interest crippled families, and the severest penalty for failing to make repayments under a type of contract called a *nexum* was death. Debtors could try to clear their debts by working for their creditors, but some were sold as slaves.

Needless to say, the plebs spotted that they suffered the most during this crisis. Through the consuls, the patricians were able to impose severe punishments, often as it pleased them.

Conflict of the Orders: A Roman class war

The result of all these grievances and tensions was the so-called *Conflict of the Orders,* the name given to the class war between the patricians and the plebeians. This conflict lasted for 200 years, and the outcome set a train of events leading up to the civil war and fall of the Republic in the first century BC (covered in Chapters 14 and 15).

The plebs waded in, not with random bouts of mob violence, but in an organised way. They took some of their ideas from Greek traders in Rome who had seen how aristocrats in their own homeland had been toppled. Greek merchants were active in a trading community on the Aventine Hill in Rome, and that's where the discontented plebs first started getting together and exchanging ideas. After the rural plebs joined in, they had the strength to start getting things changed. The plebs found various ways to flex their muscles:

- They organised general strikes to withhold their military services.

- They formed an assembly called the *Concilium Plebis Tributum* (the 'Council of Plebs Arranged by Tribes') where the plebs met in their tribes to elect tribunes to represent their interests. Unlike the Comitia Centuriata, only plebs could join the Council of Plebs. (You can read in detail how these councils and their representatives worked in Chapter 3.)

- They took an oath to protect their tribunes, come what may (this helped the power of the veto, which played a big role in expanding the plebs' power through the tribunes).

The patricians were forced to accept what the plebs had done because of the sheer force of numbers and the economic power the plebs wielded. In 471 BC, a law approved the Concilium Plebis Tributum.

One law to rule them all – the Twelve Tables (450 BC)

The plebs knew the only way to protect their interests was to demand a proper code of law that set out their rights and obligations. This law would prevent the patricians making up whatever penalties they liked and setting up unwritten precedents for arbitrary punishments. This principle is key to Roman law.

The plebs turned the heat on for a code of law in 462 BC by maintaining a barrage of demands for ten years. In 451 BC, the patricians gave in and appointed ten commissioners to draw up a law code. Doing so didn't go smoothly because the commission didn't finish its work on time, and a second one had to be formed. One commissioner, Appius Claudius, rigged his re-election to the second commission and used his position to carry on ruling as a tyrant even once the commission's work was done. The plebs had to organise a general strike to force the patricians to imprison Appius and re-establish constitutional government in 449 BC.

The result of plebeian pressure was the Code of the Twelve Tables which was finished by 450 BC. Because the patricians had drawn up the Code, they naturally made sure that their interests took priority, but writing laws down at all was a radical departure from tradition and a mark of the power plebs now had. These are some of the provisions of the Code of the Twelve Tables:

- The rights and duties of a family and its property were defined.
- Traders had a right to get together for a common purpose.
- Burials had to take place outside the city walls.
- A son sold three times into slavery by his father became free.
- Women remained in guardianship even once they reached their majority.
- A common-law wife would become her own master when her husband died.
- Only a proper law court could order the execution of a man.

The Twelve Tables fell into disuse over the centuries that followed, but they were never repealed. A thousand years later, some of the Code's original laws were preserved in the emperor Justinian's Law Code (see Chapter 21 for info on Justinian). But the patricians had clung on to some key powers:

- Consuls had the last word over things like military conscription.
- Patricians kept secret the legal jargon to be used in civil actions so that they could control how the law was enforced and who benefited from it (which was usually them).
- Marriage between patricians and plebs was prohibited, thus making sure that the patrician families would never have to share their powers.

Plebs' rights – the man with the trump card

Despite the patrician's efforts to protect their power and influence, after the Twelve Tables were passed, the plebs scored some more goals in the Conflict of the Orders:

- Any man who harmed the plebs officers, the tribunes, and/or the *aediles* (originally temple officials), would be put to death.
- The aediles became assistants to the tribunes and were elected in pairs annually.

✔ In 445 BC, the law banning intermarriage between plebs and patricians was overturned, meaning that sons of pleb women could now become patricians. The repeal of the intermarriage ban was significant because tribunes had a very important power: the veto. Through their veto, they were able to obstruct anything against the interests of the plebs. You find more about this, the tribunes, and aediles in Chapter 3.

Next, thanks to the military threats Rome faced in the fifth century, the system of having two consuls was abandoned for most of the time up to 367 BC, when it was restored. In place of the consuls, three (later six) military tribunes were elected annually. Crucially, plebs were eligible for the posts. Plebs also became eligible for a new magistracy called the *quaestorship*. Quaestors helped the consuls. Eventually plebs were even entitled to be elected as one of the consuls.

A republic came into being when laws were written down, and the patricians were forced to accept plebeian institutions and offices, creating a balance of power that worked, but only just. Rome's Republican government system was all about checks and balances. It worked so long as powers like the veto weren't abused, and also because the kind of pleb who was powerful enough and rich enough to get himself elected as a tribune knew his interests were similar to the patricians.

Chapter 11

This Town Isn't Big Enough for All of Us – Seizing Italy

. . . .

In This Chapter

▶ Rome's struggle with the Latin League

▶ Defeating the Gauls

▶ Rome's conquest of Italy

. . . .

*B*y about 450 BC, the Romans had gone a long way to setting up a political system that would define the next four centuries of their history (refer to Chapter 10 for the birth of the Roman Republic). But for the moment, Rome still didn't matter very much to the rest of the world. In the fifth century BC, Athens was the most powerful force in the Mediterranean. So much so that centuries later in the Renaissance, learned men looked back eagerly at Athens's experiments with democracy and what had happened in Greece. Egypt was now in an advanced state of decline and Alexander the Great's Macedonian Empire was still more than a century in the future. In north-western Europe, places like Gaul and Britain, which would one day be part of the Roman Empire, were just beginning to trade with the classical world.

Most of these places knew nothing at all about Rome. By 270 BC, however, despite having to deal with their own internal political problems as well as attacks by neighbours, Rome was well on the way to controlling all of Italy. Armed with the resources of the whole of Italy, Rome was poised on the brink of seizing an international empire.

What made the difference is that Rome used every setback to regroup and return to the attack. Every victory was followed up by ruthless consolidation of the territory won. Crucially, the Romans also created settled conditions in Italy that looked attractive to many of the Italian peoples. That was one of the great secrets of Rome's success – they made being ruled by Rome into a major advantage. The Etruscans and Gauls held out for a few more years, but Rome's ruthless reprisals made them give up.

Winning Over the Latin League (493 BC)

This period is one of the most complicated phases in Roman history, and many of the key details are lost to us. What seems to have happened is that there were really three power groups involved: the Romans, the Etruscans, and the Latins. When Rome pushed out the Etruscan kings, she struck a major blow. But although Rome was turning into the biggest player around, the Latin cities weren't in a rush to accept Rome's power. Getting them to do that was a decisive moment.

Fights with the Etruscans

Tarquinius Superbus was the last of the kings of Rome who, because of his tyranny and cruelty, was rather unceremoniously ousted from power (refer to Chapter 10 for the gory details). Tarquinius, an Etruscan, was naturally infuriated by this and fought a battle against the Romans to reclaim his throne, but he was unsuccessful. Not ready to give up, he went to Lars Porsenna, another Etruscan leader (he was king of a city called Clusium), for help. Porsenna seems to have had no plans to put Tarquinius back on the throne and used the invitation to start exercising his own muscle.

According to legend, Porsenna marched on Rome but couldn't cross the bridge to capture the city, thanks to a heroic defence by Horatius Cocles (which means one-eyed), who, with only two companions, held the crucial bridge long enough for the Romans to destroy it. Once the bridge was down, Horatius leaped into the river Tiber and swam home to be greeted by the cheering Romans.

Porsenna was very impressed by Horatius's display of bravery, and also by Mucius Scaevola, who crept into the Etruscan camp planning to assassinate Porsenna and, when caught, put his right hand into a fire to show how brave he and other Romans were. It wasn't just the men of Rome, either, who were tough. A woman hostage, Cloelia, held by the Etruscans, escaped back to Rome, but out of a sense of honour, the Romans sent her back. Porsenna let her go and abandoned the siege.

Thoroughly stirring stuff, designed to prove to the Romans just how honourable and brave their ancestors had been. Another version, probably more reliable, has Porsenna taking Rome, but not staying long. It seems that Rome's resistance to Etruscan control impressed other local Latin cities, creating the foundations of the Latin League.

The creation of the Latin League

In about 506 BC, determined to throw off the Etruscans for good, the Latins organised themselves into the League. The League was made up of about 30 cities (*not* including Rome) in the Latium region, including Alba Longa, Bovillae, Lavinium, Praeneste, and Tibur. These cities shared the same gods and also realised the benefits of working together to defend themselves against external enemies, mainly the Etruscans. The Latin League seems to have grown out of an earlier League of Aricia, which Rome tended to control. But Rome was left out of the new Latin League.

In response to the creation of the Latin League, the Etruscan Porsenna sent his son Arruns to teach the League a lesson, but the League defeated him at the Battle of Aricia, cutting the Etruscans off from southern Italy and permanently weakening them. It wasn't till 359 BC that the Etruscans tried again.

Rome: At odds with the Latin League

With Arruns defeated, you'd have thought that the Latins and the Romans would have spotted they had common interests, but the problem was that there were huge tensions because the Latins resented the way Rome threw her weight about, claiming to speak for various Latin cities based on the old League of Aricia.

Although the Latins had been impressed by Roman resistance to the Etruscans, they were less impressed by the prospect of Rome's growing power. The Latins were now organised in a League that left out the Romans, largely because the newly-independent Rome now claimed control of much of Latium. This claim even featured in a treaty she signed with Carthage about this time. Galvanised by their success against the Etruscans, the Latins decided to gear up for a trial of strength against the Romans.

Doing a deal with the Latins

Rome naturally wasn't prepared to back down in the face of the Latin League's resistance. Rome fought a battle against the Latins at Lake Regillus in 496 BC. Although the battle ended in a draw, it always went down in Roman tradition as a divinely inspired victory.

In reality, the Roman 'victory' had more to do with politics than divine intervention. The Latins were having trouble with mountain tribes coming down and invading their land and were forced to come to terms with the Romans to control this threat. Rome took advantage of the Latins' vulnerability and negotiated a winning deal called the *foedus Cassianum* (a treaty named after the consul Spurius Cassius) in 493 BC. It worked like this:

- The Latin League and Rome provided equal shares of a common defensive army.
- Rome and the Latin League split any spoils of war.

Rome was now a match for the Latin League. The deal had very important implications later because the Latin cities were now being drawn into the Roman system. Rome planted colonies *(coloniae)* of Roman citizens and Latins in places where the presence of a loyal town with a defensive capability would be useful. Colonists stopped being Roman citizens and became citizens of the new city, which was made a member of the Latin League. The League, incidentally, lasted till 340 BC when Rome took the opportunity to undermine it (see the section 'Meanwhile . . . the Latins strike back' later for more detail).

Crushing the local opposition

The problems Rome and the Latins faced were the Etruscan city of Veii to the north, the Aequi people to the east, and the Volscians to the south. Tradition has it that a Roman traitor called Coriolanus led a Volscian invasion of Rome. Whether this tale is true or not, the Romans did make a treaty after the year 486 BC with a people called the Hernici who lay between the Aequi and the Volsci, effectively stopping the Aequi and the Volsci from joining forces against Rome. By the late fifth century, these two cities no longer posed a serious threat.

The Etruscan city of Veii, however, stood up to the Romans. In 426 BC, the Romans defeated the Veians, and they returned in 405 BC, determined to wipe out the city once and for all. A ten-year siege, which nearly crippled Rome thanks to Veii's impregnable location, followed. Only an assault by a Roman general called Marcus Furius Camillus, who tunnelled under the walls, won the day in 396 BC.

The Romans exacted a brutal revenge on the Veians: Camillus told his troops they could kill the Veians at will and sell any survivors into slavery. The land the Romans seized was divided up amongst its poorer citizens. This sort of revenge set the pattern of Roman world-dominating brutality in later times.

Having the Gaul to Invade – 390 BC

By the early 390s BC, Gaulish Celts found their way south into northern Italy's fertile Po Valley, called by the Romans *Cisalpine Gaul*. In 391, they threatened an Etruscan city called Clusium which appealed to Rome for help. Rome warned off the invaders, but in 390 a Gaulish army reached the river Allia ten miles north of Rome.

Gaul is roughly equivalent to modern France. The Gaulish tribes were just one small group of peoples spread across central and north-western Europe and known to the Romans as *Celts*, a very loose term that doesn't mean one common cultural group, though these days it's often treated as if it does. The Celts knew about the Mediterranean world through trading contacts.

Getting sacked

In 390 BC (or 387 according to some sources), the Romans met the Gauls in battle and were totally defeated. The Romans didn't have the equipment or the tactics to face the Gauls and their long swords. The Romans might be famous today for their highly disciplined and well-equipped professional regular army, but that belongs to a later period in Roman history. In the early days, the Roman army was drawn from the ranks of citizens on an as-needed basis, and they were often not up to the job.

Rome was saved because the Gauls failed to take advantage of the open road, which gave the Romans time to build a last stand on the Capitoline Hill. When the Gauls burst into Rome, they sacked the city and besieged the Capitoline for seven months. Eventually the Romans had to surrender and pay a ransom of gold. Amazingly at that point, the Gauls went back to northern Italy. But the damage was done.

This Gallic invasion turned out to be a curious portent of Rome's future when, in AD 410, marauding tribes would once again come from northern Europe to sack and destroy Rome.

Changes at home

The invasion by the Gauls had all sorts of serious consequences. For a start, the Gauls had done a lot of damage to farmland. It took decades for Rome to repair what she had, rather than spending time on getting hold of new territory. Military service became more essential. The upshot was another economic decline.

The Tribune's image

Many years later, the Roman historian Plutarch described how the tribunes of the plebs *(tribuni plebis)* had to dress and behave like ordinary citizens, without any of the pomp and ceremony that surrounded officials like consuls. In fact, the more ordinary a tribune appeared, the more powerful he became. Approachability was essential, so his door was never locked, day or night, and he was treated almost as if he was sacred.

Another development was the growth in Roman citizenship (see Chapter 2 for more information about the benefits of citizenship). The number of Roman citizens grew for the following reasons:

✔ Latins who came to Rome and settled there could become Roman citizens with full voting rights. Foreigners, or people from other parts of Italy, who came to Rome could become 'half-citizens' – they were called *cives sine suffragio,* which means 'citizens without the vote'. Roman citizenship became a very useful device later on, awarded to certain cities other than Rome.

✔ Another source of new citizens were the families of slaves. After a slave was freed he became a *libertus* ('freedman'). He was not allowed to vote, but his sons could do so (see Chapter 2 for information about freedmen).

✔ There were also more plebs, thanks to the practice of creating colonies and also the *municipia* (cities founded by the Romans but whose inhabitants lacked the full rights of Roman citizens), and at the same time, fewer patricians. Many patricians had been killed in the fighting, and they continued to avoid marrying plebs even though that was now legal (refer to Chapter 10).

Despite the economic decline and because of the plebs' growing numbers, the plebs were gaining the upper hand. The better-off plebeians were determined to take the opportunity to demand economic and political change. (See Chapter 10 for more on the class war, the Conflict of the Orders, between the patricians and plebs.)

Economic muscle

Part of the way the plebs showed how their power was increasing came when they demanded economic measures to stave off ruin and also wanted the end of patrician privileges. The plebs forced in new laws to help debtors. The fact that they were able to do this showed the tensions between them and the patricians, and that the patricians weren't able to stop them. This is what they achieved:

✔ Maximum interest rates were fixed.

✔ Enslavement of debtors was ended.

✔ The amount of public land anyone could hold was limited, making it possible for small parcels to be distributed amongst the poorer citizens.

Political reform

Plebeians also demanded, and got, political reform. The most important reform came in 367 BC when the plebs introduced the principle that one of the two annually elected consuls had to be a pleb. In 342 BC this came into force. Because the consulship was the senior magistracy, this meant that plebs could hold any of the magistracies. After plebs started holding the consulship, they effectively became a new plebeian aristocracy. By 300, the plebs won the right of appeal against a sentence of death. In 287 came the crowning victory: the right of the *Concilium Plebis Tributum* (the Council of Plebs arranged by Tribes; refer to Chapter 10) to pass laws which bound not just the plebs, but also the patricians.

As a result of these key reforms, the Roman magistracies evolved into a career structure with a clear hierarchy. A man began with military service and then served in each of the magistracies until he reached the consulship (see Chapter 3 for the career ladder in its mature form).

Because magistracies were short-term appointments, it was the Senate that provided the underlying long-term stability. The Senate couldn't make laws, but because senators were ex-magistrates, its resolutions had so much prestige they were generally treated as laws. Certainly no serving magistrate would risk challenging the Senate.

Throughout all these changes, the Concilium Plebis Tributum was the real winner. It started out an illegal body, but by 300 BC, although it had none of the trappings or status of a magistracy, the Concilium Plebis Tributum had the power of veto over anything any magistrate did, or over any resolution of the Senate.

A new army and a new Latin League

After being defeated by the Gauls in 390 BC, the Romans were in a seriously weakened state. After having thrown their weight around for a century, all the hard-won advantage had been lost in a trice. But being Romans, they took it on the chin and set about repairing the damage:

✔ **They built walls so that no Gauls, or anyone else, would ever capture Rome again.** The new walls were 8.9 kilometres (5.5 miles) long, 7.3 metres (24 feet) high and 3.67 metres (12 feet) thick. Some of these walls, falsely said to have been built by the Etruscan king of Rome, Servius

Tullius, still stand today and are known as the 'Servian Walls'. When the Gauls invaded again in 360, the Romans made use of their new defences. In fact, they hid behind their new walls until the Gauls went home again.

✔ **They reorganised and re-equipped the army so that the Roman forces couldn't be rushed by a high-speed barbarian attack.** Instead of fighting in a solid wall of infantry, Roman soldiers were divided up into more flexible units. Troops were equipped with javelins as well as swords. The Roman army was no longer a defensive force. It was an army capable of conquest.

✔ **They reorganised the Latin League.** The Gauls' invasion of 360 BC encouraged the Etruscans to try their hand at attacking Rome again, this time in 359. In response, Rome reorganised the Latin League so that Rome took total military control instead of sharing it. The Romans thoroughly defeated the Etruscans, and by 350 had made themselves safe against possible invasion by a neighbour.

Knocking out the Samnites

The Samnites were the tribes who lived along the Appenine Mountains in central and southern Italy. Because the Romans and Latins lived in the plains below the mountains to the west and started to make inroads on Samnite territory, and the Samnites were starting to encroach on the plains, it was plain that the Romans and Samnites would come to blows.

The Samnites lived in widely-dispersed villages and had little control over any individual community's involvement in raiding or warfare. So the Samnites earned themselves a bad reputation for causing trouble. Even so, in 354 BC, the Romans accepted an offer of a treaty from the Samnites; probably both sides fearing another Gaulish invasion. But this treaty didn't solve all the problems between the Samnites and the Romans.

The First Samnite War (343–341 BC)

In 343 BC, the Samnites started hassling the city of Capua in Campania, about 350 kilometres (220 miles) south-east of Rome. Capua appealed to Rome for help. Rome saw its chance to take control over the region of Campania and promptly threw out the Samnite treaty, even though there had never been any tradition of the Romans helping the Capuans.

The First Samnite War was short and inconclusive. To begin with, the Romans drove the Samnites out of the area around Capua. But in 342, Roman soldiers mutinied because they resented being away from home on long campaigns. That could have wrecked Rome's prestige once again, but fortunately the Samnites had to retreat to defend themselves against a Greek colony called Tarentum in the far south of Italy. The result was that in 341 BC, the Romans and Samnites renewed their treaty.

Meanwhile . . . the Latins strike back

The First Samnite War wasn't a military disaster for the Romans, but it was very nearly a political one. The Latins spotted how the army mutiny had nearly scuppered Rome's ability to hold back the Samnites and decided to try their chances at gaining back parity.

The bold bid fails

So in 340, the Latins demanded a restoration of equal rights between themselves and Rome. Naturally the Romans refused. So the Latins made an alliance with the Campanians and Rome's old enemy, the Volsci (refer to the section 'Crushing the local opposition'), which looked like a good way of overpowering Rome. Except that the Romans were smarter and now used their alliance with the Samnites to defeat the Latins and Campanians.

Dismantling the Latin League

After defeating the Latins and the Campanians, the Romans offered excellent peace terms to the Campanians, who promptly left their alliance with the Latins. Now in a position of unassailable strength, the Romans simply dismantled the Latin League and forced each city to come to terms individually with Rome in a settlement of 338 BC. The Romans introduced:

- **Municipal status:** Some of the existing Latin cities were made into municipiae, divided into two types: those whose citizens became Roman citizens with full voting rights; and those where the citizens had no voting rights but still had to supply Rome with soldiers.

- **New Roman colonies:** Rome also set up colonies *(coloniae)* of Roman citizens to guard strategic locations. The city of Antium (modern Anzio), for instance, had its fleet destroyed by the Romans. It was allowed to remain in existence, but a colony of Roman citizens was planted in its territory to guard the port. Another colony called Cales was established in 334 BC to defend Capua.

The technique the Romans used to thwart the Latin League's coup is called *divide and rule*. The Romans had used it before, and they'd use it again in the centuries to come, playing off one tribe against another. Similarly, coloniae and municipia were brilliant devices that Rome would use in the future (see Chapter 2 for more on municipia). These devices left cities with their own identities and some powers of self-government, but at the same time gave the inhabitants status within the Roman system.

The Second Samnite War (326–304 BC)

Having well and truly sorted out the Latin League to its advantage (see the preceding section), Rome decided to ignore the Samnites in her settlement of 338 BC. The last straw for the Samnites was when the Romans, always looking for a way to enhance their power and influence, made a treaty with the powerful Greek trading and manufacturing city of Tarentum in southern Italy in 334 BC, while the Tarentines were at war with the Samnites.

By 327, the Samnites had made peace with Tarentum and now started trying to expand their power westwards. They placed a force of theirs into the Greek port and colony of Neapolis (Naples). The nearby Capuans objected and asked Rome for help.

Naturally, the Romans responded and sent a force down to Naples. The Roman army besieged the Samnite garrison but offered them such excellent terms the Samnites surrendered. But the Samnites hadn't given up their scheme to conquer the western coastal plains. The next few years were a stalemate. The Romans didn't dare fight in the Samnites' mountain territory, and the Samnites were held back by Roman garrisons.

The war's first phase ended in 321 BC. Impatient for a decisive action, the Romans sent an army from Capua to attack Samnium. The Samnites trapped the Roman army in the mountains at the Caudine Forks, near Capua, and forced them into a humiliating surrender. The Samnites thought they'd won, but the Romans used the peace to regroup. As usual after a defeat, the Roman army was enlarged and tactics improved.

In 316 BC, the Romans restarted the war, but things quickly went wrong. Another Roman force was defeated, and the Capuans promptly went over to the Samnites. But in 314, the Romans won back control, forced the Capuans back on their side, and set up new colonies to control the territory.

The Samnites could see they had little chance of winning under these circumstances, and in 304 BC they made peace with Rome. The Romans were keen to end the fighting and made no attempt to conquer Samnite territory. They were secure in the knowledge that, if war broke out again, they now had the upper hand with so much more territory under their control and with colonies dotted about to keep it safe.

Try, try, and try again: The Third Samnite War (298–290 BC)

Despite Rome's advantages, the Third Samnite War was a close-run thing for them. This time round the Samnites were joined by the Etruscans and the Gauls. The Samnites, under their leader Egnatius Gellus, soundly defeated the Romans at Camerinum (modern Cameria) in 295 BC. The Romans nearly lost again that year at the Battle of Sentinum (Sassoferrato), but Roman bravery (and the withdrawal of the Etruscans) turned the potential disaster into a victory. The Samnite leader Egnatius was killed, causing the Samnites to collapse. Afterwards, the Samnites' allies made peace with Rome. That's when Rome moved in to snatch a victory. By 291, the Samnites were cut off and isolated. In 290, they gave up and accepted the status of allies of Rome, and as such were forced to contribute to Rome's army. As was so often the case, Rome appeared magnanimous but had worked everything to her advantage by not seeking revenge.

Now for the Rest of Italy

The Romans had control of much of central Italy, but there was still *Magna Graecia* ('Great Greece') to deal with. Magna Graecia was the name given to southern Italy – where the Greek colonies were in control. The most powerful Greek colony was Tarentum (modern Taranto), with a wealthy economy based on wool and pottery, which enabled the Tarentines to field a 15,000-strong army, maintain a navy, and afford mercenaries to fend off their enemies, such as the Samnites, as well as their local rivals and enemies the Lucanians, a tribe who lived in part of southern Italy called Lucania.

In 334 BC, the Tarentines hired Alexander the Great's brother-in-law, Alexander of Epirus, to help them to fight off raids by the Samnites and Lucanians. Alexander negotiated a treaty with the Romans then, in alliance with the Samnites. Under the treaty, the Romans promised not to help the Samnites fight the Tarentines. The problem for the Tarentines was that the Roman alliance might have helped them hold off the Samnites, but the Second and Third Samnite Wars saw Roman armies move into the region. That worried the Tarentines, who had also realised Alexander was more interested in conquering his own empire. So they abandoned him to be defeated and killed by the Lucanians and then started deciding what to do about the Romans.

Pyrrhus arrives to show who's who

The Tarentines became more and more worried by Rome's ambitions. Rome's power was such that she was constantly being asked for help by places that felt under threat. The Greek city of Thurii was being attacked by the Lucanians, so in 282 BC, the Thurians asked the Romans for military support. As Thurii was only a few miles down the coast from Tarentum on the Gulf of Otranto, the Tarentines were worried and annoyed at the breach of Alexander's treaty (in which Rome had agreed *not* to send any of her ships into the Gulf). So the Tarentines attacked and defeated the Roman forces.

Because the Romans were still fighting off the Etruscans and Gauls, Romans asked for compensation instead of fighting back. But the Tarentines threw that out. They were feeling confident because by then they had hired King Pyrrhus of Epirus, considered to be the number one Greek soldier of his day, to make sure they could push the Romans back and encourage Rome's allies to defect.

Pyrrhus couldn't resist the opportunity to throw his weight about, so when the Tarentines called for his help, he turned up with a force of 25,000 men – a very bad omen for the Romans.

Pyrrhus won the first round in 280 BC. The Romans brought him to battle at Heraclea, not far from Tarentum on the Gulf of Otranto in southern Italy. The Roman cavalry was routed by the arrival of Pyrrhus's army of elephants. The Samnites and Lucanians promptly joined Pyrrhus, spotting their chance for revenge on the Romans. In 279, Pyrrhus beat the Romans again, this time at Asculum, but it was a hard-won victory.

Pyrrhus decided that defeating the Romans permanently would take far too long and cost too many lives. He offered peace on the condition that the Romans abandoned southern Italy, which the Roman Senate refused to do. In 278 Rome's forces were bolstered by money and ships from the Carthaginians of North Africa who were worried Pyrrhus might attack them.

Pyrrhus's victory over the Romans in 279 BC cost him so dearly he said 'another victory like that, and we're done for'. Nowadays the term *Pyrrhic victory* means any success won at so much cost it wasn't worth it.

In fact, Pyrrhus did indeed go off to attack the Carthaginians. While he was away doing that, the Romans attacked his Samnite and Lucanian allies (these battles are sometimes called the Fourth Samnite War). In 276 BC, the Samnites begged Pyrrhus to come back and help them. He did, but was roundly defeated by the Romans near Beneventum, just south-east of Capua and dangerously close to Rome.

Pyrrhus fled home and was killed two years later when a pot thrown out of a window accidentally fell on his head, which just goes to show how history can be turned around by remarkably trivial events.

By Jove, I think we've done it

With Pyrrhus gone, the way was open for the Romans. They captured Tarentum in 272 BC, which meant they'd not only seized a hugely wealthy city, but they also had control of the Italian peninsula.

The Greek cities of the south were drawn into the Roman net and became allies *(socii)*. Unlike the Latin cities, the Greek cities provided ships rather than troops. Latin colonies were planted here and there to secure strategic locations, like Paestum. The Samnite federation was permanently broken up into units that were individually allied to Rome.

More importantly, the other players on the Mediterranean saw that there was a new kid on the block. At the same time as the Carthaginians were renewing their treaty with the Romans, far to the east, the Macedonian Pharaoh of Egypt, Ptolemy II (285–246 BC), was making a pact of friendship with Rome.

Chapter 12

Carthage and the First Two Punic Wars

. . . .

In This Chapter

▶ How Rome became the biggest player in the Mediterranean

▶ Why the first two Punic Wars nearly broke Rome

▶ How Rome clung on to its allies and finished off Italy

▶ Greece falls into Rome's lap

. . . .

*I*n 264 BC, Rome was nearly 500 years old. It had grown from an insignificant cluster of villages on a few hills by the river Tiber into a world-class state. Nevertheless, Rome's expansion hadn't been an overnight success. There were constant internal political struggles, which were still far from settled, and Rome's wars with its neighbours were rarely walkovers.

Still, by 264 BC Roman rule was widely accepted throughout Italy. Instead of having only the resources of a city and its surrounding area to work with, Rome could call on the manpower and resources of all Italy. The Romans had done this by imposing more or less the same system of government throughout Italy. Armed with this phenomenally important asset, the Romans created a solid basis for their Empire. But like the previous 500 years, the next 250 years wouldn't be plain sailing.

The Sicilian Story – the First Punic War (264–241 BC)

Carthage, where Tunisia is now, was a trading colony set up in North Africa by the Phoenicians of Tyre in 814 BC (in reality, Carthage was probably founded around the time that Rome was said to have been founded). Carthage was extremely successful. Its influence spread across the western

Mediterranean, especially in Sicily and southern Italy, and it traded for tin probably as far as Cornwall. One story going around Rome was that the Carthaginian commander Hanno had even sailed all round Africa. It was inevitable that Rome's rise would matter a very great deal to the Carthaginians, and vice versa.

In fact, Rome and Carthage had made several treaties in earlier times. Under the treaty of 348 BC, the Romans allowed the Carthaginians to trade slaves in Latium and recognised the Carthaginians' monopoly of trade across the whole western Mediterranean, including Sardinia, Corsica, and Sicily. In return, the Carthaginians agreed not to set up any permanent colonies of their own in Latium. At the time, the Romans didn't have any intention of treading on the Carthaginians' toes. Another treaty, in 278, gave the Romans support from the Carthaginians against Pyrrhus (refer to Chapter 11).

By 264 BC, Rome was in full control of Italy. With Sicily only a few yards away, the situation was completely different. The Carthaginians saw that their wealth and power was under direct threat, while Rome's relentless drive to expand its land and power meant their paths were bound to cross.

The result was a series of long, drawn-out wars called the Punic Wars. They were Rome's first massive international struggle and played a monumentally decisive role in establishing Rome's power and shaping the course of history in Europe and the whole of western civilisation. In fact, the Punic Wars were a turning-point in world history. The Romans won, but had it gone the other way, this book might have been called *Carthaginians For Dummies*. Rome would have popped up in just a few paragraphs, and you and I would never have heard of Julius Caesar.

The Latin word *Punicus* is another version of the Latin *Poenicus* which comes from the Greek *Phoinikikos* (Φοινικικοζ), a Phoenician. The word comes from the Greek for purple because the Phoenicians and Carthaginians produced a highly-prized purple dye.

The Mamertines play with fire

Rome controlled Italy, but not all Italians were in Rome's service. Campanian mercenaries (from south-west Italy) had been employed by Agathocles, tyrant of Syracuse in Sicily. In 315 BC, Agathocles captured the wealthy city of Messana, just a few miles from Rhegium in Italy. After Agathocles's death in 289 BC, the mercenaries went back on their agreement to leave Sicily and out of greed captured Messana, divided it up amongst themselves, and then changed their name to Mamertines, based on their local version of Mars, the god of war, called Mamers. Not surprisingly the Syracusans were furious and attacked the Mamertines, who asked both the Romans and Carthaginians for help.

The trouble for the Romans was that, not long before, another bunch of Campanians had seized the Italian city of Rhegium, just across the straits from Messana, massacring some of the inhabitants. The Romans were disgusted by this and recaptured Rhegium. Because the Mamertines had committed more or less the same crime, the Romans couldn't decide what to do. In the end, ever practical, they put honour on the back burner and went with what was most advantageous for them: They decided to help the Syracusans. Rome's reasoning: The Carthaginians already controlled most of western Sicily. If the Carthaginians threw out the Mamertines from Messana, Carthage might get control of the eastern part of Sicily as well, and that would mean the Carthaginians were only a short hop from Italy.

Messana isn't enough: Going for Sicily

In their efforts to stop the Carthaginians from claiming more of Sicily, the Romans got off to a good start. First, they used diplomacy to break up the alliance between the Carthaginians and the Syracusans. Next, they captured a Carthaginian city on Sicily's south coast called Agrigentum and stopped the Carthaginians from sending over a bigger army.

Something changed at this point. The Romans had fallen into the Sicilian war purely because of the Mamertines in Messana. Within a year or two, the Mamertines had been completely forgotten by the Romans and the Carthaginians. The Romans saw their chance to seize all of Sicily and went to war. So began the First Punic War.

Battles and victory at sea: Becoming a naval power

Fighting the First Punic War took the Romans to a new level of military expertise because they built a naval fleet, despite having little or no naval experience, by copying the design of a Carthaginian wreck. They put the fleet under the command of Gnaeus Cornelius Scipio Asina, who trained up his naval forces. In 260 BC, although an advance force under Asina was caught out by the Carthaginians, the rest of the Roman fleet wiped out the main Carthaginian fleet off the north coast of Sicily.

The legend of Marcus Atilius Regulus

The story of Marcus Atilius Regulus (*c.* 310–250 BC) is fiction, but it was dreamed up to help create an image of Roman honour and self-sacrifice. The story goes that Regulus was leading the Roman army in North Africa. In 255 BC, the Carthaginians destroyed his army and captured him. They sent Regulus back to Rome to present the Carthaginians with terms for peace, on the condition that, if the Romans refused, he was to return to Carthage. Regulus went back to Rome and gave such an inspiring speech to reject the Carthaginians' peace terms that, of course, the Romans threw the terms out. But Regulus kept his promise, returned to Carthage, and was tortured and killed. In truth, Regulus was a real man, who probably died in prison in Africa.

The Romans realised they had no idea about naval tactics. To compensate, they built portable boarding ramps, which they threw across to enemy ships; then the Roman soldiers darted across and turned what would otherwise be a naval battle into a land battle – a very successful tactic.

Attacking Sicily wasn't going to defeat the Carthaginians for good. Rome won a second naval battle, at Ecnomus, in 256 BC using the same tactics: boarding ramps and *grappling irons* (iron-clawed hooks for seizing the enemy ships). The Romans invaded Africa with a huge army but were totally defeated by the Carthaginians in 255 BC, and the Roman fleet, which came to rescue survivors, was destroyed in a storm.

The struggle between Rome and the Carthaginians went on for another 14 years. The Romans suffered another naval disaster in 253 BC when a fleet was wrecked, and again 249 BC when Claudius Appius Pulcher took a fleet to destroy the Carthaginian navy in the port at Drepana. The Carthaginians moved out of the harbour before the Romans arrived. Pulcher sent his ships in and carried on sending them in even though the first ones were trying to get out again and chase the Carthaginians. In the mayhem, 93 out of 120 Roman ships were lost.

For some bizarre reason, despite having defeated the Romans at sea, the Carthaginians decided to take their ships out of service, completely unaware that the Romans had been busy building a new fleet, paid for by voluntary loans. In fact, they'd built two – the first was wrecked in yet another storm, but they promptly set to and built another.

Faced with this sudden resurgence of Roman naval power in 242 BC, the Carthaginians were totally wrong-footed. A new Carthaginian fleet had to be thrown together in double-quick time. In March 241 BC, the Roman fleet met the Carthaginian fleet off the coast of Sicily, and the Romans totally defeated the Carthaginians and occupied Sicily. The Carthaginians executed their admiral, Hanno, and were forced to abandon their claims to Sicily and pay compensation for the war!

Setting the stage for the Second Punic War

The Romans made a lot of mistakes in the First Punic War but they won because:

- ✔ They had so much manpower they could afford losses.
- ✔ They learned new methods of warfare from their enemies.
- ✔ They kept coming back for more battle even when they had setbacks.

After defeating the Carthaginians in Sicily, the Romans realised that Carthaginian trading wealth was up for grabs. With Carthage defeated, the Romans followed the war up by capturing the islands of Sardinia and Corsica, preventing the Carthaginians from having handy bases from which to launch assaults on Italy's west coast.

The Carthaginians, having lost Sicily, decided to make up for the loss by building up their control in Spain – a decision that led directly to the Second Punic War.

Staying busy in the interim: Capturing northern Italy

With the First Punic War out of the way, and before the Second Punic War broke out, the Romans had to deal again with the Gauls of northern Italy.

The Gauls of northern Italy last invaded central Italy in 390 BC. They'd sacked Rome but went home with a huge ransom, rather than troubling themselves to take the opportunity to destroy Rome once and for all. The Gauls were a thorn in the flesh of the Romans for much of the next century, and the Gauls even took part in the Third Samnite War (refer to Chapter 11 for details about the Gauls). Major defeats of the Gauls took place in the 280s, and a Roman colony was planted on the edge of Gaulish territory near the site of modern Ancona, in northern Italy. In 279 BC, an army of Gauls was defeated by the Greeks at Delphi in Greece.

It took more than 50 years before the Gauls finally forgot about these setbacks and for a new generation of have-a-go warriors to grow up, determined to earn themselves reputations as heroic fighters. These new Gaulish warriors joined up with other tribes from farther north and sent an army of 70,000 into Italy. Big mistake. By now the Romans had the whole of Italy at their disposal and had no trouble in sending an army nearly twice as big against the Gauls.

The Gauls were soundly defeated and the Romans decided that the best thing to do was conquer northern Italy and end the chances of another Gaulish comeback. Not that that was a difficult decision to make. Just as the First Punic War opened Roman eyes to the chances of seizing the Carthaginians' wealth, so the Gaulish invasion of 225 BC made the Romans see the attraction of holding the fertile northern plains of Italy, abundant in woodland, corn, and livestock.

Unbelievably, the Romans took just three seasons of campaigning to capture the whole of northern Italy and push the Gauls back. They built new roads and set up naval bases in the region. By 220 BC, the Romans held an area almost identical to modern Italy and controlled the whole area from the Alps to the southernmost tip of Sicily.

The Second Punic War (218–202 BC)

The Carthaginians had been well and truly bruised by the First Punic War. The loss of the rich island of Sicily made a big dent in their wealth. Their damaged prestige meant other peoples under their control tried to throw them off. To bolster Carthaginian power and reputation, the Carthaginians decided to build up their control in Spain.

Hamilcar Barca, a Carthaginian general who was busy suppressing revolts in North Africa, was the ideal man for the job. He'd spent a lot of time fighting the Romans in Sicily in the First Punic War and resented the Romans from the bottom of his heart.

Hamilcar set up new Carthaginian bases in Spain, including Nova Carthago ('New Carthage' – modern Cartagena). Hamilcar's work was carried on by his son-in-law Hasdrubal, and then his son Hannibal. The Romans didn't like what Hamilcar was doing one bit and demanded that the Carthaginians stay south of the river Ebro in north-east Spain. Figure 12-1 shows the territory controlled by the Rome and Carthage in 218 BC when Hannibal crossed the Alps into Italy in the Second Punic War.

The Carthaginians did, indeed, stay south of the river Ebro. Unfortunately for the Carthaginians, in 'their' area was a coastal city called Saguntum, a Roman ally (refer to Figure 12-1). A Roman delegation was sent to New Carthage to warn the Carthaginians to leave Saguntum alone. Hannibal (Hamlicar's son) took no notice and besieged Saguntum in 219. The city fell after eight months because the Romans were too tied up with Illyrian pirates to help (see the section 'Trouble in the East: The Macedonian Wars' for that bit of history), but by 218, Rome had defeated the Illyrians and were free to deal with the situation in New Carthage.

Rome sent a deputation to Carthage to demand that Hannibal be surrendered. The Carthaginians naturally said no and told the Roman deputation to offer them peace or war. The Roman envoys offered war and the Carthaginians accepted, which was a decisive moment in history.

The amazing march of elephants

The Carthaginian forces in Spain were miles from home and the Romans controlled the sea. The Roman plan was to use their navy to send an army to fight Hannibal in Spain. Hannibal had other ideas.

Hannibal realised that, by marching into Italy overland, he could dodge the Roman navy. In 218 BC, Hannibal crossed the Alps with his army and his elephants. The Roman force turned up too late to stop him. Hannibal was immediately joined by the Gaulish tribes who were delighted at the chance to have another go at Rome, especially as it looked as if the Romans were going to lose (refer to the earlier section 'Staying busy in the interim: Capturing northern Italy' for information on the Gauls of northern Italy).

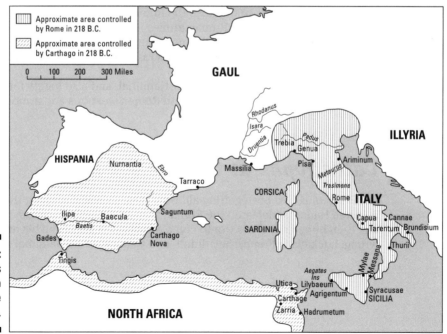

Figure 12-1: The areas involved in all three Punic Wars.

Hannibal's march over the Alps was a logistical triumph. Hannibal sent scouts ahead to plan the route and bribe the Gauls. Crossing rivers, especially for the elephants, was a big problem. Rafts made to look like a natural bridge by covering them with earth were built to lure the elephants aboard so that they could be towed across.

There's no certainty about how big Hannibal's army was. The lowest estimate was 20,000 infantry and 6,000 cavalry as well as 21 surviving elephants, but Hannibal lost a large number of men along the way (and about 40 elephants). Some of the army had refused to make the journey, while he was said to have lost 36,000 men alone after crossing the Rhône.

The Battle of Lake Trasimene – 217 BC

Despite the losses on the way, Hannibal's army was unstoppable. He fought off a Roman army in northern Italy, and the Romans fell back. The Romans thought Hannibal would come into Italy down the main road called the Via Flaminia. He didn't – he sneaked in through an unguarded mountain pass, forcing a 25,000-strong Roman army under Caius Flaminius to chase after him. Flaminius, and a large part of his army, were promptly wiped out on the banks of Lake Trasimene.

What happened at Lake Trasimene was a classic ambush. As Flaminius's force travelled by on a narrow road, warriors hurtled down the hills on either side, while cavalry attacked from behind. The ambush happened far too quickly for Flamninius to organise the Roman troops into their battle lines – the formation in which the Roman armies fought best. Out of formation, all their careful discipline and tactics collapsed. Being taken by surprise was a catastrophe. Of the 25,000 Roman soldiers, more than half were killed.

Trasimene was a brilliant success for Hannibal, and also handy for his men, who now re-equipped themselves with Roman weapons and armour. But Hannibal's plan started to go wrong.

Catastrophe at Cannae – 216 BC

Rome's genius had been getting allies on their side and keeping them there. So when Hannibal defeated the Roman General Flamninius at Lake Trasimene and then hoped the allies would come over to him and swell his army, he was wrong. Luckily for Rome, they didn't, and that meant all Hannibal's hopes of being supplied by grateful Italian cities vanished. So Hannibal bypassed Rome and tried his luck in southern Italy. The cities of the south wouldn't help him either.

At this point in the Second Punic War, Hannibal really ought to have been defeated. He wasn't able to get the help from the Roman allies that he had counted on, and by 216 BC, he had at the most about 40,000 to 50,000 men. But the Romans made a disastrous mistake. They thought that, by having a huge army, they would crush Hannibal easily. They massed an army of 50,000 and put it under the command of two Roman consuls who had no idea of Hannibal's strategy or tactics. Worse, the two consuls constantly argued, and the army threatened mutiny. Not the best way to prepare for a battle that could cost the Romans Italy. The situation was a recipe for disaster.

The Romans found Hannibal at Cannae, about 180 miles south-east of Rome. Initially, the battle went well for the Romans. They threw their main force in on the Carthaginian centre, which was made up of Gauls and Spaniards. Then the Gauls and Spaniards fell back, and the Romans found themselves trapped between the Carthaginian wings of African infantry and cavalry.

The Carthaginian wings moved in on the now-exhausted Romans and totally defeated them. One estimate put the Romans losses at 45,500 infantry and 2,700 cavalry; another put it as high as 70,000. The point is that the Roman army was wiped out, but Hannibal only lost about 6,000 troops.

Bloody and bruised, but still swinging

It hardly needs saying that after Cannae, the Romans faced total and utter ruin. Up to this point, they'd lost possibly as many as 100,000 men in Hannibal's campaign. Now Rome's allies started to defect. Capua changed sides, lured by the prospect of Rome's collapse and the chance of becoming the chief city in Italy. Overseas, places like Sardinia, Spain, and Sicily also started simmering with rebellion. One of history's great truths is that whenever a powerful state starts to look like a loser, even the most loyal friends look to the winner.

Hannibal's gamble about the Roman allies joining him didn't pay off, and most stayed loyal to Rome. Hannibal also found that Rome's persistence – even in the face of humiliating adversity – was beyond his ability to wear down. By means of heavy taxation and military conscription, Rome now threw its resources into winning the war. That included knocking out Hieronymus of Syracuse in Sicily who thought Cannae was such a brilliant victory he was easily persuaded by the Carthaginians to join in on their side in return for half of Sicily. Even though he was soon murdered by Syracusans to prevent this, they were so horrified by Roman brutality they ended up renewing the alliance with Carthage and faced an invasion by the Roman general Claudius Marcellus. The city fell in 211 BC (see Chapter 5 for the remarkable story of its defence by Archimedes against the Roman navy).

In 211 BC, Rome recaptured Capua despite Hannibal's threat to invade Rome. Rome punished Capua by lowering its status and confiscating much of its land. In 209 BC, Rome recaptured Tarentum, another defector.

When the Carthaginians sent another army from Spain to reinforce Hannibal, the Romans put together another vast army under Caius Claudius Nero. Nero's army headed off the Carthaginian reinforcements before they joined Hannibal. In 207 BC, the new Carthaginian army was totally defeated at Metaurus and its commander, Hannibal's brother Hasdrubal, was killed. Just to add insult to injury, Roman cavalry threw Hasdrubal's severed head into Hannibal's camp, which was a double shock to Hannibal, who hadn't even known that Hasdrubal had reached Italy. The game was up for Hannibal: It was obvious that despite Trasimene and Cannae, he had completely failed to capture Rome or any other Roman cities, or defeat the Romans decisively. Amazingly, the Senate wrote Hannibal off as a spent force, and he managed to hide out in the toe of Italy for four years before escaping back to North Africa to face the Romans again.

Scipio in the nick of time

Publius Cornelius Scipio was a Roman aristocrat and brilliant soldier who'd cut his teeth in the Second Punic War. He'd certainly been at the Roman defeat at Cannae and was probably at Trasimene, too. Although he was a young man – too young to be consul – he had bucketloads of military experience.

In 210 BC, Scipio was sent with an army to fight the Carthaginians in Spain. In 209 BC, taking advantage of the fact that the Carthaginians thought the Romans were a spent force in Spain and had divided their forces, Scipio captured New Carthage, the Carthaginian capital in Spain. He followed this up with a major victory against the Carthaginians at Ilipa in southern Spain in 206. With the Carthaginians knocked out of Spain, Scipio then turned to the main event, the attack on the Carthaginian homeland itself: Africa.

Meanwhile, back home in 205 BC, Scipio became Consul, despite being technically too young (the usual minimum age was 42) and was also made governor of Sicily, the perfect launch pad for an invasion of Africa. Scipio bided his time, planned the campaign to invade Africa, and made sure he had a first-class army to deliver the final blow. Scipio invaded Africa in 204 BC and set about destroying Carthaginian armies. The Carthaginians initially sued for peace, but when Hannibal came back from Italy to fight Scipio, the peace talks were abandoned.

The Battle of Zama – 202 BC

Hannibal and Scipio met at the Battle of Zama in North Africa in 202 BC. Sheer force of numbers, especially cavalry, rather than brilliant tactics, won the day for the Romans. Even so, Scipio did exactly what Hannibal had done at Cannae: He surrounded the enemy and trapped them. Hannibal surrendered, and the peace terms left the Carthaginians powerless:

✔ Their navy was cut down to ten ships.

✔ Their ally Numidia was made independent and an ally of Rome.

✔ They lost their possessions outside Africa.

✔ They had to pay 800,000 pounds of silver to Rome over 50 years.

✔ They could not wage war without Rome's permission.

Nonetheless, Carthage got over its defeat and eventually became a wealthy power again. Next time round, Rome's revenge would be total and permanent (see Chapter 13).

Scipio, little more than 30 years old, returned to Rome at the peak of his fame and popularity. He had saved Rome from its greatest enemy and recovered Rome's pre-eminence in North Africa. He took the name Africanus and celebrated with great triumph (for more on Scipio see Chapter 23).

The Romans had come to see the Carthaginians as their bitterest enemy and came to call treachery *Punica fide,* 'with Carthaginian faith'. As a result, 'Carthage' became a byword for treachery in everyday Latin.

An Italian propaganda movie, made when the Fascist dictator Mussolini ruled the nation, celebrated Scipio's victory over Hannibal. Called *Scipio Africanus: The Defeat of Hannibal* (1939), this movie features a full-scale elephant charge at the height of the Battle of Zama and the elephants' gory deaths at the hands of the Roman soldiers. The film's production was supervised by Mussolini's son Vittorio, and Mussolini himself may have taken a hand in its script.

Trouble in the East: The Macedonian Wars

Until the end of the Second Punic War in 202 BC, most of Rome's attention had been focused on Italy, the Carthaginians, and Spain. The Illyrians, people in what is now Albania and the former countries of Yugoslavia, had caused trouble before the Second Punic War, but the trouble had only been a side show (you can read the tale in the section 'A bit of background: Philip V and Illyrian pirates'). After Philip V of Macedon got involved with the Carthaginians and

Seleucids, Rome could not stand by because the campaign against Philip took Rome on a punishing journey east into Greece and beyond and eventually led Rome to conquer vast tracts of territory there: so it was a decisive moment. In 500 years, the Eastern Mediterranean region (including modern Greece, Turkey, Macedonia, Bulgaria, Turkey, Syria, Israel, and Egypt) was to become the home of what was left of the Roman Empire (see Chapter 21).

A bit of background: Philip V and Illyrian pirates

Between the First and Second Punic War, the Romans found themselves facing a problem with the Illyrians (Illyria is the coast of what used to be Yugoslavia down to Greece). This bit of trouble prompted the Romans' first foray eastwards.

The Illyrian tribes were professional pirates who made an excellent living out of stealing the valuable cargoes of merchant ships in the Adriatic. Their leaders encouraged and helped organise the piracy. In 231 BC, under their King, Agron, the Illyrians had been working as mercenaries for King Philip V of Macedon and had saved the city of Medion, under siege from a force of Aetolians (from an area farther south in Greece).

Following this victory, King Agron of the Illyrians died (he literally drank himself to death while celebrating), and his queen, Teuta, got it into her head that the Illyrians could do as they pleased. She declared that all other states were enemies and that the Illyrian navy must attack anyone and everyone. The Romans decided enough was enough. In 229 BC a diplomatic mission was sent to the Teuta. One of the ambassadors was murdered, so Rome sent a fleet over to sort the Illyrians out. Teuta immediately offered to give in, but the Romans didn't trust her and went to several Greek cities on the Adriatic coast and offered them protection in return for practical support. It was a brilliant gesture – Rome got a foothold across the Adriatic but without looking like a conqueror.

One of Teuta's supporters, Demetrius from the island of Pharos, went over to the Romans and was promptly made a Roman *amicus* ('friend'). As a result, other great Greek cities like Athens and Corinth also welcomed Roman diplomatic missions. But Demetrius blew it. Sensing the Second Punic War was brewing, he decided to return to piracy and attack the very Illyrian cities that were now loyal to Rome. Another Roman fleet was sent over in 219 BC, and Demetrius fled to Philip V of Macedon. He tried to get Philip to attack the Romans, but Philip held back.

Now back to the story.

The First Macedonian War (214–205 BC)

Just before the Second Punic War broke out in 218 BC, Rome had been trying to end the problem of the Illyrian pirates in the Adriatic. One of the players in the drama was Philip V, King of Macedon (refer to the preceding section). Philip was an opportunist. After the catastrophe at Cannae and with the impression that the Second Punic War was going against the Romans, Philip decided to make friends with Hannibal, at the time the new kid on the block in Italy (remember, this happened before Hannibal's final defeat). This was obviously a situation that Rome had to deal with, and so began the First Macedonian War.

Because the Second Punic War was using up almost all Rome's resources, the First Macedonian War didn't amount to much. Rome made an alliance with Philip's enemy, the Aetolian League led by its ally, the great Greek city of Pergamon on the west coast of Asia Minor (modern Turkey), then ruled by Attalos I (241–197 BC). The Aetolian League was a confederation of cities in central Greece formed to oppose the Macedonians. A bit of fighting took place, but in 205 BC, the Romans made peace with Philip, who had now wised up to the fact that Rome was likely to win the Second Punic War.

The Second Macedonian War (200–197 BC)

Philip, ever the opportunist, came up with another plan, one that he hoped would avoid attention from Rome. With support from the Seleucid Empire in Syria, his idea was to start attacking the Egyptians, then ruled by the boy-Pharaoh Ptolemy V, and to help himself to Egyptian possessions. The Seleucid Empire was formed in what is now Syria, Iran, and Iraq, by Seleucus, one of Alexander the Great's generals, out of Alexander's empire on his death in 323 BC. It had fallen into decline, but Seleucus's descendant Antiochus III revived its fortunes.

Thanks to the fact that Philip's forces attacked whoever they pleased in the Aegean, the Greeks got annoyed with him. Determined to protect its interests, the wealthy island of Rhodes made an alliance with Pergamon. In 201 BC, Pergamon and Rhodes turned to Rome for help after Philip's navy beat their combined forces.

Rome was exhausted and reluctant to go to war again. But when the news got out that Philip was in alliance with the Seleucids, led by the ambitious Antiochus III 'the Great' (242–187 BC), they decided they had no choice. Antiochus III had helped himself to Syria and Palestine. The Romans decided to make the war look as if it was as a campaign to protect the freedom of the Greek cities.

The Greek effect

The Romans had been fascinated by all things Greek for a long time. The Etruscans (read about them in Chapter 10) had picked up a lot from the Greeks. King Tarquinius Priscus once sent his sons to the oracle in Delphi for advice. As Rome's tentacles spread across the Mediterranean in the second century BC, the Romans became more and more impressed by the sophisticated Greek culture. Greek statues were brought to Rome and widely copied. Greek gods were matched with Roman gods. Greek literature was read and appreciated. The Roman playwright Terence (c. 190–159 BC) was translated and adapted into Latin works by the Greek playwright Menander and others for a Roman audience. The Greeks went on to influence Roman culture for centuries (see Hadrian in Chapter 17, for example).

The Second Macedonian War started when the Romans arrived in Illyria in 200 BC under the command of Titus Quinctius Flamininus. Frankly, the war got off to a slow start and stayed that way. The Romans tried to wear Philip down. Philip couldn't let that happen, so he forced a pitched battle by a ridge at Cynoscephalae in 197 BC. Racing down the hillside, Philip nearly demolished the Roman army, but Flamininus counter-attacked with his wing before the second wave of Macedonians had time to get into position. Philip was totally defeated.

The Greek cities were delirious with joy at their deliverance from Philip. At the Isthmian Games in Corinth in 196 BC, the Roman commander Flamininus proclaimed all Greece to be free. The Greeks were particularly impressed because Flamininus gave his speech in Greek. The Greeks decided that the Romans were thoroughly good types and their saviours and patrons, while the Romans indulged themselves in their love of Greek art and culture. But Greece remained a problem, and more to the point so did Antiochus III. What happened to Greece comes next (see Chapter 13 for the story about Antiochus III).

The Third Macedonian War (172–167 BC)

Philip V of Macedon died in 179 BC. The throne went to his anti-Roman son Perseus who had had his pro-Roman younger brother Demetrius executed. The Romans declared war in 172 BC on the pretext that Perseus had attacked some Balkan chieftains who were Roman allies. Perseus failed to take advantage of the general Greek back-pedalling about their love for Rome, but he still managed to defeat the Romans in 171 BC. It was the same old story – the

Romans were all the more determined to beat him. It took three more years of campaigns, but at Pydna in Macedonia in 168 BC, Perseus was crushed by the Roman army commanded by Lucius Aemilius Paullus. Perseus might have won if the Achaean League had formed an alliance with him. They certainly thought about it – until the Romans seized some key Achaean hostages to keep them on good behaviour.

After Perseus was defeated, the Romans decided they'd had enough of the Greeks and their internal disputes. Around 1,000 supporters of Macedonia in Greece were shipped to Italy for trial – 700 died in prison. In 167 BC, the region of Epirus was ravaged, and 150,000 people were sold into slavery. Macedonia was broken up into four republics.

Even so, the Romans didn't have any plans to conquer and govern the Greeks. The idea was to leave the Greeks free, but punish them so they'd never ally themselves with another enemy of Rome. The Romans even cut taxes to make themselves look like thoroughly reasonable people.

It's not really surprising that Greece wasn't Rome's greatest concern at this time. Between 151–146 BC, the Third Punic War was raging. More on that in Chapter 13.

The spoils of Greece (Achaea)

Despite Rome's plan to just punish, but not conquer, the Greeks, the last straw came with Andriscus, a pretender to the Macedonian throne claiming to be a son of Perseus, who managed to reunite Macedonia. The Romans abandoned the idea of leaving the Greeks free.

The sack of Corinth

According to the Roman geographer Strabo, Corinth was sacked partly by the Roman general Lucius Mummius because of the Corinthians' disgusting habits, such as pouring filth on top of any Romans passing by. But the main reason was to punish the city for its resistance and to wipe out a major commercial rival. The men were all murdered, and women and children enslaved. According to the Greek historian Polybius, Mummius was placed under huge pressure to be so cruel and didn't have the strength to stand up to it. He helped himself to Corinthian works of art, which were shipped back to Rome, including a painting of Dionysus which ended up in the Temple of Ceres. Polybius, who was there, watched with disgust as soldiers played dice on paintings they had chucked on the ground. A century later Julius Caesar founded a colony on the site of Corinth. The Roman colonists dug up the ancient Corinthian cemeteries and made a tidy living out of selling the terracotta reliefs and bronze vessels they found.

By 148 BC, a Roman army under Quintus Caecilius Metellus drove Andriscus off (sometimes called the Fourth Macedonian War). The Achaean League appointed Critolaos of Megalopolis their general. Refusing to negotiate with the Romans, he overran central Greece with his army. Metellus dealt with him, but Achaeans making a last stand near Corinth was destroyed by the Roman Consul Lucius Mummius.

Corinth was razed to the ground. The Achaean League was broken up. The Roman governor of Macedonia watched out for trouble, and Greece was forced to pay tribute to Rome. It was a turning point in Greek history that mirrored what had happened in Italy between 493–272 BC when the Romans systematically took control of Italian cities (refer to Chapter 11). Now the Greek city states lost their freedom; centuries of conflict, war, and destruction followed, with periods of brilliance in politics and art.

The Secret of Success: The Comeback

The Roman army didn't have a great deal of flair, but it was successful because it had a ready supply of manpower from the allies, it was the best organised, and it worked like a machine. Every soldier knew what his job was and where he was supposed to be, whether that was in camp or on the battlefield.

The setting up of colonies to guard ports, mountain passes, or major road junctions meant there was a Roman presence in crucial locations, acting as a military reserve. That colonies were laid out as if they were military camps, with institutions modelled on those in Rome, was part of the process.

Towns in allied territory continued to function much as they always had, but now under Roman supervision. All across Italy, communities found that being in Rome's orbit could be a big plus. In return for contributions to the Roman army, they received a share in the spoils of victory. The allies also benefited from stability, but without being oppressed. The Sabines, for example, had fought the Romans on four separate occasions, but instead of finding themselves sold into slavery and their settlements confiscated, by 268 BC they had been promoted to Roman citizens with full voting rights.

Chapter 13

While We're at It – Let's Conquer Everywhere Else, Too

*R*ome, having got Greece, Macedonia, and the Seleucids thoroughly under control, was by 146 BC a major power in the eastern Mediterranean (refer to Chapter 12 for details on these events). Rome's dominance was to have serious consequences for Asia Minor (modern Turkey) and Egypt. But history's never straightforward. Even though Greece, Macedonia, and the Seleucids were sewn up, Rome hadn't conquered the world – yet.

Rome still had problems, particularly in Italy, and also to the west in Spain, and in North Africa, Carthage's home. Despite being well and truly thrashed in both the First and Second Punic Wars (refer to Chapter 12), Carthage wasn't finished.

What happened between 200 and the 130s BC in the western Mediterranean and North Africa – the focus of this chapter – is the story of how Rome's power spread across the whole of the Mediterranean.

Conquering the Mediterranean was, by any standards, a simply flabbergasting achievement. No other ancient society (or any modern society for that matter) ever managed anything remotely like it. Even at the height of their power, the Egyptians had little influence beyond the Levant and Asia Minor. The Greeks, despite extensive colonisation around the Mediterranean, never had an organised political system to rival Rome's. The Greeks could hardly rule themselves, let alone anyone else. It was only thanks to the Roman fascination with Greek culture that Greek art, literature, and knowledge of Greece's experiments with democracy and philosophy were handed down at all.

How the West Was Won

Cisalpine Gaul (northern Italy) was something of a sideshow for the Romans whose main energies in the first half of the second century BC were concentrated on Macedonia and Greece. But northern Italy was still a vitally important area to the Romans. It was rich and fertile and part of the important overland route along the coast to southern France and Spain.

First stop: Northern Italy

At the end of the Second Punic War in 202 BC, Rome's first problem was to sort out and punish Rome's allies that had defected to Hannibal. Rome was in constant dread of Hannibal, fearing he planned to destroy Rome during his march through Italy (refer to Chapter 12).

Rome did what it had to do, meting out the punishment, which the defectors accepted. The turncoat city of Capua, for example, lost its right to self-government. And like other cities that had rebelled, Capua also lost much of its land as new Roman colonies were set up on Capuan territory.

Cisalpine Gaul was a different matter. No-one told the Cisalpine Gauls that the Second Punic War was over, so they carried on fighting for another ten years in an effort to fend off Roman reprisals for the help they'd given Hannibal. It took until 191 for the Gaulish Boii tribe to be knocked out. The man who did so was Publius Cornelius Scipio Nasica (a cousin of Scipio Africanus, who defeated the Carthaginians in the decisive Battle of Zama; see Chapter 12). Rome imposed heavy fines and took half the Boii's land as a punishment. What was left of the Boii drifted north-east and ended up in what is now Bohemia.

Northern Italy was resettled. Rome set up new colonies, like the one at Parma in 183 BC, and the land was broken up into individual parcels. New roads were built across the region, and within 50 years the whole area looked little different from the rest of Romanised Italy.

Relaxing by the Riviera

As usual, the Romans found that winning one bit of new territory, like northern Italy, meant that they had no choice but to take the next bit along as well. That's exactly what happened with the Italian Riviera, known as Liguria. Liguria was an undeveloped area with primitive inhabitants, but it was essential to Rome that Liguria should be under Roman control. Sailors in the ancient world liked to hug the coasts for safety and to make sure they didn't get lost. The Romans needed Liguria to guarantee the journey from Liguria to Spain was safe from enemies.

The Romans much preferred to fight great set-piece battles, but wearing down the tribes in this mountainous region meant they had to fight incessant small-scale skirmishes. After 186 BC, one Roman army after another was sent into Liguria. By 180, the tribes were exhausted by Rome's relentless ability to keep up the fight, and large numbers of tribal inhabitants gave up and moved away. Even so, it took Rome another 70 years before the coast road as far as Genua (Genoa) was completed and safe.

On the other side of Italy, the area we know as the Venetian Riviera, named after the Veneti tribe that lived there, was stable and generally friendly. The only problems came from Alpine tribes, so the Romans set up a colony at Aquileia (modern Aquila) – which became the major commercial centre of the region and the port-of-entry from Italy into Illyria, on the Adriatic.

The Reign in Spain, 197–179 BC

At first, Rome didn't have any great ambitions in Spain. But in the end, the Romans decided it was easier to take the place over to make sure that bolshie locals towed the line. Scipio Africanus had fought in Spain during the Second Punic War to stop the Carthaginians from establishing a power base in Spain that could be used to attack Italy. Hannibal had already tried to do this, and the Romans wanted to prevent him trying again (refer to Chapter 12).

Also, the Romans had been in Spain long enough to spot that the Iberian peninsula was heaving with mineral resources: tin, iron, gold, and silver. Strabo, the ancient historian and geographer, who wrote a description of the Roman world about 200 hundred years later, said Spain had the best and richest supply of metals of anywhere he knew.

Conquering Spain's tribes

In 197 BC, Rome created two new provinces: *Hispania Citerior* (Nearer Spain) and *Hispania Ulterior* (Further Spain). The locals in the new provinces didn't take too kindly to the idea of the Romans replacing the Carthaginians. Also, the nasty side of Roman administration came into play after Scipio Africanus left. The next few decades in Spain were brutal, oppressive, and unpleasant.

The Celtiberians

Celtiberians were tribes of Celtic origin living in defended hilltop centres in the Iberian peninsula (Spain and Portugal). Celtiberian was a name the Romans gave to a whole lot of different Celtic tribes living in the region, such as the Carpetani and Oretani. Like most Celts, the Celtiberians avoided fighting pitched battles, preferring to operate in small bands, using their knowledge of the local terrain to harass the Roman forces.

Constant rebellions by different tribes, especially the Celtiberians (people who lived in Hispania Citerior), followed. It took two Roman armies in 179 BC to corner the Celtiberians and Lusitanians (people from Hispania Ulterior, nowadays Portugal) into giving up the fight and accepting Roman rule. (Of course, it may have helped that the Roman commander Tiberius Sempronius Gracchus, who claimed to have captured 300 Celtiberian settlements, earned the Celtiberians' respect by his fair-mindedness.) Even so, Celtiberian guerrillas were trouble for decades to come.

Return to war

The peace Gracchus installed in Spain left the Romans in control of almost the whole Iberian peninsula (apart from the Atlantic coast), and lasted until 154 BC. The peace fell apart because, after Gracchus left, a number of Roman governors who followed abused their powers. Every time the Spanish tribes complained to the Senate, nothing was done. The Celtiberians and Lusitanians returned to war, and the situation worsened when some Roman commanders made unprovoked attacks.

The unrest in Spain became even more significant because, by 151 BC, the Third Punic War had broken out (see the section 'The Third Punic War (151–146 BC)' later in this chapter), placing greater pressure on Roman military resources. But ironically, it was the general who destroyed Carthage in the Third Punic War who brought his experience to Spain and brought the conflict to an end.

The Lusitanians were led by Viriathus, a herdsman, who through sheer force of personality became the Lusitanians' leader. From 146–141 BC, Viriathus beat the Romans every year. His success brought the Celtiberians back into the fight in 143 BC (they'd originally come to peace terms with the Romans in 153 after a year of fighting), though by 142 BC the Romans had driven the Celtiberians back to their hilltop settlements.

The Roman solution to the Lusitanians was sneaky. In 140 BC, the Roman leader, Servilius Caepio, bribed traitors in the Lusitanian camp to murder Viriathus. Without him, Lusitanian resistance collapsed in 139 BC.

All that remained were a few cities that refused to give up. Numantia, sitting between two rivers in deep ravines, was practically impregnable and managed to hold out for nine years. Despite Roman trickery and weight of forces, the siege of Numantia went nowhere until 133 BC.

The destruction of Numantia

Numantia's end came in 133 BC. The destroyer of Carthage in 146 BC, Publius Cornelius Scipio Aemilianus, the adopted grandson of Scipio Africanus (see Chapters 12 and 23 for more on Scipio Africanus, the hero of the Second Punic War), arrived at Numantia with a force of 60,000 made up of Roman soldiers, Spanish, and other allies. Aemilianus built seven forts around the town (some of which still survive), starved out the 4,000 Numantians who were sold into slavery, and destroyed the town.

Roman names are easily confused because they're often so similar, especially in the same family. Publius Cornelius Scipio Africanus got his title from his victories in the Second Punic War. His adopted grandson, Publius Cornelius Scipio Aemilianus, was also given the title Africanus for his efforts in the Third Punic War, and was confusingly called Africanus the Younger. But this man, Aemilianus the grandson, was also awarded the title Numantinus for the victory at Numantia. For Scipio Aemilianus's mysterious death, see Chapter 14.

Why the Spanish wars were different

The Roman wars in Spain were an ugly affair. They dragged on, and the Roman custom of appointing a new commanding officer each year didn't help. The Romans had a reputation, on the whole, for being magnanimous in victory and keeping their word. Not so in Spain. The Romans broke treaty after treaty, and the Senate did nothing to stop it. The sheer number of men conscripted for military service caused discontent at home in Italy and had a serious impact on Roman domestic politics.

The Third Punic War (151–146 BC)

While the war in Spain dragged on, Rome had another war on her hands: the Third, and final, Punic War. Rome had been remarkably generous in her peace terms with Carthage (refer to Chapter 12) at the end of the Second Punic War, given that Rome could have finished off Carthage as a trading power. In addition, Rome left Hannibal in power – he probably couldn't believe his luck.

Hannibal patches up Carthage

The Carthaginians soon got themselves on their feet again. In North Africa, Hannibal introduced more efficient farming and administrative reforms which meant that Carthage was able to start paying off its fines to Rome. Carthage even offered free gifts of corn to Roman armies fighting in Greece and Macedonia. Carthage had become so servile that Hannibal's political enemies decided to go to Rome and tell the Senate that Hannibal was doing deals with the ambitious king of Syria, Antiochus III (see Chapters 12 and 25 for more on Antiochus). A Roman deputation turned up to investigate, but Hannibal escaped and went to Antiochus III's court (see the later section 'Mopping Up the East' for information on Rome's problems with Antiochus).

Rome was clearly satisfied with the way things were in Carthage. But the aged King Masinissa of Numidia, Carthage's neighbour, had other ideas.

The ambitions of Masinissa: Provoke Carthaginians

King Masinissa did well in the peace at the end of the Second Punic War: The Romans made him King of Numidia. Over the next 50 years, Masinissa built up an army and improved the Numidians' standard of living. But then, like most rulers, power went to his head, and he thought his kingdom wasn't big enough. Masinissa had his eyes on North Africa where there were numerous Carthaginian settlements.

Thanks to Rome's peace terms at the end of the Second Punic War in 202 BC (refer to Chapter 12), the Carthaginians weren't allowed to defend themselves without Roman permission. Masinissa started helping himself to Carthaginian settlements and fended off Roman objections by falling over backwards to look pro-Roman by sending food and troops to the Roman armies in the East.

Naturally, the Carthaginians were provoked and in 150 BC attacked Masinissa, which was exactly what he wanted to happen. Masinissa knew the Romans had an obsessive fear of the Carthaginians and that Hannibal was Rome's ultimate bogeyman. The slightest suggestion of trouble from the Carthaginians meant that the Romans would crush the Carthaginians mercilessly.

Lucius Hostilius Mancinus's one-man show

Lucius Hostilius Mancinus was the first soldier over Carthage's walls in the campaign of 146 BC. When Lucius got back to Rome, he infuriated Scipio Aemilianus by holding live shows in the Forum telling a public audience all about the siege and his exploits. Lucius even put up a plan of the assault and displays of scenery. Lucius's one-man show was so popular that Lucius ended up as Consul at the next election.

Rome's response: Wipe out Carthage!

Marcus Porcius Cato, an 84-year-old veteran of the Second Punic War and the wars in Spain, and leader of anti-Carthaginian fervour in Rome, denounced the Carthaginians as proven treaty-breakers. Cato famously declared *delenda est Carthago,* which means 'Carthage ought to be wiped out' (for more on Cato, see Chapters 4 and 23). Cato's opponents disagreed, thinking Carthage ought to be left as it was because it presented no real threat to Rome and fear of Carthage would hold the Roman people together. But Cato won the day, though he died almost as soon as the war started (as did King Masinissa, who had started the whole thing in the first place).

A Roman army arrived at Carthage in 149 BC. The Carthaginians promptly surrendered and handed over hostages and their military equipment. But the Romans demanded more and more. To destroy the Carthaginians once and for all, the Romans demanded that the Carthaginians abandon their city and move inland, which meant that Carthage as a trading power would cease to exist.

The Carthaginians were enraged by Rome's demands. Deciding they had nothing to lose, the Carthaginians prepared for war. Unfortunately for Carthage, most of their neighbours had already sided with Rome. The Carthaginian fortifications helped to keep the Romans back, and they sent out bands of soldiers to slow up the Roman supply lines. They held out until 147–146 BC when a new campaign began. The Roman commander Publius Cornelius Scipio Aemilianus arrived and utterly wiped out the city.

The final indignity: Salt on the wounds

There was no grand battle in Scipio Aemilianus's campaign of 147—146 BC. Aemilianus simply wore the Carthaginians down, smashing his way through Carthage's outer defences. Then, inch by inch, his troops fought hand-to-hand to reach the inner citadel. Only 50,000 Carthaginian citizens were left, which came to a tiny number, given the trouble Rome thought Carthage was. The citizens were captured and sold into slavery. The city library was broken up and its books given to neighbouring African rulers. According to legend, the Romans sowed salt on the land round Carthage to sterilise it and make it into a wasteland. Whether this legend is true or not makes no difference: Carthage was finished and in ruins. The ruins which can still be seen today lie not far from the city of Tunis. Some time later, a Roman colony was founded nearby: the final insult.

Mopping Up the East

Asia Minor (modern Turkey) was only as far away from Rome as Spain. However, the difference was that Asia Minor had a long history and established cities and kingdoms. Rome first got involved in Asia Minor during the Macedonian Wars when the Seleucid king Antiochus III 'the Great' (242–187 BC) made an alliance with Philip V of Macedon (check out Chapter 12).

The ambitions of Antiochus III

Antiochus III had been seen off by the Romans in the Second Macedonian War (200–197 BC; see Chapter 12). But he remained powerful in Asia and for the moment concentrated his ambitions in the East instead. Antiochus had married his daughter to Ptolemy V Epiphanes, Pharaoh of Egypt, as part of a treaty that secured Antiochus's conquest of Syria and Palestine, and he had also added the south coast of Asia Minor to his land.

The wealthy Greek communities of the island of Rhodes and the city of Pergamon, which headed the Aetolian League in Asia Minor, were starting to get twitchy. In the aftermath of the Second Macedonian War, the Romans had guaranteed the liberty of Greek mainland cities. Now in 196 BC, Pergamon asked the Roman Senate to guarantee the liberty of cities in Asia Minor. It was an extraordinary request and shows how powerful Rome had become. It was also an amazing gesture of confidence in Rome, now seen as a benign and honourable power.

Rome protested to Antiochus III, but this wily operator brandished a new treaty he had signed with Egypt to show he was acting with Egypt's approval. So it was impossible for Rome to pretend it was acting to defend Egypt's interests. Flamininus, the Roman commander in charge of the Roman forces in Greece, fell for the story. Others, like Scipio Africanus, weren't so sure, especially as Antiochus had now been joined by Hannibal who'd fled from Carthage in 195 BC (Hannibal later committed suicide in 183 BC).

Rome carried on negotiations with Antiochus for the next few years without getting anywhere. In the meantime, Roman forces were withdrawn from Greece. By 191 BC, however, the Romans had to return to Greece.

Cramping Antiochus III's style

The Aetolian League felt cheated by the outcome of the Second Macedonian War; they'd helped out but had been prevented by the Romans from acquiring part of Greece as a reward. So the Aetolian League invited Antiochus III to invade Greece. He did, but was met by a Roman army under the command of Scipio Africanus the Elder, who soundly saw Antiochus off at Thermopylae and Magnesia with almost the total loss of the Seleucid forces. The peace of 188 BC ended Seleucid ambitions in Europe. Antiochus had to hand over most of his fleet, pay a vast fine to Rome (the biggest Rome ever imposed on an enemy), withdraw from much of his territory, and was left only with a right to defend himself. The Seleucids remained a force to be reckoned with in Asia, but the reality was that they were so damaged Rome was bound to be able to move into the power vacuum before long.

Antiochus was crushed and humiliated by the peace imposed by Rome. He had to say goodbye to his navy and pay a record-breaking fine of 15,000 talents. Antiochus had to pull out of western Asia Minor and was denied the right to hold any territory in Europe or the Aegean or have any allies there.

A *talent* was a unit of weight of gold or silver. It's hard to get an exact equivalent but suggested figures range from 25 kilograms to 42 kilograms (about 57–93 pounds) of gold for each talent. These days, gold has been hitting prices of more than £270 an ounce, which comes close to £280,000 a talent at the lowest estimate. Which means Antiochus faced the modern equivalent of about £4.2 billion in fines.

Scipio throws a sickie

Scipio Africanus threw a sickie on the day of the battle that defeated Antiochus III. The overall Commander of the Roman force was his brother, the Consul Lucius Cornelius Scipio. Probably Scipio Africanus wanted to make sure that his brother got all the credit, but on the other hand, the real reason may have been that it suited Scipio Africanus not to be there, because he had cut a deal with Antiochus who was holding Africanus's son as hostage.

The Romans then pulled out of Asia Minor. Pergamon did the best out of the peace in territorial terms, but what really happened is that the whole area was broken up into small units. By destroying Antiochus's power in the west, the Romans wrecked his prestige, and he lost some of his eastern provinces as well.

After this, the Romans only intervened occasionally in Asia Minor's affairs, despite having done a lot to destabilise the region. When Rhodes tried to act as a peacemaker in the Third Macedonian War, Rome destroyed the island's trading interests and power, and Rhodes's traditional role of policing the seas as well.

Winning the lottery: Gaining Pergamon

In 133 BC, Rome found it was the owner of Pergamon and its territory – without a drop of blood being spilled. King Attalus III of Pergamon (reigned 138–133 BC) had no heirs, and in his will he left his kingdom to the Romans on the basis that they were the only people likely to make good use of it. Because Pergamon and its other cities were amongst the wealthiest communities in the Greek-speaking East, it wasn't difficult for Rome to accept.

Pergamon became part of the Roman province of Asia, and Rome now had a gateway to the East. This gateway turned out to be

- ✔ A source of fabulous wealth
- ✔ Where some of Rome's greatest enemies would emerge
- ✔ The site for Constantinople, the new Rome, some 440 years in the future
- ✔ Where in AD 1453 the Roman Empire would fall and ultimately die

But that was yet to come. To date, Rome had faced some of her greatest trials so far, but other challenges were on the horizon. Unlike most of Rome's previous problems, these trials were to come from within Rome herself.

Part IV
When Romans Ruled the World

In this part . . .

By the late second century BC, Rome was the most
successful state in the ancient world. She had more
power and prestige than anyone else. Yet, in the next hundred years, the Roman Republic tore itself to pieces. All
the wealth and power Rome had went to the heads of several very ambitious men. Civil war nearly destroyed the
greatest phenomenon of the ancient world.

It could have been terminal but for the genius of one man:
Augustus Caesar. Augustus reinvented the Republic by
turning it into a hereditary monarchy. His genius was to
pretend that he had restored the Republic. How he did that,
and as a result made the Roman Empire more powerful
than ever before, is what you'll read about in this part. At
its climax Roman power spread from the hills of Scotland
right the way across Europe and the Mediterranean to the
remote southern deserts of Egypt.

Chapter 14

Reform and Civil War

• •

In This Chapter

▶ The bitterness of Rome's class conflicts

▶ The reformers and the new men

▶ How military dictators seized power

▶ Why the First Triumvirate came into being

▶ How the Republic dissolved into civil war

• •

*W*henever a country grows rich and powerful, it's usually the case that the rich get richer and all too often the poor get poorer. As Rome's power and wealth grew during the second century BC, all sorts of domestic political issues started to come to the front. Because the Romans hadn't planned to end up with a growing Empire, no-one had really given any time to wondering whether the now increasingly ancient institutions of the Republic were really up to coping with the new order.

Crisis in Rome

There was a sea change in Roman politics in the second century BC. The Roman Republican system was originally built around magistracies, like the consulship (see Chapter 3). The idea was that the system would roll on endlessly, year after year, with no one man becoming pre-eminent. But corruption and self-interest led to demands for reform, led by the Gracchi brothers (read about them in the section 'Enter the Gracchi', later in this chapter). Their campaigns, and the hostility from their enemies, showed how bitterly personal Roman politics was becoming. Meanwhile, the emergence of powerful generals, like Marius, who used their armies to increase their political power at Rome showed a different side to personality-based politics and led to the civil wars of the first century BC. These wars between generals with their rival armies brought the end of the Republic.

The Conflict of the Orders, the class war between patricians and plebeians, was beginning to look like a big waste of time (Chapter 10 explains how the Conflict of the Orders started). The aristocracy, which eventually included the most successful plebeian families, had ended up controlling the whole political system and held all the high offices, leaving all the other plebeians with no real power at all. This caused terrible tensions, as the plebeians and their representatives, like the Gracchi brothers, demanded reform from an aristocracy determined to do anything to stop them.

Power to the people! – Not

Unrest arose over who was going to benefit from Rome's new wealth and power. As Rome's territories increased, new tribes had been added with new voters. Since 241 BC, the Roman voting population had been divided into 35 tribes, the final total (for more on tribes, see Chapter 2). Citizens still had to do their voting through the *Comitia Centuriata,* the assembly of male citizens eligible for military service, but it just became impossible for many of the new Roman citizens to get to Rome to vote. They simply lived too far away. Only those citizens in and around Rome were able to use their vote.

Buying votes

In addition, Roman politics were getting too complicated for most Romans. It was the politically ambitious who were able to use the system to gain power. Roman society was based round rich, powerful individuals known as *patrons,* who surrounded themselves with hangers-on, their own freed slaves ('freed-men'), business associates, and so on, called their *clients.* Patrons looked after their clients in return for loyalty. This made it easy for the nobility to persuade their clients to vote for them, and buying votes became routine. Nobles simply paid clients cash for votes or, more subtly, put on free public entertainments. Case in point: A whole series of new public games were invented during the Second Punic War (see Chapter 8 for the gaming calendar).

The Roman mob was steadily getting bigger because of the influx of farm workers and smallholders to Rome. Rome's wars put these men out of work and also captured thousands of slaves who did the work instead, situations explained in more detail in the later sections 'A soldier's tale' and 'Slaves to circumstance'). Keeping this growing mob happy became more and more important to the aristocrats because of the risk of riots and disorder in Rome if the mob became hostile.

Aristocrats on top

The upshot was that all the power ordinary people had won in the Conflict of the Orders was being gradually worn down by the aristocracy. The power of the Comitia Centuriata was also weakened. Although most senators came from plebeian families, they had become known as *nobiles* ('nobles'). In theory, any plebeian could enter the Senate and hold office, but in practice, the new nobiles shut the door on aspiring plebeian senators.

Rome was now ruled by old and new aristocrats. No-one else could get a look in. By the year 134 BC, 25 families had dominated the consulship over the last 75 years. Although no individual could hold permanent political power, it was starting to look as if the family was becoming more powerful than the individual. Aristocratic families tried to hold on to their interests by forging political ties through marriage, and did anything they could to maximise their support and political strength. At the same time, they looked for any sign that a political enemy had broken the law and then set about having those enemies prosecuted.

The rise of the equestrians

The structure of Roman society was changing. Wealth was replacing birth. In the eighteenth and nineteenth centuries, countries like the USA and Britain saw the rise of families that had grown wealthy from trade, rather than from inheriting vast landed estates like the aristocratic families. These newly rich families had a dramatic effect on society, and that's pretty much what was happening in Rome.

The main beneficiaries were the equestrians *(equites),* originally Roman citizens wealthy enough to field a horse in battle. By the late Republic, this was long in the past, and the equestrians had evolved into a sort of second-grade aristocracy below the senators. There were now really two types: the 'financier equestrians' in Rome who had grown rich from trade and business, and the equestrians who belonged to local municipal aristocracies in Italian cities with Roman citizen status (refer to Chapter 2 for where equestrians fitted into Roman society and Chapter 3 for the sorts of jobs they could do).

The trouble with allies

Other tensions were simmering. Rome's allies wanted more of the rights that Roman citizens enjoyed, such as voting and the chance to take part in the colonisation of conquered territory. After all, the allies had put a lot into winning Rome's wars for her, providing around half the troops Rome had used to fight the war in Spain and the Third Punic War. Amazingly, in 177 BC, the allies were even told they were only entitled to war booty at half the rate a Roman citizen enjoyed. Insulting treatment by Romans made the allies even crosser. In 173 BC, the city of Cales banned its own townsfolk from using the baths when a Roman magistrate was staying there.

A soldier's tale

Fewer and fewer people, especially Romans, wanted to do Rome's fighting. Even the senators protested and led the way by organising draft-dodging for their sons who ended up with office jobs on a general's staff instead of fighting. Military leadership tended to be poor. Even though hardened professionals like Scipio Africanus and his adoptive grandson Scipio Aemilianus had triumphed in the Second and Third Punic Wars respectively, the Romans continued to rely on the system of sending out a new consul each year as general. This was what had contributed to the disasters of Trasimene and Cannae in the Second Punic War because there was no system of choosing men on ability or experience.

Traditionally, Rome had relied on part-time soldiers. Raised from the Roman citizenry based on a minimum property qualification, counted in the census, these men did not come from a background of solid military training and discipline. They were raised on an as-need basis, and at this time, no man could be made to serve for more than 16 years. Normally what happened is that the army was disbanded at the end of a campaign, so there was no means of creating an experienced army and keeping it together. It wasn't until the days of the late Republic and the Empire that the Romans developed a professional army (explained in Chapter 5).

This system of part-time soldiers worked well in the past, but it wasn't good for long-term campaigning abroad because as many as 100,000 men could be involved each year. Most of Rome's soldiers worked on farms. Taking them away from their land and families for years on end could mean ruin, not just for a man and his household, but also serious consequences for Roman society and the Roman economy, so it's no surprise that some men deserted.

In an effort to increase the number of available soldiers, the minimum property qualification had to be drastically lowered. But in practice, this seems to have had little effect on improving things. Nothing at all was done to build up a highly-trained, experienced, and fully-prepared army. Instead, Rome continued to call up inexperienced new troops when needed and to rely on her allies to bolster the numbers and also on her massive resources to keep pounding away until her enemies were worn down. But as Rome's power and influence grew, it became obvious this couldn't go on. It wasn't till Gaius Marius (discussed in the section 'Marius the New Man – and More Unrest') came on the scene that a professional Roman army was organised, providing the foundation of the army of the Empire, but that brought its own dangers, as you'll see.

Slaves to circumstance

Slaves were the lowest of the low in Roman society, and Rome's wars had generated thousands more of them. These slaves worked on aristocratic estates and in the city.

On the plus side, using slaves on farms helped make good the shortage of peasants who were away fighting. On the minus side, this meant that peasants came home from the wars to find they often couldn't get work on the land. This was especially true for those peasants who fell into debt while away. In addition, land speculation, which made for larger and more efficient estates, meant more slaves were needed, forcing even more free men off the land.

In Roman society, there's a difference between a 'free man' and a 'freedman'. *Free man* means someone like you and me. A *freedman*, on the other hand, is someone who was formerly a slave.

Slaves became essential to the Roman economy, but as their numbers grew, the fear of the Romans at the prospect of slave rebellions grew as well. At the same time, free men forced off the land to make way for these huge estates became more and more discontented.

Enter the Gracchi

The *Gracchi* (which is the plural of Gracchus) brothers, Tiberius and Gaius, came into the world with the perfect pedigree. Their mother Cornelia was the daughter of Scipio Africanus, hero of the Second Punic War (refer to Chapter 12). Their father, Titus Sempronius Gracchus, had been one of the more successful commanders in Spain (refer to Chapter 13). Tiberius Gracchus had fought with distinction in the Third Punic War (detailed in Chapter 13) and climbed the social ladder by marrying Claudia, daughter of Appius Claudius Pulcher, who had been Senator in 143 BC. Strange to say, Tiberius and Gaius Gracchus set out to reform the very system that had made themselves and their families powerful.

Tiberius and Gaius Gracchus tried to pass laws that would increase the Roman citizen base in Italy and make land distribution fairer, but both found themselves fighting the self-interest of the Senate and the aristocracy, who used underhand methods to undermine them. Even though the Gracchi brothers' reforms failed, they had made a name for themselves, and their violent deaths turned them into popular martyrs.

Tiberius Sempronius Gracchus

No-one knows what turned Tiberius Gracchus, a man born to privilege and wealth, into a social reformer. But while in Spain, he'd seen that Roman soldiers weren't as tough as they used to be and also noticed how free peasant farmers and farm-workers were being replaced by slaves. Tiberius had also been disturbed by how a massive slave revolt had exploded in Sicily in 135 BC, provoked by extremely harsh treatment and started by slaves working on a farm. Before long, more than 70,000 slaves had risen, murdering their masters and leading to minor copycat slave rebellions in Italy, too. It took a Roman army till 132 BC to crush the Sicilian slave revolt.

Tiberius Gracchus probably concluded that the Italian farming stock, which provided the backbone of the army, needed support with improved rights and privileges so that Rome would have a better and bigger source of soldiers for its wars, and not have to depend for agriculture on slavery, with all its dangers of rebellion. He also realised that a system where the aristocracy controlled so much of the wealth was bound to lead to civil unrest if something wasn't done (perhaps he'd looked into the future and seen the French Revolution!).

Proposing land reform

In 133 BC, Tiberius Gracchus was elected Tribune of the Plebs (see Chapter 3 for this important post). As tribune, he tried to bring in a law to distribute public land acquired since the Second Punic War more fairly to encourage the farming of land by free men rather than slaves (this wasn't an entirely new idea; his father-in-law Appius Claudius Pulcher had already suggested this). Tiberius Gracchus proposed that big landowners should be compensated and the land divided up into smaller parcels.

Because this was a slap in the face to all those senators who'd been profiteering from land over the past few decades, it's no great surprise to learn that the Senate refused to fund the commission to organise the reforms. But thanks to Attalus III of Pergamon in 133 BC and leaving his kingdom of Asia to the Romans (refer to Chapter 13), Tiberius brought in a bill to appropriate those funds instead and the commission set to work.

An ancient law of Rome held that no Roman could have more than 500 acres of land. No-one had taken any notice of the law for generations, but Tiberius Gracchus wanted the law restored in order that more people would benefit. Senators with vast estates were horrified.

A veto war, a new land law, and growing concern

The nobles, unhappy with Tiberius Gracchus's proposed change, were out to get him. They had the other Tribune, Marcus Octavius, on their side, and he vetoed Tiberius Gracchus's bill. A veto war broke out. Tiberius Gracchus vetoed all the other legislation going through at the time. Both Tiberius Gracchus and Marcus Octavius were determined not to back down.

Tiberius Gracchus finally told Marcus Octavius to abandon his veto or be thrown out of office by the plebs. Marcus Octavius refused, so he was removed by a vote of the plebs. The new land law went through, but there were deep concerns that Tiberius Gracchus had broken the law by having Octavius thrown out.

In 132 BC, Tiberius Gracchus stood for Tribune again, to protect himself and his new laws. He hoped this would make his position safe because the job of tribune was treated as inviolable. This strategy was both tactless and borderline illegal (a law of 180 BC banned holding the same magistracy two years running, though it wasn't clear to anyone if this included the tribuneship) – it was certainly bad practice, and Tiberius Gracchus lost a lot of support. A brawl broke out during the electoral meetings. A bunch of senators got out of control and, in their fury, clubbed Tiberius Gracchus and 300 of his senators to death. So much for the rule of law in Rome. The Senate went on to use the law to prosecute the rest of Tiberius Gracchus's supporters, though in reality it was more of a witch hunt.

Continuing Tiberius Gracchus's reforms: Scipio Aemilianus and Marcus Fulvius Flaccus

As a senator, Publius Cornelius Scipio Aemilianus denounced Tiberius Gracchus for his dubious actions. But Scipio Aemilianus, the great commander in the Third Punic War who'd destroyed Carthage and Numantia in Spain (refer to Chapter 13), knew how much Rome owed to its Latin and Italian soldiers. Scipio Aemilianus decided to promote the soldiers' interests, which irritated the Roman mob. Mysteriously, Scipio Aemilianus was then found dead. It was probably a natural death, but the situation had become so heated that there was talk of foul play. And the prime suspect was Scipio Aemilianus's wife Sempronia, sister of Tiberius Gracchus.

Marcus Fulvius Flaccus, Consul for 134 BC, took up Scipio Aemilianus's proposal to give the allies who wished, Roman citizenship. This was totally unacceptable to the senators who only wanted voters in Rome whom they could buy and control. The proposed extension of citizenship was a missed opportunity and started a time bomb ticking that would go off in 90 BC.

Gaius Gracchus

Gaius Gracchus, who in 123 BC became Tribune of the Plebs, followed up his brother's reforms and became one of the most important political figures in Rome's history. He was a brilliant speaker. Unlike his brother Tiberius, Gaius Gracchus was hot-blooded, but he knew what he was doing, kept cool, and avoided acting on impulse. If Gaius Gracchus got worked up, a slave calmed him down by playing the flute.

Reforms on his watch

As Tribune of the Plebs, Gaius Gracchus brought in social and economic reforms, including:

- **Land reforms:** Gaius Gracchus promoted his brother Tiberius's land reforms and arranged for new roads to be built in order that produce could be transported and sold more easily.

- **New colonies:** Gaius Gracchus founded new colonies to stimulate industry in Italy.

- **Agricultural reform:** Gaius Gracchus reorganised Rome's corn supply to prevent fluctuations in availability by arranging for storage, setting the amount for each person, and regulating prices.

- **Legal reform:** Gaius Gracchus decreed that Roman citizens could not be executed before the Roman people without a trial.

Gaius Gracchus also challenged abuses of the law, such as senators on juries who had acquitted fellow senators charged with extortion while serving as provincial governors. Gaius Gracchus's new law passed control of such juries to the equestrians, which everyone interpreted as an insult to the Senate. Senators would no longer be able to control and exploit provincial governorships. Gaius Gracchus also promoted the interests of the equestrians by making the tax collectors among them responsible for collecting revenue from the newly acquired province of Asia. By offering the equestrians so much power, Gaius Gracchus also bought their support.

Downfall of Gaius Gracchus

In 122 BC, Gaius Gracchus was re-elected tribune but with none of the trouble his brother Tiberius experienced. Wisely, Gaius Gracchus hadn't actually stood for re-election, but the people voted him in anyway. Gaius Gracchus proposed that the first overseas Roman colony be founded near the site of old Carthage. He also reintroduced the idea that the Latin allies be made full Roman citizens and the rest given Latin status. But a rival tribune called Marcus Livius Drusus, with secret Senate backing, vetoed Gaius Gracchus's ideas and offered an even more attractive package of reforms. They included 12 new settlements in Italy, open even to the poorest, and also total exemption for the Latins from execution or flogging by Roman military commanders.

Livius Drusus's laws were passed, though nothing was ever done about any of them; their sole purpose had been to undermine Gaius Gracchus, whose popularity was on the wane anyway, partly because rumours were circulating that his new colony near Carthage was encroaching on the 'cursed' site of the old city destroyed at the end of the Third Punic War in 146 BC. In 121 BC, Gaius Gracchus tried to get in as tribune for a third term, but failed.

The Senate told one of the new tribunes, Marcus Minucius Rufus, to propose annulling the law intended to create the new colony in Africa. One of the reasons was that the Senate had an abiding fear that one day a colony of Rome would end up being more powerful than Rome. After all, the original Carthage started life as a colony of the city of Tyre in Phoenicia (roughly where Lebanon is now) and had ended up totally overshadowing its mother city.

Gaius Gracchus's opponents in the Senate had a leader in the form of Lucius Opimius, a man who hated everything Gaius Gracchus stood for, and they made sure he was elected Consul. Lucius Opimius and his associates immediately started revoking Gaius Gracchus's laws. So Gaius Gracchus got his friends together to try and stop Opimius blocking his new colony by turning up at the Capitol to protest in force, but a fight broke out between the rival bands of supporters and one of Gaius Gracchus's men killed one of Opimius's servants. That gave Opimius the chance to declare Gaius Gracchus an enemy of the state, offering a reward for his capture and persuading the Senate to pass a resolution called *Senatus Consultum Ultimum* ('The most extreme Senatorial decree').

The Senatus Consultum Ultimum decreed that, when a situation was desperate, the Senate had to support magistrates bringing an action against an enemy of the state. That meant consuls could do away with someone like Gaius Gracchus and simply argue they were defending the state, and, of course, the consuls automatically had the support of the Senate.

121 BC: A vintage year

Funnily enough, 121 BC was also remembered for its excellent wines as well as the end of Gaius Gracchus. The summer of 121 BC was especially hot and sunny, producing a celebrated harvest of grapes. Two centuries later men were still drinking wine made that year and singing its praises.

In the riots that followed, hundreds of Gaius Gracchus's supporters were killed. Gaius Gracchus himself ordered his slave Philocrates to kill him, which he did, though another story has both men being caught and killed by rioters. Thousands more of Gaius Gracchus's supporters were later executed.

The aftermath of the Gracchi

With Gaius Gracchus out of the way, the Senate could do more or less as it wanted. The Senate was able to call on its new Senatus Consultum Ultimum resolution whenever it needed. Wisely, the Senate allowed most of the Gracchi brothers' reforms to go ahead, realising that any opposition would incur the fury of the people.

What the Gracchi brothers left to the world was the fact that the days when the people could reform Rome through their tribunes were over. Politicians now divided into two groups. The two groups weren't political parties as we would understand them; they were more simply ways of thinking:

- *Optimates* ('the Best Men'): These were political leaders who pursued their ambitions through the Senate and claimed moral and social superiority based on birth.

- *Populares* ('the People's Men'): These were political leaders who tried to work through the people and tribunes and claimed to defend the liberty of the people from the actions of the Optimates.

The identities of the Optimates and the Populares were easily blurred. For example, a noble starting out on his political career could serve as tribune of the plebs and use Populares' techniques like promising land and voting reforms. In the long run, this made it possible for the nobles, including emperors, to keep control.

Marius the New Man – and More Unrest

Gaius Marius (157–86 BC) had fought at Numantia in Spain (refer to Chapter 13 for more on Numantia). With the support of the Metelli family, one of the top senatorial families in Rome, Gaius Marius came to Rome to try his hand in politics as a *novus homo* ('new man'). A novus homo was a person who was able to get power, not by their wealth or birth, but through ability. As a 'new man', Gaius Marius was to become the most important military leader at the end of the second century BC.

Marius rose to the top purely because of his own talents. Marius came from a town called Arpinum, south-east of Rome, as did another brilliant new man, the orator Cicero, born in 106 BC. Both men eventually became consuls and made a permanent mark on Rome's history. Although they both came from affluent backgrounds, they couldn't rely on the network of support members of old aristocratic families and had to try much harder to get on. Such ambitious and committed self-made men were the shape of things to come. (Head to the section 'The Gang of Three: The First Triumvirate', later in this chapter, for details on Cicero's objections to the triumvirate system.)

Fighting the Jugurthine War

Masinissa's Numidia came back to haunt Rome. It was Masinissa's skilful manipulation of Rome's hysterical fear of Carthage that had led to the Third Punic War (see Chapter 13). By 118 BC, Masinissa was long dead and was so his son Micipsa, who had left Numidia to his two biological sons and an adoptive third son called Jugurtha. Jugurtha killed one of the two other brothers and defied all Roman attempts to impose a settlement between himself and the surviving brother.

So in 111 BC, Rome started the Jugurthine War. It didn't go well, which was bad news for the nobles, especially in the eyes of the Roman mob – because some senators had also been accused of corruption and accepting bribes. In 109 BC, Quintus Caecilius Metellus, a member of the vastly powerful Caecilii Metelli family whose members held many consulships and military commands, took command in the Jugurthine War. He improved discipline, but the Roman mob wasn't impressed by the slow progress of the fighting.

Gaius Marius, who was in Africa with Quintus Caecilius Metellus, seized his chance. He raced back to Rome, claiming that Metellus was dragging out the Jugurthine War for the sake of his own glory.

Marius, taking advantage of frustration in Rome at the way the Jugurthine War had not been brought to an end, severely criticised Caecilius Metellus. By presenting himself as an appropriate alternative, Marius managed to get himself elected as Consul in 107 BC, thus qualifying him to be made Commander in Africa, instead of Caecilius Metellus.

To improve the army, Marius brought in volunteers, rather than unwilling conscripts. He trained the new troops and led a highly successful series of campaigns against Jugurtha, bringing Jugurtha to Rome in 104 BC for execution. Marius became extremely popular in Rome – not surprisingly – and his military success was to have important consequences for Rome's politics.

MILESTONE

Marius's mules

Marius helped start the process of creating the first professional standing army in Rome's history. In 107 BC, he started hiring, training, and equipping volunteers from amongst Romans who were too poor to have the normal property qualifications for military service. It's possible this had happened before, but Marius turned it into a major break with the past. Crucially, his troops were loyal to Marius, their leader, rather than to Rome. Soldiers were now disciplined, mobile, and self-sufficient. Marius improved the organisation of the army by introducing centurions (see Chapter 5). Having professional soldiers meant keeping them busy when there was no fighting, rather than sending them home. Marius used soldiers to build roads and bridges. The soldiers became known as 'Marius's mules'. The professional army was to be the backbone of the future Roman Empire.

The 'Northmen' advance

As soon as Marius returned to Rome, he was promptly appointed to train up and lead another army to fend off a tribal invasion from the north. The Cimbri and Teutones tribes, known collectively as the 'Northmen', terrified the average Roman. As a result of this fear, Marius was illegally made Consul five times between 104–100 BC (there was supposed to be a ten-year gap between being consul twice), because it was generally felt that having him in charge was more important than worrying about the law. Marius ended up being the first man to be consul seven times. In 102 and 101 BC, he destroyed the Northmen threat and made himself even more popular.

Suppressing a slave revolt in Sicily

Marius then suppressed a slave revolt in Sicily. Many of the slaves there had been free men, captured by pirates and sold into Roman slavery. In 104 BC, the Senate ordered that the kidnapped men be freed, but slave owners were determined not to lose their expensively purchased labour. The owners, led by the governor of Sicily, prevented the Senate's order being enforced, so in 103 BC, the kidnapped men seized a chance to escape and start a rebellion, encouraging other slaves to join them. It wasn't until one of Marius's armies arrived in 101 BC that the revolt was crushed.

Marius's downfall

Despite his many successes, Marius totally failed to use his position as Consul to reform the Roman state. More concerned with the welfare of his soldiers, he left all the moves for land reform to a tribune named Lucius Appuleius Saturninus. The two men fixed things so that Caecilius Metellus was the only senator to oppose the reforms and forced him into exile.

Saturninus had been placed in charge of Rome's grain supply in 105 BC. This was a good job for anyone with ambition because doing well meant more votes. But Saturninus was pushed out when the grain price went up thanks to a shortage caused by a slave rebellion in Sicily; instead the job was given to someone with more experience. Saturninus took this as a personal insult and was out to get the nobility from then on. He had himself elected as tribune in 103 BC and used the position to crank up demands for reform.

To begin with, Saturninus was the perfect friend for Marius. Saturninus attracted popular support by reintroducing low-price grain handouts and arranged for land grants for Marius's veteran soldiers. Saturninus used thugs from the Roman mob to attack anyone who criticised him and made sure of his own re-election as tribune by having a rival murdered.

Unfortunately for Marius, Saturninus's plans for Marius's veterans, and the Latin and Italian allies who had also fought for Marius, turned the Roman mob against Saturninus. There was an all-out riot in the Forum of Rome between Saturninus's supporters and the Roman mob. Saturninus won, but he organised the murder of another political rival called Memmius.

Marius decided enough was enough. The Senate demanded Marius use his powers as Consul to protect the state against Saturninus. Saturninus was trapped on the Capitoline Hill, but a crowd burst in and killed him. Marius was in a no-win situation. He had lost support in the Saturninus Populares camp, but because also Marius wouldn't let Caecilius Metellus come back from exile, Marius lost any standing with the Optimates.

Marius and the eagle

Marius came up with the idea to get rid of the different standards the legions carried into battle. The emblems represented a variety of real and mythical beasts like wild boars, wolves, and the Minotaur. But Marius wanted the eagle to be the great symbol of Rome's power. He had his way, and from 104 BC each legion carried a standard with a silver eagle into battle. The idea of eagles-only didn't last – the legions later went back to their own symbols as well as that of the eagle.

The Senate overturned all of Saturninus's legislation that would also have provided for Marius's veterans. The Senate's action created a divide between the soldiers and the Senate. From now on, soldiers looked to their generals and not to the Roman state for their future security.

Metellus was allowed back from exile anyway, and Marius had to leave for Asia. Marius was a military genius and a great commander, but he was no politician. But he was far from finished, even though he'd managed to annoy just about everyone.

Fighting Your Friends: The Social War (90–88 BC)

The word for an ally in Latin is *socius* (allies: *socii*); the name given to the conflict that now broke out: the Social War. The conflict threatened Rome's very existence – and was the worst crisis that Rome had had to deal with since Hannibal's exploits more than a century before.

Wrong-footing the allies

When the Senate overturned Saturninus's law reforms (refer to the preceding section, 'Marius's downfall'), Rome's Italian allies were bitterly disappointed. The allies had made a great contribution in recent wars, and they deeply resented being excluded from becoming full Roman citizens. Italians who'd gathered in Rome to support Saturninus now looked like serious trouble. Italian resentment was growing, and before long it was bound to explode.

Marcus Livius Drusus, Tribune of the Plebs in 91 BC, started the reform ball rolling again. He had the backing of the Senate, who hoped he would clamp down on the political power of the equestrians. The plan included the following:

✔ Drusus would restore control of the courts to the Senate and, in return, 300 top equestrians would be made senators.

✔ In his biggest move, Drusus's was to give the Italian allies full Roman voting rights. He did this because he realised giving the allies Roman citizenship was inevitable, and Drusus wanted to make sure it was done on the Senate's terms.

The Senate, equestrians, and the general Roman mob joined forces in total opposition to Drusus's reform. Even Drusus was alarmed when the cities of the allies started organising 'committees of action', and even more so by a plan to assassinate the Consul Lucius Marcius Philippus, one of Drusus's chief opponents. Drusus warned Philippus, but his good faith gesture did him (Drusus) no good. Philippus had all Drusus's previous reforms thrown out and had Drusus murdered.

The allies involved in the Social War that followed were mainly from the mountainous areas and were only a small proportion of Rome's allies – but they were good fighters. These allies organised a confederation. Considering that the allies had been trained and disciplined in warfare the Roman way, they were a deadly prospect.

Extending the franchise and ending the war

The Social War went badly for the Romans to begin with, as they'd been caught off their guard. Despite fielding a massive army, by the end of 90 BC, the Romans decided they had to stop the rebellion spreading. Therefore, they gave the full franchise – that is, Roman citizenship – to loyal allies and to those allies who hadn't joined in fighting. This move had the desired effect. (One of the Roman commanders, Lucius Cornelius Sulla, also did a great deal to bring the war to an end in 88 BC by fighting with uncompromising ruthlessness. You can read about Sulla in the following section 'Think the unthinkable: A Roman captures Rome – Sulla'.) In the end, the war was said to have cost Italians more than 300,000 young men.

The upshot of the Social War is that Rome survived, but it was ironic that it had taken the conflict to bring about the franchise extension that had been such a source of unpleasantness and violence in Rome for decades. If what Gaius Gracchus and Drusus had asked for originally had been granted, war could have been avoided.

The outcome of the Social War was that by giving the allies the franchise, Rome in the long run became stronger. But the dogs of war had been let loose. The very same Roman armies created to fight and bring peace would soon tear the Republic apart.

Think the Unthinkable: A Roman Captures Rome – Sulla (88 BC)

Lucius Cornelius Sulla (138–78 BC) had a nickname: *Felix* ('Lucky'), and with good reason. But he also went down in history as one of Rome's greatest villains (see Chapter 24). Because he had fought so well in the Social War, Sulla was in the perfect position to benefit from Marius's lack of political skills.

Taking Rome and settling Mithridates

Mithridates VI, King of Pontus, without difficulty, had occupied a large part of Asia Minor and Greece, the locals having decided that Mithridates's lordship was preferable to Rome's greed and bullying. Sulla was put in command of the army to fight Mithridates, but Marius wanted the job. The Tribune Sulpicius had the command transferred to Marius, with the idea that he, Sulpicius, could use Marius's support for his reforms. Sulla gave in, but finding that he still had the loyalty of the troops, Sulla decided to gamble everything and marched on Rome.

In 88 BC, Sulla marched on Rome and seized the city – an unbelievably dramatic and illegal act for which he was forever remembered as a criminal. Even his own officers deserted in disgust. Sulla had Sulpicius killed, and Marius then fled Rome and hid out with his veterans. Sulla forced through new laws, using his army's muscle to put down opposition. The die was cast for the future: Ambitious men and their armies would control Roman politics for the decades to come.

Sulla left Rome, ignoring a summons to stand trial, and fought Mithridates. In 87 BC, the Consul Lucius Cornelius Cinna tried to start reversing Sulla's legislation. He was expelled from Rome by his colleague, the Consul Gnaeus Octavius, who practically set himself up as sole ruler. So Cinna collected an army of legionaries and Italian allies, and Marius, who came back to Italy to join in. They marched on Rome – bad news for Sulla who was obviously desperate to get back. Sulla forced Mithridates to come to terms with Rome, ignoring the fact that Mithridates had murdered thousands of Romans while conquering Asia. Mithridates became a Roman ally in return for giving up all his conquests in Asia and Greece.

Marius and Cinna fight back

Marius and Cinna marched on Rome where they carried on a reign of terror and murdered many of the aristocrats, including Sulla's supporters.

During this campaign in 86 BC, Marius died (of natural causes, believe it or not – exhausted, he had a breakdown, started drinking heavily, and got pleurisy). Cinna was left the ruler of Rome. Keen to restore order and end the violence, Cinna promptly gave Roman citizenship to the new Italian citizens in Rome's 35 tribes and cancelled their debts. This made Cinna very popular, and he was re-elected to the consulship in 86 BC without opposition. Despite the reign of terror that lead up to his rule, Cinna managed to establish peace and stability for a few years, but Sulla was still a danger. Cinna prepared for war against Sulla, but Cinna was murdered by some of his own men in 84 BC.

I'll be back: Sulla comes home

Sulla had little trouble rounding up support from the aristocracy, thanks to Cinna and Marius's campaign against them. Amongst the aristocrats who joined Sulla were two future big names:

✔ Marcus Licinius Crassus

✔ Gnaeus Pompeius (known to history as Pompey)

Sulla needed just one year of fighting to deal with the opposition to his return. Only a force of 70,000 Samnites (for Samnites, see Chapter 11) ended up standing in his way. Close to Rome, in 82 BC, Sulla's army wiped out the Samnites and butchered and tortured the survivors. Pompey wiped out any support amongst forces in Sicily and Africa who supported Marius, and earned himself the title Magnus ('the Great'), which was supposed to be one of Sulla's jokes but the name stuck. By 80 BC, all resistance to Sulla ended.

Dictator of Rome

Sulla was elected Dictator of Rome in 81 BC. He organised the murder of his opponents by declaring them outlaws, putting a price on their heads, and displaying a list of their names. Funnily enough, the idea of the list was to save unnecessary worry for anyone not on it. Imagine what it did to those who were listed – all 500 of them!

Sulla's main targets were the new breed of financier equestrians, whose wealth came from business and trade, because they'd supported Marius. Sulla seized these equestrians' money and gave it to his veterans or his friends. Sulla freed the condemned equestrians' slaves and hired them as his bodyguards. He also seized land from cities that had supported Marius and gave it to his own soldiers. This last was a smart move on Sulla's part: Sulla needed to provide for his soldiers in order to stop them turning to crime and being a threat to Sulla's rule.

Despite his brutality, Sulla knew Rome needed the return of the rule of law and did the following:

✔ Increased the numbers of the Senate by promoting members of the equestrians in the Italian municipal aristocracy (not the same as the financier equestrians in Rome, whom he hated) to replace the men lost in the fighting. The Senate now numbered 600 and crucially the new members meant much better representation for Italy.

✔ Restored the Senate's right to veto legislation passed by the *Concilium Plebis Tributum* (the Council of Plebs, see Chapter 3), wiping out most of the tribunes' power at a stroke. That meant that men like Marius could no longer use tribunes to pass laws they had failed to get the Senate to introduce.

✔ Laid down that the career structure of magistracies held by senators would be strictly fixed by age to prevent overambitious young men reaching high office too early, but their numbers were increased to take into account Rome's increasing number of provinces (magistrates like quaestors and praetors, see Chapter 3, would serve a year at Rome and then be sent out to a province).

✔ Gave the Senate the power to select magistrates for posts in provincial government and, at the same time, prohibited them from fighting wars outside the borders of their provinces to stop them trying to seize power and destabilising Rome.

✔ Increased the number of Roman provinces to ten (in Spain, northern Italy, Africa, Sardinia and Corsica, and Sicily). Naturally, this increased Rome's wealth and call on resources.

✔ Left Italy's civil and political privileges as they were and promised not to revoke any earlier grants of Roman citizenship to Italian cities, except in one or two cases. In practice, many Italian cities started voluntarily remodelling their constitutions on Rome's anyway. It just showed how influential the Roman system was.

Retiring alive and dying peacefully

Sulla was dictator for three years, which was an incredible violation of the age-old principle of the Roman Republic: that no-one could hold permanent political power. In 79 BC, Sulla resigned, retired to the country and, living up to his name of 'lucky', died peacefully the following year, which was a remarkable achievement for him and the age he lived in.

Sulla's man Lucullus

Licinius Lucullus (*c*. 100–57 BC) was related to both Sulla and the powerful Metelli family. Lucullus had marched on Rome with Sulla and also fought with him in Asia against Mithridates VI, King of Pontus. In 74 BC, Lucullus got his own military command in the East because Mithridates had broken the 88 BC settlement with Sulla and started fighting again. Lucullus's army refused to fight, accusing Lucullus of dragging out the war to get rich. He was recalled and Pompey sent out in his place. Lucullus more or less retired to private life. Apart from obstructing Pompey's settlement of Asia in 62 BC (see Gnaeus Pompeius); Lucullus became notorious for his luxury lifestyle, extravagant gardens in Rome, and famously lavish banquets.

Despite his achievements, Sulla left Rome unsettled because:

✔ Although Sulla promoted Italian equestrians to the Senate, he only did that as a one-off. He failed to introduce a regular system of bringing in Italians, which would have invigorated the Senate and given it a broader appreciation of Rome's place in Italy and the world.

✔ He missed the chance to bring in long-lasting reforms to the Republic, for example, creating permanent representation of Italian cities in the Senate or making it possible to vote in places all round Italy for Rome's magistrates.

✔ He left many enemies such as Sertorius, who was leading a revolt in Spain (discussed in the later section 'Gnaeus Pompeius (Pompey)').

✔ In the East, Mithridates VI had overturned his settlement with Sulla and gone back to war, which meant a new Roman army had to be sent out to force a new peace. But it took till 62 BC to achieve this.

✔ Sulla had dramatically shown how a single general could rise to power at the head of an army. They owed their livelihoods and their retirement grants to him and him alone, and were liable to follow other military leaders once he was gone. This was a terrible sign for the future, and it echoed down the decades to come. Any man with an eye on power could see how Sulla had done it and made sure he did the same.

Well, They Started Out As Mates: The Age of the Generals

Instead of the Roman Republic being allowed to recuperate after Sulla's rule, it was plunged into more warfare. The traditional aristocracy carried on dominating all the senior positions in the Senate and the various magistracies, but spent most of its energies on its own internal quarrels and holding on to its privileges, rather than trying to carry on any reforms. What followed was the *Age of the Generals*, which brought the Republic to its final dizzying end.

The three generals who defined the shape of Roman history down to the 40s BC were Gnaeus Pompeius, Marcus Licinius Crassus, and Gaius Julius Caesar. They all led armies, jockeyed for power, worked together and against each other depending on the circumstances. And they all had violent deaths.

The time from Sulla down to Octavian (roughly the first 70 years of the first century BC) is sometimes called the *Imperatorial Age* from the Latin word *imperator,* meaning a general.

Gnaeus Pompeius (Pompey) (106–48 BC)

Pompey was the son of a general called Pompeius Strabo. He fought with great success and bravery under his father, and he was immensely popular for his looks and manner, which did a lot to overcome the fact that he was born an equestrian. He used three legions of his father's veterans to fight for Sulla against Marius.

Pompey earned his title Magnus ('the Great') during the campaign to clear Marius's supporters out of Africa (see the earlier section 'I'll be back: Sulla comes home'). But Pompey's rise to military and political power had also been achieved in other campaigns:

- ✔ **The revolt in Spain:** In Spain, the Marian Sertorius led a highly successful revolt that involved making a pact with Mithridates VI, King of Pontus; Sertorius followed this by stirring rebellions in southern Gaul; and he even planned an overland invasion of Italy, as Hannibal had done in 218 BC. In 77 BC, the Senate sent Pompey to Spain to finish Sertorius off. Sertorius had been waging a guerrilla war with about 2,600 men, and what was left of a Roman army that had fled Italy, led by Perpenna. Between them, Sertorius and Perpenna held off four Roman armies totalling about 140,000.

  The war in Spain came to a rapid end in 73 BC when Sertorius was murdered by Perpenna. Pompey's settlement of Spain was generous and fair-minded. He even destroyed Sertorius's archives to prevent a *pogrom* (an organised persecution) of any of his associates in Rome. Because of this, Pompey's personal standing and popularity increased.

- ✔ **The slave war:** In about 73 BC a massive slave revolt broke out in Capua and spread across Italy, lasting until 71 BC. The revolt was led by a runaway gladiator called Spartacus. Marcus Licinius Crassus had defeated the slaves, but Pompey raced back from Spain with his army to help hunt down survivors and claim all the credit. That stole Crassus's thunder, much to Crassus's fury, and had given Pompey an excuse to bring his army into Italy.

  Spartacus and the slave revolt are immortalised in the famous movie made in 1960, starring Kirk Douglas as the hero. See Chapter 2 for more on the revolt, and Chapter 25 for more about Spartacus himself.

- ✔ **Making an alliance with Crassus:** Because of the bad blood between them during the slave war, Marcus Licinius Crassus and Pompey could have gone for each other's throats, but they were smart enough to realise they would be much more powerful working together. In 70 BC, Crassus and Pompey were made joint consuls and promptly gave back to the tribunes all the powers they had before Sulla was in power. It was a clever move. Crassus and Pompey depended on their armies for their power, but they knew the Senate hated this and would try to force them to give up their armies. Now the tribunes were restored to power, Crassus and Pompey could appeal to the tribunes for the necessary approval to keep their armies.

✔ **Pompey and the pirates:** In 67 BC, Pompey was given supreme command to get rid of the Cilician pirates in the eastern Mediterranean (Cilicia is where southern Turkey is now). Pompey did the job in three months, capturing 20,000 men and 90 ships, as well as huge quantities of treasure. Pompey's victory made him very popular because it at once cut the price of grain, and grain ships no longer risked piracy.

The Cilician pirates also feature in the movie *Spartacus* (1960). The pirates help the rebellious slaves by providing transport for the slaves out of Italy. There isn't a movie about Pompey and the pirates, but the movie *Ben Hur* (1957), set in the early days of Christianity, starring Charlton Heston as our hero, features a great sea battle between Roman warships manned by shackled slaves, pirate galleys, and shows how the ships tried to ram each other.

✔ **Defeating Mithridates and conquering other lands:** In 66 BC, Pompey was ordered to sort out Mithridates VI, King of Pontus. Pompey defeated Mithridates and followed that up by conquering Armenia, Syria, and Judaea. Pompey's settlement in 62 BC was brilliant: He founded colonies, gave the pirates land so they didn't need to be pirates, and set up a loyal client king in Judaea.

In 62 BC, Pompey came home and disbanded his army, to everyone's relief (and surprise). But in return, Pompey wanted land for his veterans and the Senate's approval of his settlement in the East. Pompey was frustrated by the Senate. In order to get what he wanted, Pompey joined forces with two other ambitious politicians – Marcus Licinius Crassus and Julius Caesar – in an alliance known to history as the First Triumvirate.

Pompey's victories

The victorious Pompey was a legend in his own lifetime and ever afterwards. Pompey had risen to the top through his own talents; he was merely an equestrian when his career started. Pliny the Elder (see Chapter 23) thought Pompey was quite equal to Alexander the Great, but Pliny then went over the top by suggesting Pompey was nearly as successful as the immortal Hercules. After the war in Africa, Pompey was the first equestrian to ride in a triumphal chariot. The chariot was towed by elephants, a sight never seen before in Rome. To commemorate the defeat of the pirates and his Eastern conquests Pompey paraded a costly portrait of himself made in pearls. He was later blamed for making precious stones and pearls fashionable. At the same time Pompey introduced fluorspar (calcium fluoride), translucent ornamental vessels, to Rome, as well as handing out vast sums of money to the state, his commanders, and every one of his soldiers.

Marcus Licinius Crassus (c. 115 to 53 BC)

Marcus Licinius Crassus's father had defended Rome unsuccessfully against Marius in 87 BC, and Crassus fled to Spain, later reaching Africa before returning to Italy where he joined Sulla in 83 BC. His reward was to make money out of Sulla's proscriptions against his enemies, even adding an innocent man to the list just to profit from confiscating this man's estate. Sulla never trusted him again after that, but Crassus could work a crowd and was popular with the Roman people.

After serving as praetor (see Chapter 3 for this magistracy), Crassus was made general of the army sent to defeat Spartacus and the slave revolt of 73–71 BC, in preference to sending out inexperienced consuls. He was victorious, but the way Pompey turned up at the last minute to take all the credit enraged him. Crassus's career was a constant struggle against Pompey, though they served together in the First Triumvirate (discussed in the later section 'The Gang of Three: The First Triumvirate') because he was too powerful to be left out.

The most famous Roman of them all: Julius Caesar

Gaius Julius Caesar (100–44 BC) – (see also Chapter 23), is the most famous Roman who has ever lived. Caesar's family claimed descent from Aeneas's son Anchises, known also as Iulus. Aeneas's mother was the goddess Venus; you can see what sort of pedigree Caesar was able to boast about. Caesar backed Marius's military leaderships and Pompey's restoration of the tribunes.

How Crassus got rich

Crassus was phenomenally wealthy, and it didn't all come from Sulla's proscriptions. One of the ways he got rich quick was by training up slaves to be builders and architects. When Crassus got news of a house on fire, he'd rush round and offer the owner a knock-down price.

The terrified owner usually sold up, as even a bad price was better than nothing. Crassus then had the fire put out and redeveloped the site for rent. The end result was that after a few years, Crassus owned a huge part of Rome.

Caesar was highly ambitious and extremely intelligent. He was also a brilliant leader and knew how to make himself popular. In 65 BC, Caesar became an aedile (the assistant to a tribune, refer to Chapter 3) and spent a huge amount of money (probably Crassus's money) on public works and entertainments, such as wild-beast fights and stage plays. Caesar also reinstated the trophies commemorating Marius's victories in the Jugurthine War and against the Northmen.

Caesar wasn't averse to underhand tactics. In 63 BC, he bribed his way into becoming *Pontifex Maximus* (chief priest). In 62 BC, an attempt was made to implicate Caesar in a conspiracy against the state (the Catiline Conspiracy; see the sidebar 'Marcus Tullius Cicero and the Catiline Conspiracy' for details), but Cicero proved this was impossible. The accusations against Caesar did him no harm, and Caesar was made governor of Further Spain (nowadays Portugal) in 61 BC.

The Gang of Three: The First Triumvirate (60 BC)

Triumvirate comes from two Latin words: *tres* ('three') and *vir* ('man'), and means 'rule by three men'. By the time of the Second Triumvirate, the triumvirate had become a legal Roman institution. But the First Triumvirate had no legal backing; it was a private deal between three immensely powerful men – Pompey, Crassus, and Caesar – who believed they would be even more powerful if they joined together. However, not everyone was so keen on the idea of the triumvirate, and the most conspicuous was Cicero.

 Cicero (106–43 BC), like his famous forbear Marius, was a *novus homo* ('new man'). Unlike Marius, Cicero was a man of letters and brilliant orator (refer to Chapter 1 for details of what Cicero wrote). By the 60s BC, Cicero had a brilliant reputation following his success in the trial of Gaius Verres, accused of extortion in his time as governor of Sicily (Chapter 24). Cicero championed Pompey and also exposed the Catiline Conspiracy in 62 BC. Determined to remain politically independent, Cicero refused help from Caesar and fled Rome, returning several years later. Cicero's greatest wish was that all the various political groups would work together in what he called the Concord of the Orders. Cicero thought the best way forward was for the senators and equestrians to work together. In the end, Cicero had no choice but to accept the union of the First Triumvirate.

Cicero and the Catiline Conspiracy

Lucius Sergius Catilinus was one of Sulla's side-kicks during Sulla's dictatorship. Catilinus stood for Consul in 63 BC, but was defeated by Cicero. The next year Catilinus stood on a ticket to defend anyone who was poor and discontented. Catilinus lost, and Crassus dumped him. Catilinus got together the disaffected and organised a conspiracy to take over the state, hiding out with some landless veterans. Cicero got hold of evidence implicating the conspirators, who were rounded up and executed. Catilinus fled from Rome and was defeated in battle by Cicero's co-consul, Gaius Antonius. Cicero had the remaining conspirators arrested and executed without trial, an arbitrary act that ruined Cicero's reputation. For more about Catilinus, see Chapter 24.

By 60 BC, Pompey, Caesar, and Crassus had each been frustrated in their ambitions, mainly by the Optimates. As usual in Roman politics, aristocratic internal feuds came into play:

✔ **Pompey:** The powerful Optimates Metelli family blocked Pompey's request for land for his veterans. Pompey then had to look for support elsewhere.

The Senate's rejection of Pompey's request shows just how personal Roman power politics had become. The Metellis were getting back at Pompey for having divorced his wife Mucia Tertia, a relative of the Metelli.

✔ **Crassus:** Despite Crassus achieving great fame in crushing the slave revolt in 71 BC, Pompey's victories in the East and late arrival to mop up the slaves had totally overshadowed him. Crassus's ambition involved using his money, connections, and financing any up-and-coming young man. This meant he 'owned' lots of politicians, earning him enemies amongst the Optimates. Crassus also came up against the conspirator Catilinus (refer to the sidebar 'Cicero and the Catiline Conspiracy' for that story).

✔ **Caesar:** Caesar was governor of Further Spain in 61–60 BC, where he defeated various tribes and settled disputes between creditors and debtors. Flushed with success, he set off for Rome in hope of a triumph and being elected as consul. Anyone hoping for a triumph had to wait outside Rome, but by law, a candidate for the consulship had to be in Rome. So Caesar asked to be considered for the consulship in absentia. The Senate turned him down, annoyed by this attempt to bend the law, and said he could only stand for the consulship if he came to Rome in person. So Caesar then came back to Rome.

Caesar returned to Rome and formed the First Triumvirate with Crassus and Pompey. In 59 BC, Caesar was elected consul. In practice, Caesar was also now the leader of the First Triumvirate.

Caesar, Crassus, and Pompey bombarded the Senate with their demands and, after some resistance, got what they wanted. Thanks to Caesar, Pompey got both the land for his veterans and ratification of his settlement at the end of the war with Mithridates VI. Pompey married Caesar's daughter Julia in 59 BC to bind their alliance. Caesar got the job of Proconsular Governor in Gaul together with an army, though the truth was, Caesar had awarded himself this powerful command. Crassus was sidelined for the moment and had to wait till 55 BC before he had a chance to gain himself a military reputation to rival Caesar and Pompey.

Building his power base: Caesar and the Gallic Wars

Caesar's governorship of Cisalpine Gaul gave him the best of both worlds. He was close enough to Rome to be able to remain at the centre of political developments, and he had a major provincial command with an army, which gave Caesar the prospect of conquest.

During a nine-year campaign known to history as the Gallic Wars, Caesar conquered Gaul. The war brought the huge area of Gaul into the Roman Empire, giving Rome an Atlantic and North Sea coastline. Caesar also led two expeditions to Britain (55 and 54 BC). With these exploits, Caesar gained a phenomenal level of personal prestige and box-office popularity. Reaching Britain at all was the stuff of legend, because Britain was popularly believed to be at the ends of the earth.

We know a great deal about Caesar's campaign in Gaul because he wrote a detailed account, which survives in full. Inevitably biased, because it was written as propaganda, it is still an extraordinary account of a generally highly successful campaign. Discipline, logistics, squabbling amongst the enemy, and the brutal suppression of rebellions against Roman rule, all play their part. There is no doubt, though, that the campaign was utterly ruthless, bloody, and caused colossal suffering to the Gauls – just so Caesar could make himself into a Roman hero. The final engagement against the Gaulish chieftain Vercingetorix came with the legendary siege of Alesia (modern Alise).

Some like it hot

One day, in 62 BC, publius Clodius Pulcher tried to seduce Caesar's wife. Caesar was out because his wife Pompeia was taking part in a women-only celebration of Ceres, also known as the Good Goddess *(Bona Dea)*. Clodius turned up disguised as a female lute player, but when a maid asked him who he was, his voice gave him away. Clodius hid, but was found and taken to court. Clodius declared he had been out of Rome on the day in question, but his former friend Cicero said that wasn't true. Other evidence emerged that Clodius had committed incest with his sisters. Clodius's accusers were bribed and Clodius got off scot-free. The outcome of the case was that Caesar divorced Pompeia, but Caesar refused to give evidence against Clodius. Caesar famously said he had divorced Pompeia not because of the allegation of adultery but because 'Caesar's wife should not only be free from guilt but free from any suspicion of guilt'.

Meanwhile back in Rome . . .

While Caesar was in Gaul and Britain, polishing up his curriculum vitae, tensions were mounting in Rome, where the tribune publius Clodius Pulcher had been left in control. Clodius Pulcher's actions promoted the vicious personal rivalries that characterised Roman politics at this time and showed how things were becoming more and more out of control. More importantly, Clodius Pulcher's behaviour gave Pompey an excuse to increase his power in Rome at Caesar's expense. Clodius Pulcher had

✔ Shamelessly courted the Roman mob with free handouts and kept gangs of thugs on Caesar's payroll.

✔ Used the doubtful legality of the executions after the Catiline Conspiracy to chase Cicero out of Rome, pursuing a personal vendetta (refer to the sidebar 'Cicero and the Catiline Conspiracy').

✔ Deposed the king of Cyprus in order to help himself to the treasury to pay for the free handouts.

✔ Locked Pompey up in his own house. Pompey responded in kind and organised his own gang of thugs and then passed a law which Clodius Pulcher failed to block, allowing Cicero back.

✔ Tried to seduce Caesar's wife. Clodius Pulcher was discovered, stood trial, and, through bribery and other underhand tricks, got off. (For the intimate details, read the sidebar 'Some like it hot'.)

Renewing the Triumvirate

By 56 BC, the First Triumvirate agreement between Pompey, Crassus, and Caesar was looking distinctly shaky. Pompey was asserting himself against Clodius Pulcher whose behaviour was out of control, and Crassus took the chance to bring Caesar, still on campaign in Gaul, up to speed with what was going on. A meeting was arranged at Luca (Lucca) in northern Italy to sort out all their differences and guarantee mutual support. Caesar's command in Gaul was extended, while Crassus took Syria and Pompey took Spain, all positions of enormous power.

Death of Crassus and the crumbling Triumvirate

Crassus was given a prestigious military command in the East to fight the Parthian Empire (roughly equivalent to modern Iran and Iraq). He went out in 55 BC and started off well. But in 53 BC, Crassus was defeated at Carrhae (modern Harran on Turkey's south-east border with Syria) and was killed trying to escape. The final humiliation came when the Parthians captured Crassus's legionary standards, not recovered until 20 BC when the Emperor Augustus negotiated their return.

The death of Crassus left Caesar and Pompey in open opposition by upsetting the balance of power. Unfortunately, Caesar's daughter Julia (Pompey's wife) had died in 54 BC, removing the only personal link between the two men.

Because of the problems in Rome, the Senate made various moves to recall Caesar from Gaul. In the end, an agreement was reached in which Caesar would get time to finish the war in Gaul, but he would give up control of Rome to Pompey. The problem was that Rome was dissolving into chaos. Gang warfare between supporters of Caesar and Pompey led to street riots, ending up in the burning of the Senate house in 52 BC and the death of Clodius. The Senate's solution was to give Pompey all the powers of a dictator in order to restore order.

A key turning point came in 52 BC because Pompey had just been awarded the power of *imperium* (see Chapter 3 for the power it conferred) for another five years. Everything hung on whether Pompey would support demands for Caesar's recall from Gaul, which would mean Caesar giving up his army and thereby all his power. Since Julia had died in 54 BC, Pompey was free to marry again and instead of marrying another woman in Caesar's family, he chose one from the Metelli family, cementing his new loyalty to the Optimates. Influenced by the Optimates, he supported demands that Caesar be recalled, and in 50 BC accepted command of the Roman armies in Italy. The balance of power was destroyed, and the Roman world dissolved into civil war, which is the story of the next chapter.

Chapter 15

Daggers Drawn – The Fall of the Republic

In This Chapter

▶ The rivalry of Caesar and Pompey

▶ How Caesar became master of Rome

▶ What happened on the Ides of March

▶ Why Octavian and Mark Antony fell out

▶ How an Egyptian queen nearly destroyed the Roman world

*T*he Roman Republic – based on the ideal of rule by the people – had been falling apart for years, but finally ground to an end in 43 BC. Within 15 years the Roman Empire, ruled by an emperor, came into being. Or did it? At the time, many pretended that the Roman Empire was the old Republic reinvented. What couldn't be ignored though, was that one man, the 'general', held a lot more power than anyone else.

At first, believe it or not, no such thing as a Roman emperor officially existed. A Roman emperor actually called himself *imperator,* which means 'general'. Only later did the title 'general', commander of the Roman army, come to mean what we mean by the word 'emperor' – that is, a supreme ruler like a monarch.

During the Republic, different men of high rank did various jobs: consul, quaestor, praetor, tribune, censor, and so on (see Chapter 3 for descriptions of these positions). The same set-up carried on into the Roman Empire – but with a difference, the 'general' now held more and more of the jobs.

This chapter follows explains how the Republic collapsed and how one man, Octavian (known as Augustus), refashioned the rule of the Republic in such a way that he held absolute power.

Civil War

The seeds of the Civil War were sown with the creation of the First Triumvirate. Three men – Crassus, Pompey, and Caesar – backed by their own armies, individually forced the Senate to do what they wanted (refer to Chapter 14). Their personal struggle for power became the most important force in the Roman world.

Crassus, the third member of the Triumvirate, was dead by 53 BC, and Caesar and Pompey were left in opposition to one another. Caesar and Pompey weren't enemies (yet), but they *were* rivals. By the late 50s BC, both men had *imperium:* the authority to command an army. The crucial issue of the day was whether Caesar or Pompey, or both, could be made to give up their commands. No-one, not Caesar or Pompey or their supporters, was prepared to back down.

Deadly deals

The crunch came in 50 BC when the consul Gaius Marcellus demanded Caesar's recall from Gaul. A bankrupt tribune called Scribonius Curio, whose support Caesar had bought at vast expense, vetoed Caesar's recall. Marcellus begged Pompey to save the Republic by using his army to bring pressure on Caesar to give up his command. Caesar offered a compromise: that both he and Pompey would give up their commands. The Senate rejected Caesar's offer because they thought Pompey needed his army to bring Caesar to heel. The Senate appointed new governors to the Gallic provinces. The Tribune Mark Antony tried to veto the new appointments but was threatened with his life and had to flee.

Even Cicero, who opposed the Triumvirate and was Caesar's enemy (refer to Chapter 14), tried to negotiate a deal, in which Caesar would go to Illyricum and Pompey to Spain. But the deal fell apart when the Senate granted Pompey the *Senatus Consultum Ultimum,* which gave Pompey the power to declare Caesar an enemy of the state and then get rid of him.

Crossing the Rubicon (50 BC)

The Rubicon is a river (now the Rigone) on the border between the Gallic provinces and Umbria in northern Italy. Caesar had been presented by the Senate with the option of giving himself up as an enemy of the state or of being taken by his enemies in Gaul. Caesar spent hours thinking about it and decided that he had nothing to lose. If he gave himself up to the Senate, he would have to stand trial in Rome and be condemned by a regime that had become corrupt.

Caesar did the unthinkable: In 49 BC, he took his troops from Gaul across the Rubicon and invaded Italy, an act that would be seen as a declaration of war against the Republic. This was the occasion of Caesar's famous phrase: _Iacta alea est_, 'The die is cast'.

Nowadays, the phrase 'crossing the Rubicon' is used to mean there's no going back, whatever the situation.

Cutting off Pompey at the head (48 BC)

If Caesar had had his own way, he would have preferred to negotiate power sharing with Pompey. Pompey, who tended to be indecisive, gave in to his advisors and turned down Caesar's offer of a compromise. Pompey made a bad decision amounting to a declaration of war, but Pompey's army wasn't anywhere ready. Caesar, however, was more than ready for war and hurtled down through Italy in barely two months. Pompey fell back with his soldiers, got away to the port of Brundisium (Brindisi), and shipped his army across the Adriatic to the safety of Greece.

Caesar takes Rome

Caesar had time on his side. Having planned his attack, he then seized Rome. Most of the senators had fled out of blind terror, but thanks to Caesar's rigid discipline over his troops, no looting, destruction, or murdering of opponents took place. Caesar kept his reputation for fair play intact. Caesar's other goodwill gestures included cancelling debts, bringing Italians into the Senate, and allowing back to Rome men who had been exiled by Sulla and Pompey. Caesar even recruited Pompey's soldiers who had been left behind in Rome.

African setback

Caesar's first setback came in Africa. A rebellion by the governor Attius Varus, a supporter of Pompey, was met by an army sent out by Caesar under the command of the ex-tribune Scribonius Curio. Curio had no serious military experience, and even worse, a large part of the army he'd been given was made up of Pompey's former soldiers. Curio was totally defeated. Caesar himself went to Pompey's province of Spain to fight Pompey's two deputies and defeated them in little over a month.

Pompey's plan

Meanwhile Pompey was busying himself building up a colossal army in Greece. He took Roman soldiers from frontier garrisons and ended up with a force that vastly outnumbered Caesar's. Pompey's plan was to reinvade Italy, but like most military schemes, it didn't work out. Caesar took his army over the Adriatic to Greece in 48 BC. The campaign started out badly for Caesar when he had to abandon the siege of Pompey's Adriatic base at Dyrrachium.

The Battle of Pharsalus 48 BC

Pompey could have invaded Italy without any trouble but decided instead that his real target was Caesar and chased him into Greece. Urged on by the Optimates (refer to Chapter 14) to end the conflict as fast as possible, Pompey drew up battle lines at Pharsalus in the heart of northern Greece. Caesar had 22,000 men, but Pompey had nearly 40,000.

Pharsalus was a disaster for Pompey. Caesar's infantry stood firm against Pompey's cavalry and stopped them in their tracks. Next, Caesar threw in his reserves and overwhelmed Pompey's army. Pompey fled to Egypt, and Caesar captured most of his army, having told his troops to 'spare your fellow citizens'. True to his honourable reputation, Caesar burned Pompey's papers without reading them.

The death of Pompey

Pompey's end was ignominious. He might have preferred the honourable option of suicide. He was murdered in Egypt by Pothinus and Achillas, two members of the Egyptian court of the pro-Caesar boy-King Ptolemy XIII. Caesar turned up in Egypt in hot pursuit of Pompey and was proudly shown Pompey's severed head. Ptolemy rather hoped that Caesar would support him in the dispute with his sister Cleopatra VII. He was wrong.

Caesar gets a girlfriend

Caesar was disgusted at Pompey's humiliating end and had Pothinus executed. Caesar placed Cleopatra VII on the Egyptian throne by giving the crown to her other brother Ptolemy XIV, whom she married (brother-sister marriages were normal for Egyptian rulers). Cleopatra was known to be intelligent, politically astute, and manipulative. But Caesar's action involved him in an Egyptian civil war. Fortunately for Caesar, Ptolemy was killed in an attempt to attack the tiny Roman force Caesar had brought with him. For good measure Cleopatra became Caesar's mistress and had a son by him.

Wiping out the remaining opposition

On the way to returning to Rome in 47 BC, Caesar had to settle trouble in Asia Minor. Pharnaces II, son of Mithridates and now King of Pontus, had given help to Pompey. Caesar crushed all opposition from Pharnaces in a high-speed five-day war. Caesar summed up his victory over Pharnaces in the immortal words: *Veni, vidi, vici*, 'I came, I saw, I conquered'.

In 46 BC Caesar defeated an army loyal to Pompey in Africa, the campaign ending in the bloody Battle of Thapsus. After the battle, one of Caesar's most die-hard enemies, Marcus Porcius Cato, who had been in charge of the garrison at Utica in Africa, committed suicide.

Marcus Porcius Cato

Marcus Porcius Cato (95–46 BC) was a direct descendant of Cato, the renowned veteran of the Second Punic War and champion of traditional Roman virtues, who a century before had insisted that Carthage must be destroyed (refer to Chapter 4 for information on Cato's works and Chapter 12 for details on the Second Punic War). Like his famous ancestor, Marcus Porcius Cato was a dedicated Stoic and was committed to personal integrity and intolerance of weaknesses in others. He was also a wholehearted supporter of the Optimates and their thinking (explained in Chapter 14) and therefore totally opposed Caesar.

Caesar: Leader of the Roman World

Caesar's victory in the civil war at the Battle of Pharsalus in 48 BC and the death of Pompey left him in sole charge of the Roman world. The Senate created Caesar Dictator for ten years. The responsibility for repairing the damage, restoring the Republic, settling veterans, and recreating law and order was all down to him. Caesar was determined to avoid the bloody reprisals that Sulla had carried out during his dictatorship (refer to Chapter 14). Caesar's impact on the Roman state was colossal and his reforms much more far-reaching than those of the previous century.

Caesar's new order

Caesar's reconstruction of the Republic was a model of restraint and foresight. He brought in practical solutions to restore stability in the Roman world, such as extending the Romanisation of the provinces by bringing provincials into the heart of the Roman system. Caesar's reforms included:

- ✔ Forgiving Pompey's supporters, even Caesar's arch-enemy Cicero, if they agreed to come over to Caesar.

- ✔ More than halving the number of Romans who depended on the free corn dole in order to cut the numbers of idle troublemakers. Those who were disqualified were transported to colonies overseas.

- ✔ Settling Caesar's veterans in overseas colonies.

- ✔ Setting up new colonies, such as Arles in France and Seville in Spain, and giving them Roman or Latin status.

- ✔ Awarding Roman citizenship to worthy provincial individuals, and cities and soldiers Caesar had recruited overseas.

✔ Admitting Italians, and even some Gauls, to the Senate, thus broadening the Senate's understanding of issues outside Rome.

✔ Improving road links to the port at Ostia.

✔ Giving Latin status to Transpadane Gaul.

✔ Cutting taxes and reforming collection in some provinces.

Caesar raised vast sums of money by taking land off supporters of Pompey who hadn't surrendered quickly enough, fining provincial cities that had supported Pompey, and selling privileges to eastern cities and kingdoms. The income allowed Caesar to provide handouts for his soldiers, put in place a programme of public building, and fund free public entertainments.

Hey, we didn't want a king! (44 BC)

Caesar was widely admired – not surprising really – for his reforms. Caesar had done more than anyone else to bring stability to the Roman world. The Senate believed Caesar was still going to operate within the Republican system.

But Caesar had other ideas, and with the army behind him, he could do as he pleased. He took over the job of Consul several times and the powers of a tribune. Caesar's actions went down badly with traditionalists, who thought he was trampling on the Republican system. Caesar's biggest mistake was to remind Romans of the city's ancient past. He packed the Senate with his own men and, because of this, did more or less whatever he wanted, saying his word was law.

The Julian calendar

One of Caesar's most enduring reforms was the calendar, which was named after him. The Julian calendar is still the basis of the one used today. The Roman year lasted 355 days with an odd month inserted after February to make it fit the sun's year. However, thanks to various extra days put in by priests, the whole thing became hopelessly unworkable. Caesar's solution was to make the year 365 days long and add an extra day every fourth year. His new calendar, which included a month named after him (July), lasted for centuries, until it was found that the calendar didn't quite match the earth's orbit round the sun. By 1582, the Julian calendar was ten days out. The new calendar devised by Pope Gregory XIII modified Caesar's leap year allowances to correct the error but wasn't introduced in Britain until 1752. It's the one we use now.

Caesar's talents and weaknesses

Caesar had an exceptional reputation for energy, vigour, and multitasking. He could read and write, or listen and dictate, at the same time. It was said that Caesar was able to dictate four letters at once if they were important, and seven if they weren't. He had reputedly fought 50 battles, a record, but was considered the most merciful of men – though it's unlikely the Gauls would have agreed with that. Apart from vanity and a weakness for women, Caesar also suffered from epilepsy. He had a fit during the Battle of Thapsus in 46 BC. Several Roman historians refer to his condition, which probably got worse in later life.

But Caesar let his achievements go to his head. He allowed a statue of himself to be carried with those of gods at the beginning of games and another statue of himself to be placed with those of the kings, and he issued coins with his portrait on them. Even his reform of the calendar only made some men resent his power more. In 44 BC, Caesar was made *Dictator Perpetuus* (Dictator for Life), and to make sure everyone knew this, he accepted the offer of a gilt throne in the Senate house, a triumphal robe, and laurel crown. When he was once hailed as King he said, 'I am Caesar and not King', but the mud stuck.

The fatal blow (44 BC)

Most of the Roman population only wanted stability and leadership; they probably didn't care how Caesar went about it. Caesar's reforms were practical solutions to years of chaos. But many senators were angry and didn't want change – they wanted the Republic restored to the original way of working. Cicero called Caesar a tyrant, and the idea spread rapidly. Caesar was now so convinced of his invincibility that he felt he had no need of a bodyguard. He was planning a war against Parthia, and his supporters even put it about that there was a prophecy that only a Roman king could defeat Parthia.

Caesar's enemies knew he was leaving on 18 March 44 BC and would be out of their reach – they had to strike while the iron was hot. A motley collection of patriots plotted to kill Caesar in March 44 BC. Some, like Cassius and Brutus, were supporters of Pompey pardoned by Caesar. Others had personal grievances, but there were men who were still faithful to Caesar. Cassius wanted Mark Antony killed as well, but Brutus refused.

Omens of Caesar's death

The Romans loved the idea of bad and good omens and especially liked to watch out for clues that bad things were coming. Caesar is said to have sacrificed an animal that turned out to have no heart, but much more ominously a soothsayer warned that some great danger would come to him not later than the Ides of March. The night before the Ides of March, Caesar had a dream he was in heaven, and on the morning of 15 March, he hesitated to go out. But he did and was even handed a note warning him of an impending disaster. Caesar didn't read the note and was brutally assassinated. Just after Caesar's death, Caesar's great-nephew, the emperor Augustus, saw a comet during the games he was holding to honour Venus. Augustus later built a temple in the comet's honour.

Marcus Junius Brutus was descended from Lucius Junius Brutus, leader of the conspiracy to throw Tarquinius Superbus off the Roman throne (refer to Chapter 10) and credited with founding the original Roman Republic. This probably explains why the young Brutus was dedicated to the ideals of the Roman Republic. For example, although Brutus hated Pompey for killing his father, Brutus went over to Pompey, believing that Pompey was a greater Republican patriot than Caesar, and he fought for Pompey at Pharsalus. Brutus had other reasons to hate Caesar: Amongst Caesar's many female conquests was Brutus's mother Servilia Caepionis (half-sister of Caesar's sworn enemy Marcus Porcius Cato; for him, see the earlier sidebar by the same name) and his sister Junia Tertia, supplied by her mother for Caesar's pleasure. Others included Crassus's wife Tertulla and Pompey's wife Mucia.

In Rome, on the Ides of March 44 BC (15 March), Caesar arrived at a Senate meeting at a hall just next door to the great stone theatre built by Pompey – a classic twist of fate. The conspirators pounced on Caesar and stabbed him 23 times.

A hideous mistake and the rise of Mark Antony

Caesar's murderers thought that they had liberated the people from a tyrant and would be welcomed as the saviours of the Republic. The murderers made the mistake of assuming that the clock could be turned back and the Republic could once again operate in the way it was set up back in 509 BC. They thought wrong. Brutus planned to give a speech justifying Caesar's assassination, but the senators had all cleared off. Instead of cheering crowds, the conspirators found the Forum deserted. The conspirators marched through the streets brandishing their weapons and, protected by a band of gladiators, hid out on the Capitol.

Caesar's colleague in the consulship, Mark Antony, took charge, much to Cicero's regret (Cicero thought Antony should have been killed, too). Cicero hated the way Caesar had been behaving and was utterly delighted at the news of the assassination, but thought it was a wasted opportunity because Antony took over instead.

Antony and Caesar went back a long way: Antony had been on Caesar's staff during the war in Gaul, defended Caesar's interests when Antony became tribune in 49 BC, and commanded part of Caesar's army at Pharsalus.

To please those who had supported Caesar, Antony persuaded the Senate to pass any outstanding legislation of Caesar's and to approve an amnesty for the conspirators, suggested by Cicero. Antony also asked the Senate to vote for a public funeral for Caesar.

Caesar's funeral turned into a public frenzy. The crowd went crazy at the sight of Caesar's body and ransacked the Forum for anything that could be set alight. The crowd then lynched someone they thought was a conspirator (an act of mistaken identity), and some of the crowd raced to where Brutus and Cassius lived and tried to kill them. Brutus and Cassius fled Rome.

Et tu Brute?

The story goes that Caesar said *Et tu Brute?* ('And you, Brutus?') when faced with his murderers. The original source of the story is in Suetonius's *Life of Julius Caesar.* Caesar spoke in Greek, using the words *Kai su teknon,* which means 'You also, my child?' William Shakespeare changed the phrase to *Et tu Brute* for his play *Julius Caesar* (Act III, Scene I).

But whether you hear the words in Latin or Greek, the meaning is the same: Brutus was Caesar's old friend, but now one of his assassins. So what exactly was the relationship between Caesar and Brutus? When Pompey's troops, including Brutus, were defeated at Pharsalus,

Caesar ordered his troops not to kill Brutus because of Caesar's fondness for Brutus's mother Servilia, with whom he had had an affair. Caesar was uneasy about where Brutus's loyalties lay, but he made him a friend and supported his career, making Brutus Praetor in 44 BC.

And what of Brutus's character? Was he the idealistic Republican of literature? Well, yes, but he was also ruthless. Case in point: Brutus got himself a special exemption from a cap on interest rates and then lent money at a ruinous 48 per cent to the people of Salamis. Brutus enforced repayments by murdering city councillors.

Picking Caesar's heir: Mark Antony or Octavian?

Mark Antony managed to stabilise a potentially disastrous situation after Caesar's murder. He deliberately allowed the conspirators to escape, found land for Caesar's veterans to keep them away from Rome, and arranged for the abolition of the dictatorship. Antony made Brutus and Cassius Governors of provinces. Brutus and Cassius took exception to this treatment, but Antony threatened them and they fled to the East. However, Brutus and Cassius were awarded *maius imperium* (an enhanced form of the military command, *imperium*) by the Senate, giving them power over provincial governors. Brutus and Cassius helped themselves to all the resources Caesar had put in place for his campaign in Parthia, imposed ruthless taxation, and set about building themselves an army.

Not everything was going Antony's way. In Rome, the Senate objected to the way Antony was spending money and selling privileges and immunities using forged documents, which he claimed were Caesar's. And Caesar's great-nephew, Gaius Octavius – and not Antony – was named as Caesar's heir.

Octavian's relationship to Julius Caesar is complicated but important. Julius Caesar's sister Julia married Marcus Atius Balbus, a relative of Pompey's. Julia and Marcus's daughter Atia married Gaius Octavius, who died in 58 BC. Atia and Octavius had a son born in 63 BC, who was Caesar's great-nephew: Gaius Octavius with the addition of the name Thurinus to commemorate Thurii where his family had come from. Gaius Octavius Thurinus became known as Octavianus, and we call him Octavian.

Caesar named Octavian as his heir in his will and Octavian was adopted as Caesar's son. (Caesar had a son of his own by Cleopatra, called Caesarion. When Caesar died, Caesarion, who Octavian was to deal with later, was still alive in Egypt with Cleopatra.) The 18-year-old Octavian was in Epirus (northwest Greece) on military training when he heard he was Caesar's heir, and promptly came to Rome to claim his inheritance.

The history of the last 70-odd years of the Republic has been all about the careers of a few key men: Marius, Sulla, Crassus, Pompey, and Caesar. They'd totally dominated Roman politics and war. They had all challenged the fundamental principle of the Roman Republic: That no-one was supposed to have permanent political power. Caesar had overturned that principle, and the Republic had teetered on the brink of being ruled by a monarch and a tyrant. Caesar's mightiness was the cause of his downfall. The Republic was to last for just a few more years till 43 BC and the course of world history changed.

Octavian and the End of the Republic (44–43 BC)

Octavian arrived in Rome and changed his name to Gaius Julius Caesar Octavianus, knowing this was the best way to win over Caesar's troops. Octavian was annoyed to discover that Mark Antony had been merrily spending Caesar's private fortune, as well as any public funds he had been able to get his hands on. Octavian now had to raise the money that Caesar had left as a bequest to his troops. Octavian and Antony were instantly locked in a deadly feud.

The tense situation was made worse when Cicero interfered by issuing the First and Second Philippics, (a *Philippic* was a bitter critique, and comes from the Greek orator Demosthenes's criticisms of Philip II of Macedon in the fourth century BC). Cicero slated Antony for being an opportunist who had all Caesar's criminal ambitions, but none of Caesar's skills and restraint. Cicero praised Antony for getting rid of the dictatorship, but cursed Antony for turning government into 'monstrous marketing', and for protecting himself with a band of thugs against honest men.

Meanwhile, Antony had himself made governor in Gaul and planned to move troops from Macedonia into Gaul. Antony accused Octavian of plotting to assassinate him, which led Octavian to call on Caesar's old troops to come and join him.

Back in Rome, in 43 BC, Cicero continued to stir things up by unveiling his plans to undo Antony's legislation, just when Antony was planning to attack Brutus at Mutina in northern Italy. Antony offered not to go to war if his laws were left alone, but Antony's offer was rejected, and the Senate declared him a public enemy.

By now Octavian was approaching with his army, so Antony pulled back and joined forces with the governors of Gaul and Spain.

Octavian fell out with the Senate, who wanted him to become an ally of Brutus. The last thing Octavian was ever going to do was work with the murderers of Caesar. The Senate punished Octavian by holding back money for the troops. Octavian's answer was to march into Rome, have himself elected Consul, and cancel the amnesty for Caesar's killers.

Brutus and Cassius had their own armies so civil war was inevitable. Ever practical, Octavian could see that feuding with Antony wasn't going to help. Octavian saw that the time had come to strike a deal with Antony.

The second Gang of Three: The Second Triumvirate (43 BC)

Octavian met Antony, together with Marcus Aemilius Lepidus, the Governor of Spain. Lepidus had gone over to Antony's side, but had also negotiated to come back to Octavian. The three men made a five-year legal pact known to history as the Second Triumvirate, so unlike the First Triumvirate this one was official. The power of the Second Triumvirate made the Senate no more than a rubber stamp. Octavian, Antony, and Lepidus could appoint magistrates, and more importantly, they had the absolute freedom to go to war whenever they wanted. The law creating the Second Triumvirate was passed on 27 November 43 BC and marked the end of the Roman Republic, though no-one realised it at the time.

Blood, guts, and gods

The Second Triumvirate was bathed in blood from the start. Octavian, Antony, and Lepidus drew up a list of 300 senators and 2,000 equestrians who had been supporters of Caesar's assassination and, apart from a few lucky ones, massacred them. The Triumvirate's action wasn't just about fear of their opponents. Octavian, Antony, and Lepidus had 43 legions between them, and by confiscating the estates of the massacred senators and equestrians they could pay the troops. The money wasn't enough though, and the Triumvirate had to impose heavy taxes as well.

Cicero's Second Philippic to Antony was Cicero writing his own death warrant. Octavian spent two days trying to persuade Antony to let Cicero live, but Antony refused to listen. Cicero toyed with the idea of escaping to Greece, but decided to accept his fate. Cicero was caught in his villa and murdered. His head and hands were carried to Rome and Antony displayed them in the Forum, declaring the punishment of Caesar's supporters had now ended.

Octavian upstaged Antony and Lepidus by proclaiming his close relationship to the great god, Caesar. In 42 BC Julius Caesar had been created a god and a temple was built in his honour. As Caesar's adopted son, Octavian was able to bask in Caesar's fame – without any danger of being accused of thinking he, Octavian, was a god.

The Battle of Philippi

Octavian, Antony, and Lepidus split the Roman Empire between them. Octavian had Sicily, Sardinia, and Africa; Lepidus had Spain and part of Gaul; and Antony the rest of Gaul. All three shared Italy, and Octavian, Antony, and

Lepidus joined together with the common purpose of recovering the East from Brutus and Cassius.

In 42 BC Antony and Octavian left Lepidus in charge of Italy and set out for Greece, determined to wipe out Brutus and Cassius. At the Battle of Philippi, Antony took command because Octavian wasn't much of a general. In the first engagement Antony overcame Cassius's troops and Cassius committed suicide. In the second engagement, three weeks later, Brutus also took his own life after being defeated by Antony.

Octavian had never enjoyed good health. After the Battle of Philippi Octavian was said to have spent three days sick in a marsh with dropsy.

The bust up starts

The Second Triumvirate was made up of three ambitious men so they were bound to fall out. Antony was the main player in the Triumvirate because he had done all the fighting at Philippi. Antony and Octavian packed Lepidus (whom they had previously left in charge of Italy) off to Africa, accused him of disloyalty, and helped themselves to his provinces. Octavian was left to take care of Italy while Antony headed east to build himself an empire. Octavian planned to settle his own veterans on lands he had confiscated in Italy. But Octavian's plans were frustrated by Antony's family, who promised the people whose lands Octavian had taken that Antony would soon be back to restore the Republic.

Antony returned to Italy in 40 BC. Refused entry by Octavian's forces, he blockaded the port of Brundisium in retaliation. War almost broke out, but realising this wouldn't help anyone, the three triumvirs decided to join forces once again. Octavian suppressed revolts in Gaul and even settled some of his soldiers there. In 38 BC Antony helped Octavian defeat Pompey's son Sextus, who was leading a rebellion in Sicily. The Second Triumvirate was renewed for another five years, and then Octavian showed his true colours and had Lepidus driven out from the Triumvirate. Octavian followed this up by fighting his way into the East down through Illyricum.

As you can imagine, with Octavian and Antony left fighting for power the situation just got worse and worse.

Antony and Cleopatra

Antony's big problem was recovering Rome's eastern possessions. The Parthians had invaded Syria and most of Asia Minor. Although they were driven back, Antony also wanted to carry out the invasion of Parthia that Caesar had been planning just before his murder.

Antony met Cleopatra, queen of Egypt, while preparing to invade Parthia (refer to the section 'Caesar gets a girlfriend', earlier in the chapter). Antony demanded Cleopatra's presence to explain why she had supported Cassius. Cleopatra arrived on a magnificent boat, dressed as Venus, and Antony was completely bowled over. Cleopatra had charm, intelligence, could speak numerous languages, and, of course, had plenty of sex appeal.

To complicate matters Antony had married Octavia, Octavian's sister, in 40 BC, as a way of settling the differences between Octavian and himself. The idea for the marriage came from Octavia herself. But Antony left Octavia and their children behind when he went back to the East. Antony met up with Cleopatra in Syria in 37 BC – Antony couldn't resist Cleopatra; they fell deeply in love and had children together.

Antony went on to recover most of Rome's eastern territories, but when Antony invaded Parthia in 36 BC he was trapped and had to beat a hasty retreat, losing 22,000 soldiers, although he was left with most of his army. With his forces depleted and his money disappearing, Antony became totally dependent on Cleopatra's resources. In 35 BC, Antony divorced Octavia, which meant that he had cut himself off from Octavian as well.

Throwing down the gauntlet

In 34 BC, Antony held a triumph in Alexandria where he declared Caesarion, Cleopatra's son by Caesar, to be the true heir of Julius Caesar. Sometime around 33 BC Antony had agreed to marry Cleopatra. Antony's action was a blatant insult to Octavia, whom he did not divorce until the next year. Antony set about expanding Cleopatra's kingdom by unilaterally dividing up Roman and other territory in the East amongst Cleopatra's children, which threatened the strength of the Roman Empire.

In 32 BC, Antony and Cleopatra issued a coin with Antony's portrait on one side and Cleopatra's on the other. Cleopatra's legend read 'Queen of Kings, and of her sons who are Kings', a clear statement of Antony and Cleopatra's ambitions, and a direct challenge to Octavian.

The Battle of Actium (31 BC)

The Second Triumvirate broke up in 33 BC. Octavian instantly abandoned his title and powers, and drove out the consuls and 300 senators who had planned to condemn him. The consuls and senators left to join Antony, but a rumour blew up that Antony was planning to make Cleopatra queen of Rome, and rule the Roman Empire from Egypt.

Antony's silver

Mark Antony issued vast numbers of silver coins in order to pay his troops. Each coin had a picture of a war galley on one side, and a legionary standard with a legion's number on the other (coins were issued for each of Antony's legions). To make Antony's silver go further, the coins were debased with more copper than usual. The value of the coins was reduced, making the coins less useful for melting down or saving. Because the coins weren't all that valuable, Antony's coins were in circulation for hundreds of years after his death, and turned up all round the Roman Empire. Today, Antony's coins are common and relatively cheap in the coin-collecting market.

Octavian's next step was to publish Antony's will (there was no proof that it was genuine), which reaffirmed Cleopatra's son Caesarion as Caesar's true heir. Roman cities across the West promptly swore allegiance to Octavian, who took this as approval that he could go to war against Antony. In 31 BC Octavian was made Consul, and he got the Senate to declare war against Antony and Cleopatra, who were now in Greece.

Antony and Cleopatra defeated

Antony and Cleopatra were at Actium on the north-west coast of Greece with their fleet. Octavian's admiral and friend, Marcus Vipsanius Agrippa, used the fleet to cut off Antony's supplies. Octavian's army wore Antony's soldiers down. On 2 September 31 BC Antony tried to slip away with a force of 200 ships. Cleopatra escaped with 60 ships, and Antony followed her but with only a few more vessels. The rest of Antony's fleet, and the remains of Antony's army, quickly surrendered to Octavian.

Antony and Cleopatra made their way back to Egypt. But they knew the game was up and committed suicide.

The aftermath

Octavian spared Antony's children by Cleopatra but had his own cousin Caesarion killed. Egypt now became a Roman province after being an independent state in the ancient world for 3,000 years, but a special one because it was Octavian's personal property and was passed down to the emperors who succeeded him. As Octavian was now undisputed master of the Roman Empire, no-one was in a position to argue the toss.

Chapter 16

Augustus and the Caesars – Plots, Perverts, and Paranoia

· ·

In This Chapter

▶ How Augustus created his own unique version of the Republic

▶ Why Tiberius, Caligula, Claudius, and Nero nearly destroyed the Empire

▶ How the Empire came to have four new rulers in one year

▶ Vespasian's restoration of the Empire

▶ How the Flavians made the Empire stronger

· ·

*A*fter the Battle of Actium in 31 BC (refer to Chapter 15), the government of the Republic was in tatters. Men like Marius, Sulla, and Caesar had destroyed the prestige and power of the Senate and Rome's nobility. Rome had grown too powerful, had too many possessions, and needed powerful leadership, yet the rulers of the previous century had pursued their own ambitions and, far from creating stability, had undermined the stability of the Roman world. One thing was certain, no-one wanted to go back to a monarchy.

One of the most famous books written by a Roman historian is the *Twelve Caesars* by Gaius Suetonius Tranquillus. Starting with the life of Julius Caesar, it continues with biographies of the first 11 emperors up to AD 96. The first five emperors (Augustus, Tiberius, Caligula, Claudius, and Nero) were members of the Julio-Claudian dynasty, which means they were all linked by family connections to Julius Caesar and Tiberius's father, Tiberius Claudius Nero. The next three (Galba, Otho, and Vitellius) were short-lived emperors of the civil war of AD 68–69, and were followed by the three emperors of the Flavian dynasty: Vespasian and his sons, Titus, and Domitian. The rule of the 11 emperors covers one of the most dramatic and decisive periods in Roman history.

Augustus (aka Octavian) and His Powers

Octavian arrived in Rome from Egypt in 29 BC absolutely unchallenged. His enemies were all dead. He controlled the whole Roman army. He had seized Egypt's riches. What's more, so much time had passed that no-one could remember the Republic working properly. Octavian could have become a power-crazed megalomaniac tyrant, but he didn't – and that's one of the most remarkable things about his rule.

Restoring the Republic

Octavian had a dilemma. If he gave up command of the army or shared it with anyone else, then he risked a return to more civil war. If he held onto his control, then he was flying in the face of the Republican tradition of outlawing permanent political power in the hands of one man. And he knew what had happened to Caesar.

Octavian had to find a solution. He returned to Rome, was elected Consul, and set to work. He also:

- ✔ Restored the institutions of the Republic, but under his direction, giving him complete control of the army and foreign policy

- ✔ Discharged some of his troops, gave them land, and cancelled anything illegal he'd done in the preceding years of war

- ✔ Placed day-to-day government of non-military affairs under the control of senators and the equestrians

- ✔ Got rid of unsuitable senators and came up with a list of qualifications for entry to the Senate: military service, personal qualities, and financial standing

During these first few years, Octavian ruled in a strictly unofficial way, biding his time and working out the best things to do. He got away with it because of his personal prestige and because everyone was exhausted by the chaos. He also had two extremely important friends who helped him:

- ✔ **Maecenas:** Gaius Maecenas (died 8 BC) was an equestrian and had been at the Battle of Philippi with Octavian. In 40 BC, Maecenas negotiated the settlement with Antony at Brundisium. Maecenas was often left in control of Rome during the 30s BC. His relationship with Octavian cooled in later years, because Maecenas's wife became Octavian's mistress; however, he still left his old friend Octavian all his property in his will. Maecenas was a great patron of poets and writers, and it's thanks to him that the influential propaganda poetry of Virgil and Horace praised Octavian's rule.

✔ **Agrippa:** Marcus Vipsanius Agrippa (64–13 BC) came to Rome with Octavian when Octavian claimed his inheritance after Caesar's death. Agrippa was a brilliant soldier and naval tactician, responsible for most of Octavian's military successes. Not only did Agrippa manage Italy together with Maecenas, but Agrippa was also given control of the East and later solved problems in Gaul as well. He spent lavishly on public building projects in Rome. Agrippa married Octavian's daughter Julia. Down that line, the Emperors Caligula (AD 37–41) and Nero (AD 54–68) were descended from both Agrippa and Octavian. The most remarkable thing about Agrippa is that, despite being so able, he always put Octavian's career first.

Octavian's wife Livia (58 BC–AD 29) was another important person in Octavian's life. His first wife, Scribonia, was Julia's mother, but Octavian divorced Scribonia in 39 BC, claiming he couldn't get on with her. In 38 BC, Octavian married Livia, wife of a Pompeian supporter called Tiberius Claudius Nero, in order to cement political ties with potential opponents. Octavian even got Livia to divorce her own husband to marry him. Octavian adopted Livia's son Tiberius as his heir, but Octavian and Livia had no children of their own.

The Emperor who wasn't an Emperor

In 27 BC, Octavian gave up all his powers and all his provinces to the Senate and to the people of Rome. The Senate and the people of Rome promptly (and tactfully) gave most of the power and territory back to Octavian. Octavian now held his powers as a gift from the Senate and the Roman people. It was a brilliant move: Octavian's tactic had made him the legally elected Emperor and, more importantly, the legal holder of supreme power.

Octavian was re-elected Consul annually until 23 BC. He was given control of the provinces of Spain, Gaul, and Syria with the power of *imperium* (refer to Chapter 3 for the significance of this title) and was allowed to assign the imperium to his representatives (known as *legati* – from which we get our word 'delegate') in those provinces. Octavian also held Egypt as his own property. Governors of other Roman provinces (*proconsuls;* see Chapter 3) were appointed by the Senate. The Senate became a law court.

Becoming Augustus

In 27 BC, Octavian's name was changed to Augustus (meaning 'venerable'). It was a symbolic gesture that proclaimed his status. During his reign, Octavian had acquired several titles, showing his power and position. The titles include *princeps, imperator,* and *pater patriae* (from 2 BC), reinforced by personal qualities such as *dignitas* and *auctoritas.* (The titles apply to all emperors to a greater or lesser degree; you can find them explained in more detail in Chapter 3.)

To let things settle down, Augustus left Rome for nearly three years to attend to Gaul, and campaign in Spain. Soon after returning to Rome in 23 BC, Augustus fell seriously ill, and the year went from bad to worse. Augustus's nephew and intended heir Marcellus died, leaving his wife Julia (Augustus's daughter) a widow. Augustus briefly made Agrippa his successor in place of Marcellus. Agrippa divorced his second wife and married Augustus's daughter Julia to ensure the line of succession from Augustus. But Agrippa's early death in 13 BC, and the deaths of Agrippa's sons by Julia, ruined Augustus's plans (see the section 'A son, a son! My kingdom for a son!', later in this chapter).

Defender of the people – Populares methods for an Optimate

Augustus made some clever moves. He gave up the consulship after 23 BC for the time being (he held it twice more, in 5 BC and 2 BC). In return, the Senate each year made Augustus Tribune of the Plebs for the rest of his life. He was now firmly established as the representative of the people, with the power to summon the Senate, propose legislation, and veto any laws that he thought not in the people's interest. Augustus also had the right to nominate candidates to magistracies, and the imperium over his provinces was renewed. Being a noble, Augustus belonged to the *Optimates,* but by acting as the defender of the people he had adopted *Populares* ways of operating (refer to Chapter 14 for the distinction between Optimates and Populares). Augustus's position made him popular with the people, though in reality the plebs had even less power than they had ever had.

Augustus's political genius

With patience, tact, and diplomacy, Augustus had made himself an elected official of the state, subject to the law, with powers given to him by the Senate and the people. What is remarkable is that the principles of the Roman Republic had been upheld, while at the same time, Augustus, with the approval of the Senate and the people, held all the offices of state in his own hands.

Imagine if the President of the United States was also the Chief Justice of the Supreme Court and the leading member of the majority party in both the Senate and the House of Representatives – with everyone accepting that the Constitution of the United States was still functioning legally. You get the picture. Augustus's rule worked because he didn't abuse his exceptional powers. Unfortunately, not all of Augustus's successors were as trustworthy.

Augustus: The radical conservative

Augustus was a true conservative. He made changes, but at the same time Augustus wanted the people to believe he was keeping to the old ways.

Augustus used his powers to encourage all sorts of traditional values, such as encouraging men to wear togas. He passed laws against adultery and bribery, and men and women who failed to marry were barred from receiving inheritances, even though this was unpopular. Augustus's conservatism even went as far as being reluctant to give citizenship to non-Latins, and he placed a limit on the freeing of slaves.

Augustus enhanced the Roman religion by increasing the number of priests and reviving old rites. Augustus also:

- ✔ Built and restored temples
- ✔ Revived the night-time Saecular Games, for young people
- ✔ Made himself *Pontifex Maximus* ('Chief Priest') in 12 BC
- ✔ Revived in 11 BC the office of *flamen dialis,* 'priest of Jupiter' (from Diespiter 'Day father', another name for Jupiter)

Augustus set about reviving Roman religious customs, not because he especially wanted to restore Roman religious faith, but because it was a way of strengthening Rome's image and political status. With help from his friend Maecenas, Augustus encouraged writers to set down the myths and legends of Rome's origins. Virgil's *Aeneid* not only tells the story of Aeneas's adventures, but also presents Rome's destiny, reinforcing Aeneas's descent from Venus, a lineage claimed by Julius Caesar and Augustus himself (refer to Chapter 1 for more on Virgil).

How the Aeneid survived

When the poet Virgil died, he left instructions that the *Aeneid,* his great poem about the foundation of Rome, which foretold the coming of Augustus, be burned. Augustus, knowing the propaganda value of the *Aeneid,* ignored Virgil's will. Thereafter, generations of Roman schoolchildren memorised passages from the *Aeneid* as part of their reading and writing instruction, and quotations from Virgil's epic poem entered everyday speech, much as William Shakespeare's work has influenced modern English. Manuscripts of the *Aeneid* survived and were copied by early Christian monks in the fourth and fifth centuries AD. Preserved in monasteries, these copies formed the basis of some of the first printed editions in the fifteenth century. Today, the *Aeneid* is widely available in its original Latin and numerous other languages around the world.

Coinage

Augustus knew the importance of coinage as a way of publicising his regime. Until Caesar's time, coinage had mostly only portrayed gods. Augustus issued hundreds of different types of coins, many with his likeness and featuring various appropriate virtues and subjects. There was the comet type – featuring Augustus's head on one side and the comet that appeared after Caesar's assassination in 44 BC on the other. Another coin issued was the 'For preserving the citizens' type – with the legend *Ob Cives Servatos.* Augustus's coins circulated throughout the Roman Empire and beyond. It was the first major advertising campaign in history.

Finding it brick and leaving it marble

Augustus understood perfectly the importance of a public image. Although he had been a good-looking young man, he wasn't especially tall. He was said to be spotty, had various birthmarks, a limp, and suffered from bladder stones and a variety of serious illnesses. Rome had suffered, too, and needed a thorough restyling.

The ever youthful Augustus

Statues of Augustus portray him as a handsome, imposing, and vigorous warrior. Like all the greatest heroes, Augustus never aged. By the end of his reign, in his late 70s, no statue or coin had ever shown him as an old man. It was a trick that rulers often used. Queen Victoria (1837–1901) issued coins for the first 50 years of her reign, with the same youthful portrait, until advancing age and photography made it impossible for her to get away with it. Augustus was luckier. Most people in the Roman Empire had never seen him, so he was eternally youthful in their imaginations.

Rebuilding Rome

Like Augustus, Rome needed updating. Augustus spent a huge amount of money on improving the city. He increased the number of officials looking after public buildings and services. This meant hiring large numbers of equestrians to take charge of the many jobs in finance and administration, as well as using freedmen and slaves to do the routine administrative and clerical work. Augustus created what could be called a civil service. Rome was the Washington DC or Whitehall of its day.

Augustus's proudest boast was that he had found Rome a city built of brick and left it made of marble. It was a bit of an exaggeration, but Augustus was responsible, with Agrippa, for constructing a number of magnificent public buildings that can still be seen today. Augustus and Agrippa also introduced a sort of combination fire brigade and police force *(Vigiles),* and put on more public entertainments than ever before. You can find details of what Augustus and Agrippa achieved in Chapter 6.

Sorting out the borders

Rome's wealth and prestige depended on the existence of the Empire, which provided the money and resources for turning Rome into a fabled city of marble and the proof of Rome's superiority as a military, political, religious, and moral power. So keeping it in order was a vital part of Augustus's work.

Taxing business

Augustus had to pay out large sums of money to his veterans but had huge reserves from legacies and money he'd confiscated in the provinces, especially Egypt. Taxation was another source of income, but here Augustus had to tread carefully. Antony, Brutus, and Cassius had overdone taxation to fund their wars, and look where they ended up.

Administrative reform was essential. Because of this, Augustus ordered a census (the same census written about in the New Testament at the time of the birth of Christ in Judaea). Augustus introduced a land tax *(tributum soli)* and a poll or property tax *(tributum capitis);* however, Italy and Roman citizens were exempt from the land tax and probably the poll tax. Taxes were also imposed on goods at borders, based on a percentage of the value of goods. Augustus set up a fund for retired soldiers, giving soldiers a lump sum, and he paid for it by imposing sales taxes and death duties. In his own imperial provinces, Augustus appointed equestrians as *procurators* (financial managers) to look after his personal property (as his province of Egypt was governed by an equestrian; see Chapter 3 for the role of procurators).

Colonies

In Italy, Augustus set up 28 Roman colonies alone, like Turin, and provided each one with public buildings, rights, and constitutions, really making them into mini-Romes. Cities like these could now provide new recruits to Rome's senators and equestrians. Roads were rebuilt and repaired to maintain communications with Rome. A police force was created to deal with bandits who infested the countryside. The net result was that Rome and Italy became really two halves of the same being.

The frontiers

Augustus was determined to make the Empire's frontiers strong and secure. He had no plans to conquer more territory, because Rome already had the wealthy (and conquerable) places under her control. Not only that, he also knew that if he gave a man an army and told him to conquer somewhere, then that man had all the resources he needed to challenge Augustus.

Egypt's southern borders were made safe in 22 BC after war with the Ethiopians. Fighting in Arabia gave the Romans commercial access to the Red Sea and the Indian Ocean, and Augustus was rewarded for his involvement in the area by visits from Indian ambassadors. In Asia Minor, eastern mountain robbers were beaten off and colonies established.

Augustus and his immediate successors made use of *client kings* – tame rulers in strategically important locations around the Empire whose territories made a convenient buffer zone between potential enemies of Roman territory. Client kings could rely on Roman military support in return for their loyalty; in the East, for example, client kings helped Rome by protecting the frontier with Parthia. Yet client kings weren't always reliable and could change sides without warning.

North-western Europe

North-western Europe was a different problem. In 19 BC in Spain, Agrippa finally defeated the mountainous tribes, founded colonies, and set up a permanent garrison in Spain. Gaul remained peaceful, but unlike Greece and Asia, Gaul needed to be equipped with all the trappings of a Roman province, which meant creating administrative districts, building roads, and constructing public buildings. Gaul had become so settled that Augustus established a mint at Lugdunum (Lyons) in 15 BC, which became the main source of silver and gold coins for the next half century.

Britain still lay beyond the borders of the Roman world, but Augustus interfered in tribal politics to make sure pro-Roman rulers were in charge by subsidising them. Two British rulers even dashed to Rome for help from him in their dynastic feuds.

Augustus had much more trouble with Germany and the Rhine. German tribes constantly harried the Rhine frontier. Augustus authorised an invasion beyond the Rhine to push the frontier back farther. A series of wars began against the German tribes in 12 BC, led by Augustus's stepson, Drusus the Elder. Drusus died in 9 BC and his brother Tiberius continued the wars. By AD 5, Germany was largely under Roman control, but there was a long way to go before the area could be called a Roman province.

The disaster of AD 9

It's beginning to read as if Augustus was a one-stop brilliant success story. He wasn't. Frontier control went spectacularly wrong in the year AD 9. Augustus sent out a Governor called Publius Quinctilius Varus to Germany. Varus was tactless and high-handed. He tried to impose taxation and Roman jurisdiction. Varus's actions led to a revolt by a chieftain called Arminius, who had actually been fighting in the Roman army and even been made an equestrian.

Arminius fell back into the forests, and like a fool, Varus followed him right into the trap. Deep in the Teutoburg Forest, Arminius pounced on Varus and wiped out three legions (the XVII, XVIII, and XIX) in one fell swoop. Augustus was devastated but had to make instant preparations against riots in Rome and allies defecting.

On hearing the news from Germany, Augustus was plunged into despair; *Quinctili Vare, legiones redde,* 'Quinctilius Varus, give me back my legions!' he wailed.

In AD 14, an army of revenge was sent out under Tiberius, led by his nephew Germanicus, who found the forest littered with the remains of Varus's army; the soldiers had been massacred, and some were tortured to death. Germanicus pacified the region, as well as recovering the standards of the lost legions. But that was the end of any attempt to push the frontier beyond the Rhine.

A son, a son! My kingdom for a son!

Augustus was plagued by the problem of choosing an heir. Augustus's only child, by his first wife Scribonia, was Julia. Julia's first husband Marcellus had died in 23 BC, leaving no children. Augustus was left with three grandsons by Julia's second husband, Agrippa: Gaius, Lucius, and Agrippa Postumus – but they were all too young to be named as Augustus's heir.

Tiberius, Augustus's stepson by Livia, was the only male choice left. Augustus adopted Tiberius and forced Tiberius to divorce his wife Vipsania and marry Julia. Tiberius was furious because he loved his wife and cleared off to Rhodes for seven years; Tiberius had absolutely no desire to succeed Augustus.

Gaius and Lucius died in AD 2 and AD 4, and Agrippa Postumus was banished by Augustus for his bad behaviour. Augustus also banished Julia and her daughter, also called Julia, because of their immoral way of life. That left Tiberius as Augustus's only possible heir.

The deeds of a lifetime: The Res Gestae

As well as his will, instructions for his funeral, and a statement on the condition of the Empire, Augustus left a summary of his lifetime achievements, called the *Res Gestae.*

In the *Res Gestae,* Augustus proudly listed all the things he had done. These included:

✔ The wars he had fought to 'restore liberty to the Republic'

✔ His reform of the Senate

✔ The honours and triumphs given to him

✔ The gifts he had made to the people

✔ The temples and other buildings he had constructed

✔ The funding of public entertainments

✔ His settlement of the provinces

Augustus was bragging, but he was also telling the truth. No other document like the *Res Gestae* exists, which is as it should be, because no other Roman emperor like Augustus ever lived.

In AD 4, Tiberius adopted his nephew Germanicus, and the next year Germanicus married Augustus's granddaughter Agrippina, the sister of Gaius, Lucius, and Agrippa Postumus, and the banished Julia the Younger. Tiberius did inherit the Roman Empire, but the rest of the plan didn't quite work out (see 'Tiberius – part good, part bad, part pervert').

Augustus's death

Augustus died peacefully at the age of 75 on 19 August AD 14. Not many of Augustus's successors enjoyed such a long life or were lucky enough to have a peaceful death.

Augustus is phenomenally important in Roman history because, almost single-handedly, he created a political system that lasted. Augustus was widely worshipped after his death, both publicly and privately. His successors tried to live up to him. From now on, the reigning emperor would be known as the *Imperator Augustus;* later on, an emperor's successor would be known as the *Caesar.* The most difficult thing Augustus tried to do was to establish a secure line of succession – but that was beyond even his control!

Augustus's Dynasty: Tiberius, Caligula, Claudius, and Nero (AD 14–68)

Augustus was followed by four Emperors who all belonged to the Julio-Claudian dynasty: Tiberius, Caligula, Claudius, and Nero. The last three, like Augustus, were all descended from Julius Caesar's sister Julia (that's the Julio- bit), while Tiberius was brought in by adoption when Augustus married his mother Livia. Tiberius, Caligula, Claudius, and Nero were also descended from Tiberius's father Tiberius Claudius Nero (the last three via Tiberius's brother Drusus, making the Claudian bit).

Whatever their pedigree, if you believe the Roman historians Tacitus and Suetonius, the four emperors were nothing but megalomaniacs and perverts. Up to a point, Tacitus and Suetonius were right, although they weren't altogether fair. Tiberius and Claudius had their excesses but were actually quite good rulers. Even Caligula and Nero had their better moments. But the bad things the four emperors did angered people, and many wanted to see the old style Republic restored – not just Augustus's version of it.

Tiberius – part good, part bad, part pervert (AD 14–37)

Tiberius never wanted to be Emperor. He resented having to divorce his wife Vipsania in 12 BC and marry Augustus's ghastly daughter Julia (later exiled for immoral behaviour). Tiberius spent a large part of Augustus's reign knowing perfectly well that Augustus would have preferred the succession to pass to Augustus's own grandsons, Gaius and Lucius, who had died young.

Augustus had groomed Tiberius for the succession by allowing him to share some of his own jobs. While he was alive, Augustus made Tiberius a tribune and also gave him the imperium. Tiberius won for himself a great military reputation, thanks to recovering, in 19 BC, the standards lost by Crassus to the Parthians back in 53 BC (refer to Chapter 14) and for his leadership of the campaign in Germany after the disaster of AD 9 (refer to the section 'The disaster of AD 9'). Because of this, no-one opposed Tiberius's succession.

Tiberius abroad

Tiberius, who was 56 when he became Emperor, had always had a great sense of duty. He was determined to continue Augustus's reconstruction of the Roman Empire and followed Augustus's plan to keep the Roman Empire within its existing boundaries. That meant holding back his popular nephew (and heir) Germanicus (d. AD 19) from trying to conquer more of Germany, although Tiberius gloried in Germanicus's magnificent triumph in AD 17.

Tiberius was smart. He named Commagene and Cappadocia in the East as new provinces when the client kings died, and continued Augustus's policy of Romanisation of the provinces by constructing new public buildings and roads. When a massive earthquake with an epicentre close to Sardis wrecked many of the cities of Asia, Tiberius sent relief and issued coins commemorating his generosity.

Piso and Germanicus

Tiberius made Cnaeus Calpurnius Piso Governor of Syria to keep an eye on Germanicus. Piso had a reputation for ferocity and insubordination. Before he died, Germanicus claimed he had been poisoned by Piso. Germanicus was extremely popular, and his death was greeted with despair by the Roman people. Before long, stories started to circulate that Tiberius and Piso had conspired to murder Germanicus, because Tiberius didn't like anyone else being too popular, and because Germanicus had been planning to restore the Republic. Tiberius had enemies within his own family, namely Germanicus's wife Agrippina. The stories were a gift to her, because she planned that her own sons, and not Germanicus, should succeed Tiberius. Piso later committed suicide.

Home rule

Tiberius was really quite modest in his public image. He refused to call himself Imperator, was consul only three times during his reign, and increased the Senate's powers. Tiberius saved cash by not putting on public entertainments. Imperial mines were taken over by imperial equestrian procurators (Roman financial agents) rather than being run by private individuals, and he made soldiers stay on after they should have retired. The changes weren't popular, but they did save money. The economies meant that Tiberius was able to cut taxes. When Tiberius died, he left a large surplus, even though he had provided relief for natural disasters and let people off their debts.

Flies in the ointment

Although Tiberius made some sound political moves, he lacked tact and was highly suspicious. That made his relationship with the Senate difficult. Worse, Tiberius became far too dependent on Lucius Aelius Sejanus, the Prefect commanding the Praetorian Guard in Rome (refer to Chapter 5 for the role of the Praetorian Guard). Sejanus was a man on the make who fancied himself as the next emperor. Tiberius became a recluse, preferring his villa on Capri to Rome, which meant he took his eye off the ball.

The rise and fall of Sejanus

In AD 19, Germanicus died in Syria where he had been campaigning. Augustus's scheme for Germanicus to become emperor after Tiberius had been foiled. Next in line was Tiberius's own son, Drusus the Younger. In AD 23, Drusus died, murdered by Sejanus. Tiberius, trusting Sejanus entirely, was totally unaware of his treachery. Sejanus encouraged Tiberius to stay on Capri so that he could fill the army and administration with his own men. In AD 31, Tiberius's sister-in-law, Antonia, informed Tiberius about Sejanus's disloyalty and his murder of Drusus.

Tiberius brought down Sejanus with a masterpiece of subterfuge and revenge. Tiberius appointed a soldier called Macro, then Prefect of Rome's fire brigade *(Vigiles)* to be the praetorian prefect, and got the Praetorian Guard over to his side with an offer of cash. Tiberius then sent a long letter from Capri to be read in the Senate. Sejanus listened eagerly, thinking he was to be made a Tribune. The letter started well for Sejanus, praising his virtues and achievements, but ending with Tiberius denouncing Sejanus as a traitor. Within hours, Sejanus, his family, and supporters, were all viciously killed by a mob.

Family paranoia

Tiberius's suspicious nature wrecked family relations. After Drusus's death, Tiberius had accepted his nephew Germanicus's eldest sons, Nero and Drusus, by his wife Agrippina (Augustus's granddaughter), as his heirs. Tiberius later became convinced that Nero and Drusus were conspiring with Sejanus. Tiberius had Agrippina banished and her sons killed.

Paranoia was one of Tiberius's weaknesses and made him the prey of political opportunists. Tiberius believed what he was told and used *delatores* (informers) to build up evidence against anyone said to have spoken or acted against him. The delatores stood to get 25 per cent of the property of anyone they informed against who was successfully convicted of treason *(maiestas)*. Naturally, there was a huge incentive to inform on anyone, and the richer the better.

Tiberius expires

Tiberius died on 16 March AD 37 on his way back to Capri after an abortive attempt to visit Rome. Stories were put about that Tiberius had been murdered. It was said that his great-nephew Caligula had poisoned him and that the praetorian prefect Macro (whom Tiberius had used to put down Sejanus) had suffocated Tiberius to show his loyalty to Caligula.

Caligula was made emperor, despite Tiberius's plans that his own grandson, Tiberius Gemellus, would succeed him.

Making your horse a consul is a bad idea: Caligula (AD 37–41)

Caligula, who succeeded Tiberius, was Germanicus and Agrippina's third son. His father's immense popularity helped him a great deal. But Caligula was a very different man.

Caligula's real name was Gaius. As a child he was immensely popular with his father Germanicus's troops on the Rhine frontier, and his father gave him a pair of military sandals to wear. The name *Caligula* means 'little army boot'. The name Caligula stuck, and it's what he's still known as today.

Tiberius stories

Thanks mainly to the historian Suetonius have so many stories about Tiberius's paranoia and debauchery been preserved. Tiberius's victims, half-dead from torture, were supposedly flung off a cliff on Capri where a naval unit waited below to beat them to death if, by chance, they'd survived. Tiberius had young people called *spintriae* perform perverted sexual acts for him. But it was Tacitus who painted a devastating portrait of Tiberius as a crazed recluse.

The truth is that both historians had a hidden agenda. Suetonius and Tacitus were Senators and had seen the Senate's power dwindle as the emperors ruled. Tacitus used Tiberius's hang ups as a way of getting at an emperor much closer to his own time: Domitian (AD 81–96). (More on Domitian at the end of this chapter.) Tiberius did become a recluse and was paranoid, but is now known to have been a competent ruler.

Caligula was hailed on his way to Rome as if he was a superstar. As Germanicus's son, Caligula was welcomed with open arms as emperor in Rome, especially because people hoped the money-saving and paranoia of Tiberius's reign would be cleared out. They were, but were replaced with something far worse: murderous megalomania. Unlike Augustus or Tiberius, Caligula had absolutely no suitable qualifications to be an emperor. He had no experience of the Republic's institutions, no military reputation, no idea of tact and diplomacy, and no idea how to get along with the Senate.

Despite Caligula's lack of experience, he started off well and made himself popular, by

- Reducing taxes
- Bringing back men exiled by Tiberius
- Throwing out any outstanding legal cases
- Banishing sexual perverts
- Allowing freedom of speech
- Reviving elections
- Paying out Tiberius's legacies
- Finishing public building works
- Governing conscientiously

Caligula put on endless expensive public entertainments and paid the Praetorian Guard generously. Caligula then fell ill. When he recovered, he was a changed man. Caligula turned into a tyrant and a lunatic. His expenditure became more reckless and, despite imposing a wide range of new taxes, he managed to squander Tiberius's huge cash reserves within a year. Caligula rapidly descended into madness and did the following:

- ✔ **Declared himself a god:** Caligula posed as an absolute monarch, declaring one day 'Let there be one Lord, one King!' After their deaths, Julius Caesar and Augustus had been elevated to the status of gods (Tiberius, not surprisingly, wasn't given that status). In reality, being named as a god was a political gesture, and for Caesar and Augustus, it was a way of acknowledging their great achievements as emperors. Caligula, however, decided he already *was* a god. He planned to replace statues of other gods with a bust of himself, set up a priestly cult to 'Caligula', and spent the day 'talking' to Jupiter.

- ✔ **Purged the Senate:** Caligula slated the Senate for supporting Sejanus (refer to 'The rise and fall of Sejanus', earlier in the chapter). Men were executed without trial, including Macro, and Caligula brought back the use of the *delatores* (informers; refer to 'Tiberius – part good, part bad, part pervert').

- ✔ **Acted the hypocrite:** He cursed the equestrians for being obsessed with the theatre and the arena – which, frankly, was a cheek because he was a fanatical supporter of the Green faction at the chariot-racing circus himself. He had the neighbourhood silenced so that his favourite horse, Incitatus, would not be disturbed before a race. Apparently, he even toyed with the idea of making Incitatus a consul, though it's unknown if this actually happened.

- ✔ **Was fanatically cruel:** Caligula's cruelties never stopped. He flung men of rank into the mines or the circus, and had a playwright burnt alive because the writer had dared to put an indelicate joke into one of his own plays. One of Caligula's most famous remarks was 'I wish the Roman people had a single neck' – meaning that Caligula would be able to execute the Roman population in one go.

- ✔ **Made a complete fiasco of foreign policy:** Caligula had a client king called Ptolemy (grandson of Antony and Cleopatra) of Mauretania in North Africa murdered for turning up in Rome wearing a purple cloak (that smacked of imperial rivalry). Caligula provoked Mauretania and Judaea to the point of rebellion. On the way to visit a rural shrine, Caligula got it into his head to invade Germany and, while there, gave the chief centurions the sack.

Adminius, a British warrior prince, fled to Caligula for help. Caligula then announced proudly that he had conquered Britain. Next, Caligula sent his troops to the shores of the North Sea and told the men to collect sea shells as spoils of war.

✓ **Plotted against his family:** Caligula declared his mother Agrippina was the offspring of an incestuous relationship between Augustus and Augustus's daughter Julia. Caligula had his grandmother Antonia poisoned and his cousin Tiberius Gemellus (Tiberius's grandson) murdered.

✓ **Indulged in incest:** Caligula had incestuous relationships with his sisters Drusilla, Julia, and Agrippina (the younger). He even issued a coin portraying himself on one side and his sisters on the other. Caligula carried on with Drusilla, Julia, and Agrippina despite the fact that he was married to Caesonia and had a daughter by her.

There was no way Caligula was going to die peacefully in his own bed. He'd signed his own death warrant, several dozen times! A plot implicating two of his sisters was uncovered, but another was organised involving senators, imperial freedmen, and the Praetorian Guard. On his way to a public performance on 24 January AD 41, Caligula was set upon and hacked to death, despite being protected by his German bodyguards who killed some of the conspirators.

One of the most controversial movies made about the Roman Empire is the 1979 film *Caligula,* starring Malcolm McDowell in the title role and Peter O'Toole as Tiberius. Written by Gore Vidal, the movie features scenes of extreme violence and sexual perversions, but nevertheless reflects what the historian Suetonius recorded about Caligula's reign.

The dribbling old halfwit done good: Claudius (AD 41–54)

Caligula, of course, had made no plans for the succession. Neither had his murderers, whose only concern was to get rid of a dangerous madman. (They also killed Caesonia and Caligula's daughter.)

The Senate spotted its chance and decided it was the time to throw away Augustus's principate and restore the 'good old days' of the Roman Republic. They'd forgotten, however, that for the last 150 years, the Senate had had to do whatever the generals and the army had told them to do. And that's what happened now.

In the plots against his family, Caligula left his uncle Claudius, Tiberius's nephew, unharmed. Claudius had a reputation as the family idiot because he dribbled, stammered, and had a limp. Caligula thought he was a joke, but Claudius was highly intelligent. Augustus knew that Claudius was clever and made sure that Claudius had an education. But Claudius was never allowed to gain experience as a soldier or administrator, because his physical handicaps would have been bad for Augustus's image.

Claudius was found by the Praetorian Guard hiding behind a curtain when Caligula was murdered. The Guard wrong-footed the Senate by declaring the 50-year-old Claudius their new Emperor and champion. Claudius, being a historian, was smart enough to realise that the only power that mattered was military power. If Claudius had said no to being emperor, he would probably have been killed. Claudius accepted the job and promised the Praetorian Guard a handsome sum of money in return for their support.

The making of a man: Conquering Britain

Rome's secret of success was adapting to new circumstances while clinging on to tradition, and Claudius knew this. He also knew that his personal reputation was a handicap: Claudius had to prove himself as a leader and as a conqueror. He started off by settling the war in Mauretania, made Mauretania into two new provinces, and created a client kingdom to stabilise Judaea. Claudius also added Lycia and Thrace to the Empire.

Claudius's greatest opportunity came in AD 43 when a British tribal chieftain called Verica fled to him for help. Britain, like most parts of the world ruled by tribes, suffered from endless petty dynastic and territorial disputes. The disputes weren't of much importance to Rome, but Britain was important, because of its valuable mineral resources.

Claudius mounted a major military expedition to Britain, led by the general Aulus Plautius. Caligula had left some of the preparations to invade Britain in place from his abortive effort a few years earlier. Claudius was able to take advantage of Caligula's arrangements. Julius Caesar had failed to hold on to Britain, and now Claudius was given the chance to outdo the greatest Roman of them all.

To begin with, the invasion of Britain went remarkably well. Plautius advanced inland and then sent to Rome for the Emperor. Claudius marched at the head of his army to the great tribal capital of Camulodunum (Colchester), returning to Rome after 16 days. Claudius put on a triumph, erecting arches and issuing coins to commemorate his mighty achievement. The war in Britain continued on and off for more than a century, but Claudius had achieved his goal. He was now a fully-fledged Roman emperor who had proved himself as a victorious commander. To celebrate, he named his son Britannicus.

Running the Roman Empire

In AD 48, Claudius encouraged the senators to admit leading Gauls to the Senate, a liberal gesture on Claudius's part, which gave provincials more power. Part of Claudius's original speech announcing this survives on a bronze plaque in Lyons. Claudius was also keen that the Senate felt free to express its own views, rather than just agreeing with imperial decisions.

The Druids

The Druids were a priestly caste in Gaul and Britain. The word *druid* comes from the Greek for an oak tree: δρυς, pronounced *drys*. Groves of oak trees with mistletoe were sacred to the Druids. The Druids controlled tribal religion, law, and politics, enforced with human sacrifices, which disgusted the Romans. The Druids hugely resented the Romans for denting their power. In Britain, Druids continued to lead resistance to the Roman invasion until AD 60 (see the later sidebar 'The Boudican War').

Claudius built a large new harbour for the port at Ostia to improve the grain supply to Rome, and he reformed the grain supply's administration (see Chapter 7 for information on the importance of the grain supply). He also built a new aqueduct and handed out gifts to the people.

Claudius revived Roman religious customs, discouraged emperor worship, and generally tolerated foreign cults, but only if they didn't directly challenge Roman power. Jews were allowed to worship freely, but Claudius ordered that the Druids in Gaul be wiped out.

Claudius's shortcomings

Apart from his physical handicaps, Claudius had an unpredictable temper. Sometimes he was careful and considerate, at other times thoughtless and impatient, which led to hasty judgements in the Senate. Claudius relied on his wives and freedmen for advice, which made the senators and equestrians distrustful and resentful.

Claudius's Chief Secretary Narcissus, Chief Assistant Pallas, and Examiner of Petitions Callistus were all freedmen and the most senior men in Claudius's government. Narcissus, Pallas, and Callistus wielded unprecedented influence, sold offices and privileges, and made themselves wealthy over and above the gifts they received from Claudius.

Senators and equestrians themselves hadn't been above such practices in the past. The use of freedmen and slaves was simply more efficient, and Claudius's dependence on a personal bureaucracy was probably better for the Empire.

Claudius's wives

Claudius had four wives (not at the same time), but it was numbers three and four who annoyed the Senate, more even than Claudius's freedmen. His third and fourth wives, Valeria Messalina and Caligula's sister Agrippina (Claudius's niece), both played on Claudius's fears of conspiracies. Suetonius said that thanks to Messalina and Agrippina's denunciations, 35 senators and 300 equestrians were executed.

✔ Messalina, mother of Claudius's son Britannicus, was a bigamist and a nymphomaniac. Claudius had Messalina executed in AD 48 when he discovered she had secretly married another man, Gaius Silius. Disgusted and disappointed, he was determined not to marry again, but there's no fool like an old fool, and he fell for his niece Agrippina (Caligula's sister).

✔ Agrippina ensnared Claudius easily. Claudius had the law changed to make it legal to marry his niece. Agrippina wanted her son Lucius by Cnaeus Domitius Ahenobarbus to become Emperor (he did: as Nero). Agrippina persuaded Claudius to adopt Lucius, which placed him second in line to the throne after Britannicus. Lucius's name was changed to Nero Claudius Caesar Drusus Germanicus.

The end of Claudius

Nero, still too young to succeed as emperor, fell increasingly under Agrippina's control. In AD 54, when Nero was nearly 17 (five years older than Britannicus), by a lucky chance, Claudius died. The story at the time was that Claudius had been murdered, but this was not proved. The smart money was on Agrippina, who was said to have served him up a plate of poisoned mushrooms.

Claudius's death was kept quiet until Agrippina could arrange for Nero's smooth succession. The reign of Nero, probably the most notorious in Roman history, was about to begin.

Robert Graves wrote a couple of novels, *I, Claudius* and *Claudius the God,* which trace how Claudius became Emperor and tell the story of the reigns of Augustus, Tiberius, and Caligula. *I, Claudius* is a great yarn and was brilliantly televised in a 1976 BBC series with Derek Jacobi, superb as the stammering Claudius. John Hurt as Caligula was a tour de force of hysterical menace.

Where mother went wrong: Nero (AD 54–68)

Nero was a melodramatic, ridiculous, and posturing egomaniac who had unlimited faith in his own creative, artistic, and sporting skills. In Suetonius's words, Nero was obsessed with a 'craze for popularity'. Still only in his mid-teens, Nero had been handed the whole Roman world and its resources with which to indulge himself. At that point in his life, he was still, by most standards, pretty normal. He had spent his childhood honing his interest in horses, sport, art, music, and painting.

The Boudican War

The Boudican War in Britain was no sideshow. The war nearly cost Rome a province; if Rome had lost, the Empire's prestige would have been permanently destroyed.

The client king of the Iceni in Britain, Prasutagus, died around AD 59. Prasutagus left half his kingdom to Nero in the hope the tribe would be left in peace, but Roman administrators moved in to ransack Iceni territory. Boudica, Prasutagus's wife, was famously flogged and her daughters raped. The Iceni, taking advantage of the governor's absence (he had taken a large chunk of the Roman army on a campaign to wipe out the Druids on the island of Anglesey, off the Welsh coast), rose in rebellion and were soon joined by some of their neighbours.

Although the Iceni had serious grievances, there's no doubt that many of the rebels were more interested in loot and plunder. Three Roman cities (Colchester, London, and St Albans) were burned to the ground and their inhabitants massacred. The Roman army in Britain suffered defeats until the governor, Gaius Suetonius Paullinus, forced the rebels into a pitched battle and destroyed them. In the aftermath, the Roman army moved more troops into Iceni territory and punished the rebellious tribes.

The Iceni rebellion was a devastating blow to Rome, and news of it was kept as quiet as possible to stop other provinces rebelling. No victory coins were issued. Nero had already thought about abandoning the war in Britain because of the cost, but decided it would have been an insult to Claudius and his victories in Britain. The Iceni rebellion made it impossible for Rome to withdraw from Britain. For more about Boudica, see Chapter 25.

Nero's reign in a nutshell

During the early years of Nero's reign, the Roman Empire carried on much as it had under Claudius. The efficient new bureaucracy continued to work. In the East, the general Cnaeus Domitius Corbulo conquered Armenia and installed a client king. In Britain, the war of conquest was steadily proceeding north and west with the ultimate target being the destruction of the Druid stronghold on Anglesey, off the north-west coast of Wales. But as Nero's reign wore on, his lack of ability led to instability in Rome and the provinces.

As the Roman poet Juvenal once said, 'no-one ever reached the depths of depravity all at once'. It took Nero a few years, but he got there alright. Towards the end of his reign, things got really out of control. The advisors who had held Nero in check – his praetorian prefect Burrus and his tutor Lucius Annaeus Seneca – were no longer around. (Burrus had died in AD 62 and Seneca retired.) Nero fell into a life of depravity and wild extravagance and abandoned any attempt to govern the Empire.

Nero's reign had many memorable moments. Here are some of the highlights (or lowlights):

✔ **Clearing the way:** In AD 55, Agrippina poisoned Claudius's son Britannicus, to wipe out the chance of a rival faction.

✔ **Nero killed his mother Agrippina:** He was driven to distraction by her constant interference. Nero wasn't the only one who hated Agrippina; Seneca and Burrus both resented her power and influence. Much as he loved his mother, Nero threw Agrippina out of the palace. Nero couldn't take any more when Agrippina interfered over his mistress, Poppaea. He decided to have Agrippina killed. (Seneca put it about that Agrippina was plotting to kill Nero, to stop Nero from getting any bad publicity.) But Nero didn't find the task of getting rid of Agrippina easy:

- Nero tried poisoning Agrippina, but he was foiled because Agrippina had all the necessary antidotes.

- Nero planned to have ceiling panels dropped on Agrippina while she slept, but his wicked scheme got about before he could arrange the 'accident'.

- Anicetus suggested that Nero build a collapsible boat for Agrippina so that she would drown. When Agrippina came to see Nero, she went home in the boat, but when the boat fell apart Agrippina saved her life by swimming home.

- Nero gave up and sent Anicetus and some other thugs round to beat Agrippina to death, which they did.

✔ **Rebellions in the provinces:** AD 60 and AD 61 were terrible years for Rome. In Britain, a rebellion led by Boudica, ruler of the Iceni tribe, devastated the new Roman province and was put down with great difficulty (see the sidebar, 'The Boudican War' for details). In Armenia, in AD 62, a Roman army was defeated and forced to surrender. Armenia was only brought to heel by sending in the general Corbulo with a new and much bigger army.

Nero sent out an expedition of Praetorian Guards under a tribune to Africa in AD 61, because he was planning an attack on Ethiopia. It took the soldiers around 1,000 miles beyond the Roman frontier in Egypt – probably the furthest the Roman army ever reached – but because all they found was desert, the idea of an invasion was abandoned. Given what had happened in Britain, perhaps it was just as well.

✔ **Nero killed his wife Octavia and seduced Poppaea:** Nero divorced and murdered his wife Octavia and then married his mistress Poppaea (who died in AD 65). Poppaea was the wife of Nero's friend, Marcus Salvius Otho, who had helped Nero kill Agrippina. Not surprisingly, Nero and Otho fell out, and Nero sent Otho to govern Lusitania in Spain. Otho took his revenge by becoming emperor after Nero's death, (explained in the section 'A man of many enemies: Otho', later in this chapter).

✔ **Great Fire of Rome:** In AD 64, a catastrophic fire destroyed a large part of Rome, and, as the famous story goes, 'Nero played the fiddle while Rome burned'. The disaster was a heaven-sent opportunity for Nero to regain public support and esteem by funding the rebuilding of Rome and helping out the homeless. Nero did give some help in organising repair work, but he was more interested in helping himself to a huge chunk of the land (120 acres) to build himself a palace, known as the *Domus Aurea* ('Golden House'). People seethed with resentment, believing that Nero started the Great Fire in order to fund his new palace. Nero, with the help of the new praetorian prefect Othonius Tigellinus, responded by putting about a rumour that it was the Christians who were responsible for the fire, and Nero organised a hasty round of persecutions to prove the story.

Quo Vadis (1951) is all about a general called Marcus Vinicius, who returning home to Rome, falls in love with a Christian girl called Lygia. Vinicius gets Nero to give Lygia to him, but when Nero starts persecuting Christians after the fire in Rome, Vinicius has to rescue Lygia and her family. Peter Ustinov as Nero is particularly memorable.

✔ **Nero tried people for treason on the smallest pretence:** In AD 66, a philosopher called Publius Paetus Thrasea was tried and executed for treason for mildly criticising Nero. Others, like Nero's old tutor Seneca, who had been implicated in a plot against Nero, were told to commit suicide. As time went on, Nero suspected anyone and everyone. He executed his General Corbulo, as well as other military commanders. The executions were a bad move on Nero's part. Nero had killed off men of real power and influence. Now powerful men had to choose between execution or rebellion; they chose rebellion.

✔ **Nero took a holiday in Greece at the wrong time:** Nero, ignoring all the signs of a conspiracy against him, took a vast entourage to Greece, after declaring the whole province to be free. From AD 67 to 68, Nero had a great time in Greece taking part in games he was always allowed to win, and giving musical performances to captive audiences who were literally locked in the theatre. While Nero was enjoying himself, a famine broke out in Rome because grain ships bringing corn to Rome were being diverted to take the grain to Greece instead.

Nero's coins

Not much coinage was struck by Claudius after AD 41, and the shortage continued into Nero's reign. But in AD 64, Nero ordered a massive new issue of coins to be struck, employing the finest engravers available. The new coins, especially the large brass sestertii (34 millimetres wide), carried dramatically realistic portraits of Nero.

He was shown in his late bloated and preening years, complete with designer hairstyle and stubble, bull-neck, and double-chin. In the Renaissance, scholars wondered at the coins, which so brilliantly reflect the personality of Nero described by Suetonius and Tacitus.

Domus Aurea

Nero's *Domus Aurea* ('Golden House') sprawled across a large part of central Rome. Nero employed two architects, Severus and Celerus, to design his new residence, and building was in progress from soon after Rome's Great Fire in AD 64, until Nero's death in AD 68. The Domus Aurea had an artificial lake, parks, and forests, as well as an array of buildings that included covered passages connecting the complex to the palaces of Augustus and Tiberius. Although some of the Domus Aurea was destroyed after Nero's death, a fair-sized part was later buried to provide the site for baths built by Trajan (AD 98–117) and has survived. It can still be seen today, complete with wall-plaster and ceilings.

By the late 60s Nero's reign was falling apart. To pay for foreign wars, Nero had to lower the bullion content of silver coinage. Then Nero had to send Titus Flavius Vespasianus to Judea with a huge army to suppress a rebellion. Unwittingly, by giving Vespasian the command of an army, Nero had given Vespasian the power to bring Nero down and the means of becoming Emperor himself.

The rebellions start

Out on the Rhine frontier, the Roman army had a reputation for being mutinous: The troops were sick of waiting for their pay or retirement papers. Nero let their pay get even more behind, and as they had no personal loyalty to him, it would only take a spark to start a mutiny. In AD 68, the governor of Gallia Lugdunensis, Gaius Julius Vindex, led a rebellion against Nero. Vindex was the descendent of Gallic tribal chieftains, and although he had been 'Romanised', the legions on the Rhine saw Vindex as a Gallic rebel and destroyed the rebellion.

After Vindex had been put down, the victorious soldiers were keen to march on Rome and make their own commander, Lucius Verginius Rufus, emperor. Rufus said no to the soldiers, but news of the plan reached Rome, and the Praetorian Guard's new commander Nymphidius Sabinus told the Guard that the governor of Hispania Tarraconensis in Spain, Servius Sulpicius Galba, was prepared to give the Praetorian Guard a large cash reward to make *him* emperor. The Guard promptly sided with Galba.

Nero panicked. He tried to get an escape fleet organised, but no-one would help him. Next, he considered surrendering to Galba; then he thought about making a speech in the Forum begging for forgiveness and asking for the governorship of Egypt instead of being emperor. But Nero realised he would be lynched before he got as far as the Forum. Nero was left with just a few trusty servants; one of them, called Epaphroditus, in the summer of AD 68, helped Nero commit suicide.

As Nero died, ever missing the point about what an emperor needed to be, he declared: *Qualis artifex pereo,* 'What an artist I die!'

The Year of the Four Emperors (AD 68–69)

There were, quite literally, no Julio-Claudians left to succeed Nero. The mechanism of choosing a successor by family connection to the Julio-Claudians was broken. The historian Tacitus said this was when the terrible secret of the Roman Empire was exposed: An emperor could be made in a place other than Rome. It looked like Rome was going to turn back the clock to the days of the Republican generals in the first century BC. What followed is sometimes called the Year of the Four Emperors.

Too old and too tight: Galba (AD 68–69)

Galba was chosen by the Senate to replace Nero. Galba came from an old Republican family, was 71 years old, and suffered from gout. He seemed to have all the right qualifications but started out completely on the wrong foot:

- ✔ He made himself look like a tyrant by executing Nero's supporters.

- ✔ His strict economies annoyed the mob, especially the army, which had been hoping for a large payment in return for their loyalty.

- ✔ He removed Lucius Verginius Rufinus from his command on the Rhine, infuriating the troops, and sent in two new commanders (Flaccus and Vitellius – more of them shortly) who were unable to control the troops.

- ✔ He upset the former Governor of Lusitiania, Marcus Salvius Otho, who had supported him, by making a young and untried man called Lucius Piso Licinianus the new commander on the Rhine.

The army on the Rhine swore allegiance to Vitellius, but Otho, whose hopes of being adopted by Galba as his successor had been dashed by Piso's promotion, seized his chance to become emperor.

A man of many enemies: Otho (AD 69)

Otho had himself declared emperor on 15 January AD 69 simply by offering the Praetorian Guard a large sum of money. Galba and Piso were promptly murdered.

Greedy Vitellius

Vitellius was said to have spent time with Tiberius's *spintriae* (young people who performed sexual perversions; refer to the earlier sidebar 'Tiberius stories') on Capri. Vitellius had been popular with Caligula because he liked chariot driving and with Claudius because he liked playing dice. But Vitellius is remembered most for his greed.

Vitellius used to invite himself to people's houses for dinner, forcing his hosts to spend a fortune on food, nearly ruining them. Vitellius even helped himself to food intended for religious sacrifice, and he designed a gigantic dish called the 'Shield of Minerva the Protectress' that included food from every part of the Empire.

Otho, like Galba, had a bad start. Having been one of Nero's closest friends, Otho wasn't trusted, and with the powerful Rhine armies supporting Vitellius, civil war looked unavoidable. Vitellius's forces divided into two and set out across the Alps for Italy. Vitellius's troops met Otho's army at Cremona, and thanks to the help of Batavian auxiliaries, Otho's army was defeated. Otho's troops surrendered to Vitellius, and Otho, after a reign of just three months, committed suicide. The Senate immediately declared Vitellius emperor.

The gluttonous emperor: Vitellius (AD 69)

Not a lot is known about Vitellius's family background. Vitellius's uncle, Quintus, had been involved in Sejanus's conspiracy against Tiberius (refer to the earlier section 'The rise and fall of Sejanus'). Vitellius's father Lucius had been close to Caligula, even worshipping him as a god. Lucius had also taken care of the Empire while Claudius was campaigning in Britain in AD 43.

Vitellius had been a competent provincial governor, but he had no experience on the battlefield and had relied entirely on his troops in the campaign against Otho at Cremona. After defeating Otho, Vitellius dismissed most of the Praetorian Guard as a punishment for killing Galba. Leading a triumphant march to Rome, Vitellius stopped at the battlefield at Betriacum near Cremona and, drinking plenty of wine to overcome the stench of corpses, made the tactless comment that only the smell of a dead fellow citizen was sweeter than the smell of a dead enemy.

Vitellius appointed unsuitable advisors, including an insolent thief of a freedman called Asiaticus. He also had men tortured and executed on the slightest pretext. Vitellius was on the way out soon after he got in.

The Revolt of Civilis

Gaius Julius Civilis was a Batavian tribal chieftain who had served in the Roman army and earned Roman citizenship. Antonius Primus asked Civilis to create a diversion and prevent Vitellius's troops slowing down the pro-Vespasian forces in Italy. Civilis decided to pretend to be pro-Vespasian, in order to fight a war of liberation. Various border tribes joined Civilis and, amazingly, Roman troops at Neuss. Civilis's army managed to defeat a legion, and Civilis even started striking Roman-type coinage to pay his troops. But when Vespasian sent a Roman army to put down the revolt, Civilis gave up, and no-one knows what happened to him.

The rise of Vespasian

Out East, Vespasian, with his son Titus, had been fighting a major war against the Jews in Judaea. Unlike Nero, Galba, Otho, and Vitellius, Vespasian was a trained and successful soldier and was smart enough to wait for the right moment to make a bid to be emperor.

When Vitellius had been emperor for eight months, Vespasian's army in the East declared Vespasian as emperor, making him the fourth emperor in the 'Year of the Four Emperors'. Vespasian also had the support of legions in the Danube area. Vespasian's army, commanded by Antonius Primus, set out for Italy and defeated Vitellius's forces at Cremona, almost at the same place where Vitellius's forces had defeated Otho earlier in the year. Cremona was sacked and governors across the western provinces went over to Vespasian.

Vitellius made a deal with Vespasian's brother Sabinus, who was in command of what was left of the Praetorian Guard, that he would abdicate. Vitellius's troops, however, refused to let him give up. Vitellius drove Sabinus and his supporters into the Capitol, lynching them and burning down the Temple of Jupiter. When the Danube troops who supported Vespasian reached Rome, Vitellius tried to escape in disguise, but was soon caught, tortured, and flung into the river Tiber.

Starting Well and Finishing Badly – the Flavians (AD 69–96)

The Year of the Four Emperors had changed everything for the Roman Empire. Not only was it clear that an emperor could be made outside Rome, but it was also clear that being emperor was open to people who were not from ancient aristocratic families. Vespasian (full name Titus Flavius Vespasianus) and his sons Titus and Domitian would rule as the Flavian dynasty.

From Augustus to Nero, the name 'Caesar' was a family name – the holder was a member of the Julio-Claudian dynasty. From the reign of Galba onwards 'Caesar' became a mark of rank: the title given to the named heir, or heirs, of the emperor, who were later given the title of Augustus on becoming emperor. Vespasian's sons Titus and Domitian were named as Caesars. When Titus became emperor in AD 79, he became Augustus, and Domitian remained a Caesar until AD 81, when he, too, became Augustus.

Mr Down-to-earth: Vespasian AD 69–79)

Vespasian (full name Titus Flavius Vespasianus), and his sons Titus and Domitian, ruled as the Flavian dynasty. Vespasian's family were equestrians from the Sabine town of Reate (modern Rieti), but Vespasian and his brother gained promotion to senatorial status. His father was a tax collector and banker, with a reputation for honesty. Vespasian won fame as a brilliant soldier during the invasion of Britain in AD 43 and later in Africa, and then in Judaea under Nero. Nero banished Vespasian for walking out of (or falling asleep during) one of Nero's recitals. But luckily for Vespasian, Nero recalled him because of his military abilities, and he was sent to Judaea with Titus and a large army to put down the Jewish revolt.

Vespasian was a practical man. He had no great vision like Augustus, but he was tireless, straightforward, and blissfully free of delusions of grandeur. Thanks to Vespasian, the office of emperor survived the war of AD 68–69 instead of being abandoned.

When in Rome

In AD 70, Vespasian made an important change to government by reviving the censorship. A censor's chief job was to organise a census of the population, but more importantly, a censor could nominate men to the Senate. Vespasian was able to bring men into the Senate with the right abilities and experience to serve the Empire – in fact, men like himself. Vespasian got rid of unsuitable senators, and if the right man wasn't able to fulfil the property qualification (refer to Chapter 2), Vespasian made up the shortfall in cash. Vespasian's new men included not only Italians but also men from farther afield. Vespasian took the important step of broadening the make-up of the Senate by filling it with men from backgrounds other than the Roman aristocracy.

Vespasian no longer relied on freedmen to do the clerical work as Claudius and Nero had done. He retained a few freedmen, but their duties were given to equestrians. Because of Nero's excessive spending, Vespasian had to raise taxes and invent new ones, and take back estates former emperors had given to their friends. Vespasian, though, wasn't above dubious practices; to raise cash, he sold offices and, for a price, acquitted men being prosecuted.

Vespasian had the loyalty of the army and escaped having to make extra payments to the soldiers for their support. He managed to offset opposition to his rule by organising a programme of public building, including the building of the Colosseum, Rome's famous amphitheatre, and also allowing anyone to build on sites in Rome left vacant by fire or ruin.

In the provinces

Administration of the provinces became easier when Vespasian brought in the post of *legatus iuridicus* (the judicial legate). Judicial legates were posted to certain provinces where they could take care of legal cases while the governor-proper had other things to worry about, such as in Britain, for example, where the governor was still busy conquering the west and north of the country. The settled part of Britain was recovering from the devastation of the Boudican revolt. Public buildings were being constructed, and the Britons were encouraged to adopt the Roman way of life.

Elsewhere, Vespasian brought in new provinces by taking away their liberty; for example, revoking Nero's grant of freedom to Greece meant that Greece was obliged to pay taxes to Rome.

Vespasian's heirs

Vespasian believed in omens. He was committed to establishing a Flavian dynasty and believed he had been given all the right signs. Vespasian told the Senate that only his sons Titus and Domitian would succeed him as Emperor. When Vespasian died on 23 June AD 79, the succession was clear-cut, something that had not happened since Augustus died in AD 14, 65 years earlier.

Vespasian was the first emperor to use Imperator as a title, rather than as part of his name. Legends on Vespasian's coins start 'Imperator . . .'. The fiction that Augustus had 'restored' the Republic was giving way to the hard fact that the real power now belonged to the emperor.

The much-loved Titus (AD 79–81)

Titus, Vespasian's son, was a popular young man; he had been a childhood playmate of Claudius's son Britannicus. Titus was good at almost everything, from warfare to music, and he had an exceptional memory. He had fought with his father in the Jewish revolt and then came to Rome, where he served a fellow official of his father's who was consul and tribune. But Titus wasn't perfect and could be arrogant. He had a reputation for murdering anyone he suspected of conspiracy and had a taste for all-night revels. Titus was infatuated with a Judaean Queen called Berenice and brought her back to Rome; he might have married her if it had not been for Vespasian's death.

As Titus was so clearly his father's designated heir, the succession went smoothly. Titus got rid of disreputable friends, gave up misbehaving for good, and sent Berenice, the Judean Queen, home. Titus quickly developed a reputation for fair dealing, confirmed any favours done by previous emperors rather than overturning them as previous emperors usually did, and avoided helping himself to people's estates. Titus had the *delatores* (informers) publicly humiliated and sent out of Rome. He also continued Vespasian's building projects and completed the Colosseum, which he opened with a spectacular cycle of public games and entertainments.

Dealing with disasters

Barely two months into the job of emperor, Titus faced the most famous disaster in the history of the Roman Empire. On 24 August AD 79, Mount Vesuvius erupted and devastated the Bay of Naples. Villas owned by wealthy Romans were destroyed by lava and pumice, and thousands of people were killed by poisonous fumes. Two major towns, Pompeii and Herculaneum, were wiped out. The following year a serious fire and also a plague hit Rome. Titus gave huge amounts of cash and practical aid to both disasters and tried, without success, to have a cure found for the plague.

A sudden death

Titus had made himself very popular by his generous response to the disasters, and his unexpected death caused widespread mourning. On a journey into Sabine territory, in the late summer of AD 81, Titus caught a fever and died on 13 September, leaving a daughter called Julia Titi.

Judaea and Masada

Judaea was a nightmare province, seething with resentment at Roman control. Titus was left to finish off the war that had broken out in AD 66 under Nero. This war involved fighting for every last yard until the temple and citadel in Jerusalem were destroyed. Judean rebels held out against Rome until AD 73, in the Judean hilltop fortress of Masada. An army of 7,000 legionaries beseiged the fortress for six months, until the people inside set the fortress on fire and then committed suicide. To this day, the siege works used by the Roman army are still visible at Masada, including a huge ramp that was built up one side to gain access. The conquered Judeans became Roman slaves and Jews around the Empire were taxed to pay for the new Temple of Jupiter in Rome.

Flavian propaganda

Titus, or one of his officials, had a brainwave. A whole series of coin types issued by previous emperors was revived and issued in large numbers. It wasn't a new idea, but no-one had done it on this scale before. The old coins were copied but had a legend added to them saying 'the emperor Titus restored this coin'. The new coin was a clever way of showing how the Flavian dynasty represented continuity. Augustus, Tiberius, Claudius, and Galba were included (Galba being there to show you didn't have to be a Julio-Claudian to be emperor: pretty important for the Flavians), as well as imperial family members and associates like Germanicus (Tiberius's nephew) and Agrippa (nominated by Augustus as his heir). But Caligula, Nero, Otho, and Vitellius weren't represented – they had been classed as imperial outcasts; no-one in their right mind was going to celebrate their reigns.

Paranoid fly-killer: Domitian (AD 81–96)

Domitian, Vespasian's other son, was everything Titus was not. Domitian had spent much of Titus's reign plotting his brother's downfall. Once, when Titus fell ill, Domitian ordered Titus to be left for dead. Titus left no sons, and as Domitian had been named by Vespasian as his heir, there was no opposition to Domitian becoming emperor.

Vespasian and Titus had kept Domitian under control by letting Domitian serve as consul, but Vespasian and Titus didn't allow Domitian the command of an army in case Domitian attracted a following. With Vespasian and Titus gone, Domitian had a free rein. Domitian showed all the signs of a cruel and despotic ruler. He boasted that he was the one who had placed Vespasian and Titus on the throne. He had people executed or banished on the slightest pretext; Sallustius Lucullus, the governor of Britain, for example, designed a new type of spear, but Lucullus stupidly named it after himself rather than after Domitian. As a punishment, Domitian had Lucullus executed. When Domitian became emperor, it was said that he spent his spare time stabbing flies.

Domitian as ruler

Domitian, for all his defects, was a surprisingly competent emperor. He maintained a popular programme of public entertainments and gifts, insisted on proper Roman dress amongst spectators, and encouraged the cult of his favourite goddess, Minerva. He had public buildings repaired and built new ones, but committed a public-relations crime by putting his own name on the restored buildings instead of the names of the emperors who had originally built them.

In the Piazza Navona in Rome, you can still see the outline of Domitian's stadium, which replaced a wooden one from earlier times. Parts of the brick and stone substructures of the circus (which held 20,000 people) are still visible, but the stadium was destroyed in the Middle Ages, and the bricks and stones used as foundations for houses and a church. Large parts of Domitian's palace on the Palatine Hill are still standing.

Meanwhile, on the frontiers

Domitian had money problems because of excessive public spending, and his solution was to cut back on the army and military expeditions. In AD 87, he abandoned a long-standing campaign to conquer northern Britain, including Scotland. The reality was that securing Britain's far north wasn't going to make Rome any safer, but holding the German frontier would. The Rhine-Danube frontier had never been secure in the areas where the two rivers rise, because both rivers turn southwards to their sources, leaving a large gap between them. This created a sharp 'V' in the Roman frontier, which the Chatti tribe took advantage of. Domitian's answer was to push the frontier northwards and create a network of fortifications, which made the frontier in Germany secure for generations.

After strengthening the borders in Germany, Domitian's troops were ready to go to war against the Dacians. The Dacians' chieftain Decebalus was determined to make himself an empire out of Roman territory. Domitian wasn't able to deal with Decebalus because he was distracted by a Roman general who had picked the same time to rebel. Domitian set a precedent by paying Decebalus a large subsidy to keep the peace. (See Chapter 17 for the more about the Dacians.)

Damnatio Memoriae

Domitian was convinced that he was surrounded by enemies. Despite his achievements, he was widely loathed. Domitian acted like a despot and was far too keen on the trappings of the job. He liked it when poets called him 'Master and God'. Domitian had an ongoing affair with his niece, Julia Titi, and a taste for prostitutes, which might explain why his wife Domitia (daughter of the general Corbulo, discussed in the earlier section 'Where mother went wrong: Nero') seems to have been one of the main players in his assassination. He dreamed that Minerva (his favourite goddess) had told him she could no longer protect him. On 18 September AD 96, Domitian was murdered.

Domitian's death caused mixed reactions. Most people didn't care. The soldiers, however, were furious; Domitian had increased soldiers' pay by a third, and now it was likely that they would lose the increase. The Senate was delighted to get the news of Domitian's death, so delighted, in fact, that they ordered statues of Domitian be torn down and Domitian's name chiselled off every inscription in the Empire that named him. This was a Roman punishment known as *damnatio memoriae,* 'the damnation of (his) memory' – simply a way of wiping someone from the record.

At the museum in the Roman town of St Albans, you can see an inscription with Domitian's name deleted. The text has been restored from the few surviving fragments; Vespasian's name can be seen along with that of Agricola, the Governor of Britain. The bit where Domitian's name was hacked out is plain to see.

Chapter 17

The Five Good Emperors

After Nero died in 68, the civil war and three disastrous emperors (Galba, Otho, and Vitellius), one after another, took Augustus's world to the brink. Fortunately, Vespasian came next. His common sense, patience, and hard work saved the day. Vespasian's son Titus continued to provide competent leadership and stability. When Titus died, his brother Domitian took over. Domitian might have been a bad emperor in some ways, but like his brother Titus and his father, he was really a competent ruler. Not only that, but by the end of the first century AD, no-one could really imagine the Roman world without an emperor, most of all the provincial senators who now packed the benches in the Roman Senate.

After Domitian's death the Senate had a choice: restore the Republic or pick another emperor. The Senate went for emperor, and what followed was a series of rulers called the Five Good Emperors. It was the climax of Rome's power, when the Empire was at its richest and most settled.

Edward Gibbon, the famous historian, in *Decline and Fall of the Roman Empire,* published in 1776, talked about the time of the Five Good Emperors as 'the most happy and prosperous' in all human history. Maybe Gibbon was right, but what is certain is that when Marcus Aurelius, the last of the five emperors, died in AD 180, the Roman Empire was on the long road into decline.

We've now passed the time of the last, greatest Roman historians, Tacitus and Suetonius. As the second century opened, they were busy writing down their work, much of which has survived. But no-one wrote anything quite so detailed after that – at least, nothing that has survived. So instead, we have to fall back on what's left of Dio Cassius's history, occasional other histories, biographies of emperors written hundreds of years later, inscriptions, and scattered other bits and pieces. If that sounds a lot, it isn't – at best the sources are patchy; at worst they're non-existent or chronically unreliable.

Nerva: A Good Stopgap (AD 96–98)

In AD 96, the senators got together to find a new emperor instead of fantasising about restoring the Republic. They came up with a veteran Senator called Marcus Cocceius Nerva. He was the first of what are now known as the Five Good Emperors, whose rule covered the climax of Rome's power, when the Empire was at its richest and most settled.

As a young man Nerva had been a close friend of Nero's, but he was trusted by Vespasian and Domitian to serve as consul. Nerva might have been in on the plot to assassinate Domitian. No-one knows, but as he was made emperor the same day, he must have known about it. He also must have been politically astute – perfect to calm the crisis down.

Nerva was 64 years old when he became emperor, and he was just a good stopgap. He didn't have foolish ambitions, nor did he have children, but he did have the necessary political and administrative experience for the job.

As luck would have it, Nerva and the next three emperors would be childless (or outlive their sons), giving them all the luxury to choose the right successor, rather than passing on the Empire to an unsuitable son.

Smart moves and good deeds

After the nastiness of Domitian's reign and its violent end (refer to Chapter 16), Nerva had to restore public confidence in the position of emperor. He wanted to show that an enlightened emperor could do good things for the people of Rome and Italy and make their lives better. His policies addressed the following:

✔ **Public funds:** Nerva saved on public spending by cutting back on the gladiatorial games and religious sacrifices. He sold off imperial treasure and appointed a commission to find different ways of saving money. Because of the economies, he was able to cut taxes. He also abolished the way local communities had to pay for the imperial post (the communication system introduced by Augustus; see Chapter 6 for details).

✔ **Public policy:** Nerva probably introduced the *alimenta,* a scheme to finance the education and welfare of poor Italian children, which was developed further by Trajan, Nerva's successor (see Chapter 2 for how it worked). Nerva also spent a huge sum of money on buying land to give in allotments to poor Romans. And, best of all, Nerva restored free speech.

Pliny the Younger, writing a letter to a friend, captured the mood of the times: 'Liberty was restored,' he said. Tacitus, delighted by the new freedoms, said, 'It's the rare fortune of these times that a man can think what he wants and say what he thinks.'

✔ **Public works:** Nerva appointed Sextus Julius Frontinus to sort out Rome's water supply system (described in Chapter 7).

Foiling plots and picking a successor

Nerva wasn't completely up to the job. A tactful coin issue bearing the legend *Concordia Exercituum* ('The harmony of the army') and showing a pair of clasped hands couldn't conceal the fact that he had no military credentials to impress the soldiers, and his old age meant he wasn't likely to be around for too long. So there was a danger the soldiers would hunt around for a successor of their own choosing. Told of a plot against his life hatched by a senator called Calpurnius Crassus, Nerva invited the conspirators to a public event and even offered them swords. Stunned by his coolness, Calpurnius Crassus abandoned the plan.

Nerva solved the problem of the army and the succession a year into his reign by adopting Marcus Ulpius Trajanus, then aged 41, as his heir in October 97, who was then commanding the army in Upper Germany and had just won a victory. It was a brilliant move. With Trajan's protection, Nerva could rule safely for the last four months of his life. He died on 25 January 98.

Trajan: Right Man for the Job (AD 98–117)

Nerva's selection of Trajan as his successor was a delight to the Senate and the army, but it was a good deal more radical than it first appears. If the year 68 (the Year of the Four Emperors; refer to Chapter 16) revealed that an emperor could be made in a place other than Rome, then the year 98 revealed that the emperor didn't have to be Roman or even Italian. In fact, Trajan's remote family origins were in Umbria in Italy, but his ancestors had settled at Italica in Spain, and his mother was Spanish. Unthinkable as little as a generation earlier, Trajan's succession was a major innovation.

Italica

Scipio Africanus, the great hero of the Second Punic War back in the days of the Roman Republic (refer to Chapter 12), founded Italica in Spain as a Roman colony. Scipio couldn't possibly have imagined that he had created the future home of two of the greatest of all the Roman emperors: Trajan and Hadrian (see the section 'Hadrian, Artist and Aesthete', later in this chapter), and much later the emperor Theodosius I (AD 379–395), who would hold the Empire together in its darkest days (see Chapter 21).

Trajan in Rome

Trajan didn't rush to Rome. He made sure everyone knew he was in charge and started with the army. He made certain the Rhine and Danube frontiers were safe and secure first, reduced the bounty to soldiers before having any troublesome praetorians forced into retirement or executed, and confirmed all the Senate's privileges.

Once in Rome, Trajan took care to guarantee the corn dole to the Roman mob. The alimenta, which might have been started by Nerva, was certainly operating now and improved the lot of poor Italian families. Taxes were reduced and another vast programme of public building initiated, including baths on the site of Nero's Domus Aurea, a new aqueduct, and a forum. Large parts of the Forum of Trajan can still be seen in Rome today, including its multi-level terraced shopping precinct.

War with Dacia and Parthia

Trajan paid for the tax reductions and costly building programme from the booty earned by going to war with Dacia and Parthia. Dacia and Parthia were the Roman Empire's furthest boundaries (see Figure 17-1).

Fighting the Dacians

Trajan resented the large subsidies being paid to Decebalus, the Dacian leader, to keep peace with Rome (refer to Chapter 16). In AD 101, Trajan crossed the Danube to finish off Decebalus, who was building up Dacian power.

By AD 104, Trajan had defeated Decebalus and installed garrisons in Dacia. A magnificent bridge across the Danube designed by the architect Apollodorus gave Trajan access into the Romans' newly won territory, but in AD 105, Decebalus restarted the war with Rome. Trajan marched back into Dacia and destroyed Decebalus's army (Decebalus committed suicide in shame). Trajan turned Dacia into a Roman province and took over Dacia's rich mineral mines.

Trajan's letters

Trajan was a hands-on ruler, and there's no better evidence for this than the unique series of letters exchanged by him and Pliny the Younger, governor of Bithynia and Pontus. They show that Trajan was constantly personally consulted on almost every aspect of provincial government, whether that meant enfranchising a soldier's daughter, arranging for new architects to oversee inept local building projects, or dealing with Christians who were refusing to go through the motions of paying homage to the imperial cult (for more on the tension between Christianity and the Roman state, see Chapter 9).

To make navigation on the Danube safe, Trajan's military engineers in AD 101 dug out a canal to bypass the lethal rapids of the Iron Gate gorge. The construction of the canal is just one of the Roman's phenomenal engineering achievements. No-one else was able to rival the skill of the Romans until the Industrial Revolution in the eighteenth century.

Figure 17-1: The Roman Empire in AD 116, at its greatest extent.

Parthian problems

Parthia in the East was a constant irritation to Rome. The Parthian king Osroes threw out the client king in Armenia, and Trajan set off for Parthia in AD 113 to defeat Osroes. Within a year, Trajan had recaptured Armenia and made it into part of the province of Cappadocia. By AD 115, Trajan had captured the Parthian capital at Ctesiphon; the next year, he crushed a revolt.

Trajan's legacy

As Trajan was travelling home from his victory over the Parthians, he had a stroke and died on 8 August AD 117.

Trajan never abused his power and treated his position as a privilege and a responsibility. Although Trajan spent much of his reign away from Rome, his authority was so respected that the machinery of government throughout the Roman Empire went on working efficiently without his presence in Rome.

Trajan created the archetype Roman emperor: powerful, paternal, able, and effective. The Senate awarded Trajan the title *Optimus Principorum,* 'the best of princes'. However, Trajan's territorial ambitions left the East far from settled, and the Empire was becoming overstretched. The Roman Empire had now reached its territorial limit.

'Veni, vidi, vici...'

The Vindolanda archive

Vindolanda, the British fort in Northumberland, was used during Trajan's reign, and amazingly some of Vindolanda's archives survived. The story of Vindolanda is written down on wooden writing tablets, and no other place in the Roman world has records to match the Vindolanda archive. The archive survived because the waterlogged conditions in the remote north British fort preserved the wooden tablets. Dozens of wooden tablets from Vindolanda have been dug up and studied. The Vindolanda archive gives a unique picture of Roman frontier life around the years AD 95–105. The tablets record the arrangements to celebrate a commanding officer's wife's birthday, food supplies, a list of the troops and the reasons for absence,

from sickness to being posted away, and even a complaint about poor roads. One of the units based at Vindolanda was the Ninth Cohort of Batavians, who pop up almost 400 years later as the last-ever-heard-of-unit of the Roman army in the West (see Chapter 5). You can see the Vindolanda archive in the British Museum in London.

Here's a quote from one of the tablets:

'Octavius to his brother Candidus . . . send me some cash as soon as possible . . . I would have already been to collect the [hides] except that I did not care to injure the animals while the roads are bad.' (For more on Roman roads, see Chapter 6.)

Trajan's column, one of Rome's most famous monuments, celebrates Trajan's greatness. Trajan's cremated remains were buried in its base. The column is decorated with a continuous spiralling relief from top to bottom, and illustrates Trajan's campaign against the Dacians, including Trajan's journey, warships, sacrifices, forts, battles, and prisoners. The column is one of the most valuable sources of information on the Roman army. It's hard to see detail on it today, because the surrounding Roman library with its viewing galleries has long gone, but you can go to the Victoria and Albert Museum in London and see full-size plaster casts of the column taken long ago before modern traffic pollution damaged the original. In the sixteenth century, the statue of Trajan on top of the column was replaced by one of St Peter.

Hadrian, Artist and Aesthete (AD 117–138)

Publius Aelius Hadrianus is one of the most famous Roman emperors of all. He was a highly intelligent man who took a great interest in military discipline and organisation, architecture, and Greek culture. He travelled throughout the Roman world, visiting as many provinces as possible, and made the crucial decision to end the conquest of new provinces. His reign represents a turning point in Roman history.

A dodgy succession

Like Trajan, Hadrian was Spanish and came from Italica. Hadrian's father died when he was young, and he was taken on by the childless Trajan and his wife Plotina. Hadrian took up a high-profile career, making his mark in senatorial magistracies and military posts. By AD 114, he was governor of Syria and was left in charge of the East when Trajan set out for home. But Trajan made a bad move: He never publicly named Hadrian as his successor.

Hadrian's succession was anything but smooth. The day after Trajan's death, Trajan's wife and her lover (a former compatriot of Trajan's) made an announcement that Hadrian had been adopted by Trajan on his deathbed. At the time plenty of people, including Roman historians, thought the whole thing had been made up; nevertheless, the Senate agreed to accept Hadrian as Emperor.

Hadrian was Plotina's favourite, despite other more senior men pushing to be Trajan's successor. Unfortunately, Trajan hadn't specified his intentions for the succession, and there were several other possible candidates, all of whom were more experienced. The last thing the Empire needed was a disputed succession – look what happened in 68–69 (refer to Chapter 16). Hadrian moved quickly to secure the Senate's approval. But his reign started badly because the Senate had four alleged conspirators executed on his say-so, though Hadrian blamed this on the praetorian prefect. Fortunately, civil war was avoided because Hadrian had moved so fast. Hadrian had to promise the Senate never to have anyone executed again without the Senate's approval.

Hadrian in Rome

Hadrian's rule was remarkably successful, but he faced an instant problem: tying up Trajan's affairs. Hadrian had to suppress another revolt on the Danube frontier before reaching Rome to establish himself as emperor. Arriving in Rome, Hadrian put on public entertainments, provided handouts to the mob, and gave a general pardon to debtors, celebrating his generosity by throwing all the relevant paperwork onto a bonfire in the Forum.

Hadrian, like Trajan, spent little time in Rome (his travels are detailed in the next section), but his administration was well set up and worked effectively without him. He generally carried on the work of his predecessors, for example Trajan's alimenta, and kept extortion in the provinces to a minimum. He also encouraged the use of equestrians, rather than freedmen, as administrators.

Enough's enough: Touring the provinces

Hadrian called a halt to further expansion of the Roman Empire. Augustus, more than a century before, had held the view that the Empire should stay within its borders. Conquests by Claudius, Vespasian, Domitian, and especially Trajan, had broken that rule and left the Empire struggling to maintain its frontiers.

Hadrian decided enough was enough: The Empire would expand no longer. He set out on a famous tour of the provinces, the only emperor ever to do so, reviewing the army and the frontiers. Under Trajan, there'd been a series of governors being prosecuted for extorting their provinces, so it was clearly time for some hands-on attention from the emperor. The travel was part supervisory, part sightseeing, and part military. The journey was commemorated on a remarkable, unparalleled series of coins that show Hadrian being greeted by each province he visited.

Restoring military discipline on the frontiers

Hadrian was an absolute stickler for military discipline and swept away any nice, relaxed frontier living amongst garrison troops, especially in Germany and Britain during AD 120–122 where he tightened things up and had the frontiers redesigned, building his famous Wall across Britain (see Chapter 5 for more on that). He was particularly annoyed to discover the soldiers had nice dining rooms and ornamental gardens. He had no time for fancy imperial dress himself and went about in the most basic clothing he could get his hands on.

Giving back provinces and hostages

By 123 Hadrian had headed to the East. Provinces which he decided were a step too far, like Armenia and Mesopotamia, he simply gave up. The Parthian king's daughter, taken hostage by Trajan, was returned.

When in Greece . . .

Hadrian reached Greece in 125 and visited again in 128. He loved Greece and all things artistic, as well as mathematics and architecture. It affected his dress and appearance – he grew a beard as Greeks did (though apparently this was to cover blotches on his face), a fashion followed by his successors and many men of rank throughout the Empire. He was also responsible for great building projects like the Temple of Olympian Zeus and a library in Athens.

The Bar Cochba Revolt

During AD 132–135, Hadrian had to deal with a major revolt in Judaea led by Bar Cochba. Trouble started under Trajan when Roman troops were diverted to the war in Parthia. The trouble was suppressed, and generally Hadrian was enlightened and tolerant towards the Jews. But he came up with the foolish idea of forcing the Jews in Palestine to be assimilated – in 131 BC, for example, he declared circumcision to be illegal. That provoked Jewish nationalist hopes which threatened to destabilise the Roman East. (For more on Bar Cochba himself and the revolt, see Chapter 25.) After Hadrian put down the revolt, the Jews lost their land and became nationless. The historian Dio said 'Judaea was made desolate'.

TECHNICAL STUFF

Building more than walls: Hadrian the architect

Hadrian seems to have been behind the reconstruction of the Pantheon in Rome. Built originally by Agrippa in Augustus's reign, the Pantheon was rebuilt as a magnificent domed structure with a vast pedimented façade supported by Egyptian granite columns. Agrippa's original dedication inscription of 25 BC was modestly reproduced with no mention of Hadrian. Incredibly, the building survives virtually 100 per cent intact in Rome today, having been used as a church in the Middle Ages. Hadrian also built the Temple of Venus and Rome, and a new imperial mausoleum in Rome, which survives today as the Castel San Angelo (it was turned into a castle in the Middle Ages). To the east of Rome at Tivoli, Hadrian built his vast sprawling villa covering 160 acres (65 hectares), known today as the Villa Adriani. An almost endless complex of buildings, each of which was individually designed by Hadrian to reflect his interests or the places he had visited around the Empire, it was where he spent most of the last part of his life. Today the Villa is in ruins, but large parts of it can still be seen and enjoyed.

Hadrian and Antinoüs

Hadrian, on his grand tour of the provinces, reached Egypt in AD 130. Egypt was where Hadrian's favourite, a youth called Antinoüs, had drowned in an accident. Hadrian may well have had a homosexual relationship with Antinoüs, but what is known is that Hadrian was absolutely devastated by the loss of Antinoüs and was said to have 'wept for him like a woman'. Hadrian founded a city called Antinoöpolis in Antinoüs's memory.

Hadrian was married to Trajan's great niece, Sabina. No-one knows what Sabina thought of Antinoüs. Popular gossip had it that Hadrian's marriage to Sabina was unhappy, but there's no evidence, and Hadrian granted Sabina all the usual honours, as well as striking coins with Sabina's portrait on them.

Growing ill in mind and body

As Hadrian grew older, his health began to fail. All Hadrian's travelling caught up with him. He seems to have lost his reason because there are various stories about him ordering the death of various people, including a would-be successor called Servianus (though this is impossible nonsense as Servianus was over 90 years old) and even possibly his wife Sabina. The signs had been there already though. He'd been keen for years on using imperial spies *(frumentarii)* to keep him fully informed about the private business of people in court, his friends, or, in fact, anyone.

Hadrian also suffered from oedema (a build-up of water in the body) and felt so ill that he asked a slave to stab him to death. Antoninus, the senator Hadrian appointed as his successor (see the next section, 'Choosing a successor'), stopped the slave, but Hadrian hadn't much longer to live anyway.

Choosing a successor

Hadrian, racked with illness, had to choose a successor. Like Trajan before him, Hadrian had no children. Hadrian's first choice was Lucius Ceionius Commodus (renamed Lucius Aelius Verus Caesar), whom Hadrian adopted in AD 136. Aelius was made a consul and given a governorship. Unfortunately, Aelius was a sick man and died on 1 January AD 138, after taking too much medicine.

Within a few weeks of Aelius's death, Hadrian adopted as his successor a senator and distinguished governor of Asia, with the exaggerated name of Titus Aurelius Fulvus Boionius Arrius Antoninus. In AD 138, shortly after Antoninus's nomination, Hadrian died.

The frumentarii

No self-respecting totalitarian state could do without its spies. Originally, frumentarii (imperial spies) were soldiers in charge of the corn stores, but the frumentarii ended up being used as couriers on imperial business. Emperors, by Hadrian's time, were using the frumentarii to spy on anyone and everyone. They were a gift to bad emperors, like Commodus (see Chapter 18), but the frumentarii became so unpopular that Diocletian (see Chapter 20) had to get rid of them.

Antoninus Pius: Nice and Vice-free (AD 138–161)

Antoninus succeeded as Antoninus Pius, a name he acquired either because of the honours he heaped on Hadrian after his death or because he took great care of his aged father-in-law. He certainly had to persuade the Senate to make Hadrian a god, which they were reluctant to do after all the carryings-on at the end of Hadrian's reign.

Antoninus in Rome

The most remarkable thing about Antoninus Pius is that he really was apparently without any vices whatsoever. He was the last word in decency and honesty and scrupulously respected the Senate. Even a senator who confessed he had killed his own father was marooned on an island instead of being executed. When there was a shortage of wine, oil, and wheat, Antoninus bought in extra stocks at his own expense and gave them out for free. He refused to travel abroad on the grounds that putting up an emperor and all his entourage cost the provinces far too much. He placed a maximum cost on gladiatorial games to save cash, which helped him finance new public buildings and the repair of old ones.

Antoninus adored his wife Faustina and set up an order of homeless girls called the Faustinianae in her honour. When Faustina died in AD 141, Antoninus issued a magnificent series of coins commemorating her life. How much nicer can you get?

Largely as a result of this, practically nothing of any great note happened during Antoninus Pius's reign, especially in Rome, apart from a disastrous collapse of a stadium (probably the Circus Maximus) causing the deaths of more than 1,000 spectators. There were no proscriptions, no executions, no sexual scandals, no vice. Nor were there any significant innovations in imperial government, though he did establish some important legal principles concerning inheritances, adoptions, and the treatment of slaves.

Whenever he could, Antoninus Pius avoided war. His favourite saying was that he would 'rather save a single citizen than a thousand enemies', a quote he apparently found amongst the sayings of Scipio Africanus.

On the borders

Out in the provinces life wasn't quite as settled. In Britain, a northern war led to the temporary abandonment of Hadrian's Wall and a trial new frontier made of turf called the Antonine Wall farther north. But after little more than a generation, this was given up and the garrisons returned to Hadrian's Wall. Various other risings in Numidia, Mauretania, and Egypt all had to be suppressed, and Dacia had to be divided into three provinces to settle it. None of the rebellions were very serious, but together they gave a hint that had any or all of them blown up into something really dramatic, the Empire would have been hard put to cope. That was really the key to stability under Antoninus Pius: He had the good luck to rule over a world largely at peace.

Smelling the Storm Brewing: Marcus Aurelius (AD 161–180)

Marcus Aurelius was the son of Antoninus Pius's brother-in-law and came from a family of Spanish origin. He'd been educated under Hadrian's supervision and married Antoninus Pius's daughter Faustina the Younger in 145.

Mr Sensitivity

Marcus Aurelius was, by nature, a man of peace. He wasn't paranoid like some of his predecessors, such as Domitian, who saw conspiracies everywhere. Aurelius always tried to think well of everyone. He avoided executing or imprisoning Avidius Cassius's co-conspirators (see the section 'Marcus the warrior' for details on this episode). Although Aurelius's wife Faustina had been implicated in the same plot, she died soon afterwards, and Aurelius burned all Faustina's papers to avoid reading about the plot, because it could force him to hate the conspirators. Even at the games, Aurelius couldn't bear the idea of gladiators getting hurt and made them fight with blunt weapons.

Appointing a partner

Marcus Aurelius took over smoothly, but unlike his predecessors, he promptly organised the who-comes-next problem. He appointed Lucius Verus, son of Aelius (the designated heir of Hadrian who had died in 138 before he could succeed), his co-Augustus immediately. This was a radical step, placing the Empire under the control of two emperors of equal rank for the first time.

Lucius Verus's position was enhanced when he was married to Aurelius's daughter in 164. Great scheme, but like all the best ideas, it was susceptible to things going wrong. Verus was an effective military commander but had none of his colleague's qualities. He was thought by some to be like another Nero but without the cruelty.

Marcus the warrior

Marcus Aurelius would definitely have rather spent his life poring over books and meditating rather than running an Empire. So it's ironic that much of his reign was spent in war. Aurelius sent Lucius Verus to deal with the Parthians who had invaded Armenia and Syria, and by AD 166 the Parthians were defeated. A great triumph took place in Rome, but the war had terrible consequences. The soldiers brought a plague back with them to Rome, and large numbers of people died, causing a famine.

Tribes in Britain and the Chatti in Germany took advantage of Roman troops being away to fight the Parthians and rebelled, causing trouble for Aurelius. It was now clear that Rome could not deal with multiple frontier problems; the Empire simply did not have the manpower to cover distances that would challenge even a modern mechanised army today.

Although the German and British rebellions were put down, a major invasion by German tribes in AD 166 threatened Italy. The invaders were brought to terms by AD 168, but then Aurelius faced more trouble from the Sarmatians along the Danube. Worse, Marcus Aurelius had to deal with the troubles on his own because Lucius Verus died in AD 169 after suffering an apoplexy.

Next came a revolt in 175 by Avidius Cassius, commander in the East, who thought Aurelius was dead. Aurelius had to set out for Syria before news came that Avidius had been murdered. Another German invasion, by the Quadi and Marcomanni, followed and Aurelius headed out on campaign once more in 178.

Who comes next? Picking a successor

Marcus Aurelius didn't get round to appointing a replacement successor until AD 177. Aurelius appointed his son Commodus as his co-Augustus. Commodus was fighting with Marcus Aurelius at Vindobona (Vienna), and with the war almost won, Aurelius passed away (although he took a week to do it) on 17 March AD 180, facing death like a true Stoic.

Unfortunately, Commodus didn't have any of his father's qualities, or any of those of the four emperors before Aurelius. With the death of Marcus Aurelius, the good days were over. The historian Dio Cassius said 'our history now descends from a kingdom of gold to one of iron and rust'. Dio Cassius should know – he watched the Roman Empire begin to decay with his own eyes.

Marcus Aurelius features in two epic movies: *Fall of the Roman Empire* (1964), starring Alec Guinness as the emperor (the film was a flop), and *Gladiator* (2000), starring Richard Harris as Aurelius and Russell Crowe as Maximus the Gladiator (a monster international hit). *Fall of the Roman Empire* wins the prize for historical accuracy, but *Gladiator,* which is only half true and half nonsense (Maximus didn't exist), is rather less boring.

The End of the Good Old Days

Antoninus Pius and Marcus Aurelius were good and honourable men with exceptional qualities, and their reigns were the high summer of the Roman Empire. Antoninus and Aurelius had ruled over an Empire that stretched from northern Britain to Egypt. But all things must pass.

By the time Marcus Aurelius died, Rome had been ruled by emperors for nearly 200 years. The system had survived the die-hards who wanted to go back to the old days of the Republic, the reigns of Caligula and Nero, and the civil war of AD 68–69. Along the way there had been imaginative reforms, which now meant emperors of Gaulish and Spanish origin could rule the Roman world, while the Senate was filled with men from all over much of the Empire.

The Roman Empire was far from perfect but it was truly remarkable that, despite the frontier problems, a colossal land area was kept very largely at peace for two centuries. You have only to think of all the wars that have crippled Europe and the rest of the world over the past 1,500 years to appreciate that this was no mean feat. Of course, it couldn't last, and it didn't.

Part V
Throwing the Empire Away

In this part . . .

A century of brutal thugs ruled the Roman world after Marcus Aurelius, and very few of them died in their beds. The Roman Empire even started splitting up into rival Empires as one general after another decided to try and become emperor himself. Meanwhile, war broke out constantly on the borders. As long as this went on, the very existence of the Roman world was at stake.

Along came Diocletian at the end of the third century. Diocletian's system was completely different – in an effort to keep the Roman world functioning, he tied Roman citizens to their homes and jobs. The medieval feudal system had been born. The rich grew very rich, and the poor grew poorer. But the Roman Empire was still under attack on all its borders and from within. Diocletian's new order started falling apart over the next hundred years as his successors squabbled over power and territory. It's no great wonder that the barbarians found their way in and sacked Rome. The Western Roman Empire fell to pieces. Perhaps the strangest thing of all, though, is that the Eastern Roman Empire had another thousand years to run.

Chapter 18

More Civil War, Auctioning the Empire, and Paranoid Lunatics

A Roman emperor could do pretty much what he wanted because he had the money and there were plenty of people hungry for power who'd let him. Which wasn't a bad thing, if the emperor was good at his job and didn't let it all go to his head. Nerva, Trajan, Hadrian, Antoninus Pius, and Marcus Aurelius, who ruled between AD 96 and 180 (see Chapter 17 for details), did this. They put the Empire first and didn't use the power at their disposal to pursue their own selfish ambitions. Apart from a few ructions, their reigns were the high summer of the Roman age. The Empire had never been richer, more powerful, or more stable.

The same can't be said of the emperors who followed. The men discussed in this chapter put their personal ambition first. The result was intermittent civil war as one man after another used the Empire's resources for his own ends. The good times were over.

I Think I'm Hercules: Commodus (AD 180–192)

Marcus Aurelius (whose reign is discussed in Chapter 17) lost quite a few sons, including one half of a pair of twins. The other twin, Lucius Aurelius Commodus, lived and was 17 when his father died in 180.

Marcus Aurelius hadn't planned on having Commodus succeed him. But Lucius Verus, the man he had picked to succeed him, died in 169. Marcus

Aurelius, being a Stoic (refer to Chapter 1), seems to have accepted that things were the way they were.

Like Caligula in AD 37 (refer to Chapter 16), Commodus was too young and inexperienced to be emperor. Other emperors, Hadrian and Antoninus Pius, for example, had been trained up to the job. They'd commanded army units and had served as magistrates in Rome and as provincial governors abroad. Commodus hadn't done any of those things.

Depending on which Roman historian you read, Commodus was either a simple coward who fell in with a bad lot, or he was cruel, foul-mouthed, and debauched. Either way, he certainly ended up debauched, and Rome suffered for it. Incidentally, the Latin word *commodus* means 'pleasant' or 'obliging'. Rarely was a man more inappropriately named.

Commodus and the affairs of state

Because Commodus was too busy spending his time chariot racing and carousing with his friends, he used the praetorian prefect Perennis to run not just the army but also all the other affairs of state. Perennis (an equestrian like all prefects) started making equestrians into legionary commanders, largely because Commodus hated and distrusted anyone of senatorial rank. Following Perennis's death – he was executed for treason; see the section 'Plots against Commodus and his demise' – Commodus gave a freedman called Cleander control of the Praetorians and pretty much everything else.

Cleander was an operator. Realising his master wasn't in the least bit interested in affairs of state, he turned his job into a business trafficking in jobs. He sold senatorships, governorships, and military commands, charging his customers as much as he could. He even sold 25 consulships alone in a single year – one of the lucky buyers was a man from North Africa called Septimius Severus (see the section 'Septimus Severus' later in this chapter for more on his political career). Commodus let Cleander get away with it because Cleander gave Commodus some of the cash. When a riot broke out during a famine, the crowd blamed Cleander. All this terrified Commodus, who ordered Cleander executed.

After the fall of Cleander in 189, the last three years of Commodus's reign descended into mayhem. Men he'd once regarded as favourites were murdered for their money or, in one case, simply because Commodus was jealous of his sporting skills.

Things were so bad that when plague broke out in Rome, killing as many as 2,000 in a single day, no-one took any notice. They were far more frightened of Commodus, who in a fit of egomania had decided Rome should be renamed Commodiana.

Commodus the gladiator

Commodus was obsessed with fighting in the arena, killing animals, and riding chariots. He decided he was the reincarnation of Hercules, so he dressed up like the mythical hero with a lion skin headdress and waving a club. That is, when he wasn't parading around dressed as the god Mercury. Unlike Nero, who wasn't particularly good at sport or performing, Commodus was actually quite accomplished, and one day killed 100 bears himself. He fought as a gladiator and paid himself a fortune out of the gladiatorial fund. Senators were forced to attend and watch what everyone regarded as a thoroughly humiliating spectacle. On one occasion, Commodus decapitated an ostrich and waved its head at the senators as a reminder of what he'd like to do to them.

The movie *Gladiator* (2000) begins in the reign of Marcus Aurelius. But the story carries right on into the reign of Commodus, who is one of the chief characters. Despite the way the script plays fast and loose with historical fact, the portrayal of Commodus by Joaquin Phoenix as a half-bonkers, bloodthirsty stadium and circus fanatic is really pretty good.

Plots against Commodus and his demise

Throughout his years as emperor, Commodus had to deal with a series of conspiracies against his life. The first was orchestrated by his sister. After that, Commodus was very wary of plotters and used secret police (known as *frumentarii*) to root them out. The following sections share the highlights.

Plot 1: The loving sister

When Marcus Aurelius died, Commodus was on campaign. Upon hearing the news of his succession, he abandoned the war against the German tribes, negotiated a treaty on favourable terms, and headed back to Rome with his best friend Saoterus, parading him in a triumphal chariot and kissing him. One historian said Saoterus was Commodus's 'partner in depravity'.

Commodus's sister Lucilla started a plot as a result. It was uncovered and Lucilla was forced into exile, but the commanders of the Praetorian Guard killed Saoterus anyway.

Plot 2: Rumour has it . . .

Although Perennis (refer to the earlier section 'Commodus and the affairs of state') was good at his job, the soldiers were annoyed at how he'd pushed his rival out of the way for the post of Prefect. They mutinied. A band of soldiers came all the way from Britain to Rome and told Commodus in person that Perennis was plotting to kill him.

Commodus believed the soldiers and promptly allowed the troops to kill Perennis and his family in the year 185.

Plot 3: The end of Commodus

It was unlikely Commodus would die in his bed, and he didn't. In 192, the praetorian prefect Aemilius Laetus and Commodus's chamberlain Eclectus decided to kill Commodus when news got out that the emperor was planning to execute both consuls and replace them with gladiators. While everyone was distracted by the mid-winter festival, the Saturnalia (see Chapter 8), they had Commodus fed poison by his mistress Marcia who was in on the plot. Commodus was already so drunk, he vomited the poison up, so they had an athlete strangle Commodus on the last day of December in 192.

Pertinax: The 87-Day Wonder

When Commodus died, he left no successor. Laetus and Eclectus, who had arranged Commodus's death (see the preceding section), went to see Publius Helvius Pertinax, the 66-year-old consul and prefect of Rome, who the Roman historian Dio said was an 'excellent and upright man'. The son of a freedman, Pertinax grew up to become an equestrian, before Marcus Aurelius made him a senator. He was rich and had governed various provinces including Africa and Britain. He was a stickler for discipline and tough enough to suppress a mutiny in the army in Britain where he was nearly killed, and he also put down several rebellions in Africa.

Reintroducing discipline

Before Pertinax accepted Laetus and Eclectus's offer, he sent a friend to see Commodus's body, just to make sure the story was true. He then went in secret to the Praetorian Guard and offered them a fat bonus to accept him as emperor. Pertinax said he was going to put everything right again and sort out discipline. To that end, he did the following:

- ✔ He had all the statues of Commodus knocked down and declared the dead emperor a public enemy.
- ✔ He reordered government and had himself declared 'Chief of the Senate'.
- ✔ He gave posthumous pardons to people unjustly put to death.
- ✔ He sold off Commodus's possessions to raise money so that he could pay the soldiers and the mob.

Ticking off the soldiers

After the debauchery of Commodus's reign, you'd think that everyone would be relieved to have someone competent in charge, but Pertinax's intentions worried the soldiers and the imperial freedmen, who could see all the privileges awarded them by Commodus disappearing in a puff of smoke.

Soldiers were no longer allowed to behave as they please, which had included (incredibly) hitting passers-by as they went about Rome and waving axes. Pertinax put a stop to the axe-carrying and told them to stop insulting the public. But that just made the soldiers nostalgic for the 'good old days' of booze-fuelled chaos under Commodus.

Biting the dust

To rid themselves of Pertinax, the Praetorians and Laetus started a plot to put a consul called Falco on the throne. Pertinax found out about it and pardoned Falco. To cover his back, Laetus then turned on the soldiers. Terrified that they were going to be killed, 200 of them went round to the palace and murdered Pertinax along with Eclectus.

Pertinax had managed a reign of 87 days, five less than the previous record for the shortest reign of a Roman emperor held by Otho in 69 (refer to Chapter 16).

Didius Julianus and Civil War

When Pertinax died, Didius Julianus, a former colleague of Pertinax's in the consulship who'd been exiled by Commodus, raced to the Praetorians' camp and offered them serious cash to make him emperor. He had a rival, the new city prefect Sulpicianus (Pertinax's father-in-law), and the two men competed to outbid one another in the auction of the Roman Empire. If that sounds incredible now, it was considered no less incredible at the time. It went on until Didius Julianus suddenly increased his bid by a huge amount and won the auction (see Chapter 24 for details of Didius's personality).

The people of Rome were not amused and called Didius 'Empire robber'. A mob raced to a circus and held out there, demanding that soldiers in the East under the governor Pescennius Niger in Syria come and save them from Didius. They resented Didius because they'd hoped that Pertinax would do away with all Commodus's abuses. Didius didn't care. He was having the time of his life, handing out favours, going to the theatre, and having banquets. It was bound to end in tears, and it did.

Immortalised in bronze

The Senate voted Didius a statue made of gold, but he refused because he'd noticed that gold and silver statues were always destroyed and asked for a bronze one instead so that he would be remembered forever. But as the historian Dio pointed out, the only worthwhile way to be remembered was as a man of virtue. The bronze statue was knocked down when Didius was killed. So much for immortality then.

When the soldiers in Syria, under the command of the governor Pescennius Niger, heard the appeal from Rome to come and get rid of Didius Julianus, they promptly declared Pescennius Niger emperor. Niger wasn't the only one who had such aspirations. Two other men threw their hats into the ring: Clodius Albinus, a North African who was governor in Britain (even Commodus had once considered him an heir) and Lucius Septimius Severus, another North African in Pannonia who was declared emperor by his troops.

The scene was set for an almighty civil war. Severus was the cleverest. He knew that once Didius Julianus was dead, the three of them would have to fight it out, and it was unlikely anyone would be a clear winner. And as Severus had every intention of being the winner, he came up with a cunning plan.

Severus pretended to be friends with Clodius Albinus and said that Albinus could be his declared heir. Albinus fell for the trick hook, line, and sinker, believing this meant he had a share in imperial power without having to fight for it, and waited in Britain. Severus marched on Rome where Didius Julianus tried to turn the city into a fortress. The problem was that the Praetorians were so used to easy living, none of them knew how to build fortifications properly, and some of them were going over to Severus. In the end, Didius was done for by Severus's promise that if they handed over the men who'd killed Pertinax he would protect them. The Senate assembled, approved the soldiers' action, sentenced Didius to death, and declared Severus emperor.

Didius Julianus was executed after a reign of 66 days, which was another new record for the shortest reign in the history of the Roman Empire. He cried as he was killed, 'What evil have I done? Whom have I killed?'

Septimius Severus (AD 193–211)

Lucius Septimius Severus was born in 145 at Leptis Magna, a major city of North Africa on the coast of what is now Libya. He came from a wealthy family of Punic and Italian descent, was a scholar, and his favourite childhood game was playing at being a judge. He came to Rome to finish his education and, with family backing, became a senator under Marcus Aurelius (see Chapter 17 for his reign). He bought one of the consulships sold by Cleander under Commodus (refer to the section 'Commodus and the affairs of state', earlier in this chapter). Highly superstitious, Severus was always on the look out for omens and was convinced that he was destined to be emperor because, amongst other signs:

- ✔ He once dreamed that he'd been suckled by a she-wolf like Romulus (refer to Chapter 10 for more about this mythic figure).

- ✔ When he married his second wife Julia Domna (a Syrian) in Rome in AD 173, the reigning emperor Marcus Aurelius's wife Faustina had prepared their nuptial chamber.

- ✔ An astrologer had once predicted that Julia Domna would marry a king (and, in fact, that's why Severus chose her as his wife).

- ✔ A snake once coiled itself round Severus's head but did him no harm.

- ✔ While governor in Gaul, he'd dreamed the whole Roman world had saluted him.

Securing the throne

After the death of Didius Julianus, Septimius Severus had a long way to go before securing the throne. Leaving Clodius Albinus in Britain optimistically assuming he was a permanent fixture in the new regime, Severus could safely head out East to clear Pescennius Niger off the map. Niger hadn't been wasting his time and had sewn up the whole region. But Severus defeated Niger's forces three times and caught up with him while he tried to escape towards the river Euphrates. Niger was promptly executed in 194 along with anyone even suspected of being a supporter. Severus fined cities that had supported his rival and punished them by taking away municipal status.

Pertinax's funeral

Septimius Severus put on a massive show for Pertinax's funeral before setting out to defeat Niger. An effigy of the dead man was made and treated as if it was a real man asleep, even with a slave to wave flies off. A procession of soldiers, senators, and equestrians and their families was followed by an altar decorated with ivory and jewels from India. Finally the 'body' was placed in a three-storey tower and set ablaze.

Next on Severus's list was Clodius Albinus, who'd realised he'd been stitched up and had strengthened his army. Albinus's soldiers declared him emperor and together they crossed from Britain to Gaul and set out for Rome. Severus met them near the city of Lugdunum (Lyons) in 197. The battle, supposedly involving 150,000 soldiers on each side, was a close-run thing, and Severus was very nearly killed, but he won the day. Because the last thing Severus wanted was a rival dynasty, he ruthlessly ordered Albinus executed and had his head displayed on a pike. Then he ordered the killing of Albinus's wife and children and all his supporters. Albinus's body was left to rot before it was thrown into a river.

Dividing and ruling

Severus was undisputed master of the Roman world by 197. Britain and Syria were each subdivided into two provinces so that never again would an upstart of a governor be able to call on either province's garrison to try and seize power. (Actually Severus was wrong about this, as Chapter 20 explains.)

Building a dynasty

Severus purged the Senate of any supporters of Niger and Albinus and set about establishing a dynasty, claiming to be the son of Marcus Aurelius. It was obvious nonsense, but lots of emperors over the turbulent decades to come did the same thing to appear legitimate. His eldest son was named Bassianus at birth but was now renamed Marcus Aurelius Antoninus as part of Severus's spurious lineage, pretending to be descended from the famously good emperors of the second century AD. But the boy was always known as Caracalla because he wore a hooded Gaulish cloak called a *caracalla*.

Severus was particularly dependent on his praetorian prefect, Fulvius Plautianus. Plautianus ruthlessly stole whatever he could, tortured people for information, and had so much influence he even got away with being rude to Julia Domna. In 202, Plautianus's daughter Plautilla was married to Caracalla, even though Caracalla loathed them both. When Severus's brother denounced Plautianus in 205, the game was up and Plautianus was killed (reminiscent of what happened to Sejanus under Tiberius, see Chapter 16).

Severus and religion

Thanks in part to his exotic Syrian wife, Julia Domna, his own origins, and his campaigns, Severus was very interested in eastern cults. While Severus was visiting Egypt, he worshipped Serapis (a hybrid Egyptian god made up from Osiris and Apis), and it was probably while Severus was in Britain that a legionary commander of his in York dedicated a temple to Serapis.

The Arch of Severus

The arch of Septimius Severus in the Forum in Rome is one of the most complete monuments still standing in the city. At 23.2 metres (76 feet) wide and 21 metres (68 feet) high, it's one of the biggest. It has one large central arch and a smaller one on each side and is covered with carvings commemorating Severus's campaign against the Parthians.

Dealing with the frontiers

Severus was lucky. The borders on the Danube and Rhine were peaceful, and he could afford to go and deal with the Parthian threat in the East. He dealt the Parthians a fatal blow from which they never recovered and reconquered territory given up under Hadrian. He made the city of Palmyra into a colony, and it rapidly grew into one of the greatest cities of the Roman Empire as it lay on the great trade route to the Far East.

Palmyra's growing power meant in the decades to come that the city became a huge threat to Rome's power in the East (see Chapter 19).

Dealing with the Roman Senate

Severus only came back to Rome in 202. He had no interest in pretending to co-operate with the Senate, the last bastion of the Republic. He started giving administrative jobs to the equestrians and even made them commanders of new legions, as well as putting them in charge of some provinces (a process which had begun under Commodus). He brought in many provincials from the East, which is hardly surprising given where he and his wife came from, and he must have extended Roman citizenship to do this.

Severus was keen on putting up public buildings, and he also increased military pay. Some of the cash he raised by confiscating estates from Niger's and Albinus's supporters. The rest he raised by increasing taxes and by reducing the silver content of the coinage so that he could mint more coins with less silver. That caused inflation (refer to Chapter 7) and would have a disastrous impact on Roman currency.

Beefing up his sons in Britain

By 208, Severus was off again, this time to Britain. Britain's northern frontier was a constant irritation, and he'd already had to order the repair and reconstruction of Hadrian's Wall. But the real reason was to toughen up his two sons, Caracalla and Geta, whom he was determined would succeed him. These two needed all the prestige of a great war of conquest and preferably one that didn't mean any risk for Rome.

The war was a farce. The Roman army headed into Scotland, plagued by guerrilla tribesmen who kept agreeing to peace and then breaking their word. The Romans found it impossible to fight the enemy properly, because small bands of tribesmen just lurked in swamps and disappeared into the forests and mists after attacking the Roman column. The Roman army, weighed down by equipment, got dragged farther and deeper into northern Britain.

Severus's death

After three years of fighting in Britain, Severus died, worn out with old age and gout, in the northern British city of York in 211. Needless to say, he'd seen omens of his own death – he dreamed he was being carried up to heaven and was terrified when an Ethiopian soldier said, 'You've been a conqueror, now be a god!'

Severus's reign was a sign of the future:

- ✔ He was born a long way from Rome.
- ✔ He was made an emperor in the provinces.
- ✔ He died an emperor in the provinces.
- ✔ He spent most of his reign away from Rome.
- ✔ He brought more provincials into the Roman elite than ever before.

Not Living Up to Dad's Expectations – Caracalla (AD 211–217)

Septimius Severus had the succession all nicely worked out when he died. Caracalla had been lined up as co-emperor since 198 and was joined in 208 by his brother Geta. For the first time in Roman history, there were three emperors (*Augusti*) of equal rank. It was a great plan except that the brothers hated each other, and hating each other was of far more concern to them than anything else.

As a boy Caracalla was sensitive, intelligent, and compassionate; he even restored rights to the cities of Antioch and Byzantium which his father had punished for supporting Niger back in 193. But as he grew up, he turned into an arrogant and ambitious thug who loathed his brother and fancied himself as Alexander the Great.

Getting rid of Geta and a host of others

Severus's death in 211 couldn't have come soon enough for Caracalla, who amazingly had already tried to kill his father during the campaign in Britain. Now Caracalla took care to have any of his father's closest advisers murdered, as well as Severus's doctors for not speeding up his death. Caracalla and Geta abandoned the war in Britain and headed home.

Caracalla had his own wife Plautilla murdered, too. She was daughter of his father's favourite, the praetorian prefect Fulvius Plautianus (see the earlier section 'Building a dynasty'). Caracalla had had her exiled to Sicily years before. He then told the praetorians that Geta had plotted against him and had him killed. To do this, he had to get their mother Julia Domna to summon them to her room, so that Geta would be without his bodyguards. Two soldiers rushed in on Caracalla's orders and killed Geta in his mother's arms. Caracalla forced Julia to treat the murder as a deliverance. He had to calm the soldiers down with money and then proceeded to murder any other relatives or members of Marcus Aurelius's family that looked like potential rivals. He didn't stop there and had any supporters of Geta killed, too.

Caracalla's problem was that he refused to take advice from anyone, and resented anyone who knew something he didn't. He was determined to have total power and to prevent anyone else from having power of any sort.

Universal citizenship (AD 212)

In the year 212, Caracalla made the most dramatic change to Roman society for centuries. He declared that all free men within the Empire's borders were to be Roman citizens. The edict is called the *Constitutio Antoniniana* ('the Antoninian Decree'). It finished off a process that had been going on for years, but it was a remarkable gesture, even though Caracalla's real reason for issuing the edict was to raise money.

Caracalla used to demand money with menace from anyone and everyone. He also loaded the population with more taxes – he doubled the tax on freeing slaves, for example. Caracalla desperately needed cash for the soldiers' pay rises and hand-outs to his friends and favourites. So he cancelled exemption from tax on legacies for Roman citizens. By making everyone into Roman citizens, they all became liable for the tax (refer to Chapter 3 for more on the rights and responsibilities of Roman citizens). No wonder he declared 'no-one in the world should have money except me, and I want to give it all to the soldiers!' The army changed, too – because citizenship was a qualification for being a legionary and a reward for an auxiliary soldier, the army started to evolve into a different kind of force.

Caracalla's indulgences

Caracalla had an insatiable blood lust. He loved seeing killing in the arena and even took part in the games himself. He forced senators to provide huge numbers of animals at their expense; he also made them build houses all over the place so that he could stay there if he fancied (but almost never did). He also drove around in chariots dressed in the colours of the Blue faction (see Chapter 8 for circus factions) and had a champion charioteer, called Euprepes, killed just for being a member of a rival faction.

On a journey to Gaul, Caracalla suddenly had a governor killed, and thanks to inscriptions found in Britain with a scrubbed-out name, it seems he might have ordered the execution of a governor there, too. He had four of the Vestal Virgins killed on the grounds that they were no longer virgins, even though he had defiled one of them himself (for information on Vestal Virgins, see Chapter 10).

Caracalla swaggered around with weapons he thought had once been used by Alexander the Great, decided he was a reincarnation of Alexander, and even organised a 16,000-strong force of Macedonians on the lines of Alexander's *phalanx* (a close order of Macedonian infantry). Despite that, he decimated the population of Alexandria and then built a kind of Berlin Wall to divide the survivors because he'd heard that the Alexandrians had treated him as a joke.

The end of Caracalla

Caracalla's opportunity for war came first with fighting off more threats along the Danube; then he set his sights on trying to conquer more territory in the East. He asked the Parthian king Artabanos for the hand in marriage of his daughter, which was instantly rejected, so Caracalla began a war to attack the Parthians. He met his end on that campaign in 217 at the hands of Macrinus the praetorian prefect, who murdered him – events you can read about in the next chapter.

Chapter 19

The Age of the Thug – The Third Century's Soldier Emperors

In This Chapter

▶ Why a Sun-God worshipper became an emperor

▶ How one soldier after another ruled the Roman Empire

▶ Why the Empire started splitting apart

▶ How Aurelian and Probus repaired the Roman world

*B*efore the Severans of 193–235, the emperors had ruled with the Senate, generally treading carefully and going to a lot of trouble to try and maintain a semblance of the old Republican system. Many of them had a genuine sense of duty and a belief that they had a responsibility to the state and that the state came first.

Septimius Severus (refer to Chapter 18) changed all that. He was supremely in charge. The Roman Empire became a tool he used to advance himself and his family. Severus had enough personal prestige to hold the Empire together, but the soldiers knew they held all the trump cards. Macrinus, Elagabalus, and Severus Alexander were made emperor because of the soldiers; the Senate had no choice. In any case, the Senate was unrecognisable from the one Augustus had known. There were far more senators, very few were from Italy, and most spent little or no time in Rome. These days the emperor made the laws and the Senate just rubber-stamped them.

The decisive power in the Roman world was the army. It always had been, but now it was absolutely out in the open, and the soldiers knew it. The army made and broke emperors. Because the Roman army was never a single organisation but a collection of dozens of units scattered across the Empire, there was plenty of potential for rival claims on the throne. During the next 50 years, the Roman Empire tore itself apart.

The First Thug on the Throne: Marcus Opelius Macrinus

Marcus Opelius Macrinus came from Caesarea in Mauretania in North Africa. Not much is known about him because he came from such a modest background. Even so, he'd worked his way up from nowhere to equestrian status. Despite his obscure origins, he was a lawyer with a reputation for having a healthy respect for the law. This probably explains why he was given the prestigious job of procurator in charge of Caracalla's private property (to read about Caracalla, go to Chapter 18). Macrinus was then promoted to prefect of the Praetorian Guard, a job he did so well he was more or less left to get on with it by himself.

How to take the throne

An African soothsayer announced that Macrinus and his son Diadumenian were destined to be emperors. This prophecy put Macrinus in a fright because it was inevitable Caracalla would have him killed if the story got out. So he promptly organised a conspiracy and had Caracalla murdered on campaign.

Macrinus had been clever enough to put it about that a conspiracy of soldiers had killed Caracalla, so that his own hands seemed clean. To cover his tracks even more, he made Caracalla into a god, though it's hard to think of a less deserving candidate.

Despite murdering Caracalla, Macrinus took Severus as part of his own name, added Antoninus to his son Diadumenian's name, and made him heir apparent.

Macrinus had achieved a first. Because he was an equestrian, he'd never served in the Senate, which means he'd never served in any of the posts all the other emperors had held at least some of. It was a major precedent. Many of the emperors who followed came from what would have seemed impossibly obscure origins a few years before.

How to lose popularity

Despite whatever talents he may have had, Macrinus didn't secure his position as emperor very well. Already unpopular because of his modest origins, he made several mistakes and misjudgements:

✔ **He lost Roman territory.** After killing Caracalla, Macrinus carried on the campaign against the Parthians, but after losing two battles, knocked up a compromise peace and had to hand over Armenia. It was a bad move because it made him look like a loser and meant he lost any prestige he might have earned himself through murdering Caracalla.

✔ **He failed to get rid of any other potential Severan candidates for the throne.** Macrinus had forgotten that Septimius Severus's widow, Julia Domna – who had committed suicide after Caracalla's death – had a sister (see the next section, 'How to lose the throne').

✔ **He made several unsuitable appointments.** Macrinus promoted Adventus, a former imperial spy. Macrinus made Adventus into a senator, a consul, and even prefect of Rome, despite the fact that Adventus was old and blind, had no relevant experience, and was so uneducated he knew nothing about how the Roman administration worked. The idea seems to have been to divert attention from Macrinus's obscure origins, but along with several other unsuitable appointments and acting high and mighty, all it did was provoke resentment.

✔ **His behaviour alienated the soldiers.** Macrinus had a curious taste for taking part in mime shows; he also liked walking about wearing brooches and a belt decorated with gold and jewels. As far as the soldiers were concerned, this was all too decadent and much too much like a barbarian's taste for them. The fact that Macrinus lived in luxury while they were having a tough life in forts annoyed them, too. They added all these to their list of resentments and felt that killing him was totally justified.

How to lose the throne

Macrinus was eventually deposed by Julia Domna (Caracalla's mother) and her daughter Julia Soaemias, who installed Julia Soaemias's son Elagabalus as emperor. Although Macrinus sent some troops to get rid of Elagabalus, the troops promptly changed sides. At the battle that followed, even more soldiers went over to Elagabalus, and Macrinus was doomed. He and his son escaped but were soon caught and executed.

Elagabalus (AD 218–222)

Caracalla's mother, Julia Domna, had a sister called Julia Maesa (who died in 225). Julia Maesa was massively ambitious. She was also boiling with rage that Macrinus had thrown her out of the palace when Caracalla was killed.

Julia Maesa did not let the fact that she was only related by marriage to Septimius Severus impede her (see Figure 19-1 to see the Severan family tree). She decided that her grandsons, Elagabalus and Severus Alexander, were the ideal candidates to replace Macrinus. There was also a handy rumour going about that Caracalla was the real father of Elagabalus (he looked like Caracalla, too), which Maesa encouraged because Caracalla's popularity with the troops would help her cause.

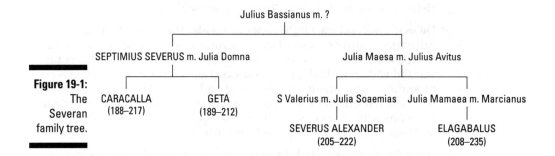

Figure 19-1: The Severan family tree.

Maesa used hard cash to buy the soldiers at Emesa in Syria, and they declared Elagabalus emperor in 218. Elagabalus took the name Marcus Aurelius Antoninus so that he could pretend to be part of the direct descent from the original Marcus Aurelius.

Thanks to all the spurious descents from Marcus Aurelius and Antoninus Pius being claimed, Caracalla's and Elagabalus's coins bear similar names to those of their so-called illustrious forbearers. Thanks to realistic portraits, the coins can be distinguished, but with imperial inscriptions sometimes it really isn't possible to tell the difference between those of Caracalla and Elagabalus.

The 14-year-old Elagabalus might have been Emperor, but the people who were really in charge were his grandmother Julia Maesa and his mother Julia Soaemias (Julia Soaemias was allowed to watch the Senate and even run her own women's senate). What they'd established was a new eastern Severan dynasty at Rome. Initially, Rome welcomed Elagabalus because he was good-looking and seemed a better bet than Macrinus, but from day one he took no notice of worrying about government. The Roman people were horrified at what followed.

Elagabalus's god

Elagabalus's real name was Varius Avitus Bassianus. He was a fanatical worshipper of the sun-god Heliogabalus (or Elah-Gabal) of Emesa, and that's how he got his nickname.

The Sun-God Heliogabalus was worshipped at Emesa in Syria where there was a black conical stone, which was generally believed to have fallen from the sky and landed on the spot. It might, in fact, have been a meteorite. Once he became emperor, Elagabalus had the stone taken to Rome.

Elagabalus had only one serious agenda: imposing the worship of the Sun-God and preventing any other cults apart from that of the Great Mother *(Magna Mater)*, another Eastern religion. To that end, he built a temple to the Sun-God.

Elagabalus's government

Rumours started circulating about Elagabalus's homosexuality, the way he posed as 'Venus' for the purposes of copulation, and his interest in well-endowed men to whom he gave all sorts of high-profile jobs. He made a barber, for example, the prefect of the grain supply and a mule-driver the collector of the inheritance tax. Elagabalus sold off any positions or privileges he could, purely to raise cash. His freedmen were made commanders of legions or governors of provinces. His favourite, whom he 'married', was an athlete called Zoticus who threw his weight about in the palace.

The difference between Elagabalus and, say, someone like Antoninus Pius (138–161), discussed in Chapter 17, is so colossal it's sometimes hard to believe it's the same Empire. Even more incredibly, Elagabalus actually took the official name 'Antoninus Pius' himself, and called himself that on his coins.

Elagabalus's women

Elagabalus's first wife in a marriage arranged by his grandmother Julia Maesa was Julia Paula, who was disgusted by him. Because she came from an old Roman aristocratic society, that's no surprise. He divorced her in 220, and she retired into private life. (In the mayhem that followed, Julia Paula was one of the few lucky ones. She lived.)

His second wife was his lover and Vestal Virgin called Aquileia Severa. Their marriage caused such outrage, even though Elagabalus claimed to the Senate any children they might have were bound to be divine, he had to divorce her, too.

Wife number three was Annia Faustina, a descendant of Marcus Aurelius. This marriage was clearly an attempt to reinforce his crumbling regime. (During this marriage, Elagabalus went back to Aquileia, whom he seems to have really liked, though this just made him more unpopular than ever.)

Elagabalus's tastes

Elagabalus devoted his life to pleasure. These are some (and only some – there are plenty more) of the things he liked:

- His pool had to be perfumed with saffron.

- He had couches made of silver and cushions stuffed with rabbit fur and partridge feathers.

- He had lions and leopards for pets.

- Presents at his banquets included eunuchs and four-horse chariots.

- He drove various chariots pulled by elephants, stags, tigers, dogs, and lions.

- He wore clothes made of pure silk – the first in Rome to do so – and never wore the same shoes twice.

- He sometimes invited eight men with the same disability to dinner, such as eight deaf men, eight one-eyed men, or eight bald men.

The end of Elagabalus

Elagabalus went too far when he decided to do in his cousin Alexianus (who succeeded as Severus Alexander, see the next section). Alexanius, adopted as Elagabalus's heir in 221, was a decent young man who was loved by the soldiers. Elagabalus seems to have had a sudden whim to order Alexanius's execution. The troops raced round, rescued Alexanius, his mother, and grandmother, and told Elagabalus that if he wanted to stay emperor he'd have to give up his favourites and all his degenerate activities.

Elagabalus pretended to make peace, but he was still hell-bent on killing Alexanius. On 6 March 222, the praetorians had had enough – Elagabalus and his mother Julia Soaemias were killed and their bodies dragged around Rome before being thrown in the Tiber. No emperor ever before, however degenerate, had been humiliated that way.

Severus Alexander (AD 222–235)

Despite the horrors of his cousin Elagabalus's reign and the distinctly unpleasant family he seemed to come from, Alexianus was a thoroughly decent boy. In fact, if he'd been born a century earlier into an altogether better time, he might have been one of the Five Good Emperors of the second century (refer to Chapter 17). But he wasn't. He was only 13 when he was made emperor, changing his name from Alexianus to Alexander and becoming Marcus Aurelius Severus Alexander.

A little stability in a sea of chaos

Back in the first century, Nero (54–68) had got sick of being dominated by his mother Agrippina and killed her (refer to Chapter 16). But Alexander didn't do that – he put up and shut up. He was under the power of his grandmother Julia Maesa until she died in 226 and then his mother Julia Mamaea who even declared herself to be Augusta, as if she was empress in her own right.

Julia Mamaea was no idiot. Realising that her and Alexander's lives would be at risk if another bout of military anarchy followed, she decided that a show of respect to the Senate would pay dividends. So 16 senators were appointed to the imperial council, and it was made possible for a senator to be Praetorian prefect. One of the greatest lawyers in Roman history, Domitius Ulpianus, was made Praetorian prefect, but in reality he ran the government of the Roman Empire under Mamaea's supervision.

If that sounds bad, it wasn't – at least, not all of it. The equestrian administrators under Ulpianus did a good job generally, and the Roman Empire was temporarily restored to stability and sanity. For a good ten years the frontiers were peaceful, hand-outs to the mob were maintained at a sensible level, cash was found to subsidise teachers, the special money *(alimentia)* for poor families was increased, and the imperial court went on an economy drive to pay for all this.

But not all is well

Despite the benefits of a more stable government, things were far from sorted. The praetorian prefect Ulpianus was murdered by his own Praetorian troops by 228. They also wanted to kill the historian Dio Cassius, consul in 229, on the grounds that he was too severe for them. Dio was saved when Alexander discharged him.

The Sassanids

By AD 224, the Parthians had ruled Persia since 247 BC. In about AD 10, a Parthian king called Artabanos II threw off Greek cultural influence and restored old Persian traditions and religion. Ardashir, also known as Artaxerxes, was descended from a man called Sassan. He overthrew the last Parthian king, Artabanos IV, in AD 224, establishing the Sassanid dynasty and restoring the ancient Zoroastrianism religion. Zoroastrianism was one of the first ancient religions to teach monotheism, the idea of a resurrection after death, and eternal life for the reunited body and soul. It still exists today in the Middle East.

And then there were the frontiers. The Parthian Empire collapsed in 230, and into the power vacuum came a Persian dynasty called the Sassanids under a king called Ardashir, who was determined to recover all the land the Persians had once ruled – which meant much of the Roman Empire in the East. Alexander did defeat Ardashir, but it cost him dearly in men, which damaged his prestige. Meanwhile, the Alamanni tribe in Germany decided to take advantage of the Eastern war. Alexander headed for the German frontier in 234, but his troops mutinied and he had to bribe the Alamanni to hold off.

The end of Alexander and Julia

The frontier trouble was the chance Maximinus Thrax ('Maximinus the Thracian') needed. He'd served in Alexander's Eastern war and was now one of the commanders in the German war. To the soldiers who were disappointed by Alexander's lack of military skill, Maximinus looked a much better bet. Alexander and Julia Mamaea were murdered in their camp near Mainz in Germany.

Blink and you'll miss them: A slew of emperors who followed Alexander

If it wasn't for the coins of the soldier emperors we'd know a lot less about them. Coins provide names, portraits, and records of some of these rulers' deeds and in a few cases are the only evidence we have at all. (But see Chapter 7 for the effect of all the instability on the coinage's quality.) Portraits of emperors on coins from the years AD 235–284 tell the story. Almost to a man they show brutal, unshaven thugs because these were the men who appealed to the soldiers. Usually men who had risen from the ranks, they cared little or nothing for the Senate or traditional Roman virtues, though, of course, they pretended they did. Hardly a single one died in his bed. While they battled it out, Rome's enemies on the borders started to move in for the kill.

- ✔ **Maximinus 'Thrax' I (235–238):** He set the pace. A huge man, he fought the Germans successfully, but he was ruthless and cruel and hated the Roman aristocracy. The Senate tried to get rid of him by supporting a coup in 238 led by the governor of Africa, Gordianus.

- ✔ **Gordianus I and Gordianus II (238):** The former Governor of Africa ruled briefly with his son, but Maximinus's friends killed them.

- ✔ **Balbinus and Pupienus (238):** The Senate made these two senators into joint emperors in 238. The Praetorians killed them, but not before Maximinus's own men had mutinied and killed him, too.

✔ **Gordianus III (238–244):** Gordianus I's grandson was made emperor. He was killed on campaign against the Persians by the praetorian prefect, a soldier called Philip I the Arab who became the next emperor.

✔ **Philip I the Arab (244–249):** Philip defeated the Persians and celebrated the thousandth year of Rome with a vast festival of games. Philip sent the governor of Lower Moesia, Trajan Decius, to suppress a rebellion amongst the Danube legions. But the rebels made Trajan Decius emperor, and he defeated and killed Philip in a battle near Verona.

✔ **Trajan Decius (249–251):** Decius lasted two years, during which he famously started a ruthless persecution of Christians. Trajan Decius was killed fighting the Goths.

✔ **Trebonianus Gallus (251–253):** He replaced Decius and ruled jointly with Decius's son Hostilian. Gallus made a humiliating peace with the Goths, but it was becoming difficult for any emperor to manage the various border threats. He also faced a devastating plague that swept across the Roman world and killed Hostilian. Gallus was killed in 253 by his own soldiers who preferred the idea of being ruled by a governor called Aemilian, who had succeeded in defeating the Goths.

✔ **Aemilian (253):** Aemilian only lasted about three months: He was murdered by Valerian, who had been gathering an army to help Gallus. Read more about Valerian in the next section.

Valerian 1 (AD 253–260) and Gallienus (253–268)

Valerian was a decent man, but he faced all the consequences of years of anarchy which had allowed frontier defences to fall to pieces. He ruled jointly with his son Gallienus, realising it was the only way to try and manage the frontier troubles and run the Empire. By 256, Valerian had set out to fight the Persian Sassanid king Shapur.

While his father Valerian was fighting in the East, Gallienus was supposed to be in charge of the western provinces of the Roman Empire; in reality, he was trying to rule an Empire rent by revolts, plagues, and famine. By 262, following hot on the heels of a catastrophic earthquake that wrecked cities in Asia and shook Rome, a plague reached Rome that, at its height, was said to be killing up to 5,000 people in a single day across the Empire. In the East Gallienus faced the rising power of the Palmyrenes, and in the West something unprecedented happened: Part of the Roman Empire broke away to create the Gallic Empire.

Valerian dies and a rebellion starts

Four years into the war against the Persians in 260, Valerian's army was crippled by plague. During peace negotiations, Valerian was captured by Shapur and died in prison. It was a spectacular and unprecedented humiliation for a Roman emperor.

An officer called Macrianus in Valerian's army promptly took his chance and proclaimed his two sons, Macrianus the Younger and Quietus, emperors in 260. The two Macriani headed west with an army to get rid of Valerian's son Gallienus.

Events in the Palymrenes

Palmyra, an oasis on the great trade route into Mesopotamia and farther east, was one of the largest and richest cities in the Eastern Roman Empire. The people had nomadic origins, a tradition they put to good use when Mark Antony tried to capture Palmyra in 41 BC just to plunder its riches. Hearing he was coming, the people carted their goods across the Euphrates, and Antony's men found the city empty. Later, Palmyra was given privileges by various Roman emperors, including being allowed to tax all traffic passing through, which made it even wealthier. Palmyra was made into a Roman colony by Septimius Severus (193–211; refer to Chapter 18). Publius Septimius Odaenathus was a member of the most important Palmyran family and declared himself King of Palmyra after Valerian I was killed in 260.

Actually, Odaenathus had done Gallienus a favour because this was the only way the East could possibly be held against the Sassanids and get rid of the usurper Quietus. Gallienus made Odaenathus 'Duke of the East' and commander of all Roman forces in the region. Odaenathus attacked and killed Quietus at Emesa in 261.

Under Odaenathus, Palmyra became the major force in the Roman East. Odaenathus recaptured Mesopotamia for the Roman Empire and was even given the title *imperator*. But Palmyra's power was growing unchecked. Odaenathus was assassinated in 267 as part of a local dynastic plot. His son Vabalathus inherited the throne, but had to share power with his beautiful, highly intelligent, and ambitious mother Zenobia. But time was running out for the Palmyrenes.

The Gallic Empire breaks away

Valerian had made Marcus Cassianus Latinius Postumus commander of the Rhine garrisons. In 259, Postumus was declared emperor at Cologne by his troops. Unlike a lot of other pretenders, he wasn't stupid enough to think he could have the whole Empire to himself.

Postumus had control of Gaul, Spain, and Britain, and he ran it like a proper Roman Empire. Today it's known as the Gallic Empire. It was truly astonishing because he adopted all the trappings of a Roman emperor and set up his own Senate with consuls and all the usual magistracies. He was a generally popular and sensible ruler who tried to reform the coinage and posed with all the proper Roman virtues. The only difference was that his empire wasn't centred on Rome, but Trier.

Gallienus's death and the next emperor, Claudius II

Gallienus was educated, interested in Greek culture, and tolerant of Christians. He preferred men of ability, which was why he used experienced soldiers who had reached equestrian status to command his legions and relied increasingly on a crack body of mobile troops to reach trouble spots.

Gallienus beat off an invasion of Greece by a Germanic tribe called the Heruli. He had left a general called Acilius Aureolus in charge of the war against Postumus, but Aureolus took his chance and headed towards Rome. Gallienus caught him up and besieged him at Milan, where Gallienus was murdered in 268 by some of his own officers, who included the future emperors Claudius II and Aurelian. Gallienus's death was a waste.

Claudius II Gothicus (268–270) was one of the conspirators involved in Gallienus's death. He earned his title after winning a massive victory over the Goths in the Battle of Naissus. His reign was short-lived, however, because he caught the plague and died in 270, a rare instance of an emperor *not* being murdered during the third century.

Aurelian (AD 270–275)

Succeeding Claudius II was a highly effective general called Aurelian. Aurelian was a rare instance of a Roman emperor in the third century who could control the army, put down rebels, hold the frontiers, and tackle domestic problems. As the sections 'Annihilating Palmyra' and 'The end of the Gallic Empire' explain, he settled the Palmyra dispute and reclaimed the Gallic Empire for Rome. During a great triumph held in Rome to celebrate his victories, he had both Tetricus of the Gallic Empire and Zenobia of Palmyra walk in the procession, but he pensioned both off and allowed them to live out their days in peace.

The ruins of Palmyra

Palmyra, which sits on top of an underground spring, means *city of palms*. Today, it's Syria's number one tourist attraction. Visitors today can see the Street of Columns, a triumphal arch, the remains of several temples, and other buildings scattered over an area of more than 6 square kilometres (2 square miles). The on-site museum has mosaics and paintings that testify to the huge wealth enjoyed by the Palmyrenes before Aurelian destroyed the city.

Annihilating Palmyra

In Palmyra, when Vabalathus was declared emperor in 271, it was the last straw for Aurelian. Aurelian headed east and defeated the Palmyrenes at Antioch and Emesa. Next he crossed the desert and besieged Palmyra. During the siege, Zenobia was captured while trying to escape and hire Persian reinforcements. She was deposed, and a Roman garrison established. Aurelian headed to the Danube to deal with the frontier only to hear that a revolt in Palmyra had killed the whole garrison. Aurelian raced back to Palmyra and wiped the city out, totally destroying it. Palmyra wasn't rediscovered until travellers from Europe made it there in the 1700s.

The end of the Gallic Empire

Everything started going wrong for the Gallic Empire in 268 when a revolt against Postumus was put down. Postumus refused the soldiers permission to sack Mainz as punishment. So they killed Postumus. A succession of very short-lived emperors followed, ending with Tetricus I (270–273) and his son Tetricus II. Aurelian, just back from wiping out the Palmyrenes, invaded Gaul in 273. The two Tetrici promptly (and wisely) surrendered, and that was the end of the Gallic Empire.

Aurelian at home

Aurelian tried to reform the coinage and end the skyrocketing inflation with modest success, but he used the money he had taken from Palmyra to pay for handouts of bread, meat, oil, and salt in Rome. He repaired the Tiber's banks and started making food and shipping guilds into semi-official organisations to improve commerce and production.

The Aurelian walls of Rome

Although he was a brilliant general, Aurelian knew only too well how real the threat was to Rome from rebels and barbarians. He ordered the building of a massive new circuit of brick and concrete walls to protect the city. Nineteen kilometres long (12 miles), they were finished under Probus (276–282) and had watchtowers and massive gates all the way round. The walls were constantly improved over the next 200 years and eventually had 383 towers, 14 gates, and 116 latrines for the guards. Large stretches survive more or less intact and are one of the most impressive sights in Rome today.

Aurelian co-operated with the Senate and involved it in his reforms though he was always ready for trouble – his nickname was *Manu ad ferrum* which translates as 'Hand on iron', meaning he was always ready to draw his sword if necessary.

The death of Aurelian

In 275, Aurelian was in Thrace, heading off to deal with the Persians once more. Along the way, he was murdered by Praetorian officers who'd been told (falsely) by an imperial secretary that they were on the list of men to be executed. Thoroughly ashamed of their actions, the soldiers asked the Senate to pick the next emperor, the first time anything like that had happened probably since Nerva's accession in 96.

The Sun-God

Interest in monotheism (belief in one god) was becoming more and more common in the Roman world. Aurelian was especially keen on the god called the 'Unconquered Sun-God' *(Sol Invictus)* and had been impressed by Sun-God worship in places like Palmyra. He built a temple to Sol in Rome and created a college of priests to man it. He posed as a priest of Sol on his coins, which was a big step towards a world in which the emperor presented himself as a divinely appointed representative of a god on Earth. Sol's feast-day was 25 December, later adapted to be the winter festival of the Christians. But Aurelian had no intention of getting rid of the old gods – he just wanted Sol to be the most important.

The Senate picked an elderly senator called Tacitus after a delay of six months. Tacitus successfully defeated the Goths in Asia Minor but died from old age after a reign of only about seven months in the summer of 276. His half-brother Florianus, the praetorian prefect, declared himself to be emperor. Unfortunately for him, he wasn't the only candidate. Probus, Aurelian's former general in the East, was also declared emperor. Florianus's troops decided Probus was the better bet and killed Florianus.

Probus (AD 276–282)

Probus was young enough, wise enough, and capable enough to have restored the Roman world. He made his way to Rome, was approved by the Senate, and promptly set out on a war to defeat German tribes. He was successful and also put down rebellions in Britain, Gaul, and Germany; he even hired some of his prisoners-of-war as soldiers to strengthen his own forces.

Probus kept his soldiers busy with public building projects and even planting vineyards when they weren't fighting. Word seems to have got out that Probus thought conditions were improving so much that soon the army, or large parts of it anyway, could be discharged. That didn't go down well amongst an army already resentful at being made to work on building sites, and as a result, Probus was murdered by troops in the provinces of Raetia and Noricum. A waste of a potentially good emperor.

The End of the Principate

Things became chaotic again following Probus's murder. The troops who murdered Probus proclaimed the praetorian prefect Carus emperor in 282. Carus (282–283) promptly appointed his sons Numerian and Carinus his heirs and set off with Numerian to finish off the Sassanid Persians. Carus defeated the Persians but had an amazing stroke of bad luck in his camp: He was struck by lightning and killed. At least that was the story put about. Another possibility is that he was killed by Numerian's father-in-law, the praetorian prefect Aper, who fancied seeing his descendants on the throne more quickly. Either way, Numerian (282–284), who preferred writing poetry to fighting, set off back to Rome but was mysteriously murdered in his litter in 284, probably also by Aper. That left Carinus (282–285) in charge.

In the spring of 285, Diocles, head of the imperial bodyguard, was chosen by the army in the East to avenge the death of Numerian. Diocles headed west and met Carinus's army near the Danube. Carinus, who was extremely unpopular, was killed by one of his own men, and his troops went over to Diocles.

Carinus's death marked the end of the principate, the system established by Augustus 300 years earlier and which had evolved over the years. It's pretty obvious it was in a very dodgy state, so it's just as well that Diocles was something of a visionary. He realised that the Roman world had changed beyond recognition. It needed a new system, it needed it fast, and he decided he was the man to bring that about.

Chapter 20

East Is East and West Is West: Diocletian and Constantine

*B*y the end of the third century, the days when the emperor could do much of his ruling from Rome, or concentrate on one war at a time, were long gone. Roman emperors, good or bad, were spending virtually all their time on campaign. Instead of just relying on well-established garrisons around the Roman world, highly mobile units had also to be created so that soldiers could race from one trouble spot to another. When the emperors weren't fighting one another, they were moving from one frontier to another, shoring up the defences, fighting back barbarians, and negotiating peace deals. The coasts of Britain and Gaul, for example, were plagued by pirates from Northern Europe, so a series of coastal fortified compounds were installed to help protect commerce, towns, villas, and farms. New fortifications were being built on new frontiers as well.

Meanwhile, society across the Roman Empire was changing. The endless parade of rebel emperors disrupted provincial government. As vast quantities of resources were being poured into the army and defences, provincials found themselves being taxed to pay for all the various rebellions as well as the legitimate army. Some lost their land and livings and formed marauding bands of landless outlaws.

This chapter tells the story of how one soldier emperor named Diocletian tried to transform the Roman world in an attempt to repair the damage before it was too late, and how another Roman emperor named Constantine issued an edict that changed Rome forever.

On the Case: Diocletian (AD 284–305)

Diocles, born around 240 to a poor family in Dalmatia, had spent a lifetime witnessing the chaos of the soldier emperors. Like so many of the emperors of the third century, he rose through the ranks of the army entirely on merit. That was how he ended up on the imperial bodyguard under the emperor Numerian (282–284) and why he was chosen to avenge Numerian's death (refer to Chapter 19 for the details on this episode).

When he became emperor in 284 (following the murder of Carinus, who ruled from 282 to 285, and the defection of Carinus's men to his side; refer to Chapter 19), Diocles changed his name to Gaius Aurelius Valerius Diocletianus. It helped echo former emperors' names.

Diocletian moved fast and decisively after getting rid of Carinus. In 285, he made his comrade Maximian his Caesar and, therefore, his heir. The next year, he made Maximian into a joint Augustus and sent him to Gaul to sort out the Bagaudae, a mob of landless peasants who were ravaging the countryside. Maximian soon defeated Bagaudae, with the help of another soldier called Carausius, who went on to become one of the most successful rebel Emperors of the time (more on him in the section 'The rebellion in Britain: Carausius', later in this chapter).

Four emperors are better than one: The Tetrarchy

Diocletian knew that the Empire was too big, too unstable, and too insecure for one emperor to run alone. Although the Roman Empire had had joint emperors before, Diocletian did something different: He split the Empire in half. Maximian would rule the Latin West, and Diocletian would rule the Greek East.

In 293, Diocletian came up with the idea of the *Tetrarchy,* in which four men would rule the Roman Empire. He appointed two junior emperors, known as Caesars: Constantius Chlorus in the West and Galerius in the East. Constantius would assist Maximian, and Galerius would assist Diocletian. Then, at an appropriate point in the future, Maximian and Diocletian would abdicate, and Constantius and Galerius would succeed them as the Augusti and appoint their own Caesars.

Tetrarchy comes from two Greek words: *tetra-* ('four') and *archos* ('chief' or 'commander'). So Tetrarchy means 'four chiefs'.

Each tetrarch had his headquarters. Diocletian ruled from Nicomedia in Asia Minor (Turkey), Galerius from Sirmium in modern Serbia, Maximian from Milan in Italy, and Constantius from Trier in Gaul. So much for Rome. Now the original city wasn't even an emperor's base. It was too far from the trouble areas.

The idea was to create a self-perpetuating system in which the succession was assured and the best men were selected for the job. On paper it looked like a brilliant system, and in the beginning, it went well. Constantius was able to deal with the rebellion of Carausius and Allectus in Britain (described in the section 'The rebellion in Britain: Carausius'), Diocletian was able to successfully deal with rebellions in Egypt, and Galerius sorted out the troublesome Persians.

Repairing the broken Empire

During the 20 years of his reign Diocletian energetically restored cities, roads, and infrastructure. Maximian, for his part, ran a major building programme in Rome. (It's a mark of just how much there was to do and the nature of the times that Diocletian didn't even visit Rome for the first time until 303, by which time he'd reigned for nearly 20 years.) But the greatest impact came from a series of major reforms.

The army

Diocletian started the process of turning the enlarged army into two halves: the mainly cavalry mobile field force called the *comitatenses* and the frontier garrisons called the *limitanei*. This system which became fully established under Constantine I (307–337). You can read more about the organisation of the army in Chapter 5.

Provinces

Provinces were divided up, roughly doubling the total, so that no individual governor would be powerful enough to start a rebellion. Britain, for example, had started life as one province, was divided into two by Septimius Severus (see Chapter 18), and was now made into four. Even Italy was broken up this way. Regional groups of provinces were arranged into *diœceses* (districts; singular *diœcesis*), 13 in total, each of which was overseen by a *vicarius* (vicar). The vicars were under the control of four Praetorian prefects, one for each of the four emperors. Provinces were no longer governed by a senatorial *legatus* (see Chapter 3); instead the position was variously called *praeses* ('protector') and *rector* ('leader').

The *diœcesis, vicarius*, and *rector* of Diocletian's new system probably look familiar. That's because the Christian church modelled some of its own government on Diocletian's system. So today bishops run dioceses, and the Anglican church's local priests are called vicars. A rector is a priest or layperson in charge of an institution like a college.

Tax reform, Roman style

The tax assessment system that Diocletian set up may seem complicated, but it isn't. This is how it worked:

1. Land was now counted across the Empire by a fixed unit called the *iugerum* (plural: *iugera*).

2. Each iugerum was measured for how much it could produce according to a fixed unit of production called the *iugum* (plural: *iuga*).

3. Iugera that produced more or higher-value crops had to pay more tax. So 5 iugera of vineyard was assessed at 1 iugum, but it took 40 iugera of poor mountain land to be assessed at 1 iugum. Likewise 40 iugera of vineyard would be assessed for 8 iuga.

Money matters

Running Diocletian's new system cost a fortune. Taxes were levied not just in cash but also in kind, meaning people found themselves obliged to hand over money as well as produce and goods that the Empire needed. So if you made woollen goods, then you paid over some of your woollen goods to the government for tax. Paying in kind helped get round inflation. To halt the roller-coaster inflation of the third century, Diocletian fixed the prices in an Edict of Maximum Prices in 301. The same year he also fixed maximum salaries.

To make taxes less painful, in 296 Diocletian changed the system of assessment so that people only paid what was fair. The idea was to get rid of an almost infinite number of different local systems. Under Diocletian's system, better land was liable for more tax, poor land for less. The number of people was counted as well, so that a poll tax could be levied. This way each farm or villa ended up with a taxable value that took into account the people who lived and worked there and how much the estate could produce. Every year, the government announced how much it needed and divided that up amongst all the *iuga* which had been counted. (If you're interested in the details of this system, head to the sidebar 'Tax reform, Roman style'.)

But Diocletian's monetary and tax reforms didn't work properly in practice:

✔ Diocletian didn't have enough gold and silver to make coinage stable. Inflation continued upwards, and many goods just disappeared from the market. Eventually the Edict on Maximum Prices had to be withdrawn.

✔ Corrupt tax assessors over-measured estates' liabilities and pocketed the difference.

✔ Tax collectors could over-collect and pocket the difference (though if they under-collected, they had to pay the shortfall).

✔ The system of assessments effectively forced people to stay where they were permanently.

The Dominate: A new order

The result of Diocletian's new world was the beginning of the totalitarian state: interfering in every aspect of people's lives, and restricting freedom and movement. The new order is called the Dominate because the emperor was now called *Dominus* ('lord'), styled *Jovius* ('Jupiter's Chosen One'), and was treated as if he was a god. Appropriately enough, he was shown in statues and on reliefs wearing a halo. It's also very striking how emperors were no longer portrayed as individuals. Each of the Tetrarchs looks like all the others – a deliberate way of making rulers into a generic type.

But unlike the madmen who came before him, such as Commodus (discussed in Chapter 18) or Elagabalus (discussed in Chapter 19), Diocletian was just creating a new imperial image rather than actually deluding himself into believing he really was a god.

Persecuting Christians

In 303, Diocletian and Maximian began a major persecution of Christians. Maximian's suppression of Christianity in North Africa was especially severe. Actually, it remains something of a mystery why this happened because the Christians had been left more or less alone ever since the last persecution under Valerian I, which came to an end in 260. Diocletian even had a Christian wife. But his sidekick Galerius was fanatically anti-Christian. Galerius must have convinced Diocletian that the Christians were subversive and dangerous, and that the new totalitarian state had no room for any religion that undermined total loyalty to the regime. The persecution involved destroying churches and confiscating any holy texts, but Diocletian ordered no bloodshed, perhaps out of deference to his wife and his personal tendency to toleration. Galerius had a deathbed change of heart in 311 (see the later section 'Issuing the Edict of Milan').

Diocletian's spies

Diocletian did away with the *frumentarii* spies (see Chapter 17), who were extremely unpopular, and replaced them with *agentes* (agents). They did much the same job, but because their main role was carrying despatches, they were probably able to operate rather more undercover.

Diocletian's palace

Diocletian built himself a huge fortified palace at Split on the Dalmatian coast of the Adriatic, now part of modern Croatia. Split was then called *Spalato*, which means 'little palace', though it was anything but small. After he abdicated in 305, Diocletian spent most of the rest of his life there. Modelled on a Roman fort, the palace had the imperial apartments in the southern half, while the north was given over to servants, slaves, and soldiers. Huge parts of the palace have survived.

The rebellion in Britain: Carausius

During Diocletian's reign an extraordinary rebellion broke out in Britain. In many ways it was the most unusual rebellion of the whole of Roman history. It was certainly the cheekiest. It was led by a man called Carausius whose breathtaking front, swaggering bravado, and creative political spin were without parallel.

The making of a pirate

Mausaeus Carausius grew up on the coast of where modern Belgium is now. He became a soldier in Maximian's army and was so successful at defeating the Bagaudae in Gaul, that he was given the job of clearing Saxon raiders who were sailing down the North Sea and attacking towns and villas in Gaul and Britain.

Carausius used a Roman fleet to attack the raiders. He was so effective at this and became so popular that Maximian became annoyed. A story circulated that Carausius was waiting for the raiders to help themselves to loot, then he attacked them and took what they'd stolen. Maximian declared Carausius a criminal and offered a bounty for his capture.

Maximian might have put the story out himself, perhaps because he was jealous. We don't know. But what is certain is that Carausius now had nothing to lose. In 286, he declared himself emperor in Britain and part of Gaul. He was clearly popular because there isn't a hint of opposition to his rule.

Carausius's cheek

Carausius was a propaganda genius. Not only did he declare himself emperor, but he also

✔ Renamed himself Marcus Aurelius Mausaeus Carausius, echoing Septimius Severus 80 years before (Chapter 18) in creating a pseudo-claim to be descended from the 'good emperors' of the second century.

✔ Issued the first good silver coinage for generations (so perhaps he had indeed helped himself to loot!) to ensure his soldiers' loyalty, which Diocletian hadn't been able to produce.

✔ Posed on all his coins as a real toughie but associated himself with all sorts of proper Roman virtues like *pax* ('peace') and *uberitas* ('fertility') and claimed to be renewing the Roman Empire.

✔ Put slogans from the poetry of Augustus's state poet Virgil, written 300 years before, on his coins (for Virgil, see Chapter 1). This was an absolutely unprecedented move because no-one, even Augustus himself, had ever done that before.

What Carausius was saying was that his regime was the new Roman Empire. He was 'restoring' all the qualities of Augustus's world but in Britain, not in Rome.

✔ Declared he was a member of the Tetrarchy, too – adding insult to injury – and struck coins showing him with Diocletian and Maximian and the legend *Carausius et Fratres Sui*, 'Carausius and His Brothers'.

As you can imagine, the Tetrarchs were spitting with anger and called Carausius 'the pirate' and other insulting names. They tried to send a fleet in 289 to destroy Carausius, but it was wrecked by a storm.

Done in by a coup: Allectus

Carausius lasted in power till 293, swaggering away in Britain to Diocletian and Maximian's fury. But Carausius was murdered in a coup in 293 by his finance minister Allectus. Allectus made himself emperor, but it couldn't last.

The Empire strikes back

In 296, a huge fleet was gathered in Boulogne on the north coast of Gaul. The praetorian prefect Asclepiodotus invaded southern Britain, fought a battle with Allectus, and killed him. Meanwhile, Constantius Chlorus took another part of the fleet and seized London. A magnificent medal was issued to celebrate the event with the legend 'restored to the eternal light', which was how the Tetrarchy modestly liked to see itself.

The rebellion was over. It wasn't the last, in Britain or anywhere else, by any means. But it was certainly the most remarkable.

Like all the best ideas: The Tetrarchy falls apart

The Tetrarchy was a good idea. Too good for the Roman Empire, as it turned out. What Diocletian hadn't taken into account was other people's ambitions.

Because Galerius and Constantius had married their respective seniors' daughters, there was the making of a dynasty. There were also other interested parties, each of whom had an eye on getting a slice of the action.

Following Diocletian's and Maximian's retirements on 1 May 305, Galerius and Constantius succeeded them just as they were supposed to. Galerius appointed his ambitious nephew Maximinus II Daia as his Caesar, and Constantius recruited a man called Severus II. In theory, the Tetrarchy was now in its next phase. But then things started to go wrong

Too many cooks

When Diocletian and Maximian retired, and the new Augusti Galerius and Constantius had appointed their own Caesars (Maximinus II Daia and Severus II, respectively), a few people were a bit disgruntled by the way things had shaken out, particularly

- ✔ **Maxentius:** Maximian's son
- ✔ **Constantine:** Constantius I's son by an earlier marriage (a lot more on him in the section, 'Constantine I, the Great', later in this chapter)
- ✔ **Licinius:** Diocletian's adopted son

If that sounds like a recipe for disaster, it was.

Succession woes

Maximian's son Maxentius took grave exception to being cut out, and so did Constantius's son Constantine.

In 306, Constantius died in York, Britain, while on campaign. His troops rejected the idea of Severus II succeeding him and promptly declared Constantius's son Constantine emperor instead. It was an act that changed the history of the world.

Galerius was furious, but was very wary of letting a civil war break out. So he offered a compromise: Severus II would become Augustus in the West, as planned, and Constantine would become Severus's Caesar and thus the heir. Unfortunately, things started to heat up. Maximian's son Maxentius, still resentful at being cut out of the deal (any deal in fact), decided to throw his hat into the ring, and then things really got wild. Here, in the general order in which they happened, are the events that kept people guessing about who was *really* in charge between 305 and 308:

1. Maxentius led a coup in Rome and recalled his father Maximian who became emperor again.

2. Galerius sent Severus II against the usurpers, but his own soldiers abandoned him, and Severus was imprisoned and killed.

3. Maximian married his daughter Fausta to Constantine and made him Augustus in the West.

4. Galerius tried to seize Rome but was forced to retreat.

5. Maximian fell out with his son Maxentius and was made to give up and go and live with Constantine.

6. A conference followed in 308, in which both Diocletian and Maximian turned up. At this conference

   • Maxentius was declared a public enemy, though he remained a serious problem.

   • Constantine was demoted to Caesar, though he refused to accept it.

   • Galerius's comrade Licinius was made Augustus in the West.

   • Maximian was told he had to stay abdicated.

So by 308, here's where things stood:

✔ In the East, the Augustus was Galerius, with Maximinus II Daia as his Caesar.

✔ In the West, the Augustus was Licinius, with Constantine as his Caesar.

✔ Meanwhile, regardless of who was in charge in theory, Maxentius was in control of Italy and North Africa.

The final death throes of the Tetrarchy

As you may have figured out by now, in Roman history, even the things that are settled are never really settled. So you can expect that things didn't go smoothly for the Tetrarchy once the dust had settled in 308.

In 310, Maximian fell out with Constantine and declared himself emperor again (for the third time). This time Maximian was forced to give up by his own men and was found dead soon afterwards, probably murdered by Constantine. The wars that followed over the next 15 years wiped out Diocletian's Tetrarchy for good and left one man in sole charge of the Roman Empire: Constantine I, the Great. His reign would do more than any other to transform the Dominate and the Roman Empire and make changes that echo right down to the present.

Constantine I, the Great (AD 307–337)

In 311, Galerius died from an agonising illness. Maximinus II succeeded him as Augustus in the East.

Constantine made an alliance with Licinius, who was Augustus in the West, and then he marched into Italy to defeat and kill Maxentius at the Battle of the Milvian Bridge on 28 October 312. (Remember, Maxentius was neither Augustus nor Caesar for any of the regions, but he had control of Italy and North Africa.) The victory meant Constantine had total control of the western Roman Empire, which set him up directly against Maximinus II in the East. What's more, the Senate declared Constantine was the senior Augustus, so it was a moment of enormous significance.

The Battle of the Milvian Bridge, at Rome, was one of the most decisive moments in the history of Europe and all Western civilisation because Constantine was convinced his victory had been caused by the Christian God. According to legend, Constantine claimed to have had a vision of Christ before the battle. In this vision, he was told to place the Chi-Rho symbol on his soldiers' shields, and he heard the words *in hoc signo vinces,* 'in this sign you shall conquer'.

Taking control of the West

After his victory at Milvian Bridge, Constantine's first job was to get shot of Maximinus II Daia, who was Augustus of the East. Constantine's motivation was simple: He had no intention of sharing the Roman world with anyone, and he was also determined to defend the interests of Christians.

Maximinus had gone back to persecuting Christians and had even tried to create a rival pagan church organised like the Christian church. As the senior Augustus, Constantine ordered him to stop. Maximinus didn't. Instead Maximinus set off to try and defeat Licinius who, in return for recognising Constantine in the West, had been awarded the right to rule in the East. Unfortunately for Maximinus, Licinius defeated him in Thrace. Maximinus disguised himself as a slave to escape; he also started trying to undo his Christian persecutions by issuing an edict of toleration. But it was too late. Before his change of heart had any impact, he died in the summer of 313.

Maximinus's death left Constantine undisputed master of the West and Licinius undisputed master of the East.

The two met in Milan in 313. Licinius married Constantine's half-sister Constantia to cement the alliance. To help their claim to rule, Constantine said he was descended from Claudius II, and Licinius said he was descended from Philip I (refer to Chapter 19 for information on both men). They also issued the Edict of Milan.

Issuing the Edict of Milan, 313

On his sick bed in 311, Galerius had orchestrated an edict with his fellow Tetrarchs that ended the persecution of Christians. All the persecutions had done was harden the Christians' resolve and divide the Roman world. The edict asked that Christians pray to their God to help the Roman state.

It was one thing to announce that Christians were free to worship, as Galerius had done in 311. It was another thing altogether to start turning the Roman state into a Christian one. The toleration of Christians was renewed in the 313 Edict of Milan, but this was a far more significant moment.

What the Edict of Milan said was that all religions would be tolerated and that anything that had been confiscated by the state from the Christians would be returned unconditionally. What the Edict didn't say was that Christianity was now the only legal religion. But it started the process that eventually led to the outlawing of paganism.

East vs. West: Fighting Licinius

A power struggle gradually ensued between Constantine and Licinius, despite their personal (and admittedly political) connections. In a way, it's reminiscent of how the First and Second Triumvirates of the late Republic fell apart around 400 years before even though their members were tied together in political and personal alliances (refer to Chapters 14 and 15). It just seems that sharing the Roman world was something few rulers could bear the idea of.

This power struggle eventually broke out into open war. Constantine was convinced he had the Christian God on his side.

Trouble brewing

Religion has a bit of a track record of being used to divide people, and that's what happened now. Constantine was also a smart operator. He used Christianity as a means of establishing a new power base. He could appoint new men to government and high rank in the army, men who owed their new status to Constantine, while old pagan families got pushed out. Constantine gave the church and its members all sorts of privileges, like exemptions from taxes, favouritism for jobs, and so on.

Licinius got suspicious when Constantine made his own brother-in-law, Bassianus, his Caesar in charge of Italy and the Danube provinces. Licinius encouraged Bassianus to revolt in 314, but the plot was uncovered and led to open war between Licinius and Constantine in 316 though the tensions between them had never gone away.

By 316, Constantine and Licinius had negotiated a truce. Part of the deal was sorting out the succession. In 317, Constantine's two sons, Crispus and Constantine II, were named his Caesars, and Licinius's son, also called Licinius, was named his. That held off the fighting for a while, but Licinius senior was still not satisfied. He believed that Constantine was using Christianity to undermine him by filling the East with Christians who were loyal to Constantine and not him. In retaliation, Licinius began to clamp down on the Church in the East, and he threw Christians out of the top jobs.

Licinius also thought Constantine was preferring his own sons for all the consulships. Although in the days of the Dominate, being consul amounted to nothing more than taking part in public ceremonials, it was a great way to promote someone. Licinius believed that Constantine was giving his own sons preferential treatment to make sure they would succeed as emperors, at the expense of Licinius's son.

The end of Licinius

In 322, Constantine entered the East, supposedly to see off another Gothic invasion. Licinius took this as a direct infringement of his control of the East, and war broke out. But Licinius had a series of disasters: In July 324, he was defeated at the Battle of Hadrianopolis; shortly afterwards the 350 ships of his fleet were destroyed by 200 ships commanded by Constantine's eldest son Crispus at the Battle of the Hellespont; and then in September Constantine totally defeated Licinius at the Battle of Chrysopolis. Licinius fled but was soon captured. He was later executed after being accused of plotting a comeback; his son's execution followed.

The Empire goes Christian

With Licinius out of the way, Constantine was left in sole control of the Roman Empire. Convinced that Christianity was the best way to hold the Empire together, Constantine began in earnest to Christianise the Roman Empire, a process that had started with the edicts of 311 and 313 (see 'Issuing the Edict of Milan, 313').

Clamping down on paganism

Constantine I's mother was Helena, said to be from Britain. She might have been Constantius's first wife, or a mistress. She was later made into a saint because she travelled to Judaea in 326 to visit places associated with Christianity. She believed she had found the major locations in Christ's life, including where he was born and where he was crucified. A dig led to the discovery of what were thought to be the three crosses and helped create a trade in fragments of the 'true cross'. Some shrines were multi-faith and were visited by pagans of all types as well as Christians. Constantine's mother-in-law, Eutropia, was horrified at one such shrine at Hebron and had Constantine destroy all the pagan monuments and install a church: Early Christianity often 'hijacked' pagan monuments and traditions and refranchised them as Christian.

The new imperial court

Constantine called himself 'Equal of the Apostles' and presented himself as the Christian God's representative on Earth. He maintained Diocletian's Dominate. The totalitarian state became more and more a fact of life. The Senate was a total irrelevance, and the old distinction between senators and equestrians was abandoned. Constantine had a council, the *sacrum consistorium* ('sacred body of those standing together'), which stood in his presence. It was all about pomp and circumstances, honorific titles, with everything being labelled *sacrum* ('sacred'). There was a vast imperial court, which was made up of Constantine's

- household staff, including eunuchs.

- his bodyguard (*scholae palatinae,* literally 'the corporation of the palace').

- ushers *(silentarii).*

- secretaries (*notarii,* from *nota* for a 'letter' or 'memo').

- ministers for the following: dealing with imperial lands (*comes rei pirivatae,* 'count of private affairs'), the palace (*quaestor sacri palatii,* 'quaestor of the sacred palace'), jobs (*magister officiorum,* 'master of jobs'; *magister militum,* 'Master of the Soldiers' – the latter becoming especially important in the late fourth and fifth centuries), and finance (*comes sacrarum largitionum,* 'count of the sacred largesse'), and their respective staff.

Celebrating Christianity in architecture

New architectural forms were developed to celebrate Christianity, like Constantine's Church of the Holy Apostles in his new capital of Constantinople, built in the form of a cross. The old pagan government basilica design, a hall with a nave and aisles, was adapted as a church design and formed the basis of all the great medieval cathedrals. The new designs appeared in Rome, too, like the first Basilica of St Peter (now beneath the modern St Peter's).

Vast statues of the emperor were carved. Fragments of two in Rome survive (one bronze, one marble), as well as one in York in northern Britain, where Constantine had been declared emperor. Totally unlike the lifelike classical statues of old, the new imperial images show an impersonal face with eyes rolled heavenward.

Christians at each other's throats

The Christians ought to have been delighted at their new-found freedom to worship. They probably were, but instead of automatically holding the Empire together, as Constantine had hoped, Christians proved as liable to squabble as – well, any other bunch of human beings. For a start, some of the Christians were as intolerant of pagans as some pagans had once been of them. This intolerance encouraged a long-term, ongoing process of bringing in anti-pagan laws banning pagan worship and temple building.

The Arian theology – it's all in a letter

The Arian schism in the end hinged on the letter 'i'. The orthodox (Catholic) Church defined their belief in the prayer called the Creed with the Greek word *homoousios,* which described how God the Father and God the Son were coeternal and coequal – in other words, exactly the same. The Arians added an 'i' and got *homoiousios* from *homoios* ('similar'), which meant God the

Father and God the Son were similar but not identical. The Creed, which comes from the Latin *credo,* 'I believe', is a statement of what Christians believe about God the Father, God the Son, and God the Holy Ghost. The Arian schism resulted in two rival versions: the Nicene (orthodox) Creed and the Arian Creed.

To many Romans, Christianity was just one more religion to add to the many available. Some dedicated Christians rejected all other religions. But many people were prepared to worship Christ alongside pagan gods. Even Constantine continued to issue coins with the Unconquered Sun-God and the Genius of the Roman People on them as well as other traditional Roman pagan symbols and personifications.

However you look at it, Christianity at this time was not one single, uniform religion. Christians fell out with one another in splits called *schisms:*

- **Catholic (Orthodox):** These Christians believed that Christ was God in his own right alongside God the Father and that while they were separate they were also one (the idea of Three Gods in One as the Trinity was still evolving). This was the teaching promoted by the leadership of the Christian church in Rome – so orthodox also means anything they said.

- **The Arians:** A North African priest called Arius declared in the early 300s that Christ was not God in his own right, but only as a creation of God the Father as an instrument to create the world. Arius soon had quite a following, including some bishops. As you can imagine, this outraged orthodox believers.

Constantine called a council at Nicaea in 325 to settle the matter. The Arians were banished, but before long, Constantine started to think the Arians might be right and started reinstating them. The furore carried on for decades after Constantine's death in 337 while various councils tried to thrash out a form of words that would satisfy everyone and hold the Church together.

- **The Donatists:** Some members of the African church objected in 311 to the consecration of a bishop of Carthage called Caecilian by Felix of Aptunga, who had given up his holy scriptures during Diocletian's persecution. As far as they were concerned, anyone who'd shown weakness during persecution should be cut no slack. So they appointed a rival, himself succeeded by a man called Donatus, who gave his name to the schism. Donatus had quite a reputation, having put up with a series of torture bouts during the persecution. A commission of 313, a synod at Arles in 314, and Constantine in 316 found against the Donatists, whose supporters rioted at the bad news. Constantine tried to suppress them but gave up in 321. Amazingly, the Donatists were around for another 400–500 years before finally fizzling out altogether.

Moving house: The capital goes to a new location

The showcase of Constantine's new order was to be his new capital. He chose Byzantium, an ancient Greek city which controlled the Bosphorus strait between Europe and Asia. He selected this site for his capital for the following reasons:

- ✔ It had a harbour.
- ✔ It could be defended by a land army and a navy.
- ✔ It was much closer to the wealthy and productive eastern provinces like Egypt and Asia.
- ✔ It was closer to the most important frontiers (the East and the Rhine-Danube).

Rome remained the Empire's first city on paper, but Byzantium was the future. It was treated to all the necessary public buildings like a senate house, a horse- and chariot-racing stadium (known as the *Hippodrome*), forum, and libraries. Various ancient sites were plundered by Constantine so that his new capital could have instant pedigree (see the sidebar, 'Instant heritage'). In 330, the city had its official opening as *Nova Roma,* 'New Rome', but was soon renamed Constantinopolis (Constantinople; today it's called Istanbul).

Instant heritage

Constantinople was kitted out with all the trappings of a great city by filching them from other places. Constantine's Hippodrome in Constantinople was decorated with four bronze horses, cast more than 700 years earlier in Greece. Around 900 years later in 1204, those same horses were taken from Constantinople in the Fourth Crusade and were installed on St Mark's church in Venice where, apart from being briefly stolen by Napoleon, they remained until the 1980s, when they were removed to a museum (replicas stand in their place). Other decorations included the fifth century BC bronze Tripod of Plataea, which had been made to commemorate the Greek victory over the Persians in 479 BC. It was brought to the Hippodrome from the Temple of Apollo at Delphi in Greece. Unlike the four horses, the Tripod (or what's left of it) is still in the Hippodrome and is known as 'the Serpentine Column'.

Managing money

Unlike Diocletian, Constantine did manage some sort of stability of the coinage. He introduced a gold coin called the *solidus* which was smaller and lighter than the old *aureus,* but it was highly successful and became a staple coin for centuries to come.

To cope with the increased costs of a vastly enlarged army and his own colossal staff, Constantine added new taxes and confiscated temple treasures. Landowners, whose responsibilities for tax assessment and collection were vital, were prevented from getting into occupations that were exempt from such work, such as senators, civil servants, and the Christian clergy. That meant landowners were condemned to stay as they were, just like the millions of ordinary people in trades and professions. Bakers and butchers, for example, were obliged to stay in their jobs, and so were their sons. Tenant farmers were stuck, too, and could even be chained to the ground to stop them leaving. The idea was to keep the wheels of the economy turning and prevent bands of landless and jobless outlaws growing up, but it was done at a terrible price. It essentially was the end of personal freedom.

Paranoia and the succession

Constantine was determined to settle the future, but in 326, he got it into his head that his wife Fausta and his son Crispus (born to his first wife Minervina) had been plotting against him. He executed both and made his three other sons – Constantine II, Constantius II, and Constans – and two of his nephews, Delmatius and Hannibalianus, into five potential successors. Constantine seems to have been under the illusion, or perhaps delusion's a better word, that they would all rule happily together after his death. Some hope.

Constantine was finally baptised a Christian on his death bed, having fallen ill while planning a war against the Persians. (Death bed baptisms were quite common in those days because it meant you could die in the purest possible form. The idea was that there wouldn't be time to sin again between baptism and death and compromise any chance of getting into Heaven.)

There's no doubt that Constantine's reign had been a truly remarkable one. He had turned Diocletian's Dominate into a workable system. The frontiers were in better shape, and the Empire's prestige as a whole was restored in the eyes of the rest of the world, even if most people in the Roman world were tied to their homes and their jobs and could only imagine how much freedom there had once been as a Roman citizen.

Constantine's loving family – not!

Constantine planned that his three surviving sons, Constantine II, Constantius II, and Constans, and his two nephews Delmatius and Hannibalianus, would succeed him. All were made Caesars except Hannibalianus, who was made King with power over the provinces of Armenia, Pontus, and Cappadocia. Considering what a taboo the idea of Roman king was, Hannibalianus's position was remarkable. They did all succeed Constantine, but not in the way he'd hoped. Unfortunately, Constantine had ignored Diocletian's plans to have successors chosen by merit and had gone for the right to inherit through birth instead.

Fighting over everything

In 337, Constantine II was about 21 years old and had already fought a successful war against the Goths. Constantius II was about 20, and Constans about 17. Not much is known about the nephews Delmatius and Hannibalianus, and it doesn't matter much either because the first thing that happened is that they were both murdered, probably on the orders of Constantius II. He and his brothers became the three Augusti, and the Empire was divided up between them, recalling the Second Triumvirate (refer to Chapter 15):

- ✔ Constantine II got Gaul, Spain, and Britain.
- ✔ Constantius II got the Eastern provinces.
- ✔ Constans got Italy and Africa.

With the stakes so high, it's not surprising that the arrangements didn't last. Arguments soon broke out, and the ante was upped by religion. The Arian controversy (see 'Christians at each other's throats', earlier in this chapter) was still simmering. The orthodox (Catholic) Bishop of Alexandria, Athanasius, had been sent into exile when Constantine I started favouring the Arians. Athanasius found refuge in Trier, which became Constantine II's capital. Athanasius was given permission to go back to Alexandria in Constantius II's territory. Constantius II was furious because he favoured the Arians and Athanasius was forced to flee to Rome in 339.

The deaths of Constantine II and Constans

Meanwhile, the imperial brothers held a meeting in 338 to sort out their differences. Constans was awarded more land: the Danube provinces, Thrace, Macedonia, Achaea (Greece), and Constantinople.

Constantine II felt hard done by, especially as he considered himself the senior emperor, and started quarrelling with Constans. In 340, he led an army over the Alps to invade Italy but was ambushed near Aquileia and killed. Constans helped himself to his brother's territories. Within three years of his death, Constantine I's five successors had been reduced to two.

The birthday party coup

The coup to topple Constans took place in January 350 when Marcellinus, chief finance minister of Constans, held a sham birthday party for his son at Augustodunum (Autun) in Gaul. Along with Magnentius and others, he had hatched the plan when Constans was out hunting. Magnentius attended along with a number of other important men and, at an appropriate moment, disappeared as if to relieve himself. He returned dressed up in purple and was promptly acclaimed as the emperor. The army instantly declared for Magnentius, and Constans had to make a hasty escape. Not hasty enough as it turned out. One of Magnentius's supporters caught him and killed him.

Constans was a committed orthodox Catholic and had even been baptised in 337. He actively supported the Church in the West and sided with Athanasius at the Council of Serdica in 342. The Empire was beginning to split down the middle between the orthodox West and the Arian East. War nearly broke out in 346, but Constans and Constantius II overcame their differences.

Constans lasted until 350. Although he was a popular emperor for his support of the Church, he had a terrible personal reputation for depravity and promoting men in return for bribes, which disastrously cost him the support of the army. In 350, he was killed in a coup led by a soldier called Magnentius.

Constantius II (AD 337–361)

After the death of his brother Constans, Constantius II might now have had the pleasure of running the whole Roman Empire, but he also had the humiliation of the rebel Magnentius running a breakaway empire in Spain, Gaul, Britain, and even Africa (refer to the preceding section). Magnentius had also killed a nephew of Constantine I's called Nepotian who had tried to seize power in Rome when Constans was killed.

The Magnentian Revolt

Magnentius, a pagan, posed as an orthodox Christian on his coins and even had the Chi-Rho symbol prominently displayed on the reverse of one type. He was using the split in the Church to rustle up support in the Catholic West against the Arian East.

Eyewitness

The historian Ammianus Marcellinus was in Rome in 357 when Constantius II visited. This is his eyewitness account of an emperor in the days of the Dominate:

'He did not stir while being hailed as Augustus by supportive acclamations while the hills resounded to the roar, and showed himself to be as calm and imperturbable as he had in the provinces. Although he was very short, he stooped to pass below high gates. He fixed the gaze of his eyes ahead and did not turn to left or right, as if his head was in a vice. He did not nod if a wheel jolted, and he wasn't once seen spitting, wiping or rubbing his face or nose, or moving his hands about – as if he was a dummy.'

War was inevitable. Constantius II made his cousin Gallus into his Caesar and put him in charge of the East so that he could go off and fight Magnentius. In 351, Magnentius and Constantius met at the bloody Battle of Mursa Major in Pannonia. It was an expensive stalemate. Constantius's cavalry defeated the Magnentian legions, but it cost Constantius 30,000 men and Magnentius 24,000. A series of engagements followed that gradually pushed Magnentius back into Gaul. In 353, Magnentius was defeated again and committed suicide.

Constantius came down on Magnentius's supporters with utter totalitarian ruthlessness. Anyone suspected of supporting the rebel was liable to be executed or at the very least be thrown into prison, his estates and wealth confiscated. The historian Ammianus Marcellinus thought Constantius was more paranoid about treachery than any other emperor of the past, even Domitian (Chapter 17) or Commodus (Chapter 18). Some of the plots were genuine ones, but where cases were doubtful, Constantius was quite happy to use torture to extract confessions.

The first Santa Sophia

In 360, Constantius II's great church *Santa Sophia* ('Holy Wisdom') was dedicated in Constantinople. Two hundred years later, it was rebuilt by the Byzantine emperor Justinian I (see Chapter 21). Although today it is a mosque, it stands as one of the most remarkable structures to have survived from the Roman world.

While at Mursa Major, Constantius had met the local Arian bishop, a man called Valens. Valens had a huge amount of influence on Constantius, who became even more dedicated to the Arian cause. Athanasius, the orthodox Catholic bishop of Alexandria, was forced into exile once again.

Gallus was summoned after reports that he was acting like a despot, but he was tried and executed before he even reached Constantius. He was soon replaced in 354 by his brother Julian who became Constantius's designated successor.

Constantius II in power

As a ruler, Constantius was relatively competent. He fancied himself as an intellectual but really hadn't any abilities, unlike in sport, military skills, and hunting, which he was extremely good at. He only promoted men in the army on merit, but avoided handing out the highest titles unless thoroughly deserved. Conversely, he was rather too quick to commemorate his own military exploits on triumphal arches, and because he was indecisive, he listened to his eunuchs, his wives, and other officials too readily. Taxes were already heavy, but he did nothing to stop tax collectors extorting people, which only made him unpopular.

Resolving the Arian versus Catholic crisis

In 359, Constantius organised a two-part council to resolve the Arian versus orthodox tussle so that Christianity could work as the state religion of the Roman Empire. The Arian bishop Valens suggested a compromise wording that glossed over the key bone of contention (whether Christ *was* God or was *like* God, see the earlier section 'Christians at each other's throats') and it looked for a bit if everyone would be happy. The orthodox diehards led by Athanasius and Basil, Bishop of Ancyra, rejected that totally. But before too long, the Arians were weakened by splitting into three groups, each of which with its own idea about the precise difference between Christ and God. Finally, a council at Constantinople in 381 ratified the decisions made at Nicaea in 325. Arianism became a legal offence and disappeared from the Empire, though it remained popular for another century amongst some German tribes.

Bringing Back Pagans: Julian II 'the Apostate' (AD 360–363)

For most of the last part of his reign, Constantius II dealt constantly with trouble on the borders. He fought on the Danube and then had to head east once more to fend off the Persians. Constantius sent his cousin Julian to clear out Germans who had crossed the Rhine and sacked Cologne.

Riots in Alexandria

Julian's restoration of paganism sometimes had unfortunate consequences. In Alexandria, the people hated their bishop Georgius, believing that he had denounced all sorts of people to Constantius. The last straw was when Georgius threatened to pull down a pagan temple dedicated to the pagan Genius of the City (see Chapter 9 for information on the Geniuses). A riot broke out, and Georgius was lynched. Other officials were murdered, and even the Christians put up with it because they hated Georgius, too. Julian was appalled but cooled the situation by doing no more than threatening severe punishments if anything else happened.

Julian's father was another Constantius, a half-brother of Constantine I, who was killed along with various other relatives as soon as Constantine died in 337. Julian was born in 332 and was educated by a eunuch called Mardonius, who taught Julian all about the old pagan gods and classical literature. It had a permanent effect on Julian. Julian had been made Caesar in 355 by his cousin Constantius II because he was one of the very few family members left.

Julian spent the next few years successfully campaigning on the Rhine frontier. He was popular with his troops and even lowered taxes in Gaul. Of course, this made Constantius II jealous. He ordered some of Julian's troops to come back, but they refused and promptly declared Julian to be the Augustus. Negotiations followed, but got nowhere. Constantius set out to deal with Julian, but died from a fever in 361 along the way.

Turning back the clock

Julian now had the Roman world to himself, and he immediately turned back the clock. Some of Constantius's men were executed, but the big change was that all anti-pagan laws were overthrown. He threw money at pagan cults and encouraged them to create the sort of organisation that had made the Christians so strong. He punished the Christians by taking away their privileges, especially the financial ones like tax breaks, and even stopped them from serving as teachers.

Julian wasn't alone in his interest in paganism. Quite a few people regarded schisms like the Arian row, the Donatist heresy, and Christian intolerance of paganism as cast-iron evidence that the Christian church was an unstable and dangerous innovation. Julian saw how his Christian cousins in the family of Constantine had committed all sorts of crimes and found it absurd that, however much a Christian sinned, all he had to do was apologise and be forgiven. Like many other traditionalists, Julian grew up believing that the old tolerance, old gods, and the old beliefs were the way to keep the Roman Empire together. He grew a beard, became interested in the Greeks, mysticism, and magic. But he was so keen on sacrificing animals that if he had lived longer it was said there would have been a shortage of cattle!

Julian in charge

When he wasn't knocking Christians, Julian was a decent emperor who tried to control inflation and reduce the vast heaving mass of imperial bureaucracy and hangers-on. He was particularly shocked when an extravagantly dressed court barber came to cut his hair. Julian discovered the barber received various food allowances and other perks of the job, and promptly threw all such attendants out of the palace. In the East, he paid for repairs to the city of Nicomedia, wrecked by an earthquake.

Julian's final great ambition was to defeat the Persians. He arrived in Antioch in 362 to start getting ready. In March 363, he set out with 65,000 men and soon reached the Persian capital of Ctesiphon. He decided to pull back and join the reserves. The Persians used the opportunity to harass Julian's army, and in one attack, he was wounded and died, probably from an infection.

As he died, Julian admitted Christianity had defeated him. *Vicisti Galilaee,* 'You have conquered, Oh Galilean [Christ]'.

History remembers Julian as the man who turned his back on Christianity, and so he is usually known as 'Julian the Apostate' (*apostasy* means to abandon Christianity). Some see him as a man who committed a crime by going back to paganism while others see him as a man of intellect and reason.

Julian the writer

Julian wrote more than any other Roman emperor. Some of his work survives, showing he was an accomplished writer in Greek. He wrote letters and speeches, as well as critiques of Christianity like his *Against the Galileans,* and a hymn to the Sun-God. He also composed a series of satirical biographies of former emperors. He installed a vast library in Constantinople, housing 120,000 books.

Chapter 21

The Barbarians Are Coming! The End of Rome

*T*his chapter is about the last act in the great drama that was the history of a city called Rome. When Julian II died in 363 (see Chapter 20), Rome was, if we accept the traditional date of its founding in 753 BC, 1,116 years old. The Roman world stretched from Egypt and the Middle East to the British Isles and the furthest tip of Spain. It had gone through colossal change, but it was still essentially 'Roman', and the city of Rome was its spiritual heart.

But for more than a century, few emperors had done much more than pass through Rome. They spent most of their time campaigning or basing themselves closer to the frontiers. They'd shown that emperors could be made and die in places other than Rome, because the only power that mattered was military loyalty to the man who led the soldiers, wherever he was.

Constantine I (307–337) had made the most symbolic, permanent change for centuries. He'd recognised that Constantinople was the key to holding on to the Roman Empire because Rome had become more of an idea, a state of mind, than a physical place. Constantine's contribution was enormous, but even he could do nothing about the mounting pressure on the frontiers from barbarians. Worse, his plan to divide the Empire between his sons led to more civil war and rebellions that only weakened the Roman world further. During the fourth century, the Western Roman Empire began to crumble under the barbarian onslaught, and in the end, Rome herself would fall.

A Rundown of Barbarians

The Romans called 'barbarians' anyone who wasn't like them – that is, civilised, living in cities, with a taste for art and architecture, literature, and polite living. These included the inhabitants of some of their own remoter provinces, like the Britons, but mostly they meant tribes beyond the Roman frontiers of the Rhine and Danube. Naturally, the Romans were biased. Some of the barbarians were highly accomplished and could create great things, but what matters here is what the Romans thought of them.

The Romans had a thoroughly ambivalent relationship with the barbarians. For centuries, they had been trying to civilise tribes along the frontiers and had hired tribal warriors to fight in the Roman army in the hope that they would be an effective force against other barbarians trying to invade. By the fourth century, many people in the Roman world – especially in the frontier provinces – had barbarians amongst their ancestors. But everyone in the Roman world was terrified by the thought of the tribes beyond who were on the march in search of new lands and who saw the Roman Empire as either a place they were determined to be part of or as a place to sack and pillage.

The important thing to remember is that, although we have names for some of these barbarians, they were in a constant state of flux, moving about from place to place, forming alliances one minute and starting wars the next, with no regular chain of command or line of succession. The information we have about them is sporadic and incomplete, not least because we rely on Roman sources, and they were often fairly confused about who they were dealing with. No wonder the Romans who ruled by a system looked at barbarians with horror: They had no idea what to do with them or how to handle them.

Following are some of the most important barbarians. Notice how they fought one another as well as the Romans, and at times even *joined* the Romans:

- ✔ **Goths:** The Goths were divided into two: the *Ostrogoths* ('Bright Goths') and the *Visigoths* ('Wise Goths'). The Ostrogoths lived where the Ukraine is today, and the Visigoths where Romania is, but they originally came from Scandinavia. By the mid-third century AD, the Goths were on the move towards the Roman Empire, pushed forward by the Alans, a tribe on the Asiatic steppes. In 251, the Gothic king Cniva killed the emperor Trajan Decius (refer to Chapter 19). Then they experimented with joining the Romans as confederates, but the Visigoths killed the emperor Valens in 378 (see the later section 'Valens in the East' for details of these events). In 410, the Visigoth chieftain Alaric sacked Rome, but after that, the Visigoths became confederates with what was left of the Western Roman Empire.

- **Vandals:** The Vandals were a German tribe who originated in Scandinavia and first turn up causing trouble under Marcus Aurelius (refer to Chapter 17) when they crossed the Danube. They fought their neighbours, the Visigoths, and the Romans as the mood took them. Apart from those who joined the Roman army (like Stilicho, discussed in the later section 'Sacking Rome'), they were really just a nuisance till 406 when, pushed forward by the Huns, they crossed the Rhine with the Alans and Suebi and laid waste parts of Gaul and Spain. The Vandals were ruled in Spain by their king Gunderic until his death in 428, after which they moved to North Africa.

- **Huns:** Outstanding horsemen, the Huns first turn up in south-east Europe in the late fourth century. They drove the Visigoths out, forcing them to invade the Roman Empire, and later pushed the Vandals into Italy and Gaul. The most significant leader was Attila (434–453), but after his death the Huns were largely a spent force.

- **Franks:** The Franks were a collection of German tribes on the Rhine who started attacking Gaul and Spain in the late third century. Julian II (refer to Chapter 20) pushed back a major invasion in 355, and until 425 the Franks served under the Romans as confederate troops, helping to prop up the frontiers. In about 425, one of the new leaders, Chlodio, started a new invasion. By the end of the fifth century, the Franks had largely taken over Gaul which now bears their name: France.

- **Alans:** The nomadic Alans lived in southern Russia, trapped behind the Caucasus. The Roman Empire frequently fought off their efforts to break out, but in the end it was pressure from the Huns that forced them out. The Alans finally reached Gaul in 406 and Spain in 409, where they met the Vandals, after which they simply merged with them and disappear from history.

- **Alamanni:** The Alamanni was a collection of Germanic tribes who crossed the Roman frontier in *c.* 260. They remained a constant problem thereafter, even though Julian managed a major defeat of them in 357 at Strasbourg. By the fifth century, they had settled in Alsace before being conquered by the Franks.

Going Downhill – Barbarians at the Door

After Julian II died in 363, the captain of his imperial guard, Jovian, was declared emperor. The first thing Jovian did was negotiate a humiliating peace to abandon all the Persian territory won since the time of Diocletian more than 60 years earlier. When Jovian later set out for Constantinople, he was suffocated in an extraordinary accident when a brazier was left burning in his bedroom. It was a bad time to lose an emperor. The barbarians were knocking at Rome's door, and the next 50 years were going to be decisive.

Breaking the Empire into East and West

Valentinian was in Julian and Jovian's army. Following Jovian's death, Valentinian was made emperor at Nicaea. For one month, he was sole ruler of the Roman world from West to East, and he was the last there ever was. After four weeks in the job, he made his brother Valens co-emperor. Valentinian took the West and Valens the East. The division was permanent. Now Rome's future depended on how the emperors dealt with the barbarians.

Valentinian I in the West (AD 364–375)

Valentinian based himself in Milan to be closer to the frontiers. He upgraded the soldiers' status, providing them with tools so that they could farm during quiet periods. That meant higher taxes, but he softened the blow by limiting tax breaks for the rich. Valentinian loathed the wealthy and privileged, especially anyone who thought himself above the law. So he was especially concerned with the lot of ordinary people and made every one of the regional Praetorian prefects appoint a Defender of the People to protect their interests. Valentinian was also determined that Christianity not oppress other religions. So in 371, he declared that all religions would be tolerated and no-one should be made to worship any god other than the one he wanted to.

It was just as well Valentinian was in Milan and improving the army. He was faced almost immediately with a dramatic series of barbarian invasions. First the Alamanni crossed the Rhine, only to be beaten off by the Roman armies. Then in 367, a 'barbarian conspiracy' burst across Britain and devastated it. Valentinian had to send Count Theodosius to rebuild Britain's defences and drive out the invaders. In 374, a swarm of Germans crossed the Danube. Valentinian fought back over the river, but when an embassy of Germans arrived to broker a deal the following year, they so infuriated Valentinian he burst a blood vessel and expired on the spot.

Valens in the East (AD 364–378)

Valens had his own problems. First he had to put down a rebellion by a soldier called Procopius who declared himself emperor. Next he crossed the Danube to head off a potential invasion by the Visigoths. Unlike Valentinian, Valens was a dedicated Arian and started a series of persecutions of orthodox Catholics.

Next the Visigoths and Ostrogoths invaded en masse, forced out of their own lands by the Huns of the North. They were allowed to settle in the Eastern Empire, but broke out into rebellion when they were oppressed and exploited. More German tribes crossed in behind them to add to the chaos.

The Aqueduct of Valens

The rebel Procopius had been supported by the city of Chalcedon. To punish Chalcedon, Valens destroyed their defences and used stones from the city's walls to build a mighty aqueduct in Constantinople. The aqueduct crossed a valley in the city between two hills, carrying water to a reservoir called the *Nymphaeum Majus* ('Great Fountain'). Eighty-six arches still stand in Istanbul today.

The Visigoths, having been pushed out of their territory by the Huns, became one of the most important threats to the Western Roman Empire. Once inside the Empire, they soon decided they wanted better land than the Balkans and headed for Italy.

Valens launched a hasty counter-attack and met the Visigoths at the Battle of Hadrianopolis in 378. Valens was catastrophically defeated and killed, and his body was never found.

At Last! Someone Who Knows What He's Doing: Theodosius I the Great (AD 379–395)

In 375, Valentinian's sons Gratian, then 15 years old, and Valentinian II, aged 4, succeeded their father in the West (the two were half-brothers). In 378, with Valens dead, too, Gratian had the wit to see he was completely unable to cope with the whole Empire because they were both too young. He chose Flavius Theodosius, the son of the Count Theodosius sent to Britain after the disaster in 367, and made him Augustus in the East. Flavius Theodosius had been born in Italica in Spain, the same place as two of the greatest of all Roman emperors, Trajan (98–117) and Hadrian (117–138), and in many ways he lived up to his predecessors' reputations. (To read about Trajan and Hadrian, two of the 'Five Good Emperors', go to Chapter 17.)

Theodosius might have been forgiven if he had turned down his new job. His father, Count Theodosius, had been executed in about 375 on a charge of treason, and he had retired to Spain. But he accepted Gratian's offer of a command on the Danube in 378 followed by promotion to being the Eastern Augustus in 379.

Hiring the Visigoths

Theodosius started out by fighting the Visigoths but found the job impossible. His solution was on the 'if you can't beat them, join them' principle, except that he had the Visigoths join the Romans rather than the other way round. The Visigoths were made into federal allies within the Roman Empire. The deal was that they were given land in Thrace and in return provided soldiers (*foederati*, 'federates') for the Roman army and farm workers for the Roman economy.

It was a clever idea, bringing desperately needed reinforcements for the army. But it established the idea of independent barbarian states within the Empire, and it cost a lot of money. Theodosius declared that anything and everything could be taxed. Just how much freedom had been lost is summed up by the fact that now a tenant who left his land could be prosecuted for 'stealing himself' away from his job. Even tax collectors could be whipped for failing to collect everything due.

Breaking it up again: Revolts

In the West, Gratian's government was really controlled by Ausonius who, as well as being a famous poet, was chief minister and also praetorian prefect over Gaul, Italy, and Africa. Gratian monitored the frontiers from his base at Trier.

In 383, disaster struck when a soldier in Britain called Magnus Maximus was declared emperor and promptly set out for the Continent to get rid of Gratian. Gratian was betrayed by his own troops, who went over to Magnus Maximus. One of them killed Gratian in 383. Maximus then added Gaul, Spain, and Africa to his new empire.

In 387, however, Magnus Maximus got too ambitious and invaded Italy. Valentinian II fled to Theodosius, who was really in charge of the Roman Empire. Theodosius marched west and destroyed Maximus at Poetovio in 388. Valentinian was made emperor of the West again, but in 392, he was throttled by his Frankish general Arbogastes.

Arbogastes wasn't stupid enough to make himself emperor; instead he found a puppet in the imperial court called Eugenius and declared him emperor, while Arbogastes controlled everything. Theodosius refused to accept a barbarian general ruling through a puppet and invaded Italy in 394, defeated Eugenius's army, and then executed Eugenius on 6 September 394. Arbogastes fled and committed suicide.

Death of Theodosius

Theodosius died four months later at Milan in January 395 from dropsy. His sons Arcadius (aged 18) and Honorius (aged 11) succeeded him. They'd already been made into Augusti. Arcadius (383–408) took the East and Honorius (393–423) the West. Being young, both were easily led by powerful men in their courts. Arcadius, controlled by a succession of Praetorian prefects, staggered on in the East until 408 when he was succeeded by his 7-year-old son Theodosius II. The real story (told in the next section), however, belongs to Honorius and his father-in-law, Stilicho.

Sacking Rome

Rome wasn't built in a day, so the saying (actually a twelfth-century French proverb) goes. It wasn't destroyed in a day, either. The end was humiliating and rather slow, but the key point is that, whereas Rome had once been the hub of the Roman world, now it was almost an irrelevance. Of course, it had tremendous symbolic importance, but in a practical sense it was a sideshow. One of the ironies is that it was the very barbarians the Romans had been trying to keep out who kept Rome going as long as it did.

Stilicho: Buying off the Visigoths

In 395 when Theodosius died, his son Honorius was only 11, so it's no great surprise that the real power lay with Honorius's Master of Soldiers and later father-in-law, a Vandal general called Flavius Stilicho.

Stilicho fought off a Visigoth invasion of Italy under Alaric in 402 at Pollentia (Pollenza), and then fought off an Ostrogoth invasion in 405 at Faesulae (Fiesole), but he was unable or unwilling to hold back the relentless Visigoths who now had their sights set on Italy. Stilicho kept letting them get away, because he had lurking ambitions to conquer the Eastern Roman Empire. His chief rival was Rufinus, one of Arcadius's officials.

In 406, a horde of Vandals and other tribes, including the Alamanni and Alans, crossed the Rhine and devastated Gaul. Stilicho did little or nothing to fight them off because he wanted to use his forces to attack the Eastern Empire. In the meantime, he agreed to hand over a fortune in gold to the Visigothic leader Alaric, one of the Visigoths that Theodosius I had allowed to settle in the Roman Empire, who was demanding to be bought off. That only gave rise to suspicions that Stilicho was using Alaric to help make his (Stilcho's) son emperor. His troops mutinied, and Stilicho was executed in 408.

During this period, the imperial court was in Ravenna in north-east Italy, protected by the swamps that surrounded the city. Ravenna's late Roman churches and other buildings are some of the most magnificent surviving monuments from antiquity. They owe their preservation largely to their remote location.

As if the battles with the Visigoths weren't enough, in 407, Britain produced yet another rebel, this time the so-called Constantine III whose sole appeal seems to have been his name, which reminded the troops of the great days of Constantine I. Spotting the chaos in Italy, Constantine III led another rebellious army into Gaul. By 409, he had seized Spain, too, but was overwhelmed by barbarians himself. He was defeated and killed by Honorius's army in 411, which was remarkable given what had been happening in Rome in the meantime (explained in the next section).

Alaric and the fall of Rome in 410

In 408, Stilicho was murdered in a palace coup when the story got around that he might be planning to make his own son emperor with Alaric's help. German troops in the Roman army, now terrified for themselves and their families, promptly joined Alaric and the Visigoths. With Stilicho dead, Alaric had no useful friends at the Roman court. He saw his chance and burst into Italy.

'And when Rome falls – the world' (Lord Byron)

The Visigoths surged down to Rome and started a series of three sieges of Rome:

✔ In 408, after Stilicho's execution, many families of federated barbarian troops were murdered. Those troops fled to Alaric, who set out to besiege Rome in September 408. Facing the prospect of starvation, the Senate ordered the payment of a huge ransom to persuade Alaric to withdraw. All Alaric wanted was official recognition by Honorius. When that didn't come Alaric besieged Rome again in 409.

✔ In 409, Alaric forced the Senate to come to terms. He put his own puppet emperor, Attalus, on the Roman throne. Attalus was hopeless, so Alaric deposed him and decided to open talks with Honorius in 410. Unfortunately, a rival Visigoth leader called Sarus used his influence to wreck the negotiations. Alaric decided that Honorius must have been responsible and set off to besiege Rome again as a punishment.

✔ In August 410, Alaric was let into Rome by traitors. For the first time since the Gauls sacked Rome in 390 BC (refer to Chapter 11), the city was captured by an enemy. Actually, the Visigoths did relatively little damage: They left churches alone and anyone taking refuge in them, for example. But they may well have burned down the Basilica Aemilia in the Forum, which was certainly destroyed about this time.

Galla Placidia's husbands

Galla Placidia married Alaric's successor, Ataulf, in 414. Honorius refused his consent, and his general Constantius drove Ataulf into Spain and had him murdered. Placidia was returned to the Romans by Ataulf's successor, Wallia. As a reward, he was allowed to set up a Visigothic state in Gaul.

In 417, Galla Placidia married the general Constantius. Their son Valentinian was born two years later. In 421, Constantius was made joint-emperor with Honorius but died later the same year. Things took an odd twist next when Honorius took a fancy to his half-sister Placidia. His public displays of 'affection' caused a public outcry and her fury, so she fled to Constantinople in 423, the same year as Honorius died.

The fall of Rome in 410 was a horrifically demoralising experience, not just for the Romans, but also for Roman citizens everywhere. It was, literally, like facing the end of the world.

Actually Alaric only stayed three days in Rome before heading off to southern Italy with Honorius's half-sister Galla Placidia. He died before he could start a planned invasion of Africa and was reputedly buried under a river (the river was diverted first so that the grave could be dug).

Abandoning Britain

The year 410 was generally a bad one. In addition to the fall of Rome, Britain was also abandoned. Honorius told the island province to take care of its own defences, though actually the frustrated Britons had already thrown out the Roman officials a year before. What few troops were left were withdrawn. The rebel Constantine III had taken most of what was left.

Staggering On

For the rest of the fifth century, barbarians from central and northern Europe steadily moved into the Roman Empire. The fact that independent barbarian states had been established within the Roman Empire anticipated the future.

During this time, the sitting Roman emperors were not always the ones who held the real power.

In the East, Theodosius II (402–450) was Augustus, but the real power was held by his sister Aelia Pulcheria (ruling as co-regent from 414). She stayed in power for the rest of her life and died in 453. A devout Christian, she took a vow of chastity to avoid being forced into marriage. Many of her decisions were affected by her Christianity; she had Theodosius send the Jews of Constantinople into exile, for example.

In the West, the struggle for power continued:

- **Johannes (423–425):** Honorius's secretary Johannes succeeded Honorius. The Eastern emperor, Theodosius II, sent an army to get rid of Johannes. A Roman general called Flavius Aetius had fetched an army of Huns to support Johannes, but they turned up too late. Galla Placidia had paid off his Huns and sent him to deal with the Visigoths and Franks in Gaul.

- **Valentinian III (425–455):** Galla Placidia's son Valentinian became Augustus of the West when they returned to Rome. Galla Placidia spent the next 12 years as regent in the West until she retired to building churches in Ravenna (she died in 450). The real power was then held by Aetius, the emperor's *Magister Militum* ('Master of the Soldiers'). There was no stopping the relentless disintegration of the Western Roman Empire. By 429, the Vandals under Gaiseric had crossed Gaul and Spain, and were conquering Africa, which they seized by 439. By 429, Aetius could do nothing about the Vandals in Africa. But he did manage to push back the Germans, suppress peasant revolts, and defeated the Burgundians.

Attila the Hun (ruled AD 434–453)

Everyone has heard of Attila the Hun. Here's the chance to find out what he did. Attila was brought up as a barbarian hostage at the court of the emperor Honorius. The idea was that he would grow up more sympathetic to the Romans, but it meant he also grew up knowing how the Roman world worked. In 432, Attila and his brother Bleda inherited control of the Huns from their uncle Ruga. They followed this up with an invasion of Persia, followed by assaults on the Roman Empire, crossing the Danube in 440 and sacking cities in Illyria. In 443, another invasion followed, climaxing in their siege of Constantinople which ended only because they hadn't any proper siege equipment to scale the walls. In 447, Attila attacked the Roman Empire again and defeated a Roman army in Moesia before fighting his way south to Thermopylae in Greece. Constantinople was saved because the damage of 443 had been repaired, but the Eastern Empire agreed to pay Attila off.

Meanwhile, the Huns had been supplying the Western Roman Empire with troops. In 450, the Eastern Empire stopped the cash payments to Attila. Valentinian III ordered his sister Honoria to marry a Roman whom she disliked, so Honoria sent her ring to Attila and begged for rescue. Attila took this as an offer of marriage and demanded half the Western Empire as his dowry. Valentinian III said no to Attila, so Attila the Hun invaded the West.

In 451, Flavius Aetius defeated Attila at the Battle of Maurica (also known as the Battle of Chalons), the only time Attila was ever defeated. Attila withdrew but invaded Italy again in 452. Aetius used his troops just to harass Attila who was busy sacking various cities and demanding Honoria's hand. Eventually a Roman embassy met up with Attila and persuaded him to give up. He pulled back and left. In 453, Attila died from a burst blood vessel. The Hun Empire collapsed as barbarian kingdoms often did because they were totally dependent on the prestige of particular leaders.

The murders of Aetius (AD 454) and Valentinian III (AD 455)

In 454, the general Flavius Aetius was murdered by Valentinian III for threatening the Emperor's court eunuch Heraclius and the powerful Petronius Maximus (twice prefect of Rome and twice praetorian prefect of Italy). This ended the life of one of the most important men in Roman history over the preceding 20 years. And this time it was actually the emperor who did the killing, stabbing Aetius. The story goes that, after the killing, someone told Valentinian 'with your left hand you have cut off your right hand', meaning that Valentinian had now ruined his chances of ruling properly.

Petronius Maximus assumed he would now become the top man at Valentinian's court, but the eunuch Heraclius told Valentinian this was a bad idea. In retaliation, Petronius hired two of Aetius's soldiers to avenge their master. In 455 they killed Heraclius and Valentinian.

Petronius Maximus was proclaimed emperor on 17 March 455 and married Valentinian III's reluctant widow, Licinia Eudoxia. But he lasted about 70 days because she sent a message to Gaiseric, the Vandal king in Africa. Gaiseric had his own designs on the imperial dynasty and had plans to marry his son Huneric to Valentinian and Eudoxia's daughter Eudocia.

When Petronius heard the Vandals were on their way from Africa to Rome, he panicked and fled. But before he could get out of Rome, a mob killed him. Gaiseric arrived and carted off both Eudoxia, Eudocia, and her sister Placidia the Younger to Carthage. They were later released, and Placidia the Younger still had a part to play in Rome's last act. (For another of Galla Placidia's legacies, see the sidebar on 'Buildings').

Valentinian III's death was a disaster for the West because it marked the end of a dynasty that could be traced back to Valentinian I and Valens, nearly a century earlier. For all its faults, the dynasty had managed some sort of central stability even though the power nearly always lay in the hands of men like Stilicho and Aetius, and the Western Empire had been steadily eroded by barbarian invasions.

Buildings

The fifth century might have been a time of increasing chaos, but some of the great surviving buildings of the Roman world date from this era. Santa Sabina in Rome, begun in 422, is an immaculate basilican church largely in its original state, with columns dividing a nave and aisles. Galla Placidia's elegant brick cross-shaped and barrel-vaulted tomb in Ravenna is one of the great sights of the city, and its interior preserves all its wall and ceiling mosaics.

The next few emperors and the rise of Ricimer

Following Valentinian III's death, a series of emperors claimed (or were persuaded to claim) the throne of the Western Roman Empire, which by that time didn't amount to much more than Italy. All had to deal with the *Magister Militum* Ricimer, a general of mixed Visigoth and Suebian descent who was the real power in the West between 455–472. Here's a quick rundown of the last Western Roman emperors:

✔ **Avitus (455–456):** The Visigothic king Theodoric II persuaded Avitus to take the throne. So crushed was the West that the new emperor resorted to stripping bronze from public buildings to pay the Goths in his army. It was too much for the Romans, who forced him to flee. He was later defeated and deposed by Ricimer, whom he had promoted.

✔ **Majorian (457–461):** Majorian, who had served under Aetius, followed Avitus. Majorian defeated the Vandals in Gaul, but thanks to treachery, his fleet, prepared in Spain to attack the Vandals in Africa, was destroyed before it left. Majorian was deposed and executed by the general Ricimer, who installed a puppet called Libius Severus.

✔ **Libius Severus aka Severus III (461–465):** The real power behind the throne was Ricimer. Practically nothing is known about Libius Severus as a result. It might have been Ricimer who killed him.

✔ **Anthemius (467–472):** Leo I (457–474), who was now the Eastern emperor, appointed Anthemius himself. Anthemius was Leo's son-in-law. He had been hoping to succeed Leo but accepted the Western throne. He reached it in 467 and was immediately proclaimed emperor; his daughter even married Ricimer. A joint West-East expedition to attack Gaiseric and the Vandals in Africa ended in disaster when Gaiseric routed the Roman fleet. Events in Gaul further complicated things: The

Visigothic kingdom had been taken over by Euric who murdered his brother Theodoric II and started planning to seize the whole of Gaul and separate it from the Roman Empire. Euric defeated a Roman army. Bad feelings between Ricimer and Anthemius followed, and Leo I sent a man called Olybrius to sort out the quarrel between the two. Ricimer, however, decided Anthemius was a lost cause and set Olybrius up as a rival emperor. Olybrius happened to be married to Valentinian III's daughter Placidia the Younger. Ricimer besieged Rome. Anthemius fled and disguised himself as a beggar but was found and executed. Ricimer died a few weeks later.

✔ **Olybrius (472):** Anicius Olybrius, a member of the senatorial Anicii family, died in 472 of natural causes only a few months after being made emperor. After Olybrius died, four months passed before anyone suitable to be made emperor could be found.

✔ **Glycerius, Count of the Domestics (473–474):** He was proclaimed emperor at Ravenna in 473 by the current Magister Militum, Gundobad (in post 472–473). Glycerius's sole achievement was to persuade invading Ostrogoths to invade Gaul instead of Italy.

✔ **Julius Nepos (474–475):** The Eastern emperor Leo I refused to recognise Glycerius and sent Julius Nepos, his wife's nephew, to be emperor instead. Gundobad abandoned Glycerius, who Nepos easily dethroned. Nepos took over in June 474. He lasted barely a year before the new Magister Militum, Orestes (475–476), led a rebellion.

The last emperor in the West: Romulus Augustus (AD 475–476)

Orestes, who led a rebellion against the emperor Julius Nepos, made his own 16-year-old son emperor. By some extraordinary coincidence, the boy's name, Romulus Augustus, recalled the founder of Rome and also its first emperor. Of course, Orestes was the real power, and he ruled what was left of the Western Empire though Romulus Augustus lasted for less than a year. In August 476, Orestes's barbarian troops rebelled, killed Orestes, and made their leader Odovacer king of Rome. Romulus Augustus was allowed to retire (he lived on till 511 at least).

It was 1,229 years since the traditional date of the founding of Rome and 985 years since the last king of Rome, Tarquinius Superbus, had been ejected.

Odovacer sent a senatorial deputation to Constantinople and declared the West no longer needed an emperor. Strictly speaking, Julius Nepos was, on paper, still the 'legitimate' emperor – if anyone could really be called that – but in Rome itself, the last one was Romulus Augustus.

The new Eastern emperor, Zeno (474–491), had no choice but to accept. He made Odovacer Magister Militum and incorporated the West into the East once more. Italy was now under the rule of Germanic kings, based at Ravenna, from 476.

Far from destroying Roman traditions, Odovacer (King of Italy 476–493) and Theodoric the Great of the Ostrogoths (King of Italy 493–526) went out of their way to preserve them. Odovacer continued the tradition of public entertainment in the Colosseum and even restored the ageing arena. Theodoric, despite fighting his way into power and murdering Odovacer, had been educated at Constantinople. He maintained Rome's institutions under a system of law and did a good job of looking civilised, while at the same time bringing in 200,000 Ostrogoths. But there's no getting away from the fact that the Roman Empire in the West was over, though Rome remained home to the pope.

What Became of Rome's Western Provinces

The history of Western Europe after the fifth century is an incredibly complicated one and the subject for another, enormous, book. But in essence what happened is that the provinces of the Roman West simply fragmented into a huge variety of kingdoms, chiefdoms, dukedoms, and fiefdoms, though that process was already well advanced by the time Rome fell in 410 and even more so by 476.

The crucial difference from the days of Roman rule is that these various states depended far more on the prestige of their individual rulers, rather than institutions of government, and they laid the foundations for what Europe is today: a collection of different countries with their own languages, traditions, and identities. Here's a rundown of what happened:

- ✔ **Italy:** In 536, the Byzantines retook Rome (see the section, 'In the East: The Byzantine Empire'), but in 568, Italy was conquered by the Germanic Lombard peoples. In 756, the Papal States, ruled by the pope from Rome, were created. By 800, Italy was part of Charlemagne's Holy Roman Empire. Italy remained part of the Holy Roman Empire, but power struggles developed with the Papal States and the independent Italian cities. By the fifteenth century, Italy was made up of the rival kingdoms of Milan, Florence, Venice, Naples, and the Papal States. It took until 1870 for Italy to become one nation again for the first time since 476.

- ✔ **Britain:** Britain had been cast off since 410. The Church remained in some control into the fifth century, but all the Roman towns, forts, villas, and infrastructure fell steadily into disrepair. It wasn't till after the Norman Conquest in the eleventh century that England became ruled as a single nation. Wales was added in the fourteenth century. In 1707, Scotland was joined to England and Wales to create Britain. Ironically, during the eighteenth and nineteenth centuries, Britain established a vast Empire that dwarfed the Roman Empire – remarkable for a place the Romans regarded as a barbaric nowhere on the edge of the world.

✔ **Gaul:** The Roman provinces of Gaul were overrun by Germanic tribes including the Franks. The Frankish king Clovis (481–511) founded a Christian Frankish kingdom with a capital at Paris, but it fell apart until Pepin the Short (751–768) reunified it and founded the Carolingian dynasty. His son Charlemagne created the Holy Roman Empire (refer to Chapter 1) in much of Western Europe.

✔ **Spain and Portugal:** In the fifth century, Visigoths and Vandals overran the Roman province of Hispania and created a Visigoth kingdom.

✔ **Germany:** Only small parts of Germany were ever in the Roman Empire. Charlemagne of the Franks took Germany into the Holy Roman Empire.

In the East: The Byzantine Empire

With the Western Empire no more, the East was left on its own. Historians call it the Byzantine Empire, from Constantinople's old name of Byzantium, though the name wasn't even coined until the sixteenth century AD, decades after it had ceased to exist. The Byzantines called themselves the Roman Empire because, as far as they were concerned, it was no more or less than a continuation of the old Empire. In fact, the East continued to behave as if Rome and the West were still a fully functioning part of the Roman world. The pope remained in Rome (in the West), and even Latin remained the everyday language of government in Constantinople despite the fact that most people in the East spoke and used Greek.

The truth is that the history of the Byzantine Empire is a whole massive story in its own right, but until someone writes *The Byzantine Empire For Dummies* the best I can offer is the briefest of brief summaries. It's a story with its ups and downs, but the relentless fact is that the Byzantine Empire spent most of its time getting smaller, weaker, and poorer. To the Byzantines' credit, it took another thousand years to come to an end.

Religious tensions

The Christian church had been good at producing reasons to split ever since Constantine I issued his Edict of Milan, which imposed religious toleration on the Roman Empire, back in 313 (refer to Chapter 20). Now was no different. Theodoric the Great, the Arian king of the West, was fairly inspired when it came to religious tolerance, but the Eastern church started to insist on everyone singing from the same hymn sheet, so to speak.

Theodora

Justinian's wife Theodora (c. 500–548) was a considerable individual and a major force behind Justinian's throne. She started life as an actress, performing nude on stage – a career regarded then as tantamount to prostitution. She became a Monophysite (she believed that Christ had a single Divine nature), gave up the stage, and went to Constantinople where she worked as a wool spinner. Justinian came across her and had his uncle Justin I change the law so that he could marry a former actress. After saving the day during the 532 riot, she encouraged Justinian's building programme in Constantinople and supported his legal and religious reforms, though she remained a Monophysite till her death from cancer in 548.

The problem came over Christ's 'nature': Did he have a single, Divine nature, or did he have a double nature, both Divine and Human (which was the Catholic Orthodox teaching)?

Monophysitism means the doctrine of 'one nature'. Monophysites believed that Christ had a single Divine nature. *Dyophysitism* means the doctrine of 'two natures'. Dyophysites believed Christ had a double nature: Divine and Human.

The Catholic Orthodox teaching (that Christ had a dual nature) held sway in Constantinople. They wanted everyone to follow suit so that the Western and Eastern churches could all operate together. The new Eastern emperor, Justin I (518–527), supported this policy. Theodoric in the West was upset by all this. Even so, Theodoric allowed Pope John I to visit Constantinople in 526, but was horrified to hear that John had been mobbed by enthusiastic crowds. When John returned to Rome, he was imprisoned and died, followed soon after by Theodoric. Theodoric's dynasty gradually crumbled over the years that followed, while Justinian I started a massive campaign to recover the West.

Justinian 1 (AD 527–565)

If he had lived 400 years earlier, Justinian (Justin I's nephew) would have been one of the great Roman emperors. As it was, he remains probably the most important Byzantine emperor and the one who did a huge amount to preserve much of what has survived from the Roman Empire.

Hopeful signs and good moves

One of the first things Justinian did was order the codification of Roman law (see Chapter 1). His *Digest* contains vast quantities of vital information about how the Roman world had run itself, while the various case histories preserve all sorts of examples of how Roman society had functioned in the days of the Republic and Principate.

Riot in Constantinople

Justinian wasn't a total success. The mob in Constantinople was divided into groups based on factions of circus supporters. They didn't like Justinian's ministers and rioted in 532, trying to set up another emperor and burning down large parts of the city. Justinian was only saved by his wife Theodora, who rallied the resistance, and by his generals Belisarius and Mundus, who attacked the crowd. Thousands were killed in the clampdown, but the destruction left room for great new building projects. This was when Constantius II's church of Santa Sophia was rebuilt into the form it survives in today.

With his general Belisarius (*c.* 505–565), Justinian started to recover the Roman Empire. In 530, Belisarius defeated the Persians, and in 532, the 'eternal peace' was signed. It didn't last, but the border was fortified. Between 533–534, Belisarius defeated the Vandals in Africa. By 535, he had taken Sicily, and by 536, he led a victorious entry into Rome. In 540, the Ostrogothic capital at Ravenna fell. Belisarius had to leave to fight the Persians again. He was back in Italy in 544 to fight the Ostrogoths, but by then Justinian had started to get suspicious of Belisarius's success. Another general, Narses, finally defeated the Ostrogoths and reorganised the government of Italy in 554. After that date, the Senate in Rome was never heard of again.

The Empire after Justinian

Justinian died in 565. He had ruled over more territory than any other emperor for 150 years. It's an irony that his reconquest of the West ended the rule of Germanic kings in Italy who'd been looking after Roman institutions. It wouldn't be until the reign of the Frankish king Charlemagne that anything remotely resembling a Roman Empire would return to the West.

As for the Eastern Empire, it lasted another 900 years. But Justinian had over-stretched its resources. Most of Italy was lost again by 570. Maurice Tiberius (582–602) managed to consolidate and hold on to the East, fighting back the Persians. But in the Balkans, he couldn't hold back the Slav and Avar peoples which severely dented the Byzantine Empire's prestige. More threats came from the Bulgars and the Muslims. In the eighth century, Leo III (717–741) and Constantine V (741–775) held back the Muslims. Constantine V also forced the Bulgars to a peace in 774. The coronation of Charlemagne as Holy Roman Emperor in the West in 800 by the pope was another blow to Byzantine prestige.

A Macedonian dynasty of emperors, started by Basil I (867–886), heralded in a time when the Byzantines recovered their position. Basil made great advances in the East towards the Euphrates and used conversion to integrate

---

The Muslims

On the death of the prophet Mohammed in 632, the Islamic religion was confined to part of Arabia. But within 25 years, Islam had spread across the Middle East and Egypt. By 750, Muslims controlled all of the former Roman provinces of North Africa, Sicily, and most of Spain. By the late eleventh century, the Muslims were in Asia Minor (Turkey) and controlled almost all of it by 1250. The Byzantine Empire spent this time fighting an increasingly futile rearguard action, and in the end, Byzantium itself would fall to the Muslim Ottomans in 1453.

Slavic peoples into the Empire. Nicephorus II (963–969) took Cyprus and Antioch, which had been out of Byzantine hands for three centuries. John I Tzimisces (969–976) defeated the Russian prince Svjatoslav and advanced into Palestine, garrisoning bases all the way. By 1025, the Byzantine Empire was made up of what is now: southern Italy, Croatia, Serbia, Bulgaria, Albania, Macedonia, Greece, Turkey, and Cyprus.

Thanks to his epileptic fits, Michael IV, the Paphlagonian (1034–1041), relied on his brother John the Eunuch to run the Empire. John was a ruthless tax collector and the Slavs rebelled. Michael defeated the rebels, but the effort killed him. Byzantine power, increasingly depending on buying in mercenaries, was declining steadily.

The Great Schism of 1054

Under Constantine IX (1042–1055), the East and West churches finally split. Pope Leo IX excommunicated the Byzantine Patriarch Michael Cerularius, who excommunicated the Roman delegates to Byzantium (a patriarch was the name given to the bishops of Rome, Alexandria, Antioch, Jerusalem, and Constantinople, the five chief sees of Christendom). The East and Western churches, now known as the Western Catholic Orthodox and the Eastern Orthodox churches respectively, came to a sort of accommodation in 1274 when Michael VIII (1261–1282) recognised the papacy in order to get support for a war against his enemy, Charles of Anjou. But the real differences remained. Both claimed to be the One Holy Catholic and Apostolic Church, and it wasn't until 1965 that the churches met and committed themselves to reconciliation, even though in the intervening centuries various members of the Eastern Orthodox Church had rejoined Rome and created the Eastern Catholic Church.

The toll of the Crusades

Under Constantine X (1059–1067), the Byzantine Empire suffered terrible setbacks but enjoyed a brief revival under Alexius I (1081–1118). The next problem came from the Crusaders. The Crusades were essentially armies that came from Western Europe to recapture the Holy Land from the control of non-Christians. That was the theory, but in practice a lot of the Crusaders were only really interested in fighting and looting. Here's a quick rundown of the four Crusades:

- **First Crusade of 1095–1099:** During this Crusade, the Crusaders recovered Jerusalem and it culminated in an alliance with the Holy Roman Empire of the Germans.

- **Second Crusade of 1144–1150:** The Western crusaders had their eyes on Byzantium itself. Although the Eastern Emperor Manuel I (1143–1180) was able to hold them at bay, in doing so, he allowed the Normans to plunder Greece. The Byzantines suffered a total defeat at the Battle of Myriocephalon against the Turks, supported by the German Empire under Frederick Barbarossa (1155–1190), who was now an enemy.

- **Third Crusade (1189–1192):** This Crusade is known primarily for one of the crusaders – Richard I of England (1189–1199) – and was intended to recapture the Holy Land from the Muslim warrior Saladin. It didn't, but an agreement was gained which allowed Christian pilgrims to visit Jerusalem.

- **Fourth Crusade (1201–1204):** This Crusade was a catastrophe for Constantinople. Funded by the Venetians, the original plan was to invade Egypt to recover holy places, but the Venetians were determined to cash in on their investment and ordered the crusaders to sack Constantinople. And that's exactly what they did. The Byzantines fled, and the crusaders established a Latin dynasty of emperors in Byzantium.

The fall of Byzantium

Even though the Byzantines recaptured Constantinople after the Fourth Crusade, the last 250 years of the Byzantine Empire was a sorry tale of trying to fend off various would-be invaders. The last gasp at restoring the Empire came in 1261 when Michael VIII (1261–1282) retook Constantinople. His biggest threat came from the Norman Charles of Anjou, King of Sicily, who was rounding up an alliance to attack the new Byzantium. Michael agreed to recognise the pope. This made the Byzantines furious (see the earlier section 'The Great Schism of 1054'), but it did mean Pope Gregory X persuaded Charles of Anjou not to attack. Charles was overthrown in 1282.

It really was the last gasp. By the mid-1300s, all the Byzantines could do was watch what was left of their Empire disappear.

The end of the ancient world

The last Byzantine emperor was Constantine XI (1448–1453). It was his bad luck to preside over the end. The Sultan Muhammed II started his assault on Constantinople on 7 April 1453. Constantine heroically held out for seven weeks, but the city fell to a new discovery the great Roman Generals of the remote past, like Scipio Africanus and Caesar, or Emperors like Augustus and Vespasian, could never have dreamed of: gunpowder. The ancient world had met the modern world. Cannon fire breached the walls and, appropriately enough, Constantine died with a sword in his hand. His Empire consisted of little more than the city of Byzantium itself.

The Roman Empire, in its last guise as the Byzantine Empire, had finally fallen, 2,206 years after the legendary founding of Rome itself.

Part VI
The Part of Tens

The 5th Wave   By Rich Tennant

LESSER KNOWN ROMAN LEADERS

Atrocious III

Lost several hundred troops conquering uninhabited islands off Asia Minor.

Marcus Delirious

Wandered for years with his followers searching for the Mediterranean Sea.

General Odious Flatus

With his battle cry of "Excuse me!", he led troops which conquered the bean fields of eastern Thessaly.

Arugula "The Crucifer"

Related to Caligula, Arugula organized the infamous salad orgies of A.D. 37.

In this part . . .

The idea behind this part is to provide you with meaty but digestibly-sized chunks of facts about the key events, people, and places that made Roman history happen the way it did. I'll freely admit it's a purely personal selection, and if someone else had written this book, he or she might have chosen a different list, but hopefully not that different!

What you'll find here is a list of ten crucial moments in Roman history when everything changed – for better or worse; ten Romans who were good or interesting people; ten award-winning villains; as well as ten anti-Romans whose opposition to Roman power made them legendary in their own time and afterwards. And finally, because I know you'll be itching to go out and see the Roman world for yourself, I've listed my top ten (actually, I've sneaked an extra one in, so make that eleven) places to start looking.

Chapter 22

Ten Turning Points in Roman History

In This Chapter
▶ Key events that changed the shape of the Roman world
▶ Wars, conquest, and social revolutions

*T*urning points are those moments in history when everything changes for a civilisation forever. The significance isn't always obvious at the time, but it is to historians, and that included Roman historians who could look back and see some of the decisive moments in Rome's past.

Kicking out the Kings (509 BC)

When the Romans turfed out Tarquinius Superbus in 509 BC, they established a principle that would last for centuries: no more kings. The Roman Republic that was created as a result defined the whole Roman system for the next five centuries, and even when Augustus became emperor, he had to make it look as though he'd done so within the Republican system. You can find the chucking out of the kings in Chapter 10, and how Augustus solved the problem of being a monarch without looking like one in Chapter 15.

Creating the Twelve Tables (450 BC)

When the plebs forced the patricians into accepting a written code of law that protected the plebs' interests, the Romans created something they'd all be immensely proud of in the long run: the idea of the rule of law, a principle most modern countries have inherited. For the Romans, it was also the opening skirmish in the Conflict of the Orders, which saw the plebs exert more and more political control through their tribunes. You'll find the Conflict of the Orders at the end of Chapter 10 and its next phase in Chapter 11.

Winning the Second Punic War (218–202 BC)

Rome's rivalry with Carthage was the greatest conflict of the age. The First Punic War (covered in Chapter 12) had nearly put pay to Carthage's ambitions and put Rome on the map. In the Second Punic War, the struggle became truly international with much higher stakes. The catastrophic defeats at Lake Trasimene (217 BC) and Cannae (216 BC) ought to have wiped Rome off the map. The fact that Rome held onto her allies, came back for more, and ended up defeating Carthage at Zama in 202 BC convinced Rome even more of her destiny and showed the world what she was capable of. The Second Punic War is discussed in Chapter 12.

The year 146 BC

This is a critical year for the Romans because it settled them as the supreme power in the Mediterranean. It marked the permanent destruction of Carthage as a rival, wiped out in a bitter and petty war of revenge that did Rome no great credit but showed what she could do if she wanted. The year also saw the end of Greece as an independent nation of any sort. With so much power, the Romans now did what so many successful states do: started falling apart as men squabbled over the riches. For more than a century, Rome was torn apart in a series of social struggles and the age of the imperators. Chapters 12 and 13 cover the climactic events that led to 146 BC, and Part III picks up what happened afterwards.

Augustus's settlements with the Senate in 27 and 19 BC

Augustus's proudest boast was that he had restored the Roman Republic. He gave up all his powers so that the Senate could give them back to him. It was the greatest political spin in Roman history and one of the greatest in all world history. Augustus clearly was a de facto emperor, but he created the brilliant fiction that he merely held positions within the Republican system and defined how Roman emperors ruled for centuries to come. The genius was that by doing this, Augustus made it possible for the Republic to survive at all. Turn to Chapter 16 to find out how he did it.

Breaking the link between the emperor and Rome (AD 68–69)

The historian Tacitus spotted the key significance of the Civil War of 68–69: Emperors did not have to be made at Rome. They could declare themselves anywhere so long as they had an army to back them. From then on, the Roman Empire was always going to fall prey to ambitious men who had the men and resources at their disposal. It's frankly amazing, then, that the next 120 years were so stable, but from the death of Commodus in 192, the revelation of 68–69 came back to define much of the rest of Roman history. The civil war of 68–69 is discussed in Chapter 16, and the chaos of 192 and later starts in Chapter 18.

Ending the tradition of conquest (AD 117–138)

Hadrian was one of Rome's most interesting emperors. An aesthete, architect, and inveterate traveller, he created some of the Roman Empire's most remarkable buildings, like the Pantheon in Rome. But he made a key decision that flew in the face of everything the Empire stood for and was based on: Realising that the Empire was too big to manage and defend itself, he pulled back and fortified the frontiers and said 'that's that'. From his reign on, the Roman Empire trod water and then went on the defensive, fighting sometimes desperately for its very existence. Hadrian comes in Chapter 17.

Dividing the Roman world (AD 284–305)

Diocletian was the last in a line of soldier emperors in the third century. But unlike so many of his predecessors, he knew the Roman Empire was going to have to change to face the challenges of the future. It had grown too big and had too many border problems for one man to rule. So Diocletian split the Empire in two: East and West. At the time, the devastating significance wasn't too obvious, but he'd created the division down which the Empire would split in the fifth century. The West would crumble, while the East would go on for another thousand years. Diocletian's radical step comes in Chapter 20.

The Edict of Milan (AD 313)

Rome's destiny had been 'preordained' by the pagan gods – a story which plays a central part in Virgil's *Aeneid* – yet the genius of Constantine I (AD 307–337) was to realise that Christianity might help to hold the Empire together. His Edict of Milan started the process that turned the Roman Empire into a Christian state by declaring that all religions would be tolerated – it was a way of letting the Christians in. The change brought its own problems, but it took Roman history into a completely new direction and defined not just the fourth century but the whole nature of power and the identity of the Eastern Roman Empire, which would last for another 1,100 years. See Chapter 20 for how he did it.

The fall of Rome (AD 410)

When Rome fell to Alaric the Goth in 410, the psychological impact was colossal. It's almost impossible for us to imagine just how devastating this event was. It wasn't just the practical implications of an assault on a city, but the mind-numbing sense that the whole foundation of the known world had turned out to be so vulnerable. The Roman world had been unnerved by decades of warfare, but once Rome fell, even though the end wouldn't come until 476, everyone no doubt knew that nothing would ever be the same again. Chapter 21 tells the story.

Chapter 23

Ten Interesting and Occasionally Good Romans

In This Chapter

▶ Men who set the standards for being Romans

▶ Dictators, emperors, politicians, farmers, and ordinary soldiers

*I*n every historical era, a few people really stand out from the rest for helping define the age they lived in. They don't always have to be the great
movers and shakers, but they're usually somehow in the centre of events.

Cincinnatus (519–438 BC)

Lucius Quinctius Cincinnatus is one of the great traditional figures of the
Roman Republic. Cincinnatus was a consul in 460 BC, but in 458 BC, while
ploughing his fields, he was made dictator and placed in charge of the war
against the Volsci and Aequi. Cincinnatus did the job in just 16 days, after
which he laid down his command and went back to the plough. In 439 BC, he
was made dictator again, despite being 80 years old, to put down a conspiracy. He gave up the post again after 21 days and turned down any rewards.
Cincinnatus sums up the Roman Republican ideal – a man of honour and
leadership who wanted nothing more than the chance to plough his fields.
The American city of Cincinnati in Ohio is named after him.

Scipio Africanus the Elder (236–185 BC)

Publius Cornelius Scipio Africanus was the great hero of the Second Punic
War. In fact, the war had been the backdrop to the whole of his early life. Not

only was he at Cannae in 216 BC, but in 211, he heard his father and uncle had been killed in the fighting in Spain. Catapulted to being head of his family at only 24, Scipio was given the unprecedented award of proconsular *imperium* at so young an age and was sent off to avenge his family. His triumphant defeat of the Carthaginians in Spain by 206 BC and then in Africa at Zama in 202 BC made him a great Roman hero. Ruined eventually by corruption charges brought by Cato (see the later section on Cato), Scipio ended up dying in exile. But Scipio went down in Roman lore as a heroic Roman of great honour and was revered for it. His family later included Scipio Aemilianus Africanus the Younger and the Gracchi brothers, whom you can read about in Chapter 14.

Marcus Sergius (late third century BC)

Marcus Sergius was said by some to have been the bravest Roman who ever lived. By the time of the Second Punic War, he'd already been wounded 23 times, including losing his right hand, and fought four battles using his left hand only. He ended up apparently unable to use his feet or his remaining hand, presumably temporarily. Hannibal captured him twice, but he escaped both times despite being banged up in chains for 20 months. Plans were made to disqualify him from the praetorship for being disabled, but Sergius was persistent and was elected anyway. He had an iron right hand made for himself and proceeded to raise the siege of Cremona in 200 BC during the war against the Cisalpine Gauls, and captured 12 enemy camps. Ironically for such a brave man and an inspiration to the Romans, his great-grandson was the arch-villain Sergius Catilinus (more about him in Chapter 24).

Marcus Porcius Cato (234–149 BC)

Cato (sometimes called 'Cato the Elder') was admired in Roman history as the ultimate stickler for traditional Roman virtues. He fought in the Second Punic War (covered in Chapter 12) while still only 17. Cato earned a reputation for ignoring any temptations to indulge himself. He stuck to water and simple meals. Cato hated luxury, decadence, and corruption of any sort and was even disgusted by Greek art, believing it would undermine the great Roman tradition of rural simplicity. You can read about his influential farmer's manual which celebrated the Roman myth of rural bliss and purity in Chapter 4. His moral strictness echoed down later generations, and Virgil even made him one of the judges of hell in the *Aeneid*. Cato sounds like a pretty dreadful person, and indeed it was Cato who called for Carthage's final destruction (described in Chapter 13). But there's no getting away from the fact that Cato summed up what some thought Rome stood for and the way Rome should have stayed.

Gaius Gracchus (d. 121 BC)

Gaius Gracchus (see Chapter 14) was a remarkable man who, like his brother Tiberius, knew that Rome couldn't possibly survive so long as the senatorial aristocracy tried to keep all Rome's wealth to themselves. Unlike Tiberius though, Gaius Gracchus was far more organised and had a much bigger programme of reform. Gaius Gracchus also understood that Rome's Italian allies needed to be rewarded with citizenship and Latin status. His legal measures to recover the liberty of the people earned him the loathing of the aristocracy, and like his brother, he paid with his life. But the Gracchi became martyrs in the cause of political reform, and the Senate had no choice but to accept a lot of what they'd done. Their violent deaths set the tone for Republican politics that lasted until nearly a century later when Augustus took power.

Julius Caesar (102–44 BC)

Caesar deserves his place in this list because he's the most famous Roman who ever lived. Let's get one thing straight: Caesar wasn't an emperor, though he's sometimes described as if he was. But he was a consummate politician who worked the mob like a genius and manipulated his rivals. He was also one of Rome's greatest generals and a brilliant leader of men. A relentless self-publicist, Caesar always had an eye on posterity and left behind his own account of some of these activities. In the end he went too far for the reactionaries who thought he was turning himself into a king. They might have killed him but all they did was cement Caesar's place in history and created a crisis which led to Caesar's nephew Augustus establishing a monarchy. Caesar himself has echoed down the ages, influencing every great military leader ever since.

Augustus (63 BC–AD 14)

Augustus is an obvious choice, but I'm making no apologies for including him here. He was no great general, but he was the winner at the end of all the ghastly civil wars of the first century BC, and instead of using his power to make himself fantastically rich and turn himself into a despot, he created the principate (the Empire disguised as a restored Republic with himself as 'first citizen' – see Chapter 16). What he also achieved was the image of the emperor himself, a kind of universal ageless identity that linked every part of the Roman world together under a single umbrella. Few of his successors were his equal in any way, and it was Rome's great and good fortune that he was the man he was. Augustus wasn't perfect by any means, but considering how some of his successors behaved, he was about as good as a Roman emperor could be.

Pliny the Elder (AD 23–79)

I love Pliny the Elder. He was fascinated by the world around him and, thank goodness, he wrote it all down for his own time and for ours. His *Natural History* is packed from end to end with what passed for Roman science, together with an endless parade of anecdotes, half-baked theories, historical facts, and yarns. It's completely absorbing, as well as amusing. Pliny's total fascination with what made the world tick makes him truly one of the first 'moderns' – if he'd lived centuries later he'd have been one of the geniuses of the Renaissance or a Victorian scientist, and he'd have got on like a house on fire with Thomas Jefferson. It's only appropriate he died when he went to view the eruption of Vesuvius at first hand in AD 79. What a truly fascinating man he must have been.

Carausius (reigned AD 286–293)

Including Carausius is blatant favouritism on my part. I'm intrigued by this man who emerged from total obscurity on the North Sea coast of Belgium to command the Roman fleet sent to clear out pirates. He ended up declaring himself emperor in Britain and part of Gaul, to the fury of Diocletian and Maximian. Simultaneously a rebel and a patriot, his revolt was just as much about frustration at the destruction caused to Rome's reputation by generations of civil war. Carausius resurrected ancient Roman traditions, myths, and literature, and declared his regime to be a brand new, restored Roman Empire. His front was breathtaking, but he's also a symbol of Rome's extraordinary impact on communities all round her Empire. He was the ultimate product of Augustus's branding and anticipated the medieval imitation Roman emperors because the Roman world had created the template for power.

Sextus Valerius Genialis (late first century AD)

Sextus Valerius Genialis was a nobody, but I'm including him because he sums up the Roman Empire. The only thing that survives of this man is his tombstone. It tells us he came from Frisia, just beyond the Rhine frontier. Genialis joined the Roman army and served for 20 years, dying at the age of 40 while on campaign in Britain in the late first century AD with a wing of cavalry from Thrace in northern Greece. His *tria nomina* (see Chapter 2 for Roman naming practices) shows that, unusually for an auxiliary, he hadn't had to wait until retirement to become a Roman citizen and was probably awarded it while in service. His name is totally generically Roman, blurring his own ethnic identity into a Roman one. Without the mention of Frisia, we'd otherwise have no idea at all where Genialis came from. Genialis is a symbol of untold millions of other men from places hundreds of miles from Rome, a city he probably never even saw, whose greatest ambition in life was to become a Roman. The fact that they wanted to and were allowed to is one of the reasons the Roman Empire became so powerful.

Chapter 24

Ten (Mostly) Bad Romans

In This Chapter

▶ Men who didn't live up to Rome's great ideals

▶ Lunatics, thugs, and crooks

*L*ike all the best history, Roman history is packed with villains. Villains make for great stories, and the Romans revelled in making sure none of their worst offenders went forgotten. I've picked ten here, but I can promise you I could have picked out ten times as many and still had room for more.

Tarquinius Superbus (535–509 BC)

In the annals of Roman history, Tarquinius Superbus (see Chapter 10) went down as one of the greatest villains of all time. Not only was he an Etruscan, but he'd only become king by arranging the murder of his father-in-law. He was called *Superbus* because of his pride and insolence (*superbus* means 'arrogant, overbearing'). He ignored the Senate and the public assemblies, so he ended up being hated by both. It was said that many of the citizens forced to work on his public sewer system tried to commit suicide, they were so exhausted. Tarquinius crucified the bodies of those suicides so that they could be eaten by animals. He emptied the treasury. When his son Sextus committed the Rape of Lucretia, it was the last straw for the Roman people. When Tarquinius was thrown out, it was the end of the rule of kings for good.

Coriolanus (527–490 BC)

Caius Marcius was the hero of the Battle of Lake Regillus in 496 BC in the war with the Latin League (refer to Chapter 11). He'd killed one of the enemy soldiers who was going to kill a wounded Roman. He took part in a later siege of the town of Corioli, which belonged to the Latin Volscian tribe. The Volscians came out to attack the Romans, but Marcius led a very small force and pushed them back into Corioli. For this he was given the name Coriolanus. But Coriolanus was a patrician and the plebs resented his attitude – he even tried to hold back a grain handout until the plebs agreed to give up their tribunes. He was forced to leave Rome and amazingly joined the Volscians and led their assault on Rome. This was regarded as the most scandalous and outrageous betrayal imaginable, guaranteeing his infamy. He only pulled back when his wife and mother came out of Rome to ask him to. One day William Shakespeare used the story for one of his most famous plays.

Sulla (138–78 BC)

Sulla (see Chapter 14) went down in history as the man who marched on, and captured, Rome. For that, he was damned to all eternity in Roman history. One of the men responsible for the fall of the Roman Republic, he rose to fame and power as the arch-rival of the general Gaius Marius (also in Chapter 14) and justified taking Rome because it was in the grip of mob rule led by Marius. Sulla was totally ruthless in his annihilation of his enemies, but it's a mark of the age that the relative order he imposed meant he was appointed dictator. Roman historians remembered his rule as a terrible time of proscriptions, arbitrary execution, banishment, and confiscations. No wonder the historian Appian (a Greek who wrote in the early second century AD) called his rule an 'absolute tyranny' of force and violence.

Sergius Catilinus (d. 63 BC)

Lucius Sergius Catilinus was one of Sulla's (see the preceding section) lieutenants, so perhaps it's not surprising he was such a bloodthirsty thug. In every sense a product of the age, Catilinus divorced his wife and married an heiress to underwrite his political ambitions. As a provincial governor, he extorted money and disqualified himself from becoming consul when placed under investigation. His conspiracy (see Chapter 14) was his solution to his money troubles and his thirst for power. He was damned by Cicero in famous speeches in which Cicero condemned Catilinus for being the kind of crook who needed to be driven out if the Roman Republic wasn't to be overrun with men like him.

Gaius Verres (c. 109–c. 43 BC)

Verres had an appalling reputation for milking dry the provinces he was sent to govern. Verres seized inheritances, passed laws to take money off farmers, took bribes to let guilty men off, and even – and this was considered the worst of all his crimes – tortured and executed Roman citizens as if they were slaves. He was absolutely the worst kind of Roman administrator imaginable, because men like him could wipe out Rome's claim she was acting for the good of the places she conquered. In 70 BC, the lawyer Cicero (refer to Chapter 14) was responsible for the prosecution of Verres on charges of extortion. Despite attempts by Verres and his associates to bribe their way to freedom, the evidence was overwhelming. So before the trial ended, Verres exiled himself and was then made an outlaw together with punitive fines. He was executed in about 43 BC by Mark Antony.

Caligula (reigned AD 37–41)

Caligula's villainy is one of the most priceless stories of the days of the Roman Empire. But let's face it, the odds were stacked against him. He was only the third emperor and had to follow in the footsteps of Augustus and all his achievements, and then the miserable Tiberius who at least had a track record as a war hero. Caligula had none of these things to offer the Roman people, and he was totally out of his depth. Add to that the fact that he seems to have become seriously ill, and it was a recipe for disaster. The rest of his reign was a cycle of manic self-delusion, perversion, crazed indulgence, and merciless brutality. The incredible thing is that the brand-new institution of the principate (the rule by an emperor, see Chapter 16) survived this devastating body-blow.

Nero (reigned AD 54–68)

Nero, the last of the Julio-Claudians, is more of a comical figure, but he was a gift to the historians Suetonius and Tacitus who positively revelled in telling the tale of this absurd posturing youth. Convinced of his own great artistic talents, Nero's adult life (once he had done away with his mother Agrippina) was a reckless cavalcade of self-indulgence, violence, narcissism, and eccentric extravagance that included building himself a vast sprawling palace in Rome and performing in Greece. No wonder the tales of his reign made him a byword for tyranny in later ages.

Commodus (reigned AD 180–192)

Commodus earns his place in this list because he was the emperor who brought to an end the Age of the Five Good Emperors. From 96–180 (see Chapter 17), the Roman Empire and most of the free people who lived in it enjoyed an amazing period of affluence and stability. It all went wrong because Commodus was Marcus Aurelius's son but wasn't up to ruling (all the other emperors had had no sons, so the best man for the job had been chosen instead). Commodus was a weak-minded fool who handed over power to corrupt officials and spent his time performing in the arena. It was a tragedy for Rome, because his violent death was inevitable and it heralded in a century of intermittent civil war and a succession of soldier emperors.

Didius Julianus (reigned AD 193)

Frankly, from Commodus's reign on, I'm spoilt for choice for bad Romans, but I've chosen one of his immediate successors. What marks Didius Julianus out is that, unlike all previous emperors, he was out for himself and his family and nothing else. He didn't even have an army of supporters. All he had was his ambitious wife Manlia Scantilla and daughter Didia Clara. In early 193, he offered 25,000 sesterces per soldier if they'd make him emperor, to the disgust of everyone. A call went out for revenge, and as a result, the Roman Empire exploded into civil war as the rival avengers fought it out for supreme control (refer to Chapter 18). Didius Julianus had taken the Empire to a new low – ironically he never paid the soldiers and was murdered after two months.

Caracalla (reigned AD 211–217)

When Septimius Severus made Caracalla and his brother Geta joint emperors and his heirs, the idea was to establish a new imperial dynasty. How wrong can a man be? Once Severus died in 211, Caracalla let rip. The brothers fell out, and Caracalla murdered Geta and his supporters, and his own wife. The rest of Caracalla's short and brutal reign was a reckless cycle of murder and intrigue as he pursued his obsessive belief that he was a reincarnation of Alexander the Great. No wonder he was murdered himself. His short, thuggish reign was the first of many similar ones that followed over the next century, and the sad truth is that he really helped the set the pace.

Elagabalus (reigned AD 218–222)

I doubt if Augustus would have bothered with establishing himself as emperor if he'd known who'd come along 200 years after his death. Elagabalus, born Varius Avitus Bassianus, was the victim of his mother's ambitions (Chapter 19). But he compounded that with his own obsessive sexual perversions, which included marrying a vestal virgin. That outraged the Romans who were equally horrified by his Sun-God cult which he celebrated by building a massive temple on the Palatine hill in Rome to their disgust. What matters, though, is that Elagabalus had absolutely no idea what being a Roman emperor meant apart from an opportunity to indulge himself with complete and utter indifference to the dignity of the position he held, the needs of imperial government, or even a sense of honour and respect. He outraged Rome and the Empire, making sure he died a violent death.

Chapter 25

Ten of Rome's Greatest Enemies

. . . .

In This Chapter

▶ Men, women, and tribes who hated Rome and everything she stood for

▶ Wars, rebellions, double-crossing, and feminine wiles

This motley collection of characters all in their own way resisted the Romans. In a way, the very fact that they did as they did was a recognition of Rome's power. If any one of them had succeeded, the history of the Roman Empire would have been very different. There's no doubt this is only a selection of Rome's greatest enemies. Like all major powers, Rome spent most of its existence facing opposition who viewed Rome with a mixture of awe, envy, and loathing.

Hannibal (247–182 BC)

The prize for Rome's ultimate bogeyman goes to Hannibal of Carthage. His father Hamilcar made him swear lifelong hatred of the Romans, and his campaigning in Spain guaranteed Rome would go to war. Hannibal's greatest years were during the Second Punic War (218–202 BC) when he led his army in an epic and legendary march across the Alps into Italy where he defeated the Romans at Trasimene and Cannae. He survived the war and remained in power in Carthage, but that only gave Rome the excuse to suspect what he was up to. He ended up fleeing to Antiochus III, but after Rome defeated Antiochus, too, Hannibal committed suicide. It was an ignominious end for a brilliant soldier whose fame and notoriety was so great that Carthage remained Rome's nightmare, leading ultimately to the vicious and gratuitous Third Punic War. To read more about Hannibal, go to Chapter 13.

Antiochus III (242–187 BC)

Antiochus III 'the Great' of Syria succeeded his father Seleucus II in 223 BC, whose reign had been a series of misfortunes, including defeat by Egypt and by the Parthians. Antiochus was determined to rebuild the Seleucid kingdom of Syria and, by 206 BC, had taken Armenia and also brought Parthia under his control. The problem for any expansionist monarch like Antiochus is that coming up against Rome was almost inevitable. So his plan to divide up Egypt's possessions with Philip V just put Rome on her guard, and when he invaded Thrace and then Greece, war ensured. It was probably Hannibal who urged Antiochus on to provoke Rome into war and also suggested that Antiochus invade Italy. Unfortunately for both of them, Antiochus was defeated at Thermopylae and Magnesia, as well as at sea, and the peace he was forced into in 188 BC destroyed the Seleucids' chances of being a force to be reckoned with in the Mediterranean. Antiochus was killed in 187 BC while trying to seize the temple treasure of the eastern kingdom of Susiana so that he could pay the annual fine to Rome. You'll find more about Antiochus's antics in Chapter 13.

Mithridates VI, King of Pontus (120–63 BC)

Rome's most relentless opponent in the East, Mithridates, was an admirer of Alexander the Great. When Mithridates V of Pontus (in Asia Minor) was murdered at Sinope, probably by his wife Laodice, Mithridates VI fled and had to hide out until he'd gathered the resources to come back. Mithridates captured Sinope, killed his brother, and slapped his mother into prison and took over the kingdom. He carried on his father's work of expanding the kingdom, but he came up against Rome when he tried his luck in Cappadocia and war broke out. Unfortunately for the Romans, ripping off provincials made Mithridates a popular alternative – when the Romans got it wrong, they often created their own enemies. Mithridates was defeated by Sulla in 85 and thrown out of Greece, but by 81 was fighting the Romans again. War broke out once more in 74 when Rome tried to take Bithynia and lasted till 63 BC when Mithridates's own oppressive treatment of his subjects generated a rebellion led by his own son Pharnaces. He was killed by a guard.

Spartacus (fl. 73–71 BC)

Spartacus was a Thracian slave who ended up in a gladiator school at Capua. He was educated and physically powerful. The revolt broke out thanks to the cruelty of the owner (lanista) of the school, Lentulus Batiatus, and Spartacus was elected one of the leaders. The slaves ran riot through Italy, defeating several Roman armies, one after another. But Spartacus found it impossible to persuade the slaves to flee Italy because they were more interested in pillage. He was finally cornered by Marcus Licinius Crassus in 71 BC and totally defeated, being killed then or amongst the survivors who were crucified. Pompey raced back from Spain to join in the hunt, which gave him the perfect excuse to keep his army together and also gain even more credit than he already had for protecting Rome.

The epic movie *Spartacus* (1960), starring Kirk Douglas as the rebel slave, Laurence Olivier as Crassus, and Peter Ustinov as Batiatus, is not only one of the greatest motion pictures set in the ancient world but also fairly authentic to the story and setting.

Cleopatra VII of Egypt (69–31 BC)

Unlike the other enemies of Rome in this list, Cleopatra played the Romans for fools rather than fighting them. She understood the Romans had colossal power and that the best thing was to harness it to her own interests. Celebrated for her looks and intelligence, Cleopatra made the most of them to beguile Julius Caesar and then Mark Antony. Caesar had become totally infatuated with the Egyptian queen even though she was only about 17 years old (he was 52). She bore him a son called Caesarion and later had children by Antony.

The affairs Cleopatra she had with both men is one of the great stories of the ancient world, and it's no surprise it was the subject of one of the most famously expensive epic movies of all time: *Cleopatra* (1963), starring Rex Harrison (Caesar), Richard Burton (Antony), and Elizabeth Taylor as guess-who. There's a lower-key and much funnier version called *Caesar and Cleopatra* (1945) starring Claude Rains as Caesar and Vivien Leigh as Cleopatra, based on the play by George Bernard Shaw. There's an even lower-key version called *Carry on Cleo* (1964) but the less said about that, the better.

Vercingetorix (fl. 52 BC, d. 46 BC)

Vercingetorix led the Gauls in a revolt against Julius Caesar in 52 BC. It was six years into the war against the Gauls, and Vercingetorix presented Caesar with an unprecedented challenge: the united tribes of Gaul. Vercingetorix destroyed farms and villages to stop the Roman army getting supplies. The

Gauls had hilltop strongholds with fortifications that were strong enough to resist Caesar's battering rams. His troops managed to burst into Avaricum (Bourges) and massacred almost 40,000 inhabitants, but Vercingetorix defeated Caesar at Gergovia which humiliated him and only helped spread the revolt. The climax came at the siege of Alesia (Alexia) where Caesar, vastly outnumbered, built massive siege works that separated the Alesians from a relief army. Alesia fell in the final battle, and Vercingetorix surrendered, being executed by Caesar in Rome in 46 BC. But he became a watchword for Gallic nationalism.

Christopher Lambert plays the hero in *Vercingetorix,* a French movie made in 2001, though the whole war is much more humorously commemorated in the *Asterix the Gaul* comic books and films created by Goscinny and Uderzo in 1959.

Caratacus (d. AD 43–51)

Caratacus led the resistance against the Roman invasion of Britain from the moment the Romans arrived in 43. Unlike most anti-Romans, he lasted a remarkably long time, considering the forces thrown against him. A prince of the Catuvellauni tribe, his domain was quickly overrun, so he escaped to the hills of Wales where he joined tribes together and held the Romans at bay in difficult upland country. He had the time of his life, giving the ancient world's superpower a monumental runaround (sounds familiar, doesn't it?). The Romans finally defeated him in a major battle, but Caratacus fled for sanctuary with a tribal queen called Cartimandua. Unfortunately for Caratacus, she handed him over to the Romans, and he was taken to Rome. Unlike Vercingetorix, however (see the preceding section), he was treated with respect by the emperor Claudius who pensioned him off. He spent his retirement in Rome, wondering why the Romans could possibly have been interested in conquering a remote and primitive place like Britain.

Boudica (d. AD 61)

In 60–61, Boudica led a destructive rebellion in Britain against Roman rule (see Chapter 16). Said to have been a powerful and impressive woman with a mane of red hair, she seems to have provided historians like Tacitus and Dio with a certain amount of suppressed erotic fascination at her dominatrix role in the uprising. Boudica and her family were the victims of oppressive Roman provincial administration. But what makes her really fascinating is how those historians portrayed Boudica as the exact opposite of Nero. It makes one wonder how true the picture is, but it tells us a huge amount about what Romans thought their rulers should be like. Nero was the effeminate man with none of the virtues a Roman leader should have, but Boudica was the masculine barbarian woman with all the virtues of leadership, bravery, and patriotism.

Boudica has been a frequent theme of television documentaries and dramatisations but oddly never a motion picture for cinema.

Simon Bar Cochba (fl. AD 132–135)

Bar Cochba's name means 'son of a star'. Because actual letters by him have been found, we now know his original name was Shim'on Ben Cosiba. He led the great Jewish revolt against the Romans in Palestine under Hadrian, the result of decades of resentment ever since the destruction of Jerusalem and the Temple in 70. Hadrian provoked the rebellion by banning circumcision and planning to build a new city on Jerusalem's site. Bar Cochba created an independent Jewish state and was even thought by some to be the Jewish Messiah. Hadrian sent a general called Julius Severus, who'd been toughened up by campaigning in Britain, and he successfully put the revolt down. Dio says the war cost the destruction of 50 fortresses and 985 villages, and the lives of 580,000 men. The figures are probably exaggerated, but it's clear it was a bloody war. When the revolt fell apart, some of the rebels hid out in Dead Sea Caves, but Bar Cochba was killed in a Roman attack on a place called Bethar. Jerusalem was replaced by a city called Aelia Capitolina.

The German tribes

As soon as Rome advanced north into Gaul and central Europe, she became exposed to the tribes of Germany. If you've seen *Gladiator* (2000), you'll remember the vicious opening battle between Marcus Aurelius's army in 180 and a horde of barbarian tribesmen. The Rhine marked the barrier, and throughout Rome's imperial history, holding that frontier was a constant nightmare on which Rome's very existence depended. The Germans started to become a real problem under Augustus, despite the efforts to integrate German tribal leaders. The catastrophe of AD 9 when three legions were lost (see Chapter 16) was psychologically devastating for Rome. One of the tribes involved was the Chatti, who later took part in the Revolt of Civilis (69–70) (also in Chapter 16). Domitian (81–96) had to fortify the gap between the Rhine and Danube to hold the Chatti back. It was largely successful, but by Marcus Aurelius's time (161–180), war had broken out on the frontier again (Chapter 17). Throughout the third and fourth centuries (Chapters 11,12 and 13), the fighting continued on and off. The Germans played their own part in the last days of the Roman Empire in the West, even annoying Valentinian I so much in 374 that he literally died of rage (Chapter 21).

Chapter 26

Ten (or So) Great Roman Places to Visit

In This Chapter

▶ Places to see that still evoke Rome's extraordinary history

▶ Towns, amphitheatres, forts, frontiers, and plenty more

There are remains of Rome's civilisation to be seen in just about every part of the world the Romans ruled. In this chapter, I list 10 (okay, I list 11; consider the last a bonus). You'll have heard of some of the places but might not be sure what there is to see. Other places you probably won't have heard of, but I've included them because they're truly marvellous and not to be missed at any price.

Rome and Ostia

Yes, I know this is an obvious one. Rome has remains of the forums, the imperial palaces, the Pantheon, original Roman bridges, and the Colosseum, of course, all of which have popped up throughout the book. But Rome has all sorts of other extraordinary remains a little off the beaten track. You can see the exceptional fifth-century late Roman church of Santa Sabina, for instance, and not far away is the amazing Monte Testaccio (the heap of Roman waste-oil *amphorae* from Spain; refer to Chapter 7). But nothing can be beat the ruins of the port of Rome at Ostia, now half an hour away by train on the coast at the mouth of the Tiber. With its streets, granaries, apartment blocks, and tombs, it evokes what everyday Rome once looked like for the ordinary Roman.

Pompeii and Herculaneum

Pompeii is the only place in the Roman Empire, apart from Ostia, where you can get a real sense of the Roman town as a functioning organism. The big sights here are the amphitheatre and the houses with their painted walls. But to get a real feel for the place, linger in the streets and look at the deeply-worn ruts in the flagstones – the evidence of real lives eked out here before the place was destroyed by Vesuvius in August 79. A few miles north are the even more outstanding, but less often visited, ruins of Herculaneum. Swamped by a pyroclastic mud flow, Herculaneum was much more deeply buried, with all sorts of organic remains preserved, right down to the carbonised bread in a street-side tavern. Here you can see Roman houses with upstairs rooms and a shop with a wooden rack for _amphorae_ pottery containers.

Ravenna

Almost forgotten in north-east Italy, Ravenna was where the imperial court of the west holed itself up in the late fourth century. Thanks to its isolation, many of the magnificent late Roman churches and other buildings have survived almost totally intact. My personal favourite is the neat little Tomb of Galla Placidia with its extraordinary vaulted roofs covered with brilliantly coloured mosaics. Perhaps the most astonishing building of all is the mausoleum of Theodoric the Great, king of the Ostrogoths (ruled Italy AD 493–526) with its vault made of a single piece of Istrian stone, 35 feet (10 metres) wide and weighing about 300 tons. These buildings, although built later than most Roman buildings, preserve examples of technique that just don't survive as well elsewhere. Go to Chapter 21 for information about Galla Placidia and Theodoric the Great.

Ephesus

Sitting on the west coast of Turkey not far from a resort called Selçuk and an hour's drive south of the major port at Izmir is Ephesus, once one of the greatest cities of Asia Minor. Once a mighty port itself, Ephesus died when the harbour silted up, and it was left high and dry. Ephesus's ancient status is reflected in the epic scale of the ruins, which include the Great Theatre, where St Paul addressed the Ephesians in the mid-first century AD, and the vast towering façade of the Library of Celsus, which has been re-erected from the ruins. But for my money what makes Ephesus so fabulous is the sheer beauty of the setting, the vast crumbled fragments of gigantic buildings, and the realisation that, however great man's achievements, in the end all things must pass.

Aphrodisias

Aphrodisias is in Turkey, and until modern excavations, little or nothing was visible. If you can get to Turkey and make your way inland to the site from the coastal port of Izmir, you'll see the magnificent theatre, the odeon, and the extraordinary Temple of Aphrodite which was dismantled and turned inside out so that the columns of a classical temple became the columns between the nave and aisles of a Christian church. Aphrodisias was the centre of a major sculpture industry, exporting its products around the Roman Empire, and some of their work can be seen in the site museum. But the most memorable sight of all is the chariot-racing stadium which has to be the best-preserved in the whole Roman Empire.

Sbeitla

In ancient times, Sbeitla was called Sufetula, and it was in what is now Tunisia in North Africa. Sbeitla was once a fantastically rich Roman province where agriculture and olive groves were in abundance. These days, the Sahara has advanced north, and it's a very different place. Sbeitla is a good day trip from the coast, and you have to drive across the desert to get there. Because the town is so remote, it's escaped the worst ravages of time, and so, amazingly, the temples of its capital are largely intact, surrounded by the tumbled down ruins of the rest of the town which include magnificent mosaics. I like it because it shows that even a minor provincial town could have major public architecture, and it's one of the few places left where you can see reasonably intact Roman buildings.

Piazza Armerina

In Sicily, you can find one of the greatest Roman villas of the Roman Empire, now known locally as Villa Romana del Casale. Built between AD 300 and 320, it includes 3,500 square metres of mosaic flooring alone in an extraordinary complex of rooms, courtyards, porticoes, audience chambers, and baths. Some of the mosaics feature popular rural pastimes like hunting boar and hare, fishing, and even catching animals in North Africa for the circus. No-one knows who owned Piazza Armerina, but it's quite possible an emperor lived there, perhaps Maximian I who 'retired' in 305 (see Chapter 20), or his son Maxentius. It's the climax of villa living, aped by other people with money around the Roman Empire.

Hadrian's Wall

Rome's greatest frontier stretches from Newcastle to Carlisle in northern England. It's quite simply the Roman world's greatest surviving military monument with an array of ruined forts, mile-castles, turrets, ditches, inscriptions, temples, altars, and all set in magnificent wild scenery. The best-preserved sections are in the central sector with the forts of Housesteads and Chesters being two of the best-preserved. Nearby, the hinterland fort of Vindolanda is the source of the Roman writing tablets, still being recovered from ongoing excavations. Great museums at Carlisle and Newcastle store some of the best finds, but the forts at Wallsend and South Shields to the east are the centres, not only of wonderful museums and excavations, but also of pioneering rebuilding. Wallsend has a full-scale set of replica working Roman baths, while South Shields has a rebuilt fort gate, commandant's house, and barracks. There's nowhere else to see anything like that.

Petra

Petra is in Jordan, once part of Roman Syria. Founded in the sixth century BC, Petra wasn't taken over by the Romans until the end of the first century AD. It's a totally spectacular location on the edge of the desert and surrounded by huge sandstone hills which give the place its sensational array of orange, yellow, and red coloured landscape. The stone is easy to carve, and the rich Petrans commissioned the most extraordinary tombs cut into the hills with ornate and beautiful classical façades. Even today, the site is quite a trek to reach, but well worth it. Petra still has to be approached through a narrow cut called the Siq which is just 16 feet (5 metres) wide. The first rock-cut façade to greet the visitor is the *khazneh* ('treasury'), and it's 131 feet (40 metres) high.

Dendara

The Temple of Hathor at Dendara is the finest Egyptian temple to have survived. The reason I'm mentioning it is that parts of the main temple and several of the surrounding temples and other buildings were actually made in Roman times. The 'pharaohs' carved on the walls of the smaller temples are Roman emperors, including Augustus and Trajan, while the hypostyle hall in the big temple was built by Tiberius. On the back wall is Cleopatra with her son by Caesar, Caesarion, so it has great historical significance, too.

It's an epic place to visit, a couple of hours' drive north of Luxor, but well worth it because Dendara sums up the brilliant way the Romans adapted. Realising that Egypt was so steeped in traditions that stretched back thousands of years, the Romans made no effort to impose their own styles of architecture or gods. Instead they 'went native' and posed as Egyptian rulers worshipping Egyptian gods on Egyptian temples, and had their names engraved in hieroglyphs.

Bath

Bath, in Avon (England), was once called *Aquae Sulis* ('the Waters of Sul'). It started life as a natural hot spring, but the Romans made it into a religious, healing, and leisure complex complete with cult temple, massive baths complex, and an array of shops and services to cater for visitors from across the Roman world. People have been doing that in Bath ever since. You can descend to the subterranean galleries where the Roman ground level of the temple precinct is exposed, walk from here past the windows where Roman pilgrims hurled their offerings to the sacred spring, read their curse tablets and dedications to the combination god Sulis-Minerva, and put your hand in the waters of the Roman baths, still hot from the underground spring which bubbles up at around 117 ° Fahrenheit (47.2 ° Celsius) all the time.

Index

• S •

Notes

Notes

FOR DUMMIES®

Do Anything. Just Add Dummies

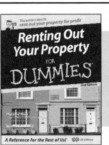

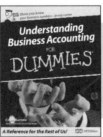

FOR DUMMIES®

A world of resources to help you grow

HOBBIES

0-7645-5232-5

0-7645-6847-7

0-7645-5476-X

Also available:

Art For Dummies
(0-7645-5104-3)

Aromatherapy For Dummies
(0-7645-5171-X)

Bridge For Dummies
(0-7645-5015-2)

Card Games For Dummies
(0-7645-9910-0)

Chess For Dummies
(0-7645-8404-9)

Improving Your Memory
For Dummies
(0-7645-5435-2)

Massage For Dummies
(0-7645-5172-8)

Meditation For Dummies
(0-471-77774-9)

Photography For Dummies
(0-7645-4116-1)

Quilting For Dummies
(0-7645-9799-X)

EDUCATION

0-7645-7206-7

0-7645-5581-2

0-7645-5422-0

Also available:

Algebra For Dummies
(0-7645-5325-9)

Algebra II For Dummies
(0-471-77581-9)

Astronomy For Dummies
(0-7645-8465-0)

Buddhism For Dummies
(0-7645-5359-3)

Calculus For Dummies
(0-7645-2498-4)

Forensics For Dummies
(0-7645-5580-4)

Islam For Dummies
(0-7645-5503-0)

Philosophy For Dummies
(0-7645-5153-1)

Religion For Dummies
(0-7645-5264-3)

Trigonometry For Dummies
(0-7645-6903-1)

PETS

0-7645-5255-4

0-7645-8418-9

0-7645-5275-9

Also available:

Labrador Retrievers
For Dummies
(0-7645-5281-3)

Aquariums For Dummies
(0-7645-5156-6)

Birds For Dummies
(0-7645-5139-6)

Dogs For Dummies
(0-7645-5274-0)

Ferrets For Dummies
(0-7645-5259-7)

Golden Retrievers
For Dummies
(0-7645-5267-8)

Horses For Dummies
(0-7645-9797-3)

Jack Russell Terriers
For Dummies
(0-7645-5268-6)

Puppies Raising & Training
Diary For Dummies
(0-7645-0876-8)

FOR DUMMIES®

The easy way to get more done and have more fun

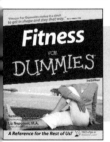
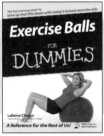
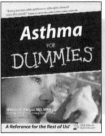

FOR DUMMIES®

Helping you expand your horizons and achieve your potential

INTERNET

0-7645-8996-2

0-7645-8334-4

0-7645-7327-6

Also available:

eBay.co.uk
For Dummies
(0-7645-7059-5)

Dreamweaver 8
For Dummies
(0-7645-9649-7)

Web Design
For Dummies
(0-471-78117-7)

Everyday Internet
All-in-One Desk Reference
For Dummies
(0-7645-8875-3)

Creating Web Pages
All-in-One Desk Reference
For Dummies
(0-7645-4345-8)

DIGITAL MEDIA

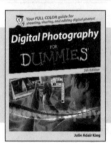

0-7645-9802-3

0-471-74739-4

0-7645-9803-1

Also available:

Digital Photos, Movies,
& Music GigaBook
For Dummies
(0-7645-7414-0)

Digital Photography
All-In-One Desk Reference
For Dummies
(0-7645-7328-4)

Photoshop CS2 For Dummies
(0-7645-9571-7)

Photoshop Elements 4
For Dummies
(0-471-77483-9)

Podcasting For Dummies
(0-471-74898-6)

Windows XP Digital Music
For Dummies
(0-7645-7599-6)

COMPUTER BASICS

0-7645-8958-X

0-7645-7555-4

0-7645-7326-8

Also available:

Office XP 9 in 1
Desk Reference
For Dummies
(0-7645-0819-9)

PCs All-in-One Desk
Reference For Dummies
(0-471-77082-5)

Pocket PC For Dummies
(0-7645-1640-X)

Upgrading & Fixing PCs
For Dummies
(0-7645-1665-5)

Windows XP All-in-One Desk
Reference For Dummies
(0-7645-7463-9)

Macs For Dummies
(0-7645-5656-8)

The Ancient Egyptians For Dummies®

Cheat Sheet

Egypt and the River Nile

For Dummies: Bestselling Book Series for Beginners

The Ancient Egyptians For Dummies®

Cheat Sheet

Egypt and the Ancient Near East

Periods of Egyptian History

You can see from this timeline that some of the dates and dynasties overlap in ancient Egyptian history, especially during the Intermediate Periods, because different kings ruled different parts of Egypt at the same time – all holding the title of king.

Predynastic Period

The Badarian period: 4400–4000 BC
Maadian period: 4000–3300 BC
The Amratian period: 4000–3500 BC
The Gerzean period: 3500–3200 BC
The Negada III period: 3200–3050 BC

Early Dynastic Period

Dynasty 0: 3150–3050 BC
Dynasty 1: 3050–2890 BC
Dynasty 2: 2890–2686 BC

Old Kingdom

Dynasty 3: 2686–2613 BC
Dynasty 4: 2613–2500 BC
Dynasty 5: 2498–2345 BC
Dynasty 6: 2345–2333 BC

First Intermediate Period

Dynasties 7 and 8: 2180–2160 BC

Dynasties 9 and 10: 2160–2040 BC

Middle Kingdom

Dynasty 11: 2134–1991 BC
Dynasty 12: 1991–1782 BC

Second Intermediate Period

Dynasty 13: 1782–1650 BC
Dynasty 14: Dates unknown. This dynasty is characterised by a few chieftains ruling one town, calling themselves kings.
Dynasty 15: 1663–1555 BC
Dynasty 16: 1663–1555 BC
Dynasty 17: 1663–1570 BC

New Kingdom

Dynasty 18: 1570–1293 BC
Dynasty 19: 1293–1185 BC
Dynasty 20: 1185–1070 BC

Third Intermediate Period

High Priests (Thebes): 1080–945 BC
Dynasty 21 (Tanis): 1069–945 BC
Dynasty 22 (Tanis): 945–715 BC
Dynasty 23 (Leontopolis): 818–715 BC
Dynasty 24 (Sais): 727–715 BC
Dynasty 25 (Nubians): 747–656 BC
Dynasty 26 (Sais): 664–525 BC

Late Period

Dynasty 27 (Persian): 525–404 BC
Dynasty 28: 404–399 BC
Dynasty 29: 399–380 BC
Dynasty 30: 380–343 BC
Dynasty 31: 343–332 BC

Graeco-Roman Period

Macedonian Kings: 332–305 BC
Ptolemaic Period: 305–30 BC

The Ancient Egyptians

FOR

DUMMIES®

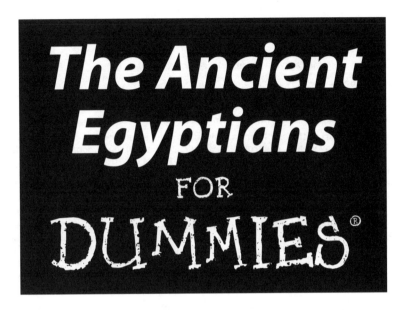

The Ancient Egyptians FOR DUMMIES®

by Charlotte Booth

BICENTENNIAL
1807
WILEY
2007
BICENTENNIAL

John Wiley & Sons, Ltd

The Ancient Egyptians For Dummies®

Published by
John Wiley & Sons, Ltd
The Atrium
Southern Gate
Chichester
West Sussex
PO19 8SQ
England

E-mail (for orders and customer service enquires): cs-books@wiley.co.uk

Visit our Home Page on www.wiley.com

For general information on our other products and services, please contact our Customer Care Department within the U.S. at 800-762-2974, outside the U.S. at 317-572-3993, or fax 317-572-4002.

For technical support, please visit www.wiley.com/techsupport.

Wiley also publishes its books in a variety of electronic formats. Some content that appears in print may not be available in electronic books.

British Library Cataloguing in Publication Data: A catalogue record for this book is available from the British Library

ISBN: 978-0-470-06544-0

Printed and bound in Great Britain by Bell and Bain Ltd, Glasgow.

Translations by James Henry Brested, B. Brier, J. and R. Janssen, Barbara S. Lesko, M. Lichtheim, C. El Mahdy, C. Nims, R. Partridge, James B. Pritchard.

With thanks to C. Banks, W. Frostick, D. Thompson, and G. Webb for their kind permission to reproduce the photographs in this book.

WILEY

About the Author

Charlotte Booth is a freelance Egyptologist who started her education at Birkbeck, University of London, with a Diploma in Egyptology. From there she went to University College London and gained a degree and a Masters in Egyptian Archaeology. She is currently studying at the University of Wales, Swansea, for a PhD, and has written a number of articles and books on Egyptology. Charlotte teaches archaeology and Egyptology in various adult education institutions including the Workers' Educational Association and Birkbeck. She is the founder of the Essex Egyptology Group.

Charlotte has worked in Egypt on the Egyptian Antiquities Information System (EAIS) project (part of the Supreme Council of Antiquities) as an Archaeological Researcher. Closer to home, she appeared on *The New Paul O'Grady Show* as the mummification expert!

Author's Acknowledgements

Over the years many people have inspired me to continue researching and writing. I would like to thank my mum for giving me the all-important first break, the good education, and for her support over the years. Thanks to my fiancé, Wayne Frostick, who knows when to offer advice and when to go and watch the football. Various Egyptologists over the years have also inspired me, including Rosalind Janssen and the late Dominic Montserrat; both were inspirational and memorable teachers. My students also help a great deal by letting me know exactly what is interesting and what is not. Apparently I get the two confused sometimes. Let's hope I have got the right blend in this book. If I have got it right, this is due to the guidance of the *For Dummies* team: Sam Clapp, Rachael Chilvers, and Brian Kramer.

Publisher's Acknowledgements

We're proud of this book; please send us your comments through our Dummies online registration form located at www.dummies.com/register/.

Some of the people who helped bring this book to market include the following:

Acquisitions, Editorial, and Media Development

Project Editor: Rachael Chilvers

Development Editor: Brian Kramer

Content Editor: Steve Edwards

Commissioning Editor: Samantha Clapp

Copy Editor: Sally Lansdell

Proofreader: Mary White

Executive Editor: Jason Dunne

Executive Project Editor: Martin Tribe

Cover Photos: © Trip/Alamy

Cartoons: Rich Tennant
(www.the5thwave.com)

Composition Services

Project Coordinator: Jennifer Theriot

Layout and Graphics: Claudia Bell, Shane Johnson, Barbara Moore, Heather Ryan, Alicia B. South, Christine Williams

Proofreaders: Laura Albert, Susan Moritz

Indexer: Aptara

Brand Reviewer: Jennifer Bingham

Publishing and Editorial for Consumer Dummies

Diane Graves Steele, Vice President and Publisher, Consumer Dummies

Joyce Pepple, Acquisitions Director, Consumer Dummies

Kristin A. Cocks, Product Development Director, Consumer Dummies

Michael Spring, Vice President and Publisher, Travel

Kelly Regan, Editorial Director, Travel

Publishing for Technology Dummies

Andy Cummings, Vice President and Publisher, Dummies Technology/General User

Composition Services

Gerry Fahey, Vice President of Production Services

Debbie Stailey, Director of Composition Services

Contents at a Glance

Table of Contents

Introduction

As a 5-year-old child, I only ever wanted to spend my Saturdays at the British Museum looking at the mummies – until my own mummy started to think I was odd. But nothing is odd about mummies (the ancient Egyptian or the parental kind). The Egyptian mummy was a fundamental part – albeit a small part – of Egyptian funerary beliefs and culture. The mummy has now become an iconic image of Egypt, and many horror films have given it a bad name. Other than questions about mummies, the first thing anyone ever asks me as an Egyptologist is 'So who built the pyramids?' or 'Was Tutankhamun murdered?' As valid as these questions are, *Egyptology* (the study of ancient Egypt) offers so many more interesting things to discover and explore than these age-old queries. (And while others have answered these questions frequently and well, I offer my plain-English answers too in this book.)

In my opinion, some smaller pieces of research in Egypt are far more impressive than the pyramids, such as examining clay objects that still bear the fingerprints of ancient craftsmen, discovering the specific diseases an individual suffered from prior to being mummified, or reading a note from a woman to her dressmaker stating she 'has nothing to wear' (we've all been there). These small insights into the lives of the people who make up a history that is now world famous better answer the question 'Who were the Egyptians?' After you know *who* the ancient Egyptians were, figuring out *how* they built the pyramids doesn't seem like such a monumental question.

The ancient Egyptians were just like modern humans: They wanted to build pyramids, so they used all their available resources and did it. No mystery. In fact, I'm sure the ancient Egyptians would have loved a book entitled *Westerners of the 21st Century AD For Dummies*, so they could learn about this futuristic society that is so primitive it can't even build pyramids!

I think it essential to stop thinking of the ancient Egyptians as some bizarre civilisation so far removed from modern life that the people are undecipherable. They were amazingly similar to us, with the same drives, motivations, emotions, and weaknesses. I hope this book goes some way to helping you make a connection with this fascinating culture and the colourful individuals who created it.

About This Book

Egyptian history has been described as a jigsaw with half the pieces missing, no picture, and no indication of how many pieces there are – it is a daunting task to try to recreate a history that makes sense. Every year, new excavations uncover information that changes or adds another dimension to the available history of this culture. What this means in regard to this book is that I present the history of Egypt *as it stands today*. In ten years' time, it may look different due to new discoveries and new interpretations of the evidence – and this book would need to be updated.

The Nile Valley (a romantic way of saying Egypt) was relatively small and only covered about a mile on each side of the Nile river, but its people achieved so much. Generals waged numerous battles and went on expeditions, priests honoured a pantheon of gods numbering nearly 1,000, and hundreds of kings with what appear to be unpronounceable names (many of them the same – for example, there are eleven King Ramses) produced great architectural feats. In addition to the pyramids, the most iconic image of Egypt, ancient Egypt featured an array of temples, palaces, villages, and subterranean tombs, all with religious elements and iconic imagery, built and added to over hundreds of years.

Hundreds of texts are available from ancient Egypt that help explain the lives and beliefs of the kings, the priests, and even the ordinary people. This book weaves together all these stories to create a complicated but beautiful tapestry of the lives of the Egyptians.

If you think you'll mispronounce all those odd names, confuse the religious practices, and get your dynasties in a diddle, relax. This book presents more than 3,000 years of history as a straightforward outline of eras and periods. To the basic sketch, I then add clusters of intriguing details about ancient Egyptian lifestyle, culture, religion, and beliefs. Further chapters layer on insights about the incredible art and buildings produced by the ancient Egyptians. It's a fascinating journey, and you're going to love it.

Conventions Used in This Book

The dating system used in ancient Egypt was complicated. Surviving records use regnal years (for example, 'year 16 of Ramses II') rather than a centralised calendar ('1450 BC'). However, the Greek traveller Manetho divided ancient Egypt's 3,000-year history into 30 dynasties, and his system is still applied today. This is what this book uses.

Ascertaining exact dates for these dynasties is difficult, but I have added accepted chronological dates to give an idea of when events happened, although I also refer to general eras such as the 18th dynasty, 19th dynasty and so on. All dates are BC (before Christ) unless otherwise stated. Many people prefer BCE (before the Common Era), but I opt for BC because it's more traditional.

The names of kings are often spelt differently from publication to publication, sometimes with Greek versions of the name being used (Cheops instead of the Egyptian Khufu, for example). As an Egyptologist, I use the Egyptian version of the name that the people themselves would recognise, except when the Greek is the better known (for example, I use Thebes rather than Waset for modern Luxor).

Foolish Assumptions

I assume, perhaps wrongly, that you:

- ✔ Are interested in Egyptology through watching popular television shows, going to movies, and visiting museums
- ✔ Know a little about pyramids, Tutankhamun, and Cleopatra, but do not know how these flashy topics and figures fit into the wider history of ancient Egypt
- ✔ Find general books on Egypt and history dry, confusing, and uninviting
- ✔ Want to find out more – as long as the journey is interesting

How This Book Is Organised

You can either read this book from cover to cover, or you can dip in and out if you prefer. You can jump from chapter to chapter as their contents interest you. You can even skip around in each chapter, because each subsection offers information on a specific, selected topic. I also provide numerous cross-references between sections and chapters so you can easily jump from topic to topic and quickly locate the parts of the book that cover the specific aspects of Egyptology that you find most captivating.

The following information gives you an idea of what you can find in each part of the book.

Part I: Introducing the Ancient Egyptians

The landscape and ecology of Egypt were fundamental to the formation of the civilisation and are essential to understanding the culture, government, and even religion that developed along the Nile river. This part looks at the foundations of the ancient Egyptian culture, including its villages, careers, and social arrangements (marriage, divorce, and more). The social structure of Egyptian civilisation was particularly important, with the king at the top and everyone else beneath him, as this part details.

Part II: Stepping Back in Time

This part is the true story behind all the monuments. It covers the personalities who built them, fought for them, and later dismantled them. I take you on a chronological journey through more than 3,000 years of history, starting at the very beginning of Egyptian civilisation in the pre-dynastic period, and travelling down the timeline to the Roman invasion at the death of Cleopatra in 30 BC. This history is pitted with battles, especially in the period known as the New Kingdom, when Egypt had its first permanent army. This part investigates the life of a soldier, including the gruesome battle techniques, the victories, and the near misses.

It also considers the role of Egypt's women – including notable queens as well as working-class wives and mothers. This part ends with the collapse of the Egyptian civilisation after a period of constant invasion and divided rule – the sobering end to a dynamic culture.

Part III: Living Life to the Full: Culture and Beliefs

The Egyptians loved life – partying, hunting, eating, dancing, and chatting with their friends. Compare the intricacies of your own social life with that of the Egyptians and be amazed at the similarities. Sadly a part of life, now and then, is disease and illness, and the Egyptians suffered many of the same ailments as modern humans – although I wouldn't recommend their cures!

When the cures didn't work, death often followed and involved a great number of funerary beliefs and practices. Nowadays, mummification is synonymous with ancient Egypt, although the Egyptians were not the only culture to practise it. Mummification practices were slow in developing, but quickly became an essential part of the afterlife of the deceased, because without a body, the afterlife is pretty dull. To further prevent boredom, all the deceased's belongings were dumped in tombs for use after rebirth.

The Egyptians loved life so much they wanted it to continue for as long as possible. However, mummification and funerary practices are not the only religious beliefs covered in this part. The temples in Egypt were closed to the public, so the Egyptians developed two forms of religion – a complex state religion with the king as a direct communicator with the gods, and an equally rich household religion with a completely new set of gods to help with specific aspects of life, such as health, fertility, and childbirth.

Part IV: Interpreting Egyptian Art and Architecture

Part IV starts with the deciphering of the Egyptian hieroglyphic language, one of the most fundamental discoveries of Egyptology. Artwork is also a substantial part of any document (and of architectural remains), and being able to 'read' artwork is as important as reading the texts. This part explains some of the fundamental characteristics of Egyptian art.

This part also includes a study of the monumental structures of the Egyptians, including temples, tombs, and pyramids. The Egyptians did nothing randomly or because it looked nice (but it has to be said it all looks nice as well). Instead, a religious ideology influences every ancient Egyptian architectural element. So as I explore these incredible structures, I also introduce you to the inspiration behind them.

Part V: The Part of Tens

This part gives you easy-in, easy-out information, including a list of ten famous Egyptologists and ten critical discoveries and milestones in the discipline of Egyptology. You meet ten Egyptian personalities who helped the culture develop, as well as examples of the top achievements of this culture. I also present my list of ten great places to visit in Egypt.

Icons Used in This Book

Egyptology gets people thinking and coming up with their own interpretations of a complex history and culture. I use a number of icons to help highlight some of the points you may be thinking about.

We're lucky to have so many written records from ancient Egypt. Where you see this icon, you know you're reading the words of the ancients.

Many beliefs about ancient Egypt aren't true or are misinterpreted. Where you see this symbol, these myths are explained away.

This icon pinpoints important information that's essential for understanding future information.

There are many aspects of Egyptian history that get the response 'No way! You're making it up!' This icon shows that the information is true, no matter how bizarre.

These are intricate details that aren't essential for understanding the section. Skip these as you wish or absorb them so you can be the nerd at the party!

Where to Go from Here

Well, tradition says start at the beginning and continue until the end; but the thing about traditions is that someone years ago made them up because they seemed good ideas at the time. New traditions can be created right here! Simply jump in and out of the following pages and read them in whatever order you like. All the information is fun and interesting (I promise!), so does it matter what order you read it in?

If you're interested in the pyramids, dash to Chapter 14, or if you want to join the troops in the military, march to Chapter 3. If you want the gruesome details of mummification, flip to Chapter 10. But if you're a stickler for tradition and want to build your understanding of the roots of this intriguing culture, simply turn to the next page.

Part I
Introducing the Ancient Egyptians

"Living on the Nile is wonderful. It brings us water, it brings us mud for bricks, it brings us fish, it brings us green pastures..."

In this part . . .

The ancient Egyptians are famous throughout the world for their pyramids and lashings of gold jewellery. However, this is only part of the story. The Egyptians were part of a large, intricate society, with the king at the top and the unskilled workers at the bottom. Rather like a pyramid, in fact.

Luckily, the Egyptians left loads of information regarding their everyday lives. This part explores the houses they lived in and with whom, their education system, and their social arrangements concerning marriage, divorce, adultery, childbirth, and the elderly.

Chapter 1

Getting Grounded: The Geography and History of Ancient Egypt

T he ancient Egyptians have gripped the imagination for centuries. Ever since Egyptologists deciphered hieroglyphs in the early 19th century, this wonderful civilisation has been opened to historians, archaeologists, and curious laypeople.

Information abounds about the ancient Egyptians, including fascinating facts on virtually every aspect of their lives – everything from the role of women, sexuality, and cosmetics, to fishing, hunting, and warfare.

The lives of the ancient Egyptians can easily be categorised and pigeonholed. Like any good historian, you need to view the civilisation as a whole, and the best starting point is the origin of these amazing people.

So who were the ancient Egyptians? Where did they come from? This chapter answers these questions and begins to paint a picture of the intricately organised culture that developed, flourished, and finally fell along the banks of the Nile river.

Splashing in the Source of Life: The Nile

The ancient Egyptian civilisation would never have developed if it weren't for the Nile. The Nile was – and still is – the only source of water in this region of north Africa. Without it, no life could be supported.

Ancient Egypt is often called the *Nile valley*. This collective term refers to the fertile land situated along the banks of the river, covering an area of 34,000 square kilometres. This overall area has not altered much during the last 5,000 years, although the course of the river Nile itself has changed, and with artificial irrigation the fertile land has been increased a little. See the Cheat Sheet for a map of Egypt.

In de-Nile: Size and scope

The Nile is the longest river in the world, running 6,741 kilometres from eastern Africa to the Mediterranean. Six *cataracts*, or rapids, caused by rock outcrops on the riverbed, separate the southern section of the Nile between Aswan and Khartoum. The first cataract at Aswan created a natural boundary for Egypt until the New Kingdom (1550 BC), when the ancient Egyptians began travelling further and further south in the hunt for gold and areas to build up their empire. (See Chapters 3 and 4 for more information about this era of ancient Egyptian history.)

The Nile flows from south to north – from the interior of Africa to the Mediterranean Sea. Southern Egypt is called *Upper Egypt* because it is closest to the source of the Nile, and northern Egypt is called *Lower Egypt*.

The northern part of the Nile fans out into a series of canals, all leading to the Mediterranean. This area of northern Egypt is known as the Delta and is primarily marshland. The zone is particularly fertile – papyrus (on which many surviving ancient Egyptian records were written) grew in abundance here.

The failing flood

During the reign of Djoser in the third dynasty (refer to the Cheat Sheet for a timeline), Egypt is said to have experienced seven years of famine because of particularly low annual floods. The king was held responsible for the situation because he was an intermediary between the people and the gods, and the famine was seen as punishment from the gods for the king not doing his job. On the Island of Sehel in the south of Egypt, Ptolemy V (204–181 BC) commissioned a stela recording this famine and Djoser's actions:

I was in mourning on my throne. Those of the palace were in grief . . . because Hapy [the flood] had failed to come in time. In a period of seven years, grain was scant, kernels were dried up . . . Every man robbed his twin . . . Children cried . . . The hearts of the old were needy . . . Temples were shut, Shrines covered with dust, Everyone was in distress . . . I consulted one of the staff, the Chief lector-priest of Imhotep . . . He departed, he returned to me quickly.

Imhotep, the builder of the step pyramid (see Chapter 14), traced the source of the Nile to the island of Elephantine and the caves of Khnum. He assured Djoser that renewed worship of Khnum would start the floods again. Khnum then appeared to Djoser in a dream:

> When I was asleep . . . I found the god standing. I caused him pleasure by worshipping and adoring him. He made himself known to me and said: 'I am Khnum, your creator, my arms are around you, to steady your body, to safeguard your limbs . . . For I am the master who makes, I am he who makes himself exalted in Nun [primeval waters], who first came forth, Hapy who hurries at will; fashioner of everybody, guide of each man to their hour. The two caves are in a trench [?] below me. It is up to me to let loose the well. I know the Nile, urge him to the field, I urge him, life appears in every nose . . . I will make the Nile swell for you, without there being a year of lack and exhaustion in the whole land, so the plants will flourish, bending under their fruit . . . The land of Egypt is beginning to stir again, the shores are shining wonderfully, and wealth and well-being [?] dwell with them, as it had been before.

Djoser awoke and was pleased at the message. He passed a decree of an increase of taxes to be paid to the temple of Khnum:

> All the peasants working their fields with their labourers and bringing water to their new and high-lying lands, their harvest shall be stored in your granary in excess of the part that used to be your due. All fishermen and trappers and hunters on the water and lion catchers in the desert, I impose on them a duty of one tenth of their catch. Every calf born by the cows on your land shall be given to the stables as a burnt offering and a remaining daily offering. Moreover one tenth of the gold and ivory and the wood and minerals and every tree stem and all things which the Nubians . . . bring to Egypt shall be handed over together with every man who comes with them. No vizier shall give orders in these places and levy a tax on them, diminishing what is being delivered to your temple.

Once these gifts had been given to the temple of Khnum, the floods would once again reach the appropriate level, restore Egypt to the agricultural haven it once was, and re-inspire the people's faith in king Djoser.

However, because this stela was written more than 2,000 years after the date of the event, historians have difficulty assessing its accuracy as a historical document. Some scholars believe the stela is a copy of an Old Kingdom example erected by Djoser; others believe it was created in the Ptolemaic period as a means of justifying new goodies for the temple of Khnum. The truth may never be known.

The inundation: Surviving and thriving

Every year for the months between July and October the Nile flooded, covering the land on both banks with as much as 2 feet of water. When the water receded, very fertile black silt covered the land. Because of this, the Egyptians called their country Kemet, which means 'the black land'. Through careful crop management and intricate irrigation canals, the Nile valley became a major agricultural area.

Although the inundation of the Nile was essential for the agricultural success of the ancient Egyptian civilisation, a risk always existed of the Nile flooding too much or not enough. Either situation resulted in crop failure, famine, and death.

Since 1830 AD, a series of dams and sluices at the southern end of the Nile have checked the floods. In 1960 AD, the Egyptians built the High Dam at Aswan, which has stopped the Nile flooding altogether. Although these new technologies create a more stable environment for the modern Egyptians to farm, the steady nature of the present-day Nile makes imagining the up-and-down aspects of ancient Egyptian life more difficult.

Meeting the Ancient Egyptians

The ancient people who lived in the Nile valley were a melting pot of many ethnic groups, with many different origins. Prior to 5000 BC, the Nile valley did not have any settled people, because the surrounding area was rich in vegetation and was inhabited by a number of nomadic hunter-gatherer tribes, which followed large animals such as lions, giraffes, and ostriches as a source of food.

However, due to climatic change in approximately 5000 BC, the area surrounding the Nile valley began to dry out and was no longer able to sustain the large animals. This climate shift meant that the nomadic tribes all converged on the Nile valley because the river was slowly becoming the only source of water in the region.

As a result, the first Egyptian population was a collection of different nomadic tribes, which slowly integrated with each other and created a new society:

- ✔ **In the south of Egypt,** the origins of the people were closer to Nubia, resulting in a darker people.

- ✔ **In the north of Egypt,** the origins of the people were more in the Near East, creating a paler people.

By 3100 BC and the start of the pharaonic period of Egyptian history, a brand new culture – the Egyptian culture recognised today – had developed from this collection of different people, cultures and languages.

Dating the ancients

One of the most confusing aspects of Egyptian history is applying specific dates to eras, reigns, and even recorded battles and ceremonies. Also, the history of ancient Egypt spans more than 3,000 years, which is a lot to get your head around.

Making matters more difficult, the Egyptians themselves did not have a centralised dating system such as the one used today (for example, BC and AD). Instead, they referred to dates in regnal years of the current king. For example year 5 of Ramses II or year 16 of Akhenaten.

This system probably worked well in ancient times, but it doesn't help modern Egyptologists a great deal – especially when a number of kings are missing from the records or the exact length of some reigns is uncertain. So, for example, dating something from year 4 of Ramses II to year 2 of Merenptah made perfect sense to an Egyptian, but if you don't know how long Ramses II ruled and you don't know whether another king came between Ramses II and Merenptah (the king historians believe followed Ramses II), ascertaining true periods is very difficult.

A passion for all things Egyptian

For centuries – millennia, in fact – people have been fascinated by ancient Egyptian culture, including its language, history, politics, religion, burial practices, architecture, and art. Indeed, even the Greeks and Romans (ancient cultures themselves by any historian's account) were intrigued by the people of the Nile, arranged sight-seeing excursions to the area, and ended up transporting Egyptian treasures back to their homelands.

Modern *Egyptology*, a discipline that blends rigorous study of ancient history and archaeology with touches of sociology, art history, political science, economics, and more, began in earnest in 1823 when Jean-François Champollion was the first to decipher hieroglyphs, which led historians to begin deconstructing the many myths and misunderstandings of the ancient Egyptians.

Check out Chapter 19 for ten profiles of noteworthy Egyptologists, including Champollion.

Today, Egyptology is bigger than ever. Many universities now offer degrees in Egyptology or Egyptian archaeology. However, the work available for professional Egyptologists is scarce, with limited opportunitites to teach in universities or excavate in Egypt. Many museums employ volunteers instead of paid staff, therefore hundreds of applicants often seek the few paid positions. Furthermore, excavating in Egypt is particularly difficult because Egyptian researchers are favoured over westerners. Many Egyptologists therefore work in other jobs and write books and articles on Egyptology or conduct field work on a part-time basis. Hard work, but someone's gotta do it.

Manetho to the rescue

Modern Egyptologists weren't the only ones who thought that the Egyptian dating system was confusing. Manetho, an Egyptian historian and priest from the third century BC, devised the *dynastic system* of dating that is still used today.

In the dynastic system, a dynasty change was introduced whenever a change occurred in the ruling family, geography, or any other continuity issue in the succession of kings. Manetho divided the kings of Egypt into 31 dynasties, subdivided into three main kingdoms with turbulent 'intermediate' periods between them.

- **Early dynastic period:** Dynasty 0–2, around 3150–2686 BC
- **Old Kingdom:** Third to sixth dynasties, around 2686–2181 BC
- **First intermediate period:** Seventh to tenth dynasties, around 2181–2040 BC
- **Middle Kingdom:** 11th to 12th dynasties, around 2040–1782 BC
- **Second intermediate period:** 13th to 17th dynasties, around 1782–1570 BC
- **The New Kingdom:** 18th to 20th dynasties, around 1570–1070 BC
- **Third intermediate period:** 21st to 26th dynasties, around 1080–525 BC
- **Late period:** 27th to 30th dynasties, around 525–332 BC

This dating system has been very useful, and Egyptologists have been able to add chronological dates to the dynasties. However, these dates do not match from publication to publication, and this discrepancy can be very confusing for beginners. For this reason, referring to dynasties rather than dates is often easier. The dates I use in this book are based on Peter Clayton's *Chronicle of the Pharaohs* (Thames and Hudson Press), a widely accepted general chronology.

Unifying the Two Lands

Despite some quirks in their dating system, the ancient Egyptians were a very organised civilisation. This is particularly obvious in their division of the country. The most important division politically was the north–south divide. This division, into Upper (southern) and Lower (northern) Egypt produced what was referred to as the Two Lands – a concept that dominated kingship ideology from the reign of the first king, Narmer (3100 BC), to the final days of Cleopatra VII (30 BC).

The Narmer Palette, a flat stone plaque about 64 centimetres tall, shows King Narmer unifying the country – the earliest recorded battle in Egyptian history. It depicts Narmer dominating Lower Egypt to become the king of the Two Lands.

From this period on, any king needed to rule both Upper and Lower Egypt in order to be recognised as a true king of Egypt. The Egyptians considered this concept such a fundamental part of kingship that they incorporated the title 'king of Upper and Lower Egypt' into two of the five traditional names that the king received at his coronation.

These names describe certain elements of the king's rule. The traditional order of these names was:

- ✔ Horus name
- ✔ He of the two ladies (under the protection of the vulture goddess of Upper Egypt and the cobra goddess of Lower Egypt)
- ✔ Golden Horus name

- ✔ He of the sedge and the bee (under the protection of the sedge of Upper Egypt and the bee of Lower Egypt)

- ✔ Son of Ra

Representing the Two Lands

In addition to the king's titles, a number of symbols and hieroglyphs in Egyptian records highlight the importance of the unity of the Two Lands. Important imagery in kingship regalia included:

- ✔ The white crown of Upper Egypt
- ✔ The red crown of Lower Egypt
- ✔ The double crown of Upper and Lower Egypt
- ✔ The sedge of Upper Egypt
- ✔ The bee of Lower Egypt
- ✔ Nekhbet the vulture goddess of Upper Egypt
- ✔ Wadjet the cobra goddess of Lower Egypt

Additionally, the following images frequently appear in architecture, especially on pillars and as temple decoration (see Chapter 12). Although these images do not represent kingship specifically, they often define the region of rule of a particular king or, if both are shown, the unity.

- ✔ Papyrus of Lower Egypt
- ✔ Lotus of Upper Egypt
- ✔ The lotus and papyrus plants tied around symbolic 'heart and lungs' of Egypt, which indicates a unified Egypt

Uniting east and west

Although the Upper and Lower Egypt division was the most important (at least where kingship was concerned), Egypt was further divided into east and west. The Nile formed the dividing line between the two sides.

- ✔ **The east bank of the Nile** was used primarily for the construction of the cult temples (see Chapter 12) and settlements. The ancient Egyptians considered the east bank to be the Land of the Living because the sun rose each morning in the east, giving hope and bringing new life.

- ✔ **The west bank of the Nile** was home to cemeteries and funerary temples and was referred to as the Land of the Dead. West was where the sun set in the evening, starting the nocturnal journey into the afterlife until rebirth in the east.

However, exceptions to these divisions existed. Some settlements were built on the west bank, while some cemeteries existed in the east.

Subdividing further

If the divisions of Upper/Lower and eastern/western Egypt weren't enough, the whole of Egypt was further divided into 42 provinces, currently known as *nomes*. In Upper Egypt, 22 nomes were present from the start of the dynastic period; the 20 nomes in Lower Egypt developed later.

Each nome (or *sepat* as the ancient Egyptians called them) was governed by a *nomarch* or mayor who answered to the vizier and ultimately the king. Ideally, only one vizier monitored the government, but many kings split the role into two – a vizier of Upper Egypt and a vizier of Lower Egypt. Each nome had a capital city and a local temple for the worship of the local deity, complete with individual religious taboos, practices, and rituals.

Each nome was represented by a *standard*, consisting of a staff bearing the statue of its local deity and a regional animal or plant. The animals and plants are often represented in offering scenes, which highlight the crops of a particular region. Nomes often took their names based on their regional animal or plant, such as the ibis nome and the hare nome.

Following the Floating Capital

Although the Egyptians were very organised with a well-established system of governmental divisions, they were not as strict about the location of their capital city. In fact, Egyptologists have identified numerous royal residences and royal burial sites in cities throughout Egypt, which indicates that the capital moved according to the whim of the reigning king. In some reigns, rulers had two capitals: a religious capital and an administrative capital.

Pre-dynastic capitals

The Egyptian civilisation had not developed in the pre-dynastic period (prior to 3100 BC), so a capital city as such did not exist.

Instead, three sites that included settlements and large cemeteries seem to dominate (see Cheat Sheet for locations):

- **Naqada** was one of the largest pre-dynastic sites, situated on the west bank of the Nile approximately 26 kilometres north of Luxor. Archaeologists have discovered two large cemeteries here with more than 2,000 graves, a number of which belong to the elite and royalty.

- **Hierakonpolis** was also used as a royal cemetery and was the base for the funerary cult of the second-dynasty king Khasekhemwy. The most famous finds from this site are the Narmer Palette (see the section 'Unifying the Two Lands', earlier in this chapter), the Narmer Mace Head and the Scorpion Mace Head. These last two items are both on display in the Ashmolean Museum, Oxford, and depict the early development of Egypt's kingship ideology.

- **Abydos** was a major site during the pre-dynastic period and remained prominent for most of the pharaonic period. The earliest settlement here dates to 4000–3500 BC, although most of the current remains are from the 19th and 20th dynasties. Abydos was a major religious centre with monuments of all the first-dynasty kings and two of the second-dynasty kings.

Moving to Memphis

The three pre-dynastic centres were abandoned as capital cities during the Old Kingdom (around 2686–2333 BC), and Memphis, near modern Cairo, became the new administrative capital. The location of Memphis provided easy access and control over both the Delta region and the Nile valley, ensuring that trade through this region was firmly under royal control.

The royal cemeteries of the Old Kingdom were also very close to Memphis, with pyramid fields at Giza, Saqqara, Dahshur, Abusir, and Abu-Roash (see Chapter 14) covering an area of approximately 35 square kilometres.

Memphis remained important throughout the New Kingdom as well. During the reigns of Sety I (1291–1278 BC) and Ramses II (1279–1212 BC), the royal harem (see Chapter 5) was located at Memphis, which shows the continuity of the city as a royal residence.

Settling in Thebes

During the New Kingdom, the major royal and religious capital was Thebes (modern-day Luxor), which was home to the powerful cult of the god Amun. This region includes the temples of Karnak and Luxor, as well as the New Kingdom funerary temples and the royal burials in the Valley of the Kings and Queens (see Chapter 13).

For the majority of the New Kingdom, Thebes was the religious capital and Memphis in the north was the administrative capital, ensuring that the king had control over both Upper and Lower Egypt.

Noting other short-lived settlements

Although Memphis and Thebes were important settlements for much of the pharaonic period, some rulers chose to have their capital elsewhere, although these locations did not maintain this important status for long:

  ✔ **Avaris:** The Hyksos rulers of the second intermediate period (1663–1555 BC) built their capital in the Delta. The settlement shows an interesting juxtaposition between two cultures: Egyptian and Palestinian (the latter where the Hyksos are thought to have originated). For more information, see Chapter 3.

- ✔ **Amarna:** This was the new capital city built by Akhenaten of the 18th dynasty (1350–1334 BC) and dedicated to the solar disc, the Aten. (Turn to Chapter 4 for more on this period of Egyptian history.) Amarna was situated half way between Memphis and Thebes in Middle Egypt and included a number of temples, palaces, an extensive settlement, and a cemetery. (Check out Chapter 18 for what you can see today.)

- ✔ **Pi-Rameses:** This city in the Delta, very close to Avaris, was built originally by Sety I (1291–1278 BC) as a harbour town and was important in controlling the transportation of goods from the Mediterranean into the Nile valley. Ramses II of the 19th dynasty (1279–1212 BC) greatly expanded the city and named it Pi-Rameses to serve as a rival to Thebes.

- ✔ **Tanis:** This was another capital in the Delta during the 21st dynasty, under king Psusennes I (1039–991 BC). Most of the city was built with reused blocks from Pi-Rameses.

These cities all had very limited lives. At the end of most of the kings' reigns, these sites declined in importance, and Thebes and Memphis were re-established as the capitals.

Populating the Nile Valley

From approximately 5000 BC, settled communities inhabited the Nile valley in an area of approximately 34,000 square kilometres. However, the population of this region was never recorded until the Roman administration of Egypt, which began in 30 BC.

Egyptologists have estimated population data based on the available area of agricultural land and the number of people it was able to support:

- ✔ Late pre-dynastic period: 100,000–200,000 people

- ✔ Early dynastic period: 2 million people

- ✔ Old Kingdom: 1–1.5 million people

- ✔ New Kingdom: 2.9–4.5 million people

- ✔ Ptolemaic period: 7–7.5 million people

The population fluctuated throughout the pharaonic period, with a marked rise during the Ptolemaic period due to an increased area of agricultural land, plus an influx of foreigners into Egypt after Alexander the Great (see Chapter 6).

Estimating the population of a warrior nation

More accurate population estimates can be calculated for specific periods of Egypt history. For example, in the period between the Saite dynasties (727–525 BC) and the time of Herodotus (fifth to fourth century BC), records state that Egypt had 410,000 warriors. Egyptologists assume that each soldier was part of a family of four, so the soldiers and their families during this time would have constituted around 1,640,000 people.

However, each soldier was given 12 *arouras* of land (1,200 square cubits or 0.63 square kilometres), a total of 4,920,000 arouras (3,099,600 square kilometres) of land for all the soldiers. This land constituted half of the agricultural land in Egypt at the time. Therefore, assuming that the other half of the agricultural land sustained the same number of people, the estimated population is $1,640,000 \times 2 = 3,280,000$ people.

Furthermore, historians believe that 2 arouras of land was able to sustain one person, so each soldier had enough land to sustain six people. This means that the population may have been higher: $3,280,000 \div 4 \times 6 = 4,920,000$ people.

Climbing the Egyptian Social Ladder

Egyptian society was greatly stratified. However, most evidence available today is only from the upper levels of society – royalty and the elite – because these individuals were able to afford to leave behind stone monuments and elaborate tombs.

The social structure of ancient Egyptian society from the Old Kingdom on was rather like a pyramid (how appropriate!). The king was perched at the top, followed by the small band of priests drawn from the elite, a slightly larger group of the ruling elite, and then the working class (including skilled trades and unskilled labour), which comprised the rest of the population.

Obviously, the majority of the population were working class. They were responsible for working on the agricultural land and producing food for the elite classes and priests. Unfortunately, Egyptologists do not know the exact number of the elite – and very little information about the working class exists in written records.

The following sections discuss the experiences of individuals at each level of ancient Egypt's social pyramid.

Being king of the heap

The most powerful person in ancient Egyptian society was the king. He was born into the position, and ideally he was the son of the previous king – although on several occasions the king was a usurper who nicked the throne from the rightful heir.

As head of state, the king had a number of functions and roles that he needed to maintain, including

- ✔ High priest of all temples in the country
- ✔ Head of the army (in the New Kingdom especially)
- ✔ International diplomat for trade and peace treaties
- ✔ Intermediary between the people and the gods

The king was considered to be an incarnation of the god Horus on earth – and therefore a god in his own right. This divine status meant that he was able to converse directly with the gods on behalf of the population of Egypt. Keeping the gods happy was also his job. If Egypt were afflicted with disease, famine, high floods, or war, Egyptians believed that the king was being punished and that it was his fault for not keeping his people happy. That's a lot of pressure for one man!

Serving the gods

The priesthood was a very powerful occupation, especially in its upper echelons (see Chapter 2 for more details). The priests worked for the temple and were able to gain honours, wealth, and titles.

The priests were privileged enough to be in the presence of the gods every day, and many people made gifts to the priests (some say bribes) to put a good word in with the gods or to ask for something on their behalf. Even the king was not immune to this gift-giving, often bestowing land, titles, and rewards on the priests. These gifts eventually helped the high priests to become very wealthy. And with wealth comes power. For example:

- ✔ The Priesthood of Amun at Karnak was the richest and most powerful in Egypt. During the reign of Ramses III, this group owned 1,448 square kilometres of agricultural land, vineyards, quarries, and mines, in addition to riverboats and sea-faring vessels. Most of this agricultural land was rented to the peasants, who paid a third of their harvest to the temple as rent.

> ✔ The *daily* income of the mortuary temple of Ramses III at Medinet Habu from its associated land was 2,222 loaves of bread, 154 jars of beer, 8,000 litres of grain, plus meat and other commodities – enough to feed 600 families.

Throughout Egyptian history, the kings felt that appeasing the priests was essential because the priests worked on the king's behalf, keeping the gods happy and keeping Egypt safe. Hardly surprising that gradually the king's presents increased and the priesthood's power grew and grew, until it rivalled that of the king.

Powering the elite

In order to alleviate some of the pressure, the king had a large number of advisers and officials who helped in decisions and activities. Royal sons who were not destined for the throne were appointed by the king to fill many of the top official positions.

The easiest role to delegate was that of high priest. Obviously the king wasn't able to carry out all the rituals expected of him as high priest in every temple in Egypt. Even though the king was a god, he wasn't Superman!

Nomarchs, get set

In the Old and Middle Kingdoms, much of the power of the king was in fact delegated to local *nomarchs*, or mayors. They were in charge of their *nome*, or province, and controlled the economy, taxes, and employment of the people living there. The nomarchs ultimately relied on the generosity of the king and needed to make regular reports and payments to the king on behalf of their nomes.

Egypt's standing army

During the New Kingdom, the king did not have to rely so heavily on the nomarchs to conscript men for war or trade, because Egypt had a permanent standing army at the beck and call of the king.

Two generals led the New Kingdom army – one for the army of Upper Egypt and one for the army of Lower Egypt. This clever ploy by the king limited how much of the army one general controlled and prevented a military coup to usurp the throne. It clearly helped if the king was a little paranoid.

Many generals in the New Kingdom army were royal princes. Some were given the title when they were small children, indicating that this was an honorary title that gave the young princes something to do – playing with a sword and chariot – as well as keeping such powerful positions within the royal family.

IN THEIR WORDS

My word is law

The tomb of the 18th-dynasty vizier Rekhmire includes one of the few inscriptions describing in full the role of the vizier, which was rich and varied and was clearly a position of great power.

The vizierate is not to show respect of princes and councillors; it is not to make for himself slaves of any people.

Behold, when a petitioner comes from Upper or Lower Egypt, even the whole land, see to it that everything is done in accordance with law, that everything is done according to custom, giving every man his right. A petitioner who had been adjudged shall not say: 'My right has not been given to me!'

Beware of that which is said of the vizier Kheti. It is said that he discriminated against some of the people of his own kin in favour of strangers, for fear lest it should be said of him that he favoured his kin dishonestly. When one of them appealed against the judgement which he thought to make him, he persisted in his discrimination. Now

that is not justice. It is an abomination of the god to show partiality.

Cause yourself to be feared. Let men be afraid of you. A vizier is an office of whom one is afraid. Behold, the dread of a vizier is that he does justice. But indeed, if a man cause himself to be feared a multitude of times, there is something wrong in him in the opinion of the people. They do not say of him: 'He is a man indeed.' Behold, this fear of a vizier deters the liar, when the vizier proceeds according to the dread one has of him. Clearly the vizierate was such a powerful position that the population feared corruption and lack of justice. (In fact, records indicate a number of instances where the viziers were accused of this.) Rekhmire himself had a mysterious end to his life: He was never buried in his tomb, and many of the images in his tomb were intentionally damaged, perhaps to prevent him from having an afterlife. Was this vandalism due to his corrupt activities? Historians may never know, but it does make you think.

REMEMBER

However, the king also relied on these nomarchs, especially in times of war or foreign expeditions. Before the New Kingdom saw the start of the full-time militia (see Chapter 4), the nomarchs were responsible for conscripting and training fit young men from their provinces to fight for Egypt or to accompany the king on foreign expeditions, either for trade or mining purposes.

Therefore the king had to keep the nomarchs on his side through payments and gifts. Otherwise these fit young men may be conscripted to march *against* the king and potentially steal the throne.

Vizier arising

The responsibilities of the vizier were varied and made him the second most powerful man in Egypt after the king.

The *vizier* was basically a personal assistant and secretary of state to the king and compiled a weekly or monthly report on all the key information for the whole of Egypt, based on daily reports from workshops and lesser officials. At times, the vizier acted as king by proxy, distributing land and the spoils of war to nomarchs or as rewards for loyalty.

Additionally, the vizier was responsible for hiring policemen and received reports from all the guard posts throughout Egypt regarding movements of enemy armies or other threatening activities. The vizier also presided over the court, dealing with the daily petitions of the ordinary people, including crimes and minor offences.

May the priest be with you

The most prominent power struggle in ancient Egyptian history took place during the reign of Ramses XI between the royal family and the high priests of Amun. At this time, the power of the throne was so diminished that a civil war broke out in order to decide who was to take over Ramses XI's throne – while he was still on it!

Throughout the first 12 years of Ramses XI's reign, the high priests of Amun held virtually the same power as Ramses and had his support because he was a particularly pious sovereign. However, the one difference between the high priests and Ramses XI is that the king had the military under his control, which gave him the edge.

However, at some point prior to year 12, one of Ramses's administrative officials – Panehsy, the Viceroy of Nubia, who was based in Thebes – came into conflict with the high priest of Amun, Amenhotep. This conflict denied Amenhotep his position for nine months, until he eventually turned to Ramses XI for help. Ramses commanded his army to destroy Panehsy, who was exiled to Nubia, and Amenhotep got his position back.

A few years later, Amenhotep was replaced by Herihor, whom the king also bestowed with the military titles that Panehsy held. For the first time in Egyptian history, one man held the top religious and military titles, making Herihor more powerful than Ramses. One gift too many, indeed!

Ramses was in a very weak position and was king in name only, while Herihor effectively ruled Egypt. Herihor showed his revered position by placing his name and high priest title in a cartouche in the manner of a king.

On the death of Herihor, his position passed to his son-in-law Piankhy, who ruled alongside Ramses in the same way as his father. At the death of Ramses, Piankhy continued to rule Thebes, while Lower Egypt was ruled by King Smendes from Tanis, who legitimised his claim to the throne by marrying a daughter of Ramses XI.

This started a period of divided rule and a dynasty (the 21st) of Theban high priests, all successors of Piankhy who held military and religious titles. Just goes to show you really shouldn't put all your eggs in one basket.

Shifting power

Although the king was the top dog in Egypt, at times lower-ranking officials such as the vizier, the military, or priests surpassed him in power. A prime example is that of Ramses XI of the 20th dynasty who was succeeded to the throne by the high priest of Amun. In fact, even throughout Ramses XI's reign, the high priests held equal or more power than he did. See the sidebar 'May the priest be with you' for more information.

The vizierate was often used as a stepping stone to the role of king, with Ay in the 18th dynasty becoming king, and Bay in the 19th dynasty being the power behind the puppet king Siptah. In fact, the 19th dynasty itself started due to a shift in power between the royal family (ending with Ay, the uncle of Tutankhamun) and the military (with Horemheb, an army general who took over the throne). Horemheb then passed the throne to his general, Ramses I, and started a new military era in Egypt.

Other lesser officials grew in wealth – and therefore power – until they overshadowed the king. Of course, this wealth came from the king in the first place, in the form of titles, land, and gifts. So at some point the king obviously gave one gift too many. This imbalance of wealth is on clear display in the tombs and pyramids at the end of the Old Kingdom. The tombs of officials were expensively carved and decorated in stone, while the royal pyramids were small and built with desert rubble.

Even historians have difficulty identifying whether various new dynasties started due to the usurpation of power by a wealthy official or a natural change when the king lacked a male heir.

During periods of political instability, when the throne did not follow the traditional line of succession, the whole of Egypt was affected, especially the economy. Any battle over the throne resulted in neglect of international trade (albeit briefly), as well as increased spending on military action, resulting in further economic problems, such as the distribution of food and the abandonment of tomb-building projects (especially in the 21st dynasty and later).

One such problem occurred in year 29 of Ramses III's reign. The workmen at Deir el Medina had not been paid for six months and went on strike, protesting before the funerary temples of Thutmosis III, Ramses II, and Sety I, which stored the grain used for their wages. The strike worked, and they were paid. But later that year when payment was again late, Djhutymose, a scribe from Deir el Medina, decided strikes were not as effective as initially thought and went with two bailiffs to collect the grain himself from the local farmers and the temples. A true vigilante.

The vast working class: Producing the essentials

Although the officials and the military were essential to the safety and stability of Egypt, those in the working classes were essential to its success. Tragically, most of the information on these people is lost. Because they were mostly poor and often illiterate, the working class did not leave stone tombs, stelae (the plural of *stela*, a round-topped stone monument), or statues. (Chapter 2 pieces together a portrait of these individuals.)

Farmers: Salt of the earth

The majority of the working classes were agricultural workers, because farming and food production were essential for survival and for Egypt to participate in trade.

While no written evidence exists from farmers themselves, some tombs of members of the elite mention farmers who worked their land, thus preserving these farmers' names for eternity. One such farmer worked for the scribe Ramose from Deir el Medina. According to tomb records, the farmer's name was Ptahsaankh, and he ploughed the land with two cows called 'West' and 'Beautiful Flood'.

Most land was owned by the state or the temples and was only rented to the farmers. As employees of the state, farmers were expected to give a specific amount of their grain yields to the landowners, plus rent and tax (tax is always there). Farmers' earnings were whatever was left. The poor were clearly working for free.

Labourers: Serving the state

During the annual flood of the Nile, many thousands of farmers were virtually unemployed because they were able to do little while their land was under 3 feet of water. In these periods, the state often conscripted farmers to work as labourers on large monumental building projects, such as the pyramids.

Commentators often say that slaves built these monuments, but in reality this wasn't the case. While working for the state, unskilled labourers were well paid and provided with housing near the building site. After the flood waters started to recede in October, workers returned to their villages to work on their farms.

Hard manual labour, such as working in the quarries or mines, was done by prisoners of war or criminals. Because this work was punishment, these people were fed, but were probably not given any spare food with which to trade. While their work was dangerous, many of these individuals probably died simply as a result of trudging through the hot desert, thirst, or encountering violent nomadic tribes.

Craftsmen: Whittling away

The only existing evidence regarding craftsmen comes from special settlements built for specific work forces, including

- **Giza,** built for the workmen who built the Giza pyramids
- **Kahun,** which housed the workmen who built the Lahun pyramid
- **Amarna,** which housed the workmen who built the Amarnan royal tombs
- **Deir el Medina,** which was home to the workmen who built the Valley of the Kings

The workmen's villages of Amarna and Deir el Medina (where most available information about craftsmen and ordinary Egyptians comes from) housed extremely privileged workmen who worked directly for the king. They were not from the ordinary working class.

Although the information from Amarna and Deir el Medina is valuable and interesting (go to Chapter 2 to find out how interesting), it only describes the experience of elite workers – not the common, non-literate members of society. No doubt many craftsmen worked throughout Egypt on non-royal projects, but sadly information about them is lacking.

Chapter 2

Examining the Lives of the Everyday Egyptians

*T*he tombs provide a wealth of information about the upper classes and the elite, but they also paint a remarkably detailed portrait of the day-to-day lives of the Egyptian masses. For instance, tomb records provide names and job titles, while mummies detail diseases and general health. Additional artefacts and remains from ancient villages give an insight into family life, religion, childhood, and old age. Given all this information, we can truly trace the lives of the Egyptians from the cradle to the grave.

One of the most important features of everyday Egyptian life is that these ancient people had the same motivations, interests, and problems as people today. From establishing homes to choosing careers, from getting married to growing old, this chapter covers the ins and outs of living as an Egyptian.

Appreciating Village Life

Most information about ancient Egypt comes from research and exploration of tombs and temples. Although these structures and the treasures they hold are truly fascinating, examining only tombs, mummies, and treasures gives a biased view of the Egyptians as a morbid nation that was obsessed with death.

Although dying was immensely important to the Egyptians, so was living! To fully understand these people, you need to look at their villages – the centres of their regular, everyday life.

Although the tombs were built of stone and meant to last forever, the villages were made of mud-brick and were not intended to last. Fortunately, researchers have identified several villages that somehow endured, providing valuable information about the Egyptian lifestyle. Unfortunately, these villages are mainly special settlements inhabited by the elite; as such they don't necessarily give an accurate overview of the life of all Egyptians, rich and poor.

The most important villages are:

- ✔ **Deir el Medina** on the west bank of the Nile at Thebes in the south of Egypt. Amenhotep I of the 18th dynasty built Deir el Medina to house the workmen who constructed the royal tombs in the Valley of the Kings. The village was occupied until the late 20th dynasty. Today the foundations of the village are still visible, including staircases, cellars, ovens, and elaborately decorated tombs, some virtually complete with mummies and treasures.

- ✔ **Kahun** in the Faiyum region dates to the Middle Kingdom and was built to accommodate the workmen who built the pyramid of Senwosret III, although it was inhabited for a number of years after the death of the king. The remains at the site are quite substantial, with three-quarters of the settlement foundations surviving, showing three styles of houses: mansions, large houses, and the equivalent of small terraces.

- ✔ **Pi-Rameses** is situated in the eastern Delta region and was the capital city of Ramses II of the 19th dynasty. The village covered an area of approximately 5 kilometres, and excavations at the site have uncovered a number of temples, palaces, and houses for the elite and their servants. The remains are very fragmentary because many building blocks were reused in later periods.

- ✔ **Avaris,** located very close to Pi-Rameses in the Delta, was the capital of the Hyksos kings from the second intermediate period (see Chapter 3). Many Asiatics (primarily from the Palestine, Syria, and Canaan region) lived at this site, which the village's style of temples and houses reflected.

- ✔ **Amarna,** about halfway between Cairo and Luxor, was the home of Akhenaten from the 18th dynasty. The village stretches for a distance of approximately 7 kilometres and included a number of palaces and temples as well as army barracks, two settlement districts, and a workmen's village similar to Deir el Medina. So many archaeological remains have been found at this site that it is often used as a blueprint for all Egyptian settlements.

You can visit Deir el Medina on the west bank at Luxor and see the layout of the whole settlement. The more adventurous tourist can visit Amarna in Middle Egypt. The archaeologists have reconstructed some sample buildings to give the gist of what it may have looked like.

Planning a village

The layout of each surviving village differs depending on whether it was built as a single project (for example, to house tomb builders) or whether it was allowed to develop naturally. Most villages needed to be near the Nile or a canal to provide a water source, and have agricultural land for food, although in the case of Deir el Medina, the state brought in water and food basics for the villagers.

Planners for single-project sites (like Deir el Medina and Amarna) built the most important building, either the temple or the palace, first, and then the elite houses were constructed around this structure. In the pre-planned villages, the streets are evenly laid out and houses arranged in neat rows. But as these towns expanded and developed, houses were extended, and new smaller houses were built among the larger mansions, destroying the grid layout.

Naturally developing settlements aren't half as tidy as planned villages. No grids divide the settlement, and the general appearance is more haphazard. Planned villages have a uniformity of house style and size, whereas in naturally developing villages the house styles are irregular because people built according to taste and need.

Housing

Houses in Egyptian villages were generally very basic. Although some were larger than others (depending on the wealth and status of the owner), the average house at Deir el Medina, Gurob, and Amarna consisted of four rooms (see Figure 2-1):

- A **front room** leading from the street, which may have been used as a meeting place for guests.
- A **living room** where the household shrine was situated. (See Chapter 9 for more on household religious practices.) The family would worship their personal gods or ancestors here.
- A **living space,** probably used as a sleeping area, with a staircase to a flat roof or upper floor.
- A **kitchen** at the rear of the house, which was open to the sky to prevent the room from filling with smoke.

Cellars underneath the rear rooms were used as storage for foodstuffs. Houses were small so each room was multi-purpose.

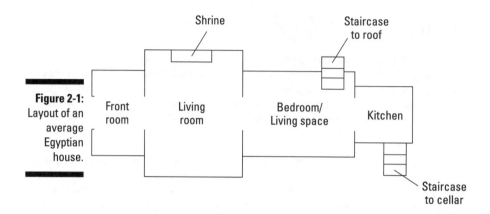

Figure 2-1: Layout of an average Egyptian house.

The houses of the elite, more appropriately described as mansions, followed a similar layout to the small houses, although they consisted of a number of small suites of rooms joined by interlinking corridors, as shown in Figure 2-2. These gave the elite owners the privilege of separating the public from the private family quarters. Many mansions also contained

- ✔ An audience chamber in which to greet visitors.

- ✔ An office in which to conduct business.

- ✔ A bathroom with built-in shower area (essentially a stone slab and a servant with a jug of water) and toilet (a horseshoe-shaped wooden seat over a bowl of sand). Some homes at Pi-Rameses also had sunken baths open to the sky – to catch some rays while bathing.

- ✔ Women's quarters, for privacy rather than confinement. These quarters provided living, dressing, and sleeping areas from the rest of the household.

All houses in ancient Egypt were nearly bursting at the seams with people. The mansions were run like estates. In addition to the owner and his family, a plethora of employees, administrators, and servants lived in these larger homes.

Small homes were even more crowded. An Egyptian couple may have had up to 15 children, all living in a single four-roomed house. When men married, their wives moved into the home as well; and when the wives had children, the children potentially also lived in the house. It was not unusual for three or four generations – as many as 20 people, mostly children – to be living in these small houses. The Egyptians truly knew the meaning of no privacy and no space.

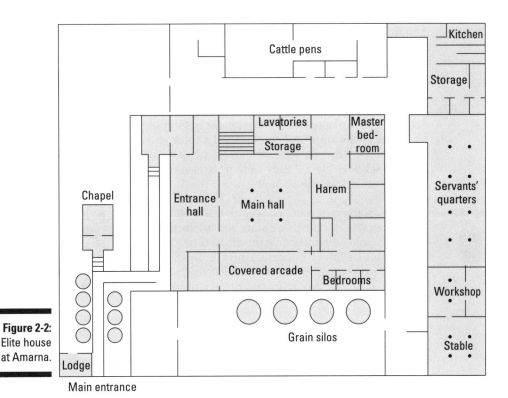

Figure 2-2:
Elite house
at Amarna.

Main entrance

Growing Up Egyptian

Preparing for – and sometimes choosing – a career was a major part of the early lives of most Egyptians, particularly boys. The following sections consider the schooling, careers, and working conditions of the vast majority of ancient Egyptians.

Educating the young

Today, most people's earliest memories are from school, and in ancient Egypt it was probably no different.

Although not every child was lucky enough to have a formal education, the oldest son in most families followed in his father's footsteps in his career choice, so he began learning his father's trade from as young as 5 years old (whether farming, sculpting, or administration). Other sons needed to be trained in a career; this inspired some elite families to educate their children.

School's out

School as you know it didn't exist in ancient Egypt, but for want of a better word I have to use the term. Egyptian schools didn't include large buildings, complete with classrooms and playing fields. There was no smell of chalk and there were definitely no uniforms.

Royalty and the upper elite were taught in temple or palace schools, which were run by the state and consisted of a tutor and a small group of hand-chosen boys. Records indicate that particularly gifted boys were accepted into the schools, even if they were from non-elite families – so the lower classes had at least some hope.

Although some girls were educated, it wasn't the norm. If a girl did receive an education, it wasn't in these state-run institutions. Because women were unable to hold administrative positions (see 'Considering the Lives of Women', later in this chapter), educating girls seemed like a pointless task to many ancient Egyptians. One Egyptian called Ankhsheshonq immortalised this idea with the following quote: 'Instructing a woman is like having a sack of sand whose side is split open.' Charming!

Some of these formal temple and palace schools taught specific trades and only accepted boys from families of certain occupations, such as scribes or magistrates. Children leaving these schools were then employed in the central government.

For boys not accepted into the elite educational institutions, local alternatives existed. Boys in most villages learned only basic literacy skills if their father was a scribe – normally in preparation for taking his place as a scribe. Village scribes also occasionally decided to teach groups of village children reading and writing as a means of boosting income.

House of Life

Although schools as you know them today did not exist, the *House of Life* was an institution that provided some education and training for a select few. A House of Life was attached to most temples. Each stored a number of texts relevant to that particular temple. The term is often mistranslated as a school, university, library, or archive. However, it was a strange institution that was all of these things and yet did not fit any of the descriptions particularly well.

Although shrouded (intentionally) in mystery, the following is known about this institution:

✔ **The House of Life stored a number of religious texts,** which were used for training priests and medical professionals (see Chapter 8 for more on the role of doctors). Being educated here was a great privilege, available to only a chosen few. However, how students were chosen remains unknown.

✔ **The priests in charge of the House of Life were responsible for conserving, copying, and storing religious texts.** The texts stored here were world famous. Later, Greek and Roman authors praised the wisdom recorded in these texts. The texts are said to include information about medicine, medical herbs, geography, geometry, astronomy, and the history of kings.

✔ **The institution was not open to the public.** The extremely restricted access only enhanced its aura of mystery. Many literary tales refer to texts stored in the House of Life that have information on how to speak the language of all animals, birds, and fish in the world, as well as a text that enables the reader to see the sun god. Powerful stuff, indeed!

School days

A number of teaching materials have survived and tell a great deal about the day-to-day education that children received. An Egyptian child typically entered school at about 5 years old and started with the three Rs: reading, writing, and arithmetic.

In Egypt, two different types of written language exist – hieroglyphs (go to Chapter 11 for more on these pretty pictures) and *hieratic* script, a shorthand version of hieroglyphs. Modern students of Egyptian history typically learn hieroglyphs first and then progress to hieratic writing, but the ancient Egyptians did things the other way round:

✔ A tutor dictated hieratic phrases and sentences.

✔ A student learned these phrases by heart.

✔ The student then wrote these phrases onto a wipe-clean wooden board through dictation and later from memory.

✔ The tutor made corrections.

✔ The board was wiped clean, and the process began again.

This intensive curriculum lasted until children were 9 years old, when they made a decision about their careers. Whatever career they chose then resulted in apprenticeships, which lasted for about ten years. Apprentices worked alongside professionals and learned the trade on the job, earning a wage (see the following section 'Checking the Balance: Wages and Values in Ancient Egypt', later in this chapter).

The ancient Egyptian proverb 'A boy's ear is on his back; he hears when he is beaten' gives an indication of how education was administered in ancient Egypt. It certainly puts my school days into a much better light!

Choosing a career

Trying to choose a career as a modern adult is difficult enough, but having to do it at 9 years old seems unreal. (At 9, I wanted to be a princess – and no amount of education can help there!) However, Egyptian 9-year-olds made this monumental decision.

In the New Kingdom, the military and the scribal profession were intense rivals for Egypt's best and brightest. For many boys, the life of a soldier seemed more glamorous than any other lifestyle. Soldiers were promised glory, foreign trips, and acknowledgement by the king, whereas the scribal profession offered knowledge, wealth, and a peaceful life with no physical strain.

In fact, one text called *The Miscellanies* appealed to the weaker, non-sporty boys who wished to join the army, but were not physically suitable, by stating:

> *Be a scribe! Your body will be sleek, your hand will be soft. You will not flicker like a flame, like those whose body is feeble. For there is no bone of a man in you. You are tall and thin. If you lifted a load to carry it, you would stagger. Your feet would drag terribly, you are lacking in strength. You are weak in all of your limbs, poor in body. Set your sights on being a scribe, a fine profession that suits you.*

Many careers were open to Egyptian children. A great text called *Satire of the Trades* lists the many occupations – and the downsides to each. As this text outlined, careers fell into four main categories: manual, administration, priesthood, and military.

Obviously some people were limited by status and wealth in what career they pursued. But on the plus side, no unemployment existed as farming and building work always needed doing.

Scribes: Leading the administration

Being a scribe was the most lucrative occupation. Scribes had many opportunities for promotion, and scribes who showed particular talent and skill could even rise to the position of *vizier*, which was second only to that of the king. If the king was weak, the vizierate could be a stepping stone to the throne.

The vizier's role was powerful and diverse; the entire palace and its internal operations was under the vizier's control. The vizier was also responsible for the safety of the king and the security of Egypt, which meant the police force was also under the vizier's control. In addition, the vizier presided over the legal court (*kenbet*) and dealt with the daily petitions of the people, normally concerning petty crimes or offences. In legal matters, the vizier acted as judge, sentencing and administering punishments on behalf of the king.

Scribes with less ambition or power were still busy because only 1–5 per cent of the ancient Egyptian population was literate. At some point, most people needed the service of a scribe for personal or legal letters, accounts, or legal petitions. Scribes were essentially civil servants and were well paid for their work.

Satire of the Trades

The *Satire of the Trades* was written by a man called Duaf for his son Khety. He is trying to encourage his son to work hard at his studies to become a good scribe. As an incentive, he describes the pitfalls of all other professions in graphic detail:

I will make you love scribedom more than your mother, I'll make its beauties stand before you; It is the greatest of all callings. There is none like it in the land.

I have never saw a sculptor as envoy, not is a goldsmith ever sent; but I have seen the smith at work at the opening of his furnace; with fingers like claws of a crocodile he stinks more than fish roe.

The jewel-maker bores with his chisel in hard stone of all kinds; when he has finished the inlay of the eye, his arms are spent, he's weary, sitting down when the sun goes down, his knees and back are cramped.

The barber barbers until nightfall, he takes himself to town, he sets himself up in his corner, he moves from street to street,

looking for someone to barber. He strains his arms to fill his belly like the bee that eats as it works.

I'll describe to you also the mason: his loins give him pain; though he is out in the wind, he works without a cloak; his loincloth is a twisted rope and a string in the rear. His arms are spent from exertion, having mixed all kinds of dirt; when he eats bread with his fingers, he has washed at the same time.

The bird-catcher suffers much, as he watches out for birds; when the swarms pass over him, he keeps saying 'Had I a net!' But the god grants it not, and he is angry with his lot. I'll speak of the fisherman also, his is the worst of all the hobs. He labours on the river, mingling with the crocodiles. When the time of reckoning comes, he is full of lamentations; He does not say 'there's a crocodile': Fear has made him blind. Coming from the flowing water he says 'Mighty God.'

Look, there is no profession without a boss, except for the scribe – he is the boss.

Most scribes were established in the village where they lived and gave their services to anyone who asked. They charged a set rate for services or a waived rate depending on the wealth of his client. Agreements were oral, so historians don't know what the fees and charges were. There could have been one scribe per village or a few scribes undercutting each other with their service charges.

The priesthood: Servants of the god

The priesthood was open to all – literate or not – although the positions given reflected the skills held. Obviously, temple scribes were literate and many worked in the House of Life, archiving, copying, and reading the numerous texts stored there.

Many priests worked on a part-time basis, only working one month in three in the temple and then returning to their villages. This arrangement was like National Service when people were called on to work for a short period.

Because many of the priests were part time, they weren't expected to be celibate. In fact the priesthood was traditionally passed down from father to son, so families were actively encouraged. Joining the priesthood was therefore not a spiritual calling, but an inheritance.

The nature of the Egyptian priesthood was very different from, say, the Christian or Hindu priesthood. Egyptian priests had virtually no contact with the population in their role as priest. They did not preach, offer advice, or try to convert people to their particular cult. The Egyptian title *Hem-Netjer* means 'servant of the god', and that is what they were. They served the god, ensuring the prayers, offerings, and incantations were carried out correctly.

A distinct hierarchy existed within the priesthood with the *first prophet* being the top dog or high priest, followed by the second, third, fourth, and fifth prophets, who all hoped at some point to have the first prophet's job. Ideally, the king was responsible for hiring the first prophet, although more often than not the king allowed the priest to name his own heir.

The lowest-ranking priests were the *wab priests* or 'purification priests', who were responsible for many of the purification rituals in the temple, carrying the *sacred barks* (small sacred boats that were used to parade statues of the gods on festival days), supervising the painters and draftsmen, and looking after other general tasks around the temple.

Military men: Dreaming of victory

Prior to the New Kingdom, no army existed, so every little boy's dream of being a soldier had to remain unfulfilled. In the earlier periods, if an army was needed, local mayors gathered likely lads from their regions and conscripted them for the duration of the expedition or campaign.

Purifying the priests

A number of purification rituals had to be performed before a priest could enter a temple. A priest anointed his hands and feet in water and then plunged into the sacred lake, which was present at every temple and represented the pure waters of the time before creation. This ritual ensured the priest was clean before entering into the presence of the god.

The Greek historian Herodotus records that Egyptian priests shaved off all (and yes, I mean *all*) their body hair to prevent lice. Some priests may even have gone so far as to pluck out their eyebrows and eyelashes just to make sure they were 100 per cent clean. They carried out this hair removal every other day. In the Ptolemaic period, any priest who forgot to shave was fined 1,000 drachmas.

Sexual intercourse was banned in the temple (quite right, too!), and priests carried out specific cleansing rituals before entering the temple after sex. In fact, it was expected that a priest about to start his working month in the temple should abstain from any contact with women for several days before entering temple service, just in case he was contaminated with menstrual blood or bodily fluids.

In the New Kingdom (go to Chapter 3 for more details), a permanent army was set up, enabling career soldiers to exist. Many autobiographies found in tombs chronicle long military careers. In fact, some soldiers rose to positions of great power; the generals Horemheb and Ramses I both became king, proving that the vizierate was not the only path to the throne.

As with all careers in ancient Egypt, soldiers started their training in basic skills, stamina, and strength young – even as young as 5 or 6.

Tomb images at Beni Hasan from the Middle Kingdom show how temporary soldiers were trained, and no doubt the training was similar for the permanent army. Training included

- Stick fighting
- Wrestling
- Weightlifting with bags of sand
- Chariot riding (although not until the New Kingdom)
- Archery
- Use of spears

A soldier's skills dictated which regiment he entered – charioteers, spearmen, or infantry.

Scribes were also an essential part of the army entourage (they get everywhere!). Scribes recorded campaign events and are often depicted in battle scenes calmly standing at the rear, recording the action. They also listed the booty gathered by the soldiers.

One particularly gruesome task of the military scribe was counting the enemy dead, which were identified by amputated right hands or penises (if they were uncircumcised). Soldiers left piles of these body parts on the battle field for the scribes to count serenely.

Manual labour

Working conditions were relatively good for the craftsmen of Deir el Medina, who were at the top of their careers and built the tombs in the Valley of the Kings, but maybe less good for the not-so-privileged members of society. These craftsmen worked long weeks with eight-hour days and only officially received one in every ten days off. Farmers and other lower class people had no days off.

However, in addition to their weekend, workers at Deir el Medina were able to take as many days off (within reason) as they needed. Surviving records from the site, known as the 'Absentee records', list an incredible range of excuses for skiving off work. Things haven't changed much in 3,500 years, as one of the most common excuses is a hangover.

The first industrial action in history?

The workmen of Deir el Medina were supposed to get paid on the 28th day of each month, and most of the time this worked fine. But on some occasions, payments were late or even non-existent.

During the reign of Ramses III, the villagers did not get paid for six months, which resulted in the workmen going on strike. Workers protested at the funerary temples of Thutmosis III, Ramses II, and Sety I, where the grain stores providing their rations were situated. Whether they had placards and chanted 'What do we want? When do we want it?' is unknown, but records describe the event as follows:

It is because of hunger and because of thirst that we come here. There is no clothing, no ointment, no fish, no vegetables. Send to Pharaoh our good Lord about it and send to the vizier, our superior so that sustenance may be made for us.

I think this message – as a slogan on a placard – is a tad long, but it does get the point across. On this particular occasion, the workers received their rations.

However, later the same year, pay was again delayed. A village scribe named Djhutymose left out the middle man (the temple) and went with two bailiffs, no doubt with large sticks, to collect the grain rations directly from the local farmers. Luckily, Djhutymose was successful, and the villagers were able to eat again.

Other excuses included

- ✔ Wrapping a deceased family member
- ✔ Burying a deceased family member
- ✔ Making libations for the deceased
- ✔ Being ill (they didn't always elaborate on this)
- ✔ Being bitten by a scorpion
- ✔ Having an argument with the wife (this one intrigues me)
- ✔ Female family members menstruating

The villagers of Deir el Medina had a resident doctor, paid by the state, which ensured that not too many days were taken off with illness or injuries. For a description of the types of medical treatments that these unfortunate villagers endured, skip to Chapter 8.

Although the ancient Egyptians have a reputation for slave labour, promoted by the Bible and Hollywood movies, the evidence shows a very positive employment programme with health care, a bonus scheme, and opportunities to earn extra income after working hours, ensuring the workmen were well fed and able to accumulate wealth.

Artists: Creating beauty

Men with artistic talent could become artists, carpenters, or sculptors and were well paid whether they had a formal education or not. Unlike artists in the modern world, ancient Egyptians did not sign their work, so identifying the work of a particular painter or sculptor is very difficult. (For more information on art, see Chapter 11.)

Most artists worked as part of a team and were responsible for one aspect of the production of a tomb or temple scene – even if they were proficient in all aspects – and would work on this skill, making it their speciality. For example:

- ✔ Plasterers prepared walls for painting.
- ✔ Stone masons prepared walls for carving.
- ✔ Outline scribes drew the outlines on the walls.
- ✔ Sculptors carved the outlines.
- ✔ Artists painted the images.
- ✔ Overseers double-checked all work and made corrections throughout the process.

The village of Deir el Medina consisted almost exclusively of artists. Although their daily jobs were to provide a tomb and goods for the king, they also used their talents to earn income outside their regular jobs. A number of working contracts survive, showing prices and services including:

- ✔ The scribe Harshire inscribed three coffins for a songstress of Amun and was paid 329 *deben* (30 kilos) of copper.
- ✔ The workman Bekenwernero made some coffins, beds, chairs, boxes, and tables and received 91 deben (more than 8 kilos) of copper.

Farmers: Working the land

With less than 1 per cent of the Egyptian population literate, many uneducated people worked at jobs that didn't require formal education. The most important of these was farming.

A large proportion of the population of Egypt worked on the land, producing food. This was hard work and essentially one of the most important jobs, because if the farmer didn't work hard, the rest of Egypt didn't eat. The state – either the temple or the king – owned the majority of agricultural land and rented it to the farmers. If farmers didn't produce the specified grain quotas, they were beaten.

The ancient Egyptians grew various crops and typically rotated their plantings each year. The following grains formed the staple of the Egyptian diet:

- ✔ Barley
- ✔ Emmer wheat (a low-yielding wheat, first domesticated in the Near East)
- ✔ Einkorn wheat (a hulled wheat with a tough husk)
- ✔ Spelt (similar to common wheat)

Many families also kept vegetable plots, and no doubt farmers grew vegetables on a large scale. Vegetables formed a large proportion of the Egyptian diet, and included the following:

- ✔ Onions
- ✔ Garlic
- ✔ Peas
- ✔ Lentils
- ✔ Beans
- ✔ Radishes

- ✔ Cabbage
- ✔ Cucumbers
- ✔ Lettuces

Many farmers also grew sesame and castor (used for oil), flax (used for the production of linen), dates (for beer flavouring and to be eaten as a fruit), and trees (fibres used in basket and rope production).

Despite the importance of the farmers' job, they were the poorest paid workers in ancient Egyptian society. Technically they didn't get paid at all! Farmers gave a grain quota to the land owner, with the addition of rent and tax (also paid in grain). Whatever they produced in excess of this they kept or sold. This arrangement worked sufficiently well for the head of a family or head farmer, but field hands were paid a pittance and no doubt couldn't feed their families well or have any excess for purchasing other goods.

Laundrymen: Airing dirty linen

One of the worst careers described in the *Satire of the Trades* is that of laundryman.

In ancient Egypt, men were always the professional launderers. They traipsed from village to village collecting the washing, which they took to the Nile. Records from Deir el Medina show that the laundrymen were allocated certain houses to collect laundry from and they were constantly moaning about the workload. Nothing's new.

After collecting the laundry, the laundryman left a 'receipt' in the form of an *ostracon* (stone flake used as note paper) with images of the clothes that he had taken. This note ensured that the household got the right stuff back – nothing's worse than someone else's loincloth being delivered among your own laundry.

The washing was done in the Nile using *natron* (hydrous sodium carbonate) and lime as soap. The clothes were crushed against stones to get the stains off, and then left in the sun to bleach and to dry.

Working in the Nile was dangerous, because of the number of crocodiles living there. A laundryman concentrating on a stubborn loincloth stain might easily disregard the log with eyes – until he had been dragged off. And if the crocs weren't dangerous enough, the Nile and its canals were rife with parasitic worms and biting insects, which could prove fatal.

Considering the Lives of Women

Although the experience of Egyptian women was not equal to that of their male counterparts, female Egyptians enjoyed a surprisingly high level of opportunity, responsibility, and empowerment.

Appreciating women's rights

Royal women had very little freedom, were used as political pawns, and were locked away from the world in the harem (see Chapter 5 for more details).

Ordinary women were much luckier. They had more freedom than most women in other contemporary societies. For example:

✔ Women were able to walk around unchaperoned. Although this is something most women today take for granted, such freedom was unusual in ancient times.

✔ Although many of the larger houses included women's quarters, women were not confined to these areas. Instead, these rooms offered privacy during childbirth, child weaning, and menstruation.

✔ Women held the same legal rights as men from the same class. Specifically, a woman could

• Own property; she could also manage her land in any way she wanted without assistance from a man

• Inherit property

• Bequeath property; in fact, landed property was passed down from mother to daughter

• Loan property and earn interest

• Bring an action of law against another person, including a man

• Bear witness to a legal document

• Be an equal partner in legal contracts; for example, in the Ptolemaic period, she could sign her own marriage contract

Furthermore, a woman did not lose her legal rights after she married and she retained her property during the marriage. While married, she could own, inherit, and sell any of her property with the same freedom as if she were single. When drawing up her will, a woman could distribute her property any way she wanted and had no legal obligation to leave anything to her children.

Taming of the shrewd

From the numerous surviving records, many clever Egyptian women are known today. One such woman was Tay-Hetem from 249 BC, who decided to help her hubbie out when he had a few financial problems. From a contract she drew up herself (all very official!), scholars know that Tay-Hetem loaned her husband 3 *deben* of silver (273 grams) from her personal store and charged him a rate of interest of 30 per cent, which was the standard interest rate of the time. She specified that the loan was to be paid back within three years.

Although it is unknown whether her husband made the payments, it would be interesting to know how far Tay-Hetem went to get her repayments. Beat him with a rolling pin? Send the boys round? Take him to court? Hopefully, he paid in time, so he never found out how far she would go.

An Egyptian widow was automatically entitled to a third of her husband's property as well as keeping all she entered the marriage with, in addition to all she accumulated throughout the marriage. (The remaining two-thirds of her husband's property was divided between his children and his siblings.) By making gifts to his wife during his life, a husband could prevent distribution of his property after death, because his wife already owned everything. Now that is my kind of arrangement!

Working women

Sure, men in ancient Egyptian society had varied opportunities and a chance of a lucrative career. But what of the women? Most women, whether married or single, spent a lot of time in the home – raising children, helping to produce family meals, or working.

Women within farming communities were also expected to help in the field during harvest time. Women are often depicted in tomb scenes helping with the winnowing of crops, grinding grain into flour, and making beer (see Chapter 7 for how).

In their spare time – although it doesn't sound like they had much! – women were able to earn money by selling the fruits of various home-making skills. Goods produced in the home, such as beer, bread, vegetables, linen, baskets, and clay vessels, were all sold at market.

Stitch in time

The linen trade was one that started in the home, but expanded to large workshops attached to the temples and even the royal harem. Flax processing and linen production was important as a cottage industry. These workshops were dominated by female workers and supervisors and produced linen for royalty and the religious cults, as well as to trade.

Royal women in the harem workshops were responsible for training and supervising the textile workers. Royal women probably carried out the delicate embroidery work themselves to pass the time.

Management positions: Ruling the roost

Although married and unmarried woman could work without social stigma, tight restrictions applied to the occupations they could actually hold.

The tightest restrictions were on bureaucratic or administrative positions, especially working for the state, although in private households women were permitted to hold positions such as:

- Treasurer
- Major doma (a female 'butler')
- Superintendent of the dining room
- Steward of the storehouse
- Steward of the food supply
- Sealbearer (a very important role, responsible for the sealing of boxes, letters and rooms)

All these positions fall under the modern title of housekeeper – ensuring the cupboards are full, meals are prepared on time, and the family's wealth remains intact.

In royal households, the bureaucratic positions held by women were all in connection with the female-oriented aspects of the royal household. These positions included:

- Overseer of the singers
- Overseer of amusements
- Mistress of the royal harem
- Overseer of the house of weavers
- Overseer of the wig shop

Whatever the administrative position, women were never in charge of the work of men, although some women held quite important positions. Indeed, the sixth dynasty included a female vizier. The Suffragette movement would have been proud.

Midwifery and wet nursing

Most girls were taught skills related to children and childbirth, and some women chose to make these skills into lucrative careers as midwives.

Most women in ancient Egypt gave birth to at least five children, so midwifery skills were often learned by helping the village women through their pregnancy and deliveries. Although the vast majority of midwives simply learned by assisting, some chose to have formal training. For example, records show that a school of midwifery existed at the Temple of Neith in Sais. Formal training enabled midwives to work for the palace or the elite members of society, thus increasing their potential incomes.

After midwives safely delivered babies, the elite and the royal family commonly employed wet nurses to help care for children. A wet nurse was viewed as a status symbol; no family worth its salt was without such a woman. Wet nurses were normally women who had just given birth to their own child and were able to feed their employers' baby alongside their own.

Market day

Ancient Egyptian market day was certainly different from a weekly trip to Tesco.

A physical market place as such did not exist, although merchants at various Egyptian port sites set up stalls to sell their goods to sailors and foreign merchants. The rest of the population had some means of selling and buying goods, possibly meeting in public squares or on the river bank, or visiting houses of people in the village and offering a service or product.

Negotiating over price is where things get complicated. Coins were not used in Egypt until Alexander came in 332 BC, so prior to this people swapped goods for goods. Relative prices in weights of copper or silver existed, and people would have been aware of these. But objects are only valuable if someone wants to buy them, and the value depends on *how* much someone wants them.

Imagine the uproar of bartering: Perhaps an Egyptian woman wants to buy some clothes for her family, but only has four unruly goats and a bad-tempered donkey to exchange! She has to traipse around until she locates a dressmaker, only to discover that the seamstress has no interest in goats or donkeys and will only exchange for a necklace. Now the poor home-maker has to look for someone with a necklace who wants one of her unruly goats and then return to the dressmaker, only to find she has already sold that must-have loincloth and kilt ensemble with the matching sandals. Blimey! Shopping would take all day – and you may have to return home with unruly goats and a bad-tempered donkey.

Infants were normally nursed for three years. Breastfeeding acted as a safeguard against pregnancy (because it is a natural – if unreliable! – contraceptive) and was a way of ensuring uncontaminated food during the most vulnerable years of the child's life.

Entertaining the masses

Some women, who were probably unmarried, chose to go into the entertainment business. The general belief is that it was unbecoming for an elite woman to perform in public. Although women sang, danced, or played instruments in private, engaging in any of these activities in public was taboo. In fact, the only time an elite woman was permitted to perform in public was if she was in the priesthood, participating in religious ceremonies and processions.

For the lower classes, however, being a performer was a respectable, lucrative career. Troupes of women and sometimes men were hired to entertain at banquets, performing with groups of same-sex dancers, singers, or musicians (see Chapter 7 for more details).

Turning tricks

Very little evidence of prostitution in ancient Egypt exists, but as 'the oldest profession in the world', prostitution was no doubt common.

Scholars have suggested that some banquet entertainers may have made a little extra income at gatherings. Records show that a particular group of dancers known as *Hn-mwt* did offer sexual favours for financial reimbursement. However, most of the evidence of prostitutes comes from the Graeco-Roman period, when prostitution was taxed and records were kept.

Some small details are also recorded about prostitutes' practices. For example, many prostitutes had alluring messages, such as 'follow me', incised into the soles of their sandals so that they left an imprint in the mud with every step. Think of it as the ancient equivalent of cards in phone boxes.

A prostitute, like a midwife, was never unemployed in ancient Egypt. Some scholars believe that most young, rich men may have visited a prostitute before marriage in order to gain some experience. But the poorer men left in the villages, who couldn't afford high-class prostitutes, had sex with each other or the farm animals.

Serving the goddesses

Many middle-class, upper-class, and royal women chose to join the priesthood, the most prestigious profession for women.

For the upper classes, the priesthood was a convenient way of occupying unmarried women – although, like their male counterparts, woman who wanted to serve the gods did not have to be celibate, and many were in fact married.

Mourning the dead

Women were regularly involved in the funerals of the elite – although not often as priestesses. Professional mourners were hired to wail, throw dust over their heads, rend their clothes, and scratch their cheeks. Such behaviour would have been unseemly for the women of the deceased's family to display.

Many non-royal tombs depict these professional mourners. Among the women are often small girls emulating their moves, which indicates that mourners were trained on the job. This profession, like many others, was probably passed down from mother to daughter.

Additionally, as with the male priesthood, the role of priestess was often passed from mother to daughter, and it may have been served on a part-time basis, one month in three.

Women were mostly employed in the priesthood of the cults of a goddess such as Isis, Neith, or Hathor – although they could hold roles in most cults of both gods and goddesses. Priestesses were primarily musicians, singers, or dancers for temple rituals and processions.

Checking the Balance: Wages and Payment in Ancient Egypt

As today, everyone in ancient Egypt worked to sustain their family and to increase personal wealth – so all looked forward to pay day. Records from Deir el Medina show that the workers were paid on the 28th day of every month, although unlike modern payday it was not in cash.

Because a monetary system was not introduced until Alexander the Great in 332 BC, wages were paid in produce or services. Quantities of grain were specified for various levels of workers. Wages depended on the position, and those in positions of responsibility were paid more than lower positions. A higher salary was approximately 422.5 litres of grain per month, which was enough to feed a family of 10–15. If an employee had a smaller family, he would have grain left over for shopping.

In addition to wages, the state gave workmen working for the king all the essentials of daily life, such as housing, firewood, fish, vegetables, water, and oil. At Deir el Medina, the workmen were often given extra rations by the state during religious festivals, or as an incentive if the king was pleased with progress on the royal tomb.

When buying and selling items, all goods had a relative value, which everyone was aware of. These relative values were based on a fairly complex system of weights, volumes, and measures:

- *Khar*: Used to measure grain; 1 *khar* was equivalent to 76.8 litres.
- *Deben*: Used as a general value for many items; 1 *deben* was equivalent to 91 grams of copper.
- *Kite*: A weight of silver; 1 *kite* was equivalent to 0.6 *deben* of copper.
- *Hin*: Used to measure liquids; 1 *hin* was equivalent to 0.48 litres and worth 1 *deben*.
- *Medket*: Used for larger quantities of liquids; 1 *medket* was worth 50 *hin*.

A number of transaction records survive from Deir el Medina, offering a good snapshot of the relative values of various goods:

- A simple wooden chair: 11 *deben*
- A bed: 25 *deben*
- A table: 15 *deben*
- A bull: 95–120 *deben* (depending on size and condition)
- A cow: 4–50 *deben* (depending on size and condition)
- A young servant girl: 410 *deben*

Christmas comes early

During the reign of Merenptah (1212–1202 BC) in the New Kingdom, the king provided a large amount of extra rations for the Deir el Medina workmen. Think of this gift as the equivalent of a nice Christmas bonus in your pay packet.

One of the village scribes, Anupenheb, recorded an inventory of the gifts: In addition to their ordinary wages, workers received extra rations consisting of 150 donkey loads of provisions, including 9,000 fish, salt for drying, ten oxen ready for slaughter, four donkey loads of beans and sweet oils, eight donkey loads of barley malt (enough for four pints of beer per person), 9,000 loaves of bread (enough for 150 per household), and eight donkey loads of natron used for soap.

The ensuing village feast no doubt produced an interesting array of aromas as the ox were slaughtered and roasted and the 9,000 fish were simultaneously gutted and dried in salt on the roofs. If the villagers did not consume all that the king provided on this occasion, they could sell any excess at market.

Tying the Knot: Marriage

A particularly important aspect of Egyptian life was marriage. Remaining unmarried was considered unusual because everyone was expected to have children.

Ancient Egyptians married young – girls sometimes as young as 10. As soon as a girl started her menstruation cycle, she was a woman and of marriageable age. Boys also married as young as 10, although a man could remain unmarried until later life (30–40 years old), especially if he had been working his way through a career.

Most people probably chose their spouses, but arranged marriages weren't unheard of, especially if the families were wealthy or important.

Exposing the truth of incestuous relationships

The Egyptians are well known for their brother-sister marriages, but this is actually a misconception. Throughout the whole pharaonic period, the practice was completely taboo for the ordinary population. Only the deities and the royal family participated in this practice – as a means of ensuring the safety of the royal line.

Unmarried princesses were dangerous because ambitious men could corrupt them. However, princesses were unable to marry outside the royal family without express permission from the king, which was rarely given. These restrictions meant that more often than not, princesses married their brothers, fathers, and even grandfathers. Sometimes these arrangements were marriages in the true sense of the word and produced children.

Evidence shows that full brother-sister marriages took place in Roman Egypt so that the marriage could take place earlier than normal and a dowry was not required, keeping family property intact.

If these marriages broke down, the couple often remained living in the same house with their parents. Evidence of this weird family set-up comes from the town of Arsinoe. A man married his sister and had two children with her before getting divorced. They remained in the same household with their two children. When the man married again, his new wife moved in to the house, and this second marriage produced two daughters. Can you imagine the tension?

Skipping formality

Although the Egyptians placed much importance on marriage, no legal ceremonies were performed, nor were any records of marriages kept. As marriage was a social event organised by the families, the ancient Egyptians had no need to formalise things.

After a couple decided to get married, the most important part was to move in together. The transport of the new wife to her husband's house may have been ceremonial, accompanied by a procession and a party, but no records of this exist.

The only records that survive involve dowries and property and what should happen in the event of a divorce. These records, however, were unusual and should not be viewed as the norm. Most marriages were between people of similar wealth and rank, with no need for pre-nuptial agreements.

Divorcing

Divorce was generally as informal as the wedding, with no formal written documentation unless financial considerations existed, such as a dowry to return or property to deal with. A man or a woman could divorce a spouse by simply stating 'I divorce you'. The woman typically then moved back to her family home.

Divorcees, both male and female, were allowed to remarry, although women over 30 did not often remarry. This was either because the women were financially self-sufficient or past their child-bearing years and thus not considered good marriage material.

Much information is missing regarding what happened to children in cases of divorce. Children may have stayed with the father or left the home with the mother. The records have not been found, but may emerge in the future.

Considering adultery

One common ground for divorce was adultery.

The penalties for adultery were harsher for women than men. For example, during the pharaonic period, divorce was the normal punishment for adultery, but some literary tales suggest that a woman could lose her life for committing adultery. Later, in Roman Egypt, a man having an affair with a married woman would be condemned to have 1,000 lashes, while the woman was mutilated by nose amputation.

Contractual arrangements

Many marriage contracts have survived, although they're from later periods when there may have been less distinction between the classes. The marriage contract of a couple called Heraclides and Demetria, from 311 BC, states:

In the seventh year of the reign of Alexander son of Alexander . . . Marriage contract of Heraclides and Demetria. Heraclides takes as his lawful wife Demetria . . . both being freeborn, from her father Leptines, . . . and her mother Philotis, bringing clothing and ornaments to the value of 1,000 drachmae, and Heraclides shall supply to Demetria all that is proper for a freeborn wife, and we shall live together wherever it seems best to Leptines and Heraclides consulting in common. If Demetria is discovered doing any evil to the shame of her husband Heraclides, she shall be deprived of all that she brought, but Heraclides shall prove whatever he alleges against Demetria before three men whom they both accept.

It shall not be lawful for Heraclides to bring home another wife in insult of Demetria nor to have children by another woman nor to do any evil against Demetria on any pretext. If Heraclides is discovered doing any of these things and Demetria proves it before three men whom they both accept, Heraclides
shall give back to Demetria the dowry of 1,000 drachmae which she brought and shall moreover forfeit 1,000 drachmae of the silver coinage of Alexander. Demetria and those aiding Demetria to exact payment shall have the right of execution, as if derived from a legally decided action, upon the person of Heraclides and upon all the property of Heraclides both on land and on water.

This contract shall be valid in every respect, wherever Heraclides may produce it against Demetria, or Demetria and those aiding Demetria to exact payment may produce it against Heraclides, as if the agreement had been made in that place. Heraclides and Demetria shall have the right to keep the contracts severally in their own custody and to produce them against each other.

Witnesses Cleon, Gelan; Anticrates, Temnian; Lysis, Temnian; Dionysius, Temnian; Aristomachus, Cyrenaean; Aristodicus, Coan.

This contract shows that even in the time of Alexander the Great, the women of Egypt were legally active and able to divorce their husbands as long as they could produce the same evidence and proof as they would have to in a similar situation today.

Although adultery was not approved of, it was acceptable for a man to have a *concubine*, a woman brought into the house to live alongside his wife and children. Having a concubine was considered a status symbol, as it reflected the man's wealth. Whether the concubine's role was purely sexual is unknown, and the difference between a wife and a concubine are not clearly defined from the ancient texts, apart from the difference in their status.

Monogamy or monotony?

Records show that a young man from Deir el Medina called Nesamenemope had been having a long-term affair with a woman in the village. Nesamenemope was married and the young woman was not. One evening an angry mob arrived at the woman's home to beat up her and her family. Luckily officials calmed the angry mob and Nesamenemope was instructed to divorce his wife and provide for his mistress before continuing with the affair.

If he didn't get divorced and still continued with the affair, the officials stated that they wouldn't prevent the crowd from beating the woman up next time, and Nesamenemope would have his nose and ears amputated before being sent to Nubia for hard labour.

Nesamenemope couldn't live without his mistress and continued the affair; although whether the threat to send him to Nubian quarries or mines was ever carried out is unknown.

Caring for the Elderly

The average age of death in Egypt was 30–35, but many people lived much longer. In surviving texts, the ideal old age is recorded as 110, although it is unlikely that many people reached this ripe old age.

Children were expected to care for their parents in old age. Girls in particular were obliged to care for their parents, whereas boys were not, presumably because a man had to care for his wife and her parents.

If a couple were childless, they quite often adopted children for the sole purpose of providing care later in life. Little is known about the adoption process, but it was normally an informal affair. However, if the adopting couple were wealthy, they sometimes signed a document before witnesses.

From Deir el Medina, limited evidence suggests that the state provided a sort of pension for the widows of the workmen still residing at the village. The records are rare and indicate that the rations distributed to widows were not enough to live on – but these did supplement the care their children provided.

Military records show that the state provided a better pension for soldiers in the form of land and *gold of honour* – jewellery and honorary priestly titles, which included a further pension.

Other than the Deir el Medina workmen and the military, no one else received a state pension. Elderly and widowed Egyptians relied solely on the kindness of friends and family.

Part II
Stepping Back in Time

The 5th Wave   By Rich Tennant

"Remember, he's known as the 'Catfish King', but never call him that to his face."

In this part . . .

The history of the ancient Egyptians is varied and colourful, and this part takes you on a chronological journey from the very beginning of the Egyptian civilisation in the pre-dynastic period to its collapse at the death of Cleopatra.

In this part I cover the battles of Thutmosis III, which were nearly lost due to the army plundering when they should have been fighting, and the spectacular stalemate of Ramses II at Kadesh that he chose to record as a great victory.

All of the military kings were supported by a great number of women, including wives, mothers, and daughters, some of whom made history in their own right such as Hatshepsut and Cleopatra who ruled Egypt without the assistance of the king. You'll find out about them in this part.

Sadly, due to constant invasions, and economic and ecological disasters, Egyptian civilisation suffered a slow decline until it was engulfed by the Romans and eventually disappeared altogether in the fourth century AD.

Chapter 3

Building a Civilisation with Military Might

. . . .

In This Chapter

▶ Sequencing the kings and their achievements

▶ Following the rise and fall of dynasties

▶ Training with the military

▶ Recording victories

. . . .

*I*n order to summarise more than 3,000 years of ancient Egyptian history, a chronology of rulers and events is necessary. One seemingly sensible place to look for this sequence is in Egyptian records of kings and their achievements.

A number of kings produced *king lists* (Egyptologists never come up with imaginative names.) These lists record the names and titles of the kings in order, in addition to reign length and major events or achievements that occurred during each reign.

Unfortunately, these lists were created to connect the king to previous rulers and therefore are selective, only listing the 'good' kings. Anyone who upset the equilibrium, was disliked, or ruled a divided Egypt was omitted from the lists. Also, the Egyptians did not have a centralised calendar. The dates chronicled on king lists are based on the years of rule of the current king (for example, year 12 of Ramses II). This is accurate unless you have no idea how long the king ruled for and when he ruled.

This chapter follows the ups and downs of centuries of Egyptian rule and change, breaking the course of civilisation into handy periods and eras. It also explores the development of a permanent Egyptian army, which had an enormous impact on the later history of ancient Egypt.

Tracing the Course of Egyptian Civilisation

Based on king lists and other historical documents and artefacts, historians organise ancient Egyptian history into the following major periods:

- Pre-dynastic period
- Early dynastic period, or archaic period
- Old Kingdom
- First intermediate period
- Middle Kingdom
- Second intermediate period
- New Kingdom
- Third intermediate period
- Late period
- Graeco-Roman period

The following sections cover Egyptian history from the pre-dynastic period through to the second intermediate period. Chapter 4 explores the New Kingdom, one of Ancient Egypt's most dynamic eras. Check the Cheat Sheet timeline so see how the periods all slot together.

Pre-dynastic period

The pre-dynastic period dates from approximately 5500 BC to 3100 BC and ends with the unification of Egypt.

During this period, Egypt was divided into two very distinct cultures: one in Upper Egypt and the other in Lower Egypt. Archaeologically speaking, cemetery sites are located primarily in Upper Egypt and settlement sites in Lower Egypt.

Comparing and contrasting Upper and Lower Egypt

For many years, archaeologists thought that the cultures of Upper and Lower Egypt were completely separate from the later Egyptian culture. Flinders Petrie (see Chapter 19) even suggested that the pre-dynastic cultures were completely foreign cultures created by an Asiatic invasion. More recent research now shows a slow progression from these contrasting cultural elements to the better-known Egyptian civilisation.

Existing king lists

Most of the existing king lists are recorded in religious or funerary contexts (although few of these lists are located in tombs and temples). Most of the lists are simply a list of royal names written in cartouches on monumental stone blocks or temple walls. The kings who commissioned them were trying to show that their lineage was an ancient one. The known king lists include:

✔ Royal List of Thutmosis III from Karnak, now in the Louvre in Paris

✔ Royal List of Sety I at Abydos

✔ Abydos King List of Ramses II, now in the British Museum in London

✔ Saqqara Tablet from the tomb of Tenroy, which lists 57 rulers

✔ Turin Royal Canon from the 19th dynasty

✔ The Palermo Stone from the fifth dynasty

✔ Graffiti from the quarries in the Wadi Hammamat, which include very short lists

Egyptologists use king lists in combination with each other, other historical records, and archaeological evidence because the lists aren't reliable on their own – they omit disliked rulers, portions of the text are damaged, or the lists only go up to a certain period.

The cultures of both areas are very different from the more traditional culture that most people associate with ancient Egypt. However, several commonalities that continued through to the Graeco-Roman period appear in the art of these earliest Egyptian cultures, including:

✔ **Smiting scenes,** or images in which the king is depicted hitting his enemy. The earliest known example comes from tomb 100 at Hierakonpolis and is dated to 3500–3200 BC.

✔ **Images of a cattle cult,** which eventually developed into the cult of the goddess Hathor (see Chapter 9).

✔ **The red crown of Lower Egypt,** which symbolised royal power in this region. The earliest image of the red crown of Lower Egypt is dated to approximately 3500 BC from a potsherd currently in the Ashmolean Museum, Oxford.

Uniting the land of Egypt

The Egyptian civilisation as it is known today started during the reign of King Narmer (dynasty 0) in approximately 3100 BC. At the start of King Narmer's reign, Egypt was divided into locally governed regions, but at some point Narmer was instrumental in unifying these regions to be governed by one man – himself.

Historians are uncertain whether this unification of Egypt was achieved by a number of small battles or one major battle, although the former is more likely.

The unification is recorded on the Narmer Palette, a ceremonial slate palette found at Hierakonpolis and now in the Cairo Museum. The palette includes the earliest battle scene from ancient Egypt as well as a number of images that continued to be used for the next 3,000 years, including

- ✔ The king hitting an enemy over the head with a mace
- ✔ The king wearing the crown of Upper and Lower Egypt
- ✔ The king as a bull trampling on captured enemies

The symbolism on the palette reinforces the idea that the king was the undisputed head of a single state. The imagery is the beginning of the kingship ideology prescribing that Egypt should never be divided. From this point on, all kings tried to maintain this ideal and all strived to rule a united Egypt.

Early dynastic period

The early dynastic period, sometimes referred to as the archaic period, covers only the first two dynasties. This period is a kind of transition between the culture of the pre-dynastic period and the Old Kingdom. Some historians contend that Narmer unified Egypt and commenced Egypt's earliest dynastic period, while others believe that the process was slow and evolutionary.

The earliest evidence of writing comes from this period in the form of

- ✔ Stone stelae (stone slabs with a curved top used in monumental inscriptions)
- ✔ Wooden and ivory labels (probably attached to grave goods in tombs)
- ✔ Pottery jars
- ✔ Clay cylinder seals (used to seal boxes, doors, and possibly accounts or correspondence)

By the end of the early dynastic period, the state was fully formed, and the kings had begun to build large subterranean tombs (see Chapter 13) with elaborate and expensive funerary goods to show the wealth they had amassed.

Old Kingdom

The Old Kingdom (2686–2333 BC) was primarily a time of royal affluence and economic strength and included the third to the sixth dynasties. The period is best known for pyramid building, which peaked during this period.

The first stone building and the first pyramid to be built was the third dynasty Step Pyramid at Saqqara (see Chapter 13 for details). King Djoser built this structure as an extension to a traditional tomb and stepped monument. The evolution of pyramids continued throughout the Old Kingdom until the culmination of the structure, the Great Pyramid of King Khufu at Giza, constructed between 2589 and 2566 BC. (For further pyramid facts, skip to Chapter 14.)

Towards the end of the Old Kingdom (the fifth dynasty), the *Pyramid Texts* were introduced. These provided some of the earliest information about the funerary beliefs of the ancient Egyptians. These texts, coupled with the biographical texts in the tombs, give historians loads of information about the bureaucracy and officialdom of the Old Kingdom.

The sixth dynasty saw a change in the economy of Egypt, with the nobility becoming increasingly more powerful and eventually growing richer than the kings. This wealth and power disparity is reflected in tombs of sixth dynasty royals and nobles; the nobles' tombs are far more elaborate. Ironically, this power swap may have been due to one too many tax exemptions granted by the king to his favoured courtiers.

The collapse of the Old Kingdom was due to a number of factors, of which the most important were a series of floods resulting in small harvest yields, famine, and eventually disease.

First intermediate period

The first intermediate period (2180–2140 BC) was a time of political unrest following the end of the Old Kingdom.

Introducing the wheel

Strangely, the Egyptians didn't really use the wheel for transportation until the New Kingdom and the introduction of the chariot. However, this is not to say that they didn't have wheels. Wheeled vehicles and carts simply weren't particularly practical forms of transportation on agricultural or desert terrain. Instead, the Egyptians of the Old Kingdom used donkeys, oxen, and boats as means of getting about.

The earliest representation of the wheel in use comes from the Old Kingdom, in the tomb of Kaemhesit at Saqqara. The image shows a scaling ladder being pushed up against a wall. The ladder has very distinct solid wooden wheels to manoeuvre it into place. The soldiers climbing the ladder are using axes to help pull themselves further up the wall. Other soldiers are blocking the wheels with a lump of wood to prevent the ladder moving and injuring those climbing up.

After the Old Kingdom collapsed (probably due to a series of bad floods and a resulting famine), the poor, who were hit worst by famine and disease, rose up against their rulers and the upper class. These uprisings are described in a long text called the 'Admonitions of Ipuwer':

> *The wealthy are in mourning. The poor man is full of joy. Every town says: let us suppress the powerful among us. The door-keepers say, 'Let us go out and plunder.' A man looks upon his son as his enemy. The wrongdoer is everywhere . . . the plunderer is everywhere. The robber is a possessor of riches, the rich man is become a plunderer. The bird-catchers have drawn up in line of battle and the farmers go out to plough with his shield.*

This text paints a picture of a horrible environment in which to live – one in which anarchy reigned and people were in constant fear for their lives. The first intermediate period seems to be proof of the saying that any civilisation is only three meals away from anarchy.

The administration of Egypt became divided again, with the eighth dynasty ruling in the Memphite region, although its power was limited to the local area. Petty chieftains who had gained control of local towns and provinces ruled the rest of Egypt.

At the collapse of the eighth dynasty, the ninth dynasty took control of Herakleopolis. This dynasty might have controlled the whole of Egypt for a short while at least, although its hold did not last long. The tenth dynasty saw a divide in Egypt again, with the dynasty ruling from the Herakleopolis area, and the trend continued with the 11th dynasty ruling from Thebes.

Losing oneself in the labyrinth

In the Faiyum, a pyramid complex built by Amenemhat III (12th dynasty) has a reputation for containing a labyrinth. Herodotus visited the site, called Hawara, and recorded that the labyrinth had a total of 3,000 rooms connected by winding passages. Based on Herodotus's description, the site of Hawara became a major tourist attraction for the Romans and Greeks visiting Egypt.

The complex was in fact relatively straightforward by Egyptian standards, with a pyramid in the north and the mortuary temple (the labyrinth) to the south. Sadly, very little remains of the mortuary temple, but enough exists to show that it was a substantial building. The mortuary temple was probably similar to the Step Pyramid complex at Saqqara, with a number of chambers, shrines, and pillared courts.

However, the temple probably consisted of far fewer rooms than Herodotus mentions; he may have been confused by numerous subterranean tomb chambers in the area. You can't blame poor old Herodotus for getting confused over the differences between an elaborate mortuary complex and a Greek-style labyrinth.

Middle Kingdom

The 11th dynasty eventually managed to take control of all of Egypt, reuniting it and starting the period called the Middle Kingdom. The unification took place during the reign of the fourth king, Mentuhotep I (2125–2055 BC).

During the 11th dynasty, the local governors increased in strength, and although the country was now ruled by a single king, this king was dependent on these governors. Thus the king needed to appeal to these governors to help him raise an army, with each region producing a number of young men to go on military campaigns, trading expeditions, or border patrols.

However, by the end of the reign of Senwosret III (12th dynasty), the king had regained enough control to raise an army without the help of the local governors.

The Middle Kingdom kings were keen on expanding Egypt's boundaries, slowly pushing further into Nubia. With each successful push, they secured the area by building a fortress. For example:

✔ Amenemhat I of the 12th dynasty built a row of fortresses in the north-eastern Delta to protect the borders from Asiatic attack.

✔ Between the reigns of Senwosret I and III, a series of 17 fortresses in Nubia – ten near the second cataract of the Nile past the boundary between Egypt and Nubia – were erected to prevent infiltration by the Nubians as well as to control the trade from the gold mines and stone quarries in the region.

Sometimes these fortresses were over-large, just to prove a point that the Middle Kingdom kings were a military dynasty and to let the Nubians know that the Egyptians were there to stay.

The ten fortresses near the second cataract share a number of architectural elements, including

✔ **Bastions** (protruding areas from the enclosure walls rather like towers) from within which soldiers could fire on the enemy.

✔ **Walls** built of mud brick with wide stone bases. The thick walls had a walkway at the top so that soldiers could patrol the perimeter.

✔ **Ditches** surrounding the enclosure walls making an obstacle for anyone trying to get into the fortress. The ditches were painted white so anyone in the ditch would be spotted from the walls.

✔ **Walled stairways** to the Nile where supplies would come in and naval attacks could be launched. The stairways were the safest part of the fortress.

Other fortresses had fortified towns and religious temples constructed nearby. The fortress of Buhen included arrow slits high up in the walls, showing that archery was the main method of defence. Written evidence from the expulsion of the Hyksos (see the following section 'Second intermediate period') suggests that the fortified enclosure walls at Avaris also had arrow slits from which soldiers could shoot without being exposed to the enemy.

In addition to standing as symbols of Egyptian power, these fortresses also provide a great deal of information about the life of soldiers, including their pay, weapons, armour, and food (see the section 'Creating an Army: A Key to the New Kingdom', later in this chapter).

Second intermediate period

The Middle Kingdom collapsed around 1782 BC in a similar way to the Old Kingdom, perhaps due to floods and a subsequent famine. Many historians contend that the descriptions of terrible living conditions in the 'Admonitions of Ipuwer' (see the section 'First intermediate period', earlier in this chapter) also apply to the second intermediate period.

For some unspecified reason, at the end of the Middle Kingdom, a large influx of people from the area of Palestine and Syria (referred to by the Egyptians as Asiatics) came to the region. This was not an invasion, but rather a small-scale migration. Some historians believe that the Egyptian government may have invited the Palestinians for their boat-making skills, and these immigrants were then housed in the Delta, which was the site of large ports and trading centres.

This influx is unlikely to have been the cause of the collapse of the Middle Kingdom, but these immigrants and the changes they brought ushered in the Hyksos period.

The Hyksos period

Towards the end of the second intermediate period (1663–1555 BC), Egypt experienced a period of divided rule, with the 15th dynasty ruling in the north from the Delta site of Avaris and the 17th dynasty ruling from Thebes in the south:

- ✔ The 15th-dynasty kings were known as the Hyksos and had risen to power from the Syro-Palestinian community living in the Delta during the Middle Kingdom.

- ✔ The 17th-dynasty kings were of Egyptian origin, but may have been *vassal rulers* of the 15th dynasty, which means that they were only being allowed to rule because they were quiet and didn't cause trouble.

The unknown soldiers

At Deir el Bahri in Luxor, a mass grave for soldiers was discovered in a site overlooking the temple of Mentuhotep I (11th dynasty), near the mortuary temple of Hatshepsut.

At least 60 bodies were discovered in this tomb, all male, with an average height of 5 feet 6 inches and aged between 30 and 40. Many of the men had a number of old wounds that had healed, indicating that they were war veterans. Most of the wounds were on the left side of the head, which is common for battle wounds, because most soldiers are right handed. The wounds were caused by:

 ✔ **Arrows:** Ten of the men were killed by puncture wounds from ebony-tipped arrows, and some fragments of these arrows were still embedded in the bodies. One soldier had an arrow embedded, while another was hit in the back from an angle that suggests he was shot from high battlements. (Most arrows were collected after battle and reused by the surviving army, but some were missed or too difficult to retrieve.)

 ✔ **Blunt objects:** Other soldiers were killed by blunt objects like stones falling from battlements, and many died from being hit with force by a blunt instrument.

This battle was clearly harsh and bloody, but these men died when there was no outside warfare, indicating that they were involved in a civil war, perhaps Mentuhotep I reuniting a divided Egypt.

The Hyksos rulers are often said to have invaded Egypt from Palestine using chariots, which had not been introduced to Egypt at this time. In fact the Hyksos kings came from the local Asiatic community in the Delta. These communities had been living in the region for more then 100 years before the start of the Hyksos period. (Also, the chariot was introduced during this period, but not *by* the Hyksos. Both the Egyptians and the Hyksos gained access to the chariot at the same time, so neither had an advantage over the other in skill at charioteering.)

Expelling the Hyksos

Near the end of the Hyksos period (around 1640 BC), Hyksos kings had gained control over the whole of Egypt, serving as the undisputed kings of Upper and Lower Egypt.

However, the members of the 17th dynasty at Thebes weren't over keen on the Hyksos kings interfering in local affairs. So Seqenenre Tao II, a 17th dynasty king, led an offensive against the Hyksos King Apophis.

Burying the evidence

The origins of the Hyksos have always been questioned, but the evidence at Avaris, their capital in the Delta, shows a juxtaposition between an Egyptian and a Syro-Palestinian culture. This mix of cultural influences is high-lighted in two of the Hyksos's most bizarre practices – servant and donkey burials:

✔ Three servant burials have been discovered alongside their master's tomb at Avaris. These servants were buried across the tomb entrance and face the door, as if waiting for orders from their deceased master. All the servants were males – an older adult, an adolescent, and a 25 year old. They all seem to have been buried at the same time as their master, indicating that they were sacrificed when their master died. This practice had been used by the Egyptians, but not for more than 1,000 years at the time of the burials, suggesting it was a foreign idea from the homeland of these Asiatic settlers.

✔ Seventeen donkey burials have also been discovered at Avaris. Donkey burial was a non-Egyptian practice. The donkeys were typically buried in pairs at the front of large tombs, possibly as a sacrifice on the deaths of the tomb owners. These donkeys may have pulled carts or funerary carriages, but no harnesses were found alongside these burials. The inclusion of donkeys was rare and only attached to very elite burials, which indicates wealth and status within the community.

The battle was not as easy as Seqenenre Tao originally thought, and he died in battle. His mummy includes numerous head wounds, indicating that this was a vicious battle. His son Kamose took up the gauntlet and continued the battle. Kamose was a little more successful and managed to reclaim most of Egypt, pushing Apopis back to the Hyksos capital of Avaris. Kamose died young, although historians are unsure how.

Kamose's brother Ahmose I took over the battle and was more successful than his brother, managing to chase the Hyksos out of Egypt entirely. Ahmose continued to pursue the Hyksos as far as Sharuhen in the Negev Desert between Rafah and Gaza, sacking villages along the way – just to show who was boss.

Ahmose then returned to Egypt and reinforced the eastern borders with a strong military presence to ensure that the Hyksos supporters did not try to re-enter the country. This successful king was the first king of the 18th dynasty and ushered in the New Kingdom. (See Chapter 4 for more on this period of Egyptian history.)

Creating an Army: A Key to the New Kingdom

The start of the New Kingdom (1555 BC) saw a number of changes in government control and organisation. But the main change – and the most successful – was the introduction of a permanent army. Prior to the New Kingdom, when the king needed an army, local governors were called on to gather likely lads from within their regions. Ahmose, however, saw the flaw in this method and introduced a full-time standing army.

As with most positions in Egypt, military roles were passed on from father to son (see Chapter 2). However, based on records of military promotions, Egyptian males, including the uneducated, were able to become soldiers and rise through the ranks. Prior to the start of a permanent army, Egyptians could gain political power or reach the throne only through bureaucracy or the priesthood.

Signing up

Training in the army started as young as 5 years old, although professional military service didn't start until the age of 20. Older recruits may have joined as part of a national service with a requirement of serving at least a year before returning to their villages. However, after training they could be called up at any time.

Just like today, new military recruits needed to get haircuts. Images of this process have been discovered in tombs. The haircuts created an element of uniformity among the ranks.

Surviving texts also describe the start of a new recruit's life in the army. New recruits received a 'searing beating' as a means of demoralising them in order to make them more pliable and susceptible to obeying orders.

The training regime was hard and included

- Weight lifting, using bags of sand as weights
- Wrestling
- Boxing
- Throwing knives at wooden targets to improve aim

✔ Sword skills, using sticks for practice

✔ Chariot riding

✔ Target practice in a chariot with a bow and arrow (see Figure 3-1)

These tasks would be hard in anyone's books, but imagine doing all of this outside in more than 100-degree heat. No wonder the Egyptian army was particularly good and greatly feared by many.

Figure 3-1:
Target
practice
using a
copper
target (Luxor
Museum).

Dividing the army

The New Kingdom was a large operation that needed a great deal of organisation to make it work well. The majority of the army was made up of infantry (foot soldiers) who were separated into divisions of 5,000 men.

Each division was named after a god and had a royal son in the position of general of the division. (Some of the princes who held this title were actually infants, indicating that it was an honorary title.) Specialist divisions included groups of charioteers, archers, spearmen, and foreign mercenaries.

For easier control, the army was further divided:

✔ A host consisted of 500 men (at least two companies).

✔ A company had 250 men (consisting of five platoons).

✔ A platoon had 50 men (consisting of five squads).

✔ A squad had 10 men.

A soldier's life

Papyrus Anastasi 3, written during the New Kingdom reign of Sety II, was probably copied from an earlier text. It describes in detail the experience of a typical soldier.

What is it that you say they tell, that the soldier's is more pleasant than the scribe's profession? Come let me tell you the condition of the soldier, that much exerted one. He is brought while a child to be confined in the camp. A searing beating is given to his body, a wound inflicted on his eye and a splitting blow to his brow. He is laid down and beaten like papyrus. He is struck with torments.

Come, let me relate to you his journey to Khor [Palestine and Syria] and his marching upon the hills. His rations and water are upon his shoulder like the load of an ass.

His neck has become calloused, like that of an ass. The vertebrae of his back are broken. He drinks foul water and halts to stand guard. When he reaches the enemy he is like a pinioned bird, with no strength in his limbs. If he succeeds in returning to Egypt, he is like a stick which the woodworm has devoured. He is sick, prostration overtakes him. He is brought back upon an ass, his clothes taken away by theft, his henchmen fled . . . turn back from the saying that the soldier's is more pleasant than the scribe's profession.

This text, as I am sure is clear, was written to try to persuade a young boy to bypass the glamour of military life and enter the scribal profession instead. You wouldn't have to tell me twice.

Tagging along

In addition to soldiers, the army included numerous other important elements, such as:

- **Musicians:** Trumpets and drums were used to help troops march in time, as well to signal tactical changes and manoeuvres during battles.

- **Standard bearers:** Military standards were an important part of the battle, because seeing where the troops were situated on the field was vital. Standards were also a source of pride for the troops.

- **Scribes:** All battle events needed to be recorded, and military scribes accompanied the military onto the battlefield. They were responsible for counting amputated body parts after a battle (a method of counting the enemy dead), as well as recording the amount of booty and number of prisoners collected.

- **Camp followers:** A number of other individuals milled around the military camps and were responsible for cleaning the officers' tents, fetching water, and cooking. These individuals often included children, who perhaps were later trained to become soldiers.

Performing non-combative duties

In addition to fighting in battles, soldiers were assigned to do a number of boring or difficult tasks:

- One of the most tedious assignments was guarding desert trading routes for up to 20 days at a time. The graffiti on some of these desert sites show that soldiers on duty were bored out of their minds, marking off the days until they returned to civilisation.

- Soldiers were also drafted for transportation of large stone blocks for the construction of sarcophagi and obelisks. Hundreds of strong men were needed, and they didn't come much stronger than the military.

- Because of their strength, soldiers helped with the harvest to ensure that it was completed quickly and efficiently. Whether they travelled to their own village to help with the harvest or were allocated to the place most in need is uncertain, but soldiers were definitely used for this important annual event.

On the march

When the soldiers were sent out on a military campaign, they probably dreamed of quiet guard duties. The journeys to get to the battles were often long and hard – sometimes as dangerous as the fights themselves.

For example, a journey from Memphis to Thebes, if travelled in daylight hours by river, took between 12 and 20 days. (Today it takes nine hours by train or about an hour by plane.) The river journey was quite hazardous, with threats from other vessels, sandbanks, and hippos.

To warn passing vessels and people that the military was on board ship, soldiers hung their cowhide shields on the outside of the boats' cabins. This may also have acted as a beacon to passing bad guys wanting to harm the soldiers.

Historians don't know how fast an Egyptian army marched, but records from Alexander the Great's army (around 336–323 BC) show that his troops covered an average of 13 miles a day, receiving a rest period every five to six days for particularly long-distance marches. On shorter campaigns, these troops covered up to 15 miles a day. The marching army also required a rest period between a long march and actually fighting, in order to recuperate their strength.

Policing and tax collecting

When not involved in military combat, soldiers were often employed in tax collecting and general policing.

One text from the reign of Horemheb (18th dynasty) tells of a court case between some soldiers and tax payers: The soldiers had gone to collect taxes and then nicked half the stuff collected and had the cheek to say they had never been paid in the first place. The king decreed that farmers shouldn't be punished for non-payment if their payments had been stolen (which is only fair, really). The soldiers were punished with 100 blows and five open wounds and were forced to return the goods they took.

In the Graeco-Roman period (332–30 BC), the military was still used for tax collection. One record shows a tax collector, Timcyenes, requesting that his boss send some soldiers to help him collect tax from a reluctant villager.

> *I have collected taxes from all the residents of the village except Johannes . . . he refuses to pay his account . . . please send two soldiers to the village where he is being held, because in that way we may be able to get the money that is owed.*

Historians don't know whether the soldiers were successful, but the record does indicate that soldiers had a certain amount of persuasive power – no doubt with the aid of big sticks.

Eating like a soldier: Military fare

Soldiers often had to carry their sustenance with them (thus increasing the weight of their packs). Alexander the Great recorded that his army of 10,000 men and 2,000 horses had a daily consumption of

- 14 tonnes of grain
- 18 tonnes of fodder
- 90,000 litres of water

Soldiers were given fewer than ten loaves of bread a day each, which they carried in bags and baskets. This bread (probably more biscuit than bread) would have grown mould, which although unknown to the Egyptians was a form of natural antibiotic.

Soldiers also carried the ingredients for making bread if they had access to ovens en route or time to fashion mud ovens while at camp.

Other food items were part of the Egyptian military diet because they stored and travelled well, and included onions, beans, figs, dates, fish, and meat. Many kinds of fruit and meat were dried, but the soldiers also caught fish. Enemy livestock was plundered for meat. Beer may have been brewed on campaign because it didn't keep for long. Drinking water was obtained from wells. Soldiers had to carry or steal wine to accompany their meals.

Because the quantity of food required for an army was so immense, the military probably stored food at numerous forts along the campaign route. The armies also made use of food storage in any town or village along the way. In fact, villages may have been legally obligated to help passing armies. Of course, feeding 10,000 men and numerous horses at the drop of a hat may have bankrupted a few of the smaller towns.

Waiting for pay day

The food that the military needed to survive formed the majority of their wages, because no monetary system existed until the time of Alexander the Great. On campaign, these wages were simply eaten, while in the barracks they were exchanged for other goods.

In addition to official wages, soldiers were able to plunder other goodies to give their wealth a boost. Plunder in the form of gold, cattle, and even women was taken from enemy camps after cities had been sacked and regions conquered. The officers obviously got the best of the booty, but ordinary infantry soldiers also returned with full backpacks.

A formal system of awards also recognised the bravest soldiers for their work. These awards consisted of golden flies (as a sign of persistence), gold *shebyu* collars for valour, 'oyster' shells of gold or shell, and even property. Not only were the soldiers made wealthy by these gifts, they also received recognition within the Egyptian community for their services.

Armed for battle

Egyptian soldiers were bedecked in weapons, equipment, armour, and even religious icons as they headed into battle.

Armed to the teeth

The weapons in the Egyptian army were varied and numerous. Soldiers did not always own their weapons, and in records from Medinet Habu, Ramses III supervises the issuing of weapons for the battle against the Sea People (see Chapter 4). The weapons were stacked in piles, swords in one, bows in another, and arrows in a third.

Weapons varied from the simple to the complicated to the downright unpleasant:

- ✔ **Sticks and stones:** Sticks were good for close combat and were used as clubs. Stones were good for long-distance combat because they could be thrown. Both were readily available.

- ✔ **Mace:** This large piece of hard stone (such as granite or diorite) mounted on a handle was used to club people to death. A New Kingdom adaptation of this weapon was to fit a sharpened curved bronze blade (see *Khepesh swords*, below) to a mace and use that not only to club but also to slice at your opponent.

- ✔ **Slingshots:** Originally used for hunting, these were adapted for military use as well. Ammunition was always available, and the slings were easy to transport.

- ✔ **Throwsticks:** These were primarily used for hunting birds, but were also effective weapons in battle. Their main disadvantage was that as soon as the sticks were thrown, the soldiers were unarmed.

- ✔ **Bow and arrow:** The Egyptian army had a large corps of archers used to protect the infantry from a distance, because arrows travelled up to 200 metres. Archers used both the *self bow* (a straight bow made from a single piece of wood) and the *composite bow* (an arched bow made from a number of small pieces of wood glued together to give greater flexibility). Archers could send arrows travelling up to 300 metres.

- ✔ **Spears:** Many of the foot soldiers were armed with spears with a 2-metre-long shaft and a metal blade. Spears were intended to be thrown, but because this disarmed the spearman, they were also used as stabbing weapons.

- ✔ **Axes, daggers, and swords:** These instruments were used in close-combat battles and were made of bronze, copper, or (in the case of axes only) stone.

- ✔ ***Khepesh* swords:** These New Kingdom weapons were normally used by royalty and featured a type of scimitar with a curved blade.

- ✔ **Shields:** These were used for body protection in place of full body armour. They measured 1 by 1.5 metres and were made of wood. Sometimes they were solid wood, which would have made them heavy; more often they consisted of a wooden frame covered in cow hide. A handle was fixed to the back, to which a soldier could attach a strap to sling the shield over the shoulder while on the march. In the absence of proper armour, Egyptian soldiers were still well protected from the showers of arrows, stones, sticks, and swords raining on them.

IN THEIR WORDS

The transport of choice

A vital item of military kit was the chariot, which was introduced during the Hyksos period (see the section 'The Hyksos period', earlier in this chapter).

The typical Egyptian chariot had a light wooden semi-circular frame with an open back and an axle with two wheels of either four or six spokes. These wheels were made up of numerous smaller pieces tied together with wet leather thongs, which shrank when dry and pulled the wheel together. A long pole was attached to the axle with a yoke for two horses.

Each chariot had a driver and a man armed with a spear, shield, or bow and arrow. The small, agile chariot allowed the army to pursue the enemy quickly as well as rain arrows down on them at the same time. Archaeologists have only discovered 11 chariots, four from the tomb of Tutankhamun, two from the tomb of Yuya and Tuya (the parents of Queen Tiye), and one belonging to Thutmose IV.

Papyrus Anastasi I from the 19th dynasty describes the adventures of an Egyptian charioteer in Canaan, including a visit to a chariot repair shop in Joppa:

> You make your way into the armoury; workshops surround you; smiths and leatherworkers are all about you. They do all that you wish. They attend to your chariot, so that it may cease from lying idle. Your pole is newly shaped. They give leather covering to your collar-piece. They supply your yoke. They give a . . . (of metal) to your whip; they fasten [to] it lashes. You go forth quickly to fight on the open field, to accomplish the deeds of the brave!

Sounds like a very ordinary visit in the life of a charioteer.

Throughout the New Kingdom, all royal sons were trained in driving chariots and firing arrows from moving chariots. Battle reliefs generally show the king alone in his chariot, often with four horses instead of the usual two, to demonstrate his great horsemanship and control.

Dressed to kill

In the New Kingdom, the introduction of bronze weapons led to a greater need for body armour. Armour was probably reserved for the elite members of the army rather than the masses of infantry, and included:

- **Scales of bronze or hard leather:** These were fixed and overlapping on a jerkin of linen or leather.

- **Helmets:** These were generally worn only by Sherden mercenaries (a foreign group who formed part of the Sea People – see Chapter 4) and had weird little horns and a round disc on top.

Ordinary soldiers probably only had their hair as a form of head protection. Some Middle Kingdom soldiers had tightly curled, heavily greased hair that created a spongy layer – a style that was difficult for the enemy to grab hold of in battle.

- **Battle crown:** The blue crown of New Kingdom kings is thought to be a royal battle helmet, probably made of leather, with silver or electrum discs fixed to it. However, no royal crowns have been discovered, so no one knows if battle crowns were worn.

- **Gloves:** Due to the climate, these were not commonly used other than by charioteers of high status. Gloves were made of leather or thick linen and prevented the reins from rubbing the hands.

- **Kilts:** Most of the army wore a single triangle of linen folded into a kilt. Some reliefs indicate that the front may have been stiffened to provide a little extra protection. A wooden model, discovered in a tomb, representing a division of Nubian archers shows them wearing red and green loincloths, which may have been made of leather for additional protection.

Soldiers wore a leather skin over the plain linen kilts. These skins were often made from a whole gazelle skin, slashed with a sharp knife to give extra flexibility. A solid leather patch over the rear provided extra padding while sitting.

Although painted reliefs only show these basic clothes, soldiers probably wore more, especially on winter nights. Tomb reliefs generally show the soldiers in their 'dress uniforms' rather than giving a realistic depiction of battle clothes. Also, during fighting, soldiers were likely to have worn as little as possible; the weather was hot, and loose clothing gave the enemy something to grab on to. Any wounds inflicted through long clothing could also get infected with tiny bits of grubby fabric entering the wounds.

Religious protection

In addition to the equipment and weapons that Egyptian soldiers carried with them (spears, shields, daggers, bows, and arrow quivers), battle reliefs and archaeological records show that the military relied not only on armour, but also on religious icons for protection.

The most prominent icon consisted of the protective wings that the king wore. The wings belonged to Horus and wrapped around the king's chest showing that he was protected by the god. A pair of these wings was discovered in the tomb of Tutankhamun. (They are, in fact, made of linen, and therefore offered no form of protection other than religious.)

Jewellery was both functional and decorative, as the king wore jewellery as a form of protection. One piece of jewellery, also found in the tomb of Tutankhamun, consists of a large collar attached to a thick band of gold scales that protected his king's torso. The collar was made of images of the king smiting enemies in the presence of the god. However, how much protection soft gold provided against a spear or arrow at speed is uncertain, and the king probably wore this type of collar in the military parades before or after the battle.

The ordinary soldiers wouldn't have had this large-scale religious protection and would have relied on amulets to protect them (Chapter 9 has more on amulets).

Recording victories

The Egyptians were very keen on their battle records as a means of broadcasting their victories. Military scribes who accompanied the army on its campaigns created these records. The records are in the form of official reports and include poetic narratives and very elaborate images.

Battle records need to be taken with a large pinch of salt because they were produced for propaganda purposes more than anything else. All battle reports claim, quite baldly, that no Egyptians ever died in battle for a number of reasons:

 ✔ They were too good at fighting.

 ✔ Everyone else was scared of them.

 ✔ All the enemy soldiers were cowards who ran away.

Archaeological evidence shows that this clearly isn't the case, with many mummies showing signs of battle wounds. I suppose that the scribes were only keeping morale up by trying to convince the troops of their invincibility.

Perusing the military annals

Many kings produced a set of annals that recorded their military campaigns. However, only two annals have survived – the Palermo Stone and the annals of Thutmose III (also carved in stone). The Palermo Stone is in fragments in the Palermo Archaeological Museum in Sicily, the Egyptian Museum in Cairo, and the Petrie Museum in London. The annals of Thutmosis III are in situ at Karnak Temple.

The Palermo stone records many events of the early kings, including battles, flood levels, and *heb sed* festivals (see Chapter 9).

The annals vary depending on what the king had achieved. For example, the annals of Thutmose III focus on his military achievements because he was a warrior pharaoh and the first empire-builder in Egypt.

Other records that describe military campaigns include

- ✔ Graffiti on campaign routes
- ✔ Autobiographical texts of army personnel in tombs
- ✔ Temple descriptions and images

Every picture tells a story

The artistic representations of battles in temple reliefs didn't change very much in 3,000 years of Egyptian history – which is a clear warning that these images cannot always be taken at face value.

Several themes recur in these surviving scenes:

- ✔ Scenes often show the king holding his enemies by their forelock as he prepares to hit them with a mace. (This was introduced on the Narmer palette in 3100 BC – refer to Chapter 1.) Regardless of whether the pharaoh is in a chariot, strolling through the battlefield, or seated on his throne, the fallen enemies are always shown in a tangled mess beneath his feet, indicating his power over them.

- ✔ The gods are often represented playing a major role in the battles of kings. In the New Kingdom, in particular, the king is counselled regarding the battle by Amun, who is shown handing the sword of victory to the king. After battle, the king is often shown parading the booty and prisoners of war in front of Amun by way of thanks for the help received in battle.

Chapter 4

Building the Empire: The Glories of the New Kingdom

The expulsion of the Hyksos (see Chapter 3) saw the end of the second intermediate period and the start of the New Kingdom. This period (1570–1070 BC) is one of the most famous, with the 18th–19th dynasties and all the popular kings, such as Tutankhamun, Akhenaten, and Ramses II. See the timeline on the Cheat Sheet for a wider chronology.

The start of the 18th dynasty saw the introduction of a permanent military (see Chapter 3) and also a change in international policy. The kingship ideology also included extending the boundaries of Egypt. This meant that each king tried to claim more land than his father, until eventually a large area of the Near East was under Egyptian control, with vassal kings who remained loyal to Egypt set up in foreign towns.

The New Kingdom was a time of renewal and empire building by some of the most powerful kings of Egypt. This chapter focuses on the people and personalities that made this era possible.

Meeting the Egyptian Napoleon: Thutmosis III

The first true empire-builder of the New Kingdom was Thutmosis III (1504–1450 BC) of the 18th dynasty, the husband and step-son of Hatshepsut (see Chapter 5).

Thutmosis III, the son of Thutmosis II and a secondary wife called Isis, was still an infant when he became king on the death of his father. Once king, he was married to Thutmosis II's widow, his stepmother and aunt, Hatshepsut. For more than 20 years, Hatshepsut and Thutmosis III ruled officially as co-regents, although for the majority of this period Hatshepsut ruled Egypt as pharaoh, pushing the young Thutmosis III aside.

Thutmosis III spent his childhood and teenage years training in the army, until the death of Hatshepsut in year 22 of their reign. At this time, he took over the throne as a fully grown adult and military leader and continued to rule Egypt for more than 20 years on his own. Figure 4-1 shows him at his most regal.

Egyptologists often refer to Thutmosis III as the Egyptian Napoleon because he spent his adult life fighting and claiming land in the name of Egypt. He left some very elaborate military records in the Hall of Annals at Karnak temple, telling of the exploits in Syria that earned him his title.

Figure 4-1: Thutmosis III (Luxor Museum).

Fighting at Megiddo

The most famous of Thutmosis III's battles was at Megiddo in Syria, in the first year of his sole rule (around 1476 BC). The King of Kadesh in Syria had slowly been gathering a number of Palestinian cities to join him in an attack against the borders of Egypt, because he wasn't strong enough to do it alone. This attacking army occupied the desirable and fortified Syrian town of Megiddo (in modern-day Israel), which was strategically placed for trade and protection.

Megiddo was the site of many battles in antiquity. The biblical term 'Armageddon' actually means 'mount of Megiddo' in Hebrew and refers to a particular battle here.

Thutmosis III and his Egyptian militia travelled from the Delta, through the Sinai, until they reached Megiddo. They laid siege to various strongholds along the way so that their line of communication (and potential retreat back to Egypt) was clear and under their control.

Three routes led to Megiddo, and Thutmosis needed to decide which one to take. Two of the longer routes were difficult to defend, whereas the shorter and more direct route left the Egyptians in a vulnerable position because they needed to travel in single file and were under constant threat of ambush from the enemy.

Thutmosis was advised to take one of the longer routes, but he decided on the shorter, more interesting route. Luckily for him, the Egyptians travelled the path with no problems and emerged a short distance from the fortified town, where they set up camp waiting for the remainder of the Egyptian army to arrive.

Time to attack

After the Egyptian army started its approach to Megiddo, the enemy forces tried to organise themselves in a very rough-and-ready fashion to guard their town. The following morning, the Egyptians paraded in full battle regalia to psych themselves up and demoralise the enemy.

Thutmosis III led the attack in a gold and electrum chariot, leading one-third of the army. Battle records state that the Egyptians were greatly outnumbered by the Syrian army, which consisted of more than 330 kings and *'Millions of men, and hundreds of thousands of the chiefest of all the lands, standing in their chariots.'*

Despite being outnumbered, Thutmosis III was valiant:

> *The king himself . . . led the way of his army, mighty at its head like a flame of fire, the king who wrought with his sword. He went forth, none like him, slaying the barbarians, smiting the Retenu (the Asiatics), bringing their princes as living captives, their chariots wrought with gold, bound to their horses.*

The Egyptian forces were too much for the skeleton army guarding the mount of Megiddo. The army at Megiddo quickly fled, leaving all its weapons, chariots, and belongings behind. The Egyptians were close on its heels, but the gatekeepers at Megiddo refused to open the doors to let the Syrians in just in case the Egyptians followed. Those inside the fort let down knotted sheets, rather like the story of Rapunzel – albeit less hairy – so that the rich and powerful among their allies could be rescued and brought within the fortress.

Missed opportunity

After the Syrians fled the mount of Megiddo, the Egyptian army had a perfect opportunity to storm the fortification before the Syrians were able to gather themselves and prepare to attack from within the fortress. However, rather than attacking straight away, the Egyptian soldiers were distracted by all the goodies left by the fleeing army and started to rummage through them. They lost their advantage over the Syrians, but filled their bags with all they could carry.

Thutmosis took control of the situation – albeit it a little too late – and organised for a wall and a moat to be built around Megiddo in preparation for a long siege of the town. It was particularly important for the Egyptians to capture the town to show their strength. They also needed to be able to defend their victory against numerous chieftains from surrounding towns who threatened to cause problems for the Egyptians and weaken the control on their empire. The siege lasted seven months before Megiddo finally fell to the Egyptians.

Giddy up

In year 30 of his reign, Thutmosis III was engaged with the Hittites in battle at Kadesh. Kadesh was particularly important because it was located on an essential trade route and gave the Egyptians access to territories in the north.

During the battle at Kadesh, the Hittites used a devious but common technique to destroy the Egyptian army. Stallions pulled the Egyptian chariots, so the Hittites sent a mare, in season, out into the field in order to distract the horses. Cunning, eh?

Luckily for Thutmosis III, his general, Amenemhab, saw and chased the mare with his chariot. When Amenemhab caught the mare, he sliced open her belly and cut off her tail, which he then presented to the king. A bit of a funny pressie really, although it obviously worked as a lucky charm because Thutmosis III won this battle and went on to fight another day.

Getting bootylicious

After the fall of Megiddo and the battle of Kadesh (see the sidebar 'Giddy up'), the Egyptian soldiers had lots of goodies to boost their salaries (see Chapter 3 for wages information). Of course, the king enjoyed the profits of war as well. Thutmosis III's annals at Karnak include booty lists that detail the following:

> *All the goods of those cities which submitted themselves, which were brought to his majesty: 38 lords of theirs, 87 children of that enemy and of the chiefs who were with him, 5 lords of theirs, 1,796 male and female slaves with their children, non-combatants who surrendered because of famine with that enemy, 103 men; total 2,503. Besides flat dishes of costly stone and gold, various vessels, a large two-handled vase of the work of Kharu, vases, flat dishes, dishes, various drinking-vessels, 3 large kettles, 87 knives, amounting to 784 deben. Gold in rings found in the hands of the artificers, and silver in many rings, 966 deben and 1 kidet [both weights of metal]. A silver statue in beaten work, the head of gold, the staff with human faces; 6 chairs of that enemy, of ivory, ebony and carob wood, wrought with gold; 6 footstools belonging to them; 6 large tables of ivory and carob wood, a staff of carob wood, wrought with gold and all costly stones in the fashion of a sceptre, belonging to that enemy, all of it wrought with gold; a statue of that enemy, of ebony wrought with gold, the head of which was inlaid with lapis lazuli; vessels of bronze, much clothing of that enemy.*

Sadly, Egyptologists don't know what happened to this booty and how it was absorbed into the Egyptian economy.

Changing His Religion: Akhenaten

Another 18th-dynasty king who has held worldwide fame for thousands of years is the heretic king, Akhenaten (1350–1333 BC). He was infamous for changing the religion of ancient Egypt from the worship of hundreds of gods to the worship of one god – the *Aten* or sun disc. Figure 4-2 shows the face of Akhenaten.

Akhenaten's bold religious changes were the product of monotheism, as commentators often state. Although the Aten was elevated to the position of supreme god, only Akhenaten and the royal family were able to worship the sun god. Akhenaten raised himself up to the position of fully fledged god, more divine than any other king – and everyone else had to worship Akhenaten! So in Akhenaten's system, there was not just one god but two.

Figure 4-2:
The face of
Akhenaten
(Luxor
Museum).

Meeting the family

Akhenaten was the youngest son of Amenhotep III and Queen Tiye. He was born under the name of Amenhotep and only later changed his name to Akhenaten ('Spirit of the Aten') as his devotion to the god grew.

Akhenaten's mother, Tiye, was of noble, not royal, birth. Some images show her as a somewhat domineering and frightening woman. She is regularly shown alongside her husband in a complementary rather than inferior position and is represented in her own right without the king, which was unheard of in earlier Egyptian history.

Akhenaten had one older brother, Thutmosis, who died before he could come to the throne, and three sisters: Beketaten, Sitamun, and Isis. The latter two were married to their father, Amenhotep III.

Marrying a mystery

Akhenaten married young, before he became king, and he married one of the most famous women in ancient Egypt – the rather serene and enigmatic Nefertiti. No one really knows where Nefertiti came from, who her parents were, and in fact who she was. But most Egyptologists believe that she was the daughter of Ay, the brother of Queen Tiye. Ay's wife held the title 'wet-nurse of Nefertiti', showing that she wasn't mum but step-mum to Nefertiti, because the title of mother would outstrip that of wet-nurse.

Nefertiti and Akhenaten had six daughters, the first born before the end of Akhenaten's first year on the throne. The daughters are often depicted with the king and queen. Their names were

- Meritaten
- Meketaten
- Ankhesenepaten (later Ankhesenamun)
- Neferneferuaten
- Neferneferure
- Setepenre

Although there is no direct evidence, it is possible that Tutankhamun was also the son of Akhenaten and a secondary wife called Kiya. Some scholars also believe that Smenkhkare, the mysterious king who followed Akhenaten on the throne for a brief spell, was the son of Akhenaten; others believe that he was the son of Amenhotep III, and other scholars think Smenkhkare and Nefertiti are the same person. What chance do the rest of us have if the experts are unable to decide?

Praising the sun god

The main focus of Akhenaten's reign was his religious revolution, which took place over a very short period. Akhenaten ruled for only 17 years, and the entire revolution was complete by year 9 of his reign. Despite the short time that this revolution took, this period is the most written about of ancient Egyptian history by modern writers.

Even stranger, for 12 years of his reign, Akhenaten was probably serving as a co-ruler with his father Amenhotep III, with his father ruling from Thebes and Akhenaten ruling from his brand-spanking-new city at Amarna in middle Egypt. Effectively, theirs was a divided rule – one of the few that was seen as acceptable in the entire span of Egyptian history (see Chapter 1).

The *Aten* is the key element in the reign of Akhenaten. The Aten was not a new deity: He was always part of the wider solar cycle and appears as an embodiment of the light that emanates from the sun disc. This light is represented in images by hands radiating from the sun disc, each ending in little hands that give an *ankh* sign (sign of eternal life, shown in Chapter 11) to the royal family. The entire image suggests that the sun provides life. All Akhenaten did was to elevate this element of the sun god to that of being the only sun god.

The favouring of the Aten over other deities started in the reign of Amenhotep III as part of a campaign to limit the power of the Priesthood of Amun at Karnak, which at the time was almost as powerful as the royal family. Akhenaten, however, went further and began to replace all the main gods with the Aten, although he didn't close all the temples until nine years into his reign, when he diverted all revenue to the new temples of the Aten.

In year 12, Akhenaten started a hate campaign against the cult of Amun. This involved carving out the names of Amun wherever they appeared – even in the name of his own father, *Amen*hotep. This had never happened before in Egypt. Kings often eliminated other kings they didn't like from their personal histories (see Chapter 3), but a king had never removed gods before. Akhenaten's actions must have upset a lot of people.

Meeting an unhappy end

Despite his unpopularity, Akhenaten does not seem to have been assassinated, which is surprising. However, the end of his reign is vague and unrecorded, so historians can only guess at the actual events.

A stream of disasters in his personal life precede Akhenaten's death and the collapse of the Amarna period:

- In Year 12 of Akhenaten's reign, his father Amenhotep III died.
- In Year 13, Nefertiti disappears from the inscriptions, so she probably died, although some scholars believe she changed her name and ruled as co-ruler.
- In Year 14, Amenhotep's daughter Meketaten died as the result of childbirth
- In Year 14, Akhenaten's mother, Tiye, died.

This stream of deaths is often attributed to a plague epidemic referred to as 'the Asiatic illness' that swept Amarna; this epidemic may have been a form of bubonic plague. This plague was viewed by the ordinary people as punishment for the abandonment of the traditional gods – which made the masses very keen to start worshipping the traditional gods again.

Akhenaten died in year 17 of his reign, when he was in his 30s. He left no known male heir, except possibly Smenkhkare, a mysterious character, who co-ruled alongside Akhenaten for three years (see the section 'Marrying a mystery', earlier in this chapter). Some believe Smenkhkare is Nefertiti, although the evidence is not conclusive. Smenkhkare then ruled alone for a few months before dying, presumably from the plague as well. (You wouldn't want to be a member of this family would you? They seem jinxed!)

At the death of Smenkhkare, only one more suitable heir existed, the famous Tutankhamun – a wee nipper at only 7 or 8 years old.

Growing Up a King: Tutankhamun

Tutankhamun is a name that conjures up images of gold and wealth, due to the amazing splendours discovered in his tomb. Prior to the tomb's discovery, very little was known about this king – and to be honest, after the tomb was opened, the world was not enlightened a great deal.

There are many gaps in the life of Tutankhamun, and most studies concentrate on the treasure from his tomb. Many of these treasures were created for the tomb and may not have featured at all in the king's life. However, the mystery surrounding this king has intrigued people since the tomb's discovery in 1922. No doubt Tut will continue to interest people for another 100 years.

Keeping it in the family

Historians think that Tutankhamun was born between years 7 and 9 of Akhenaten's reign, possibly at Amarna. Originally called Tutankhaten ('the living image of the Aten'), his name was changed when he became king.

Egyptologists are even unable to agree on who Tutankhamun's parents were. Theories include:

- Akhenaten and Kiya (a secondary wife)
- Akhenaten and Tadukhipa (a Mitannian princess)
- Amenhotep III and Tiye (making Tutankhamun Akhenaten's brother)
- Amenhotep III and Sitamun (Akhenaten's sister)

The first theory is widely accepted by most Egyptologists today.

At the start of his reign, Tutankhamun married Ankhesenepaten, who later changed her name to Ankhesenamun. Depending on who Tutankhamun's parents are, Ankhesenamun is either his half-sister or his niece. They certainly liked to keep it all in the family. Ankhesenamun was a couple of years older than Tutankhamun, and they may have been raised together at the palace at Amarna.

Sadly, despite their youth and a ten-year reign, Tutankhamun and Ankhesenamun had no surviving children. However, buried in Tutankhamun's tomb in a plain white wooden box were two female foetuses, one who was still-born and another who survived for a short while before dying. These foetuses may be Tutankhamun's children, indicating that this young couple had to endure a very trying time attempting to produce an heir to follow Tutankhamun on the throne.

Restoring the religion

The main task of the decade of Tutankhamun's rule was to restore the religion of Egypt – essentially to correct all the changes that Akhenaten had instigated. Tutankhamun started this by abandoning the new capital at Amarna and using Memphis and Thebes as the capital cities of Egypt, as was traditional and expected. Because Tutankhamun was only young, he may have been controlled by his officials: Horemheb (the general and deputy king) and the vizier, Tutankhamun's Uncle Ay.

At Karnak temple, Tutankhamun erected the Restoration Stela, which outlined some of the plans he had for re-establishing the cults and traditions of Egypt:

> *He restored everything that was ruined, to be his monument forever and ever. He has vanquished chaos from the whole land and has restored Maat [order] to her place. He has made lying a crime, the whole land being made as it was at the time of creation.*
>
> *Now when His Majesty was crowned King the temples and the estates of the gods and goddesses from Elephantine as far as the swamps of Lower Egypt had fallen into ruin. Their shrines had fallen down, turned into piles of rubble and overgrown with weeds . . . Their temples had become footpaths. The world was in chaos and the gods had turned their backs on this land . . . If you asked a god for advice, he would not attend; and if one spoke to a goddess likewise she would not attend. Hearts were faint in bodies because everything that had been, was destroyed.*

Tutankhamun needed to find trustworthy staff to work in the new temples and shrines that he was building. He employed men and women from well-known families who were loyal to the old king, Amenhotep III, ensuring that they would uphold the traditions of his time.

Death

For years, theories surrounding the death of Tutankhamun have dominated publications. He died when he was young – only 18 or 19 years old. Figure 4-3 shows the famous face of Tutankhamun.

For many years, historians thought that Tutankhamum had died from a blow to the head, because a small fragment of bone was found floating around inside his skull. However, in 2005, a CT scan was carried out on his mummy, which showed that these bone fractures happened *after* his death, probably caused by Howard Carter and his team when they were trying to remove the golden mask. The CT evidence also shows various fractures and breaks to Tutankhamum's body that may have happened prior to death and probably led to death. One new theory is that he died in a chariot accident.

Figure 4-3:
The Tutan-
khamun
death mask
(Cairo
Museum).

Lethal letters and royal drama

When Tutankhamun died, his elderly vizier, Ay, took over the throne. Tutankhamun's widow, Ankhesenamun, was still a young woman, perhaps only 21 years old, and clearly did not want to relinquish her position as king's wife and the power that accompanied it. She was not keen to marry Ay, who was the only likely candidate for marriage.

Many scholars believe that Ankhesenamun wrote a letter to the Hittite king Suppiluliumas, requesting that one of his sons be sent to her, so that she could marry him and make him king of Egypt. In a letter attributed to Ankhesenamun, she states that she does not want to 'marry a servant', which may be in reference to her prospective marriage to the elderly Ay.

My husband has died. A son I have not. But to you they say the sons are many. If you would send me one son of yours, he would become my husband. Never shall I pick out a servant of mine and make him my husband ... I am afraid.

The Hittite king was naturally suspicious and sent an emissary to Egypt to report on the political situation. The emissaries returned to the Hittite king and reported that the situation was as the queen had written. The queen, in her eagerness to marry a Hittite prince, sent her messenger to the king with another letter. The records show that the messenger, Hani, spoke on her behalf:

Oh my Lord! This is ... our country's shame! If we have a son of the king at all, would we have come to a foreign country and kept asking for a lord for ourselves? Nibhururiya, who was our lord, died; a son he has not. Our Lord's wife is solitary. We are seeking a son of our lord for the kingship of Egypt, and for the woman, our lady, we seek as her husband! Furthermore, we went to no other country, only here did we come! Now, oh our Lord, give us a son of yours.

Such a request from an Egyptian queen was very unusual, and the Hittite king did not believe that it was a genuine request. However, he was convinced by the messenger's words and eventually sent his son Zennanza to Egypt. Unfortunately, the son was murdered before he reached the Egyptian border – perhaps on the orders of Ay, who married Ankhesenamun shortly after.

Re-establishing Imperial Power: Sety 1

Whatever the cause of Tutankhamun's death, his passing was a real nightmare for Egypt. He left no male heir, so the succession to the throne was unclear.

> ✔ Ay (possibly Tutankhamun's great uncle) became king, even though Tutankhamun's army general Horemheb held the title of deputy king. However, Ay was in his 60s when he came to the throne, which was considered old, and he ruled for only four years before he died.

✔ Horemheb succeeded Ay on the throne and ruled for more than 30 years. He continued with Tutankhamun's restoration work.

Horemheb's most important action was to name Pirameses, a general in his army, as his successor. Horemheb could be called the founder of the 19th dynasty because it was he who found and promoted Pirameses (who became Ramses I on taking the throne) among his unruly rabble of military.

Tutankhamun, Ay, and Horemheb started to re-establish Egypt's borders, but the process needed to be continued. Ramses I came to the throne already elderly and ruled for only a short period (1293–1291 BC).

Fighting at Kadesh, Part 1

The reign of Ramses I's son Sety I (1291–1278 BC) saw the introduction of a number of political problems, which were to develop throughout the reigns of Ramses II and Ramses III (see the section 'Fighting the Good Fight: Ramses II', later in this chapter, for more information).

At the beginning of his reign, Sety I launched a series of campaigns to re-establish the boundaries of the crumbling Egyptian empire that had been neglected during the reigns of Akhenaten and Smenkhkare. In his first year in power, Sety embarked on a campaign across Syria, because he was told by his advisors:

> *The Shasu enemy are plotting rebellion! Their tribal leaders are gathered in one place, standing on the foothills of Khor [a general term for Palestine and Syria], they are engaged in turmoil and uproar. Each one of them is killing his fellow. They do not consider the laws of the palace [a euphemism for the king].*

Throughout the journey to Palestine, petty chieftains attacked Sety, but luckily the army had no problems repelling them. These attacks were more irritating than threatening to the king, but they still needed to be dealt with, because the chieftains' actions endangered the trade route that Egypt relied on.

The following year, Sety travelled further north to Kadesh, a fortified town in Syria surrounded by two moats fed from the river Orontes. The Hittites who were in control of the town were at the time stationed on the Syrian coast, leaving the city badly defended. The Egyptians took the city without much effort, and in fact Sety claimed to have made 'a great heap of corpses' of the enemy soldiers.

Despite this victory, Sety didn't have enough military power to put pressure on the Hittites to gain a real stronghold in Syria. The Egyptians held the area for a short while and then it reverted to the Hittites without any further military action. Sety then left, which allowed the Hittites to widen their area of control slowly, moving closer to Egypt.

One down . . . how many more to go?

After the problems at Kadesh, Sety I didn't rest on his laurels. His battle records at Karnak show that he then needed to subdue Libyans who tried to penetrate the Delta borders and squelch Nubian uprisings against Egyptian control.

The term *Libyans* was used by the Egyptians to describe Bedouin tribes of the Western Desert, rather than the inhabitants of modern Libya.

Sety and his army drove the invading Libyans away, and the Karnak relief shows Sety hitting the chief Libyan with a scimitar. That's one way to ensure he doesn't come back. However, the Libyans proved to be a thorn in the side of Ramses III in later years (see the section 'Sailing to Victory: Ramses III', later in this chapter) because they did not give up easily.

The Sety reliefs at Karnak show fortified Syrian towns surrendering to him, with the enemy soldiers fleeing to other towns or to higher ground to get away from the relentless Egyptian army. Sety no doubt led the battles, and, in one scene from Karnak, he has a captive foreign chief under each arm, showing his military prowess in the battlefield.

Fighting the Good Fight: Ramses II

Sety I was succeeded by his son Ramses II (1279–1212 BC). Ramses II has had many names and titles given to him over the centuries, including

- ✔ 'Sese' by his friends and loyal subjects
- ✔ 'Ramses the Great' by explorers of the 18th and 19th centuries AD
- ✔ 'Ozymandias' by Percy Bysshe Shelley when he wrote his poem based on a colossal statue at the mortuary temple of Ramses at Luxor (Ozymandias is a corruption of Ramses's throne name (User-maat-ra-setep-en-ra) by the Greeks)

Maybe you *can* choose your parents

Due to his non-royal origins, Ramses II made a claim of divine birth in order to legitimise his place on the throne (although in reality, because his father was king, he didn't need to).

The divine birth scene at the Ramesseum, Ramses's mortuary temple at Luxor, depicts Amun as Ramses's father. The image shows Ramses's mother, Muttuya, seated on a bed, facing Amun. Amun is holding an *ankh* sign in his right hand and is reaching for Muttuya with his left hand. This (very demurely) represents the divine conception of Ramses.

Further images at Karnak show Ramses's true divine status. In one image, Ramses is born by being moulded on a potter's wheel by the ram-headed god Khnum; in another, Ramses as a child is suckled by a goddess (this scene is repeated in Sety I's mortuary temple at Abydos).

Becoming royal

Ramses II was born in 1304 BC to Sety I and Muttuya, the daughter of the 'Lieutenant of Chariotry' Raia. Ramses II was not royal at the time of his birth because his grandfather, Ramses I, was chosen by Horemheb from within the army to be king because he had a son (Sety I) and a grandson (Ramses II). Ramses had at least two sisters, Tia and Hunetmire, and a brother, although the latter's name has been lost.

In later years, Ramses married at least one of his sisters, Hunetmire, although what she thought of this set-up would be interesting to know. Because Hunetmire and Ramses were non-royal when they were born, suddenly being married just because their family status changed was certainly strange. Luckily for Hunetmire, she bore Ramses no children; theirs may have been a marriage of convenience rather than a marriage in the true sense. (See Chapter 5 for more on Egyptian marriages.)

Marriage and family (and more family)

During the later years of his reign, Sety had named Ramses as co-regent and marked the occasion by giving him his own harem of beautiful women, consisting of 'female royal attendants, who were like the great beauties of the palace', which I imagine was an exciting yet daunting gift for a young boy still in his teens.

Ramses maintained this harem throughout his 67-year reign, and no doubt greatly enjoyed it. But his two favourite wives were Nefertari, whom he married before he came to the throne, and Isetnofret, whom he married in the early years of his reign.

Although Nefertari and Isetnofret were Ramses's favourite wives, his harem is reputed to have contained more than 300 women who bore him more than 150 sons and 70 daughters. A list of Ramses's children is recorded at Karnak in birth order – although these numbers are likely to be greatly exaggerated to show how fertile he was.

In reality, Ramses II had a maximum of 46 sons and 55 daughters. Yes, this figure is lower than his official records show, but is still an awful lot of kids!

Ramses and Nefertari had numerous children, at least ten of which have been recorded, although they sadly all died before Ramses did. Nefertari had at least six sons, whose names and occupations are recorded:

- ✔ **Amenhirwenemef** (first son) was in the army and held the title of general in chief.

- ✔ **Prehirwenemef** (third son) was a teenage veteran of the second battle of Kadesh (see the section 'Following in dad's footsteps: Kadesh Part II', later in this chapter) and was rewarded with the titles 'first charioteer of his majesty' and 'first brave of the army'.

- ✔ **Meriamun** (16th son).

- ✔ **Meritamun** (second daughter) was the consort to Ramses by year 24 and acted as deputy for her sick mother.

- ✔ **Baketmut** (third daughter) is believed to have died young, although her tomb has not been discovered.

- ✔ **Nefertari II** (fourth daughter) is presented on the façade of the main Abu Simbel temple.

- ✔ **Nebettawi** (fifth daughter) was the consort successor to Meritamun after the latter died. She is buried in QV60, which was reused in the Christian period as a chapel.

- ✔ **Henoutawi** (seventh daughter) is represented on Nefertari's temple at Abu Simbel, indicating that she was one of Nefertari's daughters, although she was dead before the temple was dedicated.

Isetnofret, Ramses's other wife, had at least six children:

- ✔ **Ramses** (second son) was a general in the army and crown prince after the death of his half-brother Amenhirkhepshef. In year 30, he was a judge at the trial of a Theban treasury officer and his wife, who were stealing from royal stores.

- ✔ **Bintanath** (first daughter) was married to her father.

- ✔ **Khaemwaset** (fourth son) was crown prince after his brother Ramses had died. Khaemwaset is the most documented of Ramses II's children. At 5–6 years old he went with his father and half-brother Amenhirwenemef to fight in a Nubian campaign. Khaemwaset then became a high priest of Ptah, a god associated with the funerary cults.

- ✔ **Merenptah** (13th son) succeeded Ramses II to the throne. In the last 12 years of Ramses's reign, Merenptah ruled Egypt as a co-ruler and then became king after his father's death.

- ✔ **Isetnofret II** married her brother Merenptah.

Ramses's other children are recorded, although their mothers' names have not been identified; it can be assumed they were born of minor wives or concubines.

The throne eventually passed to Merenptah, Ramses's 13th son born of Isetnofret.

Following in dad's footsteps: Kadesh Part II

Ramses II is well known for many things, but in particular he is remembered for his spectacular battle at Kadesh against the Hittites in the fifth year of his reign. Although Sety had won at Kadesh once, Egypt's lack of military power had enabled the Hittites to encroach on the Egyptian borders. Ramses II needed to put a stop to the Hittites before they got any closer. For the first time in Egyptian history, Egypt was the aggressor in a battle.

The Hittite king had, however, anticipated the attack and gathered a huge army in coalition with a number of neighbouring states – 16 different provinces – which included:

- ✔ 2,500 chariots, each with 3 men
- ✔ Two groups of cavalry totalling 18,000–19,000 men

The Egyptians were greatly outnumbered by the Hittite army with only 20,000 soldiers to the Hittites' 26,000 or so men. At one point, records show that the Egyptians were outnumbered three to one.

Both the Egyptians and the Hittites utilised many of the same weapons, but their styles of attack differed:

- ✔ The Hittites made greater use of hard, iron-bladed weapons than the Egyptians, who mainly used bronze and copper weapons.

- ✔ Egyptian chariots carried two people (a driver and a weapons bloke), while the Hittite chariots carried three men (a driver, a spear thrower or archer, and a shield bearer to protect the other two). While the Egyptian chariots were lighter and had more manoeuvrability, the Hittites were able to move large numbers of men at one time.

- ✔ The Egyptians also employed a group of runners to surround the chariots as they raced into the centre of the enemy amid a shower of Egyptian arrows. The runners then attacked from ground level while the enemy was recovering from the arrow attack.

The battle

Ramses II's army marched to the Levant (modern-day Israel, Jordan, Lebanon, and western Syria) and the site of Kadesh, via the Gaza Strip, in four divisions named after the gods Ptah, Ra, Seth, and Amun (Ramses II led the Amun division).

The Egyptian army forded the Orontes river 20 kilometres upstream from Kadesh, blocking the way north before entering a wooded area nearby. The army was spread over a large area, which resulted in the four divisions becoming separated.

Egyptian scouts then captured two Hittites who offered some information (a little too readily in my opinion):

> Then came two Shosu of the tribes of Shosu tribes to say to his Majesty, 'Our brothers who are chiefs of tribes with the foe of Khatti [Hittites] have sent us to His Majesty to say that we will be servants of pharaoh and will abandon the Chief of Khatti.' His majesty said to them, 'Where are they your brothers who sent you to tell this matter to His Majesty?' and they said to His Majesty, 'They are where the vile Chief of Khatti is, for the foe of Khatti is in the Land of Khaleb to the north of Tunip, and he was too fearful of Pharaoh to come southward when he heard that Pharaoh had come northward.' But the two Shosu who said these words to his majesty said them falsely.

Ramses believed that the Hittites were much further north than he anticipated. The Egyptians continued north to the city, with the Amun division full of confidence that the takeover would be easy, reaching the destination first. As the Amun division approached the city, two more scouts were captured and they revealed that in fact the Hittites were just north of Kadesh and were ready to attack.

Ramses sent an emergency warning to the Ra division behind him, but it was still 8 kilometres away. The Hittites sent 2,500 chariots to the south of the Egyptian camp, under cover of trees, and burst on them from behind. But instead of ambushing the Egyptians unawares, the Hittites came face to face with the Ra division, which was slowly approaching the site from the south. Both sides were very surprised, and as the fleeing Hittite chariots had fallen into the river, blocking it, the new Hittites had nowhere to go but towards the Egyptians.

The Hittites burst through the Ra division, which fled (some back into the woods, some to the hills, some towards the Amun division). Both the Ra division and the Hittites charged at the Amun division at the same time. The Amun division wasn't prepared for the attack and was probably somewhat surprised. Like the Ra division, Amun started to scatter and flee as the Hittites broke through the rudimentary defences of their temporary camp.

Ramses seemed to be the only one to keep his head during this whole ordeal. After saying a quick prayer to Amun, he gathered the chariots and troops nearest him and managed to hold his own against the Hittite onslaught. The texts state that Ramses was fighting the entire Hittite army single handed, which does seem somewhat unlikely – but hey, the Egyptian king *is* a god after all.

Better late than never

Luckily for Ramses, the third Egyptian division, which was travelling along the coastal route (either the division of Set or a crack force of Canaanite mercenaries fighting for the Egyptians), arrived just in the nick of time. Although still greatly outnumbered, the Egyptian army managed to repel the Hittites. (However, in reality, the Hittites only used a small proportion of their army and for some reason decided not to deploy the rest. If they had, this battle would have been the end of Ramses the Great.)

When the Hittites realised that the situation had turned against them, they fled into the fortified town of Kadesh. With the Hittites in the walled town and the Egyptians outside, further fighting was unnecessary. The Egyptians gathered their wounded, cut off the hands of the dead Hittites as an account of the battle, and travelled home claiming a great victory! (Seems more like a giant stalemate.)

Making peace

Sixteen years *after* the second battle of Kadesh, the Egyptians and the Hittites finally halted their hostilities. A peace treaty was drawn up, which is the only complete document of this type discovered in Egypt:

> There shall be no hostilities between them forever. The Great Chief of Kheta [Hittites] shall not pass over into the land of Egypt forever, to take anything from there. Ramses Meriamun [beloved of Amun] the great ruler of Egypt shall not pass over into the land of Kheta to take anything from them forever.

In addition to the Egyptian version of this peace treaty, a Hittite copy was also discovered at the Hittite capital of Hattushash in modern Turkey.

However, as ground-breaking as this treaty was, it only lasted for as long as the kings who signed it, meaning that all the fighting had to be done over again with the next set of kings.

Rushing the Borders: Merenptah

Ramses was succeeded on the throne by his 13th son, Merenptah (1212–1202 BC). Merenptah's reign saw a repeat of the Libyan problems that manifested themselves during the reign of Sety I. The war with the Libyans is recorded on an inscription at Karnak as well as numerous stelae.

In year 5 of Merenptah's reign, the Libyans joined with numerous different tribes. Numbering 25,000 men, these forces were collectively known as the Sea People. They were strong enough to penetrate the Egyptian fortresses along the western Delta and overwhelm the Egyptians on guard duty. The Sea People were clearly travelling to Egypt with a plan to occupy it, because many were accompanied by their families and all their belongings stacked on ox-drawn carts.

Merenptah marched on the Delta with the remainder of the Egyptian army, made up primarily of archers. The army's composition enabled the Egyptians to get close enough to fire hundreds of arrows from their composite bows, but not close enough for the enemy to engage in hand-to-hand combat, which was the Libyans' strength.

Ultimately, this was a victory for the Egyptians. Their records show that they killed 6,000 Libyans and took 9,000 prisoners, including the Libyan chief's wife and children.

This victory enabled the Egyptian people to live in peace once more. Records state that the Egyptians were now able to 'walk freely upon the road' and 'sit down and chat with no fear on their hearts'. Just what everyone wants, really.

Of course, sadly the peace was not to last, as Merenptah's son Ramses III was soon to discover.

Sailing to Victory: Ramses III

Ramses III's reign (1182–1151 BC) was a difficult one. It was beset by invasions, the most important being a further attack from the Libyans and the Sea People.

More battles with the Sea People

The invasion by the Libyans in year 5 of Ramses III's reign was very similar to the one that Merenptah dealt with (see the section 'Rushing the Borders: Merenptah', earlier in this chapter). A 30,000-strong army of a mixture of Libyans and Sea People faced Ramses III. Records note Ramses III killing 12,535 men and taking 1,000 prisoners – a great victory, according to the records anyway.

However, in reality, the Sea People were the first army who were strong enough to take on the Hittites and win, thus controlling trade in the Near East on both land and sea. On land, the Sea People fought in a similar fashion to the Hittites, with three-man chariots. But their seafaring vessels were smaller than the Egyptian boats, without separate oarsmen. Instead, Sea People soldiers rowed the boats, which meant that the soldiers were unable to fight and move at the same time. This was a major disadvantage against Egyptian boats, which had 24 dedicated oarsmen, protected by high sides, plus a contingent of soldiers.

Ramses III faced the Sea People on both land and sea and was successful in both areas. His naval battle is one of the earliest recorded in history. The Egyptian fleet followed the Sea People's fleet of ships into the 'river-mouths of the Delta', trapping them between the Egyptian boats and the shore, where the Egyptian archers were waiting to shower them with arrows. The Sea People didn't stand much of a chance really.

The Egyptians used fire-arrows against the Sea People's ships and killed the majority of the enemy solders. The Egyptian ships then rammed the enemy ships with their decorative prows before seizing the Sea People's ships with grappling hooks and engaging the enemy in hand-to-hand fighting. These manoeuvres finished off the Sea People once and for all. Egypt was at peace once more.

Those pesky Libyans – again

In year 11 of the reign of Ramses III, the Libyans thought they'd have another go at breaking through the borders of Egypt. Ten out of ten for determination at least!

This time, the records show that Ramses III killed 2,175 enemy soldiers and took more than 2,000 prisoners. He then drove the enemy 11 miles into the Western Desert to ensure that they didn't return straight away. (Chapter 5 describes the eventual return of the Libyans.)

At the end of the reign of Ramses III, the glory of the Egyptian empire ended. Ramses III was the last king to rule in true traditional style. Later periods were beset by invasions, divided land, and economic collapse. The empire that Thutmosis III built and Sety I and Ramses II maintained was slowly disappearing – and the Egyptian civilisation was vanishing along with it.

Chapter 5

Looking at the Power Behind the Throne: Royal Women

I once made the mistake, when being introduced to someone, of asking, 'You're Toby's girlfriend, right?' To which this person responded, 'No! I'm Clare.'

To modern women, being acknowledged by their connection to their husbands, brothers, or fathers is clearly not acceptable. In ancient Egypt though, this is exactly how women – especially royal women – were identified. This chapter uncovers the less-than-glamorous lives of these ancient mothers, wives, and sisters. (Chapter 2 has information about the lives of non-royal women.)

Nothing without Him: Considering the Roles of Royal Women

The role and relevance of royal women was defined solely by their relationship with the king. This relationship is identified by a number of titles which appear in temples, tombs, and documents of the period. Consider the titles of royal women:

- ✓ King's Principal Wife (or Great Royal Wife)
- ✓ King's Wife
- ✓ King's Mother
- ✓ King's Daughter

Without the king, royal woman had no status or role within the palace, and obviously the power associated with each role increased as the relationship with the king became closer. Each title gave different power and opportunities to the woman, although keeping the king happy was essential.

Royal weddings: Brothers and sisters

For many years, Egyptologists believed the royal line ran through the females. Thus the king needed to marry an heiress to the throne to legitimise his kingship. This theory developed as a means of explaining brother–sister marriages (common within the royal family, although a taboo for everyone else). However, because many kings didn't marry royal women, this theory has now been dismissed and it's clear that the throne ran through the male line – passed on from father to son.

Although the crown was not passed on via a woman's family, princesses had to be married. The throne ran through the male line, but this only worked if male heirs were available. If there were no male heirs, and a princess married a non-royal, the non-royal would have enough of a claim to take over the throne. Through incestuous marriages, all princesses were effectively married off as soon as possible to prevent non-royals from taking the throne. Princesses might marry their brothers, father, or even grandfather to prevent a coup. Sometimes they got lucky and their father married them to a favoured, well-trusted official – no doubt only after the king had a male heir himself. This practice set the royal family apart from ordinary people; incestuous marriages were only for royalty and gods, which indicated the royal family was truly divine.

However, with the king's express permission, the King's Sister could marry outside the royal family if the chap was accepted and of suitably noble but non-royal birth (for example, a member of the royal court, including high military and administrative officials). Ramses II, for example, allowed his sister Tia to marry an official, also called Tia, who was vetted and greatly trusted.

To make matters even more confusing, the title King's Sister was often given to a wife. This may or may not have been the king's biological sister. In ancient Egypt, 'sister' was used as a term of endearment to refer to a lover, even if that person was not related. Confusing, eh?

The Great Royal Wife and others

Being the Wife of the King – whether his sister or not – wasn't all it was cracked up to be. Wives held no power, and potentially hundreds of women were allowed to hold this title.

The only powerful queen was the Great Royal Wife, who was the equivalent of the 'first lady' in the land. (Although kings normally had only one Great Royal Wife, Ramses II had two: Nefertari and Isetnofret.)

In the Old Kingdom, the Great Royal Wife was entitled to have her own pyramid, and in the New Kingdom, her name was written in a cartouche like that of a king (see Chapter 11 for more on cartouches).

Even though the Great Royal Wife was important, the title wasn't permanent. The king could promote any wife to this position if she pleased him – normally by producing a son if the current Great Royal Wife hadn't, or at the death of the Great Royal Wife. Additionally, this queen only ever played a complementary role to the king, acting as a female counterpart who accompanied him, but never participated in royal rituals or ceremonies that the king carried out.

The king would have a number of children with his many wives, although knowing whether all his wives bore his children is impossible – especially if it was a diplomatic marriage and the woman was sent to a remote harem. In most cases, we only know the name of the Great Royal Wife, sometimes giving the false impression of monogamy. In theory, the sons of the Great Royal Wife were superior to those of lesser wives, and the eldest son would be the heir to the throne.

Burial of a queen

The tomb of Hetepheres (the mother of king Khufu, who built the Great Pyramid) was discovered in 1925 at Giza and was surprisingly intact. Hetepheres may originally have been buried at Dahshur near her husband, Seneferu. Robbers may have violated her tomb and her body, causing her son to rebury her close to his own burial at Giza. However, no tomb has been discovered at Dahshur to support this theory.

The burial chamber at Giza was certainly full of goodies suitable for a queen. In addition to the alabaster sarcophagus and canopic chest (see Chapter 10 for more on these items), the tomb included loads of furniture. The collection has been reconstructed in the Cairo Museum and includes a large canopy frame (which was originally draped with linen to give the queen privacy as she sat beneath it), a carrying chair for when the queen was out on the razz, a couple of armchairs, and a bed.

Hetepheres was also accompanied in the tomb by a number of vessels made of gold, copper, and alabaster. These were originally filled with wine, beer, and oil. Some of the queen's jewellery has also survived and consists of 20 beautiful silver bracelets, each inlaid with turquoise, lapis lazuli, and carnelian dragonflies.

Although Hetepheres's canopic chest contained remnants of her preserved internal organs, the sarcophagus was disappointingly empty. Whether the sarcophagus was empty because the queen was reburied or her remains were stolen continues to be an archaeological mystery.

Honour your mother: The King's Mother

King's Mother was a particularly important female title. A woman could hold this title alongside other titles she may have held before her son became king. In an ideal world, the King's Mother (mother of the current king) was also the King's Principal Wife (wife of the current king's dead father – showing that her son descended from a king), or God's Wife (see the section 'Marrying Amun', later in this chapter). If she didn't hold these titles before her son came to the throne, the son often bestowed them on her as honorary titles after he became king, in order to revere her and reinforce his own divinity and importance by proving he came from a line of kings.

Like the King's Principal Wife, the King's Mother was a semi-divine title and represented the female aspect of divine kingship. Both the King's Principal Wife and the King's Mother accompanied the king in rituals and the worship of the gods, although neither participated.

According to divine birth scenes depicted on temple walls, the only time the King's Mother interacted directly with the gods was when she was impregnated by the god, normally Amun, with the king. And it is probably best that her husband wasn't there to witness her impregnation by another!

Daddy's girl: The King's Daughter

The title King's Daughter was never given as an honorary title, although it was used by both daughters and granddaughters of the king. The King's Daughter was sometimes also the King's Wife, in reference to real or political marriages between the individuals, their fathers, or even their grandfathers. The King's Daughter did not hold any real power other than that from her close relationship with the king.

Some of these father–daughter and grandfather–granddaughter marriages resulted in children, which shows some arrangements were marriages in every sense of the word.

The Politics of Marriage

For royal Egyptian women, getting married was never simple – and certainly not romantic. The women had little or no say in who they married and when, and were simply pawns in a wider political game. The challenges were numerous, as the following sections discuss.

Marriage as foreign relations policy

Most New Kingdom kings had diplomatic marriages to cement alliances between two nations. Political marriages have nothing to do with love and attraction.

A number of letters have been discovered that describe two types of diplomatic marriages:

✔ If the foreign king was on equal terms with the Egyptian king, both parties referred to one other as 'brother', and the arrangements were more on equal terms.

✔ If the foreign country was a vassal state, the Egyptian king was addressed as 'my lord, my god'. These brides were regarded as booty.

Get rich quick

Ramses II had a number of diplomatic marriages. In at least one instance, the negotiation texts have survived. The Marriage Stela of Ramses records a diplomatic marriage in year 35 between Ramses and the daughter of the Hittite king. Ramses seemed quite excited at the prospect of a new wife and rather impatiently sent numerous letters to her parents enquiring as to her estimated time of arrival.

One letter is particularly surprising, as Ramses asks the Hittite queen why her daughter, and more importantly her dowry, was delayed. He even claims the absence of the dowry is taking its toll on the Egyptian economy. Queen Padukhepa, the bride's mother, was not impressed and sent a letter of rebuke back to him:

that you my brother should wish to enrich yourself from me . . . is neither friendly nor honourable

The princess, her dowry, her entourage, *and* her mother (I bet Ramses was pleased about that) eventually travelled to southern Syria, where they were met by the Egyptian authorities. The bride was described as 'beautiful in the heart of his [Ramses's] majesty and he loved her more than anything' and he celebrated the wedding with a long inscription, which gives the impression that the marriage is in fact nothing more than tribute offered by a lesser king to his master:

Then he caused his oldest daughter to be brought, the costly tribute before her consisting of gold, silver, ores, countless horses, cattle, sheep, and goats.

At least he mentioned his wife before the goats. Ramses's new wife had at least one child before being sent to live in the Faiyum region (see the section 'Earning their keep: The harem at the Faiyum', later in this chapter). A laundry list belonging to her has been found and shows that the Faiyum was her home.

This queen soon disappeared from the records, perhaps dying young. Ten years after the marriage – perhaps at her death – the Hittite king agreed to send another daughter and a large dowry to Ramses.

After these diplomatic brides entered Egypt with their entourages of sometimes more than 300 people, they were no longer allowed to communicate with their families for fear that they would give away state secrets. In fact, one letter from the Hittite king to Ramses II enquires after the Hittite king's daughter, who was sent to Egypt as a diplomatic bride, and indicates that there was no communication from her at all. (The Hittites had a large empire, with the capital in Turkey.)

Although Egyptian kings married foreign princesses, Egyptian princesses did not marry foreign princes. This distinction is made very clear in one of the Amarna diplomatic letters following a request from the Babylonian king to Amenhotep III for an Egyptian bride. The Babylonian king is told in no uncertain terms:

> From old, the daughter of an Egyptian king has not been given in marriage to anyone.

This statement would have been rather insulting to the Babylonian king, because his sister was already part of the Egyptian harem.

Vanishing wives

The problem of vanishing wives was particularly rife in the New Kingdom – although it wasn't caused by any supernatural phenomenon or evil wrong-doer. Women were frequently sent to the harem in the Faiyum (see the section 'Earning their keep: The harem at the Faiyum', later in this chapter) never to be heard of again by the king or by the wife's foreign family.

Marrying Amun

As well as marrying the king, royal women might also marry the god Amun. Amun was a solar-creator deity worshipped primarily at Thebes at Karnak Temple. From the 18th dynasty on, the title God's Wife of Amun was very important and held only by royal women.

Taking on responsibility

Ahmose I introduced the title of God's Wife of Amun as a means of honouring his mum Ahhotep (ahh, bless). He gave his wife Ahmose-Nefertari the title of Second Prophet of Amun, which was a title normally held by men only.

As Second Prophet of Amum, Ahmose-Nefertari worked as a deputy to Ahhotep, with the understanding that she would inherit the role.

The title God's Wife of Amun was initially passed on from mother to daughter, although by the 23rd dynasty and the reign of Osorkon III, these royal women were forced to be celibate and had to adopt a 'daughter' to take over the role.

God's Wife of Amun was a position of great power, especially within the temple of Karnak. In the 19th and 20th dynasties, this title enabled the royal family to possess equal power within the temple complex to the High Priests – and through bribery of local officials, that power expanded even further.

Although the names of a number of God's Wives of Amun are known, their exact duties are still unclear. From the 21st dynasty (around 1080 BC), historians know the God's Wives of Amun performed a number of tasks closely associated with kingship, reflecting the power of the role. Specifically, they

- ✔ Wrote their names in cartouches (see Chapter 11 for more information about cartouches)

- ✔ Adopted throne names (a second name after they took the title, a privilege normally reserved for kings)

- ✔ Were depicted in their personal chapels being suckled by the goddess Hathor, which shows their divinity

- ✔ Were addressed by subordinates as 'Your Majesty'

From the reign of Osorkon III (23rd dynasty), the God's Wife of Amun was the power behind the throne. Osorkon forced the High Priest of Amun to donate all his wealth to the God's Wife, diminishing the priest's power. Because the God's Wife of Amun was a relative of the king, she was under his control, which essentially gave the king the power that she held – a cunning if somewhat complicated plan.

In the 23rd dynasty, the God's Wife of Amun also held the title 'God's Hand' in relation to the creation story when the god Atum masturbated to create the next generation of gods. Whether this title had a specific role or ritual associated with it is unknown, but the mind boggles.

Enjoying the privileges

When a queen received the title of God's Wife of Amun, she also received an agricultural estate and personnel. Through these resources, she was able to produce a life-long income, which she kept for herself or used to bribe local officials.

The power associated with being God's Wives of Amun continued into the afterlife. These women were buried in their own small chapels at Medinet Habu. Their tombs were beneath the chapels and included an array of funerary goods befitting their station. Their spirits were nourished through the offering of food and drink in the chapels for a number of years after their death.

The God's Wives of Amun also constructed their own monumental chapels at Karnak temple, which is unusual, because women, royal or otherwise, didn't have their own monuments. (Women were normally depicted on tomb walls and in inscriptions of their husbands.) Yet at Karnak temple, the chapels of the God's Wives of Amun show the women standing before the image of the god Amun, as well as carrying out rituals and ceremonies that the king normally carried out.

Living with the King

Many royal women, whether siblings, wives, or children, rarely – or never – saw the king. The king lived most of the year in his palace in the capital city or travelled the country, staying at various palaces along the way. By contrast, royal women didn't always go with the king and lived in one of several harems sprinkled throughout the country (see the following section).

Harems were secure homes for royal and unmarried elite women. Each harem was a self-sufficient institution with land, cattle, and a number of male attendants (not eunuchs). The royal children lived in a part of the harem known as the household of the royal children. Harems were undoubtedly places of luxury, but royal woman had to stay where they were placed, so freedom was limited.

Location, location, location

The further away a royal wife lived from the king, the further down the royal hierarchy she existed.

The importance of each harem was in direct relation to how close it was to the main residence of the king. The location changed from king to king. A number of New Kingdom harems or women's quarters are known today from various towns in Egypt:

- ✔ Memphis in the north of Egypt
- ✔ Gurob in the Faiyum
- ✔ Malkata, the palace of Amenhotep III

> ✔ The North Palace at Amarna
>
> ✔ Pi-Ramesses, the capital city of Ramses II in the Delta region
>
> ✔ Medinet Habu (the mortuary temple of Ramses III) on the West Bank of Thebes

Each king needed a place to house his many royal wives, so more harems probably existed, although they are now lost. Ramses II is said to have had more than 300 wives, and Amenhotep III is rumoured to have had more than 1,000 women, so more harems are clearly left to find.

Living it up: The harem at Medinet Habu

The favoured wives lived at harems close to the king – such as Ramses III's harem at Medinet Habu, Thebes, the centre of the religious capital of Egypt. Thebes was a very metropolitan city in the New Kingdom – the place to be. The king spent much of his time here. The wives at Medinet Habu travelled the country with the king and stayed at other comfortable and luxurious harems on the way on a temporary basis.

The gateway of Medinet Habu is hollow and is decorated with intimate scenes of Ramses III caressing his wives. The inscriptions on the gateway don't say what it was used for, and for many years Egyptologists believed the gateway itself was the harem. However, logically speaking, the royal women are not going to live in a gateway, at danger from people outside the enclosure wall, and with the added risk of them running away.

The gateway was more probably their holiday home, because in addition to a number of chambers (none of which is a bedroom), the site included a roof complex with small structures enabling the women to sit outside and look at the scenery. From this retreat, they could see the landscape, witness processions and religious rituals, and generally watch the world go by without being seen.

The Medinet Habu women were permanently housed at the palace, firmly within the enclosure walls, which has a number of suites of rooms consisting of a bedroom, a dressing room, and a sitting room. The audience chamber has raised daises, where the King's Principal Wife sat on her throne. The palace also includes two showers, complete with drains for run-off, and a pleasure garden with a lake.

The king clearly visited this harem, as drawings on the Window of Appearances leading from the palace to the first court of the temple show. The king appeared here in festivals to bestow gold jewellery on his favoured courtiers – and then perhaps bestowed other favours on his royal favourites later.

Earning their keep: The harem in the Faiyum

Egyptologists have extensive records from the New Kingdom Faiyum harem – a harem where 'unwanted' women were sent. In this remote site the women were not a part of the king's life and would easily be forgotten. A wife would be unwanted for various reasons. Perhaps the woman was too old to bear any more children, was a diplomatic wife, or the king was simply bored of her.

Royal women must have found it terribly depressing to be sent to the Faiyum harem, because they knew they would never leave. And the king was unlikely to visit Faiyum often, which lessened these women's chances of gaining the king's favour through producing a son.

However, the women at Faiyum were quite productive and worked in the on-site textile workshop, producing linen for the other royal palaces. This activity was a means for them to earn their keep, as well as to help them pass the time. The senior women were probably involved in embroidery and close, fiddly work, as well as teaching newcomers the skills for the job. Women not involved in cloth production performed household tasks. Lower levels of the harem women were responsible for serving the King's Principal Wife and other senior wives. Probably not the lifestyle imagined by many princesses.

The Faiyum harem also had a cemetery, which means that those who lived and died there were also buried there. These women had no chance to get close enough to the king to be buried in the more prestigious Valley of the Queens (see the section 'Burying the queens', later in this chapter). Additionally, young princes were buried at Faiyum as well, showing that these males were low princes with little or no chance of ever becoming heir to the throne.

Burying the queens

The more favoured wives and children of the New Kingdom kings were given a tomb in the so-called Valley of the Queens in Luxor, very close to the Valley of the Kings. The use of the Valley changed over the years, and it wasn't used solely for queens' burials:

- ✔ From the 18th dynasty, the Valley was used for the burial of the royal sons (more than 60 burial shafts in total).

- ✔ From the beginning of the 19th dynasty, queens were buried here, the most famous Nefertari, the wife of Ramses II, who was given a richly coloured tomb.

✔ From the reign of Ramses III (20th dynasty), the royal princes were once again buried here.

✔ From the third intermediate period, the site was used for non-royal burials and continued to be used as a cemetery until the fourth century AD.

The tombs in the Valley of the Queens were smaller than those in the Valley of the Kings and less complex in design. The queens' tombs were carved in inferior rock, and many tombs were abandoned half way through construction, leaving many unfinished tombs in the valley. Those that were completed were plastered and painted rather than being decorated with carved relief. (See Chapter 13 for more on the evolution and construction of tombs.)

Plotting revenge

With a large number of women living in such confined quarters as a royal harem, trouble was bound to pop up. And trouble is certainly what happened in the reign of Ramses III when a bungled assassination attempt known as the 'Harem Conspiracy' was discovered. The trial of the main defendants is recorded on the Harem Conspiracy Papyrus, written during the reign of Ramses IV.

Fourteen men from many walks of life were called to stand as judges – rather like a modern jury. They were given the power to call for any evidence or witnesses needed to conduct the case fairly and were responsible for dispensing the verdict and punishments.

More than 40 people, all close to the king or the harem, were tried for the conspiracy. There were two plots – one to kill the king and the other to cause a fracas outside the palace at the same time, ensuring the king was not as well guarded as usual.

The chief defendant was Ramses III's minor wife Tiy, who wanted her son Pentewere to be king, even though he was not an heir. Her name is real but her son's was changed as a punishment for this crime, which made repeating his true name impossible and denied him an afterlife (see Chapter 10 for more on this funerary belief).

The papyrus records four separate prosecutions:

✔ Twenty-eight people, including the major ringleaders, were all condemned to death, possibly by public execution.

✔ Six people were condemned to commit suicide immediately in the court in front of the judges.

✔ Four people, including Prince Pentewere, were probably condemned to commit suicide within their cells after the trial.

✔ Three judges and two officers were accused of entertaining some of the female conspirators (tut tut). One judge was innocent, but the others were condemned to be mutilated by having their nose and ears cut off. One committed suicide before the sentence was carried out; clearly mutilation was too much for him to bear.

Whether Ramses III would've given the same verdicts is uncertain; he died before the verdicts were pronounced. Some say his death was a direct result of the assassination attempt – the plot thickens!

Remembering the First Feminists

Over the 3,000 years or so of Egyptian history, not many women have stood out as strong personalities or powerful individuals, because they were all overshadowed by the dominant personalities of kings.

However, a few women did make their mark, including some who worked against the system to rule in their own right, and others who had to take things in hand in order to get the job done, either due to weak kings or political circumstances.

Perhaps the following three women were products of circumstance – or perhaps they really were some of the world's first feminists.

Ahhotep: Warrior queen

Queen Ahhotep of the 17th and 18th dynasties was the first powerful royal woman of the New Kingdom, although this was more by accident than design. She was married to Seqenenre Tao II and had at least two sons – Ahmose, the founder of the 18th dynasty, and Kamose. Both Queen Ahhotep's husband and her son Kamose died in the battles against the Hyksos (see Chapter 3), and she watched her youngest son, Ahmose, follow in their footsteps.

While the men in her life were at war, Queen Ahhotep was effectively ruling Egypt from the capital city at Thebes. After her husband died and while her son Kamose was too young to rule alone, she acted as queen regent on his behalf. After her first son's death, she ruled again for her second son Ahmose. This was a very unusual role for a woman, but she was clearly a take-control kinda gal.

During such a politically unstable time, Ahhotep turned her hand to many tasks, not just the administration of the country. An inscription at Karnak goes someway to describe her role as regent with Ahmose:

> *She is one who has accomplished the rites and cared for Egypt. She has looked after Egypt's troops and she has guarded them. She has also brought back fugitives and collected together the deserters. She has pacified Upper Egypt and expelled her rebels.*

This inscription indicates that Ahhotep learnt military skills, which is feasible because the palace was probably overrun with soldiers and generals. She would have dealt with the military men because Kamose and Ahmose were too young to rule alone.

Her funerary equipment reflects these military concerns, because it included a necklace of the Order of the Fly, a military honour rather like a medal. Her tomb also included weapons, such as a jewelled dagger and a lapis axe detailed with Ahmose's cartouche in the centre of a smiting scene.

Hatshepsut: The female king

The most notorious royal woman is Hatshepsut, a queen from the 18th dynasty who eventually ruled Egypt as a king rather than a queen and upset virtually everyone in the country.

When her father, Thutmosis I, died, Hatshepsut married her half-brother, Thutmosis II, and they had a daughter before Thutmosis II died. On his death, Hatshepsut married her husband's son by another wife, and he became Thutmosis III. He was less than three years old when he came to the throne, so Hatshepsut ruled on his behalf until he was old enough to rule alone.

Hatshepsut's shopping trip to Punt

The most spectacular event of the reign of Hatshepsut was a shopping expedition to the city of Punt. The expedition was very lucrative for Egypt, and Hatshepsut was remembered for her participation – even though it was an act of a king and not a queen.

The excursion is recorded on Hatshepsut's mortuary temple at Deir el Bahri in Luxor. The location of Punt has been questioned over the years. Many places, from the Indian Ocean to Somaliland (modern Ethiopia), have been suggested as the location; the only thing that is known is that it was reached via the Red Sea.

The trading expedition was primarily for incense trees. Incense was used extensively in Egypt by the cult of Amun as well as by ordinary people as a fumigator. Because incense was not a natural resource of Egypt, it had to be imported. Ever industrious, Hatshepsut wanted to plant the trees in Egypt and make incense a natural resource.

She did indeed plant these trees along the causeway leading to her mortuary temple, and some of the pits can still be seen today.

In addition to the trees, the expedition brought back a number of other goods that were valuable to the Egyptian economy, including aromatic wood, tree gum, ebony, ivory, gold, eye paint, baboons, monkeys, hounds, panther skin, and labourers.

While in Punt, Hatshepsut's expedition was welcomed by the King and Queen of Punt, the latter depicted as being extremely obese. Images of obese Egyptians and non-Egyptians are highly unusual, so loads of discussion between scholars has developed trying to figure out whether the Queen of Punt has a disease or whether artists were trying to indicate that she was wealthy. No decision has been arrived at, and it doesn't look as if one is likely to be reached any time soon.

Initially Hatshepsut used traditional queenly titles like King's Chief Wife or God's Wife, although after a couple of years she used titles modelled on those of kings, like Mistress of the Two Lands. After seven years, she completely abandoned her queenly titles and adopted the fivefold titulary of a king. She is represented on monuments wearing the masculine attire of a king. She probably figured if she was ruling Egypt in the absence of a king suitable for the job, she wanted the power that went with it.

Many misconceptions about the images in artwork of Hatshepsut dressed as a king have persisted over the centuries – some even stating she was a transvestite! However, in order to be treated as a king in the artwork, she had to be represented as such. Kings are male, so this is how the artists presented her (see Chapter 11 for more artistic conventions). Whether she wandered around the palace in a kilt and a false beard is highly unlikely – and highly inappropriate for a royal woman.

Hatshepsut ruled as king alone for about 15 years and then completely disappears from the records when Thutmosis III took over his rightful place as king. Her body has never been found, so historians don't know if she died of old age (she was about 36 years old in the latest record) or whether she was assassinated. Either way, she made her mark on the history books – even if the later kings tried to pretend she had never existed by erasing her name from documents, monuments, and historical king lists.

Tiye: One scary lady

One woman who is often presented as a dominant individual is queen Tiye, the mother of Akhenaten. In reality, historians don't know whether she was dominant, but she was definitely prominent.

Tiye was married to Amenhotep III and gave birth to a number of children, including Akhenaten. She held the title of King's Great Wife, making her the most important royal woman in the palace.

Tiye is represented in art more frequently than any previous queen (although her daughter in law Nefertiti is depicted as frequently, if not more so – see Chapter 16 for more about Nefertiti). Prior to her reign, 18th-dynasty queens were retiring; they supported their husbands when required, but remained very much in the background. However, in images depicting scenes throughout Amenhotep III's reign, Tiye is shown alongside him in a complementary position, participating in the king's ceremonies and rituals – an unusual practice for queens. She is depicted as the same size as her husband, which indicated equality with him. She is also sometimes represented without him – also very unusual.

Tiye has a reputation for being a strong, formidable woman. Some Egyptologists believe she ruled Egypt in the later years of Amenhotep III's reign, when he was more interested in his harem than politics. Some also believe she influenced Akhenaten in his religious revolution (see Chapter 4).

The influence Tiye held over her husband and son remains unknown, but evidence does show Tiye was privy to diplomatic issues. A letter from a foreign king is addressed to her, in which the foreign king complains that since Akhenaten came to the throne, he has sent only wooden statues covered in gold rather than solid gold statues like the previous king Amenhotep III sent. The foreign king appeals to Tiye to talk to Akhenaten and persuade him to send good-quality gifts. Whether she had words with Akhenaten is not recorded, but I wouldn't have messed with her.

Both Tiye and Amenhotep III were deified in life and were worshipped at the temple of Sedinga at Nubia. Here Tiye was worshipped as the goddess Hathor-Tefnut Great-of-Fearsomeness, and is shown making offerings to herself. This title must have been chosen for a reason. Perhaps she had a fearsome reputation even then. Tiye is also shown in this temple as a sphinx trampling female prisoners, an assertive depiction that places her as a counterpart to her divine king/husband rather than in a supporting role.

Chapter 6

Following the Decline and Fall of the Egyptian Civilisation

*U*ntil the end of the New Kingdom (see Chapter 4), Egypt was a strong, economically solvent, and powerful country, with control over a large number of surrounding areas. Egypt was a country to be reckoned with.

However, by the end of the New Kingdom in the 20th dynasty (1185–1070 BC), the traditional Egyptian culture began to decline. This decline started with a division of the throne of Egypt – from one king to two (and sometimes more) ruling from separate cities. A united Egypt under one king was one of the most important aspect of kingship, so this change did not bode well for ancient traditions.

This chapter ambitiously covers more than 1,000 years of Egyptian history – from the glorious period just after the reigns of Ramses II and Ramses III all the way to the dramas of Cleopatra.

Egyptian history at this point takes numerous twists and turns – some of which modern historians are still working to understand. Try keeping your head straight by focusing on the bigger picture here. While the specifics are interesting, pay more attention to the waves of change and phases of control as led by various groups, cultures, and nations.

To give you an overall sense of the end of the ancient Egyptian empire, these 1,000-plus years can be outlined as follows:

- **Third Intermediate Period (1080–525 BC):** Characterised by numerous rulers reigning at the same time from different regions of Egypt.

- **Late Period (525–332 BC):** Characterised by foreign invasion and regularly changing dynasties.

- **Graeco-Roman Period (332–30 BC):** Began with the invasion of Alexander the Great and resulted in drastic cultural changes due to the influx of the Greeks into Egypt.

Dividing the Two Lands: Ramses XI and After

The decline of the Egyptian empire began during the early years of the reign of Ramses XI (1098–1070 BC).

The power of the king was slowly diminishing due primarily to economic problems. The priests of Amun were gaining in power and wealth. (Rather ironically, the king contributed to this increase in power through a number of gifts, offerings, and building works at the temple of Karnak in Luxor.) Eventually the priests held almost as much power as Ramses XI; the king had control of the army – a difference that kept him one step ahead.

Problems occurred when the Viceroy of Nubia, Panehsy, came into conflict with the high priest of Amun, Amenhotep. Panehsy held the upper hand for nine months, preventing the high priest from carrying out his religious duties. Amenhotep eventually turned to Ramses XI for help.

As a very religious king, Ramses fought against Panehsy. Panehsy was eventually exiled to Nubia, and Amenhotep was reinstated as high priest and remained in the position for a number of years before Herihor succeeded him.

Herihor becomes too big for his boots

Ramses XI maintained his good relationship with the priesthood of Amun and bestowed on Herihor the military titles previously held by the exiled Panehsy. This was a huge mistake, because for the first time one man held religious and military titles, making Herihor more powerful than Ramses.

Herihor made the most of the situation and took over the role of king while poor Ramses XI was still alive. It must have been clear to Ramses that Herihor was just waiting for him to die to complete the transaction. No doubt he watched his back, just in case.

Although Herihor died before he could become a true king, he adopted a cartouche (see Chapter 11) and passed on his elevated position to his son-in-law Piankhy, who also ruled alongside Ramses in the same manner. When Ramses XI eventually died, in 1070 BC, four years after Piankhy's reign started, Piankhy continued to rule Thebes as a king in his own right, albeit only for a few months.

Despite this new elevation of the priests of Amun, their power did not extend outside the Theban region – probably because of a lack of interest on the priests' behalf.

Ruling in the north: Tanis kings

While the high priests of Amun were ruling in the south of Egypt, the north was ruled by Smendes (1069–1043 BC), a man of rather obscure origins. He ruled from the site of Tanis in the eastern Delta (refer to the Cheat Sheet map), built from the remains of Ramses II's city at Pi-Rameses. Smendes legitimised his claim to the throne by marrying a daughter of Ramses XI.

Smendes was followed on the throne by Psusennes I (1039–991 BC), who allowed his daughter to marry the high priest of Amun, Menkhepere. This union indicates that a good relationship existed between the northern and southern rulers.

This generally positive relationship between the north and the south continued throughout the rest of the third intermediate and to a certain extent the late period too. The Tanis dynasty, known as the 21st dynasty, lasted for approximately 350 years, prospering during this time, and improved trade and the economy – even if only those in the north of the country experienced the benefit.

The cemetery of the Tanis kings was discovered in 1939 and included the only intact royal burial to be found in Egypt. (Even Tutankhamun's tomb was robbed in antiquity at least twice.) The artefacts in these tombs were impressive but did not get the recognition they deserved, because the media were tied up reporting the Second World War. Interesting discoveries included:

- ✔ **The burial assemblage of Psusennes I.** Psusennes's mummy featured a gold death mask and a solid silver anthropoid (human-shaped) coffin. These items were placed inside a sarcophagus that was originally used by Merenptah, the son of Ramses II, which shows that trade between the north and south of Egypt was active, despite the north and south being ruled by different kings.

- ✔ **The coffin of Sheshonq I.** Sheshonq's coffin is beautiful and unique – a silver, falcon-shaped box. In fact, silver was more valuable than gold because it was not native to Egypt. The use of silver highlights the wealth of the Tanis dynasties and indicates that their trade relations were strong.

Briefly uniting the two lands: Sheshonq I

The 21st Tanis dynasty was followed by the 22nd dynasty (945–745 BC), the members of which also ruled from Tanis but are believed to be of Libyan origin. The first king of the period is Sheshonq I (945–924 BC), who legitimised his claim to the throne by marrying a daughter of Psusennes II, the last king of the 21st dynasty.

Sheshonq seems to be a Libyan chieftain – specifically a leader of the Meshwesh, a Libyan nomadic tribe. Sheshonq held military titles and adopted the royal titles of Smendes, who had ruled more than 100 years previously. These titles gave his claim to the throne a bit of a kick start.

Although he was Libyan, Sheshonq I reunited the divided Egypt and effectively ruled both Upper and Lower Egypt, which was especially important for him to be accepted as a true king of Egypt. He managed to gain control over the south of Egypt because his son held the title of high priest of Amun, uniting the northern throne and the southern priesthood.

The end of Sheshonq's peace

Despite Shehonq I's best efforts to rule a unified Egypt and maintain the military prowess of the Egyptian nation, the end of the 22nd dynasty caused unrest and national division. Although the priesthood of Amun was now under the control of the northern king through family ties, near the end of the dynasty the high priesthood experienced a gap in succession that resulted in a civil war lasting for more than a decade.

After this civil war was over, the peace was short lived with further uprisings and hostilities that caused not only north–south divisions but even east–central divisions in the Delta between chiefs of Leontopolis (central) and Tanis (east). The harmony of the reign of Sheshonq I was slowly collapsing into chaos.

Too many kings

The problems in the Delta eventually saw a dynastic change while the seventh king of the 22nd dynasty, Sheshonq III, was still ruling from Tanis.

Three more kings ruled over the next 100 years until the end of the 22nd dynasty, but in the meantime many other rulers emerged throughout the

Delta. Notable among these was Pedibast, a local chieftain in Leontopolis, who took over the rule of the central Delta and split the rule of Egypt into three sections. Members of both Pedibast's and Sheshonq's families (east) travelled south to join the priesthood of Amun, ensuring that royal connections existed with this powerful faction.

Towards the end of the 23rd dynasty, the introduction of yet another dynasty of kings brought about further divisions:

✔ King Sheshonq III at Tanis (22nd dynasty)

✔ King Iupet at Leontopolis (23rd dynasty)

✔ King Peftjauabastet at Herakleopolis (23rd dynasty)

✔ King Nimlot at Hermopolis (23rd dynasty)

✔ King Tefnakht at Sais (24th dynasty)

Each of these kings ruled only a small area, but all took the full title of king and wrote their names in cartouches. Everyone seemed happy with the arrangement and left one another alone.

However, at the end of the period (around 727 BC), a much bigger threat emerged that stopped any further divisions from developing – the power of Nubia. In fact, this new threat encouraged the kings to join together and work in harmony.

Libyan liberator

In 925 BC, Sheshonq I went to war with Palestine and proved that Egypt's military was still a force to be reckoned with. His campaign has even been compared to that of Ramses III against the Sea People (see Chapter 4). When King Solomon died in 930 BC, his son Rehoboam ruled Judah, and Jeroboam I (the first king of the tribe of Ephraim to rule Israel) ruled Israel. These rulers were in the throws of a civil war when Sheshonq decided to prove that Egypt was still great.

The Egyptian army first marched to Judah and camped outside the walls of Jerusalem, which was governed by King Rehoboam. The Bible records that Sheshonq (Shishak) was bribed with a great deal of gold and the much coveted Ark of the Covenant so that he would not enter and sack the city.

Sheshonq continued his march to Israel until he reached Megiddo, the site where Thutmosis III fought his famous battle (see Chapter 4). Sheshonq erected a stela at this site to commemorate his victory against ancient Israel. He further recorded his victories in the quarries of Gebel Silsila and at Karnak temple.

Exerting Pressure from the South: Nubian Influences

Around 727 BC, the power and influence of the Nubians were spreading north from their homeland as far as the Theban region. If Nubians travelled further north, they may interfere with the tranquillity of a divided north. The northern kings of the 22nd (Tanis), 23rd (Leontopolis), and 24th (Sais) dynasties therefore joined forces to enable them to deal with the Nubian group of rulers (25th dynasty) to prevent the latter's power from expanding further.

Growing power

Nubia had never really been a threat to the Egyptians before. Until the reign of Ramses II (see Chapter 4), the area had been firmly under the control of the Egyptians, who exploited the Nubians' quarries and gold mines. After Ramses II's strength faded, Nubia began to distance itself from the Egyptians and managed to form its own capital city in Napata (near the fourth cataract of the Nile).

During the 21st dynasty, the high priests of Amun gained a great deal of influence over Nubia and even built a large temple to Amun at Gebel Barkal, within Nubian territory. The Nubian priests of this temple also expanded their power throughout the surrounding area and eventually usurped the Nubian kingship.

These Nubian kings used titles and cartouches in the manner of traditional Egyptian kings. After the Nubian dynasty had established itself, it started to move northwards to Egypt, where the Egyptian kingship was obviously in a weakened state because of its numerous divisions. The Nubians saw their advance as an opportunity to turn the tables and control Egypt for a change.

Egypt's the limit: Piankhy

The Nubian king Piankhy (sometimes Piye) confronted the four northern kings of the 22nd–24th dynasties in 727 BC and was victorious against them. Although he stripped them of their kingly titles, Piankhy did allow them to have a certain amount of power in their new positions as local governors, which in all honesty may not have been a great deal different from their roles as petty kings of small regions.

In order to reinforce his position as Egyptian king fully, Piankhy took over the priesthood of Amun, which gave him ultimate power over the Theban region. The kings who succeeded him maintained this connection with the cult of Amun, both in Thebes and in Nubia.

Despite this affiliation with the cult of Amun in Thebes, Piankhy chose to rule from the Nubian capital of Napata. He was buried in a pyramid at el-Kurru, north of Gebel Barkal. Later rulers were also buried in pyramids. These pyramids were very different from the Old Kingdom Egyptian pyramids (see Chapter 14) because they were small but tall and narrow. Many of the Nubian pyramids have produced a number of grave goods, including gold jewellery.

The successor of Piankhy, his son Shabaka, increased the area controlled by the Nubian dynasty to include all of Egypt from the south to the north up to the boundary of the Sais region in the Delta.

Conquering the Near East: The Assyrians

At the same time as Nubian influence over Egypt was expanding, the Assyrian empire was also expanding throughout the Near East. Several Assyrian uprisings happened close to the Egyptian borders, but the Nubian kings quashed these.

However, by the reign of Nubian pharaoh Taharqa (690–664 BC), the Assyrians and the Nubians had engaged in numerous confrontations. Both sides had gained the upper hand alternately, showing that they were equally matched. The situation must have been quite unnerving for the new Nubian dynasties that hadn't long gained the coveted prize of rule over Egypt.

In 671 BC, the Assyrian king, Esarhaddon, actually entered Egypt, gaining control of the north as far as Memphis. This meant that King Taharqa had to flee to the south of Egypt. Although they maintained their control over the Delta, the Assyrians left, only to return in 669 BC. However, Esarhaddon died on the way and was succeeded by his son Ashurbanipal, who finally gained control of Egypt.

Ashurbanipal eventually took control over Thebes in 661 BC, making him the king of Upper and Lower Egypt. This caused Taharqa and his successors to flee further south to the Nubian capital, Napata, outside the boundaries of Egypt, never to enter Egypt again.

The Saite Period: Psamtik 1 and Others

After 665 BC, the Assyrians were in control of Egypt – although they chose local people to take the role of the king, under their rule, of course. Egypt was now a vassal state of the Assyrian empire. The capital city was located at Sais in the Delta, and the kings of the Saite period formed the 26th dynasty. (Because the Nubian 25th dynasty was still in control when the Assyrians captured the north, these two dynasties occurred concurrently.)

Psamtik I (664–610 BC) of the Saite 26th dynasty was given the job of consolidating Assyrian control throughout Egypt, including Thebes. Psamtik sent his daughter Nitocris to the temple of Amun at Karnak, where she was given the priestly title of God's wife of Amun, which placed her rather high in the cult hierarchy. This combination of royal and religious power – as well as the cult's wealth – ensured that the north and south were ruled by one individual.

This unified Egypt was not stable, however, and Psamtik was forced to gather an army to deal with numerous petty chieftains who had arisen in the Delta. The chieftains all wanted a slice of Egypt to control, and the Assyrians wanted a single ruler who was easier to control.

Returning to traditions

Throughout the 50 years or so of Psamtik's reign, he brought a number of changes to Egypt. He tried to bring Egypt back to the traditions of the past, to show a continuity of the culture. To do this, he reintroduced a number of religious, artistic, and ritual elements from the Old and Middle Kingdoms.

However, being a truly traditional king in a traditional Egypt meant freedom from foreign influence. The elimination of outside influence was difficult to achieve, but that was what Psamtik I did. In 653 BC, after a number of internal problems had weakened the Assyrians, Psamtik broke free from the Assyrians and gained control of Egypt in his own right. This separation meant that Egypt was once again the driving force of the Near East.

In the navy

Psamtik's successor, Nekau II, continued to improve Egypt's status in the Near East and took control of Syria-Palestine once again. Nekau formed the first official Egyptian naval service, which included a number of Ionian Greeks. Prior to this, Egypt had been primarily a riverine nation with no real need for a navy.

During the 26th dynasty, Egypt enjoyed increased commerce with the Greeks, whose trade network was growing immensely. In order to increase the scope for trade in Egypt, Nekau began the construction of a canal joining the Wadi

Tumilat to the Red Sea – 2,500 years before the Suez Canal was formed for the same purpose. The completed canal was wide enough to navigate a trade fleet through and changed Egypt's trade relations.

Appeasing the masses

Because of increased trade relations during this period, a number of foreign immigrants settled in Egypt, primarily in the Delta region. Initially they were relatively peaceful, but throughout the reign of Ahmose II (known as Amasis; 570–526 BC), numerous civil wars flared up between different foreign groups.

Ahmose tried to limit these conflicts by giving specific trading rights to foreigners living in the Delta town of Naukratis, thus creating a sort of 'free zone' for immigrants to Egypt. Some may view this action as a little unfair to the native Egyptians living there, but at least the fighting stopped, which further encouraged trade relations and foreign immigration to Egypt.

Not even cold yet

Psamtik's separation from the Assyrians (see the section 'Returning to traditions', earlier in this chapter) led to the gradual decline and eventual collapse of the Assyrian empire, and meant that Egypt was once again the most powerful nation in the region. This status did not last long, because everyone wanted to fill the gap left by the Assyrians. The weakened Assyrian kings were under attack from many people, including:

- Babylonians under king Naboplassar
- Medes (ancient Iranians)
- Scythians (Ukrainian and Southern Russians)

The Assyrians even asked Psamtik (who had separated from them) to help with these attacks. Even so, the Assyrians lost, and in 612 BC the Assyrian empire ended with the fall of Nineveh under the attack of the Persian army.

The celebration of the collapse of this once-great empire was short lived for the Egyptians, because the Persians soon marched on Egypt, entered its borders and took over the throne in 525 BC. The inexperienced king, Psamtik III, tried to stop the Persians from gaining control of Egypt. However, Psamtik III was eventually chased to Memphis before being captured and transported to the Persian capital as a prisoner of war, leaving Egypt unguarded and without a king.

Yet again, invasion led to *another* set of kings and yet *another* dynasty (the 26th), starting the late period of Egyptian history.

Settling of the Persians

The Persian 27th dynasty lasted for more than 100 years (525–404 BC) and is recorded by Herodotus. He records three potential reasons for the Persian king Cambyses II invading Egypt in the first place, although Herodotus wasn't sure of the reliability of any of these explanations:

- ✔ Cambyses wanted an Egyptian concubine and was sent a second-rate noblewoman instead of a princess, so he invaded Egypt.
- ✔ Cambyses may have been half-Egyptian, perhaps the illegitimate son born of a daughter of the Saite king Apries.
- ✔ Cambyses made a promise as a child to invade Egypt in revenge for an insult paid to his mother.

If Herodotus wasn't sure why Cambyses invaded Egypt, how on earth can modern historians be? Whatever the specific inspiration, the Persian invasion was a nasty one, aided by the Bedouins who led the way to the Egyptian borders. After the Bedouins and the Persians arrived, they were violent and cruel and even removed the embalmed body of the Saite king Ahmose (Amasis) and set fire to it. Granted, the Egyptians were not so nice either.

In revenge for a mercenary general's betrayal, the Egyptians paraded his two sons in front of him and the Persian army and slit their throats. The blood was collected in a large bowl, mixed with water and wine, and drunk by all the soldiers. However, in the same way that Herodotus had doubts about the stories of Cambyses, perhaps this description was also an exaggerated myth. No other records exist of the Egyptians drinking human blood.

Ruling Egypt from a distance

Although Cambyses and the Persians had taken on the Greeks and the Egyptians and won, they didn't fancy staying in the country of their victory. Cambyses lived and was buried in Persia (modern Iran). During his reign (525–522 BC) he hired a provincial governor to rule in Egypt on his behalf – although he was represented in Egypt as an Egyptian with his names written in a cartouche as a traditional ruler.

However, Cambyses's successor Darius I (521–486 BC) took a lot of interest in Egypt. He built a number of temples and instigated repairs from the Delta to Aswan. Darius also continued and completed the building of the canal between the Wadi Tumilat and the Red Sea that Nekau of the Saite 26th dynasty started.

In 486 BC, despite the positive influence that Darius had on Egypt, the Egyptians revolted. This revolt was not crushed until the next king, Xerxes, came to the throne. His reign (485–465 BC) was not a peaceful one, and later in his reign the Greeks invaded Egypt.

After a short period of respite, Xerxes was assassinated amid another Egyptian revolt. This fighting went on for some time, with the Persian king being defeated by descendants of the 26th dynasty from the Delta along with the aid of Greek mercenaries.

The Egyptians were finally able to gain control during the reigns of the final two kings of the Persian period, Darius II (423–403 BC) and Artaxerxes II (405–359 BC), following a number of problems within the Persian family, which weakened their defences and left them open for attack.

Yet more dynasties

The decline of the Egyptian culture was really on the final stretch by 400 BC, with kings taking control willy-nilly and causing a great deal of confusion. Perhaps the situation was less confusing for the ancient Egyptians!

- **The 28th dynasty** (404–399 BC) consisted of only one very little-known king called Amyrtaeus, who had succeeded after six years of guerrilla warfare against the Persian kings to bring the throne back to Egyptian control. He briefly gained control of the whole of Egypt, from his capital at Sais in the Delta down to the Aswan border.

- **The 29th dynasty** (399–380) moved the capital from Sais to Mendes further south, which indicates that the Egyptian's control was still widespread. Mendes was certainly better placed for government. The two kings of this dynasty were also probably buried at this site, although they have not been discovered yet.

- **The 30th dynasty** (380–343 BC) was a little more substantial, with a total of three kings. These kings spent a great deal of time supervising building according to ancient traditions to show some continuity between their reign and the earlier dynasties.

This dynasty was also involved in a number of battles defending Egypt from Persian invasion (yet again – they don't give up!).

Nectanebo II was given a short respite from Persian attack because of more Persian internal quarrels and conflicts with the Greeks and the Levantines. In 343 BC, Nectanebo II, with the Egyptian army and 20,000 Greek mercenaries, guarded the Delta borders against a major Persian attack led by Artaxerxes III. The borders were soon penetrated, and the Delta and then Memphis fell to the Persian invaders. Nectanebo fled to Nubia, but shortly afterwards disappeared; presumably he died.

The death of Nectanebo II in 343 BC was a major blow to Egypt for a couple of reasons. First, the Egyptians were yet again under the rule of the Persian kings. Second, Nectanebo was the last Egyptian ruler to govern the country until the first president of the Republic of Egypt, General Muhammad Naguib, in AD 1953. That is a long period of foreign rule.

Another round of Persian rule

The end of the reign of Nectanebo II saw the start of the second Persian period (343–332 BC). The Persians were again a little harsh to their adopted country. The Greek records describe how the Persians razed cities to the ground, robbed temples, killed a number of sacred animals, and taxed the population until the people were broke.

Once again, the Persian kings ruled though a governor while residing in Persia. This dynasty (which some historians consider the 31st) only lasted for 10 years, with the first two kings, Artaxerxes III and Arses, being assassinated, and the cowardly Darius III opening the borders of Egypt in 332 BC to allow Alexander the Great to enter Egypt.

Invading Macedonians: Alexander the Great

The assassination of Phillip II of Macedonia in 336 BC saw the start of Alexander's attack on the Persian empire. Alexander was the son of Phillip and felt that he should continue with his father's campaign. Alexander came to Egypt in 332 BC, which instigated a further decline in the ancient Egyptian culture. If the Persians had not occupied Egypt at this time then perhaps Alexander would have left it alone, producing a very different end to the story.

Becoming divine

Alexander wanted to be accepted into the Egyptian culture. One of the first things he did was to travel to Siwa to consult the oracle of Amun (see Chapter 9 for information on oracles) in order to prove that he was the divine son of the god and therefore a legitimate king of Egypt.

Alexander's coronation was carried out in the traditional centre of Memphis, and to a certain extent he ruled in a traditional Egyptian manner. He saw the renovation of Luxor temple with some elaborate images of himself making offerings to Amun-Min.

Alexander, however, left Egypt to continue his campaigns across the Near East. Before his death in 323 BC, Alexander had extended the Macedonian empire, which included Egypt, all the way to the Indus Valley. Being part of the vast empire brought new rich and exotic imports to Egypt.

Making Egypt a home of his own

When Alexander the Great was not invading and conquering nations, he concentrated on the administration of Egypt. Specifically he:

- **Introduced a monetary system to Egypt,** which had previously relied on a bartering system. The coins introduced by Alexander bore a Hellenistic image of himself on one side and an image of an Egyptian god on the other, showing the juxtaposition of the two cultures.

- **Founded the city of Alexandria,** which became the capital of Egypt at this time. The city was built on the site of an ancient Egyptian settlement called Raqote (also spelt Rakhotis), although not much of this ancient town has survived. Alexander left the building works to his architect Deinokrates and an official called Kleomenes.

Alexandria was large – at its height it had a population of more than half a million including a large number of Greek and Jewish immigrants. It was a very cosmopolitan city and included many famous buildings, such as a library and a museum that were sadly burned down in antiquity. The later city included Roman baths, a theatre, and a gymnasium. The larger houses of the Roman settlement were even decorated with mosaics in true Roman style, as Figure 6-1 shows.

The city of Alexandria was not complete until the reign of Ptolemy II (285–246 BC). Ptolemy I (305–282 BC) started building the Pharos lighthouse in Alexandria, which was one of the Seven Wonders of the Ancient World and the world's earliest lighthouse. This structure has long since disappeared – and may be on the bottom of the sea.

Figure 6-1: Villa of the Birds, Kom el Dikka, Alexandria.

Alexander the Great died in 323 BC of a fever, leaving no obvious heir to take over his empire. His death led to the gradual collapse of the Macedonian empire, with various generals splitting to their own favoured areas.

Ending the Empire: The Ptolemaic Dynasty

Following the death of Alexander the Great and the collapse of his control over the Persian empire, many petty wars and battles ensued, fought by Alexander's generals. Everyone (especially Alexander's generals) tried to win a slice of the empire.

Ptolemy eventually returned to Egypt as governor under Phillip Arrhidaeus (323–317 BC), the successor to Alexander the Great's son Alexander IV (317–305 BC – born after his father's death). During the reign of Alexander IV, Ptolemy, his childhood friend, was effectively ruling, and on Alexander's death Ptolemy became king in his own right. By 301 BC Ptolemy had gained control of Palestine and Lower Syria, starting a small empire of his own.

However, Egypt could have done with a ruler with more imagination, as Ptolemy started a dynasty of rulers all called Ptolemy (up to Ptolemy XV), and queens called either Cleopatra (seven ruled as queens) or Berenice (four ruled as queens). Can you imagine the chaos when calling your kids in for dinner if they all answered to the same name?

The Ptolemaic dynasty was an example of the juxtaposition between two very different cultures – the ancient Egyptians and the Greeks. The rulers supported the traditional religion of Egypt and contributed to many temples, including building the temples of Dendera, Edfu, Philae, and Kom Ombo. On the walls of all these temples the kings are displayed in traditional Egyptian costume and pose, yet on the coins minted at the time they are presented in traditional Hellenistic fashion.

Sleeping with one eye open

Those in the Ptolemaic family were not a nice group of people. This may sound like a sweeping statement, but this family was obsessed with the power of the throne and did anything to keep this power. They were notorious for marrying their brothers and sisters as a means of legitimising claims to the throne or keeping the throne within the family. (Of course, many ancient Egyptian kings married within their families as well, but not all these marriages ended in children. The Ptolemaic marriages were consummated – regularly.)

Despite these very close family connections, the Ptolemaic family had absolutely no qualms about bumping off their brothers, sisters, husbands, and wives in order to rule alone – or about disposing of unpopular or unsuitable individuals.

As a member of this terrifying family, you really needed to be on your guard. A number of sovereigns and officials were murdered or died in a suspicious manner:

- Phillip Arrhidaeus was assassinated by one of his bodyguards.

- Berenice II was poisoned and scalded to death by her son Ptolemy IV.

- Ptolemy IV's wife, Arsinoe, was poisoned by the brother of Ptolemy's secondary wife, Agathoclea.

- Ptolemy VII was killed by his stepfather and uncle Ptolemy VIII (who was nicknamed Potbelly and was very unpopular).

- Memphites was murdered by his father, Ptolemy VIII, who sent the dismembered body to his sister/wife, Cleopatra II, as a birthday present. (I'm sure she'd have preferred some bath salts!)

- Cleopatra III was possibly murdered by her younger son, Ptolemy X (although, earlier in life, her older son, Ptolemy IX, was accused of plotting to murder her).

- Berenice, the daughter of Ptolemy IX, was murdered within a month of marrying Ptolemy XI. He disliked her and wanted the throne to himself. To be fair, Berenice probably didn't think much of him either.

- Ptolemy XI was lynched by the public after ruling for only 19 days, because Berenice had been very popular.

- Berenice (another one!), the daughter of Ptolemy XII, was murdered by the Romans because of her revolt against her father as she tried to take over the throne. Ptolemy XII asked Julius Caesar, dictator of Rome, for help.

- Ptolemy XIV, the brother and husband of Cleopatra VII (of Mark Antony fame), was probably disposed of by the queen so that she could promote her son Ptolemy XV to the throne, protecting him from the Romans.

The majority of these murders were about power and the throne. However, during many struggles with the Ptolemaic family, Rome was conscripted in to help sort out the arguments. Although Roman involvement ensured that someone won the arguments and had the support and power of Rome behind them, Rome did not forget the debts incurred while aiding the warring Ptolemies. And during the reign of Cleopatra VII, Roman leaders came to collect the debt – eventually leading to the final collapse of the Egyptian civilisation.

Making romantic history: Cleopatra and Mark Antony

The story of Cleopatra and Mark Antony is one of the most famous tragic love stories in the world. This story stars Cleopatra VII, born in approximately 70 BC – the daughter of Ptolemy XII (nicknamed the flute-player) and his sister Cleopatra V. Strange to think, Cleopatra's mother is also her aunt and her father is also her uncle.

Ptolemy XII was not very popular in Egypt because of his sycophantic attitude to Rome. He was also a weak and cruel ruler (which probably made him fit well into the Ptolemaic family). In 60 BC, Ptolemy XII's unpopularity had reached such proportions that he fled Egypt for the safety of Rome, while his eldest daughter, Berenice, took the throne. After a number of years, and with the support of Rome, Ptolemy returned to Egypt and reclaimed his throne. He ruled until his death in 52 BC when Cleopatra VII, aged 19 and married to her 10-year-old half-brother Ptolemy XIII, took over the throne.

Because her husband was so young, Cleopatra ruled Egypt virtually alone and even omitted Ptolemy's face from her coins. Unlike her father, Cleopatra was a popular ruler with the Egyptian people – probably because she was the only Ptolemaic ruler who had bothered to learn to speak Egyptian!

Spinning a web of deceit

Ptolemy XIII's spin doctors used the populace's affection for the queen against her by issuing a decree in her name that all available grain should be sent to Alexandria and none to Middle and Upper Egypt. This angered the Egyptian populace, and they turned against Cleopatra. Cleopatra fled in fear of her life to Ashkelon in Syria.

In 48 BC, Julius Caesar headed towards Egypt to sort out the hostilities between Ptolemy XIII and Cleopatra. At the same time, Cleopatra herself had gathered an army on Egypt's border to charge against her brother.

Caesar arrived in Alexandria determined to put Cleopatra back on the throne, until Ptolemy's courtiers brought him a gift – the head of one of Caesar's friends. This didn't exactly endear the young boy-king to Caesar, and Caesar marched into the city, seized the palace, and generally took charge.

Both Ptolemy and Cleopatra were ordered to dismiss their armies and meet with Caesar, who would settle their dispute (rather like a father and two naughty children). Cleopatra, however, was far from daft and knew that if she entered Alexandria openly, Ptolemy would have her killed. So she sneaked into the palace inside an oriental rug. When the rug was unrolled, Cleopatra fell out and Caesar fell in love.

They became lovers that night and by morning Ptolemy stormed out of the palace because he felt he had been betrayed. He was arrested shortly after, but his army laid siege to the palace. Caesar released Ptolemy, but the siege continued for almost six months and only ended when Ptolemy drowned in the Nile. Alexandria then surrendered to Caesar.

Now a widow, Cleopatra married her brother Ptolemy XIV, who was 11 or 12 years old. Julius Caesar gave them Cyprus as a wedding gift. His own interest in Cleopatra had been awakened.

Enjoying lazy summer days with Julius

The relationship between Cleopatra and Julius Caesar developed, and in 47 BC they went on a romantic Nile cruise. Cleopatra was only 23 years old and pregnant with Caesar's child, nicknamed Caesarion. The baby was born not long after they returned to Alexandria.

In the temple of Hathor at Denderah, a sculpted relief (see Figure 6-2) shows Cleopatra presenting her son Caesarion to the gods and naming him 'Ptolemy Caesar son of Julius Caesar and Cleopatra' to show that he was the heir to the throne.

Figure 6-2:
Cleopatra
and
Caesarion at
Denderah.

More brains than beauty

Despite Hollywood's depiction of Elizabeth Taylor as the Queen of the Nile, Cleopatra does not have a reputation as a great beauty. She was, however, considered witty, charming, intelligent, and bursting with sex appeal.

The Greek historian Plutarch (46–127 AD) records that Cleopatra spoke a total of eight languages, including several African languages, Hebrew, and Aramaic, plus her native Greek. She was also the only Ptolemaic ruler to speak Egyptian, which endeared her to the Egyptian population. Historians have suggested that her father taught her these languages because he was looking further afield than the boundaries of Egypt for eventual rule.

For pleasure, Cleopatra studied fragrant and protective unguents and wrote a beauty book on how to mix these substances to moisturise and protect the skin. While no copies of this book have been discovered, the Romans recorded its existence.

In 46 BC, Cleopatra, Ptolemy XIV, and Caesarion went on a holiday to Rome to visit Julius Caesar. They stayed in Caesar's villa near Rome for almost two years – now that's a holiday and a half. During this time, Julius gave Cleopatra a ton of gifts and titles and even erected a statue of her in the temple of Venus Genetrix. The Romans were horrified at this affair, and it eventually led (in part) to Julius's assassination in 44 BC.

Cleopatra, in fear for her own and her son's life, scurried back to Egypt. Before or on their return to Egypt, Cleopatra's husband Ptolemy XIV mysteriously died at age 15, possibly poisoned, leaving Cleopatra free to marry her son Caesarion and make him her co-regent, Ptolemy XV.

Enter Mark Antony

At the death of Caesar, the Roman empire was divided among three men: Caesar's great-nephew Octavian, Marcus Lepidus, and Marcus Antonius, better known today as Mark Antony.

Cleopatra had met Mark Antony when she was 15, while her father was alive, when Mark Antony had travelled to Egypt in support of Julius Caesar. The next time Cleopatra met Mark Antony, in 42 BC, she was 28 years old and he was over 40. Mark Antony had taken over the eastern section of the Roman empire and was to spend a great deal of time in Egypt over the next 16 years.

Living it up

Mark Antony and Cleopatra's relationship was a jovial one, as recorded by Plutarch:

> *She played at dice with him, drank with him, hunted with him; and when he exercised in arms, she was there to see. At night she would go rambling with him to disturb and torment people at their doors and windows, dressed like a servant-woman, for Anthony also went in servant's disguise . . . However, the Alexandrians in general liked it all well enough, and joined good-humouredly and kindly in his frolic and play.*

Over the next four years of the relationship, Cleopatra bore twins: Alexander Helios (the sun) and Cleopatra Selene (the moon). Antony acknowledged paternity of both children and actually offered Alexander in marriage to the king of Armenia's daughter in an attempt to appease a quarrel. The king of Armenia refused, and Antony attacked him in 34 BC. That taught him.

In 37 BC, on his way to invade Parthia, Antony enjoyed a rendezvous with Cleopatra, even though Octavian had married Antony to Octavian's sister Octavia as a means of preventing Antony from returning to Egypt. Despite this, from then on Alexandria was Antony's home and Cleopatra was his life. Antony married Cleopatra in 36 BC in Antioch in North Syria, where he dressed as Osiris and she dressed as Isis.

Shortly after this wedding, Cleopatra gave birth to another son, Ptolemy Philadelphus, whom Antony also acknowledged. In 34 BC, Antony made Alexander Helios the king of Armenia, Cleopatra Selene the queen of Cyrenaica and Crete, and Ptolemy Philadelphus the king of Syria.

The beginning of the end

Antony completely abandoned his Roman wife, Octavia, which upset the Romans and Octavian. After three years, Octavian decided to rule alone and turned on Cleopatra and Antony. In 31 BC, Antony's forces fought the Romans in a sea battle off the coast of Actium (northern Greece), aided by Cleopatra and 60 Egyptian ships.

When Cleopatra saw that Antony's cumbersome, badly manned galleys were losing to the Romans' lighter, swifter boats, she fled the scene. Antony abandoned his men to follow her. Although they may have prearranged their retreat, the Romans saw it as proof that Antony was enslaved by his love of Cleopatra, unable to think or act on his own.

Love does not conquer all

In 30 BC, Octavian reached Alexandria, and Mark Antony greeted him with his slowly diminishing soldiers and navy. As soon as the navy saw the Romans, they saluted with their oars and sailed over to join the other side, shortly followed by the desertion of the cavalry and infantry – leaving Antony alone. Cleopatra, now afraid, locked herself in her tomb and sent word to Antony that she was dead! Clearly, things were backfiring.

Antony, feeling somewhat unstable, tried to kill himself, only to mess it up and inflict an eventually fatal wound. While he was bleeding to death, he heard that Cleopatra was in fact alive and demanded that his body be taken to her immediately. When Antony arrived at the tomb, Cleopatra was too afraid to open the door. She and her two serving women let down ropes from a window and pulled Antony up. Distraught, Cleopatra laid Antony on her bed and he died in her arms.

Octavian, meanwhile, had invaded Alexandria and taken control of Cleopatra's palace, with the intention of taking Cleopatra back to Rome and dragging her through the streets in chains. Octavian and his men marched to the tomb, but Cleopatra wouldn't let him in. Instead they negotiated through the closed door, Cleopatra demanding that her kingdom be given to her children.

Meeting Antony for the first time

Julius Caesar, Cleopatra's lover, had just been assassinated, and Mark Antony had taken over control of the eastern part of the Roman empire. Mark Antony sailed to Tarsus (in modern-day Turkey) and summoned Cleopatra to him to interrogate her about her role in assisting his enemies.

The meeting of Antony and Cleopatra is described by Plutarch, writing between AD 46 and 127. It was the stuff of fairytales – and all from the elaborate imagination of the enigmatic Cleopatra. Cleopatra arrived at Tarsus in a boat. To be honest, this was more than a boat: It was a barge with a gilded stern, purple sails, and silver oars. Cleopatra's maids, dressed as sea nymphs, sailed the boat. Cleopatra herself was dressed as Venus, the goddess of love, and she reclined under a golden canopy, fanned by boys dressed in Cupid costumes. Antony, a simple soldier, was impressed by this blatant display of luxury, just

as Cleopatra had intended. Cleopatra refused to leave the boat and entertained Antony on the boat that night. This gave her the upper hand by ensuring that they met on Egyptian territory.

The next night, Antony invited Cleopatra to supper, hoping to outdo her in magnificence. He failed, but joked about it in a good-natured way. Like Julius Caesar before him, Antony was enthralled with Cleopatra, becoming the second great love in Cleopatra's life. First impressions clearly count.

As juicy as this story is, it needs to be taken with a pinch of salt. Plutarch, like most authors, wrote with an agenda and may have exaggerated the decadence of the story to highlight the exotic setting and the passions of Antony and Cleopatra. Of course, when Shakespeare incorporates these details into his play, all suddenly becomes fact, of sorts.

While Cleopatra was distracted at the door, Octavian's men set up ladders and climbed through the window. Cleopatra instantly tried to stab herself, but was disarmed and taken prisoner along with her children. Octavian allowed Cleopatra to arrange Antony's funeral, and Cleopatra buried Antony in royal style. After the funeral Cleopatra was so grief stricken, she stayed in bed.

Cleopatra was determined to die to be with her beloved Antony and arranged for an asp (a venomous snake) to be brought to the tomb in a basket of figs, all in secrecy without the knowledge of the Romans. The guards even checked the basket and found nothing suspicious, so they allowed it to be given to the queen. When she reached into the basket the asp bit her and she died. In her final moments, Cleopatra wrote a letter to Octavian asking if she could be buried in Antony's tomb.

Octavian ran to the tomb, but it was too late – Cleopatra was dead. The only person in the way of Octavian's control of Egypt was Caesarion, whom Octavian promptly disposed of. Egypt was now open for Roman rule.

The Romans are coming

Cleopatra's suicide in 30 BC left the path to Egypt open for the Romans to take control. However, Egypt was not made a Roman province, in the true sense of the word, straight away. Octavian (later the Emperor Augustus), used Egypt as a personal estate, governed by an official answerable to him alone. Egypt became the primary provider of grain to the Roman empire and was known in contemporary records as Rome's bread basket.

The emperors who followed Augustus on the throne of Egypt attempted to rule in traditional Egyptian fashion, building temples to traditional Egyptian gods, and even representing themselves as Egyptian kings while performing traditional rituals.

Although the Egyptian culture was unrecognisable because of the Hellenistic invasion by Alexander, many of the Egyptian cults were maintained under the Romans. In AD 394, Philae temple was still in use and in fact this carried the last inscription written in hieroglyphs in Egypt. It was to be another 1,400 years before anyone could read it again (see Chapter 11).

Part III

Living Life to the Full: Culture and Beliefs

The 5th Wave   By Rich Tennant

AT THE EMBALMERS' WORKSHOP

"Wait a minute—if this jar's supposed to hold the body's liver, what's your lunch doing in it?"

In this part . . .

The ancient Egyptians enjoyed parties, feasts, and generally living it up with their mates. Loads of evidence of these parties exist, including menus and lists of the dancers and musicians who attended. For daytime entertainment the Egyptians played board games, listened to stories, went hunting, and participated in sports.

Although relatively hygienic, the Egyptians were beset with disease and illnesses, and the doctors recorded many of the symptoms, diagnoses, and 'cures' – most of which makes our own health service look the biz. From parasitic worms, to teeth abscesses, it's surprising they could concentrate on building pyramids and temples at all!

Ancient Egyptian religion was very imaginative and diverse, with hundreds of gods, different practices, beliefs, and rituals – many dependant on the location. Although the everyday Egyptians weren't allowed to enter the elaborate temples which still dominate the landscape, they worshipped in their homes.

Many of the Egyptians' funerary beliefs were focused on prolonging life for eternity in the underworld, and they preserved bodies and possessions, enabling us to build a compelling image of their life and beliefs.

Chapter 7

Enjoying Food and Entertainment

. . . .

. . . .

*E*veryone likes to have a good time, and the same can be said of the ancient Egyptians. In an age without televisions, radios, or computers, the Egyptians had to find other ways of keeping themselves entertained at the end of a long working day.

And the working week, even for the elite and top craftsmen, was indeed long – ten days on, two days off – with the working day consisting of all daylight hours. Perhaps the poorer classes worked even longer, more difficult schedules, but because they left no records, historians may never know. Chapter 2 offers more details of the day-to-day activities of these ancient Egyptians.

Due to the heat, a midday siesta time was likely, although small details – no matter how important they were to the ancient Egyptians – are unrecorded. With these working conditions, unwinding at the end of the day or the week was extremely important.

Some of the evening and weekend entertainment for the ancient Egyptians was remarkably similar to today's pastimes. Families spent time together, friends met for a gossip and a couple of beers, and people played board games, listened to music, told stories, and enjoyed more active pursuits, such as wrestling and (during the New Kingdom) chariot racing and hunting. The following sections explore some of the most popular ways that ancient Egyptians kicked back and offer some ways in which you can relax like an Egyptian.

Nourishing the Grey Matter

Like any community throughout history, the ancient Egyptians had sporty people and more passive people. Not all Egyptians were physically active, and some chose more studious ways of passing their time, especially if they were literate.

Studious pursuits were not solely the choice of the rich, and physical pastimes were not only for the poor. In fact, the king in most periods was an active hunter. The more studious pastimes were, however, for the literate – who were primarily the elite – but that is not to say a poor illiterate member of the community did not enjoy sketching in the sand, telling stories or playing board games rather than wrestling and stick fighting!

Literacy was very low in ancient Egypt with only 1–5 per cent of the population being able to read and write. (Even today, the estimated literacy rate in modern Egypt is estimated at 25 per cent.) This is a difficult statistic for many to swallow, as the UK today is very highly literate (99.9 per cent). Many of today's pastimes depend on literacy, including reading, crosswords, sudoku, and writing.

One example of an Egyptian crossword has been discovered. Although this crossword didn't have clues, it was discovered with the grid filled in and with all the words interlocking as they do in the modern world. Although sudoku did not exist in ancient Egypt, papyri with a number of mathematical and geometrical riddles, which some Egyptian scribe may have puzzled over for many hours, do exist as well.

Of the numerous Egyptian scribes, one chap is particularly noteworthy: Kenhirkhepshef lived in Deir el Medina during the 19th dynasty (see the Cheat Sheet for a historical timeline) and had a particular interest in the past. He spent his free time, rather like me actually, researching Egyptian history. He wrote an accurate list in chronological order of all the kings of the New Kingdom. (Unfortunately, his list is unusable today because he excluded unpopular kings and those who ruled a divided country.) Researchers believe Kenhirkhepshef may have visited a number of the mortuary temples and gathered information from the priests working there.

Kenhirkhepshef was also a linguist and had a list of official governmental titles that started with 'chief'. Sadly he didn't explain what the titles entailed, and many of them are only known from this list.

Other scribes spent their evenings and weekends writing love poetry. Although some people believe these poems were written by love-sick men and women, they're grammatically correct and cleverly written with rhyming couplets and word play. As such, they're more likely to have been penned by professional scribes. Sadly the authors of this love poetry are anonymous. Some of them were probably well known at the time, and their work was probably oft repeated in the light of the fire.

Telling Tall Tales

Evidence suggests that the ancient Egyptians loved tall stories – although their methods of storytelling and the identities of these storytellers are unknown today. Storytellers did not need to be literate to tell good tales, so they may have hailed from all walks of life.

Stories were most likely told orally. The problem with any kind of oral tradition is that each time a story is told, it changes depending on the story teller's personal agenda, skills and interests – as well as the audience, which included all age groups. Oral traditions do not have rules. As a result, stories can and did take the form of poetry, sing-alongs, or even idle gossip – all of which can provide hours of entertainment.

Some scribes luckily chose to record stories that were part of this oral tradition. The scribes may have felt they were contributing to their heritage by recording these stories. A number of stories have survived, including:

- ✔ The Journey of Sinuhe, in which a man flees Egypt at the death of the king and settles in an Asiatic town, rising in power until he is a chief.

- ✔ The Doomed Prince, in which a young noble's death is foreseen as being caused by one of three fates. Throughout his life he has close shaves with these fates.

- ✔ The Tale of the Eloquent Peasant, in which a simple peasant appeals at the law courts on a daily basis, impressing the king with his eloquence. This long story illustrates that low status does not mean ignorance.

- ✔ The Shipwrecked Sailor (see sidebar), in which a sailor is marooned on an island inhabited by a divine serpent many metres long.

- ✔ The Five Tales of Magic and Wonder, which describe five separate events staged in the Old Kingdom royal court, during which magicians perform various amazing feats of magic for the king's entertainment.

- ✔ The Tale of the Two Brothers, which tells the story of the separation of two brothers because of the treachery of the older brother's wife.

- ✔ The Tale of the (other) Doomed Prince, which tells the story of a man who is foretold the method of his death. The tale recounts his journey and how he nearly comes a cropper on more than one occasion. He also strangely enough meets a princess in a tower who throws her hair down as a means of escape. Does the name Rapunzel mean anything to anyone?

The shipwrecked sailor

A young sailor encountered on the docks a sea captain who had just returned from an unsuccessful expedition. The captain was concerned about explaining himself to the king, so the sailor tried to console the captain by telling his own story of an expedition to the copper mines on a ship with 150 of the best sailors in Egypt.

One day the young sailor and his shipmates encountered a storm that destroyed the ship and killed all the crew, except the sailor who was washed up on an island. He sat alone under a tree suffering from shock for three days. When he came to, he went in search of nourishment and found that the island was abundant in figs, grain, fruit, vegetables, fish, and birds. He loaded up his arms, built a fire, and started to prepare lunch, when he was disturbed by a loud noise.

He initially thought it was a wave from the sea, but the trees shook and the earth moved. The sailor recoiled as he saw a large bearded serpent approaching at speed. Enough to spoil anyone's day!

The snake questioned the sailor as to his presence on the island, but the sailor was too scared to talk, so the snake carried the sailor in his mouth to his lair, where he questioned the sailor again. The sailor recounted what had happened to him and his crew. The snake soothed him and foretold he would remain on the island for four months before a crew he recognised would come to take him back to Egypt.

The snake then told his own story of how he came to be alone on the island. The snake originally lived on the island with 72 other serpents, including his young daughter. One day a star fell from the heavens and burnt the snakes, killing all except the gigantic serpent. He reassured the sailor that although loss hurts at first, the grief disappears with time.

After the four months passed, the sailor spotted a ship on the horizon manned by an Egyptian crew that he recognised. The crew moored, and the snake gave them lots of goodies from the island to take back to Egypt, which the crew promptly loaded onto the ship. The crew then returned to Egypt, and the king summoned the sailor to explain what had happened to his expedition. He was rewarded with land and titles for bringing the goodies from the island. And everyone lived happily ever after!

Playing Board Games

Although a good storyteller can grip a crowd for an hour or so, an evening has many hours to fill. The Egyptians spent many hours playing board games, three of which have survived. These games are known as Senet, Hounds and Jackals, and Mehen – the names surviving down the millennia.

Sadly, the rules for these games have not survived. However, some very bright individuals have come up with rules for them based on the number of squares, the nature of the dice, and the number of pieces.

Have a go at playing the following games – or develop your own alternative rules.

Senet

One of the oldest of the board games is Senet, which means 'game of passing'. Senet is a game of strategy, rather like backgammon. It was played from the Old Kingdom onwards and is often depicted in tombs.

Senet is a two-player game. To play, you need:

✔ **Two types of pieces – cones and reels.** Each player chooses which type of piece to use at the start of the game.

✔ **A senet board.** Senet boards have a numbered grid of 30 squares arranged in three rows of ten. You can draw and make a Senet board yourself or use the board shown in Figure 7-1.

✔ **A set of four 'sticks' or 'knuckle bones'.** The number of squares you move on the Senet board is determined by 'throwing sticks' or 'throwing knuckle bones' – the Egyptian equivalent of casting dice. These four wooden sticks have one plain side and one painted side. The combination of coloured sides visible when you throw the sticks determines the number of squares you move:

   • When only one painted side is visible, move forward one square.

   • When two painted sides are visible, move forward two squares.

   • When three painted sides are visible, move forward three squares.

   • When four painted sides are visible, move forward four squares.

   • When no painted sides are visible, move forward five squares.

You can make your own set of sticks by colouring or painting one side of four ice-lolly or craft sticks.

Figure 7-1:
A sample
Senet board
layout.

1	2	3	4	5	6	7	8	9	10
20	19	18	17	16	15	14	13	12	11
21	22	23	24	25	26	27	28	29	30

Players agree to play with three, five, or seven pieces each. The goal of the game is to be the first to move all your pieces from square 1 to square 30, using the sticks to determine how many spaces you can move on each turn. The following restrictions apply:

- If Player 1 lands on a square that is occupied by Player 2, the players must swap places: Player 2 must move his or her piece to the square Player 1 started from.
- All players must land on square 26 before moving off the board.

You and your partner can create other rules and restrictions to make the game more challenging. For example, you may choose to allow players to spilt a roll of 4 between two separate pieces. Or you may decide that players must roll the exact number of spaces to reach square 30 and complete a piece's trek through the board.

Hounds and Jackals

Another popular game from the New Kingdom is Hounds and Jackals – so named because one set of pieces features the heads of jackals and the other hounds. The game is also known as 58 Holes.

Hounds and Jackals is a two-player game. To play, you need:

- **A game board with two tracks of 30 holes each.** The board can be a flat piece of wood with holes drilled in it – two 'tracks' of 30 holes each. More elaborate 3-D boards are available as well. (The Louvre in Paris has a sculptural board in the shape of a hippo in its collection.)

    Figure 7-2 shows an example layout for a board. You can photocopy this image, stick it onto a ½-inch board and drill holes in each position.

- **Ten pegs.** Usually five pegs with jackals on the ends and five pegs with hounds on the ends. You can substitute pegs of two different colours.

- **A set of four sticks.** The number of squares you move on the board is determined by throwing sticks, as the rules for Senet describe.

Each player starts with five pieces (either hounds or jackals). The object of the game is to get all five of your pieces into hole 30, following the track on your half of the board. Each peg needs to go around the track twice to win.

As in Snakes and Ladders, if a player lands in

- Hole 6, he or she moves directly to hole 20
- Hole 15 or 25, he or she gets to throw again

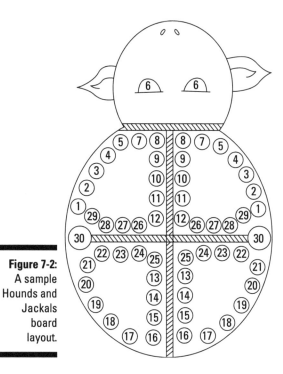

Figure 7-2:
A sample
Hounds and
Jackals
board
layout.

Like Senet, you and your partner can create additional rules and restrictions to make the game more challenging.

Leading a Sporting Life

Some members of the elite preferred more active social lives and participated in a number of sports, including wrestling and weight lifting (with sand bags). While many of these activities were part of military training, it is likely that some individuals chose to train purely to improve their physique and physical strength.

Among a number of children's toys at the town of Kahun in the Faiyum region, archaeologists discovered a few balls made of strips of animal skin stitched together and stuffed with dried grass. Whether the games that children played with these balls were ever played by adults is unknown, but I am sure some people like to think that football was not only 'the beautiful game' but also 'the ancient game'.

The following sections discuss popular forms of recreation for both the Egyptian elite and the masses.

Charioteering

The chariot was not introduced to Egypt until the late Second Intermediate Period. Kings and some noble men of the New Kingdom were trained from young boyhood in charioteering in preparation for the battlefield. See Chapter 4 for more on historical periods.

Chariots in ancient Egypt were small and light. Drawn by two horses, these vehicles carried two people – the driver and a spearman or archer. A king or nobleman was trained in both roles.

Mostly boys were trained in charioteering skills, but at the site of Amarna, the small daughters of Akhenaten (see Chapter 4) are shown on tomb and temple walls driving their own chariots – an image which is unique to this period. A small sketch in the Cairo Museum shows a queen, thought to be Hatshepsut, driving a chariot and firing arrows at the enemy, which indicates perhaps that some royal women picked up charioteering skills. At Amarna, most of the elite members of society owned a chariot, because it was their main mode of transport.

After an Egyptian mastered steering a chariot, evidence suggests that chariot races took place. Nothing of the calibre of *Ben Hur*, but racing nonetheless. Just outside Malkata, the Theban palace of Amenhotep III, is a temporary lodge called the Kom el 'Abd, overlooking a very long, straight road. The road was cleared for the use of high-speed chariot races, in which no doubt Amenhotep III participated. These races were probably semi-private events, only seen by people living at Malkata and nearby.

Target practice

After young princes or military trainees were able to drive chariots, developing archery skills was the next task. Not only was marksmanship essential on the battlefield, but it was useful in the desert while hunting game.

Before being let loose in the desert on potentially dangerous animal targets, marksmen practised in a safe environment. The typical target consisted of a copper sheet set up at shoulder height along a course. The charioteer rode at speed and tried to hit the target with arrows. A stone block in Luxor Museum shows the 18th-dynasty king Amenhotep II using one of these targets. He is particularly skilled and has hit the target with five arrows, each one hitting with such force that it protruded through to the other side.

Hunting

Tomb scenes of the elite often depict the deceased hunting in the desert for gazelles, bulls and lions as well as in the marshes for fish and birds. While these images carry a funerary symbolism of virility and fertility, they also reflect the fact that hunting and fishing were popular activities for ancient Egyptians. Additional imagery in temples depicts hunting scenes as well, indicating that these pastimes probably crossed social boundaries between the elite and royalty.

In the desert

Egypt is surrounded by land on both the east and the west bank of the Nile and supported lions, gazelles, deer, and bulls. Evidence shows that many of these animals may have been caught and housed in large pens to make the hunting safer for the king and the elite. Rather like a safari park – but not with conservation as a goal! The hunter rode along in a chariot, probably with a driver, and sometimes accompanied by pet dogs that retrieved the felled animals.

Images of the king and elite hunting normally show the kings hunting with bow and arrow, although they could possibly have hunted with spears or – if they wanted to catch the animals alive – lassoes.

A wonderful scene is depicted at Medinet Habu – Ramses III's mortuary temple in Thebes – which shows the king in the midst of a wild bull hunt. The king is riding his chariot with the reins of the horses tied around his waist, leaving his hands free to fire arrows at the animals. He has become so excited by the hunt that he has thrown his leg over the front of the chariot to give him more support while bracing himself against the force of the bow. One bull that he has hit is already collapsed in the reeds.

Most hunting was for food, and catches provided tasty meals for the king, noblemen and their families. The skins of lions were often used for luxurious throws in the palace or home. Evidence suggests that Ramses II and III actually had a pet lion, which perhaps they hunted themselves.

In the marshes

Hunting in the marshes was equally popular among the elite, particularly in the favoured holiday marshland spot of the Faiyum. This area became so popular that in the New Kingdom, a royal palace and a harem were built here so that hunters could stay overnight in luxurious surroundings. The Faiyum supported a lively array of wildlife, although visitors to the site were interested only in the fowl and fish.

Many tomb scenes depict marsh hunting scenes in which the tomb owner stands on a small papyrus skiff or boat holding a throw stick in his raised arm. To scare the birds from the marshes, a trained cat or a servant was sent into the bushes to startle the birds. As they flew into the air, the tomb owner threw the stick, felling two or three birds with each stick. The trained cat or servant then went into the marshes and retrieved the birds. (I would love to see how they trained the cat to do anything!)

Birds caught by hunting with a throw stick were prepared for eating (feathers were plucked from the bird and it was hung out to dry in the sun). However, this method of fowling was not employed on a daily basis for food production. To catch birds for food, ancient Egyptians used a large drag-net thrown over the marshland, which was pulled in and gathered birds in its path.

Fishing

The Nile and its canals were abundant with many types of fish, so fishing was a popular pastime. Fishing as a sport was carried out using spears. The fisherman stood on the papyrus skiff, waited for a fish to swim by, and at the most opportune moment thrust the spear into the water. In tomb scenes, the tomb owner is always shown with two fish on the end of his spear, showing that he can not only catch one fish but two with one thrust.

In addition to vegetables, fish was the primary food of most Egyptians. When fishing for food, the Egyptians threw large nets into the river and dragged in vast quantities of fish. Their catch was then prepared for eating by eviscerating the fish, drying them in salt, and leaving them in the sun.

Throwing Big Bashes

The Egyptians were a sociable bunch and had frequent get-togethers to share gossip and to eat and be merry. Not much information on get-togethers for the lower classes exists, but parties for the elite are well recorded.

Many images on New Kingdom non-royal tombs show the elite enjoying themselves at elaborate banquets, entertained by musicians and dancers. Although these images are of particular feasts associated with the funeral and funerary festivals, they no doubt reflect the types of parties that took place in the houses of the rich and influential.

These tomb images provide several intriguing details:

✔ Guests are seated, normally with the men and women segregated. This may be an oddity of the funerary scenes, but it is still noteworthy.

✔ Guests are given as much food and alcohol (wine and beer) as they can stomach. In fact, in one tomb there is a delightful image of a woman purging herself into a bucket after over-indulging.

✔ Teams of servants attend to guests. Everything at these banquets was designed to make the guests feel pampered and special. Servants are shown filling goblets, distributing food, and adorning the guests in floral collars and perfume cones.

Perfume cones were structures made of animal fat impregnated with scented oils. The cones were placed on guests' heads and emitted a pleasant aroma as they melted. A combination of flowers and lard – hmmm, nice! After the cones melted, servants replaced them with fresh ones.

Making music

The hosts of these parties provided entertainment, often in the form of a band – the Egyptian equivalent of the infamous party DJ. Sadly the music they played is lost, but they may have had a couple of groaners in their repertoire, on a par with today's 'Birdie Song' and 'Agadoo'.

The musicians were normally in small groups of either men or women. It was unusual for the groups to be mixed. The group played a mixture of instruments including lutes, flutes, clappers (ivory sticks tied at the end that clattered together when shaken), and harps (both small hand-held versions and full-sized examples). A small hand drum or a group of men or women clapping rhythmically kept the rhythm going.

No evidence exists suggesting that nobles played instruments in public; banquet musicians were hired especially for the occasion. However, it is possible that as a means of passing the time the elite learned to play instruments. In the sixth dynasty mastaba tomb (see Chapter 13) at Saqqara, Mereruka's wife, a princess no less, sits on her bed playing a harp to entertain her husband, who is also seated on a bed.

Dancing

An Egyptian would not have jumped onto the table and danced the night away to tunes from the party band. Music was typically accompanied by a group of dancers, who, like the musicians, were hired for the occasion.

Dancing was a very erotic form of entertainment. The performers were normally naked, except for an elaborate collar and a decorative belt or loincloth. Some dancers are shown in tomb drawings with perfume cones on their heads, indicating they also smelt nice and gave the audience a waft of perfume as they flitted by. Many dancers used their hair as a tool by flicking it from side to side; some tomb images even show weights tied into the hair, ensuring it moved in the correct way.

Perusing the party menu

Food was a major part of elaborate banquets, and fortunately a lot of information still exists.

Images of divine offering tables show what food the Egyptians considered good enough for the gods. Coupled with food left in tombs and described in offering lists, a detailed list of food that may have been on the menu at a posh party emerges.

Although for the rest of the population it was a luxury, meat was a major part of an elite meal. Some of the cuts would be distasteful to diners today; the ancient Egyptians refused to waste any part of the animal. Some of the most popular meat was ox (including the head, tongue, and entrails), goose, pigeon, and fish.

The meat was accompanied by

- Vegetables, including cucumber, onions, and lettuce
- Pulses and nuts, including lentils, chick peas, watermelon seeds, and almonds
- Herbs, including coriander and garlic
- Fruit, including figs, raisins, grape seeds, dom-palm nut (a type of fruit from the dom-palm tree), dates, and pomegranate leaves (and no doubt the rest of the fruit as well).

Baking the Hovis way

Most of the depictions of parties also show hosts serving various breads and cakes to the guests, including honey cakes and a type of fruit loaf. Bread was the staple of the Egyptian diet, and everyone, rich or poor, ate lots of it. Bread is also included on all offering tables and lists, showing that it was a food fit for the gods.

Different types of bread existed, including varieties made from emmer wheat and barley. The tomb of Tutankhamun even held fruit loaves containing berries from the Christ-thorn plant.

Egyptians baked various types of bread in different shapes (triangles and ovals were common) to make identification easier. Sadly, the exact meanings of these shapes are not known today.

To facilitate the grinding of grain into flour, bakers or women in the households may have added ground stone (quartzite or granite) or sand to their grind stones, which acted as an abrasive and produced flour in half the time. Very productive, but these inclusions in the bread caused excessive wear on the teeth of the Egyptians (see Chapter 8 for the gory details).

Brewing beer

No party is complete without a bar, and the ancient Egyptians loved their alcohol. Their parties would have been abundant in wine and beer. Beer was a staple of the Egyptian diet and was even included in the state wages and rations.

Beer was made in a similar way to bread. It was somewhat thicker than the beer or ale you're familiar with today and may have contained a number of impurities. Egyptian beer was made from stale or partially baked barley or emmer bread (a dough high in yeast), which was placed on a screen over a jar. Water was poured over the bread until it dissolved and fell into the jar, where it was left to ferment. Once fermented, the liquid was then decanted into amphora jars for storage or transportation.

The resulting beer was not overly alcoholic if drunk in moderation, but the ancient Egyptians had one too many on occasion.

Where did I get this traffic cone?

Most people at some point have had a couple of drinks too many at a Christmas party or New Year bash and have gaps in their recollection of what happened. Proving nothing is new, one chap from 19th-dynasty Deir el Medina, probably had more than the average recollection problem. Paneb had a reputation of being a womaniser, a criminal, and a drunk. From a series of legal accusations written by one of his enemies, historians can fill in some of the alcohol-related gaps for him.

On one occasion after a few beers with friends, Paneb got into an argument with his elderly adopted father Neferhotep, which ended in Paneb chasing Neferhotep home:

Charge concerning his running after ... Neferhotep, although it was him who

reared him. And he [Neferhotep] closed his doors before him, and he [Paneb] took a stone and broke his doors. And they caused men to watch over Neferhotep because he [Paneb] said 'I will kill him in the night'.

Reports also indicate that Paneb horrified a number of his co-workers at the construction site of the royal tombs. At the end of a long day, after the empty sarcophagus had just been placed into the tomb, Paneb got drunk and sat on top of the sarcophagus, singing. Although no doubt egged on by his mates, Paneb's actions would have been seen as the worst sacrilege. Now, if only his song were known! Maybe a little ditty about chariot racers?

For the more adventurous beer drinker, flavours were added to the basic mix, including dates, spices, or honey. The sugar in the dates and honey accelerated fermentation. When the Egypt Exploration Society prepared batches using the ancient recipe, the resulting beverage was found to be very sweet but not unpleasant.

Enjoying wine

Although beer was the staple alcoholic beverage in ancient Egypt, in the New Kingdom, wine was very popular, especially among the elite. Wine was a luxurious alternative to beer and was saved for special occasions.

A number of vineyards existed in this region, and many of the local farmers produced wine. Athenaeus wrote in 200 AD that Egyptian wines were 'pale, pleasant, aromatic, and mildly astringent, with an oily quality'.

Just as in the modern world, each amphora of wine was labelled with the date of the wine, the vineyard, and the vintner. Other labels from the palace of Malkata at Thebes, the home of Amenhotep III, also add what type of wine was in the jar, including 'blended', 'wine for offerings', 'wine for taxes', 'wine for a happy return', and 'wine for merry-making'. All of which indicates that the later Egyptians were truly wine connoisseurs.

The process of wine making was very similar to that in some small modern vineyards. The basic steps include

- ✔ Picking the grapes
- ✔ Treading the grapes in vats of clay, wood, or stone
- ✔ Placing the crushed mulch in large sheets of linen, which were twisted to wring out every last drop of juice
- ✔ Allowing the grape juice to ferment in pottery jars
- ✔ Transferring the fermented juice to racked jars that were stoppered with perforated seals, which allowed carbon monoxide to escape
- ✔ Enjoying the wine after a short period of fermentation

A rare variety of wine known as Shedeh was made from grapes, but was heated, like mulled wine. If served this at a party, guests knew their host was both rich and sophisticated.

Chapter 8

Staying Healthy: Diseases and Medicine

. . . .

In This Chapter

▶ Meeting the doctors

▶ Combining medicine and magic

▶ Diagnosing illnesses and diseases

▶ Curing ailments

. . . .

Disease is something that plagues every society (pun intended) – ancient and modern.

Medical papyri and mummified remains provide ample evidence of the diseases from which the ancient Egyptians suffered. These remnants also help paint a clear picture of the medical profession in Pharaonic Egypt, including some ill-conceived treatments as well as some surprisingly effective cures. By the end of this chapter, I'm sure you'll never complain about the Health Service again!

In this chapter, you meet the ancient Egyptian physicians, consult their records, and marvel at the ingenuity – and flat-out bizarreness – of many of the cures, some of which form the basis of modern medicine.

Examining Egypt's Overall Health

Numerous surviving medical records, human remains, and even a close study of the settlements can give a detailed view of the general health of the Egyptians.

By modern standards, the ancient Egyptians would be unhealthy, but much of this was due to their living conditions. In many of the settlements, people lived in very close contact, with more than ten people living in a single four-room house.

Evidence in the workmen's village at Amarna indicates the rampant presence of bed bugs, fleas, and rats – all of which aid the spread of disease. Additional evidence suggests that a plague (similar to the bubonic plague) spread throughout the city of Amarna during the 18th dynasty, killing many people including most of the royal family (see Chapter 4).

Other epidemics probably occurred due to the crowded living conditions, but they are difficult to trace in the archaeological record, especially if they weren't as fatal as the bubonic plague.

The average Egyptian had a tough life and probably suffered from one or all the following ailments:

- Dental abscesses, which resulted in tooth loss and dissolution of the jaw bone
- Parasitic intestinal worms, the most common being bilharzia
- Breathing disorders due to the sandy environment
- Osteoarthritis
- Blindness, especially among the workmen who constructed the tombs of the kings

Based on the study of the thousands of mummies from Egypt, the average age at death was only 36 years, although a number of exceptions exist. The individuals who did live into their 40s, 50s, and 60s, however, came from all walks of life, so status and wealth were not necessarily factors in life expectancy. Living to a ripe old age was more luck than judgement; the numerous fatal diseases and infections affected *all* Egyptians.

Becoming an Egyptian Physician

Becoming a physician in ancient Egypt involved study and training – in both medical procedures and religious ceremony. The following sections explore the process of becoming a doctor.

Practising magical medicine

Unfortunately, the medical practice that the ancient Egyptian people had to endure was not totally scientific. They were a superstitious population who believed that many ailments had a supernatural cause – the vengeance of a deity, an evil spirit, or the evil eye cast by an enemy.

As a result, patients turned to gods as well as physicians in times of illness. Practical medicine was very closely tied to religion and was often accompanied by religious incantations recited by medically trained priests. Most physicians were in fact priests who used magic and incantations to supplement practical medicine in an effort to appease the spirit or god. Priests were held in high esteem because they conversed with the divine on a daily basis.

The priests of some deities were more inclined than others to turn to medicine. The most important deities associated with medicine were

- **Sekhmet,** the lioness-headed goddess of war, epidemics, and plagues
- **Selqet,** the scorpion goddess, whose priests were approached to treat bites and stings from venomous reptiles, scorpions, and tarantulas
- **Thoth,** the ibis-headed god of knowledge, who was often accredited with writing the healing formulae

Most professions were passed on from father to son (refer to Chapter 2), so some priestly families who turned their hand to medicine held the profession for generations. A well-trained and effective physician was no doubt busy, well paid, and respected within the community. Neighbouring countries held Egyptian doctors in high esteem, and records show that foreign kings requested the treatment of an Egyptian doctor.

Medical training

In order to qualify as an elite physician, a young medical student was trained in the *House of Life*, an unusual institution of learning that provided medical, scribal, and priestly training, as well as housing an extensive library. See Chapter 2 for more insight into the House of Life.

Medical training and priestly training probably went hand in hand. Most House of Life institutions were attached to temples. This was the case at Bubastis, Edfu, Amarna, and Kom Ombo. The most famous House of Life was set up by Imhotep (the builder of the step pyramid at Saqqara) at Memphis; it was in use from the Old Kingdom until the Graeco-Roman period – a period of more than 2,000 years.

Although doctors were formally trained, they did not need to pass exams in order to practice. Like today's medical profession, a strict hierarchy according to ability and experience was in place:

- *Senenu* (lay physicians) were the lowest-ranking doctor. They were often scribes who could read medical texts.

- *Kherep senenu* were controllers of doctors and oversaw the work of a number of senenu physicians.

- *Sau* (magic physicians) were generally priests of Sekhmet, who were medically qualified, but only treated individuals whom the goddess had punished in some way.

- *Shepherd of the Anus of Pharaoh* was a spectacular title for the physician who gave enemas to the king.

- *Specialists* were doctors who focused on one particular ailment, much like a medical professional today. Ancient Egyptian specialties included eyes, teeth, mouth, stomach pain, and 'uncertain diseases'.

Rather than a student choosing and pursuing a branch of medicine as a career, the position was dictated by the skills held. Some doctors were therefore more qualified than others.

Equipping the physician's office

After physicians were trained, they needed to establish a practice.

Full-time priests with medical training were resident in the temples. They no doubt only had a small number of patients whom they treated in the House of Life. Other physicians who were not priests had to set up independently and treat the people in their villages, perhaps only on a part-time basis. A physician could also be employed by a rich household. Personal physician would have been a more satisfactory position to hold than village doctor.

Doctors also needed to collect a set of instruments with which to practise their art. In a sixth-dynasty tomb at Saqqara, belonging to Qar, the senior physician of the royal palace, a complete set of surgical tools was discovered, including 30 scalpels and tweezers, which seem to be the primary tools for most treatments.

The temple of Kom Ombo features an image of a complete set of medical tools, which corresponds with the items in the tomb of Qar. A corresponding list on the Edwin Smith Papyrus (a medical papyrus) contains the following items:

- ✔ A rush (a plant stem with a sharpened end, used with a knife for cutting treatments)
- ✔ A fire drill (two wooden sticks to rub together to burn growths)
- ✔ A knife/chisel
- ✔ A cupping glass to create a vacuum on the skin
- ✔ A thorn (to burst blisters)
- ✔ Heated broken glass (for eye treatments – ow!)
- ✔ Swabs, tampons, and linen material
- ✔ Knives, salve spoons, and mortars

Most of these instruments seem sensible enough and are still used today. For example, popping blisters with a sharp instrument (like a thorn) is commonplace, and burning off warts is an effective way of getting rid of them. Indeed, the only item on the list that seems slightly dubious is the hot broken glass used to treat eye conditions. It doesn't bear thinking about; even if swabs and linen pads could mop up whatever comes out, this treatment would make your eyes more than water!

Two top docs

More than 100 ancient Egyptian physicians are known by name, all of them from the elite of society. Two stand out from these known doctors:

Hesy-re is the first known physician in history, dating back to the third dynasty. Hesy-re held the title of Chief of Dentists and Physicians and was clearly a man of high position in the royal court. His tomb is located just north of the Step pyramid of Djoser.

Peseshet was the only female physician known from Egyptian history, living in the fourth dynasty. She was titled Lady Overseer of the Lady Physicians. Although no other female physicians are known until the Ptolemaic period, the fact that Peseshet oversaw lady doctors suggests enough female doctors existed to require an overseer.

To charge or not to charge?

Although loads of information about ancient Egyptian medicine and doctors exists, no surviving information explains how much certain treatments cost or how services were paid for. No evidence exists that the Government hired state physicians to treat the ailments of the populace, as British general practitioners do. The only exception to this appears to be at the workmen's village of Deir el Medina (see Chapter 2 for more on this village). The Government provided the physicians at this location to ensure only that the workmen were fit to build the tombs. The state paid the Deir el Medina doctors a lower wage than all other workers at the site. Perhaps they subsidised their low wages through charging their patients.

Egypt did not have a monetary system until Alexander arrived in 332 BC, so patients receiving treatment probably paid their doctors in grain, livestock, linen, or craft, depending on the patient's profession, wealth, and satisfaction with the cure. If only you could purchase prescriptions today with a goat and a bag of flour, the pharmacy would be a much more colourful place to visit!

Visiting the Doctor

After they were trained and equipped, new physicians could start practising.

More than 1,200 ancient Egyptian medical records have survived, giving detailed insight into what a consultation with a physician was like. These medical papyri include

- ✔ A professional medical oath, similar to the Hippocratic oath
- ✔ A description of the process of interviewing patients regarding symptoms and conducting physical examinations
- ✔ Information about pregnancy and gynaecology (see the section 'Considering Women's Health', later in this chapter, for more details)
- ✔ Descriptions of wounds and diseases of the eye, skin, and anus
- ✔ Descriptions of bites from humans, pigs, and hippopotami (the life of ancient Egyptian postmen was clearly a lot more dangerous!)
- ✔ Details of recommended treatments and prescriptions

Most of the recommended practices are exactly the same as those in use today, but some fascinating differences appear as well, as the following sections discuss.

Examining patients

There were more male than female doctors, so both men and women may have visited male doctors, although the records are silent on this. One of the medical papyri indicates that male doctors dealt with feminine problems.

The Ebers Papyrus (a medical papyrus) describes in detail the procedure for examining a patient. This method of diagnosis is similar to modern practice. The doctor began an examination with an interview, to try to understand the symptoms from which the patient was suffering.

The doctor then monitored the patient's pulse and carried out studies of bodily discharges, such as urine, stools, phlegm, and blood, noting any irregularities. Then the doctor examined the reflexes.

After all examinations were complete, the diagnosis was announced. Because not all illnesses had names, the diagnosis was normally just a statement about whether the doctor would try to treat the patient. The diagnosis came in three forms:

- An ailment that I will treat
- An ailment that I will contend
- An ailment not to be treated

Only 14 of the 48 cases on the Ebers Papyrus were seen to be hopeless and therefore not treatable. Of the other 34 patients, the physicians thought they would just have a go and see what happened.

They then prescribed whatever they felt was most appropriate. The prescriptions were very specific regarding dosage and duration, and all were adjusted according to age, giving a child a smaller dosage than an adult.

Treating patients

Egyptian physicians were more interested in trying to cure ailments than preventing illness.

Of the few surviving records of preventive methods, most seem fairly straightforward, such as bathing regularly. Physicians recommended wearing eye make-up to reflect the sun from the sensitive eye area and to prevent insects from entering the eye. They also advised the burning of incense (see the section 'Alternative methods', later in this chapter, for more on aromatherapy) to help fumigate houses and temples and keep the malaria-carrying mossies away.

Under oath

Most Egyptian physicians were also priests. Because medicine was not these people's main profession, the Egyptian version of the Hippocratic oath is somewhat abbreviated and has a moral element. The tomb of Nenkh-Sekhmet, Chief of Physicians from the fifth dynasty, includes the following declaration:

Never did I do anything evil towards any person.

To modern eyes, many of the cures and treatments used by the ancient Egyptians could be said to break this oath. But in the ancient Egyptians' mind, they were doing their best to cure whatever ailments came their way.

If an ailment was obvious, like a wound or a broken bone, the prescribed cure was purely medicinal. For example, non-infected wounds were sealed by stitching with a needle and thread, and raw meat was placed on wounds on the first day to aid with the healing. (This method is known today as an efficient way to stop bleeding.)

Although the physicians turned to the gods for aid with difficult cases, they did have a remarkable understanding of human anatomy, due to the practice of mummification. The Edwin Smith Papyrus deals with surgical techniques such as amputations, stitching, and removing rogue objects from within the body (such as arrows).

If an ailment was internal with no obvious cause, it was believed to have a supernatural origin, and the gods were addressed for a cure.

Common afflictions – and their cures

Just like today, ancient physicians seemed prepared to treat most things. Whether the prescriptions worked is open to question, but some of the ingredients used, especially for the less serious cases, form the basis of modern medicine and could have been effective. For example, the ancient Egyptians used:

- ✔ **Figs for constipation:** High in dietary fibre, figs are still consumed today to aid in digestive regularity.

- ✔ **Honey for coughs and cataracts:** In modern medicine, honey is used to treat wounds, burns, and ulcers and is effective against different types of bacteria, acting as an antibiotic.

- ✔ **Copper for cleaning wounds:** Today's scientists know that copper prevents bacteria build-up.

- ✔ **Poppies to soothe crying children:** The poppy is the basis of narcotics such as opium and morphine and would indeed have made a child drowsy.

✔ **Yeast for digestive disorders:** The Egyptians also applied yeast to boils and ulcers. Today yeast is known to be a good source of vitamin B complex and is effective as an antibiotic.

Digestive disorders

Parasitic worms were one of the most common ailments that ancient Egyptians suffered with. These critters were virtually impossible to treat, and many mummies contain evidence of worms setting up home in internal organs. Parasites included:

✔ Bilharzia, which was caught from water snails in stagnant water. It caused anaemia, loss of appetite, urinary infection, and loss of resistance to other diseases.

✔ Guinea worm, which was caught through drinking contaminated water.

✔ Trichnella and taenia, which were caught by eating undercooked meat.

✔ Tape worm, which was caught via contact with contaminated animals. It resulted in ulcers, within which the tape worm laid eggs.

Enemas seem to have been common, for the elite at least, and this may have eliminated some of the worms, but not many. The Egyptians, sadly, would just have had to live with them and deal with the symptoms.

Other diseases and disorders

For more serious cases, the cures were a little hit and miss and may not have been so successful. Because many of the following diseases are internal conditions, Egyptian doctors were unable to identify the causes and only treated the symptoms, which were pain, coughing, or physical changes. Common diseases and treatments included:

✔ **Tuberculosis:** No cure existed, but doctors eased coughing by having patients inhale mixtures of cream, carob, date kernels, and honey.

✔ **Sand pneumoconiosis:** No cure existed for this condition, caused by breathing in the sand and dust from the surrounding environment. Doctors relied on the same cough-soothing remedies as for tuberculosis.

✔ **Arthritis and osteoarthritis:** Doctors massaged patients with fragrant oils that eased pain.

✔ **Broken bones:** Wooden splints were used for mending long bones. Splints of linen were inserted into the nostril to mend a fractured or broken nose. Plaster casts – made of cow's milk mixed with barley or acacia leaves mixed with gum and water – were used to set breaks or fractures.

✔ **Cataracts:** Doctors applied a mixture of tortoise brain and honey to the eye and recited a religious incantation.

Keep ya jaw on

A treatable bone disorder in ancient Egypt was dislocation of the jaw. The cure for this is described in the Edwin Smith papyrus.

> *When you examine a man with a lower jaw that is displaced, and you find his mouth open, so that you cannot close his mouth; then you should put your finger on the end of both jaw bones in the inside of his mouth, and put your thumbs under his chin; then you must let them [the displaced joint bone]*

> *fall together in their places . . . bandage them with the imr.w [what this is, is a mystery!] and honey every day until he is better.*

None of the records specify why jaw dislocation was so common, but possibly because the biting surfaces of teeth were often very worn (see the section 'Opening Up and Saying "Agh": Dentistry', later in this chapter), many Egyptians ended up moving their mouths in strange ways to be able to chew without excessive pain. Just a theory!

Alternative methods

The Egyptians occasionally used alternative curative methods, which have experienced a recent revival in popularity.

- ✔ **Aromatherapy.** Incense was very popular in Egypt. It was burnt to sweeten the air and fumigate homes (it also acted as a hallucinogen!). It was also regularly used in temple rituals; records from 1200 BC note that at Karnak temple, 2,189 jars and 304,093 bushels of incense were burnt in a single year!

  Incense was used in *temple sanatoria*, dormitories where the ill slept overnight in order to be sent messages from the gods via dreams. The sleep was induced by burning incense that produced hallucinations. The priests then interpreted these dreams and instructed patients as to what tasks they needed to perform in order to be cured. Call me a cynic, but the priests were clearly onto a good thing – the assigned tasks inevitably financed the temple in one way or another.

- ✔ **Enemas.** One aspect of Egyptian preventive medicine that has made a comeback is the regular use of enemas and colonic irrigation. The Shepherd of the Anus was a specialist who performed enemas, which were practised as a means of maintaining general good health.

  Enemas were believed to have been introduced by Thoth, the ibis-headed god of knowledge. The ibis was often observed pushing water into its own rectum with its long beak to evacuate the bowels. The Egyptians followed suit – hopefully with a softer instrument!

- ✔ **Electroshock.** A more bizarre alternative treatment involved giving the patient electric shocks, using the electric ray *(malapterusus electricus)*, which swam in the Nile from at least the fifth dynasty.

Scribonius Largus (45 AD), physician to Emperor Claudius, records how electric rays were used in early Egyptian medicine for the cure of general pain:

> *When they come, one places a living electric ray under the foot of the patient. The patient then stands on a wet beach, covered as long as possible with water, until the foot is asleep up to the level of the knee.*

How this technique was supposed to stop pain – other than making you forget about it – I don't know. I can't decide what's worse, the pain or the cure!

✔ **Massage and reflexology.** An image from the fifth-dynasty tomb of Ankhmahor at Saqqara shows patients' hands and feet being massaged by practitioners in order to relieve aches and pains. This is thought to be the earliest image of reflexology in the world.

In a literary papyrus known as Papyrus Westcar, from the Middle Kingdom, the 110-year-old magician Djedi instructed 'his servant at his head to smear him and another to rub his legs', which indicates a form of physiotherapy which perhaps relieved some of the aches and pains of arthritis.

Satisfied customers?

Although the records don't mention the costs of medical examinations and prescriptions, patients most likely paid for a doctor's services. Because money was not used for most of the Pharaonic period, patients would have paid in goods. Whether patients paid before, after, or on the success of a treatment is unknown. However, numerous inscriptions are dedicated to various deities in gratitude for curing diseases. Whether a doctor was thanked with a gift was no doubt left to the discretion of the individual.

Opening Up and Saying 'Agh': Dentistry

The ancient Egyptians suffered greatly from dental problems, and clearly their pain threshold must have been very high considering the horrendous things festering in their mouths.

Not many dentists are known from ancient Egypt, although eight dentists have been identified from the Old Kingdom. Three of these names were discovered in three tombs in August 2006 (although the mummies had long been destroyed by looters). Three of these dentists also held the title of doctor. If dentists didn't always have a separate title, identifying them from doctors is difficult.

Wearing thin

The most common problem for all Egyptians, regardless of status or social position, was wear on the biting surfaces of their teeth. This condition was caused primarily by the quartz, greywacke, amphibole, mica, and sand in the grain, which was then ground into flour. These substances were all present in ancient bread and caused friction against the biting surface of the tooth while chewing. Whether these substances were added by the wind or intentionally is debateable – either way, the wear on their teeth was substantial.

The teeth were worn to such an extent that the enamel completely disappeared, leaving the sensitive inner pulp exposed. This exposed dental pulp then became infected, resulting in abscesses, swelling, and huge amounts of pain. In many instances, the abscesses were in the advanced stages and ate away at the bone of the jaw, resulting in tooth loss.

Little could be done to cure these abscesses other than draining the wound. The doctor or dentist used a flint knife to cut into the infection, and inserted a hollow reed to encourage the flow of pus out of the abscess. The ancient doctors knew that if they left any pus within the abscess it would recur, and they would have to go through the whole process again.

The ancient Egyptians seem to have figured toothache was normal, because the absentee records from Deir el Medina, which record excuses for days off work, show that no one took time off for toothache. (I know for a fact that if I had weeping abscesses, I would take at least a couple of days off!)

On a more positive note, the ancient Egyptians did not suffer from caries (decay) because of the very limited sugar in their diet. The elite sweetened their food with honey, but this was a luxury out of most people's reach. Only a handful of mummies show the start of dental caries, but almost every adult mummy has wear on the biting surface of their teeth.

The quest for fresh breath

With a mouth full of abscesses, the breath of the ancient Egyptians would have been somewhat ripe, to say the least.

The Egyptians did, however, do their best to clean their teeth using the frayed end of a twig. This technique resulted in the highly polished appearance of the teeth of many ancient Egyptian mummies.

The medical records have numerous prescriptions for freshening the breath, including chewing on cinnamon, frankincense, myrrh, and fragrant plants mixed with honey.

Considering Women's Health

Some of the medical papyri focus primarily on the health of women – particularly on fertility, childbirth, and health during pregnancy.

Many of the treatments are based on the idea that a woman is joined from the vagina to the head via a series of tubes. If these tubes are clear, she can become pregnant, and if they are blocked, she can't. Most treatments involve oral medicines or vaginal applications or fumigations.

Specific women's health topics included:

- ✔ **Contraception:** Excrement of crocodile dispersed finely in sour milk or honey and natron was used to avoid pregnancy. Both concoctions were used as a tampon and inserted into the vagina. And I am sure the resulting smell encouraged abstinence – a foolproof form of contraception.

- ✔ **Fertility:** The woman was advised to sit over a mixture of sweet ale and mashed dates. If she vomited, she was sure to give birth in the future; the number of times she vomited equalled the number of children she would have. If she didn't vomit, no children.

- ✔ **Pregnancy test:** The woman was supposed to urinate on barley and emmer wheat. If both of the seeds grew, she would give birth. If the barley grew first, she would give birth to a boy; if the emmer sprouted first, she would give birth to a girl. If neither grew, she was not pregnant. (When this method was recently tested, it didn't determine the sex, but, if a woman is pregnant, the grain does grow within a short period of time. When male urine was used, nothing happened.)

- ✔ **Amenorrhoea:** This is the premature stopping of the menstrual cycle and was 'cured' by giving a women a substance to drink for four days that induced vomiting. If the women vomited blood, her menstrual cycle would start again.

Chapter 9

Worshipping like an Egyptian: Religion

*W*hen looking at Egyptian religion, simply knowing where to begin can be difficult. With more than 700 different known gods, the ancient Egyptian population may seem very pious.

However, each god represents a different concept, role, or place where he or she was worshipped. And not every ancient Egyptian worshipped all the gods, all the time. They picked and chose which deity suited specific needs.

This chapter examines the many gods that the king and the priests – as well as everyday Egyptians – worshipped. I explore some of the most notable rituals and practices, including the popular practice of worshipping deceased humans.

Surveying the Pantheon of Egyptian Gods

The Egyptians were a very organised people, in religion as well as in almost everything else. Historians can divide Egyptian religious practice into two forms:

> ✔ **State religion** was closely connected with the king and his divinity. This religious practice was virtually inaccessible to most people. The state gods were worshipped in the large temples that dot Egypt, such as Karnak, Luxor, Abu Simbel, and Abydos. These temples were closed to the public; only the king and the priests were allowed to enter and worship.

✔ **Household religion** developed as a response to the exclusive state religion. Household religion involved a different set of gods. The people (without priests) worshipped these gods in their home (rather than in the temples).

Explaining all those unusual forms

Both state and household religion involved gods of somewhat bizarre form – represented as humans with animal heads, as animals, or as humans with inanimate objects for heads.

The Egyptians did not believe that these odd appearances were how the gods actually looked, however. They believed that deities were formless. The depictions represent the *characteristics* of the deity and his or her role in the pantheon of gods. The nature of the animal or object replacing the god's head gives some information about the god. For example:

✔ **Hathor** was a woman with a cow's head, which represents the mothering, nurturing nature of a cow.

✔ **Sekhmet** was a woman with a lioness's head, which represents the aggressive nature of a lioness.

✔ **Selket** was a woman with a scorpion body and human head, which represents that she is the protector against scorpion and spider bites.

Shifting roles and shapes

Like human beings, the Egyptian deities play numerous roles and take on various characteristics throughout their lives, which means that the same god can be presented in many different ways.

The sun god Ra, for example, is presented in four different ways, depending on the time of day:

✔ **Khepri** is the scarab beetle (or beetle-headed human) that represents the sun at dawn.

✔ **Aten** is the sun disc that represents the light that shines from the sun at noon.

✔ **Re-Horakhti** is a falcon-headed human with a sun-disc headdress that represents the sun on the horizon at dawn and sunset.

✔ **Flesh** is a ram-headed human that represents the sun at sunset.

Basking in the sun's rays

In a country as hot as Egypt, the sun was a particularly powerful force in people's lives. As such, the *solar cult* (worship of deities associated with the solar cycle) was particularly prominent from the Old Kingdom to the Roman period (see Chapters 3, 4, and 6 for more on these various eras).

However, rather than keeping matters simple, the Egyptians named and worshipped many different aspects of the sun god, depending on the time of day and the area where the sun god was worshipped. See the section 'Shifting roles and shapes' for more information.

Additionally, the solar gods were closely connected with the creation of the earth – the sun was the first thing to appear on the mound of creation at the start of time. This means that all solar deities are also creator gods. And as creator deities, they were also closely connected with the funerary cult and the rebirth of the deceased.

Many of the other deities wanted to get in on the solar action in order to increase their wealth and power (although in reality the power was probably coveted by the king or the priests rather than the deities themselves!). Many deities solarised their name by adding Ra to it (for example Amun-Ra). Even the kings wanted to be associated with the sun god and included 'son of Ra' in their kingly titles, showing their divine origins.

Making room for more

To add another dimension to this assortment of gods, the Egyptians were keen to mix and match their gods and make new ones. This goes some way towards explaining why the ancient Egyptians had so many gods.

For example, many gods possessed more than one characteristic and were therefore best represented by two different deities:

- ✔ **Amun-Min** was the combination of a creator god (Amun) and a god of fertility (Min).
- ✔ **Amun-Ra** was the combination of a creator god (Amun) and the solar god (Ra).

Some foreign deities were introduced and combined with an Egyptian god to make them more acceptable to the Egyptian population:

- ✔ **Seth** (the Egyptian god of chaos) combined with **Baal** (Canaanite lightning god).
- ✔ **Hathor** (Egyptian mother goddess) combined with **Anat** (Syrian martial goddess).

- **Osiris** (Egyptian god of the dead) combined with **Dionysus** (Greek fertility god).

- **Isis** (Egyptian mother goddess) combined with **Aphrodite** (Greek goddess of love).

- **Imhotep** (Egyptian god of medicine) combined with **Asklepios** (Greek god of medicine).

Deceit, murder – and forestry

One important Egyptian religious myth is that of Osiris and Seth. It serves as the basis for many of the funerary beliefs of the ancients, as well as explaining the divinity of the king.

Long ago, Osiris ruled Egypt. He was considered an ideal ruler, showing the people how to farm, worship the gods, and obey laws. His brother Seth was jealous and wanted the throne for himself. Seth devised a cunning plan to rid the world of Osiris and snatch the throne. First, he gathered all of Osiris's bodily measurements – height, width, inside leg, hair length, even toenail length. Seth then built a beautiful chest that fitted these measurements exactly.

Seth presented this chest at a banquet to which Osiris was invited and announced that whoever could fit into the chest could keep it. In true Cinderella style, everyone at the banquet tried to squeeze into the chest. Some were too fat, others too tall; some had hair that was too long or too thick. (And I'm sure someone had grotesquely long toenails!) Osiris, of course, fitted perfectly. But before he could gloat about his good fortune, Seth slammed on the lid, nailed it shut, and flung the box into the Nile, drowning the king.

When Osiris's wife Isis heard of Seth's exploits, she went in search of the chest in order to give her husband a decent burial. Her search took her all the way to Byblos (located somewhere in present-day Lebanon), where she learnt that the chest had grown into a tree that had been cut down and carved into a pillar in the palace of the king. After some time she managed to persuade the queen to let her take the pillar back to Egypt. When Isis arrived in Egypt, she lay down for a short nap. While she slept, Seth passed by, recognised the chest, removed the body of Osiris, and chopped it into 14 pieces, which he then scattered around Egypt. (Isis was clearly a very heavy sleeper.)

When Isis awoke, along with her sister Nephthys she initiated a search for Osiris's body parts. The duo were able to locate 13 of the pieces. The final part – Osiris's penis – was never found. Seth had thrown it into the Nile, where a fish promptly ate it.

Isis, however, proved herself a creative lass. After reassembling the collected body parts, she made a new, fully functioning 14th part from clay. She then transformed herself into a kite and flew over the body of Osiris. The breeze from her flapping wings gave him the breath of life, reviving him – just long enough for Isis to become impregnated with Horus. Osiris then died and was banished to the afterlife. Isis was left to raise Horus alone in the Egyptian marshes and to protect him from Seth until he was old enough to take over his father's throne.

Meeting the Egyptian State Gods

While the Egyptians worshipped more than 700 gods over the course of ancient history, several emerged as the most prevalent. This section looks at the notable figures in the state religion – primarily the king. Ordinary people worshipped a completely different set of deities at home (see the later section 'Worshipping at home: Household gods').

Identifying the main characters

Despite the large numbers of gods in the pantheon, a few stand out as the most important. The following gods were worshipped nationally, both as part of the state and household religions.

The three most important gods are

- ✔ **Osiris, the god of the underworld.** When the king died, he turned into Osiris so that he could continue to rule in the afterlife. In art, Osiris is represented as *mummiform* (wrapped like a mummy), holding the crook and flail to show his ongoing role as a king.

- ✔ **Horus (the son of Osiris and Isis), the god of order.** The king was believed to be an incarnation of the god Horus on earth. Horus is represented as a human with a hawk head.

- ✔ **Seth (the brother of Osiris), the god of chaos.** Seth was feared by most Egyptians because of his chaotic nature, although some kings adopted him as their personal god (Sety I and II, Ramses II and III). Seth is represented as a human with a strange head and a curved nose and long, erect, square-topped ears.

The three most important goddesses are

- ✔ **Isis (the sister and wife of Osiris, the mother of Horus), a general mother goddess.** Isis is presented as a beautiful woman, sometimes with wings in place of arms. She is also shown in the form of a kite to represent her role of providing the breath of life to the deceased. (See the sidebar 'Deceit, murder – and forestry' for more details.) She is shown with a throne sign on top of her head.

- ✔ **Nephthys (the sister of Isis and Osiris), a goddess closely associated with rebirth.** Nephthys aided Isis in the resurrection of Osiris and (by association) the deceased king. She is shown as a woman with wings for arms or as a kite to show similar characteristics to Isis. Nephthys is clearly identified by a semi-circle above a rectangle on top of her head, the hieroglyphs for her name.

✔ **Hathor (the daughter of the sun god Ra), a mother goddess, and deity of sex, love, beauty, fertility, and death.** Hathor is closely connected with the afterlife and the provision of food for the nourishment of the deceased. She is represented as a woman with a cow's head, a human with cow's ears and a cow-horn head-dress, or simply as a cow.

All these deities are interconnected in the same mythological stories, notably the myth of Isis and Osiris and the contending of Horus and Seth. These myths explain not only the role of the king but also the laws of royal succession.

Upholding truth, justice, and the Egyptian way: Maat

Rather than appearing in her own myths, the goddess Maat was believed to be present in absolutely everything that the ancient Egyptians did. She represented the concept of cosmic balance, justice, and truth. Although not worshipped as such, Maat was a major part of the lives of the rich and poor alike.

Maat is normally shown in human form with an ostrich feather on her head – or she is represented solely as a feather, the hieroglyphic sign for truth.

For the ancient Egyptians, the concept of Maat was present in everything – particularly in the law courts, which were overseen by judges called priests of Maat. Prayers were no doubt recited to Maat before court was in session, and a symbol of the goddess was likely in the courtroom. Judges probably addressed Maat on cases that were particularly tricky.

The most important and well-known role of Maat was in the Hall of Judgement, where deceased individuals (typically non-royals) were judged on their honesty and good deeds. The deceased's heart was weighed against Maat (represented as a feather) on huge cosmic scales. If the heart was heavier than the feather, Ammit (the devourer and a scary creature) ate the heart and denied the deceased individual rebirth and eternal life.

The weighing-of-the-heart ritual was carried out in front of Osiris, who had the final say as to who was reborn and who wasn't. Thoth, the ibis-headed god of scribes, recorded the outcome of the weighing of the heart. Fortunately, in the numerous surviving representations of this ritual, no one is ever unsuccessful.

Sibling rivalry: The contending of Horus and Seth

The contending of Horus and Seth is an ancient Egyptian myth that tells of a tribunal lasting for more than 80 years. During the trial, Seth tried to prove his right to the throne over Horus (see the sidebar 'Deceit, murder – and forestry' for details).

Horus was the son of Osiris, so the throne should rightfully have passed to him, a fact of which Seth was very much aware. The tribunal was overseen by eight divinities, including Isis and Re-Horakhty, who had tried to give the throne to Horus many times. Because Seth had never accepted their decisions, they proposed that Horus and Seth settle the argument once and for all with a series of death-defying challenges. The winner of these would be crowned the king.

Seth first suggested that he and Horus turn into hippos and submerge themselves under water for a period of three months; the one to survive wins the crown. Isis ended this task by throwing a copper harpoon into the water for fear her son Horus would die. She speared Horus and then Seth, resulting in them both emerging somewhat short of the three months. When she released them both from her spear, Horus was furious that she had freed Seth and cut off Isis's head. A somewhat extreme reaction – and certainly no way to treat your mum!

When Re-Horakhty learnt of Horus's action, he demanded that Horus be punished. Seth magnanimously offered to do it. What a hero! Seth found Horus asleep (decapitation is tiring work) under a tree and promptly plucked out both of Horus's eyes and buried them. The eyes turned into two bulbs, which grew into lotus flowers and illuminated the earth. This is mythology – go with me on this.

Seth then returned to Re-Horakhty and told him that he had not been able to locate Horus. Hathor, however, discovered Horus and healed his eyes by milking a gazelle into the sockets. She then reported Horus's injuries to Re-Horakhty, who in turn demanded that Horus and Seth stop their arguing.

After many further incidents, Horus decided to take the upper hand and offered to settle the argument with a race in stone ships; the winner gets the crown. This time, however, Horus planned to cheat. He built a boat of pine and covered it with gypsum to give the appearance of stone. Seeing Horus's boat floating in the water and believing that it was stone, Seth sliced off the top of a mountain to create his own racing ship. After the race began, Seth's boat obviously sank and rendered him the loser. Not happy at losing, he transformed himself into a hippo and attacked Horus's ship. Horus was about to throw a copper barb at Seth, but the tribunal gods stopped him.

Horus, his feathers ruffled, gathered up his harpoons and complained that he had been in the tribunal for 80 years, constantly winning battles against Seth, only to have the tribunal's decision ignored.

Eventually the deities came to the conclusion that the throne of Egypt should be given to Horus. However, although Horus was given the crown of Upper and Lower Egypt, many records attempt to maintain a sense of balance: Horus is often depicted ruling Upper Egypt and Seth ruling Lower Egypt. So everyone's a winner!

Worshipping at home: Household gods

The weighing-of-the-heart ritual (see the section 'Upholding truth, justice – and the Egyptian way: Maat', earlier in this chapter, for more information) was used primarily by non-royal individuals.

In fact, regular Egyptians worshipped a number of state deities in the home, using the same methods as in the temples – daily feeding, washing, and anointing of the statues kept in household shrines.

The following sections explore some of the more common gods and associated rituals for regular, everyday Egyptians.

The sublime cow: Hathor

Hathor was worshipped in the home as a goddess of love, marriage, and childbirth. She held spectacular titles such as 'lady of the vulva' and 'lady of drunkenness'.

She was responsible primarily for fertility, conception, and sexual love. At special shrines near the state temples, ordinary people left many offerings to Hathor in the form of necklaces, beads, and stone, clay, or wooden phalli, asking for fertility or thanking her for providing children.

Hathor was also worshipped as the

- ✔ **Goddess of the western mountain.** In this role, represented in tombs as a cow emerging from the marshes, Hathor protected the cemeteries situated on the west bank of the Nile.

- ✔ **Lady of the sycamore.** In this funerary role, Hathor provided sustenance for the deceased in the afterlife in the form of sycamore figs. She is represented as a woman emerging from a tree or as a woman with a tree on top of her head.

The craftsman: Ptah

At the village of Deir el Medina, which housed the craftsmen who built the Valley of the Kings, the creator god Ptah was worshipped as the patron deity of craftsmen.

The workmen appealed to Ptah for work-related ailments – the most common one being blindness caused by the dark, cramped, and dusty work conditions. Many inscriptions ask him to lift this affliction, which the workmen believed was caused by some blasphemous act on their behalf, rather than their working environment.

Ptah is depicted in mummiform guise, wearing a close-fitting cap rather like a swimming hat. In his hands he holds three staffs, representing stability, power, and eternal life, all of which he bestowed on his worshippers.

Attached to the external walls of some of the state temples, including Karnak, was an *ear chapel* that had a number of stelae dedicated to Ptah, decorated with a number of ears. The people whispered their prayers into the ears and the prayers went directly to Ptah himself. In some of the temples, a priest hole behind the stela allowed a priest to sit and answer the prayers. The worshippers must have believed that this disembodied voice was that of Ptah.

The happy dwarf: Bes

A number of deities were purely part of the household pantheon. Most of them are not the most attractive deities, but appealed more to the lives of ordinary folk. One of the most commonly worshipped was Bes, the god of love, marriage, fertility, and partying. He was also the protector of children and women through his noisy use of singing, music, and dance, which frightened snakes, scorpions, and all other forces of evil. If only all noisy people were as useful.

Bes is one of the only gods depicted face on, rather than in profile, which makes him really stand out from the crowd. He had a lion's head and tail, combined with the body of a dwarf with bowed legs and his feet turned outwards. His arms are often bent at the elbows, placed on his hips, or holding a musical instrument or knife. A rather odd-looking character.

Bes was often invoked during childbirth to protect the woman and newborn child, as well as to ensure a simple and safe birth. Images of Bes were placed on furniture (beds in particular), headrests, pottery vessels, eye make-up pots, and mirrors – all items that were closely associated with sexuality and fertility.

The grumpy hippo: Taweret

Another deity connected with fertility and childbirth is the pregnant hippo goddess Taweret, who is shown standing upright on her hind legs with pendulous human breasts, an abdomen swollen with pregnancy, and a mane formed from a crocodile's tail. So a real looker!

Taweret was an aggressive protector of women in childbirth and is depicted on similar objects as Bes, including head rests and cosmetic items. She also had a role in the afterlife and is depicted on various copies of the Book of the Dead.

The silent one: Meretseger

Some household deities were worshipped in particular regions, as is the case with Meretseger, who was worshipped primarily at Deir el Medina. She is represented as a cobra or as a woman with a cobra for a head, the hood open and ready to strike. She protected the inhabitants of the village from bites from cobras, scorpions, and spiders.

The Valley of the Kings, where the Deir el Medina inhabitants worked, lay in the shadow of a natural pyramid-shaped hill called Meretseger, which means 'she who loves silence'. The goddess was believed to protect the people in the same way as the mountain overpowers and protects the landscape.

Worshipping the Gods

Worship of each of the hundreds of ancient Egyptian gods – regardless of geography or function – was the same throughout the temples of Egypt. Worship in the home was similar except that rituals were carried out by the family rather than priests. The statue of the god was placed within a sanctuary in the rear of the temple, and the priest entered this sanctuary twice a day (at dawn and at dusk) to carry out the rituals:

- **At dawn,** the priest removed the statue from the shrine, washed it, anointed it with perfumes and ointments, and dressed it in a fresh linen shawl. The deity was then offered food and drink, which were placed at his or her feet. After the deity had taken spiritual nourishment from the food, it was distributed among the priests within the temple.

- **At dusk,** the same rituals were repeated and the statue was put to bed. The statue was washed, anointed with perfumes and ointments, offered food and drink, again which was placed at his or her feet. This was removed after the deity had taken spiritual nourishment from it. Then the statue was placed inside the shrine until the morning, when the rituals started again.

Throughout these rituals, the priest recited prayers and incantations, which varied in nature depending on the deity and his or her role.

Appreciating sacred geography

Although the rituals that the priest performed were the same, each cult centre had its own specific practices, including forbidden food, sacred animals, sacred symbols, and prayers.

Most of the state deities also had specific locations that served as their main cult centres (refer to the Cheat Sheet map). These sites were specifically revered:

- Ra's main cult centre was at Heliopolis. Excavations indicate that his temple was bigger than the temple at Karnak, but sadly this is currently not open to the public.

- Amun's main cult centre was at Karnak, although he was worshipped nationally. This is the largest temple complex in the world and is a must on a trip to Luxor.

- Osiris's main cult centre was at Abydos, which you can still visit.

- Isis's main cult centre was Philae, a common stop-off for tourists.

- Horus had three main cult centres; the first two are still standing and worth a visit:

  • Edfu, where he was worshipped in the image of a winged disc.

  • Kom Ombo, where he was worshipped as the son of Re.

  • Heliopolis, where he was worshipped as Re-Harakhti.

- Hathor's main cult centre was at Denderah, and you can still visit it.

- Seth's cult centres were based in the Delta region at Avaris and Qantir. These sites are not open to the public.

Participating in festivals

Festivals were an important part of worship for both state and household religion. Historical records show many festivals each month, with the most prominent ones being

- **Beautiful Festival of the Valley in Thebes.** Families visited their dead relatives in their tomb chapels to feast with them. The statue of Amun was carried in a long procession from Karnak to all of the mortuary temples on the west bank of the Nile.

- **Festival of Sokar-Osiris.** This festival was celebrated at night as a mortuary/lunar festival. People wore onions around their necks and brought offerings to the god and the deceased. The relevance of the onions is anyone's guess, but no doubt the area had a particularly pungent smell for a while afterwards.

- **Opet Festival at Thebes.** A statue of Amun was carried in procession along the sphinx avenue from Karnak temple to Luxor temple. The statue stayed at Luxor temple for a number of days before returning to Karnak temple.

- **Festival of Drunkenness at Deir el Medina.** This festival was in honour of Hathor and, as the name suggests, involved five days of drinking.

The preceding and loads of other festivals enabled everyone to have time off work to watch the processions through the streets – as well as enjoy extra food rations and lashings and lashings of beer!

Protecting the living

All Egyptians – both royal or non-royal – believed in the power of amulets to protect and strengthen their wearers, whether living or deceased.

An *amulet* is a figure made of any kind of material that can be attached to a necklace, bracelet, or ring. Hundreds of different types of amulets existed. Many featured images of specific deities; each provided specific protection from an individual god or goddess. Amulets were worn on necklaces and bracelets, alone or in conjunction with others, rather like a modern charm bracelet.

Other amulets represented aspects of mythology as well as hieroglyphic signs and included:

- **The ankh:** The sign for eternal life.

- **Scarabs:** Beetle-like creatures associated with the sun god that gave hope of new life and resurrection.

- **Eye of Horus:** A human eye with brow and markings below. The right eye was associated with the sun; the left eye with the moon. For the living, the Eye of Horus provided protection against all malicious spiritual or physical forces. Both eyes are frequently found on mummies because they have the power to resurrect.

- **Hedgehogs:** Worn for fertility and rebirth – due to the animal's reappearance after hibernation.

- **A leg:** A leg forms part of the hieroglyphic writing for 'health' and bestowed health on the wearer.

- **Two fingers:** Typically the index and middle fingers. Only found on mummies. Represents the fingers of the embalmers, ensuring that mummification took place as well as to provide extra protection for the vulnerable parts of the body.

- **Flies:** Worn for fertility and protection from persistent insects. Gold examples were a military honour, awarded by the king.

- **Frogs:** Mostly worn by women to absorb the fecundity of the frog.

- **A carpenter's set-square and plumb-line.** These symbols bestowed the wearer with eternal righteousness and stability.

Amulets worn by the living were also a means of showing wealth – the richer the material, the wealthier the wearer. Most were made of *faience* (a glass-like material), although some were made of semi-precious stones like carnelian, amethyst, and onyx.

Doing the voodoo that you do

The Egyptians may sound like a peaceful lot, but in fact some of their religious practices were flat-out vengeful.

Specifically, they believed in the power of clay or wax figures to bring destruction to their enemies – rather like the well-known practice of using voodoo dolls.

These ancient Egyptian figures came in two types:

✔ **Execration figures** were used to destroy the political enemies of Egypt and therefore only used by the king. Each figure represented a bound captive. On the captive's torso were lists of the traditional enemies of Egypt (Nubians, Asiatics, Libyans, Syrians). These figures were ritually broken and buried, representing the destruction of the listed enemies.

✔ **Curse figures** were made and used by private individuals as a way to immobilise another individual. Something horrible was typically done to the figure – burning or sticking nails in it. In order to make these figures more effective, a strand of the cursed individual's hair or a nail was moulded into the effigy. Curse figures were made of simple materials such as clay or wax. Presumably people could make their own without the need for a third party.

Although these figures were primarily used to cause harm and destruction, some people were creative and used them for somewhat dubious reasons. One figure in the Louvre in Paris (dated to 200–300 AD) depicts a female, bound with her hands behind her back and iron rods poked into her eyes and pubic region. This figure was buried with a lead tablet inscribed with a love charm that indicates that the figure was created out of love. However, according to the tablet, if the actual woman didn't fall for the charms of the man who made the figure, she would be destroyed. Let's hope she fell for him – I'm sure he had hidden depths.

Consulting oracles

In addition to interacting with the goddess Maat (see the section 'Upholding truth, justice, and the Egyptian way: Maat', earlier in this chapter), the Egyptians sought answers to legal issues and arguments in the form of *oracles*. Poor and rich alike used oracles to settle any number of disagreements, including personal issues.

People either addressed oracles within a temple or when the statue of the god was on procession through the streets. People had two ways of asking for help. They could:

- ✔ **Place a written message at the temple before the divine statue.** This would be handed to a priest who would place it before the god. The god answered the message by the use of yes/no tablets (a number of which have been found). This answer was then interpreted by the priests.

- ✔ **Address the statue through the priests who carried the sacred bark (boat containing the statue) during a procession.** People would shout out their questions, and the statue answered by varying the pressure on the shoulders of the priests who held the bark. The way the priests knelt or bowed meant different things to the people.

The genius of the oracle system was that if you didn't like the answer from one god, you went and asked another. There was no limit on the number of divine convictions.

Dreaming of deities

Although Egyptians appealed directly to the gods via oracles, the gods also appeared to people in dreams that dream priests then interpreted. These priests told individuals what they needed to do to have their prayers answered. Interpretations normally involved some contribution to the temple and were a lucrative business for the priests. (Call me cynical, but some of these divine messages may not have been genuine – and with enough greasing of palms, the interpretation could be anything that was required.)

Worshipping Humans

One of the most prominent forms of worship in the villages was the ancestor cult, in which villagers revered deceased members of the family, going back two or three generations. Living Egyptians appealed to the ancestors for help with everyday problems.

The Egyptians believed that after an individual was reborn into the afterlife, he or she became an *akh ikr en re*, or 'excellent spirit of Re' (go to Chapter 10 for more details). These individuals were thought to have the power to affect the life of the living as well as influence the gods of the afterlife. Through keeping the ancestors happy – by offering food and drink on a daily basis – Egyptians ensured that their deceased relatives supported the living members of the family.

The Egyptians embraced their ancestors and included them in their everyday lives, even incorporating false doors in their sitting rooms that allowed the spirits of ancestors to enter the house and participate in family meals and activities. Not something that would appeal to the average homeowner today.

Pocket-sized ancestors

Revered ancestors were included in religious festivals and processions through the use of *ancestral busts*. These were small (maximum 30 centimetres) portable figures of stone or wood representing a generic figure. The busts included the head and shoulders and sometimes wore large wigs. The busts rarely featured inscriptions, but historians believe that they represented male members of a family.

Egyptians placed these busts in their household shrines (see the 'Worshipping at home: Household gods' section above) and asked the departed for assistance. Small stelae (maximum 25 centimetres) sat alongside the ancestral busts in the household shrines. These stelae were inscribed with images of the ancestors as well as an image of the dedicator of the stela. Many have short prayers carved on them and invoke the aid of the deceased.

During the annual Beautiful Festival of the Valley (see the section 'Participating in festivals', earlier in this chapter), the statue of Amun was carried from Karnak in procession to the necropolis on the west bank of the Nile. Many Deir el Medina residents joined the procession with their ancestor busts. This procession ended at the tomb of the deceased, where a commemorative feast took place in which the deceased was believed to participate.

Deifying humans

The traditional household gods, concerned with fertility, childbirth, and danger from the bites of reptiles, insects, and arachnids, were not enough for the average Egyptian, who also worshipped humans, who were raised to the position of deities. This was not the same as the ancestor cult, because deified humans were often those who were revered and well-known in life. Deified humans were worshipped more widely than revered ancestors in the ancestor cult, which was limited to the immediate family.

Some deified humans were worshipped by the ordinary people and others by the kings. Deified humans were addressed for many reasons, including fertility and moral guidance.

Letters to the dead

Pottery vessels in many Egyptian tombs have a letter written on the inside. These letters to the dead were written by the remaining family and asked for help in various matters.

Families wrote the letters on a bowl, which was then filled with a tasty snack, so when the deceased ate the snack and saw the letter, they had to do what was requested because they had already accepted the bribe. Cunning, eh?

One letter of this type, written on papyrus, is particularly interesting:

To the able spirit Ankhiry. What evil have I done to you that I should land in this wretched state in which I am? What have I done to you? What you have done is to lay your hands on me, although I have done you no wrong. What have I done to you since I lived with you as your husband, until that day [of your death], that I must hide it? What is there now? What you have attained is that I must bring forward this accusation against you. What have I done to you? I will lodge a complaint against you with the Ennead in the West [the divine law-court in the hereafter], and one shall judge between you and me on account of this letter . . .

What have I done to you? I made you my wife when I was a young man. I was with you when I held all kinds of offices. I stayed with you, I did not send you away . . . 'She has always been with me' I thought . . . And see, now you do not even comfort me. I will be judged with you, and one shall discern truth from falsehood.

Look, when I was training the officers of the army of Pharaoh and his chariotry, I let them lie on their bellies before you. I never hid anything from you in all your life. I never let you suffer, but I always behaved to you as a gentleman. You never found that I was rude to you, as when a peasant enters someone else's house. I never behaved so that a man could rebuke me for anything I did to you . . .

I am sending this letter to let you know what you are doing. When you began to suffer from the disease you had, I let a head physician come and he treated you and did everything you asked him to do. When I followed Pharaoh, travelling to the south and this condition came to you, I spent no less than eight months without eating and drinking as a man should do. And as soon as I reached Memphis, I asked from Pharaoh leave and went to the place that you were, and I cried intensely, together with my people, before the eyes of my entire neighbourhood. I donated fine linen for wrapping you up, I let many clothes be made, and omitted nothing good to be done for you. And see, I passed three years until now living alone, without entering any house, although it is not fair that someone like me should be made to do so. But I did it for you, you who does not discern good from bad. One shall judge between you and me. And then: the sisters in the house, I have not entered any one of them.

The last line seems to have been written as an afterthought because it does not flow with the rest of the letter – but it is in fact the crux of the letter. The author is suffering from grief combined with guilt, which he believes is caused by his wife, whereas it is probably due to his activities with the women in the house! He obviously feels that his first wife does not approve and is punishing him.

Some notable deified humans who were worshipped by significant numbers in different regions of Egypt included

- **Imhotep,** the architect who built the step pyramid at Saqqara (see Chapter 13), was deified as a god of medicine, even though he was not a physician in life.

- **Senwosret III** was worshipped at the town of Kahun (see Chapter 2 for more details), because he was responsible for founding the city for the workmen who built his pyramid at el-Lahun.

- **Amenhotep I** was revered by the people at Deir el Medina as the founder of their village.

- **Amenhotep,** son of Hapu, was the vizier during the reign of Amenhotep III and was worshipped as a sage. He was the patron god of physicians and healing and was believed to aid with conception.

- **Horemheb** was revered by Ramses II, who set up a shrine in Horemheb's non-royal tomb at Saqqara. This worship was due to the break that Horemheb gave the family of Ramses II by choosing his grandfather to be king on his death.

People made offerings to the statues of deified humans, as well as reciting prayers and incantations to them.

Chapter 10

Exploring Funerary Beliefs and Mummification

*M*ost information from ancient Egypt comes from a funerary context, giving the impression that the Egyptians were obsessed with death and spent most of their time and wealth preparing for their earthly ends.

The ancient Egyptians were, in fact, obsessed with *life* and wanted to continue living for eternity. Although each individual no doubt had his or her own beliefs, evidence generally suggests that the ancient Egyptians believed careful preparation enabled them to make their lives after death more prosperous than their lives before. In fact, they believed that the afterlife (for ordinary Egyptians at least) was a perfect replica of Egypt, known as the *Field of Reeds*.

The Field of Reeds relied heavily on the solar cycle, and some believed the dead lay in primordial darkness until the sun god started his nocturnal journey in the afterlife. Although this landscape was abundant in water and vegetation, the provision of funerary goods, food, and elaborate tombs ensured the deceased's continuing happiness after death.

This chapter delves into one of the most frequently discussed (and often misunderstood) aspects of ancient Egyptian life – the preparation and burial of the dead through the physical and spiritual process of mummification.

Understanding the Egyptian Essence of Humanity

The Egyptians believed that a human being was made up of six elements or components. On death, these elements spontaneously separated. For a successful rebirth, all six elements were reunited through the funerary rituals, prayers, and offerings normally carried out by the priests and living family members.

The six elements were

- **The ka,** or the life force, which animated the individual – rather like batteries animate a toy.

- **The ba,** which was depicted as a human-headed bird. The ba represented the personality of the deceased.

- **The akh,** which was the name of the spirit created by combining ba and ka.

- **The deceased's name,** which was supposed to be repeated by the living for eternal life to be possible.

- **The shadow,** which is a little known aspect of the individual. It ties in with the solar cult, because without the sun, no shadow exists.

- **The physical body,** which was considered to be the combination of all these spiritual elements. The physical body was preserved by the process of mummification.

The Opening of the Mouth ceremony

The *ba* and *ka* were united in the afterlife through the *Opening of the Mouth ceremony.* This post-mummification ritual ensured the ka could see, hear, smell, breathe, and eat – all essential activities for life. For unknown reasons, the ba did not seem to need these earthly functions; when the ba was united with the ka for a length of time, it was nourished.

A *sem* priest (funerary priest) held a ceremonial *adze* (an axe-like hand tool) to the mouth of the mummy, which was believed to open the airways. The sem priest then offered prayers and anointed the mummy with oils. The ancient Egyptians considered this ceremony so important that they sometimes included images of the pots and jars used in the ritual on the coffin (examples appear on the interior of some Middle Kingdom coffins at the head end) in case the ritual hadn't been completed correctly and as a means of ensuring the instruments for this important ceremony were close to the body, thus increasing the ritual's effects.

The successful union of the ba and ka created another element of the body, the *akh* or spirit. The deceased was transformed into an eternal being of light. Although the akh was not divine, it had characteristics in common with the deities – the akh was able to intervene with the living and converse with the gods.

Cursing the Egyptologists

Mummies have inspired imaginations for centuries, causing both fear and awe. Over the decades, Hollywood has bombarded us with imaginative movies of mummies coming alive and chasing unsuspecting archaeologists around tombs. The mummies of horror movies are always evil, because of a curse placed on the tomb or the mummy itself.

The most famous curse story began during the excavation of the tomb of Tutankhamun in 1922 by Howard Carter and his team. The locals working with the team were very superstitious and believed entering the tomb would activate an ancient curse. To prevent the locals from entering the tomb at night and disturbing the excavations, the excavation team did not deny the curse, and the story was eventually picked up by an English newspaper.

From that point on, every death of a member of the excavation team was blamed on the curse, even those that happened 20 or so years later – a very slow-working curse, which included natural causes!

The only slightly odd event was an electrical blackout in Cairo at the time of Lord Carnarvon's death from an infected insect bite. (See Chapter 15 for more on Lord Carnarvon's contribution to the Tutankhamun excavation.) Of course, blackouts happened in Cairo regularly at the time – and still do, without any rational explanation. If you look hard enough, you can find significance in anything.

Of the thousands of tombs excavated in Egypt, only two have curses as such, to deter tomb robbers (the first is from the Tomb of Ursa, early New Kingdom; the second from a sixth dynasty tomb of Harkkhuf in Aswan):

> *He who trespassed upon my property or who shall injure my tomb or drag out my mummy, the sun-god shall punish him. He shall not bequeath his goods to his children; his heart shall not have pleasure in life; he shall not receive water (for his ka to drink) in the tomb; and his soul shall be destroyed for ever.*

> *As for anyone who enters this tomb unclean, I shall seize him by the neck like a bird, he will be judged for it by the great god.*

Don't worry, Egyptologists aren't in danger from these curses. They don't enter the tombs to injure, but to reconstruct, conserve, and learn about the owners and their history and culture.

For the ancient Egyptians, the repetition of a name ensured a prolonged afterlife. Through the study of the tombs and publication of the findings, Egyptologists are resurrecting the tombs' owners – which is what they desired all those thousands of years ago. Of course, debate continues as to whether placing mummies in museums (in store or on display) is appropriate.

I am sure the ancient Egyptians wouldn't be overly keen on today's flashy exhibitions. However, if modern Egyptologists didn't excavate the tombs, the ancient Egyptian's history, names and lives would be lost for eternity – the oblivion feared by all ancient Egyptians. A museum may not be the resurrection they wanted, but it is a resurrection and an eternal life of sorts.

Getting All Wrapped Up: Mummies for Dummies

The process of mummification can take two forms:

- ✔ **Natural:** The body is preserved in sand, ice, or peat.
- ✔ **Artificial:** The body is preserved by humans using a variety of hands-on methods.

Ancient Egypt offers examples of both forms of mummies.

In the pre-dynastic period (3500 BC), the Egyptians buried their dead in shallow pits dug into the sand on the desert edge. The pits were unlined, and the unwrapped bodies were placed in a foetal position, directly into the sand. Funerary goods consisted primarily of pots containing food and drink needed for the afterlife, which suggests that the Egyptians held a belief in life after death in this period.

When animals and shifting sands uncovered the bodies, the Egyptians realised that the skin and hair had been naturally preserved by the sand in which the bodies had been buried. The Egyptians began attempting to guarantee the preservation of the dead, rather than leaving it to chance. Over the years, the process of artificially preserving bodies evolved.

Experimenting on the dead

Various experimental mummification methods were introduced between 3500 BC and 2600 BC, including

- ✔ **Pot burials.** Fully grown adults were tightly flexed and placed inside large clay pots. The addition of a lid created a cocoon in which the body was sealed, buried in the ground and finally covered with sand.

✔ **Reed trays.** The body was placed on a shallow reed tray in a tightly flexed position and lain on its side. Rather than a lid, a linen cloth or animal skin was thrown over the body. This tray was then placed into a shallow pit and covered with sand.

✔ **Animal skins.** Prior to 3000 BC, the dead were wrapped in animal skins and placed into the shallow burial pits and covered with sand.

All the preceding methods resulted in the disintegration of the soft tissues, because the bodies were removed from contact with the substance that naturally preserved them – the sand. Skeletal remains are all that exist from these early attempts at preserving bodies.

Improving mummification practices

After the failure of early burial experiments, the Egyptians decided to preserve bodies before burial.

The earliest example of mummification was a royal burial of the first dynasty, belonging to King Djer. It was discovered by Petrie in the late 19th century. All that remained of this body was a mummified arm, adorned with bracelets of semi-precious stones. Unfortunately, the archaeologists were more interested in the jewellery than the arm, and the curator of the Cairo museum, Emile Brugsch, threw the arm part away. Luckily, however, they did take a solitary photograph of this early form of mummification – or rather, of how pretty the bracelets looked on the arm.

Mummification was only for the elite of society, and the multitudes of poor Egyptians were buried in pit burials, similar to the pre-dynastic examples, throughout Egyptian history. The only real difference is that mummified bodies after the pre-dynastic period were extended and not flexed.

Looking to the burial professional: The embalmer

Even though many examples of mummified bodies and tombs exist today, no written record from ancient Egypt is available that describes the process of mummification. The most complete record available is from Herodotus, a Greek historian from the fifth century BC.

Buried alive?

After the pre-dynastic period, animal skins were thought to be unclean and weren't used for wrapping the body. However, one example from the 18th dynasty, found in the Deir el Bahri royal cache, is of a young man stitched into a fleece. His hands and legs are tied with rope and no mummification is indicated on the body.

The man's open-mouthed expression suggests that he was stitched into the skin while still alive, and his presence in the royal cache suggests he was of royal blood. He was probably found guilty of a crime, although his crime is unknown. To deny him mummification and a proper burial condemned him to eternal death.

After an ancient Egyptian died, the body was taken to an embalmers' workshop, which was probably a temporary structure in the local cemetery. Because no evidence of these structures survives, historians are unsure of how many might have existed. The embalmers' workshops probably contained ready-made coffins and amulets, so the relatives could choose the appropriate assemblage according to their budget.

The senior embalmers were priests and were held in high esteem. The most senior embalmer in charge of wrapping the body wore a jackal mask, representing Anubis, the jackal-headed god of embalming.

Despite the high esteem in which embalmers were held, Herodotus records that the bodies of rich and powerful women were typically held back for a few days before being taken to the workshop, to prevent the bodies from being defiled. For example, when the 18th-dynasty mummy of Queen Ahmose-Nefertari was unwrapped, her body showed signs of decomposition of soft tissues before mummification. Although she was in her 70s when she died, her position as a queen may have rendered her desirable even after death – to someone who was that way inclined. (Of course, the sources and truthfulness of Herodotus's information are unknown.)

Stepping through the embalming process

The most expensive and comprehensive method of mummification made the deceased look like Osiris, the god of the underworld. Egyptians believed that the deceased king – and by the Middle Kingdom, deceased nobles – become like Osiris on death.

More inexpensive mummification methods were available (see 'Considering budget burials', later in this chapter, for details), but the following outlines the complete process.

Removing the brain

In the New Kingdom, the embalmers usually removed the brain first. Ancient Egyptians believed that thought processes and emotions occurred in the heart, so the brain was superfluous. (Know any people like that?)

The embalmers broke the ethmoid bone at the top of the nose and removed the brain piecemeal with a hook through the nasal cavity. However, experiments have shown that this method would have inefficiently removed the brain in tiny pieces.

To improve this part of the process, a liquid of juniper oil and a turpentine substance was typically poured up the nose and left for a few minutes to dissolve the remains of the brain, which were then poured out through the nostrils and disposed of. Remnants of dissolved and solidified brain matter have been found at the back of skulls.

Liposuction – Egyptian style

After removing the brain, the embalmers then made a cut in the left side of the lower abdomen with a flint knife and removed the whole contents of the abdomen, except the heart. The embalmer who made this initial slit was then ceremoniously chased out of the workshop, with people throwing stones, sticks, and abuse at him for defiling the body. Whether he returned to the workshop is unknown; I for one would have stayed well away.

After the organs were removed, the abdomen was thoroughly cleaned – first with palm wine and again with an infusion of pounded spices with antibacterial properties to stop the cavity from smelling.

After drying the cavity, the embalmers filled it with a mixture of aromatic substances; linen or sawdust was inserted to give the empty cavity shape. The body was then sewn up and the slit hidden by a bronze or leather leaf-shaped cover.

Preserving the innards

The viscera removed from the bodies were treated as carefully as the bodies themselves. They were dried in *natron*, a natural salt substance that came from the Wadi Natron (the Natron Valley). The dried organs were then wrapped in linen and placed inside *canopic jars*, which in turn were placed inside rectangular canopic chests made of the same material as the coffins and sarcophagi.

The canopic jars had lids in the form of four animal heads, which represent the Four Sons of Horus (the hawk-headed god of order). The Four Sons of Horus each had a specific role to play in the afterlife, because they protected a part of the body and then provided the body with its essential internal organs when the deceased was reborn. The Four Sons of Horus were:

- *Imsety*, a human head, which protected the liver.
- *Hapy*, an ape head, which protected the lungs.
- *Duamutef*, a jackal head, which protected the stomach.
- *Qebehsenuef*, a falcon head, which protected the intestines.

Drying the body

The stuffed body was then placed on an embalming table for 35–40 days with natron packed around the body, completely covering it. Examples of these long, low embalming tables have been discovered in the embalming caches. The location of these tables during drying and the security measures utilised are sadly unknown.

Optional extras

Ever ingenious, Egyptian embalmers developed additional mummification processes to further prepare the bodies of the deceased. Some interesting extras that have been discovered include:

- **Post-mortem skin treatment.** An elderly priestess, Nesitetnabtaris from the New Kingdom, was bedridden for a large proportion of her later years because of a fracture in her neck. As a result, her back, buttocks, and shoulders were covered in bed-sores and abscesses. After she died, the embalmers stitched up the worst of the abscesses with flax and covered the stitching with resin so it wasn't visible. They then covered the bed sores with a large gazelle skin stitched to the priestess's back, buttocks, and shoulders. This procedure ensured her body was reborn in the afterlife as complete and perfect – albeit with a go-faster stripe!

- **Gender reassignment.** Mummy 1770 in the Manchester Museum presented a multitude of problems for the embalmers. She died at the age of 14 in the New Kingdom and was rewrapped 800 years later; the newer wrappings are the ones that have survived. She was obviously rewrapped due to the shocking state of her original wrappings, perhaps after a tomb robbery. Before the rewrapping, embalmers did not know her name, identity, or sex. To hedge their bets, the embalmers provided gold nipple covers – to ensure lactation in the afterlife – as well as a penis made of a roll of linen bandages. The expectation was that in the afterlife she would use what she needed. The embalmers presumably thought their ignorance would never be exposed – but modern sexing techniques uncovered the blunder.

After 35–40 days, the body was removed, washed, and prepared for wrapping, which took up to an additional 30 days, ensuring the entire process took no more than 70 days in total.

Interestingly, the star Sirius, associated with Osiris, disappears for 70 days at a time. Osiris also disappeared for 70 days before his resurrection. Symbolically, the deceased becomes Osiris on death, disappearing for 70 days during the mummification process and then being reborn in the afterlife.

Wrapping the body

Wrapping the body was just as important as its preservation, and a priest wearing an Anubis mask (the god of embalming) was responsible for the job.

The priest needed large amounts of linen to wrap a body – up to 400 square metres have been discovered on some mummies, with more than 40 layers of wrappings.

Deceased royalty had their funerary linen specially made by the temple and harem workshops. Some of the wrappings of Ramses II were even woven from blue and gold thread.

Given the amount of linen required for wrappings, and its expense, non-royal bodies were unlikely to be bound in material made especially for burial, or even in linen provided by one household. Because they found different names on wrappings of the same mummy, researchers think that friends and relatives may have provided the linen required. Perhaps if someone died, the whole village donated linen to the family.

The evolution of wrapping

Wrapping styles changed over the years. The dates of mummies can be identified according to certain characteristics:

- **Old Kingdom:** Each limb was wrapped individually, including each finger and toe. The wrappings were then coated in resin. Plaster was moulded over the bandages of the face and painted in lifelike colours.

- **Middle Kingdom:** Mummies were wrapped in the traditional shape with all the limbs wrapped together. The hands were placed flat over the thighs or crossed over the genitalia. Mummy masks replaced the painted plaster, and many of these masks have full beards and moustaches, sometimes painted blue or green. Perhaps the earliest punks?

- ✔ **New Kingdom:** Additions were made to the mummies before wrapping, including eyes inlaid with onyx and crystal to maintain the shape. (However, Ramses IV was given two small onions as eyes – now that would definitely make your eyes water!) The arms of the royal mummies were crossed over the chest and the hands were often closed into fists.

- ✔ **Ptolemaic period:** Embalmers used very thin strips of fabric, arranged into intricate geometric patterns and decorated with studs and stars.

- ✔ **Roman period:** Elaborately painted portraits of the deceased in life were wrapped amid the bandages.

- ✔ **Roman era:** Elaborate mummy portraits were placed among the wrappings, representing the dead when they were alive.

Inclusions in the wrappings

From the New Kingdom onwards, texts from the *Book of the Dead* (refer to the later section 'The Book of the Dead') were sometimes written on the bandages to aid the deceased in the afterlife. These passages were appropriately placed on the relevant body parts to ensure protection.

While each limb of the mummy was bandaged, the priests recited spells from the funerary texts of the period (see 'Guiding the Dead in the Underworld', later in this chapter) to render each limb divine and ensure the deceased was reborn for eternity. No wonder wrapping took 30 days! Amid all the bandages, the embalmers placed numerous amulets that aided the deceased in the afterlife.

Considering budget burials

Cheaper mummification processes were available from the Middle Kingdom onwards, as evidenced in several surviving mummies from these periods. However, as mentioned in the preceding section, 'Looking to the Burial Professional: The embalmer', the exact process is recorded only in Herodotus' writing from the fifth century BC.

In general, these cheaper techniques did not involve removal of the internal organs. The mixture of juniper oil and turpentine was injected into the body through the anus, which was stopped up to prevent the liquid escaping (the most extreme enema!). After a period, the plug was removed and the liquid was drained, releasing the dissolved organs with it. However, the organs of some mummies did not dissolve evenly, and partially dissolved innards clogged the anus.

The body was then soaked in natron for 40 days, after which it was washed and prepared for wrapping. An even cheaper alternative involved dissolving the organs, drying the body, and returning the mummy to the relatives without wrapping.

STRANGE BUT TRUE

An ancient cover-up

The mummy of a 22nd dynasty priest from the temple of Khonsu at Karnak, Nesperenub, was the subject of a British Museum 3D exhibition in 2004. The mummy was placed in a cartonnage coffin, which was made of plastered layers of fibre or papyrus. The coffin couldn't be removed without destroying it. For many years, X-rays highlighted a strange object attached to the back of Nesperenub's head. This irregularity caused much puzzlement. With the use of CT (computerised tomography) scans and digital imaging, researchers were able to look inside Nesperenub's body in a way that had never been achieved before.

The CT scan identified the object as a roughly moulded clay bowl, complete with the potter's fingerprints. It would seem that while the embalmers were gluing the first layer of bandages to the head with resin, they placed the bowl beneath the head to catch the run-off. However, it was clearly the end of their shift, they forgot the bowl was there, and when they returned to work in the morning the resin had set solid, gluing the bowl to the head. Marks on the back of the head indicate that the embalmers tried to chisel the bowl off. They gave up and decided to include it in the wrappings. Who would ever know?

Returning to sender

After the bodies were wrapped, the embalmers returned them to the families for burial. However, bodies were not always buried straight away because family tombs were opened only every few years to limit robberies. While a mummy awaited final burial, it was stored in a room either at the embalmers' workshop for a rich family or in the home for a poorer family.

Getting dressed up: Clothes to be seen dead in

In addition to wrappings, linen clothes were also placed on or around the bodies, although whether embalmers or family members dressed mummies is unknown.

- A fifth-dynasty female had nine shirts buried with her inside her wooden coffin. Two of them were clearly designed as grave goods because they were very long (142 centimetres) and very narrow, rendering them unwearable in real life.

- A mummy dated to 2362 BC from Tarkhan, currently in the Petrie Museum, was buried with clothing that shows creasing under the armpits and on the elbows, indicating it had been worn in life and was probably a much loved outfit.

✔ Other clothing examples discovered in tombs were turned inside out and folded, which was a practice that Egyptian laundries used to indicate that garments had been laundered. These inside-out garments indicate that burial clothing was also worn in life.

Tidying up

After the embalmers completed the mummification process and the body was handed back to the family, all the material from each embalming process was buried in an individual cache. This process suggests that one cache should exist for each burial; sadly this is not the case in the archaeological record.

A number of embalmers' caches have been discovered from Thebes and Saqqara, including that of Tutankhamun. These caches include all the material that was used in the embalming process:

✔ Labelled pots and jars containing coloured powders for colouring the mummy

✔ Resins for filling, deodorising, and sanitising the mummy

✔ Linen for stuffing and wrapping

✔ Natron for desiccating

✔ Wax for covering the body and some of the orifices

✔ Various oils for curing and scenting the body, as well as making it supple

✔ Terebinth resin as deodorant and perfume

✔ Sawdust and chaff for stuffing cavities

✔ Lamps and fragments of the funerary feast held after the funeral in the tomb chapel

✔ A broom to sweep the footprints away of the last person to have been in the tomb

Some of the caches also contain the embalming table, which was a low table because most of the mummification process was performed from the squatting position. These tables are stained with natron, oils, and bodily fluids.

At the time of writing, the most recently discovered tomb in the Valley of the Kings (KV63) is being excavated. All seven coffins opened are full of embalmers' material similar to that used in the burial of Tutankhamun, including floral collars worn at funerals. A number of large storage vessels in the tomb are filled with natron, bandages, and various vessels, indicating that the tomb may have been an embalmers' workshop rather than a burial place. The new tomb may be the embalming cache for an as-yet-undiscovered tomb!

STRANGE BUT TRUE

Catching the imagination

Although the practice of mummification declined in the Roman period, mummies and the ancient Egyptians' burial processes have remained intriguing to the world ever since.

From AD 50 to the 19th century, the ideas regarding mummies were increasingly bizarre. Because mummies were between 2,000 and 4,000 years old, many believed they held the secret of eternal life. Mummies were commonly ground down to a powder, referred to as *mumia*, and eaten as an elixir of life. The King of Persia even sent Queen Victoria a small vial of bitumen (associated with production of the late-period mummies) for her health. One wonders if her long life was due to taking a little mummia with her tea!

In the late 19th century, the wealthy also frequently purchased mummies to display in their houses. Public unrollings of mummies were elite social events, at which ladies were known to faint at the ghastly sight as men looked on in scientific interest. Because the demand for genuine ancient mummies for unrolling events soon outstripped supply, the enterprising Egyptians made fake mummies, dried and aged in the sun, to sell to unsuspecting rich western tourists.

Guiding the Dead in the Underworld

Although the embalmers preserved the bodies, further precautions were included in the tombs to ensure that the deceased weren't hindered on their journey to rebirth and the afterlife.

These precautions were in the form of 'guide books' to the afterlife. Instructions were written on coffins, walls, papyri, and bandages, and gave the deceased necessary information for travelling through the afterlife and obtaining eternal life. The following sections discuss the most common guides for the dead.

The Pyramid Texts

The *Pyramid Texts* are the earliest funerary texts, and not surprisingly they are written in the pyramids from the reign of Unas of the fifth dynasty until the reign of Ibi, an obscure king from the eighth dynasty.

The texts were inscribed in the burial chamber and antechamber of the pyramid (see Chapter 14 for more on pyramid architecture) and do not include pictures of any kind. The hieroglyphs are painted green to represent regeneration.

The Pyramid Texts were initially designed for royal burials, but by the end of the Old Kingdom some chapters of the text were being used in non-royal tombs. The spells were initially concerned with the afterlife of the king and present different fates for him – all equal in importance. These fates were:

- ✔ The king can ascend to the sky to become a star amid his ancestors.

- ✔ On death, the king can become Osiris, the god of the underworld.

- ✔ The king can join the sun god in his solar bark (divine boat) and accompany him on his nocturnal journey.

Obviously, contradictions existed in the belief system concerning what actually happened after the king died. Even from this early period, the Egyptians appear to have as many ideas about the afterlife as their modern counterparts.

The Pyramid Texts were made up of three categories, consisting of a number of *spells*, or chapters. Different combinations of spells were chosen to decorate the pyramids. The three categories included:

- ✔ **Incantations,** which were of a protective nature. Incantations were use to ward off snakes and other dangers that the deceased king may come across in the afterlife that could affect his rebirth.

- ✔ **Funerary spells,** which associated the deceased with a manifestation of Osiris. These spells describe the king's journey into the afterlife and were often inscribed in the burial chamber. These words are narrated by the king's son in his role as Horus, the son of Osiris. These texts describe offerings and resurrection rituals, including the words of the Opening of the Mouth ceremony (see the sidebar 'The Opening of the Mouth ceremony', earlier in this chapter, for more).

- ✔ **Personal spells,** which the deceased was to use for his or her journey in the afterlife. These spells were placed in the antechamber and the passage leading out of the pyramid, aiding the *ka* as it left the tomb. These spells refer to the landscape of the underworld and include imagery such as crossing water and ascending a ladder to the sky.

The Coffin Texts

At the beginning of the Middle Kingdom, the Pyramid Texts evolved into the *Coffin Texts* – very imaginatively named, because the Coffin Texts were inscribed primarily on coffins (although inscriptions have been found on tomb walls, mummy masks, and papyri as well).

The Coffin Texts were similar to the Pyramid Texts, although new spells were added. They were available for both royal and non-royal individuals.

The Coffin Texts further developed some ideas introduced in the Pyramid Texts, including:

✔ The heavenly travels of the *ba* alongside the sun god in the solar bark.

✔ The idea that existence in the afterlife is reliant on the nourishment of the *ka*. The preservation of human remains is essential so that *ba* and *ka* can unite to become reborn. Because of this, the *offering frieze* was one of the most important elements of the Coffin Texts and consisted of an elaborately painted scene of all the goodies given to the deceased (food, clothes, weapons, and jewellery).

✔ Personal spells were still present, although they were incorporated into *Guides to the Hereafter*, the most common of which was the Book of the Two Ways. *The Book of the Two Ways* was an introduction to the Netherworld, accompanied by a map that showed how to gain access to it and all notable landmarks. Just what any traveller needs. These maps, dominated by two paths consisting of earth and water, can often be seen on the base of coffins.

The Book of the Dead

The New Kingdom was a renaissance for funerary texts, with many different versions being produced, including *The Book of the Dead* with its more than 200 spells compiled from the Pyramid and the Coffin Texts, plus some new, updated additions.

Text from the Book of the Dead was written on coffins, linen mummy shrouds, papyrus, tomb walls, and bandages, and was often illustrated with colourful vignettes relating to the text. (Earlier funerary texts consisted primarily of text only.)

Some noteworthy additions include:

✔ **Spell 125, which relates to the judgement of the deceased and his worthiness to receive eternal life.**

✔ **Specifications that some chapters need to be written on certain objects to obtain the best results.** For example:

• Chapter 6 should be written on *shabti figures*, servant statues that were placed in the tomb to work on behalf of the deceased. (No one wants to think eternity is filled with mundane chores!)

• Chapter 26, 27, 29b, and 30b, were to be written on *heart scarabs*, which were large scarabs placed over the heart. The scarabs were implored not to give away any naughty secrets when the deceased stood before Osiris in the Hall of Judgement.

- Spell 100 should be written on a clean, unused papyrus using a powder of green pigment mixed with myrrh and water. This sheet should be placed on the breast of the mummy without actually touching the body. If this was done, the deceased was able to board the bark (sacred boat) of Re and thus hang out with the most important of the gods! A very important spell indeed.

✔ **Indications that certain spells or sections of spells were to be read aloud by different people, including the *ka* priests, embalmers, and the deceased themselves.** Spells to read by the deceased were placed in the tomb as close to the body as possible in the burial chamber, so the *ka* would have immediate access to this information as soon as it left the body.

With so many clear specifications, not all 200 chapters of the Book of the Dead were ever written out in full in any one place.

Guides to the Hereafter

Unlike the Book of the Dead, the *Guides to the Hereafter*, which included the Book of Gates and the Book of the Amduat, were not a constantly changing collection of spells, but the first religious books whose contents were set, followed a theme, and were to be viewed in a specific order. The *Guides to the Hereafter* were only ever used by kings and were generally not even allowed in the tombs of queens. These books are currently visible in the tombs in the Valley of the Kings (see Chapter 13).

The Guides to the Hereafter were more illustrated than the Book of the Dead and followed the 12-hour nocturnal journey of the sun god, accompanied by the deceased.

In the story, the nocturnal journey starts at sunset for the sun and at burial for the deceased. The sun carries its light into the underworld and travels to the east to be reborn. Each hour of the 12-hour journey is separated by gates or portals protected by demons and serpents. The deceased needs to recite the name of the demon and the gate to pass through. Many of the hours include demons willing to harm the sun god and his companions – a real good-versus-evil scenario that would make a great film! At the end of the 12 hours, the sun is reborn into the sky, and the deceased is reborn into the afterlife.

It was not necessary to have all 12 hours inscribed on a tomb wall, coffin, or papyri, and often a representative one or two hours were used depending on the space available.

Tipping the balance

After the deceased negotiated his or her way through all the portals and gateways of the afterlife, there was just one tiny task left to perform before the deceased was left alone for eternity. This is to enter the Hall of Judgement, to stand before Osiris, the god of the underworld, and prove their worth.

The heart of the deceased was weighed against the feather of truth (*Maat*). If the heart was heavier, it was devoured by the monster (*Amut*) waiting nearby, thus preventing the deceased from being reborn and cursing the deceased to reside in eternal limbo.

Rather than leaving the weighing of his or her heart to chance, the deceased recited the *negative confession* from the Book of the Dead, which tells the 42 judges of the underworld all the things that the deceased has *not* done. Cunning really, because if you had done something, don't mention it and no one would ever know! The negative confession included the following lines:

> *I have done no falsehood.*
>
> *I have not robbed.*
>
> *I have not been rapacious.*
>
> *I have not killed men.*

The confession continues along these lines, combining trivial things and terrible crimes almost as if they are the same thing. If anything is missed out from the confession, the heart scarab (see preceding section 'The Book of the Dead') was inscribed with a prayer encouraging the scarab not to betray any wrongdoings still present within the heart.

Although the weighing of the heart sounds terrifying, the numerous examples of this scene show that not one person failed. So obviously reciting the negative confession worked.

Nourishing the ka

After the deceased was reborn into the afterlife, it was essential to maintain a *cult of the ka* to ensure he or she lived eternally. For royalty, this cult was practised within a mortuary temple and involved numerous priests. For laymen, however, if they were wealthy enough to have a tomb with a tomb chapel, family members acted as the *ka* priests and kept the cult active, or paid a priest to perform at the tomb. For poorer individuals, family members maintained the cult within the home.

Knowing was beyond even the Egyptians

Despite all the ancient Egyptians' efforts to preserve their bodies for eternity, not everyone was certain that the afterlife existed.

In some tombs from the New Kingdom, blind harpers are shown entertaining the elite at banquets. Above some of these harpers are the lyrics of the following song:

What has been done with them?

What are their places now?

Their walls have crumbled and their places are not

As if they have never been.

No one has ever come back from the dead

That he might describe their condition,

And relate their needs;

That he might calm our hearts

Until we too pass into that place where they have gone

Let us make holiday and never tire of it!

For behold no man can take his property with him,

No man who has gone can ever return again.

Clearly, the Egyptians were uncertain of the reality of the afterlife. But of course they continued with their mummification and funerary preparations, just to hedge their bets!

One of the most important elements of the cult of the ka was the constant food offerings, which were laid before a *stela* (a statue or false door) for the daily sustenance of the *ka*. These offerings consisted of bread, beer, fowl, oxen, and vegetables. Presumably the families tried to ensure that the offerings included food the deceased liked when he or she was alive. Nothing is worse than having to survive for eternity on fish heads and cabbage if you don't like them!

Accompanying these offerings were prayers and incantations, which primarily ensured that the name of the deceased was kept alive through repetition.

For royalty, these prayers and offerings were made twice daily to the *ka* statue of the king within his mortuary temple. For the rest of the community, the level of devotion was time-consuming and intrusive, so ceremonies were likely to be carried out weekly, monthly or annually, depending on the particular family and their commitments.

Part IV

Interpreting Egyptian Art and Architecture

The 5th Wave   By Rich Tennant

IN ANCIENT EGYPT, ONLY NOBLEMEN DROVE HORSEDRAWN CHARIOTS. FARMERS WERE FORCED TO USE MORE PLENTIFUL ANIMALS.

©RICHTENNANT

In this part . . .

Egyptologists are lucky because so many texts, tombs, and temples survive, giving a rounded view of the whole of ancient Egyptian culture. The major breakthrough in Egyptology as a discipline was deciphering hieroglyphs in the early 19th century. Prior to this, explorers could only look on in wonder with no real insight into the Egyptian's culture and beliefs.

The monuments of the ancient Egyptians are closely tied in with religion, and all architectural elements of a temple have a purpose. However, the development of tombs from holes in the ground to pyramids, and back to holes in the ground again has more to do with security than religion. As the tombs became more secretive they became more elaborately decorated; almost as compensation. This part takes you there.

Chapter 11

Deciphering Egyptian Art and Hieroglyphs

*E*gyptian art – including *hieroglyphs*, which are pictures that represent letters, sounds, ideas, and objects – is distinctive and appears strange to the untrained eye. However, after you begin to understand the codes behind the images, these ancient pictures start to speak and give loads of information about the places, events, and people represented, including their age, rank, occupation, and status.

Egyptian art survives primarily in the embellishments of tomb and temple architecture and in objects both beautiful and practical. See Chapter 12 for more on decorating temples and Chapter 13 for more on decorating tombs.

This chapter shows you how to carefully unravel these image-based codes and reveal the secrets of Egyptian art.

Recognising the Artists

Egyptian artists were very well trained and needed to be schooled in the many conventions of Egyptian art, which enabled the images all over Egypt to be the same.

This extensive training was carried out on the job, and like all Egyptian professions, it was passed on from father to son, starting in infancy (see Chapter 2 for more on occupations). First the apprentice practised his drawing and carving on *ostraca* – broken pieces of pottery and limestone used as scrap paper, rather like the modern sticky note. His tutor corrected these rough sketches in a different-colour ink. Many surviving examples show these errors and corrections.

Team players

Unlike the art of many civilisations, Egyptian art cannot be assigned to a particular artist due to the very strict artistic conventions of the time.

Saying that, the archaeological record *has* provided the names of artists who lived at Deir el Medina and worked on the royal tombs. Sadly, although historians know the artists' names and the tombs they worked on, all the artwork was done in close-knit teams, so specific scenes can't be attributed to an individual. From today's point of view, this anonymity and the culture's strict conventions may have been frustrating for artists because they had no means to express their individuality.

Each team was made up of approximately 30 people, including a number of different craftsmen:

- **A master craftsman** who designed the original composition and double-checked and corrected all the work of his men
- **Plasterers** who prepared the walls for painted relief
- **Stone masons** who prepared the walls for carved relief
- **Outline scribes** who drew the outline for both carved and painted relief
- **Sculptors** who carved the outlines for carved relief
- **Artists** who painted the images for both painted and carved relief

All workmen in a team worked at the same time on a sort of production line.

After the plasterers had prepared one area of wall, the outline scribes sketched the images and the plasterers moved on to another part of the wall. As soon as the outline scribes had finished one bit, the sculptors started their work and the outline scribes worked a little further along.

The entire process was well timed to ensure that the men carried out as much work as possible in the shortest amount of time. This process was used primarily on the large-scale compositions that range from one metre square to tens of metres square. The master craftsman had to prepare the entire composition in advance.

Following the master plan

Although the artists were all skilled in the various characteristics of Egyptian artistic style, a grid system was introduced to ensure the artwork was to scale and in proportion throughout a tomb or temple. This grid system was used for both painted and carved relief.

All compositions were initially sketched on papyrus and were copied and enlarged onto the walls of the tombs and temples. The master plan had a grid drawn over the images so artists could easily scale up the images through copying from the smaller grid to one drawn on the wall.

Artists created the grid on the wall by dipping string into red paint, stretching it across the surface, and then snapping it back into place to get a red line. This was repeated with multiple horizontal and vertical lines, creating a grid. These lines disappeared as the rock was carved or was painted over.

Equipping the Artists

The vibrant remains of Egyptian art in the form of tombs, temples, and carved statues are even more remarkable when you consider the very limited array of tools available at the time.

Paintbrushes were either bundles of plant fibres doubled over and lashed together at the doubled end to make a handle, or pieces of reed chewed at one end to make a frayed brush-type implement.

Paints were hand mixed and some ingredients for certain colours needed to be imported, which made paint an expensive commodity. Surprisingly, many of the colours are still amazingly vibrant, even though they were painted more than 3,000 years ago.

Through chemical analysis, researchers have been able to identify the minerals used to make the paint:

- **Red** was made from red ochre or iron oxide, which are both resources of Egypt.

- **Blue** was made from azurite, a carbonate of copper found in the Sinai and the eastern desert. The hue was also made of a combination of silica, copper, and calcium.

- **Yellow** was made from yellow ochre, iron oxide, or orpiment (a sulphide of arsenic); all are found in Egypt.

- **Green** was made of malachite from the Sinai. It was sometimes made by blending blue frit and yellow ochre, which were both available in Egypt.

- **Black** was made from soot, lampblack, charcoal, or plumbago (a blue flowering plant), all readily available in Egypt.

- **White** was made from gypsum, calcium sulphate, or whiting calcium carbonate, all natural to Egypt.

- **Brown** was created by painting red over black.

Lamps, which lit the dark tombs throughout the work, were also important. Shallow lamp dishes were filled with oil and included flax (a plant) or linen wicks. Because these light sources produced a great deal of smoke, some unfinished tombs show black soot marks on the ceiling – the most famous soot-covered tomb being that of Tutankhamun.

Figuring Out Egyptian Art

Egyptian art is not a photograph. When considering Egyptian art, modern viewers must remember that the Egyptians rarely recorded 'the truth' – a realistic depiction of an object or person.

Although the images can never be viewed as portraiture or a true rendition, every element of a composition is designed to tell you something about the person, event, or ritual. This notion explains the lack of perspective and three-dimensional qualities in Egyptian art, as well as the somewhat bizarre (to our eyes at least) representations of people, animals, and gods.

Everything in ancient Egyptian art is presented from the most recognisable viewpoint, in an effort to eliminate all ambiguity. However, modern Egyptologists aren't the intended audience for these ancient works, so an understanding of some of the key conventions is necessary even to begin to decipher the images.

The following sections explore several key conventions in Egyptian art.

Toying with views

To really understand an object, you often need to look at it from various angles or *views*, including bird's eye, front, and profile. Led by convention, Egyptian artists consistently used certain views of specific objects in their art and sometimes included more than one view of an object in a single image.

For example:

- A container is often shown with its contents on the top, even if the contents are sealed within.

- Chairs and stools are shown from a side view with two legs visible, and the seat is shown from a bird's eye view on top. If someone is seated on a chair, the cushion is draped over the seat and the back of the chair.

- Sandals and scribal palettes are always shown from a bird's-eye view to give the clearest view of the object.

- In garden scenes, a pool is shown from a bird's-eye view, but surrounding trees are shown from a front view, which gives them the appearance of lying flat on the ground. Objects in the pool, like fish, boats, or people, are drawn on top of the water with no indication of depth.

Forming an orderly queue

The ancient Egyptians were a very organised people, and their artwork reflects this.

All Egyptian art is divided into a series of registers and larger scenes or figures:

- Each register is separated by a *base line*, which often serves as a ground line for figures within the registers.

- Large figures (often the tomb owner or god/king) often occupy the end of a wall composition, covering four or five registers. The figures are, to a certain extent, overseeing the smaller scenes.

Although many tomb and temple scenes have the appearance of a comic strip, scenes next to each other don't necessarily follow in the narrative of the event. Compositions were planned well in advance, but individual scenes were often moved around to fit the space available. So a master craftsman might place a short scene on a short wall to allow the larger walls to be free for the larger scenes, regardless of chronological order. (This lack of linearity can be really confusing in tomb art depicting the 12-hour journey of the sun god, for example, because hour one is not necessarily next to hour two!)

Furthermore, registers do not necessarily join the larger scene or scenes in the composition, and in fact registers and scenes can be totally unconnected in space and time. (The ancients sure didn't make things easy!) Registers and scenes, however, are typically connected by a general theme: offering, hunting, war, and so on.

Other conventions related to registers include

- ✔ **Walking in step.** The feet of all Egyptians are typically on the base line and pointing in the same direction, even when large groups are depicted. Egypt represented its orderly, organised culture through this convention.

- ✔ **Rowdy foreigners.** Any people from outside the Egyptian borders are displayed in a more chaotic fashion, not in tidy rows.

- ✔ **Wild locations.** Any environment not within the confines of Egypt's borders – such as a desert or a foreign country – is represented through the use of undulating base lines.

Representing the human figure

The ancient Egyptian depiction of the human figure is one category of image that modern eyes find most bizarre – and most recognisable.

You have probably seen renditions of the 'Egyptian walk' – figures with one arm in front at head height and the other behind at waist height. Although comical, this image does not exist anywhere in actual ancient Egyptian art; modern artists have simply developed it over the years as an attempt to represent the Egyptians' unusual perspective of the human figure.

Ancient Egyptian artists depicted the human body in the same manner as other objects (see the section 'Toying with views', earlier in this chapter). Human figures are a collection of body parts assembled from their most recognisable viewpoints. For this reason, the human figures shown on tomb walls and decorated items stand in positions that are impossible to replicate with a real human body – without dislocating half your joints! (See Figure 11-1.)

Figure 11-1:
A typical
Egyptian
figure.

Specifically, the human figure in Egyptian art includes

- A head shown in profile – but with a single front view of an eye and eyebrow and a profile mouth.

- Shoulders shown in full front view with the nipple or breast (on a woman) in profile, often under the armpit.

- The waist, elbows, legs, and feet shown in profile; it was traditional to show both feet from the inside with a single toe, normally the big toe and an arch, although from the New Kingdom some images show all five toes on both feet.

- Hands normally shown in full view, either open (from the back showing the nails) or clenched (from the front showing the knuckles).

Although the two-dimensional Egyptian figures can sometimes look a little bizarre to us (with the hands on the wrong arms and the feet on the wrong legs), many images show careful musculature, and statues display the Egyptians' amazing artistic talent.

Hand in hand

Hands caused major problems to ancient Egyptian artists, especially if the hands held objects.

For example, convention often dictated which hands held particular staffs. Old Kingdom officials held long staffs in the left hand and short sceptres in the right hand, close to the body. If the person was looking to the left, this arrangement was no problem, and the staffs are easily depicted in the correct hands. But if the figure faces right, big problems result. The left arm with the long staff becomes the front arm and the right hand becomes the rear arm. The long staff then runs the risk of obscuring the face, which spoils the whole image. This problem was typically solved by placing the long staff in the rear arm and the short sceptre in the near arm – but still in the correct hands. The only problem was that the right hand is on the left arm and the left hand on the right arm.

The hands were also sometimes swapped over to ensure the figure always has two thumbs facing away from the body but visible to the observer. These confusions are often viewed as artistic incompetence, but the fact of the matter is the opposite. In order to place the hands in unusual positions and still maintain the recognisable characteristics and strict artistic conventions, the ancient Egyptians had to work with great anatomical drawing skills.

Depicting eternal youth

Most people in ancient Egyptian imagery are shown at the height of physical fitness – young and fit. Even those individuals who are known to be elderly when they were depicted (such as Ramses II who was more than 90 years old when he died) are shown at about 20 years old.

Ancient Egyptian depictions of people were designed to last for eternity on temple or tomb walls and other decorated objects. Who wants to be shown warts and all? Human beings want to be remembered at their best, and the Egyptians were no different.

A handful of tombs at Deir el Medina (see Chapter 2 for more details on this village) show elderly relatives with salt-and-pepper hair or fully white hair. Granted, their skin and bodies don't show the ravages of time, but their hair colour does give away their advanced years.

The only age that is easy to identify in Egyptian art is for pre-pubescent boys and girls. Egyptians below this age are depicted with totally shaved heads and a side lock down the right side of their heads. (At puberty – between 10 and 15 years old – children had their side locks shaved off as a rite of passage.)

Even among the pre-pubescent children, you can further divide them into infants and children. Infants are shown nude, whereas older children are shown wearing clothes.

Colouring their world

When depicting humans, artist adhered to various colour conventions in order to identify the ethnicity of an individual:

- ✔ Egyptian men have red-brown skin, while Egyptian women are usually shown with yellow skin.

- ✔ Nubians – people from Nubia (modern Sudan), which was under the control of the Egyptians – have dark brown or black skin and short, curly black hair.

- ✔ Near Eastern people (from the area which is now Israel, Lebanon, and Syria), are shown with yellow skin and dark, shoulder-length, mushroom-shaped hair.

- ✔ Libyans (nomadic tribes from the western desert) are sometimes shown with fair skin, blue eyes, and red hair, or have elaborate side locks down one side of their head.

If a crowd of people of the same race are shown standing together, such as a group of Egyptians or Nubians, artists vary the skin colour between darker and lighter shades so no two skin tones of the same shade are next to each other.

Considering fashion

Egyptians are also only ever shown wearing plain white clothes – either tunics or kilts – with the exception of leopard-skin cloaks for funerary and high priests.

In addition to differences in paint colour, non-Egyptians are easily distinguished from Egyptians in temple art by their style of dress:

- ✔ Nubians wear gold earrings and loincloths made of cow, giraffe, and leopard skin.

- ✔ Syrians have shoulder-length hair with a hairband around the forehead. Their long tunics are white with a red trim to indicate that their garments were made of rectangular pieces of fabric, wrapped two or three times around the body.

- ✔ Libyans have elaborate hairstyles of shoulder-length hair with plaited side locks decorated with feathers. They also wear elaborately decorated woollen cloaks with long fringes.

- ✔ Asiatics (a general term for the people of the Syro-Palestinian region) wear beards and elaborately decorated tunics and cloaks. Asiatic women also wear little booties, which were not worn in Egypt due to the climate.

Most art shows non-Egyptians being suppressed by the Egyptian king, overcome in battle, acting subserviently to the Egyptians, or bringing tribute to the king or an Egyptian official. However, many non-Egyptians lived in ancient Egypt and adopted the Egyptian way of life, including Egyptian names and the language. These individuals are presented as Egyptian in their tomb art.

Size is everything

Egyptian artists used size as a method of depicting rank and status.

As the saying goes, 'The bigger the better'. In Egyptian art, the larger the individual, the more important he or she was. In tombs, the biggest individual is normally the tomb owner; in temples, the large images represent the king or the gods.

In scenes where people are all presented at the same scale, you can still easily identify who is the more important. Individuals of higher status have their feet at a higher level through sitting or standing on a plinth or dais.

Carving Masterpieces

Egyptian sculptors created their art on two-dimensional surfaces – walls, signs, and plaques – as well as three-dimensional creations. Many of the tools used for carving stone were simply made of a harder stone than the one being cut. Other tools used include

- **Copper hand saws** were used from the Old Kingdom.
- **Metal wedges** were used for splitting stone blocks (made of bronze from the 26th dynasty, and iron from the late period).
- **Wooden wedges** were used for splitting blocks. The blocks were inserted into a gap in the stone and then made wet. As the wood expanded in the water, the stone split.
- **Blunt chisels** were made from all kinds of stone, sometimes with a wooden handle. The chisels were hammered using a stone hammer, sometimes attached to a wooden shaft.
- **Drills** with metal drill bits were used from the Old Kingdom. The bow drill was a wooden shaft with a stone or metal drill bit. The drill bit had to be harder than the stone it was carving. A drill cap at the end of the shaft enabled the sculptor to apply pressure by hand. Instead of a drill cap, weights of stones in sandbags enabled a greater weight to be applied, which was particularly useful for a hard stone.

On the march

From the 18th dynasty, the non-royal tomb of Horemheb at Memphis features many carved scenes in which Egyptian artists have carefully depicted Horemheb's military life.

In one scene, an officer is leaving his tent, which is supported by a decorative tent pole in the centre, in order to speak to his commander, probably Horemheb. His batsman is standing at the door of the tent in a respectful manner, and a young naked boy is on his way to the tent carrying water skins. On the other side of the tent, another man gestures to another water carrier with two large water jars on a yoke over his shoulders. Two additional servants are working in the tent – one is pouring water on the floor to settle the dust, while the other sweeps up with a makeshift broom made from a bundle of tied-together sticks. The tent is filled with the possessions of the officer, including a table piled with food and a folding stool, which was easy to carry from camp to camp.

Another damaged scene shows the military cooks preparing food for the soldiers. The fragmentary state of the scene makes identifying what is being prepared difficult, although a clear portion of the image shows a squatting soldier eating a raw onion like an apple. (With this as a dietary staple, it would take more than 'double-mint' to freshen his breath.) Another cook is preparing meatballs or bread by rolling a ball in his hands, and a soldier is helping himself to a bowl of pre-prepared food.

The scene continues by showing the camp on the march. The terrain has undulating base lines, showing that the soldiers are not in Egypt. The tents have been dismantled and rolled up, and soldiers are carrying one tent on their shoulders. These soldiers are wearing open-work leather loincloths with a square patch at the back to provide added comfort while sitting down. The abundance of movement in these scenes gives an insight into busy military life.

The finished statue was smoothed using sand in the same way we use sandpaper to smooth a surface. The statue was buffed to create a shine if the stone wasn't intended to be painted.

Chiselling reliefs

Both painted and carved relief are common in Egyptian art. Painted relief was obviously easier than carving and was often the chosen method if the stone was of poor quality.

For carved relief projects, sculptors used copper chisels in one of two ways:

- ✔ **Raised relief** required the background to be cut away, leaving the figures standing out. This more time-consuming technique was used mostly inside tombs and temples, because the shadows created by dim lighting were very dramatic.

- ✔ **Sunk relief** was quicker to carve and involved cutting the figures away from the background. This technique was often used on outside walls and produced very dark shadows, which were good in bright sunlight.

The carved images were then painted in many colours, which to modern, minimalist minds may seem gauche and a tad tacky. For the Egyptians, the inclusion of colour offered another opportunity to display wealth and status.

Mistakes happened – even in the distant past. Carving goofs were easily covered with thin layers of plaster. The outlines were then redrawn and carved. However, 3,000 years or so later, the plaster has come off, often revealing extra carved lines. Just goes to show that no one is perfect.

Carving in 3D

Hundreds of statues have survived from ancient Egypt that represent both royalty and officials. The Egyptians didn't really believe in having statues purely for aesthetic purposes, so all the statues have a function. Statues were placed in both temples and tombs and were all *ka statues*, vessels for the spirits of the individuals depicted. Wherever the statue was placed, Egyptians believed the deceased's spirit could participate in the rituals and offerings being carried out.

Statues were of varying sizes and of many materials, depending on the wealth of the individual. Statues were made of stone, metal, or wood; the cheaper ones with resources from Egypt, and the more expensive using imported materials, including

- Limestone from quarries at Giza and Tell el Amarna
- Red granite from Aswan
- Quartzite sandstone from Gebel Ahmar (near Cairo)
- Alabaster from Hatnub, south east of Tell el Amarna
- Cedar from Lebanon
- Sycamore from Egypt
- Copper from the Sinai and Cyprus

Statues, such as wall reliefs, followed a number of conventions to indicate rank and position. For example:

- A figure sitting cross-legged on the floor was a scribe.
- A bald figure with a leopard-skin cloak was a high priest.
- A figure in a wig with a leopard-skin cloak was a funerary priest.
- A bald figure with a long kilt tied at the chest was a vizier.
- Stylised rolls of fat on the abdomen show affluence and wealth.

Hatshepsut: Miss, Mr ... What?

Hatshepsut (see Chapter 5 for more on this ruler) started her time on the throne as a consort to her brother/husband Thutmosis II. When he died, she married her young stepson Thutmosis III and ruled as regent until he was old enough to rule alone. However, she wanted the power wielded by her young husband and took over the throne and ruled as king. Her actions caused a number of problems – both in artwork and in accompanying hieroglyphic inscriptions.

In order to be recognised in art as king, Hatshepsut needed to be displayed as such – with kingly attire including a kilt, crown, false beard, and crook and flail. This apparel has led some people to claim she was a transvestite, but this is not the case. Ancient Egyptian art was not a portrait; it displayed Hatshepsut in the *role* she held as king. In fact, some of her statues show her with a combination of kingly attire and feminine features, making her statues easy to identify because the face is clearly that of a woman. Some of the statues of Hatshepsut as king also show her with breasts, but wearing male attire.

This combination of male and female attributes also confused the scribes. In inscriptions, Hatshepsut is described as both male and female; as both the son and daughter of the god Amun. The guidelines the artists and scribes learnt while training did not work when the king was female. I'm sure they were pleased to see the end of her reign so they could get back to normal.

Reading Hieroglyphs

In order to further identify tomb and temple scenes, it is useful to be able to read some of the *cartouches* – the lozenge-shaped enclosures that contain the king's name and names of the gods.

Cartouches are composed of *hieroglyphs* – pictures used to represent letters, although the situation is not quite that simple. Hieroglyphs form a proper language with case endings, tenses, verbs, nouns, and prepositions. More than 700 hieroglyphic signs existed in the Middle Kingdom and the number grew to more than 1,000 in the Ptolemaic period. (As new foreign words were introduced, the Egyptians needed new signs to be able to spell them!)

Losing the language

The hieroglyphic language first appears in Egypt in approximately 3100 BC and the last-known inscription was at the temple of Philae in AD 394 – a history of nearly 3,500 years.

From AD 394 until 1799, with the discovery of the Rosetta Stone and the beginnings of decipherment, knowledge of this ancient language was lost, although many theories arose:

- ✔ In the 16th century, the hieroglyphic language was believed to have developed from Armenian or Chinese.

- ✔ In the 1630s, a Jesuit priest and scholar, Athanasius Kircher, tried to decipher hieroglyphs and believed each sign represented an individual philosophical concept.

- ✔ In the 1750s, people believed that priests had invented hieroglyphs to conceal sacred knowledge.

Cracking the code

By the end of the 18th century, a number of discoveries had been made:

- ✔ The Coptic language developed from ancient Egyptian and was used by the Christians in Egypt. Coptic uses the Greek alphabet for the Egyptian words.

- ✔ Hieroglyphs (picture writing), and *hieratic* (shorthand hieroglyphs used for paper documents), and *demotic* (the Egyptian script which developed from hieratic used from 650 BC) languages were connected.

- ✔ Cartouches contained royal names.

- ✔ The hieroglyph system included phonetic elements.

These breakthroughs were aided in 1799 by the discovery of an engraved stone in the town of el-Rashid (Rosetta). The granite-like *Rosetta Stone* changed Egyptology forever. The stone was written in three scripts:

- ✔ Ancient Greek

- ✔ Egyptian hieroglyphs

- ✔ Demotic (a late cursive form of hieroglyphs)

Most historians could read ancient Greek, so this part of the stone was easily translated. In the race to decipher the hieroglyphic text, two main contenders emerged:

- ✔ **Thomas Young,** who published his findings anonymously under the name ABCD in case the unrelated research affected his credentials as a physician. Young deciphered the demotic text and identified the names of Cleopatra and Ptolemy within their cartouches. He also identified that the hieroglyphic signs were phonetic and did not individually represent words or concepts.

✔ **Jean-François Champollion,** who corresponded with Young, but was in competition with him to decipher hieroglyphs. At Young's death in 1829, Champollion continued the work and made the final breakthrough in identifying the phonetic value of many signs, thus enabling the transcription of many inscriptions. He also deciphered some of the linguistic and grammatical elements of the language.

Both Young and Champollion read the Greek inscription and matched the occurrence of recognisable words like 'king' and 'god', and looked for a similar number of occurrences in the Egyptian and demotic inscriptions. Real code breakers!

Identifying the signs

The many signs in the hieroglyphic language are divided into four sign types:

✔ **Single (or uniliteral) signs,** like the alphabet, which only have one letter sound; for example *i*.

✔ **Biliteral signs,** which have a two-letter sound (for example, *mn*)

✔ **Triliteral signs,** which are three-letter signs (for example, *htp*)

✔ **Determinative signs,** which have no sound, but are put at the end of a word to reinforce its meaning. For example, the word for cat is spelt out (*miw*) and would have an image of a cat at the end to show it was a cat.

Rosetta ... again ... and again

The text on the Rosetta Stone states that there was a copy of the *stela* (the curved top stone monument with carved inscriptions) in every temple in Egypt. A number of stelas have been found, and most are currently in the Cairo Museum:

✔ One was found in Minuf (Nile Delta), being used as a bench in front of a house. The surviving text is in Greek and demotic, although it is badly damaged.

✔ A basalt stela was found near Tell el Yahudiyeh (Eastern Delta) being reused as an oil press. Only the Greek text survives, although the stela was bilingual originally.

✔ Fragments of a trilingual stela of sandstone were found at Elephantine and are now in the Louvre. The section that is badly damaged on the Rosetta Stone is complete here.

✔ A sandstone stela found at Naukratis has a number of errors and was clearly copied from an original by an inexperienced stone cutter who could not read hieroglyphs.

In general, there are no written vowels in hieroglyphs; well, at least not the same as in English. This is the reason there are so many discrepancies in the spelling of names of gods – Amun, Amon, or Amen (from *imn*) – and of kings – Amenhotpe or Amenhotep (from *imn htp*), for example.

Understanding direction and honorific positioning

You can read hieroglyphs from right to left or left to right, as well as from top to bottom.

Don't panic! An easy method tells you which way the text should be read. Look at the direction the animals and birds are facing and read towards them. So if the animals are facing to the right, read the text from right to left, and if the faces are towards the left, read the text from left to right. Simple. If the text is above an image of a person and the animals are facing the same way as the person, it is clear that the text is describing the person depicted.

In kings' names inside a cartouche, you find a hierarchy of signs, which makes reading them difficult. If a god's name forms part of the king's name (like *Ramses*), the name Ra is placed at the beginning of the cartouche, even if it is not to be read in that order. This is called *honorific positioning*, with the most important name being written first.

Hieroglyphic signs are positioned to fit within a small invisible rectangle in order to make them aesthetically pleasing, rather than placing each sign next to each other in a long line. This is done by placing horizontal signs together and vertical signs together, while at the same time keeping them in the order they are to be read as much as possible. In addition to looking good, this method of positioning enables more text to be placed in a small space. Also, no spaces or punctuation are between the words, keeping the inscription compact.

Learning the alphabet

Although hieroglyphic writing includes more than 700 signs, a number of unilateral signs can be used as an alphabet. Take a look at some of the most common unilateral signs in Figure 11-2. This figure shows you the hieroglyph and its English-language equivalent.

	A	(Vulture)		KH	(Placenta)
	I	(Flowing reed)		CH	(Cow's stomach - as in 'ich')
	EE	(Two flowing reeds)		S	(Fold of linen - both signs are used for the same letter)
	A	(Arm - gutteral as in cockney 'wa'er')		SH	(Pool)
	OO	(Quail chick)		Q	(Hill)
	B	(Leg)		K	(Basket)
	P	(Stool)		G	(Jar-stand)
	F	(Horned viper)		T	(Loaf of bread)
	M	(Owl)		CH	(Tethering rope)
	N	(Water)		D	(Hand)
	R	(Mouth)		J	(Snake)
	H	(Hut)		L	(Lion)

Figure 11-2:
Unilateral hiero-glyphics.

Figure 11-3 shows signs used to express common Western names.

Hieroglyphic writing does not include many vowels. Also, the sign at the end of each name (the determinative sign) tells you whether the person is male or female.

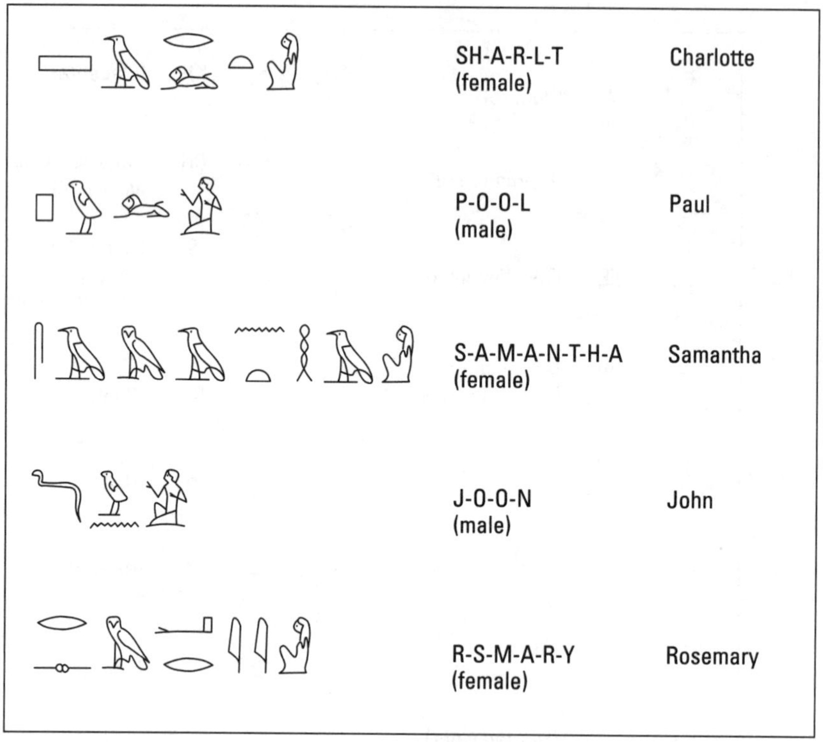

	SH-A-R-L-T (female)	Charlotte
	P-O-O-L (male)	Paul
	S-A-M-A-N-T-H-A (female)	Samantha
	J-O-O-N (male)	John
	R-S-M-A-R-Y (female)	Rosemary

Figure 11-3:
Western names expressed in hieroglyphs.

Reading the names of the divine

Most of the royal names and those of the gods are written using bi- and triliteral signs (two- or three-letter sounds). However, some of these signs are common in both royal and gods' names. Figure 11-4 shows some of the best-known gods, as well as some common kings' names that incorporate gods' names; all would appear within a cartouche.

These signs aid in identifying the gods and goddesses in artwork and inscriptions. These signs appear on the heads of figures and to identify specific gifts given to the king by the gods.

Some of these gods' names appear in the most common kings' names within a cartouche, as shown in Figure 11-5.

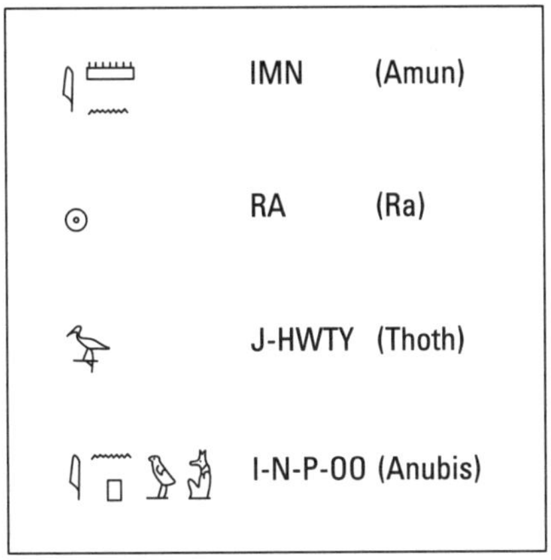

(glyph)	IMN	(Amun)
(glyph)	RA	(Ra)
(glyph)	J-HWTY	(Thoth)
(glyph)	I-N-P-OO	(Anubis)

Figure 11-4:
Common gods' names.

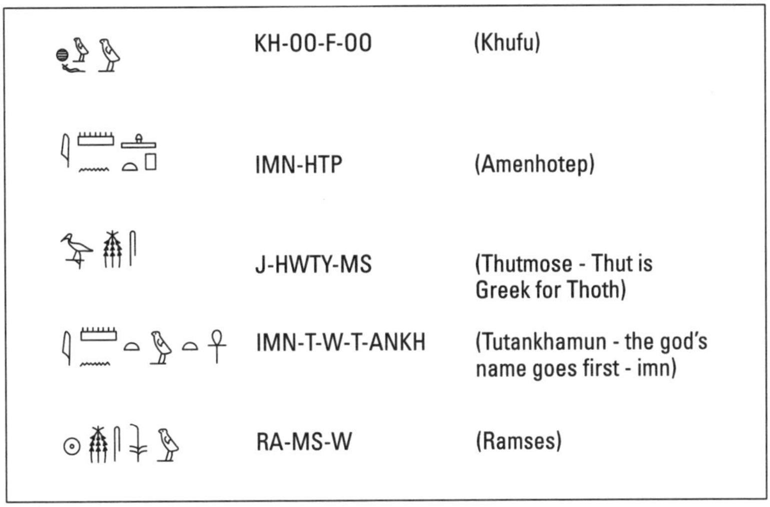

(glyph)	KH-OO-F-OO	(Khufu)
(glyph)	IMN-HTP	(Amenhotep)
(glyph)	J-HWTY-MS	(Thutmose - Thut is Greek for Thoth)
(glyph)	IMN-T-W-T-ANKH	(Tutankhamun - the god's name goes first - imn)
(glyph)	RA-MS-W	(Ramses)

Figure 11-5:
Common gods' names appear in common kings' names.

Reading Egyptian art

Hieroglyphs also appear in Egyptian art to represent concepts and gods.

Knowing some of the signs featured in Figure 11-6 can make interpreting all Egyptian art a little easier – without needing to read the long inscriptions.

Nothing in Egyptian art is random; everything has a purpose and is carefully placed within the final composition to give a clear description of what is represented.

♀	ANKH	Eternal life
⊰	WSR	Power
↑	WAS	Dominion
⌐	ST	Throne – sign for the name of Isis
𝍠	JED	Spinal column – sign for Osiris
🦅	HOOT-HOR	Horus within the palace – sign for Hathor
⚱	TYET	The Isis knot represents the goddess
꭮	MAAT	Sign for truth and justice and the goddess Maat

Figure 11-6: Common Egyptian concepts as hiero-glyphics.

Chapter 12

Touring the Temples

· ·

In This Chapter

▶ Constructing houses of worship – and more

▶ Embellishing temples with obelisks, carvings, and paint

▶ Understanding the role of temples, priests, and kings

· ·

Many temples of ancient Egypt are still standing throughout the desert – a beautiful testament to a long-dead religion and a tradition of architecture and design.

The temples dominated the ancient Egyptian landscape. They were awe-inspiring, colourful structures. However, they were closed to the public; only the priests and the royal family had free access. Although the temples were inaccessible to the ordinary people, the activities and function of the temples affected the lives of everyone.

This chapter covers the planning and construction of these buildings, the roles of the priests and royalty, and the opportunities for worship available to both royals and everyday Egyptians.

Building a Temple

The ancient Egyptians built two types of temples:

> ✔ **Cult temples,** known as houses of the god, were for the worship of a god. These structures were normally situated on the east bank of the Nile. Although the temples were often dedicated to one god in particular (Amun, for example), these gods were often part of a *triad* that included a consort and child. (In the case of Amun, his consort was Mut and his child was Khonsu.) The triad was therefore worshipped at the site too. In a large temple like Karnak, many other gods are also worshipped within the complex – although the main god was Amun.

> ✔ **Mortuary temples,** known as temples of millions of years, were for the cult of the dead king. These buildings enabled worshippers to keep the king's spirit nourished for the afterlife and were normally situated on the west bank of the Nile. Although they were built in association with the kings' tombs, the temples were often some distance away in order to keep the tombs' locations secret.

The type of worship practised in each temple type was the same, although the statue within each type was different: Cult temples included statues of gods such as Amun or Ra, and mortuary temples housed statues of kings.

The ancient Egyptians believed that architectural design – just like art, religion, and literature – was dictated in the remote past by the gods. For this reason, they believed that they should not change the design of the temples, because improving on perfection was impossible. However, the Egyptian kings still needed to feed their desire to build and therefore constructed larger and larger versions of the same designs.

Going way back: The earliest temples

Very limited evidence of religion and temples prior to 3500 BC has been discovered. The early temples that have been identified bear no resemblance to the New Kingdom monuments still standing in Egypt today. The New Kingdom temples that dominate the modern landscape of Egypt all follow a similar pattern, which took centuries to develop.

Hierakonpolis

The earliest temple in Egypt is at Hierakonpolis just north of Luxor, dating from approximately 3200 BC. Excavations show that the temple consisted of a covered court on a raised mound of sand (probably symbolic of the mound of creation), which looked onto a walled courtyard. Just outside the courtyard, a number of small rectangular buildings probably housed workshops or stores associated with the cult.

The falcon-headed god, Horus (see Chapter 9), was probably worshipped at Hierakonpolis, although no inscriptions or statues have been found at the site. Horus is closely associated with kingship and is the earliest recorded deity.

Medamud

Another early cult temple just north of Thebes at Medamud does not follow New Kingdom conventions. Unfortunately the deities worshipped at this temple are unknown, although in later periods this site was the cult centre for Montu, the god of war.

An enclosure wall surrounded this temple, and an undecorated pylon gateway marked the entrance. This entrance led to a hexagon-shaped courtyard dominated by two mounds, perhaps indicative of the primordial mound of creation. Two corridors led to the top of these mounds.

A mud-brick chamber in the centre was filled with trees. Why these were included is unknown, but the explanation probably has something to do with creation and life sprouting from the mounds of creation. Either that or it's the earliest eco-house.

Evolving design during the Middle Kingdom

By the Middle Kingdom (2040 BC), temples were very symmetrical, although sadly examples from this period are rare, because they were mostly destroyed by the construction of later monuments.

Most of the Middle Kingdom temples were replaced by the New Kingdom (1550 BC) structures, but the Middle Kingdom legacy remains in the design. For example, the Karnak temple features Middle and New Kingdom influences, which makes sense because the structure took 2,000 years to complete and is the largest religious centre in the world.

The Middle Kingdom temples were very simple in design, with an entrance pylon leading to an open courtyard. At the rear of the courtyard, doorways led to three shrines. The central shrine was dedicated to the main god of the temple, and the two others were dedicated to the god's consort and the couple's child (see Chapter 9).

The Middle Kingdom design led to the *traditional temple*. The huge elaborate New Kingdom temples were merely expansions on this design, with each king adding a little to an already complete Middle Kingdom structure.

Adhering to design conventions in the New Kingdom

After the start of the New Kingdom (1550 BC), temple builders began to follow certain rules, and a more stylised and standardised temple design emerged.

Twinkle, twinkle, little star

Rather than being oriented towards the sun or the Nile, a few surviving temples in Egypt are positioned based on a star or stellar constellation.

For example, the temple at Elephantine is oriented towards the star Sothis (the star known today as Sirius). This star's rising announced the start of the annual inundation and was also associated with Osiris, the god of the underworld.

Another stellar temple – the Middle Kingdom temple on Thoth Hill near Luxor – is particularly interesting. This temple is also dedicated to the star Sirius, but archaeological evidence shows two sets of foundations. The temple was clearly re-aligned, because over the centuries the original orientation of the temple no longer aligned with the star's position, which had shifted over time.

Aligning with the elements

One design rule that began in the New Kingdom was the orientation of both cult and mortuary temples. While orientation varies between temples, these buildings were ideally sited on an east–west axis, at a 90-degree angle to the Nile. Of course, sometimes the natural terrain made this orientation impossible, and some temples, like the Luxor and Edfu temples, completely ignore this rule and are positioned north–south to run in line with neighbouring temples.

However, east–west is by far the most common orientation. This position highlights the solar aspect of the majority of temples. The sun rises in the east, so temple entrances often face that way to greet the rising sun.

Minding the rising tides

In addition to choosing a site for a temple according to the location of the Nile, some temples were built in such a way that during the annual inundation, the temple flooded. This flooding reinforced the temple as being like the universe, and a divine place, because the floods represented the primordial waters from which the temple emerged as if created from the waters.

This annual flooding entered all parts of the temple – except the sanctuary (see the section 'Proceeding to the Holy of Holies', later in this chapter, for more information), which was the highest point of the temple. This fact may help to explain why temple decoration rarely extends all the way down to the floor, but stops a metre or so above ground level. Having to repaint the temple once a year would be a major pain in the butt and best avoided at all costs.

Strolling down the processional avenue

Processional avenues or approaches to temples – which were sometimes added years after the main temple was completed, as improvements by later kings – are more commonly known as *sphinx avenues*, because these approaches were lined with multiple sphinx statues.

The most famous of these processional avenues is between Luxor and Karnak temples. A great deal of this avenue is still visible, especially around the two temples. Although Egyptian governmental figures and historians have discussed reconstructing the avenue to allow tourists to walk the full processional way, this plan has not been realised yet.

In addition to Luxor and Karnak, many temples originally had such avenues, including Abu Simbel in Nubia and the Ramesseum on the West Bank at Luxor.

Four types of sphinxes lined the processional avenues, including

- **Ram-headed lions,** which were identified with Amun, who is sometimes shown with a ram's head. Often a small figure of the king was placed under the chin of the sphinx.

- **Falcon-headed lions,** which represented the king in the form of Horus. These are rare and are found primarily in Nubian temples.

- **Sphinxes with the head of a crocodile, jackal, or snake,** which represent the gods Sobek, Duamutef (Anubis) or the cobra goddess Wadjet. These are very rare: Examples have been found only at the mortuary temple of Amenhotep III at Luxor.

- **Human-headed lions,** which bear the face of the ruler who constructed them. These sphinxes normally wear the blue and gold nemes headdress or the crown of Upper and Lower Egypt.

Processional avenues were used during religious festivals (see Chapter 9) when the *sacred bark* (small ceremonial boat) was carried to another temple on the shoulders of the priests. The procession was shielded from the public's prying eyes by a wall behind the two rows of sphinxes with the pathway running through the centre.

Entering the temple

The area by the temple entrance was always wide and open and was the lowest point of the temple. Priests and temple workers progressed through the temple via a system of short staircases or ramps, to reach the sanctuary at the rear (see Figure 12-1).

Take a break

Along the processional route, and therefore not part of the temple proper, a number of way stations offered an opportunity for the priests carrying the statues to stop and rest the sacred bark (boat). The sacred bark often had carrying poles that rested on the priests' shoulders.

The way stations were normally only large enough to accommodate the sacred bark for a short period and did not contain anything other than an altar on which the statue was refreshed with food and drink before continuing its journey.

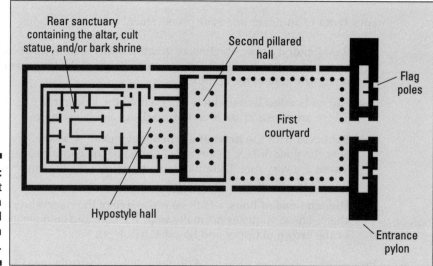

Figure 12-1:
The layout of a traditional Egyptian temple.

Because the temples were closed to the public, getting into them was a tricky business. The outside of the temple was not designed to be inviting, and in fact all temples were surrounded by large enclosure walls. These walls were generally built of mud-brick laid over a frame of wooden beams and reed matting. These walls were not for scaling and were sometimes more than 10 metres thick. Not only were these barriers efficient at keeping people out, but they also offered protection for the royal family, priests and anyone else lucky enough to be admitted during times of war or conflict.

The enclosure wall was sometimes designed to represent primeval waters. By alternating the brickwork into convex or concave sections to look like waves, this building element further associated the temple with a representation of a microcosm of the universe.

In the centre of the enclosure wall stood an *entrance pylon*. These structures, generally built of stone, were often hollow and sometimes contained staircases or rooms, or were filled with rubble – anything to create a more stable structure. The shape of the pylon represents the hieroglyph for horizon, with a depression in the centre over the door. Because the pylon was ideally in the east, the sun rose between the sides of the depression over the sacred landscape of the temple. Many pylons exist at Egyptian temples today, including ten at Karnak, three at Medinet Habu and two at the Ramesseum.

A number of flag poles were erected on the wings of the pylon, on either side of the door. The flag poles (sometimes 60 metres tall and possibly made of gold or *electrum*, a mixture of gold and silver) bore flags with the sign of the god. Figure 12-2 shows the entrance at Luxor temple. The photo clearly shows the grooves for the four flag poles, as well as a standing obelisk, which was part of a pair. See the section 'Pointing to the sun: Obelisks', later in this chapter, for more.

Figure 12-2:
The entrance pylon from the Sphinx Avenue at Luxor temple.

Entering via the back door

During processions, the gods (actually their statues carried by the priests) didn't always use the main pylon entrance. Instead, most temples included a river entrance just outside the temple walls that was approached by a landing quay from the Nile or a local canal. In times of procession, the sacred statue began and ended its journey here. The general public may have gathered here for these processions to greet or bid farewell to the god.

Getting a foot in the door: The first courtyard and hypostyle hall

Once through the pylon gateway, the first courtyard loomed ahead. This area was open to the sky and surrounded by a pillared colonnade. The courtyard may have been accessible on special occasions to carefully chosen nobles to receive gifts from the king, to address the oracle of the god, or to receive divine advice (see Chapter 9). This courtyard housed many statues of nobles, priests, and royalty, and was a means for these individuals to be forever present in the temple and in the company of the gods.

At the rear of the first pillared court was the columned *hypostyle hall*. The pillars were believed to hold up the sky and the ceiling was often painted blue with hundreds of stars to represent the night sky. The pillars represented the vegetation that grew in the primordial marshes that surrounded the mound of creation. Entering the hypostyle hall was a symbolic walk in the marshes of creation. The most impressive existing hypostyle hall is at Karnak temple; it was planned by Horemheb, started by Sety I, and completed by Ramses II.

Proceeding to the Holy of Holies

The central axis that ran through both the first pillared courtyard and the hypostyle hall led to the most important part of the temple – the sanctuary. Only the king and the high priest were allowed to enter this part of the temple.

This small chamber was known by many names:

- ✔ The inner sanctuary
- ✔ The inner sanctum
- ✔ The Holy of Holies

The floors ascended as people progressed through the temple towards the sanctuary (see the section 'Entering the temple', earlier in this chapter), and the ceiling descended. Therefore, the sanctuary was the highest point of the temple, but with the lowest roof. This dark raised room represented the mound of creation, from which all life began.

Within the sanctuary, there was an altar with a small shrine. Behind golden or bronze doors, the cult statue stood. The Egyptians believed that this statue was not merely a representation of the god, but in fact housed the spirit of the god. For this reason, access to the statue was extremely limited.

The bark shrine was often within the sanctuary or very nearby. This shrine provided a spot to house the portable bark of the deity when it wasn't needed for processions.

Going for a dip: The sacred lakes

Because the temple represented the universe, and the sanctuary the mound of creation, the complex also needed to include the primordial waters. And indeed every temple had a sacred lake.

Sacred lakes were stone lined with steps that led down into the water. They were filled by the natural water table. Since the Aswan Dam was built in 1960 and the inundation was stopped, most of these lakes have dried up.

The water in these lakes was used in ritual offerings and for the purification of both the temple and the priests. Before the priests entered the temple, they were required to plunge into the lake to be purified by the holy waters.

The sacred lake of Karnak, built by Thutmosis III, had another very creative use. A special tunnel from the lake led to geese pens some distance away. The geese were systematically pushed from the pens through the tunnel, from which they popped up into the water, as if from nowhere. These geese symbolised Amun at creation and proved that the primeval water was still creating new life from nothing.

Supporting the ceiling

Present-day visitors may have difficulty imagining what the temples originally looked like, because the remains indicate very open, bright places. This is in fact the *opposite* of how the temples looked during the New Kingdom. All the temple areas – aside from the sacred lake and first pillared hall – were closed in with heavy stone roofs.

In order to support these roofs, columns were a major aspect of most temples, and indeed of architecture in general. Columns appear in at least two areas of a standard temple – the first pillared hall and the hypostyle hall. In larger temples, pillared courtyards, corridors, and kiosks were also common.

Because pillars were such a dominant architectural element, the Egyptians varied their design. In fact, more than 30 different column designs were used during the pharaonic period.

All pillar types were elaborately decorated with painted and carved images and hieroglyphs. Popular motifs included

- ✔ Lotus blossoms, with both open and closed buds
- ✔ Papyrus bundles, with both open and closed *umbrels* (flowering heads)
- ✔ The face of the cow-headed deity, Hathor

Considering doors and windows

The doors throughout the temples were huge affairs (some more than 20 metres high). Imagine the splendour of these monumental doorways. They were made from wood, ideally cedar wood imported from the Lebanon. These large planks of wood were then inlaid with gold, silver, lapis, and many other semi-precious stones.

As beautiful as they were, the doors served an important function: They were difficult to penetrate, which kept out the public and any invading enemies.

Temples were lit not by windows, but rather by stone grilles high up in the walls or by holes cut into the ceiling blocks, which let in small shafts of light. See Figure 12-3 for an example at Karnak temple. As a result, the temples were very dark and gloomy places, and the light shed by these lighting systems was intermittent and probably very creepy. For extra lighting, the priests and other temple personnel used oil lamps, which no doubt added to the shadow-ridden corners.

Figure 12-3:
A window grill in the hypostyle hall at Karnak Temple.

False doors and ear stelae

In both cult and royal mortuary temples, the sanctuaries included false doors carved into the rear walls. These doors weren't functional but were simply decoration carved onto the wall. (False doors are also found in tombs and tomb chapels; see Chapter 13.)

In a mortuary temple, such doors allowed the spirit of the deceased king to enter freely into the temple from his burial place. The royal burial places were often a distance away from the mortuary temples in an effort to prevent tomb robberies. The tombs were very secret, with no superstructure to act as a beacon to their whereabouts. Because the mortuary temple was the site of the food offerings, the deceased's spirit needed to have access, which the false door provided.

In cult temples, the false doors often backed onto *hearing chapels*. These chapels enabled the ordinary people to speak to the gods from the exterior of the temple (they were unable to enter the temple itself). The chapel wall was decorated with *ear stelae*, stone inscriptions inscribed with images of numerous little ears.

Worshippers spoke into one of the ears – saying a prayer, thanking the god, or asking for something, such as curing of an illness – and their voices went straight to the god's ears. Some of the chapels also had a small priest hole behind the stelae, within which a priest sat and answered the prayers out loud. That would certainly make you jump if you weren't expecting it!

Building the outhouses

In addition to the main temple, a number of outbuildings, essential to the function of the temple, stood around the surrounding grounds.

The most common outbuildings were the stores, or magazines, used to house the foodstuffs that were gathered in payment of taxes and redistributed to the temple and state workers. Some of these structures may also have stored the materials and tools used within the temple.

Other buildings included kitchens, animal and fowl pens, stables, and housing for the priests who resided within the temple enclosure walls. The temple was probably a noisy, busy place – and no doubt very smelly as well. Not the quiet serenity of a modern Christian church.

Several additional outbuildings had a religious function and can therefore be considered part of the temple itself.

The mammissi

From the Ptolemaic period (332 BC), many temples had a building known as a *mammissi*, or birth house. It wasn't a useable building, like a maternity ward, but rather a sacred place that commemorated the birth of the king.

The king had to show that he had a divine birth in order to prove his right to the throne. Prior to the Ptolemaic period, kings from slightly dodgy backgrounds had divine birth scenes added to their temples in order to 'prove' their divine origins and hence their right to rule. Because none of the kings in the Ptolemaic period were Egyptian, they needed to validate their right to rule even more than most. Check out Chapter 6 for more on this era.

In temples dedicated to a male deity rather than being a mortuary temple of the king, the mammissi was symbolic of the birthplace of the deity, and his birth was depicted on the walls. If the deity of the temple was female, the mammissi displayed images of her giving birth to her divine child. A rather splendid mammissi exists at the Ptolemaic temple of Denderah, just north of Luxor.

Sanatorium

Another building common in the Ptolemaic period is the *sanatorium*. Although sanatoria were present at most temples, the only surviving example is at Denderah.

The sanatorium was a dormitory where the sick came in an attempt to be healed. These were open to the general public, although no doubt if you gave the priests a financial gift, your cure was promised to be quicker or better.

After a patient arrived in the dormitory, the priest administered a sleeping draught. When the patient awoke, his or her dreams were interpreted by the priests. Egyptians believed that dreams were messages from the gods (see Chapter 9), so whatever the message of a priest-induced dream was, it would help cure ailments. Risking being called a cynic, I believe that most of these dream interpretations ultimately benefited the temple in one way or another; many of the 'cures' involved making offerings or building shrines at the temple.

Adding Finishing Touches: Obelisks and Decoration

After a temple was completed and the statue of the god had been placed in the shrine, the temple was considered fully functioning. But this didn't mean that kings couldn't keep adding to temples as a means of improving the works of their ancestors, as well as showing their devotion to the gods.

Additions took the form of carved or painted decoration, statues, and obelisks (as well as the processional avenues described in the section 'Strolling down the processional avenue', earlier in this chapter). The following section cover these architectural add-ons.

Pointing to the sun: Obelisks

All temples had at least two *obelisks* – tall, pointing structures that are synonymous with ancient Egypt. Obelisks are characterised by their tapering needle-like shape. At the top of the shaft was a pyramidion, which was gilded in gold or electrum, and takes its shape from the mound of creation. Some of the obelisks were completely covered in gold if the Egyptian economy allowed it.

Obelisks were made from a single block of stone, often red granite from Aswan. The quarry at Aswan has an incomplete obelisk (more than 41 metres long) embedded in the rock, showing that the features (shaft and pyramidion) were carved in situ and removed when complete.

In a standard New Kingdom temple, the obelisks were normally placed in front of a pylon, flanking the doorways, or along the central axis.

Hatshepsut's obelisk adventure

At her mortuary temple at Deir el Bahri and the Red Chapel she built at Karnak, Hatshepsut records her erection of two obelisks at Karnak temple. She even shows their transportation from the quarries at Aswan where they were initially carved.

At Aswan, the obelisks were tied to wooden ledges, which were towed on large sycamore barges, more than 60 metres long, by 27 tow boats to Thebes via the Nile. These boats were rowed by 850 oarsmen – a huge number of rowers, reflecting the weight of their cargo. Each obelisk may have weighed more than 450 tonnes and stood more than 50 metres high. The obelisks were completely covered in gold and were a beautiful sight to behold.

Luckily the currents of the Nile aided the transportation process. The entire journey was accompanied by three ships of priests who chanted incantations and prayers over the boats. I'm sure the rowers appreciated their efforts. After these boats arrived at Thebes, a bull was sacrificed in honour of the event and offered to the gods. Hatshepsut then presented her obelisks to the god Amun.

The whole process from quarry to temple took only seven months and was a phenomenal achievement. Sadly, all that remains of these obelisks are the bases, as the gold and the shafts were removed and reused in antiquity.

A few years later, Hatshepsut erected a further pair of obelisks, standing nearly 30 metres high, one of which is still standing at Karnak temple and is the tallest obelisk in Egypt. Only the tops of this pair were gilded, but still they were an impressive sight.

STRANGE BUT TRUE

Journey of a lifetime

The transportation of Cleopatra's Needle to London was not an adventure-free journey. In fact it can be described as disastrous.

Cleopatra's Needle was presented to the United Kingdom in 1819 by Mohammed Ali, the Viceroy of Egypt, in commemoration of victories at the Battle of the Nile and the Battle of Alexandria in 1801. The structure remained in Alexandria until 1877 when the funding for transportation, a total of £10,000, was provided by Sir William James Erasmus Wilson. (Prior to this no one wanted to pay the transportation costs.)

The obelisk was placed in a custom-made, 28 by 4.5 metre iron cylinder, named rather unoriginally *Cleopatra*. This cylinder then floated behind the tow-boat *Olga* – a modern(ish) twist on Hatshepsut's obelisk transportation.

When the boat reached the Bay of Biscay, *Cleopatra* capsized in a storm and floated into the bay. The cylinder was rescued by an English ship and taken to Spain for repairs. It eventually arrived in the United Kingdom in January 1878 and was erected on Victoria Embankment seven months later.

In September 1917, during the First World War, German bombs landed near the obelisk, causing damage to the right-flanking sphinx. This was never repaired, in commemoration of the war, and shrapnel holes are still visible. To be honest, the British are lucky to have the obelisk at all – so what are a few holes?

New Kingdom obelisks were very tall. Due to their height, they were often the first and last point of the temple to catch the rays of the sun, and indeed the shape of the obelisk is believed to represent a sunbeam.

Of the hundreds of obelisks that once existed in ancient Egypt, only 30 are still in existence, and of those only seven are in Egypt. The others have been spread around the world:

✔ Seven are still in Egypt, two at Heliopolis, one at Gezira Island, one at Cairo, and four at Karnak.

✔ 13 are in Rome.

✔ Ten are elsewhere around the world, including Paris, London, New York, Istanbul, Florence, Urbino (a small town in Italy), Catania (in Sicily), Wimborne (United Kingdom), Arles (southern France), and Caesarea (Israel).

Temple décor

One of the easiest ways of making an impact is through decoration, and many kings decorated a wall or chamber of an existing temple and claimed credit for the building work as well. In their logic, if their name was painted or carved on the wall, then they must have built it too.

During particularly weak economic periods, or even just busy times, kings commonly usurped temples in order to reduce time and construction costs. During the New Kingdom, it became the norm for kings to nick the work of their ancestors by simply painting or carving over the cartouches of the original decorator and claiming the work for themselves. Ramses III, however, was determined that he would always be credited for the work he did – he therefore carved his cartouches so deeply into the stone that it was impossible for a later king to usurp his monument without carving half a metre into the wall.

Carvings

Two types of relief were used in temple decoration:

- ✔ **Raised (bas) relief,** in which the background was cut away, leaving the image raised. This was very time-consuming and was kept to a minimum. It was more common on interior walls.

- ✔ **Sunk relief,** in which the subject was cut away from the background. Quick to execute, this type of relief was more common, especially on exterior walls.

Ramses II devised a way of carving which looked like the finer raised relief, but was in fact the quick-and-easy sunk relief. This involved carving a very deep line around the edge of the images, which gives the impression of raised relief. Figure 12-4 shows an example of this carving technique.

After the carved images were completed, they were painted in elaborate colours. Paint also added small details, such as fabric patterns, wings on birds, and plant life.

Figure 12-4:
The image of Hathor and Isis at the Hathor Temple in Deir el Medina is a sunk relief made to look like a raised one.

Interior embellishments

Because the temple represents the universe, the ceilings were always decorated with sky-related images, and the decoration near the floor was always of marshland. Pillars often represented plants, creating a stone universe recognisable to all.

Both cult and mortuary temples featured the same categories of artistic embellishment, including depictions of

- ✔ **Ritual activities,** such as temple rituals, processions, and offerings.
- ✔ **Historical activities,** such as battles, processions (either military or religious), coronation celebrations, sacred birth scenes, and diplomatic treaties.
- ✔ **Environmental scenes,** which were applied to certain elements of the temple architecture and included depictions of the sky, marshes, flora, and fauna.
- ✔ **Making offerings to the gods.**

Although the preceding categories are nicely labelled, many surviving images actually fall into more than one category on occasions. For instance, religious processions or offerings are both ritual activities *and* historical activities because they were real events.

The images were strategically placed throughout the temple, and although artists had a lot of freedom regarding the content of the images, the location was often pre-determined. For example:

- The sanctuary had images of offerings being made to a shrine on a sacred bark.

- Shrines had images of offerings being made to various gods by the king.

- Windowsills were decorated with images of sunrays.

- Ceilings were painted with stars or birds to represent the sky.

- Food stores were decorated with images of fatted oxen ready for slaughter.

- Routes of processions showed the procession in progress.

- Pylons and external walls were decorated with violent scenes showing the king smiting enemies in battle or parading bound captives. These images were to act as a deterrent against enemies wishing to cause harm to the temple, Egypt, or the king.

In rooms that did not have a specific function, a variety of images were presented, including historical events such as expeditions, coronations, or public military processions. For example, in the temple of Edfu, the walls were used as archival documents recording the history of temple building and festival calendars.

Who's a pretty pylon?

Luckily for modern visitors and historians, many of the kings described their temple-decoration methods and meanings on temple walls and papyri. These records provide some idea of the splendour that once existed in these vast and now barren places.

For example, the decoration of the third pylon at Karnak is described by Amenhotep III and shows that paint and carving were just the beginning:

The king added a monument for Amun, making for him a very great doorway before the face of Amun-Re, King of the Gods, embellished with gold throughout. [On its door] the sacred ram-headed image, inlaid with lapis lazuli, is embellished with gold and precious stones: the like will never be done again. A stela of lapis lazuli stands on either side. Its pylons reach to the sky like the four pillars of heaven: The flagpoles thereof, embellished with electrum, gleam brighter that the sky.

The riches mentioned in this description have long since been stripped and taken away – if they ever existed. The description may be pure propaganda to inflate the piety of the king. For the ancient Egyptians, once something was written in hieroglyphs, it was considered to have been created by the gods and became reality. Now if only those kinds of pens were available in the shops today . . .

Worshipping in the Temple

The temples were busy and vibrant places. Although the temples were closed to the public, the rituals inside were very important.

Attending to the god

All temple activities revolved around the sacred statue in the sanctuary at the rear of the temple. This statue was tiny – perhaps only 30 centimetres high – and was made of gold or gilded wood. Sadly, none of these statues survives, but the shrines within which they were placed survive and give an indication of how small the statues were.

The most important ritual was the first one of the day. Just before dawn, all the temple staff rose, purified themselves, and prepared food for an elaborate breakfast for the statue. Typical duties included baking bread and honey cakes, slaughtering animals, and arranging fruit and vegetables on trays. The meal was then offered to the statue.

A similar meal-preparation ritual was repeated at dusk when the statue was put to bed; for further information see Chapter 9.

Throughout the day, the hour priest offered different hourly prayers to the god. The hour priest kept time by observing the sun and using water clocks, which were essentially bowls with holes that measured the time by the amount of water that had drained away.

Enjoying the festivities

The temple was also the site of many festivals and processions, which enabled ordinary people, typically denied access to the temple, to visit the temple and participate in worship. Records indicate that up to ten processions happened each month, enabling the people to view the sacred bark and perhaps receive blessings and guidance from the priests.

During festivals and processions, temple staff often distributed extra rations so that people could have a feast and celebrate in style, in addition to enjoying the obligatory day off work.

Not only did festivals benefit the villagers, they also benefited the smaller temples. The statues of the deities from the larger temples, like Karnak or Luxor temple, travelled to the smaller ones. To ensure that the god was suitably received, the larger temples supported the smaller temples economically, greatly benefiting the priests working there.

Getting wasted

The Festival of Drunkenness was celebrated annually at Deir el Medina in honour of the cow-headed goddess, Hathor, the lady of drunkenness (see Chapter 9). The aim of the celebration was to drink as much beer and wine as possible over a five-day period. Rather like St Patrick's Day – for the better part of a week!

Texts from Deir el Medina describe the festival in detail:

> Come, Hathor, who consumes praise because the food of her desire is dancing, who shines on the festival at the time of

illumination, who is content with the dancing at night. Come! The drunken celebrants drum for you during the cool of the night.

Sounds like the party went on well into the wee hours of the morning with lots of dancing – as is normally the case with drunk celebrants.

Egyptians, however, believed that the drunkenness associated with this festival was a means of achieving an altered state that enabled worshippers to see the divine or receive messages from the goddess. If you drink enough, who knows what can happen?

Appreciating the Roles of the King and the High Priests

REMEMBER

The king was officially the high priest of all the cults in every temple in Egypt and was expected to perform all the necessary rituals in order to maintain the cosmic order, or *Maat*. (See Chapter 9 for a further discussion of Maat.)

If the king failed to appease the gods, the land would collapse into a state of chaos resulting in famine, floods, or invasion. If I had this kind of pressure, I would delegate it – and this strategy is exactly what the king followed with his high priests. The high priest of each temple worked in place of the king. Everything the priest did was done in the king's name.

Whenever the king was present at a temple, the high priest was relieved of his role, albeit briefly, enabling the king to perform his duty as high priest.

Laying the foundations

The king's role in the temple started as soon as a location was chosen (and often he chose the location himself). As the section 'Building a Temple' earlier in this chapter explains, most temples were built on older sacred sites, which often required the dismantling of the older temple that originally stood there.

After the site was clear, the king performed the ten foundation rituals:

1. **Fixing the plan of the building by 'stretching the cord'.** This was the most important ritual and was assisted by the goddess of writing, Seshat. During this ritual, the king banged a peg into the earth at the spot where each corner was to be and then stretched cord between this peg until an outline of the temple was established.

2. **Purifying the area by scattering gypsum.**

3. **Digging the first foundation trench.** The trench was dug until the natural water table was reached.

4. **Pouring sand into the first foundation trench.** This represents the mound of creation protruding from the primeval waters at the bottom of the trench.

5. **Moulding the first bricks.**

6. **Leaving *foundation deposits* at the corners of the structure.** These deposits are varied and consist of pottery, model food, model tools, and occasionally jewellery.

7. **Initiating the building work.**

8. **Purifying the finished temple.** This no doubt involved prayers and incantations.

9. **Presenting the temple to its deities.** The king placed the statue of the god in the shrine at the rear of the temple. The statue was the focus of the whole temple. Although a temple could enable worship of numerous deities, each temple had a primary deity. (For example, although Amun, Mut, Khonsu, Montu, Ptah, Opet, and Amum are all worshipped at Karnak, the main deity is Amun. Amun's statue is therefore the most important on the site.)

10. **Making sacrificial offerings to the gods who now resided in the temple.** These sacrifices were probably in the form of geese or oxen.

Because these rituals are only recorded in list form, knowing exactly what each ritual consisted of is difficult, if not impossible.

Feeding the populace: Other temple duties

In addition to being the 'house of the god' where the priests worshipped and revered the statue of the god, the temples were the economic centres of the cities.

Monitoring the river's rise and fall

In order to calculate taxes correctly, temple personnel devised methods for predicting flood levels that helped them determine the type of harvest that was likely to result. If the flood was too high or too low, the harvest failed and resulted in famine. So through prediction, the priest prepared for agricultural abundance or shortfalls.

Each temple had a *nilometer*, which was a deep well that reached the water table. When the Nile started to flood, the priest measured the speed of the rise at the bottom of the nilometer. These measurements were recorded and compared to those made at the same date in previous years. With this information the priests fairly accurately predicted annual flood levels. Clever, eh?

Most temples were supported by their own estates, which the king or wealthy members of the community gave the temples in exchange for the blessings of the god. This agricultural land was rented to farmers, who paid the temple a third of their yields as rent. Much of this income was redistributed in the form of rations (wages) for the army, to the officials (essentially anyone who held a position in government or the priesthood), and for royal construction of temples and tombs. (See Chapter 2 for more details.)

Meeting the priests – civil (not divine) servants

Prior to the New Kingdom, a permanent priesthood did not exist. Priests worked in the temples on a part-time basis and then returned to their jobs in ordinary society. During the New Kingdom, many priests were primarily administrative officials in control of taxes and food distribution – with only a small hint of religion (for the full role of the priest, skip to Chapter 2). Even in the New Kingdom, a large majority of the priests served one month out of four.

A small core of permanent priests lived within the temple precincts, with the high priest in the most senior position. Obviously the number of personnel in a temple varied according to the size of the temple. Karnak, for example, had more than 2,000 employees, whereas most other temples had between 10 and 80 personnel.

Acting as an ancient records office

Because the temples were so involved in the Egyptian economy and the associated administration, they kept extensive records of the local regions, rather like a town hall records office. These records were stored in the House of Life (for further details go to Chapter 2) and included details of

- Locations of holy places
- Pilgrimages, which anyone could participate in
- *Cult centres* (centres of worship of particular deities) and names of personnel
- Local crops
- Local standards and deities
- Dates of principal festivals
- Taboos regarding activities or food
- Portion of the Nile present in the region
- Cultivated fields and marshy lands
- Outgoings, such as support for campaigns to foreign areas, building works, and rations
- Foreign countries and their resources

Recording the days

The priests were also responsible for devising the calendar systems. Three were in use, all for different purposes:

- **Agricultural calendar:** For day-to-day use by the majority of the population. The year was divided into three seasons of four months each – inundation (flood), time of growing, and harvest.
- **Astronomical calendar:** For ritual use and based on the movement of the stars.
- **Moon calendar:** For ritual use for *lunar cults* (cults devoted to gods associated with the moon). Careful records of the lunar phases were kept and these were tied in with religious days and rituals.

All the calendars had certain aspects in common. Each month consisted of 30 days, totalling 360 days in a year. Five religious festival days were then added to the end of the year for the birthdays of Osiris, Horus, Seth, Isis, and Nephthys (see Chapter 9). Of course, this 365-day calendar slowly veered away from the true year. Every four years, the agricultural calendar advanced one day, which meant that eventually the seasons no longer coincided with the calendar. To deal with this discrepancy, the rising of the star Sirius always coincided with the beginning of the inundation, which was seen as the New Year.

Chapter 13

Excavating the Tombs:
Houses of Eternity

*E*gypt is well known for its burial sites, whether pyramids or the elabo-rately decorated tombs in the Valley of the Kings. This chapter focuses on the history of tombs, while Chapter 14 delves into the secrets of the pyramids.

The Valley tombs are the result of years of evolution brought on by changing religious priorities and increasing security risks.

However, regardless of the tombs' design, the same fundamental belief in the afterlife is present. The Egyptians saw the afterlife as a place where the deceased was reborn and lived for eternity (see Chapter 10 for more details), the ancient equivalent of paradise. In fact, a belief in the afterlife is suggested in the earliest burials (prior to 3100 BC), before the construction of elaborate tombs, from the simple inclusion of funerary goods.

As religious beliefs became more complex, the tombs grew more elaborate and developed into status symbols – like today's Porsche!

But above all, these resting places were intended to last for eternity, as a home for the deceased in the afterlife. They were therefore referred to as *Houses of Eternity*. (It does exactly what it says on the tin!)

Burying the Earliest Egyptians

All civilisations need to dispose of the dead, and in a country as hot as Egypt, decomposition can start immediately. Therefore, in the pre-dynastic period (prior to 3100 BC), burials were simple affairs:

- The deceased was buried individually in a shallow pit dug into the desert edge, a short distance away from the settlements.
- The body was placed into the pit in a foetal position with no coffin or covering of any kind.
- The pit was filled with sand, which fell directly onto the body, preserving it naturally.

Burials were accompanied by a number of grave goods, including pottery vessels and dishes, jewellery, and cosmetic palettes. These objects were clearly connected to a belief in the afterlife and the belief that the deceased would need them again.

Enclosing the dead

Occasionally, animals disturbed the pit burials, uncovering the buried bodies and revealing the natural preservation that had taken place. The bodies sometimes even retained skin and hair, whereas at other times the preservation was not so consistent.

Natural preservation sparked a belief that in order to survive in the afterlife, bodies needed to be preserved. With that, the process of artificial preservation, or *mummification* (see Chapter 10), began. Artificial preservation also led to the development of tombs as a further effort to preserve bodies for eternity.

The earliest attempts to preserve the body artificially took two forms:

- Enclosing the body in something, such as a clay pot, reed tray, animal skin or linen shroud
- Lining the burial pits in bricks or wood

A number of early cemeteries have been discovered (Hierakonpolis; Minshat Abu Omar, 150 kilometres from Cairo; and Adaima, 25 kilometres north of Hierakonpolis) that include simple pits lined with mud brick. The walls were left undecorated, and the bottom of the burial pit was lined with reed matting tied to wooden strips, which created trays to lay the bodies on. A ledge runs around the top of the inside wall, which supported wooden roofing beams. These pits were then covered with desert rubble in order to disguise the burial locations in the desert plateau.

Tomb 100

Tomb 100 from the pre-dynastic cemetery at Hierakonpolis (around 3685 BC) was the first tomb (and the only one known from the pre-dynastic period) to contain decorated walls. Rather than a simple pit, Tomb 100 features a number of subterranean rooms separated by partition walls. In the burial chamber, these walls are plastered and painted. Depictions of men, animals, and riverboats appear in red, white, green, and black paint on a yellow background.

At least three images in Tomb 100 relate to more traditional Egyptian art, including imagery often used to represent the role of kingship. For example, one image in Tomb 100 shows a man smiting three bound captives with a mace; another shows a figure holding two wild animals in his bare hands; and another has a boat holding a figure, probably a chieftain, seated underneath a canopy with a group of men in loincloths worshipping him with their hands outstretched.

Although no texts survived in Tomb 100, these prominent figures suggest that a king, or chieftain, was probably the tomb owner. Sadly, since its discovery in the early 20th century, the location of Tomb 100 has become lost, so further examination of the original paintings is impossible. Photographs and copies of the paintings are in the Ashmolean Museum, Oxford, and the Egyptian Museum in Cairo.

Upgrading the pits

As time went by, the simple brick-lined pits weren't enough. Egyptians wanted something more impressive as their House of Eternity.

Initially the pits were modified to include partition walls, which created a number of chambers to store lots of grave goods. The largest discovered pit tomb is tomb Uj from Abydos from dynasty 0 (around 3100 BC; see the Cheat Sheet for chronology). The tomb is 9.10 by 7.30 metres and is divided into 12 rooms, nine of which contained hundreds of pottery vessels and ivory labels. This elaborate tomb most probably belonged to a local chieftain or mayor.

The Egyptians were still not satisfied, however, and wanted to extend their House of Eternity upwards. The sky's the limit, as they say.

Turning Pits into Palaces: Mastabas

By the start of the Old Kingdom, officials began building superstructures over the pits. The mounds of desert rubble piled over the pits' wooden roofs were extended upwards, making the tombs distinguishable from the surrounding landscape.

Adding superstructures

The size and design of the materials placed on top of the tombs reflected the status and wealth of the individual and no doubt led to a trend of keeping up with the Joneses – or rather, keeping up with the Amenhoteps.

Smaller, less impressive burials consisted of small uneven mounds of rubble covering the burial pit, whereas more elaborate tombs had rectangular brick superstructures built up to heights of 1 metre above ground level.

These superstructures were bench-like in shape, hence they were named *mastaba*, from the Arabic word for bench. The outside of the superstructure was painted white, while offering niches along the west wall were painted a dull red. A brick pavement led to the niches and provided a space where mourners could leave food offerings of bread, beer, and vegetables for the spirit of the deceased.

Because these superstructures were built *after* the burial had taken place, entrances were unnecessary. The lack of entrances meant mastabas were safe from most robbers, but it also meant the tombs couldn't be re-entered. This was soon to change, as family burials became the height of fashion.

Bigger, better mastabas

By the end of the Old Kingdom (2333 BC), family tombs were common, with elaborate hollow mastaba superstructures being constructed.

These superstructures contained numerous decorated chambers, including areas that functioned as funerary chapels and enabled family to leave offerings inside rather than outside. The deceased were still buried in pits beneath the ground and could be reached via a shaft in the floor of the mastaba.

As the mastabas became more impressive, the kings needed to reassert their status and wealth, which led to the design and construction of step pyramids and eventually smooth pyramids (see Chapter 14).

Stepping up: King Djoser

The first step pyramid was built for King Djoser of the third dynasty (2686 BC). The structure started with a traditional mastaba tomb at Saqqara. The burial chamber was 28 metres below ground at the bottom of a shaft and was lined with granite. This remains under the step pyramid that is on the site today.

Room for 11 more?

Just to the east of the original completed mastaba of Djoser, 11 burial shafts were sunk 38 metres into the ground. These 11 shafts each ended in a large galleried chamber and were the intended burial places of the royal family.

Although the chambers were sadly robbed in antiquity, two calcite sarcophagi have survived, one with a gilded coffin containing the remains of an 8-year-old girl.

Leading from the burial chamber are four corridors, which lead to a suite of chambers and storerooms. Some of these rooms included blue faience (a type of ceramic made from sand) tiles decorated with djed pillars, representative of the god Osiris, which is the only decoration in this burial site. The only human remains found in this step pyramid was a mummified foot, which suggests that a burial took place here.

The mastaba superstructure was constructed of desert rubble and clay, encased in limestone blocks 3 metres thick. The initial superstructure was 63 metres long and 8 metres high, which was in itself no mean feat.

At some point in the mastaba's construction, Djoser decided he wanted something more impressive and made a number of alterations:

- ✔ The mastaba was extended lengthways.
- ✔ Three more structures were placed on top of each other, creating a four-step pyramid.
- ✔ The base was extended, and two more steps were added, resulting in a six-step pyramid rising 60 metres from the ground.

This was the first building in the world to be built entirely of stone. This tomb structure was thought to be a staircase that the king would ascend to be with his ancestors, who became stars after death.

After the construction of step pyramids, the next evolution in pyramid development was to fill in the steps to form a true, smooth-sided pyramid. See Chapter 14 for more on these structures. A number of pyramids at Saqqara and Abusir started as step pyramids and were turned into true pyramids by filling in the steps.

More complex than tomb

All the tombs and pyramids built during the Old and Middle Kingdoms were not isolated monuments, but rather part of larger complexes, consisting of temples and a cemetery for nobles and officials.

The step pyramid complex of Djoser, however, is unique. Rather than building a simple temple, Djoser built an entire full-sized kingdom over which he could rule for eternity. This complex covers 146 square metres, and most of the buildings were 'dummies' with no real function.

The complex includes

✔ The king's tomb – the main, step pyramid.

✔ Family and dignitary burial tombs, buried in mastaba fields with hundreds of tombs. The closer the tomb was to the pyramid, the more important the individual.

✔ A pillared hall.

✔ An open courtyard with altars dedicated to the sun god.

✔ A festival courtyard where Djoser performed his rejuvenation ceremony, or *heb sed*, every 30 years. The ceremony involved the king running around markers representing the length and breadth of Egypt to show his strength and vitality.

✔ Two mansions for the spirit of the king to reside in. The mansions also represented his rule over Upper and Lower Egypt.

✔ A mortuary temple, which was the focus of the funerary cult of Djoser.

✔ A *serdab*, which housed a life-size statue of the king. The statue was able to observe rituals through a hole in the wall.

✔ Storage rooms to house objects used in the rituals.

The only structures in the complex with real function were the mortuary temple and the burial tombs of Djoser's family and officials. In the afterlife when the king was reborn, the dummy buildings became real and provided Djoser with the luxuries and necessities of a king – including a kingdom to rule.

Hewing in Rock

During the Middle Kingdom, the mastaba was abandoned and non-royal burials were carried out in rock-cut tombs. These were tombs cut directly into a cliff face and supplemented with a monumental façade, a sloping courtyard, and a colonnade that functioned as a chapel in which the family and friends could leave offerings for the deceased.

The colonnade consisted of a large gathering area and a small statue chamber at the rear. A shaft located cut into the floor of the chapel led to the burial chamber beneath. The walls of these tombs are elaborately decorated with painted scenes of daily life, military training, battles, and hunting scenes.

If it's not nailed down . . .

Like the pyramids of the Old Kingdom, these elaborate Middle Kingdom rock-cut tombs were security risks. Unattended goods and offerings could easily be taken and sold on the open market.

The families that owned the tombs tried to limit the danger of robbery by regularly visiting the tombs to make offerings of food and drink. They also restricted the number of times the tomb was opened for the interment of additional family members. The mummified deceased were therefore stored in houses until an annual, bi-annual, or five-yearly opening of the tomb was due. Families then conducted group funerals for all members of the family who had died during a specific period.

The practice of waiting to inter bodies continued throughout pharaonic history. People were more concerned about robberies than the hygiene issues resulting from a collection of dead bodies in the basement. Today you would be investigated by the police and possibly a psychiatrist for similar behaviour.

Continuing the trend

The concern with security, however large, did not deter the Egyptians from using rock-cut tombs well into the New Kingdom.

A number of the Theban noble tombs – at the Valley of the Nobles (Sheikh abd-el Gourna), Deir el Bahri, and the Assasif – have elaborate façades, which were prominent on the landscape.

A number of these rock-cut tombs were also surmounted by a small pyramid, which had no function other than acting as a status symbol – and serving as a beacon to tomb robbers!

Getting completely shafted: Shaft tombs

In response to the security threat, as well as financial concerns, a number of Middle and New Kingdom officials were buried in shaft tombs. These tombs were dug directly out of the desert floor and consisted of a vertical shaft, which opened into a subterranean burial chamber. If the deceased was wealthy, the subterranean burial chamber was elaborately decorated or consisted of a suite of rooms.

Eternal rest for provincial governors

The site of Beni Hasan in Middle Egypt has the best collection of Middle Kingdom rock-cut tombs. There are 39 tombs here, all carved into the rock face of the cliff. At least four of the tombs belonged to local governors of the region from the end of the 11th and early 12th dynasties, and were impressive statements of their wealth and status.

Most of the tombs follow a similar construction of an outer portico and a larger inner chamber with at least two pillars and a statue niche. The scenes on the tomb walls focus on military training, including wrestling, stick fighting, and weight lifting using sand bags. There are also scenes of warfare, with the Egyptian army laying siege to fortified buildings. Some researchers believe that these scenes depict the civil war between northern and southern Egypt during the early 11th-dynasty unification battles of King Mentuhotep II.

The tomb of Khnumhotep II includes a particularly interesting scene in which a trading party from Syria-Palestine is bringing eye-paint to Egypt. The party leader Absha is titled *heka haswt*, from which the term Hyksos developed (see Chapter 3). The depiction is one of the earliest images of the people known as the Hyksos.

The advantage of a shaft tomb was that after the burial had taken place and the shaft filled with desert rubble, it was impossible to locate, because no superstructure advertised the tomb's location.

Shaft tombs were used for the rest of the pharaonic period. Today, these tombs are often discovered intact, because even well-trained robbers couldn't find them.

Sinking to their level: New Kingdom tombs

From the start of Egyptian history, tombs evolved architecturally and ideologically – and did much more than simply provide a place to dispose of the dead.

The ideological significance of the tombs was never more apparent than in the sophisticated New Kingdom. The New Kingdom tombs were divided into three parts

- **The upper level** or superstructure represented the realm of the sun god. This level was represented by a small niche, a *stela* (a stone slab with a curved top and an inscription), or a small pyramid.

- **The middle level** included the internal offering chapels and represented the juxtaposition between the realm of the living and that of the dead.

- **The lower level** included the burial chambers and represented the realm of the dead.

The kings of the New Kingdom, however, chose to build tombs that had no visible superstructure, as a means of preventing robberies. During this period, the construction of upper levels was only applicable to non-royal tombs. The royal offering chapel (middle level) was situated some distance from the tomb in the desert on the edge of the cultivated land closer to the Nile, while the royal burials (lower level) took place in the Valley of the Kings.

Interring the Divine

The Valley of the Kings on the west bank of the Nile at Thebes (Luxor) is separated into two valleys:

- **The Eastern Valley,** which contains 63 tombs numbered in the order in which they were discovered. KV (for King's Valley) 63 was discovered in February 2006.
- **The Western Valley,** which contains five tombs.

The development of the Valley of the Kings in the New Kingdom brought about a number of innovations in tomb design. All the tombs in the Valley of the Kings are rock cut, but rather than being built into the sides of cliffs with elaborate façades, the entrances are carved directly into the floor of the Valley – or, if the entrances are carved into cliffs, they are inaccessible and hidden.

Each individual tomb is different due to a number of design features:

- The **bent axis tomb** was introduced by Amenhotep II and consisted of a long corridor that turned 90 degrees before reaching the burial chamber. This style was used for 130 years.
- The **jogged axis tomb** was introduced by Horemheb and consisted of a long corridor that ended in the burial chamber. However, the axis was not entirely straight and jogged to one side after the first hall.
- The **straight axis tomb** was introduced by Ramses IV and was a long, straight corridor cut into the floor of the valley, which ended in the burial chamber.
- The **oval burial chamber** was introduced by Thutmosis III and was representative of a *cartouche*, an oval that surrounded the royal name. Surrounding the royal burial with the same shape offered the same protection in death as the ruler received in life.
- The **shaft burial** was used throughout the period of use of the Valley of the Kings and consisted of a vertical shaft that opened out into the burial chamber at the bottom. See 'Getting completely shafted: Shaft tombs', earlier in this chapter, for more information.

Would you like a flake with your cone?

An architectural feature used in the upper level of New Kingdom non-royal tombs was a frieze of funerary cones. Funerary cones were about 15 centimetres long and made of pottery. They were rounded at one end and pointed at the other. The round end was stamped with the tomb owner's name and titles, as well as those of his wife and family.

The frieze was constructed using up to 300 identical cones in a tomb, embedded into the external wall with the stamped, rounded end visible and flush with the wall. (Archaeologists use these cones to identify any missing tombs; if the cones exist today, then the tomb must have also existed at some point.)

Funerary cones were first introduced in the 11th dynasty and continued to be used until the 25th dynasty, although they were most popular in the 18th dynasty of the New Kingdom. There has been some debate as to their ritual function, including the suggestion that they represented loaves of bread to nourish the deceased in the afterlife.

Not one of the tombs in the Valley of the Kings is actually finished. Indeed, no tomb in Egypt is complete. Some are carved completely out of the rock and are waiting to be decorated, whereas others have the outlines drawn, ready for carving. Some tombs appear to be complete, but have missing inscriptions, or the painting of the images isn't complete. The most likely reason for this is the death of the intended recipient, forcing the workmen to halt their work. Also, to finish a tomb would be to admit perfection, and that the tomb was suitable to house a god. What architect could ever seriously make that claim?

The number of incomplete tombs is, to a certain extent, useful, because it allows archaeologists to record the methods of carving and decorating the tombs.

Taking a trip to the King's Valley

The Valley of the Kings is one of the most visited sites in Egypt, and consists of 63 elaborately decorated tombs. However, the name Valley of the Kings is somewhat misleading, because not all the 63 tombs in the Eastern Valley are royal. In fact, only 23 of the 63 tombs in the Eastern Valley are tombs of kings – all the New Kingdom kings from Thutmosis I to Ramses XI (see the nearby sidebar for the complete list).

The other 40 tombs are of unknown and named princes, officials, pets, and unknown individuals.

Officials

Some revered officials were also buried at the site, both in rock-cut and shaft burials. Burial in the Valley of Kings was a great honour for any official. At least seven tombs were built for officials:

- KV13 belongs to the Chancellor, Bay, from the reign of Sety II and Siptah.

- KV36 belongs to Maiherperi, a Nubian fan-bearer from the 18th dynasty. The title of fan-bearer was one of great status, because it enabled the individual to be in the king's company and privy to all his secrets.

- KV45 belonged originally to an official called Userhet from the 18th dynasty, although it was reused in the 22nd dynasty.

- KV46 was the intact tomb of Yuya and Thuya, the parents of Queen Tiye, who was the husband of Amenhotep III and mother of Akhenaten.

- KV48 belongs to an official called Amenemopet, commonly known as Pairy, from the reign of Amenhotep II.

- KV60 belongs to Sitre-in, the wet nurse of Queen Hatshepsut, and contained a female body that has been identified as either Sitre-in or Hatshepsut.

Those who would be king

The Valley of the Kings also accommodated the tombs of some queens and princes – some kings wanted their entire family close by.

- KV3 was the tomb of an unnamed son of Ramses III.

- KV5 is the biggest tomb in the Valley of the Kings and was intended for the burials of the sons of Ramses II.

- KV14 was originally built by Queen Tawosret for her and her husband Sety II, but this was usurped by King Setnakht, who extended the tomb and removed her body.

- KV19 was built for Montuherkhepshef, a prince who later became Ramses VIII.

- KV42 was constructed for Hatshepsut Merytre, a wife of Thutmosis III.

Even though these tombs were for the royal family, being buried in the Valley of the Kings was still a privilege, because the closer someone was buried to the king, the higher status he or she held. These burials show that these wives and children were highly praised by their husbands or fathers. In the 19th and 20th dynasty, the Valley of the Queens, south of the Valley of the Kings, was constructed as a place solely for members of the royal family and contains 75–80 tombs.

Who's who in the Valley of the Kings

The Valley of the Kings may be chock full of tombs, but who's who in this upmarket resting place?

- ✔ KV38: Thutmosis I, father of Hatshepsut

- ✔ KV20: Hatshepsut (refer to Chapter 3 for more on the life of Hatshepsut)

- ✔ KV34: Thutmosis III (Chapter 4 has more details of Thutmosis III)

- ✔ KV35: Amenhotep II

- ✔ KV43: Thutmosis IV, who set up the Dream Stela at the sphinx at Giza (see Chapter 14)

- ✔ WV (Western Valley) 22: Amenhotep III, the father of Akhenaten

- ✔ WV25: Akhenaten (Chapter 4 has more about Akhenaten)

- ✔ KV55: Smenkhkare – Akhenaten's successor

- ✔ KV62: Tutankhamun, the famous boy king (see Chapter 4)

- ✔ WV23: Ay, the uncle and successor of Tutankhamun

- ✔ KV57: Horemheb, Ay's successor

- ✔ KV16: Ramses I, a general of Horemheb who ruled for a short period

- ✔ KV17: Sety I, the father of Ramses II

- ✔ KV7: Ramses II (refer to Chapter 4)

- ✔ KV8: Merenptah, the 13th son and successor of Ramses II

- ✔ KV10: Amenmesse, possibly the son of a daughter of Ramses II

- ✔ KV15: Sety II, husband of Tawosret and father of Siptah

- ✔ KV47: Siptah, who ruled alongside his mother until he became an adult

- ✔ KV14: Tawosret and Setnakht – the tomb was started by Tawosret and then completed by Setnakht and is one of the only tombs with two burial chambers

- ✔ KV11: Ramses III (refer to Chapter 4)

- ✔ KV2: Ramses IV, son of Ramses III

- ✔ KV9: Ramses VI, son of Ramses III

- ✔ KV1: Ramses VII, son of Ramses VI

- ✔ KV6: Ramses IX, who reigned Egypt for 18 years

- ✔ KV18: Ramses X, who reigned for between three and nine years

Furry and feathered friends

Like many pet owners today, the Egyptians loved their pets. A few tombs in the Valley were constructed solely for the burial of these beloved family members.

- ✔ KV50 housed the pets of Amenhotep II, including the mummified remains of a dog and a monkey.

- ✔ KV51 contained the burial of three monkeys, one baboon, three ducks, and an ibis; however, the owner of this menagerie of animals is a mystery.

- ✔ KV52 contained the mummified remains of a monkey, although again the owner is unknown.

These burials and others discovered in other cemeteries tell us what types of pets were kept by the Egyptian kings – primarily monkeys, dogs, cats, and ducks. Many of these burials consisted of a mummified animal within a coffin, and some even contained funerary goods as well. The burial of pets was not exclusive to royals, and a number of pet mummies have been discovered, including horses, cats, and birds.

Considering unknown owners

Details of the ownership of 20 of the 63 Eastern Valley tombs have not survived, and the ownership of one of the Western Valley tombs is unknown.

Based on tomb style, researchers can sometimes identify the period when a tomb was built. All the tombs were robbed in antiquity, and priests moved a number of bodies to a store in the 21st dynasty to protect them from further violation, so many of the tombs do not contain bodies or grave goods. The priests re-wrapped the bodies before placing them in the store, but they may have confiscated the riches wrapped against the body as a means of boosting the flagging economy.

Still not exhausted

As the recent discovery of KV63 suggests, the Valley of the Kings still has discoveries to offer. In February 2006, an American team discovered a tomb shaft 5 metres from the tomb of Tutankhamun. This tomb had been identified using sonar survey by the British-run Amarna Royal Tomb Project in 2000, although it took six years for the tomb to be uncovered.

The tomb was approached by a 5-metre-deep shaft, which then leads into a rectangular, undecorated burial chamber measuring approximately 4 metres by 5 metres. The tomb contained seven wooden sarcophagi and 27 large storage jars dated to the reign of Tutankhamun, identified by a seal bearing the name of his wife Ankhesenamun.

Before the tomb was cleared, a lot of publicity and speculation focused on who the tomb belonged to – suggestions included Nefertiti, Kiya, and Ankhesenamun (the stepmother, mother, and wife of Tutankhamun, respectively). Imagine everyone's disappointment when the coffins and storage jars contained only the remains of an embalmer's workshop – a lot of linen, natron, pillows, miniature vessels, resin, chaff, and floral collars. Of course, these materials raise a number of questions, as embalmers' caches are normally remains from a burial. Whose burial does this cache belong to?

In July 2006, the Amarna Royal Tomb Project announced results of further sonar surveys that indicate another possible tomb in the same region as KV63 and KV62 (Tutankhamun). Perhaps the embalmer's cache in KV63 is the remains of the burial in KV64. Who knows?

A tomb fit for kings

The largest tomb in the Valley of the Kings – and indeed the whole of Egypt – is KV5, built by Ramses II for the burial of his numerous sons (for more on Ramses II, see Chapter 4). The tomb was originally discovered prior to 1799 and then recorded in the 1820s, although only the first court was entered and deemed not worthy of excavation.

However, in 1987, Kent Weeks, while working on the Theban Mapping Project (see Chapter 15 for details of the project and Chapter 19 for the low-down on Dr Weeks), entered the tomb to assess the damage of a leaking sewage pipe and discovered the potential of KV5. Due to numerous flash floods over the centuries, the tomb was filled to the ceiling with compacted desert rubble, which sets to the consistency of concrete. Weeks and his team have systematically removed rubble and revealed more than 120 chambers and corridors on three levels. More chambers are uncovered each season, and the total number of chambers is likely to exceed 150 over the coming years.

So far, six of Ramses's sons have been discovered buried here. However, the wall decoration depicts more then 20 sons, so many more may be awaiting discovery. There are many years of work still left on this tomb, and no doubt other surprises await Weeks and his team.

A couple of these mystery tombs have stood out from the rest due to remains that were discovered within them. Although these details bring researchers no closer to identifying the tombs' owners, the remains are fascinating none the less:

- ✔ KV56 is referred to as the 'Gold Tomb' because a collection of 19th-dynasty gold jewellery was discovered within it.

- ✔ KV58 is known as the 'Chariot Tomb' because a number of chariot fragments were discovered here. The chariot or chariots were most likely moved from King Ay's tomb in the Western Valley and dumped here, probably by ancient robbers.

- ✔ KV63 was discovered in 2006 and was an embalmer's cache – although which burial this cache is connected to is unknown.

Other houses for the royal afterlife

Although the Valley of the Kings is the most famous burial site, kings of other periods favoured different cemeteries:

- ✔ The early Old Kingdom kings favoured burial at Abydos, the mythical burial place of the god Osiris.

- ✔ The late Old Kingdom kings favoured the Cairo region (Saqqara, Memphis, and Giza).

- ✔ The Middle Kingdom kings favoured the Faiyum (Hawara, Lahun, and Dashur).

- ✔ The earlier New Kingdom kings were buried at Dra Abu el Naga on the West Bank at Thebes.

- ✔ Akhenaten was buried at Amarna in Middle Egypt.

- ✔ Amenhotep III and Ay were buried in the Western Valley of the Valley of the Kings, and Akhenaten started building a tomb here before he moved the capital city to Amarna (see Chapter 4).

- ✔ Those in the Tanite (22nd) dynasty were buried at Tanis in the Delta.

Embellishing Tombs: Decoration to Die For

Many burial places from the pre-dynastic period onwards contain decorative paintings that have some function in the afterlife and are supposed to make the eternal survival of the tomb owner more bearable.

Entertaining the robbers

The burial of a baboon and a dog in KV50 is not in itself remarkable. However, when the archaeologists were excavating the tomb in 1906, the placement of these animals caused some amusement, which was attributed to an ancient robber with a sense of humour!

Theodore Davis, the excavator, describes the scene:

I went down the shaft and entered the chamber, which proved to be extremely hot and too low for comfort. I was startled by seeing very near me a yellow dog of ordinary size standing on his feet, his short tail curved over his back and his eyes open.

Within a few inches of his nose sat a monkey in quite perfect condition; for an instant I thought that they were alive, but I soon saw that they had been mummified, and unwrapped in ancient times by robbers. Evidently they had taken a fragment of the wooden monkey box on which they seated the monkey to keep him upright, and then they stood the dog on his feet so near the monkey that his nose almost touched him ... I am quite sure the robbers arranged the group for their amusement. However this may be, it can fairly be said to be a joke 3,000 years old.

Well, they say the old ones are the best.

The earliest decorated tomb was Tomb 100 from Hierakonpolis, built around 3685 BC, which is the only decorated tomb from this period. There was a gap of 1,000 years or so before the next decorated tombs, which appeared in the third dynasty in the non-royal mastaba tombs, and the fourth dynasty pyramid of King Unas, which contained the Pyramid Texts. (See Chapter 14 for more on the pyramid and Chapter 10 for more on the texts.)

Even during the early Old Kingdom, which was the beginning of the tomb-decorating trend, artisans relied on certain themes that remained popular throughout the pharaonic period for both royal and non-royal tombs. Only the artistic representation of these themes changed (see Chapter 11).

Decorating for the plebs

From the Old Kingdom mastabas to the New Kingdom rock-cut tombs, the non-royal themes in paintings focused on

- ✔ Nourishment
- ✔ Daily life
- ✔ Banquets
- ✔ Funerals

These themes were in use for hundreds of years, and never lost their meaning and importance. Only the artistic style changed – but the main purpose was consistent.

Nourishment

Scenes showing rows of servants carrying piles of food to offering tables before the tomb owner provided the deceased with nourishment for the afterlife. Agricultural scenes showing food production include animal husbandry, sowing, harvesting, winnowing, vineyard tending, fishing, and bird hunting. Some New Kingdom examples of agricultural scenes show the tomb owner actively participating in farming, indicating that the deceased will always be able to provide themselves with food.

Other scenes show the deceased residing in the *Field of Reeds*, the ancient equivalent to paradise. The Field of Reeds was an exact copy of Egypt, but Egypt at its best, with abundant crops, lots of water, and beautiful flora and fauna peppering the landscape. The deceased are often seen in their best frocks, tending the land and harvesting the constant crops.

Daily life

Scenes showing the life of the tomb owner are based on the deceased's occupation:

- ✔ For a vizier, whose role was to oversee all the workshops attached to the palace, scenes show detailed images of a number of these crafts, including jewellery making, carpentry, stone masonry, brick making, and metal crafts.

- ✔ For a military individual, the tomb included images of battles, campaigns, and training.

- ✔ For an agricultural overseer, many of the agricultural scenes described in the previous section were used.

By the New Kingdom, these everyday life scenes, especially those dealing with agriculture, are associated with the cycle of life and rebirth.

Banquets

Banquets are often depicted in non-royal tombs and show the tomb owner and his wife seated before a heavily laden offering table with a number of guests, segregated by sex, being served by servants. The servants adorn the guests' necks with floral collars and their heads with perfume cones, and keep their food and wine topped up. Singers, musicians, and dancers are often shown entertaining guests.

These banquets can represent one of two things – a depiction of the funerary feast that occurred after the funeral, or the *Beautiful Festival of the Valley*, a Theban funerary festival at which the dead were remembered. (During this festival, processions on the West Bank were followed by people visiting their ancestors' tombs to participate in a feast with the dead.)

Funerals

Images of funerals show the procession into the tomb, consisting of a number of servants carrying boxes of goods. The contents of the boxes include jewellery, clothes, weapons, statues, and furniture.

The procession is often accompanied by a group of professional mourners – a group of women hired to wail and throw dirt over their faces in an open display of grief.

The funerary rituals are also often depicted, including the *opening of the mouth ceremony* (see Chapter 10), which enabled the deceased to breathe, speak, and eat in the afterlife, as well as the *ceremony of the breaking of the red pots*, an ancient ritual of unknown meaning or origin.

Decorating for the royals

The themes of royal tomb decoration are not as flexible or diverse as the non-royal tombs. Instead, royal tomb art focuses on religious rather than personal scenes. These religious themes do, however, vary from tomb to tomb and include

✔ Scenes from funerary texts (see Chapter 10), which primarily focus on the 12-hour nocturnal journey of the sun god. The king accompanied the sun god on this journey and faced the same dangers. These funerary texts protected the king and the god until dawn and rebirth.

✔ Scenes of the king making offerings to various gods, including Re-Horakhty, Osiris, Ptah, and Hathor – all deities associated with death and rebirth.

✔ Scenes of the gods embracing the king and welcoming him to the afterlife. Often the gods are seen holding the king's hand, leading him to the realm of the dead.

One variant on this theme can be found in the tombs of the sons of Ramses III, where the king is shown leading his sons into the afterlife and introducing him to the gods.

Although kings, queens, and princes had little room to deviate from these themes, they could choose from a number of funerary texts with a large canon of images. Additionally, royals were able to change artistic representations, colours, and techniques, which allows each royal tomb to be unique despite the simple themes available. It seems that all people, ancient or modern, manage to work within the boundaries and still express their individuality!

Chapter 14

Probing the Pyramids

. . . .

. . . .

*P*yramids are synonymous with ancient Egypt. Over the years, these structures have been the topic of many discussions and books – some of a somewhat dubious nature.

The function of pyramids changed over the years, with the Old and Middle Kingdom pyramids acting as tombs designed as imposing declarations of wealth and status, and the smaller New Kingdom pyramids used to surmount a tomb, but not functioning as burial places themselves.

The history of the development of pyramids is a long one, peppered by mistakes and miscalculations before the 'true pyramid' was achieved. Even after the Great Pyramid was built, pyramid structure did not remain static. New innovations appeared in an attempt to build a perfect monument, one that was better than the ancestors' pyramids.

This chapter focuses on the development of these amazing structures during the course of more than 3,000 years of Egyptian history.

Defining the Shape

The shape of the pyramid had religious significance long before the pyramid structure itself.

So what exactly are they?

Researchers and historians now know that pyramids were tombs, even though some authors still dispute the fact. But for many centuries, people debated the function of these great monuments.

✔ Prior to the fifth century AD, the writer Julius Honorius believed the pyramids were granaries built by the biblical Joseph. This idea was also adopted by later Renaissance scholars.

✔ The Duc de Persigny (1808–1872 AD) tried to prove that the pyramids were screens against the desert sand to stop the Nile from silting up, although logically many more barriers would have been needed to create an effective barrier. Along the same lines, Arab writers of a similar period thought the pyramids were built as places where people could seek protection from natural disasters.

✔ Charles Piazzi Smyth (1819–1900) wrote two books about the pyramids, which he believed enshrined God's plan for the universe. Through mathematical measurements, Smyth believed this divine plan would be revealed and spent a great deal of time trying to decipher it. Whether he succeeded is unknown, but people are still looking for the deeper meaning to these funerary monuments.

Piles of desert rubble were initially used to cover pit burials during the pre-dynastic period. Over time, these mounds became more elaborate and developed into superstructures (see Chapter 13) and eventually step pyramids. These heaps were believed to represent of the mound of creation, from which all life began. All life started on this mound, so it obviously possessed creative powers and helped the rebirth of the deceased (see Chapter 9 for further information on Egyptian religion).

The pyramidal shape is just a stylisation of the mound of creation and was called a *benben*. As time progressed, the benben became closely associated with the sun god. The solar connection of the pyramids can't be denied – the shape was thought to resemble the rays of the sun, and the Pyramid Texts even refer to the pyramid as a ramp leading to the sky, enabling the dead king to join his ancestors, who became stars upon death.

Filling in the Gaps: Achieving the True Pyramid Shape

After the development of step pyramids (see Chapter 13), the next, um, step necessary to create a true pyramid was for the Egyptians to fill in the steps with masonry. There were, however, a few errors in the process, resulting in some interesting-looking monuments.

Indiana Jones and the temple of Meidum

The first attempt at a true pyramid was at Meidum, just south of Cairo. You can visit and explore inside this pyramid today. The pyramid of Meidum was built by Sneferu, the first king of the fourth dynasty. The pyramid was originally built as a step pyramid with seven steps, but before the fifth step was completed, the whole structure was enlarged to eight steps.

All that is visible today are the top three steps, because the casing stones have been removed. It was initially believed that this pyramid collapsed during construction, but recent excavations have uncovered no evidence of bodies, tools, or ropes, which would all indicate that the structure was indeed completed.

The burial chamber of this pyramid is at desert level and is reached via an entrance in the centre of the north face, nearly 17 metres above the ground. The entrance passage descends into the pyramid, ending in a horizontal passage that then leads to a vertical shaft, which ascends to the burial chamber. Cedar beams embedded in the walls leading to this chamber may have been used to haul the sarcophagus up to the chamber, although the sarcophagus is no longer there. This shaft is ascended today by a rather rickety wooden staircase.

The burial chamber is not complete, and it seems that a burial did not take place here – although fragments of a wooden coffin were discovered in the burial chamber. Sneferu built another two pyramids at Dahshur and may have been buried in one of these.

Gotta Dahshur

Sneferu's two pyramids at Dahshur are known as the Bent Pyramid and the Red or North Pyramid, which is only exceeded in size by the Great Pyramid at Giza. You can still visit these pyramids today.

Getting bent

The Bent Pyramid was built before the Red Pyramid and got its name from a bend half way up the structure, which was caused by a change in design that went wrong. The structure was initially built with an angle of 60 degrees (the true pyramid angle ranges from 72 to 78 degrees). While workers were building the pyramid, there was a problem with subsidence – the weight of the stone caused the foundations to sink into the ground. To counteract this, a girdle was built around the base, changing the slope at the base to 55 degrees. The top of the pyramid was completed with a 44-degree slope, creating a distinct bend in the centre, as you can see in Figure 14-1.

Figure 14-1:
The Bent
Pyramid at
Dahshur.

The Bent Pyramid is also unusual because it features two entrances, one in the north face and one in the south:

- ✔ The northern passage leads to a narrow chamber with a corbelled roof. The burial chamber, also with a corbelled roof, was directly above, probably reached by a ladder.

- ✔ The western passage leads through a series of portcullis blocking systems (vertical sliding blocks sealing the tunnel) to a second corbelled burial chamber.

Both of these burial chambers were for Sneferu as the king of Upper and Lower Egypt, with a chamber for each role. At a later date, the two chambers were connected by a passageway cut through the masonry, clearly by someone who knew the location of the two chambers – perhaps by some very sharp robbers.

The Bent Pyramid was abandoned because of weaknesses in the structure caused by the unsuitability of the desert plateau that the pyramid was built on. Sneferu was not to be put off though, and started the construction of the Red Pyramid.

In the red

The Red Pyramid is second in size only to the Great Pyramid of Khufu at Giza and was the first successful true pyramid. It gained its name from the colour of the exposed granite under the casing stones of limestone used to encase the pyramid. The capstone (also called the *pyramidion* or *benben*) was representative of the mound of creation from which all creation started, and was made of a single block of limestone, which archaeologists discovered on the site. You can still visit this pyramid at the site of Dahshur.

The entrance to the pyramid is in the north face and leads to a 63-metre descending corridor, which ends in two corbelled antechambers. High up in the wall of the second chamber is a short, horizontal corridor, which leads to the 15-metre-tall corbelled burial chamber. This burial chamber is not subterranean and is almost in the centre of the superstructure. Some human remains were discovered in the burial chamber, although whether these belong to Sneferu is unknown.

Middle Kingdom Kings at Dahshur

Kings of the Middle Kingdom continued to use Dahshur as a royal burial ground. Senwosret III and Amenemhat III of the 12th dynasty built their pyramids here.

Senwosret III's pyramid was built to the north-east of the Red or North Pyramid of Sneferu. The quality of construction had declined by this period (1878–1841 BC), and Senwosret III's pyramid was made of irregular-sized mud bricks in stepped courses, which were then covered in limestone casing stones. The entrance to the pyramid is at ground level on the west side of the pyramid and leads to a sloping passageway, ending in a store room. The antechamber lies at a 90-degree angle to the store, which then leads to a burial chamber constructed of granite. There is a granite sarcophagus in the burial chamber. Despite the discovery of a few objects in the pyramid, researchers doubt whether Senwosret was buried here.

As with all pyramids, Senwosret III's was part of a wider complex consisting of

- Seven pyramids for royal women
- A mortuary temple and causeway
- A further temple in the south

Senwosret III's son and successor, Amenemhat III, followed in his father's footsteps and built his pyramid at the same site. He also built his pyramid of mud brick with limestone casing blocks, all of which have since been removed for reuse. The son's pyramid stood 75 metres high. There are two entrances to this pyramid on the east and west sides, and the pyramid is entered via staircases rather than ramps. These staircases lead to a combination of corridors and chambers, a layout more complicated than that of any other pyramid. The complex includes

- Three burial chambers within the pyramid, one of which contains canopic equipment (see Chapter 10) of a queen named Aat, indicating she was buried here.

  The burial chamber situated just east of the central axis housed a sarcophagus, although Amenemhat III was probably not buried here.

- Several nearby underground chambers that feature a number of small chapels and a shrine.

Package tour – ancient style

One of the statue rooms of the funerary complex of Djoser at Saqqara contains graffiti showing the site was visited in later (but still ancient) periods as a tourist site. One of the inscriptions dates to the winter of year 47 of the reign of Ramses II. Two scribes of the treasury, the vizier and two brothers called Hednakht and Panakht, record their visit to the site.

The Great Pyramid of Giza was also visited as an ancient monument from the New Kingdom onwards, as attested by graffiti. Records note that Cleopatra took Mark Antony to the pyramids at Giza (they were already nearly 2,000 years old during her reign) on a romantic tour.

This structure was abandoned before completion because of unstable clay foundations and instability within the pyramid structure caused by the huge number of rooms it contains.

The Great Pyramid: Finalising the details

After the true pyramid was perfected by Sneferu at Dahshur, the next stage was to enlarge the structure, which is what Khufu did at the virgin site at Giza. The three main pyramids at Giza belong to Khufu, Khafra, and Menkaura, all of the fourth dynasty (2613–2494 BC).

The Great Pyramid of Khufu (shown in Figure 14-2) – Khufu is the son of Sneferu – is 146 metres high and was originally encased in limestone blocks, each weighing 16 tonnes. The entrance is in the north face of the pyramid and was entered via a descending passage, which led to a subterranean chamber. Near the beginning of the passage is another passage that ascended to the grand gallery, which led to the burial chamber.

The burial chamber is constructed of red granite and has five stress-relieving chambers above it that take the weight of the pyramid. Exactly placed on the central axis of the pyramid is the red granite sarcophagus, which was put in the chamber before completion because the doorway is too narrow to take the large block of stone. The burial chamber is sealed by a series of portcullis-type blocks and plugging stones that block the entrance to the grand gallery.

At the base of the grand gallery is a horizontal passage, which leads to the so-called queen's chamber and may have been a *serdab* (a chamber with a hole in the wall so that the statue can see out) designed to house the *ka* statue of the king (see Chapter 10). The burials of the bodies of the queens of Khufu took place in the three satellite pyramids to the east of the pyramid.

Figure 14-2:
The Great
Pyramid of
Khufu, Giza.

The pyramid complex was surrounded by a limestone wall standing 8 metres tall, enclosing a courtyard that could only be reached via the valley temple, causeway, and mortuary temple – all standard elements of the pyramid complex.

Following up one of the greats: Khafra's pyramid

The Great Pyramid was one of the seven wonders of the ancient world – indeed, it is the only one still standing.

Khafra, the son of Khufu, had a difficult act to follow, but he still decided to build his pyramid alongside that of his father. Because he was unable to beat the monumental splendour of the Great Pyramid, Khafra built his pyramid on a higher area of the Giza plateau, giving it the appearance of being larger, although it is in fact smaller. Cunning, eh?

There are two entrances to the pyramid, one at ground level and the other 11.5 metres (38 feet) above ground level on the northern side of the pyramid. The lower passage descends to a small chamber (which may have functioned as a serdab) and a horizontal passage, which gradually ascends to meet the descending passage of the upper entrance. This horizontal passage then leads to the burial chamber.

The sarcophagus in the burial chamber is made of black granite. The sarcophagus did contain bones, which were later identified as those of a bull. The bones are thought to have been given as an offering to the king's *ka* at a later date, after the body had been removed by robbers.

What a way to build a pyramid!

Herodotus records that Khufu was a bit of a tyrant, a reputation that the king has maintained for 4,000 years. While building his own pyramid, Khufu was also constructing pyramids for burying his queens. However, due to the expense of such huge construction works, he forced his daughter to pay for her own pyramid. According to Herodotus:

Cheops (Khufu) moreover came, they said, to such a pitch of wickedness, that being in want of money he caused his own daughter to sit in the brothels, and ordered her to obtain from those who came a certain amount of money (how much it was they did not tell me): and she not only obtained the sum appointed by her father, but also she formed a design for herself privately to leave behind her a memorial, and she requested each man who came in to give her one stone upon her building: and of these stones, they told me, the pyramid was built which stands in front of the great pyramid in the middle of the three, each side being one hundred and fifty feet in length.

At one stone per sexual encounter, she would have been a very busy lady because there are probably more than 50,000 blocks used to build her pyramid!

Bringing up the rear: Menkaura's pyramid

The pyramid of Menkaura is the smallest of the three pyramids at Giza. The bottom courses are cased with granite, and limestone was used for the top. Granite was considered a superior building material, and clearly at this time size was not the primary concern. Although his pyramid was small, Menkaura increased the size of his mortuary and valley temples.

The internal structure of the pyramid is a complicated collection of descending ramps and chambers sealed by portcullis blocks. There were two burial chambers, one of which may be a serdab, and a sarcophagus was in the larger burial chamber. Within the sarcophagus was a wooden coffin with Menkaura's name, although the coffin dates from the late period and the bones date to the Christian period, indicating that the sarcophagus had been reused at a later date.

Accessorising the Pyramids at Giza

Like any great outfit, a pyramid wasn't complete without suitable accessories. Each Giza pyramid was part of a complex consisting of a number of buildings and elements, including

✔ Valley temple

✔ Mortuary temple

✔ Queens' tombs

✔ Burial chambers – three for Khufu, one for Khafra, and three for Menkaura

Khufu also went further and included boat pits, a sphinx, and a sphinx temple. The following sections examine the boat pits and sphinx; see Chapter 12 for more on the temple.

Sailing for eternity

Five full-size boat pits were constructed near the pyramid of Khufu, two of which definitely contained boats. One has been opened and consisted of a 31-metre-long by 8-metre or so deep and 7-metre-wide pit covered with large stone blocks. A 43.5-metre-long boat, dismantled into 1,224 pieces, was placed within one of the pits. Luckily, because the pit remained watertight over the centuries, the boat survived and has been reconstructed and is now on display in the boat museum at Giza (see Figure 14-3).

Figure 14-3: Reconstructed boat from remains in the boat pit, Giza.

Dreams of the sun god

The stela (curved top stone monument) between the feet of the sphinx is known as the Dream Stela and was set up by Thutmosis IV. Thutmosis IV slept near the sphinx and dreamt that the solar god spoke to him, legitimising his claim to the throne. The voice in the dream instructed Thutmosis IV to remove the sand that had covered the sphinx up to the neck. He recorded this on the stela between the sphinx's paws;

> On one of these days it came to pass, that the king's son Tuthmosis, came, coursing at the time of mid-day, and he rested in the shadow of this great god. A vision of sleep seized him at the hour when the sun was at the zenith, and he found the majesty of this revered god speaking with his own mouth, as a father speaks with his son, saying; 'Behold me, see me, you, my son Thutmosis. I am your father Harmakhis-Kheperi-Ra-Atum who will give

to you my kingdom on earth at the head of the living. You shall wear the white crown [of Upper Egypt] and the red crown [of Lower Egypt] on the throne of the earth-god Geb . . . The land shall be yours in its length and in its breadth, that which the eye of the All-Lord [sun god] shines upon. The food of the two lands shall be yours, the great tribute from all countries, the duration of a long period of years. My face is yours, my desire is towards you. You shall be to me a protector for my manner is as if I were ailing in all my limbs. The sand of this desert upon which I am, has reached me; turn to me, to have that done which I have desired.'

Thutmosis IV removed the sand as the god requested and then ruled on the throne, indicating that he had pleased the sun god.

The entire boat was constructed using wooden pegs and ropes only. (The boat currently on display has a number of gaps between the planks of wood. The wood expanded when wet and sealed the holes, making the vessel watertight.)

Evidence suggests that the boat was used at least once, probably during the funeral of Khufu, as his body sailed from the east to the west bank of the Nile. The boat had ten oars, five down each side, a covered chamber that may have held the body of the dead king at the rear, and an open shrine at the front that may have displayed a *ka* statue of the king as part of the funerary procession.

Khufu, however, wasn't the first king to include boat pits in the burial complex:

- ✔ King Khasekhemwy of the second dynasty had 12 boat pits surrounding his Abydos tomb. Each pit contained a boat.
- ✔ Unas of the fifth dynasty had boat pits, although these pits probably never contained any boats.

✔ Senwosret III had six boat pits at his pyramid at Dahshur. These boats were believed to have a solar connection. The sun god sailed in his solar bark through the afterlife, accompanied by the king.

Phew – what a sphinx!

The sphinx is another prominent feature of the Giza plateau and is an enduring symbol of ancient Egypt (shown in Figure 14-4). Although smaller sphinxes exist, the sphinx at Giza is the only one of this size and prominence in Egypt. It is situated at the end of the causeway leading to Khufu's pyramid and was carved from the natural bedrock, which was of the right proportions and approximate shape (although, saying that, the body is in fact too long). The sphinx consists of a lion's body with a human head, wearing the *nemes headdress* (the blue and gold headcloth) in place of the mane.

The lion was both a solar symbol and a symbol of the might and strength of the king. Having a human head on a lion's body indicates that the power of the lion is governed by the intelligence and wisdom of the king. The position of the sphinx at the end of the causeway to the great pyramid suggests its function is that of guardian, as well as being a large monument representing the importance of the king.

Figure 14-4:
The Sphinx, Giza.

Evolving Further: Later Pyramids and Complexes

Over the centuries, kings continued to construct pyramids and surrounding complexes of tombs and temples.

Making up for shoddy workmanship: Unas at Saqqara

The fifth-dynasty pyramid complex of Unas at Saqqara is not as well preserved as the pyramid of Djoser at the same site. Unas built his pyramid of mud brick, but it is still a perfect example of a fully developed Old Kingdom pyramid complex. The complex included all the elements that the king needed in the next life:

✔ A valley temple

✔ A causeway

✔ A pyramid

✔ Boat pits

This pyramid at Saqqara is the first to house the *Pyramid Texts*, carved on the walls of the burial chamber and antechamber. These texts described the following:

✔ Creation myths

✔ Myth of Osiris and Isis

✔ Myth of Horus and Seth

✔ How to survive death in the afterlife

The Pyramid Texts formed the basis for the Middle Kingdom *Coffin Texts* and the New Kingdom *Book of the Dead*. See Chapter 10 for information on these funerary texts.

The causeway of Unas leading to the mortuary temple is particularly noteworthy. It shows unusual depictions of a famine, with graphic images of emaciated men, a woman rummaging in her hair for head lice in the vain attempt to find something to eat, and a child with a distended stomach begging for food. This famine may not have taken place in Egypt, as such an event was unsuitable to record for eternity. Rather, the paintings depict a famine that affected the nomadic tribes in the surrounding desert. The appearance of some of the people is very un-Egyptian, and Egypt is represented as a wealthy and generous nation, coming the aid of these earliest refugees.

Jumping on the bandwagon: More Middle Kingdom pyramids

Pyramids continued to be used as tombs well into the Middle Kingdom. All the kings of the 12th dynasty had one, with complexes at Dahshur, El Lahun, and Hawara. Some kings of the Middle Kingdom had both a pyramid and a rock-cut tomb (see Chapter 13).

In the Middle Kingdom, the Faiyum region was very popular with royalty and nobles alike for the hunting of birds and other marshland wildlife. The popularity of the site saw the construction of a number of pyramid complexes situated at

- ✔ **Lisht:** Amenemhat I and Senwosret I of the 12th dynasty built pyramids here. Amenemhat's complex includes a number of tomb shafts for the burials of the royal women. Senwosret's complex also houses nine subsidiary pyramids of his queens.

- ✔ **Lahun:** A pyramid complex built by Senwosret II of the 12th dynasty. The foundation is built of a natural outcrop of limestone and the upper part is made of mud brick. There is a double enclosure wall around the pyramid with a number of queens' shaft burials between the walls.

- ✔ **Hawara:** The pyramid here was built by Amenemhat III of the 12th dynasty and was part of a complex containing a labyrinthine building with lots of interconnecting winding corridors and dark chambers.

Growing popularity: Small pointed things

By the start of the New Kingdom (approximately 1540 BC), pyramids were no longer being used by the royal family, who were now buried in secretive rock-cut tombs. Pyramids were adopted for non-royal burials of wealthy people, albeit on a much smaller scale.

At Deir el Medina, the workmen constructed small, hollow, mud-brick pyramids over the tops of their subterranean tombs, which limited the weight that the tomb roof needed to support. The pyramidia at the top of these structures were made of limestone and were carved with images of the tomb owner.

From the 19th dynasty onwards in Nubia, small pyramids were attached to mortuary chapels built over a shaft burial beneath, combining the pyramid and the practical cult of making offerings of food and drink to the deceased. These pyramids have small bases and are tall, narrow structures.

The 26th dynasty (664–525 BC) saw the last development in pyramid evolution at Abydos and Thebes. These mud-brick pyramids have a domed interior and are similar to granaries or ovens. Attached to the side of the pyramid was a rectangular chamber, which led to the shaft burial beneath and was the focus of the funerary cult.

By this period, the 3,000-year evolution of the pyramid came to an end. These structures have remained a symbol of all things Egyptian, even though they were only a small aspect of the wider funerary beliefs.

Part V
The Part of Tens

In this part . . .

This part helps you to impress your friends and family (as well as anyone within earshot) with a whole bunch of useless but interesting facts about loads of things to do with Egyptology. You can wax lyrical about the top ten turning points in Egyptology, as well as the best ancient Egyptian achievements. Not only can you discuss ten famous Egyptologists, but also ten ancient Egyptian personalities, almost as if you knew them personally.

Then why not travel to Egypt and impress everyone in your hotel with the top ten places to visit, some off the beaten track? Start your journey here.

Chapter 15

Top Ten Breakthroughs in Egyptology

*A*rchaeological discoveries and academic breakthroughs punctuate the history of Egyptology, which makes this discipline one that is constantly changing.

Egyptology is bit like a jigsaw with an unknown number of pieces, no picture, and half the bits missing, which may make you wonder why anyone bothers with it! Egyptologists continue in their research because so many questions still need answers. Each fresh discovery opens up a whole new area of study and provides further insights into the lives of the ancients.

The greatest breakthroughs and discoveries of persevering Egyptologists – from the 18th century onwards – are the focus of this chapter.

Deciphering Hieroglyphs

All the excavations in Egypt in the early 19th century weren't half as exciting as they could have been, because archaeologists were unable to read the hieroglyphic language inscribed on walls and coffins and thus were unable even to identify who had built the tombs and temples.

This frustrating state of affairs changed in 1826 when Jean-François Champollion published the first dictionary on ancient Egyptian hieroglyphs. At last the meaning of the inscriptions on architecture and objects could be deciphered. Egyptologists haven't looked back since!

This amazing breakthrough comes down to the discovery and translation of the Rosetta Stone (see Chapter 11), a stela written in three languages: ancient Greek, Egyptian hieroglyphs and demotic (a late cursive form of hieroglyphs).

Most historians could read ancient Greek, so with a lot of hard work and logical thinking, they gradually deciphered the other two languages and established a basic alphabet and list of common words. These linguistic tools were applied *ad infinitum* to any Egyptian inscription Egyptologists could get their hands on. Finally, researchers were able to identify who built certain tombs and temples, as well as identify the gods depicted on the walls.

Only later did grammar became an important focus of hieroglyphic studies. Even now, nearly 200 years later, dictionaries, grammar, and inscriptions are being reworked to provide ever more accurate translations of this ancient language. Find out more about translating hieroglyphs yourself in Chapter 11.

Petrie's Seriation Dating System

William Matthew Finders Petrie was a remarkable archaeologist and Egyptologist (see Chapter 19) in the 19th century. Not only did he excavate some of the most interesting sites in Egypt, he also devised a relative dating system that archaeologists the world over still use.

Seriation dating assigns dates to whole assemblages of items or locations, rather than isolated objects from a specific site.

Petrie devised the system while working at Diospolis Parva, where he had excavated a number of pre-dynastic graves that he couldn't link or match to king lists to provide a chronological date. Petrie wanted to put sites and contents into chronological order, so he wrote the contents of each tomb on a slip of paper and placed the slips in a long column. He kept rearranging the sheets until he believed he had a true chronological order based on the style and decoration of the artefacts in each burial.

Although a very simple system, seriation dating is very useful because researchers can create a relative date for the tomb assemblage by stating that one object is earlier or later than another one. The system is useful for arranging sites into some form of order when no written texts or datable objects are available. However, the problem with seriation dating is that it isn't always clear how this sequence fits into the wider chronology of an area.

The Temples at Abu Simbel

Two temples stand at the site of Abu Simbel, 250 kilometres southeast of Aswan. Ramses II built both temples – one in honour of the sun god and the other in honour of Ramses' wife, Nefertari (see Chapter 18 for more information).

Traveller Jean-Louis Burckhardt discovered the temples in 1813, although all that was visible was a colossal head of one of the statues on the façade. Wind-blown sand covered the rest of the three colossi.

In 1817, Giovanni Belzoni – an engineer, turned circus strongman, turned Egyptologist (see Chapter 19) – started to clear away the sand. Unable to find workers willing or strong enough to help with the task, Belzoni, who was 6 feet 7 inches tall, was able to do a lot of the work himself. Unfortunately, every time he cleared the temple façade, the sand built up again, making the process time-consuming and frustrating. Belzoni had to leave without locating the entrance.

In 1871, when his benefactor Henry Salt financed another trip to Nubia to collect antiquities, Belzoni briefly excavated in the Valley of the Kings and then returned to Abu Simbel, where he managed to locate the entrance. Belzoni was the first modern man to enter the temple – a great achievement for anyone – where he saw the towering images of Ramses II on the pillars and the barbaric scenes of the battle of Kadesh. This must have been (and still is) an amazing sight, albeit one tinged with mystery, because, at this point in history, no one could read hieroglyphs and so Belzoni was unable to identify who built the temple.

The Royal Cache of 1881

If it wasn't for the discovery of the Royal Mummy Caches, the only New Kingdom royal mummy recovered today would be Tutankhamun. The mummies in the Royal Cache helped to fill in the jigsaw of Egyptology, providing insights into royal burial practices, diseases, and age of death. In the future, with the help of DNA testing, researchers hope to clarify family relationships among the mummies.

The caches were created in the 21st dynasty as a means of protecting the royal mummies from robberies. The priests moved the bodies from their tombs in the Valley of the Kings, re-wrapped them, and placed them together in a safe, secure place.

The discovery of the first Royal Cache was a combination of luck and detective work – and could very well never have happened at all. As early as 1874, rumours suggested that a wonderful tomb had been discovered in western Luxor, full of fabulous treasure. No one had seen this tomb, but papyri and other artefacts began to appear on the black market, clearly from a new royal tomb. Eventually the Egyptian Antiquities Service, under the leadership of Frenchman Gaston Maspero, started to investigate. By 1881, Ahmed Abd er-Rassul, from a notorious tomb-robbing family from Gourna (the village on the Valley of the Nobles), was brought in for questioning.

Maspero questioned er-Rassul vigorously, but the Egyptian denied all knowledge of a tomb; Maspero eventually let him go. He was later arrested again with his brother Hussein by the Egyptian police, who were not as gentle in their questioning as the Frenchman. Still er-Rassul and his brother denied all knowledge and were allowed to return to their village. Once they returned, disagreement reigned in the Rassul household.

The eldest Rassul brother, Mohammed, was the culprit who had discovered the tomb. Ahmed and Hussein felt they should be rewarded for their unpleasant time with the authorities, as well as enjoy a larger share of the loot from the tomb. After much arguing that eventually involved the whole village, Mohammed went to the authorities and confessed. After receiving assurance that no one would be prosecuted, he revealed the location of the tomb, secreted in the Deir el Bahri Valley, close to the temple of Hatshepsut.

Inside the tomb, the authorities discovered many New Kingdom royal mummies, including

- Ahmose
- Amenhotep I
- Thutmose III
- Sety I
- Ramses II
- Ramses III

These kings were all taken to Cairo where they are currently on display (except Ahmose, who in 2004 was moved to the Luxor Museum). In 1898, another mummy cache was discovered in the Valley of the Kings, which provided an additional ten royal mummies.

In order to get the full set of royal mummies of the New Kingdom, Egyptologists still need to find the remains of

- ✔ Horemheb

- ✔ Ramses I (The second body in Luxor Museum is believed by some to be this king, although this is not proven.)

- ✔ Sethnakht

- ✔ Ramses VII

- ✔ Ramses X

- ✔ Ramses XI

Perhaps another cache of mummies is waiting to be found, one that will uncover the secrets of these pharaohs and give Egyptologists a 'full house'.

KV55: The Desecrated Tomb

KV55, or Tomb 55 in the Valley of the Kings, has for many years caused much discussion in the Egyptological world. Edward Ayrton and his benefactor Theodore Davis discovered it in the Valley of the Kings in 1907.

A panel from a large wooden shrine that was originally used in the burial of Queen Tiye, Akhenaten's mother, blocked the entrance corridor to the tomb. This led many Egyptologists at the time to believe the tomb was Tiye's. When they later entered the burial chamber, they discovered a coffin containing a body. While some assumed the body was Tiye's, all the names on the coffin had been erased, rendering the inhabitant unidentifiable. The body was sent to Grafton Elliot-Smith (an expert in Egyptian mummies) for analysis. Rather than being the bones of an elderly woman, they were from a young man. The plot thickened!

Egyptologists began debating whether the bones were Akhenaten's or his successor Smenkhkare's. Even now people do not agree, although due to similarities in head shape, the body is often stated and widely agreed to be the brother of Tutankhamun, and therefore probably Smenkhkare. DNA testing may make this identification clearer, but testing will not be carried out until results involving ancient DNA are more accurate.

Tomb 55 was thought to have provided the missing king of the Amarna period, an era that has intrigued Egyptologists for many years. Many bodies are missing from this period (Akhenaten, Nefertiti, and their six daughters; Smenkhkare; and Ay), so any tomb from this time takes Egyptologists one step closer to a complete picture.

Tutankhamun's Tomb

Tutankhamun's tomb is one of the most famous and monumental finds in the history of Egyptology, because it is the only undisturbed royal tomb found in Egypt. All the other royal tombs were robbed in antiquity, and indeed so was Tutankhamun's. Luckily, these burglaries were small, and the majority of Tutankhamun's goods were found intact.

In 1914, Egyptologist Howard Carter and his benefactor Lord Carnarvon started excavating in the Valley of the Kings, just after another excavator, Theodore Davis, who had worked in the area for some time, claimed that 'The Valley of the Tombs is now exhausted.' How wrong can one man be?

Carter and his team did uncover a number of tombs in the Valley, and in 1917 Carter began to search for the missing tomb of Tutankhamun (a number of objects had been discovered showing the existence of a tomb in the area). However, by 1921 the team still had not discovered the tomb, and Lord Carnarvon considered withdrawing his funding. After much debate, Carter convinced him to fund one final season.

Luckily for Carter this final season was a cracker. On 4 November 1922 his team uncovered the first stone step of Tutankhamun's tomb. The next day they cleared the steps to reveal the door, complete with ancient seals showing the tomb was intact. The first doorway was opened on 23 November 1922, and the second doorway within the tomb on 26 November. At the opening of this door, Carter and Carnarvon saw for the first time the wonderful objects hidden for three millennia. These include solid gold coffins, gilded shrines, scores of pieces of golden jewellery, and the famous solid gold death mask (see Chapter 4 for a photograph of the death mask).

The first chamber was officially opened on 29 November, and the burial chamber on 17 February 1923. The cataloguing of the objects started, and on 28 October 1925 the team finally opened the coffin and gazed at the face of the king who lived and died so long ago. Cataloguing and recording all the artefacts in the tomb was finally completed on 10 November 1930, eight years after the discovery.

KV5: The Tomb of the Sons of Ramses II

The existence of KV5 in the Valley of the Kings has been recorded since the early 19th century, but the entrance had long since been lost. When early explorers entered KV5, it was filled with rubble and debris almost to the ceiling, making progress difficult. In fact the tomb was abandoned as a lost cause. If only they knew what lay beyond the rubble.

In 1989, Kent Weeks, working for the Theban Mapping Project (see Chapter 19 and www.thebanmappingproject.com), entered this long-lost tomb. Rather than seeing golden treasure like Howard Carter did on entering Tutankhamun's tomb, Weeks was faced with raw sewage, the result of a leaky pipe that had been pumping waste into the tomb for decades. Coupled with the extreme heat of the Valley, it was not a nice experience! After the sewage was cleared away, the team started the job of removing the rubble and debris and revealing the tomb beyond.

And what a tomb it was – the largest tomb complex in the Valley of the Kings and indeed the whole of Egypt. Built by Ramses II for the burial of his numerous sons, the tomb (so far) includes more than 120 corridors and chambers spread over two levels. The number of corridors is expected eventually to be more than 150.

At least six sons of Ramses II were buried in the tomb complex, and their skeletal remains have been discovered. They were originally mummified, but flash floods over the centuries aided the decaying process, reducing their soft tissues to gunk.

Every wall of the tomb was carved and painted, but over the centuries this decoration has fallen off, creating an amazing puzzle for Egyptologists to piece together. Tomb depictions on the walls show more than 20 sons, including their funerary rites, so probably more than the six discovered mummies were buried here. Many years of work remain on KV5 – along with many more discoveries to be revealed.

Akhenaten's Talatat Blocks

During the reign of Akhenaten, a new building block was introduced, called a *talatat*. This word comes from the Arabic for 'three', which is appropriate, because the blocks were two hand widths long and one hand width high. Talatats could be handled by one individual, making building work easier and quicker to execute.

Akhenaten used these blocks when building a number of temples at the complex of Karnak in Luxor. During the reigns of Tutankhamun, Ay, and Horemheb, these temples were dismantled and the blocks reused for other building projects, as a means of destroying all evidence of Akhenaten (to find out why go to Chapter 4).

However, Horemheb decided to use talatat blocks to fill the hollow areas of his pylon gateways at Karnak to give these structures more stability. He was quite methodical in his work, and as he removed the block from the temple, he placed it directly into the pylon, creating a reverse order of many of the images originally carved onto the blocks. (Little did Horemheb realise he was in fact preserving, not destroying, the memory of Akhenaten.)

Since the first excavations of the pylons at the start of the 20th century, more than 35,000 talatat blocks have been discovered. They are being kept in a number of storehouses in the Karnak complex until they can be reconstructed.

All 35,000 blocks are decorated, including some on two sides, and reconstruction has been a monumental task. In Luxor Museum, a small wall of talatat have been reconstructed and researchers are continually adding to the display as work progresses.

From the reconstructions already made by the Akhenaten Temple Project, Egyptologists, using a high-tech computer program, are about to get an idea of the buildings that Akhenaten originally constructed, including

- A temple belonging to Nefertiti, Akhenaten's wife, which had a pillared courtyard with up to 30 pillars, all bearing images of the queen.

- A temple belonging to Akhenaten, which housed colossal statues of the king.

- A possible ceremonial palace where the royal couple stayed before performing ceremonies or rituals in the temple. Images from the talatat show a *window of appearances* (see Chapter 4) at this palace, where the king and queen stood to reward their favoured officials. Sadly this window hasn't yet been discovered, but you never know.

Palace of Cleopatra

In 1997, a French team in the Mediterranean discovered the sunken harbour of Alexandria and the two cities of Herakleion and Canopus just off the coast of Alexandria. This discovery started the underwater excavations of what was the city of Cleopatra. A devastating tidal wave caused by an earthquake flooded this area some 1,200 years ago.

The ongoing excavations have uncovered hundreds of artefacts, including colossal statues of kings and queens and of Hapi, the god of the Nile flood. These remnants, as well as smaller statues and architectural fragments including pillars and architraves, hint that the royal palace and gardens were situated close to the harbour.

As excavations have progressed, the position of Cleopatra's palace, Antony's palace, and a temple have been located. Just think, the setting of their romantic story and tragic demise has been identified.

In 2006, a proposal was put forward regarding an offshore underwater museum to display the city of Cleopatra. Many of the objects found underwater are left there in order to preserve them; when removed and dried, these items could disintegrate. The proposed museum includes a plexi-glass tunnel allowing the visitor to walk underwater in the footsteps of Cleopatra, Mark Antony, and Julius Caesar. Rather like the seal or the shark tunnel at the zoo – except no seals or sharks, just the eerily silent remains of a lost city.

Smaller articles like jewellery and coins have already been removed to prevent theft, and these will be displayed separately in an on-shore building.

KV63

On 10 February 2006, an American archaeological team discovered an 18th dynasty royal tomb, 5 metres from the tomb of Tutankhamun in the Valley of the Kings – long after the Valley was said to be exhausted.

The American team was working on a nearby tomb when its members discovered a number of New Kingdom workman's huts, built for those men who created the tombs in the Valley. Beneath these huts, they found the hidden entrance to the shaft of KV63. Some of the hut floors had never been disturbed, indicating that the tomb beneath was also undisturbed. The shaft is approximately 5 metres deep and leads through a 1.5-metre-high doorway to an undecorated 4 by 5 metre burial chamber. The blocking stones in the doorway were not original, which suggests that the doorway had been opened and closed a few times in antiquity.

The chamber contained seven wooden sarcophagi piled on top of each other and 27 large pots. A few of the jars had been opened and contained a number of items, including miniature vessels, natron (salt), scraps of material, seeds, wood, carbon, chaff, resin, and minerals – all items left over from a mummification (see Chapter 10). Researchers do not yet know whose mummification took place, although considerable evidence suggests the deceased was from the 18th dynasty, at the time of Tutankhamun.

By the end of May 2006, the sarcophagi had also been emptied and much to everyone's great disappointment no bodies were found within them. Instead, researchers found a number of items, similar to those from the jars. One sarcophagus was full of linen pillows, and another contained a small golden coffinette, perhaps for the burial of a servant figure.

The whole tomb was probably used as an embalmer's store and was entered frequently. Embalmer's stores were common, and many royal burials included a cache of materials left over from mummification. If KV63 was such a store, at least one more tomb may yet be discovered. Perhaps it's the elusive tomb of Akhenaten, Nefertiti, Tutankhamun's wife Ankhesenamun, or his grandmother Tiye. Who knows? Watch this space at www.kv63.com for developments.

Chapter 16

Ten Egyptians Worth Knowing

*H*istory is made up of people, not events. Fortunately, the archaeological evidence from Egypt provides lots of information about these ancient people. Unfortunately, this evidence only relates to the upper classes, including royalty and the elite, who formed only a small percentage of society (see Chapter 1). The majority of the population – the farmers and labourers – are completely lost to modern historians.

Although the elite are very interesting – ten of the most intriguing are the focus of this chapter – the unknown lower classes were almost certainly interesting as well, adding another dimension to the history of ancient Egypt. If you want to find out more about the individuals of ancient Egypt, see *People of Ancient Egypt* by yours truly (Tempus Publishing, 2005), and John Romer's *Ancient Lives* (Phoenix Press, 2003).

Thutmosis III: The Egyptian Napoleon

Many of the kings of the 18th and 19th dynasties were military kings, but none more so than Thutmosis III. He didn't start out his rule in the most conventional way, though, and he is lucky he was able to make his mark on the military history of Egypt.

Thutmosis III was the son of Thutmosis II and a secondary queen called Isis. On the death of his father, Thutmosis III became king at the tender age of 2 or 3 years old. Because he was clearly too young to rule, he was married to his stepmother Hatshepsut, the widowed Great Royal Wife of Thutmosis II. After a few short years, Hatshepsut took over the throne as a king in her own right (see Chapter 5 for details), shoving Thutmosis III to the side. When Hatshepsut died, Thutmosis III was still only 24 or 25 years old and took over the rule of Egypt as the rightful king.

At the beginning of his sole rule, Thutmosis III started re-establishing the borders and control that Egypt had over the Near East, starting with a great campaign to Megiddo (a city in modern Israel), territory of the Hittites. With great bravery, Thutmosis marched into Megiddo via the most difficult route, catching the Hittites off guard. The Egyptians, however, lost their advantage when they stopped to loot the Hittite camp. The Hittites were able to resist the Egyptians for more than seven months, and the Egyptians eventually returned home. Refer to Chapter 4 for more on this campaign.

Thutmosis didn't give up though. During his 50 years or so of sole rule, he made 17 additional campaigns into Syria, as well as further campaigns into Nubia – some when he was in his 80s. Through his efforts, he firmly re-established Egypt as a power to be reckoned with.

Horemheb: The Maintainer of Order

Horemheb is a particularly appealing character in Egyptian history because his life is a true rags-to-riches story. He was born in a small town near the Faiyum, to a local middle-class family. He excelled at his studies and became a military scribe during the reign of Akhenaten in the 18th dynasty.

Horemheb slowly and carefully proceeded in his career and rose through the military ranks until he was a general – a powerful and influential position. But the story gets better: By the time the boy-king Tutankhamun was on the throne, Horemheb was a very prominent figure in the royal court. He is recorded as being the only person who could calm the young king down when he was having a tantrum, and he may even have taught Tutankhamun his military skills. Tutankhamun rewarded this general with the title of deputy king, meaning that Horemheb stood in for the king in some royal appointments and ceremonies.

At the death of Tutankhamun, Horemheb didn't push his right as deputy king and take over the throne. Instead he allowed the elderly vizier Ay to occupy the throne. Four years later, Ay died and Horemheb became king. A far cry from the middle-class family of his upbringing!

As king, Horemheb started the full-scale restoration of Egypt to the glory of the reign of Amenhotep III, before Akhenaten and his religious revolution (see Chapter 4). This set the standard for the 19th dynasty that was to follow, started by Horemheb's army general Ramses I. The 19th dynasty was to be an empire-building, military-based, incredibly disciplined and yet religious period of Egyptian history.

Ramses II even built a shrine at the tomb of Horemheb at Saqqara to worship him as a god. From rags to riches to divinity – can anyone hope for more?

Nefertiti: The Beautiful One Has Come

Nefertiti, the wife of Akhenaten, is one of the most famous queens from ancient Egypt, which is strange because remarkably little is known about her. Although she is mentioned frequently during the reign of Akhenaten (see Chapter 4), no record of her parents, family, or background exists.

Some Egyptologists think Nefertiti was a Mittannian (from an empire that spread from western Iran to the Mediterranean) princess sent to Egypt for a diplomatic marriage. Her name means 'the beautiful one has come', which may show that she travelled to Egypt and was given the name when she arrived. However, the wife of Ay holds the title 'wet nurse' of Nefertiti, indicating Nefertiti was in Egypt as a young infant and was therefore unlikely to be a foreign princess sent for marriage. Egyptologists now widely accept that Nefertiti was the daughter of Ay, and his wife was her stepmother, indicating perhaps that Nefertiti's own mother had died.

Nefertiti lived at Amarna and followed the religion of her husband; she is often depicted worshipping the sun disc alongside him. The most famous image of Nefertiti is a painted limestone bust. However, the bust does not have any identifying inscriptions; the identification as Nefertiti is based on the bust's crown, a design that only she is ever shown wearing.

Nefertiti and Akhenaten had six daughters but no sons, as far as the records show, and one of Nefertiti's daughters married Tutankhamun. Nefertiti disappeared from the records in year 13 of her husband's reign when she was in her 30s. Whether she died or was disgraced and banished from the king's palace to be replaced by another consort is unknown.

Although Nefertiti's life and death is shrouded in mystery, people are intrigued by Nefertiti, probably because of the lovely bust of Nefertiti in the Berlin Museum, and because she is associated with one of the most written-about kings in Egyptian history. However, we know very little, and until a body is clearly attributed to her we'll never really know who she was.

Ramose: The Honest Scribe

Ramose was a scribe from Deir el Medina, the village that housed the workmen who built the Valley of the Kings (see Chapter 2). He moved to the village as scribe during the reign of Sety I of the 19th dynasty and worked there for more than 40 years. Ramose was one of the richest and most popular men in the village. He spent a great deal of his wealth on religious shrines and temples and was particularly pious.

Unlike some of the other characters who lived in the village (see the following sections on Kenhirkhepshef, Naunakhte, and Paneb), Ramose was very honest. Available records include no accusations of corruption, bribery, or general naughtiness. He was a goody-two-shoes through and through.

Sadly, the one thing Ramose wanted more than anything was a child, and he and his wife Mutemwia tried for many years, unfortunately without success. A stela was found at Deir el Medina begging the goddess Hathor to grant them a child in reward for all their piety. This also didn't work, and Ramose and Mutemwia ended up adopting a new arrival to the village, a scribe called Kenhirkhepshef.

Kenhirkhepshef: An Ancient Historian

Kenhirkhepshef was also scribe at Deir el Medina during the fourth decade of the reign of Ramses II, and he held the position for more than 50 years. Various accusations of corruption were levelled against him, so he was not as honest as his adopted father Ramose.

Kenhirkhepshef is accused of taking bribes to cover up the misdeeds of others and forcing a number of workmen to work for him without pay:

> *The Draftsman Prahotep salutes his superior . . . Kenhirkhepshef: What does this bad way mean in which you treat me? I am to you like a donkey. If there is some work, bring the donkey, and if there is some food, bring the ox. If there is some beer, you do not look for me, but if there is work, you do look for me.*

Corruption aside, Kenhirkhepshef has other intriguing facets. He had an extensive library with papyri on various topics. These papyri contained medical texts, religious spells and hymns, letters, poetry, household hints, and dream interpretations.

Kenhirkhepshef was an early historian and had a particular interest in the history of Egyptian kings. He liked to make long lists, and one of these records the kings of the 18th and 19th dynasty in chronological order. Kenhirkhepshef also had a copy of the Battle of Kadesh report, the famous battle of Ramses II, which shows that Kenhirkhepshef had an interest in current affairs.

Kenhirkhepshef, as an elder of the village, was very firm in his beliefs and didn't seem to mind voicing them. He was particularly against alcohol, and a text from his library admonishes

> *Do not indulge in drinking beer for fear of uttering evil speech. If you fall no one will hold out a hand to you. Your companions will say 'out with the drunk', you lie on the ground like a little child.*

Naunakhte: The Property Owner

Naunakhte lived at Deir el Medina during the reign of Ramses II, and she was married to Kenhirkhepshef, the scribe. At the time of their marriage, she was as young as 12 years old while he was between 54 and 70 years old. Naunakhte and Kenhirkhepshef were married for eight to ten years, although they did not have any children. Kenhirkhepshef was more of a father figure than a husband. He probably married Naunakhte as a means of caring for her and ensuring that she inherited his possessions. As a childless widow when she was only in her 20s, Naunakhte married a workman called Khaemnum from Deir el Medina, and they were married for 30 years. She had eight children with him – four boys and four girls.

Although little has survived about the life of Naunakhte, she left four papyri recording her last will, in which she disinherits four of her children. This meant they would inherit only their father's and not her personal wealth. The reason she disinherits these children is neglect:

> *As for me I am a free woman of the land of Pharaoh. I brought up these eight servants of yours, and gave them an outfit of everything as is usually made for those in their station. But see I am grown old, and they are not looking after me in my turn. Whoever of them has aided me, to him I will give of my property but he who has not given to me; to him I will not give any of my property.*

Two of the papyri list, item by item, all the objects she owns and which of her children she leaves them to. These documents show that women were in complete control of their own property; but they also show her rather petty and pedantic nature, because each bowl or dish is listed. Ironic, considering the most valuable item today is the papyrus itself.

Paneb: The Loveable Rogue

Paneb was one of the most colourful characters from Deir el Medina. He lived there during the reign of Ramses II and probably knew Kenhirkhepshef in later life. Kenhirkhepshef was not keen on alcohol, so some friction may have existed between the two because Paneb was notorious for getting drunk and disorderly. Despite this behaviour, Kenhirkhepshef stood up for Paneb and covered some of his misdeeds.

Throughout his career at Deir el Medina, numerous accusations were made against Paneb of criminal deeds and adultery (for which he was punished). All accusations were recorded on a document known as the Papyrus Salt (because it was purchased by archaeologist Henry Salt) by a man called Amenakht, who greatly resented the position that Paneb held. The accusations were numerous and varied, including

- Bribing the vizier to gain the position of foreman
- Forcing many workmen and their wives to work for him without payment, including making a relation of Amenakht's feed his (Paneb's) ox
- Using government tools to build his own tomb
- Stealing cut stones from the tomb of Merenptah and using them in his own tomb
- Threatening to kill his father, Neferhotep, while he was drunk
- Threatening to kill another Deir el Medina foreman, Hay
- Murdering some men who were to deliver a message to the king

Despite the slowly increasing severity of these accusations, none was proven, and therefore Paneb went unpunished. The accusation of murder, in fact, seems to be hearsay, because Amenakht doesn't even bother to mention the victims' names, indicating perhaps he didn't know who they were.

However, some robbery accusations appear to be based in fact and may have resulted in punishment:

- **Tomb robbery 1:** A list of items stolen from the tomb of Sety II, includes tomb doors, chariot coverings, incense, wine, and statues. The case was brought before the vizier, and Paneb swore an oath saying 'Should the vizier hear my name again I shall be dismissed from my office and become a stone mason once more'. This oath was enough to acquit him on this occasion.

✔ **Tomb robbery 2:** According to records, Paneb 'went to the tomb of the workman Nakhmin and stole the bed which was under him. He carried off the objects which one gives to a dead man and stole them.' No punishment for this, so perhaps the accusation was false.

✔ **Tomb robbery 3:** Paneb was accused of taking a model goose from the tomb of a wife of Ramses II, Henutmire. Paneb swore he didn't take the goose, but the authorities found it in his house. This accusation was shortly followed by Paneb's disappearance from the records, so perhaps this was enough to get him executed, which was the punishment for tomb robbery.

Bearing in mind he was in his 60s when he died, Paneb lived an active and interesting life. Even at 60 he was clearly a bit of a lad, ducking and diving until the day he got caught – or died.

Mereruka: The Princess's Husband

Mereruka was a very prominent official during the reign of King Teti in the fifth dynasty. Mereruka's mother was 'the royal acquaintance', Nedjetempet, which means Mereruka came from a prominent noble family before his promotion. Mereruka held a number of important titles including

✔ Overseer of the house of weapons

✔ Overseer of the king's harem

✔ Vizier

✔ High priest of Re

These important titles show that Teti held Mereruka in high esteem, a fact the king reinforced by allowing Mereruka to marry his daughter Sesheshat. In addition to becoming son-in-law to the king, Mereruka was made 'foster child of the king', indicating that the king favoured him a great deal. So much in fact that Mereruka took the place of the eldest son, acting as Teti's funerary priest during his funeral.

Mereruka had three children with Sesheshat, and he was also privileged enough to have a secondary wife with whom he had five sons. Mereruka led a busy and varied life, and as vizier he was responsible for much of the state administration (Chapter 1). He also supervised the construction of the pyramid complex of Teti at Saqqara, and in fact he had his own huge mastaba tomb (see Chapter 13) with 32 chambers very close to the pyramid of his king.

Mereruka's is the largest tomb in the cemetery and is decorated with elaborately and beautifully carved decoration, showing that he was wealthy, prominent, and held the favour of the king. All in all a very privileged young man.

Asru: Chantress of Amun

Asru was a chantress of Amun at the temple of Karnak at Luxor in the third intermediate period. She was of noble birth and inherited the position of *chantress*, a priestly title, from her mother. Her mummified body was encased in two highly decorated coffins, and her remains tell us a lot about her life.

Fingerprints and footprints taken of the mummy show she was neither a dancer nor a musician, rather a singer who sang prayers and incantations for the worship of the god Amun. In her later years, Asru probably found singing difficult because of breathing difficulties.

Asru suffered from a number of parasitic worms, which caused nausea, dizziness, and anaemia. She probably saw blood and worms in her stools and urine. Her lungs showed evidence of sand pneumoconiosis, which was caused by breathing in sand and led to major respiratory problems. She also had a 20-centimetre cyst on her lung at the time of her death, caused by one of her worms.

When she died, Asru was 60–70 years old – elderly for an ancient Egyptian. She suffered from osteoarthritis and chronic arthritis throughout her body, which damaged the joints of her fingers. At some point in her life, she had a nasty fall that damaged her lower back, sending sciatica pains down her left leg. Her last years were painful, and walking and sitting were difficult, but as a full-time priestess she may have spent her last days in the temple teaching the younger priestesses how to continue their roles.

Nesperenub: The Priest of Khonsu

Nesperenub was a priest of Khonsu at Karnak in the third intermediate period. The temple at the time was very rich because the high priests of Amun had taken over the throne and were ruling the Theban region. This meant the priests at Karnak were well paid and well fed. But poor Nesperenub did not always have such a wealthy lifestyle. His body shows that when he was young he suffered a growth interruption, perhaps caused by poverty or disease.

As was traditional, Nesperenub inherited his position from his father; in fact generations of his family all held the same titles. He also held the title of fan bearer, and he probably fanned the god and ensured he did not overheat in the hot desert sun during processions (see Chapters 9 and 12). Nesperenub was the 'fan bearer on the right of the king', showing that he was also responsible for keeping the king cool – another very privileged position to hold.

Nesperenub was approximately 40 when he died, and a CT scan has shown he may have died from a brain tumour. A small hole on the inside of his skull may be the result of the fluids from the tumour eating into the skull. Imagine the headaches – and no ibuprofen to deal with it. The added pain and stink of the abscesses in his mouth and the wear on his teeth mean that Nesperenub was probably quite ratty.

CT scans of Nesperenub's mummy also show a rather strange object on the back of his head – a small clay bowl used by the embalmers to catch excess resin when sticking the bandages in place. Clearly the embalmers forgot about the bowl, which allowed the resin to set solid and stick the bowl to the back of his head. Damage around the bowl indicates that the embalmers tried to chisel it off. Their efforts didn't work, and they must have figured if they wrapped up the body, no one would ever know. Poor Nesperenub, destined to wander eternity with a bowl on his head.

Chapter 17

Ten Ancient Egyptian Achievements

*T*he ancient Egyptians were a very civilised nation and had many achievements to their name, including monumental buildings and extensive trade networks. They were a very busy society – constantly improving and progressing in their lifestyle and technology.

While the Greeks are attributed with most academic, scientific, and philosophical achievements, evidence shows that the Egyptians were not lacking in these departments; they just had a different approach. Everything the ancient Egyptians did had a practical purpose. They did not believe in researching for research's sake or contemplating unusable theories. Theirs was a practical rather than academic society. This chapter showcases ten of their greatest successes.

Scientific Method

As very practical people, the ancient Egyptians liked to solve problems with the least amount of fuss and general theorising. Therefore science as a discipline and as a word did not exist, because the ancient Egyptians no doubt believed they were only ever doing the necessary to continue with their work. Research for the sake of research did not seem to be carried out.

However, the Edwin Smith Medical Papyrus and the Ebers Papyrus show that the Egyptians conducted themselves according to scientific rules – they were willing to experiment within the frame of their daily work.

For example, when examining a medical patient (see Chapter 8 for details), scientific method was strictly used and included

- An interview with the patient
- Examination of bodily discharges
- Study of reflexes
- A diagnosis of the illness

Doctors then went about curing the ailment and recorded the results for future reference.

A similar scientific method was applied to building monuments, with many mathematical calculations (see the following section, 'Mathematics') being taken into account before work commenced. Sadly, little of this process has survived, but from the evidence available, the Egyptians clearly relied on multiple disciplines – such as mathematics, astronomy, geography, and surveying – when designing and planning the pyramids, temples, and tombs.

Mathematics

A few mathematical papyri have been discovered that give some indication of the advanced mathematical knowledge the Egyptians possessed.

While the Greeks are well known for their mathematical formulae, the Egyptians didn't really see the point. Instead they had a more practical collection of small calculations that produced the same answers.

This practical use of mathematical calculations can be identified in Egyptian building works – the pyramids in particular. Archaeologist William Matthew Finders Petrie (see Chapter 15) was the first to record and measure the pyramids systematically. The work of Petrie and others clearly shows that these structures were very well planned mathematically.

The Egyptians were among the first to consistently and correctly combine and utilise these techniques:

- ✔ The use of fractions (½, ¼, ⅓, and so on)
- ✔ Calculating the area of a rectangle by multiplying the length by the width
- ✔ Calculating the area of a triangle by turning it into a rectangle and then halving that area
- ✔ Calculating the area of a circle using the length of the diameter and an approximation of pi (3.16)
- ✔ Finding the volume of cylinders and pyramids based on knowledge of areas

The Egyptians were in fact more advanced in their mathematical knowledge than they are given credit for. The reason for this underrating seems to be that the ancient Egyptians' concerns were practical rather than theoretical.

Astronomy

The Egyptians were very knowledgeable about the stars and constellations. From the Middle Kingdom, constellations were often depicted on coffins as star clocks, showing the length of time stars were visible or invisible. From the New Kingdom, ceilings of tombs and temples often displayed the constellation of stars. These constellations were the same as the ones we see today, but represented differently. For example:

- ✔ Orion was represented as a man turning his head.
- ✔ Ursa Major was represented as a bull's foreleg.

Like mathematics (see the preceding section), astronomy was used by the Egyptians for many different practical uses including

- ✔ Scheduling temple-building ceremonies, which relied on the visibility of the constellations we refer to now as the Great Bear and Orion
- ✔ Setting the cardinal points for the orientation of the pyramids by observing the North Star
- ✔ Setting the New Year always to coincide with the rising of Sirius in mid-July and the annual flooding of the Nile

From the Middle Kingdom, the Egyptians were able to recognise five planets, known as stars that know no rest, which were often associated with Horus, the Egyptian god of the sky:

- ✔ Jupiter, known as Horus who limits the two lands
- ✔ Mars, known as Horus the red
- ✔ Mercury, known as Sebegu (a god associated with Seth)
- ✔ Saturn, known as Horus, bull of the sky
- ✔ Venus, known as god of the morning

The stars were not used to predict the fate of humans in Egypt until the Ptolemaic period when the Greeks introduced astrology. The most famous zodiac in Egypt is on the ceiling at Denderah and dates to the first century AD. This zodiac displays all the familiar zodiac signs, including Leo, Aries, and Taurus.

Understanding of the Human Body

The ancient Egyptians had a remarkable understanding of the human body, primarily gained through their observations during mummification. They probably didn't perform live internal surgery, but their greatest anatomical achievement was the near-discovery of circulation.

The Greeks were credited with discovering circulation in the fifth century BC, the but the Egyptians clearly understood a lot more about the workings of the human body than they're often given credit for.

The Edwin Smith Medical Papyrus, which dates back to approximately 1550 BC, discusses blood circulation through observation of the pulse, making clear that these two concepts were connected in the minds of the Egyptians. Pulse-related observations include:

- ✔ 'It is there that the heart speaks.'
- ✔ 'It is there that every physician and every priest of Sekhmet places his fingers . . . he feels something from the heart.'

Additionally, this papyrus indicates that the Egyptians knew that the blood supply ran from the heart to all organs:

- ✔ 'There are vessels in him for every part of the body.'
- ✔ 'It speaks forth in the vessels of every body part.'

Even the creation story of the ram-headed god, Khnum, who fashioned humans on a potter's wheel, reads a little like an anatomical record. For example, Khnum:

- ✔ Oriented the bloodstream to flow over the bones and attached the skin to the skeletal frame
- ✔ Installed a respiratory system, vertebrae to support it, and the digestive system
- ✔ Designed sexual organs for comfort and ease of use during intercourse
- ✔ Organised conception in the womb and the stages of labour

Not only did Khnum create Egyptians this way, his creation extended to foreigners, as well as animals, birds, fish, and reptiles. He was truly a universal creator – and a very talented potter!

Irrigation

Egypt is situated in the desert with the Nile as the only source of water. Using a complicated system of irrigation canals and water dykes, the Egyptians were able to make the most of the water available. Canals were directed to dry areas and were deep enough that they were still full when the flood waters receded.

Evidence suggests that in the Middle Kingdom the natural lake in the Faiyum was used as a reservoir. Water filled the lake during the annual inundation (flood) and was stored to be used in the drier times of the year. In addition to this lake was a canal leading directly from the Nile, which would provide a constant supply of water to the area.

In order to irrigate the land artificially, channels needed to be dug during the inundation to direct the water to areas of land in desperate need. To get water into the channels:

- ✔ In the Old and Middle Kingdoms, water was transported by hand in large vessels and then physically poured into the irrigation channels.
- ✔ In the New Kingdom, the *shaduf* was introduced. The shaduf is a wooden pole with a jar on one end and a weight on the other, which can easily lift and direct water.
- ✔ During the Ptolemaic period, the *sakkia* was introduced. The sakkia is an animal-powered water wheel that moves more water – which meant more land could be irrigated, resulting in more agricultural land and ultimately more food production.

Artificial irrigation was a necessity, and it was a major achievement. Even today, with only one water source and still situated in the desert, the Egyptian people never have hosepipe bans and water shortages!

Stone Buildings

The third-dynasty King Djoser is credited with building the first stone building in the world. This was his pyramid complex at Saqqara, dominated by the step pyramid that still towers over the landscape.

The step pyramid started from much humbler origins, however – as a pit burial and mastaba tomb (see Chapter 13), which covered a total of eleven burial shafts. Djoser's structure was gradually extended outwards and upwards until the step pyramid was created, standing 60 metres high and consisting of six steps.

Most impressively, the step pyramid was built of stone instead of the mud bricks normally used at this period. To maintain a traditional appearance, the stone blocks were of the same dimensions as the mud bricks. The outside was then completely encased in limestone blocks, giving the finished pyramid a smooth look.

The use of stone was a great achievement, particularly considering that other buildings were made of perishable materials. This pyramid complex was designed to last for eternity – and it looks like it is well on its way. After the third dynasty, buildings were built of stone more often. However, stone was only ever used for buildings that were intended to last for centuries, such as temples and tombs. All other buildings (houses, palaces, and even some shrines) were built using mud brick. We have to be thankful to Djoser – if he didn't want such an impressive monument, we might not have the stone structures in such abundance today.

A Surviving Wonder

Egypt has the only surviving Wonder of the Ancient World – the Great Pyramid of Giza (see Chapter 14). King Khufu of the fourth dynasty built this pyramid. It stands proud on a natural rock plateau and towers 146 metres into the sky. Even with modern Cairo encroaching, the Great Pyramid is visible for miles around.

The outside of the pyramid is encased in limestone blocks, which give it a beautiful white, shining appearance. The pyramid incorporates two burial chambers, one of which contains the red granite sarcophagus designed for the burial of the king. However, no royal burial seems to have happened in this pyramid; it is likely that Khufu was buried elsewhere.

The Great Pyramid has been visited for many years as a tourist attraction, with Cleopatra VII and Julius Caesar among the earliest celebrity visitors. Even Tutankhamun, Ramses II, and Ramses III almost certainly travelled to Giza to marvel at these monuments, which were ancient even then.

Glass Production

Glass was not introduced until the early New Kingdom, probably brought from Syria by Thutmosis III. The Egyptians gradually became proficient in

- ✔ Glass making from raw materials (including silica, alkali, and lime)
- ✔ Glass working from imported ready-made blocks of glass

Glass was used in clear or coloured form from the reign of Hatshepsut. Egyptians even fashioned vessels by making a core of clay in the required shape and then dipping it in molten glass. Removing the clay core was quite difficult, especially in vessels with narrow necks, so vessels crafted this way have an opaque quality.

Other methods of manufacture include

- ✔ **Moulding:** Molten glass is poured into moulds of clay.
- ✔ **Cold cutting:** Pre-moulded glass is carved as if it were stone using stone, bronze, or copper tools.
- ✔ **Core moulding:** A clay or sand core in the shape of the cavity in a vessel is dipped in molten glass and moved around until it is completely covered. Once cold, the core is scraped out.

Archaeologist William Matthew Finders Petrie (see Chapter 15) discovered a great deal of waste from glass production at Amarna, the city of Akhenaten. Other production sites were at the palace of Amenhotep III at Malkata in Luxor and the site of el-Lisht in the north of Egypt.

A more recent glass-related discovery was at the site of Pi-Rameses, the city of Ramses II in the Delta. In 2005, excavations uncovered a glass factory, showing that glass was produced in great quantity at this site. Enough of the equipment was unearthed to reconstruct the manufacturing process:

✔ The raw materials were heated in used beer jars up to temperatures of 750 degrees Celsius and then again in crucibles to as high as 1,000 degrees Celsius.

✔ The glass was coloured using natural pigments added to the raw ingredients. Sometimes a coil of coloured glass was draped around the completed vessel while soft and then blended to create waves, marble effects, garlands, and arches of feathered patterns.

Glass was a prestige item, under royal control, and was often given to foreign dignitaries as a diplomatic gift. This prestige is due to the extensive skills needed to produce quality items, and glass is used with some frequency in the artefacts from Tutankhamun's tomb. It was such a sought-after commodity that those who couldn't afford glass made replicas from wood or stone.

Female Leadership

The female pharaoh Hatshepsut is famous for many things, and many achievements punctuate her reign. The most spectacular achievement is that as a woman she took over the role of king, pushing Thutmosis III (her husband, step-son, and co-ruler) aside. This is the first time that a woman had ruled Egypt as a king rather than a queen or co-ruler. Check out Chapter 5 for more on the role of women.

Hatshepsut ruled in relative peace and spent her 20-odd years on the throne building monuments. Her funerary temple at Deir el Bahri records the transportation of two red granite obelisks – even showing the massive structures tied on Nile barges – and their erection at Karnak. These obelisks were completely covered in gold.

Other records on the walls of Deir el Bahri detail Hatshepsut's expedition to Punt. No one really knows where Punt is, and Egyptologists have never agreed on this issue. Even Hatshepsut wasn't sure, and she appealed to the oracle of Amun to give the direct route to this 'god's land'. It's a pity she didn't draw a map.

When Hatshepsut returned from Punt, she brought a number of incense trees carried in baskets on a carrying pole. She planted the trees along the approach to her temple and aspired to make incense a local product, thus eliminating the need for trade. The expedition also returned with incense bundles, animal hides, and exotic woods. These items boosted the Egyptian economy and made a number of exotic items available.

Although Hatshepsut did plant incense trees, historians do not know whether she was able to produce enough incense to prevent the need for trade. A self-contained Egyptian incense industry is unlikely; incense is often a prominent feature of later booty and trade lists.

Continuing Civilisation

The most spectacular achievement of the ancient Egyptians is the continuance of their civilisation for more than 3,000 years. The Roman Empire lasted just over 500 years and the ancient Greek civilisation was at its height for about 400 years. Ancient Egyptian society was fully developed in 3100 BC when King Narmer united Upper and Lower Egypt for the first time. From this time until the death of Cleopatra in 30 BC, the culture's religion, practices, and lifestyle did not change a great deal, making Egypt a civilisation to be reckoned with.

Even after the death of Cleopatra, the Romans did not totally destroy Egyptian culture straight away. Indeed, the religious practices continued at the temple of Philae until the fourth century AD.

Although Egyptian culture may appear to be static for 3,000 years or so, it was in fact ever changing, and this is the secret of its success. The Egyptians were ever so accommodating. They were more than happy to absorb aspects of foreign culture and religion into their own, which enabled an immigrant community to thrive in Egypt. Their religion and culture had a something-for-everyone policy; if something was missing, they simply added it.

Problems occurred when the influx of foreigners was so great that Egyptian culture could not easily accommodate the new culture or cultures. This was why Egyptian culture died a slow death with the infiltration of the Greeks from the time that Alexander the Great entered Egypt, followed by the Romans in 30 BC.

These newcomers were unprepared to adopt Egyptian culture completely, and a Hellenistic society slowly formed. After Alexander the Great and the Romans, came the Christians and the Muslims, which eventually resulted in a total loss of ancient traditions – until archaeologists started to reconstruct a portrait of this great civilisation.

Chapter 18

Top Ten Places to Visit in Egypt

· ·

In This Chapter

▶ Pyramids in the north

▶ Tombs in the middle

▶ Temples in the south

· ·

*E*gypt continues to be a marvellous travel destination, but the number of temples, tombs, and museums can be overwhelming. You may be tempted to plump for a package tour with all your trips planned for you, but they have tight schedules and often spend longer at alabaster, papyrus, and perfume shops than at the ancient monuments.

Why not plan your Egyptian trek on your own? This chapter features the top ten places to visit – some on the tourist trail and others a little off the beaten track. For locations, have a peek at the Cheat Sheet map. Armed with a guide book, camera, and taxi driver, the sky's the limit. You never know, you may even discover other sites to add to this list as must-goes.

Hundreds of guidebooks are on the market, but the best are Jill Kamil's guides (although they can be tricky to get hold of) and those published by Lonely Planet or Rough Guides. Also take a look at the Egyptian Monuments Web site at www.egyptsites.co.uk which outlines all the sites in Egypt with directions on how to get to them.

The following recommended sites are listed in geographical order, starting in the north and working your way south.

All the sites require tickets – normally costing less than LE.30 (£3 or $6) per site, with many costing as little as LE.10 (£1 or $2). You can buy tickets at each site.

Giza Plateau, Cairo

Although the prominent pyramids dominate the skyline, the Giza plateau in Cairo is teeming with places to visit. An average tour spends about an hour here, but to see everything you need at least three hours – maybe longer if you like to wander off the beaten track.

The three main pyramids were built by Khufu, Khafra, and Menkaure, and each is accompanied by satellite pyramids belonging to the kings' wives – for a grand total of nine pyramids. At least three are open to the public.

Only 200 or so tickets for the Great Pyramid are sold daily, so you must be at the ticket office when it opens at approximately 8 a.m. (check the opening time before going there, arrive early, and be prepared to sprint up the hill to beat the coaches). After purchasing your ticket, wait a couple of hours before entering the pyramid, after the crowds have lessened. The pyramid is worth the wait!

Alongside the Great Pyramid of Khufu, be sure to visit the empty boat pits (see Chapter 14) and the modern boat museum (for which you need a separate ticket), which features a reconstructed vessel from the pits. This boat was used in the funeral of Khufu and has been reconstructed according to ancient techniques. Walkways at different levels enable visitors to view the boat from all angles.

The causeway of Khafra leads from the Great Pyramid to the sphinx (made of solid rock and so only viewed from the outside), the sphinx temple (closed to the public, but you can see it from a short distance away), and the valley temple. (You can visit the valley temple, although it bears no decoration.) Between the paws of the sphinx is the Dream Stela erected by Thutmosis IV after the sun god appeared to him in a dream (refer to Chapter 14). On both sides of the causeway is the mastaba cemetery with a number of beautifully decorated structures, three of which are open to the public. The mastaba of Seregemib (which includes a lovely scene of driving donkeys) and that of Khnumenty (a two-level structure with an Indiana-Jones-type ladder to climb) are worth visiting.

Saqqara, Cairo

Saqqara is the site of the oldest stone building in the world – a step pyramid – as well as a 'dummy complex' of shrines, temples, and ritual areas designed for King Djoser to rule in the afterlife.

The site also has a number of other pyramids, including the pyramid of Unas, which appears to be nothing but a pile of rubble. Sadly the pyramid of Unas is closed to the public because it is structurally unsafe, but you can see the Pyramid Texts from Unas's pyramid in the burial chambers of the pyramid of Teti nearby.

Close to Teti's pyramid are the mastaba tombs of Mereruka (with the image of his wife on the bed playing the harp), Ankhmahor (with an image of the earliest circumcision scene), and Ti (with elaborate farming scenes and a *serdab* and statue). For more information on mastabas and serdabs, go to Chapter 13.

A short distance away stand the large underground catacomb known as the *Serapeum*, constructed for the burials of the sacred Apis bulls, which were worshipped at Saqqara. The bulls were mummified, according to tradition, and then buried with huge stone sarcophagi and canopic jars. Their mothers also received elaborate burials complete with a burial suite of their own.

The Imhotep Museum has also opened on the site and showcases archaeological finds from the Saqqara region. Highlights include a beautiful reconstruction of the wall tiles that decorated some of the chambers of the Djoser complex, as well as the infamous famine scene from the causeway of Unas, depicting emaciated people entering Egypt looking for help. This scene is very graphic and even shows one chap pulling lice from his hair and eating them.

To see everything at Saqqara takes all day, so negotiate with your driver to wait for you. Take some food with you, because there's no café at the site.

Museum of Egyptian Antiquities, Cairo

The Museum of Egyptian Antiquities (commonly known as the Cairo Museum) is soon to be replaced by the Grand Egyptian Museum and relocated near Giza, where it will be centred around the colossal statue of Ramses (moved in 2006 from Ramses Square in Cairo). The new museum is scheduled to open by 2010.

The museum as it now stands is spectacular and is bursting at the seams with hundreds of objects from 3,000 years of Egyptian history. Most package tours spend a couple of hours here but you could spend an entire day – the morning upstairs and the afternoon downstairs. The café does quite nice sandwiches and cold drinks.

Unusual objects are tucked away in every corner, from the sarcophagus of Akhenaten (in the garden to the left of the main building) to the beautiful wooden coffin of Ramses (who oversees the goings-on of the first floor). Close by is the only human-shaped shroud in Egypt, two real wigs, which are very close to a classic 'mullet' style, and a leather military kilt.

Wonder at the weight of the gold jewellery awarded to favoured officials and stare into the eyes of long-dead animal mummies. Marvel over the statue of the dwarf Seneb, seated with his wife and children, as well as the statue of Ramses III with Horus and the little-represented Seth. Spend hours discussing the anomalies of the Amarna art style on the ground floor. If you have any time left, be sure to visit the Tutankhamun exhibition and gaze on the face of the boy-king.

If you'd like to know more, take a look at the official Web site at `www.egyptianmuseum.gov.eg`.

Tell el Amarna, Al Minya

Tell el Amarna was the city Akhenaten established for the worship of the sun disc, the Aten. The city is situated in Al Minya in Middle Egypt about half way between Cairo and Luxor. Very little of the actual city is exposed because of the fragility of the remains, but British archaeologists have reconstructed some buildings. These structures include the small temple to the Aten, the north palace where Nefertiti and Tutankhamun lived, a city house that is typical of many from the site, and the bridge that joins two temples over the so-called King's Road. The King's Road would have seen the daily processions of Akhenaten, Nefertiti, and their children in their sparkling chariots. This bridge on the King's Road is also believed to be the site of the *window of appearances*, from which the royal family bestowed golden jewellery on their favoured courtiers. Visit Chapter 2 for more details on the town.

The real reason to visit Amarna, however, is to tour the two sets of tombs (the north and the south tombs) and the royal tomb. Many of these tombs are open to the public. These tombs are some of the only places where you can see classic Amarna-style art outside a museum.

Most of tombs include images of Akhenaten and Nefertiti standing at the window of appearances along with the princesses, riding in a chariot, or worshipping the Aten. A classic image of Ay can be found in his tomb here, showing him boasting to his friends about his new red leather gloves, a rare commodity in Egypt. The royal tomb is badly damaged, but trying to make out the images on the walls is interesting, and this monument once probably held the secrets to the Amarna period, which continue to elude Egyptologists today.

To make the most of Amarna and Beni Hasan (see the following section) you need to stay overnight at Al Minya. Only a couple of hotels are here – and don't be surprised if you're the only people there. You can't drive to Al Minya alone and need to organise with your driver to travel with the military convoy that leaves daily. You can travel there by train, but first check the safety issues. Your hotel in Cairo or Luxor may be able to help.

Beni Hasan, Al Minya

Near Al Minya is the Middle Kingdom burial site known as Beni Hasan. This site is formed by an outcrop of rock, high up in the cliff face. The site includes 39 rock-cut tombs (see Chapter 13) built by local *nomarchs*, or governors.

Of the 39 tombs, 5 or so are open to the public. Each tomb has an entrance consisting of a pillared courtyard. A central door leads into the tomb itself, and images and inscriptions decorate some tombs. All tombs have large open rooms with supporting pillars, and statue rooms at the rear of the chambers that housed statues of the deceased individuals. The family of each deceased individual laid offerings of food and drink at the statue to nourish the departed's spirit. (Actual burials took place at the end of a long shaft that opens out into the burial chamber under the main room; these rooms are not open to the public.)

The decoration in these tombs features lots of action. Notable images include:

- ✔ **Military training activities,** such as wrestling, stick fighting, and weight lifting with sandbags.

- ✔ **Siege warfare,** including the earliest image in Egypt of the wheel and an image of foreign diplomats travelling to Egypt to participate in trade.

    The most important of these siege scenes is in the tomb of Khnumhotep II and features the earliest depiction of the Hyksos, a rather colourful group of people bringing eye paint to trade with the Egyptians.

- ✔ **Elaborate fishing and fowling scenes,** awash with colour and detailed renderings of marsh flora and fauna.

Karnak Temple, Luxor

Karnak temple in Luxor is the largest temple ever built. Because it took more than 2,000 years to construct, Karnak temple includes a number of different shrines, temples, statues, and chapels dedicated to many different kings and gods. It covers 247 acres and many hours can be required to walk around the various monuments. Most package tours spend about two hours here, but you need at least a morning to do it justice – although even a morning won't allow time for the open air museum and the temples of Khonsu and Opet. The complex includes a coffee shop, and the Tutankhamun restaurant outside does a lovely lunch. Check with the guards when leaving the temple, because they often let you come back in after lunch on the same ticket. The temple can easily provide a couple of days' entertainment to any Egyptophile tourist!

The main temple has ten entrance pylons, each decorated with elaborate images and texts, as well as the largest hypostyle hall, consisting of 134 columns. These columns, which stand up to 21 metres (69 feet) tall, create a stone version of the primeval marshes – a most impressive sight. And if you can tear yourself away from the pillars, the surrounding walls feature images of the coronations of Sety I and Ramses II in great detail.

The Karnak complex also has two sacred lakes – a rectangular one built by Thutmosis III and a horseshoe-shaped lake built by Amenhotep III (although the latter is closed to the public and forms part of the complex of Mut outside the present enclosure walls). Within the enclosure walls are a number of small temples worth going to see, including the temple of Ptah (with a beautiful statue of Sekhmet enhanced by ancient lighting techniques), the temple of Khonsu (built with re-used blocks, many of which retain their original images), and the Chapels of the God's Wives of Amun (some of the only chapels built by and depicting women).

The complex also has an open air museum displaying a number of decorated blocks as well as a large-scale temple of Thutmosis III and three reconstructed chapels – the Alabaster Chapel of Amenhotep I, the White Chapel of Senusret I, and the Red Chapel of Hatshepsut, which includes some lovely scenes of her coronation. Don't miss a reconstructed temple gateway of Akhenaten's temple to the Aten, which surprisingly shows him in a traditional manner, smiting foreign prisoners with a large mace head. Compared with later images, this depiction of Akhenaten is completely unrecognisable.

Medinet Habu, Luxor

When in Luxor, you must visit the spectacular mortuary temple of Ramses III at Medinet Habu on the west bank of the Nile. This temple is a copy of the temple of Ramses II at the Ramesseum (which is situated further north and is also open to the public). Some of the scenes on the walls have been directly copied without any thought for reality; for example, Ramses II recorded battles with the Nubians, whereas Ramses III didn't, but copied the Nubian battle scenes as his own victory! The temple is a good means of seeing what the Ramesseum looked like, because now the Ramesseum is in a ruined condition.

The pylons at Medinet Habu depict the many battles of Ramses III, including his Libyan wars. An external wall shows the battle of the Sea People. Although these scenes are difficult to make out, it is worth the effort because they show the first naval battle in history. Don't miss the image of the world's first crows' nest, which enabled sailors to see for great distances and shoot fire arrows into the enemy ships.

To the left of the entrance pylon is a palace with a window of appearances that looks into the first court of the temple. No doubt the king himself stood in this area, so why not stand in the footsteps of the pharaohs.

The palace itself was for women. A number of three-room suites – perhaps a sleeping area, dressing room, and lounge area – are at the rear of the structure. You can also see an audience chamber complete with throne dais, a pillared court, and even two showers – the drain is still visible.

The main gate to the temple is an amazing structure – a copy of a Syrian *migdol*, or ceremonial gateway. The hollow gateway, which, sadly, isn't open to the public, contains images of the king and his royal women. Although historians once thought the site was a harem, many now believe it was a visiting place for royal women. Evidence shows patio gardens on various levels of the gateway where women sat and sunned themselves. From the windows in the gateway, the women viewed processions and activities happening outside the temple or entering into the temple itself. The decoration on the gateway retains a lot of colour. In fact, this temple is one of the most colourful in Egypt and gives visitors an idea of what it must have looked like new.

Put aside a morning for this temple. Cafés opposite the entrance provide lovely food and cold drinks – you can re-enter the temple feeling refreshed.

Deir el Medina, Luxor

The village of Deir el Medina, which housed the workmen who created the royal tombs in the Valley of the Kings, is situated on the west bank at Luxor. This site offers much to see and is well worth the trip – set aside a morning or an afternoon for this site. Check out Chapter 2 for all the details on this village.

The entire village is extant, with the foundations up to a metre high, giving a clear view of the village layout. Each house consists of four or five rooms, and many include staircases (the bottom few steps are still visible), which led to flat roofs.

Some in-built furniture, such as couches and box beds, can be seen in many houses, as well as sunken pots used for storage, and even bread ovens in some of the kitchens. In a couple of the houses, religious shrines are still standing, and you can almost imagine the incense burning and ancient Egyptians praying to their household gods.

The tombs of the workmen surround the village in the cliffs. Three of them are open to the public: those belonging to Sennedjem (with lovely farming scenes), Pashedu (showing one of the few scenes of salt-and-pepper-and white-haired ancestors), and Inherkhau (with an image of the deceased playing senet).

If the preceding isn't enough, you can also visit a number of temples built and used by the inhabitants of the village. These include a small temple to Ramses II, a terraced temple to Amenhotep of the Garden (Amenhotep I, the original builder of the village), and a large Ptolemaic temple dedicated to Hathor, built by and for tourists on the way to the Valley of the Kings. Even tourism isn't new!

Luxor Museum

The Luxor Museum has recently undergone an extension, which has improved it no end. Although it is a small museum, there is plenty to see, and the low lighting creates a great atmosphere for viewing the objects inside.

Highlights include the Kamose stela describing the expulsion of the Hyksos, and the mummy of Ahmose, the brother of Kamose, who finally *did* expel the Hyksos. Gaze into the beautiful carved face of Thutmosis III and wonder why Senwosret III looks so unhappy. Follow the Tutankhamun trail, which begins as you enter the museum with a statue of Tutankhamun as the god Amun and includes shabti figures on the first floor, each of which bears his youthful chubby face.

The reconstructed wall from the temple of Akhenaten at Karnak is still being worked on, so if your timing is right, you may be able to see archaeologists making additions. There is also a case of large ostraca (limestone flakes) used to draw the plan of a tomb and a house. The grid system is marked out on another wall to practise illustration. If all this isn't interesting enough, don't miss a number of weapons, a chariot, and a stela showing Amenhotep I in his chariot shooting arrows at a copper target.

The Luxor cache wing of the museum includes numerous royal statues discovered in the courtyard at Luxor temple, including Horemheb kneeling before the creator god Atum, a lovely red statue of Amenhotep III with rather slinky cat's eyes, and a large statue of Amun and Mut built by Ramses II. Although this last statue is damaged, many historians believe that the face of Mut is the true face of Nefertari, Ramses's beloved wife.

Visit the museum after 5 p.m. when it reopens for the evening, and plan to spend a couple of hours here.

Abu Simbel, Aswan

Ramses II built the temples of Abu Simbel at Aswan at the southernmost reaches of the Egyptian borders. The project may have taken more than 30 years to build, although the smaller of the temples is not complete. Ramses built two temples out of the cliff face, oriented to the east to meet the rising sun – one to the sun god Re-Horakhty and the other to Hathor and Nefertari. The façade of the Re-Horakhty temple is constructed of four colossal seated figures of Ramses, standing 21 metres (69 feet) high, carved directly from the rock face.

On entering the temple, a hall confronts you featuring pillars carved into *Osirid* (wrapped like a mummy) figures of the king. At the rear of the temple is a statue room with figures of Ramses, Re-Horakhty, Ptah, and Amun-Ra creating the focus of the worship in the temple. In February and October, sunlight enters this sanctuary and illuminates the faces of the gods.

Temple decoration shows Ramses II at his battle of Kadesh against the Hittites, as well as his Libyan, Syrian, and Nubian wars. The scenes are lively, brutal, and colourful, with much of the original paint still vibrant.

The smaller temple to Hathor and Nefertari has colossal figures of Ramses II and Nefertari on the façade, standing 10 metres (33 feet) tall. There are only two statues of the queen and four of the king, demonstrating that the building of this temple glorified the king as much as the queen. Within the temple, the first pillared court has Hathor-headed columns, and the sanctuary at the rear has a carved image of Hathor as a cow emerging from the marshes. Again the king is present and is standing beneath the head of the cow. Nefertari is shown throughout the temple carrying out rituals in worship of the gods, which was unusual, because queens normally played a more passive role.

Both temples were moved to higher ground in the 1960s when the Aswan dam was built and Lake Nasser submerged many of the Nubian temples. While visiting Abu Simbel, you can take a tour of the concrete support structure within the cliff face that stabilised these newly placed temples – itself a feat of modern engineering.

You can fly or drive to Abu Simbel. The drive from Luxor takes about four hours, but the road is often closed for security reasons. You can fly from Aswan, but the return flight is such that you only have an hour or so from the arrival time. I recommend staying overnight at Aswan and arranging transport with a local driver to really make the most of this site.

Chapter 19

Ten Key Egyptologists

During more than 200 years of Egyptian archaeology, hundreds of important archaeologists, scholars, and historians have contributed in one way or another to the discipline of Egyptology. This chapter looks at ten people who have made Egyptology what it is today, although many others made equally important discoveries and contributions and continue to do so – so this list is by no means conclusive.

Giovanni Belzoni (1778–1823)

The Italian Giovanni Belzoni was a tall man – 6 foot, 7 inches – which cut a fine figure in Egypt where the average height was at the time about 5 foot, 8 inches. His earliest career was as a circus strongman, touring Europe, before he turned his attention to Egypt.

Initially, Belzoni travelled to Egypt to sell a new type of water wheel (nothing to do with his strongman career). When this endeavour proved unsuccessful, he turned to the more lucrative work of excavating and transporting ancient monuments. In 1816, he started working for Henry Salt; one of his first jobs was to move the top half of a colossal statue from the Ramesseum, near Luxor. The statue today forms part of the Egyptian collection at the British Museum.

Belzoni carried out extensive excavation work and discovered, among other things, the tomb of Sety I and the temple of Ramses II at Abu Simbel in Nubia. Although his techniques of excavation were scandalous by modern standards – he often used dynamite when a trowel would have sufficed, and he had a habit of carving his name into objects – Belzoni did a lot to promote Egyptology through the exhibition of his objects.

He excavated for more than eight years. He died of dysentery in 1823 on an expedition to locate the source of the river Niger.

Jean-François Champollion (1790–1832)

Egyptologists will always remember Jean-François Champollion as the linguist who made the final breakthrough in deciphering hieroglyphs. His discovery changed Egyptology and enabled the world finally to read the ancient Egyptian language.

Champollion was always interested in language, and by 1807 (when he was 17) he had delivered his first paper on the language of ancient Egypt at the Lyceum. He spoke many languages, including Hebrew, Coptic, Arabic, Syriac, and Chaldean, when he embarked on deciphering the Rosetta Stone, a stela from Rosetta in the Delta written in three languages: hieroglyphs, demotic, and ancient Greek (see Chapter 11).

Champollion consulted with the English physician Thomas Young and compared notes until Young's death in 1817, after which Champollion continued the work. By 1822, he had worked out the key to hieroglyphs, although it wasn't until the completion of his grammar book in 1832 that he was able to read hieroglyphs with any certainty.

Between 1828 and 1829, Champollion and Ippolito Rosellini travelled to Egypt to record and survey further monuments, no doubt bringing back detailed copies of inscriptions to decipher. Champollion died from a stroke in 1832; not until shortly after were his books *Egyptian Grammar* and then *Egyptian Dictionary* published, so he never got to see the difference his work made.

Karl Lepsius (1819–84)

Karl Lepsius, a German Egyptologist, gained his doctorate in 1833 and then used the newly published *Egyptian Grammar* by Champollion to learn to read hieroglyphs. He made his first trip to Egypt in 1842 with the aim of recording the monuments and collecting antiquities, which was the norm at the time. In his career he collected more than 15,000 artefacts, which formed the basis for the Egyptian Museum in Berlin.

Between 1842 and 1845, Lepsius led the Prussian expedition to Egypt and Nubia and recorded its work in 12 volumes entitled *Denkmaeler aus Aegypten und Aethiopien*. This publication is still valuable for modern Egyptologists because many of the monuments recorded have since deteriorated, and these volumes provide clear images and descriptions of their appearance more than 150 years ago.

Lepsius founded the study programme of Egyptology at the University of Berlin and was appointed the keeper of the Egyptian collection at the Berlin Museum, which housed his growing collection from the expeditions. The Berlin Museum still thrives today and houses some of the most famous images in the world, including the painted limestone bust of Nefertiti.

Amelia Edwards (1831–92)

Amelia Edwards, an English Egyptologist, journalist, and novelist, went to Egypt in 1873 and was hooked. This trip inspired her to write *A Thousand Miles up the Nile*, a travelogue of her adventures.

Writing, however, wasn't new to Edwards: Her first poem was published at 7 years old, her first short story at 12. She was home educated and was clearly a promising student. She had written a number of travelogues prior to her Egyptian trip, recording her adventures with her female travel companion.

On her first trip to Egypt, she spent six weeks excavating at the site of Abu Simbel. In 1880, she set up an informal group to deal with the conservation and excavation issues of Egypt. In 1882, the organisation was officially named the Egypt Exploration Fund (now the Egypt Exploration Society). The society's goal, then and now, is to excavate and record the monuments of Egypt. You can visit the society's Web site at www.ees.ac.uk.

On her death, Edwards bequeathed a number of artefacts, her books, photographs, and other Egypt-related documents to University College, London, to be used as teaching aids for Egyptology students. As a supporter of the Suffrage movement, she chose University College because it was the first college to admit women as students. She also bequeathed enough money to set up the United Kingdom's first professorship in Egyptian archaeology and philology at University College, which went to W. M. Flinders Petrie.

W. M. Flinders Petrie (1853–1942)

Flinders Petrie was an archaeologist for more than 70 years. He started his Egyptological career in the 1880s when he went to measure the Great Pyramid at Giza. He then directed excavations at a number of important sites around Egypt at a time when there were still lots of things to be discovered.

Petrie was not only a famous Egyptologist but also a great archaeologist. His *seriation dating technique* is still used worldwide. This technique creates relative dates for any site through the arrangement of items into an evolutionary sequence. (See Chapter 15 for more on this technique.) Petrie also had a great interest in the less glamorous side of archaeology and collected all the bits – mostly hundreds of potsherds – that most archaeologists left behind because they weren't gold and shiny.

Over his many years excavating, Petrie collected thousands of Egyptian artefacts, some of great interest, which he sold to University College, London, in 1913, creating the Petrie Museum of Egyptian Archaeology. Petrie retired from his position as Edwards Professor at University College in 1933. He then excavated for a few years near Gaza before his death in Jerusalem in 1942.

Howard Carter (1874–1939)

English Egyptologist Howard Carter was born in Kensington in London and is famous for his discovery of the tomb of Tutankhamun in 1922.

However, Carter had a rich career *prior* to this discovery. He started life as an artist and was sent to Egypt to record the tomb decoration at Beni Hasan (see Chapter 18). He then tried his hand at archaeology alongside Petrie at Amarna, although Petrie didn't think Carter would be a great archaeologist. Just goes to show what an impressive find can do.

Carter was appointed inspector general of Upper Egypt in 1899 and was responsible for putting electric lights in the Valley of the Kings. He resigned his position in 1903 after a dispute with some drunk and disorderly French tourists. He worked as a draftsman and antiquities dealer until Lord Carnarvon offered to finance excavations, employing Carter as director. They worked for many years around Luxor and the Valley of the Kings, making many discoveries until by accident in the last year of excavating they found KV62, the tomb of Tutankhamun.

The remainder of Carter's life was filled with recording and analysing Tutankhamun's artefacts, as well as writing excavation reports and giving lecture tours around the world.

Alan Gardiner (1879–1963)

Sir Alan Gardiner was an amazing linguist and made great advances regarding the language of the ancient Egyptians. He was an expert in *hieratic*, the cursive form of hieroglyphic script that the Egyptians used for everyday writing. Egyptology students the world over are familiar with Gardiner's *Egyptian Grammar*, a comprehensive guide to Egyptian hieroglyphs with a dictionary that is still used regularly. During his career, Gardiner made trips to Paris and Turin to copy hieratic manuscripts; many translations being used today are the result of his work.

Gardiner was born in Eltham and was interested in Egypt from a young age, which resulted in his being sent to Gaston Maspero in Paris for a year to study. He then returned to The Queen's College, Oxford. From a wealthy family, Gardiner never needed to work and spent his time teaching himself all he wanted about Egypt and Egyptology and pursuing his own goals. From 1912 to 1914 he held a readership at Manchester University, after which he continued his linguistic work.

Jac Janssen (born 1922)

Professor Jac Janssen, a Dutch Egyptologist now in his 80s, has been fundamental in the work at Deir el Medina (see Chapter 2). He has held the emeritus professorship of Egyptology, University of Leiden, Netherlands, for many years and is now living in the United Kingdom where he still works to further enlighten students and historians on the workmen's village of Deir el Medina.

As a New Kingdom hieratic expert, Janssen has worked on many of the inscriptions from Deir el Medina, which has provided invaluable information regarding the day-to-day lives of everyday Egyptians.

Janssen has worked primarily on the economic side of history, publishing important books such as *Commodity Prices from the Ramessid Period: An Economic Study of the Village of Necropolis Workmen at Thebes*, which gives all the prices for various household goods. In 2006, he published a book on the economic use of the donkey at Deir el Medina called, not surprisingly, *Donkeys at Deir el Medina*.

Kent Weeks (born 1941)

Dr Kent Weeks, an American Egyptologist, is best known for his current work in the Valley of the Kings on the Theban Mapping Project, which resulted in the rediscovery of KV5, the tomb of the sons of Ramses II. The discovery of KV5 is a major achievement. The Theban Mapping Project began in 1978 with the goal of recording the locations of tombs, temples, and other archaeological sites and structures on the Theban west bank. This is a monumental task that will take many more years to complete.

Weeks has worked in Egyptology from the 1960s, and from 1972 taught at the American University in Cairo. Between 1977 and 1988 he returned to the United States as the assistant and then associate professor of Egyptian Archaeology at the University of California, Berkeley, before returning to the American University in Cairo for the professorship in Egyptology that he still holds.

Rosalie David (born 1947)

Professor Rosalie David OBE holds numerous titles, including:

- Director of the Manchester Mummy Project
- Director of the KNH Centre for Biological and Forensic Studies in Egyptology at the University of Manchester. The project was set up in 2003 to enable the unique opportunity for university training in biomedical Egyptology
- Director of the International Mummy Database (University of Manchester)
- Director of the Schistosomiasis Investigation Project (University of Manchester)

Professor David set up the Manchester Mummy Project in order to study the 24 human and 34 animal mummies in the Manchester Museum collection. Before the project was set up, mummies were X-rayed using portable equipment in galleries or in situ at the find site. Manchester now provides permanent facilities for ongoing mummy-related research. Recent successes include discovering the DNA of a schistosomiasis (bilharzia) worm found inside one of the mummies.

Manchester is also home to a tissue bank, which includes a collection of Egyptian mummified tissue from mummies held in various international museums. The tissue bank is a modern resource for DNA, which can provide information about these Egyptians of the past, and a real pioneering project.

Professor David is the first female Egyptology professor in the United Kingdom and has taught Egyptology for more than 25 years. She received an OBE from the Queen in recognition of her services to Egyptology in the New Year Honours List of 2003.

Index

• *W* •

Notes

Notes

Notes

Notes

Notes

Notes

FOR DUMMIES®

Do Anything. Just Add Dummies

PROPERTY

UK editions

Buying and Selling a Home
978-0-7645-7027-8

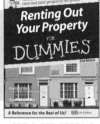

Renting Out Your Property
978-0-470-02921-3

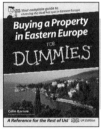

Buying a Property in Eastern Europe
978-0-7645-7047-6

PERSONAL FINANCE

Investing
978-0-7645-7023-0

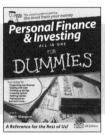

Personal Finance & Investing ALL-IN-ONE
978-0-470-51510-5

Bookkeeping
978-0-470-05815-2

BUSINESS

Starting a Business
978-0-7645-7018-6

Marketing
978-0-7645-7056-8

Business Plans
978-0-7645-7026-1

Answering Tough Interview Questions For Dummies (978-0-470-01903-0)

Arthritis For Dummies (978-0-470-02582-6)

Being the Best Man For Dummies (978-0-470-02657-1)

British History For Dummies (978-0-470-03536-8)

Building Self-Confidence For Dummies (978-0-470-01669-5)

Buying a Home on a Budget For Dummies (978-0-7645-7035-3)

Children's Health For Dummies (978-0-470-02735-6)

Cognitive Behavioural Therapy For Dummies (978-0-470-01838-5)

Cricket For Dummies (978-0-470-03454-5)

CVs For Dummies (978-0-7645-7017-9)

Detox For Dummies (978-0-470-01908-5)

Diabetes For Dummies (978-0-470-05810-7)

Divorce For Dummies (978-0-7645-7030-8)

DJing For Dummies (978-0-470-03275-6)

eBay.co.uk For Dummies (978-0-7645-7059-9)

English Grammar For Dummies (978-0-470-05752-0)

Gardening For Dummies (978-0-470-01843-9)

Genealogy Online For Dummies (978-0-7645-7061-2)

Green Living For Dummies (978-0-470-06038-4)

Hypnotherapy For Dummies (978-0-470-01930-6)

Life Coaching For Dummies (978-0-470-03135-3)

Neuro-linguistic Programming For Dummies (978-0-7645-7028-5)

Nutrition For Dummies (978-0-7645-7058-2)

Parenting For Dummies (978-0-470-02714-1)

Pregnancy For Dummies (978-0-7645-7042-1)

Rugby Union For Dummies (978-0-470-03537-5)

Self Build and Renovation For Dummies (978-0-470-02586-4)

Starting a Business on eBay.co.uk For Dummies (978-0-470-02666-3)

Starting and Running an Online Business For Dummies (978-0-470-05768-1)

The GL Diet For Dummies (978-0-470-02753-0)

The Romans For Dummies (978-0-470-03077-6)

Thyroid For Dummies (978-0-470-03172-8)

UK Law and Your Rights For Dummies (978-0-470-02796-7)

Writing a Novel & Getting Published For Dummies (978-0-470-05910-4)

FOR DUMMIES®

Do Anything. Just Add Dummies

HOBBIES

978-0-7645-5232-8

978-0-7645-6847-3

978-0-7645-5476-6

Also available:

Art For Dummies
(978-0-7645-5104-8)

Aromatherapy For Dummies
(978-0-7645-5171-0)

Bridge For Dummies
(978-0-471-92426-5)

Card Games For Dummies
(978-0-7645-9910-1)

Chess For Dummies
(978-0-7645-8404-6)

Improving Your Memory
For Dummies
(978-0-7645-5435-3)

Massage For Dummies
(978-0-7645-5172-7)

Meditation For Dummies
(978-0-471-77774-8)

Photography For Dummies
(978-0-7645-4116-2)

Quilting For Dummies
(978-0-7645-9799-2)

EDUCATION

978-0-7645-7206-7

978-0-7645-5581-7

978-0-7645-5422-3

Also available:

Algebra For Dummies
(978-0-7645-5325-7)

Algebra II For Dummies
(978-0-471-77581-2)

Astronomy For Dummies
(978-0-7645-8465-7)

Buddhism For Dummies
(978-0-7645-5359-2)

Calculus For Dummies
(978-0-7645-2498-1)

Forensics For Dummies
(978-0-7645-5580-0)

Islam For Dummies
(978-0-7645-5503-9)

Philosophy For Dummies
(978-0-7645-5153-6)

Religion For Dummies
(978-0-7645-5264-9)

Trigonometry For Dummies
(978-0-7645-6903-6)

PETS

978-0-470-03717-1

978-0-7645-8418-3

978-0-7645-5275-5

Also available:

Labrador Retrievers
For Dummies
(978-0-7645-5281-6)

Aquariums For Dummies
(978-0-7645-5156-7)

Birds For Dummies
(978-0-7645-5139-0)

Dogs For Dummies
(978-0-7645-5274-8)

Ferrets For Dummies
(978-0-7645-5259-5)

Golden Retrievers
For Dummies
(978-0-7645-5267-0)

Horses For Dummies
(978-0-7645-9797-8)

Jack Russell Terriers
For Dummies
(978-0-7645-5268-7)

Puppies Raising & Training
Diary For Dummies
(978-0-7645-0876-9)

FOR DUMMIES®

The easy way to get more done and have more fun

LANGUAGES

978-0-7645-5193-2 **978-0-7645-5193-2** **978-0-7645-5196-3**

Also available:

Chinese For Dummies
(978-0-471-78897-3)

Chinese Phrases
For Dummies
(978-0-7645-8477-0)

French Phrases For Dummies
(978-0-7645-7202-9)

German For Dummies
(978-0-7645-5195-6)

Italian Phrases For Dummies
(978-0-7645-7203-6)

Japanese For Dummies
(978-0-7645-5429-2)

Latin For Dummies
(978-0-7645-5431-5)

Spanish Phrases
For Dummies
(978-0-7645-7204-3)

Spanish Verbs For Dummies
(978-0-471-76872-2)

Hebrew For Dummies
(978-0-7645-5489-6)

MUSIC AND FILM

978-0-7645-9904-0 **978-0-7645-2476-9** **978-0-7645-5105-5**

Also available:

Bass Guitar For Dummies
(978-0-7645-2487-5)

Blues For Dummies
(978-0-7645-5080-5)

Classical Music For Dummies
(978-0-7645-5009-6)

Drums For Dummies
(978-0-471-79411-0)

Jazz For Dummies
(978-0-471-76844-9)

Opera For Dummies
(978-0-7645-5010-2)

Rock Guitar For Dummies
(978-0-7645-5356-1)

Screenwriting For Dummies
(978-0-7645-5486-5)

Songwriting For Dummies
(978-0-7645-5404-9)

Singing For Dummies
(978-0-7645-2475-2)

HEALTH, SPORTS & FITNESS

  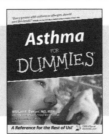

978-0-7645-7851-9 **978-0-7645-5623-4** **978-0-7645-4233-6**

Also available:

Controlling Cholesterol
For Dummies
(978-0-7645-5440-7)

Dieting For Dummies
(978-0-7645-4149-0)

High Blood Pressure
For Dummies
(978-0-7645-5424-7)

Martial Arts For Dummies
(978-0-7645-5358-5)

Pilates For Dummies
(978-0-7645-5397-4)

Power Yoga For Dummies
(978-0-7645-5342-4)

Weight Training
For Dummies
(978-0-471-76845-6)

Yoga For Dummies
(978-0-7645-5117-8)

Available wherever books are sold. For more information or to order direct go to www.wiley.com or call 0800 243407 (Non UK call +44 1243 843296)

FOR DUMMIES®

Helping you expand your horizons and achieve your potential

INTERNET

The Internet FOR DUMMIES

978-0-7645-8996-6

Search Engine Optimization FOR DUMMIES

978-0-471-97998-2

Creating Web Pages FOR DUMMIES

978-0-470-08030-6

Also available:

Building a Web Site For Dummies, 2nd Edition (978-0-7645-7144-2)

Blogging For Dummies For Dummies (978-0-471-77084-8)

eBay.co.uk For Dummies (978-0-7645-7059-9)

Web Analysis For Dummies (978-0-470-09824-0)

Web Design For Dummies, 2nd Edition (978-0-471-78117-2)

Creating Web Pages All-in-One Desk Reference For Dummies (978-0-7645-4345-6)

DIGITAL MEDIA

Digital Photography FOR DUMMIES

978-0-7645-9802-9

iPod & iTunes FOR DUMMIES

978-0-470-04894-8

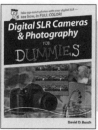

Digital SLR Cameras & Photography FOR DUMMIES

978-0-7645-9803-6

Also available:

Photoshop CS2 For Dummies (978-0-7645-9571-4)

Podcasting For Dummies (978-0-471-74898-4)

Digital Photography All-In-One Desk Reference For Dummies (978-0-470-03743-0)

Digital Photo Projects For Dummies (978-0-470-12101-6)

BlackBerry For Dummies (978-0-471-75741-2)

Zune For Dummies (978-0-470-12045-3)

COMPUTER BASICS

PCs FOR DUMMIES

978-0-7645-8958-4

Laptops FOR DUMMIES

978-0-470-05432-1

Windows XP FOR DUMMIES

978-0-471-75421-3

Also available:

Macs For Dummies, 9th Edition (978-0-470-04849-8)

Windows Vista All-in-One Desk Reference For Dummies (978-0-471-74941-7)

Office 2007 All-in-One Desk Reference For Dummies (978-0-471-78279-7)

Windows XP For Dummies, 2nd Edition (978-0-7645-7326-2)

PCs All-in-One Desk Reference For Dummies, 3rd Edition (978-0-471-77082-4)

Upgrading & Fixing PCs For Dummies, 7th Edition (978-0-470-12102-3)

The Ancient Greeks For Dummies®

Cheat Sheet

Map of Ancient Greece

The Ancient Greeks For Dummies®

Cheat Sheet

Timeline

2600 BC	Beginning of the Minoan Period
1450 BC	Development of Linear B writing
1400 BC	Foundation of Mycenaean Palaces

BRONZE AGE

1370 BC	Palace complex at Knossos destroyed. Minoan civilisation comes to an end
c.1250 BC	The Trojan War
1200 BC	Destruction of Mycenaean Palaces. Doric invasions
1000 BC	End of Mycenaean civilisation

IRON AGE

776 BC	First Olympic Games
c.750 BC	The *Iliad* and the *Odyssey* composed. Greek alphabet established. Greek colonies established in Sicily and Southern Italy
630 BC	Colony of Cyrene established
594 BC	Solon renews the laws of Athens
508 BC	Kleisthenes reforms the Athenian constitution and Athens becomes a democracy!
490 BC	Battle of Marathon: Greece versus Persia I (Greece wins!)
483 BC	Athenians discover silver in the mines at Laureion
480 BC	Battle of Thermopylae: Greece versus Persia II. Battle of Salamis

479 BC	Battle of Plataea (Greece wins . . . eventually!)
477 BC	Athens establishes the Delian League
461–445 BC	First Peloponnesian War: Athens versus Sparta (draw)
431–404 BC	Second Peloponnesian War: Athens versus Sparta (Sparta wins)
430 BC	Plague in Athens
429 BC	Death of Pericles
415 BC	Athenian expedition to Sicily defeated
399 BC	Socrates tried and executed
359 BC	Philip II becomes King of Macedonia
356 BC	Alexander the Great born
331 BC	Alexander the Great defeats the Persians at Gaugamela and becomes the new King of Persia!
323 BC	Death of Alexander the Great
322 BC	Death of Aristotle
300 BC	Ptolemy the Great founds the library at Alexandria
214 BC	Philip V of Macedonia defeated by the Romans
172 BC	Macedonia becomes a Roman province
146 BC	Romans invade Greece and take control. Ancient Greece comes to an end

For Dummies: Bestselling Book Series for Beginners

The Ancient Greeks

FOR

DUMMIES®

The Ancient Greeks

FOR

DUMMIES®

by Stephen Batchelor

John Wiley & Sons, Ltd

The Ancient Greeks For Dummies®

Published by
John Wiley & Sons, Ltd
The Atrium
Southern Gate
Chichester
West Sussex
PO19 8SQ
England

E-mail (for orders and customer service enquires): cs-books@wiley.co.uk

Visit our Home Page on www.wiley.com

For general information on our other products and services, please contact our Customer Care Department within the U.S. at 800-762-2974, outside the U.S. at 317-572-3993, or fax 317-572-4002.

For technical support, please visit www.wiley.com/techsupport.

Wiley also publishes its books in a variety of electronic formats. Some content that appears in print may not be available in electronic books.

British Library Cataloguing in Publication Data: A catalogue record for this book is available from the British Library

ISBN: 978-0-470-98787-2 (P/B)

Printed and bound in Great Britain by TJ International, Padstow, Cornwall

10 9 8 7 6 5 4 3 2

WILEY

About the Author

Stephen Batchelor has taught Ancient History and Classical Studies for a number of years to a wide variety of student groups and is currently Head of School for Creative and Visual Arts at Mid-Kent College. He has travelled extensively in the Mediterranean and worked there an archaeological tour guide. He has written book reviews for *Current Archaeology* and *History Today*. *The Ancient Greeks For Dummies* is his first book.

Author's Acknowledgements

This is my first book and there are several people that I would like to thank: Rachael and the team at Wiley for all their supportive comments and feedback, Dr Neil Faulkner for all his help over the years and his recommendation for this project, both my parents for their continued support, and my partner Samantha for putting up with so many lost weekends while I just did 'a bit more on the book'.

I'd like to dedicate this book to my father, Alan Batchelor, and thank him for absolutely everything. I know you've always preferred the Romans, but this one is for you, Dad.

Publisher's Acknowledgements

We're proud of this book; please send us your comments through our Dummies online registration form located at www.dummies.com/register/.

Some of the people who helped bring this book to market include the following:

Acquisitions, Editorial, and Media Development

Project Editor: Rachael Chilvers

Content Editor: Nicole Burnett

Development Editor: Brian Kramer

Copy Editor: Charlie Wilson

Proofreader: Rachael Wilkie

Technical Editor: Dr Ian Rutherford

Executive Editor: Samantha Spickernell

Publisher: Jason Dunne

Executive Project Editor: Daniel Mersey

Cover Photos: © Roger Cracknell 05/London/Alamy

Cartoons: Rich Tennant (www.the5thwave.com)

Composition Services

Project Coordinator: Erin Smith

Layout and Graphics: Reuben W. Davis, Stephanie D. Jumper, Tobin Wilkerson

Indexer: Christine Spina Karpeles

Special Help

Brand Reviewer: Carrie Burchfield

Publishing and Editorial for Technology Dummies

    Richard Swadley, Vice President and Executive Group Publisher

    Andy Cummings, Vice President and Publisher

    Mary Bednarek, Executive Acquisitions Director

    Mary C. Corder, Editorial Director

Publishing for Consumer Dummies

    Diane Graves Steele, Vice President and Publisher

    Joyce Pepple, Acquisitions Director

Composition Services

    Gerry Fahey, Vice President of Production Services

    Debbie Stailey, Director of Composition Services

Contents at a Glance

Table of Contents

Introduction

*W*hen I think about it, I've always been interested in Ancient Greece but I spent a lot of my time not realising that I was. When I was very young I went to Cyprus on holiday and was fascinated by the ruined statues and mosaics. As I grew a little older I loved films like *Jason and the Argonauts* and *Clash of the Titans* that were endlessly repeated on television at Christmas. What I didn't understand was the 'Greekness' of these things. I knew that I liked the great stories and scary monsters but it was only when I got older that I realised that they were just a tiny part of the fascinating world of the ancient Greeks.

What interested me most was the fact that, despite the gap of over 2,000 years, the world of the ancient Greeks seemed very real and contemporary. They had the same concerns and problems as people do today and went about dealing with them in tremendously imaginative ways. The Greeks were hugely creative and although they lived in a world with a very dominant religion, they never stopped looking for new solutions to age old problems.

About This Book

Studying the ancient Greeks can be a bit frustrating because an awful lot of their story doesn't take place in Greece but elsewhere in the Mediterranean. The other big frustration is that Greek history isn't really a continuum. By that I mean that it doesn't start at Point X and finish at Y. The Greeks were a fractious bunch, always fighting amongst themselves and with other people, so tracing their story can get quite complicated!

It's worth the effort though. The most wonderful thing about the Greeks is the legacy that they left behind, which you can see, touch, and immerse yourself in. The huge amount of archaeological evidence that still survives is breathtaking. From massive buildings like the Parthenon in Athens to the tiniest coin, each piece of physical evidence reveals something interesting about the way the Greeks lived and what they did.

Another fantastic resource is the huge amount of written evidence that's survived; plays, poems, works of history, philosophy, science, medicine, and epic poetry that read like the plot of a Hollywood action film have all survived for over 2,000 years. Throughout this book I try to quote as much as possible from these original sources because it's always best to hear it from the horse's mouth!

This book introduces you to the world of the ancient Greeks – a world part bizarre, part visionary, and part bloodthirsty. It's not an attempt to tell you *everything* about the Greeks; more a way of getting started so that you can carry on exploring their world – and there's enough to keep you going for the rest of your life!

Conventions Used in This Book

The two main issues when looking at any period of ancient history are language and dates!

The biggest of the two is language. The ancient Greeks used an entirely different alphabet to ours, and consequently the words seem strange and different, although a great many English words come from ancient Greek ones. To try to make things easier throughout the book I put any Greek word in *italics*. So, for example, when I'm talking about an elected official in ancient Athens I call him an *arkhon* because that's the word that the Greeks used.

You might find that in other books some Greek words are spelt differently (often using a c instead of a k) or that the author uses the proper Greek punctuation marks on words. Don't worry – it's still the same word but I choose to use the simpler version.

The other issue is using dates. Virtually every date that I use in the book has BC after it, meaning 'Before Christ'. That's because the bulk of ancient Greek history took place during the two thousand years or so before the accepted date of Jesus's birth. (I go into more detail about BC and AD in Chapter 1). Of course, this is our dating system, not the one that the Greeks would have used.

Oh yes, one other thing – places. I mention place names all the time. In most cases you can find the places on the map on the Cheat Sheet at the front of the book. In the case of battles, the Greeks often fought in a big open space like a field or a beach, and they'd avoid fighting near towns if possible. Pinpointing these out-of-the-way places can be really difficult so I try to refer to the town nearest the battle.

Differences of opinion

One of the exciting things about history is that it is always up for debate. Answers are never 100 per cent right or wrong and interpretation (understanding the 'why' rather than the 'when') is the most important thing. You can probably expect to read some things in this book that seem to disagree with things you've read elsewhere. When you're dealing with events that took place over 2,000 years ago there'll always be differences of opinion, just as there'll always be new archaeological discoveries that completely blow older theories away. In a few years' time whole new schools of thought on many of the issues that this book discusses might emerge. I hope so, because that's what keeps history fun!

How This Book Is Organised

This book is split into five specific parts, all covering a different aspect of ancient Greece.

Part 1: Travelling Back in Time

Part I is all about establishing who the Greeks were and where they came from, which isn't quite as straightforward as you might think – even the Greeks weren't sure! Modern historians have established that the really ancient Minoan and Mycenaean cultures were the forerunners of the ancient Greeks and I look at them in Chapter 2. After that comes the story of how the Greeks came into being and spread all over the Mediterranean. I also look at how they developed into such amazing warriors. It was just as well they did because the last chapter in Part I focuses on the wars with the Persian Empire when it seemed as if ancient Greece might actually be wiped out.

Part 11: Athens to Alexander: The Rise and Fall of Empires

Part II is a fantastic rollercoaster of a story! It looks at the period of greatest Greek success following the Persian Wars and how the city of Athens became so wealthy and dominant. However, after a difficult period a new power emerged in the north: Macedonia. Under Alexander the Great the Macedonians went on tremendous military campaigns and built up an empire that stretched as far as India. This didn't last either, as after Alexander's death the empire broke up and new kingdoms emerged. The last chapter in this part deals with how the kingdoms fought amongst themselves until they all finally succumbed to the threat of the Romans. Ancient Greece was effectively at an end.

Part III: Living a Greek Life

So what was being an ancient Greek actually like? Part III looks at life in the towns and cities of ancient Greece from the food they ate to what sort of exercises people did at the gym, to what happened when people got divorced. I include specific chapters on theatre, art, architecture, and what life was like in the countryside.

Part IV: Mythology, Religion, and Belief

One of the things that people find most interesting about the ancient Greeks is the world of mythology. The stories about gods, heroes, and monsters were dominant themes throughout Greek life, influencing their plays, literature, and art. Religion was a major part of public life, full of strange and bizarre rituals. Part IV is all about these themes with a focus on how the Greeks lived their lives surrounded by these ideas and based a lot of what they did on examples from mythology.

This part ends with a look at the Greek philosophers, the men who challenged these beliefs in gods and monsters, and set out to make sense of the world using their own powers of logic and reason. They were an odd bunch but their ideas are fascinating!

Part V: The Part of Tens

This final part has four brief chapters intended to give you an idea of where to go next to further your experience of the ancient Greeks. I include chapters on places to go and books to read. Chapter 23 is all about Greek inventions – you'll be surprised at some of the things that the Greeks came up with but they're all true, promise! Chapter 25 is about interesting but slightly dodgy characters; the people in history who are worth a second look and a revaluation.

Icons Used in This Book

Throughout the book I use a series of icons to capture your attention. I hope they're as useful to the reader as they were to the writer!

As much as possible I try to use bits of what the Greeks actually said. Reading something first-hand is fascinating and the huge amount of writing that survives from Ancient Greece makes this easy to do.

Just like urban myths today, a lot of 'facts' about ancient Greece aren't actually true. Occasionally I point them out with this icon.

This icon pinpoints important information to bear in mind when getting to grips with the ancient Greeks.

Some of the stories from ancient Greece are like the plots of Hollywood films and increasingly they are being made into them. This icon means that I'm referencing a film you may want to check out.

Sometimes I include information that's interesting but not vital. This icon highlights more complicated stuff that you can skip over if you want to.

Where to Go from Here

You can start at the beginning so that you have the historical context before you start looking at how the Greeks lived their lives. Alternatively, you can start with Part IV, all about religion and mythology and where the Greeks considered that they came from. This is just as important to understand as the historical background.

Each chapter in the book is written around a specific topic so you can really dive in anywhere. If you want to know about Alexander the Great, go to Chapter 11. If Greek drama is your thing then Chapter 16 is the one for you. I include cross-references in the chapters so if something comes up that's mentioned in more detail elsewhere, you're directed to it.

Whichever way you choose to enjoy the book, I hope you find it fun and interesting.

Part I
Travelling Back in Time

© RICHTENNANT

"Well, that was just terrific! We pull up to shore, announce that we're Minoans bearing the framework for civilisation, and you start eating houmous with your fingers."

In this part . . .

So who were the Greeks? Well, it isn't as obvious as you might think. In this part I look at where the Greeks came from and what made them Greek. I go on to look at how these people spread out all across the Mediterranean until the Greeks were living as far away as modern Spain and Turkey.

Oh yes, and I also consider the Minotaur, human sacrifice, and huge battles with the Persians . . .

Chapter 1

When, Where, What, Who?
Meeting the Ancient Greeks

. . . .

In This Chapter

▶ Exploring the land and sea of ancient Greece

▶ Organising ancient Greek history

▶ Writing and reading ancient Greek

. . . .

*M*odern Greece is very different to the Greece of the ancient world.

Today, Greece is a medium sized member of the European Union that uses the euro as its currency. To the north-east it's bordered by Macedonia and to the north-west Albania. Most people think of it as a popular tourist destination, and during the summer months people from around the world flock to the seaside resorts on the mainland and on islands like Crete and Rhodes.

For these visitors, the material remains of the ancient world are still visible. Tourists can look at ruined temples and statues while they sit drinking Mythos beer in bars and restaurants named after Greek gods and heroes. Often, they stay in towns whose names are redolent of the ancient world, like Athens, Delphi, Olympia, and Corinth.

Much like the rest of the Mediterranean, visitors to Greece find great food, friendly people with a strong sense of honour and family values, and a seductively relaxed way of life that seems to go at a slower pace than the rest of the world.

This idyllic and fascinating holiday destination, however, is in sharp contrast to the focus of this book – the Greece of the ancient world. Ancient Greece is about huge events, incredible battles, and tremendous advances in science and understanding that took place over 2,000 years ago.

In this chapter I put the ancient Greeks in historical and geographical context – answering the questions 'When?' and 'Where?'. I also address the fundamental questions about them – precisely who they were, where they came from, and why what they did is still incredibly important.

Understanding Why the Ancient Greeks Matter

Hopefully, you have already decided that the ancient Greeks are worth bothering with – otherwise you wouldn't be reading this book.

Falling for all things ancient Greek

Simply put, the ancient Greeks were amazing. Their society and culture is endlessly fascinating. If you don't believe me, try the following for size:

- ✔ Zeus, the ancient Greeks' most powerful god, changed himself into a bull, a swan, and a shower of gold so that he could make love to beautiful women without his wife finding out. Oh yes, and his wife was also his sister. (See Chapter 19 for more on Zeus and the rest of the ancient Greek gods.)

- ✔ Ancient Greeks thought that the world was an island entirely surrounded by water that looked rather like a fried egg. (See Chapter 19.)

- ✔ They invented the Olympic Games, and their greatest Olympian trained by carrying a cow around for four years. (See Chapter 16.)

- ✔ The Greeks had elaborate religious cults that participated in strange rituals, including swimming with pigs. (See Chapter 21.)

- ✔ One of their philosophers jumped into a volcano to prove he was a god. When he didn't come back, people realised that he wasn't one. (See Chapter 22.)

Noting the Greeks' contributions

Everybody goes on about the Romans and the massive advances in civilised life that they were responsible for such as central heating, straight roads, and Latin. Well, the Romans certainly did a lot, but they were preceded by the Greeks, who were pretty inventive too.

The ancient Greeks are responsible for a fascinating number of creations and inventions: money, democracy, written history, bras, satire, and musical notation are all things that the Greeks are at least partly responsible for creating. You can read more about these and other inventions in Chapter 23.

While inventions are all well and good, the most impressive thing that the Greeks came up with was civilisation itself. *Civilisation*, the whole idea of living together in large towns and cities, was a fairly new concept that the Greeks initiated in Europe.

So who were these fascinating, inventive, and civilised people?

Meeting the People of Ancient Greece

Modern Greece is very different from the Greece of the ancient world. The biggest difference is that what you may think of Greece and being Greek is nothing like the ancients' experience.

'Being Greek' in the ancient world meant that you shared a way of life with people, rather than the citizenship of a single country. Greeks lived all across the Mediterranean: Spain, North Africa, Sicily, southern Italy, Asia Minor (modern-day Turkey), the Aegean islands, and of course the land mass that folk call modern Greece. This way of life included:

- ✔ The language that you spoke (see the later section 'Talking the Talk: Ancient Greek Language').
- ✔ The gods that you believed in (see Chapter 19).
- ✔ The food you ate (see Chapter 15).
- ✔ All the other things that make up an individual's identity.

Furthermore, the Greeks of the ancient world didn't necessarily consider themselves to be Greek; rather, they classified themselves as being citizens of the towns or cities from which they came. Greeks only really considered themselves to be Greek in comparison to foreigners. So an Athenian talking to an Egyptian described himself as a Greek, whereas if the same Athenian was talking to somebody from Corinth (another Greek town), he called himself an Athenian.

Locating Ancient Greece

Ancient Greece was very spread out, which means that the people, ideas, and events that I talk about in this book came from and took place all around the Mediterranean and sometimes beyond, as Figure 1-1 shows. Eventually, there were people who considered themselves to be Greek in Spain, France, Italy, North Africa, Libya, and Asia Minor – and in Greece itself of course.

The most densely populated area was the land mass known as Greece today. It's an area that is really dominated by two things – the sea and very large mountain ranges. For the ancient Greeks, the mountain ranges meant that sections of this big slab of land were sometimes very disconnected from each other. This is one of the reasons why people tended to think of themselves in local terms rather than national ones.

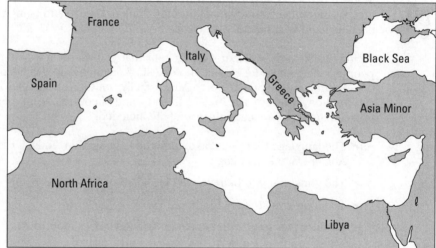

Figure 1-1:
The Ancient
Mediter-
ranean.

Greece isn't a very large land mass, and wherever you stand in it you're unlikely to be more than about 50 kilometres from the sea. The land is fertile but also very hilly, which means that it doesn't have vast plains of workable farmland. These two factors are important when considering why so many Greeks decided to leave the land mass and create new towns on the nearby islands and elsewhere in the Mediterranean (see Chapter 7).

Separating the region

You can divide Greece in two at the Gulf of Corinth, the large body of water that runs through the middle of the region:

- **To the north:** North of the Gulf was the larger part of mainland Greece, although the south was much more heavily populated. The biggest city in this part of Greece was Thebes and also located in the region was the sacred site of Delphi, which was home to the famous oracle. (See Chapter 21 for more.)

- **To the south:** Southern Greece was divided in two by the Peloponnese mountain range. Most of the famous cities of ancient Greece were here: Sparta, Olympia, Corinth, Argos, and, to the north-east, Athens.

Touring the islands and beyond

Although the Greek mainland is fairly small, bits of what historians consider to be ancient Greece were spread all over the eastern Mediterranean. All the places that people now go to on holiday – approximately 1,400 islands – were part of ancient Greece, as well other more distant lands.

Here's a brief guide to some of the most notable parts of ancient Greece:

- **Euboia:** The big peninsula that's just off the eastern coast of Greece. Its people considered themselves to be very different and separate from those on the mainland.

- **The Cyclades:** The big group of islands in the south, including places like Naxos, Paros, and Delos. The ancient Greeks called this group 'The Circle'.

- **Asia Minor:** The western coast of modern-day Turkey. During the Dark Ages, loads of Greeks from the mainland moved there and created the new Greek areas of Aeolia and Ionia (for more, see Chapter 3).

- **Thrace:** At the top of Figure 1-1, the area is now southern Bulgaria. For the ancient Greeks, this area was wild, hilly country full of warlike tribes – definitely a place to avoid!

- **Crete, Rhodes, and Cyprus:** Big important islands to the south-east that developed their own civilisations independent of the Greek mainland. In fact, civilisation started on Crete; read all about it in Chapter 2.

- **The western islands:** Important islands to the west of mainland Greece. Corcyra (modern-day Corfu), Cephallenia, Ithaca, and Zakynthos were all in this part of the Mediterranean.

- **Other islands:** Of the 1,400 islands, only about 250 were inhabited and many of those by not more than about 100 people. Each of the islands has its own fascinating stories and episodes. Islands like Lemnos, Miletus, Samos, and Lesbos are important to the story of the ancient Greeks.

You can visit these islands and many contain fascinating archaeological evidence, some of which is remarkably well preserved, from enormous chunks of ancient temples to the small personal possessions that people used in everyday life. Chapter 26 suggests several places that you might like to visit when you've finished reading this book!

Clarifying When It All Happened

The period of history that historians consider to be the time of the ancient Greeks is very big. Broadly speaking, it dates from the very early beginnings of the Minoan civilisation in Crete around 2800 BC up until the defeat of the Macedonian king Perseus by the Romans in 168 BC. That's more than 2,500 years – 500 years longer than the time that's passed between the birth of Jesus and the present day.

Clearly, a book of this size can't cover everything that happened during this vast expanse of history – and I don't intend to try! Most scholars and historians agree that the history of Greek civilisation went through several distinct phases (see the later section 'Establishing chronology'). Of these I devote most pages to discussing the period between 900 and 300 BC. That's the period that I think of as ancient Greece: Homer, the Persian Wars, Socrates, Greek tragedy, the Parthenon, and Alexander the Great all came about during this time.

Playing the dating game: BC or AD?

All the dates that I use in the book are followed by the suffix *BC*, meaning 'Before Jesus Christ'. This means that something taking place in 545 BC occurred 545 years before the year in which Jesus Christ is thought to have been born. You count dates BC backwards, so that the year 344 BC was the one that immediately followed 345 BC.

Events that took place *after* the birth of Jesus are preceded by *AD*, which stands for the Latin phrase *Anno Domini*, meaning the year of Jesus's birth (AD 1 – there's no year zero). So I'm writing this book in the year AD 2007, 2007 years after the birth of Jesus. You count dates AD forwards. So this book was published in 2008, the year immediately following 2007.

Sometimes when you read a book or visit a website about the ancient world, you see dates followed by *BCE* and *CE*, meaning 'Before the Common Era' and 'Common Era' (confusingly, also known as 'Before the Christian Era' and 'Christian Era'). This convention has come about so that people who don't recognise Jesus as the son of God can use a dating system to represent the years in question without the assumption of Christ's divinity. In this book I decided to stick with BC and AD because I've always used them and it's never done me any harm.

Figuring out dates for the ancient Greeks

Obviously, the Greeks didn't think about things in terms of BC and AD, but they also didn't think in terms of the year having a number.

- Generally speaking, people in the ancient world used major events as a method of dating rather than specifically numbered years. So, for example, an ancient Greek may describe himself as having been born five years after the battle of Marathon (see Chapter 6).

- Another common method was to date an event by its proximity to the Olympic Games. For example, 'The Spartans attacked our town two years after the 25th Olympiad'.

Of course, things were often not this simple. For a mind-reeling discussion of the intricacies of the ancient Greek calendar, check out Chapter 15.

Establishing chronology

The following is a brief chronology of the whole of ancient Greek history. Of course, the ancient Greeks themselves wouldn't have thought about their history in these terms and their ideas of how the world was progressing were very different (see Chapter 19), but modern historians generally agree on the following sequence of periods.

The Bronze Age: 2700–1100 BC

This period is the earliest of Greek history. During these years the first European civilisation appeared on the island of Crete and became known as *Minoan*. This period was strange and wonderful and seems very alien to modern sensibilities.

Civilisation soon sprang up on mainland Greece, and historians refer to this culture as *Mycenaean*. Around 1300 BC something cataclysmic happened in Crete; the Minoan period came to an end, and the people scattered. Read all about these earliest ancient Greeks in Chapter 2.

The Dark Ages: 1100–900 BC

The Dark Ages are so named because historians know very little about what was going on. Most scholars describe it as time of travelling, and that pretty much sums it up. All the people who left mainland Greece after the end of the Bronze Age travelled far and wide, setting up new towns all around the Mediterranean. As a result trade and diplomacy began in earnest too.

Archaeology: Answering the impossible

Written source material from ancient Greece reveals a phenomenal amount about the Greeks and their lives. But this source material is never truly complete. The science of archaeology has been hugely useful in understanding who the Greeks were and where they came from. A little over 100 years ago we didn't know anything about the Minoans or Mycenaeans. Now, thanks to archaeological discoveries in the early years of the 20th century we know how influential these civilisations were on the development of the ancient Greeks (see Chapter 2 for more on this). New archaeological discoveries are continually being made, producing more and more 'material culture' to sit alongside the written sources that we've always had. In this book there's a bias towards written evidence (because it really helps to emphasise points that I make!) but don't ignore the impact of archaeology!

Early Greece: 900–490 BC

This period was when Greece started to grow up. The hundreds of communities and colonies that had been established during the Dark Ages grew into new societies and what became known as *city-states*.

These city-states had different forms of government, but remarkably the market town of Athens decided upon the system of *democracy*. You can read about how it happened in Chapter 4.

All the city-states soon faced a major challenge, however, when the immense Persian Empire launched a series of attacks against them. Look at Chapter 6 to find out how they got on.

The Classical period: 490–350 BC

After dealing with the Persians, the Athenians began throwing their weight around and soon possessed an empire. The money that the empire generated was responsible for some of the fabulous culture that ancient Greece is famous for. You can read more about Athens in Chapter 7 as well as nearly every aspect of Greek life during the Classical period in Part III.

Athens's domination, of course, came to an end when the Peloponnesian War began with Sparta (see Chapter 8). After its defeat, Athens declined in influence and a whole series of squabbles between the city-states broke out with no clear winner. Until . . .

The Hellenistic period: 350–150 BC

. . . the Macedonians arrived on the scene. Under King Philip II, the Macedonians dominated the whole of Greece through both war and diplomacy. Philip's son Alexander then took things further by invading Persia, seizing control of the Persian Empire, and journeying as far as India in a quest of discovery and conquest. You can read more about this brilliant story in Chapter 11.

After Alexander died without a strong heir, his empire broke up into warring territories ruled by his former generals. Eventually, the Romans arrived in the middle of the second century BC, and what we call the Greek period came to an end.

Talking the Talk: Ancient Greek Language

The language that historians and scholars call *ancient Greek* came into being around 1100 BC and first appeared in written form around 750 BC. As I note in the earlier section 'Establishing chronology', this is a time period when all the travelling and colonisation was going on, after the collapse of the Minoan civilisation in Crete.

Developing differences

Language-wise, ancients Greek came in roughly three different types:

- **Dorian Greek** was spoken by people who lived on most parts of the Greek mainland and on the islands of Cyprus and Crete.
- **Ionic Greek** was spoken by people who lived on most of the smaller islands, as well as on the eastern coast of mainland Greece (such as the people of Athens) and the south-western coast of Asia Minor.
- **Aeolian Greek** was spoken by everybody else! This included people who lived in the northern part of the Mediterranean Sea (called the Aegean Sea) and on the north-western coast of Asia Minor.

 Just like today, people also spoke in their own localised dialect. These individuals would all have been able to understand each other, but regional differences existed, even within the three types of Greek mentioned in the preceding bulleted list. (For example, people who lived in Athens spoke a slightly different form of Ionian Greek called *Attic*.) It's the same today: Think of the differences in accent between people in Glasgow and Texas. They speak the same language but with huge regional differences.

(Not) lost in translation

You can read a huge number of ancient Greek dramatic, literary, historical, poetic, and philosophical texts in translation. Many translations are available and they often vary quite considerably. Some people argue that you can never really appreciate the true nature of these works unless you read them in the original Greek but, quite frankly, that's a load of old rubbish!

Translation of these ancient texts has been going on for centuries. It's only because of the work of medieval monks (who zealously made copies) that we still have these amazing works of literature. Modern translators are incredibly skilful at producing work that captures the spirit of ancient Greek literature while still making it accessible to readers.

Try the translations of *The Iliad* and *The Odyssey* by Homer and *The Oresteia* by Aeschylus that have recently been completed by Robert Fagles (available in Penguin Classics). They are vibrant and powerful, retaining all the chutzpah of Homer and Aeschylus while still feeling contemporary today.

In the film *Alexander* (2005), Colin Farrell, who plays Alexander the Great, speaks in his own natural Irish accent, as do all the other Macedonian officers. The more refined Greek characters (the Athenians, for example) speak standard British. This use of modern dialects was a great way of showing that, despite all speaking Greek, the Macedonians would have spoken in a slightly rougher rural dialect as opposed to the more refined Greek of the folks in Athens.

Creating the Greek alphabet

If you spoke ancient Greek, people pretty much all over the Mediterranean could understand you. Part of the reason for this is that some time around 750 BC the Greeks began to use writing to record business transactions and contracts. In doing so, they came up with a method of reproducing the sounds of their language in symbols. The result was the ancient Greek alphabet.

The Greek alphabet was made up of 24 symbols that represented letters or groups of letters, like alpha α and beta β. Figure 1-2 shows the letters of the Greek alphabet.

The ancient Greek alphabet was heavily influenced by the eastern world and ancient Mesopotamia. Indeed, initially the Greeks wrote their script from right to left, like modern Arabic. However, by the Classical period, when many of the great works of literature were produced, the Greeks had adopted the left-to-right writing style familiar to writers of English.

If you look at a modern version of ancient Greek text, it includes accents and marks to suggest where you should leave gaps for breathing when reading it out. These are all modern additions. The Greeks didn't use punctuation initially (it developed during the Hellenistic period) – just plain text. Mind you, as they invented writing as we know it, we can probably let them off for skipping the commas and full stops! The Greeks used spaces between lines of dialogue to indicate a change in the speaker. This system was known as *paragraphos* and the English word 'paragraph' comes from it.

A	B	Γ	Δ	E	Z
Alpha	**Beta**	**Gamma**	**Delta**	**Epsilon**	**Zeta**
(al-fah)	(bay-tah)	(gam-ah)	(del-ta)	(ep-si-lon)	(zay-tah)

H	Θ	I	K	Λ	M
Eta	**Theta**	**Iota**	**Kappa**	**Lambda**	**Mu**
(ay-tah)	(thay-tah)	(eye-o-tah)	(cap-pah)	(lamb-dah)	(mew)

N	Ξ	O	Π	P	Σ
Nu	**Xi**	**Omicron**	**Pi**	**Rho**	**Sigma**
(new)	(zie)	(om-e-cron)	(pie)	(roe)	(sig-mah)

Figure 1-2: The letters of the Greek alphabet.

T	Y	Φ	X	Ψ	Ω
Tau	**Upsilon**	**Phi**	**Chi**	**Psi**	**Omega**
(taw)	(up-si-lon)	(phe)	(che)	(sigh)	(oh-may-gah)

Ancient Greek was a *phonetic* language (the letters of the alphabet represented a single sound) but certain stresses were employed, especially on vowels.

Chapter 2

Encountering Prehistoric Civilisations: The Minoans and Mycenaeans

*T*hese days you can very easily find out about what happened in the past. TV, the Internet, and books like this one mean that you can very quickly and painlessly have dates and facts at your fingertips.

The ancient Greeks didn't have that ability. People living in the first millennium BC didn't know very much about what existed before them, so they filled in the big gaps in knowledge about their own past with myths and legends that explained how their town or city came to be. (See Part IV for more on the ancient Greeks' rich mythological past.)

Indeed, up until about 100 years ago, researchers were still in the dark about what existed *before* the ancient Greeks. Historians relied on myths, poems, stories, and a few ancient historical writings that mention a very successful, pre-Greek civilisation based on the island of Crete, the largest of more than 1,400 islands that lie off the coast of the Grecian mainland.

This chapter is about this early civilisation – the Minoan – as well as the Mycenaean civilisation that followed. These two unusual and hugely successful groups started the chain of events that resulted in what eventually became ancient Greece.

Starting at the Beginning: The Minoan Civilisation

At the beginning of the 20th century, archaeological digs on the island of Crete led by Englishman Sir Arthur Evans revealed the existence of a wealthy, complex civilisation that had built huge palaces. Evans named these people the *Minoans*, after the legendary King Minos (see the later section 'Mythologising the Minoans' for more info). Evan's rediscovery of Minoan culture finally provided a solution to the origins of ancient Greece.

What historians and researchers call the Minoan civilisation flourished from around 2200 to about 1450 BC on the island of Crete. The Minoans weren't Greek, but the culture that grew out of their civilisation had a huge influence on the people living on mainland Greece who eventually become the ancient Greeks.

The archaeological discoveries on Crete show that people had inhabited the island since 7000 BC. Sometime around 2600 BC a great deal of disruption and moving around seems to have happened. At this point Crete became an important centre of civilisation. Historians refer to this period (roughly 3000 to 1200 BC) as the *Bronze Age* because bronze (an alloy of copper and tin) was the most commonly used metal at the time.

Unfortunately, knowledge of the Minoans is limited because they didn't use writing in the way that the later Greeks did. Early Cretan writing seems to have been writing in pictures – like Egyptian hieroglyphics – and later developed into a more recognisable form, a series of letter-like symbols that we would think of as writing; what you might call a *script* like a letter or document. Around 3,000 Minoan tablets have been discovered, and these tablets were written in *Linear B script*, a method of writing that was used in the formation of the early Greek language (see Chapter 1). Unfortunately, because the Minoan tablets are mostly lists of goods or inventories of resources, they're very difficult to translate and don't tell much about Minoan society.

Because no Minoan texts or documents exist, historians have to use the results of archaeology to interpret and make judgements about the civilisation. Hence, the Minoan culture is considered *prehistory*, rather than history.

Organising the civilisation

Researchers do know that at the height of Minoan power (around 1850 BC) the island of Crete was divided into six different political regions, as Figure 2-1 shows. Other palace complexes were on the island, but these six seem to have been the most influential due to their evident wealth and prosperity.

Figure 2-1:
Map of
Minoan
Crete.

The remains of great palace complexes, which have been uncovered during the past hundred years or so, tell researchers that Crete was politically organised. The presence of a palace implies that a monarchy ruled a society, and the towns and cities on the Greek mainland were highly influenced by this arrangement. Later, Greek cities tended to organise themselves around a palace complex.

Of all the Minoan palace complexes, by far the biggest was constructed at Knossos on the north of the island (a 5-acre site with a main building that covered more than three acres by itself). Knossos is one of the most impressive sites that people can still view today (see Chapter 27).

Knossos wasn't just a palace; it was also a seat of government, a stronghold against invasion, and a place for storing goods and wares. The main building contained around 19 rooms, the vast majority of which were used for storage.

Wealth – and in particular the visible display of it – was a prime qualification for rulers in early societies (hence, the impressive scale of Knossos). People during the Minoan period didn't have bank accounts, so they displayed their wealth through the size and contents of their houses. The Minoans didn't have the fast cars or impressive stereo systems of today to spend their money on, so they spent it on wine, olive oil, wool, and grain. Although these items were fairly ordinary, they were vital for existence, and having a lot of them was impressive. Another reason for stockpiling so much stuff was that the Minoans made their money from trade.

Engaging in retail therapy

The Minoans were serious traders. Their economy was based on buying and selling. Have a look at the position of Crete on the Cheat Sheet map. Being down in the south-east of the Mediterranean meant that the civilisation was ideally placed to carry out lots of trade.

Human sacrifice?

One unpleasant religious practice that's often been associated with the Minoans is human sacrifice. Even today academics can't agree on whether this practice actually took place.

Several sites on Crete contain shrines with possible evidence. The best example is a shrine at Anemospilia, where a body of a young man was found in a very unnatural position on top of a platform. He was in a constricted position as if he'd been trussed up in preparation for sacrifice, and a dagger was found on top of the body. This may well have been an isolated incident. But given the fact that Minoans routinely sacrificed hundreds of animals, they could possibly have switched to sacrificing humans on occasions, perhaps when a town or city was facing major problems.

The Minoans were hugely involved in the trade of tin. They didn't mine it themselves but imported it, manufactured, and sold it on. By combining tin with copper from nearby Cyprus, they were able to make bronze. Bronze was used for everything during the Minoan period, especially weapons and tools. Bronze was also in great demand throughout the Mediterranean. A good comparison would be with how important oil is in modern society.

But tin was far from the only thing that the Minoans had for sale. Other popular Minoan products included the following:

- ✔ **Ceramics:** The Minoans produced huge amounts of pottery and decorative items that they sold all around the Mediterranean region, including Greece, Asia Minor, and as far west as Spain. These must-have items were quite simple in design – usually a dark background with decorative images such as trees, fish, and animals.

- ✔ **Gold and silver:** The most valuable of metals, gold and silver were highly prized and used only for jewellery. Wearing it was a sign of real social status. It wasn't until around 600 BC that the Greeks started using coins. Accordingly, amounts of gold and silver were used as a substitute for exchanges of high value.

- ✔ **Timber:** The mountains on Crete were thickly wooded during the Bronze Age; even more so than they are today when forest fires are still a real risk. All the available lumber enabled the Minoans to build many ships. Minoan wood was also highly prized abroad, in places such as Egypt where timber was scarce.

- ✔ **Saffron:** This rare spice was the most exclusive Minoan product. Saffron was highly prized and incredibly expensive – only the very rich could afford it. The spice had a number of uses from flavouring and preserving foods to treating various medical ailments.

✔ **Wool:** Wool has always been a central part of the Greek economy, even at this early stage. Sheep's wool was most commonly used and was taken as raw fibres straight from the sheep before being dyed and spun using a spindle.

As Crete became the leading supplier for many essentials and luxury goods, the island also developed a powerful hold on some of its customers on the nearby Aegean islands. Historians don't know exactly how the relationship between Crete and the surrounding area worked, but the ties must have been a mixture of dependency and colonisation. When the Athenians built a powerful empire more than 1,000 years later (see Chapter 7), contemporary historians made comparisons with the Minoans. Most likely, a lot of neighbouring islands became trading outposts that enabled the Minoans to take Cretan goods farther across the Mediterranean.

Trying to meet the mysterious Minoans

All their wealth and influence presumably brought the Minoan aristocracy a high standard of living, but knowing for sure is difficult. Aside from the spectacular remains of the palace complexes, historians know very little about the lives of these puzzling people.

Getting dressed, Minoan-style

Some illustrations that have survived on fragments of pottery show men wearing clothes rather like kilts or loincloths. Given the hot climate and active lifestyle it was a fairly common form of dress and can be found elsewhere at the time, such as in Ancient Egypt.

Women's outfits were slightly more unusual. The Minoans seem to have invented the bra. The women shown in paintings wear a type of girdle that goes round the back and supports the breasts while leaving them exposed. This unusual garment was certainly not passed on to the Greeks, who were incredibly scrupulous and controlling of female dress and appearance (see Chapter 15).

Worshipping

The one area in which historians do have a little more information is religion. The Minoans often represented their gods through animal symbols, in styles much like the decoration on their pottery.

The Minoans worshipped female deities that represented different aspects of life – a mother goddess who was associated with fertility and others that represented protection of cities, animals, the harvest, and households.

The bull was also an important symbol in Minoan religion and represented a male god that was associated with the sun. In fact, some Minoan art shows young men (and occasionally women) engaging in the bizarre practice of bull leaping. This trial of strength and dexterity required individuals to leap across the back of an untethered, fully grown bull – not dissimilar to the rodeo events in modern America.

Mythologising the Minoans

Of course, this talk of bulls and human sacrifice leads to the most famous story associated with the Minoans: Theseus and the Minotaur. This story is probably a very early example of how the Greeks used myths to explain the gaps in knowledge of their own history.

Theseus and the Minotaur

According to the story, Theseus was a great hero of the city of Athens. (Indeed, a huge number of stories are associated with his legend.) His mother Aethera brought Theseus up in the city of Troezen. When he became a young man, he left home to claim his birthright as the son of Aegeus, the king of Athens, and after many adventures he succeeded in becoming heir to the Athenian throne.

At the time, Minos, the king of Crete, was exacting a grisly annual tribute on the city of Athens: Seven girls and seven boys were taken to Crete and fed to the Minotaur that lurked in the labyrinth beneath Minos's palace. The *Minotaur* was the illegitimate half-man, half-bull son of Minos's wife Pasaphae. The creature fed on human flesh.

In the third year of the tribute, Theseus volunteered to go as one of the seven boys in order to kill the Minotaur and bring the practice to an end. Theseus did kill the Minotaur and was helped by Minos's daughter, Ariadne, who gave Theseus a ball of wool that allowed him to find his way out of the labyrinth and escape with her.

Separating history and 'mythtory'

The story of Theseus has many layers – indeed, I write more about it in Chapter 4. But for now, consider how much the story tells about what the later Greeks knew of the Minoans. The story includes many of the elements I talk about in this section: foreign colonisation, bull worship, large palace complexes, human sacrifice, and bulls.

You can easily see how later Greeks put together some of the elements of Minoan civilisation and came up with a great story that explained the

Minoans' previous dominance over their own part of the world. You can almost call this practice 'mythtory' – a creative filling-in-the-blanks between what you do know.

The story of Theseus shows how myths work – a topic I cover in Chapter 19. But the myth is particularly relevant at this point because the end of the Minoan civilisation certainly involved an intervention from mainland Greece.

Going out with a bang

At some point around 1450 BC, most of the large palaces on Crete were turned to rubble. With Minoan civilisation enjoying such success, why did it come to a sudden end?

The most common explanation is an earthquake, possibly tied in with a volcanic eruption on the island of Thera (modern-day Santorini), around 150 years earlier. Many people have tried to tie this event in with the legend of the lost city of Atlantis. If the volcano theory is true, it explains why so many of the palaces were destroyed around the same time but the dates don't quite match up.

However, some people argue that human intervention may have been involved. One reason for this is that Knossos, the biggest palace of all, appears to have survived for another 50 years or so, perhaps indicating that a war won by those from Knossos led to the large-scale destruction of the other palaces half a century earlier.

Whatever the reason, by 1400 BC Knossos itself had been destroyed and Minoan dominance and civilisation was at an end. The archaeological evidence suggests that human beings destroyed Knossos. If that was the case, only one likely candidate exists: the Mycenaeans, the newly dominant force in the eastern Mediterranean.

Meeting the New Kids on the Block: The Mycenaeans

The Mycenaean civilisation flourished between 1600 BC and the collapse of what's referred to as the Bronze Age civilisation, around about 1100 BC. Later Greeks considered the Mycenaeans to be a warlike people who were bent on conquest and the expansion of their territory, and they put Greece as we know it on the map.

Mycenaean civilisation was based in mainland Greece. As Figure 2-2 shows, its main centres were the cities of Mycenae, Tiryns, Pylos, Athens, and Thebes.

Historians have struggled to identify the origins of the Mycenaean civilisation. Most researchers now agree that the Mycenaens were probably originally from Crete. When the Minoan civilisation began to spread out around 1700 BC, some travellers settled in central Greece. Within a century or so, these individuals had established a new society that was very different from their Minoan ancestors.

Figure 2-2:
The major centres of Mycenaean civilisation.

Separating Minoan and Mycenaean: Trade versus conquest

The Minoan civilisation was primarily based on trade and commerce (see the earlier section 'Engaging in retail therapy'). Although the Minoans must've fought several wars, the empire that they gained was built on trade and exchange.

This wasn't the case with the Mycenaeans. Their civilisation was dominated by a warrior elite who gained status and influence through conquest. To become an important figure a man had to be a great warrior who had conquered towns and taken booty. One great example is the conquest of Crete around 1400 BC. Whether or not the Mycenaeans were responsible for the destruction of the palace of Knossos (skip back to the section 'Going out with a bang' for more), they certainly took advantage of its demise and gained control of Crete as a centrepiece of their huge empire.

One effect of the Mycenaean conquest was that the script they used, which historians call Linear B, became probably the earliest form of ancient Greek.

However, by far the greatest achievement associated with Mycenaean civilisation is the conquest of the immense and wealthy city of Troy on the north-western coast of Asia Minor (modern-day Turkey). The legendary events around this conquest became known as the Trojan War. Read more about this fantastic piece of 'mythtory' in Chapter 21.

Of course, Mycenaean civilisation was much more than just war and conquest, as the following sections explore.

When looking at the Mycenaeans, you're dealing with *prehistory* – no written records exist. Historians must rely on archaeology for most of their knowledge of this civilisation.

Burying the dead

Mycenaeans buried their nobles and warrior dead in beehive-shaped tombs, known as *tholoi*. The contents of many of these larger tombs have enabled modern archaeologists to come to a lot of conclusions about the Mycenaeans.

Nobles were often buried with a lot of *grave goods*, valuable possessions that tell about the person buried. Typical goods include jewellery, armour, gold masks, and weapons.

Conspiring religion

Historians know little about Mycenaean religious practices. The Mycenaeans apparently worshipped a number of the same gods that the later Greeks did, such as Poseidon. However, they probably didn't worship in the same way. Certainly no evidence exists of the sort of temples that cropped up in later periods. (See Chapter 21 for more information on ancient Greek religion.)

Organising socially

The way the Mycenaeans organised their society influenced Greek cities and culture for the centuries that followed.

Mycenaean civilisation was divided into several different centres. The poet Homer (described in Chapter 20), who was composing around 500 years later, said that these centres were based around the major cities, including Mycenae, Pylos, and Sparta. The Mycenaeans didn't have an overall ruler; their world was probably periodically dominated by whichever king was most powerful.

Each Mycenaean city had:

- ✔ **A king:** The king was probably the biggest landowner and most successful warrior within the local area and may well have become king by force. If you think about the fact that the Mycenaeans were descended from colonists, the leadership was probably the descendants of families that had originally grabbed the best land and became the most powerful.

- ✔ **The king's court:** These free individuals were courtiers to the king and lived in large residences around the royal palace complex.

- ✔ **Ordinary people:** These free individuals were known as the *demos.* The word 'demos' is very important; see Chapter 4 where I look at the birth of democracy. These merchants, farmers, and artisans lived outside the palace complex.

- ✔ **Slaves:** The few available Mycenaean texts list slaves as having been the property of the king and working at the palace. It's highly likely that the Mycenaeans captured slaves from their foreign wars, because this was the most common method of obtaining them.

Working for a living

Evidence indicates Mycenaean society had a far more developed set of social and work roles than what historians know of the Minoans. Farming was still the main profession for the majority of people, but in and around the palace complex some Mycenaeans worked as scribes, administrators, or artisans such as potters and smiths, depending on the king's patronage.

More interestingly, the Mycenaeans developed what modern people think of as industry. One of the biggest industries was metallurgy, particularly the production of bronze, which was essential for a warlike people like the

Mycenaeans. Some of the tablets that have survived suggest that a significant proportion of the population were involved in metallurgy in the town of Pylos, and historians assume that other towns had similar arrangements.

The Mycenaeans were also heavily involved in the production of textiles. Evidence shows they produced up to 15 different textile varieties, mostly from wool and flax. Other industries included ivory carving, stone carving, and perfume making.

A large amount of what the Mycenaeans produced was sold abroad. For example, Mycenaean vases have been found in Egypt, Sicily, Western Europe, and as far away as Central Europe and Great Britain.

Expanding in all directions

After the collapse of Minoan civilisation with the fall of Knossos (see the earlier section 'Going out with a bang'), the Mycenaeans became the big players in the western Mediterranean and took over much of what had been Minoan settlements. For example, they took over the town of Miletus, which had been a Minoan colony, and the same thing happened on the island of Samos.

But the Mycenaeans didn't just focus on trading with and taking over their western neighbours. They took a much more aggressive interest in the eastern Mediterranean than the Minoans – not only trading with these areas but also establishing outposts and colonies. Bases were set up on several islands like Rhodes and Cos, where merchants stayed and acted as middlemen, letting the industries in Pylos, Argos, and elsewhere know what the local markets required. The island of Cyprus and the ports on the coast of modern-day Syria were particularly big trading centres, but the Mycenaeans also traded with ports on the coast of Asia Minor.

Eventually, the Mycenaeans were in charge pretty much everywhere, including:

- ✔ **The crumbling Hittite Empire:** By around 1300 BC, expansion brought the Mycenaeans into contact with the other big, warlike civilisation at the time – the Hittite Empire.

  The Hittites had nothing to do with the Greeks; they were a completely different people. By the time that they came into diplomatic contact with the Mycenaeans, the Hittites had become the dominant force in Asia Minor, Syria, and as far east as Mesopotamia. The Hittites had come from north of the region and spoke a very different language. Their biggest enemy were the Egyptians, with whom they were continually fighting for control of Syria.

There aren't any records of the Hittites and the Mycenaeans having any military contests, but within a few years of coming into contact with each other in 1300 BC the Hittite civilisation had collapsed. Historians don't really know why, but some archaeologists have suggested that the Hittites may have experienced a devastating civil war.

✔ **The city of Troy:** The most famous of all the Mycenaean expansions was the destruction of the city of Troy around 1250 BC. Archaeology shows that the end of Troy was probably the work of a western Greek army like that of the Mycenaeans. I talk more about the myth and reality of Troy in Chapter 21.

With the Minoans destroyed, the Hittite Empire at war with itself, Troy conquered, and no real threat from anyone elsewhere in Greece, the Mycenaeans should have dominated the Mediterranean for generations to come. They were the dominant military power and economically self-sustaining, with a large trade network throughout the Mediterranean and beyond . . . but then something happened. Historians aren't exactly sure what occurred because it happened during the region's Dark Ages (see Chapter 3 for more info).

Chapter 3

Shedding Light on Ancient Greece's Dark Ages

In This Chapter

▶ Investigating the Dorian invasion

▶ Colonising to the east and west

▶ Inventing writing

▶ Establishing new Greek city states

*I*n around 1200 BC the whole of society in the eastern Mediterranean was in trouble. In the east the Hittite civilisation had collapsed and huge numbers of people fled west into Syria, Palestine, and as far as Egypt. Around the same time the Mycenaean world fell apart (refer to Chapter 2). After this civilisation's last big hurrah at Troy, something devastating happened back at home. All the big Mycenaean city centres were attacked and utterly destroyed. Mycenae and Pylos were burned and never fully recovered. And around 50 years later a second sequence of attacks finished off the remaining cities.

The damage was devastating and conclusive, and the Greek world was humbled by it. A huge amount of the learning and technology that the Mycenaeans had developed during the past 500 years was lost. The big cities were abandoned and left as permanent landmarks to the memory of those Mycenaeans who'd died, with vast numbers of people deciding to move and re-establish themselves in other areas of the Mediterranean.

It took 300 years for the Greek world to recover, but recover it did. Although the Mycenaean culture was gone, never to return, a new set of Greek people developed, with new cities, kingdoms, and – by around 750 BC – a new form of written language that scholars recognise as ancient Greek.

So although historians refer to the period of around 1100 to 750 BC as ancient Greece's Dark Ages, light was shining at the end of the tunnel. The changes ancient Greece experienced during its Dark Ages are the focus of this chapter.

The term 'Dark Ages' is actually quite a misleading one. The term suggests a time when nothing much happened – as you'll see from this chapter, that's not the case! The idea of a Dark Age comes from the fact that historians are uncertain about exactly what happened and who went where. The age is dark in terms of information, not innovation!

Surviving the Dorian Invasion

So what cataclysmic force overwhelmed the mighty Mycenaeans in around 1200 BC? Well, according to the Greeks themselves, the Dorians did it.

Later ancient Greek historians describe the destruction of Mycenae and the burning of other Mycenaean cities as being the work of a powerful army from the north that swept down over the Peloponnese mountains and into southern Greece.

The Greeks filled in the gaps in their knowledge with myth and stories – a phenomenon I describe in detail in Chapter 2. The Dorians may well have been an example of this process.

According to the Greeks, the Dorians were a people who came from the north and smashed the Mycenaeans. Many Greeks believed the Dorians descended from a group of people called the Heraclids. The Heraclids were thought to have been the descendants of the great Greek hero Heracles (or Hercules as the Romans called him) who'd once lived in southern Greece under Mycenaean control but had then been sent into exile. The Heraclids regrouped and eventually returned, led by King Hyllus, to wreak revenge on their former masters.

The famous Greek historian Thucydides, who was writing 500 years after the end of the Mycenaean civilisation, had no doubts about what had happened:

> *Eighty years after Troy the Dorians and the sons of Herakles made themselves masters of the Peloponnese. It was with difficulty and over a long period that peace returned.*

Many other versions of this story existed then and now, and all accounts seem to point to an invasion into Greece by a big army from the north or north-west.

Exactly who the Dorians were remains a mystery. What is important, however, is that by 1100 BC things had changed. The Mycenaeans had disappeared, many people had fled from their homes to a new life elsewhere, and the map of the region was very different.

Travelling into a New (Dark) Age

The movement of most people from mainland Greece during the Dark Ages had a huge effect on the rest of the Mediterranean. Imagine if today all the people living in a city like London suddenly left and began to look for somewhere else to live in Britain. The effect on the lives of people throughout the UK would be huge. Obviously big differences exist between life then and now, but some considerations are constant: The Greeks needed water, food, shelter, and enough land to be able to sustain themselves and their families.

Unsurprisingly the Greeks ranged far and wide in their search for new land. Some went east toward modern-day Turkey and beyond; others went west to Italy, Sicily, and, by the seventh century BC, North Africa. These big migrations during the Dark Ages are one of the reasons why the history of ancient Greece is so fragmented.

As I note in Chapter 1, being Greek during this time was more a state of mind than a nationality. Well, the migrations of the Dark Ages contributed significantly to this experience.

Heading east

A vast number of people leaving mainland Greece headed east across the Mediterranean toward Asia Minor. Traditional Greek myth/history says that these people fled to the city of Athens and then on to an area known as the Ionic Coast (see the map on the Cheat Sheet), establishing ancient Greece's roots in a matter of a few years. The official version of events soon became that this movement of people was a single event of colonisation, with one population group moving from their original home to make a new one.

As ever, the truth is slightly different. The transfer of people from mainland Greece to the coast of Asia Minor was a *migration* rather than a colonisation. This process took place over a number of years rather than in one big trip. For one thing, an adequate fleet of ships wouldn't have been available for such an undertaking. Furthermore, the stuff about Athens is just propaganda. Many years later, when Athens was building up its empire from many of these Greek towns, saying that the original inhabitants had come from Athens made for a good argument to go back and aggressively force the towns to join their empire and pay a tribute! (For more on this empire-building, see Chapter 7.)

A much more likely comparison of the process is that of the Pilgrim Fathers leaving England for America, a brave and adventurous group of people embarking on a journey of discovery without really knowing too much about the land that they were going to. Again like the Pilgrim Fathers, these on-the-move Greeks were a mixed group from all around the mainland. Whole towns wouldn't have moved at once and each successive migration would have been made up of a mixed bag of people. It was only when they made land and founded a new place to live that they became a new 'people'.

Those that had headed east became known as the *Ionian* Greeks because the coastland and nearby islands they inhabited were known as Ionia. Confusingly this region had nothing to do with the Ionian Sea, which refers to the stretch of water between Sicily, Southern Italy, and Western Greece. Although the two words look exactly the same in English, they meant different things in ancient Greek.

Meeting the neighbours

Although much of the territory of Ionia was uninhabited when the Greeks arrived, the areas to the immediate north and south weren't. These areas were called Aeolis and Doria (so-called because some Dorian Greeks had ended up living there) and they'd both been populated for some time.

- ✔ **Aeolis:** The people to the north of Ionia were known as the Aeolians. They were probably also Greeks who had left the eastern Greek mainland a little before the travellers who became known as the Ionians. Later Greek writers maintained that the Aeolians were the sons of Orestes, the son of the famous Mycenaean king Agamemnon. But this bit of genealogy is just a myth. The area known as Aeolia was very fertile, and the Aeolians seem to have spent their time as relatively contented farmers.

- ✔ **Doria:** To the south of Ionia was Doria, which was under the control of a very different people called the Carians. The Carians spoke an old language that was different from the Greek languages. They'd been in contact with the Mycenaeans and had absorbed a lot of Greek culture but they were definitely not Greek. Like the Aeolians they were, in the main, farmers.

The Greek writer Strabo describes the Carians as *barbaroi*, which gave rise to the modern word *barbarians*. Strabo's word choice came from his belief that when the Carians tried to speak Greek, they made a noise that just sounded like 'ba, ba, ba'! The Greeks used this word to describe anybody who was a non-Greek speaker.

Establishing new Greek cities

The new Ionian territory was made up of 12 major cities. Two of them were on the islands of Chios and Samos and the others, such as Ephesus and Smyrna, were on the mainland (see the Cheat Sheet map).

The Greeks learn to write

The Greeks in the east were in very close association with the Phoenicians and picked up from them something far more important than any treasures or fancy goods. At some point around 750 BC, Greeks in the east began to use the Phoenician system of language notation, which led to the Greek alphabet. Although some letters and forms varied depending on where ancient Greeks lived throughout the region, the basic underlying principles of the Phoenician-based system became standard throughout the Mediterranean. In fact, the Greek expression for writing is *phoinikeia grammata*, which means 'Phoenician writings'.

In the main, the new settlers built their settlements on peninsulas just away from the mainland. These areas were linked to the mainland by narrow causeways, or *isthmuses*. These locations were beneficial for a few reasons:

✔ The new cities enjoyed relatively cool temperatures along the hot Asia Minor coastline.

✔ The geography offered natural harbours that the new inhabitants used for trading supplies and receiving friends and relatives from the Greek mainland.

✔ The new cities were more secure from attack because they had water as a natural barrier on one side and freshly built fortifications on the landward side.

Early on, these new towns weren't particularly remarkable – but they became tremendously important later on. Constantly involved in the struggles between Greece and Persia, they were eventually used as an excuse for the invasion of the Persian Empire by Alexander the Great. (For more on Alexander the Great, march to Chapter 11.)

Soon after their foundation, the cities were nothing more than increasingly popular trading spots. The trade that they engaged in, however, brought them into contact with a culture that had a major impact on ancient Greeks – the Phoenicians.

Trading with the Phoenicians

The Mycenaeans had been adventurous traders and their kings had spent their wealth on luxuries from the east, in particular Syria and Egypt. The knowledge gained from trade routes in the eastern Mediterranean became more wide-spread on the Greek mainland and helped with the migrations that followed the collapse of Mycenaean civilisation.

The main traders in luxury goods from the east were the Phoenicians. The Phoenicians were originally from the east, possibly as far east as the Persian Gulf, and they established themselves in the city of Tyre on the Syrian coast, in the area known now as Lebanon. From there they eventually founded colonies as far away as Cadiz in Spain and most famously Carthage in North Africa.

Going west

While the great migration of people to the east took place, things continued to happen on the Greek mainland. Archaeology indicates that the tenth and ninth centuries BC (900–700 BC) was a period of great poverty on the Greek mainland. After the destruction of the Mycenaean civilisation, a great deal of the established industry and infrastructure disappeared. Society became entirely dependent on agriculture, and the number of inhabited sites decreased significantly.

The old system of Mycenaean kings was dependent on wealth, so when the kings were eliminated, society changed too. The old palace culture of the Mycenaeans disappeared (see Chapter 2), and a levelling out of social classes took place. In each community, power became shared among a group of the most influential people rather than one man. I write more about these changes in Chapter 4.

The most immediate result of these societal changes was another wave of migration. Around 750 BC new groups of people were looking to leave mainland Greece. This time, the people weren't fleeing invasion (see 'Heading east' earlier in this chapter). Instead, they were:

- Discontented nobles who'd lost influence
- Struggling farmers who were looking for new territories to cultivate

With the Ionian Greek cities firmly established to the east, these new travellers had to look elsewhere for fresh land – and they looked to the west, as Figure 3-1 shows.

Settling in Italy

One of the western-bound Greek travellers' first ports of call was southern Italy. In fact, so many early ancient Greeks migrated to Italy that the Romans later called the south of Italy and Sicily *Magna Graecia*, which was Latin for 'Greater Greece'.

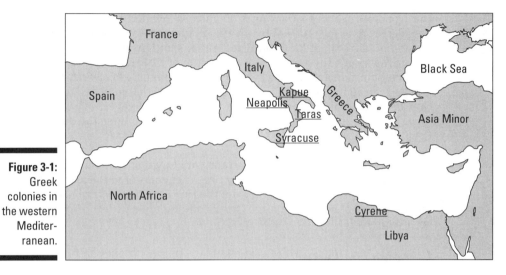

Figure 3-1:
Greek
colonies in
the western
Mediter-
ranean.

In the eighth century BC westward migrating ancient Greeks founded the
Italian towns of Neapolis (Naples), Kapue (Capua), and Taras (Taranto).
These towns became very rich and powerful thanks to their close trade links
with mainland Greece and beyond. The towns maintained their independence
for more than 500 years until the Romans finally conquered them and
absorbed them into their empire.

On the island of Sicily, the most important new town by far was Syracuse
(see Figure 3-1). Greeks from the city of Corinth founded Syracuse in around
734 BC. They were led by Archias, who named the town *Sirako* after a nearby
swamp. Due to its excellent position for trading, Syracuse grew very quickly
and became immensely wealthy. The money was spent on extending the
harbour facilities and defences and for some time Syracuse was considered
to be the most powerful Greek city in the whole of the Mediterranean.

Setting up in Egypt

Coincidence is a wonderful thing. Just around the time that ancient Greeks
were establishing more western towns and initiating trade across the
Mediterranean, the ancient civilisation of Egypt opened its doors to trade.
For thousands of years Egypt had been closed to Mediterranean society.
Egypt had no need to trade with anybody because it was so fertile and pretty
much self-sustaining. For more on the histories and mysteries of ancient
Egypt, check out *The Ancient Egyptians For Dummies* by Charlotte Booth
(Wiley).

During ancient Greece's Dark Ages, Egypt was invaded and conquered by its great rival Assyria, led by the great monarch Assarhaddon. The Assyrians ruled Egypt for several generations until Assurbanipal, one of Assarhaddon's successors, was the victim of a big revolt led by Psammetichus. Psammetichus was probably from Libya in North Africa and had raised a mercenary army from all around that included new Greeks from Ionia and Caria. After he won a tremendous victory over Assurbanipal, one of Psammetichus's first acts was to open the doors of Egypt to his new allies.

This meant that Greeks could now trade with Egypt and travel there to experience the country. As a result, many Greeks encountered the art and architecture of Egypt for the first time, and the rich Egyptian culture had a huge impact on them. For more on the Greeks' interactions with the Egyptians, see Chapter 17.

Venturing into Cyrene

Psammetichus came from present-day Libya in North Africa, and the Greeks soon established a town there too. In around 630 BC, a group left the small island of Thera and founded the town of Cyrene (shown in the map in Figure 3-1). Cyrene was in a great location, roughly halfway between Carthage and Egypt, and it very quickly became large and wealthy.

Ancient Greece's Dark Ages were actually a tremendous period of travelling and expansion, which changed the map forever. People living on opposite sides of the Mediterranean now, appropriately, claimed to be Greek and spoke a version of the Greek language. Large trade networks were building up and these new international Greeks were adopting new things such as writing.

Back on mainland Greece, however, something equally remarkable was happening: old social structures were breaking down and new rulers emerging. Read all about it in Chapter 4.

Chapter 4

Governing by Kings, Tyrants, and (Eventually) Democrats

· ·

In This Chapter

▶ Increasing the number of social classes

▶ Living under the rule of kings and tyrants

▶ Working with the Spartans

▶ Initiating Athenian democracy

· ·

*I*f you leave a group of people in a room together for long enough, they're bound to end up having an argument about something. TV these days is based around this concept. Usually the disagreement comes up because somebody feels unable to express a point because others aren't listening.

The same was true 2,500 years ago in ancient Greece. Back then the arguments were about who controlled the towns and cities that had developed after the big migrations that I write about in Chapter 3. Unlike most arguments, however, these ancient disagreements ended up producing something amazing.

This chapter is the story of how a bunch of farmers and aristocrats managed to invent the system of government that still exists throughout the world today – democracy.

Shaping the New Societies

When ancient Greece's Dark Ages came to an end in the eighth century BC, the communities that had survived in mainland Greece were very small and simple. The big expansions overseas involved thousands of people leaving the Greek mainland, severely weakening the old Mycenaean power centres (see Chapters 2 and 3).

Remembering Theseus

The shift from local governments to a centralised government took place before the Greeks started recording their own history. Without recorded history to rely on, the Greeks often turned to characters and events from their mythology to explain things.

Some later writers credited the mythological noble Theseus (see Chapter 2) for bringing the whole of the region of Attica under centralised control. He did this by setting up a council of nobles that met regularly and made decisions about the running of the area as a whole.

Of course, one man wasn't solely responsible for uniting the entire, and significantly large, territory of Attica. Still, the Athenians' mythological hero proved a very useful story to gloss over the years of fighting and plotting among several wealthy families in the region.

As a result most ancient Greeks at the end of the Dark Ages were likely to live in small villages ruled by local nobles and wealthier citizens with the most land. Life for most people was very tough, and the chances of improvement and advancement very small. Depending on who you were, you filled a certain place in society. You were born into your position, and change was virtually impossible.

As an ancient Greek at the end of the Dark Ages, your family and your *clan,* or extended family that you came from, were the most important considerations in your life. Your ultimate superiors were local lords to whom you and the rest of your community paid tribute.

Over about half a century, these very local communities began to come under central control by one town. This change probably wasn't the communities' choice; they were most likely forced into the new arrangement by threats and violence from another town in the area that wanted to expand its territory. Probably the most significant example of this was what happened in the region of Attica in western Greece (see the Cheat Sheet map) because it resulted in the formation of the city of Athens. Several important families in the region fought and plotted against each other for hundreds of years. But by the seventh century BC, the region was in the hands of an aristocratic elite.

Meeting the ruling class

In the seventh century BC the people of Attica were ruled by what they considered to be a king, but this leadership wasn't what modern people would understand as a king. The ancient Greeks used the word *basileus* to describe a king. This word translates as 'sovereign', so the individuals weren't actually kings in the sense of Henry VIII. A *basileus* was just one of a board of annually elected officials – like councillors or local government officials – called the *arkhons.* This board formed a ruling council that met at a spot known as the *Areopagus* on the Hill of Ares in Athens and exercised control over Athens and the region of Attica. Eventually the title *basileus* became used to describe an *arkhon* with special religious duties.

Although this combination of a *basileus* and an *arkhon* may sound like a move toward a more open form of government, the arrangement wasn't really much of a change. The opportunity to be an *arkhon* wasn't open to everybody – only those born into the leading aristocratic families in Athens had the right to stand for election. The elections were also only open for the aristocrats to vote in! So in a way the government was as much of a closed shop as it had been under the earlier king-led system. The aristocrats were still in control; there were just more of them.

The aristocrats themselves clearly recognised the exclusive nature of the system because they named the group the *Eupatridai*, which means 'the sons of good fathers'.

The power structures found in Athens and the Attica region during this period weren't all that different from the surrounding area. Throughout Greece and the Mediterranean at the time, the vast majority of people who ruled did so based largely on the qualifications of wealth and birth. The aristocrats were generally the oldest families who'd lived in the area longest – and therefore grabbed all the best land when they arrived. Consequently, they become the wealthiest and the most influential citizens.

Introducing the new middle class

People always find something to argue about, and the system of government in Athens was no different. Any agreement among the aristocrats held only for as long the entire ruling group agreed. If one man wanted to take all the power for himself, the system could break. Indeed, by the seventh century BC the relationships among the various aristocratic families in Athens had reached a breaking point, but another potentially bigger problem existed – the growing middle class.

As Athens had grown and expanded, it had become wealthier. In particular, people who made money from trade or successfully farmed less attractive land were frequently as wealthy as the leading aristocrats. Although these successful individuals made up Athens's new middle class, they were still born outside the noble families and had no chance of being elected to rule.

Around the same time big changes were happening to the way that the Athenians made war and fought against their enemies. The Athenians had adopted the *hoplite* method of fighting (see Chapter 5), which brought together and armed many male Athenians. Unsurprisingly this group soon realised they had enormous power at their disposal.

This mixture of middle-class discontent and burgeoning military strength was a time-bomb waiting to go off. All that was needed was an individual with the charisma and drive to take advantage of the situation and initiate massive change.

Surviving the Cycle of Tyranny

The Greeks used a word called *turannos* that means 'the rule of one' and is the source of the modern word *tyrant*. However, the ancient Greeks' notion of the tyrant didn't necessarily have the connotations of cruelty and harshness that it does today.

The earliest surviving instance of the word *tyrant* is in a poem by Archilochos. This piece of verse talks about the tyrant Gyges who reigned in Lydia in Asia Minor between 680 and 640 BC:

> *To me the possessions of Gyges rich in gold are of no concern, envy has not seized me, and I do not look with jealousy on the works of the gods, nor do I passionately desire great tyranny; such things are far from my eyes . . .*

Nevertheless, many of the tyrants who seized control in ancient Greece did go on to run repressive regimes, as the following sections explore.

Kylon: Discovering that tyranny is harder than it looks

The first attempt at tyranny in Athens was a failure. In 640 BC, Kylon tried to take advantage of the discontent in the city (see the preceding section).

Kylon was an interesting character. He was a former winner at the Olympic games (see Chapter 16 for more on the Olympics), which made him very popular with the common people who saw him as a hero. He also had the backing of his father-in-law Theagenes, who was the tyrant of Megara.

According to the historians Herodotus and Thucydides, Kylon acted on the advice of the Delphic Oracle by trying to sieze Athens during the Festival of Zeus when much of the city was otherwise engaged. Unfortunately for him the plan failed and he was forced to flee to the temple of Athena. Kylon was persuaded out by a promise that he wouldn't be harmed but then stoned to death! Although Kylon's plan was a total failure, it was a warning of what was to come.

Drakon: Changing the rules

Discontent rumbled on in Athens, and the *Eupatridai* responded to Kylon's action by attempting to tighten their control on the city. Around 620 BC, Drakon published the first-ever Athenian law code, defining the rules by which Athens would be governed. (These laws were deliberately harsh, and Drakon's name is the source of the word *draconian*.)

In particular the laws tried to break down the idea that people should look to their own family for justice and take vengeance when someone had been wronged. Drakon's laws made clear that justice was the role of the state. This might not seem like such a controversial idea to us but it was establishing the state as able to interfere in private affairs. This was a big change because previously it had been the role of the individual to protect his own household. The law particularly affected the aristocrats of Athens who'd previously acted as they wished. Drakon was attempting to get this group under state control – a laudable aim but probably for his own benefit rather than anybody else's.

Enter Solon: A Man of the People

With so many tensions pulling at the organisation of society, ancient Athens seemed about to break. The Athenians recognised how critical the situation had become and in 594 BC appointed Solon, a middle-class Athenian who'd made his money from trade, as *arkhon*. Solon is very interesting to historians because he's the earliest Greek historical figure who's famous, well-documented, and real.

In fact, Solon was the first ancient Greek to write his autobiography. It wasn't actually a book but he composed numerous poems for people to recite and so remember his achievements after he was long gone.

> *To the people I have given such privilege as is enough neither taking away nor adding to their honour. While those who had power and were famed for their wealth, for them I took care that they should suffer no injury. I stood, holding out my strong shield over both, and I did not allow either to triumph unjustly.*

Making changes

Boasting aside, Solon did have a tough job to do. Athens was in a difficult situation with all the classes feeling hard done by. As a result, Solon made some sweeping changes, including:

- **Cancelling debts:** Solon introduced legislation that he called the *seisakhtheia* or 'the shaking off of burdens'. Many peasants with small amounts of land were effectively paying protection money to members of the aristocracy from whom they rented it. If their crops failed they got further and further into debt and eventually had to vacate the land.

- **Defining new political classes:** Solon divided the city population politically based on agricultural wealth. This policy broke the exclusive power of the *Eupatridai,* and the wealthiest citizens in Athens now had the opportunity to become *arkhons* regardless of whether they came from one of the city's original families.

- **Establishing the new council of 400:** By far Solon's biggest change was the introduction of a new council called the *boule.* This assembly was made up of 400 citizens, 100 from each of the four Athenian clans, and gave an opportunity for the rest of the citizen body to participate in debate.

The reforms of Solon were publicised in an interesting way. All the individual laws were numbered and inscribed on wooden tables or *axones*. Each law was then quoted by number, like items on a take-away menu. Citizen were required to swear an oath that they would obey the new laws for the next ten years, the idea being that the laws would be revised a decade later.

Stepping out of the limelight

Solon's reforms seemed like real progress. His policies attempted to prevent the *Eupatridai* from lording over the rest of the population, reduce the economic problems of the lower classes, and give the lower classes a voice in the process of running the city.

Unfortunately Solon was one of the first people to discover that you can't please all the people all the time. His debt laws proved extremely popular with the lower classes and greatly helped poor farmers but the leaders of the aristocratic clans were hugely resentful. Nevertheless, it kept more people working on the land, which was Solon's intention. But his political reforms had an entirely different outcome as the aristocrats tried to seize back control (see the following section 'Bouncing Back to Tyranny').

Anarchy!

The whole point of Solon's reforms was to stop Athens from falling victim to tyrants. Unfortunately the same old problems soon cropped up again. The period immediately after Solon is another one for which historians don't have many sources. Researchers do know that in around 589 BC, Athens fell into a struggle among the aristocrats that was so bad no *arkhons* were elected for two years. The Greeks used the term *anarkhy* – meaning 'without *arkhons*' – to describe this time. Of course, this is where the modern word *anarchy* comes from.

Solon retired from public life. The details of his later life are sketchy. Some people say that he went travelling but it seems that he eventually returned to Athens. Unfortunately by the time he died in 558 BC he saw all his good work undone by the vengeful *Eupatridai* and other opportunists.

Bouncing Back to Tyranny

After the crumbling of Solon's reforms and a brief period of political anarchy, Athens was ripe for potential tyrants. Several people made attempts to seize power. By far the most successful was the man who dominated Athens in the sixth century BC – Peisistratos.

Peisistratos: Playing the system

While Solon had been trying to solve Athens's social and political problems, the city had been in conflict with the neighbouring city of Megara. During the conflict the Athenians had successfully attacked and captured the port of Nisaea, an ally of Megara. The leader of the expedition was called Peisistratos, and his military success encouraged him to launch a political career.

Solon's reforms and the chaos that followed had led to a split amongst the Athenian people. On the one side were the aristocrats and on the other were the *democrats*, from the Greek word *demos* which meant 'the people'. The democrats believed that Solon hadn't gone far enough in giving power to the whole population.

Peisistratos targeted the democrats as allies. In 561 BC he appeared in the *agora* or public square covered in blood and claiming to have been injured by his political enemies. He used the ensuing public outrage to his advantage and seized control of the city.

Essentially Peisistratos played Solon's system to his own advantage. Peisistratos didn't change anything that Solon had put in place; by using bribery and intimidation he just made sure that every year his own supporters were elected as *archons.* Eventually people were keen to vote for his supporters as they realised that their own prospects of advancement would be limited if they didn't. Simple really.

Out, in, and back out again

Peisistratos's grip on power was actually quite simple to break. He dominated Athens for five years until a faction of aristocrats led by a man named Megacles managed to drive him into exile in 556 BC.

However, Megacles was unable to keep hold on the argumentative elements within his own party, and within a few years, he sought to reconcile with Peisistratos, sealing the deal by arranging that the former tyrant marry his daughter. In 550 BC Peisistratos returned to Athens a hero.

Of course, Peisistratos didn't stick to the arrangement with Megacles. Peisistratos already had two sons from his first marriage, and he wanted them to take power after his death. Consequently, he treated Megacles's daughter badly and refused to recognise her as his wife so as not to weaken the position of his sons.

Unsurprisingly Megacles was upset about the situation and immediately betrayed Peisistratos to enemies. After a very brief power struggle, Peisistratos was forced into exile once again.

Regrouping abroad

In exile for the second time, Peisistratos learned from his mistakes. This second exile was much longer, lasting over a decade. During this period, Peisistratos realised that to truly dominate Athens he needed support from other powerful states throughout Greece. The benefits of this strategy were two-fold:

- ✔ The Athenians would see Peisistratos as the only person able to handle the foreign affairs of Athens.
- ✔ Peisistratos would be able to immediately build up an army to help him grasp and keep hold of power.

Noble failures – Harmodios and Aristogeiton

In 514 BC, two lovers named Harmodios and Aristogeiton attempted to end Hippias's rule by assassinating Peisistratos's other son, Hipparkhos, during a public festival. The plot succeeded, but Harmodios was killed during it and Aristogeiton was captured and died under torture.

But despite the relative failure, the two assassins became celebrated figures in Athens and were considered to be important heroes in the struggle for democracy. Unfortunately, this celebrated status wasn't quite based on truth. Harmodios and Aristogeiton were both aristocrats and wanted to get rid of Hippias so they

could replace him with another set of aristocrats. But the romance of their story ensured their fame.

Harmodios and Aristogeiton became such celebrities that several statues were erected to their memory in Athens. The rose-tinted view of their exploits was also remembered in later ancient Greek drinking songs like this one:

In a branch of myrtle I shall bear my sword like Harmodios and Aristogeiton when the two of them slayed the tyrant and made Athens a city of equal rights.

Peisistratos spent ten years building up support in Macedonia, Thessaly, and other places to the north of Athens (refer to the Cheat Sheet map). Finally, in 540 BC, he landed with an army at Marathon and swept virtually unopposed into Athens. He declared that he was the true and legal ruler of the city. He was back in power and this time he wasn't shifting for anybody.

Enjoying the benefits of tyranny

Peisistratos stayed in power for the next 13 years, and during this time Athens undeniably went through a boom period. Peisistratos's aggressive foreign policy built up Athenian territory around Greece and generated a lot of revenues.

In fact, during this time some of the earliest of ancient Greece's impressive building projects began. Virtually all of the building programmes attributed to Peisistratos are now lost but he's said to have initiated the building of several religious buildings in the *agora* (the main town square, like the Roman *forum*) as well as a large palace for himself. The knock-on effect was that artists were attracted to Athens – like artists in Renaissance Italy, creative people went where the money was. Peisistratos's other cultural achievement was the introduction of two new elements to religious festivals; the singing of *dithyrambs* (hymns sung in honour of the gods) and also tragic drama. To do so he introduced the first *orchestra* (performance space) in the city.

Hippias: Tyranny as a family business

Peisistratos's hold on power was so complete that when he died in 527 BC he was able to hand over control to his son Hippias. Unfortunately for Hippias, his father's personality had been a big part of his success. Many people who had previously supported Peisistratos turned against Hippias.

After the assassination of his brother (see the nearby sidebar 'Noble failures – Harmodios and Aristogeiton'), Hippias became more severe, and many influential aristocrats were forced to flee Athens. Those individuals who stayed needed fresh help. The people who they turned to were something of a surprise – the Spartans.

Getting to Know the Spartans

Although the Athenians couldn't have known it at the time, the Spartans were to become their mortal enemy and also the most feared and famous fighting force in the ancient world.

The city of Sparta was to the south-west of Athens in a region called Laconia (take a look at the Cheat Sheet map). The Greek term for the region was *Lacedaemon*, and that's why the Spartans are sometimes referred to as the Lacedaemonians. Their way of life was considered to be brutal and without luxury, hence the modern word *Spartan*, which means simple and non-luxurious.

Growing up Spartan

The Spartans first came to prominence after the Dorian invasions (see Chapter 3 for more details) when the old inhabitants of the region were kicked out and replaced by tribesmen from the north-west and Macedonia. Being both very warlike and very good at it, the Spartans soon gained control of the whole of Laconia. By the time that Hippias was tyrant in Athens, Sparta was the leading power in southern Greece.

Two things made Sparta very different from all the other Greeks states:

- ✔ Sparta was the only state to have a standing professional army. Read more about this in Chapter 5.

- ✔ The Spartans governed themselves. Other cities in Greece were experimenting with new forms of government and different systems (see the sidebar 'Know your ocracies', later in this chapter), but the Spartans had a form of government and social organisation that was fixed and unchanging.

Living the hellish life of a Helot

Nearly all the citizens of Sparta were involved in running the state and were brought up since childhood to perform their roles (see Chapter 5). An unfortunate group of people known as the *helots* carried out farming, labour, and all other manual work required by Sparta. These people were serfs (or workers) owned by the state. The *helots* had come to their position because their land had been incorporated into the Spartan state, and they were now forced to work for it. It was a grim existence: The *helots* worked hard for little reward and no chance of bettering their station in life.

Helots made up 90 per cent of the Spartan population. As a result, the Spartans were always worried about revolts and developed a particularly unpleasant way of keeping power over the *helots*. Because the *helots* didn't count as Spartan citizens, they could technically be considered foreigners or enemies. Consequently every year the *gerousia* would vote to declare war on the *helots* and then carry out massacres to keep the numbers down. The Spartans also considered that this brutality was a useful way of giving young soldiers practice at killing.

In short, Sparta had two kings who were the top dogs, taking the roles of generals in war and chief priests in peace. A group of elected officials called the *ephors* and a council called the *gerousia* carried out the actual administration of the state. The system wasn't particularly unusual except for the fact that many positions were for life and were full-time jobs. Thus, the aristocracy of Sparta devoted their entire lives to the official business of Sparta – which included fighting many wars.

Getting involved in Athens

The Spartans were a warlike people keen on furthering their territory, and they had a pretty brutal attitude toward violence and death – all of which makes them a surprising choice for the Athenian aristocrats seeking their help.

Yet after the failed attempt to remove Hippias, the Athenian aristocrats were forced to look to Sparta for help. According to the Greek historian Herodotus, Sparta had a reputation as being sympathetic to requests for help from states under tyranny. In addition, a prophecy from the Delphic oracle (see Chapter 21) suggested to the Spartans that they should involve themselves in the Athenian situation.

The end result was that in 510 BC, the Spartan king Kleomenes led his troops into Athens and forced Hippias and his entire family to flee. He couldn't have imagined what would happen next.

Considering Kleisthenes: The Beginnings of Democracy

When Kleomenes intervened in Athens and restored the usual form of government, fresh elections were held. One of the candidates was a man called Kleisthenes. When Kleisthenes made a series of important reforms to the Athenian constitution in 508 BC, he never imagined the impact he'd have on the history of mankind. Kleisthenes's change – arguably – created the idea of *demokratia* or 'rule of the people'.

Rather than being the product of some high-minded ideals, democracy was the result of another aristocratic squabble. Kleisthenes himself was a blue-blood Athenian aristocrat. The year before he had lost out to a fellow aristocrat, Isagoras, in the election for *arkhon*. Rather than seek revolution or look for military support, Kleisthenes appealed to the common people for support. In this case, the 'common people' were individuals who didn't really have a voice, even after the reforms of Solon; people such as traders and farmers without much land or social status.

Kleisthenes proposed new laws in the *ekklesia* that allowed all citizens to take part in the process of government. Unsurprisingly Isagoras tried to block the moves, but he didn't have enough support. As a result, Isagoras called in Kleomenes of Sparta to quell the unrest in the city.

Kleomenes and his troops turned up in Athens, but he took things a bit too far, expelling 700 pro-Kleisthenes aristocratic families from the city and then leaving Isagoras to sort things out himself. Isagoras attempted to abolish Kleisthenes's reforms, but Kleisthenes responded by returning to the city with a small number of troops and forcing Isagoras to surrender. Finally, Kleisthenes was able to complete his proposed reform.

Reforming and reorganising

In essence Kleisthenes only made one big change: He scrapped the wealth-based classes that Solon had created nearly 90 years before and instead divided the population in terms of where people lived.

To do this Kleisthenes created ten new *phulai*, or tribes. Your tribe depended on where in the city you were born rather than which class you were from or how much money you had. Each tribe was further divided into *demoi*, or *demes*. These were smaller districts, like the constituencies or wards making up a City or County Council , a few streets or a zip-code district. The *demoi* became the units in which local business was done and meant that *demoi* representatives could take the views of each local area to the *ekklesia* and get it on the agenda to be discussed.

Knowing your ocracies

Although Athens is heralded as the birthplace of democracy, many different forms of government existed in ancient Greece and democracy was just one of them. Here are some common governmental forms (and examples from ancient Greek history):

✔ **Democracy:** Literally the 'rule of the people'. In a democracy, the people make decisions about the policy and actions of their community. In the ancient world, this tended to be *participative* (people actually voted and debated themselves) rather than *representative* (where they elected somebody to do it for them). For more on democracy, see Chapter 7.

✔ **Monarchy:** Rule by a king or queen. In this form of government, an absolute ruler is unelected, and his or her authority is unquestioned. The monarch may (or may not) be able to appoint a successor. Monarchy of a type was very popular in early Greek culture and survived throughout Asia Minor and in Macedonia.

✔ **Oligarchy:** Rule by the few. In early Athens, the aristocrats descended from the region's early settlers who had claimed the best land functioned as an oligarchic governing body.

✔ **Plutocracy:** Rule of the wealthy; from the Greek word *ploutos*, meaning wealth. A minimum property or wealth requirement was usually in place for those who wanted to take part in government. Plutocracies were normally mercantile communities like several of the Greek islands such as Samos.

✔ **Timarchy:** Nothing to do with people called Tim; derived from the Greek word *time*, which meant honour or respectability. In practice, a timarchy could be anything from the strongest warrior to the most respected family ruling a region. Many people argue that Sparta was a timarchy and some Mycenaean states are good examples of warrior timarchy.

✔ **Tyranny:** Literally 'rule by one'. In ancient Greece, the individual often seized power but sometimes he was voted in. The Greek meaning didn't have the negative associations that it does in the modern world.

Throughout the ancient world these and many more systems flourished – or they were combined as suited a particular political moment. For example, the Roman Empire was essentially an oligarchy but with elements of plutocracy; at certain points it was fundamentally a tyranny!

After Kleisthenes's reform a massive section of the Athenian population that previously hadn't been able to gain citizenship now could. Theoretically the change meant that any citizen from any social status could become an *arkhon*.

In actuality, things didn't turn out like this – and it was very unlikely that Kleisthenes wanted any other result. During the next century nearly all the people that ruled Athens continued to be aristocrats.

Taking small steps toward democracy

What Kleisthenes achieved wasn't democracy in the way you think of it today. Athenian political involvement depended on citizenship, which meant no women, resident slaves, or resident foreigners were able to vote. Also, it was highly unlikely that anybody outside the aristocratic elite had the money or influence to win an election.

However, Kleisthenes did recognise the power of popular opinion (and how he could manipulate it). The changes that he made ensured that the reformers who followed him in the fifth century BC could create something truly extraordinary. I talk about how the system worked in Chapter 7.

When Kleisthenes was making his reforms at the end of the sixth century BC, the word the Greeks used for popular rule was *isonomia*, which literally meant 'equality under law' and referred to the status that the creation of the tribes brought to all citizens. The Greek word *demokratia* had a much more serious meaning and referred to the people holding all power. The Athenians would have considered that their state was a *demokratia* and would have described it as such. So *demokratia* was an Athenian invention!

Challenging the new order

The Spartans weren't best pleased with the political reforms of Kleisthenes and were quick to respond when he kicked Isagoras out. In 506 BC, Kleomenes returned with another Spartan army intent on forcing Kleisthenes and his supporters out for a second time, but the Spartan attack didn't work. The mass public support that Kleisthenes was able to call on saw the Spartans soundly defeated, and the same happened to invading armies from elsewhere the following year.

The reforms of Kleisthenes had banded the people together to a common cause in a manner ancient Greeks hadn't previously experienced.

Chapter 5

Fighting and Warring: Greece Gets Heavy

· ·

In This Chapter

▶ Outfitting warriors with armour and weapons

▶ Training like a Spartan

▶ Fighting strategically on land

▶ Battling at sea

· ·

> *Timokritos was bold in war. This is his grave.*
> *Ares the war-god spares the coward, not the brave.*
>
> –Anakreon of Teos (circa 550 BC)

*L*ike death and taxes, war is something that seems likely to always be part of being human. Even today, with much of the world at peace, wars are still going on all around. For the luckier individuals and nations, war is something experienced from afar through newspapers, TV reports, and re-creations in films. You might know people affected by war – but for many, war is not a close-to-home experience.

In ancient Greece, however, the situation couldn't have been more different. War was essentially ever-present. Depending on who you were, war was either a threat or an opportunity for glory. If you were male then, whatever your social status, your involvement was likely to be brutal, painful, and right in the thick of battle. In ancient Greece warfare was upfront and personal.

In this chapter I cover the basics of Greek warfare on sea and land, focusing on the experience of war and warfare in ancient Greece from the end of the Dark Ages (around 750 BC) through to the rise of Macedonia (around 350 BC).

I describe the activities and equipment involved in war, how various combat tactics developed, and why the Spartans (see Chapter 4) became famous for being so good at fighting.

I examine specific techniques as they relate to particular battles or time periods in other chapters. For example, Chapter 8 offers details on siege warfare, which was critical during the Peloponnesian War and when Athens was under siege by the Spartans.

Joining the Fight

When a war took place in ancient Greece it involved all men of fighting age. Most modern states have armed forces to fight wars for them, and fighting, patrolling, and eventually keeping peace after battle are these people's jobs. But in ancient Greece, responsibility wasn't divided up this way. If a town was attacked, it had to defend itself, and that meant that every male citizen who was old enough (and not too old) to hold a sword took part in the effort. Indeed, officers and (in the case of Sparta, kings) were required to fight in the front line in just the same way as common men. War was a great leveller in ancient Greece. The experience on the battlefield was the same for every man, regardless of station.

In short, the vast majority of the city states that I write about in Chapters 2, 3, and 4 defended themselves by using a citizen militia, an army made up of the male citizen population and led by officials chosen by the state or elected by the people. For example, if you wanted to stop somebody from attacking your farm and stealing your property, you had to protect it yourself. The only exception to this citizen-led system was Sparta, a city-state whose whole system was built around constructing and maintaining a fearsome standing army (a group of men who had no other responsibility than war, a professional force). See the later section 'Living for Killing: The Spartans' for more info.

One fascinating aspect of ancient Greek warfare is how little it changed over many centuries. Yes, tactics improved, as did the calibre of weapons, but if you took a soldier from 750 BC and put him in the middle of a battle with Alexander the Great in 350 BC, the basic experience was amazingly similar – even though 400 years had passed. So what I write about arms, armour, and tactics in this chapter goes for much of the historical period from 750 BC to 350 BC. (Of course, I make mention of any changes and differences whenever appropriate.)

Fighting like a Homeric hero

Ancient Greek males had to learn to fight and use weapons. Much of this was done through physical exercise in the *gymnasium* (see Chapter 16) as nearly all Greek sports were developed out of practising the skills needed to fight in war.

In particular, the Greeks considered Homer's *Iliad*, the epic poem of the Trojan War, a mine of information on all manner of subjects (for more on *The Iliad* and its influence, see Chapter 20). The only problem with using this great work of literature as a training manual is that the characters are a lot to live up to. Indeed, the Greek and Trojan warriors in *The Iliad* fight like superheroes – battling for hours and laying waste to scores of enemies, with seemingly no consideration for tactics, formations, or obeying orders.

In this typical scene from *The Iliad* the Greek hero Patroclus is tearing into the Trojan fighters.

Patroclus kept on sweeping in, hacking them down, making them pay the price for

Argives slaughtered. There Pronus, first to fall – a glint of the spear and Patroclus tore his chest left bare by the shield-rim, loosed his knees, and the man went crashing down.

In the next thirty lines of the poem Patroclus kills another ten warriors in equally unpleasant ways without even stopping to pause for breath!

Although the weapons and armour described by Homer are similar to those the ancient Greeks actually used, everything else was very different. In particular, real-life battle focused much less on one-to-one combat, and those lengthy introductory speeches before a fight began probably didn't happen.

Nonetheless, the tales in *The Iliad* and indeed those elsewhere in mythology were a great influence on later Greeks because they regarded the nobility and skill of the warriors mentioned as the ultimate example of what they should aspire to.

Dressed to kill: Hoplites

Ancient Greek soldiers were referred to as *hoplites*. Hoplites were standard infantrymen who fought in formation at a battle (see the section 'Getting tactical: Hoplite formations').

By far the most important development in Greek warfare was the discovery of iron in approximately 1200 BC. Prior to this, all metal weapons were made of bronze. Iron is tougher, more hard wearing, and incredibly strong in comparison. When wielded by a powerful warrior, an iron sword could literally split a bronze weapon in two.

By the eighth and seventh centuries BC, the hoplite's equipment (or *panoply*) had become fairly standard, as Figure 5-1 shows.

Figure 5-1:
A Greek
hoplite in
full armour.

Armour

Ancient Greek armour was heavy but not as heavy as the gear worn by an armoured knight from the Middle Ages. The Greek soldier needed to be able to run fast and be as flexible as possible, so he kept his armour to a minimum.

The most important piece of armour was called the *cuirass*. This piece protected a soldier's body but left his arms free to fight – rather like wearing a sleeveless t-shirt but much, much heavier.

The *cuirass* was made in two separate ways. One was to stitch together many layers of canvas and linen to fashion a kind of rigid shirt with strips of bronze sewn in to reinforce it. The other, much more expensive way was to cast the *cuirass* completely in bronze, muscled to fit the shape of the body.

The legs were protected by *greaves*, which were made of bronze and cast so that they fit the legs of the soldier without using any kind of straps. The greaves protected the front of the leg between the knee and ankle with a partial covering around the calves. Soldiers wore normal sandals with no extra armour or protection.

Helmet

Helmets were bronze, and many different styles existed. The most common was the *Corinthian* (see Figure 5-1), which had an opening at the front with a long strip of bronze as a nose-guard. Many soldiers wore a horse-hair crest on top of their helmet but this was purely for display rather than protection.

The arms trade

For the ancient Greeks, a complete *panoply* (all the armour and weapons I write about in this section) was really expensive. Every soldier had to buy his own panoply, and looking after this equipment was important. Only the very rich would have had somebody to tend to their equipment for them in the way that medieval knights did. For everybody else their panoply was their own concern and many men used armour and weapons that their grandfathers and fathers had bought because the cost of replacing these items was so great. Hence, the panoply that you owned in ancient Greece gave a good indication of the class you came from.

Anybody who owned a full hoplite panoply would've been from the wealthier middle or upper classes.

Although arms and armour were expensive, the poet Archilochos of Paros (circa 650 BC) made it clear what was most valuable to take from the battlefield:

> *I don't give a damn if some Thracian ape struts, proud of that shield that the bushes got. Leaving it was hell, but in a tricky spot. I kept my hide intact. Good shields can be bought.*

Shield

The shield was known as a *hoplon*, and that's where the hoplites got their name. By the seventh century BC, the typical shield was about 1 metre (3 feet) in diameter. It was round in shape, made of wood and reinforced with bronze. The inside most likely had two brackets. The soldier put his arm through one bracket and gripped the other.

Sometimes soldiers hung leather curtains from the bottom of their shields to use as a barrier against rocks, arrows, and missiles. The shield would've been really heavy, probably about 8 kilograms (17 pounds).

Weapons

Hoplites carried two main weapons into battle:

- **Spears:** These were the most important weapon and quite big and cumbersome – about 3 metres long, made of wood, and tipped with iron at both ends (refer to Figure 5-1). Given their size, they weren't thrown like javelins (covered in 'Cavalry' later in this chapter) but used for thrusting and defence.

- **Swords:** These weapons were quite small, only around 60 centimetres long and would have only weighed about 1.5 kilograms but they were very deadly at close quarters. They were made of iron with a bronze handle and carried in wooden scabbards. Another version of the sword, called a *kopis* meaning 'chopper', was longer, heavier, and used with a slashing motion – usually from horseback.

Considering other troops

Although hoplites dominated warfare in ancient Greece, other types of troops took part in battle.

Cavalry

Cavalry weren't a big feature of early Greek warfare, partly because providing and paying for horses was incredibly expensive. The endeavour was also very risky. The Greeks rode without stirrups and mostly only used cloths as saddles. Ancient Greek cavalry were excellent horsemen; they needed to be because their main weapon was the javelin – actually several javelins – that they threw while on the gallop. A cavalry soldier didn't carry a shield or wear any armour. His only covering was a broad-brimmed hat that helped keep the sun at bay.

By the time of Alexander the Great (356–323 BC), cavalry had become a vital part of the Greek war machine. For more on how the cavalry developed, see Chapter 10.

Light troops

Sometimes the Greeks used lightly armed troops for special missions, like scouting and ambushing the enemy. These troops were called *peltastai* because they carried the light shield called a *pelte*. The *pelte* was usually a goatskin stretched in a crescent shape across a wooden frame. It was incredibly light and only really useful for deflecting small missiles from the *peltastai*. *Peltastai* were most often armed with a small bundle of javelins, which they used strictly for hit-and-run operations.

Archers

Archers appear a lot in Greek mythology. The hero Odysseus was famed for his skill with the bow, and arguably the most famous of all Greek warriors, Achilles, was killed when he was hit in the heel by the Trojan archer Paris. It was this story that gave rise to the expression 'Achilles heel' because it was the only vulnerable point on his body. The most famous Greek archers were from the island of Crete.

Greek archers were very lightly armed. The bows themselves were made of cedar wood with animal sinew used for the string. The bow would usually be the only weapon carried by the archers because it was vital that they could move quickly as the battle changed, so they could attack fresh targets. Despite this, archers weren't often used in Greek battles. The Greeks felt that it was more honourable to fight face to face and archers were sometimes of little use when a heavily armed *phalanx* (see the following section) was fighting in formation. Some Greek armies did use archers that hailed from Scythia, the large region to the north of Asia Minor. Athens kept a troop of Scythian archers, which Peisistratos (refer to Chapter 4) introduced. These archers were used mostly as a police force and not in battle.

Getting tactical: Hoplite formations

Films such as *Troy* (2003) and *300* (2006) can make it seem as if a Greek battle just involved everybody charging at each other in the midst of a general punch up. This was far from the case. Greek battles were fought along rigid tactical lines that meant each man knew exactly what his job was.

The hoplite infantrymen were dominant in ancient Greek warfare at the expense of all other types of fighting because they were so effective. The strength of hoplites came down to the shield. The *hoplon* shield was lighter than the larger shields that soldiers had used previously. As a consequence, men began fighting closer together in battle, and the hoplite *phalanx* developed – a powerful battle formation in which the hoplites lined up in files (see Figure 5-2), probably eight men deep.

In the *phalanx* the troops set out in an open formation, marching or jogging alongside each other with weapons sheathed until it was time for battle.

When a battle began, these open formations closed up, so that each man occupied only about 1 metre of space. Moving close together meant that the right-hand side of each man was pretty much covered by the shield of the man to his right – and so on all along the line. Tightening their formations produced the effect of a wall of shields that the hoplites then thrust their spears over or in between. Figure 5-2 shows how close the men were to each other and how they covered the man to their left.

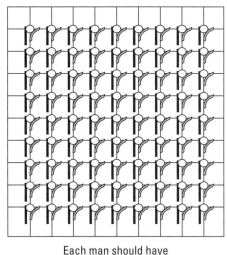

Figure 5-2:
The hoplite phalanx in battle formation.

Each man should have

| = Spear   / = Shield

Let battle commence!

Hoplite tactics were very regimented, reducing the role of the individual to that of a cog in a well-oiled machine. This was a complete departure from the super-heroes in *The Iliad* (see the sidebar 'Fighting like a Homeric hero' for more points of departure).

After battle began, the role of each hoplite soldier was to push forward against the man in front. If the man in front of you fell, you moved forward and took his place in the line.

The Spartan writer Tyrtaeus, who lived in the seventh century BC, wrote about fighting as part of a hoplite *phalanx*:

> *Everyone should close up to his man with his great spear or sword and wound and kill his enemy. Standing leg to leg, resting shield against shield, crest beside crest and helmet to helmet having drawn near, let him fight with his man with his sword or great spear.*

The key element to the battle was to push forward and at some point force the line of the enemy to break. After this happened, the fight was usually all over.

Reports of ancient Greek battles usually suggest massive casualties for the losers and only very minor ones for the victors. Although the figures are probably inflated, an imbalance between winner and loser makes sense: After the losing line broke, the victorious army would chase its men down as the soldiers fled the field, resulting in most of the killing that took place. Cavalry and light troops were also brought in at this point to chase the enemy down.

Imagining the abject terror of fighting in a battle like this may be difficult given modern warfare tactics. On the ancient Greek battlefield, you had no hiding place; you were face to face with your enemy. If you didn't kill or severely injure the man across from you first, he would kill or injure you. All around you, other men were dying of the most horrific injuries. You'd have had no time to save them or offer help.

'Are you calling me a coward?'

Any soldier who ran from the ancient Greek battlefield would drop his shield to move more quickly. The Greek word for this was *rhipsaspis*, or 'one who throws his shield away'. Calling somebody a shield-dropper was a huge insult.

Although ancient Athens didn't have an equivalent to modern laws of libel or slander, you could take somebody to court if he called you a *rhipsaspis*.

Living for Killing: The Spartans

As I note in Chapter 4, the people of Sparta were different from the rest of ancient Greece – and indeed the western world – in many respects. Their attitude was that you returned from battle *with* your shield – or *on* it (as a funeral *bier* or stretcher). The Spartans didn't believe in half-measures, and their standards of military discipline were absolute.

Military training for Spartan boys began when they were just 7 years old. At this age, boys left home and joined the education system. This comprehensive curriculum including hunting skills, physical training, and also emotional training – designed to teach bravery.

One particularly brutal element of Spartan education was called 'The Gauntlet' and involved boys running around and being continually flogged by older children until they fell down or, in some cases, died.

The final Spartan training exercise, called the *krypteia*, involved sending young men (possibly as young as 14) into the countryside alone with no food or water and requiring them to live on their wits for a month. Sometimes a *krypteia* also included the task of killing *helots* (see Chapter 4 for more on these people) found wandering the countryside.

Although these young men probably stole food to survive, stealing was considered a crime. A story from Plutarch shows the lengths that one young boy went to in order to hide stolen property:

> *The boys take great care over their stealing, as is shown in the story of one who had stolen a fox cub and hidden it under his cloak, for he endured having his stomach lacerated by the beast's claws and teeth, and died rather than be detected.*

Their training and ability to endure hardship made the Spartan army more feared than any other in Greece.

After completing their training, Spartan men became part of the army in which they had to serve until the age of 30. Between 30 and 60, they became part of the military reserve, which could be called upon at any time.

Sink or Swim: At War on the Waves

As I explain in Chapter 1, ancient Greece was very spread out, with people living as far apart as modern-day Spain and Turkey considered to be Greek. Consequently the wars that took place weren't always fought on land, and the

Greeks developed quite complicated methods of naval warfare. (I only talk about war ships in this section; you can find information on other types of sailing in Chapter 13.)

Getting on board the Greek trireme

The standard Greek fighting ship was known as the *trireme*, which comes from the Greek word *trieres* meaning 'triply equipped' or 'three oared'. The triple description comes from the three banks of oars that the crew used to propel the ship forward.

These ships were 40 metres long and about 4 metres wide – long, stream-lined, and built to travel as quickly as possible. They relied on the power of oars, although sometimes they incorporated a sail. Before going into battle, the crew lowered both the sail and mast.

The construction of this sort of ship was time consuming but followed a very specific model. The keel (central long section) was assembled first and then all the additional planking fixed to it and sealed. As you can see from Figure 5-3, the finished ship couldn't sit very low in the water because the lowest oars were only a few feet above the water. The ships were fast but not very robust and wouldn't have been suited to surviving really difficult weather.

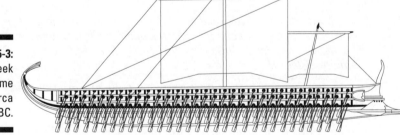

Figure 5-3: A Greek trireme circa 500–450 BC.

Meeting the crew

Each *trireme* had a crew of about 200 – a lot of people on board a small ship. The vast majority of the crew were on board to make the vessel move. Here's the crew roster:

- ✔ **Rowers (170):** Unlike in the Roman empire, the men who rowed the ancient Greek warships weren't slaves. They were well-trained citizens from the lower classes who ended up as sailors because they could not afford the panoply to be soldiers.

Rowing was hard, back-breaking work – continually digging in to heft the 4 to 5 metre (15 foot) oars. On a *trireme*, the rowers were arranged on three different levels: 62 upper rowers (*thranites*), 54 middle rowers (*zygotes*) and 54 lower rowers (*thalamites*).

✔ **Flautist (one):** Rather like the cox or skipper on a modern row boat, this flute-player helped the rowers keep time.

✔ **Marines (14):** These individuals were usually a mixture of hoplite soldiers and a few archers (probably Scythian).

✔ **Deckhands (15):** These soldiers had the vital work of keeping the ship functioning – making repairs and working the sails and tiller (steering).

✔ **The captain:** The captain of the ship was called the *trierarch*. He was responsible for everybody on board and the tactics in battle. He'd allocate duties to the various deckhands, all of whom would take turns on watch at night. Generally the *trierarch* took responsibility for navigating and setting course because that was considered a duty of command.

With all these people on board, triremes weren't particularly useful for transporting land soldiers around. The majority of Greek wars were fairly localised, so most soldiers would march to battle but if they had to be moved across the sea, they travelled on normal merchant ships, guarded by triremes.

Being nautically tactical

Fighting at sea was completely different to land battles. The great strengths of the hoplite fighters (see the earlier section 'Getting tactical: Hoplite formations') weren't very useful on the water. The two main attack methods were ramming and boarding.

✔ **Ramming:** Because the Greek ships sat low in the water, a ramming caused damage so severe that the rammed ship would sink. Surprisingly, if it was done correctly, it would cause very little damage to the attacker.

✔ **Boarding:** When fighting at close quarters, boarding was usually the preferred attack method and often took place after a ramming. Boarding usually involved grappling hooks, ropes, and other equipment to get a hold of the enemy ship. Eventually the Greeks developed something that the Romans called the *corvus* (Latin for 'raven'), which was a kind of bridge that swung onto the enemy vessel. Hand to hand fighting did take place in naval battles but the sides would have to be close enough together to do so first! The marines could only really actively engage with each other when the ships had locked together.

With both sides relying on fairly similar equipment, the Greeks had to develop attack strategies to gain an advantage over their enemies. The three main strategies, illustrated in Figure 5-4, included:

✔ The *diekplous* involved targeting one ship in the enemy line and turning it, breaking open a hole in their line. Any enemy ship that turned to aid the stricken ship ended up exposing its flank to the attackers too.

✔ The *kyklos* was a defensive formation that was used when a fleet was outnumbered or being pursued by a faster fleet. The ships formed a circle with their rams facing outwards, projecting at their pursuers.

✔ The *periplous* was an attacking move that was designed to outflank the line of the enemy.

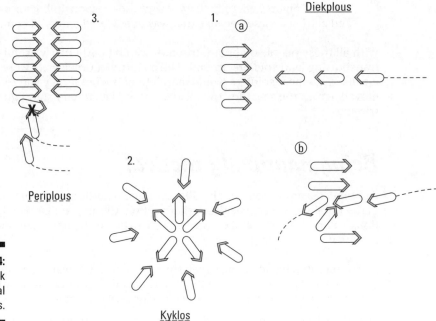

Figure 5-4:
Three Greek naval tactics.

Chapter 6

East versus West: The Persian Wars

In This Chapter

▶ Expanding the Persian Empire

▶ Joining the multi-faceted Persian army

▶ Fighting the big battles: Marathon, Thermopylae, Salamis, and Plataea

---

*P*eople in the ancient world experienced many and varied wars. Usually the fighting was more of a local thing, with neighbours acting on long-term grievances. Occasionally one city or region attempted to bring another city under its rule. Some wars, however, were massive, international events. The Persian Wars certainly come under this category.

Struggles between the west and the east are a big feature of history. The Persian Wars were followed by Alexander the Great's invasion of Asia Minor in the fourth century BC, the struggles of Alexander's successors afterwards, and eventually ongoing trouble between the Roman Empire and the Persians' successors, the Parthians.

Today, because the differences between east and west continue to cause friction and often escalate into confrontation, the Persian Wars of the fifth century BC have never seemed so relevant. This chapter introduces the ancient Persians and examines the problems they had with the Greeks.

Powering Up the Persians

The Persian Empire came into being in the sixth century BC, around the same time that Athens was going through the changes that eventually resulted in the beginnings of democracy (refer to Chapter 4). Much of the empire's early success can be attributed to King Cyrus and his progeny.

Taking charge with Cyrus

Within a period of about 40 years, the hugely successful Persian king Cyrus the Great took control of all the territory between Asia Minor (modern-day Turkey) and the Asian Steppe (modern Russia to the east of the Black Sea). A people called the Medes previously held most of this territory, but Cyrus effectively defeated them when he occupied their capital of Ecbatana in 549 BC.

Cyrus established this new Persian empire based around the city of Susa on what became known as the Persian Gulf (modern-day Iraq). As Figure 6-1 shows, this empire was absolutely vast, covering a huge geographical area of almost three million square miles.

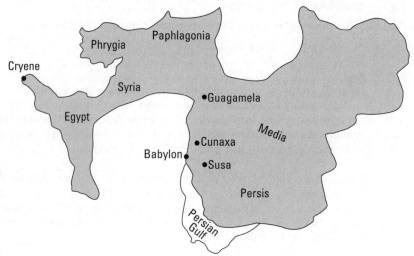

Figure 6-1:
The Persian Empire circa 500 BC.

Having gained control of such a vast area, Cyrus began to look to the west to further consolidate his territory and gain control of all the trade routes that passed through his empire to the Mediterranean Sea.

In fact, trade was what first brought the Persian Empire into contact with the Greek world. In 546 BC Cyrus fought and defeated Croesus of Lydia. During the Dark Ages, Greeks had established many new towns and settlements in Lydia (refer to Chapter 3 for more on Greek movements in the Dark Ages).

With Cyrus's victory over Croesus, the mighty new Persian power was less than a week away by sea from the Greek mainland. Furthermore, Cyrus divided Asia Minor and the newly conquered Greek mainland into provinces that were each run by a *satrap* – a local lord who controlled the area and its people and collected revenues, which he sent back to the king. The Ionian Greeks were now under foreign control.

The Greeks of the mainland were shocked to become subjects of the Persian Empire. The Ionian Greeks pondered how to respond to their new rulers, and eventually the Spartans acted. They sent an embassy to Cyrus and ordered him to leave the Ionian Greek cities alone. Cyrus's puzzled reply was, 'Who are the Spartans?' Cyrus did nothing and ignored them but confrontation with mainland Greece was inevitable.

Cyrus continued to expand the empire by attacking and conquering the fabulous ancient city of Babylon, which had remained independent of his rule to this point. After he was killed during a war in the north of the territory, Cyrus's successors continued to expand and refine the empire, and in 512 BC the Persian king Darius extended the empire's reach as far as Thrace and Macedonia.

The Greek playwright Aeschylus fought at the battle of Marathon (see the following section 'Going the Distance: The Battle of Marathon') and wrote a play called *The Persians* in 472 BC. In the play, the chorus of Persian elders give their opinion of Darius. Aeschylus was a Greek but his depiction of the Persian attitude seems authentic:

> *Alas! It was a glorious and good life of social order that we enjoyed, while our aged, all-powerful, guileless, unconquerable King god-like Darius ruled the land. Firstly, we displayed glorious armies, which everywhere administered tower-like cities.*

Rebelling with the mainland: The Ionian revolt

Greece and Persia eventually came to blows. The Persian army was much larger and more cosmopolitan than the mainland Greeks (see the nearby sidebar 'Assembling a league of nations: The Persian army'), but the main difference between the two armies was that the Greeks generally wore heavier armour and fought in a closely regulated formation (refer to Chapter 5) and the Persian troops donned light armour and were armed in a variety of ways.

Assembling a league of nations: The Persian army

The Persian Empire was huge and included many cultures; consequently its army was very diverse. Here are some of the main troops:

✔ **Persian 'immortals':** These full-time soldiers were of Persian origin and were the king's elite troops for ceremonial as well as battle purposes. They were known as the 'immortals' because of their incredible courage and fighting prowess – they fought like gods. There were always 10,000 of them and whenever their numbers dipped after a battle, more troops were brought up. The immortals' main weapons were the bow (which wasn't very effective against heavy Greek armour; see Chapter 5), short spear, and short sword. They also used large wicker shields called *gerrons* that were fairly light and quite manoeuvrable although not as strong as Greek bronze.

✔ **Mede cavalry:** Lightly armed cavalry was the Persians' other main force in battle. The cavalry's main weapons were the bow and javelins, which the horsemen fired while riding at speed. Very impressive.

✔ **Phrygian spearmen:** Recruited from Asia Minor, these were very fast spear throwers who were also highly manoeuvrable. They wore hardly any armour apart from a reinforced wicker helmet and a small round shield.

✔ **Ethiopian troops:** The vast Persian Empire even drew troops from Africa. These troops were generally referred to as Ethiopians, even though they had nothing to do with the modern country. The soldiers were very simply armed with a bow and spear and wore no armour at all.

The Persian army's mix of troops was one of its strengths, but it also inspired rebellion. During Darius's campaign in Thrace at the end of the sixth century, the contingent from Ionian Greece saved the Persian forces from defeat. The Greeks took their success in the Thrace campaign as a sign of Persian weakness and saw an opportunity to revolt.

A Greek called Aristagoras, who Darius had appointed to rule all of Ionia from Miletus, travelled to the Greek mainland to canvas support from the Ionian Greeks. The Spartans – surprisingly turning down an opportunity to be difficult and to fight – refused to join Aristagoras. The Spartan king Kleomenes apparently felt that the Persian Gulf was too far to travel for the cause of Greek liberation.

Eventually Aristagoras gained support from Athens and the city of Eretria. The revolt initially met with success, but the rebels couldn't sustain the uprising against Darius's massive forces. Darius had a whole empire to call on and could routinely devote 50,000 men to the campaign (see the nearby sidebar 'Assembling a League of Nations'). Eventually in 494 BC Darius's army attacked Miletus and razed it to the ground. The revolt ended, and Aristagoras fled to Thrace where he was eventually captured and killed while trying to drum up support for a fresh revolt. The campaign had taken over five years and Darius blamed the Greeks for it. Although the Ionian Greeks had caused the problems, Darius felt that it was the states on the Greek mainland which had been behind the uprising. His focus would now be on extending his empire west across the Mediterranean.

Going the Distance: The Battle of Marathon

In 490 BC, four years after the fall of Miletus, Darius's army crossed the Aegean Sea intent on the invasion and conquest of mainland Greece. The Persians had sent agents ahead of them to scout the land and try to arrange support from some Greek states. They'd been successful and the city of Eretria on the island of Euboia allowed the Persian army to land. From Eretria, the mainland was a simple trip by boat, landing in north-east Attica at the bay of Marathon only about 40 kilometres from Athens.

With the massive Persian army perilously close to Athens, the Athenians had to decide whether to stay in the city and face a siege in the hope that the other Greek cities would come to their aid, or go outside the city walls and march out to meet the Persians in battle.

Many believe the origin of the word *marathon* relates to an unnamed runner who brought back news of victory – the Greek word *nike* – to Athens. (This runner was also the first ever piece of product placement in history!) However, this isn't true. *Marathon* actually relates to a runner named Pheidippides who was sent from Athens to Sparta to tell the Spartans that the Persians had arrived. Pheidippides was the first Marathon runner. Only in later versions of the story was his run changed to being from Marathon to Athens.

Even though Pheidippides delivered his message, the Spartans didn't come to the Athenians' defence against the Persian invasion. The Spartans were celebrating a religious festival and refused to leave, so the Athenians were on their own. Led by the general Miltiades, they advanced to attack.

The battle: First blood to Athens

In the battle between the Athenians and Persians, the Persians were overwhelming favourites. They had a force of around 25,000 men including 5,000 cavalry. By contrast the Athenians mustered only slightly less than 10,000 hoplites (see Chapter 5 for more on the hoplites) and no cavalry at all.

The Persians made camp close to the sea in the bay of Marathon with a large marsh behind them and they marched out toward the small Athenian army with the sea to their left, as Figure 6-2 illustrates.

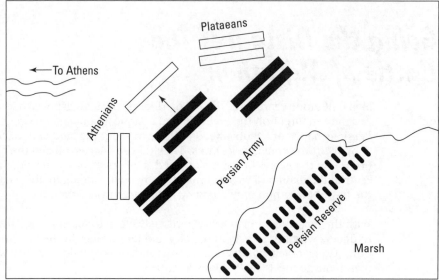

Figure 6-2:
Military manoeuvres at the battle of Marathon, 490 BC.

Additionally the Persians sent some infantry and all their cavalry by ship to Athens. The odds were almost impossible: The Athenians had to beat the Persians near Marathon and then dash back to Athens ahead of the Persian strike forces to defend their city.

The dire situation forced a bold Athenian strategy. As the Persians advanced, the Athenians ran towards the centre of its infantry line. Despite the fact that they were in arrow range, the Athenians' heavy armour protected them. The centre was the Persian army's weakest point, and it began to crumple. Many Persians were shocked and began to flee – some into the marsh and others back to their ships.

Instead of pursuing the Persians, the Athenians held their discipline and set off on an amazing forced march back to Athens, despite the fact that they'd all just fought in one of the hardest and most nerve-racking battles of their lives. They made it back about an hour before the Persian strike fleet. When the Persians arrived they saw they were outnumbered, and sailed back across the Mediterranean empty handed.

In the final reckoning the Persians lost about 6,000 men to the Athenians' 192. These few Athenian dead were buried with great ceremony in a mound that still exists. It was a magnificent victory – but the Persians would be back (see the following section 'Having Another Go: Greece versus Persia II').

Athens hits the jackpot

Marathon was a tremendous victory for Athens, but what followed was almost as important.

In 483 BC the discovery of silver in the mines at Laureion in Attica immediately brought fabulous wealth to Athens. This new wealth was a huge boom for the middle classes, but eventually the Athenians decided to spend their riches on something they desperately needed – a fleet.

The encounter with Persia showed the Athenians that mainland Greece was truly at the mercy of the Persian navy. By 480 BC the Athenians constructed a fleet of nearly 200 ships (Chapter 5 has more on Greek naval warfare). The motivator for this was the *arkhon* (elected official) Themistocles who famously told the Athenians to 'Lay hold of the sea'.

The people took him at his word as further fighting with Persian forces demonstrated.

Having Another Go: Greece versus Persia II

Darius wasn't around long enough to hold a grudge against the Athenians; he died in 486 BC. However, he was succeeded by his son Xerxes who was absolutely determined to gain revenge for his father's defeat and began to assemble a massive army and fleet.

Regrouping in Greece

The Greeks knew Xerxes would return to Athens and realised that a combined effort was required if the Greek mainland was ever to defeat the Persian forces.

In 481 and 480 BC, representatives of the major Greek cities held two big conferences at which 31 Greek states pledged to put aside their differences and join together against Persia. They erected a monument at the sacred site of Delphi as a visual symbol of their new unity. The conference also voted that the Spartans would have overall command of the joint army. For the fractious Greeks, this level of agreement was amazing.

The Greeks definitely needed to be united, because the size of the second Persian force was extraordinary. Ancient sources talk about a force of about a million, but the number was probably around 150,000 as the logistics involved in moving and feeding an army any larger than that would have made the invasion almost impossible.

Heating up at Thermopylae and Artemision

As the Greek troops made their way south, they had to choose a strategic location to make a stand against the Persians. Eventually the leaders chose a small pass in the southern Greek mainland near the mountains and the sea. The location was the famous natural sulphur springs – Thermopylae, literally meaning the 'hot gates'. It was a good choice because if they wanted to avoid going through the narrow pass, the Persians would have to take a massive diversion. Either way, they'd be held up until the Greek forces further south were fully organised.

Having chosen Thermopylae as the point at which to stand the Greeks sent their new fleet, which was mostly composed of the new Athenian ships (see the earlier section 'Athens hits the jackpot'), to Artemision, a promontory sticking out of the north-east corner of the Euboean peninsular where they hoped to stop the Persian fleet from joining up with its army.

The famous 300

Barely 7,000 Greek troops fought at Thermopylae, all under the command of the Spartan king Leonidas. The fact that only 300 of the troops were Spartan made the Greeks doubt the level of the Spartans' commitment. However, Leonidas chose the narrowest point of the pass to defend and, incredibly, he and his troops held on for two days against wave after wave of Persian attacks. Although other Greeks took part in this battle, the 300 Spartans were at the forefront, thus the famous '300' of the film!

After several attacks were rebuffed with high Persian casualties, Xerxes paid a local goatherd for information about an alternative route. This was another, even narrower track that took a longer way around the mountains. Xerxes sent a large group of his army's 10,000 immortals (see the sidebar

'Assembling a league of nations: The Persian army') on this alternate route in an effort to get behind the Greeks.

Historians don't know why, but Leonidas dismissed the vast majority of the Greek troops, leaving only his 300 Spartans and a few others. After a heroic defence that slowed up the Persian advance, Leonidas and his men were eventually overwhelmed. The Persians advanced swiftly further south but the hold up had been vital.

The heroism of Leonidas and the Spartans became legendary. The Spartan poet Simonides paid tribute:

> *Stranger, go tell the Spartans that we lie here*
>
> *Obedient to their laws.*

Simonides's lines were probably the ultimate expression of the Spartan ideals of bravery (refer to Chapter 5). Leonidas and his men had taken on a fight that they knew they could never win but had stayed and fought to the last man 'obedient to their laws'.

The action film *300* (2007) is based on a stunning graphic novel by Frank Miller and depicts the events at Thermopylae. Although the film has some fantastic elements and over-the-top scenes, the violence and brutality of the battle scenes are very accurate. It's worth seeing but is in no way a historical representation. It presents the Greeks as heroes and the Persians as evil – a very biased version. It also includes mythical beasts – none of the Greek historians mention them!

Meanwhile, at Artemision

While the battle at Thermopylae raged, the weather along the coast at Artemison was stormy, causing the Persians to lose large numbers of ships on the rocks. The Persians were further surprised by the Greek fleet, which captured several more of its ships. What remained of the Persian fleet sailed on south with the intention of meeting up with Xerxes and the land force before launching an attack on Athens.

Seeking safety in Salamis

The Greeks did exceptionally well at Thermopylae and Artemision to hold up such a massive army but it was nothing like a victory. The city of Athens was in a tricky position after these battles because it was left very exposed. The huge Persian army was moving south and looking to attack the city. The *arkhon* Themistocles realised that the city could never hold out against such vast numbers, so he persuaded the citizens to put their faith in the Athenian fleet.

The citizens of Athens abandoned their city and fled to the island of Salamis, and the Athenian fleet positioned itself near the island. The Persians took their chance and *sacked* (looted and vandalised) the empty city as the fleet travelled south. The Persian fleet then moved around the peninsular of Attica and approached the island of Salamis, but to get any farther they had to get past the Athenian fleet.

The Persians still had the advantage of numbers, but the Greeks countered with stealth and deception. The Greeks used a brilliant five-step plan:

1. They sent a false message to Xerxes the Persian king, telling him that the Greek fleet intended to flee north-east to the Isthmus of Corinth. Xerxes fell for the message and sent the Egyptian section of his fleet off to block the fake move.

2. At dawn the Greek fleet put to sea and headed north into the narrow channel between Salamis Island and the mainland. A small section of ships from Corinth went south to defend against the Egyptians who were soon to find out that they'd been conned.

3. Another small section of Greek ships hid in the small bay called Ambelaki to the south of the narrow channel.

4. The massive Persian fleet, thinking that the Greeks were fleeing, followed the Greeks into the narrow channel. The Athenians turned to face them, and the Persians were stuck. The Greeks rammed the Persian ships, and the Persian commander was one of the first casualties. Chaos ensued.

5. The small fleet hidden to the south caught the Persians as they tried to flee back down the channel, and the Corinthians (remember them from Step 2?) stopped the Egyptians from coming back to help.

The Persian fleet was *routed* (utterly devastated and incapable of recovery). They lost about 200 ships to the Greeks' 40.

Entering the endgame: The battle of Plataea

After the events near Salamis, the Persian fleet was in pieces, which meant its army was cut off from supplies. As September came – and with it the end of the sailing season – Xerxes decided to head north for the winter to rest his army and spend time organising supplies. In the event, Xerxes decided he'd had enough and headed back to Asia Minor. (He was probably worried that the Ionians may revolt again; see the earlier section 'Taking charge with Cyrus'.) Xerxes left the army under the control of his son-in-law Mardonios, who led the army south in the spring of 479 BC.

This battle really was the endgame – the Greeks faced the Persians on land in open battle. All or nothing.

The Athenians evacuated their city once more, and the Persians sacked it again. However, this second attack convinced the Spartans to finally commit to the fight (since Thermopylae their support had been in doubt). In command of the joint force was a young Spartan named Pausanias who was acting as regent for the young son of Leonidas (Leonidas was killed at Thermopylae). Pausanias led the army north into the lands around the town of Plataea.

The Persian recruitment drive

Although the Spartans had joined up again, many other Greek states refused to rally to the Athenian cause. As the Persians moved south, they were joined by contingents from Thebes, Thessaly, Phocris, and Locris, amongst others. None of the new recruits thought that the southern Greeks could possibly win. They figured they should throw in their lot with the Persians because it was odds on that the Persians would soon be their new overlords.

The battle of Plataea: A time for heroes

For a period of about two weeks, the Greeks manoeuvred around the countryside, avoiding the attacks of the strong Persian cavalry. Pausanias grew very frustrated and tried to work the Greek army into a position to attack. He attempted to make the move at night, but the plan ended in total confusion. As dawn broke the Greeks were halfway to their destination of Plataea. Mardonios, the Persian commander, sensed that this was the Persians' moment and he led an attack.

But Mardonios got it wrong. Although the Greeks had become a little split up, their hoplite training (refer to Chapter 5) kicked in as soon as they saw the Persians begin to attack. The Greeks assumed a defensive formation, which limited the effectiveness of the Persian archers' onslaught.

When the two lines of infantry came together, the Persians – despite their superior numbers – couldn't cope with the heavily armed hoplites. Slowly but surely the Greeks forced the Persians back. Mardonios was killed and soon afterwards the Persians broke, fleeing the field. As the Persians fled, the Spartans hunted and killed them by the thousands.

The Greeks scored an amazing victory against huge odds, but their success was due more to luck than wise judgement. Pausanius certainly hadn't intended to take the Greeks into battle when they ending up fighting, but at the end of the day it's the result that counts. The Persians were defeated and fled, and this time they didn't come back.

The poet Simonides recorded the epitaphs that the Athenians wrote to their dead. The following tells much about what the Greeks considered to be an honourable death:

> *If dying nobly is the greatest part of valour, to us above all others Fortune has granted this. For after striving to crown Greece with freedom, we lie here enjoying praise that will never age.*

Fighting the forgotten battle – Mykale

What happened next often gets a little bit lost in history. Marathon, Thermopylae, Salamis, and Plataea are always thought of as the biggest battles of the Persian Wars whereas it was actually at Mykale that the last act was played out.

As what remained of the Persian fleet made its way home across the Mediterranean the Greeks followed in hot pursuit and they quickly caught up. After what had happened at Salamis (see the preceding section 'Seeking safety in Salamis'), the Persians weren't keen to fight at sea, so they beached their fleet at the promontory of Mykale opposite the island of Samos, where they were joined by some Persian forces that had stayed behind in Asia Minor.

The Greeks, commanded by the other Spartan king Leotykhidas (each year Sparta had two kings), stormed the beach and burned the Persian fleet. As the Persians desperately tried to defend themselves, the Ionians who were part of Persian army swapped sides and helped the Greeks.

After Mykale, the Persian defeat was total, and the Persian Wars were at an end.

Heralding the Real Winner: Athens

The Persian Wars were huge historical events that impacted the course of western civilisation. Imagine how different things would've been if the Persians had won. Nearly everything else in the following chapters of this book would never have happened. The Olympic Games wouldn't be in London in 2012, and people wouldn't be arguing about whether the Parthenon sculptures in the British Museum (the so-called 'Elgin Marbles') should be returned to Greece. Who knows how the arts, government, and science – to name but a few critical areas – may have evolved without the Greeks' victory. History would've been very different.

Although victory in the Persian Wars benefited all of Greece, one city-state emerged particularly strong. Yes, the Spartans fought heroically to defend Greece, but the historian Herodotus gives credit for defeating the Persians to Athens:

> *And so anyone who said the Athenians were the saviours of Greece would be perfectly correct . . . they chose that Greece remain free and they roused all of Greece that hadn't medised [become a Persian ally] and played the main part, after the gods, in driving off the King.*

Athens' new fleet was without equal anywhere in the Greek world and its role at the head of the resistance made the Athenians very influential in all political and economic decisions to come. Athens' position ushered in a new era of empire building.

Part II

Athens to Alexander: The Rise and Fall of Empires

The 5th Wave   By Rich Tennant

"Okay, we've invented democracy, philosophy, and astrology. Now, Hilladius, you're working on something called pole dancing...?"

In this part . . .

The chapters in Part I look at who the Greeks were and how they forged an identity as a people by coming together to fight the wars against the Persian Empire. Well, some people did rather better out of that experience than others and in this part I look at the rise and fall of the Athenian empire and that of its ultimate successor, Alexander the Great of Macedon, who took the war to Persia. Hold on – it's a bumpy ride!

Chapter 7

Athens and Empire Building

*A*fter years of warring with the Persians, the Greeks emerged victorious (see Chapter 6) – and Athens played a massive part in the success. In the years following the end of fighting with Persia, Athens built on its successes to become the dominant Greek state in the Mediterranean with a domain comprising other cities, towns, and islands. In this chapter, I explain how the Athenians created one of history's greatest empires.

Establishing the Delian League: Athens Comes Out on Top

Although the Greeks defeated the Persians in 480–479 BC, the threat of the Persians returning to fight again was never likely to go away. All the Greek cities realised this danger, and after the celebrations of their great victories were over the big question facing the victorious Greeks was 'What do we do now?'

The Greek naval fleet continued to range around the eastern Mediterranean. In 478 BC Pausanias, the Spartan commander from Plataea, took the war to Persian-held Greek territories. First he sailed to Cyprus and managed to take control of the island. He then sailed up the Bosphorus to Byzantium (close to the site of modern-day Istanbul in Turkey) and managed to drive out the Persian garrison. Sadly, at this point Pausanius seemed to have lost the plot and was recalled to Sparta for attempting to install himself as a tyrant in Byzantium. If you want to know what happened to the power-hungry Pausanius, look at Chapter 26.

Let's stick together

Pausanius's naughty behaviour had a big effect. Despite the Spartan's military greatness (see Chapter 5), the rest of Greece began to suspect that they were not the best candidates to lead the long-term resistance against Persia. The Athenians, with their large fleet that had done so well in the recent war with Persia, seemed a much better alternative.

In the winter of 478–77 BC, ambassadors from many Greek towns and islands held a big meeting on the island of Delos. An Athenian general called Aristeides came up with the idea of a league of Greek states that worked together to protect the Greek world from the Persians – and also to financially compensate the states for damages that the Persian king had inflicted.

To prove their allegiance to this new enterprise, Aristeides proposed all the league members be required to pay an annual tribute of either money or ships to the Delian League treasury. (Aristeides himself decided how much members had to give.) Of course, the general also proposed that the Athenians supervise the entire endeavour and take on the job of treasurer, collecting and holding the cash for this new enterprise.

Essentially all the states (including Athens) were contributing for the common good because the collected resources were to be used to defend any of the member states against attack. Athens, however, was in a very strong position – having control of the entire operation made the city very powerful.

Adding another brick in the wall: Themistocles's return

Themistocles, the man who played a massive part in the battle of Salamis and persuaded the Athenians to abandon the city (refer to Chapter 6), made an even bigger contribution to Greek politics following the Persian Wars.

While the Delian League was being set up, Themistocles prompted the Athenians to begin rebuilding the walls of their city. In order to imagine the size of this undertaking, take a look at the plan in Figure 7-1. We don't know how high or thick these walls were but they were about four miles in length. Some parts are still preserved and if you go to the Naval Museum in Athens you can see a section of them.

Figure 7-1 shows Athens around 450 BC. By this point the walls of Themistocles had been joined to the 'Long Walls' that connected Athens with its port Piraeus. This meant that the city was completely encircled by defensive walls.

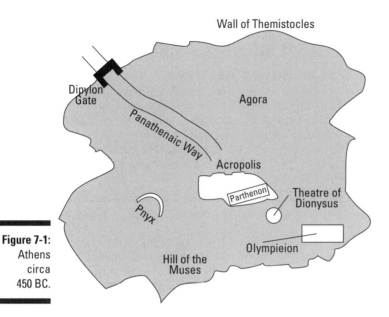

Wall of Themistocles

Dipylon
Gate

Panathenaic Way

Agora

Acropolis

Parthenon

Theatre of
Dionysus

Pnyx

Olympieion

Hill of the
Muses

Figure 7-1:
Athens
circa
450 BC.

Athens's protective walls had been destroyed during two Persian sackings (being vandalised and looted by invaders) carried out over the preceding 25 years. The move to rebuild the walls was very controversial at the time. The Spartans (who else?) protested against Themistocles's plan, claiming that it went against the spirit of the accord that brought many Greek states together to defeat Persia. Surely, the Spartans suggested, destroying the Athenian walls was a more appropriate symbol now that all Greek states trusted each other.

More likely, the Spartans were concerned about Athens's growing power and knew that large walls would make the city more difficult to defeat in open warfare because it would be more able to withstand a siege. In any case, the Athenians ignored the Spartan's protests and carried on with the building project!

Getting together the necessary amount of stone and materials was a huge task. The historian Thucydides describes the extent that some Greeks had to go to:

> *Meanwhile the entire population of the city should build the wall, sparing neither private nor public buildings which might be of some use in the work, but demolishing everything . . .*

The project took 20 years to complete. By 450 BC, walls encircled the whole city of Athens as well as the large port of Piraeus. The Athenians then went on to build 'the Long Walls', that linked the port and the city. No other Greek state boasted defences like this.

Thanks a lot, now push off!

You may think that a hero like Themistocles was guaranteed a life of fame in Athens after initiating the city's massive wall rebuilding project. No chance. Like many others, he fell foul of the chaotic political scene in Athens. Not long after the walls were finished, Themistocles's political opponents ostracised him from the city. He ended up in the town of Argos but was driven out of there when the Spartans accused him of intrigue. Themistocles finished up living at the court of the Persian king Artaxerxes, an odd place for a Greek hero to end up! He had dreamed of Athens gaining a whole Mediterranean empire – ironically that was exactly what they did after his death in 459 BC.

Athenian construction went even further, spending money on the buildings within the city. During this period the Athenians constructed the Parthenon on the Acropolis and many other buildings (see Chapter 18 for more on ancient Greek building techniques), which attracted huge numbers of artists and poets (see Chapter 17).

Expanding its Influence: The Delian League Goes into Action

Of course the Delian League wasn't just a defensive measure. Despite the fact that the league had been created to help the Greeks defend themselves against foreign threats, fairly soon after it was founded, the Greeks started to aggressively attack the Persians. The league seemed to follow the idea that attack is the best form of defence. From around 477 BC onwards the states involved in the Delian League began to launch attacks on Persian-held territories.

Representing the Delian League – or the Athenian empire?

Kimon was the man who led the new attack on Persia. He was the son of the famous general Miltiades, who had been one of the heroes of Marathon (see Chapter 5). Kimon had two significant early successes:

- ✔ In 476 BC, he captured the port of Eion, which was the last surviving Persian port on the borders of Thrace.
- ✔ In 475 BC he took control of the island of Skyros.

Holding out for a hero: Enter Pericles

By 470 BC, Athens was experiencing its 'Golden Age'. A combination of military success, financial security, and immense creativity in the arts turned this small market town in Attica into the absolute centre of the ancient world. (You can read a lot more about the achievements of Athens as well as the everyday lives of its people in Parts III and IV of this book.)

Central to a great deal of what was happening in Athens was a dominant new player on the political scene. His name was Pericles, and he made huge changes to the way that Athens looked and acted.

In many ways Pericles was a traditional aristocrat. His family was descended from the Alkmaionids, who were among the oldest and most influential aristocrats in the city (see Chapter 4). Despite this upper class background, Pericles was always very closely associated with democratic reform in Athens. (I mention several of these reforms in the later sections 'Navigating Athenian Democracy' and 'Examining the Athenian Legal System'.) And as a patron of the arts, Pericles was dedicated to turning Athens into the greatest of all Greek cities and (at the time) he arguably succeeded in doing so. It didn't last, however.

Although Kimon's victories were all well and good, other members of the Delian League began to question whether he had won the new territories in the name of the Delian League or the city of Athens. The answer soon became clear.

The island of Skyros wasn't even a Persian territory, but the Athenians claimed to have captured it for strategic reasons. Just to back their argument up even more, the Athenians enacted an impressive piece of spin-doctoring. Soon after Skyros was captured the Athenians discovered the skeleton of a very large man, and claimed they'd discovered the tomb of the hero Theseus (refer to Chapters 2 and 3). And because Theseus was an Athenian, Skyros must therefore be Athenian territory. Hmmm. This only served to increase the cynicism of the other members of the league.

Extracting protection money

The Athenians asserted their interests within the Delian League to an even greater extent over the next few years. In 470 BC Kimon used the fleet (technically the Delian League fleet) to force the Euboian city of Karystos to join the league. The city was no threat to Greece, but after the Athenians forced Karystos into the league, it had to pay dues (see the preceding section, 'Let's stick together').

Pestering the Persians

Kimon went even further in the following decade. He took the fight to Asia Minor and beyond. In 459 BC, the Egyptians revolted against Persian rule, and Kimon took 200 ships from the Delian League to the Nile Delta. The Delian League stayed in the region for five years, supporting the Egyptians' attempt to revolt.

What had started as a means of protecting mainland Greece from Persia had turned into something quite different. The military and naval strength that had been assembled to protect Greece from external attack was now acting as a kind of international policeman in foreign wars and engaging in unprovoked attacks on Persian territory. None of this was defensive and the greatest beneficiaries were the Athenians. The arrival of a new leader in Athens took things further still.

Transforming the league into an empire

Around the time that Pericles rose to prominence in Athens, the nature of the Delian League changed forever. The key event happened on the small island of Naxos in 470 BC.

Despite the continuing threat of Persian attacks, Naxos decided that it wanted to withdraw from the league. The Athenians responded by sending the fleet to attack the island and then destroy the walls of its main city. The Athenians also forced Naxos to continue paying its taxes – only this time Naxos had to pay directly to support the upkeep of the Athenian fleet.

The league was increasingly functioning more like an empire (with Athens as enforcer) rather than a mutually supportive organisation. Compared to the Athenians, the Persians weren't really that much of a threat to the people of Naxos! (A similar bit of political and military intimidation happened to the island of Thasos in 463 BC.)

Taking all: Athens in control

The Athenians effectively put the seal on the deal in 454 BC, establishing themselves as the leaders of an empire. During that year the Athenians moved the league's treasury from the island of Delos to the Acropolis of Athens. Not only did the leadership in Athens hold on to the money, but they also insisted on taking a percentage each year as a tribute to the goddess Athene (the patron deity of Athens) under whose care the money now rested.

This shift was a clear sign that Athens now considered itself the head of an empire rather than the chair of a league. The following section looks at how Athens managed to ascend to its dominant position.

Navigating Athenian Democracy

Many ancient Athenians probably considered the city's well-developed system of government to be the main reason it had become so dominant in the Greek world and Delian League by 470 BC. In Chapter 3, I examine how Athens's aristocratic system and tyrannies finally gave way to democracy. This section covers how the system actually worked.

Democracies exist throughout the world today, but they're very different from democracy in ancient Athens. Most countries today rely on some form of *representative democracy*, in which people vote for somebody (usually from a political party) to represent them in a parliament (or other governing body) and hopefully to vote in accordance with how people feel on issues. By contrast, ancient Athenian democracy was a *participative democracy.* Although the system included elected officials, government was carried out directly by the people, who voted on all major issues such as whether to go to war, build walls around the city, or start new religious festivals.

Getting organised

Athenian democracy ran via two main bodies:

- The **ekklesia,** or general assembly, which was the main body open to all male citizens over the age of 18.
- The **boule,** or Council of 500, which had a subcommittee known as the *prutaneis* to deal with emergency situations.

In addition to these two, the highest body in ancient Athens was the Aereopagus Council. This was a throwback to the old days of aristocratic rule in Athens (refer to Chapter 4), but as I explain in the later section 'Meeting the VIPs: Very important politicians', this group was due for a shake-up!

The following sections examine these bodies in much closer detail.

The Acropolis and its temples are very famous, and many think of the site as a symbol of Greek democracy. But the Acropolis wasn't actually the home of Athenian politics – this was based in various sites around the *agora.* Figure 7-2 shows the actual political areas in the Athenian public square, or *agora.*

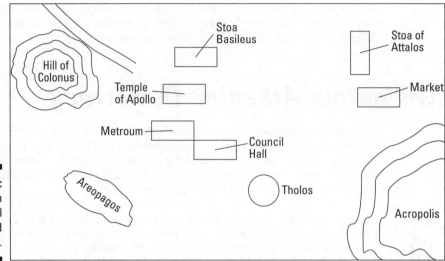

Figure 7-2:
Athenian
political
sites around
the *agora*.

Participating in the ekklesia

The *ekklesia*, or general assembly, was the main democratic body in Athens. Its job was to make major decisions and pass laws. If a male citizen registered in his *deme* (local area), he was entitled to attend the meetings of the *ekklesia*. It might seem as if this would make the meetings unmanageable but the Athenian population in 450 BC was around 250,000. Of this only around 30,000 were eligible male citizens (the rest were women, children, slaves, and resident foreigners called '*metics*'). Of these 30,000 probably an average of around 5,000 would attend *ekklesia* meetings. That's a lot but still only about two per cent of the population!

Meeting and voting

The *ekklesia* met regularly, four times a month on the big hill called the Pynx, which was located to the south-west of the city (see Figure 7-2).

Meetings were usually held early in the morning because agendas were lengthy and could take most of the day. Standing items on the agenda were defence, the election of officials, and the grain supply.

After this business was out of the way, the floor was opened by the chairman of the *ekklesia*, who was also the chairman of the *prutaneis* (see the sidebar 'Acting presidential: The *prutaneis*'). Theoretically, anybody could speak at the *ekklesia*, but matters to be voted on had to be cleared by the elected *boule* first (see the later section 'Joining the *boule*').

Votes were usually taken by a show of hands unless it was particularly close, in which case a secret ballot took place. It was a lengthy process where people dropped a stone of a different colour into a jar depending on whether they were for or against. The jars were emptied and the votes counted. The pebble and jar method was also sometimes used to decide sensitive issues such military policy and commands.

Speaking up, speaking out

Of course, some people in the *ekklesia* spoke more than others. Those people who responded most often became known as *rhetores*, which is where the words *orator* and *rhetoric* come from. Wordy modern politicians owe their name to this group of old windbags. Quite appropriate really!

The *rhetores* were regularly in attendance and became very good at speaking and quite influential. Although the *rhetores* didn't hold an official position, other attendees at the *ekklesia* looked to them to speak. Often a *rhetor* would represent a group of like-minded people, thus forming the closest thing that ancient Athens had to a political party.

Packing 'em in

So, if every male citizen over the age of 18 was eligible to attend the *ekklesia* surely every meeting was packed? Well, probably not, actually.

At the time of Pericles (circa 450 BC), estimates suggest that the citizen population in Athens was probably about 30,000. Clearly not everyone could attend the same meeting and have his say! Historians estimate that only about 6,000 people could attend a meeting of the *ekklesia* at any one time.

Citizens were unable to attend for many reasons:

- Citizens (who were mostly self-employed) lost a day's work by coming to meetings. By 400 BC, when the city was suffering after the Peloponnesian War (see Chapter 8), the Athenians instituted a system of attendance pay – citizens received 1 obol to compensate for lost earnings. For many citizens this was a mere gratuity.

- Many citizens lived all over Attica; the trip into Athens was time-consuming for these individuals.

In the middle of the fifth century, the Athenians introduced a new attendance system in which the Scythian police force (described in Chapter 15) dragged a long, red rope across the *agora* (public square) on the mornings when the *ekklesia* was meeting. People touched by the rope would already be late for the meeting on the Pnyx and that would show when they arrived with a big red stain on their clothes. They would then be fined for late attendance!

In his play *Acharnians* the Greek comic playwright Aristophanes (see Chapter 16) gives an interesting description of a day at the *ekklesia*:

> *At dawn, and the Pynx here is deserted – people are sitting in the agora and here and there avoiding the vermilion rope. Even the prutaneis haven't come, but they'll arrive late and then jostle as you might expect to try and get on the front bench.*

Despite Aristophanes's sarcasm, the Athenians loved democracy and shouted it from the rooftops. Although not every meeting of the *ekklesia* had maximum attendance, politics and the daily life of the city was on people's lips all the time in a way that may feel quite unusual to people today.

Joining the boule

The *boule*, or Council of 500, complemented the *ekklesia* as the other major element of Athenian democracy. Basically the *boule* was an administrative group that set the agenda for the *ekklesia*, where the main business was done. Subsequently, it was the responsibility of the *boule* to carry out the laws and administration that the *ekklesia* had decided on. The *boule* met in the large building to the west of the *agora* called the *bouleuterion*.

Like the *ekklesia*, the *boule* was an amateur group made up of citizens who gave their time for no financial reward. The 500 individuals who made up the *boule* had to be Athenian citizens over the age of 30. They served on the *boule* for a year at a time and couldn't serve more than twice in their lifetime.

Additionally, the 500 citizens were selected in a very specific way: Every year 50 men were elected from each of the ten tribes of Athens. This system meant that all areas of Attica were equally represented in the process.

Acting presidential: The *prutaneis*

The *boule* contained a special group known as the *prutaneis*, or presidents. This was an emergency committee that dealt with crises as and when they emerged. Serving as a president was a full-time job; citizens lived at state expense on 24-hour call in a building called the *tholos* (see Figure 7-2). The first duty for the *prutaneis* if a crisis happened was to summon a meeting of the *boule*. The *prutaneis* was a coveted position and usually only held once in a lifetime. A candidate would have to be wealthy because he needed to ensure others carried out his business or worked his farm while he served. Like other aspects of Athenian democracy, the *prutaneis* appeared to be open to all but time and money pressures meant that only the wealthy could really afford to do it.

In a sense, members of the *boule* were like a kind of civil service that administered all areas of the state. Huge numbers of people were voted in as officials on an annual basis to enforce the policies of the *ekklesia*. At points during the fifth century BC around 700 people served as registered officials although the vast majority of these posts weren't full-time and could be worked alongside the post-holder's own business.

The following are some of the more important positions:

- ✔ **The Nine:** These nine individuals (surprise) were the most senior officials. The most prominent of the Nine gave his name to the calendar year. The rest of the group dealt with public festivals, religious matters, and justice.

- ✔ **The Eleven:** Below the Nine in prominence, these eleven officials were responsible for the jury-courts and maintaining punishments and the prison (see the section 'Examining the Athenian Legal System' for more on Athenian legal matters).

Many other officials tackled other areas of civilian life. For example, some officials were elected to engage in foreign policy and foreign relations, including envoys (*presbeis*) and heralds (*kerux*), who were state-appointed.

Meeting the VIPs: Very important politicians

Despite the full democracy at work in Athens some citizens were more important than others. In many ways, the true leaders of the Athenian people were the Aereopagus Council, nine *arkhons* who were elected on an annual basis. The council was so called because it met in the space known as 'the crag of Ares' between the hill of the Acropolis and the Pynx. Although they met on their own these *arkhons* also attended all meetings of the *boule* and *ekklesia*.

Solon (described in Chapter 4) decided in 594 BC that only two people from the top two property classes were eligible to ever become *arkhons*. Dating back to the early days of Athens, any former *arkhons* had automatically become part of the Aereopagus Council. Originally, the council had administered most of the business of the city, but gradually the *ekklesia* and the *boule* took on most of these responsibilities. The Aereopagus became a court to deal with serious criminal offences.

The *arkhons* and *strategoi* (elected generals) were the most dominant people in Athens. They were very influential in the *ekklesia*, but their influence wasn't because people feared their power. Rather, the prominence of these people came from their being excellent speakers who knew how to work an audience and convince people to vote for their ideas.

One of the most notable VIPs was Pericles (see the earlier sidebar 'Holding out for a hero: Enter Pericles'). He was involved in changes that reduced the powers of the Aereopagus Council, but he also made significant changes to the other great boast of ancient Athens – the jury system.

Examining the Athenian Legal System

The legal system in ancient Athens was very complicated. I could write entire chapters – indeed books – about Athenian justice. In this section, I just give a brief guide and overview of what took place in the court of law.

The main principle of the Athenian legal system was trial by jury. The Athenians believed that, like politics, every citizen should contribute to the system of justice – and jury trials were the easiest way of doing this. Other Greek cities either decided on issues by the power of the monarch or ruling council or allowed individuals the opportunity to enact vengeance themselves. Athens was doing something really quite different.

Meeting the legal players

The *thesmothetai* – six *arkhons* who were part of the Eleven (see the section 'Identifying special roles and posts') – were responsible for administering justice, which meant staffing and running the jury-courts and ensuring that justice took place.

The jury-courts were known as the *eliaia* and were staffed by between 201 and 2,501 jurors, which the *thesmothetai* would decide upon depending on the case's significance. Immense care was taken over the selection of the jury to try and ensure that people with close relationships to those involved were not selected, but this was always difficult in such a small community.

The Athenians held a register of 6,000 citizens who were eligible for jury service. Pericles eventually introduced the system of payment for jurors, arguing that jury duty was as important as attending the *ekklesia* and so participants should be paid. The going rate was two obols a day (twice the rate of a day at the *ekklesia*). The number of cases going on meant that a juror was likely to be busy for many days of the year.

Prosecuting cases

Athens's legal system was different from modern, Western systems in that all prosecutions were brought by private citizens. The state didn't prosecute anybody. So, for example, if somebody broke into your house and stole your property, even if they were caught in the act, *you* would be responsible for taking them to court. Even crimes against the state, such as treason, were prosecuted by private individuals. When Socrates was put on trial in 399 BC for 'corrupting the youth of Athens' (Chapter 9 has the details) the charge was made by several private citizens, not the state.

Similarly, the Athenian system didn't have any lawyers, as you know them nowadays. Citizens represented themselves in court, although they sometimes got more eloquent speakers to write speeches for them – for a fee, of course!

Everything took place in front of the jury of citizens (no private discussions with a judge or meetings between lawyers). Also, trials had to be over in one day. In a sense this time limit made for a much less complicated process – although you can argue that the jury was merely swayed by clever speaking.

Determining the fitness of a witness

Given the short duration of all Athenian court cases, good witnesses were vital. In the Athenian court, witnesses merely gave their evidence; no cross-examination was allowed. The selection and use of witnesses in court was the main legal strategy employed by prosecuting citizens.

Only citizens were allowed to give evidence. This regulation meant that women and *metoikoi* (resident foreigners) weren't allowed to serve as witnesses. However, they could make a statement to a representative of the *eliaia* that a male citizen then read aloud.

Trial evidence provided by slaves was particularly controversial in the Athenian courts and was admissible only if the slave had been tortured first. This grizzly task was carried out by the Scythian archers who served as the Athenian police force and supervised by an *eliaia* official. (Indeed, the lives of these unfortunate people were in stark contrast to the experiences of citizens in highly democratic Athens; for more on slavery see Chapter 14.)

Doggone good justice

In Aristophanes's play *Wasps*, he pokes fun at the Athenian legal system and the tendency of some people to be over-litigious on trivial issues if there was any chance of gaining compensation. He stages a fake trial at which a dog called Labes is prosecuted for stealing and eating a piece of Italian cheese! The prosecuting citizen Bdelykleon sums up the charge and suggests punishment:

> Now hear the indictment. Prosecution by the Dog of Kydathenaion against Labes of Aixone that he wronged one Sicilian cheese by eating it all by himself. Punishment one figwood dog-collar!

Trying a case

At a preliminary hearing in the Athenian courts both parties stated their case. An attempt would be made to settle the issue at this point as the appointed *arkhon* would encourage both sides to negotiate. If that failed then any physical evidence was boxed up and handed to the *arkhon*, and he would set a date for the trial which could be several weeks or even months in the future.

At the trial a water-clock timed the proceedings so that neither side was allowed to dominate and both had sufficient time to make their case. Both sides presented their evidence and then the jury voted. If the jury decided on a guilty verdict then they took another vote about the form of punishment. Very often the prosecution suggested its own punishment during a case.

More often than not, the jury's punishment was a fine. The three heaviest penalties were death, exile (being expelled from the city either indefinitely or for a set period of time during which citizen rights would be lost), or *atimia*. *Atimia* involved stripping away the rights of Athenian citizenship. Although people could continue to live in Athens, they could no longer participate in any official functions. The Athenians often referred to *atimia* as a state of 'living death'. The presiding *arkhon* was responsible for ensuring that the punishments were carried out and would attend and supervise executions.

Chapter 8

Dealing with the Neighbours from Hell: The Peloponnesian War

In This Chapter
▶ Identifying the war's causes
▶ Waging the First and Second Peloponnesian Wars
▶ Surviving the plague in Athens
▶ Engaging in siege warfare

Thucydides the Athenian wrote the history of the war between Athens and Sparta . . . in the belief that it was going to be a great war and more worth writing about than any of those that had taken place in the past.

–Thucydides, The History of the Peloponnesian War

The Peloponnesian War lasted for more than 30 years. When it started in 431 BC, Athens and Sparta were pretty much unchallenged as the two dominant city-states in the whole of Greece. Athens had its international empire and dominant fleet, and Sparta had control of large sections of mainland Greece and its famous army.

By the end of the war, both sides were in a position from which they never really recovered. Essentially, their time had passed. The Peloponnesian War brought one era of ancient Greece to an end, and this chapter examines how.

Engaging in the First Cold War

A clash between Athens and Sparta was always likely. Ever since the final defeat of the Persians in 478 BC, the various Greek states had struggled for supremacy. Of all the states Athens and Sparta were the best placed to grab power. The states were rivals for several reasons:

- ✔ **Historically,** the Spartans were the military leaders of the Greeks, and the Athenians were the founding force behind the Delian League (see Chapter 7) and used this political entity to build an empire.

- ✔ **Politically,** Athens was a participative democracy (see Chapter 7), but Sparta was ruled by a dominant aristocracy and had two kings and a group of *ephors* (supervisors) that ran the state (see Chapter 4).

- ✔ **Culturally,** Athens had developed into the artistic capital of the Greek world, and Sparta was an austere, war-like civilisation that held fast to its strict and disciplined rules.

Athens and Sparta had a lot of differences but what they had in common was an aggressive foreign policy towards the other Greek towns and cities and they gained control over more and more of them when they could.

Like the US and USSR in the 20th century, Athens and Sparta had become too big to not be rivals. And just like the Cold War in the last century, any confrontation between the rivals had the potential to be brutal, final, and come at a massive human cost.

Sparta in the doldrums

The Athenians had done very nicely out of the Persian Wars – establishing the Delian League and creating a vast empire – but the years that followed 478 BC weren't as kind to Sparta.

The Spartans were the big players in what was known as the Peloponnesian League. This loose group of cities including Corinth and Elis banded together to face the Persian threat in the 480s BC. After Persia was defeated in 478 BC the league drifted apart, and the Spartans weren't able to call on league members for support in the way that the Athenians did with the Delian League.

In many ways 464 BC was Sparta's *annus horribilis* (awful year). During this year Sparta suffered a tremendous earthquake, resulting in massive damage to the town and the death of many people. Following the earthquake, the long-suffering helot population (see Chapter 4) took its chance to revolt. The Spartans managed to recover and pin down the revolting helots on Mount Ithome where they'd built a fortified encampment that eventually became a town. This was a huge problem for the Spartans because the helot population was massive – at least five times the number of Spartan citizens.

At this point the Spartans appealed to their fellow Greek towns – including Athens – for help to launch a final attack on the helot camp.

Kimon: A big fan of Sparta

Kimon was such a fan of Sparta and its constitution that he named his son *Lakedaimonios*, which literally means 'of Sparta' or 'Spartan'. Being sent back to Athens was a tremendous blow to him because he'd worked so hard for the campaign to be approved. He suffered the consequences on his return being *ostracised* (sent into exile) for ten years. Kimon tried (unsuccessfully) to return two years later but was eventually recalled in 451 BC when the Athenians needed his experience to help them negotiate a peace treaty with Sparta, and he resumed his leading role in the political life of the city.

Decision time in Athens

The dominant political figure in Athens in the fifth century BC was Pericles (see Chapter 7). He encouraged policies that saw the Athenians expand their empire and turn the city into a cultural centre. But Pericles wasn't a king and there were other speakers in the *ekklesia*, or general assembly, who disagreed with his reforms. (Chapter 7 has more info on *ekklesia*.) One of these was a man called Kimon.

Kimon was pro-Spartan in outlook, meaning that he felt the Greek states should work together for their own mutual interests. He believed that the Persians were still the biggest threat to all Greece and that the Athenians should seek to form an alliance with the Spartans that protected both cities from foreign, non-Greek threats like the Persians without coming into conflict with each other.

When the call for help came from Sparta in 464 BC, Kimon managed to persuade the Athenian *ekklesia* to vote him commander of an expeditionary force that would go and help Sparta. Kimon was hugely pleased with his new role, but his actions unwittingly kicked off the chain of events that started the brutal Peloponnesian War.

Things didn't turn out as Kimon expected. Although he was pro-Sparta many of his troops were Athenian democrats. When they arrived at Mount Ithome they upset the Spartans by expressing sympathy for the helots and their plight. The Spartans grew suspicious and sent the Athenians back home, saying that they were no longer needed. After all the debating, the Athenians never even lifted a sword in anger!

This incident at Mount Ithome was fatal to the relationship between Athens and Sparta and the divide between them became permanent. A few years later in 460 BC, the Athenians signed a treaty with the town of Argos, a sworn enemy of Sparta.

Thucydides: News from the frontline

Historians are very well informed about the Second Peloponnesian War, partly because of the work of the Greek historian Thucydides. Thucydides was born around 460 BC and lived through nearly the whole war and actually served as a commander for the Athenians. He was a relative of Kimon (see the sidebar 'Kimon: A big fan of Sparta') and a supporter of Pericles. Thucydides's book *The History of the Peloponnesian War* is the first real work of history ever written and it's written by somebody who was actually there, fighting in a war that took place 2,500 years ago. Amazing!

Enduring the first Peloponnesian War (460–446 BC)

By signing the treaty with Argos the Athenians officially became the enemies of Sparta. Over the next 15 years a war of sorts took place. Athens and Sparta attacked each other's allies on mainland Greece and close by. The war involved a lot of manoeuvring for position and short-term captures of territory.

Neither side managed to gain the upper hand, and victory was usually quickly followed by defeat. After early victories for Athens, the initiative gradually slipped away, with Sparta's allies the Boiotians and the island of Euboia revolting against Athens. In 446 BC, Pericles and the Athenian army were perilously cut off in Euboia when the Spartan king Pleistoanax had a chance to attack Athens itself. Pleistoanax didn't attack, and the war petered out. Pericles began negotiations, and eventually both sides signed a treaty declaring 30 years of peace. Unfortunately, the Thirty Years Truce, as it was known, was never likely to hold for that long. Fewer than half the 30 years elapsed before the beginnings of the Second Peloponnesian War.

Fighting the Main Event: The Second Peloponnesian War

Greek historian Thucydides was clear on the causes of the second, bloodier Peloponnesian War:

> *War began when the Athenians and Peloponnesians broke the Thirty Years Truce . . . What made the war inevitable was the growth in Athenian power and the fear that this caused in Sparta.*

Historians largely agree with Thucydides's assessment; fear of Athenian power had been partly responsible for the First Peloponnesian War (see the preceding section 'Enduring the First Peloponnesian War'.)

However, the incident that prompted the breaking of the Thirty Years Truce was a bit more interesting and took place on the island of Kerkyra.

Initiating a crisis in Kerkyra

Kerkyra was a colony of the city of Corinth. In 435 BC, the Kerkyrans revolted against Corinth, and a war raged for two years. In 433 BC, the Kerkyrans asked Athens for help, and the Athenians, sensing an opportunity, said yes and immediately became an enemy of Corinth.

Corinth was a member of the Peloponnesian League (see the section 'Sparta in the doldrums'), and when the Athenians clashed with them again over the small city of Poteidaia in northern Greece in 432 BC, Corinth complained to the Spartans about Athenian aggression. Surely, the Corinthians argued, the Peloponnesian League would defend its members' interests?

The problem was that the Athenians hadn't actually broken the peace treaty they signed with Sparta because they hadn't done anything against the Spartans' interests, so the Spartans would be the ones breaking the agreement if they took any action against Athens. During the winter of 432–31 BC, the Spartans spent days debating whether to move against Athens. One of their kings called Arkhidamos argued long and hard that the Spartans should hold back from confrontation, but the momentum was already behind war.

Really the start of the war had nothing to do with the rights and wrongs of the Athens and Corinth situation. As Thucydides wrote, the Spartans feared Athens's growing power.

Actually, in the end, neither Athens or Sparta officially started the Peloponnesian War – rather it was the city of Thebes, another influential and aggressive Greek state who were at the time allied with Sparta. Ironic really, because the Thebans ended up doing rather well following the war (see Chapter 9).

In the spring of 431 BC, a group of Thebans managed to take hold of the town of Plataia. The Plataians were allies of Athens and had refused to go over to the Spartan-dominated Boiotian League, a small group of towns allied with Sparta in the east of Greece. The Thebans' actions were a direct attack on Athenian territory and broke the peace treaty. The Plataians managed to kick out the Theban force, but it was no good. The war had started.

This early stage of the Second Peloponnesian War (the first ten years, 431–421 BC) is often known as the Arkhidamian War. Rather unfair given that Arkhidamos was a leading Spartan general who argued *against* fighting in the first place. After the war began though, Arkhidamos had to lead the Spartan troops.

Figuring out how to fight

Athens and Sparta fighting each other presented difficulties. In addition to the contrasts I describe in the earlier section 'Engaging in the First Cold War', the Spartans were the superior force on land, whereas Athens had a supposedly undefeatable navy.

These differences made actually fighting each other very difficult because:

- ✔ Pericles proposed a strategy in which Athens avoided engaging the Spartan army directly but used its fleet to harass and attack Sparta's allies, like the small towns in the Boiotian League.

- ✔ Sparta spent a great deal of time invading Attica without ever going as far as to lay siege to Athens.

The Spartan attacks in Attica were very harmful. The Spartans would attack and kill farmers and their livestock and destroy any crops. This had two big effects: First, food became scarce, and second, all the homeless people from the countryside (with the encouragement of Pericles) came to Athens.

Dealing with the plague

As the Spartan attacks continued in Attica and the area surrounding Athens, people began to pour into Athens looking for shelter and safety. The effects of this population increase soon took its toll. In 430 BC, a terrible disease took hold in the city. Many people at the time blamed the illness on a ship from the east, but the immense overcrowding and unpleasant conditions in the city can't have helped.

Thucydides, who caught the plague but survived, gives an unpleasant first-hand account:

> *The bodies of the dying were heaped one on top of the other, and half-dead creatures could be seen staggering about in the streets or flocking around the fountains in their desire for water. The temples in which they took up their quarters were full of the dead bodies of people who had died inside them.*

Life in Athens must have been absolutely horrific. Around 30,000 people died of the plague and its after-effects. The population in Attica didn't really recover for several generations.

The Athenian people put all the blame on Pericles because it had been his strategy to fight the war abroad and bring many people in Attica inside Athens's walls. He was suspended from his position as a _strategos_ (general) and fined.

Then in 429 BC Pericles himself caught the plague and died. By this point the Athenians had already reinstated him as a _strategos_ (due to a lack of alternatives). Death by plague was a sad end to the life of a great man – and Pericles's death left Athens facing a very uncertain future.

Responding to the Mytilenean revolt

The war pressed on regardless of Pericles's passing. With Athens doing badly some of her allies began to jump ship. In 428 BC, the town of Mytilene on the island of Lesbos (see the Cheat Sheet map) revolted against Athens.

The Athenian response was savage. First, an Athenian fleet was sent to blockade the island. After Mytilene surrendered, the Athenian _ekklesia_ voted to execute all the male citizens and sell the women and children into slavery.

Athens had previously done everything possible to nurture its relationship with its allies. So why the drastic change in dealing with Mytilene? Well, the death of Pericles left a vacuum in the _ekklesia_, and it was filled by what Athenian aristocrats referred to as the 'new men'. These new men weren't descended from ancient aristocratic lines like Pericles, and they rose to positions of influence through their ability to rabble-rouse and speak impressively in the _ekkleisa_ (see Chapter 7).

Chief among the new men were Kleon and Hyperbolos. Hyperbolos was so famed for his speaking that the word 'hyperbole' derives from his name which literally meant 'throwing beyond' (that is, exaggerating)! Both of these new men frequently gave inflammatory speeches that encouraged Athenians to take the harshest action. The response to Mytilene was a case in point.

Although Kleon had argued that Mytilene should be punished harshly, Athens was uncomfortable with this judgement. The issue was debated again the following day, and a majority voted for a lighter punishment. A ship was dispatched to take the news and arrived at Mytilene just in time to stop the massacre. Phew!

Athens's new men are mercilessly mocked by the comic playwright Aristophanes in his play *Knights*. Aristophanes had a particular hatred for Kleon, whom he called 'The Tanner', mocking his background in the trade of leather goods. In *Wasps* he went even further, naming characters 'Procleon' and 'Anticleon'. Procleon is written as a total braggart but a real wimp when it came to fighting:

> *'Here, here, what's coming over me? I've gone all limp, I can't hold the sword up any longer! All the fight's gone out of me!'*

Going international: A situation in Sicily

The Peloponnesian War from 431 to 428BC was so far, so Greek. But after 427 BC, the effects of the war began to spread around the Mediterranean. Other countries getting involved in fighting between Sparta and Athens may sound weird, but think about the way that the Second World War ended up being partly fought in North Africa, Japan, and the South Pacific as well as in Europe itself.

Additionally, a long history of Greek influence affected the region. For example, the Greeks had founded colonies in Sicily several hundred years prior to the Peloponnesian War (see Chapter 3). The island's many towns had close relationships with the Greek cities from which they'd originated through trade and population movement.

One Sicilian town was Leontinoi. In 427 BC, Leontinoi appealed to Athens for help against the attacks by Syracuse, and the Athenians agreed to assist. You would have thought that the Athenians had better things to do, what with the Peloponnesian War going on and everything, but Athens had hidden motives for wanting to help and got involved in another war that was entirely separate from their campaign against Sparta.

Unlike Attica and much of the Peloponnese, Sicily was rich and fertile, producing a huge amount of grain. In fact, a lot of the grain that the Greek cities consumed was imported from Sicily. Athenians probably saw aiding Sicily as a chance to get to grips with the grain supply – either by taking it all for themselves or stopping grain ships from reaching Sparta and its allies.

Perhaps the Sicilians worked out that Athens was likely to be a bigger threat than a help. When the small Athenian fleet arrived in Sicily it was sent back home again because Leontinoi and Syracuse had managed to settle the dispute themselves.

Nevertheless the Athenians kept an eye on Sicily and planned to return. (See the later section 'Attempting – again! – to take Sicily'.)

Putting up a fight for Pylos

While the Athenians were messing around and interfering with Sicily, almost by accident they struck a blow against Sparta. Incredibly, when a small group of Athenian ships on their way to Sicily passed the harbour of Sparta's ally Pylos in south western Greece, they found it virtually undefended.

The orator Demosthenes was on ship with the Athenian generals because he'd been sent to use his rhetorical skill in Sicily to negotiate terms for help with Leontinoi. He argued that they should take advantage of the situation and was dropped off and left behind with a small force to build a fort at the edge of the bay. The Spartans panicked and sent their army to fight against the Athenians. A land and naval battle ensued, and the Athenians won. Athens established a base at the closest point to Sparta. Also, 420 Spartan hoplites were left marooned on the nearby island of Sphacteria.

The immediate response of the Spartans was to negotiate peace – an offer that the Athenians rejected out of hand. A bit of a mistake really, as the Athenians were never able to really make the most of the advantage that they had gained.

The reaction in Athens was hugely critical; the populace accused the generals of not making the most of things. Chief among the critics was the demagogue Kleon, who claimed that he could've done a better job. In a shock move, one of the chief *strategoi* called Nikias said that Kleon should go and do it then!

Annoyingly, Kleon was quite successful the following year. Taking the experienced Demosthenes with him, Kleon and his men headed for Pylos and managed to capture nearly 300 Spartan prisoners at the battle of Sphacteria, who became a hugely useful bargaining tool for the rest of the war.

Swaying the north-east cities: Brasidas

Although the Athenians had an advantage through the capture of the Spartan prisoners, Sparta had been pursuing another strategy that was proving quite successful. In 424 BC some towns in north-east Greece that had previously been loyal to Athens decided to revolt. With Athens's resources stretched, it must have seemed a good time to try.

Sparta sent a large force to north-east Greece under the command of a leading aristocrat called Brasidas. He went on the equivalent of a PR tour, winning over many of these cities with his personal charm – combined with the presence of around 1,500 heavily armed hoplites.

Thucydides: Warfare's loss is literature's gain

Thucydides was one Athenian who was given command during the action against Brasidas. He was sent to defend the town of Amphipolis and prevent it from going over to Sparta. He failed to keep the city under Athenian influence – more through bad luck than anything else – and on his return to Athens he was sent into exile for an indefinite period as punishment. He resolved to travel around Greece as a result.

At this point in his life, Thucydides began collecting material for *The History of the*

Peloponnesian War, which he spent the rest of his life writing. The book wasn't published until after his death by which point those who had expelled him from Athens had fallen from power. It immediately became a standard work of history that was much admired by other Greeks for its detailed style and focus on accuracy rather than rumour. Just think, if he'd won at Amphipolis, historians probably wouldn't know nearly as much about the war!

Brasidas's campaign was hugely dangerous to Athens because when cities defected from the empire the Athenians lost both their revenues and the opportunity to call on them for military support.

The Athenians set out to stop Brasidas, and the end result was a truce that lasted for one year in 423 BC. Neither side could keep to the truce, however, and in 422 BC, Kleon took a force to the north to attack Brasidas. At a big battle outside the town of Amphipolis, the Athenians were heavily defeated and both Kleon and Brasidas killed.

Brokering a precarious peace deal: Nikias

After nearly ten years of conflict, both Sparta and Athens began to realise that neither side was going to be able to win the war – every victory came at too great a cost for the winning side to be able to take advantage.

Thus, in 421 BC, peace negotiations began, led by the Athenian *strategos* Nikias. The two sides managed to agree to a 50-year peace and also the return of the Spartan prisoners in exchange for Amphipolis. So that was all sorted then, wasn't it? Sadly, no.

Although the peace of Nikias was an excellent deal for Athens and Sparta, it enraged the other cities, including Boiotia and Corinth (see the section 'Initiating a crisis in Kerkyra') that had supported the Spartan side during the years of fighting. As far as these Spartan-supporting states were concerned, the peace deal offered nothing for them – all their grievances against Athens were unresolved.

With so much discontent the peace brokered by Nikias couldn't last.

Complicating the mix: Argos and Alcibiades

The cities that felt hard-done-by in the peace of Nikias deserted Sparta and looked to make a deal with the ancient city of Argos. Argos hadn't been involved in the Peloponnesian War up until this point; the discontented cities believed that an alliance with Argos was in their best interests. But deal-making with Argos added a third potential power to the mix and made a complicated situation even worse.

At the same time Athens was falling under a new and exciting influence in the *ekklesia* – a man called Alcibiades. This young, charming, and apparently immensely handsome aristocrat possessed a tremendous talent for swaying popular opinion. (See Chapter 26 for more on this complicated fellow.)

In 420 BC, Alcibiades managed to convince the *ekklesia* that Athens could profit from what was happening with Argos. He argued that the cities were flocking to join with Argos because Sparta was now their enemy. By logical extension, these discontented states were now Athenian allies. Brilliant!

Alcibiades won the day, and Athens made an alliance with the cities of Argos, Mantineia, and Elis. Although this technically didn't break the peace of Nikias, it certainly strained it.

Of course, confrontation soon happened. In 418 BC, the Spartan king Agis attacked Argos, which the Spartans now saw as their main threat. This attack meant that the allies of Argos had to come to the city's defence – and those allies now included Athens!

The result was a battle outside the town of Mantineia. The Spartans soundly defeated a combined force of Argos and its allies. The victory was a massive confidence boost to the Spartans, reinforcing their reputation for invincibility.

Engaging in siege warfare in Melos

After losing at Mantineia, Athens quickly fell back into the policy that Pericles had proposed – attacking Spartan allies and adding them to its empire. In 416 BC, Athens's focus turned to the island of Melos, part of the Cyclades. The siege wasn't an arduous one, but when Melos finally broke, the Athenians did to Melos what they had threatened to do to Mytilene years before: All the men were put to death and the women and children sold into slavery. (See the earlier section 'Responding to the Mytilenean revolt'.)

The Athenians' actions sound absolutely barbaric today (and have unpleasant echoes of the 'ethnic-cleansing' that took place during the last century). No excuse can justify the barbarous destruction of an entire community, but in the ancient world it wasn't unusual for a siege to end like this.

Laying siege: The waiting game

In Chapter 5, I talk about the infantry battles, cavalry, and naval warfare of ancient Greeks. The other major form of military engagement during this time was the siege. A lot of siege warfare occurred during the Peloponnesian War, and Alexander the Great (see Chapters 10 and 11) was a devil for a siege. In essence, a city that was being attacked had two choices: come out and fight, or lock the gates and try to sit it out. Consequently sieges happened very often.

Generally speaking, laying a siege was a long process. The attacking army blockaded the enemy town and then essentially sat there and waited. The siege came to an end either when the attackers managed to get in, or either party gave up.

In any siege the attacking side needed to be confident that they were able to starve out those inside the city. Thus, the attacker's supply lines needed to be excellent. They had to have enough troops to surround the city and prevent supplies getting in. When laying siege to ports, this blockade activity, known as *circumvallation*, was often done by using a fleet to intercept supply ships and guard the harbour.

Sieges were very time consuming and never guaranteed success. An attacker could waste months on a siege that then had to end because the troops were required elsewhere. The process was also grim, boring work for the attackers, and armies often became ill-disciplined.

Developing new tactics

By the time of the Peloponnesian War, the Greeks had developed some new tactics to go on the offensive. Following are five popular options:

✔ **Mounds:** This approach was quite simple really. The attackers constructed a very large earth mound with an underlying structure of
timber against a wall of the city. The timber ensured that the mound
wouldn't be ground down by the thousands of feet pounding on it. The
attackers then used the mound as a ramp for mounting infantry charges,
bringing archers closer to their targets, and manoeuvring battering
rams. Walls could be 25–30 feet high so it was often easier to bash a hole
in them than climb over!

✔ **Towers:** The attackers built siege towers, which were large wooden con-
structions from which archers provided covering fire to troops attacking
the walls. The towers would normally be slightly higher than the walls
so that the archers could shoot down onto the defenders (although the
height would depend how much timber was available). Check out
Chapter 12 for the ultimate siege tower – Demetrius's 'Heliopolis'.

✔ **Mines:** For this tactic, the attackers literally dug under the other side's
protective walls sometimes 10 or 15 feet deep. Digging mines was an
incredibly dangerous job because those doing it were liable to be
crushed by the mine collapsing or the walls themselves falling on them.
The defenders often poured water into the mines, flooding them and
drowning the attackers.

✔ **Battering rams:** This tactic was mostly used in conjunction with mounds.
Teams of men continually charged a wall, striking it with a ram made of
wood, until the wall fell. Siege towers and archers often provided cover
for battering ram teams.

✔ **Treachery:** By far the simplest way for an attacker to gain victory was to
get a message to a traitor *within* the town who then opened the gates.
Often these traitorous actions were in return for money or simply the
promise that the traitor and their family would be spared when the town
was taken. Of course, often the promised safety or compensation didn't
happen in the melee that followed.

Following a siege

After a siege broke and a town was in the possession of the enemy, what followed was often terrible. The massacre of all prisoners became increasingly
common during the Peloponnesian War, as the war itself became more and
more brutal. These killings were often prompted by a shortage of food; limited resources meant keeping prisoners was impossible. On other occasions,
the killings were to prevent the town involved from ever seeking revenge.

If a deal could be struck between attacker and the besieged citizens, it often
was. For example, the Spartan prisoners taken at Sphacteria by Kleon and
Demosthenes (see the previous section 'Putting up a fight for Pylos') were
taken only because they were a really useful bargaining tool.

Sometimes the defending city won of course. Laying siege was a lengthy, arduous process and sometimes the attackers ran out of supplies (and energy) first. However, more often than not it was the attackers that won and the defenders who suffered the consequences.

War, like life itself in the ancient world, was a harsh and brutal business. The Athenian plague of 430 BC is a good indication of how death was an ever-present possibility for the ancient Greeks. While the difficulties of just staying alive don't in any way excuse the cold-blooded murders that frequently took place, considering the difficult daily lives of the ancient Greeks does help cast a light on the type of mindset that made the life-or-death decisions on the battlefield.

Attempting – again! – to take Sicily

Soon after the Athenians' brutal siege on Melos they suffered one of the most humiliating defeats ever as part of a failed Sicilian Expedition.

Amazingly, despite his role in the policy that had ended in defeat in Mantineia, Alcibiades (see the previous section 'Complicating the mix: Argos and Alcibiades') was still extremely influential in Athenian politics. When the Sicilian city of Egesta asked for help in a local war with their neighbours Selinous in the winter of 416 BC, Alcibiades enthusiastically championed the cause.

The older statesman Nikias was more circumspect, but because the war with Sparta had eased since Mantineia, the *ekklesia* happily voted to support Egesta. The Athenians also voted that the generals in charge of the fleet would be Nikias, Lamakhos, and Alcibiades himself.

Scandal and drama: Alcibiades

Just as the Athenian fleet was about to leave for Sicily, scandal hit the city. First, people inflicted damage on some *hermai*, which were small statues of the god Hermes that were associated with bringing good luck to travellers. These *hermai* were sculpted with erect penises and vandals had snapped them all off – ouch! The connection between the statues and the upcoming Sicilian Expedition must have been obvious to the Greeks who interpreted it as an attempt to curse the mission by desecrating images of the god of travel. It was both sacrilegious and also considered a bad omen for those going to Sicily, as it proved to be.

At almost the same time, in the *ekklesia* Alcibiades was accused of the crime of mocking the Eleusinian Mysteries (a very strange, sacred ritual that I describe in Chapter 22). Alcibiades's actions seem to have merely been the result of rich, young aristocrats living it up, but the consequences were very serious. Before the Athenian fleet even reached Sicily, a messenger caught up with them to announce that Alcibiades was being recalled to face prosecution. His reaction was to leave the fleet and sail to Sparta where he became an adviser to his ex-enemies! For more on Alcibiades's colourful life, see Chapter 26.

Disaster in Sicily

The Athenian fleet did eventually arrive in Sicily – commanded by Lamakhos and Nikias. Their first move was to lay siege to the great city of Syracuse that was supporting Selinous, the town that had attacked Egesta. Lamakhos was killed in early 414 BC, leaving Nikias in sole control.

Things were progressing well for the Athenians until the Syracusans were relieved by a group of Spartans who'd been sent to Sicily on the advice of – you guessed it – Alcibiades!

The Athenians now found themselves blockaded into the harbour of Syracuse and eventually the Athenian fleet was defeated. The Athenian soldiers tried to retreat across land but were outmanoeuvred and defeated by the Syracusans in 413 BC.

The results of the defeat were catastrophic for Athens. The commanders (including Nikias) were executed and all the remaining prisoners forced to work in the stone quarries of Syracuse. The existence was appalling with death coming as a merciful release. Altogether, about 7,000 Athenian soldiers and sailors were lost to death or slavery.

Thucydides firmly believed that the failure of the Sicilian Expedition was probably the biggest catastrophe that Athens had ever suffered:

> . . . for they were utterly and entirely defeated; their sufferings were on an enormous scale; their losses were, as they say, total; army, navy, everything was destroyed, and, out of many, only few returned.

Pondering the end of Athens

The defeat in Sicily was a real turning point in the Peloponnesian War. From 413 BC onwards, the war ceased to be a struggle between Athens and Sparta and became an opportunity for others to get involved and get rich pickings.

The fat (Athenian) lady hadn't sung yet, but she was certainly warming up. However, in the end Athens's final defeat was really prompted from within – as I explain in Chapter 9.

Chapter 9

Losing Their Way: The End of Classical Greece

As the Peloponnesian War dragged on toward a finish (see Chapter 8), the era that historians consider 'Classical Greece' was also drawing to a close. The dominance of the Greek city-states like Athens, Sparta, Thebes, and Corinth didn't have long to run. By around 350 BC, a new power emerged in the north – Macedonia – and the Greek world was never the same.

In this chapter, I look at what happened at the end of the Peloponnesian War and the chaos that followed. The end of Classical Greece is a complicated – but fascinating – period of ancient Greek history!

Weathering Tough Times: Athens

The failure of the Sicilian expedition in 413 BC (see Chapter 8) was almost a mortal blow for Athens in its long battle with Sparta and its allies, which had lasted decades. At a stroke, Athens lost several thousand fighting men, three of its leading generals and a large portion of its fleet. But although Athens was down, it certainly wasn't out.

Preying on Athens: Another round of Persian intrigue

The rest of the Mediterranean was watching, including the Persians who'd waged a brutal on/off war against Greece from 490 to 478 BC. (See Chapter 6 for all the gory details.)

Unsurprisingly, the Spartans were the first to take advantage of Athens's weakened stature. In 413 BC, the Spartans actually occupied Attica by making a permanent fort outside the town of Dekeleia. The Spartans also began constructing a new fleet.

Elsewhere, Athens's empire was breaking up. Several places such as the island of Lesbos revolted, knowing that the Athenians were unlikely to be able to do anything about it.

Over-extending itself: Athens pesters Persia

At a time like this, you may be thinking that the last thing that the Athenians wanted was to get involved in another foreign war – but that's exactly what happened. They threw their support behind the rebel Amorges who were trying to bring Karia away from Persian control.

Lending support to Amorges raised Persian awareness of Athens's troubles, and the Persians began to negotiate with Sparta. In return for Spartan support, Persia made large financial contributions to help build the new Spartan fleet.

Staging a coup in Athens

By 411 BC Persia wasn't the only power that was trying to benefit from Athens's diminished status. While some of the Athenian fleet was moored at Samos, its commanders were contacted by good old Alcibiades (see Chapter 8). After doing a bunk to Sparta, Alcibiades became (unsurprisingly) unpopular with the Spartans and travelled to the Greek cities in Asia Minor, ending up as a paid advisor at the court of a Persian *satrap* (regional governor) called Tissaphernes. However, Alcibiades had his eye on returning to Athens – but on his own terms.

Alcibiades knew that returning to Athens was going to be immensely difficult. He was still technically on the run and had previously collaborated with Sparta, Athens's prime enemy. So he tried to convince the generals sent to support Amorges to go back to Athens and represent him by stirring up trouble against the current Athenian government. Alcibiades was effectively proposing that Athens stage a revolution so that he could return. He would gain support from the new regime from Persia. Say what you like about Alcibiades, but he must have been some talker!

Many of the Athenian generals rejected Alcibiades's proposal and stayed on Samos, forming a pro-democracy group, but one general called Peisandros headed back to Athens and began agitating for revolt. A mixture of violence and intimidation led to a coup taking place in Athens. A number of leading members of the *ekklesia* were killed and others were forced to flee for their safety – many of them went to the island of Samos.

A new body of 400 was established, made up of 40 men (mostly aristocrats) from each of Athens's ten tribes. (See Chapter 7 for more on the composition of Athens's legislative bodies.) These new leaders made a pledge to divert all financial resources to furthering the war against Sparta. In addition, 5,000 of the wealthiest citizens agreed to pay for their own hoplite armour (see Chapter 5) and form a fighting force.

That's the way the 'coup' crumbles

But like so many political pledges the promise initiated in the coup was never fulfilled. Vast numbers of the wealthier citizens left Athens, and the 400 new aristocrats were unable to raise the money that they needed to fund more fighting. Alcibiades fell out with Tissaphernes, so the promised Persian support never materialised either. In the end, Alcibiades ended up offering advice to the exiled democrats that had fled to Samos from Athens after the coup!

By September 411 BC the Athenians had run out of patience with the 400 new political leaders who'd failed to bring about anything in particular. The democrats that remained, led by a man called Cleophon, re-established democracy, known as the 'rule of 5,000'. It was so named because rule had been handed back to the people, rather than 400 people ruling. It wasn't that 5,000 people seized control!

By the way, Cleophon was known as the 'lyremaker' because he came, like Kleon, from an artisan background.

Thucydides passes the torch to Xenophon

Around time of the Athenian coup (411 BC), Thucydides's historical narrative *History of the Peloponnesian War* runs out. Fortunately, readers have another history that picks up almost directly after, written by a man called Xenophon.

Xenophon was a gentleman farmer from Attica who had an eventful life (see the section

'Mounting Problems in the Persian Empire' later in this chapter). In his retirement, Xenophon wrote an extensive account of Greek history during his lifetime. He is also one of the best sources that we have for the philosopher Socrates. Xenophon wrote many essays and works of philosophy based around his method of argument (see Chapter 23).

The whole coup didn't achieve much, but it did prove two things:

- ✔ Athens's devotion to democracy was surviving – even while engaged in a long war with Sparta.
- ✔ The divide between Athenian aristocrats and 'new men' (see Chapter 8) was still carrying on.

Wrapping Up the Peloponnesian War

With the return of democracy, Athens started doing rather well again. Several naval victories occurred between 410 and 407 BC – some of them involving Alcibiades (see the earlier section 'Staging a coup in Athens') who had thrown in his lot with the democrats who'd fled into exile on Samos and returned to Athens with them.

Alcibiades's success didn't last. Sparta entered into another deal with Persia. This time Cyrus, the youngest son of King Darius (who had invaded Greece in 479 BC – refer to Chapter 6), agreed to finance the Spartan fleet, and the new Spartan ships won a famous victory off the coast of Asia Minor in 406 BC. Alcibiades wasn't present at the battle but was blamed for the defeat, so he went into exile again, this time to Thrace.

Enduring great losses at Arginoussai

Athens's boost was ultimately short-lived. In 406 BC, during what had been a successful battle with the Spartan fleet near the Arginoussai islands, 13 Athenian ships were lost and 12 damaged. The two captains, or *trierarchs,* in charge were unable to pick up the survivors due to a terrible storm. Around 3,000 Athenians were left to drown.

Waiting in the wings: Going into exile

As you might have noticed, exile was a very popular punishment in ancient Greece. In essence it meant being sent away from your city of origin and losing your rights as a citizen. Exile was rarely permanent (due mostly to the fractious nature of Greek politics!) and was an obviously preferable alternative to being put to death. Finding somewhere to be exiled could be a problem because most exiles tended to be aristocrats or leading politicians, so tended to be wealthy and/or well connected. Aristocratic exiles might stay with friends in another city or set themselves up in a new town at their own expense. People must have found it frustrating to lose the opportunity to participate in the political games in their native city, but they were usually back in action again pretty soon. Two of the most famous (and frequent) exiles were Alcibiades and Pausanius; check out Chapter 27 for the full story on both of them.

Six of the *strategoi* (generals) who were in charge of the campaign were put on trial in Athens and executed. Athens could ill-afford the loss of some of its most senior military minds and the decision proved a very unpopular one.

Running out of options

The following year Athens's defeat was final. The Athenian fleet was beached at the Hellespont (between Thrace and Asia Minor) when the Spartan commander Lysander initiated a surprise attack. Almost the entire Athenian fleet was captured with only nine ships escaping. The 26-year-long Peloponnesian War was effectively over. With no fleet to protect Athens, Sparta and her allies seemed likely to lay siege to the city.

Xenophon paints a vivid picture of what it was like in Athens on the evening the lone ship *Paralos* brought news of defeat to the city:

> *It was at night when the Paralos arrived at Athens. As the news of the disaster was told, one man passed it to another, and a sound of wailing arose and extended first from Piraeus, then along the long walls until it reached the city. That night no one slept. They mourned for the lost, but more still for their own fate.*

Bowing to the Spartans: Athens after the war

After the crushing final naval defeats, Athens expected the worst from Sparta. As I explain in Chapter 8, cities that resisted siege attacks typically suffered heavily after they were finally defeated. Also, Sparta and her allies had 25 years' worth of grudges to avenge.

Socrates: Victim of a shifting society

One famous victim of the new regime in Athens was the philosopher Socrates. Many Athenian aristocrats didn't trust Socrates, and he'd refused to cooperate with the 30 tyrants. The new democracy in Athens was distrustful of anything different or against tradition. Socrates held no official post but was one of the leading intellectuals in Athens and had developed a system of philosophical argument that involved him challenging people's assumptions and questioning their beliefs. Usually this was about moral and ethical questions but he was also interested in justice and the way that the state ran. He famously said, 'All that I know is that I know nothing' meaning that he didn't claim to know any answers himself.

In 399 BC, he was put on trial for not respecting the gods and corrupting the youth of the city. These charges were trumped-up, and he was most certainly framed – nevertheless he was found guilty and sentenced to death. He died by drinking hemlock – his own choice. This was a relatively quick death but still a very painful one because a person's body would go very cold before being gripped by a seizure. It was a sad end for a great man in human history.

Living under Spartan conditions

In the end, Athens wasn't destroyed nor its population enslaved. After the best part of a year in negotiation, Athens finally agreed to Sparta's surrender terms, which included the following:

- All territories that had previously been part of the Athenian empire were set free of any obligations to Athens. They no longer had to pay tribute or supply men for military service when asked.

- Athens's fleet was to be limited to 12 ships. This number would be just about enough to guard their harbours and was a dramatic reduction of the fleet of over 100 that Athens had once enjoyed.

- The protective 'long walls' of the city (see Chapter 7) were to be demolished.

- All Athenian exiles had to be recalled.

- Athens was now a Spartan territory under Spartan control.

The surrender was a huge blow to a city that only 30 years before was the dominant force in the Mediterranean world.

Establishing the rule of the Thirty

The Spartans forced Athens to break up its democracy and go back to oligarchic rule (oligarchy means 'rule of the few'). In 404 BC, the Spartan general Lysander forced the Athenians to establish a new committee of

30 individuals to run the city (under Spartan supervision, or course). Many of 'the Thirty' were formerly exiled aristocrats who'd been involved in the oligarchic coup in 411 BC (see the earlier section 'Staging a coup in Athens') and had only recently returned to the city. The Thirty's authority was backed up by 700 Spartan troops who served as a garrison in the city.

Unsurprisingly, the Thirty had a few scores to settle in Athens, and they used their new authority to take full advantage. In his book *Politics,* the philosopher Aristotle describes what happened when the Thirty came to power:

> *But when they had firmer control of the city, they spared none of the citizens, but put to death those who were noted for their property, family, and reputation, because this removed their own fear and they wanted to appropriate their property; and in a short space of time they had done away with no less than 1,500 . . .*

No honour among thieves

So the 30 newly instated tyrants began turning on each other – and trials and executions followed. At the same time democrats who'd left when the Spartans arrived were trying to find support in other cities such as Thebes (see the later section 'Waging the Corinthian War'). Eventually, the democrats returned to Athens in force in early 403 BC. The Thirty and their supporters fought a battle against the democrats during which several of the tyrants were killed.

The Spartan king Pausanias arrived to try and sort out the mess. Rather than continue to force the oligarchy on Athens, he allowed a limited form of democracy to return. The tyrants and their supporters were allowed to leave and lived in exile in the town of Eleusis. Democracy was back but an atmosphere of distrust and plotting continued.

Winning at a cost: Sparta

Presumably the Spartans were relishing the fact that they'd won a crushing victory against their old enemy after a 26-year war? Well, not really. Victory in the Peloponnesian War proved to be almost as devastating for Sparta as defeat was for Athens.

The first mistake that the Spartans made at the end of the war was the way they dealt with the Athenian empire. Now that they controlled Athens the Spartans were technically the rulers of all the territories that had been a part of the Athenian empire. As a result the Spartans forced many Greek towns and cities to adopt new oligarchic systems of government like that in Athens.

Many of these towns had never directly opposed Sparta during the war, so they now resented the harsh treatment they were receiving. Equally resentful were Sparta's allies in the former Peloponnesian League (see Chapter 8). None of Sparta's former allies got any reward at all when Sparta took control of Athens despite the help that they'd given during the war.

Because the Spartans kept all the spoils, cities such as Thebes were happy to shelter the pro-democracy exiles who fled from Athens during the time of the rule of the Thirty. Sparta had almost become Thebes's and Athens's mutual enemy.

Mounting Problems in the Persian Empire

At the same time as Athens and Sparta's woes, trouble was brewing in the Persian empire – and it had big consequences for Sparta and the rest of Greece.

Marching through the desert with Cyrus

The Persian king Darius died in 404 BC and was succeeded by his son Artaxerxes. Artaxerxes's younger brother Cyrus decided to try and steal the crown and set about recruiting an army.

Cyrus's first port of call was Sparta, which he had helped greatly in the Peloponnesian War (see the preceding section 'Wrapping Up the Peloponnesian War'). The Spartans were pretty much obliged to help Cyrus, and they did so by sending an unofficial force to join up with the Greek mercenary army that Cyrus was putting together.

The expedition didn't go well. Cyrus was defeated and killed in a massive battle at a place called Cunaxa near the Persian city of Babylon. His army of Greek mercenaries was left stranded and leaderless in the middle of the Persian desert!

Among Cyrus's mercenary soldiers was Xenophon who'd signed up after the Peloponnesian War ended (see the sidebar 'Thucydides passes the torch to Xenophon'). Xenophon and the other officers embarked on an incredible march back through Persia and Asia Minor at the head of a force of 10,000 men. Xenophon wrote a book about the experience called the *Anabasis,* or 'march up country', which reads like a daily journal. The narrative's details are said to be so accurate that Alexander the Great used it as a travel guide when he made the journey heading in the opposite direction 75 years later. Reading these details, it's easy to see why:

On this march the army ran short of corn and it was impossible to buy any except in the Lydian market . . . where one could get a capithe of wheat flour or pearl barley for four sigli. The siglus is worth seven and a half attic obols, and the capithe is equal to three pints.

Xenophon and the other generals superbly brought 10,000 men all the way back to Greek territory (in Asia Minor), but Xenophon didn't get any thanks for it. When he returned to Athens, Xenophon was put on trial. The charge was that he commanded Spartan troops – which was true – but he was also seen as a radical and was a known associate of Socrates.

Xenophon was eventually sent into exile. Bad news for him but good for historians because during this time of enforced retirement he started writing history! He lived in Olympia for a while and then Corinth before returning to Athens shortly before he died around 360 BC.

Seeking support from Sparta

After the failure of Cyrus's campaign, many of the Greek cities in Asia Minor that had supported him worried they would be punished by the Persian king Artaxerxes. The cities appealed to Sparta for help because the Spartans had supported Cyrus and were now the dominant Greek state.

The Spartans didn't let them down, fighting a series of campaigns to defend the cities in Asia Minor. The Spartan king Agesilaos led the biggest of these campaigns in 396 BC.

Unfortunately, the Spartans were about to learn that while taking responsibility for Greeks abroad, they left the back door open at home . . .

Waging the Corinthian War

While the Spartans engaged in events in Asia Minor, the other Greek states took advantage. The main players were the Thebans who were still sore about events of a few years before when they felt they hadn't been adequately compensated by Sparta for their support during the Peloponnesian War.

Forging an alliance with Thebes

In 395 BC, Thebes made a treaty with Athens to join forces against Sparta. The partnership was a success, and they inflicted a heavy defeat on the Spartans in a battle near Haliartos during which the Spartan commander Lysander was killed. The Theban victory encouraged the other Greek states, and by the end of 395 BC, Corinth and Argos had joined the partnership too.

This new powerful alliance set about the attack of Sparta. Due to the fact that most of the action took place around the Isthmus of Corinth, the attack was known as the Corinthian War.

Everybody fighting everybody else

The few years following 395 BC were a blur of battles in Greece and abroad with the Corinthian War and Sparta still involved with Persia. In 394 BC the Spartans were very successful against their Greek enemies, and the Spartan king Agesilaos was recalled to help finish the job.

Having suffered some heavy defeats, the other Greek cities avoided open battles with the Spartans, preferring to carry out spoiling attacks on Spartan territories. At the same time the Spartan fleet was almost completely destroyed by the Persians near Knidos.

With the Spartans unable to stop them, the Persians sailed all round the western Mediterranean, kicking out Spartan garrisons from the former Athenian allies that Sparta had taken over at the end of the Peloponnesian War (see the preceding section 'Bowing to the Spartans: Athens after the war'). The Spartan hold on much of Greece and the surrounding areas had lasted just eight years.

Portending a dim future: Defeat at Lekhaion

The era of the Greek city-states was nearing an end – partly because their continual wars were weakening them all! A particularly bleak omen of the future came in 390 BC when a large Spartan force was defeated by a Greek mercenary army at Lekhaion, near the city of Corinth. Once the greatest and most feared army in the Mediterranean, the Spartans were humbled by men fighting in a different way – as lightly-armed *peltastai* (see Chapter 5). And by 338 BC, the whole of Greece came under control of new fighters from the north – the Macedonians (see Chapter 10).

Taking a breather – the King's Peace (386 BC)

The Corinthian War rumbled on throughout the next decade with neither side ever seeming likely to win a victory. (As Athens and Sparta found out before, winning a war in mainland Greece was very difficult!) In the end, diplomacy won out. In 386 BC, the Persian king Artaxerxes intervened and brokered a major peace treaty. In the so-called King's Peace:

✔ The Greeks agreed to allow Persia to control all the Greek cities in Asia Minor.

✔ All the other Greek cities were allowed to rule themselves and be free from any kind of control by another state.

✔ Any country that broke these terms faced attack by the Persian forces.

In a way, Artaxerxes was trying to put an end to all the empire building that had been going on for the past century. The idea was brave – and good for Persia too – but it was never going to last.

Forming the Athenian League

The Spartans first broke the truce set down by King Artaxerxes. Although avoiding any interference in the Greek islands, for the next ten years Sparta continually attacked the Greek towns in the Peloponnese.

The King's Peace had been designed to stop the many Greek towns from ganging up together, but in the end it had the opposite effect. In 378 BC, Athens and Thebes entered into another alliance. Others joined and the new group of allies took the name of the *Athenian League*.

This new league was very different from the Delian League (see Chapter 7). Athens's weakened position meant that the new league was a group with common interests rather than an empire. Athens took no tribute from its allies – it was a group of equals.

The Athenian League made war on Sparta for the best part of the next ten years. The Persians did nothing, despite the fact that these attacks clearly broke the terms of the King's Peace. In reality, the Persian king was perfectly happy for the Greeks to fight among themselves – they were less of a problem for him.

Figuring out the Battle of Leuktra: Greece versus Sparta – and Thebes wins!

The ensuing war between the Athenian League and Sparta – surprise! – followed the pattern of nearly all the other campaigns of the past 50 years. (The real winners appeared to be the Thebans who were building up their territory and revenues from successful battles.)

Playing in the Sacred Band

Thebes's ascent was partly due to the flexible tactics that it had shown at Leuktra, but key to its success were its new elite soldiers.

Although they sound like a Christian rock group, the 'Sacred Band' was actually 300 elite troops from Thebes trained by a man called Pelopidas. These soldiers were called 'sacred' because they were originally created to guard the sacred citadel of the city (an area like the Acropolis in Athens).

What made the Sacred Band even more unusual was that each man was paired with another who was both his companion in the battle line and his lover. The idea was that each man would be inspired to fight even harder with his lover next to him. Homosexuality wasn't thought unusual in Greece (see Chapter 15), but this was still a radical idea.

As the war ground on, Athens found the fighting a real financial burden and struggled to impose new taxes on the citizens to pay for it. The Athenians organised a peace conference at which Sparta and Thebes fell out over who would control the territories of Boiotia.

Before long Sparta and some of her allies (including Corinth which had swapped sides) met the Thebans in battle outside the village of Leuktra in Boiotia. Sparta and her allies easily outnumbered the Thebans and an easy victory was expected.

Only it didn't turn out like that. The Thebans won a stunning victory over Sparta and the Spartan king Kleombrotos was killed, along with more than 400 of Sparta's crack troops, the Spartiates.

The Thebans won the Battle of Leuktra fair and square by lining up their phalanx in a wedged formation. Traditionally, the phalanx was 12 lines deep, but the Thebans lined up 50 deep on the left to make a kind of triangle, like a wedge of cheese. This formation meant their strongest troops (on the left) heavily attacked the Spartans' right (their strongest point) before the weaker Theban troops had even joined the battle.

The Spartans reacted to the defeat in a typically strange way. According to Xenophon:

> *Also, while [the Spartans] gave the names of all the dead to the relatives concerned they told them to bear their suffering in silence and avoid any cries of lamentation. And so on the following day you could see those whose relatives had been killed going about in public looking bright and happy, while those whose relatives had been reported living . . . were walking about looking gloomy and sorry for themselves.*

Celebrating the Hegemony of Thebes

For a brief time Thebes became the dominant city in Greece, and this period from 371 to 362 BC became known as the 'Hegemony of Thebes'.

Dismantling the Athenian League

As Sparta declined, Athens used its now-restored fleet to try the same trick that it had with the Delian League (see Chapter 7). Athenian ships began sailing to islands in the Mediterranean and asking for tribute money; eventually, allies became territories.

In contrast to the era under the Delian League, Athens wasn't powerful enough to sustain this kind of policy. By 357 BC, members of the Athenian League who were refused permission to leave went into open revolt and a small war followed until 355 BC. The Athenian League eventually broke up as members drifted away.

Signalling the end of classical Greece

By the middle of the fourth century BC, the once proud city-states of Greece were in trouble. A new power, Macedonia, was developing in the north and soon its king, Philip II, had most of southern Greece under his control. Imagine – the Greek city-states that only 150 years earlier had combined to beat Persia were now about to become insignificant.

Xenophon ends his history *Hellenica* with a description of the battle of Mantineia in 362 BC. At this battle, the Thebans beat a collection of other cities, including both Athens and Sparta. He concludes by pointing out that yet another big battle had really solved nothing:

> *Both sides claimed the victory, but it cannot be said that . . . either side was any better off after the battle than before it. In fact, there was even more uncertainty and confusion in Greece after the battle than there had been previously.*

Xenophon gives a pretty good summary of everything that happened to the Greek city-states since the start of the Peloponnesian War in 431 BC. Unfortunately, the Greek city-states had nobody to blame but themselves. After all that had happened – all the wars, treaties, small empires, leagues, and broken promises – the once-great city-states were at the mercy of another foreign invader, the Macedonians, which I cover in Chapter 10.

Chapter 10

Rising Quickly to the Top: Macedonia

*B*asically, by 360 BC the Greek city-states had blown it. The constant infighting and deal breaking among Athens, Sparta, and the rest had opened the door to foreign enemies. And so, during the fourth century BC, a new power emerged – Macedonia.

In a little over 50 years, the Macedonians went from being thought of as simple, barbarous hill people to being the dominant force in Greece and beyond. This amazing ascent came down to two men: Philip II and his son Alexander the Great. Their story, as well as the history of this fascinating culture, starts here.

Meeting the Macedonians

Macedonia was (and is) the territory to the north of Greece formed by the north and north-west ends of the Thermaic Gulf. Macedonia is a hard and rugged country, and throughout its earliest history it had always existed as a tribal society. The Macedonians were Greek in origin, and they spoke a broader, rougher version of the Greek language that was related to the traditional version spoken in Athens (Chapter 1 has more on the intricacies of the ancient Greek language).

Have you seen the film *Alexander* (2004)? It's an entertaining depiction of Alexander the Great's life with some fantastically shot battle sequences. However, one element of the film that people and reviewers criticised was actor Colin Farrell's accent. Farrell spoke in his natural Irish accent throughout the movie. Viewers missed the point: The difference between Farrell's regional accent and an English accent is a really good way of showing the contrast between the ancient Macedonian and Greek cultures. I'm not so sure about Angelina Jolie's accent though. . . .

Growing very good at war

Throughout much of its early history Macedonia was a tribal society made up of a large number of competing groups who spent most of their time at war with each other. The lives most Macedonians led were quite simple – hunting and fighting, and then drinking long into the night to celebrate success in either.

The Macedonians were also excellent warriors. By the fourth century BC, they had extended their territory to the borders of Illyria in the west and Paeonia in the north.

The trouble was, as I said earlier, much like the Greek city-states during the same time period; the tribes of Macedonia were always fighting among themselves. For this reason, the country was very inward looking during much of its early history and only really interacted with other Greek states through a limited amount of trade.

Crowning a new kind of king: Philip II

The Macedonian kings traditionally ruled from a fortress in a town called Aegae. The Macedonian king didn't have absolute power over his subjects:

- ✔ The king had to observe Macedonian law and make decisions that were in keeping with it. This law had been set down generations earlier by previous tribal leaders and decisions were debated within a council of tribal leaders.

- ✔ The king's title wasn't hereditary. When the king died, the tribal leaders chose his successor although often they chose the son of the previous king.

The big change to Macedonia and its governing processes came with the death of King Perdiccas in 359 BC. Perdiccas's son Amyntas was only a child at the time of his father's death and his uncle Philip became his protector. As guardian to the heir, Philip also became temporary ruler of the kingdom until a decision was made about who should succeed. However, he didn't stay temporary for long.

Despite being only 24 years old, Philip made an immediate impact. He utterly rejected established laws and tradition and sought to establish himself as king through violence. Philip attacked in battle or murdered any other rival for the throne, and he set about securing the borders of Macedonia from the rebellious tribes of Illyria. As soon as that was done, he turned his ambitious eye to the south and Greece.

Considering Macedonian warfare

Prior to 350 BC, the Macedonians weren't really too much of a threat to the inhabitants of southern Greece. So what changed?

Building a different army

The new way in which Philip II made war on his enemies was a huge change – and a huge threat to the southern city-states. Philip II created a unique fighting force that the traditional Greek hoplite phalanx (see Chapter 5) found difficult to deal with.

Following are some of the main tricks and tactics of the Macedonian forces under Philip II:

- **Shock cavalry:** Philip's army was very large and *mixed,* meaning it contained a heavy infantry phalanx as well as cavalry and light troops. Unlike in traditional Greek armies, the Macedonians used their cavalry to charge and break the enemy line. Therefore the cavalry became the Macedonian's main offensive weapon.

- **The *sarissa*:** The Macedonian infantry was armed differently to its southern Greek neighbours. Rather than the short spear or javelin used by the southern Greeks the Macedonian's main offensive weapon was a 4.5-metre (15-foot) thrusting spear called a *sarissa*. This weapon made getting anywhere near the infantry line very difficult, particularly because the Macedonian phalanx was so well drilled it could form half a dozen different formations very quickly. See Figure 10-1 for some formation examples.

- **The *hypaspists*:** The Macedonians had their own special troops called the *hypaspists* who were used for special missions that required different tactics to a standard infantry battle. The *hypaspists* were famously fearless and took on all kinds of ludicrously dangerous tasks such as climbing cliffs to attack towns and assaulting cities at night. They were more lightly armed than the phalanx and, as such, much more mobile.

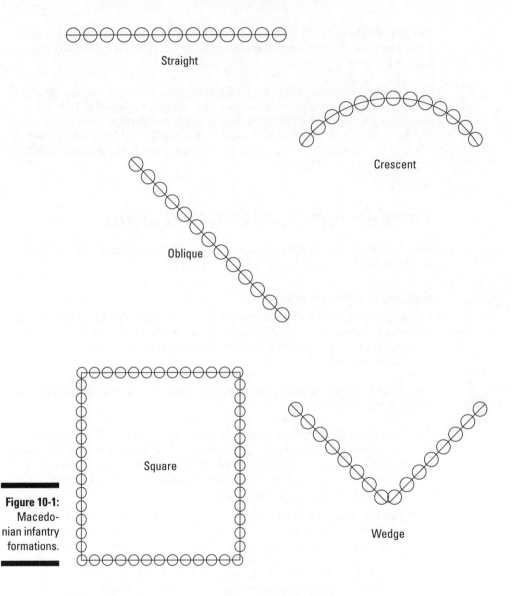

Straight

Crescent

Oblique

Square

Figure 10-1:
Macedo-
nian infantry
formations.

Wedge

Revealing the secret weapon – camaraderie

Despite all the advances and adaptations of its army, the main reason that Macedonia became so powerful so quickly was the personality of Philip II himself.

The Macedonians had always been a warrior people but had spent generations fighting each other. Philip's personality, political intelligence, and ruthlessness brought the warring tribal leaders together and focused their bravery and skill on mutual enemies.

Philip kept up a culture of hard work and hard play that involved drinking long into the night to celebrate victories. The hard work must have been exhausting – but it worked.

Taking Over: Philip's Successes

During the 350s BC, Philip II and a now professionalised Macedonian army began to seize control of large parts of Greece. In 357 BC, Philip captured the city of Amphipolis (which Athens had long thought its own), and by 352 BC virtually the whole of Thessaly in Northern Greece was under his control. The Thessalians were famous for using their heavily armed cavalry troops in a battle, and Philip quickly incorporated them into his army.

Another notable success occurred around this same time. Throughout his reign Philip regularly conducted dynastic marriages within the cities and territories he conquered. In 356 BC, he and Olympias of Epirus had a baby son whom Philip called Alexander. (Ever heard of him?) You can read a lot more about him in the section 'Taking Over the Family Business: The Rise of Alexander the Great' and in Chapter 11.

Continuing despite criticism

During the 350s BC the rest of Greece was too stunned by Philip's success to really challenge him and the Macedonian forces. The main opposition came from a new Athenian statesman called Demosthenes. Demosthenes was a great speech writer and orator – and almost the exact opposite of Philip. Like Kleon (see Chapters 8 and 9), Demosthenes came from a trade background. His father had owned a business that made cutlery and so his nickname was the 'cutler'.

Demosthenes delivered many great speeches in the Athenian *ekklesia* urging all Greeks to rise up against Philip. These orations became known as *Philippics*, a term people still use to this day to describe a character assassination delivered in the form of a speech. Indeed, 400 years after Demosthenes when the Roman orator Cicero was haranguing Mark Anthony, Cicero's speeches were called philippics.

Philip carried on with his conquest plans, regardless of Demosthenes's speeches, by making war in the north-west as far as Thrace. By 348 BC the Macedonians had destroyed the town of Olynthos and sold its population into slavery. Philip found some Athenians in town and kept them as hostages to use as a bargaining tool. He recognised that it wouldn't be long before he came into conflict with Athens and the hostages would prove useful.

Agreeing to peace (sort of)

Athens had a problem. Despite all the urging of Demosthenes, Athens couldn't afford to fight a war with Philip, and it didn't have the manpower either.

In 346 BC, a peace conference was proposed and an Athenian called Philokrates led the negotiations. Philip eventually agreed to a non-aggression treaty with Athens.

Soon after the peace conference, Philip took advantage of trouble in southern Greece where the town of Phocis had seized the sacred town of Delphi. (Turn to Chapter 22 for more on this prophecy-rich city.) The Macedonians quickly marched south, kicked out the Phocians, and earned the thanks of Delphi. Thereafter Philip tried to portray himself as a kind of peacekeeper who'd intervene if necessary to settle disputes. It's doubtful that people truly believed this but they weren't really in a position to argue with him.

Invading everywhere except Athens

Philip wasn't actually that bothered with Athens or much of southern Greece. He had other fish to fry: He had an eye on an amazingly ambitious invasion of Asia Minor.

Philip spent the years after the peace agreement concentrating on areas north-east of Athens, laying siege to the port of Byzantium on the Bosphorus. Of course, Athens viewed this attack as a threat to the cities in southern Greece because a great deal of grain came from there. The political intrigue against Philip continued in Athens which eventually spurred him into seizing the grain ships in 340 BC.

When Philip seized the ships he finally gave Demosthenes what his critic was looking for – the excuse for Athens to declare war on the Macedonians, which they duly did. The Athenians had support from some of the other major cities, such as Corinth and Thebes – all which feared Philip and felt that as rich, powerful cities, they'd be next on his hit-list.

Battling in Chaeronea (338 BC)

The Battle of Chaeronea was one of the biggest in Greek history and the last real stand of the old Greek states against the new Macedonian power from the north. The world was never the same again after this brutal fight.

The two sides – the Macedonians and the allied southern Greek city-states – met outside the town of Chaeronea in Boeotia.

The allies had a large force of more than 35,000 men from Athens, Corinth, Euboea, Megara, and Thebes, among others. Philip's forces numbered a little less at about 30,000, but he had 1,800 cavalry (see the earlier section 'Considering Macedonian warfare'), which was under the command of his then 18-year-old son Alexander.

The battle was a tough struggle, but in the end the Athenians blew it for themselves. After the two infantry lines came together, Philip's *hypaspists* feigned a withdrawal. The Athenians on the left end of the allied line bought the ruse hook, line, and sinker, and chased after the Macedonians. The allied forces' attack created a massive hole in their line, which Alexander exploited and drove the Macedonian cavalry through. Alexander was then able to surround the Thebans who were the most feared allied fighters. Game over.

Thousands of the Greek allies lost their lives at Chaeronea, and Philip took several thousand more prisoners. The famous Sacred Band was almost completely destroyed with 254 of the 300 killed. A permanent memorial was set up to honour them in the form of a large statue of a lion that still exists today.

Philip's victory was complete. Several Greek towns including Thebes were garrisoned with Macedonian troops. As far as Philip was concerned, the job was done. In terms of his own lifetime he was correct but his son Alexander would have to finish the job after Philip's death.

Enjoying Prosperity at Pella

Philip was an incredible soldier, and he also made great strides to turn Macedonia into what he considered to be a civilised power. One of his first moves was the confirmation of the second city of Pella as the base of his royal court, setting up residence there and meeting with the tribal chiefs. The city's new status meant that tribal leaders from Macedonia and beyond flocked to the city because they wanted to be close to the king and the wealth and success that he'd generated.

Not much of the city survives today. Archaeologists have found the remains of a royal palace which could well have been developed from the one used by Philip. Evidence exists of a massive *agora* (town square) that would have been filled during the fourth century by all the visitors to the city.

Along with Pella's new prominence, a new elite class soon emerged. All the sons of the Macedonian tribal leaders lived and were educated in the city. Chief among them was Philip's son Alexander. The group of young nobles who grew up with Alexander became known as his 'Companions'. They became a new generation who were both highly educated and skilled in war – a new warrior elite. Young men such as Ptolemy and Hephaestion grew up to share the amazing adventures of Alexander's adult life. See the later section 'Following in his father's footsteps' for more.

Pella became a magnet for artists and intellectuals who, like Renaissance painters, were keen to seek employment and patronage of the royal court where high fees would be paid for their skills. Some also worked as tutors to the 'Companions'. This process had already begun under previous Macedonian kings – for example, the playwright Euripides spent time in Macedonia during the beginning of the fourth century BC – but the city's stature increased tenfold under Philip.

Philip himself had no great interest in intellectual affairs, but he was happy to sponsor them because he recognised that if Macedonia was to become a truly international power its new generation of leaders would need to become more worldly. Philip had grand ambitions for Macedonia and ultimately he wanted to test its military power against the might of the Persian Empire.

In particular, he employed the Greek philosopher Aristotle (see Chapter 23) as one of Alexander's tutors.

The Greek biographer Plutarch wrote an entertaining life of Alexander in which he quotes a letter from the young prince to Aristotle. Alexander complains that Aristotle has written a book describing some of the philosophical ideas that his tutor had shared with him:

> *What advantage shall I have over other men if these theories in which I have been trained are to be made common property?*

The court at Pella gave Alexander a great training in all aspects of Greek knowledge. Combined with his obvious aptitude and first-hand experience of warfare on his father's campaigns, he grew into an amazingly confident and authoritative young man.

Taking Over the Family Business: The Rise of Alexander the Great

All things change, and in 336 BC, when Philip was at the height of his power, he suddenly and suspiciously died. His death could have been the end of a brief moment of Macedonian supremacy; instead it heralded the beginning of an era of even greater success under his son Alexander.

Slaying Philip

In 337 BC Philip had received a Greek delegation that wanted to sue for peace. The delegation ended up awarding him the title of *hegemon* ('dominant leader') of all the Greek armies. This title basically gave Philip the authority he needed to attack Persia because he would be doing so in the name of all Greece – on the premise of liberating the Greek cities in Asia Minor. (Yes, *that* old excuse again!)

In the summer of 336 BC, Philip was in Pella celebrating the marriage of his daughter when he was assassinated by one of his bodyguards. Suspicion immediately fell on his wife Olympias who'd recently been sent into exile after Philip had married again. The assassin was killed in the struggle by Alexander before he could be questioned – a fact that many people interpreted as an attempt to hush things up. Philip's death certainly had benefits for Olympias – her son Alexander became king at the age of 20.

In *Alexander* (2004), Olympias is blamed as being behind the scheme and Alexander an innocent bystander. However, I find it difficult to believe that he didn't know anything. What do you think?

Separating the man and the myth

Alexander the Great is a fascinating historical figure. He achieved incredible things in an amazingly short time. No one like him has ever existed before him – or after him. The problem with somebody like this is that he can become a magnet for all kinds of myths and stories. What Alexander did isn't really in dispute, but *how* he did it and what he was like as a person always will be.

Alexander was also quite happy to make up his own myth. As a boy and throughout his adult life he was fascinated by Homer's *The Iliad* and the heroes like Achilles and Hector that feature in it (see Chapter 21). Alexander thought of himself in the same terms and contended that he was actually descended from Achilles.

A horse and his boy

One of the most famous larger-than-life stories about Alexander concerns how he came to own Bucephalas ('Ox-Head'), the massive warhorse that he rode for most of his life.

Apparently, a trader from Thessaly brought the huge black horse to show Philip. Nobody could calm the creature enough to ride it. Alexander asked whether Philip would buy the horse for him if Alexander were able to train it, and Philip agreed. Within a few minutes Alexander was happily riding Bucephalas. Alexander had noticed that the horse was scared of its own shadow and turned him toward the sun so he couldn't see it any longer.

This story is a great example of a historical event that's probably exaggerated. Still, this story is simple and highlights Alexander's most obvious and admired characteristics – confidence, bravery, and intelligence – were present at an early age.

His mother didn't help. From an early age Olympias had told Alexander that his real father was not Philip but Zeus, the king of the gods and that various prophecies had foretold his birth. (Philip and Olympias's marriage was a less than ideal relationship, with him regularly accusing her of adultery. To be honest the family would've been perfect for *Jerry Springer.*)

As a result of this kind of upbringing, Alexander was a bit different. His family and early life explain a great deal about him – particularly his tremendous courage and drive. And his background also explains some of the strange decisions that he later made (see Chapter 11).

Following in his father's footsteps

When he assumed power, Alexander immediately began planning to do exactly what his father had intended – invade Asia Minor and attack the Persian Empire. Alexander had two distinct advantages:

✔ Alexander had all his father's old generals – men like Parmenion, Antipater, and Cleitus – around to help and advise him. Alexander spent hours on the eve of a battle planning strategy with these generals, confident that they would carry out all manoeuvres to the letter.

✔ Alexander was also part of an exceptional group of young Macedonian men who became known as the 'Companions'. As I mention in the section 'Enjoying Prosperity at Pella', these friends and peers – including Hephaestion, Ptolemy, Cassander, Nearchus, and others – had grown up with Alexander. The Companions fought alongside Alexander now; many of them riding in his companion cavalry.

Alexander, however, had a significant problem: As a new king, city-states with a grudge against Macedonia were going to try their luck against the new leadership. Before Alexander ventured off on his grand adventure to the east, he had to deal with problems closer to home.

Quieting Illyria and Thrace

The first areas to give Alexander trouble were the border regions in Illyria and Thrace. Times were tense because neither side yet knew whether the new young king would effectively take over after his father.

Alexander soon proved the doubters wrong. Within three months he invaded Thrace and utterly destroyed any opposition. While he was there, news came that the Illyrian tribes were now massing on the border with Macedonia and preparing to invade. Once again Alexander dealt extremely well with a difficult campaign.

After two difficult tests, Alexander was probably due a break – but he didn't get one. As he was finishing off the Illyrians, news came of a revolt in Thebes.

Squelching the Theban revolt

After Thebes rebelled against Philip II (see the section 'Battling in Chaeronea'), Philip left a Macedonian garrison in the city to keep an eye on the Thebans. However, while Alexander was campaigning in Illyria, a rumour began to circulate that he had been killed. Where had this rumour come from? Unsurprisingly, the source was dear old Demosthenes (see the section 'Continuing despite criticism') who produced an eyewitness who swore that Alexander had been killed. Demosthenes didn't stop there; he urged Greece to revolt and write to Persia for support.

The Greek cities saw this as a great opportunity. If Alexander was dead Macedonia would be leaderless and it would be the perfect time to strike back. In Thebes two Macedonian officers were killed and the rest of the garrison were forced to go into hiding in the citadel.

In his biography of Demosthenes, Plutarch records his opinion of the young Alexander:

> *Demosthenes now completely dominated the Athenian assembly and he wrote letters to the Persian generals in Asia inciting them to declare war on Alexander, whom he referred to as a boy, and compared to Margites.*

The 'Margites' that Plutarch mentions was a character in a comic story of the day who never really grew up and thought he knew much more than he actually did. Demosthenes and the rest of Greece were about to find out how wrong that comparison was.

Alexander's response to the Theban revolt was swift and brutal. In 335 BC, he marched quickly south, surrounded the city, and took it with little effort. The walls of the city and many of its significant buildings were burned down. Alexander's men massacred thousands of the population and sold those that survived into slavery. The city of Thebes effectively ceased to exist from this point on. Although many buildings were rebuilt, Thebes was never again a leading city.

Alexander had sent a harsh message to the ancient world: Any revolt or betrayal against Macedonia would be dealt with severely. Alexander needed to ensure that when he left for Persia he wouldn't come under attack at home.

However, Alexander made some noteworthy exceptions in his destruction of Thebes. All the temples within Thebes were left alone, as were the houses of the descendants of the poet Pindar whom Alexander much admired. These exceptions illustrate the complex character of Alexander: fierce brutality mixed with an appreciation of architecture and literature.

After dealing with the Thebans, Alexander moved south. The Athenians, especially Demosthenes, must've been seriously worried that they were about to receive the same treatment the Thebans had. A hurried meeting of the *ekklesia* was arranged, and Athens voted to send an embassy congratulating Alexander on his recent victories in the north and celebrate the just way that he'd dealt with the Thebans!

Initially, Alexander demanded that Demosthenes and the other anti-Macedonian agitators be handed over to him, but Demosthenes, as ever, managed to argue his way out of the situation. Athens received no further punishment, but Alexander ensured that an eye was kept on it.

By 334 BC, Alexander managed to get Greece back into the position it was in before his father's death. He was acknowledged as the hegemon of the Greek cities and the general of their armies. With the borders of Macedonia secure, he now needed to complete his father's project – the invasion of the Persian Empire.

Although Philip's intention (and main excuse) for attacking the Persians had been the liberation of the Greek cities in Asia Minor, Alexander ended up taking his campaign so much farther – to India and back. This incredible story is what Chapter 11 is all about!

Chapter 11

Crowning the Undefeated Champion of the World: Alexander the Great

It is my belief that there was in those days no nation, no city, no single individual beyond the reach of Alexander's name; never in all the world was there another like him, and therefore I cannot help but feel that some power more than human was concerned in his birth.

–Arrian, The Campaigns of Alexander

Arrian, a Greek who became a general in the Roman army in the second century AD, wrote the above words about Alexander's skill as a general in his book – which is still in print today. Arrian was a sober, reflective man, not given to making fanciful statements, so his assessment of Alexander is quite compelling.

Indeed, Alexander the Great was an extraordinary individual – visionary, brilliant, cruel, vengeful, and probably more than a little insane. Alexander was 20 years old when he became king of Macedonia. By the time he died, 12 years later, he'd changed the Mediterranean world. This chapter charts his incredible course.

Popping In on the Persian Empire

The Persian Empire had changed a huge amount in the 150 years after the Persian Wars (see Chapter 6 for more). By 334 BC the king very loosely ruled the massive territories that made up the empire, and local rulers or *satraps* effectively ran the show in their own territories. Central control had relaxed considerably since the days of the invasion under Xerxes in 490 BC.

During Alexander's reign, the Persian king was Darius III, who seized the throne in 335 BC after helping to instigate the assassination of his predecessor. He was a weak king, but he had the huge wealth of the Persian Empire and its massive manpower at his disposal.

Although the Persian army was huge, it did have a problem. In many ways, the Persians were the complete opposite of the unified, well-drilled, and professional Macedonian army (see Chapter 10).

With the exception of Darius's personal troops, the Persian army was drawn from throughout the empire and thrown together when needed. Many of the troops didn't speak the same language. In many cases, they had very little to fight for and were basically forced to do so.

Spin versus Reality: The Reasons for Invasion

So why did Alexander want to go to Persia? The real reason was the desire for adventure, conquest, and glory that underpinned his whole life. The idea of invading Asia Minor was originally that of his father, Philip II, who wanted the wealth that the Persian-controlled cities possessed.

The official reasons were very different. The Macedonians were seeking to 'liberate' the Greek cities under Persian control and gain revenge for the Persian invasions of Greece in the fifth century BC.

Overwhelming Persia at the battle of the Granicus River

Alexander's first real confrontation with the Persian army came at the battle of the Granicus River in 334 BC.

The Persian army that came to meet Alexander at the Granicus was made up of large numbers of troops from the most westerly parts of the Persian Empire. Darius wasn't present at the battle and the Persians were commanded by the western satraps. The Persians camped at the bottom of a hill across the river Granicus from Alexander's camp.

Alexander had to cross the river to attack with his Companion cavalry (refer to Chapter 10), breaking a hole in the Persian line. The weakened Persian line gave the Macedonian *sarissa*-wielding infantry and *hypaspists* a chance to get over and engage the centre. Fighting furiously, the Macedonians managed to surround the Persian infantry, and the other Persian troops fled the field. It was an amazing victory that owed a lot to the incredible charge by Alexander and the cavalry.

Considering a controversy

But was Alexander's attack and victory that simple? The battle of Granicus River is very controversial because the sources disagree on whether Alexander crossed the river at night to surprise the Persians with an attack in the morning, or rode straight across it in the morning as the battle began.

You may think that the time of the attack doesn't really matter, but depending on when it happened, the Granicus was either a great 'surprise attack' by Alexander or an amazing example of fighting a standard infantry battle from a situation of great disadvantage. Either is impressive but it would be great to know which it was! This discrepancy is an excellent example of how careful historians have to be when dealing with a quasi-mythical figure like Alexander.

Doling out harsh punishment

The Persian army defeated at the battle of Granicus contained a lot of Greek mercenaries. Alexander dealt harshly with them. Many thousands were killed and the rest sent back to Macedonia in chains to work in the mines. (The Athenians on the Sicilian Expedition – see Chapter 8 – suffered a similarly grim fate under Alexander's father.)

Liberating the Greeks

I mention in Chapter 10 that Alexander's main reason for attacking Persia was to liberate the Greek cities in Asia Minor. Whether they needed liberating was a bit of an open question.

The Greek cities were locally ruled by Persian *satraps*, but they were pretty autonomous and their only obligation was to pay taxes to their *satraps*. Still, the Greek cities' attitude seemed to be 'Anything for a quiet life', and they threw in their lot with Alexander as he marched south-east through Asia Minor, liberating them as he went.

A knotty problem

In 333 BC, during Alexander's trip through Asia Minor, a famous, semi-historical event happened that's a great example of the kind of mythologised stories that attach themselves to him. When Alexander arrived at the Greek town of Gordium, he was shown the famous 'Gordian Knot' that fastened a chariot to a tree. Supposedly, the chariot had been tied to the tree for hundreds of years and locals believed the man that could untie it would become the ruler of the whole world.

Based on accounts of the day and later mythologising, Alexander had a quick look, decided it was a bit tricky, and cut the knot in two with his sword. It was a logical solution that was typical of Alexander: the quickest and most expedient way to solve the problem that disregarded the traditional approach. It didn't seem to matter that he didn't untie it either – he still went on to conquer Asia and beyond.

Slipping by at the battle at Issus

After the Battle of the Granicus River, the next big confrontation between Alexander and the Persian Empire came when Alexander headed south from Asia Minor into what's known as the Levantine coast. This stretch of land includes Syria and the Holy Land and links the near Middle East with Egypt, as Figure 11-1 shows.

Alexander and his troops had been on the road for a year. Having successfully liberated many Greek cities, Alexander decided to press on into the heartlands of the Persian Empire and defeat the Persian king Darius.

However, by 333 BC, Alexander had travelled so far south that Darius now appeared to the north of the Macedonian army outside the town of Issus – cutting off Alexander from the way that he'd come. Alexander had to fight the Persians in order to protect the supply lines that he'd established in the towns and cities that he'd already passed through.

Although the Persians never defeated Alexander, the battle of Issus was a dodgy one. It was fought on a plain in between the sea (to Alexander's left) and some hilly ground (on his right). The Persians outnumbered Alexander by two to one, but many of the Persian troops had been pressed into service against their will (see the section 'Popping In on the Persian Empire').

A fierce battle raged and the Persians fell back across the river Pandarus. The Macedonian infantry really struggled against the Persians' superior numbers and the difficult terrain. In a decisive manoeuvre, Alexander took his cavalry up into the hills before veering left and charging for Darius's chariot. This was an inspired move but also a highly dangerous one – a great example of what Alexander was like. Darius wisely did a runner – and before long so did much of the Persian army.

Issus was a great victory for Alexander but not a total one. Darius was still alive and Alexander knew he'd probably face even greater numbers of Persians the next time they met.

Getting Tyre'd out

Throughout 333 BC, Alexander continued to move south down the Levantine coast. As he went, cities either welcomed him or he forced them to.

Alexander had a particularly tricky time at the siege of the ancient city of Tyre (refer to Figure 11-1). Here, the people had fled to the sanctuary of the citadel, which was on an island just under a kilometre off the coast.

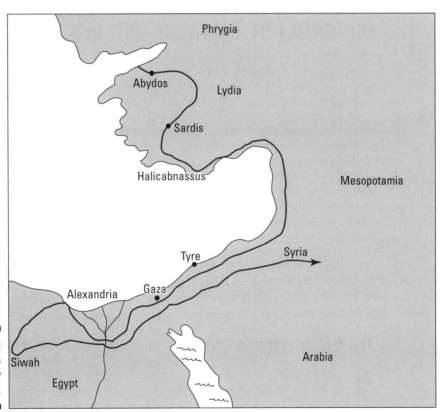

Figure 11-1: Alexander's journey south.

Alexander's solution was to build a *mole,* or causeway, out to the island. The siege required seven months of continual attacks on the island before it fell. In the end, only a combined infantry and naval assault on all four sides of the island enabled Alexander to defeat the incredibly resistant Tyrenians. More than 30,000 citizens were sold into slavery as punishment. Finally, in July 332 BC, Alexander was able to leave.

Taking a Surprising Turn: Alexander in Egypt

Given the fact that Darius was still at large and that he'd spent so long at Tyre (see the preceding section), Alexander's next step was quite surprising – he chose to head toward Egypt.

Walking like an Egyptian

By the fourth century BC, Egypt had fallen from its centuries of greatness and was part of the Persian Empire. Check out *The Ancient Egyptians For Dummies* (Wiley) by Charlotte Booth for all the details of the rise and fall of this amazing culture.

By far the most ancient civilisation in the Mediterranean world, Egypt was still something of a mystery to most Greeks – and there was no way Alexander could resist it. Alexander received a rapturous welcome when he arrived at the Egyptian town of Pelusium in 332 BC. The Egyptians saw him as a liberator who'd freed them from Darius. To show their thanks, they made him their new pharaoh. Up to this point Egypt had been under the control of a Persian *satrap* called Mazaces who surrendered as soon as Alexander arrived.

As pharaoh, all the palaces of Egypt and its immense wealth were now at Alexander's disposal. He set out on a voyage down the river Nile to visit the ancient capital of Memphis.

Turning into a god

After returning from his visit to Memphis, Alexander set out for the ancient Siwah oasis, which involved a huge trek across the desert. The journey was extremely difficult – even today the trip is incredibly hard if you go across the desert the way that Alexander did.

Alexander's reason for going to the oasis was to consult its famous oracle and, allegedly, discover whether he was the son of a god. The story goes that the oracle identified him as being the son of the Egyptian god Ammon who Greeks equated with their own god Zeus. This, of course, fitted quite nicely with what his mother Olympias had always told him (see Chapter 10) – so Alexander wasn't inclined to argue.

The events at the Siwah oasis were very controversial to the Greek mind, which clearly delineated between men and gods (see Part IV for the lowdown.) Later on, this proved a problem for Alexander and his Macedonian followers (see the section 'Going Persian'). But the notion of Alexander as a god in human form was entirely acceptable to both the Egyptian and Persian systems of belief – indeed, kings and rulers in these cultures were worshipped as gods.

Founding the first Alexandria

While in Egypt, Alexander spent a lot of time reorganising its government and appointing his own men as officials to oversee the running of his new territories. These efforts were nothing new; he'd been doing so all the way down from Asia Minor. But in Egypt he also decided to found a new city.

Choosing a spot at the mouth of the Nile, Alexander declared that it would be his new capital – called Alexandria. He recognised that the location would be a tremendous port and would link his territories in the east with those in the west.

Having drawn up a plan for the city itself, Alexander left others to build it for him. He would never return to see it completed. (For more on how the city turned out, see Chapter 12.) Never one to stop when he had a good thing going, Alexander went on to found many other Alexandrias on his travels – possibly as many as 12 spread out over the whole of the Persian Empire and as far afield as India. Only the original city was referred to purely as Alexandria; the rest were given a second name that emphasised their location such as 'Alexandria in the Caucuses'.

Hunting Down Darius

With fun time in Egypt over, Alexander returned to the hunt for Darius, and a final showdown loomed. Alexander headed west, and by the end of September 331 BC, he and his troops (around 40,000 men) were into the heartlands of Mesopotamia.

Going into the Battle of Gaugamela

Darius's and Alexander's armies met on the plain of Gaugamela in 331 BC. Darius had spent the two years since the battle of Issus building up his army. The Persians took the field with a force of well over 100,000 men and probably 15 elephants. Some sources quote up to 250,000 Persian combatants! However, such a big force faced the familiar problems of communication, commitment, and training that I mention in the section 'Popping In on the Persian Empire'.

The film *Alexander* (2004) features a brilliant depiction of the Battle of Gaugamela in all its bloody brutality. Even better though is the scene of the evening before the battle where Alexander and his generals discuss the tactics that they'll use the next day. That's exactly what they would've been doing in 331 BC.

Darius chose the spot for the showdown with Alexander with great care. In fact, he levelled out the ground so he could use his chariots. Alexander used his troops in a wedge formation. His plan was to follow a similar attack as at Issus and use the *cavalry punch tactic.* For this tactic, Alexander and the Companions rode a long way to the right of the battlefield, forcing the Persians on their left to follow. Suddenly turning back left, the Macedonians charged at the weaker Persian line, and after fierce fighting they broke through.

While this was going on, the Macedonian left was desperately holding on against the huge Persian numbers. Alexander led a charge toward Darius, and even went as far as throwing a javelin that just missed the Persian king.

Darius turned and fled again taking only a tiny fraction of his army with him. Alexander was unable to chase him because the Persians had broken through against the Macedonian left, and Alexander and his Companions had to return to support. However, as soon as news of Darius's flight spread, the Persian army followed.

Alexander had won an amazing victory against overwhelming odds. Darius was still alive – but on the run with no army. There was effectively nobody to pull together an organised response and challenge Alexander's supremacy and he and his victorious troops moved south to the city of Babylon.

Meanwhile, back at home . . .

While Alexander was away, various things were going on back in Greece and Macedonia. Alexander had left the general Antipater in charge while he was away. As you may expect, Antipater was very, very busy putting down uprisings from the Greek city-states. Even less surprisingly, Sparta, under King Agis, was the city-state that caused most of the trouble (see Chapters 5 and 8).

Burning down the house

Alexander's visit to the ancient religious capital of Persepolis in 330 BC was less successful than his time spent in Babylon. During an evening of heavy drinking, the story goes that a conversation began about the fact that the Persian king Xerxes (who built the palace that Alexander and his men were in) had burned the temples of Greece when the Persians attacked 250 years before. In revenge, Alexander set fire to the Persepolis palace. Apparently, the following morning he was very sorry. Whether or not the story is completely true isn't certain, but the palace was certainly damaged by a huge fire at that time and it seems like the sort of impulsive thing that Alexander would've done.

Things came to a head in the Battle of Megalopolis in 331 BC where Antipater crushed Sparta and her allies. King Agis died in the battle, and it was the last revolt against Macedonian control.

Moving on to Babylon

To the victor goes the spoils. With Darius defeated at Gaugamela (see the earlier section 'Going into the Battle of Gaugamela'), Alexander was free to take possession of the major cities of the Persian Empire: Babylon, Susa, and Persepolis.

Alexander was welcomed into Babylon as the new Persian king and immediately took possession of its wealth, its palaces and, among other things, Darius's harem.

The incredible wealth and opulence of Babylon must've amazed the Macedonians. It was the biggest city that any of them had ever seen. Plutarch describes Alexander's own reaction to the city's riches:

> *[Alexander] observed the magnificence of the dining-couches, the tables and the banquet which had been set out for him. He turned to his companions and remarked, 'So this, it seems, is what it is to be a king.'*

Pressing further east

By the summer of 330 BC, Alexander had a decision to make: Stay in Babylon and be content to rule his new empire from a glorious city or go farther? Unsurprisingly, he went for the latter option. His excuse was that he needed to hunt down Darius because, while Darius lived, Alexander wasn't the true king of Persia.

In fact, Darius was hunted down quite quickly; some of his own supporters had already killed him but Alexander wasn't aware of it until some scouts from his army found the body of the Persian king unceremoniously dumped onto a cart. Nevertheless, Alexander spent the next three years tearing around the mountainous regions of Bactria and Sogdiana in the north-east of the Persian Empire subduing every tribe he encountered. It was hard work, fighting guerrilla battles against fast-moving enemies in mountainous terrain.

Going Persian

Alexander experienced another difficulty during this time. Now that he was Persian king, he began to adopt certain Persian customs that his Macedonian comrades found difficult to accept.

For example, Alexander began wearing trousers and make-up – both unusual practices for Macedonians. But the custom that caused the most fuss was *proskynesis*. This traditional Persian practice required all those who met and addressed the great king to prostrate themselves before him. Although Alexander didn't ask it of them, the old generals who fought with Philip II found this new and foreign practice difficult to accept.

Unhappy campers

The mood in the Macedonian camp was further soured by the deaths of two notable Companions – Parmenion and Cleitus. (See Chapter 10 for more on the Companions.) Parmenion was killed on the orders of Alexander after an alleged plot involving Parmenion's son Philotas, and Alexander killed Cleitus after a drunken argument about, of all things, *proskynesis.*

Camaraderie had been a vital strength of the Macedonian army and culture; now it was beginning to break apart.

Taking a new queen

Alexander made another surprising decision in 327 BC. After defeating the tribal chief Oxyartes in Sogdiana, he married Oxyartes's daughter Roxanne.

The sexuality of Alexander the Great continues to fascinate people to this day. In modern terms he was probably bisexual. Alexander's relationship with his companion Hephaestion was probably sexual, and several historical writers such as his biographer Plutarch said that he also loved a Persian eunuch called Bagoas. This relationship features in the film *Alexander* (2004) and caused a furore in the final edit when much of it was cut. It's worth seeing *Alexander Revisited* (2007), Oliver Stone's second 'cut' of the film that restores much lost material.

To the end of the world and back again

Some historians believe that Alexander planned to march through India to what he thought was the edge of the world and then build a fleet. Using this, he would then sail back around the 'bottom' of the world (where India was joined to Ethiopia), find the source of the Nile, and then travel back up it to Alexandria!

It was a brilliant and fantastical idea on Alexander's part – but the geography was all wrong. Regardless of the seriousness of this plan, Alexander and the Greeks didn't know that China lay beyond India. But that was just the first of their problems. . . .

Alexander probably did find women attractive too, but it seems likely that he married Roxanne mostly because he felt it was time to father an heir to his new empire.

Alexander took a second wife, Statira, the daughter of Darius, when he returned to Babylon in 324 BC. Neither marriage was a love match, but some ancient writers allege that he took many mistresses over the course of his life.

Making a passage to India

In 327 BC, Alexander went farther than any Greek had before – through the Hindu Kush and into India itself. In doing so, he followed in the footsteps of the mythological figures Heracles and Dionysus who were said to have travelled there (see Chapter 21). Alexander was travelling toward what he believed was the edge of the world.

Having entered India, Alexander made his way to the Hydaspes (now Jhelum) River in 326 BC. He fought a furious and very difficult battle with the local king Porus, which involved his troops tackling jungle warfare for the first time.

The battle was a real struggle with great losses on both sides. (The elephants got scared and ran amok, killing scores of Porus's own men.) But Alexander was very impressed with how bravely Porus had fought. As a result, he made Porus governor of his new province of India!

Suffering a defeat – and returning home

Alexander planned to go even farther across the Indian desert, toward the Ganges River and from there to the edge of the world (see the nearby sidebar 'To the end of the world and back again'). But he suffered a revolt from his own troops who refused to go any farther.

By 325 BC, Alexander had been on campaign for nearly ten years, and many of the men in his infantry had served with Philip II for many years before that. These men were absolutely exhausted from fighting. Reluctantly, Alexander agreed to their demands.

The journey home was incredibly arduous. Alexander sent part of his army back to Persia along the land route that they had travelled a few years earlier. He also used the huge amount of timber available to construct a new fleet. With this, he sailed down the Indus River to its mouth in the Indian Ocean. To Alexander, this was the southern edge of the world.

Alexander then led the rest of his troops in a march across the Gedrosian desert. It was an appalling journey with terrible heat and a lack of food. Thousands of men and all the pack animals died before they eventually met up with the fleet, under Nearchus, on the Persian Gulf.

Returning to Babylon and Ruling the Empire

On his return to Babylon in 324 BC, Alexander set about ruling the empire he had created. He was now technically the ruler of Macedonia, Egypt, all the territories in the Persian Empire, and western India, and he was commander of all the Greeks.

Of course, such a massive area proved impossible to manage. News regularly came to his court of corrupt practices among the governors that he appointed as well as revolts by the tribes in Bactria and Sogdiana.

Creating a new master race

Alexander seems to have been well aware of the wider problems associated with ruling such a large empire. For some time he'd been incorporating young Persian men into his army and training them as replacements in the phalanx for some of his father's veterans who'd retired. After he was back in Babylon, he took this training a stage further.

Various cities that Alexander had founded from Egypt to India were already filled with a mixture of European (Greek/Macedonian) and Asiatic (Egyptian/Persian/Indian) settlers. Alexander now decided to try and settle some Asiatics in Greece and Macedonia.

Getting hitched

To realise his plans, he arranged marriages between almost the whole of his Macedonian high command and aristocratic Persian brides. Alexander himself married Statira, the daughter of Darius III. Following Alexander's lead, up to 10,000 Macedonian soldiers took Persian brides.

Plutarch describes the massive, magnificent joint wedding, which cost a fortune and certainly would've made the pages of *Hello!* these days!

> *We are told that 9,000 guests attended this feast and each of them was given a gold cup for their libations. The whole entertainment was carried out on a grand-scale and Alexander went as far as to discharge [pay off] the debts owed by any of his guests: the outlay for the occasion amounted to 9,870 talents.*

To put this in perspective, the total cost of the wedding festivities was equivalent to 97,536 kilograms of gold. Even Elton John may struggle to match that!

Boyz 2 men

Alexander had also recruited the best part of 30,000 young Persian boys when he visited Babylon in 331 BC. These males had spent the six years that Alexander was away being trained and educated in the fashion of Alexander and his Companions (see Chapter 10), and they were now ready to become the bulk of Alexander's expedition army.

Historical accounts indicate that Alexander planned future campaigns to Arabia (in the south) and even possibly to the western Mediterranean. These men would have made up his new army.

Contemplating the death of a god

Despite the great festivities and exciting new plans, Alexander's time in Babylon wasn't happy. He was constantly dealing with unrest and revolt in the empire and his loyal Macedonians reacted badly to the new Persian recruits. The death of Hephaestion in early 323 BC left Alexander stricken with grief, and he held a suitably lavish funeral with a 30-metre high pyre.

In June of 323 BC, Alexander was about to leave for his expedition to Arabia when, following a banquet to honour one of his Companions, Nearchus, he fell ill. He struggled against a high fever for a week before becoming bedridden. Finally, on 13th June 323 BC, Alexander died. He was 32 years old.

Death – or murder?

Alexander's death – by catching a fever and then dying – wasn't unusual. Alexander's companion Hephaestion died of something similar only a few weeks before. Yet rumours persist that Alexander was murdered, and several recent books have been written on exactly this subject. These books point to the unhappiness of the Macedonians at Alexander adopting 'Persian behaviour' (see the section 'Going Persian'), and his troops' unwillingness to go on another campaign now that they were fantastically wealthy in Babylon.

Others argue that Alexander had suffered a severe chest wound during one of his last battles in India. The effects of this wound, coupled with the march across the Gedrosian desert shortly afterwards, would have been severe.

It seems quite appropriate that a life so full of myth, adventure, and amazing tales should finish with death in mysterious circumstances. I still can't decide whether Alexander was murdered or not. What do you think?

Alexander's life and activities brought the world to a very different place by the time of his death:

- ✔ The traditional powers of Athens, Sparta, Thebes, and even the Persian Empire had lost their dominance.

- ✔ The continents of Europe and Asia were closer together than ever before. The old barriers between the Greek world and the Persian Empire never really existed again.

- ✔ The Mediterranean world was left in the hands of Alexander's former generals who carried out a vicious struggle for power. Chapter 12 looks at this *Hellenistic world,* as it became known.

- ✔ Almost every other dictator that's followed, from Julius Caesar to Napoleon, has regarded Alexander as a role model.

These were impressive accomplishments indeed for a mere ten years in power. In the words of the Greek general Arrian:

> *Anyone who belittles Alexander has no right to do so . . . But let such a person, if blackguard [berate or criticise] Alexander he must, first compare himself with the object of his abuse: himself, so mean and obscure, and, confronting him, the great king, with his unparalleled worldly success, the undisputed monarch of two continents, who spread the power of his name all over the earth.*

Chapter 12

What Happened Next?

Ancient Greece was never the same again after the death of Alexander the Great. In fact, historians call the period of Alexander's life (356 to 323 BC) until about 150 BC the *Hellenistic* period (meaning 'relating to Greece') because of the spread of Greek influence around the Mediterranean that happened as a result of Alexander's travelling (see Chapter 11 for all the details) and the population movements that followed. Notably, the various cities named Alexandria that Alexander founded put the Greeks in positions of power throughout the Mediterranean world and far beyond. But as this chapter explains, this prominence didn't last. Within 150 years the Greek world was effectively under the control of the Roman Empire, and that's why this period of ancient Greek history doesn't get as much space in this book as other periods do.

Still, the Hellenistic period is full of characters and events that are well worth looking into. After all, don't you want to know how the story of ancient Greece ends? Read on.

Having a Bad Heir Day: Alexander's Successors

Alexander the Great was very good at many things (see Chapter 11), but detailed planning for the future wasn't one of them. When he died in June 323 BC, he hadn't clearly stated whom he wanted to act as his successor.

The situation was complex:

- Alexander left at least one child from his marriage to Roxanne, and Alexander's mother Olympias still lived (see Chapter 11) – but neither of these women had any hope of taking over the empire because they didn't command the respect of the army and any successor would have to fight to protect their position.

- Alexander and Roxanne's small boy was named Alexander IV and was born shortly after his father's death.

- Alexander also left a half-brother in Babylon, one of Philip II's other children (see Chapter 10). Known as Philip III, this half-brother was an unfortunate man who suffered from severe mental disabilities and lived in an almost childlike state.

Auctioning off an empire

Because none of Alexander's closest relatives were capable of ruling the vast territory that he acquired during his life, a regent was required and there was precedent for this in Macedonian tradition. The general Perdiccas (one of Alexander's 'Companions') took the job and the rest of Alexander's generals divided up the empire between them.

Before long, Perdiccas was murdered along with several others. Eventually, the empire was divided up into five parts and leaders assigned:

- **Asia Minor:** Antigonus
- **Egypt:** Ptolemy
- **Eastern territories:** Seleucus
- **Macedonia and Greece:** Antipater
- **Thrace:** Lysimachus

Although these territories changed hands regularly over the next century or so, they effectively made up what became known as the *Hellenistic kingdoms.* See the section 'Raising Hell: The Hellenistic Kingdoms' for more information.

Revolting (again) in southern Greece

Here's a real shocker: Virtually as soon as Alexander had died, the southern Greeks revolted against Macedonia. Athens formed part of the revolt, and the movement was initially quite successful.

Ptolemy the body snatcher!

Ptolemy, the leader of Egypt, managed to secure his own kingdom following the death of Alexander. Alexander's body rested in Babylon for a while until the transfer to Macedonia began. The body travelled in state in a massive mobile tomb known as a *'catafalque'*. It was about 13 feet wide by 20 feet long and constructed like a mini Ionic temple (see Chapter 18) with full decoration in gold and marble. As the tomb moved through Syria, Ptolemy and his men took control of it and transported it to Memphis in Egypt. After Ptolemy and Alexander's body arrived, Ptolemy kicked out the *satrap* appointed by Alexander and declared himself ruler. Ptolemy later moved to Alexandria to supervise the city's completion and installed Alexander's body in a permanent mausoleum in Alexandria. Body snatching – so much simpler than negotiation, don't you think?

Alexander's tomb has now been lost and debate continues to this day about where it might be located.

In late 323 BC, Antipater, the Macedonian in charge of the region, marched south to meet the Greek allies and was initially forced back and besieged in the town of Lamia. However, by the summer of 322 BC, Macedonian reinforcements arrived, and Antipater was able to take on the Greek allies in a pitched battle near the town of Krannon. The Macedonian victory wasn't crushing, but the Greeks were forced to make terms – because they couldn't agree among themselves how to continue the war!

Ending democracy in Athens (322 BC)

If you've read any of the preceding chapters, you won't be surprised to find out that Antipater had to arrange peace terms separately with each city because none of the Greek allies trusted the others enough to negotiate a general peace.

As part of Antipater's peace settlement, the Athenians were required to house a Macedonian garrison that supervised a new government run by Athenian aristocrats who the Macedonians had hand-picked.

The unpleasant squabbling after the revolt and during the peace process brought democracy in Athens to an end. Nearly 200 years of democratic rule – one of ancient Greece's greatest achievements – was over, as was Athens's role as a military power.

Raising Hell: The Hellenistic Kingdoms

After the final blow to Athens, the newly established Hellenistic kingdoms (see Figure 12-1) spent about 170 years bashing each other in the hope of making some territorial gains. Nothing much ever really changed and any gains that were made were usually lost fairly soon afterwards.

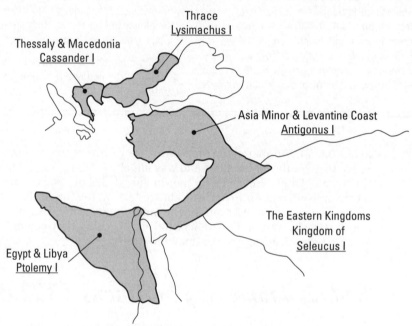

Thrace
Lysimachus I

Thessaly & Macedonia
Cassander I

Asia Minor & Levantine Coast
Antigonus I

The Eastern Kingdoms
Kingdom of
Seleucus I

Figure 12-1:
The
Hellenistic
kingdoms.

Egypt & Libya
Ptolemy I

Developing dynastic struggles

The Hellenistic kingdoms were all individually powerful, but none was powerful enough to dominate the others. Throughout the third century BC the sons of Alexander's generals fought with each other for territorial gains throughout the Mediterranean. This squabbling was very similar to the way that Greek city-states had continually fought each other throughout the century before (refer to Chapter 9).

One thing that the Hellenistic rulers did manage to achieve was the creation of dynasties that saw their descendants running the various kingdoms. The dynastic tradition was particularly true of Ptolemaic Egypt where descendants of Alexander's commander ruled all the way until Cleopatra (along with Mark Antony) was defeated at the battle of Actium in 31 BC. See the section 'Attending the greatest show on earth: Alexandria' for more on the exploits of Ptolemaic Egypt.

Laying siege on Rhodes: Demetrius

One of the more interesting successors to Alexander was Demetrius, the son of Antigonus who ruled in Asia Minor. Demetrius was known as *Poliorcetes* or 'The Besieger', although he seems to have spent more of his time eating and getting drunk.

In 304 BC, Demetrius laid siege to the island of Rhodes in a bid to expand his territory. Demetrius's main tactic was to build a massive siege tower called *Helepolis*, which was as close as the Greeks got to developing a tank. This contraption was 43 metres (140 feet) high and made up of nine storeys. Each storey contained catapults and other siege machinery operated by hundreds of men. For protection, *Helepolis* was covered with iron plates on three sides. Weighing around 150 tons, it needed more than 3,000 specially trained men to pull it.

Impressive, huh? Well, the only problem was, it didn't work. The citizens of Rhodes resisted the siege, and Demetrius left the *Helepolis* behind along with all his other siege equipment when he sailed home. The people of Rhodes celebrated Demetrius's retreat by melting down the *Helepolis* and using it to build the famous statue known as the Colossus of Rhodes, one of the original Seven Wonders of the World (and covered in Chapter 18). A much more profitable end to a bad idea. You can read more about Demetrius in Chapter 26.

The activities of Demetrius are a good example of what the Hellenistic period was like. Demetrius had no real reason to attack Rhodes other than empire building. Treaties proved meaningless as successive generations broke them and carried on fighting.

Attending the greatest show on earth: Alexandria

For all the fighting that went on throughout the Hellenistic kingdoms, Ptolemaic Egypt was relatively stable, and the new city of Alexandria thrived as a result.

City planning panache

Alexandria was ideally placed to gather the revenues from trade all across the Mediterranean, and Egypt itself was hugely wealthy due to the fertile lands surrounding the Nile. *The Ancient Egyptians For Dummies* (Wiley) by Charlotte Booth offers more insight into this exceptional city.

A gift that keeps on giving

The library at Alexandria is hugely important to historians today because the work begun centuries ago to catalogue and preserve texts started a tradition that has carried on through the medieval period and the Renaissance. This tradition is solely responsible for the fact that you and I can still read the works of Homer, Sophocles, Thucydides, and others – and that I'm able to write a book like this. Thanks, Ptolemy!

Alexandria was unusual because it was built from scratch to a definite plan for the location and design of all the major public buildings. A huge amount of money was spent on a large earth work that helped to form a double harbour and the construction of the mighty *pharos* (lighthouse) that dominated the skyline.

Checking out the library

One of the most famous public buildings in Alexandria was the library . The library was actually part of the museum of Alexandria. For the ancient Greeks, a *museum* was literally 'a sanctuary of the muses'. (The muses were Greek goddesses associated with all areas of learning; see Chapter 20 for more on these lovely ladies.)

The library of Alexandria was founded by Ptolemy and thrived throughout the Ptolemaic period. It became the new centre of learning in the Mediterranean, replacing Athens in the process. Scholars travelled from all around to work and study there. Historians believe that at its height it contained 500,000 scrolls, which catalogued nearly everything that had ever been written in the Greek language at the time.

The library flourished throughout the Hellenistic period and beyond until it suffered a terrible fire in 47 BC when Julius Caesar was laying siege to the city. Several Roman emperors subsequently lavished money and attention on the library and attempted to replace its stock, but it may have been finally destroyed during the Byzantine period when the emperor Theodosius demanded the destruction of all pagan temples in AD 391.

The museum and library weren't just about preserving things, but also about new discoveries. The Hellenistic period saw breakthroughs in science (see Chapter 26) and a new, more realistic style in art and sculpture (see Chapter 18). This new community also saw great developments in literature and distinctive poetry produced by men like Apollonius of Rhodes and Theocritus.

A cosmopolitan metropolis

One of the other great new developments in Alexandria was the cosmopolitan nature of its population. Alexandria's new ruling class was Greek and Macedonian, but many other people came to live there.

In this way, Alexandria was rather different to the other major cities of the Greek world. In Athens and Sparta, for example, citizenship and the right to reside were zealously guarded. Alexandria was much more the kind of city that Rome became later, a large metropolis with a real cosmopolitan feel where people came from far and wide to live and work.

The Greek historian Polybius became a Roman citizen and was sent as an envoy to Alexandria in 180 BC. Here he describes the city's population:

> It is inhabited by three classes of people: first the native Egyptians, a volatile group, hard to control; secondly by the mercenaries [foreign soldiers from all over the Mediterranean resident in the city]; thirdly there are the Alexandrians themselves, a people not genuinely civilised . . . for though they are mixed they come from a Greek stock and have not forgotten Greek customs.

Clearly, the cosmopolitan city wasn't to Polybius's taste! Alexandria must have been an amazing place to be, because despite the multinational feel the city was very firmly under the control of its Ptolemaic rulers.

Fading Away: The End of Ancient Greece

Greek influence on the Mediterranean during the Hellenistic period had never been stronger. But ironically, this period was exactly the same time that the Greek world began to lose its independence and get swallowed up by the emerging Roman Empire.

Meeting the Romans

The Roman Empire was the successor to the Greek world and carried on for the best part of 650 years. The Romans themselves came from what was originally a small market town in Umbria that, according to myths, was originally populated by criminals and runaway slaves. By the third century BC the Romans had come to dominate the whole of Italy and were at war with the mighty Carthaginian civilisation based at Carthage in north Africa.

Death by old lady

Pyrrhus carried on his life of adventure, and by 272 BC he was fighting in Argos. During a street battle an old woman standing on the roof of her house saw Pyrrhus attack her son. She picked up a tile from the roof and flung it at him. It knocked him unconscious and he fell from his horse and was killed in the melee. Quite an appropriate end to the life of somebody who was characterised by heroic failure.

Although Rome's rise was all going on in the western Mediterranean, the Greek world felt the impact through the Roman conquest of Sicily in 241 BC. It wasn't long before the Romans began to look east.

Tangling with the Romans: Pyrrhus of Epirus

One of the first contacts between Greece and Rome came at the beginning of the third century BC. The Romans were beginning to expand their interests and the people of Tarentum in southern Italy appealed for help against them.

Their appeal was answered by Pyrrhus, an aristocrat originally from Epirus. Pyrrhus was the joint ruler of Macedonia after driving out Demetrius (of *Helepolis* fame) – see the earlier section 'Laying siege on Rhodes: Demetrius'. But Pyrrhus had then been forced out by his co-ruler Lysimachus.

As something of a military adventurer, Pyrrhus was happy to try and further his ambitions in the west, and he landed at Tarentum in 282 BC. He brought a large army with him, including traditional Macedonian infantry with *sarissas* and about 30 elephants. Over the next three years, he fought a series of campaigns against Rome, heavily defeating the Romans on several occasions.

The problem that Pyrrhus faced was that every time he won a victory, the Romans, with all their available reinforcements, came back stronger, but Pyrrhus's own forces diminished. Despite his victories, Pyrrhus eventually lost the war, leaving to fight in Sicily in 278 BC.

His campaigns are the source of the modern expression 'a pyrrhic victory' – winning the battle but not the war.

Clashing cultures: The Battle of Cynoscephalae

In 197 BC, the Macedonian king Philip V (no relation to Philip II) became engaged with the Romans. Philip was a bit of a chancer and had spent many years fighting small territorial wars against his Hellenistic counterparts. However, in 197 BC, Philip bit off more than he could chew.

During the Second Punic War between Rome and Carthage (218 to 201 BC), Philip supported the Carthaginians and thus made himself an enemy of Rome.

The Romans used their friendship with Ptolemaic Egypt (see the section 'Developing dynastic struggles') as a reason to attack because Philip had recently helped the Seleucid king Antiochus against them. The Romans sailed across the Adriatic Sea and met Philip's forces at Cynoscephalae in Thessaly.

The battle was a real test of military strategies with new, lightly armed, and mobile Roman legions set against the formidable and old school Macedonian phalanx. In the end, the Romans won the day. They surrounded the relatively slow-moving Macedonian phalanx. When the Macedonians lifted their pikes in surrender, the Romans failed to understand the gesture and cut them down. Philip's army was destroyed, and his allies fled.

Becoming a Roman province

Commitments elsewhere meant the Romans were unable to finish the job they began against Philip V, but in 168 BC, they defeated the Macedonians again at Pydna. This time there was no coming back.

Roman forces split Macedonia into four tribal republics and placed a Roman governor in control in each region. After further trouble, the republics were eventually done away with in 146 BC. The country that had produced Philip II and Alexander the Great was made a Roman province.

Generally, the Romans were quite content to allow the Greek cities to rule themselves. The Roman governor in Macedonia kept an eye on things and (as ever!) the Greek cities were too busy squabbling among themselves to ever mount a serious threat against the Romans.

The last Greek hurrah

Following the Roman annexation of Macedonia in 146 BC, several Greek cities formed a coalition called the *Achaean Confederacy,* which rose up in revolt again Rome. Of course, the gesture was futile. The small army that the confederacy mustered never stood a chance against the professional Roman army. The confederacy was easily defeated and the city of Corinth destroyed in the process.

After the revolt, Rome more closely monitored the Greek cities from Macedonia, and in some cases, Roman garrisons were installed. Finally, in 46 BC a large part of southern Greece turned into the Roman province of Achaia. The ancient Greeks never really ruled themselves again.

Living On: Rome and Beyond

Although the Greeks as a powerful entity were no more by 46 BC, Greek civilisation thrived for hundreds of years after. The Romans and subsequent civilisations adopted many elements of Greek life:

- The Roman gods were broadly similar to Greek gods, even though they had different names.
- Greek art, architecture, literature, philosophy, and all manner of other elements of Greek society were incorporated into Roman and Byzantine life, and then rediscovered and reintegrated into Europe during the Renaissance.

Even today you're reading a book about the ancient Greeks. So the Greeks never really went away; they just stopped existing in Greece!

Part III
Living a Greek Life

In this part . . .

With all the fighting they did it's a wonder that the Greeks ever found time for anything else. In this part I look at the nature of everyday life in ancient Greece. I cover what people did in their working lives and leisure time; what they ate and drank; and the art and architecture that they enjoyed. This great cultural life is one of the things that the Greeks are most famous for, and I reveal why . . .

Chapter 13

Out in the Fields: Farming, Herding, and Travelling

- -

In This Chapter

▶ Farming and winemaking

▶ Herding livestock

▶ Getting around in ancient Greece by land and sea

- -

*T*hroughout its 2,000-year history, ancient Greece was an *agrarian society*, which means huge numbers of people spent nearly every day working the soil or tending livestock. Most Greek towns and cities started off as farming communities, and many of them remained so throughout the entire ancient Greek period. Many Greeks were involved in industry or trade (see Chapters 14 and 15 for more on city life), but the vast majority of people derived their income and kept themselves alive by what they and their animals produced.

In this chapter, I discuss what was involved in making a living from the land. I also look at how the Greeks travelled and transported things by land and sea. As you may guess, living a successful life – in the seemingly idyllic Greek countryside – demanded a lot of very hard work!

Scratching a Living

Working the land was tough in the ancient world. People worked from the moment that the sun was up until it set. In the Mediterranean, this schedule meant a 14-hour day most of the time – and they didn't even have weekends to look forward to for time off (although they did have a lot of festivals and public holidays).

The typical ancient Greek farmer worked a relatively small patch of land; a house with perhaps two or three acres that would usually have been in his family for generations.

Richer farmers owned estates that incorporated several pieces of land, sometimes in various locations. Larger farms used slaves and serfs. Serfs were paid workers tied to working on the estate, which was also their accommodation.

Working a farm was exceptionally hard work, and people were only a bad storm or a dry season away from ruin. Furthermore, if a man was called up for military service (see Chapter 5) and his relatives were unable to manage the farm during his absence, he could lose everything.

Growing crops

The basic farming traditions in ancient Greece were similar to those everywhere else in the Mediterranean at the time and they hadn't changed for a very long time. Specifically:

- Nearly all smallholding farmers grew two basic staple crops, which were the mainstays of the Greek diet:

    - **Wheat:** The most common type of wheat was basic emmer wheat, also known as farro wheat. Farmers grew other types of wheat elsewhere in the Mediterranean, and these crops were sometimes exported abroad. Wheat was ground and made into bread.

    - **Barley:** Barley was a lower grade wheat alternative that was easier to grow and was turned into a hard bread or small cakes. Generally speaking, poorer people ate barley bread because the better lands (worked by the wealthier farmers) could grow wheat rather than barley. Barley was also grown a lot in Egypt where it was used to make beer (the Greeks didn't drink beer).

- Greek farmers also grew grapes (see the later section 'Growing grapes and making wine'), olives, and vegetables (mainly pulses and beans).

- Farmers grew crops using *dry farming methods*, meaning that they were able to grow without irrigation. This was very important because of the relatively low rainfall in Greece. See the section 'Working the land' for more info.

    The ancient Greeks had no knowledge of wet-farming (using irrigation) techniques used to grow crops such as rice. However, wet-farming was practised in the near east from as early as 1500 BC, and Alexander the Great and his men probably passed through rice fields on their travels.

- Farmers usually sowed crops in autumn (September in modern terms) because the rainy season in Greece was between autumn and spring. This schedule meant that the summer was usually festival time for celebrating the harvest (June/July). The harvest needed to be successful, too, because it had to sustain the farmers all the way through until next summer.

Chapter 15 discusses more exotic foods and meal preparation.

Going underground: Persephone and Demeter

The myth of Persephone is an interesting story. The daughter of Zeus and Demeter, she was chosen by Hades (the god of the dead) to be his wife. This meant that she was taken from the living to the underworld where Hades lived. Demeter was shocked by her daughter's disappearance and searched the world for her, withholding her blessings from men. This turned the world barren and caused widespread famine. Eventually she discovered where Persephone was and whisked her away from Hades's clutches. However, Zeus ruled that Persephone would have to spend six months of the year with Hades and six with her mother. The Greeks interpreted this as the reason why the world is cold during autumn and winter when Persephone is in the underworld, and warm in spring and summer when she's returned. This is a great example of a myth being used to explain a natural phenomenon.

Honouring Demeter, the friend of the farmer

Several of the Greek gods had associations with farming and fertility, but the most relevant one was the goddess Demeter. Her main association was with wheat, and her name effectively means 'god-mother'. In myth she had a daughter called Persephone, and mother and daughter became known as 'the two goddesses' or sometimes 'the Holy Twain'.

The ancient Greek religious calendar was closely aligned with the farming year, so most celebrations of Demeter coincided with ploughing or harvesting. One of the most famous celebrations was the Thesmophoria, which occurred during sowing time. The festival was for women only; men were strictly banned from it (Chapter 21 has more details). This exclusivity was due to the fact that the Greeks saw fertility on the farm as being closely related to a woman's capacity for child bearing. This rationale is also part of the reason why Demeter was called 'god-mother'. For more on ancient Greek religious customs, see Chapter 22.

Working the land

The techniques used to work the land in ancient Greece were fairly straightforward. If they were able, farmers used the traditional method of 'half and half', which involved ploughing and working half their land every year while leaving the other half *fallow*, or unused. The following year the farmer worked the other portion, so some land always got a break and the soil was able to replenish its natural nutrients.

Unfortunately, some smallholders weren't able to rotate their field because they needed to work every scrap of land. Over time their soil became less and less fertile.

Ploughing

Given the crops the Greeks were growing (see the section 'Growing crops'), ploughing was a major farming activity. The methods for ploughing were very straightforward:

- On bigger farms, two oxen pulled a simple wooden plough. Sometimes the implement was tipped with iron to allow for more accurate ploughing.
- On smaller farms, ploughing was done by hand, which was backbreaking work. This form of ploughing didn't generally turn the soil, only broke it to allow for planting.

Sowing and growing

Similarly, sowing would have been done mostly by hand although on larger estates the number of serfs meant that the work was more evenly spread out. On a small farm the whole family would have been involved.

As I mentioned, the Greeks were dry farmers so watering and irrigation weren't really an issue. They did use manure and most farms would have had an evil-smelling dung heap that it was wise to steer clear of.

Harvesting

After the crops had grown, they were reaped with a simple curved sickle, heaped in a basket, and taken to be threshed. Farmers carried out *threshing* – separating the buds from the main plant – on a threshing floor; a cleared patch of dry ground. Sometimes they used a sled drawn by animals. Barley collecting and wheat 'winnowing' were typically done by hand with a small shovel and a basket. Not a fun job.

Crops were stored in small outbuildings. The Greeks had no refrigeration techniques so things were kept and used for as long as possible until they eventually spoiled.

Following the herd

Most ancient Greek farm estates weren't very big, so the majority of farmers didn't keep many animals. Grazing land was at a premium, so a few pigs, sheep, or goats alongside a pair of oxen were all the livestock most farms supported.

IN THEIR WORDS
ΣΩΦ

Pan: Friend of the farmer – and the soldier?

The Greek god associated with farm life was Pan. His name means 'guardian of the flocks', and he is always depicted as a young man with pipes who tends a herd of goats. However, because he was said to lead a fairly hermit-like existence, he was also associated with the unfortunate soldiers who had to perform guard duty on isolated borders. Several ancient writers suggest that he appeared in the Athenian ranks at the battle of Marathon (refer to Chapter 6). Quite handy to have a god on your side. No wonder the Athenians won!

The female Hellenistic poet Anyte, who was born in Tegea in Arcadia, not far from where Pan was supposed to have come from, writes of Pan:

Why, country Pan, sitting still among the lonely shades of the thick-set wood, do you shrill on your sweet reed?

So that the heifers may pasture on these dewy mountains, cropping the long-haired heads of the grass.

The type of animals that larger farms kept very much depended on the terrain involved. Generally, larger animals, such as cattle and oxen, tended to be kept in the north of Greece and Macedonia because these regions were wetter and more grazing land was available. In the Peloponnese and the south, sheep and goats were better choices because the land was rockier.

Goats and sheep were particularly useful to the ancient Greeks because they were used to produce milk, cheese, wool, and meat – all things that farmers could trade for other commodities at the market in town. Goats and sheep were also useful because farmers could sell or use them in sacrifice; healthy, well-kept animals fetched a very good price for religious purposes.

Hunting high and low

The other method of living off the land was the original one – hunting game. Hunting was a big part of Greek myth with boar being the most popular animal for heroes to hunt. Hunting itself was seen as an activity that helped to sharpen skills for war. These heroes usually hunted with either a spear or a bow, but everyday hunting was rather different and mostly for game such as hares using traps and snares. This was often an activity carried out by young boys.

Farming by the book

Manuals and books about farming weren't really available to the ancient Greeks (although they were developed later in the Roman Empire). Instead, many Greeks referred to a long poem first composed by the poet Hesiod around 700 BC called *Works and Days*. It's full of advice in poetic form for individuals intent on running a farm and relies on mythological examples of what could go wrong if farmers didn't follow Hesiod's advice.

Hesiod was particularly scathing about whether or not a farmer needed a wife, suggesting that a female slave might be better:

First of all you should acquire a house and a woman and an ox for the plough . . . A female slave, not a wife, who can follow the oxen as well.

Hesiod was no great fan of women in general. Later in the poem, he warns that women are not to be trusted as they are likely to want to 'steal your barn'. Clearly, he just never met the right woman.

Boar hunting did go on using hounds and (when done by the rich) on horseback in large groups. Boar hunting was still seen as a noble art and one that a man of action should be proficient in.

Growing Grapes and Making Wine

People drank a great deal of wine in ancient Greece. Grapes were relatively easy to grow because of the climate and soil, so most farms and estates included some vines.

Evidence indicates that the forerunners of the ancient Greeks, the Mycenaeans (see Chapter 2), grew grape vines and made wine, so viticulture (the growing of grapes to make wine) was fairly well established by the last millennium BC.

Despite the region's long history of wine making, little is known about the processes, and no books on the subject survive. However, historians do know that the beverage was usually mixed with water, and the alcohol content wasn't as high as with wine today.

Different varieties of red and white wine were available. Usually, the geography and climate of the region dictated what type of grape farmers grew and the sort of wine they produced. For example, the island of Ceos produced three specific types:

'High on the hill sat a lonely goatherd . . .'

Spending time tending goats day in and day out may not sound like the most romantic of jobs, but the occupation became very popular in ancient Greek art and literature – and beyond.

The idea of the Greek goatherd – and, in particular, one pining for a lost love – became a traditional feature in classical art and poetry.

Over a thousand years after the ancient Greeks, the goatherd became popular again, and during the Renaissance the idea of 'pastoral' was born. Everything from the paintings of Titian to the Symphony No. 6 'Pastoral' by Beethoven trace back to the old goatherds of ancient Greece.

- ✔ **Austeros**: A dry wine

- ✔ **Glukazon**: A sweet wine

- ✔ **Autokratos**: A variety somewhere between the two – a medium-dry, if you like.

These varieties from Ceos were established and known all over Greece (see the sidebar 'An early marketing effort'), and other cities and regions had similar specialties.

Wine was a vital part of Greek life and people drank it for a huge variety of reasons including religious celebration. See Chapter 15 and also Chapter 20, where I look at the god associated with wine and generally having a good time – Dionysus.

Getting Around in Ancient Greece

Like just about everything else in ancient times, travelling throughout ancient Greece was seriously hard work. If you were on dry land, you either travelled by horse, cart, or your own feet. On water, you had the option of riding in boats, but these vehicles weren't plain sailing (see the later section 'Venturing into Poseidon's realm: Travelling by sea').

The concept of travel for its own sake or of going on holiday wasn't really a part of Greek life. Certainly, only the very rich could've afforded the time away from work, let alone the expense of the journey. Generally speaking, the ancient Greeks travelled only if they had to. Traders, for example, were almost constantly on the move between market towns, buying local produce and selling it in the next town.

Occasionally, the ancient Greek people made massive journeys to move and set up in another place. See Chapters 3 and 4 for more on colonisation in early Greek history.

An early marketing effort

Greeks were very proud of their local vintages and had an easy system for identifying where wine came from. Each town had its own slightly different type of double-headed jug, known as an *amphora*, that exclusively held its wines. (In fact, the people of the island of Ceos were so proud of their wine that they used the symbol of their *amphora* on their coinage.) The distinctive shapes have been extremely helpful to archaeologists trying to work out where various pieces of unearthed pottery originally came from.

Going by horse

If you were able to afford a horse, riding it or using it to draw a cart was the preferred mode of transportation throughout ancient Greece. A horse was expensive – essentially another mouth to feed. Being able to maintain and equip a horse was a sign that you were financially well off. (Chapter 4 discusses the social classes in Athens.) Furthermore, riding equipment was rudimentary; stirrups didn't appear in Europe until around the ninth century AD. Add the lack of decent roads to the situation and you can see how difficult riding must have been.

Wild horses were rare in most parts of Greece with the exception of Thessaly, where large numbers of horses were tamed and bred. The Thessalians became famous for their formidable cavalry (see Chapter 11).

For those less well off an ass or a donkey was an acceptable substitute. Unlike finely bred, expensive horses, the life of a donkey wasn't happy. They were worked extremely hard as an all-purpose animal, as this little poem by Palladas suggests. Palladas was a Greek writing during the Roman era (around AD 350) but the experience of the donkey would have been exactly the same even then!

> *Poor little donkey! It's no joke being a pedant's not a rich man's moke [donkey] preened in the palace of the alabarch [official in the Jewish community].*

> *Little donkey, stay, stay with me patiently until the day I get my pay.*

Burning sandals

Most people had no transportation option other than to walk to wherever they needed to go. Consequently, people tried to limit journeys to when they were absolutely necessary.

A good example of a typical journey was the walk between Athens and the port at Piraeus, a journey of about 7 kilometres (4 miles). It would take a large part of the day to walk there and back, but some people made the trip every day, such as small farmers or people trekking in to attend the jury courts. Rich Athenian merchants often kept small houses or apartments in the port for when they needed to conduct business there before returning to their main home in the city.

Venturing into Poseidon's realm: Travelling by sea

Some journeys were only possible on the 'Great Green', as the Egyptians and Greeks called the Mediterranean Sea. The Greeks were capable and experienced sailors, and Chapters 6 and 7 describe many of their successes in naval warfare.

The Greek god of the sea was Poseidon (although many other gods and deities were associated with it). Poseidon was a violent god, and the Greeks attributed storms, earthquakes, and mishaps at sea to his rage. Making offerings to him before a voyage was seen as essential and a wise move upon returning from a successful trip.

The following passage from Homer's *Iliad* gives a great idea of how the Greeks viewed Poseidon:

> *Down Poseidon dove and yoked his bronze-hoofed horses onto his battle-car . . . skimming the waves, and over the swells they came, dolphins leaving their lairs to sport across his wake, leaping left and right – well they knew their lord. And the sea heaved in joy, cleaving a path for him.*

Another real danger in sea travel was falling overboard. Most people in ancient Greece couldn't swim. Many sailors felt that it was unlucky to learn to swim because it tempted fate and caused your vessel to be shipwrecked. Also, swimming itself wasn't a leisure activity in the way that it is now. If you were a city dweller on a sea voyage and you fell overboard, you had to hope that one of the crew swam!

Ships for trade and transport

Most military vessels were long, sleek, and powered by oars (see Chapter 5), but ships used for trade and transport were very different. Generally, they were much larger with a far greater draft (meaning they sat much lower in the water with more of the ship under the waterline) and looked a little more rounded. These larger transporters were nearly always powered by sail alone.

Pytheas: Boldly going where no Greek had been before

Despite the sea being so perilous, some Greeks attempted long journeys of discovery. The most famous of these was a man named Pytheas who in around 320 BC claimed to have sailed from the Mediterranean around Spain, into the Atlantic Ocean, around the British Isles, and even farther – almost to the Arctic Circle. When he returned home, he wrote a book about the expedition called *On the Ocean*. Nobody believed him at the time but many modern commentators think he was telling the truth.

Sails were made of linen. They were often painted and decorated with designs indicating where the ship came from or the type of cargo that it was carrying. With a decent wind behind it, one of these ships could travel at about 7 to 10 kilometres per hour (about 4 to 6 knots).

Although the dimensions and power source of trade ships meant they offered far more room for carrying cargo and passengers, the vessels were also entirely at the mercy of the weather and were also far less manoeuvrable than their military cousins.

Shipbuilding

The building of ships was a highly skilled trade that was passed down through families. Great examples of shipbuilding appear in mythology, like the construction of Jason's ship the *Argo,* which Homer's *Odyssey* describes in detail. Amazingly, the construction methods that Homer describes in around 750 BC were still being used during the Hellenistic period 600 years later.

The construction method Homer describes is known as the 'shell first' technique, where the ship begins as just a keel on to which planking and other frames are added later. This method was quite fast; ships could be built relatively quickly. Depending on how many people were involved, a ship could be put together in about a month.

Navigating

Travel by sea was highly dangerous. The sailing season was usually confined to between March and October because during the winter months the weather was too unpredictable.

The Greeks didn't have the ability to navigate by using charts, so as much as possible they stayed close to the coast or used individual islands to judge distance. Some navigation by the stars was possible on clear nights, but sailors didn't rely on this method.

The pirates of the Mediterranean

Assuming you survived bad navigation, terrible storms, drowning, or the wrath of Poseidon, you also had to watch out for pirates! Piracy was a big problem with sea travel. The ancient Greek myths are full of episodes that can be interpreted as piracy:

- Jason and the Argonauts sail to the Black Sea and steal the Golden Fleece, an obvious act of piracy.

- Many of the events in Homer's *Odyssey* are piracy, but they go unpunished and aren't criticised.

Pirates thrived because nobody (until Roman times) was able to crack down on them. Also, during wars like the Peloponnesian War (see Chapter 8), telling the difference between an act of war and an act of piracy was very difficult.

In general, pirates operated on popular trade routes using hideaways on small islands. The area around Rhodes (see the map on the Cheat Sheet) in particular was known to be a hotbed of piracy with the five harbours on the island providing rich pickings.

These navigation limitations meant that sailors only really knew a small number of local journeys and routes because they had to have specialist knowledge of local currents and how they affected the journey. So if you wanted to travel between Athens and Asia Minor you had to make a number of small journeys, hopping between islands, rather than one long trip. And you were at the mercy of the trade routes and whether somebody was going your way.

Fishing

Just like hunting on dry land, fishing was a way of getting food from the sea. Fishing was an important industry in ancient Greece, although probably not as big as you may think. Predicting the movements of heavy shoals was very difficult for Greek fishermen without the aid of modern technology, and the Mediterranean isn't as well stocked with fish as the larger oceans.

Most fishing took place close to shore with large nets. (Only the very brave fished farther out in the open sea due to navigation limitations; see the section 'Navigating'). However, the varieties of fish available in deeper, open waters were very highly prized and fetched higher prices.

The Greeks loved fish and it was a staple part of the diet for those who could afford it. For more on fish and how the Greeks ate it, see Chapter 15.

Chapter 14

Home and Family

- -

In This Chapter

▶ Organising the Greek household

▶ Appreciating the role of women

▶ Understanding marriage and divorce

▶ Raising and educating children

▶ Looking at slaves

- -

*P*arts I and II of this book cover some of the most brutal battles in all history, but this chapter looks at something you may find just as shocking – the everyday interactions of ancient Greek families. So prepare yourself: Ancient Greek attitudes about women, sex, death, and violence were very different to those held today.

This chapter (as well as Chapter 15) looks at what life was like in Greek towns and cities. For the most part, I concentrate on Athens because it was the biggest and most successful city at the time, and because of the huge amount of archaeological and documentary evidence it's the one that historians know most about.

Much of what I describe in this chapter is what you can call *social standards.* Ancient Greek social standards were very high, and an awful lot of people did not – indeed, *could not* – live up to them the whole time. You discover the Greeks' frame of mind and how they viewed the world. In a perfect world these are the standards that people expected themselves and others to live up to. However, comic plays and novels from ancient Greece indicate that people lived their lives far beneath the standards of what was supposedly acceptable. Think of it this way: Nowadays most people consider speaking with your mouth full to be rude – but many people still do it!

Appreciating the Household: The Oikos

The *oikos* was the basic unit of Greek society. In modern terms, *oikos* would probably translate to 'household', but the word meant much more than just your home. The *oikos* included:

SEEN ON SCREEN

An Ithacan's *oikos* is his castle

In *The Odyssey* by Homer, Odysseus is delayed on his return home to the island of Ithaca from the war at Troy (see Chapter 21 for more on Homer). While Odysseus is away, various local nobles turn up at his house and try to persuade his wife, Penelope, to marry them, claiming that her husband is obviously dead. Penelope is no doubt very attractive, but what these would-be suitors really want is Odysseus's land and property – his *oikos* – that come with Penelope's hand in marriage.

In the recent TV adaptation of *The Odyssey* (2000), Odysseus returns home and kills the suitors who invaded his house. He justifies killing them by saying, 'They tried to steal my world.' That's a great way of expressing what the *oikos* really meant.

✔ The physical building itself (see the following section 'Touring the typical Greek house').

✔ The people within it (see the later section 'Meeting the extended family').

✔ All property associated with the family and building.

The Greeks considered the *oikos* to be one entity, like a very small version of the *polis* or 'state' (see Chapter 4). Best to keep your hands off another man's *oikos*, or big trouble lay ahead.

Touring the typical Greek house

As Figure 14-1 shows, the average house in an ancient Greek town wasn't very big. Floor plans were simple and similar:

✔ All the rooms opened onto a rectangular courtyard, which featured a doorway to the street on one side.

✔ Each house had a main living room where family members spent most of the day.

✔ A secondary room, called the *andron* (which literally means the 'men's room') was used to receive visitors. As the name implies, this room was primarily the domain of men. Men slept in quarters adjacent to the *andron*.

✔ Women's quarters were located elsewhere in the house – usually well away from the *andron*, often on the upper level. The women would work and sleep here.

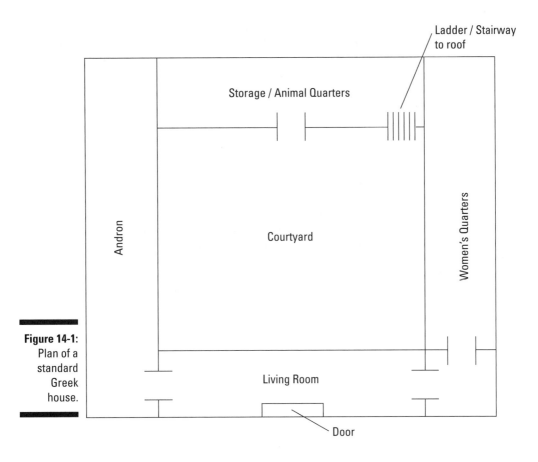

Ladder / Stairway to roof

Storage / Animal Quarters

Andron

Courtyard

Women's Quarters

Figure 14-1:
Plan of a
standard
Greek
house.

Living Room

Door

The building itself was fairly basic with walls made of mud brick or rubble and the floors most likely of beaten earth. Houses usually included a ladder (or an external stairway in wealthier houses) that family members used to access the roof, which they used as another living space.

A Greek house didn't have a specific bathroom or kitchen. Cooking would often be done outside. Washing was done with cold water in the privacy of the sleeping quarters.

No matter how much money you had, the style of house would be mostly the same. Luxury was represented by the size of the property and the quality of decoration or finish.

Meeting the extended family

In general, the concept of family was very strong. A lot of people lived within the small space of a Greek house. In addition to the modern 'nuclear family' (man, woman, and probably between two and five children), other relatives often formed part of the household. Unmarried or widowed females lived under the protection of their nearest male relatives, and grandmothers, nieces, and sisters were often legally obliged to seek shelter in an already busy household. Add to this mix several slaves, and the average household usually numbered between 9 and 12 people.

But within the family, however, equality didn't exist. Men were the absolute rulers, and women had very little status at all.

Kurios: Man about the house

The dominant male in the *oikos* was its absolute ruler. He was known as the *kurios*, which means 'the man in charge'. The *kurios* literally had the power of life and death over everybody within, including his wife and children. A man who killed his wife could be legally challenged by her relations but if she was proved to have been unfaithful he had acted legally. He carried out all the financial and legal transactions of the *oikos*. Nobody else interacted with the *oikos* in any way without his consent. A husband in a new home would automatically become *kurios* and stay in this position until he died, although in some households the eldest son would take charge if the father became too old or ill to cope.

Beyond oikos

Although the *oikos* itself was an independent unit, the concept of family was very strong and extended beyond the *oikos* to other groups:

- ✔ The *ankhisteia* was a wider network of relatives to which Greek families belonged. This network usually went as far as second cousins and comprised people's wider family.

  If a woman was widowed, her first move was to look for a new husband within the *ankhisteia*. This group also played a very big role in the inheritance process. Inheritance law was hideously complex but basically followed the rule that the nearest male relative inherited. If there wasn't an obvious heir then a male relative from the *ankhisteia* would step in and marry the widow, so inheriting the property.

- ✔ The *phratiai* were religious associations that are probably best described as brotherhoods because all the members were male, representing their *oikos*. Although the members may not have all been related, their families normally had some kind of association through marriage or business in the past.

Like the *oikos*, these other associations were very powerful. Men were expected to give absolute loyalty to them. If a man fell out with either his ankhisteia or phratiai, he was shunned by the rest and open to attack.

With all these loyalties life could become very complicated. A man's ultimate loyalty would be to his *oikos* and then his *ankhisteia* but the *phratiai* interests were strong too because they usually had a strong business or financial element. Fortunately the interests of these groups wouldn't really clash because they were all representing the same thing – the furtherance of the *oikos* and those involved in it on a wider basis.

Spending Time with the Women of Ancient Greece

Ancient Greek women were second-class citizens at best – or even less in many cities. For example, Athenian women didn't count as citizens; they were instead classed as 'Women of Attica' (Attica was the region of eastern Greece that Athens belonged to). The point was to separate the women from the city – they were associated with it but not part of its ruling class.

Women had very little liberty in ancient Greece. They were expected to spend the vast majority of their time within the *oikos* (see the section 'Appreciating the Household: The Oikos' earlier in the chapter) and were discouraged from interacting with anybody else. For example, if male guests came to the home and visited the *andron*, women were unlikely to be asked to join them. In more traditional households if women were invited, they were required to wear a veil at all times or even to sit behind a screen.

The poet – and marital advice-giver – Hesiod (see Chapter 13) had a bit of a downer on women. In his long poem *Works and Days* he's scathing about the problems that women can bring:

> *For a man acquires nothing better than a wife – a good one, but there is nothing more miserable than a bad one, a parasite, who even if her husband is strong singes him with the torch and brings him to a raw old age.*

The ancient Greeks saw women as something to be controlled and they limited the type and amount of property a woman could own. For example:

- Women weren't technically allowed to own property above the value of one *medimnos* of barley, which was about as much as it cost to feed a family for a week.

- Any property that a woman used, like clothes or jewellery, was part of the *oikos* and as such belonged to her husband.

Even when her husband died a woman wouldn't hold on to the family property – she needed to swiftly remarry (preferably to a member of the *ankhisteia*) so that the property could be taken on by another male.

Mythical monsters

Women in Greek myth and tragic plays have a hard time. Most are portrayed as untrustworthy and temperamental. Examples include:

- **Clytemnestra:** Wife of Agamemnon. She murdered her husband when he returned home from the Trojan War.

- **Medea:** The wife of Jason from the Argonauts story (told in Chapter 20). When he left her for another woman, she murdered their new children and his new bride.

- **Pandora:** The first ever woman. She was responsible for bringing all the ills into the world.

Of course, things aren't quite that simple and most men behave appallingly in myths too. But these images of women in myth affected the ancient Greeks. Men were suspicious and tried to keep women under close control.

Although restrictive, the position women were expected to adopt in ancient Greek society was somewhat manageable in wealthy households where numerous slaves ran the *oikos*. Women from poorer families, however, had to be much more active because they carried out all the tasks necessary to keep the household going. Some women even worked alongside their husbands in the family trade or at the market. Despite their hard work, women were still tied to and financially dependent on men. The only women who were financially independent were some of the more exclusive prostitutes, who I talk about in Chapter 15.

Marrying and Divorcing

Part of the reason why ancient Greek society controlled women so tightly was so as not to damage their chances of securing good marriages. Marriage was the main event of a woman's life – something that she spent her young life preparing for.

Girls married at a young age, usually about 14, to men who were considerably older, probably 25 to 30 years old. Often, women married much older men, if the men had been recently widowed.

The poet Theognis describes the challenges of marrying a young bride, particularly when the husband is older:

> *'A young wife is not suitable for an elderly husband*
>
> *For she is a boat that does not obey the rudder.*

Nor do anchors hold her; and she breaks her mooring cables,

Often at night to find another harbour.'

Getting hitched: It's all about the money

Weddings were complicated things to organise because they centred largely on property transfers. When a bride moved in with her new husband, she brought a *dowry* with her. The dowry was typically a large sum of money that represented a portion of her father's property because giving up the land itself would be very complicated. The wife didn't own her dowry and it immediately became the property of her husband – even though he may have to return it if they divorced.

Marriage took place in two stages: the betrothal (when the union was announced) and the actual (and completely unromantic) wedding itself.

The betrothal

The first part of the marriage was called the *eggue*, which is similar to the modern notion of betrothal – although the term really means something more like 'pledge'.

The coming marriage was announced publicly (read out in front of members of the *ankhisteia*) so others were able to witness both the size of the dowry the bride's father was offering and to make assurances that the girl was still a virgin. A betrothal often took place very early in a girl's life when she was still a child of maybe 5 or 6.

A young man picked his wife on the basis of status and family connections usually as a result of intensive negotiations within the *ankhisteia* carried out by his father. The couple probably never met each other before the betrothal. Romance didn't even come into the picture. The entire process was a business transaction, pure and simple.

The wedding – or moving day

The actual marriage itself was very straightforward. The girl simply entered the *oikos* of her new husband and began living with him. The couple went through a small formal ceremony to bless the union, but it was all very private. You didn't need a marriage licence because marriage was a private transaction between the two *kurioi*.

A wedding feast usually took place afterwards and sometimes went on for two or three days. All the members of the *ankhestia* would attend with the women all gathered with the bride in the women's quarters of the house. It was usually a good natured revel with much eating, drinking, and dancing – not too different from the average wedding reception today.

Packing up and moving on

Ancient Greek divorce, like marriage, was pretty straightforward: The bride simply moved out. She went back to the house of her father, if he was still alive, or to the home of the nearest male relative.

Either side of a couple could ask for divorce, but more often than not men sought divorce following an allegation of adultery. (Men commonly slept with other women and prostitutes, but wives were supposed to be entirely faithful.) Typically public proclamations were made about unfaithful wives, and the women were totally humiliated.

The other major reason for divorce was so that men could make other, more socially attractive and financially beneficial marriages. Having been married before was no barrier to marrying again – for a man or a woman – but a man had much more choice in whom he married the second or third time. Unlike other ancient cultures only one spouse was allowed at the same time!

Of course, some marriages took place that didn't conform to these well-defined social structures. The poorer and lower classes also married but without the elaborate preparations and negotiations involved in more moneyed households. Many more of these marriages would have been for love; unfortunately historians don't know too much about them because all of the evidence relates to the moneyed literate classes.

Starting Out in Life: Children

In general, the ancient Greek attitude toward children was very harsh. Some of the things that I talk about in this section are quite upsetting – so be warned.

Ancient Greek men were pretty paranoid about adultery and it partly explains their distrust and restriction of women. Part of their concern was because of the possibility of illegitimate children. Greek law around inheritance was very strict and the emergence of any illegitimate children could really complicate a situation and result in lengthy legal cases.

Clearing a difficult first hurdle: Birth

Ancient Greece had no scientific methods of contraception so women often fell pregnant. Women would be expected to give birth a number of times during their life and because they married quite young (age 14 or 15) would have had many fertile years ahead of them. Four or five children in a family wouldn't be unusual.

Oedipus: A case in point

Probably the most famous Greek play is *Oedipus Tyrannus* by Sophocles. The drama centres around the fact that, after receiving an unfavourable prophecy, Oedipus's father gives his son as an infant to be exposed. The shepherd asked to expose the child takes sympathy on Oedipus and gives him away to be adopted, starting one of the most famously tragic cycle of events ever.

The fifth-century BC audience that watched this play originally wouldn't have been shocked by the decision of Oedipus's father because they were familiar and comfortable with the ultimate power that a man had over his *oikos*. You can read more about the play in Chapter 16.

Delivery

In the vast majority of cases, birth was an all-female affair. Either experienced midwives or female friends delivered babies. Male doctors were called in only for the most difficult of cases. (See Chapter 15 for more on ancient Greek medical practices.) Birth took place in the household where the woman would have spent her entire term.

The risks to the woman giving birth were as high as they were for the child. The potential loss of blood and complications in delivery that would be manageable today were potentially fatal in ancient Greece. In many cases, one or other didn't survive the experience.

Infanticide

Although appalling, *infanticide* (the killing or leaving to die of small children) wasn't uncommon in ancient Greece. Most Athenian men wanted sons because a male was able to work in the family business and provided an heir for the *oikos*. (The poet Hesiod in his *Works and Days* poem advises that it's best to have only one son and no daughters at all.) Daughters were considered problems. They were expensive to keep and cost a lot in dowries when they married.

The Greek solution was appalling but simple. If the *kurios* of an *oikos* decided that he already had enough children, then subsequent children, especially girls, were exposed. This horrific practice involved leaving the infant out in the countryside where he or she either starved or was taken by animals.

I'm not excusing the appalling practice of infanticide, but as I mention when I discuss warfare (see Chapter 5), the everyday presence and possibility of death and disease hardened the ancient Greek people. Also, although exposure of babies is terrible, you need to bear in mind that life expectancy in ancient Greece was only around 30 years. Of course, loads of people lived to be much older than 30, but the average was brought down by the huge number of infant mortalities. Death and the loss of loved ones was a common experience, although that wouldn't make the pain of losing somebody any easier.

Getting an education

If you managed to make it through early childhood, the next stage of life was your education. This varied hugely depending on whether you were a boy or a girl.

School for boys

No age requirement existed for schooling. Many boys received some kind of formal education from 5 or 6 all the way through to adulthood (16).

Ancient Greece didn't have a state-sponsored education system. All classes were paid for by a boy's *kurios* or guardian. Wealthier families provided tutors who lived and worked in the home, giving lessons to a number of children.

Boys experienced three main strands of education:

- ✔ *Grammatistes* taught formal subjects like mathematics, reading, and writing. Boys spent a lot of their time memorising the works of Homer and other poets. The Greeks felt that the great works of literature provided moral training via the conduct of the characters in the stories.

- ✔ *Kitharistes* taught music and poetry. Boys learned how to play the lyre and perform songs and poetry.

- ✔ *Paidotribes* taught gymnastics and fitness training, most probably at the *palaestra*, or training ground. For more on this sort of training see Chapter 16.

A boy usually had lessons from all these tutors every day (apart from festival days), often travelling to different places for classes.

For the wealthy, further study was available when boys became men. Men could obtain individual tuition in a specific area or subject from teachers called *sophists* who hired themselves out for the purpose. By the beginning of the fourth century BC, Plato's Academy, and later Aristotle's Lyceum, became established as official schools of higher education. I talk more about all this in Chapter 23.

Education for the poor

Education was expensive. For families without money, education meant working in the family business or on the family farm. This education was vocational so that children could take over the business from their parents. Girls would also be involved in this work until they reached an age where they might marry. Many poorer people would have been illiterate.

Girls: They don't need no education!

Like so many things in ancient Greece, education was different for girls. It was very unusual for a father to spend money on his daughter's education. Boys were educated because they were taught the skills they needed in order to succeed in public life. Girls, by contrast, were expected to be domestic and were taught the skills of needlework and how to run a home.

Some women were highly educated and nothing stopped them learning later in life, but these more learned women were very much in the minority and never had a public role to showcase their talents.

Examining Slavery

In addition to the family members themselves, an *oikos* included the slaves within the household. Slavery formed a big part of Greek society, and ancient Athens included a huge number of slaves. Modern writers have estimated that at the beginning of the Peloponnesian War in 431 BC (see Chapter 8), about 50,000 male citizens resided in Athens. At the same time, about 100,000 slaves also lived in the city. If you consider women and children, historians contend that the total population of Athens was split about 50:50 between slaves and non-slaves. Both men and women were slaves although they fulfilled different roles, women being mostly confined to maid duties and childcare.

Defining a slave

Slaves were the property of the *oikos* and had no legal rights whatsoever. Technically and legally, a slave was exactly the same as a pot or a sheep. Whoever owned slaves had the power of life and death over them and could do whatever they wanted. If a man regularly beat and even killed his slaves, he wasn't thought of as unreasonably cruel.

As well as fighting wars and writing history Xenophon also wrote books about philosophy (see Chapter 9). In his book *Memorabilia* he recreates a conversation where Socrates discusses the appropriate punishments for slaves who are lazy and misbehave. The treatment he describes was probably quite commonplace:

Socrates: Do they not control their lecherousness by starving them? Prevent them stealing by locking up anything they might steal from? Stop them running away by putting them in fetters? Drive out their laziness with beatings?

Some people were born into slavery (as the children of slaves), but the vast majority were sold into it, mostly as a result of warfare. For example, Alexander the Great (see Chapters 10 and 11) sold the entire populations of several cities into slavery. He could only have done that if the market were thriving.

Establishing the going rate for a slave

Slave markets regularly took place in most cities, and Athens was no exception. The individuals for sale mostly came from the north in Thrace and Dalmatia but also from Asia Minor across the Mediterranean (see the map on the Cheat Sheet in the front of this book).

Following are some prices for slaves from an auction that took place in 415 BC:

- ✔ A Thracian woman: 165 drachmas
- ✔ A Syrian man: 240 drachmas
- ✔ A Scythian man: 144 drachmas
- ✔ A Carian child: 72 drachmas

To make some sense of the prices, 1 drachma was the average daily wage of a skilled worker (think of about £25 or $50). Young men were most valuable (and hence expensive) because they could be worked harder for longer and there was no risk of them falling pregnant. Older people could be expensive if they were well educated, and they were often bought to serve as tutors.

Dividing up the labour

After a slave owner bought a slave, the slave had several possible destinations and roles:

- ✔ Most households had at least one *oiketes*, or basic domestic slave.
- ✔ Some better skilled slaves were set up to work in businesses by their masters, working as potters or other types of craftsmen.
- ✔ The Athenian state also owned slaves called *demosioi* who performed official functions, such as working with coinage or serving as clerks in the courts. The Athenian 'police force' was also made up of Scythian slaves often referred to as 'Scythian Archers'.

Legal responsibilities

One of the most unpleasant aspects of being a slave was their legal position. If slaves were required to give evidence in legal cases (see Chapter 7), only statements given under torture were considered valid because it was felt that they would otherwise lie to protect themselves (being poor they were considered easy to corrupt with bribes and inducements).

Both parties in a legal case agreed to the form of torture in advance and to the compensation should the slave be disabled as a result. Typical tortures included the rack, beating, and having vinegar poured up the nose.

In general, slaves were best off claiming that they hadn't seen anything.

- ✔ Many slaves worked outside the cities on the farms owned by citizens. Some became trusted to run elements of the farm.

- ✔ The most unfortunate slaves worked in the silver mines at Laureion near Athens. Their work was hard and remorseless, and death was the only thing to look forward to.

The huge number of slaves in Athens and in Attica generally did an enormous amount of work. Their efforts made it possible for male citizens to spend so much of their time involved in the political process (see Chapter 7). It's kind of ironic that one of the major reasons that the Athenians were able to develop democracy was their system of subjugating and stripping the rights from hundreds of thousands of people.

Buying your freedom

Slaves were technically able to either buy or be given their freedom by their master, a process called *manumission.* Gaining freedom from slavery wasn't as common as in some other civilisations (like the Roman Empire, for example).

And freedom had its issues. Freed slaves were in awkward positions because they weren't able to gain Athenian citizenship and had to become *metoikoi* or *metics* (resident foreigners) instead.

Connecting with Alien Life: Metics

In addition to family and slave, the Athens *oikos* had one other possible household member: legal aliens, known as *metoikoi* or *metics.*

Metoikoi were foreigners who resided in Athens but weren't granted citizen status. Their status was slightly different to that of normal visitors to the city because *metoikoi* paid a special tax and needed to have patrons who guaranteed them while they stayed in the city. Often, guaranteeing included providing accommodation to the *metoikoi*.

Metics sometimes worked as tutors in the houses of their patrons. Several famous characters went through this process, including the following:

- ✔ The historian and traveller Herodotus performed his work for several years in Athens and was very popular, but he left when the city refused to grant him citizen status.

- ✔ The great philosopher Aristotle spent years in Athens living in a house just outside the city walls. As a *metoikos* he wasn't allowed to buy property in the city and was forced to build a house outside it.

Chapter 15

Going About Daily Life in Ancient Greece

*L*ike much of the ancient Greek experience, many things seem very close to how people live today, whereas other aspects seem very strange. In this chapter (and Chapter 16), I examine how people lived their lives on a day-to-day basis. After shedding some light on how the ancient Greeks kept track of their days, this chapter focuses on three staple elements of daily human existence: eating, drinking, and procreation. Along the way, I also touch on two other essentials: money and medicine.

Biding Their Time: The Greek Calendar and Clock

As I mention in Chapter 1, people in the ancient world most commonly dated things by events rather than an actual year. For example, they probably said 'In the year Pericles died' or 'the year after the battle of Marathon', rather than 429 BC or 479 BC, respectively.

Although this convention is very straightforward, the actual Greek calendar was really complex. The following sections cover the basics.

Figuring out the day

Part of the challenge of working with ancient Greek dates is that the region didn't operate under a single calendar. Although every city based its calendar on the lunar cycle, they named individual months and fixed dates after local gods and religious festivals.

In fact, not only did every town or city have a different name for each month, but each possibly used a different date for the start of a new year. So if you were celebrating the New Year in Athens, folks in Thebes may still be in the previous one. The dissimilarities weren't vast and probably didn't make that much difference. In the time it took to travel from Athens to Thebes it would be new year when you got there anyway!

Exploring the Athenian calendar

Because this chapter, as well as most of Part III, focuses on Athens, this city's calendar is worth examining in detail. Table 15-1 outlines the Athenian calendar.

Table 15-1	The Months of the Athenian Calendar	
Summer		
1	Hekatombaion	June / July
2	Metageitnion	July / August
3	Boedromion	August / September
Autumn		
4	Pyanepsion	September / October
5	Maimakterion	October / November
6	Poseidon	November / December
Winter		
7	Gamelion	December / January
8	Anthesterion	January / February
9	Elaphebolion	February / March

Spring		
10	Mounichion	March / April
11	Thargelion	April / May
12	Skirophorion	May / June

Each of Athens's 12 months was either 29 or 30 days long, meaning that a year usually added up to about 354 days. Except the system wasn't actually that simple. The *arkhons* designated some years as leap years and added a whole extra month. Leap years sometimes involved just repeating an already existing month, and mostly the *ekklesia* chose to have another month of Poseideon. This curious custom meant that a leap year was up to 384 days in length.

Although this was a lunar calendar and the Greeks were using the moon to calculate it, this wasn't the main reason for making changes. More often than not the changes were used to create extra time. In 271 BC the Athenians added four extra days to the month of Elaphebolion to allow more time to prepare for the City Dionysia festival (see Chapter 16). It's probably fair to assume that other cities did the same sort of thing.

What day is it again?

The days within each month were even more complicated. The Athenians didn't name the day (Monday, Tuesday, and so on) – instead, they numbered them. But even this convention wasn't as straightforward as it may seem.

A month started with the new moon and the Athenians then divided it into three parts: waxing, full, and waning. The first two parts counted forward the next 21 days. However, at the 22nd day things changed. As the moon began to wane, the Athenians counted backwards from 10 until the end of the month, finishing at day 1. This last day was known as the 'old and new' day.

So, despite having a 30-day month, the last day of Poseideon, for example, was actually the 1st. It's very confusing. It confused me when I was writing about it.

Additional calendars

Incredibly, time keeping was actually even more complicated. In addition to the calendar conventions I describe in the preceding section, the ancient Athenians used two other forms of calendar:

- ✔ A calendar for scheduling religious festivals
- ✔ Another calendar to date political documents and legislation

Phew, that was a long week!

If you read through the details of the section 'Exploring the Athenian calendar', you may wonder how the numbering system left any room for weekends. Well, it didn't. There weren't formal days of 'non-work' apart from festivals and when you worked depended on what you did. For many people, if they didn't work they didn't eat. Other wealthier farmers or business people would be able to choose what they did and when. At certain times there was more to do, particularly in seasonal work like farming.

In Athens pretty much every day was a work day except when they held religious festivals. Athenians spent about 60 days in festivals every year, and probably about another 20 days were other specified non-work days for those taking part: citizens, women of Attica, and in some cases *metics*. Slaves were mostly excluded.

With the current two-day weekend, modern folks get about 20 extra days off each year compared with the ancient Greeks – but then again, they also had thousands of slaves to do a lot of the work for them!

The various calendars were mapped against each other, and on many occasions people must have needed to be told what day it was! The public slaves, or *demosioi* (see Chapter 14), were put in charge of keeping dates and records straight.

Working from dawn till dusk

The average Athenian day began at dawn, or just before, and carried on until last light (probably an average of about 15 hours). Because most jobs and activities required light, they usually ceased by the evening, when it was time for eating, drinking, and socialising – if you were male. See the later sections for more on these good-time activities.

However, like keeping track of the specific day, telling the time in ancient Greece was tricky. The Greeks only really worked on the basis of the hour rather than minutes. The two main methods were:

✔ **Sundial:** The Greeks found out about the sundial from Babylon in Persia where the device was developed, and first started using their own less refined versions in the sixth century BC. The Greek instruments weren't terribly accurate until the third century BC when Hellenistic scholars (see Chapter 12) worked out the mathematic formula that made sundials work properly.

> ✔ **Water-clock:** At night and when no sunlight was available, some people turned to crude water-clocks that used the flow of water as a timing device. Again, these devices weren't very accurate, and the Hellenistic scholar, Ctesibius of Alexandria, refined the mechanism in the third century BC.

Greeks referred to time by using dawn, midday, and dusk as reference points and then adding hours, such as 'in the third hour after dawn'.

After you got up in the morning, what you actually did for the rest of the day was pretty dependent on who you were. Ancient Athens didn't include a wide range of occupations: farmer, artisan, labourer, or slave were the most common. For these people, most days were very similar and very hard.

More interesting are the lives of those people who were wealthy enough to be able to afford not to work every day. For them life in the city – particularly Athens – held other attractions like the *ekklesia* (see Chapter 7), the jury-courts, the gymnasium, and the theatre (see Chapter 16). The pleasures of wine, women, and song were also popular as the later section 'Acknowledging the oldest profession' explains.

Managing Your Money

Just like today, ancient Greeks had to pay to run a household and to buy products at the market, and the Greeks were the first people in the Mediterranean to introduce the actual concept of money.

Money started off as a measure for assessing how rich in possessions people were. By 800 BC the Greeks had introduced small wooden sticks called *obeloi*, meaning 'spits'. These sticks were a measure of an amount of wealth, like a modern-day cheque or a note.

Within a couple of hundred years, the Greeks moved on to using actual coins of which the main basic unit of currency was known as the *obol*. Greek coins, as shown in Figure 15-1, were made from gold, silver, or copper alloy. Their weight determined the value of the coins so this was closely regulated by officials appointed by the governing council. This caused a new trade to develop, that of the money changer who would swap coins for a hefty commission when you visited a city.

Coins were illustrated with an image on each side that indicated where they came from. Most often the coin represented a god or local deity. Demeter was very popular because she was the goddess of crops and fertility, and she was often represented by an ear of barley. (Refer to Chapter 13 for more on Demeter.)

Figure 15-1:
Example of
Greek coins.

Dining and Delighting

Some of the first written descriptions of meals in Greek literature appear in Homer's *The Iliad* and *The Odyssey*. Both poems feature multiple scenes that involve a sacrifice and a subsequent meal. The description is repeated whenever the heroes make a sacrifice and then sit down to a meal. In *The Odyssey* it's often when Odysseus and his men set down their ships on an island – think of them doing this on the beach!

> *Once they'd prayed, slaughtered and skinned the cattle, they cut the thighbones out and then wrapped them round in fat. . . once they'd burned the bones and tasted the organs they hacked the rest into pieces, piercing them with spits.*

That's right – Odysseus and his men were making beef shish kebabs!

The people of ancient Athens loved to eat, and in the fifth century BC, when Athens was a rich and successful port, a range of food was readily available. In this section, I look at what everyone ate – from basic everyday foods to the splendid feasts that took place as part of a symposium.

Putting your money where your mouth is

One of the more remarkable stories about the ancient Athenians was that they carried their small change in their mouths. Because people mostly wore clothes without pockets, your mouth was seen as a way of keeping your money safe and out of the reach of thieves. This practice gives a good guide as to how small Greek coins were. You had to be careful though – if you swallowed at the wrong time, you had to wait a day or so until you got your change!

Enjoying a simple meal

Depending on who you were in ancient Athens, most meals were pretty basic. As I write in Chapter 13, the staple of the Greek diet was cereal crops like barley and wheat. That meant that most meals involved bread in combination with other things. The Greeks described anything that was eaten with bread (perhaps cheese, honey, or another accompaniment such as being dipped in spiced wine) as *opson*.

A breakfast snack may be just some bread dipped in olive oil. A more substantial meal usually included beans, peas, lentils, or chick-peas – again with bread. A typical midday meal included honey or cheese as the *opson* – rather like a Ploughman's lunch. A huge variety of cheeses were available, the most traditional being goats 'feta' cheese but, like wine, regions had their own specialities.The ancient Greeks kept lunch simple because work continued in the afternoon.

The big meal of the day was in the evening after work. At this meal a greater variety of food was available (especially at more formal meals like a symposium – see the later section 'Sipping at a symposium'). Fish was usually on the menu. Beef, pork, and even poultry were less popular and eaten less often – people usually ate meat after sacrifices and saw it as something of a luxury food.

Favouring fish

The Athenians loved fish. The Greek word *osophegos* meant 'fish eater'. As I mention in Chapter 13, fish were quite difficult to catch in the ancient Mediterranean because the fishermen lacked modern deep sea fishing techniques. As a result, fish were highly sought after.

Greek literature is full of references to fish and where different specialities came from. Eels from Boeotia and dog-fish from Rhodes are quoted as being real delicacies. If you visit Athens today, you still find a large number of fish restaurants offering these delicacies!

In addition to fresh fish, pickled fish and fish sauce were highly prized delicacies. Often fish was used to flavour other foods, and the most expensive type of sauce, which later became known as *garum,* was popular throughout the Greek and then Roman world.

Hedylos was a Hellenistic poet from Samos who wrote mainly about food and drink. In the following poem, he describes the excitement over a special fish dinner. He also references the myth about Zeus turning himself into a shower of gold so that he could fit through the keyhole and have sex with Danae whose father had locked her away!

> *Our prize fish is done! Now jam the door-pin in Proteus! Agis the fancier of fishes might come in. He'll be fire and water, anything he wants. So lock it up . . . but maybe he'll arrive turned into Zeus and shower gold upon this Danae of a dish!*

Sampling side orders

The ancient Greek diet wasn't all just bread and fish. Some of the feasts put together for expensive formal dinners included all kinds of ingredients. A lot of vegetables supplemented main courses but people didn't usually eat veggies on their own. Vegetarians did exist but they were thought of as unusual people.

The most popular veggies were onions, turnips, leeks, and celery. (The potato hadn't been discovered yet.) Fruit was available, but mostly only grapes, apples, and figs. The Greeks didn't have bananas or citrus fruits, and they didn't have tomatoes either.

Cooking up a storm

Although not as advanced as today, the Greeks did use some cooking techniques. Baking was common practice, with bread being a staple part of the diet. Cooks usually boiled vegetables and beans, and heated other foods on a brazier (small portable stove), which was hot, sweaty work. In good weather cooking would be done outside and the food then taken in to eat.

Cooking skill was all about how a cook used sauces and spices to flavour the food. People whom the Greeks considered knowledgeable about food and cooking were those who understood the process of flavouring rather than cooking itself. Cooks often used wine to enhance the flavour of a dish, along with olive oil and the stock produced from cooking meat and fish. Marinating was a secret technique for boosting the flavour of ordinary ingredients.

Celebrity chefs

The life of a cook in ancient Greece was varied. Many cooks worked like caterers for hire to individual households, but some richer Greeks had their own cooks who were part of their domestic staff.

Some people even wrote about food and cooking. Fragments of two of the most famous cookbooks – *Gastronomy* by Archestratus and *The Art of Cookery* by Heracleides of Syracuse – still exist.

Shopping for ingredients

Most Athenians did their food shopping in the market that was located in the centre of the city. The farmers of Attica held monthly markets, bringing their wares to the city and selling them to the market traders.

Markets in Athens and elsewhere were made up of individual tables (*trapezai*) and booths rather than actual shops. The closest thing to shops were the workshops of specific artisans like potters or smiths who also did business there.

Sometimes, Athenians would travel a good distance to buy goods direct from the supplier. Fish lovers often made the half a day's walk to Piraeus to buy fresh fish from the fishing boats.

Drinking It Up

The most important accompaniment to food was drink, and drinking was a big part of Greek life. Wine was, of course, the main drink (see Chapter 13 for more on wine and viticulture), although the Greeks knew about beer because people drank it in Egypt, Syria, and the east.

Greeks drank a lot of wine, but they mixed it with water. The Macedonians were considered vulgar because they drank their wine without mixing it. The wine wasn't as alcoholic as modern wine, but ancient Greeks still got drunk and sometimes drank with the intention of doing so.

Imbibing publically – and privately

The most famous drinking sessions took place at symposiums (see the following section 'Sipping at a symposium'), but plenty of other places existed where you could sink a few. The most popular spot was a tavern or *kapeleion*.

These establishments were pretty basic places that sold only wine and their managers were called *kapeloi* – men who ran the business, mixed the wine, and dealt with any troublemakers, much like modern pub landlords.

The Greeks had an interesting take on drunkenness. In private (such as in the symposium), intoxication was entirely permissible and even encouraged. In fact, drunkenness formed a large part of many religious festivals (see Chapter 22). Public drunkenness, however, was regarded as uncouth and unpleasant.

Sipping at a symposium

Simply put, a *symposium* was a posh drinking party for men only with a bit of philosophical chat and some flute girls. Women did meet with each other but it was very rare that they attended a symposium. The only women usually present were the flute girls and possibly prostitutes. Held in the *andron* of a private household (see Chapter 14), a symposium was a two-stage evening:

- ✔ The first stage was the *deipnon*, or formal dinner.
- ✔ The following stage was the *symposion*, or session of drinking together.

Usually, a symposium involved 14 to 30 guests who drank from special wine cups, or *craters* as they were known (see Chapter 17 for more on Greek pottery). During a *symposion*, guests discussed philosophical issues. Professional performers such as poets, singers, and actors entertained the guests, and slave boys and sometimes expensive courtesans known as *hetairai* (see the section 'Acknowledging the oldest profession') attended to guests's every need.

The evening ended with a torch-lit procession through the streets known as *komos,* to show the bonding within the group that had taken place.

In one of his poems Hedylos gives a flavour of the *symposion* mood:

> *Let's drink up: with wine, what original, what nuanced, what sweet fancy speech I might hit on! Soak me with a jug of Chian, and say, 'Have fun Hedylos.' For I hate wasting time unless I'm high.*

Hedylos's boisterous words are probably a good guide to the quality of the philosophical discussion after a few *craters* of wine!

Pondering Sex and the Ancient Greeks

The concepts of love and sex were very different from that of marriage. As I mention in Chapter 14, Greek men commonly had affairs with other women –

and in some cases, younger boys (see the later section 'Contemplating homosexuality').

More often than not, the heterosexual affairs were with prostitutes or other sex workers, and sometimes these relationships were considered love affairs.

Love, sex, and wine were all linked together in the Greek mind. The following poem by Asklepiades from Samos is very evocative in its description of wine and unhappy love.

> *Wine is love's test. Nicagoras told us he had no lover, but the toasts betrayed him. His tears, yes and unhappy eyes, the tight wreath on his bent head slips out of place.*

Acknowledging the oldest profession

Prostitution was legal in Athens. Indeed, it was a thriving business that actually paid tax to the city treasury. The women involved were very unlikely to be Athenian and were most often from Asia Minor.

Although *prostitutes* is the general term used to describe these women, three distinct classes existed:

- *Pallakai* (**concubines**): These women were 'permanently' attached to a male and may even have lived in his household. Often men set up their *pallakai* in separate houses and apartments within the city and visited them regularly. These women were more like mistresses than prostitutes, although they did receive money and gifts.

- *Hetairai* (**courtesans**): These ladies were very expensive and exclusive, handpicking their clients. Often highly educated, *hetairai* had more in common with a Japanese geisha than other classes of prostitute. They were employed for their intelligence and conversation as much as their sexual attractiveness.

- *Pornai* (**prostitutes**): This term covered all types of prostitute from those who worked in brothels to more expensive girls for hire. They include the *aulos* or 'flute girls' who were invited to the *symposia*. The category also included some male prostitutes, although these were unusual.

Contemplating homosexuality

The Greeks regarded homosexuality as nothing unusual. If a man found women attractive, then there was nothing surprising about the fact that he found adolescent boys attractive also and chose to actively pursue them.

Athens does Pericles a favour

A public association with *pallakai* or *hetairai* was seen as nothing unusual in ancient Athens. Pericles, the famous Athenian politician, even went as far as divorcing his Athenian wife so that he could live permanently with a *hetaira* from Miletus called Aspasia. They had a son who couldn't receive citizen rights under Athenian law. However, when Pericles's two sons from his first marriage died of the plague in 430 BC, the *ekklesia* voted that his son with Aspasia be made a full citizen.

The normal situation was that an older man (the *erastes* meaning 'lover') pursued the affections of a younger boy (the *eromenos*, or 'beloved').

The most common place where such liaisons took place was the *palaestra* at the gymnasium where older men watched the young boys exercising. This being the case, only leisured aristocrats with time on their hands probably really engaged in homosexual affairs.

This short poem by Phanias describes his love for a boy who has grown slightly too old to be considered an *eromenos*, and it shows how quickly these relationships were considered to be finished.

> *By Themis and the wine that made me tipsy, your love won't last much longer Pamphilus. Already there's hair on your thigh, down on your cheeks and another lust ahead. But a little of the old spark's still there, so don't be stingy – opportunity is love's friend.*

That's not to say that the Greeks didn't mock homosexuality – the plays of Aristophanes are full of jokes. But their scorn was specifically reserved for men who carried on relationships with each other into middle age and those who showed any sign of effeminacy. Finding young boys attractive was entirely acceptable – a mature man allowing himself to be treated like a woman was not.

Love and sex between two women probably happened regularly in ancient Greece but it was never public and there's very little evidence of it. The most famous association is with the poet Sappho (seventh century BC) who came from the island of Lesbos (giving rise to the term 'lesbian'). Sappho wrote beautiful lyric poems about love and the goddess Aphrodite, many of which could be interpreted as being about both men and women and we know little about her actual life. The Greeks didn't recognise Sappho as being gay; only more modern readers. Sappho's poems are wonderfully evocative of the ancient times she lived in before the Greeks had begun to record their history.

Seeking Medical Assistance

So what did you do if you'd overindulged in food, drink, or sex? Consulting a doctor was relatively easy in ancient Athens, but it was also very expensive – and some of the methods were rather scary.

Doctors were professional people rather like craftsmen or artisans, and as such their methods were equally varied. Doctors travelled throughout Greece, finding work where they could. In big cities like Athens, however, they ran small businesses like a kind of shop and charged high prices.

Turning to the gods

Throughout the whole of Greek history many people believed that anger of the gods caused illness. Many gods had associations with health and wellbeing including Apollo, but the most important of all was Asclepius.

Asclepius was an interesting character who was born a mortal but became a god when he died. As the son of Apollo, he was born with miraculous healing powers, and he travelled far and wide healing the sick. In the end, Asclepius's powers didn't do him much good because, when he tried to resurrect the dead, Zeus killed him with a thunderbolt for trying to act like an immortal! Apollo intervened and Asclepius was made into a god.

Greeks all over the Mediterranean worshipped Asclepius and made offerings to him, hoping to be cured of illness. He had sanctuaries in several places but the most famous was on the island of Cos. Quite an industry built up around the shrine, and people travelled from all over the Mediterranean to visit it. The deal was that if you made an offering to the god Asclepius (such as some money, a piece of art, or the sacrifice of a small animal like a chicken), he may visit you in the night and cure you. And if he didn't? Well you obviously hadn't made a big enough offering!

Some temples offered healing services, but it was unlikely that the priests had any medical training. A large amount of belief was the best that people received.

Meeting the Father of Medicine: Hippocrates

Other people did try to cure illnesses. The most famous and influential of these was a man called Hippocrates of Cos (460–377 BC). His father was a doctor and Hippocrates followed in his footsteps. He eventually left the island of Cos and was in Athens during the Peloponnesian War, where he treated people suffering from the plague.

What made Hippocrates special was that he was one of the first ancient Greeks to argue that illness was caused by natural factors rather than being a punishment from the gods. He was keen on a healthy diet, clean conditions, and the use of herbs and pastes to treat patients. Because of his healthy lifestyle he was rumoured to have lived to be 120 years old – he didn't!

After the Peloponnesian War, Hippocrates returned to Cos and founded his own school of medicine and put together the *Hippocratic Corpus*. This massive book included 60 different essays on good medical practice, including the famous *Hippocratic Oath*.

> *I swear by Apollo Physician and Asclepius and Hygieia and Panaceia and all the gods and goddesses, making them my witnesses, that I will fulfil according to my ability this oath and this covenant.*

The *Hippocratic Oath* was written by Hippocrates as a guide for new doctors about what they should do. It includes promises not to carry out abortions, euthanasia, or any surgery that they haven't trained in, or to have sexual relations with patients. Much of the oath's language and philosophy is very out of date now, but some doctors swear by it even today!

Treating all manner of ills

Most ancient medical treatments involved the use of herbs or spices and some attempted to either cool or heat the body as a way of controlling the illness. Most doctors were keen on the idea of balance in everything and that a lack of it caused illness. So if you were too hot, you needed cooling down, and vice versa.

Surgery was rarely attempted because people knew little about the inner workings of the body. The Greeks considered the examination and dissection of corpses to be sacrilegious, and so opportunities to discover anything further after a patient's passing were slim. For example, most Greeks believed that the heart was in the head and not the body.

For anybody who contracted a serious illness, the chances of recovery were slim. Those injured in battle very often died of their wounds.

Things changed a little when the philosopher Aristotle began his study of the human body (see Chapter 23), but no major advances in medicine occurred until late in the Roman Empire through people like Galen (circa AD 200). The best advice was not to get ill!

Chapter 16

Plays and Pugilism: Enjoying Ancient Greek Entertainment

*W*hen seeking out good times, the ancient Greeks were a contrary bunch. On the one hand, they loved tragic theatre where noble heroes struggled with terrible choices and met with appalling fates. On the other, they loved comic plays chock full of nasty jokes at the expense of some of the audience and ridiculous gags about farting and sex. They also enjoyed hard, gruelling athletics, including an incredibly violent form of boxing where competitors often died.

Even more strangely, the same people enjoyed events that closely connected all these diverse activities. The games and festivals that the Greeks loved combined athletics and theatre – and they considered both endeavours to be equally prestigious.

Theatre and athletics combined a lot of themes: competition, public celebration, honouring the gods, and literature. Entertainment in ancient Greece was for everybody and enjoyed by everybody.

The type of entertainments that I look at in this chapter date from around 600 BC to the end of the Greek era in the first century BC. However, as you'll see, they had roots that went back much further into the past and their influence carries on this day.

Making Art Onstage: Greek Theatre

Going to the theatre in ancient Greece was very different from today's experience of popular long-running shows and entertainment districts with multiple theatres.

Getting in a festive mood

Opportunities to see plays and performances were quite limited in ancient Greece. When productions happened nearly everybody tried to go, because the plays and performances were part of something else, something larger – festivals.

Ancient Greek plays were performed only at certain times of the year, at the same time as specific religious festivals. These plays were massive events that involved the whole community.

The main festivals in Athens were the Lenaia in January and the Great or City Dionysia that was held in March. The dramatic performances were in government-organised competition with each other, and the rivalry was intense. See the later section 'Competing: And the winner is . . .' for more.

Touring the theatre

The key venue for the festivals was the theatre itself. In Athens the main venue was the theatre of Dionysus. The space was large and probably held an audience of about 14,000 people.

The theatre of Dionysus was one of the first permanent theatres built by the Greeks so its design was very influential. The theatre was a major public space located next to the Acropolis. A theatre of Dionysus is still in the same spot now but it's a rebuild of the original carried out by the Romans in the second century AD.

For such an important and well-attended site the actual 'building' was pretty basic. Performances took place in the open air with the audience sitting on very simple benches or sometimes just the bare ground. All the views were excellent and, with the exception of a few special seats at the front that were reserved for *arkhons* and officials involved in the competition, anyone could sit anywhere.

All social classes attended the theatre – much like the Globe Theatre in Elizabethan England where people of all classes met to watch the plays of Shakespeare, Marlowe, and other writers of the day. Entrance was either free or came at a small charge depending upon the nature of the event. It seems quite likely that women attended the theatre but they would have been very much in the minority.

The modern word 'theatre' comes from the Greek word '*theatron*', which means 'viewing place' and refers to the seated area for the audience.

The theatre of Dionysus and other ancient Greek theatres had a roughly semi-circular arrangement. As Figure 16-1 illustrates, theatres included:

- ✔ **Orchestra:** The large circle at the centre of the theatre was mostly used by the chorus (see the later section 'Dealing with a chorus of disapproval'). The Greeks often referred to it as the 'dancing circle' because the chorus spent most of their time there and their performance was full of movement and dancing compared to that of the main actors.

- ✔ **Parodoi:** Both the performers and the audience used these two entrances to access the stage and seating areas.

- ✔ **Skene:** This area was most like a modern stage. Behind the platform stood a long building with a flat roof that was used as both scenery and a place for the actors to change. It was this that was actually called the *skene* although the platform was attached to it.

- ✔ **Theatron:** These terraces were often just cut into a hill and provided seating for thousands of audience members.

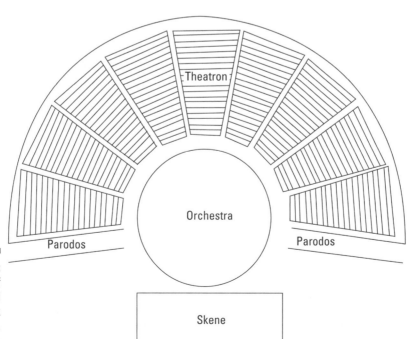

Figure 16-1:
The plan of a typical Greek theatre.

Greek theatres were *not* amphitheatres! The word *amphi* means 'on both sides', like in *amphora*, which was a double-handled jar. Amphitheatres were, therefore, double theatre spaces, making a full circle. Amphitheatres were mostly built during the Roman period (roughly 300 BC to 330 AD) and used for gladiatorial games. A good example is the Colosseum in Rome, which was originally called the Flavian Amphitheatre.

Most of the larger cities would have had a permanent theatre but smaller towns would erect a temporary structure for when performances were put on. Historians have no direct evidence that the theatres were used for other events (when plays weren't on) but given their size it seems likely that they may have been used as meeting places.

Acting up

Acting was a very specific skill in ancient Greece – and an activity that was exclusively male. Women never appeared on stage and men played all the female parts. As a result, the Greeks considered actors to be unusual in that they allowed themselves to appear like women.

Being seen and heard

The acoustics in ancient Greek theatres were tremendous. Members of the audience at the back of the theatre were able to hear every word spoken by the actors onstage, despite the fact that they were separated by around 20 metres across the orchestra and a further 80 metres to the back of the *theatron*. It required tremendous skill on the part of the actors to be audible for the length of a play (probably about 90 minutes). I've been to many Greek theatres and the acoustics still work today – you can stand in the *orchestra* and speak in a relatively clear and loud voice to be heard at the very back. Amazing!

The view was different. With no television projection technology, all the audience saw were the actors in front of the *skene* or in the orchestra. These sight limitations meant that the acting had to be very physical and not particularly realistic. Gestures were most likely large, exaggerated, and obvious.

Getting into costume and wearing masks

To accommodate the large venues, the Greek actors relied on very large costumes and masks. Masks were made of wood, brightly painted with big, obvious features meant to convey two things: the age of the character and their mood.

Masks and costumes helped male actors to play female roles and enabled the actors to swap roles if necessary. These elements minimised subtle and naturalistic acting, requiring the actors to use expansive gestures and elaborate vocalisations to get their points across to the audience. (It's no coincidence that characters in Greek plays are usually introduced and briefly described in the dialogue – it helped the audience even back then to identify who had just appeared on stage!)

Competing: And the winner is . . .

During a festival, all the plays were in competition with each other for the overall prize. First, second, and third prize were awarded to the plays and the winning poets.

The system of judging was rather strange. City officials appointed ten judges from the citizen body and they held a secret ballot at the end of the day's performances. They'd each drop a pebble into a jar, the colour of which corresponded to the poet who they'd chosen. Of these ten votes only the first five were drawn out and counted. It must have led to some very controversial results, although there are no recorded cases of anybody appealing!

As far as we know there were no material prizes; only the honour of winning. However, the winning poets could expect to be asked to perform some of their work at expensive *symposia* (refer to Chapter 15) following a victory so at the very least they'd get some decent dinners out it and would more than likely get paid as well!

The playwrights (the Greeks referred to them as 'poets') submitted their plays to the *arkhons* (see Chapter 7), who then selected three pieces for each competition. During the fifth century BC many poets wrote numerous plays, and competition was fierce. For example, out of the 92 plays written by the great dramatist Euripides, only six won first prize at a festival (although as all the works were submitted in groups of three it means that 6 out of 30 won rather than 6 out of 90). Once every five submissions!

Each poet in the competition was assigned a wealthy citizen, known as a *khoregos*, who paid for the production, including the actors, dancers, and all other expenses. Serving as the patron of a play was considered to be an extremely prestigious honour.

The poet was also assigned by lot his lead actor, whom the Greeks referred to as the *protagonist*. The poet directed the play himself.

At each festival, a poet typically presented three tragic plays and a *satyr play* – a short, comic version of a myth that provided some light relief at the end of the day. The plays weren't necessarily trilogies, although they frequently had similar themes. The audience sat through the whole offering in one day – it probably took the best part of six hours!

The vast majority of plays were produced only once because the poets didn't want to enter them twice for a festival. More popular plays were taken on tour to small rural festivals or sometimes revived many years later. For example, Alexander the Great (see Chapters 10 and 11) had a love of tragedy and regularly asked for his favourites to be performed at festivals, sometimes more than 100 years after these works were first produced.

The plays themselves took two forms: tragedy and comedy. The forms were very different but equally respected.

Delving into tragedy: Tears and fate

Tragedy was the earliest form of Greek theatre. It was probably invented in Athens in as early as 550 BC, growing out of the traditional religious hymns that the Greeks sung at festivals. These hymns known as *dithyramb* were based on a mythological and religious theme and sung solo. Over time a second voice joined the hymn, turning it into a dialogue that eventually became a play. The earliest play that survives is *The Persians* by Aeschylus, which was produced in 472 BC.

The fifth century BC was when tragedy took the form students and scholars still study today. This period is also the time when the three great tragic poets were at work:

- ✔ **Aeschylus (525–456 BC):** Wrote 80 plays of which 7 survive

- ✔ **Euripides (485–406 BC):** Wrote 92 plays of which 19 survive

- ✔ **Sophocles (496–406 BC):** Wrote 120 plays of which 7 survive

The subjects of tragic plays were very familiar to audiences because the stories were nearly all based on Greek myths. This meant that the audience was almost certain to know how a play ended before it even began. For the Greeks, the ideas of plot and suspense weren't very important. Tragic poets were much more concerned about the portrayal of the characters and the ideas that the plays were exploring. It isn't that unusual an idea to us now. Everyone knows how films like *Titanic* are going to end and they're still hugely popular. Theatre performances of *Hamlet* or *Macbeth* end in the same way – but the way that they're performed and interpreted is what the audience finds interesting.

The ancient Greeks didn't really have history as such (see Chapter 21). Nor did they have a religion that set out an ethical code of behaviour (see Chapter 22). Therefore, the myths that had existed for generations filled gaps in their knowledge and beliefs. In the tragic plays, the mythological characters explored ethical and moral issues that were relevant to the way people led their lives, providing something that history and religion didn't.

Tragedy: The Greatest Hits

Quite a few Greek tragedies still survive. Here's a rough guide to some of the best to investigate.

Play	Poet	Plot
Agamemnon	Aeschylus	Agamemnon returns home from the Trojan war and is murdered by his wife Clytemnestra and her lover Aegisthus. Orestes (Agamemnon's exiled son) then returns home and kills his father's murderers before being haunted with guilt. These plays, known as the *Oresteia*, are the only existing complete trilogy of plays.
The Libation Bearers		
The Eumenides		
Oedipus	Sophocles	The classic tragedy. See the later sidebar 'Oedipus: A complex case'.
Antigone		Oedipus's daughter strives for the right to bury her brother who's been killed fighting against their home city.
Philoctetes		Philoctetes, hero in exile, holds the famous bow of Heracles that the Greeks need to win the war in Troy. Odysseus is sent to take it from him at any cost.
Ajax		The great Greek hero Ajax is furious at being denied the armour of the dead Achilles and his anger drives him to the brink of madness.
Medea	Euripides	Cruelly spurned by the Greek hero Jason, who she helped to steal the Golden Fleece, Medea plots to avenge herself.
Trojan Women		The fate of the wives and mothers of Troy's fallen warriors is laid bare in this harrowing play.
The Bacchae		Cadmus, the king of Thebes, offends the god Dionysus and pays a terrible price at the hands of his followers.

Meeting a typical tragic hero

The main method for exploring ethical and moral issues was the role of the *tragic hero*. During the plays, tragic heroes typically underwent philosophical journeys that ended with suffering great loss and often death. Usually, the journeys are the result of mistakes or transgressions that the characters commit. Very often, the heroes are said to have a fatal or tragic flaw.

This play contains strong, bloody violence

The nature of Greek tragedy usually means that hugely unpleasant things took place: murder, suicide, mutilation, and incest, just to start with. However, all these things happened offstage (and are often vividly described by a servant or messenger who unwittingly witnesses the gruesome event) because the idea of them was thought to be terrible enough without enacting the cruel deeds.

As a result, the heroes – and the audience – know more about themselves and recognise their faults and mistakes. The Greeks referred to the process as *pathos* (suffering), *mathos* (understanding), or *anagnorisis* (recognition).

Women were often the lead characters in the plays. Characters such as Medea, Hecuba, Antigone, Clytemnestra, and Electra dominate the plays they appear in and are fascinating multi-layered characters. However, they would have all been played by men!

Dealing with a chorus of disapproval

The chorus delivers most of the commentary on the action in a tragic play. In ancient Greece, these performers generally stayed in the orchestra and commented on the things that the other characters were doing, sometimes providing the back story too. Very often the chorus is in opposition to the main character and his or her actions. Most interactions between the chorus and main actors involved the chorus leader who was the only person that spoke directly to those on the *skene*.

We don't have any evidence of the sort of music played, because none of it has survived. However, if you read a good translation of one of the plays you can see how lyrical the words are and how easily they could be chanted rather than spoken.

Aristotle wrote a book called *The Art of Poetry*. Here he sums up what good tragedy should do:

> *The tragic fear and pity may be aroused by the Spectacle [the onstage action], but they may also be aroused by the very structure and incidents of the play – which is the better way and shows the better poet.*

The gods help out at last!

In many plays a resolution is found to the terrible problems of its human characters by the appearance of one or more of the Olympian gods (which I describe in Chapter 19). Often the gods do something to tie up loose ends that humans could never do. This might seem like a bit of a cop-out but remember that the ideas rather than the plot are the important bit!

Oedipus: A complex case

Probably the most famous Greek tragedy is *Oedipus Tyrannus* (also known as *Oedipus Rex* or *Oedipus the King*) by Sophocles. Aristotle thought the play was the greatest tragedy ever written.

The story of Oedipus, the king of Thebes, goes as follows:

✔ Prior to the beginning of the play, Oedipus as a young man fled Thebes after a prophecy said that he would murder his father and marry his mother. Eventually, Oedipus returned to Thebes, defeated the fearsome Sphinx, married the widowed queen Jocasta, and became king as his reward.

✔ As the play opens, Thebes is undergoing a terrible plague. The oracle at Delphi (see Chapter 21) tells Oedipus that he has to punish the man who murdered the previous king Laius. Oedipus determines to do so despite the warnings of various people.

(During these conversations, Oedipus finds out that Laius and Jocasta had a child who was left to be exposed – see Chapter 15 – but was eventually adopted by others.)

✔ Eventually, Oedipus discovers that he in fact murdered Laius in a roadside argument – and worse, that Laius was his father and the queen, Jocasta, his mother. Grief-stricken, Oedipus blinds himself and says the following famous words:

Ah God, ah God: all come true and be known! Let this be the last time that I see the light of day. Cursed in my parents, cursed in my marriage, cursed in the blood I have shed!

Oedipus Tyrannus proves that human beings cannot escape who they are and that fate is unavoidable. Oedipus's fatal flaw is his pride and arrogance that blinds him to the warnings of others to stop his search before he uncovers the tragic truth.

The appearance of the gods like this gave rise to the expression '*deus ex machina*', Latin for 'god out of a machine' because when the gods appeared they were lowered down on a cradle at the back of the *skene*. The expression is now used to describe any situation where something unlikely happens to sort out a plot!

Considering comedy: Sex and satire

Greek comedy was very different to tragedy (see the preceding section 'Delving into tragedy: Tears and fate') but followed rules in a similar way.

✔ Comic plays were entered in festival competitions and paid for by a wealthy *khoregos*.

✔ Ideas were very important in comedy, but spectacle was too. The chorus usually wore impressive costumes and featured loud singing and intricate dancing.

✔ Comic plots are absurd. By mixing fantasy with elements of real life, the Greek comic poets virtually invented satire, the genre that involves poking fun at the establishment and criticising it using comedy. For example, in the surviving Greek comedies, men fly away to live in a land run by birds (*The Birds*), a sausage seller becomes the chief politician in Athens (*Acharnians*), and Euripides and Aeschylus have an imaginary poetry competition in Hades (*The Frogs*).

Aristophanes: Old comic genius

The most famous of Greek comic poets is Aristophanes (447–385 BC) who had an amazingly successful career and won many prizes. Quite a number of his plays still survive today.

The plays are coarse and elaborate fantasies that deal with contemporary issues and very often mock the decisions of Athenian politicians. For example:

✔ In *Lysistrata*, the women of Athens refuse to have sex with their husbands until they stop the Peloponnesian War. (This strategy seems about the only thing Athens didn't try during this long war with neighbouring Sparta; see Chapter 8.)

✔ The Athenian demagogue Kleon (see Chapter 8) tried to prosecute Aristophanes for slandering Athens in his play *Babylonians* in 425 BC. Kleon was unsuccessful, and Aristophanes took his revenge by mercilessly mocking Kleon in his next four plays. Kleon would have been in the audience for every one of them (Chapter 25 has more on this and Kleon)!

The comedies of Aristophanes had a very specific structure with key elements:

✔ The entry of the chorus (*parodos*) was always very spectacular with the actors dancing and singing while wearing extremely elaborate costumes.

✔ The following *agon* was the real meat of the play. Two sides debated issues through songs and speeches.

✔ The final key element was the *parabasis* where the chorus again took centre stage. The chorus leader directly addressed the audience and presented a long speech about the 'big issue' of the play. (The poet also usually left some room for some pleading to the judges to award him victory!)

Following is an excerpt from the *parabasis* in Aristophanes's *Wasps*, a satire on the Athenian jury-courts (see Chapter 7). The chorus leader complains that all the people that collect their jury pay don't contribute to the war effort.

It makes us wild to think that those who've never raised a hand, or risked
a single blister to defend their native land can draw their pay with all the
rest: I think that the rule should be, that if you haven't got a sting you get
no jury fee!

Aristophanes included a lot of sharp political satire, but he also appealed
to those looking for cheap laughs. His plays are full of sexual innuendo and
jokes at the expense of members of the audience. Some real-world Athenians
are mocked for being effeminate, people's wives are slandered, and foreigners
are usually portrayed with ludicrous comic accents.

Audiences at a comedy knew what they were coming to see and, in fact,
expected to see familiar elements in place. Some characters appear again and
again in the plays, in particular the crafty slave. Aristophanes even joked
with the audience about this repetition. At the beginning of his play *Frogs*, the
slave Xanthias asks his master, 'What about one of the old gags, sir? I can
usually get a laugh with those.'

The comedy of Aristophanes provided something for everybody: outrageous
spectacle, absurd plots, knowing satire, and jokes about Heracles farting after
too much pea soup. What more could you ask for?

Menander: 'Alternative' comedy

Greek comedy didn't stop with the death of Aristophanes but it did change.
The foremost comic poet after Aristophanes was Menander (341–291 BC).
Menander's comedies dropped much of the satire that was Aristophanes's
main thrust and instead were about the lives of ordinary Athenians with plots
based around mistaken identity and overheard conversations. The play that
survives in full is *Dyskolos*, a witty comedy about a cantankerous old man.

Extending to today: The influence of Greek theatre

The plays that the ancient Greeks enjoyed still have tremendous impact
on today's stage entertainment – as well as books, television, and film.

William Shakespeare was well aware of the tragic poets and their impact
on what he wrote. The mental crises and unwise actions of characters like
Hamlet and Macbeth would have been very recognisable to Aeschylus,
Sophocles, and Euripides.

Ancient Greek comedy has stood the test of time too. The broad playing to
the audience by the actors and stock characters to be found in Aristophanes's

plays carried on through the Roman theatre and the *commedia del arte* plays that were popular during the Renaissance. And satire has become an established comic tradition, showcased every day on late-night comedy shows.

Getting Physical: Athletics and the Olympic Games

Athletics was big news in ancient Greece. Physical training for boys and young men was seen as vital for their personal wellbeing and education (see Chapter 14). And as most Greek cities defended themselves with citizen militias, the bodies of the male citizens had to be kept fighting fit.

For this reason many cities, including Athens, provided a *gymnasion* (exercise area) at public expense so that exercise was available to all male citizens and *metics*. Many other exercise areas were available in the city, including the popular *palaestra*, or wrestling ground.

The *palaestra* were like private gyms where richer citizens met and exercised. They also had other uses: Older Greek men pursued the affections of younger boys and paid court to them (see Chapter 15) and important social meetings often took place, in which Greeks made political and business deals.

Working out at the gym

The modern word *gymnasium* comes from the Greek *gymnasia*. This word is derived from *gumnoi*, which means 'completely naked', because in Greece all exercise was carried out in the nude.

Unsurprisingly, only men attended the *gymnasia*. To the Greeks, athletics was hugely competitive; the word *athlon* itself means 'prize'. Whatever event you were taking part in, it was vital that you did everything for victory.

The activities at the gymnasium were fairly standard (see the later section 'The Olympic schedule') and included running, chariot-racing, boxing, wrestling, and some field events such as throwing. All these activities produced physical abilities that were very useful for fighting in wars.

The Greeks saw athletic achievement as a fitting subject for poetry, and the well-regarded poet Pindar of Boeotia (518–438 BC) wrote a huge amount about it. The following excerpt comes from a poem celebrating the achievement of a man called Timodemus in the *pankration* (an incredibly tough fighting sport) at the Nemean Games in 485 BC. Pindar compares the start of Timodemus's athletic career with the beginning of an epic poem.

> *Just as the women of Homer, the singers of woven verses, most often begin with Zeus as their prelude, so this man has received a first down-payment of victory in the sacred games by winning in the grove of Nemean Zeus.*

The spirit of competition was alive throughout the ancient Greek world, and regular international events were held. Most cities held their own games but the more important international events were the Pythian, Nemean, and Isthmian Games.

Bigger than all these, however, were the games at Olympia – the Olympic Games.

Attending the original Olympic Games

The Olympic Games were hugely influential. They are, arguably, the longest lasting single event from the ancient world. Every four years between 776 BC and AD 395 the greatest athletes in the Mediterranean (and sometimes beyond) gathered together to compete at the town of Olympia.

Like the dramatic festivals (see the earlier section 'Getting into a festive mood'), the games were held in honour of a god – in this case Zeus (see Chapter 20). The games brought huge fortune and fame to Olympia. The town eventually constructed a vast complex of temples, stadiums, and other buildings, the ruins of which you can still visit today (see Chapter 18). Thousands of people would have flocked to Olympia. They were probably wealthy because they needed to be able to afford to be away from work for a lengthy period of time.

The Greeks were so proud of the Olympic Games that they went as far as using them as a method of historical dating. Records often refer to events as having taken place in 'the year of the 28th Olympiad' rather than in a specific year.

The Olympic schedule

The events at the Olympics were fairly standard from the first games to the last. Although the Greeks added some events over time, the main ones were as follows:

- ✔ **Boxing:** This sport was similar to modern boxing but contestants didn't wear gloves and instead fought with leather strapping on their hands. It was fought until a knockout with no rounds – just one long single bout.

- ✔ **Discus:** This event was a little like the modern shot put because the ancient Greeks used flat, round stones that weighed about 4 kilograms. Whoever threw furthest won.

✔ **Equestrian:** The Olympics also featured some horse-racing events. The chariot races and horse races were most popular, but there was also a mule-cart race that featured very small carts. The Sicilian Greeks probably introduced the mule-cart race (they were good at it because of mining!), but the event wasn't popular and the Greeks dropped it after 14 games.

✔ **Javelin:** This category was an obvious test for a war-related skill, although the athletes used lighter javelins that were designed to travel a long distance rather than penetrate armour. Some sources claim that athletes regularly achieved throws of more than 90 metres.

✔ **Long jump:** This event was much harder than the modern version. Athletes jumped from a standing start holding weights!

✔ **Pankration:** This event was incredibly tough and violent and involved a fight in which any style was allowed. Only two things were barred: biting and eye-gouging. The fights were amazingly fierce, and many participants died.

✔ **Pentathlon:** This event involved the discus, javelin, long jump, running, and wrestling. It was really hard work, but if somebody won the first three events, the authorities cancelled the other two because nobody else could win.

✔ **Running:** Like the modern Olympics, running events were numerous in the original games and included:

- The *stadion,* which was the length of the stadium (about 200 metres)

- The *diaulos,* or 'there and back again', which involved running the length of the stadium and back

- The *dolichos,* which was a full 12 laps of the stadium

- One additional (and odd) foot-race which involved running the standard *stadion* sprint while wearing armour (refer to Chapter 5 for what this armour would have been like).

✔ **Wrestling:** Very different from the WWF today! Wrestling was very formal. The winner was whoever forced his opponent's back, hips, or shoulders to the ground. The successful fighter was known as the *triakter* or 'trebler' because you needed to cause three falls to win the contest.

Jam-packed competition

The Olympic Games themselves took place over only five days with an opening and closing ceremony. Each day featured a different group of events. For example, all the fighting disciplines took place on the fourth day. The final day saw the procession of all the victors to the Temple of Zeus, where they were crowned with wreaths of wild olives and showered with leaves.

Girls just wanna have fun!

Although women were excluded from the *gymnasia* in cities, they did partake in athletics and even had their own festival at the Olympic Games – The Heraea, in honour of Hera, the wife of Zeus (see Chapter 20).

The Heraea featured only one event, a foot race that was 25 metres shorter than the male *stadion*. It seems strange to cut it short in this way but it emphasises the tendency of the Greeks to put limits on opportunities for female achievement.

The inequalities didn't stop there either. Married women were banned from attending the games, in case all the naked flesh tempted them to stray! Curiously, young virgin girls were allowed to attend – perhaps so they could check out future husbands.

The laurel crown was all that the victors won – that and the eternal fame of being an Olympic victor. Sponsors of other non-Olympic events offered material and financial prizes, but nothing was prized as highly as an Olympic victory – rather like an Olympic gold medal today.

Cheats never prosper

Although the fame for winning in the Olympics was unsurpassed, the shame at being caught cheating was equally intense. The games were policed by a group of soldiers called the *alytai*, who publicly flogged anybody caught cheating. Additionally, the names of the winners were inscribed on stone tablets around the Olympic stadium, and so were the names of cheats.

Heralding the new Olympics

The ancient Olympics probably came to an end in around AD 390, when the Byzantine emperor, who was a Christian, banned all pagan festivals. Several attempts were made to revive the games, and athletics carried on elsewhere throughout the region. However, the next official Olympics held in Athens wasn't until 1896. The instigator was a French nobleman called Baron Pierre de Coubertin.

One of the main features and symbols of the Olympics nowadays is the torch and the journey that it goes on to arrive at the games from the last venue to the next (in 2008, Athens to Beijing). Most people think that this is an ancient tradition, but it isn't! The torch was only used in the ancient Olympics as a baton on a six-horse relay race called the *lampadedromia* that took place as part of the opening ceremony. De Coubertin adopted the torch because he thought it was appropriate for the revival of an ancient tradition. Remember that trivia when you're watching the next Olympic opening ceremony!

The greatest Olympian: Milo of Croton

The ancient Olympics featured many great champions, but the greatest of them all was probably Milo of Croton. A great wrestler, he won at five successive Olympic Games (a 20-year period) as well as another 25 at the other festivals.

Milo favoured a method of training that involved carrying around a four-year-old cow for a number of months to build up his shoulder muscles. Apparently, he then ate the animal – in one sitting. Another story says that Milo downed three big jars of wine (about 9 litres!) for a bet.

Unfortunately, Milo died when he attempted to split open a tree trunk with his bare hands and got them stuck. He was trapped there and in the night wild animals attacked and ate him. Whether these stories are true or not, Milo was a phenomenal Olympian and probably the greatest of all time.

Chapter 17

Depicting Men, Women, and Gods in Art

*W*hat is art? It's an eternal question that nobody can ever really answer. Today, art comes in many different forms – painting, sculpture, photography, printing, film, and digital, to name just a few. Each art form offers a way of interpreting the world. Different people find different forms important or moving for different reasons.

In ancient Greece the types of art that existed were rather more formal and subject to rules. They fell into distinct categories, or *mediums*. The most obvious examples of ancient Greek art are sculptures and painted items, including plates, cups, and vases – which I look at in this chapter. Other forms of art existed too – like interior painting – but most of this work has been lost.

Rather than forms and mediums, however, what's most recognisable about Greek art is its subject matter. The sculptures and painted works are dominated by the gods and heroes of Greek mythology (see Chapter 20 for more on this cast of characters). Other themes developed and began to appear later. By the Hellenistic period (see Chapters 10 and 11), artists began to take an interest in the ordinary world around them.

Loads of Greek art survives in hundreds of museums all over the world. In this chapter, I cover the basic forms, techniques, and details that can help you better understand the meaning behind all those 'naked men with broken noses'.

Where did *that* come from?

One weird thing about Greek art is how it changed all of a sudden around about 500 BC. As Figure 17-1 shows, it was almost as if the Greeks had decided to start producing fantastic lifelike sculptures at the drop of a hat between the Archaic and Classical periods!

For years people wondered where this sudden expertise came from. The relatively recent work of scholars and archaeologists, notably Sir Arthur Evans (1851–1941), points to the Mycenaean culture (see Chapter 2). The discovery of the Mycenaean world meant that historians could link an earlier Greek-speaking, art-producing people with the ancient Greeks. Although Mycenaean art was very different, being much less accurate in its portrayal of people and objects, the connection proved that Greek art wasn't just a sudden invention.

Defining Greek Art

The ancient Greeks didn't really have a word that meant 'art'. The closest equivalent was *tekhne,* which was more like 'skill'. So the Greeks didn't think of art as an abstract, inspired thing, more as a craft or technical ability.

In fact, many of the items that modern eyes would classify as Greek art were not really thought of as art objects back in the times when they were created. The Greeks used the plates and bowls that museums now display in glass cases to eat their dinner from, and they used the *craters* (like a cup) for drinking. In a sense, these were everyday objects to the Greeks. (Clearly, some plates are better than others, and the Greeks would've appreciated and paid more money for those with a superior design – just as you do today.)

Scholars classify Greek art into several periods, all of which date from after the Mycenaean period which finished around 1200 BC. Here's a rough guide:

- ✔ **The Geometric period (1100–700 BC):** This earliest form of Greek art consists mostly of pottery with repeated geometric patterns and few representations of people or figures.

- ✔ **The Archaic period (700 BC–480 BC):** This art is heavily influenced by Egypt and Asia. Sculptural representations of people and animals are notably Eastern-looking. See the later section 'Analysing Archaic sculpture: Naked Egyptians'.

- ✔ **The Classical period (480–330 BC):** Art from this period features idealised and beautiful representations of men and gods, very often naked with an emphasis on athletic physiques and postures. See the later section 'Contemplating Classical sculpture: Even better than the real thing'.

✔ **The Hellenistic period (330–30 BC):** Greater realism and an interest in ordinary subjects typify art from this period. See the later section 'Surveying Hellenistic sculpture: Art mirrors life'.

Surveying Greek Sculpture: Men with No Noses

Greek sculpture is the most famous form of art from the ancient world. Their big statues of men and gods with bits missing have influenced sculptors and painters for hundreds of years. Here's the story behind one of the ancient Greek's greatest artistic contributions.

Sculpting, old-school style

For the ancient Greeks, sculpting was a definite skill that was handed down through families. It was a full-time job and a very respected trade. Sculptors usually worked on their own although on large projects, such as a big statue for a temple, they might employ other sculptors to work with them.

Greek sculptors worked in two forms – marble and bronze:

✔ **Marble sculptures** were cut from large stone blocks. It was incredibly intricate work; with just a few incorrect strokes the sculptor could ruin a complete image.

✔ **Cast bronze sculptures** were even trickier than marble ones. The sculptor produced a clay or plaster model into which he poured molten bronze. After the metal cooled, he finished the piece, removing any blemishes and buffing the bronze. The final effect was very bright, shining almost like gold. Bronze statues nowadays look a little dull in colour due to the effects of time. The ancient Greeks, however, kept their bronze pieces polished and glowing. Bronze was much more expensive than marble and many popular bronze pieces were copied in marble.

These large statues were used in many ways. Some were set up in public (such as those of successful athletes); others were privately owned by rich householders. The most common use, however, was to decorate large public buildings like temples (see Chapter 18).

Analysing Archaic sculpture: Naked Egyptians

The earliest examples of ancient Greek sculpture come from the Archaic period (700–480 BC). These early Greek statues were like those the Egyptians produced, but they differed in two crucial respects:

- ✔ Greek statues were free standing, rather than sculpted onto a wall or column as is typical for Egyptian art of the time.
- ✔ The Greek figures were completely naked whereas the Egyptians preferred to show male figures wearing a kilt or skirt over their nether regions.

Take a look at the sculpture in Figure 17-1. This *kouros*, which means the naked figure of a male youth, was made around 550 BC. The human form is quite realistic and is about two-thirds the size of an actual human figure. The skill of an ancient Greek sculptor was in his ability to accurately depict the human body, its contours, and its muscles.

Figure 17-1:
A *kouros*.

MYTHBUSTER

What a beautiful fake!

Many of the Greek sculptures that survive aren't actually Greek at all. Very often these sculptures are high-class Roman copies of Greek originals. In particular, surviving marble pieces are frequently Roman versions of bronze Greek sculptures. The originals are usually lost to history as people melted down the bronze pieces to make other things. But because the originals were famous and celebrated, people wanted their own copies. Art lovers today are really fortunate that the Romans loved Greek sculpture, because at least copies exist to look at.

During this period, sculptors also produced female figures known as *korai*. These figures are much the same, apart from the crucial difference that they are fully clothed. This fits with the male Greek view that women should be modest and kept concealed (refer to Chapter 14).

REMEMBER

The pose of the *kouros* is very rigid but also very symmetrical. This positioning became the standard pose in the Archaic period. The figure's stance is particularly noteworthy – he looks like he's stepping forward. This is a significant difference from rigid Egyptian sculptures and is an early attempt at portraying movement. The depiction of the face is still very Egyptian though: large eyes and hair in ringlets. Check out *The Ancient Egyptians For Dummies* (Wiley) by Charlotte Booth for more on the Egyptian aesthetic.

Contemplating Classical sculpture: Even better than the real thing

During the Classical period (480–330 BC), the Greeks raced ahead of other ancient civilisations in their ability to portray lifelike figures. The idea of *mimesis*, or imitation of life, became an important ideal. A sculpture was considered a success if it was close to life but also represented an aspirational image of how men and women potentially looked.

The sculpture in Figure 17-2 is a copy of one created around 444 BC by a man called Polyclitus. It's a life-size representation of an athletic young man (a *doryphoros*, or spear bearer). Look at the differences between this and the Archaic kouros. The subject is the same but the treatment is completely different:

 ✔ Both sculptures convey movement in the pose, but the weight of the entire Classical figure is now carried on one leg.

✔ The muscles on the body of the Classical statue are a lot more defined – the kind of physique that it would take hours in the *gymnasium* to produce!

✔ The Classical sculpture's face is different too. He's more expressive, concentrating on something yet lost in thought. His features are much more Western than those of the *kouros*.

Figure 17-2:
Copy of
Polyclitus's
Doryphorus.

Women in art

Another important development during the Classical Period was that female figures were frequently portrayed naked, like their male counterparts. For the most part, these nude female figures represented Aphrodite, the goddess of sexual love, often shown emerging from a bath.

Other goddesses sculpted during this period (Athena, Demeter, and Hera were popular subjects) are often portrayed wearing clothes. Getting the drapery right was considered a massively important skill on the part of an artist, and the folds in the robes are incredibly realistic on sculptures from the Classical period.

Celebrity artists

During the Classical period sculptures became hugely popular as a way of decorating temples and other public buildings (see Chapter 18), and artists producing the most perfect works became celebrities themselves. Here are the most famous Greek sculptors:

✔ **Pheidias (circa 460–400 BC):** Probably the most famous of Greek sculptors, Pheidias had a permanent workshop in the sanctuary complex at Olympia for which he made the famous statue of Zeus that sat in the temple dedicated to him. The statue is long gone but Figure 17-3 shows a representation. He also worked on the Parthenon decorations (see Chapter 18). He was killed by the people of Elis who were jealous of his work at Olympia. Rather harsh critics, the Eleans.

✔ **Polyclitus of Argos (circa 460–410 BC):** Polyclitus worked exclusively in bronze and was most famous for his statues of mortals (like the *Doryphorus* in Figure 17-2). He is credited as being responsible for the creation of the standard form of depicting muscles in movement.

✔ **Myron (circa 470–420 BC):** Known as the great experimenter, Myron produced figures of gods and mortals in new and unusual poses. Myron was one of the first artists to depict people in actual movement. The best example is the *Discobolus*, or discus thrower, which is shown in Figure 17-4.

Figure 17-3:
Pheidias's statue of Zeus.

Bright-eyed and colourful

Two important elements in Greek sculpture of all periods were the use of colour and painted details. These days, when you visit a museum or look at photos of surviving figures, you see faded bronze and marble forms with big, open, sightless eyes. These sculptures were originally very different: Eyeballs and pupils were painted as well as the clothes (drapery) and any weapons or other items. Statues of the gods were meant to be intimidating; in their original painted form they would have been. Covered with red, black, and gold paint the images were meant to emphasise the awesome power of the gods.

✔ **Lysippus of Sicyon (circa 370–315):** Lysippus produced a huge variety of pieces at the end of the Classical era and the beginning of the Hellenistic. Mostly, these were new and different versions of gods, but his most famous image is the head of Alexander the Great (Figure 17-5), which ancient sources said was the most lifelike portrayal of the king.

Figure 17-4:
Myron's
Discobolus.

Figure 17-5:
The head of
Alexander
the Great,
by Lysippus.

Surveying Hellenistic sculpture: Art mirrors life

During the Hellenistic period (330–30 BC) a new aesthetic emerged. After Alexander the Great's conquests broadened the horizons of the Greek world, the subjects and representations that sculptors chose changed too. While they still produced images of heroes and gods, they also developed an interest in more human subjects of a different type, such as children and older adults, than the idealised youths of the Classical period.

Although works still reflected an accurate portrayal of the human form, depictions became less stylised and more realistic. One of the most famous Hellenistic sculptures is of a drunken old woman – a subject and treatment that would never have interested earlier sculptors.

Take a look at the bronze sculpture of a boxer in Figure 17-6. This figure was produced in the second century BC. Although he's an athlete, he looks tired after a bout – like you'd expect him to be. His physique is almost over-developed, like a WWF wrestler, and if you look closely you can see his broken nose and damaged 'cauliflower ears'. This sculpture has some of the idea of *mimesis* (see the earlier section 'Contemplating Classical sculpture: Even better than the real thing') without anything aspirational. This is a worn-out, past-his-prime boxer, after one bout too many.

Figure 17-6:
Second
century BC
bronze
sculpture of
a boxer.

Inviting the Gods to Dinner: Greek Vase Painting

Along with bronze and marble sculpture, the other major area of ancient Greek art was the painting of pottery. Clay was one of the biggest natural resources in Greece, used for roof-tiles, small sculpted figures, and house bricks. The quality of the clay varied depending on where you were in ancient Greece but the skill in using the potting wheel and correctly firing the pot was more influential on the quality of the finished product than the clay itself.

The trade of pottery was one of the most prevalent practices and the closest that the Greeks had to a modern manufacturing industry. Greek pottery was exported all over the Mediterranean. Different regions developed their own individual styles, some of which were quite sought after. Some of the vase-painters became renowned, although never as much as the sculptors because sculpture was perceived as being a much higher art form. In most cases painters also made the pots themselves.

Getting into shape

Although the patterns and designs on pottery varied, the actual objects themselves took the following forms:

- ✓ **Amphora:** This was the standard type of big vessel used to transport large quantities of wine or oil. The name came from its distinctive double-handle design.

- ✓ **Crater:** This vessel looked like a large cup, but the Greeks used it as a mixing bowl where water was combined with wine.

- ✓ **Skyphos:** This standard cup form usually featured a handle on each side. Often the bottom inside was also decorated with a painted image.

- ✓ **Lekythos:** These small delicate jars were used to keep oil or, occasionally, perfume although this was usually sold in much smaller quantities.

Many other popular pottery shapes existed during the age of ancient Greece, including numerous different types of vases such as *hydria* and even wine coolers known as *psykters*.

The beautifully decorated pieces that survive in museums are generally examples of the ancient Greeks' most precious items that probably weren't for everyday use. Think of these as the equivalent of the best dinner set that you get out for special occasions.

Vase painting basics

Just like sculpture (see the earlier section 'Surveying Greek Sculpture: Men with No Noses'), the development of Greek vase painting went through a number of very clear phases, as the following sections explain.

Early vase painting (1050–700 BC)

Like sculpture, very early Greek vases mix geometric patterns with very Eastern-looking, Egyptian-style depictions of humans and animals. Sometimes the illustrations involved fantastical creatures from mythology such as the monsters that fought with Heracles (described in Chapter 20).

Black-figure painting (600 BC onwards)

The earliest form of truly Greek painting is known as *black-figure painting*. Clay red vases from this period are decorated with figures in silhouette usually depicted in black with red or white highlighting. The artist delicately incised the details onto the painted figures and into the clay.

Modern scholars attribute the development of this style of painting to the city of Corinth (see the Cheat Sheet map) in about 720 BC. By the middle of the seventh century BC artists throughout the region used the technique.

The most popular subjects during this period are inspired by mythological stories. The images are usually depicted *frieze style,* meaning that one elaborate illustration stretches all around the pot and shows figures interacting with each other. Vivid and complex scenes capturing a range of emotions were often included in the illustrations.

Figure 17-7 shows black-figure details on an *amphora* that was painted by a man called Exekias in around 540 BC. The vessel shows the Greek warrior Achilles fighting the Amazon queen Penthesilea during the Trojan War (see Chapter 20). According to the myth, as Achilles struck the killing blow, his eyes met Penthesilea's and he fell in love with her. The painter has managed to convey this complex and poignant moment by using a simple silhouette technique.

Another thing to notice about the vessel in 17-7 is Penthesilea's very white face. During this period women were often painted with white faces, whereas men were portrayed totally in black. The reason was that upper class ancient Greek women were expected to spend most of their day indoors (see Chapter 14). Men were tanned by the heat and the sun, but women remained pale.

Figure 17-7:
Example of black-figure vase painting by Exekias.

Apelles: The lost master

The most famous of the white-ground painters was a man called Apelles of Colophon, who was active in the fourth century BC. Later writers enthuse over Apelles's genius and talent for *mimesis* (see the section 'Contemplating Classical sculpture: Even better than the real thing'), claiming that his works were so lifelike that people tried to eat the fruit he painted and horses neighed at his equine images. Sadly, modern historians must take the ancient scribes' word for it; nothing of Apelles's work survives.

Red-figure painting (circa 525 BC onwards)

Around 525 BC a new style of painting – known as *red-figure painting* – was developed in Athens. This technique was a complete reversal of black-figure painting, with the background now black and all the figures appearing in the red of the clay. This approach allowed the detailing to be much more intricate as details were now painted onto the clay instead of being incised as with black-figure work. Over time, the depictions of human anatomy and clothing become more precise – like the effects achieved by sculptors of this era.

Artists could also create much more complex scenes. Notably, red-figure painters began including more than one image on a piece, sometimes showing two or more scenes that may have some kind of linking theme.

A red-figure *skyphos* was painted around 470 BC showing the young Heracles on his way to school followed by an old woman. The image is incredibly detailed, and you can easily make out the difference in age of the two characters. Heracles stands in the style of Classical sculpture (see the earlier section 'Contemplating Classical sculpture: Even better than the real thing'), and you can even see the tattoos on the old woman, suggesting that she may be from Thrace where this was a common practice.

White-ground painting (circa 475 BC onwards)

One last style of vase painting was inspired by a technique used by painters working on large-scale interior projects. Although little of this type of *white-ground painting* survives, historians believe artists covered interior walls or wooden panels with white paint or plaster to produce a neutral background.

During the fifth century BC, some painters began to adopt this style for working on vases. The most common use for white-ground painting on vases was to decorate the *lekythos* that the Greeks buried with their dead. These *lekythos* were filled with oil and accompanied the deceased to the underworld. (See Chapter 21 for more on ancient Greek burial practices.) Most white-ground vases haven't survived very well because the vessels weren't meant for frequent handling.

Finding Beauty Elsewhere: Other Arts and Crafts

Of course, the Greeks didn't just produce pots and sculptures. They were expert at a number of other art forms:

- ✔ **Clay figures** were immensely popular. These mini sculptures followed the aesthetics of their large-scale counterparts. See the earlier section 'Surveying Greek Sculpture: Men with No Noses'.

- ✔ **Decorative bronzes** were cast in the same way as larger metal sculptures. These pieces looked a bit like small versions of the friezes and metopes (smaller sculpted scenes) on temples (described in Chapter 18).

Smaller items like these would have been used as ornaments in houses and were also sometimes given as small offerings to the gods, possibly to represent the person that was asking for help.

The following sections cover a few other artistic endeavours of the ancient Greeks.

Getting dressed: Clothing

Dress-making and fashion weren't really art forms in ancient Greece, but the garments Greeks wore while going about their daily business had a beauty and simplicity that continues to inspire designers even today.

Materials

Most ancient Greeks – male and female, rich and poor – wore pretty much the same items of clothing. What did vary was the quality of the material used.

Most garments were made of wool, although in some cases linen was used. (Linen was more common for tunics or underclothes; wool must have been a bit itchy for a hot day on the plain of Attica!) White was the standard colour but the Greeks also dyed their wool (Chapter 13 has more details). Wealthier Greek women could afford to wear silk, which was imported from Asia Minor on the silk route from the East.

Types of garment

Nearly all clothes took the form of a cloak or mantle – a single piece of material that could be worn in different ways. This garment was always sleeveless, but often during cold weather it was worn over the top of a tunic that served as an undershirt.

The standard garment for women was the *peplos*, which was a kind of combined cloak and tunic. It was a large, square piece of cloth, the top third of which the woman folded over and pinned on her shoulders. Most surviving artistic depictions of goddesses show them formally attired in peploi.

Women also often wore veils when they were outside to modestly hide their faces from men. The ancient Greek word for veil literally means 'little roof'; even though women were outside, they were still kept inside the *oikos*, or home.

The Greeks didn't wear trousers and thought them effeminate when worn by men. They were popular in the Persian Empire, and when Alexander the Great began wearing them after conquering Persia (see Chapter 11), this fashion choice proved unpopular with his Macedonian generals.

By the Hellenistic period both men and women wore simpler formal garments known as an *himation*. The *himation* was a very long piece of material (up to 3 metres by 2 metres) that you draped around the body and usually supported over the left arm. The gods in the Parthenon sculptures (see Chapter 18) wear them and the Romans later based the *toga* on this versatile garment.

Looking sharp: Jewellery

In addition to sculpture and vase painting, the other great manufacturing craft in ancient Greece, and elsewhere in the ancient world in general, was the production of jewellery.

The Greeks used precious metals (gold and silver) and semi-precious stones such as bezels in large quantities to produce rings, earrings, necklaces, and bracelets in designs that are still very recognisable today. The fashion for setting a precious stone in a metal band (like a modern ring) became fashionable only around the end of the fifth century BC.

Golden combs and hair slides were also very popular. Sometimes they featured small scenes of tiny figures not much more than a few centimetres high. Incredibly skilled and detailed work, these combs were very expensive.

A great number of examples of this work still survives in museums around the world. They're hugely delicate and personal items that give a real sense of having been touched and cared for by people from 2,500 years ago.

Chapter 18

Building Beautiful Greek Architecture

*T*his chapter is about more than the types of structures and building materials favoured by the ancient Greeks; it's about architecture. *Architecture* is the art of building, the design and construction of buildings that ensure that they're technically correct and aesthetically pleasing. In other words, architecture is about making sure that buildings look good and stay up.

Of all the things that the ancient Greeks left behind, their buildings are the most obvious. You can find great big chunks of these structures – some still in surprisingly good condition – lying around all over the Mediterranean. And museums around the globe have enshrined several buildings or portions of buildings.

Even more apparent than the physical remains is the influence of Greek architecture on subsequent buildings. Indeed, many buildings in some of the world's most famous cities instantly remind you of Greek temples – such as the White House in Washington for example.

In this chapter, I look at how the Greeks built temples and other public structures, why they built them, and what to look for when you're standing in front of one.

Building for the Masses: Ancient Greek Temples

The Greeks loved building – and building temples in particular. The council of government (refer to Chapter 4) usually paid for these elaborately decorated structures, which were used to make political statements. The Greeks tended to build smaller private buildings like houses or shops out of whatever was available and not to any particular design. See Chapter 14 for more on these day-to-day structures.

Appreciating the role of the temple

The temple was a vital part of the Greek *polis* or city. A temple's main purpose was to honour the god that it was dedicated to, such as Zeus, Poseidon, or Apollo. Each temple normally contained a large cult statue of the god within the central room, or *cella*. The statue was much bigger than life-size and could be as tall as 10 or 15 metres (see 'Going back to the temple's beginnings' later in this chapter for a plan of a typical ancient Greek temple).

The temple was literally thought of as the house of the god. When you entered the temple, you were in the presence of that deity. That's partly why the Greeks used such massive statues – to create feelings of awe and fear. Temples were open to all and people would flee there for sanctuary in times of crisis.

Festivals, sacrifices, and ceremonies all took place at the temple. Temples were often part of a whole *sanctuary complex* in which they stood alongside *treasuries*, or small buildings used to house gifts made to the gods. A good example of a sanctuary complex is the Acropolis in Athens, which was home to four different temples (dedicated to Athena and Poseideon) and also served as the stronghold of the city in times of trouble.

Despite the temple's civic functions, each building was really about the worship of the god to which it was dedicated. In a way, the vast expense of building a temple was a kind of tribute to the god to start with. Greek religion was based around the idea of giving gifts to the gods and hoping that good things happened to you as a result. You can read more about these spiritual beliefs in Chapter 22.

Going back to the temple's beginnings

Greek architecture developed very much along the same lines as Greek history. The Minoans (covered in Chapter 2) were great builders but they didn't tend to build structures exclusively for religious purposes. During the Dark Ages the Greeks seemed to build very few massive structures. It wasn't until the seventh century BC that the Greeks began the large scale construction of temples.

Between 650 and 500 BC the classic form of the Greek temple started to emerge as towns and cities throughout the Mediterranean began to construct their temples in fairly uniform style. The temples that were built during this period were all classified as *hekatompedon*, which meant 'hundred footer'. As temples were a great source of local pride, building anything that was smaller was unthinkable. The temples also all followed the same plan of a box within a box, as Figure 18-1 shows.

The temple in Figure 18-1 is a rectangle surrounded by massive round columns. Within the rectangle is another smaller rectangle that made up an interior room. This area was called a *cella* and was where the business of the temple took place. Often the *cella* had an external porch leading into it, like the one in Figure 18-1. It was the innermost sanctum of the temple where offerings were made.

Figure 18-1:
A basic
temple plan.

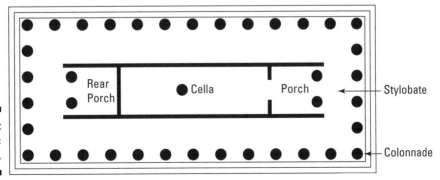

The Seven Wonders of the Ancient World

Some Greek buildings were so impressive that they even made it onto the list of the Seven Wonders of the World! Various ancient writers made lists of seven wonders, including the Greek historian Herodotus (see Chapter 22). In fact, the word the Greeks used to describe these wondrous buildings was *thaumatai*, which literally means 'must see'! Here's Herodotus's list in full:

✔ Colossus of Rhodes

✔ Great Pyramid of Giza

✔ Hanging Gardens of Babylon

✔ Mausoleum of Maussollos at Halicarnassus

✔ Pharos (Lighthouse) of Alexandria

✔ Statue of Zeus at the Temple of Zeus in Olympia

✔ Temple of Artemis at Ephesus

As you can see, after the Great Pyramid and the Hanging Gardens, the Greeks feature quite heavily in the list with five entries. Then again, it was a Greek who compiled the list!

Most interesting for historians is the Temple of Artemis at the Greek city of Ephesus on the coast of Asia Minor. Today, only the base and a few columns of this structure survive, but this temple was considered to be the best example of its kind.

This basic format remained pretty much unchanged for the whole of Greek history. Part of the reason for this consistency was the building techniques involved (see the later section 'Making it happen: Building tools and techniques').

Other forms of temple design did develop and the Greeks introduced new materials, but this rectangle-within-a-rectangle plan was the standard. Originally, these temples were probably constructed out of wood, but by the early sixth century BC the Greeks were using stone, most commonly marble.

Evolving style: Three architectural orders

Although the design of Greek temples was incredibly regular, room still existed for expansion and elaboration of the basic form. In fact, any big temple project was a chance for a city to show off its wealth and artistry. The way that temples were decorated and adorned led to the development of three notable styles, or architectural orders: Doric, Ionic, and Corinthian.

Doric and Ionic were based around the two major regions of Greece (see Chapter 3). *Doric* mainly referred to the mainland of Greece, and *Ionic* was 'Ionian' and referred to the western coast of Asia Minor. The *Corinthian* style was attributed to a sculptor and architect called Callimachus who was active in the fifth century BC and was alleged to have come from the city of Corinth.

These styles developed during the fifth and fourth centuries BC. They weren't strict ways of building but rather styles that architects of the day felt able to experiment with.

As you can see by the three temple columns shown in Figure 18-2, the differences between the Doric, Ionic, and Corinthian styles are fairly clear. The biggest design differences are in the *capital* (the top portion of the column) and the *entablature* (the structure that sits on top of the column):

- ✔ **Doric** columns feature a very simple stone capital in two pieces that looks like a bowl with a flat block on top.

- ✔ **Ionic** columns include a carved, curling block that looks a bit like the horns of a ram. Underneath this block is a decorative pattern that some people call 'egg and dart'.

- ✔ **Corinthian** columns have a far more ornate design that mimic the look of sprouting Acanthus leaves. The thinner column is more like Ionic than Doric.

So, after you decided to build a temple and picked the order that you wanted to style it in, how did you go about building it? Read on.

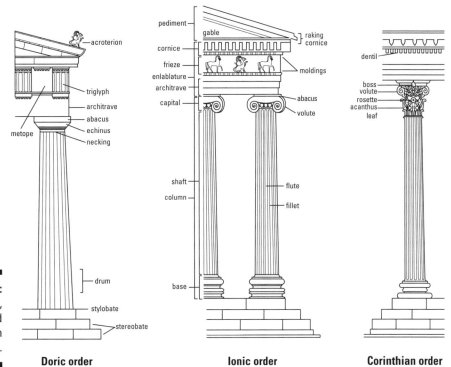

Figure 18-2:
Doric, Ionic, and Corinthian columns.

Doric order   **Ionic order**   **Corinthian order**

Constructing Temples

The most important thing about any new temple project was choosing the site. Usually, the Greeks built a new temple in a sacred place like a sanctuary complex (a site with a lot of temples and religious buildings), but it was often also the most conspicuous place in the city.

The greatest temple in Athens was the Parthenon dedicated to Athena and built on the site of the Acropolis, on a massive hill that dominated the landscape. Similarly, the Greeks built many temples in Greece and Asia Minor overlooking the sea or in other commanding and beautiful locations.

Bearing the cost

Building a temple wasn't cheap. The cost was met by the public purse and sometimes donations from rich citizens. For a temple to be built in ancient Athens, the *ekklesia* (refer to Chapter 4) had to approve and budget for the project before the builders broke a single stone. The *ekklesia* then set up a supervisory committee for the project and appointed a chief architect.

For an idea of the costs involved, consider the Parthenon in Athens. This building cost 469 silver talents to build. To give you some context, the cost of building and equipping a *trireme* warship such as those in the Athenian fleet was 1 silver talent. Ouch!

Selecting an architect

The role of the architect was crucial. The position was a hugely responsible one, combining the roles of designer, foreman, and accountant. Not only did the architect design the building, but he also supervised its construction on site, hired the workforce, purchased materials, and ensured that the whole thing came in on budget.

But despite their enormous responsibilities, the Greeks still viewed architects as artisans rather than artists.

Finessing the design

Architects designed temples according to mathematical calculations rather than modelling. For example, if the temple required more columns or wider gaps between them, the architect simply had to adjust his calculations accordingly. Another major issue was the *entasis*, or contour, of the columns (in basic terms, how much wider the columns were at the bottom than the top). Architects had to go through careful calculations to ensure that the columns could support the weight of tons of stone. And if the architect got his sums wrong, the temple would fall down!

Of course, construction wasn't quite that haphazard. The fairly standard form of temple design (see the earlier section 'Going back to the temple's beginnings') meant that architects worked within fairly standard guidelines.

Hiring the workforce

Architects managed hundreds of different workers in a temple-building project. They hired skilled artisans and craftsman, along with manual labourers and prisoners of war used as forced labour.

When a major project was under way workers came from far and wide because they knew that work would be available for years to come. The Parthenon was proposed in 447 BC, and 15 years later it was finally completed!

Animals were used to transport materials and equipment. For example, during the building of the Parthenon around 400 oxen a day were used to transport materials.

Making it happen: Building tools and techniques

Ancient Greek tools and building techniques were pretty basic – which makes it all the more impressive that they managed to erect such huge, elaborately embellished edifices.

One issue that all ancient Greek builders dealt with was the lack of concrete (it wasn't discovered until early in the Roman period, during the first century BC). That's why Greek architects were so keen on columns; these structures helped support the massive weight of the buildings' roofs.

Just getting the materials together was difficult enough. Every temple required thousands of cubic metres of stone to be quarried and, given the weight and transportation difficulties, the quarry needed to be close by. The Greeks preferred to use marble, but this could be ruinously expensive. More often they used plain stone and then covered it with painted plaster so that it resembled marble.

Each individual block had to be prepared (that is, shaped for its purpose by carving and hammering) on site and then slotted together. Instead of being fabricated of one long tube of stone, columns were made of different blocks called *drums* that were fixed together with plugs coated with lead to fill any gaps. This work had to be spot on, otherwise the curvature would be wrong and the column wouldn't be able to support weight.

Moving the stones was difficult and dangerous. For the most part, a human-powered crane involving fairly simple pulley systems and lots of manpower lifted the stones into the appropriate area, and then men levered them into position.

Getting your message across through decoration

After the temple structure was up, part of the building's statement was made: The size and spectacular position of the building no doubt impressed many people. However, the Greeks conveyed more clever messages via the decoration of the temple.

Intriguing entablatures and more

Like everything else to do with architecture and temple building, the decoration of temples followed a fairly uniform set of rules. The main areas of decoration were above the columns in the series of sections known as the entablature. Figure 18-2 earlier in this chapter shows two examples of entablature.

The major decorative areas were as follows:

- **Frieze:** On Ionic temples the frieze often displayed a long, relief sculpture that showcased a consistent theme such as a procession or a continuous battle scene.

- **Metope:** On Doric temples this space was occupied alternately by *triglyphs* (triple-grooved panels) and empty panels that could be filled by relief sculptures called *metopes*. Often each end of the temple featured a different theme.

- **Pediment:** The pediment was often used as a space for large scale sculptures, usually massive, larger-than-life versions of the gods.

Like the sculptures I discuss in Chapter 17, the temples were colourfully painted – even if they were constructed of marble. The backgrounds of the metopes and pediment sculptures were painted, as well as the *triglyphs* and some details on the columns. The paints' bold colours (probably brighter colours like red, gold, yellow and lighter blue) would have contrasted beautifully with the stark white of the remaining marble or stone.

The Parthenon: 230 feet of propaganda!

The decorations of the Parthenon are a great example of ancient Greek architecture, construction, and decoration. The Greeks constructed the building over 15 years during Athens's greatest period of supremacy, immediately before the start of the Peloponnesian War (see Chapter 7). They built the Parthenon to replace a temple burned down by the Persians in the fifth century BC (refer to Chapter 6). This new building celebrates the superiority of the Athenian empire and its leading role in defeating the Persians at Marathon and elsewhere. It's a brilliantly conceived programme of decoration.

Everything about this amazing building fits with the purpose of the temple as a place of worship and also as an expression of Athens's wealth and superiority.

- The temple was dedicated to Athena, the patron goddess of Athens, and a massive statue of her dominated the inner building within the *cella*.

- Because the Parthenon is a Doric temple it doesn't feature an external frieze, but the inner building had a frieze running around it that depicted the Panathenaiac festival that took place in honour of Athena every four years.

- The building's pediment sculptures honoured Athena as well. At one end of the temple, a scene showed all the Olympian gods at rest, and the other end showed a scene from the story where Athena battled with Poseidon for the right to be patron deity of Athens.

- The *metopes* show various scenes of Greeks fighting foreign mythological enemies like Amazons and Lapiths. These images are a not-so-subtle demonstration of Greek superiority over foreigners.

You can still see the Parthenon in a fairly good state. The ruins of the temple are there in Athens although much of the decoration has been taken off and is preserved in the Acropolis Museum in Athens and the British Museum in London.

Building More than Temples

As Greek cities developed, so did the types of public buildings that were designed and constructed. Although temples continued to dominate, the Greeks did build other communal structures.

When you look at some Greek ruins today, you may have difficulty telling the difference between temples and other buildings. The similarities are because Greek architects used many of the same techniques from temple-building to construct other types of building, including *agoras*, *stoas*, stadiums, and theatres.

Agoras

The *agora* was the centrepiece of a Greek city. The word doesn't have an exact translation – the closest modern equivalent is 'town square'. (In the Roman world, the *agora* became the *forum*.)

The *agora* was where the citizen body gathered to talk, buy, and sell, and sometimes to protest or vote. Essentially, it was a large open space, but over time buildings were added because the activities that went on needed space for administration and so on. So despite originally being a big empty space, the term *agora* came to stand for a group of buildings – if you see what I mean!

Stoas

As the *agora* developed into a building, the architectural elements that surrounded it, or *stoas*, came to resemble a colonnade, like a roofed street with columns.

Over time, these *stoas* became quite ornate and complicated buildings in their own right. Some examples of *stoas* feature more than one level. Effectively, they became a kind of precinct, with small booths used for shops and businesses as well as a street that linked the *agora* to other areas of the city.

Some *agoras* and *stoas* are still partially in existence all around the Mediterranean. The ancient religious town of Delphi contains some particularly good examples (Chapter 24 has more).

Stadiums and theatres

The other major public buildings were those the Greeks used for entertainment (see Chapter 16 for all the fun). Ancient Greek athletic competitions and theatrical performances took place in the open air, so the buildings constructed didn't have roofs. Neither type of building required much in the way of architectural design; rather the key was picking the right spot to begin with. These structures were usually just cut into a hillside with acoustics being the greatest concern in the case of theatres.

Part IV
Mythology, Religion, and Belief

The 5th Wave   By Rich Tennant

AT HOME WITH ZEUS

"You know, I wish you'd be more careful about where you leave these things laying around!"

In this part . . .

In this part I explore the fundamentals of Greek mythology and how these translated into practical religion and worship. Some of the mythology, beliefs, and cults are very strange indeed. I also look at the Greek philosophers; the men who dared to disagree with the established tradition and come up with their own unique answers to the meaning of life, the universe, and everything.

Chapter 19

Going Back to the Beginning: Myths and Gods

. . . .

In This Chapter

▶ Appreciating the role of myths in Greek life

▶ Distinguishing between myth and history

▶ Explaining creation and more

▶ Getting to know the Olympian gods

▶ Differentiating between Greek and Roman gods

. . . .

Of all the things that have survived the passage of time between ancient Greece and today, the Greek myths are probably the most enduring. First adopted and altered by the Romans whilst the Greek world was still in existence (around 300 BC), the myths and their thrilling cast of gods, mortals, and creatures have proven to be a huge inspiration to Renaissance artists, English poets, and 20th-century movie makers – to name just a few.

The ancient Greek myths are stories of love, jealousy, rage, heroism, cowardice, and nearly all other human states. In short, they're brilliant – and this chapter looks at why.

Demystifying Myths

Myths were central to Greek life. They dominated the ancient Greeks' religious practices, adorned temples and buildings, and appeared in nearly all literature and poetry. The reason for the prominence of myth in ancient Greek culture is simple: Myths helped the ancient Greeks to understand who they were.

Herodotus, Thucydides, and Xenophon were the first Greek historians. Before them, the Greeks didn't really have history as such. They still had to explain the world around them – as well as the things they couldn't see or understand.

Initially, the Greeks used myths to answer the big questions – like how the world came into being and where men and women came from. Without any scientific notions to fall back on, the Greeks came up with some surprising explanations! (See the later section 'Starting Out: Greek Creation Myths' for all the fascinating details.)

Passing on myths

Before around 750 BC the Greeks didn't have writing (see Chapter 1), so they passed on all mythical stories by word of mouth, generation by generation. Eventually, these stories became part of an accepted system of belief. The gods and heroes described in them became as real to everyday folk as their local potter or innkeeper.

Myths that went beyond man's origins eventually sprang up. Gods and heroes dominated and were involved in incredible stories of adventure. The storytelling about these characters became more involved and developed into songs and poems.

Poets and epics

By the eighth century BC the Greeks began to record their oral poetry in written form. The works of poets like Homer (see Chapter 20) and Hesiod were written down, and the stories that they told became a kind of mythical fact – 'mythtory', if you like!

In many cases, the stories that the great poets produced were *epic cycles* – long stories about heroes' whole lifetimes as well as what happened to their families for generations afterwards. These stories became a kind of mythtory too, explaining the period of time before real history was written and also served as inspiration to later playwrights, poets, and artists.

Keeping track of everything

Of course, one of the problems with myths that developed through an oral tradition was that everybody had his or her own slightly different version. Often, these differences were geographical, with many towns claiming to be the birthplace of a hero or the place where a famous event took place. A good example of this confusion is the god Pan (see Chapter 13). At least 14 different mythological characters are referred to as being his father!

Collating all these many stories and their many versions was a big job, but some writers did try and do it. Not many of their works survive, but the following are two notable contributions:

✔ The *Theogony* by Hesiod (refer to Chapter 13) is literally a book about 'god-birth'. This long poem describes the earliest elements of Greek mythology and how the Olympian gods came into being. Several translations are available online and in published form.

✔ *The Library of Greek Mythology* by Apollodorus, a scholar who lived in Alexandria during the second century BC, is an expansive survey of myths. Translations of Apollodorus's work are still published and widely available today.

Starting Out: Greek Creation Myths

So how did it all begin, then? Unsurprisingly, ancient cultures offer various versions of the myth of creation – and the ancient Greeks have several of their own takes on the story.

Hesiod's version

The Greeks called the creation stories *cosmogony*, or how everything came into being. The most common cosmogony was the one that Hesiod describes in the *Theogony*:

> *Chaos was first of all, but next appeared broad bosomed Earth, sure standing place for all . . . From Chaos came Black Night and Erebos and Night in turn gave birth to Day and Space whom she conceived in love to Erebos.*

The idea is that first there was nothing but a void (Chaos) from which sprang Earth (also known as Gaia), Love (Eros), and other elemental beings. Eventually, Gaia gave birth to Uranos who became the sky; he in turn fertilised Gaia and she gave birth to more children – the *Titans*.

All fairly trippy stuff. Notice how the Greeks personified certain things which modern folks consider to be abstract notions. For example, love and the sky have humanlike qualities and even genders. The ancient Greeks relied heavily on *anthropomorphism*. They believed the creation of the world could be explained by the interaction of various forces, and these forces were best understood by making them like humans. See the later section 'Defining the gods' for more on anthropomorphism.

Other versions

Of course, Hesiod's is just one version! Loads of others pop up throughout Greek literature. Here are a few good ones:

- ✔ The earliest creation myth is called the *Pelasgian* and may have been a foreign tradition that predated the Greeks. According to this version, Eurynome produced a massive egg. Her son Ophion sat on it and hatched it. From the egg came the whole universe, including the humans and the gods.

- ✔ In Homer, the coupling of two of the Titans – Tethys and her brother Ocean – produced all the gods.

- ✔ In later versions, the first deity was Night (known as Nyx). She either produced an egg (like Eurynome) or gave birth to all gods and humans.

These three versions (plus Hesiod's explanation) are a great example of how fluid Greek mythology was and how similar stories were told in many completely different and alternative ways.

Remembering the Titans

In Hesiod's version of the creation myth, Gaia (Earth) and Uranos (the sky) gave birth to a whole range of different characters known as the *Titans*. Like a mythological version of a musical, the Titans were made up of six males and six females.

Crafty Kronos

Chief amongst the Titans was the wily Kronos, who was married to his sister Rhea. He had his eyes on power and plotted with his mother Gaia. While Uranos slept, Kronos crept up on him and sliced off his genitals with a scythe! They fell from the sky into the sea and bobbed along, until they came to the island of Cyprus where they caused a rather surprising result. According to Hesiod:

> *The genitals, cut off with adamant and thrown from land into the stormy sea, were carried for a long time on the waves. White foam surrounded the immortal flesh, and in it grew a girl . . . and there the goddess came forth, lovely, much revered, and grass grew up beneath her delicate feet. Her name is Aphrodite among men.*

The final lines inspired the Renaissance artist Botticelli's famous painting *The Birth of Venus* – but you can see why he didn't choose to depict the first part!

What goes around comes around

Kronos became the ruler of the Titans, but he feared that one of his own children would usurp him. To protect his power, every time his wife Rhea gave birth, he grabbed the child and ate it!

Eventually, Rhea swapped her latest child (a boy called Zeus) for a stone wrapped in a blanket, which Kronos gulped down. She then gave Kronos a poisoned drink that caused him to vomit up his other children. Zeus then got his siblings together and challenged Kronos to fight. Zeus and his siblings won the war: the Titans were defeated and sent down to the abyss (an empty chasm beneath the earth also known as Tartarus). The heavens had new rulers – the Olympian gods! (See the later section 'Meeting the Olympians: X-Rated Deities' for all the details on this motley crew of immortals.)

Bridging the gap between gods and man

The ancient Greeks thought that the events of the Titans happened a long time before their own day. While they passionately believed that gods existed, they considered that they only experienced the gods' actions in the form of storms and so on.

To bridge this gap between Titans and everyday experience, the Greeks believed that another age had existed in between – an age when the gods and men had existed side by side.

Of course, the Greeks being Greeks, matters weren't that straightforward! They divided this period between the Titans and everyday ancient Greek existence into various ages. Here's a quick guide:

- **The Golden Age:** This was a peaceful time when men and women existed in harmony alongside the gods, who were ruled by Kronos. This was an age of plenty when all lived easily off nature.

- **The Silver Age:** When the Golden Age human race died out another race replaced them. But this race was foolish and wicked, and Zeus decided to destroy it (see the following section 'Figuring out where it all went wrong').

- **The Bronze Age:** During this age humans discovered war and became so obsessed with it that they ended up destroying themselves.

- **The Age of Heroes:** This period was when the great Greek heroes – including Heracles, Theseus, and Achilles – flourished. These individuals fought each other and went on incredible adventures. For more on this age, see Chapter 20.

- **The Iron Age:** This was the period that the ancient Greeks considered themselves to be living in. It was an age where men were forced to work hard for a living.

The ancient Greeks firmly believed that their own period (the Iron Age) was a time of great hardship and that life had been much better during the Golden Age. In his poem *Works and Days* Hesiod gives a lovely picture of what that golden era was like:

> *And like gods they lived with happy hearts, untouched by toil or sorrow. Vile old age never appeared, but always lively-limbed, far from ills, they feasted happily. Death came to them as sleep, and all good things were theirs; ungrudgingly, the fertile land gave up her fruits unasked. Happy to be at peace they lived with every want supplied.*

Sounds pretty good, doesn't it? Then again, it isn't unusual for any society to have a romantic view of the past and complain about its own time.

Figuring out where it all went wrong

So if the relationship between men and gods was perfectly happy during the Golden Age, why did the Greeks fear and respect the gods in their time? The difference is explained by the Silver Age, where Zeus became enraged at the wicked behaviour of the race that he'd created and decided to wipe it out.

Deucalion's ark

Zeus's choice of Armageddon weapon was a flood. Much like in the Old Testament story of Noah, only one man and his family had a chance to survive Zeus's flood. In the Greek version, a Titan called Prometheus took pity on humans and warned a man called Deucalion.

Deucalion and his family built an ark and survived the rain for nine days before coming to rest on the top of Mount Parnassus near Delphi. Zeus relented and allowed Deucalion and his family to create a new race of men and women. One of the sons was called Hellen, who gave his name to the race that the Greeks were descended from – the Hellenes. Although this was a widely held mythological belief, no historical evidence for it exists. (For my theories on where the Greeks actually came from refer to Chapters 2 and 3!)

Prometheus: Always in trouble

Prometheus also helped the new race of Hellenes by defying the wishes of Zeus and giving men the gift of fire. Interestingly, Prometheus's name means 'forethought', although he didn't show too much here because Zeus's anger was considerable.

Zeus punished Prometheus by having him chained to a cliff and sending eagles to attack him. Every day the eagles tore out Prometheus's liver. The wound magically healed every evening and the punishment was repeated the next day. Eventually, Heracles freed Prometheus when he passed by on the way to one of his labours. (Chapter 20 has more on Heracles.)

The story of Prometheus is a great example of the savage punishments that the ancient Greeks believed their gods were capable of. The tragic playwright Aeschylus (see Chapter 16) wrote a trilogy about Prometheus from which the first play, *Prometheus Bound,* still survives. In the following fiery excerpt, Prometheus defies Zeus's worst punishments:

> *Let hurricanes upheave by the roots the base of the earth, let the sea-waves' roaring savagery confound the courses of the heavenly stars. Let him lift me high and hurl me into black Tartarus [the deep abyss beneath the earth] on ruthless floods of irresistible doom: I am one whom he cannot kill!*

The story of Prometheus is very much a fantastical myth but it does reinforce the way the Greeks felt about the relationship between man and the gods. People who defied the gods would be justly punished. Greek tragic plays are full of examples of characters who have pushed too far, been too bold, or too arrogant, and suffered terrible punishments as a result.

Putting the Gods in Their Place

The ancient Greeks loved gods, absolutely loved them. The Greeks had loads of gods, and through their rich mythology they turned the most surprising things – such as rivers and mountains – into gods. This section examines the various powers and responsibilities of the gods, from the perspective of an everyday ancient Greek citizen. Get ready for some surprises!

Understanding the role of gods

The gods played a vital part in how regular ancient Greeks lived their every-day lives, including what they thought, what they built, what they painted, and what they composed poems, plays, and songs about.

At the same time, people lived in great fear of the power of their gods and made sacrifices and offerings to them in the hope of receiving good fortune in return.

In the film *Clash of the Titans* (1980), the gods are depicted in quite a classical way: sitting around a temple in flowing robes, watching the world from afar and playing a game like chess with human lives. Although the special effects are pretty cheesy, the notion of the gods as beautiful and fabulous but capable of wielding enormous power is a decent depiction of these deities.

Worshipping many

After Zeus's revolt against his father Kronus and defeat of the Titans in a war (see the earlier section 'Remembering the Titans'), the gods that the ancient Greeks recognised came into existence and continued to rule for all eternity.

Ancient Greek religion was *polytheistic,* which means it consisted of many gods or deities. This is in contrast to Christianity, for example, which has one god and is therefore a *monotheistic* religion.

Greek religion had a specific *pantheon,* or collection of gods, that comprised the most important deities. I look at these top tier gods in the later section 'Meeting the Olympians: X-Rated Deities'.

Defining the gods

The Greek gods were *anthropomorphic.* This means the Greeks imagined their gods in their own terms – looking and speaking like men and women, although being fabulously powerful and magical.

Anthropomorphism is quite a reasonable thing for humans to do. (The Jewish, Christian, Muslim, and Hindu religions all include anthropomorphism in various ways.) The Greek philosopher Xenophanes summed the idea up quite nicely in his comment that '*If horses could draw, they would draw horse gods*'.

Super powers

Despite taking human form, the Greek gods were awesome in their abilities. Specifically, they were

- Able to resist wounding and disease
- Able to transform into other beings or creatures at the drop of a hat
- Blessed with eternal youth
- Capable of flight

In a way, they were like modern superheroes.

Do as I say, not as I do

Of course, the Greeks also imagined that their gods acted with some of the same motivations as normal people and experienced the same emotions. This belief meant that the Olympian gods often acted in cruel, childish, and immoral ways. In the myths, they commit adultery, rape, and murder on a seemingly daily basis and very often appear to revel in the cruel and inhuman punishments that they inflict on poor, defenceless humans.

To the Greeks there was nothing strange about the gods' actions. The Greeks didn't look to Zeus or Apollo as exemplars of good behaviour or for moral guidance. And that's just as well really! The Greeks didn't have a concept of sin or wickedness that came from religion. All the restrictions placed on people's liberty to act were based on legal or social conventions rather than religious instruction.

Visiting Olympus – a home fit for the gods

According to mythological tradition, the gods lived at the very top of Mount Olympus in northern Greece. This was where they spent a lot of time in near continual feasting and revelry, eating ambrosia and drinking nectar. It was vital for them to do this because the magical properties of these foodstuffs renewed their divine blood and kept up their powers.

Despite this seeming idyllic existence, the gods often roamed around, visiting parts of the world and interacting with their human subjects. A good example of this god/human interaction happens in Homer's *The Odyssey* when the other gods hold a sneaky meeting while Poseidon is away visiting the Ethiopians. The gods decide to help Odysseus (whom Poseidon is angry with) get home. The Greeks thought Ethiopia (their name for all of Africa beyond the Nile) was the farthest place in the world. So far, in fact, not even Poseidon could see what was happening in the Mediterranean while he was in Ethiopia!

Working like a god: Attributions and divine job descriptions

When they weren't feasting or misbehaving, the Olympian gods did have responsibilities. Each god had his or her own area of expertise, which I think of as their *attributions*.

Nearly every area of human experience had a god that oversaw it. For example, Demeter looked after farming, Poseidon sea travel, and Asclepius medicine and healing.

Inspiring ladies: The Muses

The immortals who were most closely associated with their area of expertise were the Muses. These nine female deities were led by Apollo (patron god of the arts) and each represented an area of artistic endeavour:

- Calliope: Epic poetry
- Clio: History
- Erato: Lyric poetry
- Euterpe: Flute-playing
- Melpomene: Tragedy
- Polymnia: Hymns
- Terpsichore: Dancing and the chorus
- Thalia: Comedy
- Urania: Astronomy

The ancient Greeks believed that the relevant Muse directly inspired artists working in these fields. For this reason, all epic poems traditionally begin with a request by the poet to be inspired by the Muse Calliope. Hesiod's *Theogony* is a good example; he starts the poem by describing the encounter that he had with the Muses that inspired him: 'With the Heliconian [resident on Mount Helicon] Muses let us start our song.'

The Greeks believed that the Muses lived on Olympus and spent their days entertaining the gods. Occasionally, they came down to earth and literally filled an artist with their inspiration. Hopefully, Clio paid me a visit while I was writing this book!

In many cases, gods had more than one attribution. Some, like Apollo and Athena, had loads. And yes, these attributions sometimes clashed with each other. For example, Athena was the goddess of handicrafts, wisdom, and war. Not the most obvious combination!

The way that a god got his attribution was this: People adopted a god as the patron deity of some area of human experience. It's impossible to know why the gods were given their attributions although they were usually relevant to an incident in mythology (such as Poseidon being given the sea as his realm by Zeus). Individuals honoured the god and made offerings, hoping for benefits in return. In the case of individual trades (such as medicine or shipbuilding), having a designated god led the Greeks to form guilds and organise public festivals and celebrations in honour of their deities.

Have you seen the film *Xanadu* (1980)? It probably doesn't immediately strike you as relevant to the ancient Greeks but it does feature the Muses masquerading as rock band 'The Nine Sisters'. It also features Zeus, Cliff Richard, and ELO – perfect for a Sunday afternoon!

Separating fate from dumb luck

The ancient Greeks believed that they had to worship the gods to ensure that their lives progressed happily and that bad things didn't happen to them. This philosophy may suggest that the Greek believed the gods controlled their destinies – but this isn't the case.

In addition to the gods, the Greeks believed in the idea of *fate* – that their lives were planned out and followed preordained paths. Thus, the time of your birth and the time of your death were fixed by a group of three female deities called, surprisingly enough, *the Fates*.

According to Hesiod, the Fates were very ancient goddesses who were the daughters of Nyx (Night); see the earlier section 'Starting Out: Greek Creation Myths'. These sisters spun out the thread (or the fabric) of a life and then one of them, Atropos, cut it when it was time for the human to die. The Fates existed apart from the other gods, and some accounts go as far as to state that the Olympian gods feared them.

The role of the gods was to *administer fate* as it came to pass. In *The Iliad* Homer describes Zeus as having a set of scales on which he weighs the fates of the heroes who are in combat, deciding who'll live or die that day. But although Zeus administers these fates, he can't actually do anything to change them, which is highlighted when his own mortal son, Sarpedon, is killed in battle. For a moment Zeus considers trying to prevent his son's death but then he realises that he can't.

The Odyssey includes an even better example of the gods' relationship with fate. Athena states:

> *But from the great leveller Death: not even the gods can defend a man, not even one they love, that day when fate takes hold and lays him out at last.*

Accordingly, people rarely asked the gods for anything related to their deaths or how long they would live. The Greeks generally accepted that the gods controlled what happened in your mortal life, not when it ended. I look at the Greek attitude towards death in Chapter 21.

Mocking the gods

Despite the awesome power that the Greeks thought the gods wielded, people still often treated them as figures of fun and amusement in art, literature, and theatre. For example, in *The Iliad* the childish and comic affairs of the gods act as a kind of counterpoint to the remorselessness of the fighting and death going on in the Trojan War.

Comic plays (see Chapter 16) frequently poke fun at the gods. In *Frogs* by Aristophanes, two of the central characters, Dionysus and Heracles, are immortals and they're lampooned just as much as the rest of the cast. In one scene, Dionysus asks Heracles for travel tips on the journey to Hades (the underworld):

I wondered if you could give me a few tips: any useful contacts down there, where you get the boat, which are the best eating houses, bread shops, wine shops, knocking shops . . . And which places have the fewest bugs.

Fun and games aside, I must make two important points about Aristophanes's comic musings about the gods:

- ✔ He isn't mocking any aspect of the gods' awesome powers as gods; rather he's making fun of them acting like humans.

- ✔ He's picked two relatively minor gods – he isn't mocking Zeus or Apollo.

This careful fun-poking reveals that the Greeks had something of a hierarchy for their gods. So without further ado, the next section looks at the most important ones!

Meeting the Olympians: X-Rated Deities

Probably the most important factor to remember about the Olympian gods is that they were, for the most part, related (see the section 'Starting Out: Greek Creation Myths' for the odd genealogical details). For example:

- ✔ Zeus, Poseidon, and Hades were all brothers.

- ✔ Hera was their sister and was married to Zeus. (The Zeus/Hera relationship was more than fit for an episode of *Jerry Springer*!)

- ✔ Apollo, Artemis, and Hermes were just a few of Zeus's many children.

Like all families, the gods had their ups and downs. Many of the stories about the Greek gods are born out of their petty jealousies and squabbles. It's like a kind of immortal soap opera – so meet the cast of Olympian gods.

Zeus, the king of the gods

Zeus was king of all the gods. When he defeated his father Kronos (see the earlier section 'Starting Out: Greek Creation Myths'), he became lord of everything. He mostly appears in myth as a great philanderer, sleeping with many mortals and immortals. Zeus regularly transformed himself into other creatures to do this: a swan (Leda), a bull (Europa), and even a shower of gold (Danae)!

Poseidon, the earth-shaker

Poseidon was the brother of Zeus. When Zeus became supreme, Poseidon was made the god of the earth (thus he was responsible for causing earthquakes) and the sea. Poseidon was also the god of horses and he impregnated the demon Medusa. When Medusa was killed by the hero Perseus, the famous winged horse Pegasus was born from her neck!

Hades, the king of the dead

Zeus's other brother Hades was given the underworld to rule and he became king of the dead. The Greeks (and more frequently the Romans) also referred to him as Pluto, meaning 'wealthy', because of the richness and fertility that come from underneath the earth.

Hades is mainly known for his abduction of Persephone (daughter of Zeus and Demeter), who he took to the underworld to be his wife. Zeus forced Hades to allow Persephone to return to mortality for six months of the year, bringing with her return to the land of living the warm weather of spring and summer.

Hera, the queen of heaven

Hera was the older sister of Zeus and also his wife. She was the goddess of marriage and the Greeks honoured her in this way. In myth and literature she spends most of her time being offended by Zeus's philandering and cruelly punishing his mortal lovers. She bore Zeus three children, including Ares the god of war. She also makes regular appearances in the stories of Heracles (setting him his tasks) and Jason (helping him to steal the Golden Fleece).

Hestia, the quiet one

Another sister of Zeus, Hestia was an intriguing, lesser-known immortal. She was the goddess of the hearth and home and is often depicted tending an eternal flame or fire. She renounced sexual love and lived a life of chastity – and consequently she never really features in any myths at all!

Despite her low profile in literature, Hestia was probably the most worshipped goddess because she was the protectoress of every household, typically receiving the first offering of every sacrifice made in a Greek home.

Apollo, lord of the silver bow

Apollo was the male twin born of Zeus's coupling with Leto, the daughter of one of the Titans (Artemis is Apollo's twin sister). Apollo was the patron god of archers and had many names like 'the far shooter' and 'lord of the silver bow'. Apollo is the god of prophecy and is also heavily associated with the sun and light. He was famed for establishing the Delphic Oracle (see Chapter 21) and is always depicted in Greek art as the epitome of male beauty and perfection.

Aphrodite, the goddess of sexual love

The goddess of beauty, attraction, and sexual love, Aphrodite was married to Hephaestus, but they had no children, and she was frequently unfaithful. Her most famous myth is that of her birth (see the earlier section 'Crafty Kronos'). She frequently appears in other stories, meddling in human relationships, sometimes with her son Eros. She plays a critical role in setting up the conflict that launched the Trojan War; see Chapter 20.

Ares, the god of war

Ares was the son of Zeus and Hera, and he was a truly terrifying god. Not only the god of war, Ares actively enjoyed the fear and chaos of battle and was credited with inspiring blood lust and savagery in mortals. He had two sons – Phobos ('Terror') and Deimos ('Fear'). He was also the father of Eros, a god of lust, love, and intercourse, as a result of a long-term liaison with Aphrodite.

Athena, the intelligent one

Athena was the daughter of Zeus and was identified with both war and handicrafts. This may seem a strange combination, but these were identified as the chief male and female occupations of the day. Unlike Ares, Athena's association with war was with the sober, correct use of it to defend cities.

Athena was also closely identified with intelligence and is often shown with an owl. The patron deity of the city of Athens, she was also the great protector of the hero Odysseus in *The Odyssey*.

Artemis, the hunter

The daughter of Zeus and the twin sister of Apollo, Artemis was the goddess of hunting and of women – with a particular focus on childbirth. Her role as huntress encompassed all wildlife, and she was seen as being wild and untamed in this way. She's often depicted in art carrying a bow and arrows and wearing animal skins.

Hephaestus, the god of the forge

Hephaestus was the god of fire and metalwork. He was the son of Hera and born crippled. In some versions, he was born without a father, developing out of Hera's rage for Zeus's infidelities. Hera was so ashamed of him that she flung him from Mount Olympus, and several myths exist about the extravagant revenges that he took upon her.

Married to Aphrodite, Hephaestus spent most of his days in his forge where he famously created a wonderful shield for the hero Achilles. Eventually, the Greeks revered him for all industry and manufacturing activities.

Hermes, the messenger god

One of the many sons of Zeus, Hermes was the messenger and herald of the gods. He appears in myth wearing winged sandals that enable him to fly at great speed to deliver messages from Olympus. Unsurprisingly, he was also the god of travellers; people made offerings to him before setting out on long journeys. He was also known as a cunning trickster – probably not the one to ask directions from then!

Demeter, the life-giver

Demeter was the goddess of corn and accordingly considered to be the sustainer of life. She was the sister of Zeus and bore him a daughter called Persephone. Due to her association with the harvest, she was very heavily worshipped by the Greeks and central to their most famous cult, the Eleusinian Mysteries (described in Chapter 21).

Dionysus, the god of good times

Dionysus was another son of Zeus and the god of wine and intoxication. Drunkenness was seen as a good thing because it helped to banish the cares of the world. Drinking and revelry fitted well with his other role as god of the theatre, where people could wear masks to change their identity. Dionysus spent his time roaming the countryside with his drunken crew, including his crazed female followers known as *maenads*.

The preceding is just a tiny introduction to the top-tier Olympian gods and their most famous stories. The myths about them are incredibly complex and contradict each other all the time. What's most important is the associations the gods had because that's why Greeks worshipped them. (See Chapter 21 for more on how the ancient Greeks went about worshipping.)

Not all fun and games

Although the gods all sound like tremendous fun, they were actually violent and unpredictable. Dionysus is a particularly good example. He sounds like a god who inspired good times and revel, and he did. But he also turned people mad. Under Dionysus's influence, people did awful and terrible things.

In Euripides's play *Bacchae,* Dionysus turns Pentheus (the king of Thebes) insane after he attempts to stop Dionysus's followers from worshipping him. Pentheus is torn to pieces by the *maenads* when he blunders in on their rites.

Here Dionysus sets out how Pentheus had broken the rules.

> *No god can see his worship scorned, and hear his name profaned, and not take vengeance to the utmost limit. Thus men may learn that gods are more powerful than they.*

Although they may act like fools and make human mistakes in many of the myths, the gods were to be feared and the Greeks worshipped them through fear as much as devotion.

The third section of Disney's *Fantasia* (1940) is an animated piece that accompanies Beethoven's Sixth Symphony 'The Pastoral'. The Greek gods on Mount Olympus are all in it. The blend of music and animation is wonderful and I can never hear that music without thinking about Greek mythology.

Transitioning from Greek to Roman

The Romans adopted gods very close to the Greek ones as their own. Greek and Roman gods were very similar and had the same attributions, but had different names. It can sometimes get quite confusing so Table 19-1 serves as a quick guide.

Table 19-1	Greek and Roman Deities	
Greek Name	*Roman Name*	*Greek Attribution*
Zeus	Jupiter	Sky, weather, storms, and lightning.
Hera	Juno	Marriage and childbirth
Poseidon	Neptune	The ocean and earthquakes
Hades	Pluto	Death and the underworld

Greek Name	Roman Name	Greek Attribution
Hestia	Vesta	The hearth (or home)
Apollo	Apollo	Prophecy, divination, the arts
Aphrodite	Venus	Beauty and erotic love
Athena	Minerva	War and handicrafts
Hephaestus	Vulcan	Fire and metalworking
Ares	Mars	War
Hermes	Mercury	Messages and travel
Demeter	Ceres	Corn
Artemis	Diana	Hunting and women
Dionysus	Bacchus	Wine and intoxication

The Roman and Greek gods aren't exactly the same but they had similar attributions, so the Romans adopted the Greek gods completely as they absorbed Greece into their empire (refer to Chapter 12).

One thing that did change in the transition from Greek to Roman was the importance of some gods. Mars (Ares) was incredibly important to a warlike people like the Romans, and Vesta (Hestia) came to prominence as the founding deity of the famous Vestal Virgins, a hugely influential cult in Rome that trained young women to be priestesses.

Chapter 20

Blending Myth and History: Troy, Homer, and Heroes

. . . .

In This Chapter

▶ Reliving the glories of the Trojan War

▶ Searching for facts about Troy

▶ Appreciating Homer's epic poems

▶ Taking stock of other heroes and their adventures

. . . .

The myth of the Trojan War is very famous. For generations people have enjoyed plays, stories, novels, and films about the exploits of Achilles, Odysseus, Helen, and many other fascinating Greek characters.

You may have seen the film *Troy* (2004). It was great fun and gave the impression of an epic struggle between huge armies led by handsome, physically well-developed heroes who fought over a fantastical city for possession of one beautiful woman. When the film was released a lot of people quibbled over whether the events shown were a 'true' version of what had gone on. They were missing the point. The story shown in the film – recounted in the poetic source material, Homer's *The Iliad* – never really took place; it is a *myth*.

For the ancient Greeks, however, the Trojan War was hugely important. Their versions of the war were massively influential on the way in which they lived their lives.

This chapter is all about the Trojan myth: understanding the stories, getting to grips with its impact on ancient and subsequent Greek life, and looking at the archaeological evidence now available. It's also about introducing Homer and *The Iliad* – the man and the poem that dominated intellectual life in the Greek world.

Separating Myth and History

As I mention in Chapter 3, early Greek history is very difficult to separate from mythology. The Trojan War is a perfect example of this combining of fact and fiction.

The Greeks readily accepted the idea of what they called the Trojan Cycle (see the following section 'Mining the myth of the Trojan War') although there were various versions of it. The ancient Greeks considered the stories true and did not require any evidence. Modern minds, however, find Troy more difficult to accept unquestioningly. Historians try to balance the evidence of archaeology (see 'Seeking out the facts of Troy') with information in the original literary works, including Homer's epic poems (see 'Preserving – and Pumping Up – the Story of Troy: Homer').

Mining the myth of the Trojan War

The myth of the Trojan War encompasses a huge number of characters and incidents set vaguely around the time of the Mycenaean period (see Chapter 2), probably about 1300–1200 BC. The Greeks referred to the whole collection of stories as the *Trojan Cycle*.

Highlights of the story include the following key players and events:

- **A war spurred by love:** While on a diplomatic mission to the court of the Spartan king Menelaus, Paris, one of the sons of the Trojan king Priam, falls in love with Menelaus's beautiful wife Helen and elopes with her back to Troy. (For more on Troy's assumed geographic location, see the following section 'Figuring out the facts of Troy'.) This causes a major international incident as Menelaus's brother is Agamemnon, Mycenaean king, and the most powerful and influential of all the Greek leaders.

- **The personal becomes political:** Menelaus calls on all the other Greek nobles who owe him allegiance to join in an assault on Troy in an effort to avenge the insult to him. Agamemnon assembles a mighty fleet that sets sail from Aulis on the eastern coast of Greece, landing on the shore outside Troy (modern-day western Turkey; see the Cheat Sheet map). And thus, Helen becomes 'the face that launched a thousand ships'.

- **Larger than life warriors:** Both the Greeks and Trojans assemble armies full of the leading heroes of the age. The Greeks' superstar is Achilles, whose goddess mother bathed him in the river Styx in Hades to make him (almost) invulnerable. The Trojans' greatest warrior is Hector, King Priam's eldest son.

- **A brutal battle:** War rages between the two sides for ten years. The gods and goddesses both help and hinder each side; each deity chooses individually which army to support (see Chapter 19). Many heroes on both sides lose their lives, including Hector who is killed by Achilles. Paris then shoots Achilles in the heel (his one vulnerable spot) with an arrow, and he dies.

- **One tricky pony:** Eventually, the end to the war comes with a cunning plot devised by Odysseus, the Greek king of Ithaca. The Greeks construct an enormous horse, leave it outside the gates of Troy, and then appear to depart for home. Thinking that they've won, the Trojans take the horse inside the city and begin to celebrate. Shortly afterwards some Greeks who are concealed inside the horse slip out and open the gates for their comrades. In the bloodshed that follows, Troy is utterly destroyed, never to recover.

But the Trojan Cycle doesn't end with the war. The stories about the various characters continue. Most notably:

- Menelaus is reunited with Helen.

- Agamemnon returns home and is murdered by his wife Clytemnestra. Aeschylus's trilogy of tragic plays, known as *The Oresteia,* dramatises this veritable soap opera of deception and power.

- Odysseus spends a further ten years wandering the Mediterranean before returning home to his wife Penelope in Ithaca. See the section 'Returning home: The Odyssey' for more on Odysseus's outrageous journey.

The preceding is just one version of the myth. For the ancient Greeks, myths changed depending on who you were and where you lived. Another version of the Trojan story has Helen spending the whole war hiding in Egypt with only a ghost version of herself at Troy!

The film *Troy* (2004) was criticised because in it Paris and Helen leave Troy together and Achilles is present at the fall of the city. Critics missed the point. Many Greeks believed and told varying versions of the Trojan cycle so why shouldn't Hollywood?

Figuring out the facts of Troy

So what do historians actually know of the city of Troy? Unfortunately, facts are difficult to come by. What historians now know is based on a mixture of archaeological evidence and educated speculation. Despite some debate, historians generally contend the following:

- ✔ **When:** The ancient Greeks believed the Trojan War took place during *The Age of Heroes*, a period before the Greeks began recording history when they believed the great escapades of heroes like Heracles, Theseus, and the fighters at Troy to have taken place. The historian Herodotus thought that the war took place about 800 years before his time, or around 1200 BC.

- ✔ **Where:** The site historians now regard as Troy had been an important fortress throughout the Minoan and Mycenaean periods. The city was built on a low hill about eight kilometres west of the Aegean coast and just a little farther south of the Hellespont (see the Cheat Sheet map). Troy was in a superb position for trading at two coastal points and with the whole of Asia Minor and the east. Consequently, the city must have been very wealthy.

As I explain in Chapter 2, historians rely on archaeology for almost all their knowledge of the Minoan and Mycenaean periods. During the 19th century a German archaeologist called Heinrich Schliemann carried out a huge amount of excavation at sites around both Troy and Mycenae.

When Schliemann excavated at the spot that historians now think was the site of Troy, he discovered the ruins of an ancient town that was built on seven different levels.

- ✔ The earliest of these levels contained a huge amount of gold and other precious finds.

- ✔ The more recent levels were farther away from the centre, as you'd expect from a city that grew and expanded.

- ✔ Twentieth-century excavations found that these most recent levels showed evidence of having been destroyed through some cataclysmic event around the time of 1300 BC.

Schliemann was convinced that his site was Troy of the Trojan Cycle and that the treasure that he found belonged to the mythical king Priam. He announced to the world that he had found the site of Troy and proof that the Trojan War had taken place.

However, Schliemann's discoveries were problematic. Further excavations have shown that an earthquake, rather than an invading army, damaged the more recent areas. Signs also indicated that people lived in the recent levels once more very soon after the damage – not the hallmarks of a city razed to the ground by Agamemnon's army.

Other evidence for the Trojan War is literary (see the next section) and in the form of Greek art where the stories from the Trojan cycle were always a popular subject for sculptors and vase painters (Chapter 17 has a good example of a black-figure vase with a Trojan theme). However, these artefacts can't really be taken as proof of the war itself, rather as evidence of a continued interest in the Trojan cycle during later Greek history.

Ultimately, the general consensus is that the city found by Schliemann is the most likely site of ancient Troy. You can visit the site today although the fairly nondescript ruins are very difficult to relate to the story of the war. However, historians are no nearer to an answer about whether the Trojan War truly took place.

Passing On – and Pumping Up – the Story of Troy: Homer

The poet Homer and his poems *The Iliad* and *The Odyssey* had a huge impact on almost every aspect of Greek life. Modern folks often have difficulty appreciating quite why this was the case because the attitude to poetry today is very different. In ancient Greece *The Iliad* and *The Odyssey* were the first works of Western literature.

What makes the poems even more amazing is that they are huge, complicated, and lengthy works. Every succeeding historical period has acknowledged the poems as masterpieces, and people still consider them to be astounding examples of literary construction and story telling

The ancient Greeks presumed that the author of the two poems was one man – an author of genius called Homer. For centuries scholars have loudly debated his identity, despite the lack of any real evidence. One popular theory is that Homer was blind and ancient portrait busts of him (made hundreds of years after his death) often show him in this way. The most likely reason for this is the character of Demodocus the bard who appears in *The Odyssey* and performs a song about the Fall of Troy. Because he is blind some people have suggested that Homer put himself in the poem. It's a good theory anyway!

Sharing stories: The oral tradition

Part of the problem in identifying who Homer was comes from the fact that nothing Homer himself wrote actually exists!

Writing didn't develop in Greece until around the eighth century BC (see Chapter 1). Early Greeks composed and delivered poetry orally, and Homer was probably part of this tradition. (This tradition has continued around the world even to modern times, in places as far apart as Serbia and the Congo.)

Oral poets lived an itinerant life travelling around from town to town and performing their work. Ancient sources mention other epic poems such as one about the myths associated with the city of Thebes, but none of these poems survive and none of them had the influence of Homer's epics.

The skill of the poet

The *oral tradition* involves techniques such as using formulas or repeated phrases. You can see these techniques in the works of Homer. Characters are given *epithets* (words that describe their innate qualities or abilities) such as 'swift-footed Achilles' or Hector 'tamer of horses' and these are repeated throughout.

Some key scenes are repeated wholesale. A particularly good example is the description of heroes making a sacrifice and eating the meal that followed. This whole passage is repeated many times throughout both *The Iliad* and *The Odyssey*. You can find a quotation from this scene in Chapter 15.

Part of the reason for these techniques is that ancient Greek poets designed their work to be performed rather than read. The formulas and repetition enabled poets to keep the ideas and stories in their heads in order to present the works to audiences.

Fascinating rhythm

Equally important to the poems is the rhythm in which they were originally composed and that translators work hard to maintain in their modern versions. The original Greek rhythm is *dactylic hexameter*, a form virtually impossible to reproduce in English. Bearing this in mind helps you to remember that these works are poems, despite the many prose translations available today.

The Iliad, for example, is a very long poem of around 17,000 lines. Scholars estimate that the entire work would require roughly 24 hours to read aloud. When it was performed to the ancient Greeks, the poem was most likely presented in sections rather than as a whole.

The length and complexity of the poems have led most people to conclude that they were probably composed some time in the late eighth century BC and then written down around 650 BC. The written versions were more than likely the work of a group of poets but based on a tradition that started with one man, Homer.

Doing battle: The Iliad

I mention *The Iliad* a lot throughout this book, and that's because it's probably the most important work of literature that the Greeks ever produced. The ancient Greeks considered *The Iliad* to be more than just a huge poem about a mythical war. Rather, it was the closest that the Greeks had to a historical record and moral guide. It was a kind of bible; something they turned to for advice on all sorts of issues.

What about the Trojan horse?

One thing that isn't in *The Iliad* – or any of Homer's works for that matter – is the story of the Trojan horse. Although this clever ruse was well established as part of the Trojan myth, it doesn't feature in the poem which comes to an end before the fall of Troy. The incident is frequently mentioned in *The Odyssey* but isn't discussed in any real detail.

By far the best ancient version of the story of the Trojan horse is told in *The Aeneid*, a much later poem by the Roman poet Virgil (first century BC). *The Aeneid* details the story of the Trojan prince Aeneas and his travels after the war.

Historians have no idea if a Trojan horse ever actually existed but the version in *The Aeneid* is very affecting in its description of the tragedies that occurred as Troy fell.

Getting down to details

The Trojan War lasted for about ten years (see the section 'Mining the myth of the Trojan War' for an overview), but the story of *The Iliad* covers only about two weeks of battle.

The central character is the great Greek warrior Achilles, who withdraws from the fighting after an argument with Agamemnon, his commander. While Achilles is out of action, the Trojans get on top in the fighting. The Trojan prince Hector kills Achilles's great male friend (and possibly lover) Patroclus. Grief-stricken, Achilles returns to the fighting and eventually kills Hector before the poem ends with the funeral of Patroclus and the athletic competitions that followed it (a tradition following the death of a warrior).

Heroism, handicrafts, and history

Of course, *The Iliad* is about much more than Achilles seeking vengeance for Patroclus's death. The ancient Greeks considered the poem to be a source of information on:

- **The concept of the hero and the way that heroes behave:** To modern eyes, the characters in *The Iliad* seem unusual and probably quite petulant, but the Greeks loved the way these heroes were totally devoted to their sense of honour. In the world of *The Iliad* a man can preserve his honour only by fighting and killing enemies, and collecting the enemy's armour after battle serves as a visible sign of the hero's honour and skill.

- **Practical procedures:** Several scenes in the poem describe sacrifices and ceremonies that were heavily influenced the way that later Greeks conducted them. (See Chapter 21 for more on ancient Greek religious practices.)

Another good example of how *The Iliad* details everyday life comes when the god Hephaestus makes an incredible shield for Achilles to use during his return to the fighting.

At first Hephaestus makes a great and massive shield, blazoning well-wrought emblems all across its surface, raising a rim around it, glittering, triple-ply with a silver shield-strap run from edge to edge and five layers of metal to build the shield itself.

To modern readers, this passage (and the dozens of lines that follow it) may seem an over-elaborate description. But *The Iliad* and *The Odyssey* are full of details like this and that is why the Greeks regarded the poems as something like compendiums of knowledge.

✔ **Historical figures:** Homer also includes lines and lines of verse devoted to charting the histories of all the characters he introduces. Book 2 of *The Iliad* is often called the Catalogue of Ships; it's basically a long list of virtually all the fighters that were involved in the war. Many ancient Greeks would have regarded this book as the most impressive of the entire poem because of the knowledge that it contains.

For a travelling oral poet the Catalogue of Ships would also be a good way of impressing the audience: the sheer number of heroes mentioned in Book 2 meant that somebody relevant to the town that he was visiting would get a plug. This was a great way of getting the audience onside early in a performance!

Returning home: The Odyssey

In addition to *The Iliad*, the other great work that historians attribute to Homer is *The Odyssey*, which tells the story of what happened to Odysseus, the king of Ithaca, when he tried to return home after the Trojan War. Most scholars believe *The Iliad* was the first of the two poems, with *The Odyssey* being something of a sequel.

Getting down to details

Odysseus's journey takes a very long time because the gods punish him for allowing his men to kill and eat the sacred cattle of the sun god. His ship destroyed and his crew lost, Odysseus ends up stranded on the island of the sea-nymph Calypso for seven years. Along the way, Odysseus has loads of adventures with giants, clashing rocks, sea monsters, and a sorceress called Circe.

Arriving back in Ithaca, Odysseus finds that the local nobles presumed that he was dead and moved into his palace in the hope of wooing his wife Penelope. Teaming up with his son Telemachus, he kills many of the nobles and drives them from the house, finally reuniting with Penelope after 20 years away from home!

Rhapsodes: A load of know-it-alls!

Knowledge of Homer was considered to be vital to a person's education in ancient Greece (see Chapter 14), but some people went even further than that.

Rhapsodes were professional reciters of poetry, most commonly *The Iliad* and *The Odyssey*. Unlike Homer they weren't actually poets themselves but performed other people's work for a fee and often competed in games and competitions. Due to the fact that Homer's poems contained so much knowledge of the world, the Greeks saw the *rhapsodes* as authorities on almost any given subject. A little bit like a kind of walking Internet!

The Odyssey is a fantastic story and reads much more like a modern novel than *The Iliad*.

Despite the drama of the tale, the poem hasn't ever really been successfully turned into a film. The most modern effort was a mini-series from 1997 that starred Armand Assante and Greta Scacchi. It's a good effort with some great Mediterranean scenery and a particularly unpleasant set of suitors led by Eric Roberts. Otherwise try *O Brother, Where Art Thou?* (2001) starring George Clooney. Although set in the deep south of America it's a loose reworking of the story and it can be fun to try and work out the references to Homer's poem. John Goodman's character is the cyclops Polyphemus!

The rules of friendship

One lesson that the ancient Greeks took from *The Odyssey* is the concept of *xenia*. *Xenia* means 'guest-friendship', and it's the regulated system of greeting guests followed by virtually all the characters in *The Odyssey*. In short, *xenia* means you let people relax, eat, and refresh themselves when they arrive at your house before asking them any questions about who they are or what they want.

Here's a great example of the rules of *xenia* in action. In Book 4 of the poem, Menelaus welcomes Odysseus's son Telemachus and a warrior called Mentes (who's actually the goddess Athena in disguise!) into his house without knowing who they are, saying:

> 'Help yourselves to food, and welcome! Once you've dined we'll ask who you are. . . .' With those words he passed them a fat rich loin with his own hands, the choicest part, that he'd been served himself.

Nearly all the characters in the poem follow these rules – and all who don't (like the suitors in Odysseus's house) suffer violent punishments as a result. Consequently, the poem almost sets a moral code for the ancient Greeks. The idea of hospitality and offering guests food and drink was a key part of the ancient Greek mindset. As a regular visitor to Greece I've found this to be a tradition that continues to this day.

Meeting Other, Earlier Heroes

Although the Trojan Cycle that *The Iliad* and *The Odyssey* describe dominated Greek literature and mythology, hundreds of other heroes and stories are associated with the Age of Heroes. In many cases, these individuals were part of an earlier time than the age of Troy. In *The Iliad* the old warrior Nestor of Pylos says that none of the men fighting at Troy can compare with the earlier generation of heroes like Theseus (see the later section 'Theseus: Founder of Athens'). So these earlier heroes must have been pretty impressive! (See Chapter 19 for more on the ancient Greek's conceptualisation of the history of man.)

When ancient Greek literature talks about a *hero,* it doesn't mean somebody who does amazing things to help others like Superman or Spiderman. The ancient Greek concept of a hero is somebody who achieves amazing feats or shows incredible strength and endurance. Most of the time, these heroes aren't very nice and they do a lot of unpleasant things – very different to the modern version of a hero.

The following sections serve as a short guide to some of the other major heroes in ancient Greek mythology and literature, and what they did.

Heracles: A hard worker!

Heracles (or Hercules as the Romans called him) is pretty much the ultimate Greek hero. He was the son of Zeus (see Chapter 19) and a mortal woman called Alcmene.

Virtually from birth, Heracles was famed for having extraordinary courage and strength – as well as a terrific appetite and a terrible temper! A huge number of myths are associated with him, most famously 'The Twelve Labours'. Eurystheus, the king of Tiryns (whom the Delphic Oracle told Heracles to serve), sets up 12 near-impossible tasks for Heracles. There's never been a really satisfying explanation as to why he was given this much to do. Some scholars believe that it was just a clever way of bringing together some of the many stories about Heracles into one big tale.

Table 20-1 outlines and explains the 12 labours.

Table 20-1	The 12 Labours of Hercules
Labour	**Explanation**
The Nemean Lion	Kill the famous lion and bring back his skin.
The Lemaean Hydra	Kill the many-headed serpent.
The Ceryneian Hind	Capture a deer that was sacred to Artemis (see Chapter 19).
The Erymanthian Boar	Capture a savage wild boar.
The Augean Stables	Muck out stables full of years' worth of dung! Nasty!
The Stymphalian Birds	Rid a town of a plague of vicious birds.
The Cretan Bull	Capture a wild bull.
The Mares of Diomedes	Capture some man-eating horses.
The Girdle of Hippolyte	Steal the belt from the queen of the Amazons.
The Cattle of Geryon	Journey into the unknown to capture some cattle.
The Apples of the Hesperides	Steal the golden apples that grew at the end of the earth.
Cerberus	Journey to Hades and capture the triple-headed dog that guarded its entrance.

After all these labours, Heracles still isn't done. Many more stories tell of his exploits. When he finally dies, he is taken up to Olympus where he lives with the gods as one of them. That alone makes him the greatest of Greek heroes.

Theseus: Founder of Athens

As I mention in Chapter 4, many ancient Greeks believed that Theseus was:

- ✔ The son of Poseidon (covered in Chapter 19)
- ✔ The founder of many of the institutions of the city of Athens
- ✔ The hero who went to Crete and defeated the Minotaur

Of course, loads of other stories are associated with Theseus; not least journeying to fight the Amazons alongside Heracles. By the fifth century BC the Greeks thought of Theseus as the founding figure of justice, and he appears in several tragic plays as a very noble figure.

Perseus: Medusa slayer

Perseus was the son of Zeus and the mortal woman Danae. (Zeus turned himself into a shower of gold to impregnate this lovely lady!)

Perseus's most famous feat was killing the snake-haired Gorgon called Medusa who turned men to stone with one look. He also saved Andromeda from being eaten by a sea-monster. These adventures and more feature in the film *Clash of the Titans* (1980).

Jason: Leader of the Argonauts

Jason is famous for one really big feat. His wicked uncle Pelias denied Jason the throne of Iolcus, and set him the task of travelling far to the city of Colchis to steal the Golden Fleece, the skin of a ram with magical powers. On his ship called the *Argo*, Jason was joined by a famous crew of heroes, the Argonauts.

The most complete version of the myth is the *Voyage of Argo* by Apollonius of Rhodes, written in the third century BC.

Bellerophon: Mystery man

Historians and scholars often consider Bellerophon to be the forgotten man of Greek myths whose stories haven't survived as well as some of the others. A son of Poseidon, Bellerophon is sent on various impossible tasks, rather like Heracles. These tasks include fighting the terrifying Chimaera monster and battling single-handed against the Amazons. The flying horse Pegasus aids him in these tasks.

Where heroes go to die

Given that these heroes all achieved such amazing things in their lifetimes it's no surprise that myths suggested that they were equally special in death. Mortals just went to the grim underworld of Hades (see Chapter 21) but the fate of heroes was rather different.

According to mythology heroes went to a place called *Elysium*, also known as the 'Elysian Fields' or 'Elysian Plain.' This was a special section of Hades where heroes could spend all eternity feasting and hunting in a beautiful paradise. So it was worth carrying out all those heroic tasks after all!

Building them up – to knock them down

Just like historical figures and the Olympian gods (see Chapter 19), the early heroes of Greek mythology are very open to interpretation. Later Greek writers reinterpreted them in quite different ways. For example, Heracles is often shown in comedies as a drunkard and a glutton. The phrase 'a Heracles supper' evolved to describe an event that goes on long after it should have finished.

The tragic playwrights took heroes and portrayed elements of their character from very different viewpoints:

- In Sophocles's play *Philoctetes*, Odysseus is something of a villain, using his cunning to hurt others.

- In Euripides's *Medea*, Jason is proud, selfish, and arrogant.

Chapter 21

Practising Everyday Religion: 'A God Put It in My Heart to Say'

. . . .

In This Chapter

▶ Dying and travelling to the underworld

▶ Participating in ceremonies and sacrifices

▶ Using divination and seeking signs

▶ Frolicking in festivals and joining cults

. . . .

Chapter 19 introduces the many varied ancient Greek gods, and illustrates the roles specific gods were believed to have in the mythical past. In this chapter I look at how the ancient Greeks worshipped their gods and other mythical heroes in their daily lives. Get ready to uncover some strange and unusual rituals – at least for modern eyes.

Greek religion was actually very formal and full of big public rituals in the same way that modern religions make requirements on people to be in places at certain times of day and week. Public religion is the major focus of this chapter – understanding the private, spiritual beliefs of the ancient Greeks is very difficult because historians don't really have any record of them. The closest that we get to it is in understanding their cults, which were a slight departure from everyday religious practice.

Everything that I talk about in this chapter is what *most* Greeks accepted and did in their daily lives. Just like today, each ancient Greek man or woman had different, individual ideas about the gods, but by and large they carried out similar religious practices and ceremonies.

Dying – In Theory and Practice

Death and dying may sound like a gloomy subject, but the ancient Greeks had some intriguing – and perhaps inspiring – notions about what happened to humans after they passed away. Modern anthropologists often say that you can tell a lot about a society by the way that it deals with death because it proves what people thought was valuable. I think that idea is probably true of ancient Greece.

Venturing into the underworld: The mythological take

The Greeks believed that when people died, their bodies decayed, their souls (or 'shades' – like a kind of ghost version of the person) travelled to Hades (the name of both the god of the dead and the underworld) to exist for eternity.

When 'shades' entered the underworld, they first had to cross the river Styx (or Lethe) on a ferry piloted by the famous ferryman Charon. When people died, their friends or family placed a coin in their mouths so that they were able to pay Charon his fee. If a person died and didn't have the proper funeral rites, he or she would spend eternity unable to cross the river.

While crossing the Styx, the hand of the 'shade' fell into the water and the magical power of the river drained all memories from the body, allowing the deceased individual to be content to exist in the underworld without continually mourning for those they left behind.

Despite the gloomy subject matter, the Greeks were able to poke fun at the dying process. Aristophanes's play *Frogs* is set in the underworld, and Charon appears as a rather comical character.

> *Any more for Lethe, Blazes, Perdition, or the Dogs? Come along now, any more for a nice restful trip to Eternity? No more worries, no more cares, makes a lovely break!*

Other theories about the underworld and the experiences of the dead existed. For example, in *The Odyssey* (see Chapter 20), Odysseus has to travel to the underworld to speak with the prophet Tiresias. The souls that Odysseus meets are deeply unhappy and remember *everything* about their previous lives. Indeed, they spend eternity drifting around in grief and must consume sacrificial blood before they can speak to Odysseus. Yuck!

The ancient Greeks appear to have placed no value judgement on people's lives, and had no equivalents of heaven or hell. Everyone went to Hades regardless of the lives they'd led and stayed there for eternity. The only exceptions were the mythological heroes who were fortunate to have ended up in *Elyisum* (refer to Chapter 20).

Dealing with the dead: Practicalities

Mythology aside, the ancient Greeks had very specific ways of dealing with death. Indeed, the Greeks were obsessed with receiving proper burials because they believed that if bodies didn't receive proper funeral rites from relatives, then the souls of the dead were prevented from travelling to the underworld (see the preceding section 'Venturing into the underworld: The mythological take').

Funerals could be expensive affairs with all kinds of musicians and performers required and many people attending the formal meal, which all the family attended before the burial. As I examine in Chapter 14, the ancient Greeks were really obsessed with the idea of familial and friendship ties, so funerals were big events.

Poorer people had to make do with what was available. They'd still strive to ensure a proper burial, even if they weren't able to afford the attendant functions. After all, a family meal could just involve some wine, cheese, and olives.

Ancient Greece was mainly an *inhumation culture*, which means that bodies are buried, rather than a *cremation culture* in which they're burnt. Most families had a family tomb that they filled with generations of corpses.

Every year the surviving family members gathered at their tomb or grave to honour those who had died, a bit like an annual memorial service. Normally these rites would involve saying prayers and making offerings to the gods.

Often, the tombs included gravestones featuring epitaphs carved in the stone. These words were sometimes in verse form, produced by a poet for hire. One such poet was Simonides (circa 500 BC). Following are two of his best efforts!

> *Drinker, glutton supreme, supreme defamer of men. I, Timokreon of Rhodes, now lie down here.*

> *Someone is glad that I, Theodorus, am dead. Another will be glad when that someone is dead. We are all in arrears to death.*

Worshipping the Gods

Throughout their whole lives, ancient Greeks were continually involved in some kind of religious ceremony or ritual. Social life, business deals, marriage, war, and cultural entertainment all involved ritual practices focused on one or several gods in the pantheon (see Chapter 19).

Rituals were important because they allowed the ancient Greeks to ask the gods for help, approval, or a guarantee. All rituals involved a kind of bargaining: The humans provided the gods with something in exchange for their help. See the later section 'Sacrificing: Giving the gods gifts' for the fascinating details.

Seeing the gods in person: Idols

Many aspects of Greek religion took place inside temples (see Chapter 18). Within each temple was a statue that depicted a specific god. The ancient Greeks believed that the god was actually present inside the temple – or if many temples to a specific deity existed, they believed that the god always visited their temple at some point during the year or at least that they could see what was going on in many temples at once.

The belief that gods were present within the temples meant that the Greeks actually worshipped the statue within the temple – a practice that modern folks would call *idolatry*. (See Chapter 17 for more on the process of creating metal and marble statues.) In contrast, worshippers in a Catholic church for example, aren't honouring a statue but the figure that the statue represents.

As worship, the Greeks made small offerings and prayed to the gods. They sometimes dressed the statue with ribbons known as *stemmata*. The statues must have ended up being quite pretty and well-covered because a large number of people visited the temple on a daily basis.

When to worship

The ancient Greek calendar was full of official religious days and festivals (refer to Chapter 15). The Greeks didn't have a specific holy day but engaged in religious rituals during the many festivals.

This meant that normal worship at the temple took place whenever a person wanted. Individuals could worship alone or as groups and families and a temple priest would always supervise whatever activities they were carrying out. Men, women, and children were all allowed to attend temples but would probably do most of their personal worship in their home.

Having gods in your home

The Greek household (*oikos*) was itself a sacred place with its own rituals and requirements (see Chapter 14). The main protector of the household was

Zeus, known in this instance as *Zeus Herkeios*, or the Guardian. Zeus was also responsible for the concept of *xenia*, the proper treatment of guests (see Chapter 21).

The household itself was sacred to Hestia, goddess of the hearth (see Chapter 19). Every house kept a fire constantly burning in honour of the goddess, and this hearth was the centrepiece of the home. This was the spot where the *oikos* ate all meals and received guests.

The ancient Greeks also chose their own deities who they looked on to protect their houses. People placed images of the selected gods on the gates or doors of houses or somewhere within the home. Gods such as Apollo and Hermes were popular choices.

Sacrificing: Giving the gods gifts

Sacrifices and offerings were the main ways of honouring the gods. A sacrifice was the killing of an animal, whereas an offering was a gift of wine, food, money, or other item. These practices weren't Greek inventions; the tradition went back a long way into the past. The idea behind them was that you gave the gods some of your food – that which kept you alive – and in return the gods would either just continue to look after you or perhaps aid you in some way such as blessing a married couple with children or ensuring a good harvest for a farm.

Sometimes offerings were quite simple – fruits, grain, or special cakes. The more famous sort of sacrifice was livestock or farm animals, such as oxen, bulls, cows, sheep, pigs, goats, or other animals.

Little, everyday sacrifices

Although formal sacrifices and offerings (see the following section 'Big sacrifices') were part of religious life, the ancient Greeks believed that the gods could see everything and would pick up on any slight acknowledgement. Consequently people would make small, almost superstitious offerings throughout the day.

Additionally, the Greeks thought rivers, forests, and other natural phenomena were touched by the gods. By dropping pebbles or very small offerings of food in the river or wherever, people believed they were acknowledging the power and pervasiveness of the gods.

The belief that the gods were everywhere went even further. The Greeks believed that occasionally the gods walked the earth in human form to check on mankind. They also explained the fact that they occasionally blurted out something stupid with the expression, Some god put it in my heart to say'. Try using that explanation next time you say something embarrassing!

Purity is everything

Ritual purification was an essential part of any ancient Greek religious ceremony. This process literally meant washing, and in most cases just washing your hands was enough. The idea of purification probably comes from the fact that most Greeks were farmers (or had originally been farmers), and by washing you were removing the dirt from yourself and putting work aside before worshipping the gods.

Sometimes the purification rituals were extreme (see the sidebar 'The Delphic oracle') and involved a person cleansing themselves of an awful act – like a murderer 'washing the blood from their hands'.

Big sacrifices

At the temple, ancient Greeks cut the throats of the sacrificial animals. (The resulting blood was often presented as an additional offering.) These activities wouldn't take place inside the temple itself but in the grounds around it. The Greeks had two ways of making sacrifices:

- ✔ **Sacrificing some part of the animal, and serving the rest.** Sometimes people roasted the animal, and offered a portion to the gods. They used the remaining meat to make a formal meal for those attending the ceremony. This kind of barbeque-like sacrifice was the most common. In Greek poetry, the gods are often described as enjoying the smell of roasting meat as it drifts up to Olympus.

- ✔ **Completely burning the entire animal.** The total burning of an animal was usually reserved for a specific purpose. Most often people were trying to appease the gods. For example, in a case of murder, ancient Greeks considered the burned animal to count as a 'one-for-one' offering to replace the victim.

So what was the point of sacrifice? The most literal way of understanding the concept is that you were giving a gift to the gods. Animals were expensive, so killing a cow or goat was a significant financial offering. Of course, this also meant a good feed for everybody else involved too!

Pondering and Predicting the Future

Despite the mystically tinged scenes in lots of Greek plays and even more modern-day movies, the Greeks did *not* use prophecies to predict the future. Instead, they turned to the gods and asked for help in the future or advice on what to do in the present.

Divination, or what the Greeks called *mantike*, involved asking the gods questions to try and ensure a happy and prosperous future. The following sections look at these aspects of Greek religion.

Consulting oracles

The ancient Greeks believed that the gods were involved in a person's *fate*, and ensured that what was meant to happen to them did happen. The gods didn't create a person's fate but it was their responsibility to make sure that what was fated to happen actually took place.

One of the most popular ways for an ancient Greek to figure out what to do to follow their fate was to visit an *oracle*, a place where the Greeks believed they could ask someone questions and receive answers from the gods. An oracle was a place, not a person, and could be anywhere where the gods 'touched the world' such as a stream, a bush, or the inner sanctum of a temple.

Talk to the man

Usually, the person at the oracle was a priest, or *hiereus*, who was employed by the shrine or temple. The Greeks didn't think that the priest had any kind of magical powers, just the knowledge and skills required to do the job.

In addition to a priest, the temple or shrine sometimes used the services of a *seer*, or *mantis*, to understand the answers of an oracle. A seer wasn't tied to any religious institution and worked for private hire.

Many Greeks were cynical about the service that seers provided because it was pretty much in the interests of the seer to give a client the answers that they were looking for! In mythology, seers are often presented as figures who can actually see into the future, and who are beloved by the gods and in possession of magical abilities. In everyday Greece, it's unlikely that most people regarded seers in this way.

Yes, no, er . . . maybe!

Consulting an oracle wasn't quite as straightforward as it may sound. Oracles didn't predict the future. Instead, they gave advice on what to do in the present. The Greeks believed that the future was already set out, or *predetermined*. Therefore, they didn't ask to change it, but rather how to interpret what they saw around them to help predict how things may be.

So, for example, a man didn't visit an oracle and ask how many children his prospective wife would have. Instead, he asked for advice on whether he should marry her. If the oracle suggested he should marry, and he did and they subsequently had children, then the oracle developed a reputation for being able to predict the future. Of course, if the same man married the woman and the couple didn't have children, then the ancient Greeks thought the man had misinterpreted the answer!

In general, oracles provided answers that were supportive – telling people what to do to ensure a happy future rather than explaining what that future would be.

Because an oracle's response was sometimes quite problematic, the special skills of a seer were often required to interpret it.

Looking to signs

The Greeks were very superstitious and saw signs and portents in all kinds of everyday activities. The flight of birds (known as *bird lore*), the movement of leaves, and the flow of running water were all used as methods of interpreting the will of the gods. Just as with the pronouncements of oracles, a priest or seer was required to interpret these signs.

Interpreting bird lore was particularly complicated. This inscription from Ephesus in Asia Minor (dated at about 550 BC) is one of the only surviving examples of what certain flight patterns meant – and it isn't exactly straightforward!

> *. . . if the bird flying from left to right disappears from view the omen is favourable; if it raises its left wing, flies away, and disappears the omen is unfavourable; if flying from left to right it disappears on a straight course the omen is unfavourable; but if after raising its right wing, it flies away and disappears the omen is favourable.*

One of the most popular sources of signs was examining the *entrails* (inner organs) of recently sacrificed animals. The condition of these organs, especially the liver, was a method of testing whether the gods supported a course of action. People often made major decisions about war and diplomatic negotiations after examining a sacrifice's entrails.

Taking Oaths: 'I Promise!'

Just as the Greeks used divination and oracles to seek advice about what to do in life, religion was also a big part of any decisions or deals that they made. Decisions often took the form of oaths that the Greeks swore, using the gods as their witnesses.

The Delphic oracle

The most famous ancient Greek oracle of all was the one at Delphi in central Greece (see the Cheat Sheet map). The oracle at Delphi was extremely old and dated back to around the ninth century BC. The oracle was dedicated to Apollo and the centrepiece of the sanctuary was a large temple devoted to him. Both cities and individuals – including virtually every famous figure from ancient Greek history – asked for the Delphic oracle's advice.

Conferring with the Delphic oracle required a complicated process of purification and sacrifice (see the earlier section 'Sacrificing: Giving

the gods gifts'). The whole thing was supervised by the *pythia*, or priestess of the temple. When asked a question, the priestess went into a trance and then babbled incoherent sentences, which arose from her communication with the god Apollo. The answers were famously ambiguous, but the Greeks believed that the gods spoke clearly; any misinterpretations came down to human stupidity!

You can still visit Delphi; it's a beautiful little town and a fabulous site which I describe in Chapter 26.

Swearing of an oath (*horkos*) meant that you were promising to do something, such as paying for goods or marrying somebody. Characters in Greek tragedy often swear oaths, particularly oaths of vengeance where they promise to avenge a wronged or slain relative and this was fairly common practice in ancient Greece too. Additionally, if you didn't do what you promised, you accepted the punishment of the gods.

Given that the Greeks only really started using writing in around 750 BC (see Chapter 1), oaths were also used as a form of verbal contract in business deals. Merchants entered into trade deals and called upon the gods Hermes or Poseidon to be the arbiter.

Having Fun with the Gods: Festivals and Cults

Most Greek cities had highly defined religious calendars based around big public festivals. (See Chapter 15 for the intricacies of the ancient Greek calendar.) Some celebrations were massive and went on for days, and others were held only by a particular town region (*deme*).

Private healthcare: The sanctuary at Epidauros

Asclepius, the god of healing, had one of the most famous places of worship dedicated to him at Epidauros. Greeks visited the shrine and asked for advice on curing their illnesses. Asclepius didn't have any real connection with Epidauros, but the priests there invented one; the site became second only to Delphi (see the sidebar 'The Delphic oracle') in visitor numbers.

Despite its popularity, people didn't expect instant cures from the sanctuary at Epidauros. As at Delphi, all answers from the gods had to be interpreted by the priests, who weren't doctors. What the priests advised usually went against what Hippocratic doctors of the time would have prescribed. Nevertheless, a huge amount of money was spent in asking the priests' advice!

Additionally, smaller religious groups gathered together in the form of *religious cults* that worshipped particular individual divinities. The rules and regulations around these cults were as strict as they were bizarre. See the later section 'Getting cultic: Swimming with pigs and other oddities' for more.

Observing the religious year

I discuss the complex Athenian calendar in Chapter 15, but the typical religious calendar of a city was even more complicated. For example, Athenians gave over 130 days of the year to specific festivals, although many more small festivals and celebrations also took place. Roughly speaking, something related to a festival or celebration probably occurred every other day.

Athenians celebrated about 30 large festivals during the religious year. The month of *Pyanopsion* (September/October) featured an impressive six festivals in honour of Apollo, Theseus, Demeter (twice), and Athene (twice).

Some of these festivals were massive; for example, the big drama festivals like the Country and City Dionysia both went on for several days and took the form of a major public holiday. Visitors came from far and wide to take part in these celebrations.

As I mention in Chapter 16, festivals included all types of activities: dramatic performances, athletic games, singing and dancing competitions, and large amounts of feasting and drinking. The public purse and donations from wealthier citizen paid for these events.

Although religious celebration was the main point of festivals, they weren't sober and restrained events – quite the reverse! All sorts of ribaldry took place with much drinking and carousing. If you want a modern equivalent, try New Year's Eve crossed with the Glastonbury Festival!

Two notable festivals: The Panathenaia and the Thesmophoria

One of the biggest festivals in ancient Athens was the *Panathenaia*, which celebrated the city and its patron goddess Athena (see Chapter 19). The festival was held every year in the month of *Hekatombaion* (June/July) and was effectively a new year celebration. The Athenians made huge processions, and the main one involved the transporting of a robe (*peplos*) for the goddess Athene. The procession is depicted in the frieze of the Parthenon, parts of which are on display in the British Museum.

The *Panathenaia* was a very nationalistic festival and was rooted in the idea of celebrating Athenian supremacy over other Greeks. The Athenians made the celebration even bigger once every four years and called it the Great Panathenaia.

One of the more notorious festivals was the women-only *Thesmophoria*, which was held throughout Greece in the autumn. Men were banned from the festival, which was held in honour of Demeter. Only married women of cities were allowed to attend and they left town and held secret rites away in the countryside. These activities were usually very mysterious and are mocked by Aristophanes in his play *Thesmophoriazousai*, in which the women spend a lot of time drinking. (Okay, there's probably some truth in this!)

The Olympian gods (refer to Chapter 19) each had a sacred day every month as well. Often these holidays included ceremonies that were specific to a particular *deme*.

On lesser religious holidays, things were often simpler. Just one relatively small sacrifice to a specific god may be required.

Getting cultic: Swimming with pigs and other oddities

These days the idea of a religious cult has slightly sinister overtones. The word is currently used to describe unusual groups that shut themselves away from the world. In ancient Greece, however, the idea of a *religious cult* was very aspirational. Joining a cult was a sign of social status because membership was very closely guarded.

All the other festivals and ceremonies that I mention in this chapter were public experiences; everyone could join in, and participation occurred in the gathering areas of town and cities such as the *agora* (see Chapter 18). Cults were different. Although cults may involve a large number of people in a ceremony, the experience of the individual was intended to be quite personal. This was the nearest that ancient Greek religion got to the notion of a spiritual experience.

The Eleusinian Mysteries

By far the most famous cult was the Eleusinian Mysteries. Even now, historians don't know precisely what went on during the cult's festivals. At the time, the secrets of their ritual were closely guarded, with dire penalties for those who broke the rules. Scholars do know that the cult was based around the myth of Persephone and Demeter (see Chapter 13) and involved a process that recreated the journey into Hades. The final ceremony apparently revealed a glimpse of the afterlife to the initiates.

The ritual took place during late summer (probably during *Boedromion*) in the *deme* of Eleusis in Athens. The ritual was open to anybody Greek-speaking, although they had to pay hefty fees to take part. The purification and initiation rituals were very complicated. Every participant had to wash a young pig in the sea and then sacrifice it, and they also had to wear special clothes and fast from certain foods. The whole experience took several days and was regarded by the ancient Greeks as a life-changing one.

The following excerpt comes from one of the so-called 'Homeric Hymns', religious songs in the style of Homer (see Chapter 20). The song deals with Demeter, Persephone, and the mysteries.

> *To all Demeter revealed the conduct of her rites and mysteries . . . dread mysteries which one may not in any way transgress or learn of or utter . . . Happy is he of mortal men who has seen these things. . . .*

Because the spiritual experience of cults was considered to be so extraordinary, the various cults were incredibly closely organised with very strict rules. This inscription from the site of the Spring of the Nymphs at Delos gives a good idea of how respectful people had to be of cult places – in this case a spring.

> *Do not wash anything in the spring, or swim in the spring, or throw into the spring manure or anything else. Penalty: two sacred drachmas.*

Major cults like the Eleusinian Mysteries were open to all but others might be restricted to people in a certain trade or guild (for example, a group of tradesmen like potters or ironmongers). Equally, the nature of the rites might prove prohibitive to some people because of the costs involved. It seems certain that more exclusive and bizarre cults took place amongst the mega-rich but unfortunately historians don't really know anything about them.

Chapter 22

Trying to Figure Everything Out: Greek Philosophy

. . . .

In This Chapter

▶ Pondering existence with the early Greek philosophers

▶ Chatting with Socrates and Plato

▶ Getting scientific with Aristotle and others

. . . .

A t first glance, Greek philosophy can seem quite intimidating. Most books on the subject have front covers with pictures of marble busts of serious, slightly angry looking men with big bushy beards. What's inside these books can seem just as intimidating – but a lot of the time, the ideas, insights, and explanations are actually quite simple.

In this chapter I look at how the very idea of philosophy developed in ancient Greece and share what some of the major figures thought about all manner of topics, including existence, morality, and the nature of the universe. The ancient Greek philosophers are a strange bunch with some weird and outlandish ideas – but they're quite fun too!

Making the Case for Philosophy

In Chapters 19, 20, and 21, I look at the mythical gods and heroes and how the Greek religion dominated virtually all aspects of ancient Greek life. Their religion gave the Greeks a pretty closely defined idea of what their world was like and where it came from – but for some people unanswered questions still existed.

Greek philosophy grew out of the earliest philosophers' desire to explain the world around them, including such major issues as:

> ✔ Where everything came from.
>
> ✔ What the world was made of.
>
> ✔ What happened when you died.

The word used to describe the philosopher's drive is *reason*, a desire to understand and explain things instead of accepting religious or spiritual explanations. And as I discuss in Chapters 19, 20, and 21, ancient Greek religion was full of holes and logical gaps; the gods that filled its ranks were frequently vengeful, childish, and downright unpleasant. Some folks hungered for different – and hopefully better – answers.

Writing in the fifth century BC, the philosopher Xenophanes sums up the problem.

> *Both Homer and Hesiod have attributed all things to the gods, as many as shameful and a reproach amongst mankind, thieving and adultery and deceiving each other.*

So if the gods weren't the answer to everything, then what was? *Philosophy* came into being when some the ancient Greeks tried to work it all out.

The term philosopher means 'lover of wisdom' and comes from the Greek word *sophia* meaning wisdom. Greek philosophers were all men from varied backgrounds. Philosophers like Socrates and Plato were aristocrats and a full-time philosopher would need to be wealthy to be able to spend all day pontificating!

Other people were interested in philosophy too, though, and discussion was very fashionable amongst the educated classes.

Meeting the Early Greek Philosophers

Scholars generally refer to the earliest Greek philosophers as the *pre-Socratics* because they were around before Socrates, the most famous figure in Greek philosophy. See the later section 'Creating the 'New Philosophy' with Socrates' for more on this great Greek.

The pre-Socratics weren't really philosophers in the sense that you might think of a philosopher today. Most of them didn't write books or engage in lectures or teaching. Really, these men just asked questions and looked for answers in the world that they saw about them. They were unhappy with the explanations that mythology provided (see Chapter 19), and looked for alternatives in the natural world and its elements. Truly they were 'lovers of wisdom'.

Although the pre-Socratics didn't really come up with definite answers, they started the process of enquiry, encouraging others to explore different questions and challenge orthodox beliefs.

One of the problems with looking at the pre-Socratic philosophers is that very few sources are available. Some of the earliest philosophers didn't write anything down at all, whereas the books of others are now lost. This dearth of original texts means that modern scholars must rely on later Greek writers (such as Xenophon and Aristotle) who compiled large compendiums of philosophy that include fragments of the early philosophers' work. Happily, enough material is available to get a good idea of their theories.

This section is just a small survey of what I regard as some of the most important pre-Socratic philosophers. Loads of others – including Zeno, Anaxagoras, Melissus, Philolaus, Leucippus, Democritus, and many more – are well worth looking into if you want something interesting to think about! Using the online encyclopedia Wikipedia (at www.wikipedia.co.uk) is a great place to start but if you're looking for a book try *Early Greek Philosophy* edited by Jonathan Barnes and published by Penguin Classics.

Using their eyes: Thales and Anaximander

Two of the earliest notable pre-Socratic philosophers were Thales and Anaximander. They both came from the town of Miletus on the south-western coast of Asia Minor and were active around 580 BC.

Although historians aren't fully certain, Thales's work seems to have come first, and Anaximander appears to have been a pupil or follower of Thales.

It's probably no coincidence that these earliest philosophers came from Miletus because the town received visitors from all over the Mediterranean and the east. The mixture of ideas and theories that must have been present among the population makes the location a natural place for enquiring minds.

Both of these men's investigations were based on looking at the world around them and drawing conclusions from what they saw in nature. Modern scholars call this process *observational philosophy*.

Water, water everywhere

Both Thales and Anaximander were concerned with the idea of the *four key elements*: earth, air, fire, and water. Their idea was that everything in the world was in some way made up of these four things.

Thales's big concern was water. He seems to have looked at the world around him and decided that just as the land he stood on was surrounded by water, the whole of the earth must be too. This notion was in line with the old Greek view that the earth was an island entirely surrounded by water, rather like the yolk in a fried egg (see Chapter 19).

Thales took his speculation further though. He thought that water was the essential element of all things. Humans, plants, and animals all need water to survive; therefore, according to Thales, water was the essential stuff of life and what everything was made from. The Greeks referred to this concept as the *arche* meaning 'first principle' or 'beginning'.

Thales also came up with interesting theories about other things, among them the idea that a magnet must have a soul. He based this idea on the fact that a magnet can make things move; therefore, it must have intelligence and, accordingly, a soul.

Getting cosmic

As a pupil or follower of Thales, Anaximander went on to investigate further and and more widely than Thales. Anaximander was alleged to have been one of the first people to draw a map of the inhabited world and to come up with a theory as to how the universe and the heavens were formed. This subject was known as *cosmology*, and many argue that Anaximander invented it.

The cosmology that Anaximander came up with is a bit trippy and mad! It involves all four key elements working together to produce large flat discs (of which the earth is one) that make up the universe. All natural things like humans, animals, and the weather are created when the elements stop working together and separate.

Thales and Anaximander were interesting, if misguided. Still, they were celebrated by subsequent ancient Greeks for being the two men who first thought differently and encouraged other people to theorise about big important questions. You may say that their biggest discovery was the process of philosophy itself.

Pondering existence: Parmenides, Heraclitus, Pythagoras, and others

After Thales and Anaximander opened the philosophical floodgates, many other people began to ask difficult questions about the world around them.

Some of the later pre-Socratics took huge steps forward by trying to ask questions about the nature of existence itself. What did it mean to live and die; to exist and then to stop existing?

A bit of a show-off

One of the first philosophers to ask about existence itself in detail was Parmenides, who came from Elea, a Greek town in southern Italy. Like many of the other pre-Socratics, precise birth and death dates aren't available, but he was alive and probably visited Athens in about 450 BC.

Parmenides's big concern was to answer the question of how something comes into existence and then later ceases to be. He discussed this question in a long poem called the 'Way of Truth', which seems a little like showing off:

> *How, whence, did it grow? That it came from what is not I shall not allow you to say or think – for it is not sayable or thinkable that it is not. And what need would have impelled it, later or earlier, to grow – if it began from nothing?*

In the end Parmenides decided that everything exists and that anything that you can imagine comes into existence after you imagine it. So, for example, while you're reading this book, if you imagine me, the author, riding a giant dragon, then that dragon exists because you imagined it. Blimey! A handy trick, indeed!

Further to this notion, Parmenides believed that everything that exists always has done and always will do in some form or other. This theory was known to the Greeks as *the Immutable One*.

Constant change

Across the other side of the Mediterranean in Ephesus was another philosopher called Heraclitus (circa 525–475 BC). His theory about existence was very different to Parmenides. In fact, it was the absolute opposite.

Heraclitus's major theory was that everything is in a constant state of change, or *flux*. Everything needs to move or change in order to progress and grow. Heraclitus's view was also the opposite of Anaximander's idea that the four elements had to be in order for the universe to work (see the preceding section 'Using their eyes: Thales and Anaximander').

A great example of Heraclitus's state of change theory is that, if you put your foot in a river, by the time you take it out again the water has flowed over it and the river has changed. If you put your foot in again, the river is no longer the river that you put your foot into originally. The constantly changing experience of a river is, in essence, what Heraclitus thought about the whole nature of existence.

Reincarnation: 'I think I've been here before'

Parmenides and Heraclitus tackled the question of existence and came up with some answers. In both cases, they were really motivated by a desire to explain what happened before birth and after death.

Other pre-Socratic philosophers looked at this question from another perspective. If what Parmenides said was true about all matter always existing now and in the future, then what happened to the soul, or *psyche*, after the body died? One idea that was very fashionable was the idea of reincarnation.

Reincarnation was not a purely Greek idea, having first been discussed in places as far away as Egypt and Mesopotamia. Still, several pre-Socratic philosophers promoted this concept. This quote from Empedocles (circa 450 BC) sums up reincarnation nicely.

> *For already I have been born as a boy and a girl and a bush and a bird and a dumb fish leaping out of the sea.*

The man who popularised the notion of reincarnation was Pythagoras, probably the most famous of all the pre-Socratic philosophers and a hugely controversial figure. Active in the sixth century BC, Pythagoras originally came from Samos but spent a large part of his life in southern Italy. He was also rumoured to have magically appeared in many other cities in both southern Italy and Greece.

Pythagoras is credited with a huge number of discoveries and theories, including a particularly famous geometric principle (see the nearby sidebar 'The Pythagorean Theorem: Maths and stuff'). However, because he wrote nothing down, historians know very little about him. Scholars have pieced together the following:

✔ Pythagoras's big theory was based around the idea of *metempsychosis*, which means the movement of the soul between physical bodies, a particular kind of reincarnation. One story suggests that Pythagoras stopped a man beating a puppy because he recognised the dog as one of his old friends by its bark!

✔ Pythagoras was famed for his wide knowledge, and some people attributed him with magical powers. He was rumoured to have had a thigh made of gold and to have killed a poisonous snake by biting it first.

Whatever the actualities behind these stories, Pythagoras built up a huge following. His followers became a kind of cult and closely guarded the details of their lifestyle. They built their lives around his teaching, on principles based on music, harmony, and a very proscriptive diet – such as eating beans to keep you regular! These individuals continued to work on Pythagoras's principles long after his death (or reincarnation?).

Perhaps Pythagoras's biggest achievement was to boost the interest in philosophy in those that followed him.

Jumping into the flames

One of Pythagoras's most famous followers was Empedocles (circa 490–460 BC). Indeed, Empedocles's writings preserved many of Pythagoras's ideas.

The Pythagorean Theorem: Maths and stuff

You're probably familiar with Pythagoras because you were taught his famous *theorem* at school:

> *The square on the hypotenuse is equal to the sum of the squares on the other two sides.*

Many of the pre-Socratics (as well as later philosophers) were intensely interested in mathematics and used it to work out many of their theories. The study of mathematics and particularly geometry was a very important concern in ancient Greece, and the work of people such as Euclid was responsible for real discoveries.

I don't delve into ancient Greek mathematics in this chapter because I think philosophy is very different from maths. What's interesting to me are the tremendous leaps of imagination that these various philosophers took in thinking about the world and nature of existence. Another reason is that I'm rubbish at maths!

Like Parmenides (see the preceding section 'A bit of a show-off'), Empedocles wrote in verse form. His long poem called *The Purifications* was one of the first attempts to align philosophy and Greek religion. In it, he introduced an element of moral philosophy that was very important to later thinkers (see the following section 'Creating the 'New Philosophy' with Socrates').

Empedocles was convinced of the idea of metempsychosis (see the preceding 'Reincarnation: 'I think I've been here before'); particularly that the soul was immortal (and thus like a god). According to a long-held tradition, Empedocles set out to prove this idea by throwing himself into the volcano of Mount Etna in Sicily, telling his followers that he would return in another form. As far as I know, the world is still waiting for his reappearance!

Creating the 'New Philosophy' with Socrates

Socrates is one of the most famous of the ancient Greeks, partly because of his terrible execution by Athens in 399 BC (see Chapter 9), but mostly because he was responsible for creating the new kind of philosophy that was developed in Athens in the fifth century BC.

Like Pythagoras (see the preceding section 'Reincarnation: 'I think I've been here before'), Socrates never wrote anything down. Modern readers are reliant on his followers (mostly Plato and Xenophon) for what survives about Socrates's philosophy today.

Socrates's major interest was different from that of the pre-Socratics. He wasn't really interested in cosmology and questions of reincarnation. Instead, he was far more concerned with why people acted the way they did. His theory was that people should always try to do well and do the right thing. This stance is why he's credited with being the person who invented *moral philosophy*.

Talking with Socrates: Socratic dialogue

In addition to his focus on moral philosophy, Socrates's method of enquiry was also quite different. The process basically involved asking questions of people and challenging their assumptions. Socrates always did this questioning in the spirit of finding out an answer, because he didn't think he knew everything. Indeed, he's famously attributed for saying, *'All that I know is that I know nothing.'*

These conversations between Socrates and his educated friends – *Socratic dialogues* – began with Socrates asking a question of the person who he was talking to and then interrogating (and eventually overturning) that person's answer.

Usually, the question was about some kind of moral quality such as bravery or friendship, although Socrates seemingly discussed absolutely everything.

In this dialogue called *Charmides* (recorded by Plato), Socrates talks about the issue of keeping to doing one's own job and whether doing so shows self-control. Have a look at the way the conversation goes – the process of the discussion is more important than the subject.

> *'Well then,' I [Socrates] said, 'do you think a state would be well run by a law like this, which commands each person to weave his own coat and wash it, and make his own sandals and oil-flask and scraper and everything else on the same principle of each person keeping his hands off what is not his own, and working at and doing his own job?'*
>
> *'No, I don't,' he replied.*
>
> *'Nevertheless,' I said, 'a state run on the principle of self-control would be run well.'*
>
> *'Certainly,' he said.*
>
> *'Then,' I said, 'self-control would not be doing one's own job when it's of that sort and done in that way.'*

This is a typical piece of Socratic dialogue. Socrates asks an opinion and then fleshes it out with examples, each of which chip away at the original opinion until the idea is shown to be worthless or affirmed in some way. The whole conversation is presented very nicely and he isn't antagonistic, but if you saw Socrates in the street, you'd probably cross the road to avoid him!

Getting better at being good

Many of Socrates's dialogues argue about moral qualities: courage, self-control, reason, knowledge, and so on. These are all qualities that you can improve by practice. Socrates argues that by getting a better understanding of what bravery is, you can act in a braver fashion. It's an interesting point of view.

It's difficult to know what Socrates actually believed himself. All the outcomes of the dialogues are exactly that – the conclusion of a conversation. Scholars and modern readers can't accept the resolution of Socratic dialogues as being Socrates's beliefs. The only real belief that becomes consistent is a true desire for knowledge and to find answers. Like the pre-Socratics before him, Socrates was a true 'lover of wisdom'.

Eventually, asking too many questions made Socrates unpopular and led to his death (see Chapter 9). He died a martyr and was responsible for fundamentally changing ancient Greece's – and indeed the world's – ideas of philosophy.

Selling philosophy: The sophists

Socrates also influenced the development of the sophists. *Sophists* were essentially philosophers for hire, although many of them had no real interest in philosophy.

Sophists took the principles of Socratic dialogue (for instance, disproving an idea) and turned them to profit. They sold their services to people who were about to go to court and needed coaching in how to represent themselves. Some people alleged that sophists had no interest in the truth, merely in winning arguments.

Some sophists also provided training in speaking and argument to the sons of rich men who wanted to enter politics. These skills were tremendously useful in the *boule* and elsewhere to gain the votes of the *demos*.

Unfortunately, all the surviving sources on sophists are very biased. People like Plato (see the following section 'Leaving Philosophy to the Professionals: Plato') wrote about the sophists but hated them for what they did with Socrates's form of philosophy. Still, some ancient Greeks must have used the services of sophists for truly philosophical purposes.

One particularly big piece of anti-sophist and anti-philosophy propaganda is Aristophanes's play *The Clouds*. In it, Socrates is portrayed as running a 'School for Sophists' in which he teaches young men not to believe in the gods. None of this was true! Socrates was no sophist and he also never ran a school. Then again, Aristophanes never let the truth get in the way of a good joke!

Leaving Philosophy to the Professionals: Plato

After Socrates died in 399 BC, Greek philosophy went from strength to strength. The next great figure was Plato (circa 428–347 BC).

Historians know very little about Plato's life, and many of the facts about him are highly disputed. However, scholars agree that:

- Plato was originally a follower of Socrates.
- After Socrates's death, Plato left Athens and travelled around the Mediterranean, returning when he was about 40 and founding the famous school of philosophy known as the Academy.
- Plato's Academy flourished for the best part of a thousand years until it was finally closed by the Byzantine emperor Justinian in AD 529.

Aside from establishing the Academy, another reason that Plato became so famous was the huge number of philosophical works that he wrote and published, many of which still survive. Nearly all of them are written in dialogue form with Socrates as the main character. They explore a wide range of subjects, although Plato's favourite themes were justice, *epistemology* (the theory of knowledge), and theories about art.

Living in an ideal world: The Republic

Probably Plato's most famous work was *The Republic*, a very long dialogue based around the idea of creating an ideal state. The dialogue starts with a discussion about the true nature of justice. In Greek the word for justice is *dike* and it has a rather wider meaning; something along the lines of rightness or correctness is one version. To try to define what justice actually is , Socrates sets out what he sees as a potential ideal society.

The model he comes up with is one with a very regulated class system. People are born into the system and do jobs according to their classes. A group known as the *Philosopher Rulers* govern the state, because only they possess the wisdom and self-control to make objective decisions for the good of the whole community.

This model was a fairly controversial set of ideas because it rejected the democratic system that Athens had at the time in favour of rule by the few – an *oligarchy* (see Chapter 4).

But why did Plato only trust the rule of philosophers?

Exploring the Theory of the Forms

The main reason Plato advocated a group of Philosopher Rulers comes from his big theory of existence known as *the Theory of the Forms*. In this theory Plato argues that everything you see around you isn't actually the real world but only a shadowy copy of it. *The Forms* are the one true version of everything. Only a philosopher is able to comprehend and understand the Forms, so only a philosopher is fit to make decisions for a whole city or state.

Plato illustrates his Theory of the Forms in *The Republic* by using the simile of the cave. He describes a group of people held in a cave who see only the shadows made by reflections on a wall; this is their whole world. These reflections are of real life going on outside the cave. Eventually, a few break free and go outside into the light while the rest remain in the cave. Those who go outside are the philosophers searching for truth. The rest are inside, still watching the shadows and believing them to be real.

If this all sounds a bit like *The Matrix* film trilogy where the character of Neo suddenly becomes aware that his whole life has been a fabrication and another, 'real' world exists, you're right. Fortunately, not even Plato is as complicated as *The Matrix* movies!

Plato was so keen on philosophers because he regarded them as the only people who were totally objective and focused on discovering the truth. Thus, only philosophers were able to make decisions that weren't corrupted by their own vice or prejudice. This quote from *The Republic* sums up the idea:

> *The society we have described can never grow into a reality or see the light of day, and there will be no end to the troubles of states, or indeed my dear Glaucon, of humanity itself, till philosophers become kings in this world, or till those we now call kings and rulers really and truly become philosophers. . . .*

At least Plato was true to his word. His whole life was spent searching for the truth and helping teach others to do so. Later in his life he spent some time in Sicily and when he died he was buried in his academy.

Meeting the Man Who Knew Everything: Aristotle

One of the most famous graduates from Plato's Academy was Aristotle (384–322 BC), the final great figure in Greek philosophy. (Aristotle also pops up briefly in Chapter 10, working as tutor to Alexander the Great.)

Aristotle originally came from Stageira in the north of Greece. Although he spent a great deal of his life in Athens, he was never granted citizen status and lived there as a *metoikos* or resident alien (see Chapter 14). He established his own school – known as the *Lyceum* – outside the city of Athens.

Thinking scientifically

Two things made Aristotle very different from the other philosophers that came before him:

- ✔ Aristotle was much more interested in knowledge gained by the five senses than by intellectual reason.

- ✔ Aristotle was interested in absolutely everything – all areas of human endeavour including politics, botany, medicine, ethical philosophy, literary criticism, and more.

In many ways, Aristotle's method was like a combination of the pre-Socratics (see the earlier section 'Meeting the Early Greek Philosophers') and the philosophers who followed. Whatever the topic, Aristotle took the same method of scientific enquiry. He became known as an *empiricist* (meaning someone having an interest in studying all aspects of human endeavour), and his methods formed the basis of scientific study that followed for centuries.

Checking out some of Aristotle's greatest hits

The sheer volume of work that Aristotle produced in his lifetime is difficult to calculate. His major works include:

- ✔ **Physics**: On nature, life, and how the mind works.
- ✔ **Metaphysics**: On logic and reason.
- ✔ **Ethics**: On ethical dilemmas and doing the right thing.
- ✔ **Politics**: A survey of all political systems and their problems.
- ✔ **Poetics**: On plays on poetry and their themes (see Chapter 16).

Aristotle also wrote books on plant and animal life, medicine, the true nature of the soul, and rhetoric. Talk about a busy guy!

Venturing into Aristotle's Ethics

With so many different books by Aristotle, choosing just one is difficult. That said, *Ethics* is a really good introduction to Aristotle's style of enquiry. Like Socrates, Aristotle believed that virtues are skills that you can improve with practice; so if you make a constant effort to be generous to others, eventually you do it without thinking, as a matter of course.

Generally speaking, Aristotle decided that good behaviour takes place when you avoid extremes and exercise moderation. Take this example of the dangers of being either vulgar or, at the other end of the scale, boorish and sour.

Those who go too far in being funny are regarded as buffoons and vulgar persons who exert themselves to be funny at all costs and who are set upon raising a laugh than upon decency of expression and consideration for their victim's feelings. Those who both refuse to say anything funny themselves and take exception to the jokes of other people are regarded as boorish and sour.

In the end Aristotle decides that the best course is to take the middle path, exhibit good taste, and be 'nimble-witted'. He comes to similar conclusions with almost all ethical issues. Later writers refer to this idea as *the Doctrine of the Golden Mean* ('mean' meaning average, or the middle path), although Aristotle never called it that.

Moving On: Hellenistic Science and Beyond

One of the impacts of both Aristotle and the conquests of Alexander the Great (see Chapter 11) was a huge upsurge of interest in the sciences during the Hellenistic period. The rich kings who succeeded Alexander spent huge amounts of money on scientific development and sponsoring the foundation of academies and libraries.

- ✔ **Geometry and mathematics** were areas of interest to such notable men as Euclid (325–265 BC) and Archimedes (circa 287–212 BC; see Chapter 24). Some principles that the two men defined last until this day.

- ✔ **Astronomy** was another area of interest, particularly the study of the position of the earth in relation to the stars. The father of astronomy was Hipparchus (circa 190–120 BC), who constructed the first celestial globe, a model of the universe as he understood it.

The discoveries of these scientists and others were very influential. Although much of their work was lost during the medieval period, Renaissance scientists like Galileo rediscovered and expanded upon significant portions.

And Greek philosophy didn't stop with Aristotle – far from it. During the Hellenistic and early Roman periods, philosophy expanded and definite schools emerged – in particular, a rivalry developed between the *Epicureans* and *Stoics*. Throughout the Mediterranean, figures of learning tended to classify themselves into one of these two groups, despite the fact that they believed in very similar things. But that's a story to check out in *The Romans For Dummies* by Guy de la Bedoyere (Wiley).

Part V
The Part of Tens

The 5th Wave   By Rich Tennant

"I'm just saying, if we're able to make all these advancements in engineering, architecture, and the sciences, you'd think someone would find a way of putting pockets in a tunic."

In this part . . .

The rest of this book will have hopefully whetted your appetite for all things Greek. Here are four brief chapters giving you an idea of what Greek stuff to look at next – places to go, books to read, inventions to find out about, and slightly dodgy characters who are probably worth a second look. Enjoy!

Chapter 23

Ten Great Greek Inventions

*T*hroughout Parts I to IV, I mention all sorts of things that the ancient Greeks were the first to come up with, discover, or bring into being. In this chapter I pick out ten of the best! Subsequent generations definitely owe the Greeks a big thank you for the following.

Archimedes's Inventions

Archimedes himself wasn't an invention – but he was an incredibly prolific inventor, in addition to being a mathematician, physicist, and astronomer.

He was born in Syracuse on the island of Sicily in 287 BC and spent most of his life there. A huge number of inventions are attributed to him. Many of them are military-based and were used by the Sicilians to fight naval battles against the invading Romans. Specifically, Archimedes invented:

✔ A fearsome claw that attackers used to fix their ships onto that of their opponents. (See Chapter 5 for more on ancient Greek naval techniques.) It really worked and helped the Syracusans fight the Romans.

✔ The *Archimedes screw*, a device that was used for raising water from a low-lying source to higher ground; Archimedes screws are still found in irrigation systems today. According to the old story, Archimedes got the idea for this invention in the bath and shouted 'Eureka!' meaning 'I have discovered it!'

Much of the rest of his life was spent on mathematical calculations, particularly developing ideas about spheres and cylinders. He died in Syracuse when the Romans finally conquered and sacked the city in 211 BC. He was buried in a tomb designed according to his own principle (that a sphere has two-thirds the volume and surface area of the circumscribing cylinder – phew!). What a man.

The Railway

Yes, it's true. The ancient Greeks did have a railway – of sorts.

The first version was just a rutway with tracks dug in the ground to move heavy carts more easily, but in 600 BC a man called Einander of Corinth developed a trackway paved with hard limestone. It was used to haul ships across the Isthmus of Corinth, allowing people to avoid the long journey by boat around southern Greece when travelling from the west coast to the Aegean. The railway doesn't exist any more and ships use the Corinthian canal instead.

Modern historians have classified this trackway as a railway, although it wasn't used for public transport. Just as well because no Greek came up with a solution to the problem of leaves on the line.

The Steam Engine

Crazy as it may seem, the Greeks came very close to creating a working steam engine! The man behind this enterprise was the aptly-named Hero of Alexandria. He was born in AD 10 when Egypt was under the control of the Roman Empire. Yes, he is a little out of period of ancient Greece covered in this book, but I'm going to include him anyway!

The device that Hero came up with was a ball fixed onto a pivot over a cauldron. When the contents of the cauldron boiled, the ball span – creating a steam engine. Unfortunately nobody really knew what to do with Hero's invention.

Vending Machines

This invention comes from Hero of Alexandria as well. He invented a machine that responded to having a coin dropped into the slot at the top. The wooden device dispensed holy water into a cup placed underneath by those visiting a shrine. If only he had invented the Mars Bar as well – he could've made a mint!

Writing

Around 750 BC the Greeks began to use a system of notation that eventually developed into the Greek alphabet and from then on into the first European language. See Chapter 1 for more details on this life-changing invention.

Writing varied hugely from place to place within the ancient Greek world, but by the fifth century it had developed into a common language. It's probably fair to say that I wouldn't be writing this book in English if the Greeks hadn't invented Greek. Well done them!

History

Okay, so the ancient Greeks didn't invent history – it's all around, happening all by itself, after all. But they did invent writing about history.

Before the Greeks had their language, events and history were passed down verbally, but eventually history began to be written down too.

Herodotus's *Histories* (written 431 BC–425 BC) were the first attempt to write down the history of Greece and are an entertaining if unreliable read. History writing really began with Thucydides's *History of the Peloponnesian War* (written in 431 BC), a lengthy historical text about a big event (see Chapter 8), written by someone who was actually there.

Comedy

Like history, comedy has always been around, but the ancient Greeks were the first to turn it into a genre.

The comic plays of writers like Aristophanes (circa 456 BC–386 BC), took contemporary political situations and mixed them with farce and fantasy to produce satirical comedies that influenced subsequent sources of laughter in everything from *commedia del arte*, pantomime, modern satire, and even late-night sketch comedy. Aristophanes's greatest plays are still translated and performed today.

Later comic writers like Menander (circa 342–291 BC) removed the satirical elements and produced a kind of comedy of manners that influenced later playwrights from Shakespeare to Noel Coward.

Money

Coinage was a very definite ancient Greek invention. The Greek towns in Asia Minor began to use formal coinage in about 600 BC, replacing the old system of bartering with goods. Initially only a few varieties of coin were used but by the Hellenistic period (from 350 BC onwards), systems of paper money transfer had been developed.

The Romans eventually took over all these monetary systems in order to exact punitive taxes on their colonies. So the Greeks are in part responsible for your council tax bill. Thanks very much!

Musical Notation

Music was a very important part of Greek life, accompanying all religious ceremonies, celebrations, and dramatic performances. The theory behind music was of great interest to both philosophers and mathematicians, in particular Aristoxenus of Tarrentum (circa 350 BC).

In around 300 BC the Greeks developed a system of melodic notation that enabled music to be written down. Two different systems were developed: one for vocal music and one for instrumental, using signs developed from letters of the alphabet. This system didn't really record melody and rhythm in the way that the modern system of eight tones in an octave does, but for the simpler music of ancient Greece it worked perfectly well and became standard throughout the ancient world up until around the fifth century AD.

About 50 scores have survived from the ancient world from various inscriptions and manuscripts. When performed, it's a spare delicate music played on only a few instruments and is quite reminiscent of traditional Japanese music.

Democracy

Whether the democracy developed in Athens was the first in the world is a controversial issue. Many scholars have come up with other examples of representative government that took place earlier in areas as far away as Africa.

In a sense the exact chronology of democracy doesn't matter. The Athenian Greeks didn't know about other regions' governmental practices but still decided through a lengthy process of social change that the whole city should vote on issues of government via a participative democracy.

Athenian democracy wasn't a perfect system (see Chapter 7). It denied any role to women, for example, but it was the first European democracy and one that many others have claimed as an inspiration.

Chapter 24

Ten Things to Read Next

*A*t this point, maybe you've nearly finished reading this book – if so, congratulations and thanks for sticking with it! Or maybe you're just starting to get to know the ancient Greeks. Wherever you are in the process, one of best ways to explore the ancient Greeks is through their own words, in the plays, poetry, and prose they left behind.

So if you've enjoyed *The Ancient Greeks For Dummies* or you want to gain a better understanding of some the topics, events, or people I cover in this book, here are ten things to try next.

When reading ancient Greek literature the translation is vitally important! Many translations are available of all the works that I mention in this book but I always recommend choosing the Penguin Classics. A real attempt has been made to capture the spirit of the originals in the translations. Also, all the editions have excellent introductory notes and many have indexes.

If possible, get an audio version of Homer's works. Both *The Iliad* and *The Odyssey* were originally composed to be listened to. Only when you hear the words spoken do you get a real sense of the poetic devices and tremendous powers of plotting and construction that the poet had.

The Iliad: Homer

As I state in Chapter 20, *The Iliad* is the most important work of Greek literature. The ancient Greeks looked to Homer for guidance on the widest possible range of issues – everything from fighting and shipbuilding to hospitality and honourable behaviour.

Although a relatively simple story, the poem is a treasury of mythological characters and human and deity relationships. The central figure of Achilles, the greatest Greek warrior, is powerfully dramatic as he sits out the fighting and struggles with his own pride and anger before personal tragedy brings him back into the war.

Interesting Fact: Book Two 'The Catalogue of Ships' is often a difficult read for modern readers, but the ancient Greeks regarded it as the most impressive of the entire poem for its tremendous listing of warriors and their families.

The Odyssey: Homer

The Odyssey is the companion piece to *The Iliad*. You can read one or the other individually, but reading them together brings Homer's genius to light.

In many ways, *The Odyssey* is a better story than *The Iliad* and reads much more like a modern novel. The poem is full of great stories and characters and is very evocative of a mythological time when almost anything could happen. And the dramatic conclusion, when Odysseus returns home to Ithaca to deal with the arrogant suitors that have taken over his home and are making a play for his wife Penelope, must be read to be believed.

Interesting Fact: Many modern critics have suggested that the last two books of *The Odyssey* aren't by Homer! They're slightly different in tone compared to the preceding 22 books and deal with the fallout after Odysseus has retuned and defeated the suitors. I'm not sure myself – have a read and see what you think.

Oedipus the King: Sophocles

If you read just one Greek tragedy, try *Oedipus the King*. In many ways the play is the archetypal story of how a man who is too proud is brought down by the gods. Important questions about destiny, fate, and the role of the gods are examined in detail – and aside from this the play is brilliantly constructed.

Oedipus the King is also most likely to give you the full experience of the ancient Greek dramatic concepts of *pathos* (suffering) and *mathos* (gaining understanding) because you already know the ending and therefore can give your full concentration to the process.

Interesting Fact: Aristotle regarded this play as the most perfect of all tragedies and used it to scientifically analyse the process of writing tragedy in his *Poetics*. See if you agree with him!

The Histories: Herodotus

Herodotus's *Histories* are a fantastic read. Setting out to explain the reasons why the Persian Wars started, Herodotus ends up writing a history of Greece up until his own times. (See Chapter 6 for my take on the Persian Wars.)

Histories isn't historical writing as scholars regard it today. Herodotus's text mixes history, mythology, and hearsay – sometimes even in the same paragraph! But Herodotus was incredibly widely travelled and he's sometimes the only surviving source for some of the places and events he mentions. *Histories* is a perfect holiday read because you can pick up it up, dip into it, and find some interesting place or story.

Interesting Fact: Early in his life, Herodotus was involved in an attempted revolt in his home city of Halicarnassus. The revolt failed, Herodotus went into exile, and began his travelling. Politics' loss was history's gain!

Parallel Lives: Plutarch

Plutarch (circa AD 50–120) was a Greek who lived in the Roman Empire and wrote about the lives of great men from history. He wasn't a historian in the conventional sense but more like a modern biographer whose interest was in the characters of the individuals he wrote about.

Plutarch's life of Alexander the Great is a particularly good place to start, but he also wrote lives of many other Greek figures such as Alcibiades, Pericles, and Demosthenes.

Interesting Fact: All of Plutarch's biographies were originally published as *Parallel Lives*, in which the biographies of two men are contrasted with each other, such as the lives of Theseus (Athens's mythological founder; see Chapter 20) and Romulus (Rome's equally mythological founder).

Early Socratic Dialogues: Plato

This recommendation isn't actually a book by Plato but a collection of some of the earliest of Socrates's dialogues that he wrote down. It's an interesting and accessible collection of discussions that give a really good idea of the way that Socrates's method of discussion worked (see Chapter 22).

Topics include the difference between love and friendship and the true nature of aesthetic beauty. These dialogues are a really good introduction to Plato's style and a great place to start if you want to eventually read his book *The Republic*.

Interesting Fact: All the dialogues are named after the friends of Socrates who took part in the discussions such as Lysis, Charmides, and Euthydemus. These folk don't get much of a word in edgeways after Socrates gets going, so it's nice that they get their tribute in the title at least!

The Ethics: Aristotle

The Ethics is by far the best introduction to Aristotle's style of philosophy and scientific method. Aristotle sets out to establish what makes some people good and others bad and then tries to argue why happiness through doing good should be everybody's goal. It's a cheerful argument, well illustrated by a number of sections that try to define qualities such as modesty, prudence, and generosity.

Interesting Fact: The book includes a table of virtues and vices that also incorporates a suggestion of the middle course between them that readers should take. You have no excuse for bad behaviour after you read this classic!

Frogs: Aristophanes

Frogs was produced in 405 BC and won first prize in the Lenaea comedy festival (see Chapter 16). The comedy is typical good, riotous fun from Aristophanes. The plot involves the god Dionysus travelling to the underworld to bring back the dramatist Euripides. On the way Charon the Ferryman, a greedy Heracles, and the other great Greek dramatist Aeschylus all make comic cameos. Nearly 2,500 years old and still very funny, *Frogs* is a great introduction to Aristophanes and Greek comedy. Even better, try to see a production. The most recent was a revival of Stephen Sondheim's version that played on Broadway in 2004.

Interesting Fact: The play gets its title from the chorus of frogs that live in the swamps around the entrance to Hades. Their rhythmic songs are one of the best examples of how musical the comedies were when they were originally performed.

The Idylls: Theocritus

Theocritus (circa 300 BC) was born in Syracuse but spent most of his life in Alexandria. Not a great deal of his work survives, but *The Idylls* are beautiful, sensitive examples of a very different type of poetry to the epic poetry of Homer. Set in the Greek countryside and the world of shepherds and goatherds, *The Idylls* are said to be the first examples of the *bucolic* genre. Very lovelorn and quite melancholic, the poems show a personal and sensitive side of Greek literature. (The beautiful poems of Sappho are worth looking at for the same reason.)

Interesting Fact: The selection of poems also contains a comic dialogue between Alexandrian women making their way to a festival. Very different from the rest of Theocritus's surviving work, this conversation is quite amusing and a nice snapshot of life in ancient Alexandria.

The Romans For Dummies: Guy de la Bedoyere

The companion book to *The Ancient Greeks For Dummies*, this book introduces you to ancient Rome and its incredible story. Although the Romans may seem like the bad guys who brought glorious ancient Greece to an end, they were actually responsible for adopting and then preserving a huge amount of Greek culture. The story of Rome is amazing – take a look!

Interesting Fact: During the second century AD, it became very fashionable among the Roman aristocracy to develop a big cultural interest in all things Greek. This was partly motivated by the emperor Hadrian. The name given to such an individual in Latin was a *philhellenicus*.

Chapter 25

Ten Dodgy Ancient Greek Characters

*T*he history of ancient Greece is full of interesting characters – individuals who got into some sticky situations or rose to great heights but whose motivations were sometimes dubious.

This chapter is a short list of people about whom you may be interested in finding out more sordid details!

Alcibiades (451–403 BC)

The ultimate dodgy character, Alcibiades was an Athenian general and politician who changed sides so often that keeping up with his allegiances is difficult.

Alcibiades was a young playboy about town who everyone thought was destined for great things. He was the main mover behind the idea of the disastrous Sicilian Expedition during the Peloponnesian War (refer to Chapter 8). He never made it to Sicily because a message reached him that he was being charged in his absence with blasphemy, including drunkenly mocking the secrets of the Eleusinian Mysteries (decribed in Chapter 22). These charges were probably true; throughout his life, he lived to excess.

Hearing of these charges, Alcibiades literally jumped ship, escaping in a fishing boat, and went to Sparta and worked as an advisor to his former enemy. But the Spartans soon distrusted him too, and Alcibiades ended up at the court of a Persian *satrap*. Eventually he was welcomed back to Athens and fought successfully for the Athenians for a number of years. After a defeat in 406 BC, he retired to live in Thrace. His was not a peaceful old age – the new regime in Athens assassinated him two years later.

Alcibiades was a great man who arguably dominated his era, but you wouldn't lend him a fiver!

Odysseus

Yes, that's right – I'm including Odysseus, the great Greek hero of Homer's *The Iliad* and *The Odyssey*, on my list of dodgy characters!

Homer calls Odysseus the 'master of cunning stratagems' and throughout the myths about him, Odysseus continually lies, cheats, and cons. It was Odysseus who came up with the plan of the Trojan horse, as well as many other cunning schemes. On several occasions in *The Odyssey,* he adopts disguises given to him by the goddess Athena to work some kind of con.

The ancient Greeks recognised these traits in Odysseus's character, and later portrayals of him emphasise his untrustworthiness. In Sophocles's play *Philoctetes*, for example, Odysseus is shown to be cunning and amoral in his treatment of a wounded archer when he tries to steal the archer's bow.

Odysseus was also famed as a teller of tales. Undoubtedly they weren't all true!

Pausanias (died circa 450 BC)

Pausanias was a Spartan general who earned a possibly undeserved reputation for treachery. He was the commander of all the Greek forces at the battle of Plataea in 479 BC and claimed sole credit for the victory – an act that didn't exactly make him popular. The following year he commanded a Greek fleet that captured the Persian city of Byzantium but was afterwards accused of treachery. Back in Sparta he was acquitted and unwisely headed back to Byzantium where he was again accused of treachery! Put on trial several further times, Pausanias was eventually convicted of trying to organise a *helot* (slave worker) uprising in Sparta. He fled to avoid execution, eventually starving to death in the Spartan acropolis.

Strangely, several years later the Spartans voted that Pausanias be made a hero and a cult was established in his honour. Two statues to him were eventually constructed. So was he a traitor – or just the victim of powerful enemies? It's unlikely that we'll ever know.

Demetrius (336–283 BC)

Demetrius was the son of Alexander the Great's successor Antigonus I, king in Phrygia in Asia Minor. Demetrius grew up a playboy in the Alcibiades style with a taste for military adventure.

Demetrius spent many years campaigning like a pirate around the Aegean and earned the entirely undeserved nickname *Poliorcetes*, or 'Besieger of Cities'. He was responsible for the design and construction of the '*Helepolis*' siege engine (refer to Chapter 12) during his illegal and unsuccessful attack on Rhodes.

Eventually Demetrius was defeated in 285 and surrendered his army to Seleucus (the king of the Seleucid kingdom in Mesopotamia). He spent the last two years of his life under house arrest at Seleucus's court where he indulged his other two great passions – and effectively ate and drank himself to death.

Theseus

Like Odysseus, Theseus is another great example of a classic ancient Greek hero with two sides.

- ✔ On the plus side Theseus travelled to Crete and killed the Minotaur and was one of the greatest kings of Athens.
- ✔ On the debit side he dumped Ariadne (daughter of King Minos) on the island of Naxos when she was pregnant with his child and according to another myth kidnapped the young Helen (of Troy fame) and tried to force her to be his wife.

Theseus is a perfect example of the way that the Greeks regarded a 'hero' as somebody who did amazing things, rather than helped other people selflessly. (For more on heroes refer to Chapter 20.)

Olympias (circa 370–316 BC)

As the wife of Philip II of Macedon and the mother of Alexander the Great, Olympias was always going to have an important place in history, but she's famed as being one of the great villains of ancient Greece.

Many historians believe that Olympias was behind the murder of Philip while she was in exile. Whether that's true or not, Olympias certainly ordered the deaths of Philip's second wife and her infant daughter on her return. After Alexander's death, she tried desperately to cling on to power and was responsible for several more deaths until she was executed by relatives of her previous victims in 316 BC.

To be fair to Olympias, she lived in a court where the choice was to kill or be killed. And she was just very good at killing!

Alexander the Great (356–323 BC)

Alexander the Great – a bit dodgy? A controversial choice, but a good one, I believe:

Alexander was responsible for some of the greatest military achievements in the ancient world and created population movements that ushered in the Hellenistic Age (see Chapter 11). He founded great cities and travelled farther and wider than anybody else before.

But, during his campaigns, thousands of people were either killed in battle or executed and thousands more had their homes and lives destroyed. Alexander had several of his friends killed who he suspected of treachery – at least one by his own hands. His savagery to those who resisted him was legendary. Also, his name was used as a kind of bogeyman to scare children in eastern countries for centuries after his death. 'Go to bed when I tell you, or Alexander will get you!'

So, visionary or mass-murdering maniac? You have to judge all of these people by the standards of their age. History is all about opinions. The choice is yours!

Diogenes the Cynic (circa 412–321 BC)

Diogenes was a philosopher whose controversial methods made him famous throughout the ancient world. At various times in his life he lived in a barrel, was captured by pirates, and was expelled from the town of Sinope for 'defacing the currency' – spoiling coins in an attempt at rejecting the material world. Diogenes ended up in Corinth and lived the life of a beggar, rejecting all social conventions including marriage and cleanliness. He was known as the 'cynic' because he was credited with being the founder of the 'cynic' branch of philosophy, which disdained conventional life. The word 'cynic' comes from the Greek word *kynikos* which means 'dog like'. Diogenes believed people could learn a lot from living like dogs – he did!

Although Diogenes was a proper philosopher who wrote many books, treatises, and several tragic plays, undoubtedly the best story about him concerns his meeting with the young Alexander the Great. When the young king asked Diogenes if there was anything that Alexander could do for him, Diogenes replied, 'Yes, you can move slightly to the left, you're standing in my sunlight.' A brave man indeed!

Jason

Another ancient Greek hero with a dark side, Jason is the celebrated warrior who journeyed to the Black Sea and stole the Golden Fleece from King Aietes, along with his daughter, the sorceress Medea (refer to Chapter 20 for the full story).

However, the stories about Jason's return aren't as flattering as his early exploits. Eventually he ended up living with Medea in the city of Corinth where they had two children. In Euripides's play *Medea*, Jason dumps Medea (who, because she was a non-Greek, had no legal status as his bride) to marry Glauce, the daughter of the king of Corinth, so that he would gain social status. In an act of revenge, Medea kills both Glauce and her own two children before fleeing.

For his part, Jason eked out the rest of his life alone in Corinth, eventually dying when timber from the rotting hulk of his ship, the *Argo*, fell on him. An unheroic end!

Kleon of Athens (died 422 BC)

Kleon gets a bit of an unfair press because the only descriptions that survive of him are from Aristophanes and Thucydides – neither of whom liked him at all and (in the case of Aristophanes) continually publicly lampooned him.

Kleon was one of the first demagogue politicians (see Chapter 7), whose rabble-rousing political style clashed with old-school Athenian aristocrats like Pericles. In 426 BC he tried to prosecute Aristophanes over his play *The Babylonians*, which he claimed defamed the city of Athens, but the case was thrown out.

At the same time Kleon was a brave general who won several victories and died fighting near Amphipolis. However, most people regard him as being one of the first to exploit Athens's new democracy for his own personal glory.

Chapter 26

Ten Great Places to Visit

In This Chapter

▶ Touring museums

▶ Walking the sites

▶ Searching online

▶ Sampling the art and culture

*R*eading books is all well and good, but if you really want to experience some ancient Greek culture up close and personal, this chapter suggests ten places that are full of it. Visit these locations and you're sure to feel a real connection to the world of 2,500 years ago.

Of course, hundreds of other interesting sites with connections to the ancient Greeks exist, but you have to start somewhere. These just happen to be some of my favourites.

The British Museum, London

The British Museum has a superb collection of ancient Greek objects and artefacts in some really big galleries. The museum houses a great collection of vases and sculpture from all ancient Greece's artistic periods (see Chapter 17), plus many Roman copies of famous Greek originals. The fantastic Nereid Monument, transplanted from Asia Minor, gives a good idea of the scale of some of the building work that went on during ancient Greece's prime (refer to Chapter 18). You can also see some wonderful everyday objects that allow an insight into what normal Greek lives were like.

Best of all are the so-called 'Elgin Marbles', the Parthenon sculptures that were taken from Athens by a British adventurer, Lord Elgin, in around 1800. These are great examples of the metopes, frieze, and the pediment sculpture, which I discuss in Chapter 18. The Elgin Marbles are all presented with an excellent display that features reconstructions of what the original temple looked like and how it was built. In recent years there have been attempts to force the British Government to return the sculptures to Athens – so go and see them while they're still in the British Museum!

The Acropolis, Athens

Of course, Athens is loaded with things to see, but the Acropolis really is a standout. The Parthenon, the largest temple on the site, is amazingly impressive, but the other temples – such as Athena Nike and the Erectheum – are also stunning.

Just next to the Acropolis is the Theatre of Dionysus (described in Chapter 16). The current theatre is actually a Roman rebuild of the Greek original, but it still gives you a sense of the size of the performances that used to take place.

And at a really basic level, simply walking along the streets and through the gathering spaces where Pericles, Socrates, and all the others once trod is fantastic! Local guides are available to take you round but a good guidebook will suffice. Plan to spend most of the day there and get there early – the Acropolis can get appallingly hot around lunchtime, a good time to get something to eat!

Knossos, Crete

The site of Knossos on the island of Crete feels very different to the other sites I list in this chapter. As I say in Chapter 2, the Minoans, while technically Greek, were very different to the ancient Greeks who followed them.

Knossos was discovered and controversially restored and rebuilt by Sir Arthur Evans in 1900, but the site that remains is undeniably impressive. One of the highlights is the superb Royal Palace with its beautiful dolphin decorations. Equally interesting are the workrooms in the east wing. You get a real sense of a different, earlier time and age. But be warned, walking around the site in Cretan summer temperatures that can hit over 100 degrees can be hard work!

Crete itself is a fascinating island and worth visiting on its own. It's an overnight journey on the ferry from the Greek mainland and quite a distance to Knossos once you arrive. A visit needs to be part of a planned trip but it's well worth the effort.

Delphi

The site of the sanctuary complex at Delphi is amazing. A small town hidden away in the Peloponnese, Delphi is one of the most beautiful places that you can visit, boasting spectacular views from the sanctuary, which is built into the hillside. (Head to Chapter 21 for more on the historical and religious details about this site.)

A lot of buildings still remain at Delphi, including many treasuries and a large portion of the base of the Temple of Apollo. At the very top of the site are the remains of the athletic stadium where the Pythian games (held at Delphi in honour of Apollo) took place. You can also visit an excellent museum that includes a wonderful bronze sculpture of the Delphi charioteer.

Delphi is a little isolated but you can easily book a coach trip from Athens. It's worth staying over (plenty of hotels are in town) because the sunrise looks spectacular across the valley.

Olympia

Olympia is a famous Greek town that's well worth a visit. The town has become a bit more touristy than Delphi, but its archaeological site is just as impressive.

The ruins of the Temple of Zeus are still near Olympia, along with the workshop of Pheidias, where this legendary artist constructed the massive statue of the god that was considered to be one of the Seven Wonders of the World (and shown in Chapter 17).

The site gives you a very good idea of what the original Olympic games were like, as well as just how much of an event they were (see Chapter 16). If you're feeling suitably energetic, you can even run a lap of the stadium – although be careful, I fell over when I did it! Like Delphi you'll need to book a trip to Olympia (or travel there by public transport) and there are many hotels in town.

A Greek Play

The only way to really get a sense of what the Greek theatre was like is to see a performance of a Greek play. Any play – tragedy or comedy – will do. In addition to professional and regional shows, consider attending a university or community theatre production of these great works. You may even be able to find a production that's staged outdoors. (Pack a picnic and bring a bottle of wine just like the ancients!)

Greek plays aren't as action-packed as some modern theatre. In fact, you may be surprised to see how still the performers are (if the play is performed in a traditional manner). On-stage, you also have the opportunity to see the way that the chorus is used to support and comment on the action of the central characters.

Many modern productions update the play to the present or change the setting to somewhere different. But just as with Shakespeare, the modern touches usually still allow the brilliance of the original work to shine through.

Samos or Another Greek Island

If you want to get a sense of Odysseus's travels in Homer's epic poem *The Odyssey*, visit a Greek island and drink in the atmosphere. The history is great – and the peace and quiet is pretty wonderful too!

It's difficult to pick a single Greek island to visit because there are hundreds, but I'm recommending Samos because it is the one I most recently visited! The closest Greek island to modern Turkey, Samos was a hive of trade and activity during the heyday of ancient Greece, and the island still has a reasonable amount of archaeology to look at.

More than touring remains, however. Samos and many of the other islands give you a real sense of the independence of these small islands and their distance from elsewhere. You can easily see how men like Herodotus broke new ground by travelling to these areas and sharing their stories with Greeks on the mainland. You can also appreciate how each community grew and developed its own versions of myths and relationships with the gods.

Google Images

This recommendation may seem obvious, but if you want to see more examples of Greek art and architecture, go to the Internet!

A quick search (I like `images.google.com`) reveals a huge number of photos and drawings. You can very quickly assemble a good library of pictures.

Check out Chapter 17 for an introduction to Greek art and then seek out some more examples of different types of sculpture. Searching under 'Hellenistic Sculpture' or 'Red Figure Vase Painting' brings up loads of examples, each with its own story. The world of ancient Greek art is at your fingertips!

The National Gallery, London

The National Gallery may seem like an odd choice of place to visit for ancient Greek culture, but if you want to see how the Greeks influenced the people who followed them, then an art gallery is a good place to start.

Many Renaissance paintings feature scenes from Greek mythology based on written sources that were rediscovered during that historical period.

The National Gallery is a good place to start because it features Titian's fantastic *Bacchus and Ariadne* (1520–23 AD), an amazing, colourful picture that shows the abandoned Ariadne being surprised by Bacchus and his swaggering crew of followers. Look for paintings by Titian, Botticelli, Della Francesca, Veronese, and Rubens – all of whom loved using classical mythology as a source.

All the Renaissance paintings are idealised, but looking at somebody else's interpretation of the myths is still quite inspiring. Go along and let your imagination run riot! *Art For Dummies* by Thomas Hoving and *Art History For Dummies* by Jesse Bryant Wilder offer further insights into the connections between ancient Greek and later artists.

The Agora, Athens

Still relatively well preserved, Athens's original town centre was the busiest part of the greatest of Ancient Greek cities. If you go, take a classical text with you and sit and read it for a while. The ancient Greeks were having conversations about the same text 2,500 years ago, probably in the same spot! You'll also be sitting in the place where Plato debated with Socrates; Pericles discussed the Peloponnesian War with his generals; and Alcibiades intrigued and flirted. Their sandalled feet trod the same ground that you'll be standing on. You can't get much more Greek than that.

The Agora is in the very centre of modern Athens and is surrounded by modern market stalls. It gives you a sense of the hustle and bustle that must have been part of city life in the days of ancient Greece. Take a walk around and pick up something to eat from one of the street vendors – just as an average Athenian would have done on his way to the assembly 2,500 years ago!

Index

• D •

Notes

Notes

Notes

Notes

Notes

Notes

FOR DUMMIES®

Do Anything. Just Add Dummies

UK editions

BUSINESS

978-0-470-51806-9

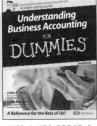

978-0-470-99245-6

978-0-7645-7026-1

FINANCE

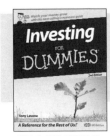

978-0-470-99280-7

978-0-470-99811-3

978-0-470-05815-2

PROPERTY

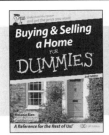

978-0-470-99448-1

978-0-470-51502-0

978-0-7645-7054-4

Body Language For Dummies
978-0-470-51291-3

Building Self-Confidence For Dummies
978-0-470-01669-5

Children's Health For Dummies
978-0-470-02735-6

Cognitive Behavioural Coaching For Dummies
978-0-470-71379-2

Counselling Skills For Dummies
978-0-470-51190-9

Digital Marketing For Dummies
978-0-470-05793-3

Divorce For Dummies
978-0-7645-7030-8

eBay.co.uk For Dummies, 2nd Edition
978-0-470-51807-6

Emotional Freedom Technique For Dummies
978-0-470-75876-2

English Grammar For Dummies
978-0-470-05752-0

Fertility & Infertility For Dummies
978-0-470-05750-6

Genealogy Online For Dummies
978-0-7645-7061-2

Golf For Dummies
978-0-470-01811-8

Green Living For Dummies
978-0-470-06038-4

Available wherever books are sold. For more information or to order direct go to www.wiley.com or call +44 (0) 1243 843291

FOR DUMMIES

A world of resources to help you grow

UK editions

SELF-HELP

978-0-470-01838-5

978-0-7645-7028-5

978-0-470-51501-3

HEALTH

978-0-470-99456-6

978-0-470-51737-6

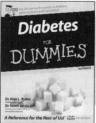

978-0-470-05810-7

HISTORY

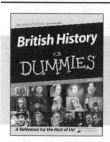

978-0-470-03536-8

978-0-470-51015-5

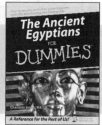

978-0-470-06544-0

Hypnotherapy For Dummies
978-0-470-01930-6

Inventing For Dummies
978-0-470-51996-7

Job Hunting and Career Change
All-in-One For Dummies
978-0-470-51611-9

Motivation For Dummies
978-0-470-76035-2

Origami Kit For Dummies
978-0-470-75857-1

Patents, Registered Designs, Trade
Marks and Copyright For Dummies
978-0-470-51997-4

Psychometric Tests For Dummies
978-0-470-75366-8

Raising Happy Children For
Dummies
978-0-470-05978-4

Starting and Running a Business
All-in-One For Dummies
978-0-470-51648-5

Sudoku For Dummies
978-0-470-01892-7

The British Citizenship Test For
Dummies, 2nd Edition
978-0-470-72339-5

Time Management For Dummies
978-0-470-77765-7

Wills, Probate, & Inheritance Tax For
Dummies, 2nd Edition
978-0-470-75629-4

Winning on Betfair For Dummies,
2nd Edition
978-0-470-72336-4

FOR DUMMIES®

The easy way to get more done and have more fun

LANGUAGES

978-0-7645-5194-9

978-0-7645-5193-2

978-0-7645-5196-3

MUSIC

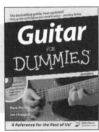
978-0-7645-9904-0

978-0-470-03275-6
UK Edition

978-0-7645-5105-5

SCIENCE & MATHS

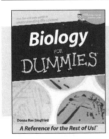
978-0-7645-5326-4

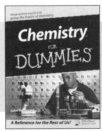
978-0-7645-5430-8

978-0-7645-5325-7

Art For Dummies
978-0-7645-5104-8

Baby & Toddler Sleep Solutions For Dummies
978-0-470-11794-1

Bass Guitar For Dummies
978-0-7645-2487-5

Christianity For Dummies
978-0-7645-4482-8

Filmmaking For Dummies
978-0-7645-2476-9

Forensics For Dummies
978-0-7645-5580-0

German For Dummies
978-0-7645-5195-6

Hobby Farming For Dummies
978-0-470-28172-7

Jewelry Making & Beading For Dummies
978-0-7645-2571-1

Judaism For Dummies
978-0-7645-5299-1

Knitting For Dummies, 2nd Edition
978-0-470-28747-7

Music Composition For Dummies
978-0-470-22421-2

Physics For Dummies
978-0-7645-5433-9

Sex For Dummies, 3rd Edition
978-0-470-04523-7

Solar Power Your Home For Dummies
978-0-470-17569-9

Tennis For Dummies
978-0-7645-5087-4

The Koran For Dummies
978-0-7645-5581-7

U.S. History For Dummies
978-0-7645-5249-6

Wine For Dummies, 4th Edition
978-0-470-04579-4

Available wherever books are sold. For more information or to order direct go to www.wiley.com or call +44 (0) 1243 843291

FOR DUMMIES®

Helping you expand your horizons and achieve your potential

COMPUTER BASICS

978-0-470-24055-7

978-0-470-13728-4

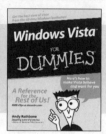

978-0-471-75421-3

DIGITAL LIFESTYLE

978-0-7645-9802-9

978-0-470-17474-6

978-0-470-17469-2

WEB & DESIGN

978-0-470-08030-6

978-0-470-11193-2

978-0-470-11490-2

Access 2007 For Dummies
978-0-470-04612-8

Adobe Creative Suite 3 Design Premium
All-in-One Desk Reference For Dummies
978-0-470-11724-8

AutoCAD 2008 For Dummies
978-0-470-11650-0

C++ For Dummies, 5th Edition
978-0-7645-6852-7

Excel 2007 All-in-One Desk Reference For
Dummies
978-0-470-03738-6

Flash CS3 For Dummies
978-0-470-12100-9

Laptops For Dummies, 2nd Edition
978-0-470-05432-1

Mac OS X Leopard For Dummies
978-0-470-05433-8

Macs For Dummies, 9th Edition
978-0-470-04849-8

Networking All-in-One Desk Reference For
Dummies, 3rd Edition
978-0-470-17915-4

Office 2007 All-in-One Desk Reference For
Dummies
978-0-471-78279-7

Search Engine Optimization For Dummies,
2nd Edition
978-0-471-97998-2

Second Life For Dummies
978-0-470-18025-9

The Internet For Dummies, 11th Edition
978-0-470-12174-0

Visual Studio 2008 All-in-One Desk
Reference For Dummies
978-0-470-19108-8

Web Analytics For Dummies
978-0-470-09824-0

Windows XP For Dummies, 2nd Edition
978-0-7645-7326-2

**Available wherever books are sold. For more information or to order direct go to
www.wiley.com or call +44 (0) 1243 843291**